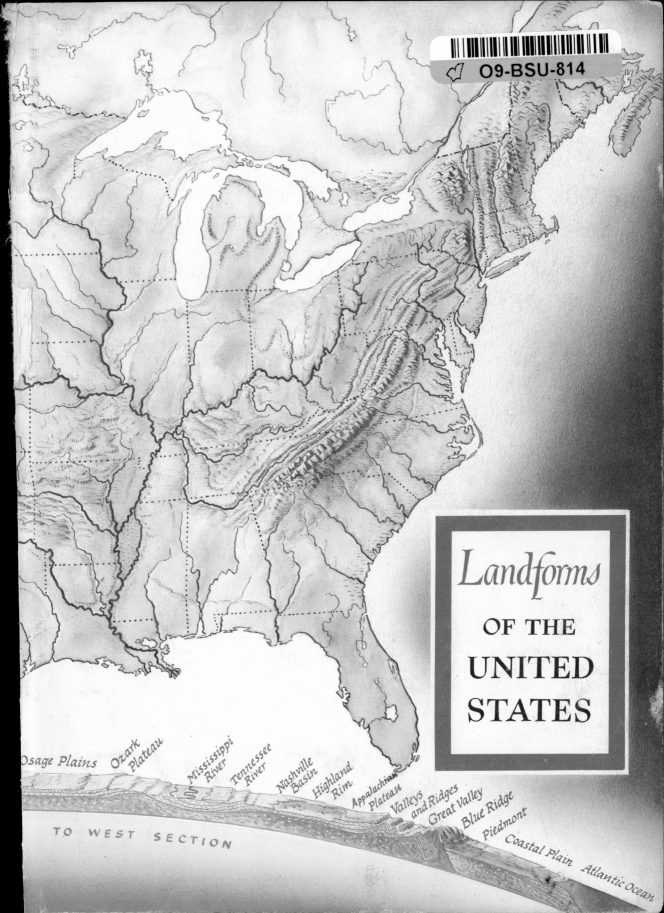

O9-BSU-814

Landforms
OF THE
UNITED
STATES

Osage Plains Ozark Plateau Mississippi River Tennessee River Nashville Basin Highland Rim Appalachian Plateau Valleys and Ridges Great Valley Blue Ridge Piedmont Coastal Plain Atlantic Ocean

TO WEST SECTION

THE

FEDERAL UNION

THIRD EDITION

A History of the United States TO 1877

JOHN D. HICKS

THE UNIVERSITY OF CALIFORNIA, BERKELEY

HOUGHTON MIFFLIN COMPANY The Riverside Press Cambridge

TO

LUCILE CURTIS HICKS

COPYRIGHT © 1957, BY JOHN D. HICKS
COPYRIGHT 1952, 1948, 1937, BY JOHN D. HICKS

*All rights reserved including the right to reproduce
this book or parts thereof in any form*

The Riverside Press
CAMBRIDGE · MASSACHUSETTS
PRINTED IN THE U.S.A.

CONTENTS

Section *I* · THE MORNING OF AMERICA · 1492–1763

Section *II* · FOUNDING THE NATION · 1763–1787

Section *III* · EVOLUTION IN DEMOCRACY · 1787–1818

Appendix

PREFACE TO THE THIRD EDITION

The Third Edition of *The Federal Union* differs from the Second mainly in that it contains a new chapter on Reconstruction, a subject that many colleges and universities now find it desirable to include in the work of the first semester. This chapter overlaps Chapters 1–3 of *The American Nation*, the second volume in this series, which will continue to cover the subject of Reconstruction. Teachers will thus find it possible to choose either 1865 or 1877 as the breaking point in their course. Since the comprehensive "List of Books Cited," available in the Appendix of *The American Nation*, 3d edition, contains nearly all the titles listed in the bibliographical note at the end of the new chapter, it has seemed unnecessary to repeat these titles in the Appendix of this volume.

JOHN D. HICKS

BERKELEY, CALIFORNIA

PREFACE TO THE SECOND EDITION

For nearly fifteen years *The Federal Union* has remained in use as a college text, with only minor revisions and without changes in pagination. As far as the content is concerned, this status might perhaps have continued indefinitely, but with the old plates wearing out, and with fashions changing in the making of text-books, it has seemed worth while to bring out a new edition which embraces "the new look." While I have taken advantage of this opportunity to remedy some oversights in the first edition, to make some rearrangements, and to change my mind now and then, the general outline remains the same. I have attempted, also, in the bibliographical notes appended to each chapter, to keep abreast of current book publications relating to the period under review.

Among the innumerable acknowledgments that I could, and perhaps should, make, there are two that I cannot in good conscience overlook. I owe a deep debt of gratitude to the efficient editorial staff of Houghton Mifflin Company, which is responsible for the handsome format of the volume, and for a prodigious amount of labor on its maps and illustrations; most especially, to Miss Joan Mackenzie, who has shown real artistry in the selection and interpretation of the illustrations. I am also deeply indebted to my editorial assistant, Mrs. Helen B. Gray, who has given me the most helpful co-operation at every stage of the work. If we can maintain the team-work we seem to have established, we hope within a few years to bring out in similar format a new edition of *The American Nation*, the companion volume to *The Federal Union*, which covers the history of the United States from 1865 to the present.

JOHN D. HICKS

BERKELEY, CALIFORNIA

PREFACE TO THE FIRST EDITION

FOR eighteen years it was my good fortune to "give" a survey course in American history for university students. When at last, with some reluctance, I surrendered this privilege to a junior member of the staff, there was no particular reason why the "course" should not be turned into a book. At least the fear that students might have to listen to the same phrases in lecture that they read in their text need no longer serve as a deterrent.

It is interesting to speculate (no other word will do) upon the sources of information that contribute to the making of such a book as this. That "sources" in the technical historical sense have alone been consulted would be an idle boast. One's store of data begins, doubtless, with the notebooks, once deeply cherished but long since turned to ashes, that were acquired while "taking" certain courses as a graduate student, or even as an undergraduate. Certainly my deep obligation to four great teachers, James Alton James of Northwestern University, Winfred T. Root of the University of Iowa, the late Carl Russell Fish of the University of Wisconsin, and Frederic L. Paxson of the University of California cannot properly be overlooked. Probably one is influenced also, consciously or unconsciously, by the textbooks he has required his students to buy, and has himself out of a distressing sense of duty felt obliged occasionally to read. In this manner I must have absorbed a great deal from Fish's *Development of American Nationality*, Muzzey's *United States of America*, West's *Story of American Democracy*, and Hockett and Schlesinger's *Political and Social History of the United States*. As for the rest, the sum total of one's reading and experience would not be too much to cite. . . .

In the writing of this book Professor Frederic L. Paxson has been my constant adviser. He has read critically both the manuscript and the proof. His riper judgment and wider knowledge have pulled me out of many pitfalls. He it was, indeed, who encouraged me to undertake this task. . . .

A few other acknowledgments remain to be made. Two of my colleagues, Professor Curtis P. Nettels and Professor William B. Hesseltine, have read the parts of my manuscript in which they were most interested, the colonial and the national periods, respectively, and have made valuable suggestions. Professor Max C. Otto, Wisconsin's beloved philosopher, generously gave me the benefit of his criticism on Chapter XXV [2nd ed., XXIV]; Mr. Herman R. Friis, a graduate student in geography at the University of Wisconsin, furnished much needed aid in the preparation of maps; and Mrs. Frances Fries, a graduate student in history, worked long and faithfully over the index.

JOHN D. HICKS

MADISON, WISCONSIN

SECTION ONE

THE

MORNING OF AMERICA

1492 - 1763

The United States, alone among the great powers of the World, has a background of dependency upon another power. The colonial period lasted a long while. From the founding of Jamestown to the Declaration of Independence was as many years as from the Declaration of Independence to the end of the Second World War. The imprint of the Mother Country, England, upon the American nation was therefore deep and abiding. After the union with Scotland in 1603 it is proper to speak of the nation on which the American colonies were dependent as Great Britain, rather than England, but the predominant part played by England and Englishmen in laying the colonial foundations well justifies the continued use of the words England and English. The English language became the American language. English ideas on government and politics, on religion and morality, on literature and art, on business and education, long dominated American thought.

It is a mistake to assume, however, that the United States was solely the offspring of England. Not Great Britain alone, but all the nations of western Europe were seized about the same time with the same urge for expansion, and for many years the competition for colonies in America was keen. The Spanish and the Portuguese long claimed a monopoly of the New World, but the defeat of the Spanish Armada in 1588 broke this grip, and ushered in a period of unbridled competition. As a result, the domination of Spain and Portugal was gradually restricted to most of South America and parts of southern North America, while the English, the French, the Dutch, and even the Swedes fought for the rest. The marks left by these various colonial conflicts have never been fully erased. The United States has within its limits today descendants of all these early colonial groups, and the institutions they brought with them from the continent of Europe have indelibly affected the institutions of English-speaking America. There have been many immigrants, too, of non-English blood, and the first great wave of such immigration came in the late colonial period from northern Ireland and the German Palatinate.

One conspicuous difference between the English colonial foundations and those of their chief competitors was the greater emphasis of the English upon individual initiative. The English colonies in North America were not founded by the government directly, but by trading companies or individuals (proprietors), armed with authority by the state. Oddly enough, the stock-holders and the proprietors generally lost heavily on their investments, but their activities provided the first great impetus to settlement in British North America.

Geography had much to do with the course of early American development. The fact that there were so many different colonies stemmed in part from the broken character of the Atlantic coastline, which invited separate establishments. Good harbors promoted trade, forests supported shipping, the ocean highway maintained connections with the Mother Country. Geography also helps account for sectionalism. The colonies had too varied economic interests for all of them to develop along the same lines. The tremendous possibilities of western expansion made for further differences. The frontier first became a section in its own right, then as one frontier succeeded another, the West became a series of new sections. The Appalachian barrier held back the advance of the English settlers for a time, but when they finally did break through, the sparse and scattered French had no chance to turn them back. The constantly shifting environment did much also to modify Old World institutions, and to emphasize more and more the difference between Englishmen and Americans.

It never occurred to the English settlers who came to America, or to their descendants, that because they lived outside England they had lost their traditional rights as Englishmen. Colonial governments grew up in the same pattern as the English model, with only such changes as the new environment and new conditions seemed to require. The colonists demanded from their governments, and for the most part received from them, the same privileges and immunities that they would have enjoyed had they lived in England. Each colony tended, indeed, to think of itself as a little England, and to resent, sometimes to the point of obstruction, British efforts at control. But British officials, who were interested in achieving a well-coordinated and economically self-sufficient empire, took a different view. They claimed for their government full imperial rights, and induced it, particularly through the Navigation Acts, to lay down the most painstaking regulations for the Americans to follow. Consciously or unconsciously, the Colonists weighed the irritations of British control against the benefits of British protection. As long as the French remained in Canada, the need of aid from the British government in the emergency of war was great, and imperial control was accepted as a necessary make-weight for imperial defense. But when French rule in North America came to an end with British victory in the French and Indian War, the scene was set for a change.

1

The Opening of the New World

Physiography of North America — Europe in the Middle Ages — The Italian monopoly on Asiatic trade — The search for new routes to Asia — Discovery of America — Spanish and Portuguese colonization — Defeat of the Spanish Armada — European rivalry for America — Motives of English colonization

THE civilization that has grown up in the United States was begun a little more than **Europe in** three centuries ago by groups **America** of European emigrants, mostly English, who crossed the Atlantic in search of new homes in the western world. They were the representatives of a culture that was already ripe, and their task, great as it was, required mainly that they adapt to the new environment a manner of living already well developed in the old. The mingling in America of these representatives of many diverse peoples, the successful efforts they and their successors and descendants put forth to conquer the continent, and the development out of their great variety of traditions and experiences of an essentially new civilization constitute the main stream of American history.

America before the time of Columbus had developed no great civilization of its own. **Lack of** The Mayas and the Aztecs in **a native** Mexico, and the Incas in Peru, **civilization** shone brilliantly in comparison with other American tribes, but not in comparison with the best that Europe and Asia had produced. Racial traits may account in part for this failure, but the importance of the environment cannot be overlooked. A primitive civilization, if it is to survive the attack of savage neighbors, must have the protection of encircling mountains or seas, such, for

example, as nature afforded the Greeks and the Romans. America offered few such settings. Its coast-lines were regular, its islands small and few, its peninsulas hard to defend, its mountain fastnesses inhospitable, its plains too unbroken. Such obstacles proved to be difficult enough for the transplanted Europeans; for the Indians they were insuperable.

And yet that portion of the western world that became the United States was potentially well fitted to sustain a **Natural** great nation. Its location wholly **resources** within the temperate zone freed its inhabitants alike from arctic cold and from tropic heat, but because it possessed every other variety of climate, every degree of rainfall, every texture and composition of soil, its agricultural possibilities were limitless. Abundant forests gave to shipbuilders the masts, spars, and naval stores they needed, and to pioneers the timbers for houses, barns, and fences. Wild life offered to hunters and trappers a paradise, and mineral resources of incalculable value awaited exploitation.

The Indians themselves were a great natural resource. They were incapable of serious resistance, and they taught the Europeans how to live in America. From the experience of natives the colonists learned what seeds to plant, what soils to cultivate, what trails and streams to follow into the interior, what manner of craft to launch upon the inland waters; in short, what wealth the land possessed, and how best to take it.

The fact that America lay so much closer to Europe than to Asia determined that the **Connections** inhabitants of the New World **with Europe** would be Europeans, not Asiatics, and that for many centuries to come the relations between America and Europe would be closer than the relations between America and Asia. The ease with which sailors soon learned to conquer the Atlantic made that ocean less a barrier between the two continents than a highway. Colonies could thrive in America because during their infancy the all-essential connections with the mother country could be maintained; indeed, dependence upon Europe was so natural that the colonists learned with difficulty to depend wholly upon themselves. The American people remained British subjects for almost as many years as they have been citizens of independent states, and neither the Declaration of Independence nor the American Revolution sufficed to break the cultural and economic ties that bound the New World to the Old.

Had the Atlantic coastline of North America been as little indented as the Pacific, **The coastal** doubtless the number of British **plain** settlements would have been fewer. As it was, ideal sites for colonies could be found on the shores of sheltered bays and landlocked harbors all along the coast. Very often these inviting arms of the sea turned out to be also the mouths of rivers which gave access into the interior for trade with the Indians and for the expansion of settlement. The British were thus led to found many colonies instead of a single colony; and each colony, while maintaining close connections with the mother country, tended to develop independently of every other. American political institutions still reveal the influence of this early geographic environment. The thirteen colonies could not surrender their separate political life merely because they had broken with Great Britain. They became thirteen independent

states, and the system of government they worked out provided for a federal union, not for a consolidated republic.

The Appalachian mountain barrier also played an important part in determining the future of the American nation. **The Appa-** Lying inland at varying dis- **lachians** tances from the sea, these mountains extend from Nova Scotia almost to the Gulf of Mexico. They offered no protection from the Indians, for they were neither high nor difficult to penetrate, but as a restraining influence against too rapid extension of settlement they were of real significance. Because of this mountain barrier the English settlements tended to densify along the coast before the conquest of the interior was begun. When finally the westward movement swept through and across the mountains, it had behind it the driving force of a permanent and substantial population. The French, on the other hand, let through to the West too readily by the Valley of the St. Lawrence and the waters of the Great Lakes, dissipated their energies over too extensive an area. Sooner than the English they sensed the part that the Mississippi Valley must play in the future of America, but when the final contest for its possession came their scattered villagers were no match for the more numerous and more concentrated English.

The Appalachian mountain barrier served also to promote the development of a strictly American nationality. From the southern border of New York southward the mountains lie in parallel ranges, with fertile valleys in between. Into these valleys and along the foothills, or "piedmont," to the east of the mountains pushed pioneers from the northern colonies and newly arrived immigrants from Europe to mingle with such of the Southerners as had adventured into the interior, and with each other. Separated by the mountains and forest from the people of the seacoast, these men of the "back-country" became a race apart — a new people, not much concerned with local loyalties, and citizens of one nation rather than of individual states. These "backwoodsmen"

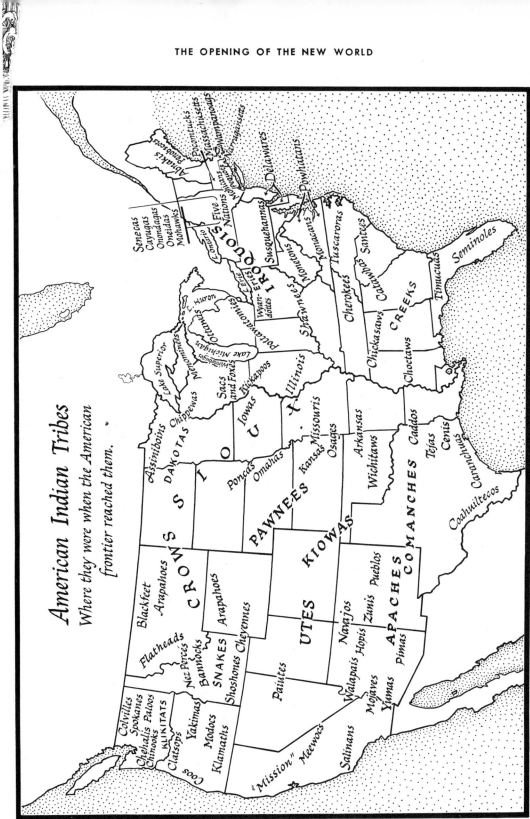

American Indian Tribes
Where they were when the American frontier reached them.

began early to restrain the particularistic tendencies of eastern Americans, and they bequeathed a common legacy of blood and custom to all future generations of western pioneers.

The interior basin of the North American continent is a vast, undulating plain, **The Missis-** bounded on the east by the Ap**sippi Valley** palachians, on the west by the Rockies, on the south by the Gulf of Mexico, and on the north, so far as the United States is concerned, by the Great Lakes. The one great river system which drains this region gives it remarkable unity and a name, the Mississippi Valley. Here lies nearly half the land now contained within the national borders, and far more than half the arable land. Once pioneers began to enter the Valley in numbers, it was inevitable that they should spread all over it. The only mountains to impede their progress were the Ozarks in Missouri and Arkansas, and they were far from formidable. The forests in the northern and eastern reaches were neither impenetrable nor indestructible, and the great central plains offered no more serious obstacle to settlement than an old pioneer prejudice against land that would not grow trees.

Here in the Mississippi Valley the process of amalgamation, already begun in the troughs of the Appalachians, was long continued. Here, too, Northerners met Southerners, here travelers from afar met those who had come from regions near by, and here foreigners met natives, all to be absorbed rapidly into a single national group. A pronounced similarity of type and culture still exists among the people of the Mississippi Valley. They speak a common language; their institutions vary but slightly from place to place; and their local loyalties, in part because of an enduring mobility, remain weak.

A striking physical feature of the North American continent is the great Cordillera or Rocky Mountain system of the **The Rockies** West. The plateau from which the ranges of this system rise is everywhere from five to ten thousand feet above sea-

level; it extends southward into Mexico and Central America and with considerable change of character northward through Canada into Alaska; it spreads out within the United States to a width of a thousand miles, and its peaks rise to magnificent heights. For all their prominence, however, these mountains lack the significance in American history that attaches to the Appalachians, or to most of the other great physical features of the continent. They possessed immense mineral wealth, they offered valuable grazing facilities, and their valleys could by means of irrigation be made agriculturally productive; but they were unfitted to shelter a large population, such as the Mississippi Valley naturally invited, and they were entered only when the formative period in the life of the nation was over.

As for the Pacific slope, it too had relatively little to do with the making of American civilization. The narrow- **The Pacific** ness of the western coastal plain, **slope** and the scarcity of its harbors, precluded such developments as took place along the Atlantic. Spanish settlements there were, but they began only when the English colonies were ripe for revolution, and they unloosed few forces of permanent significance. In due time man conquered notably the obstacles that nature here placed in his way, but not until the habits of the American people were already well set, and the nature of the American nation well defined.

The original discovery of America was made, anthropologists believe, by Asiatics who found their way across the **The** Bering Strait to Alaska, or pos- **Norsemen** sibly crossed on an isthmus which has long since disappeared beneath the sea. From them, or from others who came by the same routes, the Indians were no doubt descended. The first Europeans to reach America, however, seem to have been the Norsemen, whose bold sea-farers had discovered the Faroes and Iceland as early as the ninth century, and had come within sight of the coast of Greenland. Late in the tenth century Eric the Red, an exile from Iceland, planted in

Greenland an Icelandic colony which lasted for five centuries, then disappeared. In the year 1000 King Olaf of Norway sent Leif Ericsson, a son of Eric the Red, on a mission to Greenland, but Ericsson's ships missed their course, and before they reached Greenland had touched on some point of the North American continent. Other Norsemen soon visited the new region, which they called Vinland because of the great profusion of grapes it produced. They also reported "self-sown" wheat (more probably, wild rice), and they seem to have made some attempt at settlement, possibly in Nova Scotia or New England. But the Norse colony evaporated without leaving a trace. As Professor Channing puts it: "The history of America would have been precisely what it has been if Leif Ericsson had never been born and if no Northman had ever steered his Knorr west of Iceland." There is a possibility that the Norsemen came to America again, for in 1898 a stone with a runic inscription was discovered near Kensington, Minnesota, which proclaimed that some Norse explorers, fourteen days journey from the sea, had camped in that locality in 1362. Opinions differ as to the authenticity of the Kensington Rune Stone, but these discoverers, if indeed they did exist, like those who came to Vinland, made no slightest impression upon the course of American history.

Except then for a few Norsemen, Europeans, throughout the entire Middle Ages, **Medieval Europe** were singularly unaware of the existence of a New World beyond the Atlantic. Eastern Europe lay static under the blight of Byzantine rule, while western Europe, after the decay of the Roman Empire, descended gradually into feudalism. Feudalism meant isolation, isolation not only for the peasants who were bound to the soil, but scarcely less for the lords who were bound to their fiefs. While feudalism lasted, each rural community took care of its own simple wants; trade and commerce languished; towns and cities almost disappeared; travel became as unnecessary as it was unsafe. But beginning with the eleventh century a great change came over western Europe. The simple agricultural economy of an earlier age gave way to a city-dominated civilization, the very life of which was industry and trade. Wealth increased, and those who had it demanded better standards of living, sometimes even the luxury of a little learning. Politics reflected the new age, and city governments, or "communes," won by force or purchase their independence of local lords. Isolation broke down, and travel, whether for business or pleasure, became increasingly common and relatively safe.

Because Italy had suffered less from the barbarian invasions than the rest of western Europe, many Italian cities had **The Italian cities** managed to survive the fall of Rome, and even to maintain throughout the

The runic characters on this stone found in Minnesota presumably record the presence there of Scandinavian explorers in 1362.

"dark ages" a precarious trade with the Eastern, or Byzantine, Empire. Naturally these "Italian cities" played a leading part in the commercial revival of the later Middle Ages. By the eleventh century such cities as Venice, Genoa, and Pisa had emerged as vigorous city-states, possessed of considerable wealth and population, and virtually independent of outside control. From ports in the eastern Mediterranean they obtained carpets, sugar, and spices, while from their own workshops came leather, fabrics of linen, silk, and wool, and such articles as glass, paper, and soap. All this produce they sold for good profits to other Europeans. Galleys a hundred feet in length plied the Mediterranean with Italian wares, and Italian traders, seeking markets, found their way by sea far around the coasts of western Europe, and by land deep into its less civilized center.

The Crusades, which began in the eleventh century and continued intermittently for

The Crusades nearly two hundred years, gave a great impetus to the growth of the Italian cities, and brought prosperity to the merchant class throughout all western Europe. The ostensible purpose of the Crusades was to rescue from the infidel Turks the holy places where Jesus had lived and died, but the real motives were not so pious. The Popes who urged the Crusades were eager to get warring Christians out of western Europe, both for the peace their going would promote and for the ease of mind it

would give churchmen who aspired to temporal power. The knights who "took the cross" had often no higher inspiration than the love of adventure and the hope of spoils. Business men looked with favor upon projects which meant for them a profitable trade in arms and supplies. Shippers foresaw that men and provisions would have to be transported by sea as well as by land. Success for the Crusaders promised still greater wealth and prosperity. Colonies would be established in the Holy Land to maintain a lively commerce with the West, and a friendly people would supplant the warlike Turks at the gateway to oriental trade.

The Crusaders were not successful in wresting the Holy Land permanently from the infidel, but for the scheming tradesmen of Italy they did all that was expected of them, and more. Italian traders secured valuable concessions in the towns along the Levantine coast. Their agents were exempt from the usual tolls, held their own courts, and formed in fact if not in name actual colonies of the mother city. The Crusades accounted also for an increased western demand for eastern goods. Returning Crusaders brought back with them the higher standards of living they had learned in the East, and taught these standards to their neighbors. In an age that knew nothing of refrigeration, spices such as pepper, cinnamon, nutmeg, cloves, and ginger won immediate favor for the seasoning of foods. Those

Medieval traders leaving the Orient and returning to Europe with their purchases are represented simultaneously in this drawing from a 14th-century French manuscript.

Medieval Trade Routes

who could afford it turned also to display. Prosperous city merchants purchased from Arab middlemen rubies, sapphires, pearls, and diamonds, wondrously wrought rugs and tapestries, "cloths of silk and gold," and all the fineries of the East to adorn themselves, their churches, and their palaces. Kings and prelates caught the spirit, and struggled not to be outdone. So vigorous was the trade thus established that it continued even after the fall of the Latin Kingdom of Jerusalem in the thirteenth century. The victorious Mohammedans did not scruple to give nor the Italian traders to accept the same quarters and the same privileges that they had enjoyed under Christian rule.

Like the Italians, the Levantine traders were middlemen who bought from the East **Asiatic trade** and sold to the West. Many of **routes** the articles in which they dealt came from distant lands in Asia, and they were brought to the Mediterranean usually by one of three main routes. The southernmost of these routes was by water from India and the farther East across the Indian Ocean and through the Red Sea. Caravans completed the journey to Alexandria or Cairo, where the European traders found the goods. The northern route was a tedious relay journey by caravan from the hinterlands of China and India to the Black Sea, and thence to the Mediterranean. The central route was both by sea and by land. Chinese junks, or other native craft, brought the wares to the Persian Gulf, whence Arab traders took them by way of Bagdad to Antioch or Jaffa or occasionally to some Egyptian port. Whether at Alexandria or Constantinople or Antioch the Arab traders were met by Italian merchants. Competitors from outside Italy had little chance because of the greater proximity of the

Italian cities to the eastern markets, and because of the special privileges that the Italians had obtained. As middlemen for all the rest of Europe their prosperity was prodigious, and so complete was their monopoly of the eastern trade that the various Italian cities warred for commercial advantages not with others but among themselves.

Efforts on the part of cities outside Italy to break the Italian monopoly could not long be postponed. Italian prices were deemed exorbitant; moreover, the gold and silver with which to pay them was hard to find. Western Europe then produced for itself only the bare necessities of life, and it had little to offer in exchange for the coveted oriental luxuries. Its slender stock of gold was therefore constantly diminished to redress an unfavorable balance of trade. The Italian merchants made sure profits, but the rest of Europe suffered seriously from this situation. Especially unfavored were the people of Spain and Portugal, of France and England, who were far from the Mediterranean trade centers and habitually bought much more than they sold. To these new Atlantic nations commercial vassalage was all the more humiliating because they were no longer feudal states, but centralized monarchies whose kings hoped for self-sufficiency and whose people knew the meaning of national pride. Small wonder that the sailors of these nations dreamed of new routes to the "Indies," routes which the Italian profiteers could not control. These dreams were encouraged by such tales as Marco Polo, the Venetian, told of his long sojourn in Asia during the thirteenth century. According to these tales the original cost of eastern wares was only a fraction of the Italian price, and in the Orient gold itself was easy to obtain. The hopes of sailors were further encouraged by important inventions, the compass and the astrolabe to aid in the navigation of ships, printing presses set with movable type to make available the maps and guide-books of other

Jealousy of the Italian monopoly

travelers, and guns and gunpowder to use in warding off the attacks of savages.

The Portuguese were the first to take up the search for a new route to the East. Their theory was that by sailing around Africa they could reach the eastern markets, and thus break the Italian monopoly. Prince Henry the Navigator (1394–1460), a younger son of the King of Portugal, is usually credited with arousing his countrymen to this possibility, although his interest was really in the trade of Africa rather than that of Asia. Under his encouragement sailors proceeded farther and farther down the African coast each year, and before he died the vicinity of Sierra Leone had been reached. These ventures were profitable in themselves, for the African coasts yielded gold, ivory, and Negro slaves, but the Portuguese sailors, searching always for greater returns, pushed southward until they passed the Equator in 1472–73, the mouth of the Congo in 1484, and under the valiant Bartholomew Diaz rounded the Cape of Good Hope in 1487. By this time they had the Indian Ocean and the trade of Asia definitely in view, but John II, the King of Portugal, fearing that the route around Africa might never prove feasible, sent out three other expeditions. One was to go by way of Egypt and the Red Sea to Abyssinia, another was to try an overland journey across Africa from the mouth of the Senegal, and a third was to seek a northeast passage around Europe to Asia. These efforts came to nought, and it was not for ten years that the work of Diaz was followed by a successful voyage to the Indies. Finally, in 1498, after completing the long journey around Africa, Vasco da Gama landed at Calicut, erected a monument to commemorate his discovery of the new route, and returned to Portugal with spices, jewels, silks, and tapestries, in proof of his accomplishment. The new route, which eliminated the profits of so many middlemen, was soon in use, and as a result the prices of eastern wares in western markets dropped to much lower levels. The Italian merchants suffered acutely from the

A new route to Asia

Christopher Columbus, as a seafaring youth, left his home in Genoa for Lisbon, then a center of interest in navigation, and the residence of his brother, Bartholomew, a chartmaker. Believing he could prove that India lay in sailing distance to the West from Europe, he sought assistance from the rulers of Portugal,

England, and France, all in vain, but finally, as "Lord Admiral of the Ocean Sea," he sailed under the Spanish flag, the first of a long procession of explorers whose collective activities furnished the data for this Map of the New World, published in the Münster edition of Ptolemy's *Geography,* 1540.

---

new competition, while to add to their distress the Turks grew steadily more powerful and less tolerant of Christian traders. Slowly but surely the splendor of the Italian cities was dimmed, and the commercial leadership of western Europe shifted from the Mediterranean to the Atlantic.

While the Portuguese were first in the field, they were not alone in their desire to **Columbus** find a new route to the East. The Spanish government was convinced through the arguments of a Genoese navigator, Christopher Columbus (*ca.* 1451–1506), that the Indies might be found by sailing directly west. Columbus was a well-informed sailor who had lived in the Madeira Islands, had sailed to the north as far as England and perhaps as far as Iceland, and had doubtless heard the gossip of distant lands across the Atlantic, then current among sailors. The common people of the time believed that the earth was flat, but medieval scholars knew well enough that it was round, and possibly one of them, a Florentine named Toscanelli, had some correspondence with Columbus on the feasibility of a western route to the East. Columbus, by underestimating the size of the earth, argued convincingly that this

directly western route would be shorter than the route around Africa that the Portuguese were then still seeking, but for a long time he had great difficulty in securing the support of anyone who had means enough to finance a voyage of discovery. At last he won over King Ferdinand of Aragon and Queen Isabella of Castile, the joint rulers of Spain, and under their patronage he set sail in August, 1492, with three small ships and fewer than a hundred men. The Spanish monarchs provided him with letters of introduction to the great Khan of Cathay, and a grant of authority to govern such unappropriated lands as he might discover.

When on the twelfth of October, 1492, Columbus reached one of the small coral islands of the Bahamas, he re- **Discovery of** joiced in the belief that he was **America** near the coast of Asia. Exploring farther, he visited Cuba and Haiti, but he failed to reach the mainland, and he failed too to find the spices and jewels and rich fabrics he had sought. But his conviction that he had reached the Indies was unshaken; he called the natives he met Indians, and he returned to Spain to announce that the new route had been found. Columbus made three other voyages of exploration to the New World, but he died in the belief that it was a new route to the Orient, not another continent, that he had discovered.

Further explorations, including voyages by one Americus Vespucius, whose name was **Other ex-** given to the New World, soon **plorations** revealed how mistaken Columbus had been, but trinkets of gold which the Indians displayed were sufficient to maintain

Conquest of Mexico, easily effected by Cortez' overwhelmingly superior armed strength, is represented here in 16th-century Indian drawings.

Spanish interest in the new land. Moreover, it seemed reasonable that there must be somewhere an opening through which the journey to the Indies could be continued. For a long time this latter idea fascinated adventurers, French and English as well as Spanish, but early in the sixteenth century it was learned that Asia was far more than a few days' journey from the new land. In 1519 a navigator named Magellan set sail from Spain, discovered and passed through the straits that bear his name, and crossed the Pacific. Magellan himself was killed by Philippine Islanders, but in 1522 one of his ships sailed on by the Portuguese route around Africa to Europe, the first ship to complete a voyage around the world.

Magellan's voyage blasted the Spanish hope of a route to the East that would rival the Portuguese route, but the **Conquest of** discovery of America led to an **Mexico and** even more valuable source of **Peru** wealth. In 1519 a Spanish soldier, Hernando Cortez, pushed his way to central Mexico and defeated Montezuma, Emperor of the Aztecs. The Aztecs proved to be the most civilized race in North America, and from the rich mines of Mexico they had gathered fabulous treasures of gold and silver. Cortez and the Spanish first robbed them, and then forced them as slaves to work the mines for the benefit of their conquerors. What Cortez did to the Aztecs was repeated about 1531 by another Spaniard, Pizarro, who conquered the equally rich and even more enlightened Incas of Peru. Thereafter for many years Spain drew a tribute from the New World which made her easily the first nation of Europe. Colonies followed conquests, and the Spanish empire in America became the marvel and envy of the whole civilized world.

In keeping with the times the Spanish aimed from the first at a national monopoly of all that their sailors had dis- **Line of** covered. When the Portuguese **Demarcation** King, professing to believe that Columbus had in reality only touched upon the coast of Africa, threatened to use his fleets against

Spanish trespassers, Ferdinand and Isabella hurriedly obtained from Pope Alexander VI, himself a Spaniard, full confirmation of their rights. By a proclamation issued May 4, 1493, the Pope declared that all heathen lands which lay beyond a north and south line one hundred leagues west of the Azores were by right of discovery the property of Spain. This line was much less than satisfactory to the King of Portugal, who finally persuaded the King of Spain to abandon it in favor of the famous Demarcation Line of 1494, a meridian three hundred and seventy leagues west of the Cape Verde Islands. The new line was intended to divide the whole world, outside Europe, between Portugal and Spain, and was formally approved by the Pope in 1506. Thus by papal pronouncement and by treaty agreement between the two nations it was stipulated that all discoveries east of this line were to go to Portugal, while all to the west of it were to go to Spain. It happened that the easternmost tip of triangular South America lay on the Portuguese side of the Demarcation Line; hence, when some years later a Portuguese ship was blown out of its intended course down the coast of Africa and touched instead upon the coast of Brazil, the Portuguese King could, and promptly did, claim that part of the New World for his own. Otherwise, the Spanish monopoly on America was for many years practically unchallenged. A Venetian named John Cabot, sailing in 1497 under authority of Henry VII of England, did indeed explore the north Atlantic coast of North America, and in 1535 a Frenchman, Jacques Cartier, carried the French flag up the St. Lawrence to the site of Montreal. But the claims made by these explorers were not immediately followed up. On the other hand, when in 1562 some French Huguenots attempted to found a colony in Florida, Spanish troops under Menendez brought the venture to a bloody end.

The profitable monopoly of the New World by the Spanish and of the new route to Asia by the Portuguese aroused at length the opposition of the English. England un-

der the rule of Queen Elizabeth had achieved a stable government, a satisfactory religious settlement, and a state of domestic tranquillity *English rivalry with Spain* that tempted her merchants and sailors to look well beyond the national confines for new fields to conquer. On every hand they encountered monopolies: the Italians in the Mediterranean; the Portuguese in Africa and Asia; the Spanish in America. One English sea-captain, the pious John Hawkins, defied both the Portuguese and the Spanish by procuring slaves in Africa and selling them at a great profit to the Spanish in the West Indies (1562–68). Others, in a day which knew nothing of international law, attacked the Spanish treasure-ships and brought back rich booty. One such, Francis Drake, in 1577 sailed down the eastern and up the western coasts of South America, plundering as he went, and after advancing as far north as Drake's Bay,[1] on the California coast, turned westward, crossed the Pacific to the East Indies, rounded the Cape of Good Hope, and in 1580 returned to England, the first of his race to circumnavigate the globe. In 1586–88 Thomas Cavendish duplicated the exploits of Drake, taking many prizes along the Spanish Main and in the Pacific. And then followed a veritable epidemic of piracy.

Long before mere piracy had turned to recognized war Queen Elizabeth was giving her private approval to buccaneers whose raids on Spanish commerce she must publicly denounce. She believed, as did her people, that Philip II, the Spanish King, aimed at the domination of all Europe. He had tried to control England by means of a marriage alliance, and had succeeded in winning one

---

[1] At Drake's Bay, by way of claiming the land he touched for the Queen of England, Drake caused a brass plate, appropriately inscribed, to be nailed to a "firm poste." More than three centuries and a half later, in 1936, such a plate, marked exactly as Drake had claimed, was found near the shores of San Francisco Bay, where apparently it had been only recently discarded. Experts believe that the plate is genuine, and was picked up and then thrown away by someone who had no notion of its historical value.

ARCTIC CIRCLE

NORTH

AMERICA

1497

Cartier 1534

Azores Lisbo

Madeira Is.

TROPIC OF CANCER

Cape Verde
Is.

Pacific

EQUATOR

SOUTH

Ocean

AMERICA

South

TROPIC OF CAPRICORN

Atla

Demarcation
Line -1494

Voyages of Discovery

Spanish   Portuguese

Strait
of
Magellan

ENGLISH
John Cabot, 1497~98
FRENCH
Voyage 1, Cartier, 1534~35
        2,   1535~36

SPANISH Portuguese

SPANISH EXPLORERS

Voyage 1 · 1492-93
  " 2 · 1493
  " 3 · 1498
  " 4 · 1502
  Columbus

Hojoda, Cosa and Vespucci · 1499
Magellan and Elcano · 1519-22
Spanish Trade Routes

PORTUGUESE EXPLORERS

Diaz · 1486-87
Vasco da Gama · 1497-98
Cabral · 1500
Vespucci · 1501-02
Portuguese Trade Routes

English queen, Mary Tudor, to be his bride. When Mary died young and childless, Philip sought to repeat his tactics and proposed to her successor, Elizabeth. But the new Queen shrewdly rejected his offer, and thus freed the English nation from that particular menace. Philip's ambitions worked out more to his liking with reference to Portugal. He was closely related to the Portuguese royal house, and when in 1580 the Portuguese King died without a direct heir Philip successfully laid claim to the vacant throne. He thus became head of the two greatest empires in the world. Meanwhile his designs on France, then torn by the so-called wars of religion, became increasingly apparent, and he gave even the more remote states of western Europe occasion for alarm.

There was also a religious aspect to the approaching conflict between England and **Protestant** Spain. The Protestant Reform-**Reformation** ation, which had swept over most of northern Europe earlier in the century, found its bitterest enemy in the King of Spain. Philip, as a devout Catholic, naturally looked with horror upon the spread of heresy, but he understood also that the expansion of his own domains must proceed hand in hand with the restoration of loyalty to the Pope. If the Bishop of Rome, as the sole spiritual ruler of Christendom, could not recover his authority, what chance would there be for Philip to secure the temporal supremacy that he craved? If the peoples of Europe would not brook the idea of a spiritual overlord, how much less likely that they would be willing to accept a temporal overlord. It was partly with a view to reviving the rule of Rome in England that Philip sought a marriage alliance with two successive English queens; it was partly because England had proceeded too far along the road of national religious independence to be willing to turn back that Elizabeth refused him. More and more, as the power of England grew, the Protestants of Europe looked to Elizabeth as their champion quite as the Catholics looked to Philip as theirs. A decision must soon be reached. Could Philip, supported by the wealth which he drew from his colonies, obtain for himself the temporal, and for the Pope the spiritual, overlordship of the world? Or could England preserve her own independence in politics and religion, help other nations to preserve theirs, and contrive at the same time to break the Spanish-Portuguese monopoly on all new trade routes and all new lands?

The clash came finally toward the end of the sixteenth century. The Netherlands,

A brass plate, found in California, proclaims that Sir Francis Drake takes "possession of this kingdome . . . to bee knowne as Nova Albion."

which by a succession of royal marriages
The Spanish and births had fallen under the
Armada Spanish yoke, revolted in 1566
against the oppressive rule of Philip's agents,
and in the later phases of the struggle that
ensued received aid from Queen Elizabeth.
This interference by the English in the
Netherlands, coupled with the wholesale
depredations upon Spanish commerce by
English seamen, led Philip to dispatch
against England his "Invincible Armada" of
one hundred and thirty ships, manned by
eight thousand sailors, and carrying an army
of invasion of nineteen thousand men. The
Spanish fleet reached the English coast, but
its great galleons were no match for the
smaller and more skillfully managed ships of
Drake and his kind. The Armada was disastrously defeated (summer, 1588), many
of the Spanish ships that escaped the English
were destroyed by tempests in the North
Sea, and less than a third of Philip's splendid
fleet ever got back to Spain. Several years
later England sent forth a "counter-Ar-
mada," which successfully attacked the
Spanish port of Cadiz and destroyed a great
quantity of enemy shipping (1596). From
this time forward it was England, not Spain,
who was the "mistress of the seas."

Philip's defeat revealed to all the world
that the Spanish-Portuguese commercial and
European colonial monopoly need no
rivalry for longer be respected. Among the
America first to take advantage of this
situation were the Dutch, whose "sea-
beggars" helped themselves to Portuguese
holdings in Africa and the East Indies, and
whose traders cast covetous eyes toward the
New World. In 1609 the Dutch East India
Company sent Henry Hudson, an Englishc-
man, to search for a sea-route through North
America to India. Hudson sailed as far as
Albany up the river which now bears his
name, but he found no northwest passage.
What he did discover was an opportunity for
fur trade with the Indians, and a Dutch
trading-post was soon established on Manhattan Island. Dutch sailors also wrested
from the Spanish some valuable Caribbean

islands and a strip of territory along the
northern coast of South America. The
French, whose sixteenth-century explorations gave them a claim to the St. Lawrence
Basin, were almost as active as the Dutch.
They, too, discovered the possibilities of the
fur trade, established in 1608 a post at Quebec, and in 1610 another at Port Royal. In
the West Indies, they occupied Guadeloupe,
Martinique, and many minor islands. Even
the Swedes, who for the moment had attained a place of prominence in European
affairs, planted a colony in 1638 at the mouth
of the Delaware, a settlement which the
Dutch soon absorbed. Meantime the English, whose defeat of Spain had made all this
possible, had not been idle.

The motives which led to the founding of
the English colonies in North America were
numerous and diverse. A little **Motives**
must be credited to the unique **of English**
pioneering spirit of the age. **colonization**
Sheer love of adventure led English seamen
of the sixteenth and seventeenth centuries to
embark in tiny craft for the search of unknown seas, and many landsmen, moved by
the same spirit, went along to explore the
lands beyond the seas. These adventurers
sought gold, it is true, and they sailed often
as the agents of commercial companies, but
for gold and trade alone they would hardly
have risked so much. Their *wanderlust*, so
apparent on every page of Hakluyt's *Voyages*, was a striking characteristic of the
times, a natural reaction, perhaps, from the
insularity of an earlier age.

Nor can the religious motive be overlooked. Protestant England, with the enthusiasm of the novice for her creed, regarded
the New World as a legitimate missionary
field; and the fact that Catholic Spain, the
chief national rival of England, had already
won many converts to Catholicism furnished
an added incentive. Moreover, there were in
England many dissenters from the Established Church whose presence, in an age of
religious intolerance, was deemed a menace
to the safety of the state. For such as these
the New World might prove a haven of

Early Colonies and Trading Posts

refuge; for the government their going would afford profound relief. What better use could be made of dissenters than to permit them to carry Protestantism and the English flag to heathen lands?

Hard times and fancied overpopulation also account for much of the English enthu-

Hard times and unemployment

siasm for colonies. One writer of the period maintained that "unless the three great Imposthumes of the World, namely Wars, Famine and Pestilence, do purge the great body, all kingdomes and countries become very populous, and men can hardly live in quiet or without danger." Such a condition of affairs England seemed to have approached. Peace with Spain (1604) left many discharged soldiers and sailors to seek in vain for new employment. The increasing popularity of sheep-raising within consolidated enclosures threw many farmhands out of work. Henry VIII's dissolution of the monasteries had made objects of charity of the very monks and nuns who in an earlier age had been charged with the care of the poor. The flow of wealth from the New World to the Old had not proved an unmixed good, for the inflation of the currency by means of American gold and silver had greatly increased prices, while the abundant labor supply kept wages down. "If the people of this kingdom were numbered," declared one observer, "I am persuaded there were never more people, never less employment, never more idleness, never so much excesse. . . . The poor starve in the streets for want of labor." Such writers doubtless exaggerated greatly, but their opinions were used as arguments in favor of founding colonies. If the excess of English population could only be drawn off to other lands, those who remained behind need not fear for lack of work.

All such reasons, however, were secondary to the desire of merchant and government alike to promote English trade. Owing partly to the invigorating effect of gold and silver **Trade and trading companies** from the New World, English commerce had taken on new life. The well-to-do required now such luxuries as spices, sugar, and tea. They built ostentatious mansions for which they must have the costliest furnishings of the East. They paid high prices cheerfully, and merchants made good profits. Capital for commercial enterprise was thus easily amassed, and with seemingly sure profits ahead it became extremely venturesome. Dozens of trading companies were chartered by the government for the purpose of establishing commercial relations with some foreign region. Perhaps the most successful of these enterprises was the English East India Company, formed in 1600 to exploit the trade of India; but many others, such as the Levant Company, which built up a prosperous trade with the eastern Mediterranean, and the Muscovy Company, which dealt with Russia, paid handsome dividends. America seemed to furnish another such business opportunity, and companies were soon organized to make profits from the American trade.

The generous charters which trading companies received from the English crown reveal a kind of alliance between government and business that is not difficult to explain. The companies' ships left England with cargoes of English manufactures which they proposed to exchange for the raw materials of undeveloped regions. To the business man this meant merely profits; to the government, inspired as it was by the mercantilistic theory of the age, it meant security. According to the mercantilists, the chief measure of a country's strength was the amount of gold and silver it could amass. The trading companies, by exchanging expensive English manufactures for cheap raw materials, might be counted upon to produce for England a "favorable balance of trade," because of which a steady stream of precious metals would flow into the country. By just so much the strength of the nation would be increased. The urgent necessity of promoting national self-sufficiency was another reason why the government gave special privileges to trading companies. At a time when wars were regarded as the normal state of international affairs, and peace only an interlude between wars, each nation naturally aspired to be able to care for itself without dependence on any other. Indeed, economic dependence might easily lead to the loss of political independence.

To thoughtful English officials America seemed ideally fitted to become an independent national source of sup- **Need of a source of supply** ply. The Spanish had found abundant wealth in the New World, why should not also the English? One of Hakluyt's voyagers declared that "gold, silver, copper, leade, and pearls" were available in great quantities along the unsettled coasts of North America. With an independent supply of precious metals England would no longer be wholly at the mercy of a precarious balance of trade. Staple commodities, now purchased from rival nations, were also to be found in America. For naval stores England depended upon the Scandinavian countries, an unfortunate situation which might easily be remedied by the exploitation of the vast American forests. Potash, essential to the woolens industry, came likewise from Baltic lands, but this too might be obtained in America. English fishermen could supply only about one third of the national demand for fish, and the other two thirds had to be bought outside, mainly from the enterprising Dutch. Why should not English colonists in America draw upon the rich fisheries of the western Atlantic? Fisheries seemed particularly deserving of stimulation, for it was already a truism that fisheries and sea-power went hand in hand, and upon sea-power the safety of the English nation must depend. Whatever else England did not produce in sufficient quantity there seemed reason to hope that America could supply. Moreover, sailors still talked of a northwestern passageway around America to the Orient. If this should materialize, American establishments could serve also as halfway stations to the East, and an all-English route to the Orient would complete the emancipation of the English from any dangerous dependence upon their neighbors.

One other consideration weighed heavily in favor of colonies. England was rapidly becoming a nation of manu-facturers, and she was in need of expanding her markets. But other nations, in conformity with the popular doctrine of national self-sufficiency, raised up just such barriers against her exports as she also raised up against theirs. Clearly England needed independent markets, markets to which the trade of other nations should not be open, and why could these not be found in a colonial America? Even if the balance of trade occasionally went against England, which seemed unlikely, it would be English colonists who were enriched, not prospective enemies. Freedom of trade for the colonies was, of course, never considered. It was assumed that each colony would send its produce to the mother country, and would make all necessary purchases from English manufacturers.

Need of national markets

It is worth noting, however, that the English government, although deeply interested in having colonies founded, never seriously considered founding colonies itself. One reason for this was the fact that the government lacked the means for such undertakings; but far more important was the current conception of colonies as strictly commercial enterprises. Colony founding had to do with the expansion of trade and the making of profits, and so it was considered, for good reason, merely a type of business. The government, according to prevailing economic theories, might foster and regulate every type of business all it chose, but it must not engage in business. It might properly, in order to promote the general welfare, encourage private capital to seek profits from colony planting, but it could not plant colonies.

Why Englishmen, most of whom expected to remain in England, favored the founding of colonies in America is one thing; why certain Englishmen chose to become colonists is quite another. Doubtless the love of adventure, the false hope of gold, the need of a refuge from religious persecution, and the lack of employment at home all sent their quotas to America. But probably no other motive weighed so heavily as the desire for land. In England, and indeed throughout all Europe, land-holding was a test of gentility; ordinary people might not even hope to own land. In the New World land was equally open to all. The younger sons of nobles, left landless by the rule of primogeniture, turned to America for recompense; the peasants and artisans, destined if they stayed at home to remain what they were for life, saw in the colonies their only chance to become landed proprietors. Cheap land was the magnet which drew immigrants across the Atlantic to America, just as it was later to draw their descendants, step by step, across the continent.

The call of free land

Bibliography

On the geographic setting of American history, N. S. Shaler, "Physiography of North America," the introductory chapter in volume 4 of *Narrative and Critical History of America*, edited by Justin Winsor (8 vols., 1884–1889), is admirable. This series is an early, but still useful, cooperative project. The effect of the physical environment upon American history in general is sometimes somewhat overstressed in such books as Ellen C. Semple, *American History and its Geographic Conditions* (new ed., 1933); N. S. Shaler, *Nature and Man in America* (1891); A. P. Brigham, *Geographic Influences in American History* (1903); and R. H. Brown, *Historical Geography of the*

United States (1948). The sectional character of the North American continent is well portrayed in W. W. Atwood, *The Physiographic Provinces of North America* (1940); and in C. L. White and E. J. Foscue, *Regional Geography of Anglo-America* (1943). F. J. Turner, *The Frontier in American History* (1923), finds in the conquest of the continent a principal influence in the shaping of the American character, and W. P. Webb, *The Great Plains* (1931), shows how the pioneering process had to be modified when the farther West was reached. H. R. Muelder and D. M. Delo, *Years of This Land* (1943), is an entertaining effort to write a geographical history of the United States. George R. Stewart, *Names on the Land* (1945), draws into a fascinating historical narrative the origins of American place names.

Students should have easy access to a good historical atlas. Among those most generally available are: C. O. Paullin, *Atlas of the Historical Geography of the United States* (1932); J. T. Adams, *Atlas of American History* (1943); Clifford L. and Elizabeth H. Lord, *Historical Atlas of the United States* (1944); A. B. Hart and H. E. Bolton, *American History Atlas* (1949). R. V. Coleman, *The First Frontier* (1948) describes with the aid of maps and illustrations the earliest Atlantic penetrations.

A book of readings which includes the most important documentary sources of American history is also indispensable. Perhaps the best of these are *Documents of American History*, edited by Henry Steele Commager (5th ed., 1949); *The Shaping of the American Tradition*, edited by L. M. Hacker and Helène S. Zahler (1947); *Readings in American History*, Volume I, edited by R. L. Biesele (1952). But there are many others, among them: *Democracy, Liberty, and Property: Readings in the American Political Tradition*, edited by Francis W. Coker (1942); *Selected Readings in American History*, edited by T. C. Pease and A. S. Roberts (1940); *The Democratic Tradition in America*, edited by Col. C. E. Wheat (1943).

Indian society is well described in Livingston Farrand, *Basis of American History* (1904). This volume is the second of *The American Nation: A History*, edited by A. B. Hart. The twenty-eight volumes of this series are still unsurpassed as a general history of the United States. Of merit also is Ellsworth Huntington, *The Red Man's Continent* (1919), which is the first of a set of fifty-six entertaining volumes, *The Chronicles of America*, edited by Allen Johnson.

The circumstances which led to the discovery of America are admirably set forth in many books on medieval history, such for example, as G. C. Sellery, *The Renaissance, its Nature and Origins* (1950); G. C. Sellery and A. C. Krey, *Medieval Foundations of Western Civilization* (1929); Carl Stephenson, *Medieval History* (1943); and Lynn Thorndike, *The History of Medieval Europe* (3d ed., 1949).

On the baffling problem of the Norsemen in America, see A. M. Reeves, *The Finding of Wineland the Good* (1890); H. Hermannsson, *The Problem of Wineland* (1936); W. Hovgaard, *The Voyages of the Norsemen to America* (1914). H. R. Holand, *The Kensington Stone* (1932), and by the same author, *Westward from Vinland* (1940), accept the inscriptions on the Kensington Rune Stone as valid, but Milo M. Quaife, "The Myth of the Kensington Rune Stone," *New England Quarterly*, 7:613–645 (1934), takes the opposite point of view.

The best biography of Columbus is Samuel E. Morison, *Admiral of the Ocean Sea* (2 vols., 1942). Henry Vignaud, *Toscanelli and Columbus* (1902) maintains with much learning that the famous Toscanelli letter, which was supposed to have motivated Columbus, was a forgery. E. P. Cheyney, *European Background of American History* (1904), treats every important phase of the subject, and E. G. Bourne, *Spain in America* (1904), covers in detail Spain's activities in the New World.

An excellent account of explorations in America is in the first volume of Edward Channing, *A History of the United States* (6 vols., 1905–30). Channing's six volumes, constituting as they do an admirable synthesis of all the critical scholarship available at the time they were written, are indispensable to the serious student. William C. H. Wood, *Elizabethan Sea-Dogs* (1918), gives a sprightly account of the earliest English adventurers. Non-English white penetration of the continent is the theme of H. I. Priestley, *The Coming of the White Man* (1929). This is the first of a series which now runs to thirteen volumes, *A History of American Life*, edited by A. M. Schlesinger and D. R. Fox. The purpose of the series, admirably fulfilled, is to survey the non-political activities of the American people. Carl L. Becker, *Beginnings of the American People* (1915), contains an unusually perspicacious account of the partition of the New World.

2
Virginia and New England

Gilbert and Raleigh — The Virginia Companies —
The Jamestown Colony — The Pilgrims and the Puritans — The Plymouth Colony — The Company for
Massachusetts Bay — The Great Migration — Puritan
intolerance — The Beginnings of Rhode Island — Connecticut — New Haven — New Hampshire and Maine
— The New England Confederation

Two early colonial ventures which failed made it evident to Englishmen that the **Gilbert and Raleigh** exploitation of America was not to be undertaken lightly. In 1578 Sir Humphrey Gilbert was authorized by Queen Elizabeth to hold and govern such lands in America, not already appropriated, as he might choose to colonize. Gilbert was one of those who believed in the existence of a northwest passage, and his goal was an American colony on the way to Asia. But his first expedition was defeated by the Spanish, who were as yet unhumbled, and his second, bound for the inhospitable shores of Newfoundland, was defeated by a storm. Gilbert's efforts were followed up by his half-brother, Sir Walter Raleigh, who secured a new charter in 1584, and after some preliminary investigations decided to plant a colony along the reputedly rich shores farther to the south, which Elizabeth, the Virgin Queen, now chose to call Virginia. During the next few years Raleigh wasted his fortune on the project. The colony which he had intended to locate in the vicinity of Chesapeake Bay was by a series of blunders established instead on Roanoke Island, an unfavored site from which the colonists fled to the mainland only to lose their lives to the Indians. The ill-fated experiments of Gilbert and Raleigh showed, among other things, that the private resources of any one

man were likely to prove inadequate for the financing of so great a venture. Raleigh realized this himself, and in 1589 he organized a company of "Associates" to carry on the work; but he soon lost favor with the Queen, and when in 1603 he was convicted of treason his rights in America were annulled.

The profits of trading companies designed to exploit regions other than America were so good, however, that a group **The** of investors was soon formed to **Virginia** begin where Raleigh had left off. **Companies** If the initial difficulties could only be overcome, why should not a Virginia company prove to be the success that the East India Company, for example, had become? Investors in that enterprise were said to have realized profits in a single year equal to the principal they had risked. Accordingly, in 1606, King James I, who had succeeded Elizabeth on the English throne, was persuaded to issue a charter to some London and Plymouth merchants who had in mind the establishment of new outposts of trade in Virginia. By the terms of this charter the stockholders were subdivided into two companies, the London Company (whose coat of arms appears at the head of this chapter) and the Plymouth Company, each of which was promised a tract of land along the Virginia coast a hundred miles in width and extending a hundred miles into the interior. The charter stipulated further that the land of the London Company should be located somewhere between the thirty-fourth and the forty-first parallels, while the land of the Plymouth Company should lie farther north, between the thirty-eighth and the forty-fifth parallels. Neither company might establish a colony within one hundred miles of any colony established by the other.

The London merchants were the first to take advantage of this grant. In December, 1606, they sent out three shiploads of colonists, who the next spring founded Jamestown at a point thirty miles inland from the mouth of the James River. Thereafter for seventeen years the Company continued to send a steady stream of colonists and supplies to Virginia. Of profits there were none, but the stockholders hopefully invested in the project a sum which today would be reckoned at not less than five million dollars.

The mortality among the early colonists was frightful. Out of the one hundred and **The James-** four adventurers who reached **town colony** Virginia in the spring of 1607, only thirty-eight were alive that fall, and for many years one half to two thirds of any given lot of immigrants were doomed to death within a few months from the date of their arrival. Captain John Smith, one of the world's most picturesque characters, stands out in these early years as the man who, more than any other, furnished the common sense that saved the little colony from extinction; but as late as 1616, by which time over sixteen hundred emigrants had left England for Virginia, the population of the colony was only about three hundred and fifty. In spite of the unfavorable odds, however, including an Indian outbreak in 1622 which took a heavy toll, the number of Virginians grew, and by 1624 there were probably as many as twelve hundred people in the colony.

During these years the Virginia experiment was carried on as a strictly business enterprise. The local managers, or "governors," acted as agents for the company

John Smith, explorer and writer, published in 1616 a Map of New England, on which this cartouche appeared.

and directed the work of the company "servants," who constituted the great majority of the settlers. These servants had often been paupers or convicts in England. They came to Virginia under "indentures" or contracts which bound them to work for the company from four to seven years in return for their passage across the Atlantic and the prospect of receiving a small tract of land when their term of service came to an end. Such supplies as were brought from England and such provisions as the plantations themselves produced were kept in common storehouses, and were doled out to the settlers as needed. Almost from the first a few commodities, such as lumber, dyestuffs, and sassafras, were sent back to England in the company's ships to help pay expenses; but it was not until tobacco culture became the chief business of the colony that much was produced worth shipping away. Towards the end of the company's rule

Land Grants by Virginia Charters

several innovations, designed in part to keep the colonists contented and in part to attract new settlers, were introduced. (1) The right to private ownership of land was conceded, and liberal grants were made to indentured servants whose period of service had expired, and to all freemen. (2) The harsh laws deemed necessary during the first hard years of the colony were abrogated; and (3) a representative assembly "freely elected by the inhabitants," to consist of two representatives from each "plantation," was authorized to share in the making of the laws.

For a time the affairs of the infant colony aroused much interest in England, and many **Charter revisions** prominent men bought stock in the venture. In order to increase the power of the company and to enlarge its territory, the original charter of 1606 was twice revised, once in 1609 and again in 1612. The new land grant was especially generous, for it gave the company a frontage along the coast of two hundred miles north and two hundred miles south of Old Point Comfort, while inland the company's rights were to extend "west and northwest" from sea to sea. Unfortunately King James I regretted the liberal powers of government he had permitted the company to exercise, and he especially disliked the concessions to

popular rule that it had made. He accordingly obtained in 1624 from a subservient court an annulment of the charter. All governmental rights now devolved upon the King, and Virginia became a royal colony. By this change the Virginians lost the help they had been accustomed to receive from the London Company, but they were permitted to retain their land titles, and, after some hesitation on the part of the King, their representative assembly. As for the investments made by stockholders in the company, they were a total loss.

The success of tobacco culture was what enabled the Virginia colony to survive. When the Jamestown settlement **Tobacco** was made, the use of tobacco **culture** was already known in Europe, but the tobacco Europeans first learned to like came from the Spanish colonies in America. Virginia tobacco was regarded as inferior and undesirable until about 1616, when a new method of curing it was discovered. From this time on the Jamestown colonists had a product that would yield them a profit, and the colony soon began to prosper. Land was easy to obtain under the so-called "headright" system, by which each immigrant and each person who paid for an immigrant's passage received fifty acres. The more prosperous planters came to own many headrights, and even in the seventeenth century the tendency toward large plantations was already marked.

The prosperity of the colony was reflected in the rapid increase of its population during the middle decades of the seven- **The labor** teenth century. Many new- **problem in** comers came in response to an **Virginia** insistent demand for more labor. Tobacco planters who could afford to do so imported indentured servants, of whom some had criminal records, but most were merely poor or unfortunate. English children of the lower classes were sometimes kidnaped and sold into servitude, and frequently political prisoners were sold under indenture. The indentured servants in due time became free, obtained plots of land along the western fringe of settlement, and shared with other citizens whatever prosperity the New World had to offer. Beginning in 1619, Negroes were brought into the colony, either as servants or as slaves, although the number of such persons in early Virginia was very small. Unlike the white indentured servants, the Negroes could not be easily assimilated into the free population, and their status, if, indeed, it was ever anything less, passed quickly from servitude to slavery. Ultimately their presence produced a problem that led to the American Civil War. During the middle decades of the seventeenth century war broke out in England between the adherents of the King, or "Cavaliers," and the supporters of Parliament, or "Roundheads." When in 1649 the "Roundheads" triumphed and executed the King, Charles I, many "Cavaliers" sought safety in Virginia. By 1652 the population of the colony was estimated at twenty thousand.

The Civil War in England was not without its repercussions in Virginia. Sir William **Bacon's** Berkeley, who served as gover-**Rebellion** nor of the colony from 1642 to 1677, was a strong partisan of the King, and after 1660, when Charles II was restored to the English throne, sought to set rigid limits on popular rule. Berkeley's favoritism for the eastern planters, coupled with an extreme indifference for the welfare of the common people, particularly those who lived at some distance from the seaboard, aroused much criticism, and his failure to deal firmly with an Indian disturbance along the frontier led to open revolt. The leader of this movement was Nathaniel Bacon, a well-born and Cambridge-educated young English emigrant, who in 1676, without authority from the governor, put himself at the head of an expedition which adequately chastised the savages. Berkeley was outraged at this act of insubordination, but the temper of the public was such that he feared to punish Bacon, and felt obliged to call for long-overdue legislative elections. To the governor's chagrin, Bacon was chosen as the representative of an interior constituency, and became

the leading spirit in the new assembly. This body, after authorizing many reforms obnoxious to Berkeley, voted to send Bacon on another expedition against the Indians, a project which Berkeley approved only with the greatest reluctance. While his opponent was away on this mission, however, the governor raised an army against him, so that on his return Bacon found himself obliged to lay seige to the city of Jamestown. The seige was successful, Berkeley fled across the Chesapeake, and Jamestown was burned. But at the very moment of victory Bacon fell sick and died. Deprived of their leader, the rebels were no match for the irate governor, who took bloody vengeance, and, according to Charles II, "hanged more men in that naked country than I have done for the murder of my father." As a result of these excesses Berkeley in 1677 was recalled to England in disgrace, and conditions in Virginia gradually became normal. Bacon's efforts, a hundred years before the Revolution, "to establish a real democracy in place of the rule of the planter aristocracy" failed to achieve their objective, but this rebellion served notice on English officials that tyranny was as certain to provoke revolt from Englishmen overseas as from Englishmen at home.

The next successful English experiment in colony planting was at Plymouth, on the coast of what later became **The English** Massachusetts. Here the re- **dissenters** ligious motive undoubtedly assumed commanding importance. The church establishment which had been worked out in England under Queen Elizabeth occupied a place midway between extreme Catholicism and extreme Protestantism. All connections with Rome were severed, the sacraments were reduced in number, services in Latin were discontinued, and the head of the state became the head of the church; but many of the old forms of Catholicism, such as the vestments of the clergy, the elaborate ritual of worship, and the hierarchy of priests, bishops, and archbishops, were retained. Inevitably many Englishmen were dissatisfied

"THEIR MANNER OF GETTING GOLD FROM THE RIVERS."
Engraving by Theodore de Bry, 1590.

ADVERTISING FOR
SETTLERS, 1609.

Life in America, as dreamed about by prospective colonists, and as it actually was, presented striking contrasts. English adventurers, remembering all too well the success of the Spanish quest for gold, long held to the hope that they, too, would thus find wealth. Planters in search of colonists told tall tales of the riches of the New World and the ease of passage to it. But the harsh realities may be better judged from the appearance of this early New England housing project.

"ENGLISH WIGWAMS." Indian style shelters at the Massachusetts Bay Colony, 1636, reconstructed at Salem.

with these halfway measures and wished to go further in the direction of Protestantism. Of these "dissenters," some, known as "Puritans," desired only to reform the existing English church in such a way as to bring it into closer harmony with the teachings of John Calvin; others, less numerous and influential, were called "Separatists" because they were ready to sever all connections with the established church. Neither group was seriously persecuted during the reign of James I, but there was enough threat of persecution to make all dissenters uneasy. A little band of Separatists from Scrooby,

England, furnished the nucleus for the Plymouth settlement. They went first from England to Holland and later, in 1620, some of them, after returning to England, set sail in the *Mayflower* for America. Not all who went to Holland came to America, and not all of those who came to America had been in Holland. Indeed, when the *Mayflower* set sail from England, about half its passengers had never been outside their country before.

If the religious motive was the dominant thing in inducing these "Pilgrims," as they have usually been called, to emigrate to America, it is equally true that their

TRADING WITH THE INDIANS. Representational illustration, 1722.

THE JAMESTOWN MASSACRE, 1622. Unauthenticated view engraved by Theodore de Bry, 1634.

AN ENGLISH MUSKETMAN. Illustration in a manual of arms, 1637.

Rest your Musket.

Indian relations were not always as cordial as they might have been. According to an ancient saw, the colonists first fell upon their knees, and then upon the aborigines. Indian attacks upon the whites were rarely unprovoked. Sometimes, as in the case of the Jamestown massacre of 1622, the whites got the worst of it, but usually their use of firearms and armor gave them a decided advantage. Traders tended to get along better with the Indians than settlers, for the traders rarely wished to take from the Indians their lands and hunting grounds.

The Pilgrims journey to the New World was made possible by capitalists who hoped for profits from the enterprise. An unincorporated joint-stock company was formed, in which both emigrants and investors held stock. Each person over sixteen who emigrated was the recipient of one share of stock valued at ten pounds, and he might buy additional stock if he chose. The greater part of the capital, however, was furnished by some London merchants. In the interest of the investors it was stipulated that the emigrants must work for a period of seven years as the servants of the company. During this time whatever they produced was to go into a common warehouse, and their needs likewise were to be met out of supplies held in common. A complete settlement was to be made at the end of the seven years, by which time, it was hoped, the colonists would be able to discharge their debts with interest.

On December 21, 1620, the *Mayflower* landed an exploring expedition at Plymouth harbor. Anticipating difficulty **The** in controlling the action of some **"Mayflower** of the more turbulent members **Compact"** of the group, the Pilgrim "Fathers," or at least forty-one of them, affixed their signa tures while still on shipboard to the famous "Mayflower Compact," by which they bound themselves together into a "civil body politic" for their "better ordering and preservation." They chose John Carver as their first governor, and as a pure democracy faced the unknown trials of the New World. The first winter took a toll in dead of over half the company, but the survivors stayed on, and with the help of a few more immigrants they were able to found an enduring settlement. Farming, fur-trading, fishing, and lumbering furnished their chief occupations. In 1627 the heavy debt still owing to the London merchants was taken over by a few of the Pilgrim leaders, and was ultimately paid off from the profits of the fur trade. In 1628, with the London merchants now entirely excluded from the enterprise, the Pilgrims divided up their moveable property and voted to each colonist for private ownership twenty acres of land.

The title of the Plymouth colony to the land it had occupied was for some time **The Plym-** clouded. The Pilgrims had per- **outh colony** mission from the London (or Virginia) Company to settle within the borders of its grant, but the *Mayflower* was blown out of its course and the location at Plymouth Bay was accepted almost of neces-

Massachusetts, Rhode Island and Connecticut Settlements
----- *Plymouth Colony, 1630*
----- *Present boundaries*

sity. This site lay within the territory granted to the original Plymouth Company, which, after an unsuccessful effort in 1607 to plant a colony on the coast of Maine, had practically ceased to function. Reorganized in 1620 as the New England Council, with a sea-to-sea grant, the Plymouth Company stood ready to hand over to the Pilgrims the land they coveted. In 1630 William Bradford, who had succeeded Carver as governor of Plymouth, obtained title as trustee for the colony to the land about Plymouth Bay, and when finally in 1641 the debts owing to the London merchants were fully paid, the governor formally transferred to the people the rights he had acquired.

The government of the Plymouth colony was extremely simple. At first all the men who signed the Mayflower Compact, meeting together as an assembly, chose the governor, made the laws, and ad- **Democracy** mitted such newcomers as they **at Plymouth** saw fit (in practice nearly all) to the full privileges of citizenship. Later, as the number of separate settlements grew, a representative assembly, or "General Court," was instituted to take care of matters pertaining to the whole colony, while local affairs were left to "town meetings." All efforts to secure royal approval of these governmental privileges through a charter failed, so the Pilgrims and their successors were left to govern themselves as a self-constituted commonwealth until 1691, when William III arbitrarily joined their colony to that of Massachusetts Bay. The Plymouth colony was never large — at the time it was annexed to Massachusetts its population numbered only about seven thousand — but it played a significant rôle in pointing for other dissenters the way to the New World.

Chief among those to follow the example of the Pilgrims were the founders of the colony of Massachusetts Bay. These **The English** were Puritans rather than Sep- **Puritans** aratists, but under King Charles I, who in 1625 succeeded James I on the throne of England, they had reason to believe that the "purification" of the English church was a vain hope. With the King's consent Archbishop Laud prosecuted dissenters vigorously, deprived Puritan pastors of their parishes, and showed himself in complete sympathy with the "high-church" party. The Puritans fought back with spirit. They knew that the issue between them and the King went deeper than religion. Their leaders were well-to-do members of the middle class, men who aspired to places of influence in the government, and who were unwilling to submit any longer to the unfair taxes and other discriminations that the King, supported by the landed gentry, was accustomed to place upon their class. When the Puritans succeeded in winning a majority of the House of Commons, it appeared for the moment that they, and not the King, would have their way. But the King boldly dissolved Parliament, arrested the Puritan leaders, and entered upon a period of personal rule that lasted from 1629 to 1640. During these years he levied taxes arbitrarily, and encouraged Laud to deal more harshly than ever with the dissenters, for whom now the situation became intolerable.

Persecution stirred many of the Puritans to armed revolt, and at length under the **Massachusetts-Bay Company** leadership of Oliver Cromwell the "Roundheads" defeated the King; but in the meantime many others, despairing of England as a fit home for freemen, turned their eyes to America. It chanced that the way for a great migration had already been prepared. A group of English merchants, some of whom were Puritans, had been attracted by the possibilities of the New England fisheries, and in 1628 had obtained from the New England Council title to all land lying between the Charles and the Merrimac Rivers. Next year this "Company for Massachusetts-Bay" obtained a charter from the King which confirmed the grant of land, and authorized the company to exercise the usual governmental privileges over settlers. Two expeditions, one in 1628 and another in 1629, established Salem as a village of several hundred settlers with John Endicott, a well-

John Winthrop, great Puritan statesman, also provided posterity with a *Journal*, much used as an historical source.

known Puritan, as the civil head of the community, and Francis Higginson, a Puritan minister, as the chief religious leader. Here was the nucleus for a Puritan commonwealth in the New World. If Plymouth could succeed under the Separatists, why could not Salem, and perhaps many other villages also, under the Puritans?

The Puritan leaders laid their plans carefully. They wished to establish in the New World an ideal Puritan commonwealth where a really "purified" church might thrive. The government **The "Great Migration"** of the new colony must, therefore, be wholly in their hands. If they could secure complete control of the "Company for Massachusetts-Bay," and could take its charter with them to America, what better means could they ask for the accomplishment of their purpose? The scheme worked out as planned. A majority of the stockholders in the company voted to send its charter to America, and those who wished to stay at home sold out to those who wished to go. In October, 1629, the able and prominent John Winthrop was elected governor of the company, and next year, taking the charter with him, he led the vanguard of the migration.

Before the summer of 1630 was done, seventeen ships had landed a thousand settlers in Massachusetts, and several villages, among them Boston, Dorchester, Watertown, and Roxbury, had been founded. Thereafter, as the troublous times continued in England, other emigrants came also, until by the year 1640 no less than twenty-five thousand refugees had found their way to Massachusetts. About that time the tide of battle began to turn against the King in England, and the "Great Migration" came to a close.

In spite of the steady flow of immigrants, it was no easy matter for the Puritans to **Suffering of** make their colony a success. As **the colonists** in Virginia and Plymouth, the percentage of deaths among the newcomers, especially during the early years of the migration, was alarmingly high. Life on the New England frontier turned out to be a bitter struggle against unyielding soils, cruel winters, ever-recurring disease, and constant privation. Hundreds of the faint-hearted returned to England at the first opportunity. And in spite of the Puritan saying that "God hath sifted a nation, that he might send choice grain into this wilderness," not all of those who stayed comported themselves well. In general, however, the seed was good. Most of the immigrants were uneducated farmers or humble artisans, but they were ready to make the best of their new environment, and they were ably led.

Soon the evidences of a less primitive society could be observed. Livestock was imported and bred; mills to grind the grain, brick kilns and sawmills to produce better building materials, and even ironworks to turn out a few household necessities began to appear. Trade with England came about naturally, for the colonists were quick to discover that with such articles as fish, furs, lumber, and potash to exchange, they could obtain from the mother country some of the many things for which they stood in need.

As for government, the Puritan leaders had little difficulty in making over the charter of the Company for Massachusetts-Bay into the kind of constitution they wanted.

All power, according to the charter, rested with the stockholders, or "free- **Puritan** men," who were authorized to **government** elect as a kind of board of directors a governor, a deputy governor, and eighteen "assistants"; also to meet four times each year to admit new freemen, elect new officers, and pass such regulations for the government of the company as they saw fit. Only twelve freemen had come to America, and every one of them, as governor, deputy governor, or assistant, was an officer of the company. This group, by neglecting to choose new freemen, at first kept all authority in its hands, but such arbitrary procedure did not long escape criticism. In the fall of 1630 one hundred and nine of the settlers asked to be made freemen of the corporation, and the ruling officers did not dare to refuse so reasonable a request. They maintained, however, that the sole privilege of the freemen was to vote for new assistants whenever vacancies should occur, and that all real authority lay with the assistants, who might hold office during good behavior, choose the governor and deputy governor, and make all the laws. Such an interpretation of the charter was wholly unwarranted, but the deception was not discovered for several years. Thus the Puritan leaders still kept in their own hands the direction of the colony's affairs.

Their avowed purpose was "to build a City of God on earth." What such a city should be like they determined **Church and** from the teachings of John Cal- **state** vin, from much reading of the Bible, and from their experience in the New World. On leaving England they had regarded themselves as members of the English church, the doctrines and practices of which they had merely sought to purify. But on establishing themselves in America they were content to become as definitely Separatists as the Pilgrims in Plymouth. They soon refused to recognize Church of England ministers as duly ordained, and they referred theological disputes to their own ministers sitting together as synods. They held that the church must set up standards of conduct as well as principles of theology, and they branded anything that savored of lightness or frivolity as a sin. Moreover, they had no intention whatever of tolerating views and practices in conflict with their own ideas. As they saw it, one of the first responsibilities of government was to punish all departures from orthodoxy in theology or from propriety in behavior. Laws were passed to make the way of the transgressor hard, and the worst offenders were punished by expulsion from the colony. Church and state worked together, each to uphold the other, the state sustaining the decisions of the church, and the church proclaiming through its ministers the supremacy of the state. Early Massachusetts was not a democracy; it was an aristocratic theocracy.

The attempt of the governing few to ignore the great majority of the settlers in **Democratic** matters of state was not wholly **reforms** successful. In 1632 the freemen of the corporation boldly took into their own hands the election of the governor and assistants, and voted that each town should choose two representatives to act with the assistants in the levying of taxes. In 1634, just before the spring meeting of the General Court, a committee consisting of two men from each of the eight towns in the colony demanded of Governor Winthrop that they be permitted to see the charter. Winthrop reluctantly consented, and the committee discovered that the law-making power was in reality vested in the freemen and not in the assistants. Thereafter each town chose delegates to meet with the assistants and to participate, not only in the levying of taxes, but in the making of all the laws. Moreover, at the first opportunity the newly constituted General Court ousted Winthrop from the governorship, fined some of the assistants for abuse of power, and in other ways showed its determination to play an important part in the government. But the colony was still far less than a democracy. The number of freemen admitted to the corporation was cautiously restrained, only church members

being deemed eligible, and not all of them being chosen. Since the deference of the common people for ministers and magistrates was so strong, the will of the leaders was rarely contested. Even Winthrop was soon recalled to the governorship by the very freemen whose rights in the government he had once curtailed. Ultimately, following the precedent of the English Parliament, the Massachusetts General Court divided into two houses, one composed of representatives from the various towns, and the other composed of the assistants, who together with the governor were chosen annually by the votes of the freemen.

The intolerance of the Massachusetts government in all matters of belief and conduct provoked some irritation. Deportations for religious offenses were numerous, and harsh punishments were laid upon those who failed by ever so slight a margin to conform to the strict Puritan standards. The careers of Roger Williams and Anne Hutchinson, both of whom challenged the accepted order, serve to illustrate two facts, first, that dissent in Massachusetts Bay did exist, and second, that the dissenters usually lost in their conflicts with the ruling caste.

Roger Williams was a godly but disputatious minister who came from England in 1631, and after short stays at **Roger** Boston and Plymouth became **Williams** the pastor at Salem. He soon startled the authorities by declaring that the state had no right to punish an individual for his personal habits and opinions. If a man did wrong to his fellowmen, then, according to Williams, the state should punish him; but if a man merely held uncommon religious views, or departed from the customary practice in a small matter like Sabbath-breaking, then his offense was no affair of the state. Williams's doctrine was really revolutionary, for if carried to its logical conclusion it would have withdrawn the power of the state from the support of the church and would have wrecked the whole Puritan experiment. Accordingly the General Court voted in 1635 to expel him from the colony. The sentence

Roger Williams and *Anne Hutchinson* professed opinions that the intolerant Puritan leaders of Massachusetts Bay would not brook. But driving out these heretics served only to promote the establishment of thriving liberal centers in nearby Rhode Island.

required his return to England, but he escaped to the Narragansett Indians, with whom he spent the winter, and next spring with the help of a few adherents he began the settlement on Narragansett Bay that developed into Providence, Rhode Island.

Anne Hutchinson, according to John Winthrop, was "a woman of a ready wit and a bold spirit" who "brought over with her two dangerous errors." Just what these errors were, or the "many branches" that grew from them, would mean little to a non-theological age, but among other things she insisted that some ministers were definitely superior to others because they were under a "covenant of grace" rather than merely a "covenant of works." Roger Williams had comparatively few followers, but Anne Hutchinson attracted by her eloquent and logical arguments many adherents, among them young Henry Vane, governor of the colony, John Wheelwright, a prominent minister, and a large majority of the Boston congregation. Soon the colony was in an uproar over her teachings, although, except in Boston, her

Anne Hutchinson

doctrines were far more opposed than favored. Faced by this critical situation, the conservatives acted promptly and drastically. They removed Vane from the governorship and replaced him with the more dependable Winthrop; then they brought Mrs. Hutchinson and Wheelwright to trial before the General Court. The verdict of the Court stated succinctly the Puritan theory of intolerance, that "two so opposite parties could not contain in the same body without hazard of ruin to the whole," and banished the offenders from the colony. Some of those who believed in Mrs. Hutchinson's teachings recanted, but many others were compelled to leave. Mrs. Hutchinson, accompanied by a group of her sympathizers, founded a settlement at Portsmouth (1638), near Roger Williams's town of Providence, and also within the borders of what later became Rhode Island.

These are by no means the only instances of persecution within the Massachusetts Bay colony. The air was full of intolerance. The attitude of the Puritan leaders toward heretics was not unlike the attitude of present-day health officers toward the carriers of **Religious intolerance** contagious diseases. For the safety of the state the contaminated must be placed where they would have no power to do harm. Two Quaker women who came to Boston in 1656 were promptly deported. When other offenders of the same sect insisted on entering the colony and even on returning to it after having once been sent away, four offenders were actually executed. The harshness of this penalty gave some offense, however, and in 1661 the General Court, in a spirit of moderation, provided that unwelcome Quakers should merely be tied to a cart and whipped from town to town until they had passed the borders of the colony.

Just as religious intolerance in England had a part in bringing settlers to Massachusetts, so religious intolerance in **Beginnings of Rhode Island** Massachusetts helped along the formation of colonies elsewhere in New England. Rhode Island is the most striking case in point. At Providence Roger Williams and his followers, after purchasing land from the Indians, instituted a secular government which left the individual free in religious matters to follow the dictates of his conscience. At Portsmouth Anne Hutchinson's adherents took the Bible as their guide of life and conduct, but disagreed on so many minor matters that a group of "come-outers" soon established themselves at Newport (1639). A fourth Rhode Island settlement at Warwick (1643) was the work of Samuel Gorton, a refugee from Massachusetts whose views were so heretical that even the liberal-minded Williams refused to permit him to settle permanently at Providence.

The four Rhode Island communities wasted little love on one another, but their common fear of Massachusetts, whose leaders deeply resented such near-by nests of heretics, drew them together. In 1644 Roger Williams secured from the English Parliament a "patent" which permitted the settlers on Narragansett Bay to govern themselves so long as their laws were in harmony with the laws of England; and in 1647 repre-

sentatives from the various Rhode Island towns organized a political system not unlike that of Massachusetts. Church membership was not a qualification for voting, however, and the right of religious liberty was definitely safeguarded, "notwithstanding our different consciences touching the truth as it is in Jesus." In 1663 a formal charter was secured from King Charles II in which the Rhode Island system of representative government was accorded full approval, and the Rhode Island principle of "liberty in religious concernments" was definitely accepted.

The "soul liberty" for which Rhode Island stood was not without its disadvantages. The colony soon came to be known as a paradise for **"Soul liberty"** "cranks," and a "dumping ground for the disorderly and eccentric elements" of all New England. Roger Williams admitted that if heretics disturbed the peace they might be punished for it, but he maintained steadfastly that the state had no right to "punish any for declaring by words their minds concerning the ways and things of God." Many protests came from Massachusetts against the way in which heretics from Rhode Island passed the borders of their own colony to preach heresy in orthodox lands, but in spite of all such obstacles Williams and his associates held out tenaciously for tolerance.

Meanwhile, out in the lower Connecticut Valley, another offshoot from the Massachusetts Bay colony had appeared. Fertile lands had more **Beginnings of Connecticut** to do with the founding of Connecticut than religious dissensions. The soil around Massachusetts Bay was hard to work and the harvests were not copious; hence, tales of better lands to the southwest made a strong appeal. Thomas Hooker, minister at Newtown (later Cambridge), and John Haynes, a former governor, were the chief promoters of the Connecticut project. Neither could be branded as a heretic, although Hooker was mildly liberal in his views and somewhat disgruntled with the aristocratic character of the Massachusetts government. But he was not forced to leave. Indeed, the Massachusetts authorities considered forbidding the migration to Connecticut, and in the end they consented to it only with great reluctance.

In the years 1635 and 1636 about eight hundred settlers from Newtown, Watertown, and Dorchester pushed through the forests to the Connecticut Valley. They knew that the Dutch claimed this region, and that they themselves had no legal title whatever to it, but they unhesitatingly took possession of the land they wanted and founded three towns, Hartford, Wethersfield, and Windsor. Some settlers from Plymouth had already established a trading-post not far from the site of Hartford, and some Puritans from England, acting under a grant of land from the Council of New England, had sent over a small force under John Winthrop, Jr., son of the Massachusetts governor, to found a colony at the mouth of the Connecticut River. Here Winthrop, in spite of threats from the Dutch, erected Fort Saybrook. Another settlement in the Connecticut Valley was made at Springfield by a Roxbury congregation, but the site was discovered later to be within the jurisdiction of Massachusetts.

Progress towards the establishment of an orderly government for the Connecticut River towns was rapid. In 1639 **The "Fundamental Orders"** representatives from Hartford, Wethersfield, and Windsor met at Hartford to draw up a plan of union. The result was the Fundamental Orders of Connecticut, a document usually regarded as the first constitution to be written in America. The Fundamental Orders copied the governmental practices of Massachusetts, although the prerogatives of officials were somewhat more limited. The governor for example, had no veto, he was ineligible for re-election, and he might not arbitrarily dissolve the General Court or prevent it from meeting when it so desired. As far as the relations between church and state were concerned, the Massachusetts system was deemed satisfactory. The Orders stated plainly that "the discipline of the Churches, which according to the truth of the said gospel is now practiced amongst us," must be maintained.

Meanwhile on Long Island Sound another Puritan colony, New Haven, was in process of evolution. Its founders were **The New Haven colony** John Davenport, an English Puritan minister, and Theophilus Eaton, a well-to-do English Puritan merchant. These men visited Massachusetts in 1637, but decided to found an ideal Bible commonwealth and trading center outside the confines of any existing colony. At New Haven their dreams of commercial success failed to materialize, but with their small settlement as a beginning several other towns, Guilford, Milford, and Stamford, were soon founded. In government and religion the New Haven colony, like Connecticut, repeated with slight variations the Massachusetts experiment; indeed, no other colony was more circumspect in its Puritanism than early New Haven. Its separate existence came to an end in 1662 when the English King, Charles II, was induced, mainly through the efforts of John Winthrop, Jr., to unite the Connecticut River towns and New Haven into the one colony of Connecticut under a liberal charter. Probably the ease with which both Rhode Island and Connecticut obtained their charters of self-government was due to the dislike Charles II felt for the Puritans of Massachusetts, whose whole-hearted opposition to his father, Charles I, was almost equaled in intensity by their distaste for other colonial establishments in New England. Charles II wasted little sympathy on the people of Rhode Island or Connecticut, but he enjoyed the discomfiture that his recognition of their rights gave the Massachusetts Puritans.

The secessions from Massachusetts to the southwest, which furnished the main impetus for the founding of Rhode Island **New Hampshire and Maine** and Connecticut, were matched by similar movements toward the north into the regions known as New Hampshire and Maine. Here, however, settlers from Massachusetts were by no means the first on the ground. In 1623 two English gentlemen, Sir Ferdinando Gorges and Captain John Mason, had obtained from the New England Council a patent to all the land lying between the Kennebec and the Merrimac Rivers. They first called their grant Laconia, but presently, on determining to divide it between them, Mason took the western half and called it New Hampshire, while Gorges took the territory along the coast and called it Maine. Both men tried to establish settlements within the confines of their grants, but their successes were slight. Some trading-posts were founded, such as Portsmouth, Kittery, Dover, Exeter, and York, which eventually developed into towns, but most of these settlements owed nothing to the efforts of either Mason or Gorges; nor were these proprietors, as they styled themselves, able to maintain their control in the face of the steady influx of settlers from Massachusetts. These newcomers were exceedingly reluctant to acknowledge any other authority than that of the Puritan commonwealth in which they had lived, and finally the Massachusetts government, on the pretext that its land grant really entitled it to do so, extended its authority first over the New Hampshire towns, and finally over those in Maine. New Hampshire remained a part of Massachusetts until 1679, when Charles II made it a separate royal colony, but Maine was not accorded a separate existence until by the well-known Compromise of 1820 it became a state in the Union.

The advance of the New England frontier brought on at an early date trouble with **Indian difficulties** the Indians, particularly the Pequots, whose holdings were seriously jeopardized by the founding of Connecticut. Attacks on isolated settlers resulted in a general Indian war, during which the Massachusetts colony gave valuable aid to the Connecticut pioneers. It is a striking fact that the Protestant English, unlike the Catholic Spanish and French, showed little interest in the souls of the Indians. Englishmen in England often

Maine, Vermont and New Hampshire Settlements 1620 - 1681
---- Present boundaries

dreamed that the founding of colonies in the New World would lead to the conversion of the heathen, but Englishmen in America, although deeply enough interested in their own salvation, rarely showed much missionary zeal towards the Indians. Instead, they made whatever efforts were necessary to dispossess the Indians of their lands, and in this respect the methods of the Puritans were as ruthless as any on record. By 1637, for example, most of the offending Pequots were either dead or enslaved.

The Indian menace, coupled with the thinly veiled hostility of the Dutch in New York and the French in Canada, **New England Confederation** aroused the New England leaders to the necessity of combining their forces, and as a result the New England Confederation, consisting of Massachusetts, Plymouth, Connecticut, and New Haven, was formed in 1643. Two commissioners from each of the four colonies were entrusted with the management of the common business, which was restricted in the main to matters of military defense; but the Articles mentioned also the desirability of protecting common religious interests, presumably against such heretics as were located in Rhode Island, and provided for some other

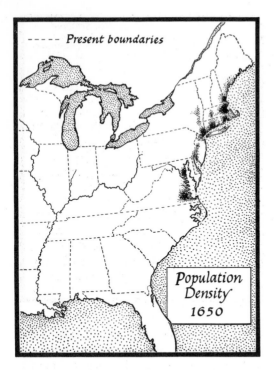

----- *Present boundaries*

Population Density 1650

prises made possible, it is hard to see how the original ventures could have made headway. Investors in the London and Plymouth Companies, in the unincorporated joint-stock company that backed the Plymouth colony, and in the Massachusetts-Bay Company could and did furnish the means that mere religious enthusiasm would have been powerless to obtain. For nearly three hundred years each new American frontier was to begin existence under a burden of debt to the adventurers of older communities who financed it.

On the other hand, it is clear that the religious motive was cogent in producing emigration, particularly to New **The religious** England. Men did come to **motive** America in order to establish colonies where they might have freedom to worship as they pleased, and for this same reason they sometimes left the original settlements to found others. In general, the colonies as commercial ventures were failures, but as new homes for emigrants they were successes. The men who came to Virginia or New England found, if they searched far enough, a religious environment that suited them; and they found also, if they survived and could work, a certain degree of economic prosperity. As havens of refuge in an intolerant age the colonies were important; as experiment stations in the art of self-government they were extremely interesting; but as places where ordinary men could acquire property, especially in land, and could make a decent living they had their greatest significance.

intercolonial relations. The Confederation lasted until 1684, and in 1675 it was of material assistance in waging another war against the Indians, generally known as King Philip's war.

The obvious contrasts between New England and Virginia during these formative **Commercial** years should not obscure the **motives in** fact that in their origins both **colonization** regions owed a great deal to the activity of trading companies. Without the financial backing which the current belief in trading companies as profit-making enter-

Bibliography

The colonial period has been the subject of several monumental works. Probably the best of these is C. M. Andrews, *The Colonial Period of American History* (4 vols., 1934–38), which embodies the lifelong research of one of the greatest of American historians. Among the older, but still dependable works, is John A. Doyle, *English Colonies in America* (5 vols., 1882–1907). Infi-

nitely detailed, but useful principally on that account, is H. L. Osgood, *The American Colonies in the Seventeenth Century* (3 vols., 1904–07). *Original Narratives of Early American History*, edited by J. F. Jameson (19 vols., 1906–17), is a valuable collection of sources.

There are many excellent one-volume treatises on the colonial period, most of them designed for text-book purposes. Curtis P. Nettels, *The Roots of American Civilization* (1938), is particularly valuable on social and economic aspects of the period. H. E. Bolton and T. M. Marshall, *The Colonization of North America, 1492–1783* (1936), is comprehensive, but too strictly factual. E. B. Greene, *The Foundations of American Nationality* (1922), is skilfully written and erudite, but mainly political. O. P. Chitwood, *A History of Colonial America* (1948), is a good general synthesis. More on the interpretative side are Max Savelle, *The Foundations of American Civilization* (1942), and F. J. Klingberg, *The Morning of America* (1941). Brief and always to the point is C. M. Andrews, *The Colonial Period* (1912).

On the reasons that lay back of the English migration, G. L. Beer, *The Origins of the British Colonial System, 1578–1660* (1908), makes an outstanding contribution. This is further elaborated in Klaus E. Knorr, *British Colonial Theories, 1570–1850* (1944). Marcus Lee Hansen, *The Atlantic Migration, 1607–1860* (1940), also sets forth, with admirable scholarship, the conditions that led to emigration.

On the beginnings of settlement, the best general treatise is T. J. Wertenbaker, *The First Americans, 1607–1690* (1927). This account may be supplemented, especially on the political side, by L. G. Tyler, *England in America, 1580–1652* (1904), and Edward Eggleston, *The Beginners of a Nation* (1896). Robert Beverley, *The History and Present State of Virginia* (1947), reissues a book originally printed in 1705. Early Virginia is best described in the numerous books by P. A. Bruce. Among them are *Economic History of Virginia in the Seventeenth Century* (2 vols., 1935); *Social Life of Virginia in the Seventeenth Century* (1927); *Institutional History of Virginia in the Seventeenth Century* (2 vols., 1910). The first decades of colonial history furnish the theme of M. P. Andrews, *The Soul of a Nation: The Founding of Virginia and the Projection of New England* (1943). On Bacon's Rebellion, the best account is T. J. Wertenbaker, *Torchbearer of the Revolution: The Story of Bacon's Rebellion and its Leader* (1940). More readable than scholarly are the works of John Fiske, *Old Virginia and her Neighbours* (2 vols., 1897), and *The Beginnings of New England* (1889). All Fiske's works have been collected into one series, *The Historical Writings of John Fiske* (12 vols., 1902). J. T. Adams, *The Founding of New England* (1921), is brilliant, but definitely anti-Puritan in point of view. C. M. Andrews, *The Fathers of New England* (1919), is an excellent short account. J. G. Palfrey, *History of New England* (5 vols., 1858–90), continues to be usable, although written long ago. W. F. Craven, *The Southern Colonies in the Seventeenth Century, 1607–1689* (1949), is an excellent synthesis of modern scholarship.

The colonies have naturally tempted much individual treatment. Among the many works of this kind that might well be cited are: S. E. Morison, *Builders of the Bay Colony* (1930); I. B. Richman, *Rhode Island, Its Making and Meaning* (2 vols., 1902); G. L. Clark, *A History of Connecticut* (1914); C. H. Levermore, *The Republic of New Haven* (1886); Isabel M. Calder, *The New Haven Colony* (1934); W. H. Fry, *New Hampshire as a Royal Province* (1908); H. S. Burrage, *The Beginnings of Colonial Maine, 1602–1658* (1914).

The biographic approach has also been fruitful. Outstanding in the record of American historical achievement is the *Dictionary of American Biography*, edited by Allen Johnson and Dumas Malone, 21 vols., 1928–44). This work provides excellent short biographies of practically all Americans of consequence. Book length biographies of varying merit, but all pertinent to this chapter, are: C. K. Shipton, *Roger Conant: A Founder of Massachusetts* (1944); L. S. Mayo, *John Endicott: A Biography* (1936); S. H. Brockunier, *The Irrepressible Democrat: Roger Williams* (1940); E. J. Carpenter, *Roger Williams* (1909); Edith Curtis, *Anne Hutchinson* (1930).

Dictionary of American History, edited by J. T. Adams (6 vols., 1940), is useful at every point. See, for example, Vol. IV, p. 252, on the "Pequot Wars," and p. 330 on the "Praying Indians." Richard Frothingham, *The Rise of the Republic of the United States* (10th ed., 1910), also contains lengthy discussions of the Indian troubles, and of the New England Confederation.

Come all ye Saints that would for little Buy,
Great Tracts of Land, and care not where they lye,
Deal with your Quaking Friends, they're Men of Light,
The Spirit hates Deceit and Scorns to Bite.

3

The Proprietary and Island Colonies

Proprietors as colony founders — The Baltimores in Maryland — The Carolina grant — New Netherland under the Dutch — New Netherland becomes New York — New Jersey — William Penn and the founding of Pennsylvania — Delaware — Georgia — The Bermudas — British West Indies — Jamaica — Other English outposts in the New World

THOSE English colonies that did not spring, directly or indirectly, from the activities of trading companies were usually the work of individuals, commonly called proprietors. Sir Humphrey Gilbert and Sir Walter Raleigh were the forerunners of this type of colony founder, but neither their unhappy experiences nor the profitless aspect of the trading company ventures in America sufficed to deter other individuals from making similar experiments, particularly after the restoration of the Stuarts to the English throne. During the restoration period the favor of the royal family was ordinarily all that was needed to enable one to obtain a proprietary grant of land from the King, together with the right to rule its inhabitants. Some of these proprietors were impecunious nobles who merely aimed to sell or let out their lands on advantageous terms, and if possible to exact from their subjects the feudal dues common to an earlier age in England. A few coveted political power such as the Old World lords were no longer permitted to possess, and others, while by no means indifferent to the prospects of financial and political rewards, sincerely desired to found havens of refuge for the oppressed.

The earliest of the successful proprietary provinces was Maryland. The launching of this colony was the work of George Calvert and his son Cecilius, more commonly known as the first and second Lords Baltimore. George Calvert was a man of means who had long been interested in colonial projects. He was a member of the London Company and of the Council for New England; and under a charter granted by James I in 1623 he had also made an independent but unsuccessful effort to establish a colony in Newfoundland. Convinced by a visit to this region in 1627 that its intolerable climate would always be an insuperable obstacle to colonization, he asked and received from King Charles I the promise of a grant of land farther to the south. Calvert, meantime, by embracing the Catholic faith, had cut himself off from all chance of political preferment in England, although the King, whose religious leanings were also in the Catholic direction, bore him no grudge and even made him an Irish peer with the title Lord Baltimore. The first Lord Baltimore died before the King's promise of a new charter had been redeemed, but in 1632 the grant was made to his son, Cecilius, who was also a Catholic. By its terms the territory from the south bank of the Potomac northward to the fortieth parallel and inland to the source of the river was handed over to the Baltimore family as an hereditary estate. Two arrows and one fifth of all the gold and silver mined in the

Proprietors as colony founders

The Baltimores in Maryland

province must be paid each year to the King, but otherwise the proprietor was left as free to govern in America as the King in England. This meant, however, an important limitation on the proprietor's power, for he could make laws and raise taxes only with the advice and consent of the freemen, or landowners, in his colony, or of their representatives.

The second Lord Baltimore greatly desired to make of Maryland a place where his **A Catholic** Catholic co-religionists might **refuge** worship without fear of oppression, and, perhaps because of an unrecorded understanding with the King, the royal charter offered no opposition to such a course. But the number of prospective emigrants among English Catholics was limited, and Baltimore was too good a business man to propose the exclusion of Protestants, who were cordially welcomed and from the first seem to have outnumbered Catholics. The *Ark* and the *Dove*, two small ships which Baltimore sent to Maryland in the fall of 1633, carried about twenty gentlemen and two hundred laborers to the new colony. Most of the gentlemen were Catholics, but most of the laborers were Protestants. Two Jesuit priests and one lay brother accompanied the expedition and labored with great earnestness but little success to convert the Protestant settlers and the Indians to Catholicism.

The beginnings of Maryland reveal no such suffering and hardship as accompanied **Early** the founding of the earlier col- **settlements** onies. The passage of the *Ark* and the *Dove* was long and trying, and it was not until February, 1634, that the Potomac was entered, but St. Mary's, the site selected for the first settlement, turned out to be healthful, and the usual depredations from disease were not recorded. Lands which had already been cleared were peacefully acquired from the Indians, and the economic life of Virginia was closely copied. Baltimore's land system contained one unique feature. He proposed to grant a manorial estate of a thousand acres to any adventurer

Cecilius Calvert, second Lord Baltimore, although the first Proprietor of Maryland, remained in England to defend his charter against legal attack.

who would transport five men to Maryland. But such "lords of the manor" were never numerous, although large estates mainly given over to the cultivation of tobacco did develop. All land was granted by the proprietor, who charged a small quit-rent. This feature of the land system, while producing for the proprietor a fair revenue when it could be collected, was by no means popular, and it accounts in part for the relatively small population which Maryland acquired in the seventeenth century. Elsewhere in the colonies lands were obtainable on easier terms.

Cecilius Calvert did not himself come to America, but sent instead as lieutenant governor his brother, Leonard Cal- **Popular** vert. While recognizing the **government** right of the people to a voice in making the laws, the proprietor and his lieutenant sought at first to hold popular participation in the government to a minimum. This was not long possible, and in Maryland as elsewhere a representative assembly soon developed. One of the most significant of its early acts, passed in the face of the rising power of Puritanism in England, was the Toleration

Maryland
- - - Maryland boundary
according to Baltimore's
interpretation of Charter
of 1632

-·-·- Present boundaries

Act of 1649. While this act threatened with death all non-Christians, including Jews and Unitarians, it guaranteed that no person professing to believe in Jesus Christ, shall be in any wise molested or discountenanced for his or her religion. Persecution of Catholics, however, did break out in Maryland during the later years of the seventeenth century, and the Church of England, in spite of the Catholic origin of the colony, became the established church.

Several other proprietary colonies of the Maryland type were founded shortly after the restoration of the Stuarts in 1660. The successes of the Baltimores, such as they were, inspired emulation on the part of the courtiers of the new king, Charles II, in whom they found a sympathetic and helpful friend. The national interest in colonization, which had died down somewhat during the period of the Civil War, now revived.

Among the regions in America that were still at the disposal of the King was the ter-

The Caro- ritory south of Virginia and
lina grant north of Florida. For this land, called first Carolana, then Carolina, eight

prominent nobles now successfully petitioned the King. Their plan was to make of Carolina an ideal feudal state, and they induced John Locke, the most prominent political theorist of his time, to prepare an elaborate set of fundamental laws through which this purpose should be carried out. The scheme of government which Locke devised contemplated among other things several ranks of nobility above the ordinary freemen, while the latter were to be virtually stripped of political power. Agents of the proprietors, sent to America for the purpose, formally proclaimed the new government in operation, but they made little headway in their attempt to apply the medieval features of Locke's carefully drawn scheme. The idea of a colonial nobility proved to be particularly inapplicable.

As early as 1654, well before the Carolina proprietors received their grant, settlers from Virginia had found their **North** way to the vicinity of Albemarle **Carolina** Sound. These pioneers and others who soon followed them were for the most part men of small means who had found life in proximity with the more prosperous Virginia planters far from pleasant. Albemarle democracy was of the unqualified sort, and the unsolicited efforts of the Carolina proprietors to assert authority in this region were ignored, or even resisted. Toward the end of the seventeenth century the Albemarle settlements came to be known as North Carolina. Here, as in Virginia, the colonists raised tobacco and foodstuffs, and they traded a little with New England and the West Indies.

The Carolina proprietors were decidedly more interested in the southern part of their
South Carolina holding, where they had expected to establish a tropical colony similar in its economic life to the islands of the West Indies. In 1670 they sent out an expedition under William Sayle which founded Charleston, or Charles-Town, as it was first called. Other immigrants soon came in, most of them, however, without any help from the proprietors, and within ten years Charleston had about twelve hundred inhabitants. The new settlements, soon called South Carolina, took on rapidly a cosmopolitan tinge. French Huguenots began to arrive about 1680, and emigrants from Ireland, New England, and the West Indies, especially Barbados, were numerous. The

New Netherland and New Jersey
Present boundaries

planters used indentured servants for labor when they could, but, as in Virginia and Maryland, they bought Negro slaves when the supply of white servants was deemed inadequate. They raised foodstuffs as well as tobacco, and beginning about 1693 they introduced the culture of rice. The excellent harbor at Charleston greatly facilitated trade with the outside world. In government both South Carolina and North Carolina tended to develop along the lines already marked out in Maryland.

The Carolina settlements were designed, in part, to act as buffers against the Spanish
New Netherland in Florida. But the Dutch colony of New Netherland, on the Hudson, was an even greater menace to the English than Spanish Florida. New Netherland actually antedated most of the English settlements, for Dutch merchants had planted a trading post on Manhattan Island as early as 1612, while the Dutch West India Company, which in 1621 had taken over the exploitation of the region, actively promoted settlement from that time forward. Most of the wealth of New Netherland came from the fur trade, but the company offered small tracts of land to freemen who would agree to settle on it as farmers, and large

North and South Carolina
--- Present boundaries

estates to "patroons," or landlords, who as a condition of their grant must bring over fifty tenants. The semi-feudal powers accorded to the patroons were not popular in a region where land was abundant, and most of the patroonships did not last long; but the promoters of the Dutch colony induced so many of their countrymen to come to America that a sparse Dutch population was soon settled in the Hudson Valley all the way from New Amsterdam, founded on Manhattan Island, in July, 1625, to Fort Orange, the present site of Albany. Many settlers from the English colonies also entered the Dutch territory. Some of them were refugees from religious persecution, others were pioneer farmers eager to accept the generous land terms offered by the Dutch, and still others were former indentured servants in full flight from the scene of their servitude. Thanks to these accessions, and to the absorption in 1655 of a small colony the Swedes had founded in 1638 on the Delaware, the population of New Netherland had risen before the English conquest to about ten thousand.

The presence of this Dutch colony in America was naturally distasteful to the

Dutch and English rivalry English, whose holdings it cut squarely in two. Furthermore, the success of the Dutch as traders, not only in America but also in Europe, Asia, and Africa, led to a period of intense commercial rivalry between the two nations, during which the same sort of antagonism that English sailors had once concentrated on the Spanish was turned against the Dutch. The last half of the seventeenth century was marked by three wars between England and the Netherlands, and in 1664, on the eve of one of them, the English King, Charles II, sent an expedition across the Atlantic to take possession of New Netherland. To his brother, the Duke of York, he granted proprietary rights over the whole province.

In spite of the evident superiority of the English force, the Dutch governor of New Netherland, Peter Stuyvesant, would have offered resistance, but the burgomasters of New **'Conquest' of New Netherland** Amsterdam, who recognized the futility of such a course, restrained him. Colonel Richard Nicolls, whom the Duke of York had sent over as his agent, was allowed to take peaceable possession of the town of New Amsterdam and the colony of New Netherland, both of which were renamed New York. The Duke of York's power, according to the terms of his grant, was almost absolute, and the "Duke's Laws," which Nicolls soon proclaimed, accorded to the inhabitants only an insignificant part in the government. Not until 1683 was an

New Amsterdam, on the tip of Manhattan island, was a Dutch trading center for over forty years before it was captured by the British in 1664.

elective assembly authorized, and then it was quickly suppressed. Throughout the seventeenth century progress toward popular rule in New York lagged perceptibly behind that of every other English colony in America.

The Duke of York disposed of a part of his holdings to two nobles, Lord John Berkeley and Sir George Carteret, who **New Jersey** were interested in the Carolina project also and who still hoped for riches from the sale of their lands in America. These gentlemen were given proprietary rights to the territory lying between the lower Hudson and the Delaware, a region which they called New Jersey, after Carteret's home in England. Here a few Dutch settlements had already been established, and the new proprietors, by offering land to newcomers on easy terms, succeeded in attracting many emigrants from New England and from all parts of the British Isles.

It is probable that the grant to Berkeley and Carteret was not intended to carry with it the full governmental authority that the proprietors promptly assumed. In 1665, however, they sent out as governor Philip Carteret, a relative of Sir George, the proprietor. Governor Carteret was instructed to establish a completely separate government for New Jersey, and to call a legislative assembly; and in spite of repeated objections from the authorities in New York, he carried out his instructions to the letter. The proprietors found out, however, that their subjects were hard to satisfy. The New England Puritans, whose ideals of government were already well formed before they reached New Jersey, were particularly bothersome. When an attempt was made in 1670 to collect a halfpenny quit-rent for each acre of land granted, the authorities were openly defied, and two years later the New Jersey citizens actually expelled their legal governor in order to choose one of their own. The proprietors soon regained control, but the collection of quit-rents had to be indefinitely postponed.

Down to 1674 the two proprietors held New Jersey jointly, but in that year Berkeley, now thoroughly discour- **Division of** aged, sold his holding to two **the colony** Quakers, John Fenwick and Edward Byllinge. A division of the colony into two parts was then effected. Carteret retained as his portion the settlements in the northeast adjacent to New York, or East New Jersey, while the Quakers took the region to the south and along the Delaware, or West New Jersey. Byllinge and Fenwick had acquired their title with the intention of establishing a Quaker colony in America, but they were unable to agree upon the details of its management, and they soon sold out to a group of Quakers, among whom the most influential was William Penn. The new proprietors promptly promulgated a liberal constitution, and they promoted settlement with marked success. Within a few years several new towns had been founded and the population of the colony had increased by about fourteen hundred.

East New Jersey also fell into Quaker hands. In 1679 Carteret died, and shortly afterwards his trustees sold his grant in America to William Penn and eleven other Quakers. New partners were soon admitted to the enterprise who were not Quakers, among them some Scottish Presbyterians who worked with energy and success to persuade a number of their countrymen to emigrate to New Jersey. Quakers came from England and Scotland, Puritans from New England, and somewhat later Scotch-Irish Presbyterians from the north of Ireland. Under the beneficent rule of Robert Barclay, a Quaker preacher who in 1682 became governor for life, the colony prospered greatly. The population of East New Jersey was probably twice that of West New Jersey, and in its economic character it closely resembled New England, whence so many of its settlers had come. West New Jersey, on the other hand, tended to copy the manner of life adopted by the settlers along the Chesapeake. Small holdings were the rule, but large plantations, worked in part by Negro slaves, were not unknown.

By the end of the seventeenth century the two Jerseys together had a population of about fifteen thousand.

The name of William Penn (1644–1718), which appeared prominently in the early **William** history of New Jersey, is associ- **Penn** ated even more conspicuously with the founding of Pennsylvania. Penn came naturally by his interest in colonization. By birth and training he was associated with the nobles and courtiers who in the last half of the seventeenth century were so often engaged in colonial projects, while by religion he was affiliated with a persecuted sect for which the New World seemed to offer the only secure refuge. Penn's father, Sir William, had been a high-ranking officer in the navy under Cromwell, but he somehow managed to retain and even to improve his status under the restored Stuarts. He was on friendly terms with King Charles II, with his brother the Duke of York, and with many of the nobles who had received proprietary grants of land in America. Young Penn, while still a student at Oxford, was impressed by the teachings of a Quaker preacher, and he soon became a member of the Society of Friends, as the Quakers called themselves. Penn's father was deeply distressed at his son's action, for the Quakers adhered to doctrines that were immensely at variance with the prevailing views of the time. They rejected all the sacraments, refused to pay tithes toward the support of the established church, denounced war unstintedly, declined to do military service, and in a great variety of ways put themselves entirely outside the pale of seventeenth-century respectability. Persecution under such circumstances was inevitable, and Penn, as one of the most prominent members of the sect, advanced the idea of founding as a retreat for the oppressed members of his faith a Quaker commonwealth in America.

Penn's experience with West New Jersey led him to conclude that, in order to establish the kind of colony he desired, he must have a charter direct from the crown. It chanced that part of the estate which the elder Penn had bequeathed to **Pennsylvania** his son was a debt owed by the King, amounting to sixteen thousand pounds. The Quaker leader now asked that, in return for the cancellation of this debt, he be granted full proprietary rights to the lands along the Delaware north of Maryland; and March 4, 1681, his request received the sanction of the King. Unfortunately the description of Penn's holding was stated so vaguely that boundary disputes with both New York and Maryland long marred the relations between Pennsylvania and her neighbors.

The early history of Pennsylvania centers about the efforts of its conscientious proprietor to establish a liberal **Representa-** government, to guarantee re- **tive govern-** ligious freedom to all settlers, **ment** and to induce emigrants to leave the Old World for his colony in the New. Penn's charter left to the proprietor much liberty of action with regard to the form of government to be established, but it did require him to obtain the advice and consent of the freemen in making laws. Penn was in full accord with this idea, and his liberal intentions were revealed in the "Frame of Government" which he promulgated for the colony in 1682. This system proved to be too complicated to work well, and it was quickly succeeded by another of simpler nature. Penn visited America in 1682 and again, 1699–1701. On these occasions he observed at first hand the conditions of life in Pennsylvania, conferred directly with the leading colonists on governmental problems, and finally after his second visit issued a "Charter of Privileges" that proved to be generally satisfactory. The government of Pennsylvania retained until the time of the American Revolution a few unique features. It had an appointive council, for example, which was never recognized as a co-ordinate branch of the government, but was distinctly inferior in power to the elective assembly.

Penn was a devout Quaker, but he had no notion of limiting in any way the privileges

William Penn early showed an interest in independent religious ideas. On this account he was expelled from Oxford University in 1662, and several years later was imprisoned in the Tower of London (near the place of his birth). After his release he twice visited the continent as a missionary, but his thoughts soon turned to America. His "Holy Experiment," Pennsylvania, proposed toleration in religion, popular participation in government, and fair dealing with the Indians. The head shown here is taken from an Irish portrait of Penn at the age of twenty-two. *Penn's Treaty with the Indians, 1682* (an idealized painting by Benjamin West, 1771), depicts one of his several efforts to establish in this way good relations with the natives.

Freedom of worship of Pennsylvania colonists who were not Quakers. One of his first measures was to guarantee full freedom of worship for such law-abiding persons as "acknowledged one Almighty and Eternal God to be the Creator, Upholder, and Ruler of the World." This guaranty went much further than the famous Toleration Act of 1649 in Maryland, for the latter discriminated against Jews and Unitarians, whereas the former did not. And yet, even in Pennsylvania, the ideal of religious freedom was not for a long time fully attained. Neither Jews nor Catholics were in practice accorded the full freedom to worship in their own way that was freely given to Protestants. Offices were limited from the first to professing Christians, while later, at the insistence of the English government, all Catholics were disqualified. Happily the great bulk of the people who came to Pennsylvania were less interested in holding offices than in escaping persecution. Not only Quakers, but members of various other oppressed sects also, looked upon the Quaker colony as an ideal retreat.

The adoption of religious toleration in Pennsylvania had an advertising value which Penn did not hesitate to exploit. **Non-English immigrants** In Germany, particularly, where many radical denominations lived under the constant shadow of persecution, Penn's agents pointed out the advantages of emigration to the Quaker colony. The terms upon which land could be obtained were made easy, both for speculators and land companies who desired large tracts, and for immigrant farmers who desired small tracts. Penn's advertising campaigns, which featured his generous land terms, his policy of religious toleration, and his liberal government, got a ready response. Bad economic conditions in Germany also helped him, and led to the emigration to Pennsylvania of German Lutherans and Catholics as well as members of the minor sects. A few Dutch and a few French Huguenots came also, and many English, Welsh, and Irish settlers, most of whom were Quakers. Some of the English settlers adhered steadfastly to the Church of England, and objected strenuously, although for the most part ineffectively,

Pennsylvania
and Delaware

-·-· Present boundaries

to Penn's "holy experiment" in toleration.

The growth of Pennsylvania was remarkable. Its population, which had reached
Rapid about twelve thousand by 1689,
growth was in a short time larger than
that of any other English colony in North
America. Its capital, Philadelphia, which
Penn himself laid out in squares, soon became the largest and busiest city in the
English overseas possessions. Part of this
success was due to the fact that Penn and
his settlers could profit from the experiences
of the earlier colonists. The heavy mortality
that had characterized the settlement of
Virginia and New England was not repeated
in Pennsylvania, nor were there such costly
mistakes as the first American pioneers made
in dealing with the Indians. Penn did not
profit as much financially from his colonial
venture as the prosperity of his colony
seemed to warrant. Quit-rents were hard to
collect, and the cost of promoting emigration
was great. Nor was the Pennsylvania proprietor more rewarded in the devotion of his
subjects than was the rule elsewhere. They
heaped criticisms upon him that would have
embittered a less religious spirit. Penn's
heirs and successors were even less popular,
although they retained their proprietary
rights, except for a brief interlude, until the
time of the American Revolution.

Delaware was at first a part of New York,
then later for a long time a part of Pennsylvania. Penn was determined to
have for his colony free access **Delaware**
to the sea, and in order to effect this purpose
he obtained from the Duke of York in 1682
the territory lying immediately to the west
of the Delaware River. When the "Charter
of Privileges" was issued in 1701, these
"lower counties" were accorded the right to
select an assembly of their own. This they
soon did, but the Penns continued as proprietors, and the relations between Delaware
and Pennsylvania remained close.

Georgia was the last of the English colonies to be established on the mainland of
North America. Its founder, **James**
James Oglethorpe, who had **Oglethorpe**
been for thirty years a member of the House
of Commons, shared the current jealousy of
French and Spanish colonial expansion. One
unappropriated region that might conceiv-
ably be claimed by any one of those three nations lay south of Carolina, north of Florida,
and east of Louisiana. Here Oglethorpe
wished to plant a colony that would pre-empt
for the English the territory in question, and
would act as a buffer state against French or
Spanish aggression. He had also a humanitarian desire to found a haven of refuge for
the large number of Englishmen who, under
the existing laws, would ordinarily be sent to
prison because of inability to pay their debts.
Many of these people, Oglethorpe believed,
would prove to be ideal colonists. Apparently, too, he and his associates hoped that
the colony might furnish a similar retreat for
persecuted Protestants from continental
Europe.

Governments by proprietors were by this
time out of favor in England, but the advantages of founding such a colony
as Oglethorpe planned were so **Georgia**
appealing that in 1732 a group of trustees, of
whom Oglethorpe was the most active, secured from George II title to the land lying
between the Savannah and Altamaha Rivers, and westward from their headwaters to
the Pacific. The grant, however, was sub-

James Oglethorpe's humanitarian plans for Georgia appealed to many Europeans, among them a group of Lutheran exiles who are shown here leaving their home in Salzburg in 1732.

ject to unusual limitations. The trustees, as individuals, were expressly forbidden to acquire any lands in the colony, or to make any profits from their connection with it, and at the end of twenty-one years their governmental privileges were to revert to the crown. In the meantime the officials they appointed, and the laws they made, had to receive the approval of the King.

In January, 1733, Oglethorpe brought over about a hundred settlers and founded Savannah. Other immigrants soon **Slow** came, Salzburgers, Highland **development** Scots, Scotch-Irish, and Welsh, as well as English. At first the terms on which land could be obtained were unusual. Not more than five hundred acres could be taken by any one person, and all such grants were entailed to male heirs. The proprietors also prohibited slavery, on the assumption that the near-by Spaniards might incite the slaves to revolt, and forbade the importation of rum. These provisions were extremely unpopular, and they checked somewhat the growth of the colony, although they were not long retained. English debtors were not

sent to Georgia in as great numbers as Oglethorpe had hoped, and by 1760 the total population of the colony was not more than nine thousand. Of this number about one third were Negro slaves whose presence was demanded when the economic interests of Georgia began to approximate those of the other southern colonies.

Because the history of the English colonies in North America is ordinarily written as a prelude to the history of the United States, the attention of American historians has naturally centered upon the "continental colonies," and particularly upon the thirteen which eventually won their independence. But Englishmen of the seventeenth and eighteenth centuries, when they thought of the English settlements in America, included also the "island colonies," which seemed in many ways even more important than those on the mainland.

Among the island colonies were the Bermudas, which at first were regarded as a part of Virginia. English interest in **The** the Bermudas began in 1609, **Bermudas** when a Virginia supply ship was wrecked on

Georgia
1735

one of the islands, and its commander, Sir George Somers, observed their possibilities as a field of colonization. Somers, on returning to England, formed a company known as the Somers Islands Company, which in 1612 began to send out settlers, and in 1614 received a charter with full governmental rights. At this latter date the population of the colony was already about six hundred, and since tobacco growing soon proved to be even more profitable than in Virginia, other settlers came in rapidly. The rule of the company was never popular, even though representative government was early conceded, and in 1679 the Bermudas were taken over by the crown as a royal colony. By this time they possessed a population of about three thousand.

The British also had possessions in the West Indies, centering for the most part **British West Indies** about St. Christopher, which was colonized in 1623, and Barbados, which was occupied in 1625. These two islands, together with others of the Lesser Antilles, were granted to the Earl of Carlisle as proprietor in 1627. Tobacco-raising was at first the chief concern of the settlers, but presently the production of sugar-cane proved more profitable and became the leading industry. For nearly a

hundred years Great Britain obtained most of her sugar from these islands, a circumstance that contributed immeasurably to their prosperity. By 1639, when the population of Virginia was only about seven thousand, there were twenty thousand people in Barbados alone. In 1661 the proprietor lost his rights, and ten years later the colony was divided, Barbados and the Windward Islands constituting one colony, and the rest, under the name of the Leeward Islands, another.

Jamaica was conquered by the British in 1655 during a war with Spain. Its possibilities as a "sugar island" had by no means been fully exploited **Jamaica** under Spanish rule, but once the British assumed control, business-minded settlers flocked to the island. The sugar plantations were worked mainly by slave labor, and the importation of Negroes went on so rapidly that soon the blacks outnumbered the whites many times over. Slave insurrections were common until well into the eighteenth century, and sometimes interfered considerably with the prosperity of the island. The gov-

Population
Density
1700

Eastern
North America
after
The Treaty of Utrecht
1713

British
French
Spanish

FIG. I.

FIG. V.

FIG. IV.

FIG. II.

FIG. III.

FIG. VII.

FIG. VI.

The slave trade was carried on in overcrowded ships like the *Brookes*, the plan of which is here shown.

ernment of Jamaica was such as existed in any royal colony, and the constitutional problems that arose were not unlike those which led the colonies on the mainland to revolt.

These island colonies contributed far more to the economic prosperity of the British Empire than did the continental colonies. They offered extraordinary opportunities for the investment of British capital. Their constant demand for slaves helped along the British slave trade to a pleasing prosperity. Moreover, because they stood ready to exchange their sugar and molasses for foodstuffs and other supplies from the continental colonies, they played an important part in making the colonies on the mainland a success.

Less important were the feeble British outposts in the Bahamas, Guiana and Honduras; but far to the north the stations of the famous Hudson's **Other English outposts** Bay Company, chartered in 1670, tapped another important source of the fur trade. By the Peace of Utrecht in 1713 the British acquired clear titles to the Hudson's Bay region, to Acadia, which they renamed Nova Scotia, and to the island of Newfoundland, but the interests of English fishermen in the waters adjacent to some of these regions dated as far back as the first half of the sixteenth century.

The British possessions in America were thus at the outset of the eighteenth century a far-flung empire, stretching from the northern coast of South America to the Arctic Circle. Meantime the British had acquired still other possessions in Asia, Africa, and elsewhere. A great variety of peoples, a wide diversity of economic interests, a hopeless expanse of geography confronted the British statesman who turned his attention to colonial affairs. It is not surprising that the task of integrating such an empire proved to be too great for eighteenth-century British statesmanship, and that the relatively homogeneous continental colonies of North America chose presently to work out their destiny apart from the rest.

Bibliography

In addition to the general works on colonial history cited for the preceding two chapters, all of which cover also the subject matter of this chapter, there are many useful special studies that throw light on the history of a given area, a given colony, or a given period.

The southern colonies as a whole are given brief and breezy treatment by Mary Johnston, *Pioneers of the Old South* (1918). On early Maryland the best accounts are Bernard C. Steiner, *Beginnings of Maryland* (1903); and Matthew P. Andrews, *The Founding of Maryland* (1933). Two old books, W. H. Browne, *George Calvert and Cecilius Calvert* (1890), and, by the same author, *Maryland, The History of a Palatinate* (1904), also provide much authentic detail. N. D. Mereness, *Maryland as a Proprietary Province* (1901), is especially concerned with the evolution of government in the colony. There are several similar studies dealing with North Carolina: J. S. Bassett, *The Constitutional Beginnings of North Carolina* (1894); C. L. Raper, *North Carolina, A Study in English Colonial Government* (1904); S. A. Ashe, *History of North Carolina* (2 vols., 1908–25). On South Carolina, see Edward McCrady, *The History of South Carolina under the Proprietary Government, 1670–1719* (1897); and R. L. Meriwether, *The Expansion of South Carolina, 1729–1765,* (1940). On Georgia: J. R. McCain, *Georgia as a Proprietary Province* (1917); A. A. Ettinger, *James Edward Oglethorpe* (1936); V. W. Crane, *The Southern Frontier, 1670–1732* (1929); E. M. Coulter, *Georgia, A Short History* (1947).

The middle colonies, especially New York, have received even more generous attention. John Fiske, *The Dutch and Quaker Colonies in America* (2 vols., 1899), exhibits well the author's extraordinary capacity for brilliant narrative and faulty detail. Maud W. Goodwin, *Dutch and English on the Hudson* (1919), is sketchy but dependable as far as it goes. Christopher Ward, *The Dutch and Swedes on the Delaware, 1609–1664* (1930), is satisfactory. Amandus Johnson, *The Swedish Settlements on the Delaware, 1638–1664* (2 vols., 1911), is exhaustively detailed. S. G. Nissenson, *The Patroon's Domain* (1937), concentrates on the Dutch influence in New York. G. T. Hunt, *The Wars of the Iroquois* (1940), covers an aspect of New York history too often neglected in the text-books.

The Quaker colonies, likewise, have had no dearth of historians. An adequate summary is available in Wayland F. Dunaway, *A History of Pennsylvania* (1935). Good reading and good history is provided in the various books by S. G. Fisher, *The Making of Pennsylvania* (1932); *Pennsylvania; Colony and Commonwealth* (1897); *William Penn, A Biography* (1932); and *The Quaker Colonies* (1919). Quaker doctrines and accomplishments receive similarly admirable treatment at the hands of R. M. Jones, *The Quakers in the American Colonies* (1911); and *The Faith and Practice of the Quakers* (1927). On William Penn, see also W. W. Comfort, *William Penn, 1644–1718* (1944), and the older, but still useful George Hodges, *William Penn* (1901). A good monograph on the beginnings of New Jersey is E. P. Tanner, *The Province of New Jersey, 1664–1738* (1908). The vexing problem of quit-rents is treated fully in B. W. Bond, Jr., *The Quit-Rent System in the American Colonies* (1919).

Howard Robinson, *The Development of the British Empire* (new ed., 1936), gives an adequate account of the island as well as the continental colonies. H. E. Egerton, *A Short History of British Colonial Policy, 1606–1909* (9th ed., 1932), views the subject from the angle of the mother country. L. J. Ragatz, *The Fall of the Planter Class in the British Caribbean* (1928), treats the later history of the island colonies.

4
Colonial America

Sectionalism in the colonies — The Plantation Area — New England — The Middle Colonies — The frontier — Antagonism between back country and coast — Everyday life in the colonies — Colonial houses — Lack of conveniences — Colonial cities — Amusements — The colonial aristocracy — Intellectual interests — Jonathan Edwards — Benjamin Franklin

WHILE each of the thirteen colonies has an important separate history, parallel conditions often existed in several colonies, and sometimes in all the colonies. It is possible, therefore, to ignore colonial boundaries to some extent, and to treat the development of the colonies more or less collectively. Until recent years, particularly in textbooks, this method of treatment was rare, and the reader who wished to gain a knowledge of colonial America was compelled to follow through at least thirteen separate narratives.

But it is quite impossible to overlook the fact that the colonies were divided into three **Sectionalism in the colonies** or four well-defined sections. The British settlements in North America extended from a region of long winters and short summers to a region of short winters and long summers. They comprehended within their boundaries extensive areas of mountains and high hills, and other extensive areas of broad valleys and fertile plains. Moreover, there were differences in the types of settlers who came to possess the various parts of English America. The plantation area, which included Maryland and Virginia and the colonies to the south of them, came early to be recognized as a section apart. The colonies of New England, also, had an identity of characteristics that drew them together, and at the same time separated them from the rest. The

Middle Colonies — New York, New Jersey, Pennsylvania, Delaware — had much in common with the sections northeast and south of them, but were yet different. Finally to the west of the more thickly settled areas, with boundaries less clearly defined than the other sections, lay the frontier, a region in which new settlements were constantly being made, and in which the conditions of life were apt not to vary greatly even from north to south.

The type of civilization which developed in the plantation area was due in considerable part to the existence there **The Plantation Area** of a wide coastal plain, indented frequently with spacious bays, unnumbered harbors, and wide-mouthed navigable rivers. Near the banks of the rivers a rich alluvial soil made for successful agriculture, although a little distance in from the waterline the soil was not so good. Owing to the fact that the tides swept far up the rivers, the coastal plain was frequently spoken of as the Tidewater. At varying distances into the interior waterfalls blocked navigation, and the Falls Line — that is, an imaginary line drawn from north to south through these waterfalls — marked approximately the end of the Tidewater. Between the falls and the mountains lay a rough, hilly country, known as the Piedmont.

Tobacco became the staple crop in most of

the tidewater area, although in the Carolinas rice and indigo were also important products. Experience proved that the easiest road to prosperity was to raise these crops, particularly tobacco, for an outside market. In exchange for them the planter could obtain from Europe the articles he desired to make life agreeable in the New World. Of necessity the plantation owner maintained lively commercial relations with the Old World, most especially with the mother country. The Virginians and their neighbors raised all the tobacco they could raise, loaded it at their own or near-by wharves for shipment, usually to England, and in return brought in all the goods they could buy.

Tobacco

As it turned out, tobacco culture led naturally to the development of large plantations. With no thought of rotation of crops, it was soon discovered that however fertile the soil might be, the constant growing of tobacco exhausted it. More and more acres must therefore be acquired if the yield was to be kept up. It was observed, too, that if lands were allowed to lie fallow for a time, they could again be put in cultivation. This the large landowner could manage much more easily than the small landowner. Moreover, the fall in the price of tobacco that followed inexorably as the supply increased did its share to promote the expansion in size of the plantations. With the decline in the price of tobacco, the prosperous tobacco-raiser who had built himself a fine house and had established himself on a somewhat lavish scale of living found his income decidedly inadequate. The only way to make good this loss was to acquire more acres and raise more tobacco, and this he promptly did if he could. If he could not, he sold out to those who could afford to buy his land and possibly dropped into the small farmer class, where his disadvantages were numerous. The great planter could own his own wharf, from it ship tobacco to England, upon it receive goods in return. The small planter, on the other hand, had to use the great

Large plantations the rule

Colonial Plantation Area
_·_·_ Present boundaries

planter's wharf — substantially, he had to buy and sell through the great planter on whatever terms the latter chose to exact. Nor could the small planter compete with the great planter in the ownership of indentured servants and slaves. As the price of tobacco went down, the price of servants and slaves went up. Only the prosperous could afford to own them in sufficient numbers to make their possession profitable. The British rule of primogeniture in the inheritance of land, which was applied in Virginia and elsewhere, did much toward keeping together large estates, once they were created.

The successful southern planter was apt to have frontage on some winding stream such as the James, York, Rappahannock, or Potomac. If he were fortunate he might own a whole neck of land jutting out into the river. The size of the ordinary great planter's holding was about three thousand acres, but many planters —

Plantation life

TOBACCO WHARF. Cartouche from a map of the region, 1775.

Tobacco before Columbus was unknown to the world outside America. The Indians believed in its medicinal value, and taught the Whites its use and cultivation. In the economy of the colonial South, tobacco was the chief source of wealth, although indigo, while costly in terms of labor and land, was an important export item.

EARLY ENTHUSIASM FOR TOBACCO. An English doctor's report, 1659.

PREPARATION OF INDIGO, 1780. Cutting the dried blue extract into squares for shipment.

"STRATFORD," WESTMORELAND COUNTY, VA., 1725. Plantation house, kitchen, and servants' quarters.

for example William Byrd of Westover, Virginia, who bequeathed to his son an estate of twenty-six thousand acres — held more. The headquarters of each plantation made a little village. The planter and his family lived in a large and usually well-appointed house, near which were clustered the workhouses in which the cooking, weaving, carpenter work, blacksmithing, and other activities of the plantation were carried on. Still other houses served as dwellings for the servants and slaves, or furnished shelter to the livestock. In so far as it was possible each plantation was a self-sufficing economic unit. Most of the food consumed on the plantation was produced upon it, and much of the wearing apparel and other necessities also. Such articles as tools, which could not easily be manufactured locally, and luxuries — fine clothes for the master and his family, expensive wines, furniture, and even building materials — were imported in return for the tobacco shipped abroad. Once a year these exchanges were made, ships bringing from England the orders sent over by the planters the year previously, and taking back with them the annual salable output of the plantation. Nearly always the planter overestimated the value of his crop, and in consequence over-ordered. Debts to British merchants began therefore to accumulate almost everywhere in the plantation area, and on the eve of the Revolution the irritation that the existence of these debts aroused helped materially to sever the ties that had bound the colonies and the mother country together.

During the eighteenth century slavery came to play a more important rôle in the **Slavery and** life of the southern plantation **servitude** than had been the case in the seventeenth century. Adequate numbers of indentured servants were hard to get, and with an inviting wilderness to the West were harder still to keep, whereas Negro slaves were fairly cheap and endured the work of the plantations with fair contentment. In the rice-growing regions of South Carolina, where the climatic conditions were bad and white laborers quickly succumbed, Negro laborers were able to survive and to make good profits for their masters. By the close of the colonial period there were about four hundred thousand Negro slaves in the colonies. Three-fourths of this number lived in the South, where they constituted two-fifths of the entire population. In South Carolina they outnumbered the white population two to one. In the early years slaves were treated with extreme harshness, even cruelty; but as time went on the relations between masters and slaves greatly improved.

The plantation system left little chance for the development of towns and cities in the South. Annapolis, Williamsburg, and Wilmington, the capitals respectively of Maryland, Virginia, and North Carolina, were hardly more than villages except when a legislature met, or a court convened. Norfolk and Baltimore attained some importance as ports, and Charleston became a thriving little city, but these were exceptional instances. The life of the South was decidedly rural rather than urban in character.

In consequence, when it came to the establishment of local political units in the South the example offered by **Local** rural England rather than ur- **government** ban England was followed. In **in the South** the plantation area the parish was the smallest political division. Its boundaries included the residences of all the communicants of the parish church. A vestry, in practice consisting of the more important planters, governed the local church, cared for the poor, levied taxes to obtain necessary funds, and looked after the affairs of the parish generally. In theory, members of the vestry were supposed to be chosen by the parishioners, but in fact the vestrymen themselves filled vacancies in their membership, and became thus a "close corporation." A county usually consisted of several parishes, although sometimes the boundaries of a county and a parish were coterminous. In each county from eight to twenty justices of the peace were appointed by the governor from among the planters, and these justices held county court, usually monthly, but not less than four times a year. At such times they administered justice, chose constables and highway surveyors for the various precincts, ordered the building of roads and bridges, and assessed taxes. Orders of the county court were executed by the sheriff and the county lieutenant, the latter being the commander of the local militia. These officers, as well as new justices of the peace, were appointed by the governor, but usually only on nomination of the county court. The county seat at which sessions of the court were held was often of hardly enough consequence to be spoken of as a village. Sometimes it was only a "courthouse" at a county crossroads.

Once in two years, ordinarily, the voters of the county assembled to choose members of the colonial legislature. In Virginia each county was entitled to two representatives in the House of Burgesses. Property tests for voting were universal, but they did not exclude the small farmer from the suffrage. The elections were boisterous affairs, and by way of electioneering the opposing candidates usually treated the voters liberally to liquor. While the small farmers probably outnumbered the great planters nine or ten to one, the representatives were almost invariably chosen from the great planter class.

In religion as in government the plantation area of the South was not unlike rural England, where the strength of the Established Church was always great. In every southern colony, from Maryland to Georgia, the Church of England was by law established, and its ministers were held to be as much entitled to their pay as any other officers of the state. They were appointed, sometimes by the governor, sometimes by the proprietor, and sometimes, as missionaries, by an English organization known as the Society for Propagating the Gospel in Foreign Parts. These ministers were usually good men who took their duties seriously, but an occasional rake appeared among them whose conduct was injurious to the reputation of the Episcopal

Religion

clergy as a whole. Unfortunately there was no bishop of the English Church resident in America, and the Bishop of London, under whose spiritual guidance the American Church was placed, never visited America. In consequence matters of discipline were extremely difficult to handle; moreover, the only way Americans could enjoy the rites of ordination and confirmation was by either themselves or the bishop making a trip across the Atlantic. The lack of an American bishop was an unending source of complaint, and contributed its share toward the general discontent with British control that lay back of the Revolution. Dissenters existed in every southern colony, and well before the end of the colonial period their practices, if not always officially licensed, were at least generally ignored. But the bulk of the population in the tidewater area remained loyal adherents of the Established Church.

Schools were a rarity in the South, and only the children of planters were adequately educated. Very frequently these children were taught at home by tutors, although "pay schools" were not unknown; then later, if the means were at hand, the boys were sent to England for further education. One of the leading colonial colleges, William and Mary, founded in 1693, was located in the South and was liberally supported by the ruling class. But even so important a center as Charleston lacked both colleges and public schools.

Education

With virtually a monopoly on education, and "to the manner born," the great planters of the South, while actually a small minority in the population, played the principal rôle in southern history. They managed the affairs of their great estates with considerable ability, and they used the talents thus sharpened in discharging the political duties that fell to their lot. They were naturally averse to governmental interference in their private affairs, and were quick to resent injustices, especially when the source of trouble lay as far away as England. They fancied themselves extremely democratic because in reality the first families were very democratic among themselves, given to much visiting back and forth, and fond of showing hospitality. They possessed a charm of manner and a distinction of bearing that distinguished them clearly, even from the élite of the northern colonies. They took a paternalist interest in the affairs of the lower classes — the yeomen and the slaves — that was for the most part beneficial to all.

In New England, as in the South, physiographic conditions had much to do with **New England** shaping the course of development. The early settlers of New England found the topography exceedingly irregular, with high hills or mountains, rising in clusters rather than ranges, not far from the sea. In an earlier age the whole region had been glacier-swept, and the surface, even in the level places, was apt to be covered with boulders. The soil, where it could be found, was good, but required infinite patience and endurance to work. Rapidly flowing rivers plunged at frequent intervals into the sea, and waterfalls furnished the power that one day would turn factory wheels, but for the moment merely made penetration into the interior more difficult. Natural harbors dotted the coast-line, and foretold commerce, while heavy forests were everywhere available to furnish naval stores, masts, spars, and timbers for the builders of ships.

The inhabitants of this "stern and rockbound coast" were a fairly homogeneous group. Probably ninety-five per cent of the emigrants to colonial New England had come from England, and furthermore, in spite of their distinguished middle-class leaders, most of them had come from little peasant villages where they had worked as artisans or from which they had gone out each day to till their land. If they were not always Puritans on coming to America, as a rule they or their children soon fell in with the dominant religious faith.

Emigration to New England proceeded usually in groups. A congregation, led by its minister and financed by some wealthy Puritan, would come to America as a unit, establish a new town, sometimes **Group** named after the town in Eng- **migration** land from which the group had come, and continue to live thereafter in much the same fashion as in old England. This procedure was closely approximated, also, in the extension of the coast settlements into the interior. Actuated perhaps by some minor religious difference, and interested at the same time in seeking out new economic opportunities, a large number of families would put out together to found another town or another site. In the formative period New-Englanders showed little disposition to settle as individuals upon separate farms. Long-established custom, aided by the great desirability of having a church easily accessible and the necessity of protecting themselves against hostile Indians, kept the settlers together in villages. The New England town thus came to be the social and economic unit around which all New England life tended to center.

Furthermore, the town was also a natural, almost inevitable, political unit, and, as it turned out, a self-governing **The New** unit. The practice among the **England** Puritans with respect to church **town** government was to allow to each congregation the complete right to choose its minister, its deacons and elders, its tithing men. Even with respect to matters of doctrine the decision of the congregation was final. In the government of the town, these same ideas of democracy prevailed. All matters of importance related to local government were at first brought before the town meeting, to which usually all the church members, or perhaps even all the citizens, were entitled to come. The levying of taxes, the distribution of land, the establishment of schools, the passing of local ordinances of government, all were brought before this meeting. Between meetings "selectmen," duly elected for the purpose, carried on the government, and as time went on the unwieldy nature of the town meeting made it necessary to hand over to this smaller group many of the duties first performed by the meeting itself. The town was also the unit from which members were chosen to the lower house of the colonial legislature, and for this purpose, ordinarily once each year, the voters convened.

Agriculture was a necessity in colonial New England, for the people had to live.

Agriculture Fields were cleared of timber and of stones, the latter being used extensively for the construction of stone walls to serve as fences, and crops of many sorts were planted. Individual land holdings were early introduced, and generally each farmer tilled his own land. Labor was scarce, for virtually anyone might acquire land of his own, hence the holdings, in contrast to the southern plantations, tended to be no larger than one man and his family could work. Lacking money with which to buy, farmers fell back upon their own ingenuity, and fashioned for themselves the tools they used, the shoes they and their families wore, the furniture that they needed, the very houses in which they lived. The women spun wool or flax into threads, wove cloth, and made the clothes that the family wore. Habits of thrift and frugality were established which persisted down through many generations.

Agriculture was supplemented by fishing and commerce. The New England coasts

Fishing and commerce were themselves rich in fish, and the banks of Newfoundland, which had long been famed as fishing grounds, were not far away. Fishing led directly to commerce, for far more fish could be taken than could be consumed locally. According to reliable estimates not less than three hundred thousand cod were exported by New England fishermen in 1641, and by the year 1675 no less than six hundred vessels and four thousand men were engaged in the cod fisheries alone. New England fishermen found ready markets for their wares in the West Indies and in the Catholic countries of Europe.

Commerce, once opened up, diversified rapidly. Foodstuffs of various kinds were carried to the West Indies, not only from New England, but also from ports farther down the coast where the Yankee **The West** traders stopped to complete **Indian trade** their cargoes. In return for these commodities molasses, sugar, ginger, and other insular products were obtained, and in addition bills of exchange which could be used in the purchase of manufactured articles in England. At first the West Indian trade was confined mainly to the British islands, but by the eighteenth century trade with the Dutch, French, and Spanish islands was also common. From these sources came a good share of the money that found its way to the colonies. In 1697 the slave trade, which had for some time before been monopolized by a few English trading companies, was opened to all British subjects, and an interesting "triangular trade" developed. Molasses, brought from the West Indies to New England, was manufactured into rum, which was shipped to the African coast, where it was used in the purchase of slaves. The slaves were then brought to the West Indies and there exchanged for more molasses, which was then brought back to New England to make more rum, to acquire more slaves, to exchange for more molasses, and so on. Not all of the rum, however, was exported. The New England fishermen themselves used it liberally, and other New-Englanders, even some of the very "elect," developed a keen taste for it. Rum was useful also in the prosecution of the fur trade, which furnished yet another item for export.

Shipbuilding went hand in hand with fishing and commerce. Skillful craftsmen early contrived to build fleet and **Shipbuilding** sturdy ships which not only withstood well the battering of the elements, but frequently outran revenue vessels, and made an art of smuggling. Especially was this the case after the British began to collect duties under the Navigation Acts. Indeed, on the eve of the American Revolution smuggling became an industry in itself, comparable in some ways to the bootlegging industry of the Prohibition era. Timbers for

WASHINGTON STREET, SALEM, MASSACHUSETTS. Anonymous painting, about 1785.

JAMES TILLEY, ESQUIRE. Portrait of a prosperous New England merchant-shipper by John Singleton Copley, 1757.

FISHING IN THE NORTH ATLANTIC. Representational illustration, about 1720, showing "ye manner of fishing for, curing, and drying cod."

Colonial New England, as it reached maturity, produced port cities that compared well in architecture, business activity, and general culture with cities of similar size anywhere in the world. Salem, Massachusetts, with an interest in the fisheries, in ship-building, in the India trade, and on occasion, in privateering, prided itself in its many handsome buildings. In near-by Boston, Copley, the artist, charged high prices for his portraits. Life was cruder in the backwoods, but the rich lumber resources of the interior contributed greatly to the general prosperity.

SAW MILL AND PROTECTIVE BLOCK HOUSE IN THE NEW ENGLAND BACKWOODS.

shipbuilding were obtained in plenty from the easily accessible forests, and such items as barrel-staves, clapboards, and naval stores were early added to the list of exportable commodities. Yankee ships and Yankee seamen came to be seen and known all over the world, while the superiority of Yankee seamanship and the shrewdness of Yankee salesmen also received general recognition. Many New England merchants, the owners of ships and dealers in foreign wares, made comfortable fortunes; and the active business life that centered in the principal posts caused the villages so located to grow into sizeable cities. Before the Revolution, Boston, with less than thirty thousand inhabitants, was the largest city in New England and the second largest in America, but many other towns, such as Salem, Newport, and New Haven, had passed well out of the village class.

Religion played a far greater part in the life of New England than in the life of the

Calvinism

plantation South, and the theology of Calvin made a profound impression upon the New England character. The cardinal doctrine of Calvinism was predestination. As Calvin conceived it, God had created man in his own likeness and image, and had given him all the blessings of life in the Garden of Eden on condition that he must never eat of the fruit of a certain tree. But man, tempted by woman, broke the contract thus implied, and thereby lost not only all title to the joys of Eden, but also all hope of happiness in the world to come. Nor did the punishment stop here, for not only the original parents but also their children, and their descendants forever, being conceived in iniquity and born with the taint of original sin upon them, were in justice outside the pale of God's forgiveness. But God, in his infinite mercy, sent his Son into the world to suffer in the place of those who had been chosen to be saved. By the sacrifice of Christ on the Cross all those whom God had predestined and foreordained to be saved were freed of the punishment that rightfully should have fallen upon them. Only such

persons as God had "elected" to be saved, however, could benefit from the sacrifice of the Son. All the rest of mankind, including even unborn infants, were "elected" to be damned.

This hard doctrine, morbidly dwelt upon by the long-winded Puritan divines, was driven deeply into the marrow of the thoughtful New-Englander. Was he of the elect whom God had chosen to be saved? One might never know, and yet the behavior of a man should show to some degree at least whether or not he had been deemed by God worthy to be saved. Those who were religiously inclined watched their conduct and searched their souls for evidences of the divine will toward them. They displayed also a not unnatural interest in the spiritual welfare of their neighbors. Who of those they knew were to be saved, who were to be damned? Village life with its intimate associations gave ample opportunity for observation to those who wished to scrutinize closely the details of their neighbors' lives. The injunction to be one's brother's keeper was cheerfully obeyed, and buttresses against temptation were erected in the shape of "blue laws" that regulated closely the behavior of the individual. Church attendance in some of the New England colonies was long required by law, and on Sundays, according to one somewhat dubious chronicle, "no one . . . could make mince pies, dance, play cards, or play any instrument of music, except the drum, trumpet, and Jew's harp."

Toward the end of the seventeenth century, too close concentration on what Cotton Mather called the "wonders of **The** the invisible world" almost **"witchcraft** swept the little settlement of **delusion"** Salem Village, Massachusetts, from its moorings. At this time the existence of witches, or persons endowed with supernatural powers of evil, was still taken for granted on both sides of the Atlantic. The Hebraic law had accepted the idea, and in the Old Testament (Exodus xxii, 18) there was a direct command: "Thou shalt not suffer a witch to live." Furthermore, a fif-

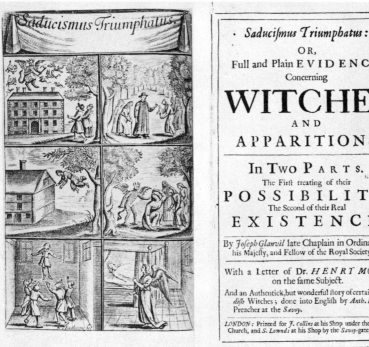

Saducismus Triumphatus:
OR,
Full and Plain EVIDENCE
Concerning
WITCHES
AND
APPARITIONS.
In Two PARTS.
The First treating of their
POSSIBILITY,
The Second of their Real
EXISTENCE.

By *Joseph Glanvil* late Chaplain in Ordinary to his Majesty, and Fellow of the Royal Society.

With a Letter of Dr. *HENRY MORE* on the same Subject.

And an Authentick, but wonderful story of certain *Swedish* Witches; done into English by *Anth. Horneck* Preacher at the *Savoy.*

LONDON: Printed for *J. collins* at his Shop under the *Temple*-Church, and *S. Lownds* at his Shop by the *Savoy-gate, 1681.*

WITCHCRAFT PROVEN. A treatise not uncommon in England, 1681.

PURITANS BEING PUNISHED IN THE STOCKS IN ENGLAND. After a drawing by William Hogarth.

Religious intolerance was long taken for granted on both sides of the Atlantic. The same Puritans who had themselves suffered grievous persecutions because of their opinions saw nothing wrong, on coming to America, in persecuting those who disagreed with them. Witchcraft was accepted as a fact, and at Salem, Massachusetts, in 1692, there occurred a violent persecution of alleged witches.

teenth-century pope had even issued a bull on the subject, while during the sixteenth and seventeenth centuries secular courts, first in Europe and then in America, had sentenced to death persons convicted of being witches. The "witchcraft delusion" was thus no mere invention of the Puritan mind; it was based on long-standing tradition. During the spring of 1692 some Salem children, insisting that certain individuals whom they named had bewitched them, began to act queerly, even having, or perhaps feigning, fits. Soon, not only in Salem, but elsewhere

in the colony also, ministers and magistrates were giving serious attention to these accusations, and were demanding that something be done about them. Finally the governor appointed a special court of distinguished judges to try the cases, and the whole colony debated the evidence that was laid before the court. Arrests multiplied, convictions were obtained, and by the end of September no less than nineteen persons had been hanged, and many others imprisoned. Then a reaction set in, and soon even among the leaders of the frenzy there was abject repentance.

A few years later one of the judges before whom the trials had been held, and a number of the jurymen, openly confessed their error, and asked forgiveness. The Salem executions were not actually the last for witchcraft in America, but there was never again a comparable outburst.

The "New England conscience" that was born of the austere doctrines and practices of **The New England conscience** the Puritans, endured long after some of the Calvinistic tenets that produced it had lost their binding force. Scrupulous observance of the moral law, rigid self-control carried even to the length of self-denial, earnestness of purpose, and firm belief in the righteousness of God's way with man set the conscientious New-Englander somewhat apart from other Americans. His conscience was apt to carry over into business and politics, both of which he took with great seriousness. In these realms, however, the contract idea, so firmly embedded in Calvinistic theology, was not without its helpful side. A bargain was a bargain, and a contract once signed had to be obeyed. It behooved the maker of business contracts to watch carefully the terms laid down, and mercy was not always vouchsafed to the careless. Governmental charters and constitutions were likewise held to be sacred covenants, and the principals, whether kings, lords, or commoners, might justly be held to the last letter of their plighted word. Nor was the law of the land, duly made and recorded, to be lightly ignored.

Education was taken much more seriously in New England than elsewhere in the colonies. This was due in part to **Education** the religious interest which made it seem worth while for every individual to be able to search the Scriptures on his own account, and in part to the existence of towns where schools and the means of education could be easily maintained. Five years after Boston was founded, it had a school, and in 1642 the General Court of Massachusetts passed a law requiring that all parents should see that their children learned how to read and how to ply some trade. Another Massa-

chusetts law, passed in 1647, proposed the establishment of free public schools throughout the colony, an ideal that was not soon attained. But schools of one kind or another, sometimes private and sometimes public, were the rule rather than the exception throughout New England. The common schools taught reading, writing, and arithmetic; Latin or grammar schools prepared boys for college; and academies, which admitted both boys and girls, offered a somewhat wider course of study. Religion received much attention in most of the schools. Pupils were taught the catechism at an early age, they read selections from the Bible as exercises in reading, and such textbooks as came into use were strongly impregnated with the Scriptures and Calvinistic theology. Discipline was extremely severe, and any wanton tendencies toward self-expression on the part of the pupils were promptly and thoroughly suppressed. Colleges, designed primarily for the purpose of training ministers, presently put in their appearance. Harvard College was founded in 1636, Yale in 1701, Brown in 1764, and Dartmouth in 1769.

New-Englanders believed genuinely in their own ways, and carried them along wherever they went. Into New **New England propagandism** York, New Jersey, Maryland, and other neighboring colonies streamed New England emigrants carrying with them the New England conscience and the institutions New-Englanders held dear. Indeed, in the settlement of the whole of the American West, New-Englanders were invariably present to reproduce as best they could in their new homes the civilization they had left. The typical New-Englander was exceedingly intolerant of customs that diverged to any great extent from his own. Advocates of innovations were apt to be frowned upon heavily, and in the middle seventeenth century such total nonconformists as the Quakers were sometimes grievously persecuted. In eighteenth-century New England the narrowness in religious matters that had been so characteristic of the formative period was much less in evidence.

By this time Episcopalians and even Catholics were treated with consideration, and many such communicants were to be found, particularly Episcopalians, in all the urban centers.

The Middle Colonies rested upon a geographic foundation that combined the chief **The Middle Colonies** characteristics of New England and the South. Here there was a coastal plain and a piedmont, but the plain was narrower than in the plantation area, and the piedmont was wider. Toward New England, in New York, the mountains were in great glacial-ground clusters, but toward the south, in Pennsylvania, the long parallel ridges of the Alleghanies began to rise. The rivers of the central area were fewer in number, comparatively, than in the other sections, but they were longer and furnished more convenient highways into the interior than could be found elsewhere along the Atlantic seaboard. Indeed, three great river systems, the Hudson, the Delaware, and the Susquehanna, furnished the chief key to the development of the region. Each of these rivers flowed, generally speaking, from north to south, each was entered through a spacious harbor, and each was navigable even by ·ocean-going vessels for a considerable distance into the interior. In each river valley a distinctive civilization developed, and in due time a great city marked the point where each river reached the sea. New York commanded the trade of the Hudson Valley, Philadelphia of the Delaware, and Baltimore of the Susquehanna. Even in colonial times the spirit of rivalry between these growing towns was much in evidence.

The Dutch influence left a lasting impression upon the people of the Hudson Valley. **Dutch influence** The hopes of those who invented the patroon system were never fully realized, but the pretensions of the system did tend to mark off from the other elements of society an aristocratic caste of great landowners. One patroonship, Rensselaerswyck, which was founded near Albany by Kiliaen van Rensselaer and came to embrace many thousands of acres,

worked out much as the original plans had contemplated; and a number of other estates, while by no means so closely approximating the feudal pattern, at least reached large dimensions. On some of the great estates of the lower Hudson tobacco was raised much as in Virginia. In a country where free land was so plentiful, however, and where even in the days of Dutch control emigrants were practically given all the land they could im• prove, it was difficult to maintain a tenant class. The great estates might exist, but many of their acres remained unworked. Nevertheless their owners came to constitute a distinguished upper class of "Vans" and "velts," who, in spite of being overwhelmingly outnumbered by small free farmers, exerted a preponderant influence in the affairs of the colony.

Dutch governmental practices also left some traces upon the subsequent English colony of New York. During **Absence of** the period of Dutch control very **democracy** little was permitted the colonists by way of a voice in their government. New England emigrants protested vigorously against being thus deprived of rights to which they had long been accustomed, and on the eve of the British conquest Peter Stuyvesant, the Dutch governor, actually called together a representative assembly, which failed, however, to reach any important agreements. Thus, except for a limited amount of local self-government permitted in the Dutch villages, the English conquest found the colony wholly lacking in democratic political institutions. After the conquest, with the colony now under the rule of the reactionary Duke of York (later King James II), the introduction of democracy was still delayed. Richard Nicolls, the first British governor, was an astute diplomatist, and managed to keep discontent with such a system at a minimum, but his successor, Edmund Andros, had little such skill.

In 1683 the proprietor felt obliged to yield to the pressure for a representative assembly, but the Assembly adopted a charter of Liberties and Privileges which nettled him, and when he became king a year later he went back on his bargain. New-Yorkers ultimately won the right to participate in the control of their colony, although only a privileged few were granted the right to vote, and the government of the colony was distinctly less democratic than that of any other. New York politics, down to the American Revolution, tended to be little more than a series of factional fights among the important families to see whose influence would be strongest.

With respect to religion some Dutch survivals may also be noted. The Dutch adhered generally to the Dutch Reformed Church, which was as definitely Calvinistic in its teachings as even the Puritan congregations of New England could have asked. The Dutch, however, fed their souls less upon the doctrine of predestination than did the Puritans, and they were a little more content to rely upon God's abounding grace. With them religion played no such dominant rôle as in New England. Religious toleration, moreover, was a Dutch tradition, and the emigrant who came to New Netherland was rarely bothered about his faith. Peter Stuyvesant made some trouble for the Quakers, he once expelled a Baptist minister from the colony, and perhaps he discriminated unfairly against the Lutherans, but these acts were not so much an expression of Dutch policy as an expression of the personal predilections of Peter Stuyvesant. When New Netherland became New York, the Church of England supplanted the Dutch Reformed Church as the official church of the colony. But the number of Anglican communicants remained small for a long time, whereas, besides the members of the Dutch Reformed Church, there were on Long Island and elsewhere many Puritans from New England. Inasmuch as the proprietor, the Duke of York, was known to be a Catholic, it seemed expedient to carry over the Dutch spirit of toleration into the new régime, and this was done, although later some harsh anti-Catholic legislation was enacted.

Religion in New York

The Delaware Valley became the seat of a civilization quite as distinctive as was to be found along the Hudson, for it was here that the Quaker influence was preponderant. But democracy was inherent in the Quaker teaching. Quakers believed that God spoke to men directly by a voice that reached their hearts, and this "inner light" was denied to no man or woman. Since anyone might thus be in direct contact with the divine will, there was no room for ministers, or bishops, or ecclesiastical foundations. Even the Bible as a guide of faith and conduct suffered somewhat, for the "inner light" furnished quite as convincing an authority. All men were equal before God, so why should there be the distinctions in dress and manners that marked the aristocracy apart from the common run of men? Good Quakers called no man master, and used simply the word "Friend" by way of address. They objected to the use of the formal "you" when speaking to an individual, and employed instead the democratic "thee." They kept their hats on their heads even in the presence of kings, and they wore a plain, standardized garb that was designed to deny all social distinctions. Since the "inner light" came to women as well as to men, women were accorded the same privileges, at least in a religious way, that men enjoyed. Women spoke their minds freely "in meeting," notwithstanding the injunction of Saint Paul to "let the women keep silence in the church." Slavery the Quakers deeply deplored.

Quakers on the Delaware

Faith in such democratic principles as these could not but affect markedly the development of the Quaker colonies. Their tolerance of many varieties of religion, their unwillingness to propagandize in the Puritan fashion, and their generous land terms attracted great numbers of settlers. The valley of the Susquehanna, however, quite as much as the Delaware, was to profit from these inviting practices. To the Susquehanna came a mixed population, including many colonials from other regions, but in far greater num-

Religious toleration

bers emigrants from Europe, in particular the so-called "Pennsylvania Dutch" and the Scotch-Irish.

The "Pennsylvania Dutch" were not Dutch at all, but Germans who had left their homes for many good reasons. For one thing, the wars that Louis XIV of France prosecuted in his attempt to attain for his country its "natural boundaries" not only drew the adjacent German states into the struggles, but made of them a periodic battle-field. For emigrants from this region, who sought relief from the brutalities of war, the Quaker doctrine of pacifism had a peculiar charm. Economic pressure furnished another motive. Petty feudal lords exacted heavy dues, required annoying services, and collected burdensome tithes for the support of state churches. Even in German Switzerland, where the ravages of war seldom touched, such exactions as these made many of the lower classes look with favor upon emigration to America. Religious persecution also played a part, for each prince of the Holy Roman Empire was left free to determine as he might choose the religious faith of his people — *cuius regio eius religio.* Catholics were in consequence subject to persecution in Lutheran states; Lutherans in Catholic states; and the minor religious sects, which came to have a great vogue in Germany, in all the states. Particularly oppressed were the sects, such as the Mennonites, who objected to military service. Penn's agents advertised persistently the advantages of America among the distressed Germans, and in 1709 the British Parliament, glad enough of the opportunity to stimulate outside immigration into the British Empire, passed a law for the naturalization of foreign Protestants.

Some German immigration reached the colonies late in the seventeenth century — Germantown, Pennsylvania, was founded in 1683 — but the great bulk of the German invasion came toward the middle of the eighteenth century. A few settled at Newbern, North Carolina; others settled in New York, where they were generally called Palatines, and acquired lands as far inland as the Mohawk Valley; and still others in New Jersey, Maryland, and Virginia; but in the main the German immigrants found their way to Pennsylvania, where they picked for themselves choice lands usually well up the valley of the Susquehanna, for the English colonists already had the Delaware. They came in such numbers that the provincials began to be alarmed, and the Pennsylvania legislature even passed laws restricting immigration. But these laws were invariably vetoed by the governors, and the Germans continued to come. It is estimated that, at the time the American Revolution broke out, about one third of the inhabitants of Pennsylvania were German. Living together as they did, they retained their own language, established their own schools, printing presses, and newspapers, and continued for many years to be a people apart. Indeed, many of their descendants in central Pennsylvania still speak and write a patois known as "Pennsylvania Dutch."

The Pennsylvania Germans were not the only immigrants from Europe to enter the Susquehanna Valley, for they were soon followed by the Scotch-Irish, with somewhat similar reasons for migration. These Scotch-Irish newcomers were from the north of Ireland, but they were really not Irish at all. Most of their ancestors had been lowland Scots, some of whom had been colonized on lands taken from the Irish during the reigns of Queen Elizabeth and King James I, and others on the Irish lands confiscated by Oliver Cromwell during the Protectorate. The Scotch-Irish troubles in Ireland were numerous. They could not get on well with the native Irish to whom they seemed to be mere trespassers. Also, being Presbyterians of the most unbending variety, they scorned the Catholicism of their Irish neighbors, who in turn had little pleasant to say about Scottish Presbyterianism. As dissenters, they resented stoutly the legal requirement that they pay tithes to the Anglican Church. They suffered also many economic grievances. The tenant system was peculiarly harsh upon them, since most of their landlords were absentees, and were not only unconcerned about the oppressive rentals, but were also often unaware of the still more oppressive methods of collecting them. The English government, moreover, in its efforts to protect the interests of English citizens, passed laws against the importation of important Irish products, such as dairy cattle and woolen goods, and placed discouraging regulations upon the production of linen. Bad harvests and frequent famines added to the Irish discontent.

As was the case with the Pennsylvania Germans, some Scotch-Irish colonists **Scotch-Irish settlements** reached America before seventeen hundred, but the great majority did not arrive until toward the middle of the next century. Some of the Scotch-Irish settled in New England, New York, and New Jersey, but most of them penetrated into the back country of Pennsylvania by way of the Susquehanna and its tributaries. Coming a little later than the Germans, the Scotch-Irish went a little farther into the interior to find lands. They spoke English, and hence were not bothered in their relations with the native Americans by the language barrier that so often perplexed the Germans, but they were harder to deal with than the Germans. When some of them were accused of holding lands without legal title they replied that it was "against the laws of God and Nature, that so much land should be idle while so many Christians wanted it to labor on." There were fully as many Scotch-Irish as German emigrants to America, and probably more. At the time the American Revolution broke out, Pennsylvania was no less than one third Scotch-Irish.

Diversity of population elements was thus an important characteristic of the Middle **Other nationalities** Colonies. In addition to the Hudson Valley Dutch, the English Quakers, the Pennsylvania Germans, and the Scotch-Irish, although in no such numbers, there were here French Huguenots, Irish from the south of Ireland, Scots from Scotland, a few Welshmen, and a few Jews. The Jews were most numerous in New York, whither they had come from South America, Holland, Germany, and Poland during the Dutch occupation. Coupled with variety in population elements was a variety of religious denominations. The Middle Colonies were thus a hodgepodge of races and creeds, and a natural hotbed for factional politics. It should occasion no surprise that this region gave rise to a group of astute politicians, quick to compromise and ready to shift their ground as each new emergency appeared.

Local government in the Middle Colonies borrowed a little from the New England colonies and a little from the colonies to the south. Counties **Local government** appeared after the fashion of the plantation area, but they were usually subdivided into townships that were reminiscent of New England. In New York the influence of New England was more marked than elsewhere in the Middle Colonies, but well before the end of the seventeenth century a county board of supervisors, composed of representatives from the various towns, had absorbed many of the important functions of local administration. In Pennsylvania the townships were even less important than in New York. The combination of town and county government in the Middle Colonies proved to be of greater than local significance, for it was this example that most of the States of the West were to follow later on.

Public schools existed in the Middle Colonies from an early date, but the chief responsibility for educational establishments was here generally **Education** left with the various religious denominations. Colleges were relatively numerous by the time of the Revolution. The Anglicans founded King's College (later Columbia) in New York under a charter obtained in 1754; the Presbyterians established the College of New Jersey (Princeton) as early as 1746; and Rutgers, opened in 1766, ministered to the educational needs of the Dutch Reformed faith. Benjamin Franklin led the way for the opening at Philadelphia in 1751 of an "Academy," free from sectarian influences, which later (1791) became the University of Pennsylvania.

Farming furnished occupations to most of the inhabitants of the Middle Colonies, *The "bread colonies"* where the production and exportation of foodstuffs gave rise to the name of "bread colonies." Indian corn, or maize, and other grains, livestock, particularly among the Germans who understood the necessity of caring for domestic animals in winter, and vegetables, most of which were native to America and did not need to be acclimated, were produced in ever-increasing quantities. Nuts, fruits, and berries were abundant, and required little or no cultivation. Hemp and flax were also grown.

Manufacturing quickly sprang up, especially in Pennsylvania and New Jersey after *Manufacturing* the coming of the Germans, among whom there were many skilled workmen. Iron, textiles, glass, and paper were among the articles commonly made in these regions. According to one observer, the inhabitants of Germantown were mostly manufacturers who were able to "make everything in such quantity and perfection, that, in a short time, this province will lack very little from England, its mother country." Weavers, tanners, metal workers, and printers plied their respective trades with good success. Sawmills furnished excellent lumber for building purposes, but good bricks were also made and in Philadelphia and New York brick houses abounded. Mills were numerous, and the flour they produced was as good as could be made anywhere in the world.

In commerce the Middle Colonies were not far behind New England, and the merchants *Commerce* of Philadelphia and New York prospered no less than those of Boston. Philadelphia, indeed, toward the close of the colonial period came to exceed Boston in size. Grain, flour, and other provisions were exported in great profusion,

Colonial Colleges

mostly to the West Indies. New York by the middle of the eighteenth century numbered among its items of export no less than eighty thousand barrels of flour a year. Here the fur trade, which had been greatly fostered by the Dutch during their control of New Amsterdam, continued under the English as an important industry and an incentive to commerce. Shipbuilding was a natural accompaniment of overseas trade.

Interior from the seacoast, cutting across the boundaries of every other section and of most of the colonies, lay the colonial "West" — the frontier. *The frontier* Its limits were necessarily shifting; indeed, at some time every settled area in America had been frontier. But by the end of the colonial period the "back country," as the western settlements were then generally called, could be marked off fairly distinctly from the rest. In the South the piedmont and mountain valleys, in the Middle Colonies the upper reaches of the Susquehanna, the Delaware, the Mohawk, and their tributaries, in New England much of what is now

Vermont, and except for settlements near the coast, of New Hampshire and Maine also, belonged to the frontier. Fur-traders, who almost invariably led the English advance upon the West, cattle-growers, who especially in the South were attracted by the free grazing lands of the interior, and soldiers, who in one or another of the wars against the Indians had seen the western country, revealed the possibilities of the regions they had visited, and presently settlement followed.

Various conditions worked together to promote the rapid expansion of the frontier. **Why people went West** Colonial families were large, and the natural increase in population provided many pioneers. The exhaustion of the eastern lands by poor methods of farming, particularly in the tobacco-growing areas, provided others. Still others came from the ranks of the indentured servants, who, once they were free, did not often linger long near the scene of their servitude. Frequently dissenters from the locally approved or established churches of their communities sought homes in the West where they would not be looked down upon because of their religious faith. Immigrants from the Old World, who found themselves unpopular when they tried to settle in the older American communities, turned quickly to the more hospitable frontier. To all who would listen, the call of cheap western lands had an inviting sound. Speculators there were in plenty who acquired for almost nothing great holdings in the West and searched eagerly for settlers to whom they might sell them. But so abundant was the land that those who were too poor or were not too particular need pay little attention to the acquisition of land titles.

The conditions of life along the frontier were hard. Practically all the lands **Frontier conditions of life** were heavily timbered, and the "clearings" upon which crops could be planted were made possible only through infinite labor. Luxuries were unknown. The pioneer had no money with which to buy them, but even if he had,

the difficulty of transporting goods from east to west held down such trade to the barest necessities. Along the "cutting edge" of the frontier, Indians were ever in evidence, and almost never wholly peaceful. Here pioneer families were accustomed to select some well-located farmhouse for a "station," and to build about it a stockade, duly equipped with shelters and storehouses, to which they could flee when an Indian attack seemed imminent. All good frontiersmen were adept with the axe and the rifle. With the former they cut the trees, fashioned the logs of which they built their houses, and smoothed down the planks from which they made benches, tables, and other household necessities. With their rifles they not only fought off the Indians, but also kept the family larder filled, and provided the skins from which many of their garments were made. Each pioneer cabin was apt to be on the farm that the pioneer owned, or hoped to own, and at a considerable distance from any other dwelling. Pioneer life was therefore lonely, particularly for the pioneer housewife, and the opportunities for such privileges as churches and schools were decidedly limited.

The society which was thus established in the back country differed markedly from that to be found in the older and **Differences from coast society** more settled areas along the coast. For one thing, it was extremely cosmopolitan in character. Here English emigrants from the colonial East met Pennsylvania Germans, Scotch-Irish, and a variety of other foreigners, and not merely met them, but mingled freely with them. The frontier thus became a great "melting-pot" out of which a new and distinctively American race was to come. Furthermore, the frontier settlements, cutting across colonial lines as they did, tended to break down local peculiarities and to lay the foundations of a truly national point of view. Geographic considerations greatly favored this process, for the mountain valleys from Pennsylvania down lay parallel to the coast, and access to them was difficult except at favored points. In North Carolina not only mountains, but eighty miles of pine barrens also, separated the frontier outposts from the settled areas. Population entered the mountains mainly from Pennsylvania, and, spreading slowly southward, presented everywhere the same characteristics, often in striking contrast with the institutions and the traditions that bound the colonists who lived closer in toward the coast.

The genuine equality of conditions that existed among the frontiersmen bred a vigorous spirit of democracy. One man could not by the very nature of pioneer life be particularly above his neighbors. He owned about the same amount of land, lived in the same kind of house, worked with the same primitive tools, dressed in the same crude fashion as his fellows. If he possessed education it was not important in the West. If he had illustrious ancestors he might as well forget them, for his neighbors surely would. If on the other hand his ancestors were unpleasant to remember, or if he himself had a past, those were things, too, that could easily be put out of mind.

Frontier democracy

This emphasis upon democracy in the West was paralleled by an equally marked emphasis upon individual freedom. Each pioneer was practically a law unto himself, and he came to set high store by the privilege which the wilderness gave him of managing his own affairs in any way he chose. The interference by government in anything that seemed to him his own business was apt to be met by wrathful opposition. He objected to hampering regulations with regard to the acquisition of land, and he resented bitterly every attempt to impose upon him a religious establishment to which he did not subscribe. The Scotch-Irish, so many of whom found their way to the West, added a contentious note to frontier individualism. They or their ancestors had argued as well as fought for their rights both in Scotland and in Ireland, and the habit of mind so developed was not lost by migration to America.

Individualism

The contrasts between the people of the back country and the people of the coast led inevitably to some antagonisms. Men of the East still valued class distinctions and were careful to safeguard the rights of property. Men of the West had foresworn aristocracy, and to them the rights of the debtor were no less a matter of concern than the rights of the creditor. The strong foreign infusion in the western blood was another source of difficulty. The older elements of society feared that the institutions they held dear would not be safe in the hands of such people. The Westerners, on the other hand, saw little significance in national differences, and resented the suspicions of the East. Differences of opinion developed also on such matters as religious freedom, the right to hold slaves, the assessment of taxes, the control of the Indians. Skeptical of the political wisdom of the backwoodsmen, colonial legislatures under eastern control rarely accorded to the frontier counties their proportionate share of representatives. The echoes of these conflicts could sometimes be heard as the American Revolution ran its course.

Antagonism West and East

The lives which American colonials lived seem slow and humdrum in comparison with the lives of Americans today. Transportation was difficult. The colonies were at least six weeks from Europe, and often, with contrary winds, the passage was longer. The coast towns communicated with one another most easily by sea; indeed, the Atlantic Ocean and the navigable rivers which emptied into it furnished perhaps the strongest of the ties that bound the colonies together. Even so, coastwise travel was far from speedy and sometimes it was far from safe. Roads existed between the principal cities, but elsewhere they were rare, and usually they were incredibly bad. Not a single hard-surfaced turnpike could be found anywhere in the colonies. By the middle of the eighteenth century horse-drawn carriages and stagecoaches were in common use, although travel

Everyday life in the colonies

by horseback was still very popular. At convenient distances taverns and inns of a sort could be found where the travelers found lodging and where local patrons found diversion. These inns were in a sense the social clubs of the time. Here, often amidst much drinking and gambling, but unhampered by the hurry and bustle of modern life and the noise of traffic and factories, public opinion took form.

The houses in which colonial citizens **Colonial** lived had progressed from the **houses** crude thatch-roofed affairs of wattle or planks stood on end, used by the earliest settlers, to roomy dwellings usually of Georgian design. In the seventeenth century the imprint of Dutch, Swedish, and German as well as English architectural ideas could be discerned in various parts of America, but after about 1720 the Georgian, or as it is now generally termed "colonial," style won its way into every section, except perhaps, the frontier, where log houses were well-nigh universal. Glass windows replaced oiled paper at about the same time, and among the well-to-do merchants of the North and the great planters of the South there was much striving after good architectural effects. The houses were mostly rectangular two-storied affairs, built usually of wood, painted white, with green shutters. Sometimes, especially in New England, where the snows were deep in winter, outbuildings were attached to the main house one after another in a long procession. A little before the time of the American Revolution tall-columned porticoes, such as Washington's home at Mount Vernon possessed, became very popular. Houses of stone and brick were also common, and numerous chimneys, made necessary because of the many fireplaces, broke the roof-lines. Churches, in much the same style as the houses except for their tall spires, were everywhere abundant.

Within the most sumptuous of the houses, however, there were few conveniences, judged by present-day standards. The fireplaces rarely provided enough heat for comfort in severe winter weather, adequate screening against flies and in- **Lack of** sects in summer was impossible, **conveniences** and such items as cookstoves, refrigerators, bathtubs, and plumbing were totally unknown. Water was obtained from springs or surface wells that were easily contaminated, and this accounted for much of the disease common in colonial times. Candles usually furnished light at night, although whale-oil lamps were not uncommon in fashionable circles. Food was obtainable everywhere in great abundance and even in the cities at low prices, but often the fare was severely plain. Corn bread, hominy, and salt pork furnished the chief items of subsistence for the poorer classes, particularly in the South. Whiskey, beer, hard cider, and rum were manufactured locally and were available in great profusion, but only the upper classes could afford the finer wines and brandies that had to be imported.

The colonial cities compared fairly favorably with cities of similar size in Europe. Philadelphia was built on a plan **Colonial** worked out by William Penn, **cities** with wide paved streets, crossing one another at right angles. Here the houses were mostly of brick, and sometimes they were as many as three stories in height. Sidewalks were plentiful, and street lamps made the lot of the night traveler easy. Both Boston and New York were noted for their general planlessness and their narrow crooked streets, but some of the more important streets in both cities were paved, and they were usually kept clean. Charleston, as the favorite resort of the South Carolina planters, enjoyed a lively social life not found elsewhere; but its method of garbage disposal was primitive, for buzzards were here protected by law as necessary scavengers. In all the cities ashes and garbage were dumped into alleys and on vacant lots, and in most of them hogs running at large in the streets served the purpose expected of the buzzards of Charleston. Sanitary conditions were bad, and the resultant prevalence of disease was little checked by the physicians that the times afforded. Bleeding was still in common use, and the herbs and drugs prescribed were of dubious value. Shortly before the outbreak of the American Revolution medical colleges were opened, one in New York and one in Philadelphia. These were the first of their kind in the colonies. Since commerce was the chief concern of all the colonial cities, the noise attendant upon modern industrial life was wholly lacking. Creaking carts loaded with merchandise were perhaps the chief offenders against the ear.

Attendance at church, public meetings, "Thursday lectures" (mostly theological) in New England, and in the less strait-laced communities dances

Amusements

and theaters furnished a large share of the amusement the people were permitted to enjoy. Lavish hospitality was a point of honor with the southern planters, and the constant visiting back and forth made life for the younger generation a succession of what today might be called house-parties. Dancing was a favorite amusement with all classes in the South, and despite the frowns of the godly was a common pastime nearly everywhere. Theaters existed in the large cities only, but by the time of the Revolution the American stage was definitely established. Gambling, horse-racing, cockfighting, and fox-hunting were major activities with the young bloods, especially in the South, but lotteries to raise money for churches, public works, and even college endowments were conducted without censure in Puritan New England, and were in especial favor with the clergy. Out in the rural districts, particularly along the frontier, "log-rollings," house-raisings, husking bees, weddings, and funerals furnished relief from the ordinary tedium of life. Courtship was officially surrounded with many hampering conventions that have since been wholly eliminated, but the habit of marriage was strong with the colonials, and ways seem to have been found. Bachelors and widowers were under great social pressure to marry, and sometimes laws which discriminated against the unmarried were added to the incentive of public opinion.

There was no such thing as a colonial nobility — even among the Cavaliers who came to America there were very few of noble birth — but **The colonial aristocracy** throughout the colonial period there was a well-recognized aristocracy which held itself definitely above the common run of men. To this class belonged most of the English officials resident in America, the ministers and magistrates, the well-to-do merchants, the owners of great estates in the central colonies, and the great planters of the South. Members of the aristocracy sought to distinguish themselves from the lower classes by their manners, their superior education, and particularly their mode of dress. Indeed, during early colonial times laws were actually passed in some colonies forbidding "men and women of mean condition" to "take upon them the garb of gentlemen." Wealthy men wore silk stockings, breeches of velvet, silk, or other expensive goods, and frock coats made of imported broadcloth and richly trimmed. Wigs were also quite generally affected during the eighteenth century. The colonial dames were likewise gorgeous with dresses of costly silks, duly amplified by the use of hoopskirts. The garb of the lower classes more closely resembled the garments universally worn today. Homespun fabrics were in general use, although on the frontier the men preferred leather jackets and breeches. The slow breakdown of class distinctions reflects the essential conservatism of the people who emigrated to America. They were accustomed to caste lines in Europe, and they naturally brought to the New World what they had known in the Old. Ultimately the equality of opportunity in America, duly emphasized by the existence of cheap lands along the frontier, tended to wipe out artificial class barriers. But even the aristocratic mode of dress lasted for many years after the Revolution.

Intellectual interests were for the most part confined to the upper classes. Newspapers, however, had come into vogue during

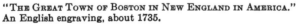

"THE GREAT TOWN OF BOSTON IN NEW ENGLAND IN AMERICA."
An English engraving, about 1735.

GEN. WALDO OF MAINE.
Portrait by Feke, 1748.

MISS HALL OF VIRGINIA.
Portrait by Williams,
1766.

"WESTOVER," CHARLES CITY COUNTY, VIRGINIA. Estate
of William Byrd, II, designed by him about 1730.

FASHIONABLE TRANSPORTATION. Detail from
a view of Harvard College, 1726.

Colonial culture, long before the Revolution, revealed
a mounting interest in the finer things of life. The tall
spires of numerous churches and public buildings
dominated the skylines of the coastal cities. Early colonial artists, mostly itinerant painters, produced handsome portraits of the well-to-do painted in the English
manner. Pretentious dwellings, especially on the
southern plantations, copied the current styles in
British architecture. The difficulties of inland transportation have no doubt been exaggerated; even the
fashionable coach-and-four was by no means unknown.

SALON OF THE POWEL HOUSE, PHILADELPHIA, 1768.
American and imported furnishings.

GRANDFATHER'S CLOCK.
Built by Benj. Cheney,
Hartford, about 1760.

SILVERWORK.   Part of a service
by Paul Revere, about 1770.

CABINET MAKING.   Trade card of Benj. Randolph, about 1770.

Early American housefurnishings, like early American houses, were of simple but sturdy construction, with greater emphasis on usability than on beauty. By the later eighteenth century, however, American craftsmen had begun to reflect the best taste of Europe, and, at least in furniture, to strike out occasionally along new and original lines. Competent cabinet makers were available in all the cities, and silversmiths such as Paul Revere vied with the best craftsmen of Europe in the excellence of their art.

"THE END OF THE FOX HUNT." American school painting, about 1750.

TOURING ENGLISH THEATER. Mrs. Hallam's acting was widely applauded in colonial American cities about 1750.

Colonial amusements, *especially in the tidewater South, included the English mounted fox-hunt, complete with a parson's blessing of the hounds. In the cities the theater flourished, often with English stars as guest artists. Both music and the theater were opposed in certain religious circles, but psalm singing had a considerable vogue in New England. The hornbooks and primers used in teaching the young laid great emphasis on Bible lore.*

CHILD WITH A HORNBOOK. From a 17th-century painting.

PSALM SINGERS. Engraving by Paul Revere for a book of Psalms, 1770.

THE NEW ENGLAND PRIMER. Familiar throughout America for over a century after 1690.

the eighteenth century, and on the eve of the American Revolution they were widely read. Books were far from numerous, although among the great planters of the South it was quite the fashion to have a library. Libraries of semi-public nature also existed, strangely enough more in the South than in the North. Benjamin Franklin was instrumental in establishing in 1731 the first public library of Philadelphia, an example that was quickly followed in other northern towns and cities. Light literature was not very common, and books on theology and law such as Calvin's *Institutes*, Blackstone's *Commentaries*, Locke's *Treatises on Government*, and Montesquieu's *Spirit of the Laws* had a wider appeal than would seem reasonable today. The Bible was everywhere read with much diligence.

Intellectual interests

Although literary achievement was not yet within the reach of most Americans, the intense theological interest of New England had not failed to produce visible results. Probably most able of the theological writers was Jonathan Edwards (1703–1758), whose expositions of Calvinistic doctrines rivaled in logic and lucidity the works of Calvin himself. Edwards was the only son of a learned Connecticut clergyman, who himself prepared his boy for college. Jonathan turned out to be unusually precocious, and at fourteen read Locke's *Essay on Human Understanding* with unfeigned delight. He was among the first to attend Yale College, where Newtonian science also made a profound impression upon him. Graduated from Yale in 1720, he was soon hard at work as a Congregational minister, proclaiming and expounding the Calvinistic doctrines that his soul had learned to love. Predestination, which once had appeared to him a "horrible doctrine," quickly won his intense admiration. As Edwards saw it, the right to bestow salvation wherever He chose was an essential attribute of divine sovereignty. No man could paint more clearly the dire vengeance that was to overtake the damned, or make

Jonathan Edwards

Jonathan Edwards, eminent Calvinist theologian, helped pave the way for the later revivalists by his ardent evangelistic sermons and writings. Portrait by Joseph Badger, about 1750.

less promising the prospect of being saved, yet he set greater store than the earlier theologians on the importance of the individual, and became the foremost American preacher of the "Great Awakening," a religious movement that spread from Europe to America in the middle of the eighteenth century. He was a successful revivalist, and counted his converts by the scores.

Edwards lived a life of great austerity. He rose at four o'clock each morning, studied and wrote thirteen hours each day, and even when he sought recreation by walks through the woods carried with him a notebook in which he jotted down his thoughts. He wrote many books, most of which had long theological titles. In 1754 he published *A Careful and Strict Enquiry into the Modern Prevailing Notions of that Freedom of Will which is Supposed to be Essential to Moral Agency, Vertue and Vice, Reward and Punishment, Praise and Blame*. On this work rests much of his fame as a philosopher. Shortly before his death he accepted the presidency of the Presbyterian College at Princeton, New Jersey, but his period of

Want of care does us more damage than want of knowledge.

For want of a nail the shoe was lost, and for want of a shoe the horse was lost.

Benjamin Franklin was the outstanding colonial of his time. He was as well known in the Old World as in the New, and was honored for his contributions to science and philosophy even more than for his contributions to government and politics. Scientists everywhere applauded his demonstration, in 1752, that lightning and electricity are one and the

same. His well-nigh universal interests are revealed in the unmistakable imprint he left upon such varied fields as journalism, literature, education, and humanitarian reform. The head shown here is after a portrait by Mason Chamberlin. At the right is one of a series of pictures from *Poor Richard Illustrated*, published in England in 1798.

---

office was too short for him to make a profound impression upon that institution.

More palatable to present-day readers are the writings of Benjamin Franklin (1706–**Benjamin** 90), who, in the opinion of many **Franklin** historians, ranks as the first American of his time. Franklin's span of life, like Edwards's, lay entirely within the eighteenth century, and his keen zest for living contrasts markedly with the otherworldliness of the great Puritan theologian. Franklin was a Bostonian by birth, and for a short period attended a Boston grammar school. His father was a tallow chandler, but since Benjamin had no liking for that trade he was apprenticed when twelve years of age to his half-brother James, a printer. Before long the apprentice was mainly responsible for the publication by his brother of a newspaper known as the *New England*

Courant, which was so indiscreet in what it printed that in 1722 James was jailed for a month. Shortly afterward Benjamin left his brother's employ and went to Philadelphia. Here he established himself as a printer of merit, and in due time began to publish much that he himself had written. His *Poor Richard's Almanack,* which appeared from 1732 to 1757, presented in homely garb the wise sayings of all the ages, and won almost universal acclaim in America as well as wide recognition in Europe. The *Pennsylvania Gazette,* with which Franklin was long associated, furnished another outlet for his pen, and it was here that some of his earliest scientific observations were set down. He was interested in a great variety of natural phenomena, but won recognition as a scientist chiefly through his experiments with electricity.

Franklin wrote only one book, his *Autobiography*, and it was never finished, but his numerous occasional articles, written in a severely plain, yet remarkably effective style, made him easily the literary leader of America. Franklin was not merely a writer, but lived an exceedingly full life. He was interested in business, he had a remarkable flair for inaugurating or helping along such projects as appeared likely to improve the lot of his fellow men, he was many times called upon for political service, and he spent years together on various errands abroad. He wrote only when he had some definite purpose to serve by his writing, but perhaps this is one of the reasons why he wrote so well.

Bibliography

Attempts to portray colonial civilization as a whole rather than colony by colony are more common than formerly. Compare, for example, R. G. Thwaites, *The Colonies* (1891), one of the volumes of the original *Epochs of American History*, edited by A. B. Hart, with M. W. Jernegan, *The American Colonies* (1929), a later offering by the same publishers in this series. The first volume of H. J. Carman, *Social and Economic History of the United States* (2 vols., 1930–34), contains an admirable section on colonial society. C. M. Andrews, *Colonial Folkways* (1919), is entertainingly written, and based on first-rate scholarship. Edward Eggleston, *The Transit of Civilization from England to America in the Seventeenth Century* (1901), is old, but extremely suggestive. L. B. Wright, *The Atlantic Frontier: Colonial American Civilization* (1947), is a recent re-evaluation. Carl Bridenbaugh, *Cities in the Wilderness: The First Century of Urban Life in America, 1625–1742* (1938), emphasizes the urban origins of American culture. Merle E. Curti, *The Growth of American Thought* (1943), begins with the colonial heritage and carries through brilliantly to the recent past. Sidney Kobre, *The Development of the Colonial Newspaper* (1944), studies one important aspect of colonial culture. See also the books listed for the preceding three chapters, particularly Wertenbaker, *The First Americans;* Nettels, *The Roots of American Civilization;* and Chitwood, *A History of Colonial America.*

The Pageant of America, edited by R. H. Gabriel and others (15 vols., 1929), is a successful effort to produce a pictorial history of the United States. The first volume is devoted to the colonial period. Marshall Davidson, *Life in America* (2 vols., 1951), accomplishes much the same end in shorter compass.

On the plantation South, P. A. Bruce, *The Colonial Period, 1607–1763* (*History of Virginia*, I, 1924), is excellent. T. J. Wertenbaker, *The Old South: The Founding of American Civilization* (1942), stresses the intellectual and artistic achievements of the Chesapeake colonies. W. E. Dodd, *The Old South: Struggles for Democracy* (1937), is more concerned with political developments. Julia C. Spruill, *Women's Life and Work in the Southern Colonies* (1938), deals with a subject all too frequently neglected. E. L. Goodwin, *The Colonial Church in Virginia* (1927), covers adequately the religious aspect of Virginia society. A. H. Hirsch, *The Huguenots of Colonial South Carolina* (1928), deals with a small but important immigrant group. A. O. Craven, *Soil Exhaustion as a Factor in the Agricultural History of Virginia and Maryland, 1606–1860* (1926), exploits a factor of basic importance to the social as well as the economic life of the South. Carl Bridenbaugh, *Seat of Empire: The Political Role of Eighteenth Century Williamsburg* (1950), gives an admirable picture of Virginia society as a whole. See also references for chapters 1, 2, and 3, on Virginia and the South).

On New England, J. T. Adams, *Revolutionary New England, 1691–1776* (1923), continues the anti-Puritan bias of his *Founding of New England*, already cited, and should be tempered by comparison with the more orthodox K. B. Murdock, *Increase Mather, The Foremost American Puritan* (1925). W. B. Weeden, *Economic and Social History of New England* (2 vols., 1891), is a work of enduring merit. V. L. Parrington, *The Colonial*

Mind, 1620–1800 (Main Currents in American Thought, I, 1927), opens with a brilliant account of the Puritan heritage. Alice Morse Earle, *Customs and Fashions in Old New England* (1893), combines much that is really important with much that is merely trivial. Similar books by the same author are *The Sabbath in Puritan New England* (1891); *Colonial Dames and Goodwives* (1924); *Stage Coach and Tavern Days* (1935); *Home Life in Colonial Days* (1913); *Child Life in Colonial Days* (1899). Perry Miller, *The New England Mind; The Seventeenth Century* (1939), centers on the cultural beginnings of the region. See also T. J. Wertenbaker, *The Puritan Oligarchy: The Founding of American Civilization* (1947). Anne B. MacLear, *Early New England Towns* (1908); Melville Egleston, *The Land System of the New England Colonies* (1886); Lois Kimball Mathews [Rosenberry], *The Expansion of New England* (1909); L. J. Greene, *The Negro in Colonial New England* (1942). See also references listed on page 37.

On the Middle Colonies, Thomas J. Wertenbaker, *The Founding of American Civilization: The Middle Colonies* (1938), is excellent. Carl and Jessica Bridenbaugh, *Rebels and Gentlemen; Philadelphia in the Age of Franklin* (1942), reveals the social handicaps of the common man. C. C. Van Doren, *Benjamin Franklin* (1938), catches admirably the spirit of colonial Philadelphia. Of great value, also, is Franklin's own *Autobiography*, the best edition of which is *The Life of Benjamin Franklin Written by Himself*, edited by John Bigelow (3 vols., 1874), and *The Letters of Benjamin Franklin and Jane Mecom*, edited by Carl Van Doren (1951). Other books worth mentioning are: C. C. Van Doren and others, *Meet Dr. Franklin* (1943); and V. W. Crane, *Benjamin Franklin, Englishman and American* (1936). T. J. Wertenbaker, *The Golden Age of Colonial Culture* (1942), centers on the six leading colonial cities. Somewhat on the lighter side are D. R. Fox, *Yankees and Yorkers* (1940); J. T. Faris, *The Romance of Old Philadelphia* (1918); Alice Morse Earle, *Colonial Days in Old New York* (1896). See also references to the Middle Colonies on page 51.

In the Colonial Frontier, Turner, *The Frontier in American History*, already mentioned, contains a significant chapter on "The Old West." F. L. Paxson, *A History of the American Frontier, 1763–1893* (1924); and R. A. Billington, *Westward Expansion* (1949), trace chronologically the suc-

cessive American frontiers. On the frontiers of the southern colonies there are two highly entertaining accounts: Archibald Henderson, *The Conquest of the Old Southwest, 1740–1800* (1920); and Constance Lindsay Skinner, *Pioneers of the Old Southwest* (1919). There are useful chapters, relating to the frontier and to the immigrants who helped people it, in A. M. Schlesinger, *New Viewpoints in American History* (1922). Other books that deal with foreigners on the frontier are: Fredric Klees, *The Pennsylvania Dutch* (1950); A. B. Faust, *The German Element in the United States* (2 vols., 1909); Lucy F. Bittinger, *The Germans in Colonial Times* (1901); J. L. Rosenberger, *The Pennsylvania Germans* (1923); A. D. Graeff and others, *The Pennsylvania Germans* (1942); W. F. Dunaway, *The Scotch Irish of Colonial Pennsylvania* (1944); H. J. Ford, *The Scotch-Irish in America* (1915); C. A. Hanna, *The Scotch Irish* (1902); G. S. Klett, *The Scotch-Irish in Pennsylvania* (1948); S. H. Cobb, *The Story of the Palatines* (1897).

Perhaps the best general treatise on economic aspects of American colonial life is to be found in the first volume of Joseph Dorfman, *The Economic Mind in American Civilization, 1606–1865* (2 vols., 1946). Other more specialized studies include: S. E. Forman, *The Rise of American Commerce and Industry* (1927); R. M. Tryon, *Household Manufactures in the United States, 1640–1860* (1917); R. B. Morris, *Government and Labor in Early America* (1946); Stella H. Sutherland, *Population Distribution in Colonial America* (1936); Carl Bridenbaugh, *The Colonial Craftsman* (1950).

The importance of religion to colonial Americans is attested by a long list of books. W. W. Sweet, *Religion in Colonial America* (1942), is perhaps the most useful in the present connection, but, by the same author, *The Story of Religion in America* (rev. ed., 1950), should not be overlooked. S. H. Cobb, *The Rise of Religious Liberty in America* (1902), deals with a subject of great significance. A. L. Cross, *The Anglican Episcopate and the American Colonies* (1902), reveals the difficult problems of absentee church administration. See also G. S. Klett, *Presbyterians in Colonial Pennsylvania* (1937); G. G. Atkins and F. L. Fagley, *History of American Congregationalism* (1942); T. E. Drake, *Quakers and Slavery in America* (1950); W. W. Sweet, *Methodism in American History* (1933); and, by the same author, *Revivalism in America* (1944). On the "Great Awakening" of the eighteenth century, see the admirable volumes by Ola E. Winslow, *Jonathan Edwards, 1703–1758* (1940); and Perry Miller, *Jonathan Edwards* (1949). On the origins of modern evangelism, see A. D. Belden, *George Whitefield, the Awakener* (1930). And on witchcraft, see Marion L. Starkey, *The Devil in Massachusetts: A Modern Inquiry into the Salem Witch Trials* (1949). On literature, K. B. Murdock, *Literature and Theology in Colonial New England* (1949).

J. T. Adams, *Provincial Society, 1690–1763* (1927), concentrates on social aspects of the colonies during the eighteenth century. Harvey Wish, *Society and Thought in Early America: A Social and Intellectual History of the American People through 1865* (1950), covers the colonies, as well as the early national period, in satisfactory detail.

'Tis Death to counterfeit.

5

Colonial Self-Government and Imperial Control

The English pattern of government — The corporate colony, Massachusetts — The proprietary colony, Maryland — The royal colony, Virginia — British vs. American views on colonial government — Efforts to establish imperial control — The four Navigation Acts — The Glorious Revolution in England and in America — The policy of "salutary neglect"

CONTRARY to a common concept, not many of the colonists came to the New World with unique political ideas and a burning desire to set up new forms of government. They came, for the most part, from the British Isles; they were familiar, or at least their leaders were familiar, with the British type of government; and in their various attempts to solve the problems that soon confronted them they sought merely to adapt to New World conditions the institutions which they already knew.

At the head of the English government stood the King, who at the time the Amer-

The English government ican colonies were founded could still claim that he ruled by divine right. This was the more plausible inasmuch as the King's title to the throne rested in no way upon popular consent, but exclusively upon the fact that he was the nearest living relative to his predecessor. He had powers of no mean sort; indeed, under the Tudors and the early Stuarts his authority tended to dwarf almost to insignificance the power of Parliament. For advice the King relied mainly upon his Privy Council, a group which varied in number from twenty to forty, and included many of the high officials of state. The "King in Council" kept an eye on all the affairs of the realm, and sometimes issued

orders that were as much legislative as executive in character.

The English Parliament was a bicameral body, and consisted then, as now, of the House of Lords and the House of Commons. The House of **Parliament** Lords was a comparatively small body, with perhaps fifty "Lords Spiritual" and "Lords Temporal," the former entitled to their seats by virtue of the high ecclesiastical offices they held, the latter by the right of birth. The House of Commons was a much larger body than the Lords, with a total membership of no less than five hundred. Each shire, or county, was entitled to two members in the Commons, and some three hundred towns were entitled to one or two members each. This distribution of seats was historic merely, and not at all in proportion to population. Great cities were wholly without representation, and "rotten boroughs," which for centuries had been without inhabitants, sometimes returned two members. The suffrage was rigorously limited, more so in some boroughs than in others, but practically always by property qualification. The whole system was well designed to throw the control of Parliament into the hands of the upper and middle classes. In theory, however, Parliament represented "all the men of England," and while there was a wide difference of opinion among seventeenth-century Englishmen as to exactly how far its powers went, the right of Parliament to a voice in the levying of taxes and in the making of all important laws was generally conceded.

The national courts of justice also occupied an important place in the English plan **The English judiciary** of government. All judicial officers, from the justices of the peace to the judges who sat on the highest courts of the realm, were appointed directly by the King and were directly removable by him. In medieval times the King's judges had formed the habit of traveling about the country on circuit duty, and had gradually supplanted the feudal and ecclesiastical courts, whose powers had once been great. The King's judges developed for both civil and criminal cases precedents and principles that came to be known as the "common law." For example, a defendant had the right of trial by jury, and no man might be deprived of life, liberty, or property without due process of law. Such rights as these the courts stoutly defended, and in general the judiciary was independent of interference either by the King or by Parliament. There were, however, numerous exceptions to this rule.

Such was the government with which the colonists were familiar when they established **The colonial governments** themselves in America; and such was the model after which their governments were patterned. The colonial governments, however, were not all alike. Some of the colonies operated under charters of incorporation that were little constitutions in themselves, and were therefore often spoken of as "corporate" colonies; others had proprietors into whose hands governmental authority had been placed, and were usually called "proprietary" colonies; still others were under the direct supervision of the English government, and were called "royal" colonies. But the influence of the English pattern was strong in each case; furthermore, the types of government instituted in America did not differ as much from one another as the names used to describe

British Parliament in session. Sir Robert Walpole is shown addressing the House of Commons in an engraving by John Pine, 1741–42.

them would seem to indicate. This can be made more apparent by the examination of a typical colony from each of the three forms of American colonial government.

The corporate colonies enjoyed the greatest degree of self-government and departed most from the English prece- **Massachusetts, a corporate colony** dents. Of these Massachusetts, in spite of the fact that her charter was drastically altered in 1691, is the natural example; for during the formative years Massachusetts led the way in working out a plan of self-government that could be applied successfully in the New World. Although the original Massachusetts charter was designed to fit the needs of a joint-stock company rather than a self-governing commonwealth, it served, with certain adaptations, not only as a satisfactory constitution for Massachusetts, but also as a model after which the other self-governing colonies could pattern.

The Massachusetts governor was elected by the freemen, or voters, at first in primary assembly, but later, when the **The governor** size of the colony had made this impracticable, by ballots taken in all the towns. The governor thus obtained his office by the vote of the people, and not by divine right as was the case of the King of England, but the voters in selecting him were limited nevertheless by the prevailing opinion that only men of the highest rank should ever be considered for this office. The governor had no veto power, and since elections were held annually he might be retired after a single year. In practice, however, he possessed tremendous influence, and compared favorably with the English King in power.

The General Court, or legislature, of Massachusetts was a two-house body after **The General** 1644, and laws could be passed **Court** only by the consent of both houses. Assistants, who constituted the upper house, were elected in the same fashion as the governor, but here again the weight of custom restrained the voters to a limited choice. The number of assistants was small, and in practice they were chosen from among the leading citizens, men of wealth and high standing in the colony. Furthermore, it was customary to re-elect assistants year after year, so that once having attained that office the incumbent was likely to hold it for life. Two members of the House of Deputies were chosen by each town entitled to representation. While there was a rule that a man might not serve as deputy who was not orthodox in religion, there was no such high standard of qualification for the Deputy as for the assistant. The governor was presiding officer for the assistants, while the deputies elected a speaker of their own. Obviously the General Court of Massachusetts was closely analogous to the English Parliament.

The judicial system of the colony was slow to develop, but it followed, at least vaguely, **The judicial** the English model. The gov- **system** ernor and assistants, to begin with, exercised full judicial authority, but as the population increased provision was made for a system of county courts. For this purpose a number of towns were joined together into counties, and court was held for each county by the local assistants and such other assistants as they could get to sit with them. Or sometimes citizens nominated by the freemen of the county and

approved by the General Court sat with the assistants. Appeals could be taken to the Court of Assistants and then to the General Court. These magistrates were by no means always learned in the law, and they were guided as often by their own judgment or by the precepts of the Bible as by the English common law. The uncertainty of decisions so arrived at led in 1641 to the preparation and adoption by the General Court of a code of laws known as the "Body of Liberties." Some of the provisions of this code would seem harsh today, but in general the "Liberties" marked a distinct advance on the prevailing practice of the time. Magistrates were no longer permitted to inflict punishment at their discretion, but only on the basis of specific law; jury trial with the right of "challenge" was provided; while the "Liberties of Women" and the "Liberties of Children" were safeguarded in varying degrees. A married woman, for example, was to be free from bodily correction by her husband, "unless it be in his own defense upon her assault."

Maryland was the first continental colony in the government of which a proprietor figured, and is fairly typical **Maryland,** of the rest. Lord Baltimore, **a propri-** by the grant of power received **etary colony** from the King, was authorized to govern his province as he chose, except that in raising taxes and making laws he must obtain the advice and consent of the freemen or their representatives. This was exactly the situation in which the English King found himself, and no doubt it was intended that the proprietor should rule in Maryland just as the King ruled in England. The proprietor, however, chose not to come to America, but instead to assert his authority through a governor, whom he appointed to represent him, and a council, whom he appointed to advise the governor.

The development of the legislature in Maryland came slowly, with the proprietor contesting every step. Balti- **The legis-** more assumed that he had the **lature** sole right to propose laws, and that the "ad-

THE STATE HOUSE, BOSTON, MASSACHUSETTS, BUILT IN 1748. Engraving from *The Massachusetts Magazine,* July, 1793.

INDEPENDENCE HALL, PHILADELPHIA, 1732–35. Engraving by J. Rogers.

Colonial capitals were characterized by public buildings noted for their symmetry and simplicity of design. One such capital, Williamsburg, Virginia, has been restored to its original eighteenth century character. Its buildings and museums provide a remarkable glimpse into the colonial way of life. Independence Hall (usually pictured from the front) and the Boston State House show Georgian architecture at its best.

THE CAPITOL, WILLIAMSBURG, VIRGINIA, ABOUT 1720. Photo of the reconstructed building.

vice and consent" of the freemen meant only what the words implied. Accordingly, when an assembly of the freemen, which he had authorized his governor to call together, took a different view, and passed laws on its own initiative, the proprietor promptly vetoed all of them. Ultimately, however, the proprietor had to give way, and permit the assembly approximately the same right in the making of the laws of Maryland as the English Parliament had in the making of the laws of England. At first all the freemen, which in Maryland meant the landowners, met together as the assembly, but in due time, as the colony grew, the representative principle was adopted. Division into two houses came in 1650, when the members of the council began to sit separately as an upper house, and the elected representatives sat as the lower house. Both the governor and the proprietor maintained a veto over all legislation, and the governor was authorized to dissolve the assembly at will. But the proprietor and his agents learned to exercise their prerogatives sparingly, and the assembly insured its frequent meeting by voting supplies for only a year at a time.

The administration of justice in early Maryland lay in the hands of the governor **Courts of** and his council, but in due time **justice** county courts were instituted to care for minor cases, and the governor and council sat as a provincial court with appellate jurisdiction and original jurisdiction in the more important cases only. As time went on the personnel of the provincial court came to consist largely of judges who were not also members of the council. Circuit courts were also presently instituted, with the judges of the provincial court doing circuit duty in the various counties. There was much shifting of jurisdiction among these courts and the circuit courts were for a long time abandoned, but the pattern eventually became clear. All judges were commissioned directly by the governor and held office during his pleasure. In civil cases the "rules by which right and justice used and ought to be determined in England"

were followed, but in criminal cases much was left to the discretion of the judges. The following penalties, all of which were prescribed by the Maryland assembly during the eighteenth century, illustrate the state of public opinion in the matter of punishment for crime:

A person convicted of embezzling, impairing, razing, or altering any will or record within the province . . . was to forfeit all his goods, chattels, lands, and tenements, be set in the pillory for two hours, and have both his ears nailed thereto and cut from off his head; a person convicted of stealing that which was valued at less than one thousand pounds of tobacco was to pay fourfold, be put in the pillory, and given not to exceed forty lashes; a person convicted of fornication was to be fined 30 s. or six hundred pounds of tobacco; a person convicted of adultery was to be fined £3 or twelve hundred pounds of tobacco; a person convicted of wilfully burning a courthouse was to suffer death without benefit of clergy; a person convicted of blasphemy was for the first offense to be bored through the tongue and fined £20 sterling, or, if unable to pay the fine, be imprisoned for six months; for the second offence, to be stigmatized by burning in the forehead with the letter B and fined £40, or, if unable to pay the fine, be imprisoned for one year; and for the third offence to suffer death without benefit of clergy.[1]

In Virginia, after 1624 when it became a royal colony, the colonial form of government most closely approximated **Virginia, a** its English prototype. The **royal colony** governor was now appointed directly by the King and held office at the King's pleasure. He was charged with the duty of carrying out such instructions as might be sent to him by the English authorities, and he must also execute the laws passed by the colonial assembly. He commanded the local military and naval establishments, supervised religious affairs, presided over the council, and with its consent appointed justices of the peace and other court officials. He could call the assembly together, could propose measures for its considerations, could pro-

[1] N. D. Mereness, *Maryland as a Proprietary Province* (1901), pp. 277–78. By permission of The Macmillan Company.

rogue or dissolve it at will, and could disallow any or all of the laws it passed. He could remit fines and pardon criminals. He was, indeed, a little king in America.

When the Virginia Company lost its charter, there was some doubt as to whether

Representative government

or not the representative assembly would be continued, but perhaps because of the earnest insistence of the Virginians themselves the assembly was presently recognized by the King. At first governor, councillors, and burgesses all sat together, but as in the other colonies division into two houses was soon agreed upon. The council was chosen by the King on nomination of the governor from among the leading men of the colony — only the richest and most prominent were considered eligible. Councillors held office indefinitely, and usually received new commissions whenever there was a new king in England or a new governor in the colony. Two burgesses were chosen from each county, and one from each of several towns, by the qualified property-holders. A miniature parliament was thus produced, with the council equivalent to the Lords, and the burgesses to the Commons.

As in Maryland, the governor and council were charged also with certain judicial

The judicial system

duties, and when sitting together in their judicial capacity were known as the General Court. Before them came all major criminal cases and all civil cases involving above sixteen pounds sterling. The county courts had jurisdiction in criminal cases not involving "peril of life or limb," and in civil cases of as much as twenty-five shillings. Lesser suits came before single justices. Appeals were allowed to the General Court, and during most of the seventeenth century a further appeal might be taken to the assembly itself. This practice was discontinued, however, about 1680. Another practice that fell into disuse was the custom of permitting councillors to sit, when they chose, as judicial members of county courts.

Government in the colonies, it thus appears, followed closely after the English model. A single executive, corresponding to the King, a two-

The colonial pattern of government

house legislature, corresponding to Parliament, and a judicial system, less pretentious and less complicated than the courts of England but roughly on the same plan, appeared in every colony. It follows also that the government in one colony did not differ markedly from the government in any other colony, whether the colony had a charter of self-government, or shared the powers of government with a proprietor or with the King. The citizens of every colony, moreover, enjoyed the same personal rights as Englishmen that would have been their privilege in the mother country — jury

Vigorous criticism of the colonial governor was openly expressed by John Peter Zenger in this newspaper which he established in 1733.

trial, freedom of speech, freedom from arbitrary imprisonment. These were privileges, moreover, that were not enjoyed in like measure by the colonists of any other nation. A degree of governmental censorship was usually taken for granted, but an important victory for freedom of the press was won in 1736 when a New York jury, contrary to instructions from the court, freed a local editor, John Peter Zenger, from the charge of libel.

It was natural that many Americans should come to think of the colonies as

British view of colonial governments practically separate and independent units of the British Empire, but English officials generally looked upon the colonial foundations as mere dependencies of the English government which were entitled to the privileges they enjoyed only by its sufferance. It was quite in harmony with the English view, therefore, to suppose that the colonies should be subject to such regulations on the part of the mother country as the home government chose to establish. But for many reasons a definite policy of colonial control was slow to develop. The English government lacked experience in dealing with colonies; indeed, the American colonies were practically the first of the kind it had ever had. Moreover, during much of the seventeenth century English governmental machinery was itself in bad order. The attempts of the early Stuarts to expand the royal prerogative were bitterly resisted by Parliament, and for many years the boundaries between the rights of the King and the rights of Parliament in respect to colonial affairs were in heated dispute. The existence of Civil War in England during much of this period also paralyzed such feeble efforts at control as the English authorities attempted. The colonies were thus left free during the formative period to work out their destinies in their own way with a minimum of outside interference.

With the restoration of the Stuarts to the throne of England in 1660 it was possible to give more definite attention to the colonial problem. A committee of the Privy Council was created, known at first as **Efforts to establish control** the Council for Foreign Plantations, but later, with its membership somewhat altered, as the Lords of Trade or the Board of Trade and Plantations. This committee was authorized to inquire into colonial affairs and to recommend to Parliament and to the Privy Council such legislation and such administrative policies as it saw fit. The committee took its duties seriously, for a time at least, and soon began to make suggestions. It accepted the prevailing theory that the colonies were to be regarded as primarily foreign plantations established for the purpose of giving to the mother country a national source of supply in staples that she might otherwise have to obtain outside the Empire. The colonies should be encouraged, therefore, to produce those commodities in which England stood in greatest need. They should plant vines to relieve the English of dependence upon the French vineyards. They should produce spices and tropical fruits to replace the business now done with the English in those commodities by the Dutch and the Portuguese; they should supplement the English fisheries; they should destroy the Scandinavian monopoly on the production of naval stores. The colonies should also be encouraged to buy English goods; if possible, to be better buyers than sellers, so that a steady flow of gold to redress the trade balance might find its way from the colonies to the mother country. Gold and silver mines, it was long hoped, would be abundant in the colonies, and of use toward this end.

The Committee on Trade and Plantations was never able to carry its theories into full effect, but it sincerely wished to **The imperial system** make England the hub and center of a self-sufficient Empire. It recommended that the colonists should preferably sell all their products to England; they should, if they could, buy from England or through England only; they must not devote themselves to manufacturing, since that was England's interest; they must be required to seek, not merely their own individual good, but rather the common imperial good.

Legislation looking in this direction actually anticipated the recommendations of the Committee on Trade and Plantations, for during the Protectorate period Parliament had passed a law, aimed primarily at the Dutch carrying trade, which forbade the products of Asia, Africa, and America to be carried to British ports except in English-owned and English-manned vessels, and forbade European goods to be brought to colonial ports except in English ships or in ships belonging to the country in which the goods were produced.[1] The colonies were thus left free to buy wherever they pleased, but they might not legally make free use of foreign shipping. This act was restated and expanded in 1660 as the First Navigation Act, and its purpose, no less than that of its predecessor, was to encourage English shipping rather than to vex the colonists. England needed a large navy, and in time of war trading ships could easily be converted into warships. Hence there was wisdom in building up a strong merchant fleet and in preventing the Dutch, whose ships it was believed carried altogether too much of the colonial trade, from building up their navy at the expense of the English. Specifically the First Navigation Act required that only English or colonial-owned ships with English captains and crews three fourths English might engage in the colonial trade. A little later it was further stipulated that the ships must also be built in England or the colonies (not including Ireland). These provisions were not seriously damaging to the colonists. Temporarily there was some shortage of ships, and freight rates rose, but there was compensation in the fact that the law tended to stimulate the shipping interest in the colonies quite as much as in the mother country; furthermore, Parlia-

First Navigation Act

ment remained deaf to all English pleas that this colonial competition be eliminated.

The First Navigation Act also contained a list of "enumerated articles" — sugar, tobacco, cotton-wool, indigo, ginger, dye-woods — that might be sold only to England or to another colony. This list was later expanded, but for the time being it contained only one item, tobacco, that seriously affected the continental colonies. Moreover, the intent of the English government to benefit the colonies as well as the mother country was indicated by the fact that the growing of tobacco in England, and the purchase of tobacco from foreign colonies for use in England, were forbidden.

Enumerated articles

The Second Navigation Act, passed in 1663, affected the continental colonies decidedly more than did the earlier law. It provided that most imports from Europe to the colonies must pass through England. This was designed to prevent the trade and the products of the colonies from passing to other countries, although by smuggling freely the colonists managed to avoid any serious restrictions. It was supposed, too, that the profits of English merchants would be somewhat enhanced by the routing of foreign goods through England. Duties, both import and export, were charged by the English government, but an elaborate system of rebates, or drawbacks, enabled the colonists to buy foreign goods through England about as cheaply as Englishmen themselves could buy them. Some items, for example Dutch and German linens, the colonists, thanks to the rebates, could buy even more cheaply than could Englishmen.

Second Navigation Act

The Third Navigation Act, otherwise known as the Plantation Duty Act, was passed in 1672 (effective 1673), and was meant to bear directly upon the colonists. There had been much evasion of the law requiring the "enumerated articles" to be shipped only to England or to another colony. Colonial shipmasters carried such goods from one colony to another,

Third Navigation Act

[1] The union of the English and Scottish crowns was accomplished in 1603, when James VI of Scotland became James I of England. But Scotland kept her own Parliament until 1707, so that it was the English, not the British, Parliament which legislated for the colonies in the seventeenth century.

perhaps across the Potomac from Virginia to Maryland, then, deeming the law fulfilled, shipped the goods where they chose. The Third Navigation Act required that a duty equal to the English import duty should be collected *in the colonies* unless the ship captain would bind himself to carry the cargo to England. This law meant the appointment of a considerable number of colonial collectors who were directly responsible to the English commissioner of customs. These officials soon made themselves obnoxious to the colonists not only because of their efforts, usually unsuccessful, to enforce the law, but also because of the constant complaints they registered with their English superiors on the unwillingness of the Americans to co-operate with them. Perhaps the most unpopular of the English collectors was Edward Randolph, who headed the imperial customs service in New England. At all events, the law was more honored in the breach than in the observance.

This tendency on the part of the colonists to pay attention to the British regulations **Efforts to** only when they chose to do so **discipline** was in large part responsible for **the colonies** a very determined effort on the part of James II and his advisers to reform the colonial governments. The attitude of New England toward the Acts of Trade was regarded as particularly reprehensible. Most of the New England governors were elected officials who made little or no effort themselves to enforce the disagreeable laws of Parliament, and refused to give adequate support to the tax-collectors appointed from England for this purpose. Finally the Committee on Trade and Plantations brought suit for the annulment of the Massachusetts charter, and in 1684 won its case. The way now lay open for a series of radical reforms. In the interest of efficient imperial control royal colonies were to supplant corporate or proprietary colonies, small colonies were to be consolidated with their larger neighbors, and royal officials — governors and councillors — were to have their duties enlarged and their powers strength-

ened. These changes, it was supposed, would be of material assistance, also, in solving the problem of colonial defense.

Between 1684 and 1688 the policy of colonial consolidation went on so rapidly that by the last-mentioned year **Dominion** the eight northernmost colonies **of New** had been thrown together into **England** one, the "Territory and Dominion of New England," with Sir Edmund Andros at its head. All the New England colonies — Massachusetts, New Hampshire, Plymouth, Rhode Island, and Connecticut — were included in the combination, and in addition New York, East New Jersey, and West New Jersey. New Hampshire and New York were already royal colonies, and the Plymouth colony had no embarrassing legal rights to be overthrown; but legal proceedings had to be brought against the governments of the remaining colonies. Andros, however, asserted his authority over them all, regardless of charters and grants of authority. Colonial assemblies were abolished, quit-rents were demanded of the owners of land, taxes were levied without the consent of any representative body, and religious worship according to the rites of the Anglican Church was given official encouragement.

These drastic changes, enforced as they were by a stubborn and tactless governor, would doubtless have led to **The Glorious** revolt in the colonies had there **Revolution** been no "Glorious Revolution" in England. But the efforts of James II to free himself from the control of Parliament had aroused as deep resentment in the mother country as the arbitrary acts of Andros had aroused in America. The King, moreover, was at heart a loyal Catholic, and he had married for his second wife a Catholic Italian princess, Mary of Modena. In 1688 the birth of a son, who presumably would be brought up as a Catholic and would succeed to the throne, was announced. This was a serious blow to English Protestants, Anglicans and dissenters alike, for they had counted on a Protestant daughter of James

II, Mary, the wife of William, Stadholder of the Netherlands, as the next in line of succession. Without bloodshed and almost by common consent James was therefore deprived of his royal rights, and by act of Parliament William and Mary were invited to mount the throne of England as joint sovereigns. The "divine right of kings" was thus summarily disposed of. James II fled with his family to France, and the kings of England thereafter owed their title to the throne solely to the will of the English people as expressed in Parliament. To leave no doubt in the matter this doctrine was presently recorded in the famous Bill of Rights and also in the Act of Settlement, passed in 1701.

The Glorious Revolution in England was followed promptly in America by the imprisonment of Andros and the collapse of the pretentious "Dominion of New England." The once self-governing colonies of New England now resumed their former boundaries and privileges, except that Massachusetts temporarily held on to New Hampshire; New-Yorkers submitted with what grace they could to the dictatorship of a tactless leader named Leisler, who had frightened Andros's lieutenant, Nicholson, into leaving the colony; and the proprietors in the Jerseys re-established their control. In the colonies where the rule of Andros had never been felt there was much less excitement, except in Maryland. There the occasion was seized upon to overthrow the rule of the proprietor, who, it was claimed, had refused unfairly to permit an increase in the membership of the assembly, had filled the appointive offices with his relatives, and had been over-generous in his treatment of Catholics.

When the English government was free to turn its attention once more to America, it abandoned the principle of consolidation, which James II had so strongly favored, but it did not hesitate to establish royal colonies in preference to any other type wherever that could conveniently be done. New Hampshire was again cut off from Massachusetts, and given a royal governor. Massachusetts was given a new charter (1691), according to which the governor was appointed by the crown instead of being elected by the people as formerly. Connecticut and Rhode Island were allowed to keep their old charters, but the Plymouth Bay Colony and the settlements in Maine were now joined to Massachusetts. In New York a royal governor backed by English troops presently took charge, while Leisler and his chief lieutenant were hanged. Maryland became a royal colony with a Protestant governor, and the rights of the proprietor were not restored until 1715. Penn's friendship with the fallen Stuarts was held against him, and in 1692 Pennsylvania became a royal colony with the governor of New York as its head. Two years later, however, Penn got back the rights he had lost. For the time being the Jerseys, since they were regarded as of small consequence anyway, were left to their proprietors, but in 1702 they were united as the royal colony of New Jersey, although until 1738 they had the same governor as New York.

These changes in America were somewhat less significant than the Glorious Revolution in England. The pretensions of Andros were eliminated, but by the multiplication of royal colonies the way was paved for closer control by the mother country than had been possible before Andros's rule began. In England, on the other hand, not only was "divine right" given a shattering blow, but the power of Parliament began to rise. William III was an important factor in the English government, but his successors were weaklings who allowed the royal power to fall into disuse. Before many years the English King reigned, but ministers, responsible to Parliament rather than to the King, really ruled. For America, however, no such transformation was in sight. It made little difference whether royal governors were appointed on the recommendation of the English ministers or at the whim of the English monarch. In either event the source of authority lay entirely outside the colony, and the right of the people to control their executive, a right which, as the power of Parliament grew, was coming more and more to be recognized in England, was largely denied in America. Colonial assemblies could, and sometimes did, sway royal governors by refusing to grant funds unless specific grievances were abated, but the power of these English officials was still great. The following diagram will perhaps make clearer the contrast between the English and the American results of the Revolution of 1688:

THE ENGLISH AND THE AMERICAN GOVERNMENTS

Before 1688

ENGLAND	AMERICA
God	King or Proprietor
↓	↓
King	Governor
———	———
Parliament	Assembly
↑	↑
People	People

After 1688

ENGLAND	AMERICA
King	English Government
↑	↓
Ministers	Governor
↑	———
Parliament	Assembly
↑	↑
People	People

Neither did the Glorious Revolution mean any abatement of the English determination to control the trade of the colonies in the interest of the mother country and of the Empire as a whole. Indeed, the Navigation Act of 1696 was designed to make more effective than ever before the enforcement of the three Navigation Acts passed during the reign of Charles II. According to the law of 1696 all colonial governors, whether royal governors or not, must take a strong oath to enforce the English regulations, and in case they failed to do so, or failed to live up to their oaths,

Another Navigation Act

they were made liable to heavy fine and removal from office. Governors not directly appointed by the crown had to receive the King's approval — a difficult requirement for the self-governing colonies to meet. Provisions were also made for tightening up the colonial customs service, and colonial laws out of harmony with the acts of trade were declared null and void. Furthermore, after the passage of this act admiralty courts were established in the colonies to enforce the English regulations. Inasmuch as these courts were patterned after the Roman law, they were not embarrassed by the necessity of holding jury trials; hence colonial juries, ever a source of difficulty in the enforcement of English law in America, could be avoided.

The determination to enforce commercial regulations upon the colonies continued unabated during the early years of the eighteenth century. The list of enumerated articles was lengthened by the addition of rice, molasses, naval stores, ship timbers, copper, and beaver skins. Even non-enumerated articles might not be sent to Ireland or Scotland except after payment of the regular import duties in England. Colonists were forbidden to carry wool, or articles manufactured of wool, from one colony to another. But the most unpalatable of all such measures, however, was the Molasses Act of 1733, which was aimed at the profitable trade carried on between the continental colonies and the non-English colonies of the West Indies. In order to insure that the former should buy West Indian produce from the English islands exclusively, practically prohibitive duties were placed on all sugar, molasses, rum, and spirits imported from foreign plantations. This was a stupid piece of legislation, for the continental colonies had more to sell than the markets of the English West Indies could absorb, and would have suffered acutely had the law been enforced. Furthermore, much of the hard money that found its way to the continent and ultimately went to England to redress

New regulations of colonial trade

an unfavorable balance of trade came from the foreign West Indies, and thus English traders and manufacturers stood a good chance to lose should the law be enforced. But as a matter of fact the Molasses Act did little harm, for from the date of its passage it was cheerfully ignored.

In various other ways, also, the British government undertook to control the behav-
Other efforts at control ior of the colonies. Manufacturing, it was assumed, could best be done in England, and colonial manufactures were therefore discouraged. A law of 1732, for example, placed a limit upon the number of apprentices that colonial hat makers might employ, and a law of 1750 restricted rigorously the right of the colonists to manufacture iron goods. Paper-money issues by colonial legislatures were severely frowned upon, and excesses along this line were prohibited either by law of Parliament or by disallowance of the colonial laws involved. For the latter purpose royal governors were instructed to veto or to suspend such colonial enactments as might run counter to British policy, and the Privy Council reserved for itself a further veto, which was exercised usually only on recommendation of the Board of Trade. Appeals were also taken from colonial courts to the Privy Council, and many colonial laws as a result of this process were finally set aside. Since royal governors were more easily controlled than those chosen by proprietors or by the people there was a marked tendency to eliminate as many proprietary and self-governing colonies as possible. Misgovernment in the Carolinas gave an excuse to withdraw the privileges of the proprietors there in 1728, whereupon both colonies received royal governors. When Georgia became a royal colony in 1752, there were left of the corporate colonies only Connecticut and Rhode Island, and of the proprietorships only the holdings of the Penns in Pennsylvania and Delaware, and of the current Lord Baltimore in Maryland.

It must not be supposed, however, that British interference in American affairs was unduly burdensome. Sometimes, as in the case of tobacco, the legal **Privileges accorded the colonies** restriction actually ran against the mother country and in favor of the colonies. When naval stores and ship timbers were placed on the enumerated list, bounties were made available to encourage their production. Colonial agents, among whom the most notable was Benjamin Franklin, appeared in England to lobby against proposed Parliamentary measures that might be damaging to American interests, and to argue the American case when a dispute came before the Board of Trade. Colonial governors, even when they were appointed from England, tended to place a high valuation upon American public opinion, and to interpret unpopular obligations as narrowly as possible. The fact that in most cases they were paid out of money appropriated by a colonial assembly also kept them fairly respectful of the will of the people they governed. Even the British revenue-collectors sometimes absorbed the American point of view. Many Americans could see, too, that the protection given to colonial trade by the British navy and by British treaties far more than outweighed the damage suffered by commercial restrictions; and for this protection the Americans were taxed not a cent.

Finally, it should not be forgotten that the British will to maintain restrictions on the colonies often lagged seri- **"Salutary neglect"** ously. Sir Robert Walpole, who was the virtual head of the British government for more than two decades (1721–42), believed that more was to be gained for the mother country by encouraging colonial trade than by restricting it, since trade of any sort would make the colonies prosperous and better able to buy British goods. This opinion was shared also by the Duke of Newcastle, who had much to do with colonial affairs during Walpole's supremacy, and continued powerful even after Walpole's fall. Indeed, Newcastle's frankly admitted policy of "salutary neglect" was not seriously amended until the close of the French and Indian War.

Bibliography

Among the many treatises on various aspects of the English constitution, the following may be cited as particularly useful in this connection: F. W. Maitland, *The Constitutional History of England* (1908); A. F. Pollard, *The Evolution of Parliament* (1920); C. H. McIlwain, *The High Court of Parliament and its Supremacy* (1910); Wallace Notestein, *The Winning of the Initiative by the House of Commons* (1924); G. P. Gooch, *English Democratic Ideas in the Seventeenth Century* (1927).

The constitutional side of colonial development receives elaborate treatment in H. L. Osgood, *The American Colonies in the Seventeenth Century* (3 vols., 1904–07); and, by the same author, *The American Colonies in the Eighteenth Century* (4 vols., 1924–25). Channing, *History of the United States*, Vols. I, II, already cited, is also excellent. C. M. Andrews, *Colonial Self-Government* (1904), and E. B. Greene, *Provincial America* (1905), likewise summarize effectively the main features of colonial political development. Useful monographs on certain aspects of colonial government are: Ella Lonn, *The Colonial Agents of the Southern Colonies* (1945); G. L. Chumbley, *Colonial Justice in Virginia* (1938); Raphael Semmes, *Crime and Punishment in Early Maryland* (1938); E. S. Griffith, *History of American City Government: The Colonial Period* (1938); E. B. Greene, *The Provincial Governor in the English Colonies of North America* (1898).

On the crucial subject of the relations between the mother country and the colonies, the leading authority is G. L. Beer, whose *The Commercial Policy of England toward the American Colonies* (1893) opened a series which ultimately included also: *The Origins of the British Colonial System, 1578–1660* (1908); *The Old Colonial System, 1660–1754* (1912); *British Colonial Policy, 1754–1765* (1907). Broader in scope, but featuring also the ties that bound the Empire together, is the monumental work by L. H. Gipson, *The British Empire before the American Revolution* (7 vols., 1936–49). L. A. Harper, *The English Navigation Laws* (1939), revises materially traditional views on the subject of his study. O. M. Dickerson, *American Colonial Government, 1696–1765: A Study of the Board of Trade in its Relation to the American Colonies* (1912), is excellent, but should be supplemented by W. T. Root, *The Relations of Pennsylvania with the British Government, 1696–1765* (1912). Viola F. Barnes, *The Dominion of New England* (1923), is admirable for the time and region covered. C. P. Nettels, *The Money Supply of the American Colonies before 1720* (1934), is a work of great merit on a subject of great importance.

6

The Winning of the West

The French in America — Rivalry with the English
for the Mississippi Valley — The forks of the Ohio —
Braddock's defeat — The French and Indian War —
Treaty of Paris — The Proclamation Line of 1763 —
Pontiac's Conspiracy — British vs. American plans for
the West — Watauga — Kentucky

As THE English settlements expanded farther and farther into the West, it presently became apparent that in the course of time a struggle with the French must ensue to determine definitely which nation, England or France, should control the interior of the continent. Should the English colonies end at the crests of the Appalachians, with France in possession of the lands beyond? Or should the great Mississippi Basin become the next swarming-place of the English? Clearly it was a case in which the fittest would survive, and the answer to the question might easily have been read in a comparison of the existing French and English foundations.

The French settlements in North America dated back to 1608, when Samuel de **New France** Champlain founded Quebec on the St. Lawrence River. In due time other French settlements appeared at Three Rivers and Montreal. The location of the colony was not a happy one. The soil was poor and the climate was hard. The seacoast was far away, and for fully half a year ice floes in the St. Lawrence River blocked communication with the mother country. Moreover, the way to the West was temptingly easy. No such formidable barrier existed as the mountains that lay back of the English settlements, and the pathways of the lakes and rivers invited explorations. Such Catholic missionaries as Father Marquette, and such intrepid traders and explorers as Joliet and La Salle, soon penetrated far into the Mississippi Valley.

La Salle's imagination took fire, and he dreamed of a magnificent French dominion that would extend from Canada to the Gulf of Mexico; in 1699 an adventurer named d'Iberville actually established a French outpost at Biloxi, near the mouth of the Mississippi. Somewhat earlier, in 1691–92, Fort St. Louis had been built near the mouth of the Missouri River, and here, as well as across the river in the "Illinois country," French settlements soon developed. Thus while the English colonies along the seacoast were densifying in population, the French were dissipating their energies in a vain attempt to conquer half the continent.

The rank and file of the people who came to New France lacked much of the individual initiative and determination to **The** succeed that was so marked **habitants** among the English colonists. The French habitants came, for the most part, not so much for reasons of their own as because the national government was determined to build up an American colony. This project enlisted the support in turn of such powerful figures as Henry IV, Cardinal Richelieu, and Colbert, the efficient minister of Louis XIV. Every effort was made to increase the population of New France. Bounties were offered for immigrants; shiploads of unmarried women were sent over to become the wives of the excess male population; unmarried individuals were ostracized socially; and official rewards were offered for large families. But still the French population in America refused to grow rapidly. By 1750, when there were a million and a half English colonists in America, the French numbered only eighty thousand. The English Americans as a whole were alert and self-reliant; the French were relatively unprogressive, and still in a state of semi-dependence on the mother country. The situation might have been somewhat different had the French government permitted the Huguenots, who were driven from France after the revocation of the Edict of Nantes (1685), to come to Canada. But Roman Catholicism received as much official favor in the New World as in the Old, and many of the exiled French Protestants went instead to swell the stream of immigration into the English colonies.

Government of New France The government of New France contrasted markedly with the government of the English colonies. Instead of many colonies there was only one,[1] and since France was an absolute monarchy, it followed naturally that an absolute government should be established over her possessions in America. New France was governed about as one of the French provinces was governed. A royal governor, usually a nobleman or at least a man of some importance, was civil and military head of the province. The extent of his power depended in part upon his personality, and in part upon the nature of the times in which he ruled. During periods of active warfare the governor's power tended to increase, while in times of peace his power waned. Count Frontenac, who was sent to America in 1672, was doubtless the most influential of all the French governors. The legal and financial ruler of the province was the intendant, an official of lesser rank but often greater power than the governor. The intendant, a lawyer, was at the head of the judicial system of the colony; he was entrusted with public expenditures; and he

[1] Louisiana had a separate government; hence to be entirely accurate one should speak of the French colonies as two in number. But the Louisiana colony was too weak to play any considerable part in the contest between the English and the French for the Mississippi Valley.

reported directly to the King, thus acting as a sort of check on the governor. The spiritual head of the province was the bishop, but his temporal power as the ruler of the church made him one of the triumvirate by which the colony was governed. In theory a "superior council," consisting of the three officers named and a number of resident councillors appointed on recommendation of the governor and the intendant, was the chief governing body of the colony; but in practice the governor, the intendant, and the bishop were able to control the rest. Local self-government was unknown, and many of the personal rights cherished by Englishmen everywhere were freely denied. "It is of the greatest importance," one official declared, "that the people should not be at liberty to speak their minds." There was, moreover, continual interference in colonial affairs from Versailles, "where a fickle-minded monarch and a corrupt court played fast and loose with their often misguided colony."[2]

The seignorial system With the possible exception of the patroonships in New York, the land system of New France differed from anything to be found in the English colonies, where every man was permitted to own his own land, with at worst a nominal quit-rent. In the French colony an attempt was made to maintain the old feudal system of land tenure. Nobles held large estates or seigniories with a wide expanse of river front; and the peasants who worked the land were supposed to pay to the nobles such dues and fees as contemporary French practice required. The maintenance of such a system of land tenure in the face of the plenty of lands in America was foredoomed to failure, but the effort was made. In general French peasants, or habitants, paid their dues only when they felt like it; and if the exactions of agriculture proved too burdensome they took to the fur trade, where they might live more as they chose.

French industries compared most unfavor-

[2] R. G. Thwaites, *France in America* (1905), p. 128. Quoted by permission of Harper and Brothers, Publishers

ably with those of their English neighbors.

Economic conditions Agriculture was sickly, and fishing, although encouraged in various ways by the government, was not notably successful. Fishing villages did spring up, however, especially those on the coasts of Newfoundland and about Port Royal in Acadia. But for the bulk of its prosperity New France relied upon the fur trade. The French Canadians, it turned out, got along well with the Indians, intermarried freely with Indian women, and in the quest of pelts scattered willingly over the whole interior. They competed on even terms for the northern fur trade with the enterprising agents of the English Hudson's Bay Company. They generally outdistanced the English traders on both sides of the Great Lakes and in the Valley of the St. Lawrence; and they took their share of furs from the upper Mississippi Valley in spite of both Spanish and English opposition. Supplementing the work of the traders regularly licensed by the government, independent or illegal traders known as *coureurs de bois* roamed the wilderness without much fear of punishment, so long, at least, as their catch went to New France and not to the rival English.

In one matter the French in America possessed a decided advantage over the

Military efficiency English. When it came to the problem of defense they were not embarrassed by a multiplicity of authorities; instead, there was unity of command and unity of action. Furthermore, the French government expected little military assistance from the colonists themselves, but kept French ships and soldiers available for their protection. The English government, on the other hand, assumed that the English colonies in America would take care of the defense problem themselves except in cases of great emergency. When attacked by the Indians or the French, the English colonies ordinarily had recourse only to their own raw militia levies. Moreover, there was not only much conflict of authority but also not a little evasion of responsibility, espe-

cially on the part of those colonies whose borders were not directly threatened. To be sure, the British fleet stood ready to guard the high seas, and no colonial navy was required, but the British army was reserved for use only when the colonists had already exerted themselves to the limit and stood a chance to fail without help. But events proved that the greater immediate effectiveness of the French military power was not sufficient to outweigh the other notable advantages possessed by the English.

The rivalry between the French and the English, first for European hegemony and then for world empire, lasted **Rivalry** many years and involved the **with the** two countries in numerous wars. **English** The earlier of these struggles, "King William's War" (1689–97), "Queen Anne's War" (1702–13), and "King George's War" (1744–48), to use the American names for these conflicts, involved no serious test of strength between the French and English in America. In each of them Indian raids promoted by the French disturbed the peace of the New England and New York frontiers, and in some of them privateering was a source of much annoyance on both sides. During King George's War an expedition under the command of Governor Shirley of Massachusetts and supported by British ships took the French fortress of Louisbourg on Cape Breton Island; but the conquest was restored by the treaty of peace. These three wars left the status of French and English rivalry in America relatively unchanged. The final contest, the French and Indian War, actually began in America two years before its European counterpart got under way, and it was fought primarily to determine whether the French or the British were to have the right of way in North America.

The struggle for the continent was precipitated by the ambition of some Virginia gentlemen, with whom a few **The Ohio** Englishmen were associated, to **Land** form a settlement west of the **Company** Appalachian mountains. For this purpose,

CHAMPLAIN AND THE ALGONQUINS FIGHTING THE IROQUOIS, 1609. Illustration from Champlain's *Voyages*, Paris, 1613.

LA SALLE LANDING AT MATAGORDA BAY (TEXAS), 1684. Engraving in Father Louis Hennepin, *Nouveau Voyage*, 1698.

New France was spread thinly over the wilderness of Canada and the Mississippi valley to Louisiana, intrepid explorers such as Champlain and La Salle having laid claim to half a continent in the name of France. French fur-traders generally got on well with the Indians, although Champlain won for New France the undying hostility of the powerful Iroquois by leading his forces against them in aid of the local Quebec tribes. In Louisiana the French colonists, with the assistance of imported Negro workers, attempted sugarmaking as well as indigo, cotton, and rice culture.

FISHING AND FUR-TRAPPING. Representational illustration from Carolus Allard, *Orbis Habitabilis*, 170?.

SUGAR MANUFACTURE IN LOUISIANA, 1751. Illustration from *Report of the Commissioner . . . for 1867.*

an Ohio Land Company was formed, and in 1749, royal consent to a grant of two hundred thousand acres of land below the "forks" of the Ohio was obtained. Next year Christopher Gist, a well-known surveyor and land prospector, was sent out to prepare the way for the coming of settlers, upon whose purchases of lands the company hoped to realize a handsome profit.

The Forks of the Ohio
--- Present boundaries

This project immediately alarmed the French, who recognized at once the peril to **French alarm** their Ohio Valley fur-trade interests in case English settlers were allowed to come in; hence, in 1749 the governor of New France dispatched Céloron de Blainville to the contested area to plant leaden plates on which was inscribed the claim of the King of France to the region the English now sought to possess. Céloron buried a plate near the source of the Allegheny River on July 29, 1749; and then as he progressed down the Allegheny and down the Ohio planted others. He turned back only after having passed the mouth of the Miami River. The leaden plates did little to deter the English advance, but three years later, when the Marquis Duquesne de Menneville became governor of Canada, a more vigorous policy was inaugurated. Indians friendly to the French were induced to attack Indians friendly to the British, and French forts made their appearance in the disputed area, one on the southern shore of Lake Erie, another on French Creek, and a third where French Creek joins the Allegheny.

Warned of the new developments, the British Secretary of State for Colonial **Washington and Gist** Affairs sent word to the colonial governors in America that while they must not take the offensive against the French, they were at liberty to "repel force by force." Armed with this authority Governor Robert Dinwiddie of Virginia determined to warn the French that they must withdraw from the Ohio Valley. George Washington, an enterprising youth of twenty-one years, whose elder brother Lawrence had been one of the founders of

the Ohio Land Company, was selected to carry the message, and in the fall of 1753, accompanied on the latter part of the journey by Gist, he pushed through to the post on French Creek and delivered Dinwiddie's ultimatum. The French commandant, however, had only defiance for an answer, and with this reply Washington returned to Virginia.

Meantime, some Virginians had been sent to erect a fort at the junction of the Allegheny and Monongahela Rivers, **The forks of** the "forks" of the Ohio; and a **the Ohio** small detachment of troops under Washington and a certain Colonel Fry were sent out to their aid. But the French ousted the British from the forks before Washington's force arrived, and completed the fort themselves, naming it Fort Duquesne, in honor of their new governor. Washington, understanding well the difficulties that lay before him, halted at Great Meadows to build a stockade. Near-by, on May 28, 1754, he surprised and annihilated a French reconnoitering party, but his attempt to advance

General Edward Braddock and *George Washington.*
Washington, an aide on Braddock's staff during the ill-fated expedition of
1755, is portrayed here as a colonel of the Virginia militia in 1772, by
Charles Willson Peale.

farther was soon blocked by superior forces
of French and Indians. Hastily he turned
his stockade at Great Meadows into "Fort
Necessity," only to be attacked and defeated, July 3. Next day he was allowed to
abandon his post with honors of war, and the
French and Indian War had begun.

When the news of this frontier fighting
reached Europe the governments concerned
Braddock's decided to regard it as a strictly
expedition local affair, and to postpone a
general war as long as possible. But the
gravity of the situation was fully recognized,
for the French promptly sent reinforcements
to America, which the British navy tried in
vain to intercept, while the British sent two
regiments of regulars under General Braddock to co-operate with the Virginians in
the capture of Fort Duquesne. Braddock's
column, consisting of over two thousand
men, less than half of whom were colonials,
advanced toward Fort Duquesne from Fort
Cumberland on the upper Potomac, along
the same route Washington had taken previously. Washington, whom Braddock took
along as an aide, complained that the
British "were halting to level every molehill,
and to erect bridges over every brook."
But Braddock worked his way to within

about ten miles of Fort Duquesne, where on
July 9, 1755, he met an unexpected, and
perhaps undeserved, defeat. He himself
was mortally wounded. One historian has
claimed, however, that "Braddock's defeat"
might better be termed "Braddock's victory," for the road he built became a highway later on for the English migration that
conquered the Ohio Valley; but at the time
the defeat was keenly felt. Indians under
French influence harassed the frontier, and
Washington, with a little army distributed
among a score of forts, found himself
almost powerless to beat them off.

By the year 1756 England and France
were in an open state of war, and for some
time the advantage in America **Open**
seemed to lie with the French. **warfare**
One reason for this was to be found in the
personality of the French commander, the
Marquis de Montcalm, who took charge of
the Canadian forces the year war was declared. Montcalm not only possessed great
ability as a general, but he was able also to
communicate to the Canadians much of his
enthusiasm for the task before them and his
optimism as to the ultimate outcome. The
English in America, on the other hand,
lacked nothing else so conspicuously as com-

petent leadership. British officers sent to America were too often, like Braddock, unacquainted with colonial traditions, unversed in frontier methods of warfare, and unable to command respect. Colonial officers were deficient in training, and whenever projects were undertaken that required the co-operation of troops from two or more colonies, they were much given to quarreling with respect to priority of rank.

For this latter situation the lack of any intercolonial organization was in large part **The Albany conference** responsible. But all efforts to unite the colonies, even in the face of the French menace, seemed doomed to failure. In 1754, the British government called a conference at Albany to discuss the Indian problem, particularly with reference to the near-by Iroquois. Representatives from seven colonies attended, and, realizing that the problem before them involved the larger problem of colonial unity, they sought earnestly to devise some scheme which would insure colonial co-operation, particularly essential in view of the impending war with France. Benjamin Franklin was a member of the Congress, and the "Albany Plan" which it presented was largely his work. Had this plan gone through there would have been established an intercolonial council composed of forty-eight representatives, apportioned among the colonies with regard to their wealth and population, and elected by the several colonial legislatures. Also there would have been a president-general for all the colonies, appointed and paid by the crown. Subject to veto by the president-general, the council was to have had the right to control Indian affairs, raise and pay armies, build forts, and levy the taxes necessary for these purposes. But this plan was promptly rejected by the colonial assemblies, who objected to any such curtailment of their own prerogatives, and who possibly feared also that such an inter-colonial organization would transfer too much responsibility for the winning of the war from Great Britain to the colonies. A counter-proposition submitted by the

English Board of Trade met a similar fate. The British plan contemplated the establishment of a council composed of one commissioner from each colony; these commissioners might then agree by majority vote upon the necessary military forces and their apportionment among the colonies. A commander-in-chief for all the colonial forces would have been appointed by the crown.

The failure of these plans left each colony free to support the war as much or as little as it chose. The colonies that **Colonial support of the war** were in greatest danger from the French did most; those that were far removed from the scene of conflict did least; and in general there was much waiting to see what the other planned to do. Suggestions from England that taxation of the colonies for their own defense might be undertaken by the authority of Parliament met a chilly reception in America, and were never acted upon.

William Pitt, who was called to the British ministry in the fall of 1756 and next year virtually took charge of the war, **Pitt's requisition system** worked out a requisition system which secured perhaps as much colonial assistance as was possible under existing circumstances. Pitt's plan left with the colonies the responsibility of levying, clothing, and paying provincial soldiers. The British government, however, under-

Colonial unity was strongly urged by Benjamin Franklin through his newspaper, *The Pennsylvania Gazette*, where this famous device first appeared in 1754.

JOIN, or DIE.

took to furnish the colonial troops with arms, ammunition, and provisions, and promised further to compensate the colonies later for their outlays in accordance with the vigor of their actions. The amount of the compensation actually paid by Great Britain to the colonies was equal to about two fifths of the expenditures the colonies made. Spurred on by this appeal, as well as by the real menace of the French and Indian attacks, the New England colonies supported the war with becoming zeal; in New York and Pennsylvania, however, quarrels between governor and legislature prevented anything like adequate support of the war; Virginia did only fairly well, considering how great she assumed her stake to be in the outcome; and most of the other colonies scarcely participated in the war at all.

Pitt's plans, so far as America was concerned, did not stop at debarring the **French successes** French from occupying territory claimed by the British; he would expel the French entirely from North America. But in carrying through such an undertaking he had to reckon with no mean adversary in the person of Montcalm, the French commander-in-chief. Soon after his arrival in America Montcalm had blocked one British approach to Canada by the capture of Fort Oswego on the southern shore of Lake Ontario. The next year (1757) he blocked another approach by the capture of Fort William Henry at the lower end of Lake George. And in view of the fact that the British efforts to dislodge the French from their fortress at Louisbourg on Cape Breton Island had so far failed, a British expedition up the St. Lawrence seemed out of the question. The year 1758 opened with the advantage all on the side of the French.

But the tide soon turned. Pitt replaced incompetent officers ruthlessly, and elevated **Turn of the tide** promising young men to positions of great responsibility. By this means the task of capturing Louisbourg was taken away from Lord Loudoun, whose ineptitude had been adequately demon-

strated, and handed over to two younger officers, Jeffrey Amherst and James Wolfe. With the assistance of Admiral Boscawen, a naval commander of genuine ability, the siege of Louisbourg was finally brought to a successful termination. In the Lake Champlain region the British under Abercrombie attacked the French outpost at Ticonderoga, only to be beaten off; but farther to the west a small British force composed mostly of colonial troops took Fort Frontenac on Lake Ontario, and thus cut the French communications with the West. Thereupon the French abandoned Fort Duquesne, and the British under General Forbes quickly occupied it. The crowning event of the war came next year when Admiral Saunders and General Wolfe successfully advanced up the St. Lawrence, and forced Montcalm to fight a decisive battle (September 13, 1759) on the Plains of Abraham overlooking Quebec. Both Wolfe and Montcalm lost their lives in the struggle, but the British victory was complete. Next year Montreal surrendered to Amherst, and the conquest of Canada was at an end.

Other British victories took place in America in spite of tardy support to the French from the Spanish, who **British conquests** entered the war in 1761. Guadaloupe and Martinique in the West Indies were taken from the French, and Cuba from the Spanish. On the other side of the world a British fleet captured Manila. On the Continent the armies of Frederick the Great, the chief ally of the British, had won decisive victories. Everywhere the British flag was supreme on the high seas.

By 1763 the French gave up the struggle, and at Paris, on February 10, signed a humiliating peace. Canada and all the French possessions east of the Mississippi River (except the New Orleans region), most of the French stations in India, and some of the French West Indies were ceded to Great Britain. Some of the British leaders would have been willing to return Canada to France in return for a cleaner sweep of the French West Indies, but, won

The
French and Indian Wars
1689~1754   1755~1763

over perhaps by the arguments of Benjamin Franklin, the conquest of Canada was allowed to stand. The Philippines and Cuba were returned to Spain; but the English demanded and received Florida. This somewhat unwarranted Spanish loss was made good by the cession of Louisiana and the Isle of Orleans from France to Spain; and thus the French possessions on the continent of North America were entirely wiped out.

In bringing about this happy solution of their difficulties with New France the colo- nies had played a considerable part; and yet to most Eng- lishmen conversant with the situation it seemed that the Americans had done far less than their full duty. They had depended upon British regulars when colonial levies might well have been materially increased; they had refused to unite under the Albany Plan, or any other plan, for their common defense; and they had been guilty of almost

Colonial indifference

wholesale trade with the French in utter defiance of the will of the imperial government. British orders to stop all commerce with the enemy had been met in the colonies by the smuggling of great quantities of colonial stores, particularly foodstuffs, both to Canada and to the French West Indies, and because of this illicit trade the war had been appreciably prolonged.

One unforeseen result of the conflict was to drive England and her colonies farther apart than they had ever been before. The disloyalty and disobedience of the colonists embittered many Englishmen against the Americans, and led to an agitation in favor of closer control of the colonies by the mother country. On the other hand, the removal of the French menace in America removed also the necessity of British assist- ance to confront it, and on this account left the colonies less disposed than ever to submit to British control. The disruption of the ex- panded empire lay only a short distance ahead.

Hudson Bay

HUDSON'S BAY COMPANY

LABRADOR

QUEBEC

NEWFOUNDLAND

L. SUPERIOR

Sault Ste. Marie

Quebec

Miquelon — St.Pierre
French

NOVA SCOTIA

L. MICHIGAN

L. HURON

Montreal

Ft. Ticonderoga

RESERVED

L. ONTARIO

L. ERIE

Detroit

Ft. Niagara   Ft. Stanwix   Albany   Boston

FOR INDIANS

OHIO R.

New York

Vincennes

Philadelphia

MISSISSIPPI RIVER

SPANISH

MISSOURI R.

St. Louis
Kaskaskia

CUMBERLAND R.

APPALACHIAN MTS.

ARKANSAS R.

TENNESSEE R.

LOUISIANA

Wilmington

Line of 1763-1767

WEST FLORIDA

Charleston
Savannah

RIO GRANDE

New Orleans   Biloxi   Pensacola

EAST FLORIDA

St. Augustine

Gulf of Mexico

Bahama Is.

Havana   CUBA

Belize

JAMAICA

Caribbean   Sea

HISPANIOLA

Puerto Rico   St.Thomas (Dan.)

Mosquito Coast

Curaçao
(Dutch)

Guadeloupe (Fr.)
Dominica (Br.)
Martinique (Fr.)
St. Lucia (Fr.)
St. Vincent (Br.)
Grenada (Br.)

Eastern North America and the Caribbean 1763

British

Spanish

French

Proclamation Line · 1763

The French and Indian War, so far as the colonists were concerned, had been fought primarily to insure that the region west of the mountains should be opened to settlement, and the terms of the treaty of Paris seemed to indicate that this object had been attained. The war was hardly over, however, when grave obstacles to the expansionist program began to appear.

For one thing, the Indians of the trans-Appalachian region were soon engaged in a **Pontiac's conspiracy** dangerous uprising against the British known as Pontiac's Conspiracy, which became at once a most effective check on pioneer ambitions. Inevitably there were differences between the rule of the English and the rule of the French, and these differences from the Indian point of view all appeared to be to the discredit of the new régime. The British garrisons in the captured French posts were not given to fraternization; the British traders drove hard bargains; and the interest of the English colonists in settlement rather than trade was all too evident. French renegades held out hopes that the time would soon come when the French would send an expedition to reconquer their former possessions, and, spurred on perhaps by vague promises of this sort, Pontiac, an Ottawa chief with far more organizing ability than was common among the Indians, induced most of the western tribes to join him in his great "conspiracy." A concerted attack upon the British military outposts began in May, 1763, each Indian tribe attacking the nearest fortified post, and within a few weeks only four out of twelve were left in British hands. At Detroit, where the whites retained control, a siege was instituted which lasted for five months before the Indians gave up. Attacks were also made upon the outlying settlements, and the whole frontier was thrown into a panic. But the Indian victories had been won chiefly through the element of surprise, and the war which resulted could end in only one way. In 1764 two strong expeditions were dispatched into the Indian country. As a result Pontiac

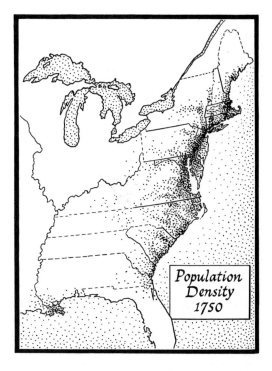

Population Density 1750

and his allies were defeated, and finally in July, 1766, at Oswego Pontiac agreed with Sir William Johnson to a treaty of peace and amity.

As a result of the Indian troubles, the British government seemed disposed to hold in check, at least temporarily, the ambitions of those colonials who wished to push farther into the West. It was plain to be seen that the colonies, working independently of each other, would never be able to devise a consistent Indian policy, and since all admonitions looking in the direction of a colonial union had proved futile, the imperial government now decided to take the whole matter of Indian relations under its direct control. On the assumption that a little delay in western expansion could do no harm, and that assurance against the invasion of their land might induce the Indians to give up their warlike behavior the British government ordered that the crest of the Appalachians should mark for the present the farthest west that settlement might be permitted to go. Beyond the sources of the rivers flowing into the

Atlantic, grants of land were not to be made; and even the settlers who had already entered the forbidden region were ordered to return. The Proclamation of 1763, which on October 2 announced this policy, thus closed the very door which the war had been fought to open. Further, it ignored utterly the western land claims of those seaboard colonies whose original charters had contained "sea to sea" grants.

That the British government had no intention of forever withholding the region **British plans** west of the Proclamation Line **for the West** from settlement was soon fairly apparent. Two treaties were negotiated in 1768, one with the Iroquois at Fort Stanwix, and the other with the Cherokees at Hard Labor. These and subsequent treaties gave the British a title, defective, perhaps, since all the tribes who asserted claims to the region concerned were not consulted, to a large strip of land extending west of the mountains into the upper Ohio Valley. Probably the government hoped to establish a neutral zone from which as a precaution against future troubles both whites and Indians should be excluded. But that some of the lands so acquired would be opened to new settlement was clear from the support given by the Board of Trade to a project which contemplated the creation of a new colony in the West to be known as Vandalia. For this purpose a British-American syndicate was formed which numbered among its membership such prominent men as Benjamin Franklin and Sir William Johnson, and much pressure was brought upon the Board of Trade to agree to the necessary land grant. After considerable dissension a patent was made out in favor of the petitioners which would have handed over to them most of what is now West Virginia and eastern Kentucky. But by the time consent to this grant had been fully won, the American Revolution was on, and the project lapsed.

Nevertheless, the settlement of the Vandalia region had already begun. Even before the French and Indian War thousands of pioneers had found their way into the eastern part of this district, and **The upper** while most of them had been **Ohio frontier** compelled to get out during the war, many promptly returned as it came to an end. After the war was over, with the help of Braddock's road from Fort Cumberland to the Ohio, and the road Forbes had cut through Pennsylvania to Fort Pitt (the British name for Fort Duquesne), migration into the upper Ohio region was made relatively easy. Regardless of the Proclamation of 1763 and the absence of regular land titles, settlers pushed out along the mountain trails, and as early as 1767 permanent settlements on the upper Ohio and its tributaries were beginning to appear. Before the Revolution broke out both Pittsburgh and Wheeling were sizeable villages.

During these years other irregular settlements west of the crest of the mountains were being made farther to the **The** south. In 1769 pioneers from **Watauga** the back country of Virginia **settlements** pushed southwestward across the watershed into the Watauga Valley, which they supposed to be within the limits of Virginia, although actually it was a part of North Carolina. Two years later they were joined by a number of "Regulators" from the back country of North Carolina, who were compelled to seek safety in flight because of an unsuccessful revolt they had waged against the domination of the colony by the eastern propertied class. James Robertson, who led this latter migration into the West, and John Sevier, a Virginian of French Huguenot descent who came to Watauga in 1772, furnished the little settlement with unusually effective leadership.

A survey of the boundary line, made in 1771, between Virginia and North Carolina revealed to the Watauga pioneers that their settlement lay in North Carolina rather than in Virginia. With the nearest North Carolina settlements almost a hundred miles distant, and with the Regulators indisposed to acknowledge the supremacy of the North Carolinian government in any case, the

CANADIAN SOLDIER ON SNOWSHOES.
From Potherie's *Histoire*, Paris, 1722.

THE TAKING OF QUEBEC, SEPT. 13, 1759. The entire day's activities are depicted in this engraving from *The London Magazine*, 1760.

THE DEATH OF GENERAL WOLFE. After a painting by Benjamin West, 1771.

The French and Indian War was fought to determine whether the French or the English should have the chance to exploit the American West. Soldiers on both sides, sometimes fighting in trackless wilderness, performed prodigious feats of valor that later artists sought earnestly to portray. Wolfe's defeat of Montcalm near Quebec, which cost the victorious general his life, was one of the decisive battles of history. With the French menace at an end, pioneers from the English colonies poured into the trans-Appalachian West.

OHIO INDIANS IN CONFERENCE WITH COL. BOUQUET, 1764. After a sketch by Benjamin West, 1766.

DANIEL BOONE LEADING SETTLERS INTO THE WEST, 1775. George Caleb Bingham's legendary painting of the famous pioneer at Cumberland Gap.

Wataugans found themselves practically outside any colony. They set to work, therefore, to form a government of their own. With Robertson and Sevier as leaders they held a mass meeting at Robertson's station, and adopted Articles of Association by which in the future they agreed to be governed. A convention of thirteen delegates — one from each of the thirteen stations — was elected by manhood suffrage, and the convention in turn chose a court of five members to rule the community. As an independent and totally unauthorized government the Watauga Association lasted on until 1778, when Watauga became Washington County of the revolutionary state of North Carolina.

The rapid advance of the white frontier, particularly in the valley of the upper Ohio, **Lord Dunmore's War** led to the outbreak of another Indian war in 1774. The failure of Pontiac's conspiracy had left the northwestern Indians with a deep-seated grudge against the whites, and the further penetration of country which until recently the Indians had regarded as exclusively their own added fuel to the smouldering fire. The Shawnees first took the warpath along the Virginia frontier, but their example was soon followed by many neighboring tribes. Lord Dunmore, the last royal governor of Virginia, was not slow to act. Two expeditions were organized at once for the relief of the frontier, one under the governor himself, which advanced to Fort Pitt and thence down the Ohio, the other under General Andrew Lewis, which marched through the wilderness to the mouth of the Kanawha River. It had been intended that the two columns should meet, but Dunmore changed his plans, and it fell to Lewis with a band of valiant but none too well-disciplined frontiersmen to do the bulk of the fighting. In the battle of Point Pleasant, fought near the mouth of the Kanawha, Lewis's men won a bloody victory, and

Cornstalk, the Shawnee chief, was forced to give up. Lord Dunmore's War, as the Virginians called this struggle, was of great significance, for from it the Indians learned that they might not hope to stay the white man's advance across the mountains.

The whites were quick to follow up their victory. The treaty which Cornstalk signed with Dunmore gave up the Shawnee title to all lands south as well as east of the Ohio River, and the former region had already aroused great interest among the whites. As early as 1769 Daniel Boone, a frontier hunter who regarded himself as "ordained of God to settle the wilderness," had been impressed by the possibilities of Kentucky, and in a few years the whole frontier was aware of the existence in central Kentucky of a bluegrass region where game abounded and natural clearings made easy the task of the pioneer. The cupidity of the speculator was also aroused, and Judge Richard Henderson of North Carolina dreamed the not unusual dream of another colony to the west with himself as chief financial beneficiary. Accordingly in 1774 he formed a partnership known as the Transylvania Company, and next year purchased from the Cherokees whatever title they claimed to the region between the Kentucky and the Cumberland Rivers. To promote settlement Daniel Boone was set to work with a party of

Kentucky

thirty men to cut a road through from the back country of North Carolina to the bluegrass region in Kentucky. By the first of April, 1775, Boone and his men, having cleared their "Wilderness Road" from the Holston River through Cumberland Gap to the Kentucky River, began the settlement of Boonesborough. Near-by at Harrodsburg other settlers, led by James Harrod of Pennsylvania, were already on hand, and the Kentucky pioneers were soon numbered by the hundreds.

Henderson tried to organize a government for Transylvania, and for the purpose held an open-air convention of delegates from the various settlements, May 23, 1775. The convention met under a giant elm, and adopted a simple plan of government not unlike that devised for Watauga. But Henderson's land title was obviously defective, his hope of securing royal support for his project was ended by the outbreak of the Revolution, and the petition which he sent to the Continental Congress that Transylvania be recognized as one of the united colonies was denied. In December, 1776, the Virginia legislature, acting at the request of the Harrodsburg settlers, acknowledged Kentucky as a county of Virginia, and the Transylvania project broke down. But the settlers stayed on and prepared to defend themselves against the Indians, whose ruthlessness, when they heard the news of war in the East, was abundantly apparent.

Bibliography

New France was fortunate in having as its historian one of America's most brilliant writers, Francis Parkman, whose *Pioneers of France in the New World* (1865), and *LaSalle and the Discovery of the Great West* (2 vols., 1879), tell the story of the French colonial beginnings. His *Count Frontenac and New France under Louis XIV* (1877); *A Half Century of Conflict* (2 vols., 1892); and *Montcalm and Wolfe* (2 vols., 1884), cover the period of rivalry with the British, and his

The Conspiracy of Pontiac (2 vols., 1886), the Indian uprising that followed the French and Indian war. A centenary edition of *The Works of Francis Parkman* (12 vols., 1922), includes all of the above titles and many others. The activities of the French missionaries who played so large a part in the early history of New France are reported in great detail in *The Jesuit Relations, 1610–1791,* edited by R. G. Thwaites (73 vols., 1896–1901).

The brilliance of Parkman's writing and the

painstaking character of his research put a heavy burden upon subsequent writers in the same field. Some of them, however, have made admirable contributions. R. G. Thwaites, *France in America* (1905), provides a useful summary of the whole subject. G. M. Wrong, *The Rise and Fall of New France* (2 vols., 1928); and, by the same author, *The Conquest of New France* (1918), introduces the results of much recent scholarship. Other useful general accounts include: Herbert I. Priestley, *France Overseas through the Old Regime* (1939); Morden H. Long, *A History of the Canadian People* (1942); Donald G. Creighton, *Dominion of the North: A History of Canada* (1944); Carl Wittke, *A History of Canada* (1941); John Fiske, *New France and New England* (1930). Grace Lee Nute, *Caesars of the Wilderness: Médard Chouart, Sieur des Groseilliers, and Pierre Esprit Radisson, 1618–1710* (1943), is based on the most meticulous scholarship, and draws upon evidence Parkman did not use. To a lesser extent the same can be said for Louise P. Kellogg, *The French Régime in Wisconsin and the Northwest* (1925). W. B. Munro, *The Seigneurs of Old Canada* (1914), describes the effort to transplant feudalism from the Old World to the New. Howard H. Peckham, *Pontiac and the Indian Uprising* (1947), restudies to good advantage the famous Indian uprising.

On the British side, C. W. Alvord, *The Mississippi Valley in British Politics* (2 vols., 1917); and *The Illinois Country, 1673–1818* (*Centennial History of Illinois*, I, 1920), are brilliant and perspicacious. They may be supplemented by Thomas P. Abernethy, *Western Lands and the American Revolution* (1937); and Theodore C. Pease and Ernestine Jenison, *Illinois on the Eve of the Seven Years' War, 1747–1755* (1940). Washington's

early exploits are reported in Rupert Hughes, *George Washington, The Human Being and the Hero, 1732–1762* (1926); and Charles H. Ambler, *George Washington and the West* (1936). A. B. Hulbert, *Braddock's Road* (*Historic Highways of America*, IV, 1903), is written from an interesting point of view. A. T. Mahan, *The Influence of Sea Power upon History, 1660–1783* (1890), is a book of epoch-making importance. Max Savelle, *The Diplomatic History of the Canadian Boundary, 1749–1763* (1940), studies admirably a particular set of problems. G. L. Beer, *British Colonial Policy, 1754–1765*, already cited, provides an excellent discussion of British policy toward the colonies during the French and Indian war.

On American expansion into the West, Theodore Roosevelt, *The Winning of the West* (4 vols., 1894–96), grasps fully the spirit of the frontier advance, even if in point of scholarship it is open to criticism. H. A. Bruce, *Daniel Boone and the Wilderness Road* (1910), is written from the Boy Scout point of view, but provides the essential facts. R. G. Thwaites, *Daniel Boone* (1902), is better history but less entertaining. Kathryn H. Mason, *James Harrod of Kentucky* (1951), preserves the family tradition of Harrod's exploits. There are also numerous excellent monographs, among them: A. T. Volwiler, *George Croghan and the Westward Movement, 1741–1782* (1926); W. S. Lester, *The Transylvania Colony* (1935); K. P. Bailey, *Thomas Cresap, Maryland Frontiersman* (1944). R. G. Thwaites and L. P. Kellogg have edited from the Draper Manuscripts of the State Historical Society of Wisconsin a valuable *Documentary History of Dunmore's War, 1774* (1905).

FOUNDING THE NATION

1763 - 1787

There are few stories more thrilling than the story of how the thirteen continental colonies of Great Britain in North America broke the ties that bound them to the Mother Country, and achieved for themselves both independence and federal union. All this was accomplished in a period of twenty-four years. During the ten years that elapsed between the French and Indian War and the American Revolution there was constant bickering and wrangling between the Americans and the British over the problem of imperial control. When the contenders failed to achieve a successful settlement of their differences, there followed eight years of war. But victory in war, as so often happens, failed to bring the tribulations of even the victors to an end. The union that the new American states had achieved for the purpose of winning the war proved to be totally inadequate for winning the peace. It took another six years for the thirteen states to achieve under the Constitution that "more perfect union" which later served them so well.

Had the British only realized it, the American colonies were too large and too important to remain dependencies. There were about one-fourth as many Americans as there were British. The American colonies were too far away from Great Britain, too far beyond the reach of remote control. And they had less need than formerly for British assistance in diplomacy and defense. The expulsion of the French from continental North America was from one point of view a great mistake on the part of the British. With the French out of the way, the colonists could argue their case for complete autonomy with far less concern than formerly. When the British refused to see that they could not enforce imperial control by laws and regulations, but must trust solely to loyalty based on mutual self-interest, even autonomy proved not to be enough, and the colonies insisted on complete independence.

The Revolutionary War was not easily won. The Americans had to operate with a hastily devised central government, with an improvised military establishment, and with much opposition from a minority that took the British side. They could hardly have won without outside assistance. Taking advantage of the hostility for England on the Continent of Europe, they eventually won as allies France, Spain, and the Netherlands. France gave them the most aid. In spite of the fact that France was an autocracy with a government quite out of sympathy with the democratic aims that the American revolutionists professed, this aid was not only gladly received but was earnestly sought. Further, English opinion was itself badly divided on the issues of the Revolution, and the reluctance with which many Englishmen supported the war was an inestimable boon to the American cause. At the end of the war the friends of America actually controlled the British government, and made with the new United States a remarkably favorable treaty of peace.

In spite of its weakness and inadequacy the Confederation government had a few notable achievements to its credit, particularly with respect to the West. It laid down the principle of equality with reference to the new states to be created, and turned its back definitely upon the idea of an eastern imperialism, designed to throttle the wishes of the West, as British imperialism had throttled the wishes of the colonies. Given a little more time, the Confederation might have graduated into a successful central government, but it lost the confidence of the well-to-do upper classes, and was soon replaced by a new government under the Constitution. This document may not have been, as Gladstone once said, "the most wonderful work ever struck off at a given moment by the hand and purpose of man," but it embodied within its short compass what the Americans had learned from their experience in government, and it made skillful use of the ideas they had imported from Europe. It is not without significance that the Constitution of the United States is today the oldest written constitution in existence anywhere in the World.

7

A Decade of Controversy

British opinion on the colonies — The Sugar Act of 1764 — Paper-money regulation — The Stamp Act and its repeal — The Townshend duties and their repeal — Committees of Correspondence — The tax on tea — Boston Tea Party — The Intolerable Acts — First Continental Congress — The Continental Association

THE FRENCH and Indian War had brought to the attention of the British government

British opinion on the colonies

a variety of problems with reference to America that might otherwise have escaped serious notice. British officers reported with considerable feeling that the customs service in the colonies was hopelessly defective. Smuggling was rife, and trade with the enemy existed during the war in spite of stringent British regulations against it. Moreover, the cost of collecting the customs was out of all proportion to the amount of revenue taken in. It seemed apparent also that the Navigation Acts, most of which dated back to the seventeenth century, were in many ways obsolete. They permitted, according to some critics, altogether too free trade with the foreign West Indies, they failed to take into consideration the numerous additions that had been made to the Empire since the time of their passage, whatever the letter of the law might have been, and they did not in practice restrict the markets of North America wholly to British merchants. Most obvious of all was the laxity of the colonists in dealing with the problem of defense. Unity of colonial action had proved to be utterly unattainable, and only by the flattering promises of Pitt's requisition system were any of the colonies induced to do their duty in the raising of troops.

Nearly two years before the close of the French and Indian War William Pitt had resigned from office because he wished to pursue a more aggressive policy against Spain than the Cabinet was willing to approve. Pitt

Grenville succeeds Pitt

understood American affairs better than most Englishmen, and his absence from the government at this juncture was extremely unfortunate. When the war ended it fell to the lot of George Grenville, Pitt's brother-in-law, but the leader of a faction far less friendly to America, to deal with the colonies. Grenville had long been a member of the Cabinet, but in April, 1763, as Chancellor of the Exchequer and First Lord of the Treasury, he became its head. He was a man of great obstinacy, but little talent, who made a fetish of efficiency. Not well versed in American affairs, he was nevertheless convinced that reforms in colonial administration were necessary and that he must carry them through at once. He began the work by tightening up the customs service. Commissioners of customs for America were notified that they should proceed at once to the colonies, instead of remaining in Great Britain, as was customary, and hiring substitutes to do their work. Still more important, relentless war was declared upon all smugglers, first by authorizing the commanders of British men-of-war on duty in American waters to act as customs officials and seize offenders, secondly by enlarging the jurisdiction of the admiralty courts, whose verdicts did not depend upon the whims of local juries, and thirdly by issuing strict orders to colonial governors that they must enforce the navigation acts.

Grenville also pushed through Parliament the famous Sugar Act of 1764, by which he **The Sugar Act** proposed not only to regulate trade between the continental colonies and the foreign West Indies, but also to raise a revenue. This measure took the place of the Molasses Act of 1733, the provisions of which had never been seriously enforced. Ostensibly the new law was milder than the old, for it reduced from 6d to 3d a gallon the duty charged against molasses imported from the foreign islands. But the old duty, had it been enforced, would have been prohibitive, whereas the new duty was so low that its enforcement would mean only a curtailment of the West Indian trade, and would raise a revenue. The act also provided for new and in some cases higher duties on refined sugar, coffee, pimento, indigo, and other West Indian commodities, while the importation from these islands of rum and spirits was strictly prohibited. A curiously phrased statement in the act required that all the duties paid under it must be paid into the "receipt of His Majesty's Exchequer." Many Americans argued, probably incorrectly, that this statement meant that for these duties only gold and silver would be received, and that the colonies accordingly would soon be drained of all their hard money.

As if to leave no stone unturned to vex the colonists, the same year that the Sugar **Paper money regulation** Act was passed saw the enactment of a law prohibiting the use in the colonies of paper money as legal tender, and requiring that colonial issues of paper be payable in a reasonable time. Since the American colonies did not have and never had had an adequate supply of metallic currency, and since the inevitable tendency was for such hard money as they did obtain to be drawn to England by an unfavorable balance of trade, the Americans regarded this measure as extremely ungracious. It was designed, of course, to check the normal tendency of a debtor community to resort to money inflation as a means of scaling down debts. And for this very reason the law was especially unpopular among the people who found the most difficulty in meeting their financial obligations. The Sugar Act particularly angered the rich merchants; the limitations placed upon paper money issues angered the ordinary citizen.

Grenville was nothing if not thorough, and the problem of colonial defense remained to be solved. Pontiac's Con- **Colonial** spiracy had shown that this **defense** problem was not brought to an end by the happy outcome of the French and Indian War; it would recur at intervals as long as whites and Indians were in contact. It was with a view to lessening the amount of such contact that the Proclamation of 1763 had been issued; but if the Proclamation Line or any other line was to be defended, more adequate provision for the purpose must be made than the colonists had so far shown themselves willing to undertake. According to the British version, colonial troops had been found undependable during the French and Indian War, colonial levies could be secured only after much wheedling, and colonial unity of action was utterly out of the question. Grenville proposed, therefore, that the imperial government, as the only central and effective agency, should take over completely the problem of defense and that a permanent garrison of ten thousand British soldiers should be stationed in America. Incidentally, the presence of these troops might strengthen the hands of British officials charged with the duty of putting an end to smuggling.

But Grenville had no notion that the entire cost of defending the American frontier should be borne by the **The Stamp** British government. Part of **Act** the burden, he insisted, should fall upon the colonies. The cost of maintaining the requisite number of British troops in America was estimated at about £360,000 per year, and according to Grenville's plan one third of this sum should be raised by taxing the colonists. Assuming that the revenue to be collected under the Sugar Act would amount to about £45,000, Grenville saw the need of raising £75,000 more by the imposition of a new tax. This tax, he decided, might best be a stamp tax levied upon newspapers and upon the various official and legal documents through which colonial business, both of a private and public nature, had to be transacted. Knowing full well that the colonists would raise objections to any such tax, Grenville gave notice of his intention a full year in advance, and even suggested that if the colonial assemblies should present a better plan he would consider it. But the colonists seemingly could think of nothing better than the requisition system used during the recent war, and Grenville, recalling how unsatisfactory that system had been, put his Stamp Act through Parliament early in 1765 by a good majority in the House of Commons and without opposition from the Lords.

It took some time for American sentiment on the question of the stamp tax to crystallize. Franklin, who, while the **American reaction** act was under consideration, was in London representing the colony of Pennsylvania on another matter, opposed such a tax in principle, but assumed that if the act were passed the colonists would have to obey it. James Otis, in a pamphlet entitled *The Rights of the British Colonies Asserted and Proved*, argued that the taxation of the Americans without the consent of their own representatives was contrary to the English constitution and irreconcilable with the rights of the colonists as "British subjects and men." But he, too, assumed that if Parliament chose to act in this highhanded and illegal fashion, there was nothing that the Americans could do about it. As time went on, however, and the full import of the various policies initiated by Grenville began to be realized, American resentment grew. Grenville's program seemed admirably designed to cripple in the most effective manner the economic life of the colonies.

Patrick Henry won fame as a lawyer by defending the tobacco planters against efforts of the clergy to collect back tithes.

The Proclamation of 1763, granted that it could be enforced, would stop migration to the West just as hard times in the East, following close on the heels of the French and Indian War, had made the search for new homes in the West all the more essential. The Sugar Act would not only hamper trade with the foreign West Indies; but since those colonies were better buyers than sellers, it would interfere also with the normal flow of hard money from the islands to the continental colonies, and would make increasingly difficult the payment of balances owed by New England merchants to London. As if this were not sufficiently embarrassing, colonial paper issues were outlawed by the Currency Act, and the Stamp Act demanded more money when money was harder than ever to obtain. The colonies were poor, and the debts that they had incurred, or that some of them at least had incurred, during the French and Indian War seemed heavy; yet this was the time the English government selected to restrict their trade, remodel their monetary system, and tax them for a kind of protection that they did not want and thought that they did not need.

The most vulnerable point in the Grenville program, and the one which therefore drew the heaviest fire, was the Stamp Act. This, from the colonial point of view, was a clear case of taxation without representation. Patrick Henry, the leader of a group of insurgents in the Virginia House of Burgesses, forced through that body a set of resolutions that denounced the act in language so extravagant that the more conservative members were deeply concerned; and in the heat of debate Henry uttered his famous defiance of the British King: "Caesar," he said, "had his Brutus, Charles the First his Cromwell, and George the Third——" Here cries of "Treason! Treason!" arose from the House, while Henry continued, "may profit by their example. If this be treason, make the most of it."

"Taxation without representation"

The Virginia resolutions, one of which asserted "that the general assembly of this colony have the only and sole exclusive right and power to lay taxes and impositions upon the inhabitants of this colony," were given wide currency throughout the colonies, and served as topics of much discussion. There was a fair consensus of opinion that Parliament had definitely exceeded its authority. Most Americans were willing to admit that external taxes in the shape of duties on imports might be levied on the colonies by Parliament in the course of regulating imperial trade. But internal taxation without the direct sanction of popular representatives was "taxation without representation." Some of the northern merchants agreed among themselves that they would cease importations from England as long as the law held, and the general court of Massachusetts sent out a circular letter inviting all the colonies to participate in a conference at New York on the first Tuesday in October through which an appeal for relief might be made to the British government.

The date set for this conference made it impossible for some of the colonial assemblies to select delegates, but with nine colonies represented the Stamp Act Congress, as it was generally called, presently convened. This Congress repeated the argument of the Virginia resolutions, and held that since the only persons who might legally represent the colonies were those "chosen therein by themselves," the British Parliament, in which not one American sat, was wholly without authority to enact such a measure as the Stamp Act. Moreover, the resolutions that it adopted not only denounced the Stamp Act but objected also to the use of admiralty courts as a device to circumvent the traditional right of trial by jury, and described the restrictions on American commerce as unduly "burthensome and grievous."

The Stamp Act Congress

Opposition to the Stamp Act, however, went much further than the adoption of resolutions. An organization known as the Sons of Liberty directed an active campaign of intimidation against the stamp agents which made their lives so miserable that nearly all of them resigned. At first, refusal to buy the stamps required to be affixed upon clearance papers kept many ships in port, and the same attitude toward stamps on legal papers caused court sessions to be suspended in every colony but Rhode Island. But open defiance soon reigned. Newspapers refused to buy the stamps, official business was transacted without them, and legal papers that showed no evidence of having paid the tax were issued freely. Many deeds of violence occurred, the worst of which probably was the burning of Chief Justice Thomas Hutchinson's house by a Boston mob. Extremely effective upon English public opinion was the decline in American importations from England. Nonimportation agreements multiplied, and English merchants began to complain bitterly of their loss of trade.

Faced by this situation, there seemed nothing for the British government to do but back down. Fortunately for the American cause the course of factional politics in England had thrown Grenville out of office in June, 1765, and a new ministry had been

Repeal of the Stamp Act

COLONIAL RESENTMENT. Editor William Bradford's announcement of the *Journal's* suspension due to the Stamp Act.

"THE STAMP." From a colonial document, 1765.

The Stamp Act, passed by Parliament in 1765, introduced a period of bad relations between the mother country and the colonies that one writer has described as "ten years of wrangling and eight years of war." The colonies were too wealthy and populous, too far distant from England, too accustomed to independence to submit to outside rule.

REPEAL, OR THE FUNERAL OF MISS AME-STAMP. Pro-colonial British cartoon on the death of Grenville's Act, 1766.

formed under the Marquis of Rockingham which could yield on the Stamp Act with less loss of face. "I rejoice that America has resisted," said William Pitt, and many other Englishmen agreed with him that the colonists had the better of the argument. They had before them, also, the testimony of Benjamin Franklin, who appeared before the House of Commons and stated the colonial case with great lucidity, that the colonists would never submit to any internal taxes levied by Parliament. The repeal did not come without a struggle, however, and the American theory of taxation came in for unsparing denunciation. To the argument

that the colonists were unrepresented in Parliament because they had no direct representation there, the theory of "virtual representation" was advanced. "There can be no doubt, my lords," said Chief Justice Mansfield, "but that the inhabitants of the colonies are as much represented in parliament, as the greatest part of the people of England are represented; among nine millions of whom there are eight which have no votes in electing members of parliament." As for the distinction the colonists sought to draw between internal and external taxes, the Chief Justice found it equally invalid. A tax laid upon tobacco "in the ports of

Virginia or London," he argued, "is a duty laid upon the inland plantations of Virginia, a hundred miles from the sea, wheresoever the tobacco may be grown." When the repeal was finally accomplished (March 17, 1766) Parliament did not surrender to the American arguments, but to expediency. To make this perfectly clear a Declaratory Act was also passed which stated that the King and Parliament had "full power and authority" to legislate for the colonies "in all cases whatsoever."

The repeal of the Stamp Act was received in America with much enthusiasm, and the menacing gesture of the Declaratory Act was scarcely noticed. According to John Adams the decision of the British government to abandon the stamp tax had "hushed into silence almost every popular clamor, and composed every wave of popular disorder into a smooth and peaceful calm." Popular protestations of loyalty toward the mother country were common, and such a spirit of good-will existed that only a little tact seemed necessary to avoid for the future all such outbreaks as had just occurred.

The good relations thus happily restored might possibly have been maintained but **George III** for three unfortunate circumstances. In the first place, George III, the British King, cherished fond hopes of acquiring great personal power in the direction of national affairs. In order to accomplish this end without undue violence to the British constitution, however, he proposed to control Parliament rather than to overthrow it. Members were induced by the gift of honors, pensions, or offices, and by every other means of corruption then current, to become the "King's friends," and to vote as he chose to have them vote. On the subject of American affairs, unfortunately, the King was both ignorant and prejudiced. He was opposed to the repeal of the Stamp Act, and was ready at any time to see Parliament defy American opinion. Accordingly, as his followers grew in number the chances of

good relations with the colonies correspondingly declined.

Another unfortunate circumstance was the illness of William Pitt (now the Earl of Chatham), who was the real, **Illness of** although not the nominal, head **Pitt** of a new British ministry which was formed in the summer of 1766 and lasted on until 1770. The new ministry did not represent any particular party. Indeed, it included members chosen from a great variety of factions, both Whig and Tory, among them several of the "King's friends." Party government was never at lower ebb in England, and the talents of Pitt might well have been insufficient to hold so composite a group to an even reasonably consistent course. As it turned out, Pitt because of illness practically retired from the Ministry; and left thus without a leader each minister tended to do as he pleased within his own domain. The result, at least so far as it related to American affairs, was one colossal blunder after another.

The third unfortunate circumstance was that the Chancellor of the Exchequer, Charles Townshend, to whom **Charles** fell the task of finding an ade- **Townshend** quate revenue, was distinctly hostile to the colonies, and did not hesitate to take advantage of his position to translate his feelings into deeds. He speedily got into an unnecessary quarrel with New York. British troops were still kept in America, and as was customary requisitions for their supplies were made to the colonies in which they were stationed. The New York legislature, however, scaled down one such requisition in protest against so many British troops being routed to or through that colony. In answer, Townshend pushed through Parliament a law suspending the New York legislature until it should show itself ready to yield. He proposed, also, to continue the war which Grenville had begun against smugglers. A Board of Commissioners of the Customs with headquarters at Boston was created, and was given ample authority to enforce the Navigation Acts. Also writs of assistance, that is, general search warrants in which the premises to be searched need not be specifically mentioned, were formally authorized. Such writs had been issued during the French and Indian War, and in 1761 they had been declared legal in spite of the efforts of James Otis as counsel for some Massachusetts merchants to prove that they were a violation of the constitutional rights of British subjects. Townshend's reopening of the subject was therefore as unnecessary as it was provocative.

Furthermore, Townshend was determined to revive the contest with the colonies over **The Town-** taxation. Without so much as **shend duties** consulting his colleagues, most of whom, like Pitt, appear to have been friendly to the Americans, he gave out that he intended to raise a revenue from the colonies, and soon presented in fulfillment of his promise an act imposing duties upon all tea, paper, glass, painters' colors and lead to enter American ports. The Townshend Duty Act, as this measure was called, did mock deference to the supposed distinction between internal and external taxes, for it was a strictly external tax; but the preamble definitely stated that the law was designed to raise a revenue rather than to regulate trade, and that the revenue so obtained might be used at the discretion of the government to pay the salaries of colonial governors and colonial judges. The law was in fact, and was meant to be, a challenge to the Americans — a challenge to them to defend if they could their theory of taxation and their practice of disciplining governors and judges by withholding salaries. But probably neither Townshend nor the members of Parliament who voted to support him realized fully the serious nature of the challenge they had made. Townshend died soon after the acts that bore his name were passed, but his successor, Lord North, one of the King's friends, attempted for three years to enforce them.

The Townshend Acts aroused in America the resentment that might have been expected. The suspension of the New York legislature struck at the very roots of colonial self-government, for if the **Opposition** lawmaking body of a colony **in America** had to make appropriations whenever the British government told it to do so, or else lose its life, there could be no such thing as legislative independence in America. Indeed, all the colonial legislatures might be suspended permanently on one pretext or another. Townshend's reorganized customs service likewise led to bad feeling, particularly in Boston, where lax enforcement of the Navigation Acts had been treated as a sort of vested right, and rigorous enforcement might prove ruinous to business. The Duty Act was denounced generally as an unwarranted and unconstitutional measure. Some said that an external tax that was designed primarily to raise a revenue was no less an instance of taxation without representation than an internal tax, such as the Stamp Act had been. Others held not merely that taxation without representation was tyranny, but that all legislation by the British Parliament for America was unconstitutional. For the slogan, "No taxation without representation," these extremists would substitute the slogan, "No legislation without representation."

The most widely read of the arguments against the Townshend Acts was a series of pamphlets entitled *Letters of a* **"Letters** *Pennsylvania Farmer* published **of a** by John Dickinson. Dickin- **Pennsylvania Farmer"** son did not deny the legislative supremacy of Parliament, nor did he object strenuously to reasonable measures in regulation of colonial trade and manufacture. But he did argue in simple and convincing language that the new acts were unfair to the Americans, contrary to the best interests of the British themselves, and fit only to be repealed. While opposed, except as a last resort, to the use of violence in attempting to put an end to the Townshend system, he suggested that the Americans, as a means of making their power felt, might well proceed with a boycott on British goods.

In Massachusetts opposition to the

Samuel Adams was the skilled propagandist who, more than any other individual, paved the way for the Revolution. Portrait by John Singleton Copley.

he had ranked fifth, socially, in a class of twenty-two. His father was a man of some means who tried Samuel Adams to establish his son in business and left him one third of the family estate. It soon became apparent, however, that Samuel Adams was not designed for a successful business career. He ran through his property and remained forever after impecunious. But however unfit he may have been in the management of his own affairs, he early demonstrated a remarkable talent for managing the affairs of the public. By the time the controversy over the Townshend Acts broke, Adams had risen from the level of town-meeting politics to be the chief radical leader in the colonial House of Representatives. He was not a merchant and never could have been one for long, but he united all classes of malcontents in opposition to the vexatious Duty Act. He displayed rare skill as a writer, and not a little aptitude as a thinker. He maintained that the British constitution, like the constitutions of all free peoples, was "fixed in the law of Nature and of God," and that "neither the supreme legislature nor the supreme executive" could alter it. In various documents adopted by the Massachusetts House, Adams's views were set forth, and finally in a *Circular Letter*, which he drafted, all the colonial assemblies were invited to join with Massachusetts in resisting the policies of the British government. This act deeply offended Lord Hillsborough, Secretary of State for the Colonies in the British Ministry, and he promptly ordered the Massachusetts House to rescind it; when this order was defied the governor of the colony, acting according to instructions from London, dissolved the assembly. In spite of the threat that the same fate would befall any assembly which dared discuss the *Circular Letter*, legislative halls throughout the colonies rang out repeatedly with resolutions supporting the position of Massachusetts and deploring the act of the British government. The Virginia Resolves of 1769 are famous, not only for their statement of the

Townshend Acts was particularly determined, for there an unsettled state of the public mind already existed which made easy the work of agitators. The aristocratic clique which ran the affairs of the colony had long been in bad odor with the common people — the farmers and the artisans — who believed that their interests had often been betrayed by their rulers. Orthodox Puritans, already fearful because of the growing influence of Anglicans in colonial affairs, took added fright at the talk of establishing an Anglican bishopric in America. The royal governor had quarreled tactlessly and needlessly with the legislature about many things. The merchant class, which because of its wealth might under ordinary circumstances have been counted upon to be conservative, was on edge lest too rigorous enforcement of the Navigation Acts might bring it to grief. Small wonder that Samuel Adams (1722–1803), the astute leader of the popular party in the Massachusetts legislature, became at once the man of the hour.

Adams was of such good family that when as a boy he had attended Harvard College

American case, but also because they were introduced by George Washington himself.

The weapon by which the colonies might defend their rights had already been forged **Non-importation agreements** during the controversy over the Stamp Act. Once more non-importation agreements were entered into by the merchants of the leading cities, a program which many southern planters also chose to adopt. British trade began to fall off; British merchants began to protest; and the wisdom of Parliament's taxing the sale of British goods overseas, whatever the revenue involved, was called into serious question. The British government had little choice but to back down once again. Accordingly, Lord North, the King's friend who became in 1770 the head of the British Ministry, moved the repeal of the duties except the tax on tea "to keep up the right."

Meantime two regiments of British soldiers had been transferred from Halifax to **"The Boston Massacre"** Boston to overawe the radicals in that port. The presence of the troops was deeply resented, and they received scant courtesy from the townsmen. On the same day that Lord North asked Parliament to repeal the Townshend duties (March 5, 1770) seven British soldiers under the command of Captain Preston were so irritated by a mob of fifty or sixty jeering men and boys that the soldiers fired into the crowd. Five citizens were killed, and news of the "Boston Massacre," duly exaggerated, spread like wildfire through the colonies. Captain Preston, on the ground that he had ordered the men to fire, was indicted for murder, and demands from Samuel Adams and his friends forced the governor to quarter the troops outside the city. But saner heads saw that the mob was quite as much to blame for the outrage as the soldiers, and John Adams, a rising young lawyer distantly related to Samuel Adams, in spite of his many misgivings as to the effect of such a course upon his future, defended Preston and his men in the trial that followed. Preston

was acquitted, but two of the soldiers were given slight punishment for manslaughter.

The news that the Townshend duties had been repealed tended once more to restore good relations be- **Good relations restored** tween the colonies and the mother country. Non-importation agreements were generally rescinded or were reduced in scope to oppose merely the importation from England of tea, which, it was well understood, could be smuggled in from Holland without much difficulty, and even the boycott on tea was not well observed. The fact that the British government had not backed down on the right of Parliament to tax the colonies troubled very few, for most Americans cared less about the theory of taxation than about the practice, and in practice the British attempt to tax the colonies had failed.

It would not be correct to say, however, that the fires of discontent had gone out; they were merely burning low. Evidence that they might flame up again at any time was not difficult to find. The enforcement of British trade regulations was a never-ending source of irritation, and sometimes led to violence. When, for example, a revenue schooner, the *Gaspee*, ran aground on the Rhode Island coast, her captain and crew were overpowered by a mob of colonists and the vessel burned (June, 1772). Efforts on the part of the British to bring the culprits to trial proved futile, for no trustworthy witness could be found who would give evidence against them; and British talk that suspects might be taken to England for trial made a bad situation worse.

In Massachusetts Samuel Adams continued with strong backing his attacks upon the aristocratic control of **Committees of correspondence** the colony, now admirably personified in the new governor, Thomas Hutchinson, who was appointed in 1770. With some asperity the two set forth in detail their conflicting notions on the sovereignty of Parliament. In 1772 Adams, who had heard that the King intended to pay Massachusetts judges out of money col-

BRITISH TROOPS LANDING AT LONG WHARF, BOSTON, 1768. Detail of an engraving by Paul Revere.

"THE BLOODY MASSACRE AT BOSTON, 1770." Prints of Paul Revere's highly inaccurate report were in wide circulation within a few days of the famous riot.

The Boston Massacre resulted from the stationing of British troops in Boston, beginning in 1768, to aid in the enforcement of the Townshend Acts. Their presence was a taunt to the American radicals, who lost no opportunity to ridicule the "red-coats." The snow-balling of a British sentry, March 5, 1770, wound up as a riot that cost the lives of several colonials. Among those killed was a Negro, Crispus Attucks.

lected from the colonial customs, organized the radical elements of the colony through "committees of correspondence," which were charged with the duty of informing one another of the current state of affairs. Next year some of the back-country radicals in the Virginia House of Burgesses, led by Patrick Henry, Richard Henry Lee, and Thomas Jefferson, decided that intercolonial committees of correspondence would be a good thing, and induced the House to appoint such a committee for Virginia. Radicals elsewhere soon took up with the idea, and presently a network of radical committees came into existence through which, when occasion should demand, revolutionary sentiment might easily be fomented and revolutionary action taken.

At a time when the British government might well have been exerting itself to main-

The tax on tea tain good relations with the colonies, it blundered most unfortunately by passing a Tea Act which was well designed to revive once more the old controversy over taxation. The East India Company, it chanced, was in sore straits financially and a fitting object for governmental solicitude. It had on hand in English warehouses a large quantity of tea which it had found difficulty in marketing, partly, no doubt, because too many Americans drank tea smuggled in from Holland. To help save the company from bankruptcy by finding a market for its tea, the British government now agreed to remit the twelvepence a pound duty charged in England on all tea imported, and to allow the tea to be reshipped to America, where it would pay only threepence duty (May, 1773). Since the cost of transportation would not be great, it seemed evident that tea could thus be landed and sold in the colonies for less than it could be sold in England, where the twelvepence duty still held, and probably for less even than the Americans would have to pay for smuggled tea. For the most part the measure was designed merely for the relief of the East India Company, but the hope that cheap tea might induce the Americans to forget their scruples on taxation was by no means absent. As Lord North said, "the King meant to try the case in America."

The Tea Act was extremely annoying to colonial merchants who had grown rich **Colonial** from smuggling, and it furnished **resistance** Adams and his radical following with a new and attractive grievance. It proved easy to organize resistance to the landing of the tea, and a variety of unpleasant receptions were arranged for the tea ships now dispatched for all the more important colonial ports. So much opposition to the sale of the tea developed that many of the agents appointed to receive it were afraid to carry out their commissions, and resigned. The ships sent to New York and Philadelphia returned to England with their cargoes intact. Tea was landed at Charleston, but since no one was on hand to pay the duty it was stored in government warehouses and left there until after the Declaration of Independence, when it was sold at auction for the benefit of the patriot cause. At Annapolis a mass meeting decided that the tea ship should not be permitted to land its cargo, and forced the owner to set fire to his ship.

Boston was thus not alone in refusing entry to British tea; but the Boston Tea Party attracted more attention **The Boston** than all the other colonial acts **Tea Party** of insubordination put together. The Boston agents, close relatives of the governor, Thomas Hutchinson, refused to resign, and Hutchinson refused to permit the tea ships to return to England. On November 29, 1773, a mass meeting of citizens held in the Old South Church voted that the tea should not be landed, and a few weeks later (December 16), following another mass meeting, fifty or sixty men, faintly disguised as Indians, boarded the ships and threw the tea into the harbor. In Boston a large

The Tea Act of 1773, focus of the issue of England's right to tax the colonies, aroused the indignation of many Americans who saw it as a device to bribe them into obeying the law, and caused a storm of active — sometimes violent — protest from American radicals.

BOSTONIANS PAYING THE EXCISEMAN. Anonymous cartoon, 1775. The Boston Tea Party is represented in the background.

PATRIOTIC LADIES OF NORTH CAROLINA PLEDGING TO DRINK NO MORE TEA. British cartoon, 1775.

crowd looked on approvingly while the tea was destroyed, and elsewhere in the colonies, when the news was known, there were many to commend the act. Some Americans, among them Benjamin Franklin, regretted what had been done, and nearly all Englishmen, including as consistent a friend of America as William Pitt, regarded the Tea Party as an outrage. Why Americans should refuse to buy tea for even less than Englishmen could buy it seemed to many of the latter almost beyond comprehension.

The British government under the circumstances could hardly fail to attempt **The "Intol-** retaliation. Early in 1774 five **erable Acts"** measures, usually called by the Americans the "Intolerable Acts," were passed by Parliament, an intended rebuke, incidentally, to the theory held by some Americans that the British Parliament had no right to legislate for the colonies. The Boston Port Act ordered that the port of Boston should be closed to all commerce, regardless of consequences, until the tea destroyed had been paid for. The Massachusetts Government Act reformed the government of that colony by increasing the power of the governor, by making the council, or upper house of the assembly, appointive instead of elective, and by suppressing town meetings — "hotbeds of sedition" — except as the governor might permit. An Act for the Impartial Administration of Justice enabled royal officials who were accused of capital offenses in Massachusetts to be sent for trial to England or to another colony whenever, in the opinion of the governor, a fair trial in the local courts would be difficult to secure. The Quartering Act, which applied to other colonies as well as Massachusetts, authorized colonial governors to requisition such buildings as might be needed for the use of royal troops stationed within the boundaries of a given colony. The Quebec Act, which to the Americans seemed quite as "intolerable" as any of the rest, was not designed by the British government as a punitive measure. It was based upon several years' experience in attempting to govern the terri- **The Quebec** tory in America recently ac- **Act** quired from France, and showed a spirit of accommodation toward the French subjects of Great Britain that was all too rarely in evidence when the British government dealt with its English colonists. The French, unaccustomed to participation in the affairs of government, were given once more an autocratic régime. French rather than English legal traditions were permitted to govern in the trial of civil suits, thus eliminating the use of juries in such cases; and the religion of the French, Roman Catholicism, including the right of priests to collect tithes, received full legal recognition. Less defensible was the extension of the boundaries of the province to include the territory north of the Ohio River and east of the Mississippi, although Canadian furtraders operated throughout this region and several French villages were located in the Illinois country. The passage of this act suggests that the British government did not consider the western land claims of the seaboard colonies to be worthy of much respect.

These five measures could scarcely have been better calculated to arouse to the highest pitch the spirit of resist- **American** ance in America. General Gage, **resentment** who now replaced Hutchinson as governor of Massachusetts, appeared in Boston with four regiments of troops to enforce the acts designed for special application there; and he discharged his duty with such thoroughness as to leave no doubt about the seriousness of the British intentions. What was happening to Boston and Massachusetts might at any time happen to other ports and other colonies. Colonial charters might be altered or abolished at the whim of the British Parliament. The expansion westward of such of the colonies as had claims to western lands was definitely blocked by the Quebec Act. That ill-timed measure seemed, indeed, to threaten American liberties in more ways than one. Did the British government intend that the autocratic government established in Canada should be the pattern to which all the American colonies must conform? Were such fundamental rights of Englishmen as trial by jury on the wane in America? Was Roman Catholicism to be encouraged as a counterweight to New England Puritanism? It was true enough that the Intolerable Acts were denounced by some outstanding English liberals such as Burke and Chatham (William Pitt), but they pleased the King, and the King's power was on the rise.

The network of committees of correspondence that Samuel Adams had inaugurated **The First Continental Congress** now began to function, and Massachusetts was soon assured that she had the sympathy and support of the radical element throughout the colonies. A plan for concerted action was soon devised. When the Virginia House of Burgesses adopted a resolution naming June 1, the day Boston harbor was to be closed, as a day of fasting and prayer, the royal governor dissolved the House for its impudence; but the members, meeting unofficially afterwards, adopted a resolution calling upon all the colonies to send delegates to a Continental Congress, to meet in Philadelphia the following September. This resolution, which was industriously circulated by the committees of correspondence, received a hearty response, and delegates to the proposed Congress were speedily selected. Sometimes they were chosen by the committees of correspondence themselves, sometimes by self-appointed committees of safety, sometimes by provincial mass meetings, and in a few cases only by colonial legislatures. In the main the more radical opponents of British policy controlled the selection of these delegates. Conservatives were not interested or were not consulted.

The years of controversy with Great Britain had divided colonial society more or **Radicals vs. conservatives** less definitely into two schools of thought. There was general agreement that the British government had dealt unfairly with the colonies, but there was a wide divergence of opinion as to how best to meet the situation. The radicals were determined never to yield to the British pretensions. They meant to stand firmly by the rights Americans had always enjoyed and to gain new rights if they could. But the conservatives, who saw more clearly the great benefits of British trade and British protection, favored conciliation. The colonies, they thought, could even afford to give up some of their cherished rights rather than lose the advantages that their status within the British Empire gave them. In general the lower and middle classes inclined more toward the radical point of view, while the well-to-do upper classes were conservative. There were, however, many interesting deviations from this division. Many rich colonial merchants were so greatly outraged by the course of the British government that they were willing to make common cause with the radicals. So also were the bulk of the planter aristocrats of the South, intense individualists almost to the last man, who regarded with extreme disfavor both the regulations of the British government and their own embarrassing indebtedness to British merchants. Class lines were still further shifted by the fact that to many

Congressional delegates from New York were nominated by the local Committee of Correspondence, to be approved by the citizenry, as advertised in this broadside.

ADVERTISEMENT.

THE Committee of Correspondence in New-York, having on Monday Night laſt proceeded to the Nomination of five Perſons to go as Delegates for the ſaid City and County, on the propoſed General Congreſs at Philadelphia, on the 1ſt of September next; the five following Perſons were nominated for that Purpoſe,

Philip Livingſton,
James Duane,
John Alſop,
John Jay,
Iſaac Low.

The Inhabitants, therefore, of this City and County, are requeſted to meet at the City-Hall, on THURSDAY next, at 12 o'Clock, in order to approve of the ſaid five Perſons as Delegates, *or to chooſe ſuch other in their Stead, as to their Wiſdom ſhall ſeem meet.*

By Order of the Committee,

ISAAC LOW, CHAIRMAN.

TUESDAY, 5th July, 1774.

Americans, particularly those of the interior and the "back country," "home rule" was of rather less consequence than "who should rule at home." In New England and some of the Middle Colonies, revolt against British control and revolt against the local governing aristocracy were practically one and the same, for an end to British domination would be the surest means of undermining the power of the local aristocrats. In Virginia, back-country farmers and tidewater planters postponed their local differences to make common cause against the more pressing dangers of British misrule; but in the Carolinas the pioneer farmers generally took the British side, for they found it difficult to understand how there could be any good in a cause which won the support of so many tidewater aristocrats.

The First Continental Congress, which began its sessions in Philadelphia September **Galloway's** 5, 1774, was attended by fifty-**plan** six delegates representing every colony except Georgia. It was soon apparent that the radicals were in the majority; indeed, considering the methods used in selecting the delegates, there could have been no other result. Nevertheless a plan of compromise that was proposed by Joseph Galloway of Pennsylvania came within one vote of adoption. Galloway's plan suggested that a grand council should be constituted which would consist of delegates chosen by the various colonial assemblies and would have authority to deal with such matters as might concern both Great Britain and the colonies or more than one colony. A president-general, appointed by the crown, was to possess an absolute veto on all measures passed by the council; and the consent of both the British Parliament and the colonial council was to be required to give validity to imperial regulations touching America. In time of war the council might levy taxes independently.

But the radicals were eager to avoid any **Declaration** appearance of yielding to the **of Rights** British contentions, and succeeded presently in pushing through a far less conciliatory program. A Declaration of Rights was adopted which stated the American case against taxation without representation as clearly as the somewhat conflicting opinions of the delegates on that subject would permit, branded the "Intolerable Acts" as "unpolitic, unjust, cruel and unconstitutional," and demanded their repeal. The language of the Declaration was deferential enough, but the statement of the American case was thoroughly unyielding. To insure that words would be backed by deeds, the Congress went on to frame a continental "Association," by which the delegates bound themselves and, so far as they could, those whom they represented, not to import or use any British "goods, wares, or merchandise whatsoever." Also, the slave trade was to be discontinued, and if the British government failed to come to terms with the Americans inside of a year, American exports to the British Isles and to the West Indies were to be stopped. The enforcement of this measure was to be turned over to popularly elected local committees, who should make it their business to publish violations of the agreement, seize goods imported in defiance of its terms, and maintain a united front against the British. And after the lapse of a year a second Continental Congress should meet to observe the progress of events.

The actions of the First Continental Congress were essentially revolutionary. Without any constitutional au- **Work of the** thority whatever the Congress **Association** had to all intents and purposes passed a law and provided the means for its enforcement. For the Association proved to be singularly effective. In nearly every colony radical committees were organized which resorted, when it was deemed necessary, to such acts of violence as tarring and feathering to secure obedience to the regulations of the revolutionary Congress. Radical spokesmen urged also with some success that such home industries as might serve to diminish dependence on Great Britain be patronized, and that as a fit precaution against further

British injustices militia companies be formed and munitions of war collected.

These measures had much the same effect upon British opinion as Americans had **English opinion** learned by previous experience to expect. Burke and other English liberals urged that the various repressive acts be repealed, and that the status which the colonists had enjoyed at the close of the French and Indian War be restored. Pitt believed that a bargain could be struck with the colonists by which they would agree to acknowledge the legislative supremacy of Parliament in return for the promise that Parliament would not construe its power to include the right to tax the colonies. Merchants in London and elsewhere, who were losing heavily from the American boycott, petitioned Parliament to conciliate the Americans and reopen trade. But this time the ministry, strongly supported by the King and by a majority in the Parliament just elected, refused to yield to the clamor. Instead it placed closer limits on New England trade and voted to send more troops to America. Lord North's "Conciliatory Proposition," which offered immunity from parliamentary taxes to any colony which would agree to assume of its own accord its fair share of imperial expense, was generally regarded in America as merely a device to promote dissension among the Americans, and probably was so intended.

Meantime party lines in America became more and more definite. The day of temporizing was soon over, and **Growth of radicalism in America** wavering citizens were gradually forced to decide what course they meant to support. For some time even the radicals were not precisely of one mind. All were agreed that no concessions should be made to the British point of view, but the more moderate, who hoped to avert the use of force unless in case of extreme necessity, viewed with some misgivings the military preparations under way. Similarly the conservatives disagreed among themselves. Some thought that resistance, so long as it was strictly peaceful, might well be continued in the hope of ultimate success; others were eager for conciliation and compromise. Ultimately the conservatives parted company. The extremists, preferring the British connection to anything that resistance to the mother country had to offer, became the "Tories" or "Loyalists" of the American Revolution. The moderates, on the other hand, gradually drifted over to the radicals, and ultimately joined with them as "Whigs" or "Patriots" to take up arms and to win independence. Doubtless a minority in the beginning, the radical extremists through their effective organization and aggressive tactics ultimately won over a majority to their way of thinking. But probably as many as a third of the colonists were openly or secretly loyal to the mother country throughout the Revolution.

Bibliography

C. H. Van Tyne, *The Causes of the War of Independence* (1922), is still one of the best books by an American writer on the background of the Revolution, but J. C. Miller, *Origins of the American Revolution* (1943), incorporates the results of more recent scholarship. Klingberg, *The Morning of America*, already cited, covers admirably the eve of the Revolution, and continues also into the early national period. A. M. Schlesinger, *The*

Colonial Merchants and the American Revolution, 1763–1776 (1917), brings out clearly the motives that actuated the merchant class. Other books of great value in this connection are: C. M. Andrews, *The Colonial Background of the American Revolution* (1924); G. E. Howard, *Preliminaries of the Revolution* (1905); H. E. Egerton, *The Causes and Character of the American Revolution* (1923); Carl L. Becker, *The Eve of the Revolution* (1918).

On the intimate connection between the French and Indian War and the Revolution, much light is shed by E. I. McCormac, *Colonial Opposition to Imperial Authority during the French and Indian War* (1911). Less dependable, but suggestive, is W. S. McClellan, *Smuggling in the American Colonies at the Outbreak of the Revolution* (1912). See also Channing, *History of the United States,* III.

The constitutional aspects of the Revolution have naturally attracted much attention. An excellent summary is to be found in A. M. Schlesinger, *New Viewpoints in American History*, Ch. VII, but this should be compared with C. H. McIlwain, *The American Revolution; A Constitutional Interpretation* (1923). C. E. Merriam, *A History of American Political Theories* (1936), gives a good brief statement of the American contentions. Other useful books in this connection are: L. B. Namier, *England in the Age of the American Revolution* (1930); Reginald Coupland, *The American Revolution and the British Empire* (1930); R. L. Schuyler, *Parliament and the British Empire* (1929); G. H. Guttridge, *English Whiggism and the American Revolution* (1942); Lynn Montross, *The Reluctant Rebels: The Story of the Continental Congress, 1774–1789* (1950). See also W. E. H. Lecky, *The American Revolution, 1763–1783*, edited by J. A. Woodburn (1898), which is a selection from the author's eight-volume *History of England in the Eighteenth Century* of all "chapters and passages relating to America."

Among the many biographies of men who had a part in the making of the Revolution, the following may be cited: R. V. Harlow, *Samuel Adams, Promoter of the American Revolution* (1923); J. C. Miller, *Sam Adams, Pioneer in Propaganda* (1936); C. J. Stillé, *The Life and Times of John Dickinson* (1891); J. K. Hosmer, *The Life of Thomas Hutchinson* (1896); M. C. Tyler, *Patrick Henry* (1917); W. W. Henry, *Patrick Henry* (3 vols., 1891). The often overlooked prominence of George Washington in these events is the theme of an excellent study by Curtis Nettels, *George Washington and American Independence* (1951). See also Catherine D. Bowen, *John Adams and the American Revolution* (1950).

On certain local problems, including the attitude of the back country residents toward those of the seacoast, see C. H. Lincoln, *The Revolutionary Movement in Pennsylvania, 1760–1776* (1901); C. A. Barker, *The Background of the Revolution in Maryland* (1940); Oscar Zeichner, *Connecticut's Years of Controversy, 1750-1776* (1949); and Adams, *Revolutionary New England*, already cited.

8

Revolution

Lexington and Concord — Second Continental Congress — Bunker Hill — Washington chosen Commander-in-Chief — The first year of war — Declaration of Independence — British capture of New York and of Philadelphia — Burgoyne's defeat — The French alliance — Valley Forge — The war in the West — The war in the South — Surrender of Cornwallis

EVENTS were now moving rapidly in the direction of that appeal to arms which many observers on both sides of the Atlantic had long foreseen. In Massachusetts the authority of Governor Gage was openly defied; "minute men" were being drilled upon the village commons, and stores of munitions were being collected at strategic spots. Neither side wished to precipitate hostilities, but as a necessary measure of self-defense Gage finally felt obliged to seize the military supplies that the radical leaders had accumulated at Concord, and to arrest, if possible, the arch-conspirators, Samuel Adams and John Hancock.

With these ends in view a small detachment of troops left Boston on the night of **Lexington and Concord** April 18, 1775. The Governor had counted on surprise, but his opponents had been on the lookout, and thanks to the activities of Paul Revere and others the whole countryside was soon aware of the coming of the "redcoats." When, early on the morning of the nineteenth, the troops entered Lexington, they found a company of armed militia drawn up on the meeting-house green, presumably with intent to oppose the British advance. Thereupon Major Pitcairn, in command of the British, rode forward and ordered the Americans to disperse. Captain John Parker, who led the colonial militia, observing that his men were badly outnumbered, also ordered them to withdraw.

But from some quarter, whether British or American will never be known, a shot was fired, after which the firing became general. Resistance to the British troops proved futile, as Parker had foreseen, and leaving the Americans to care for a number of dead and wounded, Pitcairn marched on to Concord. There he found and destroyed some American supplies, but he scored no further triumphs. On the return to Boston his troops were the target for farmers and militiamen who lined the roads, and from behind stone walls, rocks, and trees picked off so many of the redcoats that the retreat to Boston ended in a humiliating rout. The news of this long-awaited clash soon penetrated to every village and hamlet throughout the colonies. From all New England armed militiamen collected around Boston to lay siege to the city, and patriotic resolves from far and near assured the Massachusetts radicals that in the course they had chosen they would not lack for support.

On the tenth of May following the affairs at Lexington and Concord the second Continental Congress began its sessions at Philadelphia. The new Congress was a far more radical body than its predecessor, partly because the colonial governors had received instructions from England to prevent the election of delegates to another Congress, and the choices had therefore to be made by strictly revolutionary groups. There were mode-

Revolutionary War 1775

← British – April 19, 1775,
▬ American Lines 1775~1776

1 2 3 4 5
MILES

rates present, however, such as John Dickinson of Pennsylvania, and they not only prevented an immediate declaration of independence, but they also succeeded in inducing the delegates to appeal once more to the King for redress of grievances. But the tide of revolution could not be stemmed for long. On June 15 Congress took over the troops gathered near Boston as the Continental Army, and assumed authority to direct the course of the war. At the suggestion of John Adams, it gave the command of these troops to George Washington, the well-known Virginia aristocrat. While this selection was designed in part to flatter the South and in part to placate the upper classes of every section, probably no wiser choice could have been made.

Washington was present in uniform as a delegate to the Continental Congress from Virginia when he was chosen to head the army. He set out at once to join his command, but before he

Bunker Hill

could complete his journey another battle had been fought. Reinforcements had brought the number of British soldiers in Boston to about ten thousand men, and General Gage, fearful lest the Americans should gain possession of the hills that surrounded the city and open on him with cannon fire, planned to occupy some of the hills himself. But the Americans anticipated him, and sent twelve hundred men under Colonel William Prescott to occupy Bunker Hill in Charlestown, although Prescott's command went beyond Bunker Hill to Breed's Hill, and began fortifications there. It would have been easy for the British to entrap the Americans, since the heights in Charlestown were connected with the mainland by only a narrow neck of land. But Gage, instead of attempting to cut off Prescott's chance of retreat, ordered a direct assault up the hill from the bay. Twice the colonial lines held, and twice the British after heavy losses retreated to re-form their lines. On the third assault, the Americans gave way, for they had run short of ammunition. But the battle of Bunker Hill, as it has always been called, fought June 17, 1775, proved alike to the British and to the colonists that as soldiers the raw American militia were not wholly to be despised.

Nevertheless the colonial troops about Boston, numbering perhaps twenty thousand, that Washington now undertook to command were less an army than a mob. Organization was lacking, bickering over precedence in military rank was rife, supplies were woefully inadequate, desertions were dangerously numerous. Washington's ability to draw order out of chaos never showed itself to better advantage. The troops were drilled and taught to obey, desertions were checked, and a better plan for the siege of Boston was evolved. All summer and fall and far into the winter, the American army watched and waited, while the British within the city, now under the command of General Howe, hesitated to attack. At length, on the fourth of March, 1776, Washington occupied Dorchester Heights, to the south of Boston, and trained his cannon on the city. Faced by this dire threat, Howe hastily embarked his troops for Nova Scotia, taking with him also nearly a thousand Loyalists who feared to face the American occupation.

Washington in command

The cannon that Washington used to make Boston untenable for the British had been dragged overland from Ticonderoga, a captured British fort at the southern end of the Lake George–Lake Champlain approach to Canada. This post and Crown Point, which lay farther to the north, were made the objectives of two expeditions, one led by Ethan Allen, who held a Connecticut commission, and another led by Benedict Arnold, under the authority of Massachusetts. The two expeditions combined, and on the very day that the second Continental Congress opened, Ticonderoga surrendered without the firing of a gun. With Crown Point also taken, the pathway to Canada seemed open, and Congress,

The attack on Canada

Revolutionary War 1775 ~ 1776

hoping that the French there might be induced to join in the revolt, authorized Richard Montgomery and Benedict Arnold, with separate commands, to continue the northward advance. In November, 1775, Montgomery took Montreal and then cooperated with Arnold, who had made an heroic march through the Maine woods, in the attack on Quebec. But an assault made December 31, 1775, which cost Montgomery his life, was unsuccessful, and the winter siege that followed proved equally futile. With the French showing no desire to help the Americans, and the British ably commanded by Sir Guy Carleton, Montreal was abandoned and Arnold's troops were soon forced back to Crown Point.

The only other military activity of consequence during the first year of the war occurred in the Carolinas, where the British made a bid for the support of the back-country Loyalists. An expedition was dispatched by sea to attack

The Carolinas

Wilmington and Charleston, but before the fleet reached Wilmington a clash at Moore's Creek Bridge, February 27, 1776, between North Carolina Patriots and Loyalists gave a complete victory to the former. General Clinton, in command of the British expedition, then gave up hope of taking Wilmington, and went on to Charleston, where he met such stiff resistance that he abandoned the entire project and retired (June, 1776).

The first year's fighting thus ended in a kind of stalemate, with the Americans repulsed in their effort to conquer Canada, and the British equally unable to secure a foothold anywhere in the colonies. But American opinion during this period had not remained stationary. At the outbreak of hostilities, only a few extremists were ready to go the whole length of separation from Great Britain; the great majority thought of the conflict as merely a civil war conducted to maintain American rights within the British Empire. Indeed, such was their sentimental attachment for the mother country that many colonials took up arms against her with extreme reluctance. They counted on the aid of powerful English liberals, such as Burke and Pitt, to bring the British government to a more conciliatory point of view and they hoped devoutly that the fighting would not last long. But the events of the year seemed to belie their hopes. George III had turned down the American petition for the redress of grievances, had branded the Americans as rebels, apparently with the full support of Parliament, and had even begun to hire German troops — "Hessians" — to assist in the vigorous prosecution of the war. Furthermore, there were changes in America. The old colonial governments had crumbled away, and to forestall anarchy new political foundations had had to be laid. Revolution had thus taken place in fact if not yet in name. Also, American trade was suffering acutely, and since seemingly trade with Great Britain could not be reopened — was now forbidden by an act of Parliament —

Sentiment for independence

other outlets for American trade must be found. Such outlets only an avowedly independent nation, fully competent to make treaties for itself, would be able to obtain. And, since the war must needs continue, expediency demanded that help be sought from the traditional enemies of Great Britain, particularly from France. But what foreign nation would care to exert itself merely to secure a redress of grievances for Americans within the British Empire? On the other hand, if the disruption of the Empire was the American goal there was plenty of outside interest in that.

At precisely the right moment there appeared a pamphlet by Thomas Paine, entitled *Common Sense*, which stated simply and effectively the American case for independence. Paine had only lately come from England to America, but he was a lover of liberty, and the opportunity to strike a blow in its behalf appealed to him strongly. He ridiculed the idea of personal loyalty to the King, of which so much had been made in American protests against the tyranny of Parliament, and called George III a royal "brute." He saw "something absurd in supposing a continent to be perpetually governed by an island," since "in no instance hath nature made the satellite larger than the primary planet." He branded reconciliation as "a fallacious dream," and found a potent argument for separation "in the blood of the slain." The pamphlet sold by the hundreds of thousands, and in the early months of the year 1776 was read and quoted everywhere in America. Neither its logic nor its language was above reproach, but the common man liked both, and the sentiment in favor of independence grew accordingly.

Paine's "Common Sense"

That Congress was in a mood to respond to the shift in public opinion soon seemed evident. As early as April, 1776, the North Carolina delegates received instructions to work for independence, and the next month Virginia openly proclaimed her own secession from the British Empire. On the seventh

THE TORY'S DAY OF JUDGMENT. From John Trumbull's *M'Fingal*, 1795.

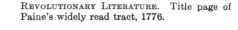

COMMON SENSE;

ADDRESSED TO THE

INHABITANTS

OF

AMERICA,

On the following interesting

SUBJECTS.

I. Of the Origin and Design of Government in general, with concise Remarks on the English Constitution.

II. Of Monarchy and Hereditary Succession.

III. Thoughts on the present State of American Affairs.

IV. Of the present Ability of America, with some miscellaneous Reflections.

Man knows no Master save creating HEAVEN,
Or those whom choice and common good ordain.
THOMSON.

PHILADELPHIA;
Printed, and Sold, by R. BELL, in Third-Street.
MDCCLXXVI.

REVOLUTIONARY LITERATURE. Title page of Paine's widely read tract, 1776.

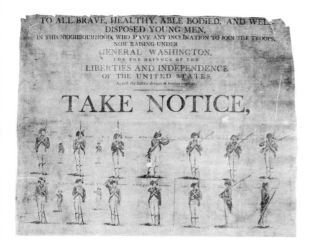

TO ALL BRAVE, HEALTHY, ABLE BODIED, AND WELL
DISPOSED YOUNG MEN,
IN THIS NEIGHBOURHOOD, WHO HAVE ANY INCLINATION TO JOIN THE TROOPS,
NOW RAISING UNDER
GENERAL WASHINGTON,
FOR THE DEFENCE OF THE
LIBERTIES AND INDEPENDENCE
OF THE UNITED STATES,

TAKE NOTICE,

RECRUITING NOTICE. Broadside advertising for men to "embrace this opportunity of spending a few happy years . . . in the truly respectable character of a soldier," 1776.

The American Revolution was the logical result of a growing spirit of independence in the colonies. When trouble came, that spirit manifested itself in many diverse ways — the hanging of Tories to "liberty poles," the writing of anti-British tracts such as Thomas Paine's Common Sense, *recruitment of a patriot army, and the solemn decision of Congress in favor of separation.*

CONGRESS VOTING INDEPENDENCE. Painting by Pine and Savage, 1785.

of June, Richard Henry Lee, seconded by John Adams, offered a resolution "that these United Colonies, are, and of right ought to be, free and independent states." Doubtless this resolution expressed the sentiments of an overwhelming majority of the delegates, but to satisfy a small minority it was agreed, June 10, that the vote should be delayed three weeks. Not until July 1, however, was the debate resumed, and at this time a vote in committee of the whole showed only nine states favorable. But when the formal vote was taken next day, every state save New York, whose provincial convention gave its assent a week later, was for independence.

Meantime a committee headed by Jefferson had been at work upon an appropriate declaration through which to convey to the world the decision that it was confidently believed Congress would reach. On July 2, the same day that Congress voted for independence, this committee presented its report. After striking from this document a passage which censured the British people as well as their rulers, and another which severely arraigned the King for forcing the slave trade upon the colonies, the remainder of the Declaration of Independence that the committee had formulated was adopted, July 4,

The Declaration of Independence

1776. Two weeks later Congress decided that the document should be engrossed on parchment and signed by all the delegates; and this was done. On August 2 the members of Congress who were present affixed their signatures, and later as occasion offered those who had been absent were given an opportunity to sign their names.

The Declaration of Independence, which was written almost entirely by Jefferson, borrowed heavily from Locke's *Second Essay of Government*, and asserted in language already familiar the natural rights of men, including the right of revolution. It differed markedly from earlier American protests in that it directed its attack primarily against the King rather than against Parliament. Hitherto the Americans, while they had denounced Parliament unsparingly for assuming powers unwarranted by the British Constitution, had been content to acknowledge the King as a common sovereign, and to protest their loyalty to him. But if, as many of the American leaders had come to maintain, the only bond of union with the mother country lay through the King, then to break that bond their attack would have to be directed against George III himself, rather than against Parliament. The Declaration of Independence even blamed the King for the "acts of pretended legisla-

Declaration of Independence. Jefferson's rough draft of the revolutionary document shows corrections and changes written in by Benjamin Franklin and John Adams.

tion" to which he had given his assent, and found in the long list of grievances it recited a kind of breach of contract on the part of the monarch which gave the colonies the right, if they chose, to become free and independent states.

The appearance of unanimity which accompanied the Declaration quite belied the **Loyalists vs. Patriots** facts. Not less than a third of the Americans would have preferred that the colonies retain their membership in the British Empire, and in the course of the next few years probably as many as fifty thousand of these "Loyalists" proved their sentiments by fighting with the British forces and against the "Patriots." So numerous were the pro-British Americans in some localities that Washington's forces, rather than his adversaries, sometimes suffered the disadvantage of fighting in enemy territory. Naturally the Loyalists, unless they were fortunate enough to live where they could receive the protection of British troops, came in for as severe persecution as the Patriots could inflict. Many Loyalists saw their property destroyed or confiscated, they often suffered great personal violence, and they were driven by the thousands to take refuge in Canada, the West Indies, or England.

Nor had complete political unification been achieved in America. When the thirteen separate colonies became thirteen separate and independent states, the difficulties of union that had been so overwhelming before the Revolution were by no means eradicated. The new states did indeed co-operate through Congress in a way that they had been unable to agree upon before; but the Articles of Confederation which were presently presented and adopted as a codification of the existing practice merely provided for a loose alliance that only the necessities of war could hold together. Congress was sadly lacking in authority, and often proved to be a debating society when what was needed was a powerful and efficient central war office.

Over against these political dissensions in America, however, the British were unable to present a united front. The King's party, which strongly favored the war, was supported by the upper classes generally — the ministers, the nobility, the **British opinion on the war** majority in Parliament, the leading lawyers, the clergy of the established church, and even a few of the dissenting clergy such as John Wesley, the founder of Methodism. But the opposition party was far from enthusiastic at taking up arms against the Americans. Liberal leaders, long convinced that such a step was as unnecessary as it was unwise, reflected that failure to win the war would serve their ends well by discrediting the personal power of the King and causing the downfall of his satellites in the ministry; merchants desirous of retaining American trade longed for normal times and were not too particular about how they should be restored; dissenting ministers very generally lined up against the King and the established church; the common people, who were practically without voice in politics, showed their resentment against being required to fight far from home and against Englishmen by refusing to enlist; and there was the customary trouble in Ireland.

The inefficiency of the British government as a war-making machine was also a handicap. The King's friends in the ministry were often of little merit as administrators. Lord George Germain, Secretary of State for the Colonies, had himself been cashiered from the army, and was sorely lacking in talent. Lord Sandwich, in charge of the Admiralty, was a notorious corruptionist. The American Congress with its defective organization and its lack of experience was at times not more inept in the direction of affairs than the British government under these incompetent leaders.

In the comparison of armed forces, the odds told more heavily against the Americans. The number of enlist- **The Patriot army** ments in the Continental Army was great, reaching perhaps ninety thousand

American Generals Ethan Allen, Horatio Gates and Nathaniel Greene all played roles of considerable consequence in the revolutionary armies. Ablest among them was probably Greene, who, like Washington, was often defeated, but managed somehow to achieve most of his objectives.

in the year 1776, but this was due to the fact that short-term enlistments, often for only three months, were permitted. Washington rarely had as many as sixteen thousand men under his command at any one time, and at Valley Forge his forces had dwindled to a paltry two thousand. As the war wore on the difficulty of obtaining enlistments increased, for the soldier's wages, low enough in any event, were always in arrears, while work was plentiful and brought a much higher and surer reward. Moreover, the American troops were never adequately supplied with munitions, and they were often clothed only in rags. Supplementing the Continental Army which Congress created was the state militia. These troops sometimes fought well when defending their own homes and firesides, but otherwise they were exceedingly undependable. Practically none of the American volunteers had had anything like adequate training in military tactics, thanks to the short-term enlistments, and the American officers were forced to whip a new army into shape for practically every battle. For all their shortcomings the American soldiers were as individuals hardy and resourceful; some of them had profited from military service during the French and Indian War, or other Indian wars; and at

least a small nucleus were deeply enough devoted to the cause for which they fought that they stood together regardless of all difficulties.

To oppose the Americans the British had a well-drilled regular army of perhaps sixty thousand men, most of whom **The** were needed on garrison duty **redcoats** somewhere in the far-flung British Empire. What might have amounted otherwise to an embarrassing shortage of troops was made up for by the use of "Hessians," of Loyalists, or "Tories," and of Indians. The British commanders in America were, on the whole, adequately supplied with troops. Clinton's army in 1781 reached a total of thirty-four thousand men. While Howe was at Philadelphia he had under his command about seventeen thousand men. The British redcoats, moreover, were not "summer soldiers and sunshine patriots," but were enlisted for long terms, were rigorously disciplined, and were adequately supplied with the materials of war. They were backed also by almost unlimited naval power, for Great Britain was the clearly acknowledged mistress of the ocean. Even with the assistance of the French, the efforts of the Americans to challenge British sea-power were painfully inadequate. And yet all this superiority

Foreign Generals Lafayette, Pulaski and von Steuben gave invaluable aid to Washington's armies. Of chief importance was Lafayette, who, like many young Frenchmen of this period, was fascinated by the radical doctrines of the Revolution.

was not enough to enable the British to win. Their armies were three thousand miles away from home; their attack had to be delivered along a thousand miles of seacoast; and they were confronted, once they had penetrated into the interior, with a trackless wilderness where conquest was virtually impossible as long as the will to resist endured.

In point of military leadership, thanks mainly to the solid qualities of Washington, **Washington the general** the Americans were superior to the British. It cannot be demonstrated that as a commanding officer Washington was a genius. He was not thoroughly versed in military tactics, and he might have had great difficulty in commanding large armies. But whatever the limits of his ability, he proved equal to the existing emergency. His obvious integrity, his unflinching courage, and his dogged determination inspired his men with confidence and paved the way to ultimate victory. He was a master of the strategy of retreat, and understood thoroughly that while he had an army in the field the Patriot cause was not lost.

Unfortunately most of Washington's immediate subordinates were of mediocre or even inferior abilities. Charles Lee, with perhaps more military experience than Washington himself, proved to be untrustworthy and insubordinate. Benedict Arnold, with all his dash and brilliance, lacked something of fundamental importance in the way of character. Horatio Gates, a favorite of the politicians, disappointed even their expectations. Possibly Nathanael Greene, who had had virtually no military experience prior to the war, was the ablest of Washington's lieutenants. The contribution of a number of European officers who joined the American army was highly creditable. Chief among these were the two Germans, Steuben and Kalb, whose up-to-date knowledge of military tactics was an invaluable asset to the Americans; the two Poles, Kosciusko and Pulaski, who brought enthusiasm as well as ability to the defense of the American cause; and the young Frenchman, Lafayette, who so spectacularly displayed the interest that many of his countrymen felt in the success of the Americans.

The British commanders were not well chosen. Neither Howe, who was placed in command at the outset of the **The British** war, nor Clinton, who succeeded **commanders** him, were first-rate men, and both of them for reasons that are more or less unaccountable failed to do even the best that might have been expected of them. There is some truth in the assertion, frequently made, that

Howe should share equally with Washington the credit for the final American victory. Probably this lack of vigor at the outset was due in part to his hope that a reconciliation between the mother country and the colonies could be obtained, but with respect to the later period of his command there was much more than humor in Franklin's remark, "Philadelphia has taken Howe." Clinton's task was more difficult than his predecessor's, but he too was dilatory, and by his failure to take full advantage of his opportunities more than once seemed to give the game away. The British commanders, and their subordinates also, far outmatched the Americans in the matter of technical knowledge, but the unusual character of the fighting in America sometimes turned this seeming advantage, as for Braddock before them, into a liability.

From the outset the financial situation in America was well-nigh hopeless. The **American finances** colonies were not rich in taxable resources, and such opportunities for taxation as existed could not be fully exploited. The unpopularity of taxes in general had not a little to do with the American revolt, and the new revolutionary governments dared not risk their permanence by demanding heavy levies. Nor did they find it either easy or expedient to borrow great sums. As for Congress, it lacked any power of taxation whatever, and it had little credit upon which to rely for loans. Very early, therefore, it resorted to paper money issues. By the end of 1778 one hundred million dollars in "continental currency" had been placed in circulation, and within the next year Congress issued one hundred and forty-three million dollars more. In consequence, by 1780 continental currency had fallen in value to two cents on the dollar. Jefferson had to pay one hundred and twenty-five dollars for a quart of brandy; Washington complained that it took a wagonload of currency to buy a wagonload of provisions; and an enterprising Philadelphia barber used the continental issues to paper the walls of his shop. Once just

before the battle of Princeton, Washington in order to keep his army from disintegrating, had to pledge the soldiers his private fortune to convince them that the money due them would be paid. Robert Morris, upon whom Congress placed the chief burden of financing the war, also borrowed heavily upon his own personal credit, while Haym Salomon, a refugee from Poland who had espoused the American cause, made such liberal advances in specie, and invested so generously in government securities, that his finances were ruined and he died almost penniless.

The British government was in none too comfortable a financial state, but it represented at least three times the total American wealth and population, and it had the double advantage of good credit and a well-established system of taxation. British gold was available at all times in America to purchase needed supplies for the British forces — often to make difficult also the purchase of supplies for the American army, for Washington usually had only paper and promises with which to pay. Indeed, the presence of the British soldiers, while menacing to American liberty, did much for American prosperity. Farm prices kept at a high figure, labor brought good returns, and manufacturers throve as never before.

When General Howe abandoned Boston it was with the intention of striking a blow later on at some more strategic point. For several reasons, the logical place for the delivery of this blow seemed to be New York. That city was located midway between the northern and southern colonies, it possessed the best harbor on the coast, and its inhabitants were notoriously Tory in sympathy. Furthermore, by controlling the Hudson Valley, to which New York City was the gateway, the British hoped to separate the New England colonies from the rest. Also, by the Lake Champlain route, land connections with Canada might possibly be established.

Accordingly, after a short stay in Halifax,

General Howe embarked a formidable army
Howe takes — twenty-five thousand British
New York and eight thousand Hessians —
for New York. Anticipating his move,
Washington had abandoned Boston, and
with perhaps eighteen thousand men under
his command had prepared to defend New
York. Probably his decision to oppose
Howe's effort to take the city was unwise,
for the Americans suffered several discouraging defeats, and in the end the
British succeeded in their attempt. Most
of Washington's troops were stationed on
Long Island, and after the battle of Brooklyn Heights, August 27, 1776, in which the
Americans were badly defeated, only the
dilatory tactics of Howe and the aid of a
friendly fog which enabled Washington to
ferry his troops across to New York prevented an overwhelming disaster.

Perhaps Howe might have been more
aggressive had it not been a part of the
British policy to make peace with the Americans if possible. Indeed, Lord Howe, the
general's brother, who commanded the
British fleet at New York, had definite
instructions to offer liberal terms if the
Americans would only lay down their arms.
After the battle of Brooklyn Heights he
conferred with a committee appointed by
Congress, John Adams, Franklin, and Rutledge, but nothing could be accomplished
because the Americans insisted on independence, and Howe was not authorized to go
that far. Washington found himself unable
to prevent the landing of Howe's troops on
Manhattan Island, and presently retreated
across the Hudson to New Jersey. New
York was held by the British until the close
of the war, and furnished a haven of refuge
for Loyalists from every part of America.
Here the tables were turned, and the
Patriots were the sufferers from persecution.

During the winter of 1776–77 Washington's army dwindled down to as few as three
Trenton and thousand men, and had Howe
Princeton been more aggressive he would
certainly have had a fair chance to bring the

Revolutionary War
1777
Northern Campaigns

war to an end. But he twice, at Trenton
(December 26, 1776) and at Princeton
(January 3, 1777), permitted Washington to
inflict stinging defeats upon isolated British
detachments, after which, with amazing
indolence, he allowed the American army to
remain unmolested at Morristown for the
rest of the winter.

The year 1777 saw two major movements
on the part of the British, one a shift of base
on the part of Howe from New **The British**
York to Philadelphia, the other **occupy**
an advance down the Lake **Philadelphia**
Champlain–Hudson Valley route by troops
under the command of General Burgoyne.
Howe chose not to proceed directly overland
against the rebel capital, but sent his troops
most of the way by sea. To avoid the
American defenses on the Delaware, the
ships sailed up Chesapeake Bay as far as
possible, and then marched the remaining
distance. Before Philadelphia as before New
York, Washington attempted against overwhelming odds to make a defense, and at

Brandywine he suffered a severe defeat. Thereupon (September, 1777) Howe entered Philadelphia, and shortly afterward won another victory when Washington attacked an outlying detachment of British troops at Germantown. The occupation of Philadelphia was a great blow to American pride and caused much rejoicing among the British and Loyalists, but its military significance was slight.

Historians are still at a loss to explain adequately why Howe did not, instead of taking Philadelphia, send help to Burgoyne, who was at the very time advancing toward New York from Canada with reinforcements intended for Howe's use in the campaign against Washington. Howe seems to have been well advised as to Burgoyne's plans, and had he so desired, he might have rendered that luckless commander invaluable assistance. Without it Burgoyne's position soon became desperate. He had counted on aid from some Mohawk Valley Loyalists and Indians under the command of Colonel St. Leger, but the back-country Patriots, many of them Germans, furnished such effective resistance that St. Leger's troops never got through to Burgoyne at all, and St. Leger himself went back to Canada. Moreover, the small detachment of regulars with which the Americans hoped to block Burgoyne's advance was swollen by accretions of local militia until the American force numbered twenty thousand men — several times as many men as Burgoyne commanded. In the second of two battles, both fought at Freeman's Farm, near Saratoga, the British suffered a disastrous defeat, and on October 17, 1777, with his army entirely surrounded, Burgoyne surrendered his force of fifty-eight hundred men to General Gates. This was the most notable victory that the Americans — or for that matter, either side — had yet won. It gave the Patriots good reason to hope that in spite of their difficulties they might eventually win the war.

The surrender of Burgoyne made possible also the consummation of the greatly desired alliance with France. Early in 1776, Congress had sent Silas Deane to Paris with instructions to obtain whatever aid he could from France. A little later he was joined by Arthur Lee and Benjamin Franklin. Deane's services to his country were substantial, but he was presently recalled and, smarting under what he deemed to be unjust treatment, ultimately came to question the righteousness of the American cause. Lee proved to be of value, but in Franklin the Americans found an ideal representative. His venerability — he was now seventy years old — his achievements in the realms of literature and science, his simplicity of manner and of speech made him a natural social lion, and he soon captivated the French. Louis XVI's minister of foreign affairs, Vergennes, was fortunately favorable to the idea of assisting the Americans. He wished to get even with the British for the losses they had inflicted on France at the close of the French and Indian War; and he was possessed of an unreasonable fear that unless France intervened with aid for the revolting American colonies, she and her ally Spain might lose their possessions in the West Indies to whichever power won the war, England or America. So even before Franklin appeared, there was a secret but very helpful flow of arms and other supplies from France to the Revolutionists.

With the news of Burgoyne's defeat to support his argument that with a little help the Americans could win, Franklin pressed successfully for an alliance, and on February 6, 1778, two treaties were signed between France and the United States. By one of these treaties the two nations opened their ports freely to each other's commerce; by the other they united in a military alliance to effect the independence of the United States. France agreed, when peace with Great Britain should be made, not to ask for additional territory on the mainland of North America, and the United States in turn promised to guarantee to France indefinitely the French West Indies. Neither

Surrender of Burgoyne

The French alliance

party was to make peace without the full consent of the other.

There was much that was anomalous about this alliance between an absolute monarch and a people fighting for freedom from aristocracy; but there was also much that was natural about it. France and England were traditional enemies; each could be counted on to take every advantage of the other's distress. Then, too, there was already popular sympathy in France for the same ideals that motivated the Americans. The French Revolution was not far away, and the doctrines that lay back of it were as well known and in certain circles were as well received in France as anywhere on earth.

The value of the alliance to the American cause can hardly be overestimated. The **French aid to America** loans obtained from the French government supplied the funds which enabled Washington to keep his army intact and in some degree prepared to fight. French officers helped in the training of American troops, and on some occasions, particularly at Yorktown, French soldiers co-operated with the Patriot army. Most significant of all was the aid of the French navy. Before France entered the war the Americans had encouraged privateering, with results that were often extremely annoying to the British; but in spite of some praiseworthy efforts on the part of Congress and the various state governments it could hardly be said that an American navy existed. French sea-power supplied this fundamental lack, and the freedom to use French ports greatly expanded the opportunities of American sea-captains. The exploits of John Paul Jones, for example, whose *Bonhomme Richard* took the *Serapis* (September, 1779) in a naval battle justly famous, would have been impossible but for the backing of the French. Even though British superiority on the high seas was at no time fully overcome during the war, French fleets hampered the British movements of troops along the American coast, threatened an attack on England that drew attention

from America at a critical time, and held the British fleet at bay during the later phases of the war.

Since Spain was bound firmly by the "family compact" in an alliance with France, the entrance of France **Spain enters** into the war practically insured **the war** the entrance of Spain also. The Spanish government refused, however, to make a formal alliance with the United States. Possessed of an extensive colonial empire of its own, Spain was naturally loath to encourage the idea of colonial revolts, and she viewed with some misgivings the American successes. But in Great Britain, Spain, like France, had a traditional enemy; Britain's possession of Gibraltar was a standing national insult. Secretly some financial aid was given the Americans before the outbreak of war between Spain and England; and after that event, which occurred in 1779, the Spanish navy co-operated constantly with the French.

Late in the war (1781), Holland, whose merchants hoped to succeed the English in the exploitation of American **Holland** trade and were adepts at smuggling war materials into America, irritated the British government into a declaration of war. The increase of naval strength which resulted from the addition of Holland to the list of Britain's enemies had much to do with the outcome of the war. John Adams, who was dispatched to Holland to represent America there, succeeded also in obtaining helpful loans from the Dutch bankers, and in 1782 a treaty of commerce. Great Britain had also to deal with the "Armed Neutrality," a combination of neutral nations, effected by Catherine II of Russia in 1780, which objected strenuously to the regulations which the British navy imposed upon neutral trade. Holland had been a member of the Armed Neutrality before her entrance into the war, and just how soon Russia and her allies — which included Denmark, Sweden, Portugal, and Prussia — might also exchange the status of neutrality for the status of war was a matter of con-

Revolutionary War
1778
The Central Campaigns

jecture. It is important to remember that in the later years of the Revolutionary War the British were fighting not only against the United States, but also against a powerful European combination which might at any time become even more powerful by the addition of new members.

Unaware of these bright prospects, Washington held his army in winter quarters at **Valley Forge**, near Philadelphia, during the winter of 1777–78, and wondered how long resistance could be maintained. During these dark days the Patriot army almost vanished, and thanks to the inefficiency of Congress, which listened to intrigues against Washington when it should have been at work supplying his men with the necessities of life, the handful of soldiers who remained true to the cause suffered incredible privations. Howe in Philadelphia, meantime, was faring sumptuously. British gold brought in

supplies from the outlying country which Washington, with only worthless promises-to-pay as currency, found himself unable to command. But fortunately for the Patriot cause Howe took his ease, and Washington's little army, in spite of its suffering, was allowed to come through the winter still an army.

Next spring the British government, visibly shaken by the news of the French alliance, was ready to offer the Americans all that they had originally taken up arms to obtain. Independence was not yet to be thought of, but a royal commission was sent to Philadelphia with terms of peace that included amnesty for those who had fought against Great Britain, the cessation of Parliamentary taxation, the restoration of the Massachusetts charter, and perhaps, if the Americans wanted it, actual colonial representation in Parliament. But Congress was as much cheered by the news of the French alliance as the British government was depressed; hence terms of peace that would have been regarded as highly satisfactory two years before were now refused consideration.

With a close eye to what the French navy might be able to do, the British government now ordered General Clinton, who succeeded Howe as commander of the British army in America, to abandon Philadelphia and concentrate his forces at New York. This movement was accomplished by a march across New Jersey, with Washington's army, infused with new life by the turn which events had taken, in close pursuit. At Monmouth, June 28, 1778, the Americans attacked the British and should have won, but the cowardly disobedience of General Charles Lee, who ordered his troops to retreat when he had been commanded by Washington to attack, cost the Americans all hope of success. Clinton got safely into New York, and Washington's army once more stood guard about that city. The British also held Newport, Rhode Island, which the Americans, counting on the assistance of a French squadron, now attempted unsuccessfully to capture. But the next year (1779) Newport also was abandoned by the British. From this time on to the close of the war no major military movements took place in the North. The British conducted many raids along the coast adjacent to New York, but these raids had little significance except, perhaps, that they diminished the prosperity of the region and intensified the opposition of its inhabitants to British rule.

Meantime the feeble American settlements along the frontier had been suffering acutely from marauding bands of Tories and Indians. Sentiment among the traders was definitely anti-American, for the success of the revolutionary forces was sure to mean an advance of the agricultural frontier and a consequent curtailment of their opportunities. The Indians, too, were well aware of the bearing of this situation on their future;

Clinton succeeds Howe

Frontier fighting

they listened willingly to Colonel Henry Hamilton, in command of the British post at Detroit, and to other British officers who encouraged them to make war upon the frontier settlements. In 1778 the Wyoming Valley of Pennsylvania and the Cherry Valley of New York were the scenes of terrible massacres; and well before that date constant fighting had brought the pioneer outposts in Kentucky to the very verge of extinction.

It was at this point that George Rogers Clark, a young Kentucky land speculator who realized fully the gravity of the situation, obtained leave from Patrick Henry, the governor of Virginia, to organize a retaliatory expedition. Clark realized that the old French towns in the Illinois country, Kaskaskia, Cahokia, and Vincennes, although seemingly indifferent to the outcome of the war, were actually havens of refuge for hostile Indians and breeding-places for conspiracies. He planned, therefore, to capture them, and if possible also the British post at Detroit. With much difficulty he succeeded in organizing a few hundred frontier militia, with which in the summer of 1778 he set out down the Ohio for the Illinois towns. From the mouth of the Cumberland he marched overland, and taking the inhabitants by surprise captured Kaskaskia, and Cahokia, without a blow. Vincennes, also, with the connivance of the French residents in the captured towns, readily accepted Clark's control.

News of these events greatly exercised Colonel Hamilton at Detroit, who determined at once to repossess Vincennes, and from that vantage-point the next year to advance against the other French towns. He succeeded without difficulty in retaking Vincennes, but he was again surprised by Clark, who marched his troops overland through midwinter cold and ice to attack and capture Vincennes once again (February, 1779). Hamilton himself was sent, none too tenderly, as a prisoner to Virginia. This

George Rogers Clark

The War in the West

Revolutionary War
in the West
George Rogers Clark Expedition · 1778

exploit greatly cheered the frontiersmen, for Hamilton, it was commonly reported, had made presents to the Indians in return for scalps, and the downfall of the "hair-buying general" was no small comfort. Clark never succeeded in capturing Detroit, but his activities greatly diminished the frontier difficulties with British and Indians, and probably saved the Kentucky settlements. In order to punish the Indians for their part in the Wyoming and Cherry Valley massacres of 1778, the following year Washington sent an expedition into the Iroquois country, which succeeded fairly well. Frontier fighting did not cease, but the menace from this quarter was distinctly lessened.

From 1778 to the close of the war practically all of the important fighting took **The War in** place in the South. In this re-**the South** gion there were many Loyalists whose services the British leaders, hard-pressed for troops to face an ever-expanding list of enemies, wished to enlist. Moreover,

with sentiment so badly divided in the South, victories in that quarter presumably would come easily, and the successful conquest of a number of states might serve as a wholesome warning to the rest. Accordingly Clinton dispatched an expedition by sea late in 1778 which captured Savannah, and with the aid of troops brought up from British Florida soon brought the whole of Georgia under British control.

Events now moved slowly, for the war in Europe occupied the major attention of the British; but the next year an American effort to recapture Savannah with the aid of a French fleet was thwarted, and in May, 1780, the British took Charleston, making prisoners an entire Patriot army of five thousand men whom General Lincoln, the American commander, found it impossible to extricate. A small army under General Gates, sent by Congress to the assistance of the beleaguered southern Patriots, was poorly led, and was badly defeated by

Cornwallis at Camden (August 16, 1780). South Carolina, like Georgia, now seemed lost to the Patriot cause, although irregular bands of Patriots under such leaders as Sumter, Marion, and Pickens kept close watch on the British, and seriously impeded their every movement of troops.

North Carolina was the next British goal, and Cornwallis began preparations for its conquest by sending Major Patrick Ferguson through the back country to recruit Loyalists. This action was somehow interpreted by the Watauga pioneers from across the mountains, most of whom were Patriots, as a threat against their settlements, and possibly Ferguson had it in mind to teach them a lesson; in any event, they crossed the mountains in force and in October, 1780, with the assistance of such other Patriots as cared to join them, won a barbaric victory over Ferguson at King's Mountain. As a result the British advance into North Carolina

King's Mountain

was delayed until 1781, and by that time the Patriots were able to offer strenuous resistance. General Gates had been succeeded by General Nathanael Greene, a far abler leader; and Greene's chief subordinate, Daniel Morgan, soon proved his mettle by defeating a British and Loyalist force under Tarleton at the Cowpens (January, 1781). Greene himself, however, was defeated at Guilford Court House (March 15, 1781) by Cornwallis, but the British victory was so hardly won that Cornwallis temporarily gave up his advance and retired to Wilmington.

All this time Washington's main army had been kept in the vicinity of New York to prevent Clinton from expanding his lines. An atmosphere of deep gloom, which affected even Washington himself, pervaded the American camp. In addition to the dispiriting news that came from the South, there were troubles from a worthless currency, from an insufficient supply of food and clothing, from backbiting and incom-

Revolutionary War in the South 1776-1781

THE BATTLE OF LEXINGTON GREEN. British regulars are depicted, center, as "the party who first fired on the Provincials." Engraving by Amos Doolittle, 1775.

THE BATTLE OF BREED'S HILL. Colonial fortifications are shown upper left; Charlestown appears in flames behind the British lines. Engraving by B. Romans, eyewitness.

American fighting methods, according to British standards, were cowardly and unsportsmanlike. British battle tactics, as the illustrations indicate, called for parade-drill formations, which the Americans rarely used. At Bunker Hill, one British officer complained, the Americans "were entrenched up to their eyes," and "kept up a constant fire with little or no damage to themselves."

petent members of Congress, and, hardest of all to bear, from the treason of Benedict Arnold.

Arnold, far more than Gates, had deserved the honor of bringing about Burgoyne's **Benedict** surrender, but after that time a **Arnold** serious wound, acquired near Saratoga, had kept him out of active fighting. He joined Washington at Valley Forge, however, and he was stationed at Philadelphia when Howe abandoned that city. Here he married a social favorite, lived far beyond his means, and even fraternized with British sympathizers. Naturally such conduct provoked criticism, and to clear himself of numerous petty charges Arnold demanded and received a court martial. On some of the charges, however, the court found him guilty and sentenced him to receive a reprimand. But Washington, in de-

livering this reprimand, did not fail to call attention to Arnold's great services in the American army, and later, at Arnold's request, did not hesitate to give him the command of West Point, a position of great strategic importance on the Hudson.

In the meantime Arnold, deeply involved in debt, and unable to collect from Congress for expenditures he had made during the campaign against Quebec, had turned informer. Through him, from the early summer of 1779 on, Clinton had been fully apprised of the American plans and movements of troops, and Arnold had asked for West Point only because he wished to betray it to the British. Fortunately, however, Major André, through whom negotiations for the surrender of West Point were being conducted, was captured within the American lines, bearing papers that revealed the

THE BATTLE OF PRINCETON. Painting by William Mercer, 1786–90.

NAVAL DARING. "Capt. Paul Jones shooting a sailor who had attempted to strike his colours in an engagement." English mezzotint, 1780.

American successes, such as Princeton and Yorktown, proved the mettle of the Patriot troops and their officers, while on the high seas John Paul Jones and others, by a variety of means, kept the American flag afloat. This behavior pattern fitted in badly with a British general's opinion that "the native American is an effeminate thing, very unfit for and very impatient of war," and a British politician's lament, "We are still a little disappointed, indeed, at their fighting at all, which was not in our calculation."

SURRENDER OF CORNWALLIS AT YORKTOWN. Detail of a painting by Van Blarenberghe.

Revolutionary War
1781
Virginia Campaigns

plot (September, 1780). Arnold promptly fled to the British, and André was executed as a spy.[1] The loss of West Point, which would have cost the Americans control of the whole Hudson Valley, was avoided, but the whole episode was a sad blow to American morale.

Clinton believed that a policy of ruthless raids would bring the war home to noncombatant Americans and lead to a demand for peace, and he found work for Arnold to do in laying waste the Virginia plantations. Early in

British raids

---

[1] Arnold claimed that he was genuinely converted to the British point of view, and possibly he was. But there is good reason to doubt the story, commonly repeated, that this end was accomplished through the influence of his wife and her Loyalist relatives. Arnold's father-in-law seems to have favored the Americans. Probably Arnold was influenced somewhat by his disgust at the alliance with the French, whom he hated and had fought; but his hurt pride and his great need of the sixty-three hundred pounds he received from Clinton as the price of treason must suffice in the main to account for his change of heart.

1781 Cornwallis, leaving Greene to the South, joined Arnold in Virginia and gave chase to a small force of Americans under the "boy" Lafayette. But the "boy" successfully eluded his pursuers. Arnold returned to New York in June, 1781, to lead another marauding expedition, this time against New London, Connecticut; and Cornwallis, at Clinton's suggestion, fortified himself in the village of Yorktown on the tip of the peninsula made by the York and the James Rivers.

Washington now saw an opportunity to strike the British a telling blow. His own resources had recently been supplemented by the landing of several thousand French regulars under Rochambeau, and he felt justified in detaching a strong enough force to march into Virginia and trap Cornwallis. This plan would require the co-operation of the French navy, however, and both Rochambeau and Washington urged the French naval commander, de Grasse, whose fleet was in the West Indies, to bring his ships north to the mouth of the Chesapeake. With some reluctance de Grasse consented, whereupon Washington, taking care to make Clinton believe that an attack on New York was imminent, started southward to join Lafayette in Virginia.

The allied plan worked out perfectly. On August 30 the French fleet under de Grasse anchored within the capes that guard the mouth of Chesapeake Bay, and a week later the French beat off the attack of a British fleet under Admiral Graves. A few days more and Cornwallis found himself not only cut off from retreat by sea, but hemmed in also by an allied army of sixteen thousand men, more than twice the number of British in Yorktown. He held out for several weeks, but on October 19, 1781, surrendered his entire command. Only two days later Admiral Graves reappeared, this time bringing reinforcements from Clinton, but the damage had already been done. Admiral de Grasse, in spite of Washington's urgent request that

Surrender of Cornwallis

he attack New York or Charleston, sailed back to the West Indies, where the next spring, after a terrible battle, he was defeated by the British fleet under Admiral Rodney (April 12, 1782). The war ended with England still in command of the seas.

But the French and American victory at Yorktown practically assured the independence of the United States. Lord North took the news of this setback, according to an eyewitness, "as he would have taken a ball in the breast, for he opened his arms, exclaiming wildly, as he paced up and down the apartment during a few minutes, 'Oh, God! it is all over,' words which he repeated many times under emotions of deepest agitation and distress." The charges of wholesale corruption and inefficiency in the prosecution of the war that had continually been brought against the King's Ministers could now be pressed with good effect, and in March, 1782, Lord North bowed to the inevitable and resigned. His downfall ended the personal rule of George III, and brought into power a ministry under Lord Rockingham (succeeded presently by Shelburne) that included several of the ablest of the men who had defended the colonies during the long-drawn-out contest over taxation. The British public was by this time weary of war, and Rockingham's ministry favored peace with all the enemies of England. Indeed, after Rodney's victory in the West

Indies the British could look forward to reasonably good terms as far as their European adversaries were concerned. As for America, the colonies would be welcomed back within the British Empire on their own terms if they would come; but if they would not come, they might have their independence.

Bibliography

Many of the books cited for the preceding chapter are useful also on the period of actual warfare. S. G. Fisher, *The Struggle for American Independence* (2 vols., 1908), is in many respects the most satisfactory general account of the period. Strongly sympathetic with the American cause is Sir George Otto Trevelyan, *The American Revolution* (4 vols., 1905–12); and *George the Third and Charles Fox* (2 vols., 1912–14). John Fiske, *The American Revolution* (2 vols., 1891), has not stood the test at every point of recent critical

scholarship, but is extremely interesting. Three of the best books on the war are by C. H. Van Tyne, *The American Revolution, 1776–1783* (1905); *The Loyalists in the American Revolution* (1902); and *The War of Independence* (1929). Van Tyne clears the "Tories" of many of the charges made against them by the "Whigs" and believed by later generations. See also E. A. Jones, *The Loyalists of Massachusetts* (1930). E. C. Burnett, *The Continental Congress* (1941), emphasizes the part played by Congress during the War (1943). Philip Davidson, *Propaganda and the American Revolution, 1763–1783* (1941), studies the propaganda techniques of the period. Another specialized study of merit is M. C. Tyler, *The Literary History of the American Revolution, 1763–1783* (2 vols., 1897). *The Era of the American Revolution,* edited by R. B. Morris (1939), is a series of scholarly essays by the students of E. B. Greene. J. C. Miller, *Triumph of Freedom, 1775–1783* (1949), rewrites interestingly, but without documentation, the whole history of the Revolution.

The Declaration of Independence has naturally and properly been subjected to the closest scrutiny. The best such study is Carl L. Becker, *The Declaration of Independence: A Study in the History of Political Ideas* (1922). But see also Herbert Friedenwald, *The Declaration of Independence: An Interpretation and an Analysis* (1904); J. H. Hazelton, *The Declaration of Independence: Its History* (1906); and Edward Dumbauld, *The Declaration of Independence and What it Means Today* (1950). Adrienne Koch, *The Philosophy of Thomas Jefferson* (1943), is useful in this connection. See also Marie Kimball, *Jefferson; The Road to Glory, 1743 to 1776* (1943); C. G. Bowers, *The Young Jefferson, 1743–1789* (1945); Dumas Malone, *Jefferson, The Virginian* (1948). The last mentioned is the first volume of a proposed series entitled *Jefferson and His Time.*

On the strictly military side of the struggle, F. V. Greene, *The Revolutionary War* (1911), is excellent, but many other books devote much attention to this subject. G. M. Wrong, *Washington and His Comrades at Arms* (1921), is mainly military. A. C. McLaughlin and others, *Source Problems in United States History* (1918), presents the principal documents needed to study the controversial phases of the Battle of Lexington. Justin H. Smith, *Our Struggle for the Fourteenth Colony: Canada, and the American Revolution* (1907), describes well the Montgomery-Arnold campaign of the first year of the war. The character of the Patriot army is well portrayed by L. C. Hatch, *The Administration of the American Revolutionary Army* (1904); C. K. Bolton, *The Private Soldier under Washington* (1902); Allen Bowman, *The Morale of the American Revolutionary Army* (1943). For the British army a similar service is done by E. E. Curtis, *The Organization of the British Army in the American Revolution* (1926); and J. W. Fortescue, *A History of the British Army* (13 vols., 1899–1930),

III; T. S. Anderson, *The Command of the Howe Brothers during the American Revolution* (1936), weighs the evidence well, with none too complimentary results for the British officers. Naval matters are further studied in: C. O. Paullin, *The Navy of the American Revolution* (1906); A. T. Mahan, *The Major Operations of the Navies in the War of American Independence* (1913). Willard M. Wallace, *Appeal to Arms: A Military History of the American Revolution* (1951), is an excellent treatment of the whole American war effort.

Diplomatic and international aspects of the war are most comprehensively covered in S. F. Bemis, *The Diplomacy of the American Revolution* (1935), but the numerous general histories of American diplomacy are also useful at this point. The two best of these are S. F. Bemis, *A Diplomatic History of the United States* (3d ed., 1950); and T. A. Bailey, *A Diplomatic History of the American People* (4th ed., 1950). Other general books of merit include J. H. Latané and D. W. Wainhouse, *A History of American Foreign Policy* (1940); C. R. Fish, *American Diplomacy* (1938); J. B. Moore, *The Principles of American Diplomacy* (1918); R. W. Van Alstyne, *American Diplomacy in Action* (1944). Relations with France are fully covered in E. S. Corwin, *French Policy and the American Alliance* (1916); J. B. Perkins, *France in the American Revolution* (1911); Bernard Faÿ, *The Revolutionary Spirit in France and America* (1927).

Biography furnishes a convenient vehicle for much excellent history of the Revolution. Rupert Hughes, *George Washington, The Rebel and the Patriot, 1762–1777* (1927), and *The Savior of the States, 1777–1781* (1930), are full of colorful detail. Bernhard Knollenberg, *Washington and the Revolution* (1940), is a useful re-evaluation. The trilogy by Louis Gottschalk, *Lafayette Comes to America* (1935), *Lafayette Joins the American Army* (1937), and *Lafayette and the Close of the American Revolution* (1942), present a uniquely intimate view of one of the great characters of the Revolution, and largely supplant such books as Charlemagne Tower, *Marquis de La Fayette in the American Revolution* (2 vols., 1895); and Brand Whitlock, *La Fayette* (2 vols., 1929). J. A. James, *The Life of George Rogers Clark* (1928), is the best of the many biographies of the "Washington of the West." See also, by the same author, *Oliver Pollock; The Life and Times of an Unknown Patriot* (1937). Other biographies of merit are: Malcolm Decker, *Benedict Arnold, Son of the*

Havens (1932); D. D. Wallace, *The Life of Henry Laurens* (1915); George Pellew, *John Jay* (1917); J. T. Morse, Jr., *John Adams* (1917); Bernard Faÿ, *Franklin, The Apostle of Modern Times* (1929); E. P. Oberholtzer, *Robert Morris* (1903); W. G. Sumner, *The Financier and the Finances of the Revolution* (2 vols., 1891); S. W. Patterson, *Horatio Gates: Defender of American Liberties* (1941); H. E. Wildes, *Anthony Wayne* (1941); S. H. Holbrook, *Ethan Allen* (1940); Miecislaus Haiman, *Kosciuszko in the American Revolution* (1943); Lincoln Lorenz, *John Paul Jones* (1943); Richard Barry, *Mr. Rutledge of South Carolina* (1942); Eleanor Young, *Forgotten Patriot: Robert Morris* (1950); J. R. Alden, *General Charles Lee, Traitor or Patriot* (1951).

Useful regional studies include Esther M. Dole, *Maryland during the American Revolution* (1941); F. H. Hart, *The Valley of Virginia in the American Revolution* (1942); Leonard Lundin, *Cockpit of the Revolution: The War for Independence in New Jersey* (1940); R. O. De Mond, *The Loyalists in North Carolina during the Revolution* (1940); C. L. Mowat, *East Florida as a British Province, 1763–1784* (1943); Cecil Johnson, *British West Florida, 1763–1783* (1943); E. A. Jones, *The Loyalists of New Jersey* (1927). S. C. Williams, *Tennessee during the Revolutionary War* (1944); T. P. Abernethy, *From Frontier to Plantation in Tennessee* (1932); T. J. Wertenbaker, *Father Knickerbocker Rebels: New York City during the Revolution* (1948).

9

Political and Social Reorganization

The Treaty of Paris — The colonies become states — State constitutions — Plans for a national government — The Articles of Confederation — Powers of Congress — Reserved powers of the states — Maryland and the Western land claims — Social changes — New views on landownership — Industry and commerce — Religious adjustments — The revolution in thought and feeling

THERE were many anxious months for the Patriot leaders after Yorktown, for the British with thirty thousand troops in America continued to hold New York, Charleston, and Savannah; and the war-weariness of the Americans was no less marked than that of the British. Congress seemed less effective than ever, the unpaid army was sadly depleted and almost mutinous, and irregular fighting between bands of men who called themselves Loyalists or Patriots, but were often in reality mere adventurers, caused a needless loss of life and property.

Peace commissioners had been selected even before Yorktown: John Adams, Benjamin Franklin, Thomas Jefferson, John Jay, and Henry Laurens; but only three of them served. Jefferson declined the appointment, and Laurens, whom the British held captive in the Tower of London, was released too late to play any important part in the proceedings. With needless timidity Congress instructed the commissioners to work for the Mississippi River boundary rather than to demand it, and to take no step of any consequence without the knowledge and concurrence of the French, by whose advice and opinion they should ultimately be governed.

The Peace Commission

The negotiations began at Paris in the spring of 1782, when Franklin was the only American delegate present. Jay, who had been the American agent to Spain, arrived in June, and several months later Adams came over from Holland. At the insistence of Jay, the British envoy, Richard Oswald, was authorized to treat with the "Thirteen United States of North America"; hence independence was conceded at the outset. But the ambitions of the United States and of Spain for territory west of the Appalachian Mountains were in sharp conflict, and Vergennes, the French foreign minister, was somewhat put to it to satisfy both his country's allies. Vergennes' private secretary, Rayneval, actually proposed that the trans-Appalachian West be divided at the Ohio River, and that the northern half be assigned to Great Britain, while the southern half be left to the Indians under the protection in part of Spain and in part of the United States. Probably Vergennes feared also that the United States might become too powerful if it were given the Mississippi for its western boundary. The British, on the other hand, who wished to make friends with the new nation and hoped to avoid the Spanish as near neighbors, seemed entirely willing to give up to the

United States the region north of the Ohio that Rayneval would have joined to Canada.

Jay strongly suspected that Vergennes was planning to sacrifice the interests of the United States to Spain, and he proposed, therefore, that the American delegation should ignore the instructions of Congress in order to deal directly with the British. To this policy Adams willingly consented, and with some difficulty the two won Franklin over also. The British government was delighted to contribute all it could to discord among its opponents, and on November 30, 1782, agreed to a preliminary treaty between Great Britain and the United States which should be incorporated in the final treaty of peace. This preliminary treaty gave to the United States the boundaries of the Great Lakes and the Mississippi. It was not clear at the time, however, whether the British would retain Florida or re-cede it to Spain; hence a secret provision was adopted whereby the boundary between the United States and Florida should be drawn at the

The Treaty of Paris

thirty-first parallel in case Spain received Florida, but at a line nearly a degree and a half farther north in case Great Britain retained it. The final treaty, signed September 3, 1783, accepted the terms of the preliminary treaty, and since later on Spain received Florida, the United States regarded its southern boundary as thirty-one degrees. Since the British ceded Florida to Spain without definition of boundaries, however, the setting was arranged for a boundary dispute that was to last for many years. Vergennes was much annoyed at the success of the American diplomats, and was amazed at the generosity of the British terms. "The English," he wrote to Rayneval, "buy peace rather than make it. Their concessions . . . exceed all that I could have thought possible."

Several other provisions were included in the treaties. Citizens of the United States retained the same rights to fish off the coast of Newfoundland and in the Gulf of St. Lawrence that they had enjoyed as British subjects; the navigation of the Mississippi

A British cartoon, favoring Charles James Fox's hope for a generous peace treaty with the Americans, depicts France and Spain attempting to prevent the "reconciliation." Published in London, May, 1782.

The RECONCILIATION between BRITANIA and her daughter AMERICA.

River was to be open alike to the commerce of Great Britain and of the United States; suits might be instituted for the collection of unpaid debts contracted by Americans of British subjects before the outbreak of the war; and the restitution of confiscated property was to be recommended by Congress to the several states. The last two provisions were in the nature of compromises. At first the British insisted that the payment of private debts owing to British subjects and the indemnification of the Tories should be guaranteed by the United States; but the Americans pointed out that the states rather than the nation had jurisdiction in such matters, and after long discussions the provisions as stated were accepted by both sides. Since many of the debts had actually been confiscated and the money had been collected into various state treasuries, the provision governing this subject proved virtually unenforceable; and ultimately, under the terms of the Jay Treaty of 1794, the central government agreed to pay them off. As for the misused Loyalists, confiscations continued even after the treaty of peace was signed, and laws which discriminated against them remained on the statute-books of some of the states until after the close of the War of 1812.

The treaty of peace was a magnificent victory for American diplomacy, but the terms were not free from criticism in America. An enduring hatred for the Loyalists made the clauses on that subject unpopular as well as unenforceable; the lack of an adequate commercial treaty, particularly to reopen the important West Indian trade, was keenly felt; and the failure of the commissioners to obey their instructions was unduly lamented. But with barely a quorum on hand for the purpose, Congress ratified the treaty, January 14, 1784.

Whether the American Revolution was merely one revolution or thirteen separate **The colonies** revolutions will probably never **become** be settled to the complete satis- **states** faction of even the closest students of the period. Certain it is, however,

that the outbreak of war not only brought into existence a new and revolutionary central government, but also resulted in the establishment of new and equally revolutionary governments within the several colonies — or, as they were soon more properly called, states. The first serious hostilities caused most British officials, including governors and judges, to make "sudden and abrupt departures," while the numerous members of the colonial councils, whose sympathies usually lay with England, were often not far behind. Tory members of the lower legislative chambers were also soon eliminated, and the whole business of maintaining government thus devolved upon the remaining Patriot members, who either carried on directly, or helped in the organization of provincial conventions or committees of safety to take over the reins of authority. In only two instances, Rhode Island and Connecticut, where liberal charters of self-government existed that needed only to be renamed to become constitutions, were the old forms of government retained. Elsewhere drastic changes were necessary, although in Massachusetts an effort was made for a time, in spite of the absence of a royal governor, to adhere to the terms of the colonial charter.

These transformations, which began well before the Declaration of Independence, put an end to the operation of the British bureaucracy in America, and left the colonists, or at least such of them as had joined in the revolt, in control of their own governments. Irregular bodies of one kind or another made laws, levied taxes, and raised troops. There was much about the situation, however, to cause grave concern to the more conservative opponents of British rule. Legally constituted courts could not be convened, and the more turbulent members of society took advantage of the situation to indulge in deeds of violence. In order to safeguard personal and property rights, local committees sometimes assumed authority that they did not legally possess, but conditions at best were far from satisfactory, and several states applied to Congress for advice on how to deal with the problem.

In response to such a request from the provincial convention of New Hampshire, Congress recommended that representatives of the people should be chosen to "establish such a form of government as in their judgment will best produce the happiness of the people and most effectually secure peace and good order in that province, during the present dispute between Great Britain and the colonies." New Hampshire and South Carolina promptly acted on this advice and formed provisional constitutions. A little later, May 15, 1776, in a general recommendation Congress again urged the formation of constitutions, but this time omitted all reference to the temporary nature of such governments, a change of front, which, according to John Adams, bespoke "absolute independence." In Virginia, the decision to form a permanent constitution for an independent state was reached before the action of Congress was known, and by the end of June, 1776, the new frame of government was duly adopted. In the course of the next few years all the other states, save only Rhode Island and Connecticut, followed the advice of Congress and the example of Virginia.

New constitutions

The methods by which the new constitutions were framed and adopted followed no definite pattern, although in many instances the procedure was precisely the same as might have been used in the passing of an ordinary law. This was the case in Virginia, although Jefferson pointed out that the state constitution, if it was to be distinguished from an ordinary law that any legislature might repeal at will, ought to be submitted to the people for their ratification. In Delaware the procedure was somewhat more modern. There a convention was chosen for the specific duty of drawing up a constitution; but once its work was done, the convention put the constitution into effect without delay. In Massachusetts the will of the people was carefully ascertained. The

Assembly first sought, and eventually obtained, permission of the towns to authorize it in going forward with the work of framing a constitution; but the town of Concord protested that so fundamental a document ought not to be written by a mere legislature, only by a convention chosen for that specific purpose. The reasonableness of this idea made many converts, and when the Assembly proposed a constitution that lacked altogether a bill of rights, the voters rejected it by an overwhelming majority. The legislature then accepted the Concord idea, and after ascertaining from the towns that they wanted a constitutional convention, provided the necessary legislation, stipulating, among other things, that every freeman over twenty-one years of age should be entitled to vote for delegates. Accordingly, in 1779, a constitutional convention, directly chosen by the people, formulated a constitution and submitted it to the towns for approval. Not until June, 1780, after more than two thirds of the towns had voted to approve, was the Massachusetts constitution put into effect. In New Hampshire much the same procedure was followed as in Massachusetts.

It was natural enough that the Americans should wish to have written constitutions. In the past most of the colonies had been able to point to some specific document according to which their government had been carried on, and the new states were merely following precedent when they replaced the old document with a new one. Moreover, the contract theory of government was then generally accepted, and in setting up such a relationship, between the people on the one hand and those who were to be placed in authority over them on the other, there was an obvious advantage about a plainly worded written statement. There seems to have been no disposition whatever to follow the English example and permit an accumulation of precedents to grow into an unwritten constitution.

Not only did every new state feel obliged in some fashion or another to acquire a written constitution, but the constitutions so acquired were also remarkably alike. This was due in the main to the fact that in the establishment of the new governments colonial traditions were followed as far as possible. Indeed the question has sometimes been raised whether or not the name "revolution" should be applied to what happened in America during these years, since the changes made were so conservative. What the colonists really desired, according to this argument, was not revolution but the prevention of revolution. It was Britain with her innovations in the way of taxation who was threatening to overthrow long-established American rights, and the colonists fought merely to preserve and maintain the institutions they had always had. Certain it is that the men who drew the new constitutions showed no considerable interest in experimentation, and since the colonial governments had been remarkably alike, whether classified as royal, proprietary, or corporate, it followed that the new state governments were also remarkably alike.

Similarity of state governments

By means of bills of rights, many of the new constitutions ordinarily paid their respects to the same political theories that were maintained in the Declaration of Independence. These bills of rights re-emphasized the doctrine then commonly accepted in America that the powers of government were limited, and that there were certain inalienable rights of men upon which government might not trespass. Such notions came not merely from the teachings of political philosophers like Richard Hooker and John Locke, who argued strongly in favor of the "natural rights" of men, and were well known in America; they owed something also to colonial experience. Colonial governments had always been limited in scope and authority, and by colonial charters the rights of Englishmen had often been specifically guaranteed to Americans. The new constitutions therefore followed both theory and practice when they listed those individual rights that

Bills of rights

government must leave inviolate. Such matters as freedom of speech and of religious belief, freedom from arbitrary arrest, the right of an accused person to trial by a jury of his peers, immunity from cruel and unusual punishments and from excessive bails and fines appeared to Americans not merely as privileges that a good government wisely extended to the people over whom it ruled, but rather as items that lay entirely beyond the limits of governmental interference. The theory that the powers of government were unlimited, or, as specifically applied in Great Britain, where Parliament was fast becoming supreme, that the powers of Parliament were unlimited, was thoroughly distasteful to Americans, as much before as after the Revolution. With respect to religious liberty the declarations in the various constitutions sometimes went further than actual practice. In many states discriminations were still made against Catholics, religious qualifications for office-holding were not wholly eliminated, and state-supported churches continued to exist.

The framers of the first constitutions assumed that there should be three branches of government, executive, legislative, and judicial, and that each should be kept as distinct as possible from the others. Here again their opinions were based upon both theory and practice. Many of them knew well the writings of Montesquieu, who eulogized the principle of the separation of powers; and they all knew that in the colonial governments this situation had been foreshadowed. The British government, which Montesquieu thought so fine an example of the separation of powers, was actually in process of evolution toward an all-powerful Parliament, but the American governments, thanks mainly to the control of the mother country over governors and to some extent over judges also, had made little progress in this direction. The new constitutions merely codified colonial experience when they provided for a single executive, to be known as

The separation of powers

the governor, a two-house legislature, and an independent judiciary.

Late unpleasant relations with royal governors, however, tended to keep the powers of that official at a minimum.

Governors In ten states he was elected for a year only, and in eleven states he had no veto power. Only in New England was he chosen by popular vote; elsewhere he was elected by one or both houses of the legislature. Pennsylvania at first had no governor, but tried out a plural executive in the form of a council of five, one of whose members was termed president. But this innovation worked badly, and was soon abandoned in favor of the traditional single executive. As British governors receded further into the background, the lack of confidence in the executive disappeared, and the powers he had normally exercised were restored.

Since confidence in the legislature had not been impaired by the events leading up to the American Revolution,

Legislatures the tendency was to expand the powers of this branch of the government. In most of the states, for example, the appointive power ordinarily vested in the governor was transferred to the legislature. Frequent elections, however, were deemed a necessity. In six states new legislatures were chosen every year; in two states they were chosen twice a year. Four states adopted the plan now in common use of selecting the upper house for a longer term than the lower house, but in only one instance was the lower house chosen for as long a period as two years. Pennsylvania and Georgia experimented for a time with single-chamber legislatures, but eventually gave their adherence to the usual plan.

The courts were complicated and varied. The judges were usually chosen by the legislatures, and were bound by the

Courts precedents already set during colonial times. The right of a court to declare unconstitutional an act of the legislature was neither asserted nor denied, but in colonial times judges had frequently refused to enforce laws which they found to be out of harmony with the colonial charter or contrary to the laws of Parliament. Probably the doctrine of judicial review was not yet foreseen, but the case of *Trevett vs. Weeden,* in which a Rhode Island court declared a law duly passed by the legislature to be null and void because it was out of harmony with the state constitution, came during the confederation period.

In spite of their revolutionary surroundings, the men who framed these constitutions were fairly timid when it came **Limitations** to entrusting full authority to **on democ-** the people. The upper house of **racy** the legislature was invariably constituted in such a way as to insure that it would represent the well-to-do upper classes rather than the common people. Outside of New England, ordinary voters were in no case entrusted with the selection of high officials, such as governors and judges. Oftentimes the upper house of the legislature was chosen by the lower house instead of directly by the voters. Property qualifications for those who were to exercise the suffrage were maintained in every state, and in a few instances a man had to be a landholder to be eligible to vote. The property qualifications were sometimes graded, so that the man who was entitled to vote for a member of the lower house of the legislature might not be entitled to vote for higher officials. In North Carolina, for example, any taxpayer might vote in elections to the lower house, but only the owners of at least fifty acres of land might vote in elections to the upper house. The same state also prescribed far higher property qualifications for officeholders than for voters, and required of some office-holders higher property qualifications than of others. It is abundantly clear that the framers of these constitutions did not include within the natural rights of men the right to vote or the right to hold office. Probably the adoption of universal manhood suffrage would have expanded the electorate fourfold.

That the future might hold something of

the sort in store, however, might have been judged from the constitution **Vermont** adopted by the more or less irregular state of Vermont. In colonial times the region north of the Massachusetts border and west of the Connecticut River had been claimed by both New Hampshire and New York. When the Revolution broke out the frontier inhabitants of the disputed territory took advantage of the unsettled situation to organize a government of their own. At first they relied upon "the laws of God and Connecticut," but in 1777 they adopted a constitution that, unlike those of the thirteen states, granted the right of suffrage to all men over twenty-one years of age. But Vermont was not accorded official recognition for many years.

The constitution-makers of the Revolutionary epoch must have thought well of their work, for they made quite inadequate provisions for future changes. As often as not they overlooked the matter of amendments altogether; and when they did include a clause on the subject it was rarely well thought out. In Delaware and Pennsylvania the process of amendment was too difficult to be workable, while in some of the other states an amendment to the constitution could be made in about the same way that a new law could be passed. Massachusetts and Georgia alone made adequate provision for the calling of subsequent constitutional conventions.

The various states assumed for themselves without question all rights of sovereignty, **State sovereignty** and paid scant attention to the Continental Congress, through the work of which a central government was being evolved. Loyalty to state, indeed, was probably far stronger than loyalty to nation, and it is not surprising that the idea of state sovereignty died hard. Nevertheless the exigencies of war required that there be unity of action, and the problem of union, always evaded in colonial times, now had to be faced.

The Continental Congress, which in 1775 had taken over the direction of the war, was quick to recognize that it had little if any legal authority for the powers it **Plans for a national government** was forced by the logic of events to exercise; and in June, 1776, with independence imminent, it appointed a committee, headed by John Dickinson, to draft a plan of confederation. Dickinson's committee, in undertaking this task, was not without precedents for its guidance. Most important, of course, was the Continental Congress itself, and the work it was actually doing, with or without authority; but there had been much talk of union before, and fully matured plans were available, particularly the one Franklin had presented at Albany in 1754, and with suitable modifications had brought to the attention of Congress in 1775. There seems to have been no thought, either on the part of Franklin or on the part of Dickinson's committee, of replacing the existing *de facto* government with something decidedly different. The sufficiency of this type of central government seems rather to have been taken for granted; all that was deemed necessary was to write in the details and obtain the necessary grant of powers from the states. Franklin would have preferred that the states be given voting strength in Congress according to their population, but this innovation was easily blocked by delegates from the small states who insisted on preserving the principle of complete equality. Dickinson's committee undertook merely to ascertain what problems were common to all the states, and to clothe Congress with authority to deal with them.

Shortly after the Declaration of Independence, Dickinson's committee made its first report, but Congress, faced by **The Articles of Confederation** the more pressing problems of the war, acted slowly, and it was not until November 15, 1777, that the Articles of Confederation were recommended to the states for adoption. They provided for just such a Congress as already existed. It was to be composed of delegates, not less than two nor more than seven, from each of the thirteen states. These delegates were more like diplomatic agents than representatives, for they were paid by the states that sent them, and, while they were chosen annually, were subject to recall at any time. Regardless of the number of delegates it sent to Congress, each state had only one vote. A curious, and as it proved a most unfortunate, provision required that any delegate might serve only three years out of each six. Another provision, even more unfortunate, required the consent of two thirds of the states to pass any measure of importance. To cast the vote of a state at least two delegates must be present and in agreement. If a state delegation divided equally on any matter, then the state lost its vote. Otherwise, a majority of the delegation determined the vote of the state.

The listed powers of Congress gave it complete control over foreign affairs and some **Powers of** control over interstate relations. **Congress** Congress might make peace or war, send and receive ambassadors, make treaties and alliances, govern trade relations with the Indians, determine the standards of coinage (the states might still coin money) and of weights and measures, and organize a postal service. These were powers which in colonial times had been exercised to a large extent by the imperial government, and in assigning them to Congress the states in reality denied themselves few privileges that they had ever held as colonies. The Articles specifically stated, however, that a state might not, without the consent of Congress, make treaties with foreign powers, send or receive ambassadors, or engage in war. It was intended that within these spheres the Congress should be unhampered by state interference.

Congress had only such powers as were definitely assigned to it; the states had all **Reserved** the rest. It was natural enough **powers of** that in making such a division **the states** the new states should wish to retain as their own the prerogatives for which they had made war rather than yield them to the mother country. The right of taxation was one of these; hence only the

states might levy taxes. If Congress wanted money, it might requisition funds from the states. This the British Parliament in its day might also have done without raising the question of constitutionality, for the colonies would have been left free to meet requisitions or not just as they chose. So, too, under the new system there was no way to compel the states to pay. The regulation of commerce was another power fully reserved to the states. Indeed, the Articles in this respect withheld from the central governing body some privileges that the British Parliament had been accustomed to exercise; the states alone might levy tariffs and tonnage taxes, and Congress was denied the right of laying down even the most general sort of regulations. Only through the incidental provisions of treaties could Congress control commerce in any way, and while it was given full permission to make commercial treaties, only the states might retaliate against a foreign country which discriminated against American trade. Nor did the states concede to Congress any authority whatever over interstate commerce.

There was no room for doubt as to where sovereignty lay under the Articles of Confederation, for they pointedly declared that each state retained its "sovereignty, freedom, and independence." Congress in a sense was merely an assembly of diplomats to whom had been entrusted the control of certain common problems. It derived its authority wholly from the states, as whose agent it acted. It was in no sense responsible to the people of the United States, nor could any of its actions bear directly upon them. Changes in the Articles could be made only after the approval of Congress and ratification by every state legislature.

It seems surprising that a document so conservative, and so in line with experience, as the Articles of Confederation **Maryland** should have been delayed in **and western** adoption. And yet such was the **land claims** case. One by one, the various states gave their consent until only Maryland remained. Her objections, shared by some of the other

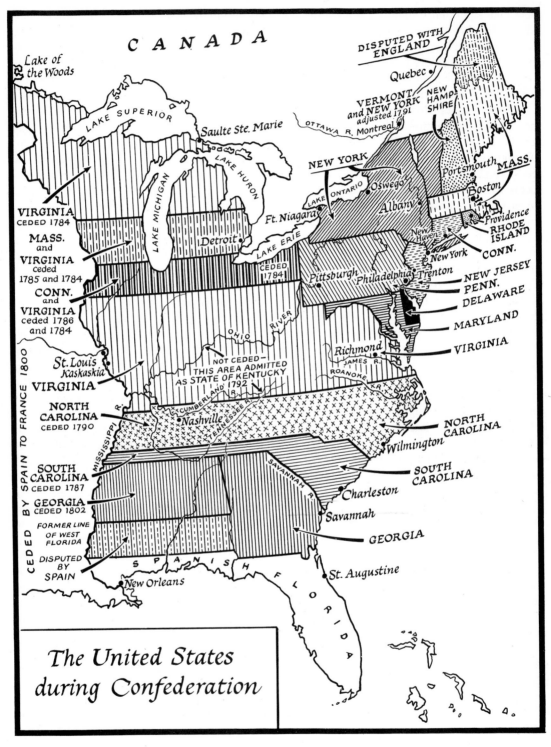

The United States
during Confederation

"small states," had to do with the ownership of western lands. Were these the property of the individual states who claimed them, or were they the property of all the states collectively? The Articles of Confederation seemed to favor the former assumption, for according to that document no state might be deprived of territory for the benefit of the United States. Six states — Massachusetts, Connecticut, Virginia, North Carolina, South Carolina, and Georgia — had claims to western lands based upon early grants from the crown. New York had a shadowy title, based on an Indian treaty, to some lands in the upper Ohio Valley. The other six states had no western claims of any kind. Maryland, always fearful of her powerful neighbor, Virginia, had urged upon Congress, even before the Articles were adopted by that body, that "the back lands, claimed by the British crown, if secured by the blood and treasure of all, ought, in reason, justice, and policy, to be considered a common stock, to be parcelled out by Congress into free, convenient, and independent Governments, as the wisdom of that body shall hereafter direct." When Congress refused to accept this advice, Maryland refused to accept the Articles, and, with both justice and expediency favoring her contention, she finally won out. Thomas Paine wrote an article "The Public Good" supporting the Maryland contention, Congress reversed itself and urged such a policy "for the common good of the United States," and public opinion gradually veered around. There was no better claim than that of Virginia, which was now based not only upon the original grant, but also upon the military exploits of George Rogers Clark, so when Virginia agreed to relinquish her claim to Congress, Maryland was content. On March 1, 1781, more than two years after every other state had agreed to the Articles, Maryland also ratified, and at last they went into effect.[1]

In some respects the Articles registered a definite step in advance. The various states agreed, for example, to permit to the citizens of all the other states the same privileges that their own citizens enjoyed. National citizenship was thus brought a step nearer. Also the extradition of fugitives from justice who had fled from one state to another was made possible, and the public records and judicial proceedings of each state were given full faith and credit in every other. As an. experiment in federation the Articles are not to be despised. They were weak enough, to be sure, but they were destined at least soon to demonstrate their shortcomings and thus to speed the way to a closer union.

The Articles left Congress free to work out as best it could a plan for the discharge of its executive duties. The committee system was first given a trial, but by the close of the Revolution three executive departments had been created, with individuals at the head of each: Robert Livingston as Secretary of Foreign Affairs, Robert Morris as Superintendent of Finance, and General Lincoln as Secretary of War. A naval department was also provided for, but remained unorganized. It is interesting to speculate on how far this course of development might have gone, had the Confederation continued, in the direction of evolving for the United States the cabinet system of government already fairly well defined in Great Britain.

The Articles failed, also, to establish a well-rounded national system of courts. Congress, however, was authorized to act as a court of appeal in cases of disputes between the several states, and it was given authority to provide, on request, for the creation of special committees to try such cases. It might also select certain state courts in which piracies and felonies on the high seas might be brought to trial, and it might establish appellate courts for the rehearing of prize cases. Had the Confederation lasted longer, it is not beyond belief that these grants of authority might have been so interpreted as to make possible an adequate system for the handling of such business as

The executive authority

[1] Virginia's concern over the ratification of the Articles was greatly increased by the Cornwallis invasion. See p. 146.

The spirit of liberty that was released by the American Revolution manifested itself in a great variety of ways. Popular participation in government tended to increase, and sometimes, as in the illustration, to precipitate tense scenes between the holders of opposing ideas. Many individuals saw and deplored the fact that slavery was inconsistent with the equalitarian doctrines of the Revolution.

DISSENSION IN TOWN MEETING. Illustration by Tisdale for Trumbull's *M'Fingal*, 1795.

THE GENIUS OF AMERICA ENCOURAGING THE EMANCIPATION OF THE BLACKS. Painting by Samuel Jennings, 1792, in which Liberty is shown displaying the arts and sciences to the Negro.

could not readily be disposed of by the state courts.

Congress was most seriously handicapped by its lack of power to tax, its absence of authority to control commerce, and its inability to act directly upon the people of the states rather than merely upon the states themselves. Even so, had the process of amendment been less difficult these defects might have been remedied. It is by no means certain that, given better times and a longer term of life, the Confederation might not have developed into a fairly satisfactory form of government.

While the leaders of the American Revolution were no doubt chiefly interested in bringing about political changes, the trans-formation that actually took place in American life during this eventful period was by no means confined to politics. As one distinguished historian observes, "Who shall say to the waves of revolution: thus far shall we go and no farther?" It is a fact that "many economic desires, many social aspirations were set free by the political struggle, many aspects of colonial society profoundly altered by the forces thus let loose." Nor was this social revolution ended with the conclusion of the war, for the forces making for change merely gathered momentum with each successful assault upon the older order.

The downfall of the colonial aristocracy was far more than a political phenomenon.

The Revolution, socially considered

MOVING A HOUSE IN PHILADEL-PHIA. The Walnut Street jail is shown in the background. Engraving by William Birch, 1799.

PHILADELPHIA WATERFRONT. The Arch Street ferry slip is shown in the foreground. Engraving by William Birch, 1800.

Life and labor in the United States was not for some time markedly different from life and labor in the colonies. Port cities looked invariably toward the waterfront, where ships were constantly loading and unloading. Foreigners visiting in America gazed with amazement upon the phenomenon of house-moving, common enough in rapidly changing America, but almost unknown to the more static society of Europe.

Making due allowance for exceptions — and there were many — the Patriots represented in the main the common people, and the Loyalists the upper strata of society. The victory of the former, together with their studied persecution of the latter, made it possible for men who in colonial times had been regarded as of low degree to hold high office and enjoy important privileges. Common men came naturally to hold themselves in higher esteem, and their superiors in lower. Many, indeed, read into the Declaration of Independence, with its emphasis upon the equality of men, a demand for the emancipation of the slaves, and in all the northern colonies the abolition of slavery followed fairly promptly upon the attainment of independence. Even in the South emancipation societies were common, and the gradual disappearance of slavery was generally expected.

The trend towards small independent holdings of land, which was marked even in colonial times, was greatly accelerated by the Revolution. **Land-ownership** Many of the largest estates, the property of Loyalists, were confiscated and sold out in small tracts to free farmers. The old feudal rules of primogeniture, which provided that property in land should descend to the eldest son, and of entail, which held such property in the family by prohibiting its owner either to sell it or to give it away, were quickly abolished. Quit-rents, always regarded as a nuisance and rarely paid without protest, became a thing of the past. Moreover, such British restrictions upon the advance of the agricultural frontier as the Proclamation of 1763 and the Quebec Act lost their meaning, and cheap lands to the West were available for all who wished them, particularly for those veterans of the war who had been granted land bounties as a part of the inducement to enlist. Landownership no longer served as a test of gentility, and, even as a qualification for voting, it extended the suffrage, so one conservative asserted, "to every biped of the forest."

Changes with respect to landownership were closely paralleled by changes in indus-**Industry and** try and commerce. American **commerce** manufactures, always hampered to some extent by British restrictions and still more by the habit of buying manufactured articles from England, were immensely stimulated by the war. Far more attention was given than formerly to the making of such necessary articles as firearms, gunpowder, nails, salt, paper, and cloth, and the occupations of the people shifted accordingly. Commerce, on the other hand, suffered acutely from the war, although much successful privateering kept the sailor's art alive, as the speedy return of American ships to the sea at the close of the war abundantly attested. Freedom from the British restrictions on colonial trade opened up some new opportunities to American skippers, but this advantage was probably more than offset by the loss of trade privileges that the colonies had once enjoyed as a part of the British Empire.

Independence served also to force a series of readjustments with respect to the religious **Religious** life of the Americans. The **adjustments** union of church and state that existed in nine out of thirteen of the colonies was promptly attacked, although with varying results. In the South, where the state church was the Church of England, disestablishment was naturally associated with revolution, and was early accomplished. Here the demand for religious freedom met its most vigorous resistance in Virginia, but in 1786 the legislature of the Old Dominion asserted, in words penned by Jefferson, that "no man shall be compelled to frequent or support any religious worship, place, or ministry whatsoever, nor shall be enforced, restrained, molested or burthened in his body or goods, nor shall otherwise suffer on account of his religious opinions or belief; but that all men shall be free to profess, and by argument to maintain, their opinion in matters of religion, and that the same shall in no wise diminish, enlarge, or affect their civil capacities." In New England, where, except for Rhode Island, the Congregational Church was supported by the state, patriotism could not so easily be invoked on the side of religious freedom, and the struggle lasted far into the nineteenth century. In Massachusetts, the strongest citadel of Puritanism, disestablishment was not voted until 1833.

After the Revolution most of the American denominations undertook to reorganize their systems of church government. With this in mind, the American Anglicans, when they failed to obtain the co-operation of English church officials, persuaded the non-juring bishops of Scotland to consecrate in 1784 an American bishop, Samuel Seabury. With an American episcopate thus assured, the Protestant Episcopal Church of the United States was organized. About the same time the separate status of the American Catholic Church was recognized by a decree from Rome, and in 1790 Father John Carroll was made Bishop of Baltimore. At the close of the Revolution John Wesley, the English founder of the Methodist Church (who himself never left the Church of England), sent Thomas Coke, another Englishman, to the United States as general superintendent of the American Methodists. On arriving in America, Coke promptly associated himself with Francis Asbury, the leading spirit among the American Methodists, and in December, 1784, at a conference of the

Religious Statesmen. Samuel Seabury, Father John Carroll, and Francis Asbury became bishops of their respective churches in the United States, and worked successfully to achieve national unity for their denominations.

church held in Baltimore, the two were designated joint superintendents. Asbury and his successors, contrary to Wesley's wishes, assumed the title of bishop, and the denomination over which they presided was officially known as the Methodist Episcopal Church. Other denominations, although freer from overseas connections than these three, generally redefined and elaborated their systems of government.

Of still greater significance was the revolution in thought and feeling that came over **Revolution in thought and feeling** the American people during the period of war. Religion, in the more formal sense, suffered disastrously, for churches were destroyed, religious ties loosened, standards of morality lowered, and traditional beliefs swept away. On the other hand, the revolutionary ideals of liberty and equality were deeply impressed upon the minds of the people. The inhuman penal codes of the eighteenth century were more frequently denounced, and imprisonment as a means of punishment for debt sometimes received the ridicule it deserved. A change could be noted, also, in the popular concept of education. The colonial schools, such as they were, had been virtually destroyed by the years of Revolution, and new systems had to be devised. In an age that exalted the rights of the common man, pressure upon the state to accept the obligation of popular education steadily increased. Prophetic of the future was the provision in the first constitution of the unrecognized state of Vermont that a school system, beginning with the towns and including a state university, should be established. Systems of this sort were slow to develop, and seven of the original state constitutions made no mention whatever of education; but when, in the nineteenth century, the American school system did take form, it was under secular, not religious, control, and its right to public support was still defended on the grounds Jefferson had stated years before. "Above all things," he had written, "I hope the education of the common people will be attended to; convinced that on their good sense we may rely with the most security for the preservation of a due degree of liberty."

Bibliography

On the transition from colonies to states the best general treatment is Allan Nevins, *The American States during and after the Revolution, 1775–1789* (1924). This may be supplemented by such useful special studies as the following: H. A. Cushing, *History of the Transition from Provincial to Commonwealth Government in Massachusetts* (1896); W. C. Abbott, *New York in the American Revolution* (1929); J. T. Adams, *New England in the Republic, 1776–1850* (1926); R. L. Brunhouse, *The Counter-Revolution in Pennsylvania, 1776–1790* (1942); M. B. Jones, *Vermont in the Making, 1750–1777* (1939); C. M. Thompson, *Independent Vermont* (1942); P. A. Crowl, *Maryland during and after the Revolution* (1943); W. F. Dunaway, *A History of Pennsylvania* (1935).

The Confederation Period is taken as the beginning point for two monumental works on American history: J. B. McMaster, *A History of the People of the United States from the Revolution to the Civil War* (8 vols., 1883–1913); and James Schouler, *History of the United States of America under the Constitution* (7 vols., 1880–1913). McMaster leaves few subjects of consequence untouched, but Schouler's chief interest lies in political history. A. C. McLaughlin, *The Confederation and the Constitution* (1905), is particularly good on the problem of union. A. W. Small, *The Beginnings of American Nationality* (1890), features the work of the Continental Congress. John Fiske, *The Critical Period of American History* (1916), is generally accounted the best of Fiske's books, but in point of view needs the cor-

rective treatment it (as well as other older books on the period) receives at the hands of Merrill Jensen, *The Articles of Confederation* (1940); and by the same author, *The New Nation: A History of the United States during the Confederation, 1781–1789* (1950).

On non-political aspects of the period, the most comprehensive treatment is E. B. Greene, *The Revolutionary Generation, 1763–1790* (1943). R. A. East, *Business Enterprise in the American Revolutionary Era* (1938), opens a fruitful field. Dixon Wecter, *When Johnny Comes Marching Home* (1944), explores the postwar activities of veterans, beginning with those of the American Revolution. J. F. Jameson, *The American Revolution Considered as a Social Movement* (1926), stresses especially the revolution in thought and feeling that came with independence. Dixon Ryan Fox, *Ideas in Motion* (1935), contains a number of entertaining essays, some of which have a bearing on this period. J. B. McMaster, *The Acquisition of Political, Social, and Industrial Rights of Man in America* (1903), focuses upon the growth of American liberties. J. K. Morse, *Jedidiah Morse; A Champion of New England Orthodoxy* (1939), is useful on the religious transformations of the period.

On the treaty of peace that ended the Revolutionary War, there is a good chapter in C. E. Hill, *Leading American Treaties* (1922). See also the references on diplomacy following chapter 8, p. 148.

10

The Confederation: Successes and Failures

A period of depression — Confederation finance — Efforts to amend the Articles — The problem of the West — The Northwest Ordinances — The Northwest posts — Adams's mission to England — Spanish-American relations — *Trevett vs. Weeden* — Shays' Rebellion — Growth of radicalism — Demands for a stronger government — Forces making for union

THE Confederation Period coincided closely with a period of economic depression that **A period of** came in the wake of the Revo-**depression** lutionary War. The waste and over-expenditure of those eight years had been a serious drain on the resources of a country which at best was far from rich, and the war was not long over before the new nation was made fully aware of the heavy price it had paid for freedom. Also, separation from the British Empire made necessary a set of painful readjustments. If American commerce suffered somewhat in the colonial period from British regulations, it had also the advantage of British trade treaties and British protection. As a new and independent nation, the United States now had to make its own way in such matters. Being outside the British Empire was in itself a serious handicap, for, contrary to a common impression, the British government did not, as a result of the American war, give up immediately its efforts to promote imperial self-sufficiency; and the United States found itself deprived of trade privileges which the colonies as members of the imperial family had freely enjoyed. Then, too, the removal of the British troops from America, while a source of much satisfaction to good patriots, eliminated also the gold supply from British payments to Americans for foodstuffs and other necessities. With commerce at low ebb, and with an inadequate market for farm produce, unemployment became common, radical doctrines found a ready hearing, and criticism of the government grew by leaps and bounds.

To meet this critical situation the new nation had only a makeshift government, lacking even in the all-important **Confedera-** power of taxation. The finan- **ion finance** cial embarrassment of the Confederation government was always acute. To meet its ordinary expenditures it required an income of about a half million dollars a year, and this sum made no provision for payments, either of interest or principal, on the public debt. Altogether the United States had incurred an indebtedness of well over forty million dollars during the prosecution of the war. About six million dollars had been borrowed from France, and perhaps another two millions from other foreign sources. The remainder, mostly in the shape of back pay for soldiers and certificates of indebtedness to those who had furnished supplies for the army, was owing to the citizens of the United States.

The means by which the government could raise money to discharge its financial obligations were strictly limited. It might resort to paper-money issues, but during the war this source of revenue had been dried up by overuse. It might also indulge in further borrowing provided creditors could be found to lend, and some funds were actually obtained in Holland for use in paying the interest on the foreign debt. A small sum was realized from the sales of public lands, and the post-office brought in ten or fifteen thousand dollars a year. In the main, however, Congress had to rely upon requisitions levied upon the states for money it needed to meet obligations of every sort and kind. The requisition system proved to be entirely inadequate. Requests for funds were honored by the states only in so far as they chose to honor them, and probably not more than one tenth of the sums asked for by Congress was ever paid in. Much of the money that was obtained, moreover, was of uncertain value, for the states also had their financial difficulties, and many of them had resorted to overissues of paper currency. Plans for the compulsory collection of the sums levied upon the states were considered, but none seemed practicable enough to warrant giving it a trial.

On two occasions Congress made an earnest effort to obtain alterations in the Articles of Confederation that would make possible an independent source of revenue for the central government. **Efforts to amend the Articles** The first request (1781) was for a five per cent ad-valorem duty on imports, from the proceeds of which the interest on the national debt might be paid and a beginning made toward the payment of the principal. This modest proposal, while agreeable to most of the states, met with serious objections, and was defeated. The Revolution had been fought in part as a protest against taxation by an outside agency, and to many citizens Congress seemed quite as much beyond the control of the individual state as the British Parliament itself. Moreover, with unpleasant memories of the activities of British tax-gatherers still fresh in mind, there was much skepticism as to the wisdom of allowing the agents of Congress to enter a state for the purpose of collecting taxes within it. Rhode Island refused outright to consent to such a tax, and Virginia withdrew her consent after it had been given; and since the Articles of Confederation could not be amended without a unanimous vote the proposal came to naught. Congress then modified its request (1783), and sought the power to levy duties on imports for twenty-five years only, the states themselves to appoint the revenue officers. But again Rhode Island refused, New York gave only a qualified consent, and several other states failed to take action in the matter. It seemed evident, therefore, that while the Articles of Confederation endured the central government must depend for its financial support upon the unsatisfactory requisition system.

The financial impotence with which it was cursed soon made the Congress of the Confederation a joke. The men **Impotence of Congress** best qualified to serve as delegates refused to risk their reputations or waste their time in such futile labor, and the states were compelled to send second-rate men to represent them. Some states preferred to send no delegates at all. Moreover, the delegates chosen often neglected to attend the sessions of Congress. Only twenty-three members were present to ratify the treaty of peace by which the Revolution was brought to an end — the opposition of a single state could have defeated ratification. Washington's resignation as head of the army was presented to Congress when only twenty delegates were present. The Northwest Ordinance of 1787, doubtless the most notable of the acts of Congress under the Confederation, was passed with but eighteen delegates present.

Of all the problems with which it was required to deal, Congress did best with the problem of the West. That this **The problem of the West** section would play a part of great importance in the history of the nation seemed evident enough in the light of recent events. The French and Indian War had been fought primarily to determine whether the English or the French should have the opportunity to expand into the Ohio Valley. The Revolutionary War itself had been brought on in no small part because of western problems. It was the determination that the colonies must help pay for the defense of their western frontier that had led to the passage of the ill-fated Stamp Act. It was the fear that England wished to cut off expansion into the West that had made so many Americans resent deeply the Proclamation Line of 1763 and the Quebec Act. It was discontent with the rule of the East that made many back-country settlers support the war against Great Britain, for out of the Revolution against British tyranny they hoped also to achieve freedom from the tyranny of eastern aristocrats.

The cessions of western lands to Congress by the states claiming them were not completed until 1802, when Georgia at last surrendered her claim, but after the adoption of the Articles of Confederation in 1781 it was apparent that the nation rather than the states must deal with the West. Here a number of permanent settlements had already been made. Farthest in the interior lay the French villages that George Rogers Clark had conquered, which together with Detroit and other centers of fur trade had a population numbering several thousands. On the upper Ohio around Pittsburgh, in the valleys of the Holston and Watauga Rivers, in the blue-grass region of Kentucky, and now also along the Cumberland in central Tennessee were other settlements of varying sizes, all of which were growing rapidly.

That attention must be given to the needs of these western communities by the central

Western independence government was soon made evident. In the region south of the Ohio River, where new settlers were entering more rapidly than anywhere else in the West, there was a marked tendency to disregard the authority of the present states to the east. New western states that might willingly acknowledge the supremacy of a national government, but would not forever remain content to be merely western divisions of eastern states, were in the making. As for the region northwest of the Ohio River, Congress, thanks to the insistence of Maryland, had

full control there, and full responsibility.

Among the states that followed the lead of Virginia in the cession of western lands was North Carolina, which in 1784 passed an act to hand over its transmontane territory to the United States, provided that Congress accept the gift within twelve months' time. The region ceded included the Watauga settlements, which had been made first into one and then into several counties of North Carolina only a short time before, and now contained probably more than ten thousand settlers. There was reason to believe that the North Carolina legislature felt that it was exhibiting considerable shrewdness in getting rid of these western counties. Their inhabitants paid very little into the state treasury, and yet on western insistence the state had made expensive treaties with the Indians to acquire more lands. With the cession of the territory in question to Congress it was assumed that the state of North Carolina would be under no obligation to continue the payments to the Indians that the treaties provided; and much to the dissatisfaction of the Indians, who promptly threatened to take the warpath, these payments were discontinued.

Already the Wataugans had known what it was to govern themselves without the aid of North Carolina, and they **State of** now promptly took steps to set **Franklin** up once more a wholly independent government. Possibly they might become a new state in the United States, or failing that, at least they would be in a better position to meet the Indian menace. Following a series of conventions, the state of Franklin was created, with John Sevier as governor and the laws of North Carolina as a legal guide of conduct. For some time the new state charted its own course; but the North Carolina legislature was quick to repent its action and to repeal the cession act, and by 1788 the western counties had returned, with some reluctance, to their former allegiance. Meantime Congress had taken no action whatever on the matter.

By this time still another settlement had

Pioneer leaders, John Sevier and James Robertson were young men in their twenties when they took their families to the remote frontier, in what is now eastern Tennessee. Sevier became the first governor of the state of Tennessee.

been made in the western land claimed by North Carolina. For this ven-**Cumberland settlements** ture, Richard Henderson, the same that had attempted the Transylvania project in Kentucky, was chiefly responsible. When his rights in Kentucky were taken over by Virginia, Henderson sent James Roberston with a few companions into central Tennessee to found a colony along the Cumberland. Willing pioneers came in from Watauga and from the Virginia frontier, and under the guidance of experienced leaders they soon provided themselves with a temporary form of government. In May, 1780, at Nashborough (or Nashville) all adult male settlers, two hundred and fifty-six in all, affixed their signatures to an agreement that amounted to a constitution. Following the Watauga precedent a court of twelve judges was to be chosen by manhood suffrage to represent the several stations; but it was expressly stipulated that whenever North Carolina should be ready to take over the government of the "Cumberland settlements," no impediment should be placed in the way. For a few years this temporary government functioned smoothly, but in 1782 the Assembly of North Carolina

recognized the new region by the creation of Davidson County.

The most populous of the western areas of settlement, however, was Kentucky. Here thousands of pioneers came in **Kentucky** during the closing years of the Revolution, so that by the end of that struggle the total population of the bluegrass region was probably not less than twenty-five thousand. Soon the growing western communities had one thing in common, an increasing interest in trade down the Mississippi to New Orleans. Here, at a very early date, they began to seek markets for their produce, and on their return journey sometimes to make use of a hazardous land route from Natchez to Nashville, known as the Natchez Trace. Bound to the West, as they were, by ties of transportation, they all showed signs of restiveness under the rule of the eastern states, but the size of the Kentucky settlements, which continued to grow rapidly during the entire Confederation period, made their protests seem the most important. Kentuckians objected strenuously to the inaccessibility of courts, which in some cases could not be reached without crossing the mountains, and to the lack of local authority to call out the militia and otherwise deal with the Indian problem. Numerous conventions were therefore held — ten of them in all — in the interest of separate statehood for Kentucky. Virginia proved generous, and three times voted to give the Kentuckians what they desired. But during the Confederation period Congress failed to take the necessary steps to make Kentucky a state.

Nevertheless, the strong sentiment in the Southwest for separate statehood and the **The Northwest** willingness of its residents to rely upon the national government for protection and support seem not to have been wholly lost upon Congress. In the territory northwest of the Ohio River, where the title of the national government to the land was already clear, some provision for the future had to be made, and with this end in view Congress passed a series of "Northwest Ordinances" which showed a sympathetic appreciation of the problems of the West. Whether the attitude of Congress was directly affected by the situation in the Southwest is not entirely clear, but the Ordinances safeguarded in a most satisfactory way the right of settlers to adventure into the West and to establish states with the same privileges as were enjoyed by the old.

The initiative in this matter was taken by Thomas Jefferson, who was a close student of the problems of the West, and **Ordinance of 1784** realized more fully than most men of his time that provision must be made for the development of a great country. In 1784 he introduced into Congress a plan for the organization of the West. He proposed, first, that certain fundamental guarantees should be made for the guidance of future legislators. The new states to be created in the West should remain forever a part of the United States. They should remain subject to the central government as the original states were subject; they should be

State of Franklin and the Cumberland Settlements 1779~1796

State of Franklin ~ shaded

East versus West soon became as chronic a problem in American history as North versus South. Did one cling to the prosperous, or once-prosperous, estates of the East, or did one sell out and buy speculators' land in the West?

For SALE, or BARTER,
A Quantity of L A N D in Patents,
from 250 to 1000 Acres, situate in Botetourt and Mononga-hela Counties, Virginia, will be sold very low for Cash, Produce, any Kind of Certificates, or Indents, good Bonds, Land, or other Property in the State of Maryland. For Terms, apply to

J. Williams.

Annapolis, May 12, 1789.

LAND SALES. Advertisement for land in the western counties of Virginia. From *The Maryland Journal*, June, 1789.

EASTERN FARMING. "View of the Seat of the Hon. Moses Gill, in the County of Worcester, Mass." Illustration in *The Massachusetts Magazine*, Nov., 1792.

liable for their portion of the federal debt; they should have a government republican in form; within their borders slavery should not exist after the year 1800. Jefferson also worked out a mechanical division of the West, marking it by lines of latitude and longitude into prospective states, ten of which he named, somewhat fantastically, Sylvania, Michigania, Cherronesus, Assenisippia, Metropotamia, Illinoia, Saratoga, Washington, Polypotamia, and Pelisipia. As for the plan of government, he suggested three stages. First, the settlers should meet together to establish a temporary government by the adoption of the constitution and laws of any one of the original states; secondly, whenever a given division could show that it had twenty thousand free male inhabitants it might establish a permanent constitution and send a delegate to Congress; thirdly, whenever its population should equal that of the smallest of the original thirteen it should be admitted to full statehood. Jefferson's ordinance, shorn of the pedantic names and the anti-slavery clause, passed Congress, but it was purely preliminary and tentative. In most of the territory under consideration the Indian titles had not yet been extinguished, and north of the Ohio River, except in the French villages, white population had not yet begun to come in.

Jefferson also believed that the lands of the West should be made to yield a revenue for the sorely depleted treasury **Ordinance** of the Confederation, and to pay **of 1785** off obligations owing to soldiers who had fought in the American Revolution. Treaties with the Indians which would make these ends possible were speedily signed, one at Fort Stanwix in 1784, and one at Fort McIntosh in 1785. These treaties opened up to sale and settlement a tract of land im-

No. 16   MIAMI LAND-WARRANT.

THIS entitles *Jonathan Dayton* his Heirs or Assigns, to locate one Section, in which the Fee of 640 Acres shall pass, subject to the Terms of settlement.

Dated the *first* Day of *May* A. D. 178

Signed by *John Cleve Symmes*

Counterfigned by

Western settlers did not always locate their land titles promptly, and sometimes such warrants as the one shown here circulated almost as money. Hostile Indians, both in the Southwest and the Northwest, long remained a great deterrent to the advance of settlement.

LAND WARRANT. Issued in 1787 by John Cleve Symmes for land in the area where the present cities of Dayton and Cincinnati, Ohio, now stand.

FRONTIER DANGERS. An Indian attack on a Tennessee station, about the time of Tennessee's admission to the Union as a state, 1796.

mediately to the west of the upper Ohio. Before the land should be finally disposed of, however, Congress, again accepting Jefferson's leadership, passed the famous Ordinance of 1785, which set forth the system of survey and sale to be followed. Instead of permitting the location of tracts as the whims of purchasers might direct, the Ordinance of 1785 provided for the "rectangular" or "rectilinear" system of survey, so familiar to western Americans of later generations. Parallel lines were to be drawn at six-mile intervals, both north and south, and east and west, as nearly as the sphericity of the earth would permit. Each of the squares so described was to be called a township, and each north and south tier of townships was to be called a range. Further subdivisions of the townships were to be made by east and west as well as north and south lines surveyed at intervals of one mile,

so that each township would be marked off into thirty-six "sections." The sections, each of which was thus a mile square and contained approximately six hundred and forty acres, might then be divided into "halves" and "quarters," the "quarters" into "half-quarters" and "quarter-quarters," and so on indefinitely. Jefferson would have preferred a township ten miles square rather than six miles square, but Congress thought the lesser unit more practicable.

This elaborate and systematic method of survey came as the result of many unhappy experiences with colonial land surveys, in which, as a rule, there was no orderly system of survey whatever. A grant of land, or deed, would ordinarily describe the plot under consideration by reference to trees, streams, rocks, or other natural markers, many of which might vary in location from time to time, and some of which were nearly sure to disappear altogether. Under such circumstances boundary disputes between the owners of adjacent property inevitably clogged the colonial courts. Moreover, there was a tendency for individuals to acquire titles to only the more choice lands in a given area, leaving in the hands of the state quantities of irregular, unsalable bits of "waste land." Under the system adopted in the Ordinance of 1785 the purchaser would have to take all the land of a section, or subdivision thereof, regardless of the fact that some of the land almost certainly would not be as desirable as the rest; but he would be insured against the annoyance of uncertain boundaries and the expense and irritation of boundary disputes.

The Ordinance of 1785 also made provision for the sale of the lands to be surveyed. In accordance with a New England precedent, section sixteen of each township was to be reserved as a bounty to public schools, but the rest of the land was to be offered for sale to the highest bidder in lots of a section or more. The minimum price was fixed at one dollar per acre, but it was hoped that by holding auctions in each state competitive bidding would result in a considerably higher average price being paid.

Congress, faced by dire calamity because of its lack of an adequate income, may well **Revenue** be pardoned for seeking to ob-**from public** tain a revenue from the public **lands** lands, although in a sense such a policy was a reversal of colonial precedent. Throughout the colonial period the lands of most of the colonies had been so administered that the pioneer farmer obtained his holding practically as a reward for his venture. The fees charged against him were usually nominal, and they were not always collected. It was assumed that in advancing the frontier and in contributing his share to its defense against the Indians, he was rendering a service of sufficient value to the colony that he was entitled to the lands he needed. To be sure, land speculators did acquire large tracts of land, and they sometimes disposed of them at a profit; but such a grant was

usually made on the theory that it would promote the rapid colonization of the West, and the colony itself rarely made any money out of the project. Under the terms of the Ordinance of 1785, however, the poor man was virtually deprived of the opportunity to buy lands of the United States, for he could rarely amass as large a sum as six hundred and forty dollars; and the chief purchases were to be made by speculators who would buy in order to resell their land to actual settlers for a profit.

Congress authorized in 1785 the survey of seven ranges of townships west of the western boundary of Pennsyl- **The Ohio** vania, and ordered Captain **Company of** Thomas Hutchins, Geographer **Associates** of the United States, to proceed with the work. Among the surveyors assigned to assist him was General Benjamin Tupper of Massachusetts, who was eager to see the West, and promptly took up his residence at Pittsburgh. General Samuel Parsons, another citizen of Massachusetts, was named as commissioner to treat with the Indians for further land cessions beyond the Ohio, and went as far west as Louisville. Both Tupper and Parsons saw the boundless possibilities of the West, particularly the opportunity for speculation that the almost certain rise in land values would permit. Already some Massachusetts officers who had served in the Revolutionary Army had considered a plan for accepting western lands from Congress in lieu of the debts the nation owed them, and now, spurred on by the glowing reports of Tupper and Parsons, the project was revived. At a meeting held in Boston, March 1, 1786, at the Bunch of Grapes Tavern, the Ohio Company of Associates was formed for the purchase of a tract west of the region being surveyed. The purchase price was to be subscribed by Massachusetts veterans of the Revolution in the depreciated paper currency — now considered worthless — with which they had been paid. It was hoped that a total of one million dollars might be subscribed in this way, of which no individual might contribute more than five thousand dollars. The scheme had its good points. Congress might in this way discharge an obligation which otherwise would probably never be met; and for virtually nothing at all the Ohio Associates could obtain title to a large tract of valuable land.

Congress had yet to be persuaded as to the feasibility of the proposition, and with this object in view General Parsons made a trip to New York, where Congress was then holding its sessions. His efforts were unavailing, and the company next selected the Reverend Manasseh Cutler, minister at Ipswich, Massachusetts, to try his hand. Cutler proved to be an admirable choice. He found Congress diffident because of its uncertain future, but used his persuasiveness on individual congressmen with good effect. He pointed out that the settlement of the company's lands would stimulate interest in the West, would lead to other settlement, and eventually would lead to the sale of more of the lands which Congress held. Finally, as a last resort, he agreed that a group of congressmen and their friends, to be known as the Scioto Company, should be let in on the deal. To the Ohio Company Congress would sell a million and a half acres of land at two thirds of a dollar an acre; to the Scioto Company it would give an option on the purchase of an additional three and a half million acres adjacent to the Ohio Company tract. Cutler also gave up his original intention of making General Parsons governor of the new territory, and accepted the suggestion of members of Congress that this office should go to General Arthur St. Clair, whose duties as President of Congress were soon to end. Assured of these concessions, Congress promptly chartered both companies; and Cutler, still making himself useful, succeeded in inducing the Scioto Associates to advance some $143,000 to further the work of settling up the Ohio Company's lands.

Meantime Congress was at work on the famous Ordinance of 1787 for the govern-

Manasseh Cutler

ment of the territory northwest of the Ohio River. On July 13 the Ordinance was adopted. Like the Ordinance of 1784, which it supplanted, it provided for three stages in the evolution of government. During the first stage a governor, a secretary, and three judges, all appointed by Congress, were to adopt and enforce such laws of the older states as might seem appropriate to the new territory. Whenever the district could show five thousand free male inhabitants, however, the freeholders might choose a representative assembly, which on coming together would nominate ten persons, from whom Congress would choose five to be a legislative council, or upper house. The two-house legislature thus established might then enact whatever laws it chose, subject to the governor's veto. Furthermore, a delegate to Congress might be chosen, who might speak and introduce bills, but might not vote. The Ordinance presumed that ultimately the territory northwest of the Ohio River would be divided into not less than three nor more than five states, and whenever a given district had attained a population of sixty thousand free inhabitants it should be admitted "on an equal footing with the original states in all respects whatsoever," and with full "liberty to form a permanent constitution and state government."

Ordinance of 1787

The promise of ultimate statehood and a number of other declarations were set apart from the rest of the Ordinance as "articles of compact between the original states and the people and states in the said territory" which were to remain forever "unalterable, unless by common consent." Freedom of religious worship, freedom from arbitrary imprisonment, and the right of trial by jury were thus solemnly guaranteed; schools and the means of public education were to be forever encouraged; the utmost good faith was always to be observed toward the Indians; the settlers in the new territory were to be required to pay their share of the federal debts and the expense of federal government; the prospective territorial or

Fort Miami
Fallen Timbers
Fort Defiance
Fort Wayne
Fort Recovery
Fort Greenville
Fort Jefferson
Fort St Clair
Fort Hamilton
Fort Finney
Cincinnati
SYMME'S PURCHASE
Chillicothe
Gallipolis
O H I O
GREENVILLE TREATY LINE 1795
ADMITTED 1803
Zanesville
SCIOTO RIVER
MIAMI RIVER
MUSKINGUM
OHIO CO.
SEVEN RANGES
Fort Laurens
Pittsburgh
Fort Steuben
Wheeling
Marietta
Fort Harmar
Blennerhassett I.
LAKE ERIE
Cleveland
WESTERN RESERVE
ST. JOSEPH R.
MAUMEE RIVER
WABASH R.
ST. MARYS R.
K E N T U C K Y
O H I O   R I V E R

The Ohio and Scioto Company Tracts

state legislatures were never to interfere with the administration of the public lands by the United States; the navigable waters of the West were to remain forever free for use without tax or duty by all citizens of the United States from whatever state; and there should be "neither slavery nor involuntary servitude in the said territory, otherwise than in punishment of crimes whereof the party shall have been duly convicted." By this last clause Jefferson's plan to exclude slavery from the Northwest, which had barely failed of adoption in the Ordinance of 1784, was now revived and accepted.

The Ohio Company lost little time in beginning the work of colonization it had **Marietta** planned. The tract of land it selected lay along the Ohio River just west of the Seven Ranges, and at the mouth of the Muskingum River. In the spring of 1788 the first settlement, Marietta, was begun. Forty-seven colonists had been sent out from New England the preceding fall, had spent the winter at the forks of the Ohio, had constructed there a

flatboat which they named appropriately the *May-Flower*, and in April, 1788, had floated down the Ohio in five days' time to the site selected. Other settlers, attracted by the low price of the land and the offer of free transportation, soon followed. Before many months Marietta was a village of many log cabins, surrounded by numerous clearings, and possessed of the customary "blockhouse" for defense against the Indians. In due time churches, schools, and an academy — the Muskingum Academy (1797), eventually to become Marietta College — also made their appearance.[1] The Ohio Company did not prove to be the money-making project that its founders had hoped, and it was able to redeem only a fraction of the land to which it was entitled according to its original contract with Congress.

The Scioto Company, in spite of the fact that it owned no land whatever, attempted to obtain settlers for the region upon which

[1] Ohio University, which opened its doors at Athens in 1809, was the first institution of higher learning to be established northwest of the River Ohio.

it held an option. Fearful, perhaps, lest Americans might examine into its land titles too closely, it sought to interest foreigners, and for this purpose sent Joel Barlow, the poet, to France. Barlow associated himself with an enterprising and none too scrupulous Englishman by the name of Playfair, and between the two many thousands of purchasers of Scioto Company lands were found. In 1790 some six hundred French settlers actually reached the Ohio and founded the village Gallipolis some distance down the river from Marietta. It turned out, however, that the settlement had been made on Ohio Company land, and to make matters worse for the French immigrants, the Scioto Company was never able to take up its option. The sufferings of the residents of Gallipolis, who were at best unaccustomed to American pioneering, ultimately led Congress to donate them a tract of land sufficient for their needs.

Gallipolis

Another early settlement in the Ohio country was made by a well-to-do citizen of New Jersey, John Cleves Symmes, who in 1788 was granted permission to purchase a million acres of land between the Great and the Little Miami Rivers. Symmes advertised for settlers with some success, and within a short time the villages of Cincinnati, Columbia, and North Bend were founded in what came to be called the "Symmes tract." Like the Ohio Associates, Symmes was never able to buy all the land that he had contracted for, and the size of his tract had to be cut down materially.

Symmes

By 1790 the Northwest Territory had nearly forty-three hundred inhabitants — perhaps thirteen hundred in the vicinity of Cincinnati, a thousand at Marietta, and two thousand in the old French villages. There was need, therefore, of the government which, under the terms of the Ordinance of 1787, had accompanied the settlement. When Marietta was about three months old Arthur St. Clair had appeared as governor, and had instituted

Governor St. Clair

the type of autocratic rule that the Ordinance had made provision for during the period of sparse settlement. St. Clair's difficulties, however, were many and great. The inhabitants tended increasingly to resent his assumption of arbitrary powers, and the Indians, many of whom refused to concede that the land being settled was ever legally ceded to the whites, indulged freely in scalping parties and in other ways showed their hostility. To meet the Indian menace and to keep a watchful eye on the French in the Illinois country, St. Clair soon moved his capital to Cincinnati. The confederation period had ended, however, and the new government under the constitution was in effect before the Indian problem in the Northwest came to a head.

A serious problem of Anglo-American relations arose out of the fact that many of the British posts in the Northwest, despite the treaty of peace which gave the region south of the Great Lakes to the United States, were still held by British troops. The reason for this lay in the fact that the fur trade, upon the profits of which Canada depended so largely for its prosperity, desired to retain as long as possible the advantages it enjoyed in American territory. The military posts south of the lakes at Oswego, Niagara, Detroit, and elsewhere were sources of comfort and security to the fur-traders, as well as centers of anti-American influence among the Indians. It was important to the fur trade that the settlement of the Northwest be held back, for wherever settlers came in fur-bearing animals did not long survive. Every encouragement therefore was given to the Indians to resist the encroachments of the whites, and the presence of British soldiers, whom the Indians could regard as potential allies in their attacks upon the American pioneers, seemed to the fur-traders highly desirable. Among the Americans the retention of the Northwest posts by British garrisons, with an unmistakable tendency to give moral support to the Indians, was regarded as an inexcusable breach of faith.

The Northwest posts

Coupled with this failure of the British to live up to their treaty obligations was their **Trade with the British Empire** even more serious failure to take any steps toward the re-establishment of normal commercial relations with their former colonies. For the new nation trade with Great Britain, and with the British West Indies, was greatly to be desired. American trade had always flowed naturally to Great Britain, and once the interruption of war was at an end probably half of the American exports went once more to the mother country, while at least three fourths of the American imports were from British sources. But the treaty of 1783, generous as it was with respect to political matters, was not a treaty of commerce, and American shippers soon found that they could not always count on the same privileges in English ports that they had once been accorded. Particularly trying was the exclusion from English ports of American fish-oil and whale products. Americans found, too, that the British commercial policy which restrained the West Indies from purchasing outside the Empire, except in case of necessity, cut off a large share of what had been in colonial times a most lucrative trade. For example, citizens of the United States were no longer permitted to share in the West Indian carrying trade, or to send their surplus salt-meat and fish to the West Indies even in English vessels. The loss of these markets disrupted the famous "triangle" trade, and deprived the Americans of a traditional source of supply for the bills of exchange with which in colonial times they had been accustomed to redress their balances in London. It seemed essential, therefore, to secure a trade treaty with Great Britain which would put an end to discriminations against American commerce in British ports, and would reopen the West Indian markets to American products.

To deal with these problems of commerce and the frontier, John Adams was dispatched to London in 1785, but his mission failed miserably. As for the commercial treaty, it was apparent that the English could count on whatever American **Adams' mission to England** trade they wanted without it. Congress lacked the power to make or enforce any such trade discriminations as might have brought the English to terms, and Adams was taunted by the query, Did he represent one nation or thirteen? Indeed, many Englishmen believed that the new United States might yet see the error of their way and beg to be restored to their former status as British colonies. With reference to their retention of the Northwest posts the British had good excuses to offer. The treaty of peace had promised that no legal obstacles should stand in the way of the collection of private debts owing by Americans to British subjects before the war, but the debts nevertheless could not be collected. Furthermore, the persecution of Loyalists outlasted the war and the treaty, and the promised restoration of confiscated Loyalist property was virtually a dead letter. If the Americans themselves disregarded important clauses in the treaty of peace, how could they expect the British to do otherwise? In 1788 Adams returned to the United States with the objects of his mission wholly unobtained.

Scarcely less important than the difficulties with Great Britain were those that existed between the United **Spanish-American relations** States and Spain. There was the same problem of trade discrimination in Spanish ports that confronted the Americans when they sought entrance to British ports, and there was the same special need of a free interchange of commodities with the Spanish possessions of the West Indies as with the British. There was difficulty, too, about the Florida boundary, which in the British cession to Spain had been left undefined, and there was a complete difference of opinion with regard to the rights of American citizens to the free navigation of the Mississippi River. In this latter dispute, the American contention was based on a clause in the Treaty of 1783 between the United States and Great

Britain which gave to the citizens of both nations full freedom of navigation of the Mississippi River to its mouth. The Spanish contested the right of the English to grant any such privilege, for the lower Mississippi, by any interpretation of the international boundaries, lay wholly within Spanish territory.

The Mississippi The free navigation of the Mississippi River was a matter of great consequence to the growing settlements of the American West, for almost the sole outlet for western produce was by means of flatboats down the river to New Orleans. To cut off this trade, as the Spanish claimed they had a perfect right to do, was to strike a body blow at the growth of the West. This power the Spanish hoped to use in such a way as to give them control of the greater portion of the trans-Appalachian West. They let it be known through their agents, chief among whom was James Wilkinson, a former officer in the Revolutionary Army, that the western communities could find an easy solution for their difficulties by seceding from the United States and joining forces with the Spanish; and they negotiated directly with the United States government to secure its admission that the American claim to the navigation of the Mississippi was invalid. They also sought to restrain the too rapid growth of the American population by encouraging the southwestern Indians to resist the advance of the American frontier.

The Jay-Gardoqui negotiations The first Spanish minister to the United States, Don Diego de Gardoqui, arrived during the summer of 1785. John Jay, who in 1784 had been charged by Congress with the conduct of American foreign affairs, soon entered into negotiations with Gardoqui for a settlement of the outstanding difficulties between the two countries, and for the formulation of the trade treaty so much desired by the United States. It speedily became apparent to Jay that his country had very little with which to bargain. Threats of commercial discrimination or of war were of no avail; for in the one case Congress lacked the necessary power, and in the other the people lacked the will to fight. Jay therefore was tempted to secure what he could from a bargain that Gardoqui proposed whereby the United States should receive a favorable trade treaty in return for giving up for a period of twenty-five or thirty years its claim to the right of navigation of the lower Mississippi. Such an agreement would be of great value to the northeastern states, and, as Jay reasoned it out, would hardly damage the West, for that region, he supposed, was destined at best to grow very little in population during the next quarter-century.

Jay was able to secure the support of seven states in Congress for this compromise, but he needed nine, and so the negotiations came to nothing. The northern states, which would have profited most by the trade treaty, supported him; but the southern states, whose representatives knew better the problem of the West than the Northerners, voted the proposition down. Virginia was still in possession of Kentucky, so her western boundary reached the Mississippi; while North Carolina, South Carolina, and Georgia had not yet surrendered their claims to western lands. These states were thus vitally interested in the welfare of the West, and were opposed to a measure which might hamper its growth. They knew, too, that the independent spirit of the West would never brook such restraint as the treaty proposed, and would find a means to use the Mississippi even at the cost of secession from the United States.

The Confederation thus failed miserably in its dealings with England and Spain, and it showed an equal lack of ability in negotiating with other foreign powers. A few trade treaties were signed, notably those with Sweden and Prussia, but they turned out to be relatively unimportant to American commerce. The treaties with France and Holland, signed during the war, were maintained and renewed, but they too failed to attract American trade away from its normal pre-revolutionary channels, while the good relations between the United States and her former allies in the Revolutionary War were continually imperiled by the inability of the American government to pay its foreign debt.

The state governments were confronted by problems almost as difficult as those **State tariffs** which embarrassed Congress. They possessed the power to levy tariffs which Congress so much coveted, but its exercise by so many different agencies resulted in serious complications. Promptly at the close of the Revolution, British merchants began to unload their excess goods upon the American market, almost regardless of price. American manufactures were ruined, and retaliatory tariffs were demanded. But to secure genuine retaliation, thirteen different sets of tariff regulations would have had to be brought into general agreement, and nothing of the sort could be done. Imports tended to arrive at the ports of low-tariff states rather than high-tariff states, with smuggling as an inevitable concomitant. Rhode Island, for example, profited greatly from the fact that her tariff was relatively low, whereas the tariffs of some of her neighboring states, especially New York, were relatively high. Endless confusion and much bad feeling was added by the states' levying duties against each other. New York taxed farm produce from New Jersey at a very high rate, and New Jersey in retaliation taxed a lighthouse built by the New-Yorkers on Sandy Hook. Connecticut taxed goods from Massachusetts more than she would have taxed the same goods if imported from England.

Then, too, the financial difficulties of the states actually rivaled those of the central government. Much of this **Paper money** trouble came from the almost inevitable tendency to resort to paper-money issues. This was nothing new to America, for before the Revolution the colonies had frequently yielded to a similar temptation, and had resented deeply the efforts of the British government to restrict their activities along this line; one might almost say that the Revolution was caused in part by a difference of opinion between the mother country and the colonies on the paper-money question. During the Confederation period the lack of gold in the United States, always a chronic complaint of the continental colonies, became an acute menace. Neither gold nor silver was mined anywhere within the United States; hard money was difficult to obtain from the Spanish colonies in the West Indies because of the existing restrictions on commerce; the reward of privateering that had brought

Foreign Affairs for the new government established by the Articles of Confederation were conducted from this building on Sixth Street, Philadelphia. Watercolor sketch after C. A. Poulson.

some precious metals into the country during the Revolution could no longer be reaped; and the gold left by the British army was soon drained off to meet an unfavorable balance of trade. Furthermore, the debtor classes within each state, more articulate than ever as a result of the Revolution, urged paper money because of the blessings that an inflated currency would bring to them; and in many states the more conservative propertied classes, who opposed inflation, were outvoted.

The records of Rhode Island and Massachusetts on the paper-money question give **Trevett vs. Weeden** a fair understanding of the situation. In Rhode Island the paper-money faction got the upper hand in the legislature, and multiplied issues until the currency was almost valueless; then, when "legal-tender" paper money was refused, passed a law making its refusal a punishable offense without so much as requiring a trial by jury for the offender. The attempt to enforce this law led to one of the most important judicial decisions in American legal history, for in the case of *Trevett vs. Weeden* the state supreme court held that the law just cited was out of harmony with the Rhode Island charter and therefore unconstitutional. This decision was attacked by the legislature, which summoned the judges before it and voted unsatisfactory the defense of their action that they made. Furthermore, at the next election three out of the four judges concerned were retired. But the precedent set was not overthrown, and the later power of the courts over legislation which they deemed unconstitutional owed much to this decision.

In Massachusetts the contest over paper money took the form of a test of strength **Shays' Rebellion** between the coast towns, which were relatively prosperous from what commerce still endured, and the small farmers of the interior, who found it difficult during the prevailing hard times to pay their debts and taxes. As a measure of debt relief the rural classes demanded liberal paper-money issues, but the legislature was under the control of the coast towns and refused to comply with the farmer's demands. Instead, heavy taxes were levied to pay off the war debt, and sheriffs' sales were multiplied. In the summer of 1786 open rebellion broke out. Bands of insurgents, composed of farmers, artisans, and laborers, marched on the courts in several districts and prevented them from sitting. Daniel Shays, a veteran of Bunker Hill, with an insurgent army of about two thousand men forced an adjournment of the court at Springfield and made wild threats. "My boys," said one of his men, "you are going to fight for liberty. If you wish to know what liberty is, I will tell you. It is for every man to do what he pleases, to make other people do as you please to have them, and to keep folks from serving the devil." Shays' Rebellion, as this outbreak was called, was put down by militia led by General Lincoln and paid by means of a loan to which well-to-do citizens, fearful that a wholesale attack upon property rights was imminent, subscribed generously. But the enduring power of the debtor classes was demonstrated in the next state election when Governor Bowdoin, under whom the "Rebellion" had been suppressed, was defeated for re-election by John Hancock, who was still the idol of the radicals.

Not only in Rhode Island and Massachusetts, but in practically all the states the conservative property owners **Growth of radicalism** were genuinely frightened by the growing power of the agrarian and unpropertied classes. The new state constitutions, while by no means radical documents, had added much to the power of the masses, and the Revolution itself had unsettled traditional habits of deference to those in authority. Extremists reasoned that if it had been right and proper to revolt against England because of one type of tyranny, it was now equally right and proper to revolt against local governments or practices that seemed equally tyrannical. If debts owing to British merchants could be legislated out of existence, why not also debts owing to American merchants? Grievances that

John Hancock, a rich Boston merchant, was President of the Continental Congress when the Declaration of Independence was adopted. Portrait by John Singleton Copley, 1765.

ever; it could not regulate commerce; it had no taxing power; and it was at best a mere creature of the states utterly incapable of acting directly upon individuals. Worst of all, amendments to the Articles of Confederation required a unanimous vote, and experience seemed to prove that on this account any strictly legal change would be impossible. Clearly a stronger central government was needed, and toward that end the propertied classes began to direct their efforts. Such men as Alexander Hamilton, Peletiah Webster, and Governor Bowdoin openly proclaimed their belief in the necessity of a closer and more powerful union.

Nor was this agitation confined merely to words. In the spring of 1785 a joint commission composed of delegates from Virginia and Maryland met at Alexandria, Virginia, to find a way out of the perplexing difficulties **The conference at Alexandria** that had arisen between the two states because of conflicting regulations with regard to navigation of Chesapeake Bay and the Potomac River. This proposition greatly interested George Washington, who as the owner of perhaps thirty thousand acres of western lands hoped especially for improvements in the navigation of the Potomac that would make it a better highway to the West, and at Washington's invitation the convention adjourned to Mount Vernon. On the particular points at issue the two states reached an agreement, but the legislature of Maryland suggested that a conference on commercial matters that would include the neighboring states of Pennsylvania and Delaware might achieve even greater results. This idea found support from the Virginia legislature, which promptly issued a call for such a convention to meet at Annapolis the first Monday in September, 1786. The Virginia call, however, was not restricted to the four states suggested by Maryland; instead every one of the thirteen states was invited to send delegates.

Nine states named representatives to attend the Annapolis Convention, but from only five, Virginia, Delaware, Pennsylva-

might ordinarily be overlooked were magnified because of the existing hard times and unemployment, and a spirit of discontent bordering faintly on anarchy was abroad in the land. Acts of violence, such as boycotts, tea-parties, the terrorizing of tax-collectors, had characterized the outbreak of the Revolution; Shays' Rebellion indicated that more of the same thing, this time directed against the upper classes in America, might be in store.

Confronted by this menacing situation, conservative men of property began to cast about for some means of checking the democratic tendencies that were so painfully in evidence. **Demands for strong government** What seemed to be needed was a government strong enough to maintain order at home and if possible also to protect American rights abroad. Clearly the state governments could not be trusted to do these things; their authority was limited, and in some cases the lower classes already had control. As for the central government, its impotence under the Articles of Confederation was abundantly demonstrated. It was without an effective executive, and its feeble gropings in that direction had so far proved unavailing; it had no judiciary whatnia, New Jersey, and New York, did the delegates chosen actually attend.

The Annapolis Convention

With the representation so inadequate it soon became apparent that the convention could make little progress with the matter it had in hand, but it nevertheless managed to do something very much more important. It adopted a report from the able pen of Alexander Hamilton which pointed out some of the conspicuous defects in the Articles of Confederation and called upon the states to send delegates to a new convention through which a remedy for these defects should be sought. The date set for the new convention was the second Monday in May, 1787, and the place of meeting suggested was Philadelphia. Hamilton represented the extreme conservative opinion of the country and sincerely hoped for a strong central government that would represent the propertied classes, but he dared not in this document openly advocate the overthrow of the Confederation. His report merely suggested that the convention confine its efforts to such provisions as seemed necessary "to render the constitution of the federal government adequate to the exigencies of the union." He also pointed out, by way of assuring the radical element, that whatever amendments to the articles were adopted at Philadelphia would have to be submitted to all the states for their approval.

Hamilton's proposal was transmitted not only to the various state legislatures, but

Another convention called

also to Congress, and on February 21, 1787, the latter body joined in the call for the Philadelphia Convention. In doing so, however, Congress stated that the purpose of the convention was merely to propose amendments to the existing Articles of Confederation. The clear inference was that only by the subsequent ratification of all the thirteen states could any such amendments be adopted. It is interesting to note that ultimately the convention disregarded this interpretation of its mission, and submitted a new constitution which, instead of awaiting the unanimous consent that the Articles of Confederation would have required, was to take effect when ratified by only nine of the thirteen states. It is also interesting to note that there is no way of demonstrating that the complete abandonment of the Articles of Confederation was necessary to the attainment of a vigorous national government. Could the existing Congress have been assured more power over commerce and an adequate revenue, it is possible that the other defects would have been remedied with the passage of time. The heads of the executive departments, already established or to be established, might eventually have become a responsible cabinet, and the development in the United States of the same type of parliamentary government that was already beginning to operate in England and was later to become so common elsewhere might not have been so effectively and perhaps unfortunately forestalled. Indeed, the old government under the Articles of Confederation, with all its defects, might not have been so unsuccessful had the times been prosperous. But with the country in the depths of an economic depression all through the period of its existence, the Confederation government had no chance to show what it could do under normal circumstances.

Many of those who were most interested in making the Philadelphia convention a success were yet skeptical of its outcome. Forces had long been at work, however, to insure

Forces making for union

that ultimately the hope of a stronger union would be realized. The very isolation from the rest of the world that the thirteen American states shared with one another tended to force them together. Their inhabitants were for the most part of a common racial stock, spoke a common language, read much the same books, and had inherited practically the same traditions. Every part of the new nation had, at some time not far removed, gone through the frontier process — a process which did not differ markedly from place to place or from time to time, and tended therefore to supply a common mold for the formation of American traits. The frontier of the 1780's itself acted as a binding tie. In the mountain valleys of the Appalachians and in the new communities still farther to the west there was a continual mingling of settlers from many different states and even from the Old World. Here state boundaries were freely passed, and old loyalties were soon forgotten. Democratic frontiersmen might fear for the moment the attempt of an aristocratic group in the East to form and dominate a strong central government, but potentially at least the West was inescapably nationalistic.

Moreover, the problems that faced the American states were increasingly national in character. The conflicting interests of debtors and creditors cut across state lines. In the back country the debtor point of view dominated; along the coast the creditors tended to maintain their control. Commerce vied with agriculture, but most of the states were neither strictly commercial nor strictly agricultural; the commercial classes everywhere tended to present a solid front against an almost equally united agricultural interest. Even in matters pertaining to religion there was a tendency to divide along national rather than along state or local lines. In the East adherents of the old settled faiths, Congregationalists in New England, Quakers in Pennsylvania, Dutch Calvinists in New York, and Episcopalians in the South, found themselves drawn together in defense of the old ways against hordes of upstart Presbyterians, Methodists, and Baptists, who challenged church establishments wherever they found them, overturned timeworn customs, and demanded complete religious freedom as the right of every man. Such common problems as these revealed lines of cleavage within the nation as a whole rather than within the individual states. Efforts to solve these problems nationally tended to draw together radicals from every state and section no less than conservatives, and to prophesy the speedy formation of a closer union.

Bibliography

Most of the books listed for the preceding chapter are applicable also to this. On the western settlements F. J. Turner, *The Significance of Sections in American History* (1932), has a chapter on "Western State-Making in the Revolutionary Era." Justin Winsor, *The Westward Movement* (1897), recounts the course of events, but misses some of its significance. S. C. Williams, *History of the Lost State of Franklin* (1924), tells of the political transformations that befell the Watauga settlements. Biographic studies of pertinence to the same area are J. R. Gilmore, *John Sevier as a Commonwealth Builder* (1887); and F. M. Turner, *Life of General John Sevier* (1910). R. M. McElroy, *Kentucky in the Nation's History* (1909), contains chapters on the period of early settlement, and the statehood movement. F. A. Ogg, *The Old Northwest* (1919), is a sprightly but rather thin account of settlement north of the Ohio. B. A. Hinsdale, *The Old Northwest* (1888), is principally concerned with legal and constitutional beginnings. Beverly W. Bond, Jr., *The Civilization of the Old Northwest* (1934), contains much social history. Walter Havighurst, *Land of Promise; The Story of the Northwest Territory* (1946), is a recent attempt at synthesis. An excellent state history that begins with this period is *The History of the State of Ohio*, edited by Carl Wittke (6 vols., 1941–44). Of great importance, also, is the monumental collection edited by C. E. Carter, *The Territorial Papers of the United States* (17 vols., 1934–50). Louise P. Kellogg, *The British Regime in Wisconsin and the Northwest* (1935), covers in scholarly fashion the period from the French and Indian War to the War of 1812.

On the important subject of the public lands, one should refer to Herbert B. Adams, *Maryland's Influence upon Land Cessions to the United States* (1885). Amelia C. Ford, *Colonial Precedents of our National Land System as it Existed in 1800* (1910), is a study of basic importance. P. J. Treat, *The National Land System, 1785–1820* (1910), covers in great detail the subject of early land disposals. Two excellent general accounts deal with the whole history of our national land policy: B. H. Hibbard, *A History of the Public Land Policies* (1924); and R. M. Robbins, *Our Landed Heritage: The Public Domain, 1776–1936* (1942). J. A. Barrett, *Evolution of the Ordinance of 1787* (1891), is a useful study that, unfortunately, is available in only a few libraries.

On the diplomatic history of the Confederation see the general histories listed on page 148; also L. M. Sears, *A History of American Foreign Relations* (1938); and J. W. Foster, *A Century of American Diplomacy* (1900). On Spanish-American relations during this period, consult A. P. Whitaker, *The Spanish-American Frontier, 1783–1795* (1927); F. A. Ogg, *The Opening of the Mississippi* (1904); *Spain in the Mississippi Valley*, edited by Lawrence Kinnaird (3 vols., 1946–1949). E. W. Lyon, *Louisiana in French Diplomacy, 1589–1804* (1934); Caroline M. Burson, *The Stewardship of Don Esteban Miró, 1782–1792* (1940). On diplomatic relations with Great Britain, Adams gives an account of his fruitless mission to England in *The Works of John Adams*, edited by C. F. Adams (10 vols., 1850–56), III.

See also such special accounts as R. C. Downes, *Council Fires on the Upper Ohio* (1940); and, by the same author, *Frontier Ohio, 1788–1803* (1935); A. L. Burt, *The United States, Great Britain, and British North America from the Revolution to the Establishment of Peace after the War of 1812* (1940); Arthur B. Darling, *Our Rising Empire, 1763–1803* (1940); Wayne E. Stevens, *The Northwest Fur Trade, 1763–1800* (1928); Ida A. Johnson, *The Michigan Fur Trade* (1919); Nelson V. Russell, *The British Régime in Michigan and the Old Northwest* (1939).

On financial problems of the Confederation, consult, in addition to the general works on the period, D. R. Dewey, *Financial History of the United States* (1903, 12th ed., 1936). This book has gone through numerous editions, and still retains its usefulness. General economic histories all have chapters on the Confederation: H. U. Faulkner, *American Economic History* (1949); F. A. Shannon, *America's Economic Growth* (1940); R. C. McGrane, *The Economic Development of the American Nation* (1950). A contemporary view of Shays's Rebellion is given by George R. Minot, *The History of the Insurrections in Massachusetts in the Year 1786* (1788).

11

The Constitution

By THE end of the Confederation Period the line of cleavage in the new nation between **Classes in America** the possessors of considerable property and the common people was clearly drawn. The merchants and importers, the shipbuilders and shipowners, the possessors of landed estates, the speculators and money-lenders were set apart by their economic interests from the small farmers, the artisans, and the nonpropertied classes generally. Among men of property the fear had grown almost to the proportions of panic that the lower classes would eventually secure control of all the state governments (as they already seemed to have done in Rhode Island), and that as a result property interests everywhere would suffer perhaps even to the point of confiscation. Out of this state of mind came the agitation in favor of a strong central government — a government which would be independent of state control, and would possess the will and the power to protect the rights of property. The movement for the Philadelphia Convention was thus primarily an upper-class affair, and when the time came for the choice of delegates it was the interested upper class that determined the selections.

Fortunately for the well-to-do, the call for the Philadelphia Convention did not designate the method by which delegates should be chosen, and the selections were made, therefore, by the various state **Conservatism of the** legislatures, in most of which the **delegates** men of property still had comfortable majorities. Rhode Island refused to choose delegates, but from the other states a total of seventy-three men were elected, of whom only fifty-five ever put in their appearance at the convention. These men were typical representatives of the conservative upper class. They were almost without exception men of financial and social standing, well prepared for their labors by education and by previous governmental experience. One may fairly say that the small-farmer-artisan class was not represented in the convention at all.

When May 14, 1787, the day for opening the convention arrived, there were too few present to organize, but on May **Philadelphia** 25 twenty-nine delegates met in **Convention** Independence Hall and chose George Washington to be their presiding officer. For three and a half months the sessions continued, usually with not many more in attendance than appeared the first day. The convention at once decided that, to promote freedom of discussion and to avoid outside interference, its sessions must be held behind closed doors and all proceedings carefully guarded from the public. This decision was adhered to with great consistency. Indeed, only the barest details of business were recorded in the official journal kept by the convention, and for a more intimate account of what went on the historian must turn to the notes kept by individual members, particularly to James Madison's *Journal* in which the Virginia delegate recorded a careful summary of every important speech he heard.

The seriousness of the situation in which the conservative men of property felt themselves to be probably had much to do with the care they exercised in their choice of delegates. Undoubtedly, the best men they could send to the convention were actually chosen to go. The presiding officer, George Washington, was even then probably the most respected and revered of Americans. Benjamin Franklin had for many years been known as America's most distinguished scientist and literary light. Alexander Hamilton, in spite of his youth, had already exhibited genius of high order in the realm of finance. Of nearly every delegate who sat in the convention something similar could be said. The list included George Mason and Edmund Randolph of Virginia, James Wilson and Gouverneur Morris of Pennsylvania, Charles Pinckney and Charles Cotesworth Pinckney of South Carolina, Roger Sherman and Oliver Ellsworth of Connecticut, John Dickinson of Delaware, Luther Martin of Maryland, and William Paterson of New Jersey.

Leaders in the convention

These men had little faith in democracy; indeed, one might almost say that it was their fear of democracy that had brought them together. Their problem was how to make a government democratic enough to be adopted but not so democratic as to constitute any menace to upper-class control. Again and again during the convention this attitude on the part of the delegates found forceful expression. Once when Roger Sherman was protesting against the election of members of the House of Representatives by direct vote of the people he remarked that "the people imme-

Fear of democracy

diately should have as little to do as may be about the government." Elbridge Gerry held that the evils from which the country suffered were due mainly to an "excess of democracy." Edmund Randolph, the brilliant young governor of Virginia, took occasion to deplore the turbulence and follies of democracy. John Dickinson felt that a limited monarchy was "one of the best governments of the world," and hoped that the Senate might be made "as nearly as may be like the House of Lords of England." Such statements could be multiplied almost at will.

The convention was quick to conclude that the mere strengthening of the Articles of Confederation would never produce the kind of government desired by men of property. It decided, therefore, without much hesitation, to form an entirely new constitution. Some writers tend to feature the differences of opinion that developed in the convention and to emphasize chiefly the difficulty with which decisions were reached. It is true enough that many conflicting views had to be reconciled, and that innumerable compromises had to be made. But an even more striking fact is that on so many of the essentials the delegates were in almost complete accord. They agreed perfectly as to the fundamental ends that the new government was to accomplish; they accepted with little debate many of the precedents set by the English Constitution and by the constitutions of the new states; and they evinced a remarkable willingness to arrange compromises on all matters of minor detail.

It was not easy, however, to adjust the relative weight of states and nation in the new government. The extreme nationalistic point of view was embodied in the so-called Virginia Plan, which had resulted from the daily meetings of the Virginia delegation. The plan proposed a two-house legislature, the lower house to be chosen by the people of the several states in such a manner as to give small states like Delaware and Rhode Island only one representative and large states like

The Virginia Plan

Adoption of the Constitution at the convention in Philadelphia, September 17, 1787. Washington, the presiding officer, is shown at the right in this 19th century reconstruction of the scene, painted by J. B. Stearns.

Massachusetts and Virginia sixteen or seventeen representatives, and the upper house to be chosen by the lower house. Separate executive and judicial departments were to be established, but the holders of both executive and judicial offices were to be selected by the legislature, which would also be given authority to veto state laws out of harmony with its own. The two obvious defects in this plan from the small-state point of view were the absence of any provisions guaranteeing the equality of states, and the uncertainty that the small states would secure any representation whatever in the upper house of the legislature. Moreover, the Virginia Plan really implied the formation of a consolidated national government which could and probably would relegate the states to the position of mere administrative units. The Virginia Plan was presented to the convention May 29 in a brilliant speech by Edmund Randolph, and for two weeks clause by clause was earnestly debated.

This debate served to bring out the most important line of cleavage that the convention **Large states vs. small** developed. The Virginia Plan satisfied the large states, Virginia, Pennsylvania, and Massachusetts, fairly well, and was supported also by North Carolina, South Carolina, and Georgia, states

in which the possibilities of growth were great. But the small states, New Jersey, Delaware, Maryland, Connecticut, and New York (which then meant little more than the Hudson Valley) were profoundly agitated at the prospect of large-state tyranny, and feared even that the small states might ultimately lose their separate identity. Thanks to the system of voting by states in the convention, the small states had great weight in the deliberations; indeed, but for the failure of Rhode Island to send delegates and the tardy participation of New Hampshire, whose representatives did not arrive until July 23, the small states would have been in the majority. It was natural enough, therefore, that they should present a plan of their own as a substitute for the plan suggested by the Virginians.

The small-state point of view finally found expression in a report by William Paterson of New Jersey, commonly called **The New** the New Jersey Plan. It pro- **Jersey Plan** posed to retain the states as equal, and perhaps sovereign, units. There would be no change in the organization of Congress, although a genuine executive and an independent judiciary were contemplated; but the powers of Congress were to be expanded to include the right to levy tariffs, to regulate commerce, and to force a state to pay requisitions made upon it by the central government. The New Jersey Plan was debated for a week, and then, to the great chagrin of its defenders, was set aside. The small-state men did not leave the convention, however, but sought instead to modify the Virginia Plan, to which the convention now recurred, in such a way as to emphasize the federal rather than the strictly national idea.

Ultimately a solution was found which in a measure, at least, satisfied both parties. The "Great Compromise" In accordance with the Virginia Plan the convention voted to establish a two-house legislature, with the membership of the lower house to be apportioned according to population. It then left to a committee on compromise the composition of the upper chamber. This committee, upon which sat some of the ablest men of the convention, including Franklin, finally recommended that the national character of the lower house, whose membership was to be apportioned among the various states according to population, should be offset by an upper house in which the states should be equally represented, two members to be chosen by each state. On July 16 this report was accepted by the convention, and the "Great Compromise," so called, became a fact. Thereafter the suspicions that had kept the large states and the small states so far apart tended to disappear. Ultimately it was decided that representatives of the lower house should be elected by the people for a period of two years, and that two senators were to be chosen for six-year terms by the state legislature in every state.

There remained, however, many adjustments to be made, and one may say that The "Three-Fifths" Compromise almost every line of the constitution that was written came as the result of some compromise. Even on the matter of representation in the lower house a serious dispute arose. Should the slaves, so numerous in some of the southern states, be counted in apportioning the number of representatives to which the states were entitled? Or should these slaves be regarded as property rather than persons? These questions were the more perplexing in view of the fact that the convention had already agreed to assess direct taxes upon the states in accordance with the population. The northern states were unwilling to allow the South to count its slaves in determining the representation a state should have in the lower house of Congress, but desired to count them when direct taxes were to be assessed; the South, on the other hand, wished to count its slaves when the question of representation in Congress was up, but not when taxes were to be levied. A reasonable, if utterly illogical, solution was found in the decision to count five slaves as equal to three whites both in the apportionment of representatives and in the assessing of direct taxes.

During the debate that led to the "Three-Fifths" Compromise the question of the part that new western states were to Provision for new states be allowed to play in the new government also came to the fore. Gouverneur Morris argued earnestly that the rule of representation ought to be so fixed as to secure to the Atlantic states a prevalence for all time in the national councils. The new frontier states, he said, would know less of the public interest than the old, and in particular might involve the nation in wars with the Indians and with neighboring nations that would have to be paid for by the maritime states. Representing as he did the conservative property-holding classes of the East, Morris maintained that if the untutored and irresponsible small farmers of the West got the power into their hands, they would ruin the Atlantic interests. Even Elbridge Gerry of Massachusetts, one of the least conservative members of the convention, feared that the Westerners, if they were given the opportunity, might use it to "oppress commerce and drain out wealth into the Western Country." He suggested that the number of representatives to be chosen from the West should never exceed the number chosen by the Atlantic states.

Fortunately for the good of the country and for the permanence of the constitution, the narrow view expressed by Morris and Gerry did not prevail. Instead, the convention took the advice of Wilson of Pennsylvania, who insisted that "the majority of people, wherever found, ought in all questions to govern the minority. If the interior Country should acquire this majority, it will not only have the right, but will avail itself of it whether we will or no. This jealously misled the policy of Great Britain with regard to America." Probably, however, many members of the convention comforted themselves with the thought to which Roger Sherman gave expression, that the number of future states would probably never exceed that of the existing states anyway.

The sectional character of the dispute over representation came out again when the convention discussed the extent to which Congress should have authority over commerce. The northern states, in which commerce was a dominant interest, were ready to clothe Congress with ample regulatory power, but some of the southern states feared that this power might be used to revive the tyranny that England had been guilty of in passing the Acts of Trade. If, for example, Congress should require that all American products should be carried in American-built and American-manned ships, it would greatly stimulate the shipbuilding and commercial interests of the northern states, but it would almost certainly increase the expense and the difficulty of the agricultural South's getting its produce to market. Some of the southern states, particularly Georgia and South Carolina, were also concerned lest Congress might tax heavily or even forbid the importation of slaves, and thus strike at what in their section was still believed to be an essential labor supply; consequently they insisted that there should be no tax on exports or upon "such persons" as the several states should "think proper to admit," and they demanded that navigation acts should be passed only by a two-thirds vote of both houses of Congress. To resolve

these differences, the northern states yielded to the South on the prohibition of export duties, and agreed also that the importation of slaves should not be forbidden before the year 1808, although Congress might levy a tax of ten dollars per head for each person imported. The southern states, thus reassured, gave up their insistence on a two-thirds vote in Congress for the passage of navigation acts.

The convention early decided that the national government should have only "enumerated powers"; hence one of the most important sections of the Constitution was that which listed the powers of Congress. In this enumeration many provisions of the old Articles of Confederation were taken over almost intact. Such, for example, were those which authorized Congress to borrow money on the credit of the United States, to declare war, to maintain an army and navy, and to establish post-offices and post-roads. Extremely significant, however, were the new powers, especially those which gave Congress authority to lay and collect taxes, duties, imposts, and excises, to regulate commerce with foreign nations and among the several states, to pass naturalization and bankruptcy laws, and "to make all laws which shall be necessary and proper for carrying into execution the foregoing powers." The last-mentioned provision, spoken of later as the "elastic clause" of the Constitution, made it possible to stretch the grants of power specifically enumerated to lengths that the members of the constitutional convention would scarcely have deemed possible. To insure obedience to the central government, Congress was also authorized to provide for the calling forth of the militia to execute the laws of the Union and to suppress insurrections and repel invasions.

Hardly less important than the delegation of powers to the national government was the withdrawal of certain powers from the states. States were forbidden to coin money, to emit bills of credit, to make anything but gold and silver legal tender in payment of debts, to have direct relations with foreign countries, to levy duties on imports or exports (without the consent of Congress), "to pass any bill of attainder, ex post facto law, or law impairing the obligation of contracts, or grant any title of nobility." Most of these provisions were designed to prevent the radical non-propertied classes, in case they should win control in any of the states, from passing legislation hostile to the interests of the propertied classes. For example, while the national government was left free to print paper money, and even to declare it legal tender, the states were expressly forbidden to exercise these powers.

Following closely Montesquieu's interpretation of the English Constitution and **The separation of powers** the actual practice of government in the American colonies and states, the delegates to the Philadelphia Convention agreed without hesitation to the principle that the legislative, executive, and judicial powers of government ought to be separated as completely as possible. Bent as they were upon establishing a powerful central government, they therefore assigned to the executive and to the judiciary powers that compared well with the powers of the legislature. Indeed, it was an old theory that each of the three branches of government should be strong enough to act as an effective check or balance to the others, and that in this fashion the danger of tyranny or error on the part of any one should be measurably cut down.

The creation of an executive department caused the convention a great deal of trouble. **The executive** Extreme conservatives were in favor of a single executive chosen by Congress for life, or at least for a very long term. Some, however, felt that such a plan was too closely akin to monarchy, and argued for a plural executive, or at least for short terms and frequent elections. The idea of a plural executive was quite out of harmony with British and American experience, and was quickly voted down; but many delegates held that the possibility of re-election might stimulate an executive to faithful performance of his duties. The objection to frequent elections was that in case Congress thus held the right to continue the executive in office or to dismiss him, his independence would vanish. Obviously the method of escape from this dilemma was to find some way to elect the executive other than by vote of Congress. Popular election seemed the natural alternative, but the judgment of the people was sorely distrusted by the great majority of the delegates, and this idea was hastily thrust aside. Election by popularly chosen electors suffered from the objection that such a system would give undue power to the large states, and was also voted down.

For a time it seemed as if the long-term system with election by Congress would have to be adopted, but toward the **The electoral college** close of the convention a way out was discovered. A committee appointed to solve the problem reported in favor of a modified electoral system, and the committee report, somewhat amended, went into the Constitution. The President was to be chosen for a term of four years, and was to be eligible for re-election. As many electors were to be named in each state as the state had senators and representatives, and the method of choosing the electors was to be left for each state to determine for itself. The electors were to vote for two candidates for President, and if anyone should receive the votes of a majority of the electors he was to be declared elected, while the candidate receiving the next highest number of votes, whether a majority or not, was to become Vice-President. It was assumed, however, that unless there were some outstanding candidate, such as in the first election General Washington was sure to be, an election by a majority of the electoral college would be impossible, and each state delegation would merely cast its vote for some favorite son. To meet this contingency it was provided that in case the electoral college failed to choose a President, the duty should devolve upon the House of Representatives, where for this purpose each delegation might have only one vote. This arrangement involved a subtle compromise. Since the House could choose only from the five highest names on the list voted for by the electors, it appeared that the large states would ordinarily nominate the candidates, while the more numerous small states would hold the balance of power in the election to follow. The committee report left this choice to the Senate, but because so many powers had already been conferred upon that body it was decided that the election of the President should be the prerogative of the House, voting by states. Needless to say, the delegates failed completely to foresee the subsequent practice of presidential elections.

There was little hesitation about granting extensive powers to the President. He was **Powers of the President** made the commander-in-chief of the army and navy and also of the state militia whenever it was called into national service; he had the power to make treaties with foreign nations "by and with the advice and consent of the Senate . . . provided two-thirds of the Senators present concur"; he could with the consent of the majority in the Senate name ambassadors, ministers, consuls, judges of the federal courts, and all the other officers of the United States not otherwise provided for; he might call Congress into extraordinary session when he believed such a session necessary; he must "take care that the laws be faithfully executed"; and he had the right to veto bills passed by Congress, with the qualification that a two-thirds vote of both houses might make the bill a law without the President's signature. As a safeguard against executive usurpation or other misbehavior a method of impeachment was devised, with the House bringing the indictment and the Senate sitting as a court. A two-thirds majority of the Senate was required to convict and remove from office.

The importance of a federal judiciary was **The judiciary** not underestimated, but there was surprisingly little debate on the subject during the convention, and the section on the judiciary that was finally written is very brief. That there should be a supreme court was generally agreed, but many believed that the existence of state courts made inferior federal courts unnecessary. This difference of opinion was compromised by providing merely that Congress might establish inferior courts if it chose to do so, but nothing was put into the Constitution to require their establishment. The appointment of judges occasioned some debate, and at first was made the duty of the Senate; later it was decided that the President should have the right to appoint them, subject to confirmation by the Senate. The judicial power of the federal courts was so defined as to extend to all cases arising under the Constitution, the laws of Congress, and the treaties to which the United States was a party; to all cases affecting ambassadors, other public ministers, and consuls; to all cases of admiralty and maritime jurisdiction; to controversies to which the United States was a party; and to controversies between two or more states, between a state and citizens of another state, and between citizens of different states. The supreme court was given original jurisdiction over cases affecting foreign ministers and cases to which a state was party; otherwise its jurisdiction was appellate only.

Curiously, the Constitution itself says nothing with regard to the power which the judiciary soon assumed of de- **Judicial review** claring invalid such laws as in its opinion were contrary to the Constitution — a power which ultimately was to become the most characteristic feature of the American judiciary, as well as its most effective weapon. It was plainly stated, however, that "the constitution, and the laws of the United States which shall be made in pursuance thereof; and all treaties, made or which shall be made, under the authority of the United States, shall be the supreme law of the land; and the judges in every state shall be bound thereby, anything in the constitution or laws of any state to the contrary notwithstanding." Many leading members of the Philadelphia Convention felt that the federal judges would as a matter of course have the right of declaring null and void laws out of harmony with the Constitution, and so expressed themselves time and time again during the debates. To James Madison, for example, it seemed perfectly obvious that "a law violating a Constitution established by the people themselves, would be considered by the judges as null and void." Indeed, a proposition to give the supreme court a qualified veto over laws of Congress was voted down partly because the federal judges would probably exert some such authority anyway. Thus the doctrine of judicial review can hardly be regarded as the usurpation of a power that the framers of the Constitution never intended the courts to exercise.

The three-headed system of government, with its separate legislature, executive,

Checks on democracy and judiciary, provided numerous opportunities for preventing those excesses of democracy which were so much feared by the framers of the Constitution. The powerful judiciary was designed to act as a check on the President and Congress, while the executive would also check the legislature, and the legislature the executive. A number of provisions for the direct operation of this principle were written in; such, for example, as the power given the Senate to reject treaties and appointments made by the President, and the right of the President to exercise a qualified veto over the acts of Congress.

Democracy was still further qualified by the insistent emphasis upon the representa-

The representative principle tive principle in the new government. As little as might be was left to the people themselves to do; and the powers of government were handed over instead to representatives removed once or twice from the popular will. The judges were appointed by the President for life, the President was elected by electors who might be chosen directly by the people, but if the legislature of a state so determined might be chosen indirectly; the Senate was chosen by the legislatures of the various states; the only officers of the central government chosen directly by the people were the members of the House of Representatives. Probably some qualifications on the right of citizens to vote would also have been set up had it not seemed necessary to leave this matter to the states themselves. Because of the great variety of election laws in the several states, it was finally decided that in choosing representatives to seats in the national House the qualifications for voters should be the same as were set up by a given state for the election of the most numerous branch of its legislature. In time this particular clause came to have a decidedly leavening influence, for as the suffrage was widened in the states the qualifications of those who could vote for members of the national House of Representatives were correspondingly scaled down. Nevertheless the national government was designed to be, and to this day remains, a representative system. The people have the right to vote; but their representatives make and execute the laws. In theory, at least, and probably also in fact these representatives of the people were supposed to be even more conservative than the voters who chose them, and thus, according to the framers of the Constitution, more trustworthy and dependable.

While from the American point of view the Constitution was, and was meant to be, an eminently conservative docu- **Radical** ment, when compared with the **features** forms of government that existed in the rest of the world it fell little short of radicalism. It continued the doctrine of popular sovereignty that had formed the philosophic background of the American Revolution, and was yet to find support from the results of the French Revolution. Thus in a day when nearly every other government adhered to the principle of monarchy, with its implied belief in the divine right of kings, the American government was strictly republican in form. Unique also was the effort to establish a dual or federal type of government. Undoubtedly the framers of the Constitu-

Beheld'a Fabric now to Freedom *rear'd,*
Approv'd by Friends, and ev'n by Foes revrd,
Where Justice*,too,and* Peace*,by us ador'd,*
Shall heal each Wrong,and keep ensheath'd the Sword
Approach then, Concord, fair Columbia's Son,
And faithful Clio, write that WE ARE ONE.

A salute to the unity achieved by the states
through the Constitution. An allegorical cartoon
from *The Columbian Magazine,* 1788.

tion believed in the divisibility of sovereignty, and they sought to hand over certain
sovereign powers to the federal government
while retaining for the states certain other
sovereign powers. Time proved that either
the nation or the states must be supreme,
and ultimately a civil war had to be fought
to decide the issue. But the attempt to establish two entirely separate agencies of government, each operating upon the same individuals, turned out to be as successful as it
was unusual. Furthermore, the federal Constitution, like the state constitutions, took
cognizance of the reserved rights of individuals upon which government might not
tread. Since the central government was
designed to be one of strictly specified powers, it was not deemed necessary to include

an extensive bill of rights such as had characterized the early state constitutions. But
such specifications as that the privilege of
the writ of habeas corpus should not ordinarily be suspended, and that bills of attainder and ex post facto laws should not be
passed, showed the same determination to
set limits beyond which in its dealing with
individuals the government might not go.
Early amendments to the Constitution went
much further in the direction of stating
definitely the "rights of man" upon which
government was forbidden to transgress.

Forewarned by the difficulties they had
experienced in their efforts to amend the
Articles of Confederation, the   Amend-
framers of the Constitution did   ments made
not omit to provide for a means   possible
of amendment. Probably they felt that
many changes would surely be necessary, and
that in a relatively short time the whole document would have to be supplanted. Accordingly Congress was given authority,
whenever two thirds of both houses should
deem it necessary, to propose amendments
to the Constitution; or in case the legislatures
of two thirds of the states should demand it,
Congress was required to call a special convention for proposing amendments. All
amendments, however proposed, must be
submitted for ratification or rejection either
to the various state legislatures or to conventions in each state called for the purpose,
and the approval of three fourths of the
states was necessary to complete the process.
The convention system of proposing amendments has never been used, and ratifying
conventions were called for the first time
when the eighteenth (or prohibition) amendment was repealed.

The last article of the original Constitution
provided that the ratification of the conventions of nine states should be   Method of
regarded as sufficient for the   ratification
establishment of the Constitution among the
states so ratifying. This was completely out
of harmony with the original call for the convention, which took for granted that anything done by that body would be submitted

as an amendment to the existing Articles of Confederation, and hence would require for adoption the ratification of all the states. To this extent the Constitution actually proposed, and the formation of the government under its terms before unanimous ratification had been achieved, actually constituted a revolution. So weak, however, was the sanction under which the Articles of Confederation still operated that this procedure drew no protest from Congress. The Constitution, indeed, was first submitted to that body, and by it was formally submitted to the states.

Ratification was not accomplished, however, without a struggle. The men who had **The contest over ratification** framed the Constitution and those who now favored its adoption were representatives of the propertied classes, and the strong central government which they proposed to set up would presumably be in their hands. Such popular leaders as Patrick Henry, Richard Henry Lee, and Samuel Adams expressed their emphatic disapproval of the way in which the new Constitution proposed to curtail the power of the states, and the whole debtor class looked with particular disapproval upon the clause which forbade the states to issue paper money. Westerners feared that their freedom to use the Mississippi outlet might be bargained away to Spain, just as Jay had attempted to do a few years before. Philosophic liberals, most of whom were earnest champions of the doctrine that all men were possessed of certain inalienable rights, deplored the absence of a formal bill of rights to guarantee individuals as well as states against undue oppression on the part of the central government.

The defenders of the Constitution, fearful of the offense they might give by calling themselves Nationalists, chose to be known instead as Federalists. They made an admirable case for adoption. The Constitution, they argued, was the only alternative to anarchy. Its provisions might leave much to be desired, indeed few if any of its defenders could say truthfully that they liked it all,

THE

FEDERALIST:

A COLLECTION

OF

ESSAYS,

WRITTEN IN FAVOUR OF THE

NEW CONSTITUTION,

AS AGREED UPON BY THE FEDERAL CONVENTION,
SEPTEMBER 17, 1787.

IN TWO VOLUMES.

VOL. I.

NEW-YORK:

PRINTED AND SOLD BY J. AND A. M'LEAN,
No. 41, HANOVER-SQUARE,
M,DCC,LXXXVIII.

The Federalist, as originally published in 1788, was primarily a propaganda tract favorable to the proposed Constitution.

but if this Constitution, made as it was by the best talent the country could produce, could not be adopted, what hope, they asked, could there be for relief from the chaos of the Confederation? The Federalists had an advantage over their opponents in that many of their leaders had been members of the Philadelphia Convention and already knew well the arguments which had resulted in the adoption of the various provisions of the Constitution. The anti-Federalists, as opponents of the Constitution came to be called, had on the other hand to begin their study of the Constitution after the document was made public.

Both sides filled the press with propa-

REDEUNT SATURNIA REGNA.

On the erection of the Eleventh PILLAR of the great National DOME, we beg leave moft fincerely to felicitate " OUR DEAR COUNTRY."

Rife it will.

The foundation good—it may yet be SAVED.

The FEDERAL EDIFICE.

ELEVEN STARS, in qnick fucceffion rife—
ELEVEN COLUMNS ftrike our wond'ring eyes,
Soon o'er the *whole*, fhall fwell the beauteous DOME,
COLUMBIA's boaft—and FREEDOM's hallow'd home.
Here fhall the ARTS in glorious fplendour fhine !
And AGRICULTURE give her ftores divine !
COMMERCE refin'd, difpenfe us more than gold,
And this new world, teach WISDOM to the old—
RELIGION here fhall fix her bleft abode,
Array'd in *mildnefs*, like its parent GOD !
JUSTICE and LAW, fhall endlefs PEACE maintain,
And *the* " SATURNIAN AGE," *return again*.

The Federal Edifice is hailed in an editorial cartoon celebrating the ratification of the Constitution by the eleventh state, New York. From *The Massachusetts Centinel*, August 2, 1788.

ganda, and numberless pamphlets upholding **"The Federalist"** or attacking the Constitution found their way to the news-stands. Among the most illuminating of these writings were the arguments in defense of the Constitution made by Hamilton, Madison, and Jay, in a series of anonymous essays. These articles, collected together and published as a book, *The Federalist*, still constitute the best commentary available on the Constitution as its framers intended it to be interpreted. One of the strongest of the Federalist arguments was that the new Constitution would pave the way for a return of prosperity. Its provisions for dealing with foreign nations, together with the new powers over commerce to be given the central government, were cited as evidence that a more vigorous trade between the United States and foreign countries could be expected once the Constitution went into effect. Possibly some wise heads foresaw that the prevailing hard times would not last forever, and that the adoption of the Constitution on the eve of a revival of prosperity would be a shrewd stroke of policy.

The Federalists did not have to depend wholly upon their arguments to secure results. In every state restric-**Ratifying** tions on the suffrage existed **conventions** which made the conventions chosen to pass on the Constitution far more favorable to adoption than the attitude of the general public would seem to have justified. In some states, Pennsylvania for example, the back country, which was especially hostile to the Constitution, was given far less representation in the ratifying convention than it should have received in view of its population. Some of the elections were held with undue haste so that anti-Federalists would have insufficient time to organize their forces and distribute their propaganda. Nearly everywhere the Federalists included within their numbers the more astute and experienced politicians who knew how to make the most of the opportunities that came their way.

By the end of the year ratifications were being recorded. Equality of representation in the Senate seemed to satisfy most of the small states, for several of them were among the first to ratify. The ratification of Delaware came December 7, 1787, by a unanimous vote. Five days later Pennsylvania ratified by a vote of 46 to 23. Pennsylvania was one of the large states, but her central location and her composite population both pointed in the direction of nationalism. The ratifications of New Jersey on December 18, 1787, and of Georgia on January 2, 1788, were both unanimous. Connecticut voted to ratify, 128 to 40, on January 9. In Massachusetts there was a determined fight, which the Federalists won only by promising to favor amendments to the Constitution that would guarantee the rights of individuals. John Hancock, who was a power in the convention and for a time none too friendly to ratification, may also have received the impression that he was slated to be chosen Vice-President at the first election. Even so the victory for the Federalists was achieved, February 6, 1788, by the narrow margin of 187 to 168. The ratification of Maryland came April 28, 1788, by a vote of 63 to 11; that of South Carolina, May 23, 1788, by a vote of 149 to 73. In New Hampshire the first session of the convention failed to reach a decision, but the second session ratified, June 21, 1788, by a close vote, 57 to 46.

Since New Hampshire was the ninth state to ratify, the Constitution could now be put **Virginia and** into effect, but it was conceded **New York** on all sides that the new government could not hope to succeed without the support of Virginia and New York. In both states the opposition was strong. The back-country farmers of Virginia, led by Patrick Henry, fought valiantly to prevent ratification, and almost succeeded. The landowners of the Hudson Valley, fearing heavier taxation in case the United States rather than the state of New York should collect the duties on imports at New York City, made an equally hard fight. In the end, the arguments of Madison and John Marshall persuaded the Virginia convention to ratify, June 25, 1788, by a vote of 89 to 79; while Alexander Hamilton, aided by the fact that the Constitution would surely be given a

trial anyway, brought the New York convention to a half-hearted ratification, July 26, 1788. The New York victory was won by a vote of 30 to 27, the narrowest margin thus far accorded in any state. The North Carolina convention postponed ratification until steps should actually be taken to amend the Constitution by the inclusion of a bill of rights. The state of Rhode Island showed as little interest in the adoption as in the framing of the Constitution, and for the time being failed even to hold a ratifying convention.

The success of the Federalists in securing the ratification of the Constitution by enough states to give it a trial does not **Ratification** prove that there was any great **with reservations** popular mandate in its favor. **vations** Five states, Pennsylvania, Virginia, Massachusetts, New York, and South Carolina, had ratified only with reservations, most of which demanded the adoption of an adequate bill of rights. This much the Federalists were willing to concede, but even so, according to as prominent a Federalist as John Marshall, there was good reason to believe that "in some of the adopting states, a majority of the people were in the opposition. In all of them," he added, "the numerous amendments which were proposed, demonstrate the reluctance with which the new government was accepted; and that a dread of dismemberment, not an approbation of the particular system under consideration, had induced an acquiescence in it." There was great relief, however, that the long dispute over the government was at an end, and among the bitter opponents of ratification there were many who were ready, now that the Constitution was actually adopted, to give it a fair trial. The old Congress of the Confederation, even before the ratification of New York had been received, in acknowledgment of the fact that its authority had been supplanted, ordered the states to choose presidential electors, senators, and representatives, and set the first Wednesday in March, 1789, as the date for the New Congress to convene.

Bibliography

Two admirable collections of the documents relating to the formation of the Constitution have been made: *Records of the Federal Convention of 1787*, edited by Max Farrand (4 vols., 1911–37); and *Documents Illustrative of the Formation of the Union of the American States*, edited by C. C. Tansill (1927). See also *History of the Formation of the Union under the Constitution*, edited by Sol Bloom (1940), especially the excellent account by D. M. Matteson on the formation of the new government. From the many authoritative books on the framing of the Constitution, the following are selected: Carl Van Doren, *The Great Rehearsal: The Story of the Making and Ratifying of the Constitution of the United States* (1948); Max Farrand, *The Framing of the Constitution of the United States* (1913), and *The Fathers of the Constitution* (1921); Charles Warren, *The Making of the Constitution* (1928); R. L. Schuyler, *The Constitution of the United States* (1923). Homer C. Hockett, *The Constitutional History of the United States, 1776–1876* (2 vols., 1939), traces admirably the evolution of the Constitution during the formative years.

Many members of the constitutional convention have attracted biographers, among the best of which are: E. M. Burns, *James Madison, Philosopher of the Constitution* (1938); R. S. Boardman, *Roger Sherman, Signer and Statesman* (1938); Ellen H. Smith, *Charles Carroll of Carrolton* (1942); Sister Mary Virginia Geiger, *Daniel Carroll: A Framer of the Constitution* (1943).

Some of the arguments advanced against the Constitution are in *Pamphlets on the Constitution of the United States*, ed. by P. L. Ford (1888). For the struggle over ratification, see *The Debates on the Federal Constitution*, edited by Jonathan Elliot (5 vols., 1827–45). Two monographs useful in this connection are C. E. Miner, *The Ratification of the Federal Constitution by the State of New York* (1921); and S. B. Harding, *The Contest over the Ratification of the Federal Constitution in the State of Massachusetts* (1896). See also O. G. Libby, *The Geographical Distribution of the Vote of the Thirteen States on the Federal Constitution* (1894).

C. A. Beard, *An Economic Interpretation of the Constitution of the United States* (1913), is a work that has profoundly affected the thinking of most students of American history. Beard's flair for brilliant interpretation is also given free rein in Charles A. and Mary R. Beard, *The Rise of American Civilization* (2 vols., 1927). Studies that particularly relate to the powers assumed by the Supreme Court are C. A. Beard, *The Supreme Court and the Constitution* (1912); E. S. Corwin, *The Doctrine of Judicial Review* (1914); H. L. McBain, *The Living Constitution* (1927). Opposition to the Constitution is featured in two biographies: Helen D. Hill, *George Mason, Constitutionalist* (1938); and E. W. Spaulding, *His Excellency, George Clinton, Critic of the Constitution* (1938). E. C. Mason, *The Veto Power* (1890), centers on one important aspect of constitutional development.

SECTION THREE

EVOLUTION IN

DEMOCRACY

1787-1818

It was one thing to draw up a good constitution, but it was quite another thing to make it work. In inept hands, the Constitution might not have succeeded any better than the Articles of Confederation. Fortunately in George Washington and the men who surrounded him the new republic had leaders of exceptional competence. Their sure-footedness saved the day. The Constitution was a short document and stood in need of elaboration. In order to carry its provisions into effect, Congress had to enact innumerable laws, and administrators had to set precedents of far-reaching consequence. All this was done with a minimum of error.

The rock on which the Confederation had foundered was finance, and the Constitution, but for the guidance of Alexander Hamilton, Secretary of the Treasury, might easily have gone down the same way. Hamilton was a conservative, a nationalist, and a partisan of the well-to-do. But he was also a financial genius. He established the national credit on a firm basis; he made full use of the taxing power; he created out of whole cloth a national banking system and a sound national currency. With these things accomplished, the new government could live.

There was need also of a foreign policy. The United States had an alliance with France, dating back to the Revolution. But was this alliance to draw the infant republic into every European war in which France became involved? When Great Britain and France went to war early in the 1790's, Washington and his Cabinet decided on a course of neutrality. Eventually this policy developed into what is sometimes called the Doctrine of Isolation. The United States was a tiny nation, surrounded by the outposts of great European empires. It could not risk its independence by involvement in their wars. Eventually, when the United States grew up, and itself became a great power, the Doctrine of Isolation became obsolete, but in its time it was the course of wisdom and statesmanship.

Washington had hoped that the United States might avoid the hazards of party politics, but his hopes were not to be realized. For a time he kept men of such divergent views as Hamilton and Jefferson in his cabinet. But the two could not see eye-to-eye, for Hamilton was ever the spokesman of wealth and privilege, whereas Jefferson's interest lay in the welfare of the common man, in whose capacities he earnestly believed. Hamilton also spoke for the commercial interests of the Northeast, whereas Jefferson favored agriculture, and saw in the small free farmer of the South and West the ideal citizen. Hamilton favored the greatest possible centralization of power in the hands of the national government, whereas Jefferson championed the rights of the states, and believed firmly in the adage "the less government the better." Around the views of these two men parties took form, the Federalists reflecting Hamilton, and the Republicans, Jefferson. With the Revolution of 1800 the Republicans, by electing Jefferson President, took control of the government away from the Federalists, and began the process of liberalizing the Constitution, a process which has continued, with only occasional reverses, ever since. But American democracy was much more than a political manifestation. The Revolution of 1800 symbolized the rise of the common people to a much higher level in thought, culture, and self-expression than they had ever known before.

Under Jefferson and his successors the United States greatly expanded, both in population extent and in national boundaries. The Purchase of Louisiana opened the way to the Trans-Mississippi West, and the explorations into the Far West that Jefferson encouraged gave a further hint as to what was to come. The hope of expansion, quite as much as the demand for freedom of the seas, led to the War of 1812, with its temporary abandonment of the position of neutrality that Washington had counseled. Except for the fact that the Indians were humbled, the dream of expansion was not much furthered by the War. Canada, which the West had hoped to take, remained, and was to continue to remain, a part of the British empire. But the tension with the Mother Country soon came to an end. After the war was over, a series of agreements between the United States and Great Britain worked out a peaceful solution of their principal areas of conflict, and left the United States free to continue its growth in democracy and its expansion to the West.

12
Launching the New Government

The first President — The first inauguration — The establishment of precedents — Democratic misgivings — Alexander Hamilton as Secretary of the Treasury; his policies — The "Whiskey Rebellion" — The southwestern frontier — McGillivray — Indian war in the Northwest — Admission of new states — War in Europe — Establishment of American neutrality — Election of 1792

ONE of the arguments in favor of the Constitution that carried conviction to many minds was the undoubted fact that George Washington would be the first President. No other American leader has so captured the confidence of his contemporaries as did Washington, and the certainty that his solid judgment and rugged honesty would be at the command of his countrymen during the experimental period allayed many misgivings. In the first presidential election every elector cast a vote for Washington, and there is every reason to suppose that, had the Constitution permitted it, the people would gladly have elected him President for life.

Washington's hold on the public imagination was somewhat dimmed during the later **The first President** years of his term of office, but the criticisms that had then assailed him were mostly forgotten once he retired to private life. Upon his death the Washington legend began to take form. Weems's *Life of Washington*, an early and popular biography, yielded to every temptation of the hero-worshiper, and in glowing words of praise pictured such a boy and man as never could have lived. The portraits painted by Gilbert Stuart, likewise, which were obviously designed to make Washington look as godlike as the father of his country should look, were accepted by later generations at face value. The popular estimate of Washington thus set was long continued,

and only recently have biographers sought to skim off the fancy from the fact in order to present the first President more nearly as he was. In their efforts to destroy what was merely legend, however, some recent writers have overreached the mark, and have unfairly denied to Washington the greatness that was really his.

George Washington (1732–99) was born in tidewater Virginia, the son of a moderately well-to-do planter who **The youth of** owned several estates. Wash- **Washington** ington's father had gone to school in England, but this privilege was denied George, whose education was somewhat limited. He took an interest in mathematics, and at an early age knew the rudiments of surveying. When he was only sixteen years old he accompanied a surveying party into the Shenandoah Valley, and after his return became surveyor-general for Fairfax County. His frequent surveying trips into the back country gave him a glimpse into the possibilities of the West that he was never to forget. His career as surveyor was cut short when his elder brother Lawrence died in 1752, and left to George the management of the estate at Mount Vernon. A few years later Washington married Martha Custis, the widow of a wealthy planter, and her property, added to his own, made him for the times a very rich man. For many years he lived the usual life of the prosperous southern planter, enter-

199

tained lavishly, participated actively in parish affairs, and sat for his county as a member of the House of Burgesses.

Washington's trip to the West in 1753 to warn the French from the forks of the Ohio, **His military** and his subsequent exploits in **career** the French and Indian War, drew him into the limelight as a military leader. If a southern aristocrat was to be chosen to lead the American forces in the Revolutionary War, Washington, as John Adams so wisely observed, was the natural choice. The events of the war proved that no mistake had been made. Washington's knowledge of military tactics was no doubt defective, but it was sufficient to meet the needs of the situation. He never commanded a large army, and perhaps he could never have commanded a large army well, but with the limited supply of troops he was able to obtain he did effective fighting. He understood clearly the necessity of preserving at all costs the little army he had, and he invoked frequently the strategy of retreat. He was fertile in new ideas, and always ready to take a promising chance. Unlike most commanders, he often had to help raise his own army, and he nearly always had to struggle against odds to keep it together. By the end of the war his military exploits had won the admiration, not only of Americans, but also of his British opponents, and of such a master-strategist as Frederick the Great.

Washington's success as a soldier was no guaranty that he would not fail as a political **His states-** leader, but in this respect also **manlike** the people trusted him. Time **qualities** proved that they were right. As an administrator he possessed the ability, so strikingly absent in some men, to make up his mind, and to make it up before the time for acting had passed. He was an unusually keen judge of men, and surrounded himself with an able group of subordinates. He knew how to ask and to take advice, and he rarely made any important decisions without consulting others. His judgment as to what the future held in store was right a surprisingly large number of times. He saw clearly the important part that the West was to play in the history of the nation, he recognized the dangers involved in a growing sectionalism, he understood better than most men of his time the menace of slavery, and he realized fully the wisdom of diplomatic isolation from Europe until the nation he had helped to create could get securely upon its feet. Few statesmen have a clearer record on so many important matters. Washington could hardly be called brilliant, but his character was unassailable, he possessed much sound common sense, and he could do many things well.

On the fourth of March, 1789, the day designated by the old Congress of the Confederation for the new govern- **The first in-** ment to go into operation, only **auguration** eight senators out of twenty-two and thirteen representatives out of fifty-nine had arrived at New York, the temporary capital. This was not wholly due to indifference; roads were bad, streams were swollen by the spring rains, and for those who came by sea the winds were not always favorable. It was the sixth of April before a majority of the members in each house required by the Constitution for a quorum were on hand. The electoral votes were then counted, and the election of Washington to the Presidency, and of John Adams, who had the next highest number of votes, to the Vice-Presidency, was announced. Word was then sent to Washington of what had transpired, after which the President-elect journeyed, much of the way on horseback, to New York. The trip was an ovation all the way, and so consumed eight days. It was April 30 before the inauguration actually took place.

Nor was the new government then fully launched. The Constitution was a relatively short document, and much legislation had to be passed in order to make it effective. Laws had to be enacted, for example, to create departments of state, of war, and of the treasury, to establish a judiciary, and most important of all to provide for the levying and collection of taxes. Once the essential laws were enacted the President still had

George Washington of Virginia, first President of the United States, took office, he said, "in the evening of a life nearly consumed in public cares." He was reluctant "to quit a peaceful abode for an ocean of difficulties," and doubted whether he possessed "that competency of political skill, abilities, and inclination, which are necessary to manage the helm." One observer described Washington at this time as "in stature about six feet. . . . His frame would seem to want filling up. His motions slow rather than lively.

. . ." The portrait is by Peale, 1783, the last painted from life. At right is a woodcut from a Lancaster, Pa., almanac, 1779, the first printed reference to Washington as the "Father of his Country."

to select the officials to carry them into effect, and the Senate had to pass on the President's appointees. It was months, even years, before the actual machinery of government was fully constituted.

In many matters important precedents had to be set. Among the most vexing of these, at least to certain members of Congress, was the question of titles. Should not the President be decorated with some resounding title such as His Excellency, or His Elective Majesty? Should not senators, and possibly even representatives, be styled Honorable? Ultimately democratic simplicity won out, but the failure of important officials to obtain high-sounding titles rankled in some breasts for a long time. Nor did the Constitution make fully clear the powers of the Vice-President as presiding officer in the Sen-

The establishment of precedents

ate, and the Speaker as presiding officer in the House. Very largely because of the personalities involved the Vice-President came to be a mere moderator, whereas the Speaker soon came to play such an important rôle in the affairs of the House that for over a century he was regarded as second only to the President himself in power. Out of the clause in the Constitution which provided that the President might ask for the opinions of heads of departments in writing, grew the Cabinet as the official board of advisers upon whom the President was to lean. The free use of the veto power by the President, negotiation of treaties in advance of asking the "advice and consent" of the Senate, and many other modes of procedure came about as mere customs based on precedent rather than upon any requirement of the Constitution.

COURTLY LIFE. Lady Washington's Reception, painted by Daniel Huntington.

GRAY'S FERRY, PHILADELPHIA. Triumphal arches erected for the reception of General Washington, April 20, 1780. Engraving by Trenchard after Peale for *The Columbian Magazine* May, 1789.

Democratic misgivings arose early in Washington's administration when the veneration of the first President reached proportions usually reserved for royalty. Washington's journey to New York for the inauguration was marked by celebrations such as might have been given a king. The President's wife was often called "Lady Washington," and her receptions were likened to a court by democratic gossipers.

Extreme democrats, such as William Maclay, one of the senators from Pennsyl-

Democratic misgivings vania, were alarmed almost at the start at some of the undemocratic tendencies they witnessed. The President to some extent, and the Vice-President to a great extent, seemed concerned about the matter of titles. The behavior of the British House of Lords and House of Commons was much cited. The President, instead of receiving callers in true democratic fashion, held levees like a king. How long would it be at this rate before a monarchy would exist in fact? Conservatives were almost equally worried at the openings which the new Constitution gave to democracy. There was not much to be hoped for at best. Probably Fisher Ames expressed the mingled feelings of many observers, as they saw the

new government take form, when he said: "A monarchy is like a merchantman. You get on board and ride the wind and tide in safety and elation but, by and by, you strike a reef and go down. But democracy is like a raft. You never sink, but, damn it, your feet are always in the water."

The Confederation had failed largely because it was unable to solve the problem of finance. If the new government was not also to go on the rocks, clearly its financial policy must be wisely conceived. Washington recognized this fact when he chose as his Secretary of the Treasury Alexander Hamilton, a young man only thirty-two years of age who had already displayed remarkable talent along financial lines.

Hamilton (1755–1804) was a West Indian by birth, the son of a Scottish father and a

Alexander Hamilton

mother of English descent, not French Huguenot as was once thought. His birth date, long given as 1757, was actually, according to trustworthy West Indian records, two years earlier. He was sent to school in New Jersey when he was only eighteen years of age, and later attended King's College in New York. Here, although New York was a Loyalist center, he absorbed the American point of view on the quarrel with England, and when war broke out joined the army. Washington made use of him for staff duty so that he had little opportunity to distinguish himself in the field, but he emerged from the war a lieutenant-colonel, and the husband of a daughter of General Philip Schuyler, whose influence in New York politics was great.

Hamilton was early interested in financial matters. During the war he wrote Robert Morris a letter on the state of the nation's finances that described fully the evils of an inflated currency and urged that a halt be called on such a policy. Later he advocated the contraction of the currency, and the negotiation of a foreign loan to be used in starting a bank. During the Confederation period his interests were varied. He studied law and was admitted to the bar, served for a time as a member of Congress, tried hard as receiver of taxes for New York to obtain money for the central government, served in the Philadelphia Convention which framed the Constitution, and also in the New York state convention which so reluctantly ratified it. He was, in spite of his youth, an ultra-conservative. He believed that the rights of property must be protected at all costs, and he never doubted that government, to be really effective, must be the monopoly of the upper classes. "Take mankind in general," he told the Federal Convention in 1787, "they are vicious."

As Secretary of the Treasury, Hamilton concerned himself first and foremost with the establishment of the nation's credit. To make sure that there could be no doubt about the determination of the United States to pay its

Funding the national debt

just debts, he proposed that all outstanding loans be funded at their face value. The United States had borrowed from abroad about twelve million dollars, and against the meeting of this obligation in full there could be no valid complaint. But the domestic debt, which amounted to nearly forty-two million dollars, seemed to many honest men a totally different matter. Probably the original obligations incurred far exceeded the returns in services, supplies, and depreciated paper currency that the government had realized on them; moreover, they were now as a rule no longer in the hands of the original owners, but had fallen to speculators who had purchased them for a fraction of their face value. Since these securities were worth on the market about twenty-five cents on the dollar, there were many who thought that for the government to purchase them back at that price, or a little above, with a new and valid issue would be an entirely respectable procedure. But Hamilton was determined to win the enthusiastic approval of the moneyed class, and he ultimately succeeded in having his own way. The entire debt was funded at par, and the speculators, including some members of Congress, who as they voted for the funding bill were not unaware of the opportunity it gave them to profit, reaped a rich harvest.

Hamilton's plan did not end, however, merely with the funding of the debts owed by the United States. He wished also to take over such of the debts incurred by the states themselves for the cause of independence as they had not yet paid. His object, again, was to place the creditor class under deep obligation to the central government, and thus to win its hearty support. But the assumption of state debts by the central government was not accomplished without a struggle. It was all very well to argue that these debts were incurred for a common cause and should be paid out of the common treasury, but the fact remained that some states had large obligations to pass over and some did not. Virginia, for example, had

Assumption of state debts

financed the war to a great extent with paper money issues that had either been redeemed in western lands or had ceased to have any value. The South in general opposed the scheme, and it was finally put through Congress only after Hamilton, working through Jefferson, the Secretary of State, had struck a notable bargain. The South was exceedingly desirous of securing the capital, and Hamilton now offered to use his influence in favor of a southern site if Jefferson would help find the votes to pass the assumption bill. The bargain worked, Congress agreed that the new capital should be located at Philadelphia for a period of ten years, and thereafter on the Potomac; and it voted also the assumption by the central government of some eighteen million dollars' worth of state war debts.

Still further to bind the moneyed classes to the government, Hamilton proposed, in **Bank of the United States** December, 1790, that Congress should authorize the establishment of a Bank of the United States similar to the Bank of England. He could give many sound arguments in favor of such a measure. The bank would constitute a safe depository for government funds, and through branch banks would provide for their easy transfer from place to place; it would make possible the issuance of a national currency which would have the same value in one part of the country as in another; it would greatly facilitate the sale of national bonds; and it would provide a cheap and easy means of exchange for all the people. But those who had raised their voices against the funding bill and the assumption of state debts were even more vociferous in their opposition to the bank. Where, indeed, would this devotion to the interests of the aristocracy of wealth end? Hamilton proposed not only to quadruple by his funding measures the value of government securities, but also to offer to men of means stock in a national bank as another safe and attractive investment.

Men who looked askance at this frank alliance between the government and the well-to-do urged that the Constitution gave no such authority to Congress as Hamilton asked it to exert. James Madison, who knew the motives of the **"Broad" vs. "strict" construction** framers of the Constitution at least as well as any other man, held this view. But Hamilton was willing to interpret the "necessary and proper" clause in the Constitution broadly enough to include the creation of a bank in which to deposit the tax money which clearly the Constitution authorized Congress to raise. Thus began the battle over the broad construction and the strict construction of the Constitution that was to go on for many years. Hamilton's interpretation of the Constitution looked clearly in the direction of a powerful central government which should make a special effort to care for the needs of the moneyed classes. Jefferson and Madison, representing the agrarian element, which had no use for an elaborate financial structure and feared the taxes and the tyranny of a strong central government, stood earnestly by the doctrine of strict construction, and maintained that Congress had power to do such things as the Constitution specifically authorized it to do, and no other.

Once more Hamilton won out, this time with the support of the President himself, and Congress voted to charter a Bank of the United States. This institution was to have a capital stock of ten million dollars, for the time a very large sum. Of this amount one fifth was to be subscribed by the United States, and the other four fifths by private individuals. Into the bank went all the deposits of the United States, and this fact, coupled with the fact that the national government also owned a large part of the bank stock, tended to win for the institution the confidence of the public. The bank had the right to issue paper money, and these notes were made receivable for public dues. Investors were quick to take advantage of the opportunity offered them, and the bank was soon doing business. For twenty years it prospered to such an extent that those who held bank stock realized on an average about

Alexander Hamilton, although of humble origin, became the foremost conservative of his time. As a youth he developed his talent for political theory by arguing the American case against Great Britain, but he soon had his doubts about the common man. "Take mankind in general," he said, "they are vicious, their passions may be operated on." He believed in representative government, however, provided the suffrage could be properly controlled and the central government could be given ample powers. Among his many actions toward this latter end was the creation of the first Bank of the United States at Philadelphia, shown at the right in an engraving after Klinckostrom. The portrait of Hamilton is by John Trumbull.

---

eight and one half per cent annually on their investment.

Hamilton's plan for funding the debt cost money, and the modest tariff that Congress **The whiskey** had levied as one of its first **excise** measures was unequal to the emergency. In consequence, the Secretary of the Treasury offered yet another suggestion. The Constitution clearly authorized Congress to levy an excise tax, and this power, Hamilton felt, should be used. Not only was money needed, but in addition the people should become accustomed to the taxing power of the central government. When it came to choosing the item upon which to place the tax, however, Hamilton took care not to offend the moneyed men whose goodwill toward the government he deemed so essential to its success. Instead, he suggested a tax on whiskey which would hit the small farmers of the back country who had opposed the adoption of the Constitution, and who were still doubtful as to whether the new government merited their support. There was then no odium attached to the manufacture and sale of whiskey. Thrifty farmers who lived far from market turned their surplus grain into whiskey in order to solve easily the problem of transportation, and the sale of this commodity brought them almost the only ready cash they knew. An excise tax on whiskey was as sure a way to arouse their wrath as could possibly have been devised. Hamilton knew this full well, but he considered it right and proper to levy the tax, if for no other reason than to show that he could collect it by force, if necessary, and thus prove to those who were least friendly toward the central government that they had to obey it whether they wished to or not. Congress, with a comfortable majority now completely under Hamilton's influence, passed the bill.

Washington had hoped that the new government might be carried on without the development of political parties, **Opposition** and he had not hesitated to **to Hamil-** place men of such divergent **ton's policies** views as Jefferson and Hamilton side by side in his Cabinet. But the financial program

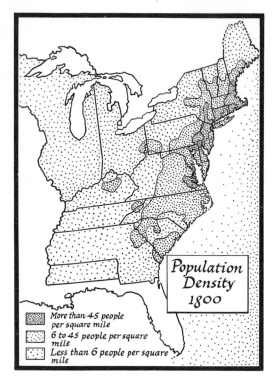

Population
Density
1800

More than 45 people
per square mile

6 to 45 people per square
mile

Less than 6 people per square
mile

brought on the trouble that Hamilton had foreseen. Wherever it was collected, the tax was resented, but the chief center of opposition developed in western Pennsylvania in the Pittsburgh area. The tax was offensive, not merely for the money it took, but also because of its prying nature. The pioneer farmer set high store by his personal freedom, and he felt outraged at the behavior of tax-collectors who pried into his private business, and told him what he must and must not do. As early as 1791 popular meetings of protest were held at which speakers urged the farmers to resist the excise. During the next two or three years bands of "Whiskey Boys" raided stills that paid the tax, handled roughly the tax-collectors, and ultimately succeeded in setting the law completely at nought in a number of western counties. Albert Gallatin, a highly respected resident of western Pennsylvania, tried to counsel moderation, but the people showed more interest in the writings of one "Tom the Tinker," who urged uncompromising resistance. Particularly burdensome was the system of enforcement, which required for the accused an expensive trip across the mountains to Philadelphia, where the delays of justice might detain the victim of the law for months.

At length smouldering resistance broke into open revolt. On August 14, 1794, a convention was held to remonstrate, and even before that date two thousand armed militia threatened to attack a small detachment of regulars stationed at Pittsburgh. Washington had already warned the law-breakers to change their ways, and now he prepared to use force. Again testing a power derived from the Constitution, he called out fifteen thousand militia from the states of Virginia, Maryland, and Pennsylvania, and ordered them to march to the scene of trouble. The troops were forthcoming, and the overwhelming strength of the army sent against the revolters made them more willing to listen to Gallatin's admonitions than they had been before. When the troops reached

The "Whiskey Rebellion"

that Hamilton carried through Congress was so clearly designed to benefit a favored class that those who were not of that class were certain to be in opposition. The creation of a powerful central government which at all times could be counted on to serve the interests of the well-to-do aroused the deep resentment of the agricultural classes generally. The merchant, the manufacturer, the shipbuilder, and their dependents might profit much, directly and indirectly, by Hamilton's policies; but the small farmer and landowner would not. For them the Hamiltonian system meant the multiplication of taxes and the curtailment of liberty no less than the British government had once planned. The agrarian interests tended, therefore, to join hands under the leadership of Jefferson and Madison. Hamilton's friends called themselves Federalists, so their opponents were often called anti-Federalists. But before long the opposition took for its party label the more significant term, Republican.

The attempt to enforce the excise tax soon

their destination late in 1794, all resistance had vanished. A number of men who had been leaders in the "Whiskey Rebellion," as the episode was called, were arrested, and eighteen were sent to Philadelphia for trial. Of these only two were convicted, and they were pardoned by the President. But the power of the government had been amply demonstrated, and thereafter distillers of whiskey generally paid the tax. Politically this strong show of force was probably a mistake. Not only the residents of western Pennsylvania but many others also were aghast at the ruthless power that the Federalists in control of the government chose to wield. In consequence they gave their support the more willingly to Thomas Jefferson and the Republicans.

The revolt in western Pennsylvania was not the only western problem that the new government was called upon to solve. Still farther to the west were other pioneers whose troubles with the Spanish in the Southwest, with the British in the Northwest, and with the Indians in both regions were even more perplexing than they had been in the time of the Confederation. As the West grew in population, the uncertainty of trade down the Mississippi became constantly more serious. The Spanish remained sullenly unwilling to open the river freely to trade from the United States, they continued to urge their claim to a boundary for Florida much farther north than the United States was willing to concede, and they placed no obstacles in the way of Indians under their control who moved to attack the southwestern frontier. In the Northwest the British continued to hold on to their posts south of the Great Lakes, and Canadian fur-traders gave aid and encouragement to the Indian tribes of the Northwest who had already gone on the warpath against the pioneers in Ohio. Washington realized fully that the loyalty of the West to the central government would be sorely tried if the frontier was not relieved. Moreover, the prestige of the nation was at stake.

The southwestern frontier

Realizing that he was sure to become involved in war with the northwestern Indians, Washington resolved to try diplomacy with the Indians of the Southwest. The leading Indian chief of this region was a half-breed Creek named Alexander McGillivray, who had fought with the British during the American Revolution, and still cherished a deep hatred for the United States. Washington succeeded in persuading McGillivray to pay a visit to New York, where he was received with every courtesy. An agreement was reached whereby McGillivray received one hundred thousand dollars for damages he claimed to have sustained at the hands of the Patriots during the Revolution, in return for which he promised to use his influence to keep the Indians at peace. McGillivray's word proved to be of little worth, and the attacks on the southwestern frontier continued. At length the Tennesseans took matters into their own hands, and extensive raids conducted in 1783–94 by local militia under Sevier and Robertson brought better results than came from Washington's negotiations with McGillivray.

McGillivray

The Indian troubles of the Northwest resulted ultimately in no less than three extensive campaigns. The United States during the Confederation period had made two treaties with the northwestern tribes, Fort Stanwix (1784), and Fort McIntosh (1785), by which a large section of land west of the western boundary of Pennsylvania and north of the Ohio River was supposedly to be cleared of Indians in preparation for the coming of white settlers. But the Indians, while they had signed the treaties, had little understanding of what they meant. The white man's concept of private land-ownership was quite beyond the Indian's comprehension, for the only kind of ownership he understood was tribal ownership. In consequence serious friction developed between roving groups of Indians and white settlers, who viewed all such visitors with alarm and looked upon them as trespassers. Indian democracy constituted

The northwest Indians

Northwest Indian Wars 1790-1795

another barrier to good relations between the races, for Indians who had not been present when the treaties were signed held that they were not bound by anything other Indians had done for them. The Indian memory of treaty terms, moreover, was short, while the presence of white men drove away their game and interfered seriously with the trapping of fur-bearing animals. It seemed evident to the red men that the white advance at all costs must be turned back.

Indian resistance was immensely strengthened by the existence of the British forts and **Harmar's expedition** fur-trading posts south of the Great Lakes. Here the talk was all against the further invasion of the West by American settlers. Canadian fur-traders saw in the expansion of the American frontier a corresponding decrease in their business, and they did not hesitate to provide the Indians in the course of trade with the weapons and ammunition they needed to drive back the whites. The Indians, emboldened by this support, committed so many depredations that by the time Washington took

office drastic retaliatory measures had to be taken. In 1790, therefore, Washington dispatched General Harmar in command of about fifteen hundred militia to destroy the Indian villages on the Maumee. This task Harmar accomplished, but on his return from the Indian country his troops were ambushed and he was forced to make a humiliating retreat.

Next year Governor St. Clair took the field himself in command of about two thousand militia. He sought to **St. Clair's** profit by the mistakes of his **failure** predecessor, and advanced deliberately, building as he went retaining posts about a day's journey apart. But this procedure proved too slow and uninteresting for the frontier militia he commanded, which preferred action to work, and resented any pretense at discipline. Wholesale desertions depleted his ranks, and on November 4, 1791, his expedition was ambushed by the Indians and utterly overwhelmed. The uncertain frontier militia fled precipitately from the scene of the action, only to be pur-

GEN'L. WASHINGTON AT FORT CUMBERLAND. Painting by F. Kemmelmeyer, about 1794. Characteristically in some so-called "primitive" art, the central figures vary in size according to their relative importance instead of being in natural perspective.

INDIAN TREATY OF FORT GREENVILLE. Detail of a painting by an unidentified artist, about 1795.

Frontier problems caused the Washington administration much anxiety. The picture above shows the first President reviewing the militia assembled at Fort Cumberland in 1794 for use in putting down the Whiskey Rebellion. The other, reputedly painted by one of "Mad" Anthony Wayne's men, shows the leaders of the Northwest Indians bargaining for peace after their defeat at Fallen Timbers.

sued by the Indians so successfully that not more than one third of the whites escaped uninjured.

It is said that when Washington received the news of St. Clair's defeat his rage knew no bounds. It was necessary now at all costs to redeem the reputation of the government. Who next to send against the Indians was a matter of grave concern, and the choice finally fell upon "Mad" Anthony Wayne, the hero of Stony Point. Wayne demanded as the terms of his acceptance that he be permitted to enlist twenty-five hundred volunteers for a period of two years, and there was nothing for Washington to do but to accept. Wayne took his time, drilled his troops carefully, hired Indian scouts, and when at length he began his advance had a force that he could depend upon. Wayne

"Mad" Anthony Wayne

followed St. Clair's plan of building forts as he advanced, and at one of these stations, Fort Greenville, far in the Indian country, spent the winter of 1793–94. In the spring he was joined by sixteen hundred mounted troops from Kentucky, and began a relentless campaign. The Indians counted heavily on British support and retreated toward an outpost on the Maumee that British soldiers were erecting. But, confident that they would defeat Wayne as they had defeated Harmar and St. Clair, they attacked the Americans south of the British post at a place known as Fallen Timbers, only to be disastrously defeated. Realizing Wayne's strength, the British now refused to give the Indians further succor, their villages and winter supplies were destroyed by Wayne's soldiers, and they were left no choice but to treat for peace. In the summer of 1795 at

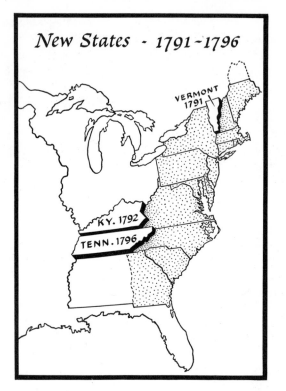

New States - 1791-1796

VERMONT
1791

KY. 1792

TENN. 1796

Fort Greenville a treaty was signed. The Indians now ceded vast stretches of land in central Ohio to the whites, and agreed to bury the hatchet. So stinging was the defeat they had been dealt that they gave the United States no further trouble for many years to come.

No less gratifying to the people of the West was the willingness of the new government **Admission of** to admit frontier states into the **new states** Union. Vermont had carried on a state government since the beginning of the Revolutionary War, but was left outside the Confederation. In 1791, however, Congress agreed to accept Vermont as a fourteenth state. The pleas of Kentuckians also were given favorable consideration. In 1789 Virginia gave full consent to the separation from the Old Dominion of the Kentucky counties, and in 1792 Congress allowed Kentucky to become a state. In Tennessee matters moved more slowly toward the same end. The state of North Carolina finally ceded her western lands to

Congress in 1790, whereupon a Southwest territory was set up similar to the territory established northwest of the Ohio River by the Confederation. In 1796 this territory gave way to the state of Tennessee. The constitutions of these new western states all showed a tendency toward greater democracy than was yet the rule in the original thirteen states. Especially were they willing to expand the right of suffrage. Vermont and Kentucky went the whole length of universal manhood suffrage, and Tennessee closely approximated it.

Meantime the outbreak of the French Revolution had started a train of events in Europe that was to prove of **The French** tremendous interest to citizens **Revolution** of the new republic across the Atlantic. A week after Washington's inauguration, the French Estates-General that Louis XVI had found it necessary to call had begun its sessions. In a short time the evolution of a more democratic government for France had begun. Most Americans sympathized wholeheartedly with this development, and the country took pardonable pride in seeing the principles of the American Revolution accepted by one of the greatest, if not the very greatest, of European powers. Superficially the two revolutions had many things in common. Both were fought to redress longstanding grievances against an autocratic king; both maintained steadfastly the right of any people to a voice in levying the taxes they were called upon to pay; both attacked privilege and proclaimed lustily the doctrine of the rights of man. Moreover, Lafayette, a hero of the American Revolution, was no less a hero of the new régime in France.

Even European nations were for quite different reasons constrained to look at first with some satisfaction upon what was happening in France. Rival European monarchs were not altogether unhappy to see Louis XVI in trouble at home. The British nation rejoiced to see the decline of its hereditary foe. Austria, Russia, and Prussia, busy for the moment with the final partition of Poland, were glad to be rid of the danger of French interference. This smug satisfaction gave way to alarm, however, when the French Revolution grew definitely more radical and more propagandist. If the outbreak of democracy in France was to become in fact "a war of all peoples against all kings," something would have to be done about it. By the Declaration of Pillnitz (1791), Emperor Leopold II of the Holy Roman Empire and King Frederick William of Prussia agreed to act together in case either should be attacked by France. In April, 1792, France declared war on Austria, and the French Revolution was no longer an internal affair.

In the conflict which followed, French arms by a miracle began to win. American **Sympathy for France** opinion tended still to be overwhelmingly pro-French, and the victory of the revolutionary army at Valmy (September 20, 1792) was celebrated in Boston by a great civic feast in which all parties joined. But when a short time later the French actually put their king to death, and issued declarations of war against both Great Britain and Spain, more conservative Americans began to have grave doubts as to the course France was pursuing. The United States was bound by a treaty of alliance to France. Would another war with Great Britain have to be fought, and perhaps also a war with Spain? Any such development might mean the death of American commerce, which ran mostly with England and Spain, and it might mean the loss of American independence as well. Hamilton did not disguise his disgust for the French Revolution, and to most of the Federalists it now seemed that Great Britain was fighting for the preservation of civilization while France had become a public enemy. But Jefferson and the Republicans took a very different view of the situation. Representing as they did mainly the agrarian interests, they were not so immediately concerned as the Hamiltonians for the safety of American commerce. Great Britain was the traditional enemy of American democracy, and she still unlawfully held on to the northwest posts.

Spain was an even older antagonist, and was now planted at the mouth of the Mississippi to dispute the right of western farmers to the use of that river. Republican clubs, many of which had already been formed out of sympathy for France, multiplied amazingly, particularly in the South and West. Many of the Republicans were ready to make common cause with France in a war against the British in Canada and the Spanish on the Gulf of Mexico. To Jefferson the French Revolution was still "the most sacred cause that man was ever engaged in."

With public opinion thus divided, Washington received with many misgivings the news that the revolutionary **"Citizen" Genêt** government had dispatched a minister, "Citizen" Edmond Charles Genêt, to the United States. The President at once put certain questions that perplexed him to his Cabinet. Should Genêt be recognized as the rightful minister from France to the United States? Were the French treaties, made before the outbreak of the French Revolution, still binding on the United States? If so, could the United States, in spite of them, maintain an attitude of neutrality? The last question was particularly perplexing, for the United States had guaranteed to France her West India possessions, and had agreed that French prizes captured at sea might be brought into American ports for adjudication. Privateers, also, were to be reciprocally admitted into French and American ports. On the question of the French treaties Hamilton and Jefferson divided sharply. Hamilton took the ground that the treaties were with the King of France, and the King's government being done away with, they were no longer binding. Jefferson took the more correct view that treaties were between nations, and that the existing French government had the same claims upon the United States that the King's government had had. All agreed that for the present, at least, neutrality was the only possible course. Washington decided to issue a proclamation of neutrality before Genêt should arrive at the American capital, and

TRIUMPH GOVERNMENT. The stately Federal chariot moves on despite obstructions, while stalwart troops of "volunteers" form to prevent the invasion of "cannibal" Republicans. Anonymous cartoon, about 1793.

THE ANTIFEDERAL CLUB. Jefferson's followers are depicted as an unsavory group of visionaries, pirates, French revolutionaries, drunkards, and the devil. Anonymous cartoon, 1793.

Federalist cartoonists delighted in portraying anti-Federalists, or Republicans, as disreputable characters and obstructionists, always ready to overthrow order and decency. In the cartoon above, Jefferson and Genêt are trying to "stop de wheels of de gouvernement"; at the right, Jefferson is represented standing on a table exhorting his followers to subversion of the government.

to live up to the treaties as well as he could without involving the United States in war. He would recognize Genêt as the rightful minister of France, but make clear to him that the United States did not intend to participate in the war.

Genêt was a young man of great enthusiasm, a fair representative of the visionary Girondin faction for the moment in control of the French government. On April 8, 1793, he landed at Charleston, South Carolina, a center of pro-French sentiment, and was given a great ovation. Without thought of being hampered by American neutrality, he planned to begin hostilities from the United States as a base against the Spanish in Florida and Louisiana, and also to make use of American ports in a campaign of privateering against

Genêt's projects

British commerce. In South Carolina these projects were popular, and Genêt found no difficulty in finding plenty of volunteers to serve in a campaign against the Spanish, and plenty of sea-captains to accept his commissions as privateers. In due time he progressed by land to Philadelphia, now the seat of government. The route he chose led through the interior, where the sentiment was strongly pro-French. Genêt passed from triumph to triumph, and when at last he reached Philadelphia he had no doubt that the whole of the American people were with him. Had he landed at Boston, and gone overland from that port to Philadelphia, he might have gained a far different impression.

Genêt was duly received by Washington, although without much cordiality, and

was given to understand that the procla-
American mation of neutrality meant what
neutrality it said. The young Frenchman
had no notion, however, of giving up his
plans. Already he had not only taken the
initial steps toward organizing an expedition
from South Carolina and Georgia against
Florida, but had also accepted an offer
made by George Rogers Clark, who proposed
to organize another expedition from Kentucky to float down the Ohio and the Mississippi and attack New Orleans. Both these
projects required financial assistance, and this
Genêt meant to get from the United States
government by discounting the debts it
owed France in return for immediate payments. Washington held, however, that any
other plan of payment than the one already
agreed upon would constitute a breach of
neutrality, and so Genêt found himself
totally without funds. The expedition
against Florida was given up, but George
Rogers Clark took his commission as an
officer in the "French Revolutionary Army
of America" seriously, and found a few Westerners who were sufficiently eager to dislodge
the Spanish from the mouth of the Mississippi to be willing to serve as his "Revolutionary Legion of Kentuckians" regardless of
financial reward. Had they known that
Genêt also hoped to separate the back country from the rest of the United States in
order to make it over into a republic under
French influence, their attitude might have
been different.

Meantime Genêt got into trouble with
Washington over his plans for privateering.
The Little The President was willing to
Democrat live up to the letter of the treaties of alliance as he interpreted them, but
he insisted that they did not authorize the
use of American ports as bases of operation
for privateers, and he would not countenance
the sending into American ports for sale of
the prizes that the French privateers took
at sea. Genêt was much disappointed at
this attitude, and in spite of it proposed to
convert a prize, the *Little Sarah*, into an
armed ship, and send her out to sea. He was

warned that this must not happen, and promised not to allow the *Little Democrat*, as he
had rechristened the ship, to sail without
notice. Within a few days Genêt broke his
word. After discussing the matter with his
Cabinet, Washington asked the French government to recall Genêt, and announced that
thereafter all French prizes and privateers
would be denied access to American ports.
By this time the French Revolution had
progressed another step in the direction of
radicalism, and Genêt was already out of
favor at home. A new minister, Fauchet,
was appointed, who was instructed to send
his predecessor home under arrest. Genêt
realized that his return to France might cost
him his life, so he asked permission of Washington to stay on in the United States.
Washington mercifully consented.

After Genêt's retirement the President
learned of the activities of George Rogers
Clark, and ordered the governor of Kentucky to put an end to them. The governor
took his time about it, but Fauchet, anxious
to redeem the reputation of his nation with
Washington, also denounced the project,
and nothing more came of it.

It soon became apparent that neutrality
was not altogether without its rewards. The
export trade, particularly in **The profits**
provisions bound for the warring **of neutrality**
nations, grew by leaps and bounds. The
American carrying trade also prospered, for
neutral vessels were safer than the merchant
ships of nations flying enemy flags. Particularly lucrative was the trade between the
French West Indies and France, which had
hitherto been a monopoly of French traders,
but was now opened to vessels from the
United States. Prices responded to the increased demand for American produce, sailors' wages rose, and shipbuilders as well as
shipowners reaped a rich harvest. Congress under these circumstances backed the
President strongly in his policy of neutrality.
It established by a law of 1794 definite rules
of neutrality, emphasizing particularly the
duties of neutrals, and it appropriated
seventy-five thousand dollars to be used if

needed in enforcing the law. With the public, the policy of neutrality came to be better appreciated, and for the time being there were not many who would have preferred war.

Prosperity, indeed, seemed to be an accompaniment of the new government. Prob-**Election of 1792** ably the period of depression that had coincided with the years in which the Articles of Confederation were in effect had by 1789 about run its course, and doubtless better times would have come regardless of the form of government. But to a great share of the public it seemed that the adoption of the Constitution had brought about the change, and by the end of Washington's first administration there were comparatively few who regretted the establishment of the new government. There were many, however, who felt that the Federalists had gone too far in the direction of centralization and had granted un-

reasonable favors to the propertied interests. To remedy this defect they were already considering the wisdom of placing the government in other hands. Had Washington retired at the end of his first term, as he had wished to do, undoubtedly there would have been a hard fight between the Hamiltonian and Jeffersonian factions over the choice of his successor. But Washington was persuaded to stand for re-election, and there was none who would oppose him. When it came to the Vice-Presidency, which John Adams held, the Republicans had fewer scruples, and gave their votes to George Clinton. In the election of 1792, Washington again received a unanimous vote, but Clinton, who carried New York, Virginia, North Carolina, and Georgia, and took one vote in Pennsylvania, received a total of 50 votes to 77 for Adams. It was clear that in the course of time a real party struggle for the control of the national government would be staged.

Bibliography

The central figure in the new government, George Washington, has naturally received extensive biographic treatment. The best complete biography of Washington is N. W. Stephenson and W. H. Dunn, *George Washington* (2 vols., 1940). H. C. Lodge, *George Washington* (2 vols., 1889), is wholly laudatory, but contains much good history. D. S. Freeman, *George Washington* (4 vols., 1948–51), supplies an extensive reevaluation. Rupert Hughes, *George Washington* (3 vols., 1926–30), emphasizes the human qualities of Washington, while W. E. Woodward, *George Washington, The Image and the Man* (1926), is full of indiscriminate denunciation. J. H. Morgan and M. Fielding, *The Life Portraits of Washington and their Replicas* (1931), reproduces elaborately every known portrait of Washington. Among the many one-volume biographies worth citation are: J. C. Fitzpatrick, *George Washington Himself* (1933); P. L. Ford, *The True George Washington* (1903); W. R. Thayer, *George Washington* (1922); L. M. Sears, *George Washington* (1932).

Biographies of the men who surrounded Washington are also important, but especially with respect to Hamilton and Jefferson biographers find it difficult to write without a bias. H. C. Lodge, *Alexander Hamilton* (1917), and J. T. Morse, Jr., *The Life of Alexander Hamilton* (2 vols., 1876), find little fault in the first Secretary of the Treasury. Claude Bowers, *Jefferson and Hamilton* (1925), tips the scales heavily in favor of Jefferson and against Hamilton. Somewhat more critical are W. G. Sumner, *Alexander Hamilton* (1890); and H. J. Ford, *Alexander Hamilton* (1920); Nathan Schachner, *Alexander Hamilton* (1946). L. K. Caldwell, *The Administrative Theories of Hamilton and Jefferson: Their Contribution to Thought on Public Administration* (1944), is an original concept, well executed. L. D. White, *The Federalists: A Study in Administrative History* (1948), also concentrates on this much-overlooked subject. *The Journal of William Maclay*, edited by E. S. Maclay (1890, new ed., 1927), is a delightful bit of American literature that throws much light on the organization of the new government. *The St. Clair Papers*, edited by W. H. Smith (2 vols., 1882), reveal the reasons for many of the new administration's troubles in the Old Northwest. Henry Adams, *The Life of Albert Gallatin* (1879, new ed., 1943), is useful for the troubles in western Pennsylvania. Gilbert Chinard, *Honest John Adams* (1933), is discriminating.

All of the extensive general histories cover this period in great detail. Channing, IV, begins here, and McMaster, I, ch. 6. J. S. Bassett, *The Federalist System* (1906), is the relevant volume in the *American Nation* series; and H. J. Ford, *Washington and his Colleagues* (1918), serves for the *Chronicles of America*. J. P. Gordy, *Political History of the United States with Special Reference to the Growth of Political Parties* (2 vols., 1903), is still an excellent guide to early American politics. Of fundamental importance on presidential elections is Edward Stanwood, *A History of the Presidency* (2 vols., 1898, new ed., 1916). G. H. Haynes, *The Senate of the United States: Its History and Practice* (2 vols, 1938), is painstaking and enlightening. C. G. Haines, *The Role of the Supreme Court in American Government and Politics, 1789–1835* (1944), presents an anti-Federalist view.

There are books on a great variety of special subjects pertaining to the period. C. A. Beard, *Economic Origins of Jeffersonian Democracy* (1915, new ed., 1949), continues the argument begun in his *Economic Interpretation of the Constitution*, already mentioned. L. D. Baldwin, *Whiskey Rebels, the Story of a Frontier Uprising* (1939), is excellent. F. J. Turner, *The Significance of Sections in American History* (1932), contains two useful essays on the diplomatic relations between the United States and France during this period. Louise B. Dunbar, *A Study of "Monarchical" Tendencies in the United States from 1776 to 1801* (1923), reveals the strength of conservative thought in the new nation. On the social side, J. A. Krout and D. R. Fox, *The Completion of Independence, 1790–1830* (1944), is outstanding. A close-up view of urban life during this period is F. Monaghan and M. Lowenthal, *This was New York: The Nation's Capital in 1789* (1943). Of interest particularly on problems of the West is J. R. Jacobs, *The Beginning of the U.S. Army, 1783–1812* (1947). The evolution of political parties in a single state is the theme of H. M. Tinkcom, *The Republicans and Federalists in Pennsylvania, 1790–1801* (1950).

13

The Freedom of the Seas

English violations of American neutrality — The Embargo of 1794 — Jay's Treaty with England — Pinckney's Treaty with Spain — French violations of American neutrality — Indiscretions of Monroe — Party politics in the United States — Election of 1796 — John Adams — A mission to France — The X Y Z affair — Naval War of 1798

WITH the establishment of the government under the Constitution, American shipping interests took a new lease of life. In 1789 a navigation act was passed which placed a duty of fifty cents per ton upon ships built and owned by foreigners, and thirty cents per ton upon ships built by Americans but owned by foreigners. Ships that were both American-built and American-owned paid only six cents per ton. The result of the legislation was to stimulate greatly the carrying of American imports and exports in American ships. During the Confederation period it was the exception when an American ship carried goods either to or from America, but a few years after the adoption of the Constitution it was the rule.

An overwhelming proportion of American overseas trade was still with Great Britain, **Trade discriminations** although the British government as yet gave no evidence of willingness to sign a trade treaty with the United States, or to relax any of the discriminations against American trade that had been laid down at the close of the Revolutionary War. American ships entering British ports were faced by heavy port duties, and such American trade with the British West Indies as was permitted had to go in British ships. To remedy this situation, Madison proposed in 1789 that discriminatory tonnage duties should be levied against the ships of any nation with which the United States did not have a commercial treaty. Madison's proposal was not adopted,

but the threat worried the British, and an unofficial agent, Major Beckwith, was sent to the United States from Canada to find out what the new government proposed to do. Instead of dealing with Jefferson, the Secretary of State, Beckwith made contact with Hamilton, the Secretary of the Treasury. In 1791 the British for the first time sent a minister to the United States, George Hammond, and the United States sent Thomas Pinckney in the same capacity to England. But Beckwith stayed on in America to keep the ear of Hamilton, and to act as a go-between for him and Hammond. The Secretary of the Treasury was deeply solicitous about the maintenance of good relations with the British, and from him Beckwith soon gained the impression that the Federalists would never allow a war to break out between the two countries. Hamilton believed sincerely that war with Great Britain would mean the destruction of American commerce, and that in preference to such a blow peace should be maintained at any price.

The outbreak of war between Great Britain and France precipitated a situation that put a serious strain upon American **War in Europe** neutrality. One of the first war measures of the French government was to open to neutral nations the trade between the French West Indies and France. Ordinarily this trade was a French monopoly, but the possibility that the British navy might cut the communications between the

French islands and the mother country was great, and so in time of war the French government stood ready to countenance trade which in time of peace it strictly forbade. The French officials fully expected that Americans would assume the trade thrown open, and they doubtless hoped that such a development would mean trouble between Great Britain and the United States.

As foreseen, American ships soon flocked to the French islands, and the prospect of **The "rule of 1756"** splendid wartime profits seemed great. But in June, 1793, the British government announced that it would adhere to the so-called "rule of the War of 1756," according to which trade not open to a nation in time of peace could not be opened to that nation in time of war. All vessels and cargoes found to be engaged in any such trade were ordered to be seized. The news of this regulation, and the ruthless way in which it was enforced, filled Americans with dismay. Hundreds of American ships were taken, and American seamen and passengers were subjected to the grossest indignities. To make matters worse, the British government soon announced that all ships engaged in carrying the private property of French subjects would be confiscated when captured, but the American protests against this order were so sharp and so well justified that it was soon modified. Ships carrying French produce to Europe remained liable to capture, but the normal trade between the French islands and the United States was allowed to go on.

At best the rights of neutrals were subject to much dispute. The British government, **Neutral rights** accustomed for centuries to naval pre-eminence, tended to multiply the privileges that a belligerent power might exercise, while the Continental nations, with their less formidable navies, were disposed to challenge the British point of view and to defend the rights of neutrals. The United States, naturally enough, preferred the Continental way of thinking, and saw in the British practices indefensible violations of international law.

As time went on the disagreements multiplied. The United States held that neutral ships made neutral goods; hence, French goods on American ships should have been free from molestation. But the British orders flouted this doctrine. The United States held that foodstuffs were not to be regarded as contraband of war. The British argued that, inasmuch as imported provisions were essential to the French in their prosecution of the war, such cargoes might lawfully be taken over by the British and paid for. The United States adhered emphatically to the principle that a blockade to be legally binding must be effectively maintained by a blockading squadron off port, but the British did not hesitate to establish paper blockades of many French ports, or to capture neutral ships, bound for a forbidden destination, anywhere on the high seas. The United States held that the British had no international sanction whatever for their "rule of 1756." The British contended that it was unfair for France to monopolize trade with her colonies in time of peace, when her ships ran no risk, and then to expect that the same trade in time of war could enjoy immunity under a neutral flag.

The difficulties attendant upon enforcing the British regulations brought out still other differences. It was agreed on **Visit and** all sides that a belligerent ship **search** might in certain cases visit and search a neutral merchantman. On the extent to which the search might go there was complete disagreement. The United States contended that the boarding party had no right to do more than examine the ship's papers. The British insisted that such a search was no search at all in view of the ease with which fraudulent papers could be obtained. British boarding parties, therefore, examined the cargoes of suspected ships to see what was really carried.

Another difficulty was the disposition shown by these boarding parties to impress seamen into the British service. **Impress-** In the eighteenth century im- **ment** pressment from British merchant vessels was

CROWNINSHIELD'S WHARF, SALEM. High adventure and great wealth attended the rich shipping trade that sailed from Salem to every part of the world. Painting by George Ropes, 1806.

Shipping and commerce, *so fundamental to the welfare of the colonies, continued to play a vital part in the life of the new nation. While American trade ran principally with Great Britain, American produce also found markets elsewhere in Europe, and, in spite of hampering British and French regulations, in the West Indies. The* Empress of China, *which sailed from New York for Canton, in 1784, was the first United States merchantman to visit China.*

THE CHINA TRADE. Chinese fan presented to the Captain of the *Empress of China* by the Cantonese, showing the American ship, left, anchored at Whampoa, 1784.

TONTINE COFFEE HOUSE, NEW YORK. The shipping wharfs are visible at the end of the street at the right. Painting by Francis Guy, 1800.

a perfectly normal and legal method of recruiting the royal navy; hence, when British sailors were found on American ships, it seemed reasonable enough that they should be taken off and made to serve under the British colors. Sometimes the men so impressed were actually British subjects, and sometimes they were American-born. In the latter event they were usually returned, after suffering much hardship and inconvenience. But impressed sailors who were British-born, whether naturalized by the United States or not, were never returned, for the British government still held to the doctrine, "Once an Englishman, always an Englishman." The United States never conceded the right of impressment, and later on this abuse caused much friction between the two countries. For the moment the American government seemed less concerned about the rights of men than about the rights of property.

The British attack on American commerce gave to the pro-French Republicans an opportunity to urge drastic measures of retaliation. They pointed out that commercial reprisals had brought the mother country to terms in the years preceding the Revolution, and that England was in as great need of retaining the American trade now as then. Madison, speaking for Jefferson, advocated that whenever a foreign nation restricted American commerce, whether by duties, by tonnage taxes, or by the exclusion of our ships from her ports, the President should be empowered to return discrimination for discrimination.

Embargo of 1794

While this particular plan was not adopted, the illegal acts of the British so aroused public opinion in the United States that something spectacular had to be done. An embargo on foreign trade for one month (later extended to two months) was therefore authorized. For this space of time American ships were excluded from the high seas, and all foreign ships were excluded from American ports.

The embargo was a mere stop-gap, designed to call attention to the seriousness of the problem, and to give the government time to decide on a better plan. Nevertheless, many Republicans favored its continuance and argued that to abandon it would be to give the appearance of yielding to the British. Subsequently they brought forward a non-importation bill, directed specifically at British commerce, but it failed of adoption by the casting vote of the Vice-President. Extremists even suggested that debts owing to British creditors by Americans be seized — an act that could hardly have failed to provoke war. The strengthening of the military forces of the country was voted enthusiastically.

The Federalists, meantime, guided by the reasoning of Hamilton, had decided that a far safer policy than any that the Republicans proposed would be to seek concessions from Great Britain by treaty, and they finally persuaded Washington to send the Chief Justice, John Jay, to London for this purpose. Jay's instructions explicitly required him to obtain (1) evacuation by the British

John Jay, first Chief Justice, complained that the Supreme Court lacked "energy, weight, and dignity." Portrait by Gilbert Stuart.

of the military posts they held south of the Great Lakes, (2) compensation for their illegal seizures of American ships, (3) a satisfactory commercial treaty, which must embody, among other things, the American position on disputed points of international law. If such a treaty seemed unattainable, Jay was told to seek the co-operation of the northern nations of Europe in a joint effort to maintain neutral rights. He was then to report to his government for further instructions.

Jay should have been able to obtain a good treaty. His mission to England was a **Jay's negotiations** plain avowal that the United States would not be drawn into the war against the British if such a course could be honorably avoided, and that friendly treatment by the British might ultimately array the Americans on the British side against the French. Also, the threat that the United States might join with the northern neutrals of Europe in an armed neutrality ought to have had some weight in the negotiations. But Hamilton did much to undermine Jay's strength. He gave Hammond to understand that the

United States could neither be provoked into war nor into co-operation with any armed neutrality that the northern neutrals might propose. Jay was thus handicapped more than he knew, and perhaps under the circumstances he did as well as could have been expected. His decision to ignore his instructions is hard to defend, but, as one writer has pointed out, the treaty he negotiated should really have been called "Hamilton's treaty."

Jay succeeded in arranging in a fairly satisfactory way the disputes that had arisen out of the settlement of the Revolutionary War. The news of **Jay's treaty** the battle of Fallen Timbers had made a deep impression in England, and the British now agreed to withdraw their military posts from south of the Great Lakes. Plans were also made for the establishment of two joint commissions, one to settle the non-payment by Americans of their pre-Revolutionary War debts to British subjects, and the other to straighten out the disputed boundary line between Canada and Maine. This time the British lived up to their agreement with regard to the northwestern posts, and in 1796 their troops were withdrawn. In due time, also, a settlement of the debts controversy required the United States to pay British claims amounting to $2,664,000, and a compromise boundary line was recommended.

On commercial matters the treaty left much to be desired. A commission on spoliations was established to determine what payments the British should make for their recent illegal seizures of American ships and cargoes, and *vice versa*. Ultimately a balance of $5,705,654 was awarded to the United States. A trade treaty, to remain in force for a period of twelve years, was also agreed upon. It recognized at last the "most favored nation" principle in all trade relations between the United States and the "dominions of his majesty in Europe."

Colonial trade was separately considered. It was agreed that both nations should be permitted to use freely for trade purposes the "rivers, lakes, and waters" of the American continent, except within the limits of the Hudson's Bay Company's monopoly. The United States was also given generous trade privileges in the British East Indies. But the provisions that applied to the British West Indies fell far short of what Americans expected Jay to obtain. Article XII stipulated that American small sailing-vessels (not over seventy tons) might trade without discrimination in West Indian ports *on condition that* the United States would forbid American ships to carry molasses, sugar, coffee, cocoa, and cotton from the West Indies to any other country than the United States, *or from the United States to any part of the world except the United States.* British vessels, however, might freely enjoy the West Indian trade with the United States, and discriminations against them were expressly forbidden. These extraordinary provisions were designed to remain in force until two years after the close of the war between Great Britain and France, when they might or might not be renewed.

On the subject of neutral rights Jay gained very nearly nothing at all. He promised that the enemies of Great Britain should not be permitted to fit out privateers in American waters, as Genêt had once attempted, and that Americans who accepted commissions to serve against the British might be treated as pirates. On such important matters as visit and search and impressment, the treaty was ominously silent.

Although deeply displeased with Jay's failure to carry out his instructions, Washington, after some hesitation,
Ratification decided to submit the treaty to the Senate. There the terms that Jay had made, particularly with reference to the West Indian trade, almost defeated ratification; only by voting to strike out the obnoxious Article XII was a two-thirds majority obtained. Also, the President himself, because the British government had issued a new order for the seizure of provisions bound for France, seriously considered the advisability of halting the progress of the treaty. Finally, however, he decided to accept it if the British government would withdraw her

provisions order, and would agree to the elimination of Article XII. On this basis ratifications were ultimately exchanged. From the moment its terms were known, the public heartily denounced the treaty. Jay was excoriated at every turn, and Washington himself was not spared in the general disapproval. When Congress met in December, 1795, the House of Representatives almost refused to appropriate the funds necessary to carry the treaty into effect, but capitulated ultimately to the argument that, bad as it was, the treaty was preferable to its alternative, war.

Time seemed to show that the acceptance of the treaty was no mistake. It eased somewhat the obstacles confronted by American trade, and in conjunction with the treaty of Fort Greenville it opened the way for a new advance of settlement into the Northwest. Most important of all, its adoption greatly facilitated negotiations between the United States and Spain for the settlement of their long-standing difficulties over the southwestern frontier.

By 1795 Spain had withdrawn from her alliance with Great Britain, and had revived her normal friendship with France. The news that the United States had just signed an agreement with Great Britain disturbed the usual serenity of Count Manuel Godoy, then the most powerful statesman in Spain, who feared that Jay's treaty might be only the prelude to an alliance between the two English-speaking nations. Should such an alliance be formed, Spain stood a chance, in case of war, to lose Florida, and perhaps even more of her American possessions. As an offset to Jay's treaty, Godoy determined, therefore, to sign an even more generous treaty with the United States. Suddenly Thomas Pinckney, in charge of the American negotiations at Madrid, found his difficulties at an end.

In the resulting Treaty of San Lorenzo, or "Pinckney's treaty," as it is sometimes called, the Spanish King con- **Pinckney's** sented to the thirty-first parallel **treaty** as the northern boundary of Florida, conceded to Americans the navigation of the Mississippi "in its whole breadth from its source to the ocean," and agreed to allow citizens of the United States the right to deposit at New Orleans, duty-free, such merchandise as they planned to export. This "right of deposit" at New Orleans was to run for three years; thereafter the Spanish monarch promised renewal, but, if he chose, at some suitable site other than New Orleans. Thus, within a few months' time the most critical problems of the Northwest and the Southwest seemed to be solved. With trade freely opened down the Mississippi, the rapid growth of the West was assured.

So far as the relations between the United States and France were concerned, the signing of Jay's treaty had most unfortunate results. The treaty specifically denied that any of its provisions were meant to violate the French treaties, but the French government assumed, not without some reason, that the closer relationship established with Great Britain was in reality designed as a blow at France. Early in 1796 the French foreign minister taunted the American minister to France, James Monroe, with the statement that the agreement with the British had nullified the French treaties.

Already the French had developed what was known as the doctrine of retaliation. **French retaliations** They held that a neutral nation was obliged to defend its rights. If it failed to do so, then it was actually aiding the belligerent power from which it permitted mistreatment. Accordingly, the opposing belligerent had the right to retaliate on the erring neutral by doing the same things that the other belligerent did. In accordance with this doctrine, French seizures of American ships had taken place for a long time, but after the adoption of Jay's treaty French sea-captains were definitely ordered to treat American ships in the same way that American ships were being treated by the British. If, for example, the Americans permitted the British to seize provisions as contraband, the French might also seize provisions as contraband. The interpretation

of this order naturally varied somewhat according to the whims of the individual French commanders, but before long French violations of American neutral rights began to be about as offensive as anything the British had ever done.

In spite of these depredations, the French government felt that it could count on the friendship of the Republican **Monroe's** Party in the United States. Re- **indiscretion** publicans were usually bitter in their denunciation of Jay's treaty, and firm in their devotion to the French treaties. Moreover, the Republican minister from the United States, James Monroe, showed plainly that his sympathy lay with the French. Inadequately informed as to the real purpose of Jay's mission to England, he had done nothing to prepare the French for the treaty, which shocked him as deeply as it shocked them. In this frame of mind, he neglected to present the official explanation of the treaty that he had belatedly received, and he may have dropped the hint that after the next presidential election things would be different in the United States. For his indiscreet conduct he was promptly recalled, but the French government truculently refused to receive the reliable Federalist, C. C. Pinckney, whom Washington sent to replace him.

By the time the election year of 1796 had arrived, Washington had made up his mind not to accept another term. **Jeffersonian** This meant that a clear-cut **Republicans** party conflict could no longer be forestalled. Jefferson, out of the Cabinet since 1793, had built up a strong following among the common people, with which he meant to wrest control of the government from the Federalists. The small farmers, deeply offended by every item of Hamilton's financial program and by the forceful suppression of the Whiskey Rebellion, were readily induced to follow his lead. The states'-rights element was also with him, for the Supreme Court, in one of its first important decisions, *Chisholm vs. Georgia* (1793), had held that a state might be sued by a citizen of another state. No more complete denial of the doctrine of state sovereignty could have been devised, and the decision was promptly recalled by the submission and ratification of the Eleventh Amendment. Federalists as well as Republicans favored the amendment, but Republicans blamed the Federalists for the decision, and maintained that they repudiated it only because they dared not do otherwise.

The whole anti-British element in the population tended to favor Jefferson. Such persons denounced the truckling attitude of the Federalists toward Great Britain and the humiliating treaty that it had brought forth. They professed still to admire the French Revolution, and to believe that in the war with Great Britain France was battling against autocracy on behalf of "liberty, equality, and fraternity." Supported by a bitingly sarcastic press, and surrounded by a group of efficient lieutenants, Jefferson was ready to make his bid for the Presidency. For strategic reasons his choice for Vice-President fell on Aaron Burr, a leader in the New York democracy.

The Federalists, meantime, had lost ground. Their concern for the commercial classes and the well-to-do, however much it might make for the prosperity of the country, was totally lacking in popular appeal. They had been long enough in office for numerous grievances against them to accumulate, and for dangerous internal dissensions to appear. They were unable to nominate their ablest leader, Hamilton, who, notwithstanding the fact that in 1795 he had followed Jefferson's example in leaving the Cabinet, had retained a powerful voice in the administration. A caucus of the Federalist members of Congress, fearful that Hamilton's ultra-conservatism might cost the party votes, chose John Adams to be the Federalist candidate for the Presidency, and Thomas Pinckney for the Vice-Presidency. Thereupon Hamilton, knowing well that his influence over Adams would be slight, intrigued to throw the election to Pinckney. Hamilton's plan came out during the campaign, and revealed a rift in the party that almost cost the Federalists the

Federalist losses

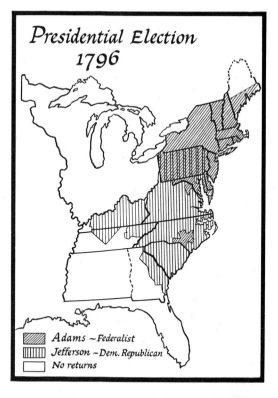

Presidential Election 1796

Adams ~Federalist
Jefferson ~Dem. Republican
No returns

election. Also, it left Adams with an abiding distrust of Hamilton.

The French government, quite unintentionally, came to the aid of the Federalists. Its attack on American commerce, although undoubtedly designed to heighten dissatisfaction with the Jay treaty and thus to help the Republicans, merely added to the anti-French feeling in the United States, and strengthened the Federalists. The French government also, in protest against the Jay treaty, ordered Adet, the French minister to the United States, to give up his office; but it unwisely permitted him to remain in America to work for the election of Jefferson. Adet tried to induce American electors to support the Republican candidates by the threat of a war with France in case the Federalists were not turned out. Undoubtedly the chief result of the French efforts to interfere in the election was to turn many voters to Adams who might otherwise have supported Jefferson. The American people were then, and still

Election of 1796

are, deeply resentful of any attempt on the part of a foreign nation to influence their internal political decisions. By a narrow majority, 71 to 68, Adams was chosen over Jefferson. Hamilton's scheme to elect Pinckney to the Presidency was foiled by the action of many New England electors who voted for Adams, but refused to support Pinckney. The curious outcome of this procedure was that Pinckney received fewer votes than Jefferson, and the Vice-Presidency fell to the leader of the defeated party.

Washington left office with far less popularity than when he assumed it. His dream of avoiding the formation of political parties in the United States had been shattered, and he had been forced, alike by his temperament and by his convictions, to ally himself with the Federalists. This display of partisanship exposed him to many bitter attacks. Even his Farewell Address, which later generations came to revere so much, was published on the eve of the election of 1796, and was construed by the Republicans as a campaign document. He urged loyalty to the Union, cautioned against an "irregular opposition" to government, and warned against the entanglements that might result from a too active participation by the new nation in European politics. From the Republican press there was little but rejoicing when the first President laid down the reins of office. After March 4, 1797, he retired to Mount Vernon in order to take up again the life of a Virginia planter. For the most part he kept carefully away from the stir of politics, and even before his death, in 1799, he had regained much of his former popularity.

The new President, John Adams (1735–1826), looked the part of greatness less than his predecessor. During the debate on titles in the Senate his short, stout figure caused some wit to suggest that a suitable title for the first Vice-President would be "His Rotundity." But Adams was one of the ablest men ever to occupy the presidential chair. He had been a lawyer of more than local fame before the Revolution, and his rôle during that eventful

John Adams

struggle was always an important one. He served as minister to England during the Confederation period, and it was no fault of his that his mission did not succeed. He assumed the duties of Vice-President with some pride, only to write a little later in disillusionment to his wife: "My country has in its wisdom contrived for me the most insignificant office that ever the invention of man contrived or his imagination conceived." Subsequent Vice-Presidents have usually agreed that Adams was right, and with better reason than he; for the early Senate was often evenly divided, and the casting vote of the Vice-President gave Adams real power. In spite of the radicalism of his Revolutionary War utterances, Adams was a thoroughgoing aristocrat, and supported willingly the policies of Washington and Hamilton. But he was never anybody's man but his own. Vain of his own ability, and often irritable to the point of anger when crossed, he was nevertheless, in the words of Jefferson, "as disinterested as the being who made him." His decisions with regard to national policy were invariably the result of his best judgment, and were wholly disregardful of the political fortunes of John Adams. Few men have ever served their country so well.

He was soon called upon to show his mettle. The result of the election of 1796 still further alienated the French, **Anti-French** whose spoliation of American **sentiment** commerce in no wise abated. As a crowning insult James Monroe, the Republican, was shown exceptional courtesies in France, while Pinckney, the Federalist, was not only refused recognition as minister but was also pointedly informed that a French law forbade aliens to remain in the country longer than two months without permission. When news of this outrage reached the United States, many Federalists were ready to sever all relations with France, even at the risk of war. But Adams, for the time being supported by Hamilton, knew that the United States was in no position to take such a stand. Public opinion was badly divided, with many of the southern states still overwhelmingly pro-French, and the nation was utterly unprepared for war. Adams urged instead that a mission to consist of three envoys be sent to France to treat for the restoration of good relations.

With the help of the more moderate Federalists, Adams got his mission. Two Federalists, C. C. Pinckney and John **A mission to** Marshall, and one Republican, **France** Elbridge Gerry, were appointed, and in the fall of 1797 they appeared in Paris. The French Directorate was then at the height of its glory, with the unsavory Talleyrand as its foreign minister. Corruption ruled the day. Talleyrand probably meant to treat with the Americans, but seeing no harm in obtaining a bribe as the price of opening negotiations, he instructed three of his subordinates, later known as X, Y, and Z, to call upon the American envoys and so inform them. When the Americans explained that they were not authorized to offer a bribe, and tried to talk of other things, one of the agents exclaimed: "Gentlemen, you do not speak to the point. It is money; it is expected that you will offer money." To which Pinckney, who was a little deaf and was loath to believe his ears, at length replied, "No, no; not a sixpence." The envoys then drew up a full statement of the American case and delivered it to Talleyrand. Two months later the French minister stated the French contentions, and insulted the American delegation by expressing his desire to continue conversations with the Republican, Gerry, but not with the Federalists. Thereupon Pinckney and Marshall left the country. Gerry had the bad judgment to stay on, although in a private capacity only, until Adams peremptorily ordered him back to the United States.

The "X Y Z dispatches," as the report on the French negotiations came to be called, **The "X Y Z** were not at once made public. **dispatches"** Adams's Cabinet was for war to avenge the insult, but Adams, still supported by Hamilton, was determined to avoid war if he could. Ultimately Congress asked to see the correspondence and Adams released

John Adams

THE SECOND PRESIDENT of the United States, Adams was the first distinguished member of a family which, through four generations, contributed spectacularly to the making of American history. Historians have made great use of the writings of both Adams and his extremely capable wife, Abigail, who expressed their thoughts freely on many matters. Portrait by Gilbert Stuart.

it, reserving only the names of the French agents, X, Y, and Z. Members of Congress were as shocked as Pinckney had been and voted for the publication of the dispatches in full. The result was great excitement throughout the country, and Pinckney's refusal to consider a bribe, liberally translated, yielded a brilliant slogan: "Millions for defense, but not one cent for tribute." Adams himself declared that he would "never send another minister to France without assurances that he will be received, respected, and honored as the representative of a free, powerful, and independent nation." Congress voted liberal appropriations to strengthen the national defense, but following Adams's sensible leadership it kept cool and made no declaration of war. The treaties with France were repealed, however, and the alliance with France was thus brought formally to an end.

The defense program included the establishment of a separate navy department, and the addition to the navy of twelve armed ships and ten galleys. Three powerful frigates which had already been authorized, the **Prepared-** *United States* and the *Consti-* **ness** *tution*, of forty-four guns each, and the *Constellation*, of thirty-six guns, were now made ready for battle. Merchantmen were permitted to carry guns for use in their own defense, and over four hundred privateers were released. The ships of the national navy, as fast as they could be commissioned, were ordered to seize French privateers wherever found, and to take whatever measures were necessary for the protection of American commerce.

The new navy gave a good account of itself. The *Constellation* attacked, outfought, **Naval war** and captured *L'Insurgente*, a **of 1798** French frigate that had seized many American merchantmen, and stood off the superior French ship, *La Vengeance*. The *Boston* took the *Berceau*. Many minor engagements occurred, and altogether the Americans captured eighty-four French ships, most of them privateers. American losses were also heavy. For over two years this period of "armed neutrality" continued, but the existence of a state of war went unrecognized by either nation.

Meantime there was much wrangling about the establishment of an army. France was far away, and was unlikely to send an invading force across the Atlantic, so that the use to which this weapon could be placed was problematic. Nevertheless Congress authorized the enlistment of a new regiment of artillery and gave the President authority to raise ten thousand volunteers. The command of this army became immediately a matter of public discussion. All agreed that Washington should be commander-in-chief, but the age of the ex-President precluded his taking an active part in campaigns. Who, then, should be second in command? Hamilton, it soon developed, burned with a great desire for the place, and intrigued to get it. Unfortunately Adams had kept Washington's Cabinet, most of whom were still under the influence of Hamilton, and in the end Hamilton had his way. Probably he dreamed of active service against the Spanish

in America. He was in close touch with Don Francisco de Miranda, a Spanish-American who wished to enlist the aid of the United States in the cause of independence for the Spanish colonies, and he still had means of private communication with the British government. With British naval assistance and a small American army, dazzling possibilities lay open, among them the conquest of Florida and Louisiana for the United States, and the formation of a great Spanish-American republic, whose trade relations with the United States would be intimate.

But the army was slow to materialize, for Adams did not much believe in it. "Regiments cost money," he told his **The army** Secretary of War, when the latter complained of the slowness of the President in exercising the power Congress had given him. And money was hard to raise. Tariff receipts, owing to the troublous times on the high seas, were going down. Congress therefore levied new excises, and attempted with as little success as under the Confederation to collect a direct tax from the states. In the end heavy loans had to be floated. It was the spring of 1799 before recruiting actually began, and by that time the war fever had cooled off. "The army is progressing like a wounded snake," said one observer.

All the while Adams was eager for peace, although Hamilton, with high hopes of glory and combat for himself, now **A second** wished for war. Unofficial in- **mission to** formation that the French gov- **France** ernment did not really desire war came to the President from several sources, and finally Talleyrand opened communications through the French representative at The Hague with our minister to Holland, William Vans Murray. In due time Murray informed Adams that Talleyrand was ready to receive a minister from the United States should one be sent. Adams's cabinet, in close harmony with Hamilton, was against any such action, for clearly it might lead to peace. But in February, 1799, when Hamilton was bending every effort to recruit an army, Ad-

PREPARATION FOR WAR TO DEFEND COMMERCE. Building the Frigate *Philadelphia*, 1797. Engraving by William Birch.

THE NAVAL WAR. The *Constellation* and *L'Insurgente* in battle. February 9, 1799. Engraving by Edward Savage.

CINQUE-TETES, OR THE PARIS MONSTER. A cartoon of 1799 depicting the five-headed Directory demanding money, the three American negotiators replying, "We will not give you six pence."

The undeclared war of 1798 between the United States and France kept the country in a turmoil for many months. The navy was enlarged and improved, and its ships saw much real fighting. In general, public opinion strongly supported the war, and looked with suspicion upon the persistent efforts of the President, John Adams, to promote peace. Nevertheless, when Adams succeeded in negotiating a settlement, there were few to regret that hostilities had ended.

PEACE CONVENTION. Signing the pact between the French Republic and the United States at Mortefontaine, Sept. 30, 1800. By F. Piranesi, after J. Barbieri, 1800.

ams sent to the Senate the nomination of William Vans Murray as minister to France. The more warlike Federalists were shocked beyond measure, but with the country less and less inclined toward war they dared not oppose the President. They urged a commission, however, instead of a minister, and on that the President gave in. Adams appointed Oliver Ellsworth, W. R. Davie, and Murray as the commission, but before he would send them he asked and obtained from Talleyrand a direct promise that they would be properly received.

By the time the envoys reached Paris, the star of Bonaparte was in the ascendancy. **Peace restored** Under his leadership the new French government was eager to make peace, not only with the United States, but also as nearly as possible with all nations. With Bonaparte posing in the rôle of peacemaker, the task of the Americans was easy. By a convention signed September 30, 1800, France agreed to the abrogation of the earlier treaties, and accepted the principle that neutral ships make neutral goods. The United States, on the other hand, waived indemnities for illegal seizures by the French of American shipping. When the treaty reached America, the country was entirely over its war mood, and however much some of the Federalists disliked the

prospect of peace, the treaty could not be turned down. The Federalist Senate accorded it only a conditional ratification, but once the Federalists were out of power the new Republican Senate, on December 19, 1801, ratified it without reservation.

John Adams was much criticized by some members of his party for keeping the country out of war, but there are few now who would not concede that he was right. By his course those embarrassing entanglements with European nations that Washington had advised against were avoided, and the policy of permanent American neutrality with regard to European wars was given an added impetus. What the schemes of Hamilton might have brought forth had he actually commanded an army in time of war, one can only surmise. Adams at length revolted against the Hamiltonian influence in his Cabinet, and reorganized that body with John Marshall, a moderate Federalist, as Secretary of State. A less conscientious man would have taken such action years before. Adams was never forgiven by the extreme Federalists for his unwillingness to lead the country into war, but years later he said that as his epitaph he could ask nothing better than "Here lies John Adams, who took upon himself the responsibility of peace with France in the year 1800."

Bibliography

The American Secretaries of State and Their Diplomacy, edited by S. F. Bemis (10 vols., 1927–29), is a co-operative work that covers in detail the history of American foreign relations. See also the two excellent textbooks on American foreign relations, already mentioned: Bemis, *Diplomatic History of the United States;* and Bailey, *Diplomatic History of the American People.* J. B. Moore, *The Principles of American Diplomacy* (1918), treats in chronological fashion the principal subjects of American foreign policy. R. W. Van Alstyne, *American Diplomacy in Action: A Series of Case Studies* (1944), is also topi-

cal, and attempts to write diplomatic history as a guide for current diplomatic problems. C. M. Thomas, *American Neutrality in 1793* (1931), is an illuminating monograph. S. F. Bemis, *Jay's Treaty: A Study in Commerce and Diplomacy* (1923), covers the problems that led to Jay's mission, as well as the formation of the treaty. It is invaluable on this episode of American diplomacy. Much the same can be said for *Pinckney's Treaty* (1926), by the same author. Both subjects are reviewed in an excellent biography, Frank Monaghan, *John Jay, Defender of Liberty* (1935). See also B. W. Bond, Jr., *The Monroe Mission to*

France, 1794–1796 (1907). G. W. Allen, *Our Naval War with France* (1909), covers the period of hostilities adequately. J. F. Rippy and Angie Debo, *The Historical Background of the American Policy of Isolation* (1924), is useful. See also Merle Curti, *The Roots of American Loyalty* (1946).

The Selected Writings of John and John Quincy Adams, edited by A. Koch and W. Peden (1946), presents in documentary fashion the important roles of the second and sixth Presidents in American diplomacy. J. T. Adams, *The Adams Family* (1930), contains discriminating appraisals of the two Presidents and several other prominent members of the family.

A. J. Beveridge, *The Life of John Marshall* (4 vols., 1916–19), is not only a biography of Marshall, but is also a brilliant history of the period from a conservative point of view.

14

The Revolution of 1800

Alien and Sedition Acts — Kentucky and Virginia Resolutions — Federalist dissension — Election of 1800 — Judiciary Act of 1801 — Why the Federalists lost — Jefferson — The new capital city — Economic conditions — Borrowings from Europe — Science in America — Education — Literature — Deism — Unitarianism — Orthodoxy — Revivalism — Art and architecture — Need of better communications — The West

THE victory of the Federalists over the Republicans in 1796 was won by an extremely **Pro-Federalist sentiment** narrow margin, and Adams was always sensitive to the taunt that he was "President by three votes"; but the threat of war with France tended both to strengthen his hands and to give courage to the diminished Federalist majority in Congress. In part to guard against the danger of anti-war activities within the United States, and in part to insure against the calamity of a Republican victory at the polls, the Federalist leaders pushed through Congress during the summer of 1798 an extensive program of legislation known as the Alien and Sedition Acts.

Unhappily for the Federalists, most of the foreigners who came to the United States during this period joined the Republican Party. Many of them were refugee Frenchmen who had been thoroughly indoctrinated with the theories of the French Revolution. Others were Irishmen or Englishmen whose radicalism had made it expedient for them to emigrate. Among the newcomers were many highly educated men who, as pamphleteers or editors of newspapers, gave no quarter to Adams and the party he represented.

Three of the Federalist measures dealt with the problem presented by these aliens. A naturalization law extended **The Alien Acts** the period of residence in the United States preliminary to citizenship from five to fourteen years. Another law, the Alien Friends Act, which dealt with aliens in time of peace, authorized the President to order any alien whose presence he regarded as dangerous to leave the country. Should the alien refuse to obey, he might be imprisoned for three years; or should he return after having left, he might be imprisoned for as long a term as the President saw fit. A third act, the Alien Enemy Act, designed to apply to aliens in time of war, gave the President the right to order such persons out of the country, or to imprison them at will. The Alien Acts were never applied. Their purpose was probably to frighten pro-Republican Frenchmen out of the country, and undoubtedly they served their purpose well.

Another thorn in the flesh to the Federalists was the intemperate criticism to which the President, Federalist members of Congress, and all other Federalist leaders were subjected by the Republican "rabble." Such criticism was often libelous, and it nearly always passed the bounds of truth. Scurrilous editors delighted in multiplying epithets, and pamphleteers stopped at nothing. Federalists as well as Republicans could call their adversaries names, but the leading office-holders were Federalists, not Republicans. Furthermore, Federalist measures as well as men were assailed, and the drift toward war with France was bitterly denounced.

A fourth repressive measure, the Sedition Act, was designed to subdue all such criticism of the administration. It

The Sedition Act defined as a high misdemeanor, punishable by a fine of not more than five thousand dollars and imprisonment for not more than five years, any combination or conspiracy to oppose the legal measures of the government, or to interfere with their execution. The publication of any false or malicious writing directed against the President or Congress, and designed to stir up hatred against them, was made a misdemeanor, conviction of which carried a fine of not more than two thousand dollars and imprisonment for not more than two years.

The Sedition Act, like the Alien Acts, accomplished more by the threat it made than by any actual enforcement. A large number of indictments were returned, but only a few persons, most of them prominent Republican editors, were brought to trial. When trials were held, however, the methods of the prosecution were as ruthless as the law under which the charge was made, and Federalist judges sometimes laid themselves open to the charge of partisanship. In general, the law proved to be a boomerang to the Federalists. Republicans who were convicted were regarded by their fellows as martyrs to the cause of free speech, and the process of enforcement was held continually before the people as an example of what might be expected if Federalist rule were to continue.

To offset the Alien and Sedition Acts, which the Republicans regarded as unconstitutional, Jefferson and Madison soon put forward their famous Kentucky and Virginia Resolutions. **Kentucky and Virginia Resolutions** These measures proposed that the states should assume the right to decide when Congress had exceeded its powers under the Constitution. Some pointed to the Supreme Court as the logical place for this authority to reside, but the case of *Marbury vs. Madison*, by which the Court first clearly declared itself on this question, was several years in the future. The reso-

Congressional Pugilists. Republican Representative Lyon and Federalist Representative Griswold engaged in "royal sport" on the floor of Congress during the debates on the Alien and Sedition Acts. Anonymous drawing, 1798.

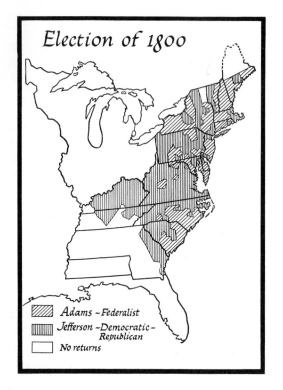

Election of 1800

Adams ~Federalist
Jefferson ~Democratic~
        Republican
No returns

lutions of the Virginia legislature, which Madison had drafted, stopped with an assertion that the states might properly "interpose" their authority against such "palpable and alarming infractions of the constitution" as were contained in the Alien and Sedition Acts, but those which the Kentucky legislature adopted, and which had secretly come from the pen of Jefferson, went much further. They called upon the other states to join Kentucky in declaring the Alien and Sedition Acts "void and of no force, and . . . in requesting their repeal at the next session of Congress."

The Kentucky and Virginia Resolutions were not echoed by the legislatures of other states, and probably their authors had no such expectation. The chief purpose of the resolutions was to furnish Jefferson a platform on which to make his race for the Presidency in 1800. He meant to drive home to the electorate the dangers of Federalist rule. If the Federalists chose to violate the Constitution in one way, why

not in another? And if a halt were not called soon, how long would it be before some Federalist administration, supported by a strong army and a strong navy, would choose to obliterate the rights of the states themselves as well as the rights of individuals? But the remedy that Jefferson had in mind was not really nullification. It was the election of Thomas Jefferson to the Presidency.

When Adams kept his country out of war he did so at the expense of his own chance of re-election. In 1798, with **Federalist** war seemingly imminent, the **dissension** determination of the voters to stand by the President was so strong that the Federalists made almost a clean sweep of the mid-term congressional elections. Had Adams then made war rather than peace, it seems reasonable to suppose that he might have retained the support of the people until after the election of 1800 was over. Furthermore, the Alien and Sedition Acts would have aroused less resentment in time of war, and could have been used far more successfully to silence the opposition. But the Federalists, instead of being united in the support of a popular war, again found themselves handicapped by factional strife. Hamilton, thoroughly disgruntled by Adams's peace policy, denounced the President vigorously in a pamphlet intended for private distribution among selected Federalist leaders. The pamphlet naturally fell into the hands of the Republicans, who used it to good advantage in the campaign. Hamilton also revived his scheme of four years before to defeat Adams by throwing the election to C. C. Pinckney, whom the Federalists intended to make Vice-President. But all such efforts, as in 1796, worked only in the interest of the Republicans.

The result of the election was a clean-cut victory for the Republican candidates, Jefferson and Burr. Seventy- **Election** three Republican electors were **of 1800** chosen, as against sixty-five Federalists. The strength of the Republicans lay mainly to the south of the Mason and Dixon's line,

Thomas Jefferson of Virginia, third

President of the United States, should normally have been a conservative, for he was "well-born, well-educated, and well-to-do." Instinctively, however, he championed the common people against the aristocrats. In his youth he shared the gay life of the first families of Virginia, but even then was strongly interested in the rights of man. In his maturity he first created a political party in opposition to the Federalists, then with consummate skill led it to victory. The portrait of Jefferson is by Rembrandt Peale, 1805. At right is an early view of the University of Virginia, largely Jefferson's creation, where many of his ideals of equalitarian education were put into practical use.

where they lost only the votes of Delaware, one half the votes of Maryland, and one third the votes of North Carolina. The Republicans also carried New York, thanks mainly to the activities of Burr, who succeeded in uniting all factions opposed to the Federalists in that state; and they won eight votes out of fifteen in Pennsylvania. The only solidly Federalist territory was New England, New Jersey, and Delaware. Probably the trend of the masses toward the Republicans would have shown even more clearly had there been fewer restrictions upon the suffrage. It was particularly significant that the new western states, Kentucky and Tennessee, voted for Jefferson, and that nearly every state with a considerable frontier element either voted for Jefferson or gave him more votes than it gave Adams. Already the leavening influence of frontier democracy had begun to work.

Unfortunately, the election was not decided when the electoral college had registered its will. The provision in the Constitution which permitted each elector to vote for two candidates for the Presidency had made Jefferson Vice-President in 1796 when a majority of the electors were against him, and it now almost cost him the Presidency. A thoughtful New England Federalist threw away a vote on Jay, so that Pinckney got one less vote than Adams, but the Republican electors with greater zeal than foresight voted unanimously for Jefferson and Burr. These two having, therefore, an equal number of votes, it fell to the strongly Federalist House of Representatives, elected in 1798, to choose between them. A Federalist caucus decided to support Burr rather than Jefferson, but this decision was disobeyed by enough southern Federalists to deadlock the House. For thirty-five ballots there was no choice. At last, acting on the advice of Hamilton, who disliked Jefferson but knew Burr to be a rogue, the Federalists relented sufficiently to give the Presidency to Jefferson. Once the Republicans were in power they lost no time in amending the Constitution so that each elector should thereafter vote separately for President and for Vice-President.

Washington, the new capital city, was laid out after a plan drawn by Major Pierre Charles L'Enfant, a young French engineer and architect who had served in the Patriot army, and after the war had remained in the United States. L'Enfant's plan was too ambitious for his time, but its worth was eventually recognized, and its ideas have governed the recent development of the city.

THE PRESIDENT'S HOUSE. Engraving by N. King, 1801.

L'ENFANT'S PLAN. Engraving by Thackara and Vallance, 1792.

The sullen reluctance of the Federalists to bow to the popular will was shown again in the passage after the election of a new Judiciary Act. To make **Judiciary Act of 1801** sure that the Supreme Court would not pass from Federalist control for a long time, the law provided that the next vacancy on the Court should not be filled, so that thereafter the number of Supreme Court justices would be one less than formerly. Also, the old practice whereby Supreme Court justices on circuit duty sat with district judges as courts of appeal was discontinued, and a whole new panel of circuit judges was authorized. Then, in spite of the fact that the duties of the district judges were thus reduced, their number was increased from thirteen to twenty-three. The evident and expressed intent of the law was not so much to reform the judiciary as to give the outgoing President the chance to pack it with Federalist judges who could be trusted to thwart the Republicans in the years to come. Adams, who on internal matters was as narrowly partisan as anyone, had already bequeathed to the Jefferson administration his Secretary of State, John Marshall, as Chief Justice, and he carried out the terms of the law in the spirit of its framers.

It is not surprising that the Federalists went down to defeat. They failed to recognize that in a democracy the opinions of the masses must be considered. They persisted too long in their assumption that government could be monopolized by the well-educated and the well-to-do. They proceeded too rapidly in their endeavor to build up a powerful centralized government, and they paid far too little attention to the strong state loyalties that had grown so naturally out of the separate status of the various colonies. Moreover, they were led by men who were for the most part commercially minded, and ignored the fact that the vast majority of the American people got their living from the soil.

Why the Federalists lost

Nevertheless, the Federalists in many important ways had served their country well. They had succeeded in making the new government work; the Constitution, and many of the precedents they had set, were destined to endure. They had successfully avoided entanglements in European affairs when a contrary policy might well have been fatal to the new nation. They had established the credit of the United States at home and abroad, and had given a praiseworthy example of honest and frugal administration.

Thomas Jefferson (1743–1826), whose election to the Presidency ushered in what he was pleased to term the "Revolution of 1800," was, like Washington, a Virginia planter, but with that similarity ends. Jefferson's father was from Albemarle County, which at the time Thomas was born was properly regarded as "back country." Jefferson's mother was a

Jefferson

Randolph, and hence from one of the first families of Virginia, but this aristocratic connection did not in the least undermine the sturdy, frontier democracy of her husband, nor prevent the development of her son into perhaps the outstanding theoretical democrat of all time.

Jefferson's formal education was much better than Washington's. The former attended William and Mary College, where he learned Latin, Greek, and French, and acquired such facility with languages that he soon added to his accomplishments Spanish, Italian, and Anglo-Saxon. He had also a good familiarity with mathematics, especially the calculus, and his knowledge of natural sciences was unusual for his day. His whole life long Jefferson maintained his thirst for learning. He was interested also in music and the arts, played the violin well, and knew enough about architecture to design his house at Monticello. After leaving college he studied law, and for a number of years he practiced that profession. The death of his father, however, gave him an estate to manage, and its management interested him more than the law. So also did the fascinating game of politics.

On the eve of the American Revolution, Jefferson's liberalism was beginning to assert itself. In 1774 he wrote *A Summary View of the Rights of America* which was widely read both in England and in America, and the philosophy of this pamphlet was later given classic expression in the Declaration of Independence. He was ill when the First Continental Congress met, but sat in the Second until after his work on the Declaration of Independence was done. He then resigned in order to accept a seat in the Virginia legislature, where he hoped to make his influence felt in liberalizing the laws. Jefferson did not need to read Rousseau and Montesquieu to become a thoroughgoing believer in the doctrine of the rights of man. He read them, but he was no more influenced by the writings of Europeans than by his own experience in the democratic West. On the strength of his own observations he urged his fellow Virginians to do away with such medieval relics as entail and primogeniture, to guarantee every one complete freedom of conscience, to abolish state support of an established church, to set up a system of public education, and to substitute for the existing cruelties of the penal code more reasonable and humane punishments. He even championed, well before the Revolution, the emancipation of the slaves. Some of his reforms were deemed too radical for even a revolutionary generation to adopt, but eventually practically all of them were accepted.

His public service continued through the closing years of the Revolution, when he succeeded Patrick Henry as governor of Virginia, and into the Confederation and Constitutional period. His influence upon the famous Northwest Ordinance has already been noted. As Secretary of State he respected Washington, and sometimes influenced him, but he came to look with increasing alarm upon the ascendancy of Hamilton, whose disdain of popular rights and determination to centralize the government were so out of harmony with the democratic principles for which Jefferson had come to stand. He left Washington's Cabinet to organize the opposition to Hamilton's policies, and even as Vice-President he kept at his work, although sometimes under the cloak of secrecy. Jefferson understood the popular whims and fancies better than most politicians, and possessed great talent as an organizer. He was not an orator, but he wrote with exceptional skill, and most of the documents he produced had an irresistibly popular appeal. If Hamilton's sympathies were with the commercial classes, Jefferson's were as definitely agrarian. A society consisting exclusively of small free farmers would, from Jefferson's point of view, have very closely approximated the ideal.

This was the man who became President **The new** on the Fourth of March, 1801. **capital city** He deplored the sham of pomp and ceremony, so the inauguration of Re-publican rule took place in a setting of extreme simplicity. The new President even walked from his boardinghouse to the Capitol to deliver his inaugural address. Elaborate ceremonies might have been difficult to stage, however, if they had been desired, for Jefferson was the first President to take the oath of office in the new capital city on the Potomac, appropriately named Washington. An admirable plan for the city had been devised by a Frenchman named L'Enfant; but the streets were unpaved and most of them unopened, the public buildings were as yet unfinished, and only the distances between them were magnificent. The wisdom of laying out a new city to serve primarily as the political capital of the nation has since been amply justified, but many of those who surveyed the scene for the first time at Jefferson's inauguration undoubtedly thought otherwise.

And yet the capital city, in which great possibilities were only faintly realized, was not unlike the nation as a whole. **Census** The United States, with a popu- **of 1800** lation of only 5,308,473, according to the census of 1800, was still a small nation. Nine tenths of these people lived to the east of the mountains; the other tenth, as far removed relatively from the rest of the population as the White House was from the Capitol, occupied the territory on both banks of the upper Ohio and of its more important tributaries in Kentucky and Tennessee. Nor had American society as yet shown many signs of sophistication.

But the new nation was growing with phenomenal rapidity. In 1790 the population had been listed at 3,929,214; hence the total increase during the decade had amounted to about thirty-five per cent. This is the more important in view of the fact that the number of Europeans who had come to America during the decade was relatively insignificant — on an average probably not over four thousand a year. Indeed, not since before the Revolution, when the Scotch-Irish and the Germans came, had there been any considerable amount of

PHILADELPHIA, 1799. Second Street, looking north from Market. Christ Church is visible a few doors from the corner. Engraving by William Birch and Sons.

Scenes from Philadelphia, long America's leading metropolis, reveal convincingly the slow tempo of the times. This merchant's counting house depicts well an air of decorum and deliberation. Street traffic, in spite of numerous highwheeled carts and an occasional horseback rider, proceeded at pedestrian speed, and even Fourth of July celebrations seemed not to get out of hand. Church spires still rose to greater heights than most secular buildings, although some of the latter were quite impressive.

TRADE CARD. The merchant's shipping business is represented above, his counting house below. Published by T. Dobsen, 1790's.

JULY FOURTH AT THE WATER WORKS. Opened in 1801, the Philadelphia public water system, which employed one of the few existing steam engines in America successfully to pump river water into the city through hollowed logs, was condemned as an impossible dream when first proposed by its designer, Benjamin Latrobe. Painting by J. L. Krimmel, 1810.

Rural life in America, as depicted in these scenes, was by no means devoid of beauty, grace, and fun. Not all farms were as well appointed as David Twining's, but the artist's obvious devotion to realism indicates that such farms did exist. Women's place may have been in the home, but home activities were not wholly drudgery. For the men, trips to country stores and mills gave frequent opportunity for fraternization.

PENNSYLVANIA FARM. The residence of David Twining, about 1787. Painting by Edward Hicks.

A COUNTRY STORE. Early 19th-century woodcut by Alexander Anderson.

WOMEN AT WORK. A community sewing bee. Early 19-century woodcut by Alexander Anderson.

A COUNTRY MILL. View near Bergen, New Jersey. Engraving from *The New-York Magazine*, November, 1794.

NEWS! NEWS!!

AARON OLIVER, *Post-Rider*,

WISHES to inform the Public, that he has extended his Route ; and that he now rides thro' the towns of *Troy, Pittstown, Hoosick, Mapletown*, part of *Bennington* and *Shaftsbury, Petersburgh, Stephentown, Greenbush* and *Schodack*.

All commands in his line will be received with thanks, and executed with punctuality.

He returns his sincere thanks to his former customers ; and intends, by unabated diligence, to merit a continuance of their favours.

O'er rugged hills, and vallies wide,
He never yet has fail'd to trudge it :
As steady as the flowing tide,
He bends about the NORTHERN BUDGET.
June 18, 1799.

NEWS AND MAIL DELIVERY. Post-rider's notice announcing extension of his route, printed in the *Northern Budget*, Troy, N.Y., 1799.

TRAVEL BY STAGE NEAR TRENTON, N.J. Watercolor by a Russian visitor to the United States, P. Svinin, 1811–13.

Travel and communication in early America had not yet progressed far beyond the horseback level. Jefferson complained in 1801 that of eight rivers between Monticello and Washington, five lacked both bridges and ferries. In the more populated areas there were stage-coach connections, though roads were uniformly poor, and the mails brought to even the most remote communities such universally familiar literature as Mother Goose *and the* Farmer's Almanack.

Mother GOOSE's Melody. **37**

JACK and *Gill*
Went up the Hill,
To fetch a Pail of Water ;
Jack fell down
And broke his Crown,
And *Gill* came tumbling after.

Maxim.

The more you think of dying, the better you will live.

ARISTOTLE'S

MOTHER GOOSE'S MELODY, OR SONNETS FOR THE CRADLE. A page from the second Worcester edition, Isaiah Thomas, 1792.

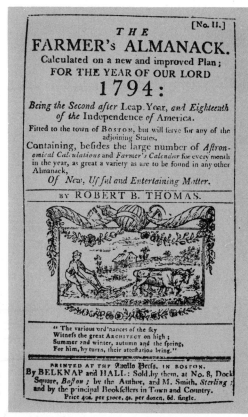

[No. II.]

THE FARMER's ALMANACK.

Calculated on a new and improved Plan ; FOR THE YEAR OF OUR LORD

1794:

Being the Second after Leap Year, *and Eighteenth of the* Independence *of* America.

Fitted to the town of BOSTON, but will serve for any of the adjoining States.

Containing, besides the large number of *Astronomical Calculations* and *Farmer's Calendar* for every month in the year, as great a variety as are to be found in any other Almanack,

Of New, Useful and Entertaining Matter.

BY ROBERT B. THOMAS.

" The various ord'nances of the sky
Witness the great ARCHITECT on high ;
Summer and winter, autumn and the spring,
For him, by turns, their attestation bring."

PRINTED AT THE *Apollo Press*, IN BOSTON.
By BELKNAP and HALL : Sold by them at No. 8, Dock Square, *Boston* ; by the Author, and M. Smith, *Sterling* ; and by the principal Booksellers in Town and Country.
Price 4d. per groce, 4s. per dozen, 6d. single.

THE FARMER'S ALMANACK. "New, useful and entertaining matter," published by R. B. Thomas, Boston, for 1794.

foreign immigration into America. The increase in population was thus due almost exclusively to increase in the native stock. Marriages were early and families were large.

The variety of European races in America, as they mingled more and more, was beginning to develop a distinctively American type. English blood furnished nearly everywhere the dominant strain, and except in a small part of Pennsylvania, where the "Pennsylvania Dutch" still clung to their patois, the English language was practically universal. But the absorption of the Hudson Valley Dutch, the French Huguenots, the Scotch-Irish, the Scotch Highlanders, and the Pennsylvania Germans, not to mention the "Hessians" whom the British had hired to fight the Americans in the Revolution, but many of whom remained in America to found American families, was producing a new American race, no longer purely English, and not wholly uninfluenced by the minor ingredients. English political ideas, English legal concepts, English notions of literary and cultural excellence generally won out, but only rarely without modification. Particularly in the West, where environment was so important a factor, the variation from the original English type was becoming more and more marked.

Economic conditions had not as yet changed greatly from colonial times. New **Economic** England still devoted her chief **conditions** energies to agriculture, the fisheries, shipbuilding, commerce, and merchandising. Her greatest profits came from her overseas trade, and the wealth of some of her merchants and traders was for the day considered great. The middle states, once called the "bread colonies," still produced great quantities of foodstuffs, and owing to the persistence of the wars in Europe these commodities brought good prices. Here, too, were carried on nearly all the activities upon which the prosperity of New England depended, and "infant industries," such as the manufacture of iron, grew increasingly numerous. In the South the large planters sometimes made money,

but nobody else had a chance. The old colonial staples, tobacco, rice, and indigo, produced by the labor of over a million slaves, were still the chief sources of prosperity for those who had it. In 1793 Eli Whitney invented the cotton gin, and the resulting change in the status of cotton was already slightly in evidence. By 1800 the country exported twenty-five thousand bales of cotton, but the later significance of cotton-growing in southern economy was as yet hardly foreseen. Free farmers in the West made a living for themselves, and enjoyed sometimes a little prosperity from trade down the Mississippi in flatboats, or, in spite of Hamilton's tax, from the distilling of whiskey. Speculators in western lands were almost as numerous as the hills, and they sometimes took good profits. Many Easterners were interested in this business, and on account of their western holdings they often became the most ardent champions of western rights. The rôle of the land speculator in American history has not yet been given its just due.

Americans still lived in the country rather than in the city, and the danger that Jefferson most feared, a city proletariat, seemed too far away for any but theorists to worry about. Philadelphia with 70,000 people was the most populous of American cities. New York came next with 60,000; Baltimore had 26,000; Boston, 24,000; Charleston, 20,000. These "cities" still wanted what would today be called "all modern conveniences." Sewers were conspicuously absent, and as in colonial times, hogs ran loose in the streets to dispose of the city's garbage. The country was as primitive as the city. The farmers' tools were much the same type as in the days of Ruth and Boaz, and small children had no reason to inquire what was meant by such Bible verses as "Take my yoke upon you: for my yoke is easy."

The new republic was provincial, intensely provincial, and yet the course of American history had been bent, **Borrowings** far more than the ordinary **from Europe** man realized, by the thinking of those few

AGRICULTURE. A water-lifting wheel suggested for use in irrigating "the interior parts of the United States," by William Tatham, 1801.

NATURAL HISTORY. A portrait of the artist in his museum, by Charles Willson Peale.

Science in America at the beginning of the nineteenth century was following closely in the wake of the progress being made in the Old World. American ingenuity was already at work, adapting the knowledge of Europe to the conditions of America, and had produced a few promising inventions. Charles Willson Peale, although famous principally as a painter, took great interest in natural curiosities, and gathered a collection that was long housed in Independence Hall.

WHITNEY'S COTTON GIN. Model of the original invention for mechanically removing the seeds from cotton.

PLAN OF A STEAM BOAT. Designed by John Fitch in 1786, the steamboat was considered an impracticable idea for many years. Engraving in *The Columbian Magazine*, December, 1796.

Americans who were in touch with the thinking of Europe. Beginning in the sixteenth century, when Copernicus, the Polish astronomer, had shown that the earth was not the center of the universe, but only another planet revolving about one of many suns, the blows to the old medieval traditions had come thick and fast. By the early eighteenth century Isaac Newton, an Englishman, discoverer of the law of gravitation, had made plausible the theory that the entire universe was governed by law — the immutable law of Nature — and that everything, even in the realm of human relationships, could be explained in terms of cause and effect. Philosophers were soon talking of the natural man, humanitarians of natural rights, theologians of a natural religion. The ideas of the Enlightenment, as the new system of thought came to be called, were given wide publicity by Diderot's *Encyclopaedia*, published in France shortly before the American Revolution. The contributors to this work, often called the Encyclopaedists, tried to base their findings only upon what they could prove by observation and experiment, or upon what they were sure they could demonstrate by the use of human reason, something they held in high esteem. The result was a kind of "manifesto of radicalism" that had tremendous repercussions on both sides of the Atlantic. Ideologically, both the American Revolution and the French Revolution owed a tremendous debt to the apostles of the Enlightenment.

Certainly as a scientist, and in many other ways also, Benjamin Franklin was in his time the ablest exponent of the Enlightenment in America (see ante, p. 76). But he was not without important successors. Dr. Benjamin Rush (1745–1813), a Philadelphia physician, was imbued not only with the scientific spirit of the day, but also with its practical idealism. To anyone of his views, mankind was composed of rational and worth-while beings, whose welfare was important to themselves and to the world. Rush therefore devoted

Science in America

himself to such humanitarian projects as public hygiene, the abolition of capital punishment, the emancipation of the slaves, the reform of prisons, and the promotion of temperance. In throwing over outworn medical ideas, he was sometimes guilty of adopting others equally untenable, but he had no compunctions about breaking with the past. He has been called "the father of modern chemistry," and "the pioneer worker in experimental physiology in the United States." His *Medical Inquiries and Observations upon the Diseases of the Mind*, published in 1812, was in some degree prophetic of present-day psychiatry. There were other exponents of the new science in America; for example, Joseph Priestley, discoverer of oxygen; Benjamin Silliman, founder of *The American Journal of Science and Arts*: Benjamin Waterhouse, pioneer in vaccination. This is not to say that the scientific spirit had percolated through to the common man; he was still all too prone to fall for every type of quackery, to hold fast to his superstitions, and to distrust every innovation. But the leaven was present, and it was beginning to work.

It took a long time for the new learning to make its dent upon American education. In the country as a whole it was still true that only the exceptional person could read and write. One might easily argue that since colonial times, especially on the lower levels, much ground had been lost. The war, and in its wake the hard times of the Confederation period, had undermined the foundations of the old educational systems, and had left the people with little interest in restoring them. Nor did the relative prosperity of the last decade in the eighteenth century do much to improve the situation. New England still had some flourishing public academies, some short-term elementary schools, and colleges of a sort, but from New England to the South or West educational opportunities grew progressively worse. Harvard College in 1800 put its faith in a president, three professors, and four tutors. The educational

Education

diet of the colleges, moreover, tended to remain traditional, with Latin, Greek, and Mathematics dominating the curriculum. Benjamin Franklin, in his day, had made notable headway with innovations at the Philadelphia Academy, which by 1791 had become the University of Pennsylvania, and the leading scientific center in the New World. Franklin's views were strongly seconded by Benjamin Rush, who railed at the old system during the 1780's, and even published a tract called *Thoughts upon the Mode of Education Proper in a Republic.* There should be a great national university, he contended, with the emphasis upon training for public service. Instead of Latin and Greek, he would emphasize history. "To spend four or five years in learning two dead Languages, is to turn our backs upon a gold mine, in order to amuse ourselves catching butterflies." But Rush's ideas, which included even education for women, were far ahead of his time, and found few followers. Jefferson tried in somewhat similar vein to liberalize the curriculum of William and Mary, but he was discouraged by sectarian obstacles and eventually turned his attention to building up the University of Virginia. Even so, there were premonitions of better times to come. Benjamin Silliman was appointed Professor of Chemistry and Natural History at Yale in 1802, the first such appointment in the history of the college. Thomas Cooper (1759–1839), an able but tempestuous scholar who for his radical views had been obliged to flee the Old World, brought the latest in science from Europe to a series of American colleges. Modern languages, especially French, began slowly to encroach on the exclusive preserves of the ancient classics. The teaching of law received greater recognition, as, for example, when James Kent (1763–1847) was elected to a professorship at Columbia in 1793. Schools of medicine increased in number and efficiency, while separate schools of divinity left the liberal arts colleges free to lay greater emphasis on secular things.

There were even stronger stirrings in American literature. For the most part colonial Americans who read at all **American literature** read foreign books — Dryden, Milton, Locke, Swift, Montesquieu, Voltaire, Rousseau. Diderot's *Encyclopaedia* was also widely known and read in America. But by the closing decades of the eighteenth century the absorption in theology that in earlier years had so restricted the offerings of American writers had begun to break down; furthermore, American life was less exclusively rural than it once had been, and there now existed city dwellers with wealth enough and interest enough to act as patrons of literature and the arts. There was also plenty to write about. The American Revolution was a subject of endless interest — almost every literate participant felt obliged to record his part in it, and the more thoughtful were at pains to defend the course of action the colonies had taken, or, more rarely, to oppose it. The French Revolution furnished another exciting topic for exploitation by those with a yen to write. It had exalted the common man, and brought down the mighty; it had deliberately set out to overthrow all the cherished sanctions of the past and it had well-nigh succeeded; it was a far more radical affair than the American Revolution, and had produced a society which, at least when viewed from a distance, was stripped of privilege and dedicated to the rule of the people. Literary opinion in America was hopelessly divided. Was all this good or bad, and what lessons did it hold for America? Whatever view one took, there was always something worth while to write about, something on which Americans seemed compelled to an opinion. In addition, the local American scene presented a very genuine challenge of its own. The westward movement, already in full swing, was something to conjure with. The almost limitless possibilities it was opening up aroused mingled feelings of joy and fright, joy on the part of the Jeffersonians who saw in the new West an ally, fright on the part of the Hamiltonians who saw in it an enemy. The existence of this great and growing

West sharpened and intensified the contest between agriculture and commerce for the control of the new republic. The followers of Jefferson, with victory seemingly assured, might well rejoice; while the followers of Hamilton, forseeing the destruction of all that they held most dear, were filled with the direst forebodings.

One trouble with the early literary outpourings of independent America was that **Emphasis on politics** they smacked so strongly of politics. In a sense the old blight of theological disputation was replaced by a new blight of political polemics. Playwrights, eager to break down the old religious animosity toward the theater, chose political subjects, and curried favor by vindicating the United States in all it had done. Thus Royall Tyler (1757–1826), poet and novelist as well as playwright, opened his play *The Contrast* with a kind of ode to democracy:

Exult, each patriot heart! — This night is shewn
A piece which we may fairly call our own;
Where the proud titles of "My Lord! Your
    Grace!"
To humble Mr. and plain Sir give place.
Our Author pictures not from foreign climes
The fashions or the follies of the times;
But has confin'd the subject of his work
To the gay scenes — the circles of New York.
On native themes his muse displays her pow'rs;
If ours the faults, the virtues too are ours.
Why should our thoughts to distant countries
    roam,
When each refinement may be found at home?

The personnel of the play presents a Revolutionary War hero, ever ready to sacrifice his all for his country, an Anglomaniac villain bent on money-grabbing, and a Yankee servant full of homespun wisecracks. Royall Tyler was by no means the only American playwright of his time. There were others of note also, among them William Dunlap (1766–1839), the author of sixty plays, and sometimes called the "Father of the American Drama." But Dunlap's plays in order to succeed were often obliged, like his *André*, for example, to glorify the revolution, to exalt the idea

of nationalism, to preach patriotism toward the new republic. Steeped in the learning of the time, he nevertheless took occasion to point out America's need of Europe:

From Europe shall enriching commerce flow,
And many an ill attendant; but from thence
Shall likewise flow blest Science, Europe's knowl-
    edge,
By sharp experience bought, we should appro-
    priate.

American poetry no less than American drama tended to reflect the political heat of the times. In the post-Revolutionary period the so-called "Hartford Wits," including such men as John Trumbull, Timothy Dwight, Joel Barlow, and others, took an extremely conservative point of view. In *The Anarchiad*, to cite a single instance, they railed at the debtor-minded government of Rhode Island, which printed paper money in profusion:

Hail! realm of rogues, renown'd for fraud and
    guile,
All hail! ye knav'ries of yon little isle.
There prowls the rascal, cloth'd with pow'r,
To snare the orphan, and the poor devour.
The crafty knave his creditor besets
And advertising paper pays his debts.

Thomas Green Fessenden (1771–1837), in *Democracy Unveiled, or Tyranny Stripped of the Garb of Patriotism* (1805), vented his rage on Jefferson and all his works, warning his countrymen of the excesses to which the French Revolution had given rise:

Such principles, alas, will flood
Columbia's "happy land" with blood,
Unless kind Providence restrain
These demons of the hurricane.

But the Jeffersonians were not without their defenders. Philip Freneau (1752–1832), had he been able to **Freneau** direct his talents consistently toward subjects of a more poetic nature than politics, might have ranked as one of America's really great poets. As it was he quite surpassed all others of his time, and his stinging rebukes to the Hamiltonians drove them into a frenzy. He had a fine gift of satire, which frequently betrayed itself even in the subjects of his verse: *To all the Great Folks in a Lump: To Atlas* (Hamilton); *To a Select Body of Great Men* (the Senate); *To a Would-be Great Man* (John Adams). Writing *On False Systems of Government,* he had this to say:

> How can we call those systems just
> Which bid the few, the proud, the first,
>   Possess all earthly good;
> While millions robbed of all that's dear
> In silence shed the ceaseless tear,
>   And leaches suck their blood.

Freneau was not the only poetic defender of democracy. There were many others, among them Joel Barlow, one of the "Hartford Wits," who abandoned the conservatism of his youth, and fought valiantly for the Jeffersonians. But Freneau was the best of the Republicans, and with him on their side they had little to fear from the poetic barbs of the Federalists.

It was on the subject of religion that the ideas of the Enlightenment caused the most

Deism

commotion in America. The people at large stood by the old time religion, and many of them hardly knew that anyone had challenged the tenets they so long had cherished. But a very vocal few took up with the rationalistic concepts of the European Deists, and sought earnestly to undermine the faith of those who believed in revealed religion. Deism had had a long, slow growth in Europe and early in the eighteenth century it had received classic statement in a book by Matthew Tindal, *Christianity as Old as the Creation or the Gospel a Republication of the Religion of Nature* (1730). The Deists regarded God as the First Cause, and the Supreme Architect of the Universe, but the machine he had created was so perfect that once it was finished it ran itself through natural law. The Deists rejected all the cherished doctrines of Christendom. They made light of the idea of the Trinity. To them Jesus was man, not God. Original sin

was a figment of someone's imagination. There had been no atonement, nor need for an atonement. Revelation came only through man's discovery of the laws of the Universe, not directly from God to man. Such views as these reached America before the American Revolution, and were even then taken up by Franklin and others. They were given further encouragement by the leaders of the French Revolution, who for a time actually enthroned and worshipped a "Goddess of Reason". Ethan Allan, a hero of the Revolution, wrote a tract, *Reason, the Only Oracle of Man,* which stated in 1784 the Deist's position, but it was a book by Thomas Paine, *The Age of Reason,* published a decade later, which really touched off the debate. Paine's views do not sound as strange today as they did then, but for their time they went the very limit of radicalism, and among the orthodox they aroused the greatest alarm. If these views should win out, the very foundations of Christian authority would be shaken. Here is Paine's "confession of faith":

> I believe in one God, and no more; and I hope for happiness beyond this life. I believe in the equality of man, and I believe that religious duties consist in doing justice, loving mercy, and endeavoring to make our fellow creatures happy. I do not believe in the creed professed ... by any church that I know of. My own mind is my own church. ... All national institutions of churches ... appear to me no other than human inventions set up to terrify and enslave mankind and monopolize power and profit. I do not mean ... to condemn those who believe otherwise. They have the same right to their belief as I have to mine. But it is necessary to the happiness of man that he be faithful to himself. ... It is impossible to calculate the moral mischief ... that mental lying has produced in society.

The Deists in America numbered among them many notables, and their views made tremendous headway in all the colleges, notably Harvard, Yale,

Unitarianism

and the University of Virginia. Some of them were passive in their "infidelity," and were even opposed to unsettling the minds

LUTHERAN SCHOOLROOM. The language and customs of the first Lutheran settlers being taught in York County, Pennsylvania. Water color by Lewis Miller, 1805.

Religious diversities in America reflected both the variety of European nationalities represented in the population, and the needs of the new environment. Some sects clung tenaciously to their Old World doctrines and practices; others accepted freely such innovations as seemed desirable. The Moravians, unlike the first Puritans, were great lovers of music, and their settlement at Bethlehem, Pennsylvania, founded in 1741, began almost at once to hold annual music festivals, events which have continued down to the present time.

QUAKER MEETING. Illustration from von Helle, *Nord-Amerika*, 1800.

CAMP MEETING IN A WESTERN FOREST. Such meetings of large groups, led by itinerant preachers, and often comprising several faiths, were increasingly common in the back settlements where clergy and churches were few. 19th-century engraving.

MORAVIAN MUSIC FESTIVAL. Illustration from a German text, 1757.

of the unlettered. More or less indirectly, however, they helped along the promotion of Unitarianism among the Calvinists of New England, where Newton's third law, that for every action there is an equal and contrary reaction, seemed in process of social demonstration. The harsh doctrines of the Puritans were an easy target for the disciples of rationalism, and the concept that man's instincts were righteous rather than evil hit at the very vitals of predestinarianism. Soon the American Congregational Church was hopelessly split between those who held fast to the old theology, and those who held that Jesus was the son of God, but not God himself; that man's natural instincts were good, not evil, that the way of salvation was available to all mankind, and not to the elect alone. In taking this stand American Unitarians tended to follow the exposition of like ideas in England. They did not go as far in their rejection of Christian theology as the Deists, and they sought confirmation for their views in the Bible itself. Great preachers, such as William Ellery Channing of Federal Street Church, Boston, and great teachers, such as Henry Ware, professor of Divinity at Harvard, gave the movement their powerful support. Not only in New England, but among the intellectual classes throughout the nation Unitarianism made headway, while some who called themselves Universalists went a step further, and argued that salvation must sometime, somehow, come to all men. Few Protestant denominations were unaffected by the new concepts. Even when they adhered to the old theology, they softened the old interpretations, dwelling less on man's total depravity, more on God's infinite mercy and good will toward men.

But revealed religion had too much to offer mankind to be dethroned by any mere appeal to reason. Most men **Orthodoxy** preferred to believe in a supernatural power, above and beyond the ability of mere human beings to understand. Not many could throw off the fear of punishment in the next world for the wrongs they had done in this. They wanted a kind of miracle religion that would set them free from the guilt they felt in their hearts, and would assure them happiness in the life to come. Convinced that humanity, bereft of such a faith, would descend to the lowest depths of depravity, the orthodox leaders fought the new heresy with every weapon at their command. The dethronement of the "Goddess of Reason" in France, and the failure of the French Revolution to overthrow traditional Christianity, gave them courage and a weapon. But the determining factor was the eagerness of the people, Jeffersonians no less (and perhaps even more) than the Federalists to hold fast to the faith of their fathers.

Piety, or the pretense of piety, suffused New England, although the Congregational monopoly had long since been broken. In the cities the Epis- **Revivalism** copalians had a strong following, in Vermont there were many Quakers, and in Roger William's Rhode Island the Baptists were numerous. In the middle states there were many sects: Quakers, Presbyterians, Lutherans, Episcopalians, Dutch Reformed. In the South along the coast the Episcopalians were dominant, although in Maryland there were many Catholics and some Congregationalists. The back country and the frontier, during and for some time after the year 1800, was experiencing one of its chronic revivals. Here the Methodists, with their intense emotionalism and their democratic doctrine that salvation was equally open to all, set the pace; but the Baptists, the Presbyterians, and numerous minor sects were not far behind. The great revival swept like wildfire through the West, and the pioneer people, always sorely in need of an emotional outlet, attended the camp-meetings by the thousands and the tens of thousands.

At first appearance, those meetings exhibited nothing to the spectator, but a scene of confusion that could scarce be put into human language. They were generally opened with a sermon; near the close of which, there would be an unusual

AN AMERICAN PORTRAIT. "Roger Sherman," by Ralph Earle.

EUROPEAN POLISH. "The Staircase Group," by Charles Willson Peale, about 1795.

HOME-CRAFTED ART. "Hope." Wooden sculpture for ship decoration by Simeon Skillin, early 19th century.

Early American artists included many itinerant painters, woodcarvers and silversmiths who considered themselves primarily skilled craftsmen. Their art was more indigenous than that of the great painters, such as Stuart, Peale, and Trumbull, who owed much to European training. Young American artists studying abroad could count on the help of Benjamin West, an American painter who lived in England after 1763 winning fame for his "ten-acre canvases" on such historical themes as "Penn's Treaty with the Indians," and "The Death of Wolfe" (see pp. 45 and 105).

outcry; some bursting forth into loud ejaculations of prayer, or thanksgiving for the truth; others breaking out in emphatical sentences of exhortation; others flying to their careless friends, with tears of compassion, beseeching them to turn to the Lord. Some struck with terror, and hastening through the crowd to make their escape, or pulling away their relations. — Others, trembling, weeping, and crying out for the Lord Jesus to have mercy upon them: fainting and swooning away, till every appearance of life was gone, and the extremities of the body assumed the coldness of a dead corpse. — Others surrounding them with melodious songs, or fervent prayers for their happy resurrection in the love of Christ. — Others collecting into circles around this variegated scene, contending with arguments for and against. And under such appearances, the work

VIRGINIA STATE CAPITOL, RICHMOND. Completed by Benjamin Latrobe after Jefferson's plan. Contemporary engraving.

MASSACHUSETTS STATE HOUSE BOSTON. Designed by Charles Bullfinch and completed in 1800. Engraving after a painting by A. J. Davis.

Public Architecture in America was strongly influenced by the Revolution. The old colonial designs seemed out of place in the new republic, and under the guidance of Thomas Jefferson, an admirer of the classical revival in France, a strong classical vogue set in. Among the architects whom Jefferson encouraged was Charles Bullfinch, whose Massachusetts State House, with its famous dome and portico, was long "the most conspicuous public building in the United States."

would continue for several days and nights together.

The orthodox doctrines of the revivalists set the pattern of religious belief in most of the United States for many generations to come. The men who professed these views, and their descendants, were destined to conquer the West and to expand their religious ideas across the continent. Their approach to religion, and, as it turned out, to politics also, was emotional and evangelical rather than rational.

Americans cared relatively little for art, yet in an age which knew nothing of photography they could at least see **Portrait painters** point to the painting of portraits. Gilbert Stuart (1755–1828), whose skill would have won him recognition in

any age, is best remembered for the great number of Washington canvases he left. He painted portraits of many other well-known Americans also, among them most of the early Presidents. Charles Willson Peale (1741–1827) portrayed famous Americans of the same generation with less technical excellence, perhaps, than Stuart, but with greater simplicity and fidelity to truth. Peale was also interested in cultivating an American interest in art, and furnished much of the inspiration which led to the founding of the Pennsylvania Academy of Fine Arts (1805) and the National Academy of Design (1826). John Trumbull (1756–1843) discovered that historical paintings had an appeal for Americans that was almost as hard to resist as that of portraits. He discreetly admitted that the occupation of painting as a rule was "frivolous, little useful to society, and unworthy of a man who has talents for more serious pursuits. But to preserve and diffuse the memory of the noblest series of actions which have ever presented themselves in the history of man, is sufficient warrant for it." And so, along with his portraits, he left many colorful representations of scenes in the American Revolution — paintings deeply esteemed by many subsequent generations of patriots. It is proper to point out, however, that all the early American artists owed most of their proficiency to European training. Some of them, like John Singleton Copley (1738–1815), lived as much of the time in Europe as in the United States.

In architecture, too, there were some worthy American beginnings. The practi **The classical** cality and good taste of the old **revival** colonial and Georgian designs were not forgotten, but shortly after the Revolution a classical revival set in which had pronounced results. Thomas Jefferson, whose variety of interests had not failed to take in architecture, was the leading exponent of this new trend. He used classical traditions in designing a house for himself at Monticello, houses for his neighbors and friends, a new capitol for his state, and a building plan for the University of Virginia that has since been called "the finest example of classical architecture in America." Throughout the country, but especially in the South, the more pretentious private dwellings with their high column-supported porticos reflected clearly the classical influence, and many public buildings also, such as the White House, the Bank of the United States, and the Philadelphia Library, were similarly designed. New

churches still adhered closely to colonial tradition.

The country stood in great need of better means of communication. Sailboats plied slowly and without schedule **Need of** from point to point along the **better com-** coast, while stage-coaches, trav- **munications** eling at about four miles an hour, connected the principal cities. In the South the roads were frequently unsafe for vehicles, and over-land travel was ordinarily on horseback. Inns were as primitive as in colonial times. The rivers of the interior, even above the falls line, were much used by all kinds of crude boats, and the "western waters" furnished alike the easiest means of expanding the frontier and the chief outlet of frontier trade.

The West was already "the most American part of America." Here the melting-pot had fused racial elements more **The West** completely than elsewhere; here the difference between American ways and European ways was most pronounced. Here cheap lands, almost literally, opened opportunity equally to all. Here democracy was practiced as well as preached, and here each citizen believed himself to be as good as anyone else. Here people looked out for themselves, and the ideal of individual freedom held universal sway. The society of the West was crude and rough, and the "men of the western waters" were mostly uncouth and illiterate, but they had begun the conquest of a continent, and they had little time for anything else. Out of their experiences were to come many of the guiding principles of American democracy. Jefferson understood these men, believed in them, and thought that, as President, he fully represented them.

Time and Distance
1800

6 WEEKS
5 WEEKS
4 WEEKS
2 WEEKS
3
7
6
5
4
3
2
1 DAYS

Boston
Albany
New York
Detroit
Pittsburgh

1
2
3 DAYS
4
5
6

Vincennes

St. Louis

Richmond

Nashville

Wilmington
1 WEEK

Charleston

2 WEEKS
St. Augustine

New Orleans

3 WEEKS

5 WEEKS
4 WEEKS

Bibliography

For the closing years of the Federalist regime, many of the books cited for the two preceding chapters, pages 214 and 228, remain useful. Channing, IV, and McMaster, II, are particularly helpful. E. D. Warfield, *The Kentucky Resolutions of 1798* (1887), is an old, but reliable, special study. H. M. Tinkcom, *The Republicans and Federalists in Pennsylvania, 1790–1801: A Study in National Stimulus and Local Response* (1950), covers the evolution of the party system in Pennsylvania. John C. Miller, *Crisis in Freedom: The Alien and Sedition Acts* (1951), restudies a familiar theme.

Biographies of Jefferson, the dominating figure of this period, are numerous. Some have already been mentioned in connection with ch. VIII, p. 147, and ch. XIII, p. 228. The series begun by Dumas Malone will be of inestimable value when the narrative reaches this period. The same may be said for the series by Marie Kimball, now three volumes along: *Jefferson: The Road to Glory, 1743 to 1776* (1943); *Jefferson: War and Peace, 1776 to 1784* (1947); and *Jefferson: The Scene of Europe, 1784 to 1789* (1950). Also illuminating is Adrienne Koch, *Jefferson and Madison: The Great Collaboration* (1950). One-volume works not hitherto mentioned include: Gilbert Chinard, *Thomas Jefferson* (1929); D. S. Muzzey, *Thomas Jefferson* (1918); A. J. Nock, *Jefferson* (1926); J. T. Morse, Jr., *Thomas Jefferson* (1924); S. K. Padover, *Jefferson* (1942). Probably the best complete study of Jefferson's career is Nathan Schachner, *Thomas Jefferson: A Biography* (2 vols., 1951).

Among the general treatises devoted to this period and after, Henry Adams, *History of the United States of America during the Administrations of Jefferson and Madison* (9 vols., 1889–1891), remains unsurpassed. There is an abridged edition of this work, entitled *The Formative Years: A History of the United States during the Administrations of Jefferson and Madison*, edited by Herbert Agar (2 vols., 1947). Edward Channing, *The Jeffersonian System* (1906), is one of the best of the volumes of the *American Nation* series.

Allen Johnson, *Jefferson and His Colleagues* (1921), covers the same period for the *Chronicles of America*. Claude Bowers, *Jefferson in Power* (1936), brilliantly defends Jefferson at every turn. D. J. Boorstin, *The Lost World of Thomas Jefferson* (1948), seeks to reproduce the climate of thought in which Jefferson and his contemporaries lived.

On social and intellectual history, the first volume of Henry Adams contains an admirable survey of American society in 1800. Many of the books cited for Chapter IV, p. 77, also continue useful, particularly Curti, *Growth of American Thought*, and Carman, *Social and Economic History of the United States*, Vol. I. R. F. Butts, *The American Tradition in Religion and Education* (1950), is an interesting attempt to fuse into one synthesis two not always related subjects. F. L. Mott, *Jefferson and the Press* (1943), is a brief exposition of Jefferson's views on a single significant subject. Ferris Greenslet, *The Lowells and their Seven Worlds* (1946), views the passing scene through the eyes of a well-placed family of intelligentsia.

There are a number of books dealing with the growth of evangelical religion. R. G. Torbet, *A History of the Baptists* (1950), is concerned with an important denomination on both sides of the Atlantic. *The Baptists* edited by W. W. Sweet (1931), deals with the expansion of the sect in America. W. C. Barclay, *Early American Methodism, 1769–1844* (1949), is concerned with another revivalistic denomination. See also W. B. Posey, *The Development of Methodism in the Old Southwest, 1783–1824* (1933); Catharine C. Cleveland, *The Great Revival in the West* (1916); and, a contemporary account, Richard McNemar, *The Kentucky Revival* (1807).

On art and architecture: J. T. Flexner, *America's Old Masters: First Artists of the New World* (1939); C. C. Sellers, *Charles Willson Peale* (2 vols., 1947); Virgil Barker, *American Painting: History and Interpretation* (1950); Howard Major, *The Domestic Architecture of the Early American Republic* (1926).

15
Jefferson in Power

JEFFERSON was a man of simple tastes who hated affectation of every sort, and he made short work of the pretentiousness with which the Federalist Presidents had surrounded themselves. Partly because he lacked fluency in speech, he substituted a written message to Congress for the formal address that preceding Presidents had felt obliged to deliver. He refused in social matters to recognize any rank whatever, and he persuaded his Cabinet to agree that "when brought together in society all are perfectly equal, whether foreign or domestic, titled or untitled, in or out of office." This rule confounded the diplomatic agents, who set great store by precedence, and almost led to international complications. The weekly levees, which Washington had instituted as a kind of imitation of the British court, were discontinued, and the President lived as nearly as possible in the same manner as if he were a private citizen.

Neither Jefferson's simplicity nor his devotion to the rights of the ordinary man could **Jefferson's** disguise the fact that he was **appointees** himself as much a member of the upper stratum of society as any Federalist. Nor did Jefferson choose to surround himself with men from the lower walks of life. He believed in the good sense and the solid judgment of the people, and depended on

these qualities in them to insure that the offices would go to able men. For his Secretary of State Jefferson chose James Madison, the "father of the Constitution," and like himself a Virginian of good position. For Secretary of the Treasury he chose Albert Gallatin of Pennsylvania, a Genevan by birth who had excellent family connections in Europe and had taught at Harvard College. Nathaniel Macon, Speaker of the House, was, like the President, an able southern planter in politics. John Randolph, who, as chairman of the powerful House Committee on Ways and Means, was the chief financial spokesman of the administration, also represented the southern planter class. In general, the "Revolution of 1800" meant the transfer of leadership in government from men who were principally interested in commerce and finance to men whose chief concern was agriculture; and it was rare indeed when high office, even under Republican rule, fell to a man of low estate.

Jefferson really wished to win over the rank and file of the Federalists to his party. His inaugural address was designed primarily to reassure them "that though the will of the majority is in all cases to prevail, that will to be rightful must be reasonable." The two parties, he contended, were "brethren of the same principle. We are all Republi-

253

cans, we are all Federalists." When it came to the removal of Federalist office-holders, the new President acted with extreme caution. Under Washington, who by 1795 had made up his mind that it was "political suicide" to appoint his adversaries to office, and under Adams, whose partisanship from the beginning had been thoroughgoing and complete, the offices had gone to the Federalists. Jefferson made a few removals on the ground of offensive partisanship, and a few others for misconduct in office. Vacancies were filled as a rule by Republicans, but vacancies were rare. "Those by death are few," the President complained, "by resignation none." Some of Jefferson's followers were much disappointed at his conservatism in the matter of removals, but by the end of his first administration a majority of the office-holders were Republicans.

"A wise and frugal Government, which shall restrain men from injuring one another, **"The less government the better"** shall leave them otherwise free to regulate their own pursuits of industry and improvement, and shall not take from the mouth of labor the bread it has earned" — this was the ideal that Jefferson set for himself and his party when he took office in 1801. To his way of thinking the national debt, which Hamilton had gladly assumed and the Federalist régime had steadily increased, ought

to be paid, not perpetuated for the benefit of wealthy investors. But such a policy presented difficulties, since the Republicans, to carry out their campaign promises, were compelled to repeal the excise tax at a cost of six hundred and fifty thousand dollars annually to the treasury. The Secretary of the Treasury, Albert Gallatin, was equal to the emergency. He recommended that drastic reductions be made in all public expenditures, and particularly in appropriations for the army and navy. This plan of retrenchment, while unpopular with many politicians of both parties, was pushed through Congress with Jefferson's hearty support. The President seemed wholly unconcerned about the national defense, and in place of a national navy suggested that small gunboats, to be manned when needed by naval militia, be supplied to the harbors along the coast — "mosquito fleets," his opponents called them.

Gallatin succeeded admirably with the reduction of the national debt, and had conditions remained normal it **Case of the Polly** might have been eliminated, as he predicted, in sixteen years. Increased purchases abroad, due to the growing wealth and population of the country, led to corresponding increases in the tariff revenues. Help came also from an unexpected quarter. In 1800 Sir William Scott, a British judge, held in the case of the *Polly* that

Burning the "Philadelphia" in the harbor of Tripoli, 1804. This engraving of Stephen Decatur's daring exploit is the work of an eyewitness, F. Kearney.

American ships engaged in the French West Indian trade might proceed without molestation to France, provided that they had first landed their cargoes at an American port and paid the duty. Thereafter American ships engaged in this once forbidden trade not only made good profits for themselves, but also piled up revenues for the American government. Except for a brief interlude, from March, 1802, to May, 1803, the European war raged on, and before the end of Jefferson's administration Gallatin, aided by the advantages of American neutrality, had retired as much of the national debt as was due and payable. His achievement was the more remarkable in view of the unforeseen expense attendant upon the purchase of Louisiana and the Tripolitan War.

The Tripolitan War probably saved the American navy from extinction. It had long **The Tripolitan War** been the habit of European nations to pay tribute to the piratical rulers of the maritime states of northern Africa — Morocco, Algiers, Tunis, and Tripoli — sometimes known as the Barbary States. In this practice the new United States, whose trade relations in the Mediterranean were of some consequence, soon joined. Nevertheless, in May, 1801, the Pacha of Tripoli, claiming that he had not received his proper share of the tribute, dramatically declared war on the United States by cutting down the flagstaff at the American consulate in Tripoli. Six days later, Jefferson, quite unaware of the Pacha's insolence, ordered a naval squadron to Mediterranean waters. The new President and his Secretary of the Treasury resented the expenditures necessary to maintain a navy, but they resented even more the idea of paying tribute money to pirates.

For the next three years American squadrons fought with varying success in Tripolitan waters. Jefferson and Gallatin had even to consent to an increase in the size of the navy. But when an American ship, the *Philadelphia*, was lost, and Congress voted to have it replaced, Gallatin, ever jealous of his revenues, refused to pay out the money until Congress had levied a special duty, called the "Mediterranean Fund," for the purpose. The war was finally brought to an end, less perhaps by the exploits of the navy than by the Pacha's fear of a small overland expedition from Egypt, headed by a pretender to the Tripolitan throne. An American citizen, William Eaton, entirely on his own authority, had stirred the pretender to action. The Pacha, faced by enemies on land and on sea, agreed to require no further tribute from the United States. His submission had a good effect upon the other Barbary rulers, who thereafter were far more tractable, but for many years a strong American squadron had to be retained in the Mediterranean, and the practice of paying tribute did not wholly disappear until 1815.

The Republicans made haste to rid the country of much Federalist legislation. The period of residence for naturalization was again set at five years. The Alien and Sedition **Repeal of Federalist legislation** Acts were in part designated to last for two years only, and they were of course not renewed. The Bank of the United States, chartered in 1791 for twenty years, was performing a needed service well, and was left alone. The Judiciary Act of 1801, however, and the "midnight appointments" Adams had made under its terms, were attacked mercilessly. This measure, passed hurriedly in the closing days of a Congress that the people had already repudiated at the polls, is a classic example of what Americans came to call a "lame duck" bill. It was designated, according to one critic, to act as a "hospital for decayed politicians," or in the language of today for "lame ducks" who had been defeated for re-election. The rank partisanship of such a bill was easily attacked, but the Republicans claimed also that it called for needless extravagance, and replaced it with a measure of their own, which added a new justice to the Supreme Court, and restored circuit duty to Supreme Court justices. Circuit courts were to consist of one justice of the Supreme Court and one district judge; in case of disagreement an appeal was to be taken to the Supreme Court. For fifty years longer this system of courts, which the Federalists had repudiated in 1801 as out of date, continued to work fairly well. As for the new judges that Adams had just appointed, they were left without duties and without salaries.

The Federalists at once charged that the Republicans had violated the Constitution, for federal judges were supposed to hold office "during good behavior." They maintained further that the Supreme Court might take a hand in the matter by declaring the Republican changes in the judiciary null and void. No such action was taken, but Marshall soon let it be known that the Court under his leadership could, if it chose, declare a law of Congress unconstitutional and refuse to enforce it.

Political polemics, about 1800. "Mad Tom in a Rage," an anti-Republican cartoon, is typically devoid of subtlety.

Marshall selected with skill the case upon which to announce this doctrine. One of Adams's midnight appointments had gone to a certain William Marbury, who had been commissioned a justice of the peace in the District of Columbia. But Marbury's commission, owing to the press of time, was not delivered before the fourth of March, 1801, and after that date Madison, the Secretary of State, refused to deliver it. Marbury then asked the Supreme Court to issue a mandamus compelling Madison to deliver the commission. From the Federalist point of view such a victory over the new administration was not to be despised. But Marshall, after reading Madison a lecture on his dereliction of duty in failing to deliver the commission, held that the Court could do nothing about it, and denied Marbury's request. The reason assigned by the Chief Justice for this startling decision was that the Supreme Court lacked the authority to grant such an order, even though it might wish to do so. The law, to be sure, gave the Court abundant authority, for it specifically stated that the Supreme Court might issue precisely such writs as the one Marbury now desired; but in giving this authority to the Supreme Court, Marshall held, the law went beyond the power delegated to Congress, for according to the Constitution the only original jurisdiction the Supreme Court might enjoy was in "cases affecting ambassadors, other public ministers and consuls, and those in which a state shall be party." With the law and the Constitution thus in direct conflict, the Chief Justice maintained that the Constitution must be followed and the law disregarded.

The "doctrine of judicial review," as the rule of law laid down in *Marbury vs. Madison* (1803) has come to be called, placed a powerful weapon in the hands of the Federalist judiciary. It might now, on the theory that the law and the Constitution were in conflict, set aside when opportunity offered such laws passed by the Republican Congress as

Marbury vs. Madison

The doctrine of judicial review

the Court could construe to be unconstitutional. But Marshall's reasoning was logical and quite in line with precedent. In colonial times judges on both sides of the Atlantic had held invalid colonial laws out of harmony with colonial charters or with the laws of Parliament. Subsequently the state supreme courts had frequently done the same thing with state laws that contravened a given state constitution. Probably it was supposed by most of the framers of the Constitution that the Supreme Court would act ultimately in precisely the way Marshall had acted. But it is nevertheless true that this rule of law placed in the hands of the Supreme Court of the United States a degree of authority not then enjoyed by any similar body of men anywhere else on earth.

What use to partisan ends the Court might make of its power was a question, and the **Impeachment of judges** Republicans were at once in search of a weapon of defense. They might rid themselves of obnoxious inferior judges by abolishing the offices that these judges held, but the Supreme Court was set up by the Constitution, and its justices held office for life unless impeached by vote of the House and removed by a two-thirds vote of the Senate. Apparently, then, in impeachment lay the only hope of remedy. Some actions along this line by the Republicans of Pennsylvania, who had successfully impeached and removed from office Judge Alexander Addison, had already been taken; and in 1804 a federal district judge, John Pickering, was impeached and removed when it was clear that he had become insane. Could impeachment be used against a Supreme Court justice who was guilty of grossly partisan actions? The Republicans meant to find out, for the adoption of such a policy would mean that Federalists on the bench must either restrain their partisanship or else run the risk of removal from office. Associate Justice Samuel Chase, a Federalist and a hero of the Revolutionary War, gave the Republicans the chance they craved to bring a trial case. In an address to a Baltimore

grand jury, Justice Chase denounced the introduction of universal suffrage, and excoriated those who were ruining the nation by making the people think that all men were entitled to enjoy equal liberty and equal rights. His attack was obviously partisan, and since there was no other way to remove judges than by impeachment the Republicans should have rested their case on that ground alone. Instead, they added irrelevant and unprovable charges of misconduct. The Senate refused to convict (1805), and a precedent was established that a man could not be impeached for anything for which he could not also be indicted. As partisanship was no crime, the Federalist justices were now free to go as far as they liked; but in the face of the growing popularity of Republican rule they conducted themselves with greater discretion.

When Jefferson took office it appeared that most of the problems of the West had been solved. By Jay's treaty the English posts in the Northwest had been abandoned; by Pinckney's treaty the Mississippi outlet had been opened to western trade; by the treaty of Fort Greenville the Indian frontier had been thrown back; by the admission of new western states the right of the West to local self-government and to full participation in national affairs had been duly recognized; and, finally, by a law passed in 1800 the West had been given nearly everything it desired by way of land legislation.

In the attempt to develop a national land policy two points of view were early apparent. Easterners, for the most **National land policy** part, wished to administer the lands in such a way as to obtain from them the maximum amount of revenue. Their point of view was well set forth by Hamilton, who, as Secretary of the Treasury, made a report on the public lands. Hamilton believed that the most money could be realized by persuading speculators to purchase the land in large tracts. He was therefore ready to give two years' credit to the large purchaser, but not to the small. Also, he wished to abandon the rectangular system of survey, so that the better lands might the more easily be separated from those less promising. While he recommended the survey of land in small tracts as well as in large, he obviously expected that the small purchaser would buy from the speculator rather than from the government. Westerners, on the other hand, tended to resent the idea that the public lands should be used to produce a revenue. They maintained that, instead, the real object of the government in disposing of its lands should be the development of the country. To this end the needy should be permitted to acquire farms on the easiest possible terms.

Hamilton's plan was ignored by Congress, and not until after the treaty of Fort Greenville had opened to settlement much new territory in central Ohio was a land law passed. In 1796 Congress authorized the sale of single sections (six hundred and forty acres) at a minimum price of two dollars per acre, but provision was also made for "wholesale" disposals. Townships were first to be divided equally, after which one of the halves was to be further subdivided into sections, while the other half was left for the speculative purchaser to subdivide as he chose. Two western land offices were opened, one at Pittsburgh and one at Cincinnati, where purchasers were allowed to pay one twentieth of the purchase price down, nine twentieths at the end of six months, and the remaining half within a year. The law did not work well. It provided for too large minimum tracts, and it placed the price of land at what for the time was a prohibitive figure. Under its terms only forty-eight thousand acres of land were sold. Settlers preferred to buy state lands south of the Ohio, or, in case they chose to locate north of that river, either to take possession of public lands without title, or to buy on whatever terms they could get from speculators. Some of these speculators had acquired lands already sold by Congress at bargain rates; others had bought up titles in the Virginia Military District, centering about Chillicothe, where the state of Vir-

ginia, when ceding its lands to Congress, had reserved an area for the benefit of its Revolutionary War veterans; still others had obtained land from the Connecticut Land Company, which held a grant in the Cleveland area, known as the Western Reserve, a district which the state of Connecticut had originally owned, and had set aside for such of its citizens as had suffered from British depredations during the Revolution.

Under these circumstances Congress was willing to listen to the arguments of William Henry Harrison, who in 1799 **Land Law** became the first territorial dele- **of 1800** gate from the Northwest Territory; and the Harrison Land Law of 1800 made notable concessions to the western point of view. Four local land offices were established in the Northwest instead of two; tracts as small as three hundred and twenty acres were offered for sale; and credit was extended to all purchasers for a period of four years, one fourth of the purchase price to be paid down, and one fourth with interest each succeeding year. As a concession to those who wished to obtain the maximum revenue from the lands, the law provided that auctions should be held for a period of three weeks whenever a new tract was opened for sale, but after the auction was over unsold lands were to be equally open to all at the minimum price, two dollars per acre. Congress also refused to agree to the so-called "right of preemption," according to which the trespasser on government or Indian land claimed that he should have the first chance to purchase the land he had settled upon, but did not own. In 1804 Congress reduced the minimum unit of sale to one hundred and sixty acres, so that thereafter a man with eighty dollars in cash could make the first payment on a frontier farm.

Migration to the West was definitely stimulated by the Land Law of 1800, and the population of the Northwest **Admission** Territory increased so rapidly **of Ohio** that by 1802 Congress voted to admit the new state of Ohio. The "enabling act" by which this decision was made effective set

THE TRAPPER'S RETURN. Illustration by Alexander Wilson in *The Port-Folio* magazine, 1810.

THE SETTLED FRONTIER. Plan of a newly cleared farm, illustrated in Patrick Campbell, *Travels Through . . . North America*, 1793.

LEWIS AND CLARK IN COUNCIL WITH THE INDIANS. Illustration in Patrick Gass, *Journal* (of the Lewis and Clark Expedition), 1812.

Jefferson's West presented a vast and varied scene. Across the Appalachians, frontier farmers were cutting down the forests, building houses, barns, and fences, preparing the way for civilization. Along the fringes of settlement everywhere, trappers and fur-traders gathered their spoils. Still farther to the west, explorers such as Lewis and Clark opened new worlds to conquer, while at the mouth of the Mississippi the proud old city of New Orleans fell an easy prey to manifest destiny.

NEW ORLEANS, LA., 1803. Painting by J. I. Bouquet de Woiseri.

two important precedents: (1) national aid to public education, and (2) national aid to road-building. The law redeemed the promise of the Ordinance of 1785 by handing over to the new state one section of land out of every township in aid of education; and it provided also that five per cent of the proceeds of the sales of public lands within the state should be "applied to laying out and making public roads" in Ohio, and from Ohio to the "navigable waters emptying into the Atlantic." In return for these favors the state of Ohio agreed to leave untaxed for a period of five years all lands of the United States sold within its borders. Under a constitution that included many democratic provisions, the new state was formally admitted in 1803.

When Jefferson became President the only state that still retained its western lands was Georgia. By its original charter the colony of Georgia had had the usual sea-to-sea grant, but this title was somewhat clouded by revisions in the Georgia boundaries that the British government had ordered after the Proclamation of 1763. The state of Georgia claimed, nevertheless, that its domain extended westward to the Mississippi River. The situation was further complicated by the secret agreement over the Florida boundary that the United States and Great Britain had made during the negotiations that led to the Treaty of 1783. According to this understanding, the international boundary would have been located much farther to the north than the thirty-first parallel had Great Britain retained Florida instead of ceding it to Spain. Thus the United States had a reasonable claim of its own to the lands in the disputed area.

But the state of Georgia not only refused to relinquish its claims to the United States; it also undertook in 1795 to sell over thirty million acres in the **The Yazoo Land Companies** disputed area to the so-called Yazoo Land Companies. The price required

Georgia Land Grants 1789-95
Yazoo Land Company Tracts

South Carolina Yazoo Co. 1789
Virginia Yazoo Co. 1789
Tennessee Co. 1789
Georgia Co. 1795

Georgia, Mississippi Co. 1795
Upper Mississippi Co. 1795
Tennessee Co. 1795

was five hundred thousand dollars, or approximately one and one half cents an acre. Among the stockholders in the companies were many prominent citizens, including, it developed, all but one of the members of the legislature that voted the Yazoo grants. The charge of fraud was promptly made, and the next legislature declared the Yazoo contracts null and void. In the meantime, however, many innocent purchasers had bought Yazoo stock, and they as well as the original holders were unwilling to concede that the land titles were invalid.

In 1798 Congress voted to set up a territory in the disputed region, and authorized the President to appoint three commissioners to treat with a like number from Georgia for a final settlement. Action was delayed until Jefferson became President, when an agreement was reached that Georgia should cede its lands to the United States on condition that the state be allowed $1,250,000 from the proceeds of the sale of the lands. Other conditions of the agreement provided that the northern and western boundaries of Georgia should be fixed as at present; that the United States should extinguish the existing Indian titles to land within the state of Georgia; that the ceded territory might be admitted as a slave state when its population reached sixty thousand; and that five million acres might be set aside to satisfy the Yazoo claimants. The agreement was duly ratified, and ultimately it went into effect.

The indemnification of the Yazoo claimants, however, was long delayed, for John **John Ran-** Randolph of Roanoke set him- **dolph and** self the task of blocking the nec- **the "Quids"** essary legislation in Congress. In this stand he was opposed by the President, for many of the claimants were northern speculators, and Jefferson was eager to strengthen his party in the North by conciliating them. Over this and other differences with the administration Randolph led a small faction of the Republican Party into open revolt. The "Quids," as these insurgents were sometimes called, claimed that Jefferson had forgotten the states'-rights doctrines of 1798, and had in reality become a Federalist. In 1810 the Supreme Court held in the case of *Fletcher vs. Peck* that the state of Georgia had no right to invalidate its original contract with the Yazoo companies; and in 1814, with Randolph temporarily out of Congress, eight million dollars was voted for the settlement of the Yazoo claims.

Meantime the problem of the Mississippi had been unexpectedly revived. In 1800 Napoleon Bonaparte, tempo- **Napoleon's** rarily dazzled by a scheme **American** of Talleyrand's for the revival **projects** of the French Empire in America, had required of Spain the retrocession of Louisiana. For some time the Treaty of San Ildefonso, by which this transfer of title had been arranged, was kept secret, and the Spanish officials in Louisiana were not dislodged. The reason for this delay seems to have been Napoleon's decision that the long-standing revolt against French authority in Santo Domingo must be crushed before the French occupation of Louisiana could begin. But General Leclerc, who was sent with ten thousand men to pacify Santo Domingo, found more opposition than Napoleon had counted on. The islanders fought valiantly under the leadership of the brilliant Toussaint L'Ouverture, and the yellow fever proved to be an even greater obstacle to French success. Repeatedly reinforcements had to be sent, and General Leclerc himself succumbed to the fever.

Less than a year after the Treaty of San Ildefonso was signed, Jefferson had learned of Napoleon's intentions toward Louisiana. In a letter dated April 18, 1802, he expressed his deep concern to Robert R. Livingston, the American minister to France:

Of all nations of any consideration, France is the one which, hitherto, has offered the most points of a communion of interests. From these causes, we have ever looked to her as our natural friend, as one with which we never could have an occasion of difference. Her growth, therefore, we viewed as our own, her misfortunes ours. There is on the globe one single spot, the pos-

The Triumph of Toussaint L'Ouverture. Leader of a revolt against French rule, L'Ouverture, once a Negro slave, was known as "the Bonaparte of Santo Domingo."

sessor of which is our natural and habitual enemy. It is New Orleans, through which the produce of $\frac{3}{8}$ of our territory must pass to market, and from its [the West's] fertility it will ere long yield more than one half of our whole produce, and contain more than half of our inhabitants. France, placing herself in that door, assumes to us the attitude of defiance. The day that France takes possession of New Orleans . . . we must marry ourselves to the British fleet and nation.

Jefferson's worst fears seemed confirmed when he learned a few months later that **Jefferson's** the "right of deposit" at New **reactions** Orleans had been suspended. The West, now also aware of the secret treaty, was immediately in a furor. Potentially the West was the most nationalistic part of America, but western loyalty depended, as Jefferson knew full well, mainly upon the ability of the United States to serve western interests. Not many years before, the West had listened to the blandishments of Spanish agents; still more recently it had shown its sympathy for George

Rogers Clark's expedition down the Mississippi; and only in 1798 a Kentucky legislature had willingly accepted Jefferson's own resolutions in defiance of the central government. Two possibilities, neither of them agreeable to a President who was by nature a pacifist, seemed open. The West might seek, with or without the aid of the central government, to dislodge the French from the mouth of the Mississippi; or it might leave the Union and join in the formation of another New France. The choice of either alternative meant war for the United States, a war in which Great Britain and the United States must be allies.

Faced by this situation, Jefferson was not slow to act. He ordered Livingston to suggest the purchase by the United States of the Isle of Orleans and West Florida, and he sent James Monroe to France as minister extraordinary, clothed with authority to offer as much as ten million dollars, if necessary, for the coveted territory. Meantime Napoleon, irritated by the losses in Santo Domingo and weary of military inaction for himself, had decided to abandon expansion overseas in favor of expansion on the continent of Europe. Inevitably this meant a resumption of the war with Great Britain. Since, for the time being at least, the British would have control of the seas, the French could not hope to take possession of Louisiana. Why not sell it to the United States for cash to be used in the war? Even before Monroe arrived, Talleyrand had startled Livingston by asking him what the United States would be willing to pay for the whole of Louisiana.

Once Monroe had arrived, the bargain was quickly struck. For eighty million francs, or about fifteen million dollars, **The pur-** the United States was to pur- **chase of** chase the whole of Louisiana. Of **Louisiana** this sum one fourth was to go to the payment of French debts to American citizens which had been recognized by the convention of 1800. Neither of the Floridas was included in the purchase, for the simple reason that Napoleon had not acquired title to them. The Americans secured a verbal promise,

Louisiana Purchase
1803

however, that France would never attempt to take over Florida from Spain. As to the boundaries of Louisiana, Napoleon agreed that they should be the same "that it now has in the hands of Spain and that it had when France possessed it." When Livingston tried to find out more definitely what this clause meant, Talleyrand refused to commit himself, saying merely, "You have made a noble bargain for yourselves, and I suppose you will make the most of it." As a matter of fact Talleyrand, in his instructions to the first French governor of Louisiana, had already defined the Louisiana boundaries as the river Iberville on the east and the Rio Grande on the west.

Jefferson was greatly astonished when he learned what his ministers had done, but he had no disposition to renounce the bargain they had made. He did feel, however, that there was no constitutional authorization for any such act, and he hoped to see the Constitution so amended as to make the purchase legal. As a matter of fact, the right to acquire new territory could easily have been implied from the treaty-making power, or from the war-making power, or from the fact that the United States was a nation, just as other nations, and had a right to do what nations ordinarily did. But Jefferson was committed to the doctrine of strict construction, and wished to hold himself within the letter of the law. A suggestion from Livingston that Napoleon might change his mind seems to have resolved the President's doubts. He submitted the treaty to the Senate, where it was promptly ratified by a vote of 26 to 5. The sentiment in the House on the measure was shown when that body authorized the funds necessary to carry the treaty into effect by a vote of 90 to 25.

Seemingly Jefferson's conscience was not in the least troubled by what Napoleon had done. That unscrupulous ruler had sold Louisiana to the United States in direct contravention of a provision in the French constitution, and he had also violated his pledge to Spain never to sell Louisiana to a third power. The French had not so much as occupied Louisiana at the time the treaty was ratified, and the French agent of Napoleon, Laussat, handed the province over to the United States only seventeen days after he received it from the Spanish governor. In a sense the United States had acted as the receiver of stolen goods. Napoleon took Louisiana from Spain because he had the might to do it, and he sold Louisiana to the United States in order to get money for his impending war against Great Britain. Viewed from any angle it was not a pretty proceeding, but it proved to be of vast importance to the United States, whose territory was expanded by the purchase not less than one hundred and forty per cent.

The government of the new territory raised some interesting questions. Some of **Government of Louisiana** the Federalists, alarmed at the growing political power of the strictly agricultural sections of the country, favored keeping Louisiana in a perpetual state of dependency. This, however, was probably contrary to the treaty, which guaranteed to the inhabitants of the ceded area "the enjoyment of all the rights, advantages, and immunities of citizens of the United States"; and it was certainly out of harmony with Republican sentiments. It was decided instead to adapt the Northwest Ordinance to the Louisiana territory, and to permit the formation from its area of new western states. At the outset, however, even a limited extension of the American system of self-government seemed impossible. The French and Spanish inhabitants of Louisiana were unaccustomed to democratic institutions and were unready for them. As a temporary expedient, therefore, the President appointed all territorial officers, including the governor, secretary, judges, and thirteen members of a legislative council. French civil law was permitted to remain in force. This autocratic régime did

not last long, and the process of breaking up Louisiana into territories and states was soon begun. In 1812 the state of Louisiana, with its present boundaries, was admitted to the Union.

With their appetites now whetted for expansion, the Republicans cast longing eyes on Florida. Jefferson decided **Florida** that the eastern boundary of Louisiana was the Perdido River, a somewhat fantastic claim in which, however, Congress promptly backed him up. This boundary pushed American territory far over into West Florida, and Jefferson, both by intriguing through Talleyrand and by negotiating with Spain, tried to acquire more. Congress was induced to appropriate two million dollars for the purchase of the Floridas, but Spain, although helpless to defend her rights against either the United States or France, remained defiant, and Napoleon found no occasion to betray Spanish interests to the Americans again.

Except among the more conservative elements of the Northeast, the purchase of Louisiana aroused tremendous **Election of 1804** enthusiasm, and served to increase the good-will felt toward Jefferson's administration. Under the circumstances the result of the impending presidential election of 1804 was never in doubt. Some northeastern Federalists, rather than face the prospect of continued agricultural control of the government, were ready to break up the Union. In the Vice-President, Aaron Burr, they found a willing tool for their plots. Back in 1800, when the Federalist House was attempting to choose between Jefferson and Burr for the Presidency, Burr had seemed willing to accept the office if Congress should so decide. For this breach of loyalty Jefferson never forgave him, and as Vice-President, bereft of presidential patronage, his control over the Republican factions in New York gradually ebbed away. When a number of Federalists suggested that he become their candidate for governor of New York in 1804, he was not averse. Their plan was to elect Burr, and then under his leadership to take New York and New England out of the Union. Fortunately Hamilton learned of the plot, and by exposing it caused it to fail. Burr, now completely discredited, challenged Hamilton to a duel, and on July 11, 1804, mortally wounded him. In the election the Federalists, compelled now to defend themselves against the charge of treason, were overwhelmed. George Clinton, Burr's chief rival in New York politics, became the Republican vice-presidential candidate and helped, as Burr had done four years before, to carry that state for Jefferson. Even New England, with the exception of Connecticut, went Republican. The electoral vote stood 162 for Jefferson to 14 for C. C. Pinckney, the Federalist candidate.

The purchase of Louisiana insured the ultimate loyalty of the West to the Union, but there was no certainty that the purchase would bring peace. The boundaries of Louisiana were left vague, and Jefferson had promptly opened a dispute with Spain over West Florida. Already hostile Indians were using Florida as a base of operations against the American frontier, and as a haven of refuge. Many Westerners were ready, also, by force if necessary, to push the southwestern boundary of Louisiana far into Spanish territory. Moreover, the creole population of Louisiana was restive under the rule of William C. C. Claiborne, a frontier politician whom Jefferson had sent to New Orleans as governor. Actually a greater menace, however, was General James Wilkinson, in charge of American troops in Louisiana. Wilkinson was a spy and a turncoat who was at the time and had been before in the pay of Spain. How long trouble could be averted in Louisiana under such circumstances, no one knew.

The possibilities of the situation were not lost on Aaron Burr, whose career in the East **The Burr** seemed ruined. What he really **conspiracy** intended to do will never be known, for he told so many conflicting tales about his plans. His story to Merry, the British minister, was that with one hundred

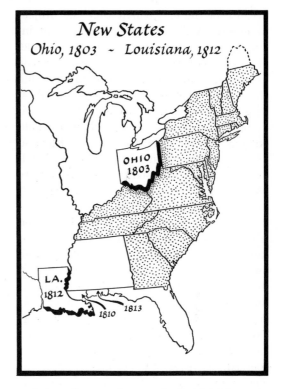

New States
Ohio, 1803 - Louisiana, 1812

OHIO
1803

LA.
1812

1810   1813

and ten thousand pounds in British cash, and the assistance of a British fleet to take New Orleans, he would assemble a thousand men on the Ohio, float them down to the mouth of the Mississippi, get the Louisiana legislature to declare for independence, and form a new state under British control with himself at its head. He let the Spanish minister think that his purpose was merely to set up a buffer state midway between Louisiana and Mexico. He made a trip to the West and talked freely of his plans. To some he said merely that he was going out West to make a new start in politics. To others he spoke of carving a Mississippi Valley Confederacy out of the possessions of Spain, or of the United States, or both. With consummate skill he suited the degree of treason to the taste of each listener.

Burr's "conspiracy" was well received by many Westerners. The feeling that Spain might still be a menace to the West persisted, and Burr's brave words of an attack on Vera Cruz or even Mexico City won much support. Some were interested merely because of the excitement that the project promised. Wilkinson, a past master at intrigue, was easily attached to the scheme. Harmon Blennerhassett, a rich Irishman who lived in splendor on an island in the Ohio River near what is now Parkersburg, West Virginia, was the most useful of Burr's converts, for on the assumption that he would one day become Burr's minister to England he allowed his island to be made the headquarters for a proposed river expedition to New Orleans, and he gave the "conspirators" money, boats, and supplies.

Whether or not Burr actually plotted treason is a question upon which historians cannot agree. Wilkinson said that he did, but Wilkinson's word was less trustworthy than Burr's. The fact that Burr's preparations were so open argues in his favor. At any rate, he collected boats at Blennerhassett's Island, and set a date, November 15, 1806, for his departure. His start was delayed, however, by an unsuccessful attempt to indict him for treason in Kentucky. Had he left at the time he originally planned, he would have found on his arrival in New Orleans that Wilkinson's troops, perhaps by prearrangement, were far to the west of the city, and that the first elective legislature of the territory had just convened. With good luck he might have started his new state. As it was, Wilkinson, for reasons best known to himself, supplied the President with the information necessary to charge Burr again with treason. Meantime the "expedition," consisting of only thirteen flat boats carrying sixty men, had started; but before he reached Natchez, Burr learned of Wilkinson's duplicity, and fled, only to be caught and sent to Richmond, Virginia, for trial.

The case was not decided strictly on its merits. Jefferson's eagerness to convict his **Trial of Burr** former lieutenant gave grounds to the charge that the defendant was being tried less for treason to his country than for treason to his party. On the other hand, Chief Justice Marshall, before whom on circuit duty the trial was set, was the bitter political foe of the President,

and was ready to discredit him at every turn. In the course of the trial the Chief Justice ruled that to be guilty of treason a man must be present when the overt act is committed. Since the overt act was held to be the starting of the expedition from Blennerhassett's Island, and since Burr was not present at that time, but joined the expedition later, his acquittal followed as a matter of course.

The case is also interesting for its constitutional implications. By bringing about Burr's acquittal the Chief Justice successfully stopped all efforts on the part of the executive to use the courts as instruments of political persecution. On the other hand, when the Court summoned Jefferson to appear during the proceedings, and to bring certain papers with him, Jefferson ignored the summons. The President could not be at the command of the courts. It was a drawn battle in which each department of government stoutly and successfully maintained its independence of the other.

Jefferson's interest in Louisiana antedated many years its acquisition by the United States. As a dabbler in natural, science he was deeply interested, long before he became President, in its geographic secrets, its fauna and flora, and its opportunities **The Lewis** for trade. In January, 1803, **and Clark** while the news that the Spanish **Expedition** had withdrawn the right of deposit at New Orleans was still fresh, he sent a message to Congress asking authority to send an exploring expedition into the far Northwest. At the time this authority was asked, all of the territory to be explored was outside the United States, but there is nothing to prove that Jefferson had any ulterior designs upon it. Congress granted the President's request, and in the winter of 1803–04 a small party of soldiers made ready, under the command of Meriwether Lewis, the President's private secretary, and William Clark, the brother of George Rogers Clark, to penetrate the Northwest. The expedition was commissioned to ascend the Missouri River to its source, to cross over

Lewis and Clark Expedition 1804~1806
and Pike Expeditions 1805~1807

the Continental Divide, and then to descend the Columbia to its mouth. The explorers were to make careful notes on the geography of the region, the native tribes they encountered, the animal and plant life of the West, and the evidence they found of valuable mineral deposits.

At St. Louis in the spring of 1804, Lewis received for his government the formal transfer of the upper part of Louisiana to the United States, and on May 14, with a party of forty-five, he began the ascent of the Missouri. It took six months for the expedition to reach the Mandan villages near present-day Washburn, North Dakota. Five months more were spent in camp among the Mandan Indians, and another seven months brought the expedition to the mouth of the Columbia, where the winter of 1805–06 was spent. Then by approximately the same route the explorers returned, arriving in St. Louis in September, 1806, after an absence of nearly two and one half years. The

Journals of Lewis and Clark, published in part in many editions, record with meticulous detail the doings and discoveries of the party. They show Lewis and Clark to be resourceful leaders, and they also give considerable credit to Sacajawea, the Indian wife of a somewhat undependable French guide and interpreter.

Lewis and Clark brought back much new information for the mapmakers, and themselves gave names to several rivers of the Northwest. They reported also that the Indians of the regions visited were numerous and friendly. These savages, hungry and destitute, might and often did steal, but if well treated they were ordinarily peaceful. As for the future of the country, Lewis and Clark said little to tempt settlers beyond the Missouri. Traders might go there; indeed, the evidence was abundant that they already knew much about it; but white settlers, never. The expedition also gave the United States a claim by right of exploration to the region beyond the Rocky Mountains, a region which could not by any stretch of the imagination be regarded as a part of Louisiana.

In 1805 General Wilkinson sent Zebulon Montgomery Pike on a similar expedition to Pike's ex- seek out the source of the Mis- peditions sissippi River. The experiences of Pike and his party were in every essential particular similar to those of Lewis and Clark. Pike thought that he had reached his goal, but later explorations proved that he had not. By April, 1806, he was back in St. Louis, but the following August he was off again under orders to penetrate far into the Southwest, as Lewis and Clark had penetrated into the Northwest. He reached the base of the Rocky Mountains at a point about where the city of Pueblo, Colorado, now stands, and then, with a part of his force, struck out into New Mexico. At length he was picked up by the Spanish, his papers were taken away from him and he and his men conducted back to the United States.

Of the men whom Pike had left behind on his trail, one party, by pre-arrangement, descended the Arkansas and returned to St. Louis, while most of the others, after capture by the Spanish, also found their way home. Pike published an account of his explorations soon after his return that rivaled in interest the *Journals of Lewis and Clark*. Over a hundred years later the documents the Spanish had taken from him were found in the Mexican archives by an American investigator, and published. Except in minor details they confirmed all that the young explorer had reported.

No doubt Jefferson was responsible for the expeditions of Pike, although there is no direct evidence to prove it. Certainly his interest in the expansion of the United States struck a responsive chord in the hearts of most of his countrymen. When he left office he could at least count on the loyalty of the West, not only to the United States but also to the Republican Party.

Bibliography

The books on Jefferson and Jefferson's administration cited for the preceding chapter, p. 252, continue useful. On problems of politics and administration, C. R. Fish, *The Civil Service and the Patronage* (1905), is illuminating. H. C. Hockett, *Western Influences on Political Parties to 1825* (1917), deals with a subject of considerable significance.

The Barbary Wars are covered adequately in Gardner W. Allen, *Our Navy and the Barbary Corsairs* (1905); C. O. Paullin, *Commodore John Rodgers* (1910), and *Diplomatic Negotiations of American Naval Officers* (1912).

The expanding power of the Supreme Court is dealt with in great detail in Beveridge, *Life of Marshall*, III. See also E. S. Corwin, *John Marshall and the Constitution* (1919); and Charles Warren, *The Supreme Court in United States History* (2 vols.; 1937). H. S. Commager, *Majority Rule and Minority Rights* (1943), expresses doubts on the constitutional justification of the doctrine of judicial review.

On the subject of the public lands, three books already cited are fundamental: Treat, *The National Land System;* Hibbard, *A History of the Public Land Policies;* and Robbins, *Our Landed Heritage.* To these may be added Thomas C. Donaldson, *The Public Domain, Its History* (1884), a useful compilation of official data, somewhat marred by omissions and inaccuracies.

On the evolution of Ohio, the books already cited for chapter X, p. 182, continue useful. Others worth noting include Rufus King, *Ohio: First Fruits of the Ordinance of 1787* (1888); E. O. Randall and D. J. Ryan, *History of Ohio* (5 vols., 1912); R. C. Downes, *Frontier Ohio, 1788–1803* (1935); E. H. Roseboom and F. P. Weisenburger, *A History of Ohio* (1934).

Besides the general histories and the biographies of Jefferson, all of which devote a generous amount of space to the Louisiana Purchase, the following special works should be consulted: Charles E. Hill, *Leading American Treaties* (1922); E. W. Lyon, *Louisiana in French Diplomacy,*

1759–1804 (1934); T. L. Stoddard, *The French Revolution in San Domingo* (1914); A. P. Whitaker, *The Mississippi Question, 1795–1803* (1934); J. K. Hosmer, *The History of the Louisiana Purchase* (1902). There is also an excellent book by E. W. Lyon, *The Man Who Sold Louisiana, The Life of François Barbé-Marbois* (1942). On a related subject, I. J. Cox, *The West Florida Controversy, 1798–1813* (1918), is excellent.

Several colorful characters of the period have attracted competent biographers. W. C. Bruce, *John Randolph of Roanoke, 1773–1833* (2 vols., 1922; new ed., 1939), is scholarly, and based in large part on manuscript sources. Henry Adams, *John Randolph* (1917), is one of the best of the *American Statesmen* series, although quite unsympathetic toward Randolph. G. W. Johnson, *Randolph of Roanoke, A Political Fantastic* (1929), draws heavily on Bruce, but is more readable. Aaron Burr is another character much written about. On the critical side is S. H. Wandell and Meade Minnegerode, *Aaron Burr* (2 vols., 1925); more favorable are W. F. McCaleb, *The Aaron Burr Conspiracy* (1936); and Nathan Schachner, *Aaron Burr: A Biography* (1937). James Wilkinson is yet another: J. R. Jacobs, *Tarnished Warrior: Major General James Wilkinson* (1938); and M. R. Werner and T. R. Hay, *The Admirable Trumpeter: A Biography of General James Wilkinson* (1941).

On the explorations of the period the sources make better reading than the secondary works. *Original Journals of the Lewis and Clark Expedition,* edited by R. G. Thwaites (8 vols., 1904–05), are fascinating. So also is Pike's own story: *The Expeditions of Zebulon Montgomery Pike . . . during the Years 1805–6–7* (3 vols., 1895). See also H. E. Bolton, "Papers of Z. M. Pike, 1806–07," *American Historical Review*, XIII, 798–827; *Zebulon Pike's Arkansaw Journal,* edited by S. H. Hart and A. B. Hulbert (1932); and John Bakeless, *Lewis and Clark, Partners in Discovery* (1947).

16

The Struggle to Maintain Neutrality

British interference with American trade — Monroe's proposed treaty — Napoleon's Continental System — British orders in council — The *Chesapeake* affair — The Embargo — Election of 1808 — Repeal of the Embargo — James Madison — Nonintercourse — Macon's Bill Number 2 — Napoleonic decrees — The Cadore letter — Drifting into war

For all the growing interest in the West, the United States during Jefferson's administration was still bound by close commercial ties to Europe, and particularly to England. The era of American self-sufficiency had not yet arrived, and great quantities of manufactured articles still had to be imported. The United States as a producer of raw materials, particularly foodstuffs, was still heavily dependent on outside markets. During part of Jefferson's first administration, Europe was at peace, and this trade went on in normal fashion. But war between Great Britain and France was resumed in 1803, and from that time forward the twofold task of American diplomacy was to keep the United States out of the war, and at the same time to defend her rights as a neutral.

The customary difficulties with the British government were soon in evidence. By 1805 **Case of the Essex** Napoleon's best-laid plans to secure the control of the seas had come to naught at Trafalgar, and thereafter the British fleets were free to tighten their control over commerce. They now found inconvenient the decision that Sir William Scott had handed down in the case of the *Polly*, and another judge, Sir William Grant, held in the case of the *Essex* (1805) that a French-owned West Indian cargo could not be shipped by way of the United States to Europe unless the owners could show that their original intent had been to leave the goods in the United States. This,

of course, could almost never be shown; indeed, the American customs officials, to encourage the trade, had adopted the policy of granting drawbacks upon goods brought in with the obvious intent of reshipment, and in the case of the *Essex* such a drawback had been taken. Sir William's decision enabled the British to use their judgment as to what part of the West Indian trade in neutral ships to permit, and what part to restrain.

Unfortunately the commercial clauses of Jay's treaty were to expire in 1807; hence, after that date, the trade of the **Efforts to** United States would be com- **treat with** pletely at the mercy of the **England** British squadrons. In the belief that a threat of commercial restrictions might bring the British to terms, the Republicans pushed through Congress in 1806 the so-called Nicholson Non-Importation Act, which prohibited the importation of such British goods as the United States was able to manufacture for herself, or could buy from other nations than Great Britain. Armed with this threat, William Pinkney of Maryland was sent to aid James Monroe, the regular minister from the United States to Great Britain, in obtaining a new and satisfactory trade treaty. Pinkney carried explicit instructions. The British must promise to abandon the practice of impressing sailors from American ships; they must restore West Indian trade to the favorable conditions laid down in the *Polly* decision; and they must pay an indemnity for the captures they had made under the *Essex* ruling. On other matters the envoys were free to use their own judgment. It was understood that, in case the British consented to a sufficiently favorable treaty, the Non-Importation Act would never go into effect.

The American envoys, according to well-established precedent, departed from their instructions, but they negotiated a treaty that might not have worked so badly had the British been willing to live up to the terms they had made. According to the treaty the British refused to give up the right of impressing British subjects from American ships, but they promised to take greater care in the future not to impress American seamen. They refused indemnity for captures made under the *Essex* decision, but they were willing to legalize much of the lucrative West Indian trade on condition that the goods carried must actually be American-owned, and must have paid a duty in American ports of one or two per cent. Unfortunately, before Monroe and Pinkney had affixed their signatures to the treaty they were told that the British would not consider themselves bound by it unless the United States agreed to resist the terms affecting neutral trade that were contained in Napoleon's recently issued Berlin Decree. The American envoys were foolish enough to sign anyway, but Jefferson refused under the circumstances to submit the treaty to the Senate, and recalled Monroe, who for the second time came home from a foreign mission in disgrace.

The struggle in Europe had now reached a degree of intensity in which neither side cared much what happened to neutral rights. Napoleon, hopelessly foiled in his efforts to control the high seas, had resolved to bring Great Britain to terms by other means. The English, he reasoned, were a nation of shopkeepers, whose livelihood depended upon their trade with the outside world. Europe was England's chief customer, and Napoleon could, or at least thought that he

Napoleon's Continental System

could, control most of Europe. His Continental System was devised to stop as nearly as might be all imports into European ports from England. He would rob England of her markets and by an unfavorable balance of trade drain her of her gold supply. He would also, in so far as he could accomplish it by threats or violence, prevent trade between England and her customers outside of Europe, particularly the United States.

Indulging his taste for the dramatic, Napoleon issued from foreign capitals the decrees by which this policy was set forth.[1] The Berlin Decree, November 21, 1806, laid a paper blockade about the British Isles, and forbade all trade in British merchandise. All private property of British subjects was declared good prize. Ships coming from England or from the British colonies were not to be received in any French-controlled port, and the falsification of a ship's papers in an effort to evade the decree was to result in the confiscation of the ship. A year later this drastic and unprecedented series of regulations was followed by the Milan Decree, which dealt more specifically with neutrals. All neutral ships that had permitted a British boarding party to visit them, or had paid the duty in a British port, or were bound to or from a British port, were to be confiscated. The Berlin and Milan Decrees were meant to forbid every known kind of trade between Great Britain and the rest of the nations of the world. Napoleon knew that he could not enforce his decrees fully, but he believed that he could stop much trade to the continent of Europe, and, even with the limited sea-power he possessed, he thought that he might interfere somewhat with trade between Great Britain and the neutral nations.

The British government replied to Napo-

[1] Napoleon found in an inept British proclamation known as "Fox's Blockade" the pretext he needed for this action. Through the instrumentality of Charles James Fox, the British foreign minister, a British blockade of the entire coast of northwestern Europe from Brest to the Elbe was proclaimed on May 16, 1806; but, as Napoleon well knew, orders to British naval officers were that the blockade was to be enforced only from the Seine to Ostend, leaving neutral trade wide open elsewhere.

United States of America.

No. 3160

I William R. Lee, Collector for the District of Salem and Beverly, do hereby certify, that John Wallis an American Seaman, aged Nineteen years or thereabouts, of the height of five feet two ½ inches, and of a Dark complexion. Was born in Salem in the State of Massachusetts

has this day produced to me proof, in the manner directed in the Act entitled, "An Act for the Relief and Protection of American Seamen," and, pursuant to the said Act, I do hereby Certify, that the said John Wallis is a Citizen of the United States of America.

In Witness whereof, I have hereunto set my Hand and Seal of Office, this Nineteenth day of January in the year of our Lord one thousand eight hundred and Eleven

William R. Lee, Collector.

SEAMAN'S PROTECTION PAPER. Issued Jan. 19, 1811, in Salem, Massachusetts.

AN AMERICAN SAILOR BOY. From a broadside containing a song sung by impressed American seamen, 1814.

Impressment of American seamen by the British occurred with such frequency before the War of 1812 that the United States government issued certificates to native-born sailors, testifying to their American citizenship. British searching parties, however, paid these documents scant respect, claiming that they were often purchased from their rightful owners by British subjects.

leon's decrees with a series of Orders in Council that were quite as careless of neutral rights as the decrees themselves.

British Orders in Council

The first, dated January 7, 1807, forbade trade from one port to another, "both which ports shall belong to or be in the possession of France or her allies." Neutral ships were to be warned of this order, and if they violated it were to be seized. A second Order in Council, dated November 11, 1807, established a blockade of "all the ports and places of France and her allies, or of any country at war with His Majesty." This meant that neutral trade with Europe, from Trieste to Copenhagen, was forbidden; although the British navy, strong as it was, obviously was unequal to the task. The blockade, therefore, was, like Napoleon's, a "paper" blockade. The British hoped by these orders to hamper the movement of foodstuffs to Europe to such an extent that Napoleon would withdraw his decrees.

The plight of American shipping was now a sorry one, indeed. Ships destined to France or to any of the nations controlled by France, which then meant most of Europe, were subject to seizure by the British. Ships sailing to any British port were subject to seizure by the French. The only trade with Europe left fully open to American ships was with Russia, Sweden, and Turkey; and for a time Napoleon even won the co-operation of the Tsar. Nor did the British Orders in Council serve to deter Napoleon from his purpose. He was never able to prevent all trade between England and the Continent, and he had frequently even to license it himself, but the rest of his career was a sustained effort to make the Continental System work. To put down opposition to it he engaged in his costly expedition into Spain; to win back support for it from the apostate Tsar he undertook the disastrous invasion of Russia.

Both the French and the British enforced their illegal blockades by captures on the American side of the Atlantic, where privateers and warships took what prizes they could. The French naturally took fewer, for their ships were less numerous and were themselves in danger of capture by the British. Admiralty courts in the West Indies, both French and British, decided against the captured American ship. British impressments of sailors from American ships occurred more and more frequently, and were sometimes carried out with unbecoming brutality. American resentment against this practice, particularly among the people along the coast whose friends and relatives had been victimized, grew steadily more intense.

The supreme outrage occurred in June, 1807, when a British man-of-war, the **The Chesa-** *Leopard*, attacked an American **peake affair** frigate, the *Chesapeake*, and took off four members of her crew. This untoward incident followed shortly after the escape of a boatload of sailors from the sloop *Halifax*, which, together with several other British warships, had put in at Lynnhaven Bay, near the mouth of the Chesapeake. The commander of the British squadron had noted that an American warship, the *Chesapeake* was preparing to leave the harbor for a cruise in the Mediterranean, and he hastily concluded that the deserting British sailors must be upon it. Accordingly, while signifying at the same time his willingness to grant a similar privilege to American captains in pursuit of deserters, he gave orders that the *Chesapeake* should be searched. Inasmuch as American sailors were not then deserting to the lower pay and stricter discipline of the British service, this offer was a mere gesture.

When the *Chesapeake* finally put out to sea, she was followed by the *Leopard*, which, on the pretense that she had dispatches to deliver, asked and received permission to send a boarding party to the *Chesapeake*. But the purported dispatches consisted merely of the British commander's order for search of the *Chesapeake*, and a note from the captain of the *Leopard* demanding that he be accorded that privilege. On the approach of the *Leopard*, Captain Barron of the *Chesapeake* had failed to take the normal precaution of preparing his ship for action, but he refused nevertheless to permit the search.

Thereupon the *Leopard* opened fire, and the unready *Chesapeake*, after firing one gun, hauled down her colors. For his carelessness Captain Barron was later court-martialed, and sentenced to five years suspension from the service without pay. Three Americans were killed during the fray, and eighteen wounded. The British then boarded the *Chesapeake* and took off four deserters, only one of whom, it transpired, was an Englishman. The others were Americans who had previously suffered impressment into the British service, and had then deserted. With their object accomplished, the British permitted the *Chesapeake* to put back to port.

The news of this outrage caused the most profound excitement throughout the United States. British depredations **Popular** against American merchantmen **reaction** had long been common, but in this instance it was an American national ship that had been attacked. The colossal effrontery of the British commander, who in spite of the incident did not hesitate to return to an American port, was even more galling. The country was in such a belligerent mood as the sinking of the *Maine* and the *Lusitania* aroused in later years, and had Jefferson wanted war undoubtedly he could have had it. But the President chose to keep the peace if he could. By proclamation he forbade British warships to take on supplies in American ports, and ordered them out of American waters. He also demanded reparations from the British government, including adequate punishment for the offending British commander; and he set a date, somewhat distant, to be sure, for a special session of Congress.

When Congress convened, Jefferson proposed an embargo on all commerce with the outside world as the most effec- **The Em-** tive means of defending Amer- **bargo Act** ican rights. He genuinely believed that the warring nations of Europe, rather than suffer long the loss of American trade, would withdraw their obnoxious regulations. Naturally the commercial interests of the country were extremely skeptical of such a policy, but

EMBARGO. "Ograbme the American Snapping Turtle." Cartoon by Alexander Anderson, about 1808.

KING QUILLDRIVER'S EXPERIMENTS, 1808. Jefferson is represented inside a fortress of proclamations, while Napoleon blows the breath of war at a windmill on Jefferson's hat

By the Virtue, Firmness and Patriotism of

JEFFERSON & MADISON,

Our Difficulties with England are settled—our Ships have been preserved, and our Seamen will, hereafter, be respected while sailing under our National Flag.

RESTORATION OF TRADE. Detail from a broadside of Madison's proclamation of the Erskine Treaty, suspending the Embargo Acts, 1809.

Jefferson's foreign policy aroused the ridicule of his enemies and brought embarrassment to his friends. In the eyes of the Federalists he was a warrior who fought only with a quill-pen sword, and became the willing tool of Napoleon. His defenders at first pictured his Embargo, spelled backwards as "Ograbme," as an effective weapon, but they could not long be sure who was being grabbed. Had the Jeffersonian policies brought peace with honor? Or, had Jefferson stripped himself, and his nation's defenses, bare?

NON-INTERCOURSE, OR DIGNIFIED RETIREMENT. Jefferson, in rags, is saying, "I have stript myself rather than submit to London or Parisian fashions!... It never Suited me. They are always wrong in their Measures!" Cartoon by "Peter Pencill," 1809.

resentment over the *Leopard-Chesapeake* affair was still strong, and the President had his way. An Embargo Act, passed December 21, 1807, prohibited all ships, except foreign ships in ballast, to depart from the United States for any foreign port. Ships engaged in the coasting trade were required to give heavy bond that they would land their cargoes in the United States.

Time proved that Jefferson had greatly overestimated the results that the embargo could obtain. The American flag did not disappear, as he had hoped, from the high seas. Many of the American ships that were at sea when the law went into effect kept out of American ports, and plied between foreign ports. Moreover, in spite of repeated enforcement acts, it was impossible to prevent ships from leaving port in defiance of the law; and sometimes they were aided by the very officials that were charged with this enforcement.

Nevertheless, the law was sufficiently effective to disrupt completely the economic life of the country. Shipowners and importers took heavy losses, while thousands of sailors, shipbuilders, sailmakers, and other artisans were thrown out of employment. Commodities that the United States had long been accustomed to import from abroad were lacking, and the inferior substitutes that American manufacturers began to produce cost high prices. Even agriculture soon began to feel the effects of the embargo, for the crops of 1808 found the gateways to market closed, and farm prices dropped precipitately. Under such circumstances the law became increasingly unpopular, and the Federalists, who opposed it, gained ground.

Election of 1808 The election of 1808 showed the changing temper of the country. Jefferson was importuned to stand for re-election again, but he declined with such emphasis as to set a precedent that long remained unbroken. He did not hesitate, however, to throw the "succession" to his Secretary of State, James Madison. The Federalists supported C. C. Pinckney, and

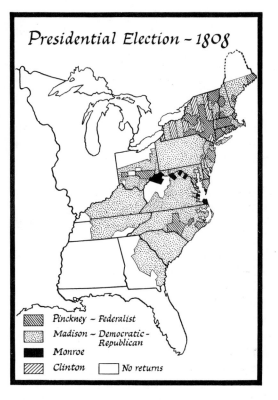

Presidential Election ~ 1808

Pinckney – Federalist
Madison – Democratic- Republican
Monroe
Clinton   No returns

by emphasizing the unpleasant features of the embargo, they won back many voters who had deserted them for Jefferson four years before. In the electoral college Madison received 122 electoral votes to 47 for Pinckney. Six electors cast their ballots for George Clinton, the Vice-President, whose claims to the succession Jefferson had overlooked. Congress remained Republican, although by a much-reduced majority. It is significant that New England, with the exception of Vermont, now returned to the Federalist fold, although this was the time that John Quincy Adams, senator from Massachusetts and son of the second President, chose to leave the Federalists and become a Republican.

Repeal of the Embargo Act The results of the election made it abundantly apparent that the Republicans must repeal their embargo or witness an even more embarrassing revival of Federalist strength. The endurance of the country was at an end. Probably the United States had not suffered much more from the embargo than Great Britain, where sales to the United States had dropped off one half, and manufacturers, already handicapped by Napoleon's decrees, had suffered acutely from the loss of American customers. But the British had shown great energy in opening up new trade with Latin-American countries, and in picking up the carrying trade that formerly had gone in American ships. The British public, moreover, was inured to the sufferings of war; the embargo was merely one unpleasant thing among many. When two nations resort to commercial retaliations, the one that can stand the most punishment wins. England was distressed by the embargo, but she was willing to put up with it as a necessary accompaniment of her war against Napoleon. The United States was also distressed by the embargo, and having no great urge to continue this self-inflicted punishment, she repealed it. After the election, Jefferson left the determination of future policy to his successor, and with Madison's approval Jefferson signed a bill a few days before he left office bringing the embargo to an end. It was with some humiliation that he was thus compelled to confess his favorite project a failure.

James Madison (1751–1836), the fourth President, was another representative of the **James** Virginia planter class, although **Madison** from his youth he was more the politician than the planter. Only a few years out of Princeton and still undecided as to his life work, the outbreak of the American Revolution determined his course for him. Successively he served as a member of the local committee on public safety, of the convention that drew up the first Virginia constitution, of the Continental Congress, of the Virginia House of Delegates, of the Convention that framed the Constitution of the United States, and of the national House of Representatives. For eight years he was Jefferson's Secretary of State and close adviser. Certainly his political apprenticeship had been ample.

Unlike Washington and Jefferson, who possessed powerful physiques, Madison was small and of delicate health. He was a better scholar along some lines, particularly constitutional history, than Jefferson, but he was not so many-sided. In spite of his long political career, he had had less administrative experience than any of the Presidents who had preceded him, and he was less able than they to recognize and withstand the pressure of designing politicians. As Secretary of State, he had of necessity been dominated by the views and personality of Jefferson, and as President he had some difficulty in shaping a course of his own. His wife, "Dolly" Madison, a woman of great personal charm, brought needed grace and beauty to White House society.

For a time Madison had toyed with the idea of continuing the embargo for a few months longer, and then follow- **The Non-** ing it up with war; but op- **Intercourse** position to such a course was **Act** strong, and a far less dramatic policy was adopted. In the place of the embargo a Non-Intercourse Act was substituted which closed American ports to the ships of Great Britain and France and forbade the importation of goods into the United States from either of those nations, or their colonies or dependencies. American ships were permitted to leave American ports, provided only that their destinations were not French or British. The act also carried with it an offer to the offending belligerents. In case Great Britain would withdraw her Orders in Council, the President was authorized to suspend non-intercourse with Great Britain; and in case Napoleon would withdraw his decrees, to suspend non-intercourse with France.

Meantime the British government had been making some half-hearted efforts to restore good relations with the **Rose's** United States. Shortly after **mission** the *Chesapeake* outrage, the British admiral who had authorized the action was recalled from his command, and a special envoy, George Rose, was sent to Washington to arrange a settlement satisfactory to the

James Madison of Virginia, fourth
President of the United States, is properly remembered more for his work during the Federal
Convention that framed the Constitution than
for his subsequent activities. With good reason
he has been called the "Father of the Constitution." No doubt he knew better than any other
man what the framers of that document intended
it to mean. As Secretary of State he was over-
shadowed by Jefferson, and as President he was
confronted by problems that would have baffled a
political genius. The portrait is by Gilbert
Stuart; at the right, Madison is shown addressing
the Virginia Constitutional Convention of 1829–
30. Watercolor sketch by George Catlin, 1830.

United States. But the British showed no
disposition to abate their policy of impressments from American merchant ships, and
Rose's instructions demanded that Jefferson's order forbidding British warships the
use of American ports be withdrawn. Rose
also refused to return the seamen that the
Leopard had impressed unless the United
States would agree to condemn Captain
Barron for encouraging desertions — something Barron had been very careful not to
do. Diplomatically considered, the net result of Rose's mission was exactly nothing
at all. He returned to England, however,
with the impression that the Republican
policy of commercial coercion was extremely
unpopular in New England, and he even
believed that under sufficient pressure that
section of the United States might be
brought back into the British Empire.

The adoption of the Non-Intercourse Act
led to another friendly gesture on the part
of Great Britain. Canning, the British foreign minister, was at least willing to consider
the withdrawal of the British Orders in
Council in return for the opening of American trade and some other favors. Accordingly he instructed Erskine, the British
minister to the United States, to prepare
the way for a treaty that would settle all
outstanding differences between the two
countries. Erskine's sympathies, unfortunately as it turned out, were too wholeheartedly with the United States. He was a
Whig, and as such he disapproved of the
truculent attitude his government had taken
in its handling of American affairs; and he
was married to the daughter of a distinguished veteran of the American Revolution,
General John Cadwalader of Philadelphia.
Moreover, Erskine was a young man, comparatively new to the diplomatic service,
while his antagonist, James Madison, had
age and experience to guide him.

Erskine's instructions were explicit. He
was told that the British government was
ready to disavow the act of the **Erskine's**
Leopard and to offer redress in **"treaty"**
case the United States would agree to the
equal treatment of French and British warships in American ports, and to the exclusion
of foreign seamen from American ships.
Also, the British Orders in Council might be
withdrawn if the United States (1) would
reopen trade with Great Britain while keeping up non-intercourse with France, (2)
would agree to abide by the rule of 1756, and
(3) would acknowledge the right of British
ships to seize American merchant-vessels
found to be disobeying the law forbidding

intercourse with France. These instructions, literally interpreted, really precluded all possibility of settlement, but Erskine chose to believe that they indicated a great desire on the part of the British government to restore good relations with the United States, and interpreted them most liberally.

In this frame of mind he quickly reached an agreement with Madison. With regard to the *Chesapeake* affair the United States consented to withdraw its request for the punishment of the British admiral responsible, while the British promised full redress for the damage done. Restrictions on trade between the United States and Great Britain were to be mutually withdrawn, although trade between France and the United States was to remain closed only as long as Napoleon continued to enforce his decrees. Erskine failed also to secure acceptance by the United States of the rule of 1756, and he got no acknowledgment that British vessels might be permitted to enforce the American law against trade with France. It was little short of amazing, therefore, that he assumed the authority to declare, June 10, 1809, that the Orders in Council would be withdrawn in so far as they applied to the United States. Nor did Madison show much foresight when he issued a proclamation restoring intercourse with Great Britain, and permitting American ships to sail for British ports.

As might have been expected, Canning repudiated the Erskine agreement at sight, and recalled Erskine for having violated his instructions. American ships that had left port were allowed to proceed unmolested to their destinations, but the Orders in Council were continued in force, and Madison had no choice but to issue a proclamation restoring non-intercourse with Great Britain. To make matters worse, Canning sent over in Erskine's place the notoriously ill-tempered Francis James Jackson, with the promise that he might stay in America for a full year. Jackson's behavior was so offensive that, after a few exchanges, Madison announced that no further communications from him

would be received. When his year was up he was recalled.

Non-intercourse left the way open for a revival of American commerce. Doubtless some new avenues of trade were **Macon's Bill** opened up, as the law intended, **Number 2** but the old connections were restored to a great extent in spite of the law. It was impossible to tell, once a ship cleared from an American port, what her destination would be, and many ships, in defiance of all regulations, departed directly for Great Britain or France. Even Napoleon winked at his own prohibitions, and issued licenses for trade that his decrees pointedly forbade. Within a year after the adoption of non-intercourse the Republicans were willing to admit that this policy was as great a failure as the embargo. They would not concede, however, that the principle of commercial coercion was wrong, and they tried once more to apply it. Nathaniel Macon of North Carolina, chairman of the House Committee on Foreign Affairs, now reported out a bill that provided for the importation of French and British goods in American bottoms only. This measure had Madison's support and passed the House, but the Federalists, aided by a disgruntled minority of the Republicans, defeated it in the Senate; whereupon Macon's committee presented a new bill that Macon himself disliked, but that was always known as Macon's Bill Number 2. It repealed the Non-Intercourse Act outright, and tried to bargain with the contending European powers for their favor. If Great Britain would repeal her obnoxious Orders in Council the United States would revive non-intercourse with France; if France would withdraw her offensive decrees, the United States would revive non-intercourse with Great Britain. On May 1, 1810, this bill became a law.

The embargo had fitted in well with Napoleon's policy of crippling British trade, although he took advantage of **New** it to issue his famous Bayonne **Napoleonic** decree, April 17, 1808, which **decrees** ordered the seizure of all American ships found in French ports. Such ships, Napoleon argued trickily, could not be truly American, for the embargo forbade American ships to leave American ports. Non-intercourse, however, was far less satisfactory to the Emperor than the embargo, for it opened the way to a far greater amount of illicit trade between the United States and Great Britain; besides, it ordered the confiscation of French ships found in American ports. Somewhat in the spirit of retaliation, and with an eye to the profits, Napoleon now issued the Rambouillet Decree, March 23, 1810, which ordered the seizure and sale of all American shipping that had entered French ports since the date set for the Non-Intercourse Act to go into effect. Napoleon knew full well that, after Canning's repudiation of the Erskine agreement, the United States could not be irritated into friendship with Great Britain and he hoped for a restoration of the embargo.

When, instead, the American policy of commercial coercion was practically abandoned by the passage of Macon's Bill Number 2, Napoleon **The Cadore letter** had to change his tactics. He proposed to take advantage of the offer that the United States would resume non-intercourse with Great Britain in case France withdrew her decrees. Accordingly, his foreign minister, the Duke of Cadore, wrote a letter to General Armstrong, the American minister to France, which stated that the Berlin and Milan Decrees were revoked to take effect November 1, 1810, "it being understood that, in consequence of this declaration, the English shall revoke their Orders in Council . . .; or that the United States, conformably to the act you have just communicated, shall cause their rights to be respected by the English." Madison should have paid more attention to these conditional clauses than he did. The law authorized him to restore non-intercourse with Great Britain if France withdrew her decrees, but it said nothing about the United States causing "their rights to be respected by the English." But the President, perhaps beguiled by honeyed phrases — "His majesty loves the Americans," the Cadore letter had said, "their prosperity and their commerce are within the scope of his policy" — or more likely in sheer desperation, accepted Napoleon's repeal as valid, and reinstituted non-intercourse with Great Britain. Thereupon Napoleon, having accomplished his purpose, laid down new regulations against American shipping in French ports that were quite as distressing as the decrees he had repealed.

The relations between the United States and Great Britain went steadily from bad to worse. The British were not deceived by Napoleon's pretense **Relations with Britain** that he had repealed his decrees, and William Pinkney, the American minister to Great Britain, could get no pledge that the British Orders in Council would be withdrawn. Moreover, since Jackson's return to England, the British government had sent no one to take his place. On this latter ground Pinkney, acting under instructions from his government, left England in 1811. Thus the two nations had reached a diplomatic *impasse*. Nevertheless, the British, feeling the need of American goods and desirous of using their entire energy against Napoleon rather than against irrelevant neutrals, were now ready to adopt a more favorable attitude toward the United States. A new minister, Augustus J. Foster, hastened across the Atlantic to settle the *Chesapeake* affair, and to pave the way for more amicable relations.

By the time Foster arrived, the people of the United States had tasted battle and had found that they liked it. Because a British frigate, the **The President and the Little Belt** *Guerrière*, operating off Sandy Hook, had repeatedly impressed American sailors, an American frigate, the *President*, was ordered to the vicinity to protect American commerce. Some ten days later the *President* sighted a British man-of-war, and, thinking it was the *Guerrière*, determined to inquire about the impressed seamen. The British ship fled, however, and it was sundown before she was overtaken and hailed. Then a shot from the Britisher started a battle which lasted fifteen minutes and ended in a complete victory for the *President*. To his chagrin, the American captain found that he had beaten the *Little Belt*, a ship half the size of his own, instead of the *Guerrière*. But the country was not so particular, and the people rejoiced immoderately that the *Chesapeake* insult had at last been avenged. Foster, the British minister, found the American government likewise unconcerned about the *Chesapeake*. What the government demanded was the immediate withdrawal of the Orders in Council, and on that subject Foster had no authority to treat.

The British government was slow to realize the changed temper of the United States, **Drifting** and Foster, in closer touch with **into war** the Federalists than with the Republicans, was for a time no great help. Again and again the British refused to withdraw their Orders in Council unless assured that France had genuinely repealed her decrees, not for the United States alone, but for all nations. But at last the evidence began to compound that stubborn refusal to

repeal the orders would mean an American war. For this the British, engaged in a life-and-death struggle with Napoleon, had no stomach. Moreover, British manufacturers had suffered about all they could stand from the loss of American markets, and the British people stood in desperate need of American food. On June 16, Castlereagh, speaking for the British ministry, announced in the House of Commons that the Orders in Council had been withdrawn. Actually the American policy of commercial coercion, plus a little show of fight, had won; for when Castlereagh made this announcement he did not know that at the very moment the American government was pushing a declaration of war through Congress. On June 1, 1812, Madison sent in his war message; on June 4, the House by a vote of 79 to 49 declared for war; and on June 18, just two days after Castlereagh's announcement, the Senate, by a vote of 19 to 13, concurred.

But to understand fully the change in American sentiment that made war possible it is essential to take note of a series of developments in the American West.

Bibliography

The various histories of American diplomacy are all useful at this point, especially Bemis, *Diplomatic History of the United States;* and Bailey, *Diplomatic History of the American People*. Bemis (ed.), *The American Secretaries of State*, III, contains admirable sketches of the Secretaries of State who served under Jefferson and Madison. Henry Adams, *History of the United States*, covers this period, possibly better than any subsequent work. Other works of special value are A. T. Mahan, *Sea Power in its Relation to the War of 1812* (2 vols., 1905); and F. A. Updyke, *The Diplomacy of the War of 1812* (1915). R. D. Paine, *The Fight for a Free Sea* (1920), is a convenient summary.

There are numerous monographs on special subjects, among the most helpful of which are the following: F. E. Melvin, *Napoleon's Navigation System* (1919); F. L. Nussbaum, *Commercial Policy in the French Revolution* (1923); W. F. Galpin, *The Grain Supply of England during the Napoleonic Period* (1925); J. F. Zimmerman, *Impressment of American Seamen* (1925); L. M. Sears, *Jefferson and the Embargo* (1927); Harry Bernstein, *Origins of Inter-American Interest, 1700–1812* (1945); A. L. Burt, *The United States, Great Britain, and British North America from the Revolution to the Peace after the War of 1812* (1940).

There are several lives of Madison, but none entirely satisfactory. Among the best are A. E. Smith, *James Madison, Builder: A New Estimate of a Memorable Career* (1937); Gaillard Hunt, *The Life of James Madison* (1902); S. H. Gay, *James Madison* (1884). A new comprehensive series is beginning of which two volumes have been published: Irving Brant, *James Madison*: Vol. I, *The Virginia Revolutionist* (1941); Vol. II, *The Nationalist* (1948).

17
The War of 1812

FOR a long time after the Treaty of Fort Greenville was signed, the northwestern In-

The frontier advance   dians fell back helplessly before the advance of the white fron-

tier. By the year 1809 they had agreed to as many as nine separate treaties of cession, and, in addition to the territory of Indiana, which Congress had created in 1800, two other new territories, Michigan (1805) and Illinois (1809), had been marked out as goals for the ambition of restless pioneers. In the Southwest the Indians, also duly chastened, watched with apprehension but with little show of opposition the encircling of their lands by settlers on the Yazoo tracts and in the valley of the lower Missis-sippi. Whether to the North or to the South the natives were keenly aware of the disas-trous consequences of the white pressure upon them. The Indian economy was hunt-ing and trapping supplemented by agricul-ture; the white man's economy was agricul-ture supplemented by hunting and trapping. The two modes of life were hopelessly incom-patible. The whites settled thickly, cut down the forests, destroyed the game, and made existence difficult for the adjacent In-dians; and the Indians, debauched and de-praved by contact with the white man's vices, degenerated into a perpetual nuisance to the frontiersmen. The power of the whites was great, and for a long time Indian resistance seemed out of the question.

On only a few occasions has Indian leader-ship approached the level of statesmanship, and the eve of the War of 1812 was one such occasion. During

Tecumseh

these years the outstanding Indian chieftain was Tecumseh, in whose person, according to tradition, the blood of northern and south-ern tribes was united, for his father, this tradition held, was a Shawnee and his mother was a Creek. Whatever his ancestry, Tecumseh had not only the Indian's natural dignity and persuasive eloquence, but he had also a keen understanding of human nature, whether of red men or of whites, and unlike most Indians he could devise and execute far-flung plans. Tecumseh understood clearly the difficulties that confronted the Indians in their dealings with the whites, but he saw also that much of the strength of the whites lay in their unity, and he therefore preached the same doctrine among the Indians. Tribe by tribe they might never hope to stem the advance of the white frontier, but united into a great Indian confederacy, embracing pos-sibly all the tribes of both North and South, their chances would be immeasurably im-proved. All Indian land, he argued, should be under the joint control of all the tribes; and only by the consent of a warrior's con-gress might it be alienated. For Tecumseh challenged also the Indian tradition of fol-lowing the lead of the old chiefs. The warriors were the men who must carry out the orders of the councils; let the warriors themselves decide.

Battle of Tippecanoe
1811

In 1810 Tecumseh, with four hundred armed warriors to defend him, visited Harrison at Vincennes, the capital of Indiana, to deliver the Indian ultimatum. In a dramatic speech the Indian chief proclaimed that his people were "once a happy race, but now made miserable by the white people, who are never contented, but always encroaching. They have driven us from the great salt water, forced us over the mountains, and would shortly push us into the lakes — but we are determined to go no further."

The next year Tecumseh made a visit to the South to secure greater support from the tribes of that section for his program. He had notified Harrison of his departure, and had asked that all matters be left as they were pending his return. Harrison made no pledges, however, and as soon as Tecumseh was well out of the way set out with a strong force for Prophet's Town with the avowed intention of destroying it. His march met no resistance, and he was in sight of his goal when an Indian delegation appeared and asked for a parley. Harrison should have been wise enough to push on at once for the attack, but he agreed to a council set for the next day, and encamped his command on a knoll about a mile from the Indian village.

A careful sentry was set, and about four o'clock the next morning (November 7, 1811) the inevitable Indian attack was disclosed. The whites, who had **Tippecanoe** slept on their arms, fought as well as they could in the darkness, and when day broke beat off the Indians, but Harrison had lost sixty-one killed and one hundred and twenty-seven seriously injured, while the enemy losses had been slight. The battle of Tippecanoe was hailed, nevertheless, as a great victory for the whites. The Indians did not return to the attack, and Prophet's Town, which they had abandoned, was duly destroyed. With much difficulty because of his many wounded, Harrison returned to Vincennes, only to learn a few weeks later that Tecumseh, back from the South with the news that he had won much support in that region, had rebuilt Prophet's Town and

Tecumseh did not wish for war against the whites, although he hated them, but he did **The "Prophet"** hope to unite the Indians into a confederacy so strong that the cessions of land could be stopped. In 1808 he joined with his brother, a medicine man generally spoken of as the "Prophet," to found near the mouth of Tippecanoe Creek on the banks of the Wabash a headquarters soon known as "Prophet's Town." To and from this center came many young warriors whose great hope was the realization of Tecumseh's dream. Gradually Indian resistance stiffened, and when, in 1809, William Henry Harrison, the governor of Indiana Territory, exacted a cession of several million acres of land in the lower Wabash Valley, it was evident that a crisis was at hand. Tecumseh frankly repudiated this cession, but he was eager to avert war, and for some time he was able to restrain his followers.

For two years the northwestern frontier lived under the shadow of impending war.

revived the drooping spirits of his followers. The great Indian chieftain still counseled peace, but after Tippecanoe Indian depredations along the northwestern frontier occurred with ever-increasing frequency. An Indian war had in truth begun.

When Harrison reported the battle of Tippecanoe he complained bitterly that the Indians were well supplied with powder and guns obtained from the British in Canada. Possibly these supplies did not come from the King's stores as Harrison thought, but the fact that Tecumseh was in close touch with the British authorities was a matter of common knowledge. Almost the same situation existed in the Northwest that had confronted Washington when he entered the Presidency. To be sure, the British had removed their military posts to the Canadian side of the boundary, but these posts still existed, and their garrisons were as much concerned as ever with the protection of the fur trade south of the Great Lakes. Tecumseh's plan for organized Indian resistance to the advance of the farmer's frontier fitted in well with Canadian needs. Should the Indians make good their efforts, the northward flow of pelts from the unsettled western lands of the United States might still continue. To the Westerner it appeared that the Canadian fur-trader and the Indian, with identical interests, were merely preparing once more to join forces for the protection of those interests.

It was only natural under these circumstances that the people of the West should

Western clamor for war applaud vigorously each step taken by the national government in the direction of war with the British. They knew, certainly as early as 1811, that a war with the Indians was sure to come, and they believed implicitly that to make war against the Indians without fighting an accompanying war against the allies of the Indians in Canada was to leave the task half-done. Strong in their devotion to the doctrine of the rights of men, the Westerners resented undoubtedly such violations of this principle as the im-

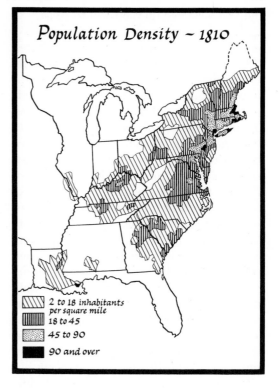

Population Density ~ 1810

2 to 18 inhabitants per square mile
18 to 45
45 to 90
90 and over

pressment of American sailors by the British, but there is room to question whether western resentment against these outrages would have been so great had there not been other and more local grievances against the British. The congenital appetite of the West for expansion was also easily whetted. If war with the British was to come, why not make it a war for the conquest and annexation of Canada? Upper Canada was as logically athwart the path of the American westward movement as the Michigan peninsula, and the need of the West for more lands was perpetual. With the British held at bay in Europe by Napoleon, what was more reasonable than that the United States should seize the opportunity to eliminate the British from North America and thus end for all time the menace of the British-Indian alliance?

In the Southwest there was less certainty of immediate war than in the Northwest, but the preaching of Tecumseh had aroused the latent forebodings of the southern tribes and had bolstered up their will to resist. In

The south-western frontier this region, despite the cession of Louisiana to the United States, the Spanish were still the traditional enemies of the Americans and the natural allies of the Indians, for Florida remained in Spanish hands, and the boundary dispute was still alive. As the southwestern frontier expanded, its residents saw with increasing clarity the necessity of ousting the Spanish from the adjacent seacoast. Through the Florida panhandle ran many of the rivers by which the produce of the new Southwest could most easily find access to the sea. Along the coast of Florida were nests of dangerous pirates that the now enfeebled rule of Spain was powerless to destroy. Hostile Indians took refuge within the borders of Florida, and mingled with the runaway Negroes and renegade whites to produce bands of ruffians as unsavory as were to be found anywhere on the American continent. In 1810 Madison, carrying out Jefferson's policy of acquiring West Florida, ordered the governor of Louisiana to extend his territory peacefully over that portion of the Spanish province adjacent to the Mississippi River, but the southern expansionists wanted more. They were ready, if it were necessary, to fight another Indian war; they saw in a war against Great Britain the prospect of the greatly-to-be-desired war against Spain, now the ally of Great Britain; and they were willing to help the Northwest acquire Canada on the assumption that the Northwest in return would help the Southwest acquire Florida.

Thus from the interior, whether to the north or to the south, every strongly

The "War Hawks" anti-British stand of the administration in Washington was received with unbounded enthusiasm, while every sign of weakening was unsparingly denounced. In the elections of 1810 and 1811 the weak-kneed policy embodied in Macon's Bill Number 2 received a thoroughgoing rebuke. Nearly half the congressmen who had voted for that measure were left at home, and a new generation of politicians

seized the reins of power. Among them were John Sevier and Felix Grundy from Tennessee, John C. Calhoun from the back country of South Carolina, and young Henry Clay from Kentucky, whom the newcomers banded together to make Speaker of the House. These young patriots and their followers were eager for war, and quickly won for themselves, from the erratic John Randolph of Roanoke, the designation, "War Hawks." They defended more stoutly than any Easterner the rights of American sailors and American commerce on the high seas; they denounced in unmeasured terms the assistance that the British in Canada were giving to marauding bands of Indians on the frontier; and they pointed out as the chief prize to be won from the war the easy acquisition of Canada. "I am not for stopping at Quebec," said Clay, "but I would take the whole continent." In vain were the efforts of conservatives who sought to restrain the clamor for war, and in vain also were the continued tongue-lashings of Randolph who denounced the "agrarian cupidity" of the War Hawks, and taunted them for the "whip-poor-will" monotony of their battle-cry, "Canada! Canada! Canada!" Even Madison himself, alive to the meaning of the recent elections, capitulated to the War Hawks.

Nevertheless, the vote for war that the administration obtained from Congress in 1812 was far from unanimous. **The vote** The commercial interests of the **for war** Northeast were desperately opposed to the measure, and their sentiments were reflected by a majority of the congressmen from that section. Nor were the opponents of the war all Federalists, for a large section of the Republican Party either voted against the declaration or refused to vote at all. Many thoughtful citizens of both parties felt especially humiliated to see the United States throw in its lot with the hypocritical Napoleon, whose fair words only faintly disguised quite as ruthless mistreatment of American commerce as ever the British had inflicted. Moreover, the ambition of

Napoleon turned increasingly toward an ever-expanding military despotism, whereas Great Britain and her allies were fighting not only to preserve separate national independence, but also to maintain what little Europe then knew of constitutional government. There was actually as good reason for a declaration of war by the United States against France as against Great Britain, and so far as neutral rights were concerned, such a policy might have proved ideal. The British government, in belated negotiations conducted after the declaration of war, did definitely block the way to peace by refusing to give up the right of impressment, but it seems reasonable to suppose that even this knotty problem might have been solved as the price of American aid against France. With British assistance the United States might have fought against Napoleon a really successful war on behalf of neutral rights. But the frontier, ably seconded by the South, was far less interested in a war to avenge wrongdoing on the high seas than in a war against Great Britain to insure a settlement of the Indian problem and the conquest of Canada. From the four frontier states, Vermont, Ohio, Kentucky, and Tennessee, every vote but one was cast for war. Most of the rest of the majority came from the South.

In spite of its name, the "War of 1812" was barely begun in the year 1812, and the **Should the war be fought** news that the British were willing to repeal their decrees would have presented a valid excuse for withdrawing the declaration, had the country so desired. With the British Orders in Council repealed, the only technicality that lay in the way of peace was the British refusal to abandon impressments. Americans who had opposed the War Hawks while the country was at peace now turned their attention to the task of preventing the war that had been declared from being fought. The presidential election of 1812 was made to hinge on this issue. Since Madison, now completely committed to the program of the War Hawks, sought re-elec-

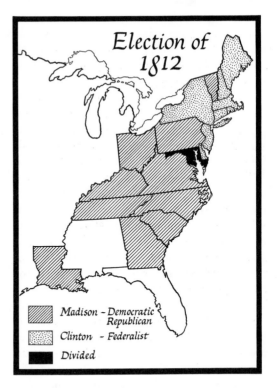

Election of 1812

Madison – Democratic Republican
Clinton – Federalist
Divided

tion with the avowed intention of seeing the war through, peace men among the Republicans advanced as an opposing candidate DeWitt Clinton of New York, whom the Federalists were also induced to support. The issue was clean-cut: a vote for Madison meant a vote for war, and a vote for Clinton meant a vote for peace.

The results of the election made further manifest the responsibility of the West for the war. New England, with **The election** the exception of Vermont, cast **of 1812** 43 electoral votes for Clinton and peace, while the middle states (including Maryland and Delaware) preferred Clinton over Madison by a vote of 46 to 31. The South voted solidly, 59 to 0, for Madison and war. Thus the seaboard states — the original thirteen — were as nearly equally divided as possible, with a vote of 90 for Madison to 89 for Clinton, certainly too narrow a margin upon which to wage a war. But the five states that had been admitted to the Union by act of Congress — Vermont, Kentucky, Tennessee, Ohio, and Louisiana (admitted in 1812)

— broke the balance by casting their entire vote for Madison, who was thus elected, 128 to 89. It was another victory of the West, aided by the dominantly agricultural South, over the commercial Northeast.

Most of the War Hawks had little or no understanding of the serious financial prob-

End of the Bank of the United States lems that the fighting of a war entailed, and they actually allowed the Congress that had declared the war to adjourn without voting the war taxes for which Gallatin, still Secretary of the Treasury, had asked. They refused also to take cognizance of the crippled state of the nation's banking and currency system. Hamilton's Bank of the United States had been chartered for twenty years in 1791, and had therefore to be rechartered in 1811 or allowed to die. Opposed alike by states'-rights Jeffersonians of the old school and by Westerners who preferred the easier credit facilities that state banks were sure to offer, the Bank of the United States was eliminated at the very moment that the nation needed more than ever before the stable currency and the machinery for floating loans that it could provide.

Moreover, the taxation system of the country was already in bad repair, and

Taxation Gallatin had predicted a deficit for the year 1812, even without the abnormal expenditures of war. Nearly all of the revenue upon which the national government depended for its support came from the tariff, and receipts from this quarter had been seriously impaired by the unstable state of commerce during the preceding months and years. Congress voted to double the tariff rates, and enough importations continued in spite of the war to make this measure a fairly fruitful source of revenue. Internal taxes were at first indignantly spurned as "unrepublican," and Gallatin was heartily denounced for recommending them; but before the war was over both an excise tax and a stamp duty had been laid. Inasmuch as a completely new system for the collection of these taxes had to be worked

out, the war was nearly over before they began to yield an appreciable revenue. In 1813 Congress also tried to levy a direct tax upon the states in spite of the fact that a similar effort, made during the war scare of 1798, had brought highly unsatisfactory results. Since no power existed on the part of the nation to coerce the states, payments of such a tax were made, or were not made, quite as each state saw fit.

From all tax sources together not more than one third enough income was realized to pay the expenses of the war, **War loans** and the remaining expenditures had to be met by loans. This proved to be an exceedingly difficult matter, for the moneyed classes of the country, with a few exceptions, did not favor the war. Gallatin succeeded in raising over eighty million dollars from loans, but in order to attract investors he was compelled to sell government securities at a serious discount, and to pay interest rates sometimes as high as seven and one half per cent. New England capital practically refused to support the war; altogether only three million dollars' worth of war bonds were sold in that section. By the end of the war the government was virtually bankrupt.

From the angle of military preparedness the United States was likewise little justified in assuming the burdens of war. **Lack of preparedness** The regular army consisted of not more than seven thousand men, all of whom were needed for garrison duty. An increase in this number was ordered, but in spite of such inducements as better pay and land bounties, recruits were hard to obtain. For the most part the administration had to rely upon state militia to do the fighting. Presumably there were about seven hundred thousand enrolled militia, and a nation of nearly eight million people should surely have found little difficulty in putting an army of two or three hundred thousand men in the field. But the requisitions on the states for troops were half-heartedly filled, and sometimes flatly refused. At no time during the war did the goverment have in actual service more than thirty or thirty-five thousand men; and on occasion whole detachments of the militia refused to fight outside the boundaries of their state. Nevertheless, this slight show of strength should have been sufficient for the conquest of Canada, for the armies that the Canadians could muster were even less formidable. But unfortunately the United States was woefully lacking in capable military leaders. The old officers were, as Winfield Scott said, "decayed gentlemen" who were "utterly unfit for any military purpose whatever," and the West Point Academy, although authorized in 1802, had not yet begun to bear fruit. Madison thus had a meager field from which to pick, but even so he could hardly have done worse than he did. All the high ranking officers were in their late fifties or sixties, and only one or two of them had ever commanded a regiment in battle.

In an administrative way also the war found the government unfit for duty. The President, James Madison, was built for peaceful and harmonious times. His Cabinet was probably the weakest that the nation had yet known, and the one really strong man in it, Albert Gallatin, was crippled in effectiveness because of the bitter opposition he had incurred from members of his own party. The Secretary of War, William Eustis, and the Secretary of the Navy, Paul Hamilton, were weak-kneed politicians whom Madison, had he been himself a man of action, would have dismissed at once. Robert Smith, Madison's notoriously incapable Secretary of State, had been replaced in 1811 by James Monroe, whose talents were considerable, in spite of his previous diplomatic blunders; but generally speaking the direction of the war lay in the hands of men who had not the wit to plan nor the energy to act.

In spite of the sparseness of Canada's population, the military strength of the province was not to be despised. At the time the war broke out, four British regiments were stationed in Canada, and the Canadian authorities had, on the whole, better luck in enlisting troops to resist an invasion than the Americans had to make one. The Canadians moreover, were far more ably commanded than the Americans, and they could count on the assistance of Tecumseh's adherents in the Northwest. It is not surprising that, from the American point of view, the war got off to a poor start.

The American plan for the conquest of Canada, to which all other considerations were subordinated, was to attack the border defense in three concerted movements. Henry Dearborn, the senior major-general, was to advance northward by the Lake Champlain route toward Montreal; Stephan Van Rensselaer, relying mainly upon New York militia, was to attack the British at Niagara; and William Hull, the governor of Michigan Territory, was to launch from Detroit an invasion of Upper Canada. Unfortunately not one of the three officers mentioned was in the least fitted to cope with the situation that confronted him.

The American plan of campaign

A week before the American declaration of war, Hull received orders to march, and with fifteen hundred men he succeeded in reaching Detroit, although his attempt to send his baggage from Toledo Bay by boat resulted in its capture by the enemy. For this misfortune the American commander was not wholly to blame. By the time it happened war had been officially declared, but Hull was left in complete ignorance of the fact, whereas his British opponents knew all about it. Hull pointed out to the government the difficulties involved in trying to conduct an invasion of Canada without first securing control of Lake Erie, but he was compelled nevertheless to begin his campaign without naval support. On July 12 he crossed the Detroit River and marched timidly toward the British post at Malden. His doubts and fears multiplied as he observed the hostility of the inhabitants, the poverty of their country, and the evidence that a strong force was concentrating at Malden to oppose him. When finally the news came that Tecumseh and a band of

War of 1812
Northern Frontier Campaigns
1812 ~ 1814

Indian warriors had joined the British, Hull's courage completely evaporated, and he fell back to Detroit. Had he followed his own judgment he would have retreated even farther, for he believed, probably correctly, that with the British in control of Lake Erie Detroit was untenable; but his men objected to any further retreat, and he awaited with much anxiety the British attack.

General Isaac Brock, the British commander, was a man of great energy and **Surrender of Detroit** resourcefulness who soon had Detroit surrounded. Hinting broadly that he could not be sure what the Indians would do, once the fighting had begun, Brock demanded that Hull surrender without a struggle. Paralyzed with fear and foreseeing only a horrible massacre if he refused to comply, Hull acceded to the British demands, August 16, 1812. A month earlier the American garrison at Michilimackinac had been forced to surrender, and the day before Hull gave in the garrison at Fort Dearborn had been massacred by the Indians. Thus the two months' time that,

according to many of the War Hawks, was to have been more than ample for the conquest of all Canada ended with the Americans on the defensive, and the northwestern frontier forced back to the line of the Wabash and Maumee Valleys. For his conduct at Detroit Hull was later courtmartialed and sentenced to be shot, but because of his creditable record in the American Revolution the President pardoned him.

The attacks on Canada from the Niagara frontier similarly miscarried. With Detroit safely in British hands, Brock quickly transferred his activities to Niagara, and made ready once more to receive an American invasion. In a preliminary skirmish led by Captain John E. Wool, a few American regulars crossed the Niagara River on October 13, 1812, and attacked Queenstown Heights, at first with marked success. In this engagement Brock himself was killed, and a notable victory might have been won had the New York militia been willing to co-operate. But when reinforcements were ordered up from the American side of the river, the militiamen were filled with terror and refused to move. They had been called into service to defend their state, they maintained, and not for an attack on Canada. The British forces were soon strengthened, however, and the attacking Americans were driven back to the river, where, within sight of a thousand armed militiamen on the other side, they were surrounded and compelled to surrender. After this Van Rensselaer in disgust resigned his command. He was succeeded by General Alexander Smyth of Virginia, who issued many bombastic proclamations, but after a few feeble feints lost his nerve entirely and ordered his men into winter quarters. By the time he could be superseded, it was too late in the season to continue the campaign.

Meantime Dearborn, the senior major-general, charged with the duty of advancing **Dearborn's** on Montreal, had collected at **failure** Plattsburg on Lake Champlain a stronger force than either Hull or Smyth had commanded. But he, too, lacked most of the qualities needed to make an efficient officer, and he delayed his forward movement until late in November. Finally, on the nineteenth of the month, he marched his command twenty miles to the Canadian border, only to discover that his militia also was unwilling to leave the country. Still further disheartened by the news of an advancing British column and by a minor military reverse, he gave up his plans entirely and marched his troops back to Plattsburg. Dearborn should have been removed at once for his incompetence, but Madison weakly allowed him to hold his post for several months longer.

Had the American officers possessed sufficient ability to make careful plans for the co-ordination of their movements, and had the American militia stood ready to obey orders, it seems reasonable to suppose that the invasion of Canada in 1812 might not have ended so disastrously. All three movements should have been in progress at the same time, not in slow succession, and a workable plan for the union of the whole American army before Montreal should have been devised. Moreover, the necessity of American naval preponderance on the Great Lakes should not have been overlooked. As matters stood, the year ended with the Americans balked in New York, and defeated in the Northwest.

Fortunately on the high seas American captains and crews were giving excellent accounts of themselves. The **The high** navy that the Federalists had **seas** begun during the last years of the preceding century had been strengthened during the Tripolitan War and numbered now some sixteen ships-of-war, together with a fair number of smaller craft. This was an insignificant force to oppose the one thousand or more ships that composed the British navy, nearly a hundred of which were assigned to trans-Atlantic duty, and the scorn of a London journalist for the "fir-built" American frigates "manned by a handful of bastards and outlaws" was a fair sample of British opinion. As a matter of fact the men who manned the American ships were well-paid and competent volunteers, while the captains who commanded them were veterans of the Tripolitan War. The "fir-built frigates," moreover, were carefully constructed to carry more guns and sail than the corresponding units in European navies. Thus in ship-for-ship engagements the Americans stood a chance to win, although the ultimate outcome of a war in which the forces were so unevenly matched should have been as apparent to citizens of the United States as it was to the British.

Before the end of the year 1812 a number of ship duels had been fought in which the Americans came off victor. On **American** July 11, Captain David Porter **sea victories** of the *Essex* captured the *Minerva* and two days later in a ten-minute engagement forced the *Alert* to surrender. On August 19, Captain Isaac Hull of the *Constitution* atoned for his uncle's surrender of Detroit three days earlier by thoroughly outmaneuvering and outfighting a British frigate, the *Guerrière*, in what was probably the most

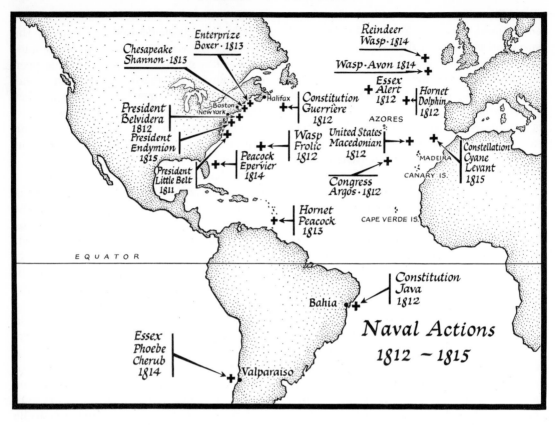

Naval Actions
1812 – 1815

brilliant American victory of the war. On October 18, an American sloop, the *Wasp*, took the evenly matched *Frolic* in a bloody conflict during which the British casualties exceeded those suffered by the Americans eight or nine to one. On October 25, Captain Stephen Decatur of the *United States* defeated the British frigate *Macedonian*, and in December brought her back to New London as a prize. The luck of the *Constitution* continued under a new captain, William Bainbridge, who on December 29 so shattered the *Java*, another British frigate, that she could not even be brought to port, and had to be blown up. It was this battle that won for the *Constitution* the name "Old Ironsides." On February 24, 1813, Captain James Lawrence of the *Hornet* sank the *Peacock* after a combat that lasted only fifteen minutes. Meantime American warships and privateers were also taking a frightful toll of British commerce.

The uninterrupted series of naval victories tremendously lightened the gloom that **British** the military blunders along the **astonishment** northern frontier had cast over the American people, but the effect on the British public was even more marked. For centuries British sea-captains had been accustomed to win against whatever odds confronted them, and the defeats by Americans seemed beyond comprehension. Commenting on the loss of the *Java* the London *Times* exclaimed:

The public will learn with sentiments which we shall not presume to anticipate that a third British frigate has struck to an American. . . . This is an occurrence that calls for serious reflection; this, and the facts stated in our paper of yesterday, that Lloyd's list contains notices of upward of five hundred British vessels captured in seven months by the Americans: five hundred merchantmen and three frigates! Can these statements be true? And can the English people hear them unmoved? Anyone who had predicted such a result of an American war this time last year would have been treated as a madman or a traitor. He would have been told, if his opponents had condescended to argue with him, that long ere seven months had elapsed the American flag would have been swept from the seas, the contemptible navy of the United States annihilated, and their marine arsenals rendered a heap of ruins. Yet down to this moment not a single American frigate has struck her flag.

But the American luck on the high seas was not to last. With the spring of 1813 the **The British blockade** British established a tight blockade of the American coast, and from that time forward American ships of war scarcely dared to leave port. When the *Chesapeake*, now commanded by Captain Lawrence, accepted the challenge of the *Shannon* to come out of Boston Harbor and fight, the British ship won a notable victory (June 1, 1813), and Lawrence lost his life. On the same day a British squadron chased the *United States*, the *Macedonian*, and the *Hornet* into the port of New London, where they were compelled to remain until the end of the war. The *Essex* was destroyed the next year (March 28, 1814) by two British ships in a battle off the coast of Chile, and a

few days after the peace treaty had been signed the *President* failed to make good her escape from a British squadron of four, and was captured. Four or five American warships, including the *Constitution*, managed to continue intermittently on the high seas until the war was over, and some of the American privateers took good prizes to the very end; but as a fighting weapon for either offensive or defensive purposes, the American navy had ceased to function. New England, which from New London northward was exempted by the British from the blockade because of its notorious opposition to the war and its readiness to sell to the enemy, could still carry on a fair export trade, but elsewhere shipments from American ports were held down to nearly nothing. In 1814 not more than $200,000 worth of goods left the ports of New York, and hardly $17,500 worth left the ports of Virginia.

In the spring of 1813 American war policy called for another attempt at the invasion of Canada. The disaster at Detroit, however, had convinced the administration that the control of the Great Lakes must no longer be left to the British, and during the winter of 1812–13 the Navy Department began the construction of a small fleet on

Brother Jonathan "administering a salutary cordial to John Bull," (pear juice, a popular drink), in honor of Perry's victory. Cartoon by "Yankee Doodle," about 1813.

Lake Erie. With great difficulty the youthful Captain Oliver Hazard Perry, who was placed in control of the half-built squadron on March, 1813, succeeded in equipping and navigating his ships; most of his ordnance, sail, and other supplies had to be hauled across the mountains by wagon, and his lack of adequate numbers of sailors had to be overcome by a detail of one hundred Kentucky militiamen. At Put-in-Bay, on September 10, 1813, Perry found the British squadron, and mainly because the American ships threw a greater weight of metal than the British, won a most significant victory. Perry's terse report to Harrison, who commanded the adjacent American army, has lived deservedly: "We have met the enemy and they are ours: two ships, two brigs, one schooner, and one sloop."

To William Henry Harrison, the hero of Tippecanoe, fell the task of retrieving the **The invasion** defeats of 1812 in the North-**of Canada** west. Under his leadership a winter campaign against Detroit was begun, only to be frustrated when a detachment of Harrison's army under General James Winchester was disastrously defeated, January 22, 1813, near Frenchtown, on the Raisin River. General Henry Proctor, in command of the British and Indian army that had won this victory, made no effort to protect the five hundred American prisoners he had taken, and the night after the battle they were massacred to the last man by the savages. Infuriated by this atrocity and by the numerous scalping parties that were let loose upon the frontier, the western states supported the war in the spring and summer of 1813 with a vigor they had not shown before. With a far larger army than Hull had commanded, Harrison made ready to attack Detroit and invade Ontario. Had Perry lost, doubtless Proctor would have attempted to force the fighting on the American side of the boundary, but the loss of Lake Erie convinced him that a British retreat was necessary. Accordingly he burned both Detroit and Malden, and attempted to withdraw his army from the dangerous western salient. But on October 5, 1813, Harrison overtook the retreating British, and on the banks of the Thames River won a signal victory. Tecumseh himself was slain, and Proctor had to flee for his life. The battle of the Thames not only recovered the ground lost by the surrender of Detroit the year before, but it definitely ended the menace of the northwestern Indian confederacy that Tecumseh had worked so hard to achieve. Harrison's invasion of Canada did not proceed much farther, but the war ended with the Americans definitely in control of the northwestern frontier.

Meantime, two other American campaigns, one on the Niagara front and the other before Montreal, had achieved far less gratifying results. In April, 1813, General Dearborn led a successful raid on York, the capital of Upper Canada, later known as Toronto. During this episode American soldiers wantonly set fire to the two houses of the provincial parliament, an act which their officers deplored, and which later gave the British an excuse to burn the government buildings at Washington in retaliation. York had to be abandoned by the Americans, for, although making strenuous efforts to wrest the control of Lake Ontario from the British, they had not yet succeeded in doing so. Other severe fighting, mostly of negligible military significance but destructive alike of life and property, occurred during the year on both sides of the Niagara frontier, and on December 30, 1813, the British took Fort Niagara. As for the second advance on Montreal, it was quite as feeble and futile as the first.

Up to the end of the year 1813 the American war had been, from the British point of view, a mere side issue; the main **Plans for** thing had been the defeat of **counter-** Napoleon. But with the spring **invasion** of 1814 the downfall of Napoleon's empire was an accomplished fact, and the British were free to turn the full strength of their victorious army and navy against the United States. British opinion strongly favored the thorough chastisement of the Americans for heir attack upon Great Britain at a time when the British people were standing almost alone against the tyranny of Napoleon, and there was much feeling, too, that the American naval successes must not be allowed to go unavenged. Accordingly, the British government decided to send over ships enough and troops enough to overwhelm the Americans. The military attack, adequately supported by the navy, was to be delivered from three points, Niagara, Lake Champlain, and New Orleans.

Had the British been able to attack in this fashion in the early stages of the war, the result might have been disastrous to the Americans; but by 1814 most of the incompetents among the American officers had been removed from high command, and the undependability of raw militia levies had been so fully demonstrated that chief reliance was placed on regulars. On the Niagara front General Jacob Brown got into action before the British reinforcements from Europe had arrived, and by the fourth of July had set a force of five or six hundred men across the Niagara River. On the same day he took Fort Erie, and on the next day the advance guard of his army under Winfield Scott won a hard-fought battle at Chippewa. The culmination of the campaign came about three weeks later (July 25) at Lundy's Lane, close to Niagara Falls, when two thousand American troops outfought a superior British force, but were compelled to fall back when news came that the British had received reinforcements. Although Brown was forced to retire to the American side of the river, he had demonstrated that an American army could and would fight well, even on Canadian soil.

The British plan was for their first serious blow to be delivered down the Lake Champlain route through New York, possibly with the idea of cutting off New England from the rest of the Union and reannexing it to the British Empire. For this purpose Sir George Prevost was given about eleven thousand soldiers, more than five times as many as General

McDonough at Champlain

Alexander Macomb, his American opponent, had on hand at Plattsburg. The Prevost campaign depended, however, upon the elimination from Lake Champlain of a small American flotilla under the command of Captain Thomas Macdonough, and the British squadron that had been made ready for this purpose, although seemingly far superior to Macdonough's in strength, proved utterly unequal to the task. The naval battle fought off Plattsburg Bay was a fight to the finish, in which the superior seamanship of the Americans won the day. The American losses were startling, but every British ship was either sunk or else was compelled to strike its colors. Prevost, in dismay, led his army back to Canada without risking a battle.

The British navy on the high seas, meantime, was able to terrorize the American cities and villages along the Atlantic coast at will. To insure against adequate assistance being sent by the American government to the Lake Champlain front a particularly active demonstration was planned against Washington and Baltimore, and a detachment of four thousand British troops under General Robert Ross was sent over to cooperate with the navy. President Madison learned of this plan several weeks before it was put into execution, and made desperate efforts to assemble an army for the defense of the capital. He managed to find troops enough, so far as numbers went, but they were nearly all militia, and they were commanded by a totally incompetent officer, General William Henry Winder. The British were allowed to land unopposed on the west bank of the Patuxent River, which flows into the Chesapeake southeast of Washington, and to march their column to within five miles of the capital.

Here the Americans, adequately supported with artillery, were drawn up in a strong position to receive the enemy **Capture of** attack. Winder's superiority in **Washington** numbers gave the American officials an undue sense of security, and the Presidene, accompanied by some of his Cabinet, camt

THE BRITISH IN MARYLAND.
Admiral Cockburn plunder-
ing and burning Havre de
Grace, June 1, 1813. Watercolor by William Charles.

THE DEATH OF TECUMSEH. The Battle of the Thames,
illustrated in Brackenridge, *History of the Late War*, 1817

The War of 1812 *means to many
Americans a succession of American
victories in naval duels on the high seas,
but this phase of the struggle did not
last long. The British navy soon won
control of American waters, and British
landing parties began to make trouble
for exposed American seaports. On
Lake Erie, however, Perry's famous
victory brought much-needed encouragement, and prepared the way for the
Battle of the Thames, in which Tecumseh was slain.*

VICTORY ON LAKE ERIE. Captain Perry transferring his flag to the *Niagara* during
the battle, September 10, 1813. Engraved from a painting by Thomas Birch.

THE SIEGE OF WASHINGTON, AUGUST, 1814. Engraving published by I. Ryland.

The War of 1812 *brought its greatest humiliation to Americans when a British landing party captured Washington. The same raiders, however, failed to take Baltimore. During the bombardment of Fort McHenry, one of Baltimore's defenses, Francis Scott Key, then a prisoner on a British ship, wrote "The Star-Spangled Banner." The Battle of New Orleans, although fought after the war was over, did much to restore American moral.*

THE BOMBARDMENT OF FORT McHENRY. An eyewitness report "taken from the Observatory," showing British shells descending on the Fort, September 13, 1814

THE BATTLE OF NEW ORLEANS. Jackson's brilliant victory, January, 1815, painted by P. L. Debuccoup.

Chesapeake Campaigns - 1814
Washington and Baltimore

out from Washington prepared to witness a telling victory. Instead the American militia broke and ran after firing a few shots, and only a handful of marines and sailors under Captain Joshua Barney were left to dispute the field. Barney's men fought bravely, but were soon overpowered, and the British marched triumphantly into Washington (August 24, 1814). A dinner prepared at the White House for President and Mrs. Madison was eaten by British officers, and the President himself narrowly escaped capture. In retaliation for the vandalism of the American troops at York the preceding year, the British officers ordered their men to set fire to all the American public buildings, but they prevented a general looting of the city, and the amount of private property destroyed was slight. Their purpose accomplished, the invaders withdrew. The military significance of the episode was negligible, but the blow to American pride was great.

The British attack on Baltimore did not fare so well, and the boast of Ross that he

intended to spend the winter in the city even if it "rained militia" proved vain. The harbor was well defended by Fort McHenry and by sunken hulks, while the people of the city and state had collected about fourteen thousand men to resist the invaders. A naval demonstration against the city proved futile, and the first skirmish on land cost the life of General Ross himself. Thoroughly discouraged, the British gave up the attack, and soon sailed off to join in the campaign against New Orleans.

The final phase of the war was fought in the Southwest, where, as in the earlier phases, both Indians and British **The Fort** were involved. In spite of the **Mims** preachings of Tecumseh, south- **massacre** ern tribes had abstained from war as long as they could. In 1813, however, some hotbloods among the Creeks attacked a stockade known as Fort Mims, on the lower Alabama River not far from Mobile, and massacred several hundred pioneers who had gathered there for protection (August 30, 1813). Already Tennessee troops, commanded by Andrew Jackson, were making ready for an attack on Spanish Florida, but they now had a more satisfactory objective. With thirty-five hundred troops under his command, Jackson advanced southward in search of hostile Indians. No better commander of frontier militia had ever taken the field. Jackson somehow overcame the lack of discipline among his men, he found by one unusual means or another the supplies that they had to have, and on March 27, 1814, at Horseshoe Bend, he thoroughly avenged the Fort Mims massacre. A few months later at Fort Jackson (August 9, 1814) the chastened Creeks were compelled to sign a treaty which handed over to the whites thousands of acres of their choicest lands.

Jackson was now placed in command of all the American operations in the Southwest, and upon his shoulders fell the **Battle of** task of warding off the final **New** British attack of the war. When **Orleans** the British sought to use Pensacola in Spanish Florida as a base of operations, Jackson, with equal disregard of neutrality, occupied and burned the town. The British then sailed off to the attack of New Orleans, and Jackson soon learned that he must face there an army of ten thousand invaders. Undaunted, he hastened to the city with all the troops he could obtain, and made vigorous preparations for its defense. Sir Edward Pakenham, an experienced officer and a brother-in-law of the Duke of Wellington, was in command of the British expedition. Fortunately for the Americans he held militia soldiery in great contempt, and after his dependable regulars were landed he pursued a plan of battle that he would not have considered tenable had he respected his opponents. Jackson, however, was neither a Hull nor a Winder, and from behind hastily improvised defenses, consisting partly of cotton bales, he received the ill-advised attack. On January 8, 1815, the inexperienced frontier commander won the most notable victory of the war, and one of the most remarkable victories in history. General Pakenham himself was killed, and against British casualties of nearly two thousand the Americans could count losses of only thirteen. Thus defeated and humiliated, the British expedition withdrew. Naturally Andrew Jackson was the hero of the hour, but curiously his great victory was won after the war was over. Had the means of communication been available in 1815 that were known less than half a century later, the battle of New Orleans would never have been fought, for on December 24, 1814, a treaty of peace had been signed by British and American plenipotentiaries at Ghent.

During the dark days of 1814 the loyalty of New England to the Union was put to the
New England discontent test, although in point of fact New England suffered far less from the war than some of her people seemed to think. Until the last year of the war the British avoided blockading the coast of New England, and thus practically all American imports that entered the country had to pass through the hands of

Southwest Campaigns
1813 – 1815

New England merchants. Moreover, the serious check that the embargo and the war had given to New England commerce was not unmixed with good. With British manufactures excluded, far-sighted men saw a great opportunity for Americans in this field, and the number of New England factories, textile mills in particular, increased during the war most amazingly. Nevertheless, the injured commercial interests pointed to the war as proof positive that agriculturalist control of the nation would ring the death-knell for northeastern prosperity. With new Indian territory opening up for settlement in the West, and with the Louisiana Purchase available to be carved up into new agricultural states, many New-Englanders held that for their section the Union had lost its attraction. Some talked freely of secession, and the British hope that New England might even return to its colonial allegiance was not without justification.

Curiously, raids made by the British in 1814 along the coast of New England aroused among New Englanders even greater resentment against the government at Washington than against the British themselves, and on October 5, 1814, the legislature of Massachusetts voted to call a convention to meet at Hartford, Connecticut, for the purpose of voicing the opinion of New England on the state of the Union. Rhode Island and Connecticut responded to the call, and on December 15, 1814, the Hartford Convention, representing these two states and Massachusetts, assembled. Two delegates chosen by popular meetings in New Hampshire, and one by the town of Windham, Vermont, were also admitted. Some of the extremists among the delegates would gladly have followed the advice of Timothy Pickering to prepare the way for "the separation of the northern section of the states" from the rest of the nation. But the more moderate wing of the Convention, led by Harrison Gray Otis, prevented any precipitate action being taken, and lodged instead a dignified protest against the "multiplied abuses of bad administrations" and the "acts of Congress in violation of the Constitution." In language definitely reminiscent of the Kentucky and Virginia Resolutions, the Convention maintained "the right and duty of a state to interpose its authority" in cases of "deliberate, dangerous, and palpable infractions of the Constitution, " but insisted also that it would be unwise "to fly to open resistance" upon every offense.

The report of the Hartford Convention favored neither nullification nor secession, but referred back to the states concerned, for proposal to Congress, a list of seven suggested amendments to the Constitution. These amendments, had they been adopted, would have limited the power of Congress to make war, to admit new states, to lay embargoes, and to restrict commerce. Also, as a blow against the "Virginia dynasty," they would have declared a President ineligible for re-election, and would have prevented the choice of successive Presidents from the same state. In order to limit the power of the agricultural South, one amend-

The Hartford Convention

ment proposed to set aside the "three-fifths" compromise of the Constitution, so that only the white population might be counted in the apportioning of representatives. In adjourning, the Convention voted to meet again at Boston on call of its president, presumably so that if, in the meantime, Congress failed to agree to its demands the adjourned session might advise a more radical course of action. The happy termination of the war and the subsequent prosperity of New England naturally ended all danger of a northeastern revolt; and it also made those who had preached such doctrine exceedingly regretful of their words. Since the Hartford Convention had been primarily the work of Federalists, it was possible, after the war was over, for the Republicans to charge the whole Federalist Party with treason — a charge which, duly pressed, had much to do with the elimination of the party of Washington and Hamilton from the American political scene.

Almost from the beginning of the War of 1812 there had been negotiations of one kind or another that looked in the direction of peace. As previously stated, there was at the outset much feeling, both in Great Britain and in America, that the war had been prematurely declared and need not be fought. As early as September, 1812, the Russian government, seeking to take advantage of this sentiment, offered mediation. This action was easily understandable, for almost at the very moment that the United States decided to throw in its lot with Napoleon, the Tsar of Russia went over to the British side. Still friendly to the United States and now an important ally of Great Britain, he hoped to iron out the difficulties that estranged the two English-speaking nations and weakened the alliance against Napoleon. Madison was quick to accept the Russian offer, and promptly dispatched James A. Bayard and Albert Gallatin to aid the American representative at St. Petersburg, John Quincy Adams, in the quest of peace. But the British government rejected the Tsar's offer,

Peace negotiations

although expressing a willingness to undertake direct negotiations with the United States. Unfortunately it was not until January, 1814, that Madison learned that this offer of direct negotiation had been made. Thereupon he dispatched Henry Clay and Jonathan Russell to join the three commissioners already in Europe, but it was not until August that the American and British commissioners finally met at Ghent.

The American peace delegation was as able as the country could command, and the commissioners themselves felt aggrieved when three British subordinates were detailed to meet them. The British government intended, however, to keep close watch on the proceedings at Ghent, and its best talent was required to effect the European settlement soon in progress at Vienna. As it turned out, the superior ability of the Americans was a great advantage to the United States, while the obligation felt by the British delegation to refer every important matter to London for decision was by no means helpful to Great Britain.

The British demands were set forth at the outset in the form of an extraordinary ulti-
The British ultimatum matum: (1) the boundary between the United States must be "rectified" by the cession to Great Britain of a part of Maine and strategic ports along the Great Lakes; (2) all Indian land cessions in the Northwest made since 1795 were to be annulled, and an Indian buffer state was to be created in that region into which the whites must never go; (3) the British interpretation of the rules of warfare on the high seas, against which the United States had for so many years protested, was to remain unaltered; (4) the United States must give up the rights it had acquired by the Treaty of 1783 in the Newfoundland fisheries, must relinquish to Great Britain the navigation of the Great Lakes, and must continue the British right of navigation of the Mississippi River. The American delegation received these demands with great dismay, and prepared to leave. "Such terms were prescribed," wrote Bayard, "as put an end to all hope of peace. . . . The terms will certainly be rejected and the negotiation will terminate in a few days."

The instructions which the American commissioners had received were by no means modest. They were told **American** to secure if they could: (1) recog- **demands** nition of the American position on maritime law, although on impressments the United States might be willing to forbid British-born sailors the right to serve on American ships; (2) indemnity for illegal prizes taken by the British; (3) the cession of "the upper

The Hartford Convention. "Leap, No Leap," a cartoon by William Charles, 1814, depicts Massachusetts urging Connecticut and Rhode Island on to "this leap of frightful size" from the United States into the waiting arms of England.

parts and even the whole of Canada to the United States"; (4) the exclusion of the British from the Great Lakes. The American terms, however, were not presented as an ultimatum, and the American delegation had full authority to make whatever concessions it saw fit without referring to Washington for advice.

In spite of Bayard's fears, the negotiations at Ghent proved to be of long duration. The American commissioners were able to convince the British agents that the terms asked were out of the question, and modifications were sought and obtained from the British government in London. Undoubtedly the attitude of the Ministry was greatly influenced by the Duke of Wellington, whom Lord Liverpool, the British Prime Minister, had asked to take command in America, "with full power to make peace, or to continue the war with renewed vigor." To this request Wellington replied:

I have already told you . . . that I feel no objection to going to America, though I don't promise to myself much success there. . . . That which appears to me to be wanting in America is not a General, or General officers and troops, but a naval superiority on the Lakes. . . . I suspect that you will find that Prevost will justify his misfortunes . . . by stating that the navy were defeated. . . . The question is, whether we can acquire this naval superiority on the Lakes. If we can't I can do you but little good in America; and I shall go there only to prove the truth of Prevost's defense, and to sign a peace which might as well be signed now. . . . In regard to your present negotiations I confess that I think you have no right from the state of the war to demand any concession of territory from America. . . . You have not been able to carry it into the enemy's territory, notwithstanding your military success, and now undoubted military superiority.

Wellington's arguments also fitted in with the temper of the British public. The wave **Treaty of** of enthusiasm for the American **Ghent** war that had followed the defeat of Napoleon soon subsided. With war a thing of the past in Europe, British merchants and traders were less interested in the punishment of America than in the complete restoration of normal peace-time trade. In consequence the British demands were gradually toned down until terms were offered that the Americans could accept. As finally signed, the Treaty of Ghent reflected well the state of the military situation. It provided, according to Adams, for "a truce rather than a peace. Neither party gave up anything; all the points of collision which had subsisted between them before the war were left open. . . . Nothing was adjusted, nothing was settled — nothing in substance but an indefinite suspension of hostilities was agreed to."

While the Peace of Ghent merely restored for the time being the *status quo ante bellum*, it did make provision for the **Subsequent** future settlement of some of the **agreements** outstanding differences between Great Britain and the United States. Stimulated in part by these clauses in the treaty and in part by the mutual desire to clear up misunderstandings, there thus came about several important agreements between the two nations. On July 3, 1815, a commercial convention was signed by which trade discriminations, except for the exclusion of American trade from the British West Indies, were mutually withdrawn. Not until Jackson's administration did the United States obtain the West Indian trade privileges it so long had sought. On April 28, 1817, the justly famous Rush-Bagot Agreement provided for complete disarmament by both nations on the Great Lakes. A few gunboats were permitted for police purposes only. The agreement could be denounced by either party on six month's notice, but it still endures, and in effect has been extended to include complete disarmament all along the boundary between Canada and the United States. The difficult question of the northeastern fisheries was treated in a convention signed October 20, 1818. The British had claimed that all rights to the fisheries acquired by the United States under the Treaty of 1783 were annulled by the declaration of war in 1812, and following the war American fishermen had suffered considerable molestation. The new agreement "acknowledged" the right of American citizens to fish along the coasts of Newfoundland and Labrador, and to dry and cure their fish on unsettled shores, but the meaning of the agreement was in some respects so obscure that trouble over the fisheries continued for many years to come.

The same convention that dealt with the fisheries question also attempted to draw a **The northwestern boundary** boundary line between the possessions of the United States and of Great Britain in the Northwest. The Treaty of 1783 had determined the boundary as far west as the Lake of the Woods, and from thence "on a due west course to the river Mississippi." Such a line could not be drawn inasmuch as the source of the Mississippi lay well to the south of the Lake of the Woods. Moreover, the undetermined boundaries of Louisiana had to be taken into consideration. The Convention of 1818 sensibly adopted the forty-ninth parallel as the dividing line between the United States and Canada as far west as the "Stony" mountains. Beyond the mountains neither side was willing to acknowledge the other's pretensions, and the dispute was left open by an agreement that the subjects of both nations might occupy the region jointly.

A precedent in favor of arbitration was set by reference to the Tsar of Russia in 1818 of an American claim for the restitution of slaves captured by the British during the war. The Tsar decided that the slaves need not be restored, but that they should be paid for, and by an agreement reached in 1826 the amount of compensation to be paid by Great Britain was set at well over a million dollars.

It is not surprising that the War of 1812, which was at best a drawn battle, settled into the American consciousness as a telling victory. The news of Jackson's magnificent triumph at New Orleans was quickly followed by the news of peace, and the unthinking public naturally, although wholly mistakenly, assumed that between these two **American impression of victory** impressive events there was the relation of cause and effect. Furthermore, the defeat of the Indians, both in the Northwest and in the Southwest, together with the death of Tecumseh, opened the way for an unprecedented advance of the frontier. No real need had ever been felt for the lands of Canada, and the failure of the War Hawk program of conquest and annexation was quickly forgotten. With peace in Europe restored, American commerce on the high seas was no longer molested, and American patriots were not above imputing to the battle of New Orleans a happy situation that was in reality the result of Leipzig and Waterloo. Pride in the achievements of the American frigates during the early part of the war soon obscured their helplessness in the face of British superiority at its close. American manufacturers, moreover, had benefited greatly by the trade restrictions that preceded and accompanied the war, and their successes had promoted a degree of economic independence from England that the United States had never known before. From the political point of view it is absurd to speak of the War of 1812 as the "Second War for Independence," for political independence had been won in fact no less than in theory by the American Revolution; but from the economic point of view it is abundantly clear that the second war with Great Britain markedly accentuated the divorcement of the two countries. Possibly this situation served for a time to accentuate the ill-feeling that the war had engendered between the British and the American peoples; but the principal causes of tension had been removed, and the way lay open for a prolonged era of peaceful relations.

Bibliography

On the western and southern causes of the War of 1812, J. W. Pratt, *Expansionists of 1812* (1925), is of fundamental importance. Dorothy B. Goebel, *William Henry Harrison* (1926), contains a good analysis of the situation that produced the clash at Tippecanoe. For the massacre at Fort Dearborn, see M. M. Quaife, *Chicago and the Old Northwest, 1673–1835* (1913). The activity of the "War Hawks" is well set forth in Bernard Mayo, *Henry Clay, Spokesman of the New West* (1937), and J. H. Parks, *Felix Grundy, Champion of Democracy* (1940). These accounts should be read in connection with the opposing views of John Randolph, well set forth in H. J. Eckenrode, *The Randolphs, The Story of a Virginia Family* (1946).

For a general history of the war years, Henry Adams, *The War of 1812* (1944) is unsurpassed. This book consists of the appropriate chapters drawn from Adams' nine-volume work. K. C. Babcock, *The Rise of American Nationality* (1906), also covers adequately the war years. On military aspects of the war, see C. P. Lucas, *The Canadian War of 1812* (1906). For the Canadian point of view, see William Wood, *The War with the United States* (1915). J. R. Jacobs, *The Beginning of the United States Army, 1783–1812* (1947), reveals the military unpreparedness that preceded the war. Chapters in Fortescue, *History of the British Army*, VIII, IX, X, give the British side. C. F. Adams, *Studies Military and Diplomatic, 1775–1865* (1911), contains a critical account of the battle of New Orleans. *Memoirs*

and Letters of Dolly Madison, edited by Lucia B. Cutts (1911), contains some interesting sidelights.

On the exploits of the navy, Theodore Roosevelt, *The Naval War of 1812* (1882), is most detailed. Other useful accounts are to be found in Harold and Margaret Sprout, *The Rise of American Naval Power, 1776–1918* (1939); Fletcher Pratt, *The Navy: A History* (1938); C. S. Alden and A. Westcott, *The United States Navy: A History* (1943). C. L. Lewis, *The Romantic Decatur* (1937), is more factual than romantic. See also Mahan, *Sea Power in the War of 1812*, already mentioned; *American Sea Power since 1775*, edited by Allan Westcott (1947); and Fletcher Pratt, *Preble's Boys: Commodore Preble and the Birth of American Sea Power* (1950).

On the Hartford Convention the following works will be found useful: S. E. Morison, *The Life and Letters of Harrison Gray Otis* (2 vols., 1913); H. C. Lodge, *Life and Letters of George Cabot* (1877); Theodore Dwight, *History of the Hartford Convention* (1833).

The peace negotiations are set forth fully in Adams, IX, McMaster, IV, Channing, IV, and Schouler, II. See also W. A. Dunning, *The British Empire and the United States* (1914); R. B. Mowat, *The Diplomatic Relations of Great Britain and the United States* (1925); *The Cambridge History of British Foreign Policy*, edited by A. W. Ward (3 vols., 1922–23), Vol. I. Edgar W. McInnis, *The Unguarded Frontier: A History of American-Canadian Relations* (1942), is a useful synthesis of one aspect of the post-war developments.

THE JACKSONIAN ERA

1818 - 1837

The War of 1812 ended in a stalemate, although the impression of victory was strong in the United States, and much affected American thinking. In the wake of the war came a great wave of national fervor that left no doubt of the fact that the United States had arrived as a nation. Legislation exhibited a strongly nationalistic tinge, the Supreme Court exalted the Nation above the States, the rise of manufacturing freed the country from too great dependence on Europe, and the American people took on peculiar characteristics that marked them as a separate and distinct nationality. Foreign travelers in America were quick to notice the departure from the English pattern. "What then is the American, this new man?" asked Crèvecœur in his *Letters from an American Farmer*, published in 1782. Even that early the foreign observers had noted the mixture of European stocks that made the American so like Europeans, but so different. But it was not only the medley of heritages that made the difference; environment also played an important part, and the American environment during the two decades that followed the War of 1812 was changing at a phenomenal rate of speed.

This was the era of the rise of the New West — six new states entered the union in as many years, 1816 to 1821. It was the era in which northern versus southern sectionalism was brought into sharp focus over the question of slavery in Missouri — the era of the Missouri Compromise. It was the era in which "manifest destiny" began to get out of hand — during these years Spain surrendered Florida to the United States, and acknowledged the existence of a Spanish-American boundary line all the way to the Pacific. It was an era of great diplomatic achievement — by the Monroe Doctrine the United States sought to free itself from the hazards of European intervention so that the westward march of settlement could proceed without molestation. It was an era of great transportation changes — of turnpikes and canals, steamboats and even railroads. It was an era of party evolution — an era in which politicians figured out how to build national

303

parties that could operate across sectional lines. It was an era of developing democracy — both within the States, and in the nation as a whole, the idea that the people should rule took a firm lead over the idea that the aristocrats had any special privileges that anyone need respect. It was an era of cultural growth — the Jacksonian era in politics was paralleled by an era of intellectual striving and humanitarian reform such as the Nation had never known before.

Andrew Jackson, whom the common people of all sections had elected to the Presidency in 1828, gave his name to the period, and well reflected the views of the American people in his principal activities. As President he made greater use of his powers than had been deemed proper by any of the six Presidents who had preceded him. The President, he seemed to realize, alone among elected officials, represented *all* the people. Why, therefore, should the President not lead? Jackson led, although he was frankly and brazenly partisan, and used the full power of his office to further the interests of his own party at the expense of the opposition. When the state of South Carolina challenged the supremacy of the Union by resort to Calhoun's Doctrine of Nullification, Jackson stood by the Union, and did what was necessary to prevent its dissolution. When the President of the Bank of the United States was so unwise as to raise the issue, Who has the greater power, the President of the United States or the President of the "BUS," Jackson met the issue head-on, and destroyed the Bank.

Jackson's leadership was not without its disadvantages. His knowledge of banking and finance left much to be desired, and his destruction of the Bank of the United States helped along those forces that were pushing the nation toward economic depression. Not without help from the President's policies, state banking, land speculation, money inflation, and luxury buying opened a wide road for the Panic of 1837. But for the most part, Jackson in his unwisdom reflected the American people quite as completely as he reflected it in his wisdom. This was one of the great eras of American democracy, even if in it the faults of democracy were no less clearly revealed than its advantages.

18

The New Nationalism

A new era — Growth of manufactures — Agriculture — Foreign travelers in America — American traits — Religious freedom — Education — Magazines and newspapers — Nationalism in politics — Second Bank of the United States — Tariff of 1816 — The Cumberland Road — The Bonus Bill — The Supreme Court under Marshall

THE War of 1812 marks a definite turning-point in the history of the United States. **A new era** Prior to that conflict the American people, for all their political independence, were in their economic life still tributary to Europe, and most especially to England. The factory system was slow to take root in America, for it was cheaper to import goods from England, where manufacturing on a large scale was already well established, than to make them in America. Moreover, the commercial connections of colonial times had been promptly resumed at the close of the Revolution, and at the beginning of the nineteenth century there were no stronger vested interests in the country than those concerned with the importation and distribution of foreign goods. Planters and farmers, likewise, were accustomed to depend heavily upon foreign trade. Their excess produce was sent to Europe quite as consistently as during colonial times, while the continual wars of the French Revolution and the Napoleonic period forced the prices of American raw materials and foodstuffs to high figures. With a steady trade flowing both ways, there was little difficulty in making exports balance imports in value.

The embargo, non-intercourse, and the War of 1812 upset completely this scheme **Growth of manufactures** of things. American commerce was for the time being almost destroyed, and the opportunity to import foreign goods was reduced to a mini- mum. Naturally enough, much of the capital that had formerly been invested in commerce turned now to manufactures, for which the existing situation was equivalent to a heavy protective tariff. Manufacturing, moreover, became a patriotic duty which states, counties, municipalities, and societies sought to encourage by offering attractive bounties. As early as 1810 Gallatin reported to the House of Representatives a surprisingly long list of items in which American manufacturers were already able to supply the American demand. Throughout the period textile mills for the production of cotton, linen, and woolen cloth increased rapidly in number, and even more rapidly in the volume of their output. Facilities for the manufacture of such significant articles as paper, leather goods, woodenware, iron, and iron goods multiplied until the most urgent needs of the American market were fully met. By the end of the war American manufacturing was definitely established, and the shortage of European imports was no longer keenly felt.

New England promptly took the lead among the sections in the shift toward manufacturing. Not only was there **New England factories** occasion here to offset with some other interest the decline in commerce; in a variety of ways New England was ideally fitted to assume the manufacturing rôle. Power to turn the wheels of the new machinery was abundantly supplied by the swift-flowing streams and their numerous waterfalls, shippers and shipping were available to send the products of the loom and factory down the coast to the other American states, and an abundant and intelligent labor supply was at hand. Workers in the New England factories consisted mainly of farmers and their families, who were only too willing to give up the unequal struggle with the hard climate and the unyielding soil to accept the more certain financial rewards of the mills. They brought with them a degree of dexterity and ingenuity, acquired through years of self-dependence on the farm, that placed them among the most capable, although possibly not among the most tractable, factory employees anywhere in the world.

But the interest in manufacturing was by no means confined to New England. As far south as the Chesapeake the new opportunity for American manufacturers was producing results. If New England led in the production of textiles, Pennsylvania, New York, and New Jersey excelled in the production of iron ore and the manufacture of iron goods. In this region coal could be obtained cheaply to supplement water-power, and by the end of the War of 1812 bituminous, and even anthracite, coal was being used by occasional manufacturers with good success. In the South there was talk of establishing factories and putting the slaves to work in them, but practically nothing of the sort was actually accomplished. Instead the South turned to cotton-growing, and became a heavy purchaser of northern goods. In 1814, according to one estimate, New England bankers received on an average a half million dollars a month from the banks of the South, practically all of which was drawn northward in payment for factory products.

The period of enforced divorcement from Europe had witnessed many changes also in **American agriculture.** American agriculture. The growth of the woolen industry made sheep-raising profitable as never before. In the back country of New England and in the middle states, where with the decline of the export trade foodstuffs had become a drug on the market, there was a noticeable trend in the direction of wool-growing. In the South the production of cotton took on ever-increasing significance. Before Eli Whitney's invention of the cotton gin in 1793, only the long-staple cotton grown in the lowlands could be profitably raised. But the cotton gin, by reducing immensely the cost of separating the seed from the cotton, made practicable the growing also of the short-staple cotton which throve well in the uplands. The results were revolutionary. The output of southern cotton, which in 1791 had amounted only to about two million pounds, had grown by 1801 to forty million, and by 1811 to eighty million pounds. Until the period of commercial restriction began, the bulk of this cotton had found its way to foreign markets, and only the establishment of the northern textile mills saved the southern cotton planters from deep disaster. Once the war was ended, both foreign and domestic manufacturers clamored for cotton, and the spread of cotton culture was more rapid than ever before. The increasing cultivation of sugar-cane in Louisiana, and to some extent elsewhere in the South, added another commodity to the list of articles that could be supplied within the borders of the United States.

Much was therefore achieved toward that national self-sufficiency which economists of the eighteenth century had regarded as so vital to the life of a nation. Accompanying this development the discerning observer might have noted also the rapid emergence of an American national type. When the Revolution ended, the typical American was still essentially an English colonial whose tastes and aptitudes were definitely reminiscent of the Old World. By the end of the eighteenth century some notable changes were already in evidence, but in the years following the War of 1812 a new nationality, with new and different characteristics, was clearly in the making. The

COTTON PROCESSING. The Hogden Holmes gin, a later development of Whitney's revolutionary invention.

IRON AND STEEL MANUFACTURE. The Rowland Steel Works, Philadelphia, 1816.

MASS PRODUCTION IN TEXTILES. Calico printing in Slater's mill, Pawtucket, R. I., 1836.

Industrial development proceeded with marked rapidity during the troubled years that culminated in the War of 1812. Cut off from normal contacts with Europe before and during the war, American manufacturing, helped along by American ingenuity, grew by leaps and bounds. Then, when the war was over, the spirit of nationalism, with its insistence on helpful protective tariffs, kept the infant industries alive and expanding.

decline of commerce, and the consequent lessening of contacts between Americans and Europeans, undoubtedly stimulated the divergence of American from European ways, but probably the unique opportunities of the New World, now better realized than ever before, account for most of the changes. America had become pre-eminently a land of "opportunity." To the resident of the Northeast the newly introduced factory system brought to employers and employees alike undreamed-of avenues to prosperity. To the southern planter, and to the southern small farmer who hoped to become a planter, the revolutionary possibilities of cotton culture seemed to point the way to sure success.

To the restless of every section came with renewed vigor the call of the West. Almost for the first time the boundless possibilities of the new nation were fully realized. Now anyone could see that future generations of Americans had before them a task no less inviting than the conquest and exploitation of half a continent. The lure of rich rewards, whether in industry, in cotton culture, or in the development of the West, captured the imaginations of Americans and determined their characteristics. Small wonder that they saw little reason to imitate or esteem the ways of an Old World where opportunity was limited, but paid deference instead to whatever qualities in themselves seemed best

THE COUNTRY FAIR. Painting by John A. Woodside, 1824.

Agriculture and commerce made parallel progress during the early decades of the nineteenth century. At country fairs, if the artists of the times are to be trusted, the results of careful livestock breeding were proudly displayed, together with the newest developments in farm implements. Improved post-roads made stagecoach travel less formidable, while the steamboat era, with all its marvellous transformations, burst suddenly onto the American scene.

THE STEAMBOAT. "Fulton's Folly," the *Clermont,* passing West Point on the Hudson River, about 1810. Lithograph by Berthaux.

COMMERCIAL
MAIL STAGE,
☞ IN THIRTY-NINE HOURS,
From Boston to New York,
☞ *CARRYING ONLY SIX PASSENGERS.*

Runs by the way of Worcester, Stafford Springs,
Hartford, Middletown, New-Haven to New-York....Leaves Boston every day at 1 o'clock, P. M.---arrives at Hartford at 7 o'clock, A. M.---arrives at New-Haven 5 o'clock P. M.---arrives at New-York, 6 o'clock, A. M.

Returning......Leaves New-York for Boston
every day at half past seven o'clock, A. M.---leaves New-Haven at 10 o'clock, P. M.---leaves Hartford half past 5 o'clock, A. M.---arrives at Boston half past 11 o'clock, P. M.---making *Thirty-nine hours,* it being seven hours sooner than ever performed before.

The Proprietors solicit the Patronage of the Public, and pledge themselves that every exertion shall be made for their accommodation.

Fare to be paid in Boston, New Haven and New-York.

☞ For Seats apply at the Stage Office, Exchange Coffee-House, entrance in Congress-Street—Boston—Col. Reuben Silex, Worcester—Bennett's Coffee-House, Hartford,—Butler's Hotel, New-Haven—Cumberland-Street, No. 1, New-York.

☞ For Seats in the *Accommodation Stages,* apply as above.

BOSTON, *February,* 1815.

PUBLIC TRANSPORTATION. Boston-New York passenger service to be made in thirty-nine hours, "seven hours sooner than ever performed before." Broadside, 1815.

calculated to insure success in the new undertakings.

Fortunately for the historian, there came to America during the years following the **Foreign travelers in America** War of 1812 a procession of foreign travelers who wrote down freely what they saw — or what they thought they saw. Some of these visitors, as the official or unofficial agents of European governments, were in search of an outlet for European emigration. The Napoleonic wars had left a train of economic distress in their wake, and most European nations were faced by an acute unemployment problem. Why not send their excess population to America? Those who visited the United States in search of a land of opportunity for emigrants found what they wanted to find, and wrote glowing reports. But there were many other travelers who came to America in a purely private capacity, not so much to chronicle the opportunities they saw as to criticize a nation that flaunted its "democracy." These travelers were drawn mostly from the classes of the well-to-do and the socially élite, who found much to confirm their long-established prejudices, but were nevertheless able to see clearly many things that an American observer would have overlooked. It is chiefly upon this travel literature that the historian must rely when he seeks to set forth the traits that were peculiar to Americans of this age.

All accounts agree that the typical American was very "provincial." To some **American traits** extent this was only another way of saying that he differed from the typical Englishman or Frenchman, or other European. But it was also a fact that most Americans knew little or nothing about the world outside America, and oftentimes they cared even less. Somewhat on the defensive because of this ignorance, Americans were inclined to be boastful, both about themselves and about their country. They were particularly proud of the American experiment in democratic government, and they would neither admit that mistakes had been made, nor that any other form of government was half so good. Patriotism became almost a national obsession.

In one respect, at least, foreigners were quick to consent that American boastfulness was justified. The ordinary American was truly remarkable for his ingenuity. He could turn his hand with considerable skill to almost any problem that confronted him. He was not precisely inventive, but he was a natural-born jack-of-all-trades whose adaptability rarely left him baffled by a new situation or defeated because of an unanticipated need. The American practice of moving houses, for example, struck foreigners with peculiar force. Houses in Europe usually stayed where they were built; in America one might meet them coming down the street.

American ideas as to good manners did not always conform to European standards. Such crudities as normally accompanied the unrestrained use of chewing-tobacco excited the amazement of travelers, and sometimes for good reason their anxiety as well. The American's habit of bolting his meals in record time also induced comment, and to gouty Europeans who set much store by the leisurely disposal of food the popularity of the American "quick lunch" quite passed belief. The restlessness and nervousness of the Americans also annoyed the foreigners. Americans resented delay, and were forever in a hurry. This quality, incidentally, marks a pronounced change from the habits of colonial Americans — habits for which their descendants could have found no more appropriate adjective than "lazy." Some observers blamed this restlessness on the American climate, which, they avowed, exhibited a greater variety of conditions in a given space of time than could be found in any other country on earth. Others thought that the American diet was enough to account for it, and for the sallowness of the American complexion as well. But probably the real reason why Americans were such "hustlers" was that they were so keenly aware of the challenging opportunities that confronted them. With riches seemingly a

FOURTH OF JULY, 1819. Public celebration in Center Square, Philadelphia. Note the patriotic posters over the tent doorways. At the left is a print of the *Chesapeake-Shannon* battle carrying Lawrence's words, "Don't give up the ship!"; at right, the Battle of New Orleans. Painting by J. L. Krimmel.

CHESTNUT STREET, PHILADELPHIA. Saunderson's Franklin House at the left. Detail of an engraving by J. R. Smith, about 1820.

American behavior attracted the attention of foreigners and artists alike. Native enthusiasm for America and its democratic system, "the best that the sun of heaven ever shed his genial rays upon," seemed to overflow at the slightest provocation, especially on the Fourth of July. West Point, even in time of peace, was the object of national pride and interest. City streets reflected the hurry and bustle that seemed to European visitors so characteristic of America.

WEST POINT, 1817. A view of "Exercises on the Plain." Illustration from Milbert, *Itineraire Pittoresque du Fleuve Hudson,* 1828.

sure reward for enterprise, the typical American felt that he had no time to waste. He took it for granted that to get his share he must work hard; indeed, he idealized work, and had great disdain for those who sought to avoid it. The existence of a "leisure class" anywhere in the world he viewed with undisguised contempt.

Optimism was another by-product of opportunity. In America there was room for all

Optimism to prosper. Unemployment for the physically fit was a matter of disposition, not of necessity, for the supply of labor was rarely up to the demand. America had neither slums nor poor in the European sense of those terms, and the most worthless sort of person could at least make a living. Faith in the future sometimes overshot the mark and tempted to speculation. "Stock-watering" was often not so much a matter of fraud as of great expectations — the profits of the company were sure to grow. The misrepresentations of land speculators were more frequently than not a fair statement of what they genuinely believed: that land values would assuredly go up. Overissues of bank currency were not all made with dishonest intent — more money was needed to care for the natural demands of a growing country.

Equality of opportunity had much to do with the turn that democracy was taking in

Equality of opportunity America. The equalitarian doctrine of the Declaration of Independence was in its day merely the statement of an ideal; fifty years later it was not far from a correct description of American society. To be sure, an aristocracy still existed in every part of the country, except possibly in the West, but the new aristocracy, whether of industrial New England or of the cotton-planting South, was an aristocracy to which now even the lowliest might aspire. Caste lines were ever more loosely drawn, and family trees counted for less and less. Not by birth, but by material success, was one marked as a member of the upper class, and the road to success was equally open to all. As if in deference to this new definition of aristocracy, the old distinction between the dress of the aristocrat and of the common man disappeared, but it was the aristocrat who gave up his furbelows, not the common man who put them on. The status of women in the new democracy seemed also to be rising toward a frank admission of equality with men. In the place of the obsequious and condescending chivalry which Europeans of the better class were accustomed to exhibit toward their own class only, all Americans, to the consternation of some foreign observers, tended to treat women of whatever class with marked respect and courtesy.

For a people that set great store by its government, this democratic trend was sure to be reflected in politics. The

Democracy new western states on admission to the Union unhesitatingly established universal manhood suffrage, and the older states of the East soon followed their example. In the latter it did not follow at once that the common people held the offices, for the old colonial tradition that candidates should be chosen only from the better classes died hard. In the West, however, there was no authentic aristocracy from which to choose, and the common people themselves held the offices. It was not to be long before this excess of democracy should be in evidence throughout the land. Travelers could observe even then a growing intolerance of superiority which in time would turn into a kind of worship of mediocrity. To elect one's betters to office was to admit that one had betters. To throw one's betters out of office was to rebuke for their pretensions those who thought themselves superior, and to prove that the people really ruled.

The abundance of opportunity in America opened the way to an almost unrestrained individualism. With the chances

Individualism for success everywhere so great, anyone with an ambition to fulfill rushed forward to achieve his goal by whatever means seemed good to him. He asked only to be let alone. Fortunately there was room enough for all. The New England

An Urban Drawing Room. "The Tea Party," painted by Henry Sargent, 1825.

The Park Theater, New York. A play by Moncrieff is in progress. Painting by John Searle, 1822.

Public Schoolroom. To accommodate larger numbers of pupils in over-crowded classrooms, an "usher," one of the older pupils, would take over a younger group and repeat to them the lesson he had just done. Illustration from Pierpont, *The Young Reader*, 1831.

Culture and refinement were earnestly sought after in America. Elegant salons were common in the cities, and the socially prominent were eager patrons of the arts from abroad. But the American ideals of self-betterment and social equality were in evidence in both country and city. An increasing interest in education for all meant an ever-growing demand for more and better public schools.

Dance in a Country Tavern. Painting by J. L. Krimmel, 1820.

manufacturer who expanded his mills need not necessarily destroy his competitor; with abundant markets the two might expand and prosper side by side. If new machinery threw employees out of work, more likely than not other jobs, equally good, soon appeared. As for the increasing number of farmers and farm laborers, cheap lands and a fertile soil beckoned them to the West, where as pioneers they might achieve a greater success and a greater degree of independence than they could ever have known anywhere else. Throughout the West individual freedom was a frontier heritage much prized by all. Pioneers made their way in the world by their own efforts, and they took pride in the work they had done. They made a fetish of their freedom, and would brook few restraints, whether of government or of society. All this was possible, however, only because of the abundance of opportunity in America. Three quarters of a century later, when lands and markets had become more limited, individual freedom ceased to be an unmixed blessing.

Ever since colonial times religious freedom, as a natural corollary of individual freedom, **Religious freedom** had made steady gains. During the American Revolution the number of church establishments in the United States had been greatly reduced; in 1786 Thomas Jefferson had won his notable victory for the complete divorcement of church and state in Virginia; and in the first amendment to the Constitution of the United States Congress had been forbidden to pass a law "respecting the establishment of religion or prohibiting the free exercise thereof." Nevertheless, the feeling that religion must somehow be supported by the state was slow to die. The new western states would have nothing to do with church establishments, but in New England, where the Congregationalists were strongly intrenched, the last citadels of conservatism were not broken down until after the War of 1812. In New Hampshire the reform was delayed until 1817, in Connecticut until 1818, and in Massachusetts until 1833. But

by this time the complete separation of church and state in the United States had become a fixed principle. This was one of the evidences of American superiority that the typical American could point out to travelers from abroad with confidence and pride.

With the great multiplicity of religious sects, mutual toleration for all and special privileges for none were well-nigh inevitable developments. To the Congregationalist, Dutch Reformed, Quaker, Catholic, and Episcopalian denominations of the seaboard were added the Presbyterian, Lutheran, Baptist, and Methodist churches of the back country, not to mention literally scores of minor religious units. Each denomination was now organized on a national basis, usually with a type of church government strongly reflecting the political institutions of the United States, and with as complete separation from Old World churches as was consistent with its theology. The western denominations, such as the Methodists and the Baptists, were growing with far greater rapidity than those of the East. This was due in large part to the democratic appeal that the frontier churches were willing to make. They did not insist upon an educated ministry, but were generally willing to accept as preachers all those who felt that they had received the divine "call." They were democratic in church government, they rekindled at every opportunity the revival fervor that had swept the country in the early years of the century and in their camp-meetings they preached a gospel of salvation for the many rather than merely for the few. Even in conservative New England, where the Unitarian revolt was still in full swing, the leaven of democracy was taking hold. Calvinistic theology, with its emphasis upon the unworthiness of man, a creature "conceived in sin and born in iniquity," was losing steadily before the attacks of the Unitarians, who held that man was the noblest work of God, born in his Maker's image, and endowed with no less spiritual possibilities than were given to the man

Jesus himself. From the religious point of view there could be no greater exaltation of democracy than was implicit in the commonly made assertion that in every man there was a spark of the divine.

Afraid as they were to confess a shortcoming, Americans generally made light of their cultural deficiencies, and featured instead their great success in dealing with the practical problems that confronted a rapidly growing nation. But there is much reason to believe that they had a secret regard for the sophistication they associated with older civilizations, that they would have rejoiced to be less completely outdone in this respect. As a matter of fact, in such realms as education, journalism, and literature the new nation already had considerable progress to its credit.

One reason for the lack of popular interest in education was the slowness of the schools to adapt themselves to the needs **Education** of a democracy. For the most part they still operated on the theory that it was their business to educate the leaders of society only, and to ignore the needs of the masses. This concept of education, however, was breaking down, and the popular prejudice against education was being correspondingly undermined. Free elementary schools were sometimes starved for lack of financial support, but the people were quick to acknowledge, especially in their new state constitutions, the duty of the state to provide such instruction at public expense. Private academies designed to meet the educational needs of children whose parents could afford to pay flourished in the East, and were available in surprisingly large numbers even in the West. Higher education was still left mainly to the churches, but between 1810 and 1820, while the number of American colleges was being doubled, evidence also accumulated that the strictly classical and theological training of an earlier age would not endure. Thanks mainly to the work of Jefferson, the curriculum of the College of William and Mary now included such subjects as law, history, political economy, and modern languages, while the University of Virginia, opened in 1825, not only adopted an unusually liberal course of study, but also made the entrance requirements easier, and allowed students great freedom in their choice of subjects. The democratic ideal of education for citizenship was clearly supplanting the older ideal of religious education.

American writers who were interested in the exploitation of American themes found a ready outlet for their efforts in **Magazines** the rapidly increasing numbers **and news-** of newspapers and magazines **papers** that were appearing. By 1810 there were no less than three hundred and fifty newspapers in the United States, as against only forty at the close of the American Revolution. The increasing popularity of magazines is shown by the fact that in 1800 there were not more than a dozen such publications in the whole country, whereas in 1825 there were nearly a hundred. Newspapers still emphasized political news and political arguments, but the magazines, although by no means unconcerned with politics and actually at great pains to defend the new republic against foreign critics, presented more varied offerings. Both newspapers and magazines had as a rule only small and local circulations, but the *North American Review*, which was founded in 1815, soon gained well-deserved notice even outside the United States.

Although the first real flowering of American literature is usually associated with a somewhat later period, the **Literary** names of at least two notable **lights** American writers, Washington Irving and William Cullen Bryant, were known even before the War of 1812. Curiously, both men opened their literary careers with attacks on Thomas Jefferson. Irving's *Knickerbocker History of New York* was less a satire on the Dutch in early New Netherland than on the policies of Jefferson's administration, while the *Embargo*, from the pen of the thirteen-year-old Bryant, disdained subtleties:

Go, wretch, resign the Presidential chair,
Disclose thy secret measures, foul or fair;
Go, search with curious eye for hornéd frogs
'Mid the wild wastes of Louisiana bogs,
Or, where Ohio rolls his turbid stream,
Dig for huge bones, thy glory and thy theme.

A little later the still youthful Bryant was penning his striking lines *To a Waterfowl*, and his immortal *Thanatopsis*. Another great name in American literature won prominence when James Fenimore Cooper published *The Spy* (1821), a story of American life during the Revolution.

The multiplication of books and libraries during these years testifies eloquently to the growing literary interests of Americans. They might pretend that there was for such a race of practical men as they professed themselves to be no charm whatever in learning and culture, but six thousand tons of paper, according to estimates made for 1816, were required annually to make the books they bought. Many Americans took great pride in assembling libraries. The largest private libraries in the country were probably those of John Quincy Adams and Thomas Jefferson, each of which ran to over five thousand volumes, but practically every prominent citizen aspired to own a library and busied himself with the collection of books. Public libraries also were becoming increasingly common, and the manufacture of books in America had reached the point where works on nearly every known subject were printed on this side of the Atlantic.

The ultranationalism of the United States after the War of 1812 is in no way more em-**Nationalism in politics** phatically portrayed than in the program of legislation which Congress, once the war was at an end, made haste to adopt. President Madison in his annual message of December 5, 1815, showed plainly that as far as he was concerned the era of narrow particularism and states' rights was over. He urged upon Congress the necessity of a strong military establishment, a uniform national currency, a tariff to protect the new American industries, a national system of roads and canals,

and a great national university. On every point save the last his recommendations were accepted. These facts are the more striking when it is remembered that the President had once been, next to Jefferson himself, the most prominent critic of Federalist centralization, while the Congress which now followed his lead had an overwhelmingly Republican majority in each house. The Republican Party, which during its fifteen years of power had gradually moved over to the positions once occupied by the Federalists, had discovered that with each move in the direction of nationalism its popularity with the voters had increased. Moreover, the new generation of Republicans had never known devotion to the doctrines of early Jeffersonianism. Madison, although somewhat changed by time, represented after all the earlier age and shifted ground with some reluctance, but such newcomers in national politics as Henry Clay of Kentucky and John C. Calhoun of South Carolina had little concern for party tradition, and felt free to follow current trends of thought.

The experiences of the war gave abundant point to Madison's plea for a strengthening of the national defense. **The national** In the place of the old feeling **defense** that a standing army might endanger the liberties of the people, and that an unscrupulous President might use it to make himself a dictator, there was frank recognition of the need of a dependable fighting weapon, and complete confidence that an American President would make no effort to overthrow the Constitution. A standing army of ten thousand men was authorized, and an appropriation of eight million dollars was voted for the construction of fifteen new naval units. The Military Academy at West Point, which had been established in 1802, was reorganized with a view to greater efficiency, and was given increased support. Thus the nation willingly embarked upon what was for the time a notable preparedness program.

An even more significant revelation of the

nationalistic trend of the times is to be found
in the act to establish a second
Bank of the United States.
With the disappearance of the
Hamiltonian bank in 1811 the banking business of the country had been turned over completely to the state banks, each of which operated under a private charter granted by a state legislature. These banks had served an important purpose even while the first Bank of the United States was in existence, for the national bank issued notes only in large denominations, and the smaller currency of the country was mostly supplied by the state banks. They were able also to do a flourishing local business that was beyond the reach of the Bank of the United States, and accordingly their number and strength steadily increased. Whereas there were all told only four state banks in 1790, there were eighty-eight of them in 1811. The prerogatives of the state banks varied greatly, but they were universally banks of issue, and most of them printed as much paper money as they dared. In the Northeast, state banking was carried on along conservative lines, but in the South and West, particularly after 1811, the paper issues were excessive, the currency was inflated, and speculation, which ordinarily took the form of speculation in land, was dangerously stimulated. Moreover, except in New England specie payments were wholly suspended by the state banks during the War of 1812, and the purchasing power of their notes exhibited bewildering variations.

It was partly with a view to correcting these evils that a new national bank was proposed in 1816. Such a bank could put out a national currency, which, unlike the state bank currency, would have the same value anywhere in the nation. Also, the second Bank of the United States could use its power, as the first had done, to check the "wildcat" tendencies of the state banks, and to force them to do a more conservative business.

The committee of seven which framed the bank bill was headed by John C. Calhoun,

and had only two members from the non-slave-holding states. Nevertheless, it decided in favor of establishing precisely the sort of bank that southern states'-rights Republicans had once opposed so vigorously. The new bank should have a capital stock of $35,000,000; the United States government should subscribe one fifth of the stock, private individuals the other four fifths, and the directors should be similarly apportioned; the bank should have a monopoly on the business of the United States and the national banking business; it might establish branch banks throughout the several states; and it might continue in operation for a period of twenty years. For the valuable privileges the bank was to enjoy it was required to pay to the government of the United States a bonus of $1,500,000.

This measure received the ardent support of Calhoun, who dismissed all doubts as to its constitutionality by the argument that the Constitution had delegated to Congress full control of the monetary system of the country, and that for this purpose a national bank was essential. Henry Clay, who had argued in 1811 against the constitutionality of a national bank, had greater difficulties to surmount, but he was equal to the occasion. Congress, he maintained, had power to make such laws as were "necessary and proper" to carry out the powers set down for it in the Constitution, and whereas a national bank was by no means "necessary and proper" in 1811 it had become so by 1816. In general the views of Calhoun and Clay represented fairly their respective sections, but from New England there came opposition. Daniel Webster was against the measure. He made no attempt to oppose it on constitutional grounds, but he argued that the state banks, if properly managed, could take care of the nation's business. The banks of his section were safe and sound, and he reflected their fear that a national bank under western and southern management might become a source of danger rather than of strength. The opposition which Webster voiced was insufficient to block passage of the bill, and the second Bank of the United States was chartered. To insure a return on the part of the state banks to specie payments, Congress also resolved that dues payable to the United States should be received only in specie or in the notes of banks which, like the Bank of the United States, stood ready to redeem their currency issues in specie.

Further evidence of the national spirit that characterized the times is to be found in

Tariff of 1816 the Tariff Act of 1816. The first tariff law, passed at the beginning of Washington's administration, had been amended upward by 1812 to a level of approximately twelve and one half per cent. These duties were doubled during the War, but with the understanding that they should be dropped to the normal peacetime level a year after its close. It became clear soon after the War was over that the peacetime duties would not be high enough to keep out foreign goods; indeed, English manufacturers, long cut off from their accustomed markets, soon began to "dump" their accumulated surpluses upon American importers at such ridiculously low prices that American manufacturers were greatly perturbed. If the degree of self-sufficiency that the country had lately attained was not to be lost, high enough tariffs to shut out the cheap foreign goods must be levied. To most Americans continued industrial independence was well worth this price. Calhoun pointed out also that the tariff would serve to bind the various sections of the country together more closely, for they would henceforth be dependent for necessities upon other parts of the United States instead of upon other parts of the world.

A tariff bill which maintained or increased the wartime duties was carried by a two-to-one majority in the House and by a four-to-one majority in the Senate. From the point of view of the commercial interests, whose hope of profits lay in the complete resumption of overseas trade, this tariff measure was a sad mistake. In defense of their interests Daniel Webster and a small group of

Federalists opposed the tariff, although within a few years these same men were to become the chief champions of protection. Nor could even a majority of the southern Republicans be brought in line for the bill; only twenty-three votes were obtained from the South for protection, while thirty-four Southerners voted against it. For this latter group John Randolph of Roanoke was the most effective spokesman. "No," he said, "I will buy where I can get manufactures cheapest, I will not agree to lay a duty on the cultivator of the soil to encourage exotic manufactures; because, after all, we should only get much worse things at a higher price." The tariff bill was intended, even by its friends, to remain on the statute books only temporarily; as soon as the infant industries could stand alone protection should be withdrawn. But to manufacturers who profited from high duties the time for their repeal was never to seem ripe.

Madison's recommendation of a national program of internal improvements was somewhat guarded. No man knew better than he what the framers of the federal Constitution had meant when they listed the powers which Congress was to exercise, and the power to build a national system of roads and canals had been deliberately omitted. Madison suggested, therefore, that Congress should take steps to enlarge its powers by proposing an amendment to the Constitution definitely permitting it to undertake works of internal improvement. In the meantime he saw no objection to its making use of its "existing powers," whatever they might be. The subject was touched upon first in his message of 1815, and when Congress failed to act upon his suggestion at that session, he renewed his recommendation a year later.

Congress was as ready to go ahead with internal improvements as with the bank or the tariff, and the younger Republicans were unaware of any constitutional obstacles. The **The Cumberland Road** Cumberland Road, designed to connect the East and the West along the route Braddock had taken in the French and Indian War,

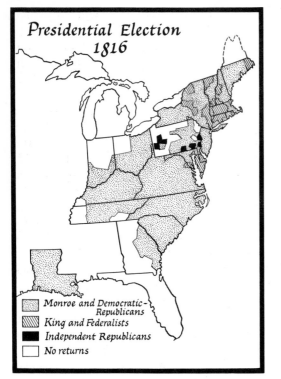

Presidential Election
1816

Monroe and Democratic-
    Republicans
King and Federalists
Independent Republicans
No returns

was already in process of construction at national expense, and its completion was a matter of good faith. When Ohio was admitted to the Union in 1803, Congress had promised that such a road would be built in return for assurance that the new state would not attempt to tax federal lands within its borders, and five per cent of the receipts from Ohio land sales had been definitely allocated to this purpose. Contracts were let in 1811 for the beginning of construction, and in spite of the war other contracts were let in 1812, 1813, and 1814; but with only twenty miles actually finished by the end of the war there remained much to be done. Neither Madison nor his successor, Monroe, made any effort to prevent appropriations being made for the continuation of this road, and Congress regularly supplied whatever funds were needed. By 1818 the road was completed to Wheeling, Virginia.

Congress was willing to stretch the Constitution further than the President could follow, however, in the adoption of a program of internal improvements. Calhoun,

the leader of the nationalists, introduced in December, 1816, a bill to pledge **The Bonus** to the promotion of internal **Bill** improvements the bonus of a million and a half dollars that the newly chartered Bank of the United States was to pay into the treasury. The constitutionality of the Bonus Bill, as this measure was called, was stoutly defended by Calhoun, who held that the Constitution "was not intended as a thesis for the logician to exercise his ingenuity on; that it ought to be construed with plain good sense; and that when so construed nothing could be more express than the Constitution upon this very point." Opponents of the Bonus Bill in Congress questioned, nevertheless, whether money might properly be raised and spent for internal improvements under the "general welfare" clause, and some of those who hailed from New England or the lower South thought that, regardless of constitutionality, the states through which the roads were to be built should bear the expense. The strongest demand for internal improvements came from the middle and western states, and since these states would profit most from the building of the roads why should they not pay for them? As for Madison, he had no objection to national expenditures for internal improvements, but he believed that on this subject the Constitution granted no such latitude to Congress as Calhoun and his followers seemed to think. The Bonus Bill passed Congress, but was vetoed by the President. The young Republicans tried in vain to pass the measure over the President's veto, but they were not discouraged. They meant to continue the policy of national improvements that the building of the Cumberland Road had begun, and they were unwilling to risk the delay and uncertainty of a constitutional amendment to give Congress the power which in their opinion it already possessed.

The election of 1816 found the Federalists out of touch with the nationalistic spirit that pervaded the country as a **Election** whole, and still further handi- **of 1816** capped by their bad war record. The Republicans, on the other hand, were assured of victory, although by no means certain as to whom they should nominate. This matter was decided, according to custom, by a caucus of the party delegation in Congress, but the caucus system of making nominations had begun to arouse criticism. Some felt that it gave Congress too great power over the choice of the chief executive; others that the sitting President could wield too much influence over the caucus. Much to the dissatisfaction of those who held these views, Madison made no secret of his wish that James Monroe, his Secretary of State, should succeed to the Presidency. When the customary caucus was held, Monroe won the nomination over W. H. Crawford of Georgia by the narrow vote of 65 to 54. The Federalists did not even trouble themselves to name candidates, and in the election which followed they carried only three states, Massachusetts, Connecticut, and Delaware, whose electors cast 34 votes for Rufus King of New York. Monroe's vote from the other states reached 183.

Like three out of four of his predecessors, James Monroe (1758–1831) was a Virginia planter. His family, however, was by no means of the first families of Virginia; it was rather of the western, small-planter class, and included in its family tree many Scottish and Welsh ancestors. Monroe was just beginning his college work at William and Mary when the Revolutionary War broke out, and although he was only sixteen years of age he promptly joined the Patriot army. He had an honorable record in the war, and emerged from it, in spite of his youth, with the rank of lieutenant-colonel. Later he studied law under Jefferson, and inevitably absorbed the political principles of the older man. Monroe never became the scholar that Jefferson was, or for that matter, Madison, and to many of his contemporaries it seemed that he was hardly of presidential calibre. But his political experience was more than ample. By the time he reached the Presidency he had served in the Virginia Assembly, in the Congress of the Confedera-

James Monroe

THE FIFTH PRESIDENT of the United States, Monroe long favored a strict constructionist interpretation of the Constitution. His term of office coincided, however, with a period of rising nationalism, and he gradually adjusted himself to the prevailing temper of the times. His name is associated with the Monroe Doctrine, long a cardinal principle of American foreign policy. Portrait by Gilbert Stuart.

tion, and in the United States Senate; he had represented his country on important missions to France, Spain, and England; he had been governor of Virginia for several terms; and he had been at one time both Secretary of State and Secretary of War.

Firmly grounded in the states'-rights principles of early Jeffersonianism, Monroe found it somewhat difficult to keep abreast of the nationalistic trend his party had taken. He and Jefferson were openly at odds over this subject when the latter left office, and Monroe was no more able than Madison to accept as constitutional the ambitious program of internal improvements at national expense that the young Republicans were beginning to preach. He allowed the Cumberland Road to be finished, but in 1822, when a bill passed Congress to provide funds for its repair by establishing toll gates and collecting tolls, he interposed a veto. The exercise of such power by Congress, he claimed, implied a "power to adopt and execute a complete system of internal improvements," and

The Cumberland tolls veto

for this he found no constitutional warrant. He believed, however, that a change in the Constitution to permit the United States to build "great national works" would be desirable, provided that "all minor improvements" should be left to the states.

While Madison and Monroe were struggling to adjust their consciences to the new nationalism, the Supreme Court under the leadership of another Virginian, John Marshall, was doing all it could to help them. "The judiciary of the United States," wrote Thomas Jefferson in 1820, "is the subtle corps of sappers and miners constantly working underground to undermine the foundations of our confederate fabric. They are constantly construing our constitution from a co-ordination of a general and special government, to a general and supreme one alone. They will lay all things at their feet, and they are too well versed in the English law to forget the maxim, *'boni judicis est ampliare jurisdictionem.'*" Thomas Jefferson had done his part as President toward exaggerating the power of the central government, but there can be but little doubt that the Supreme Court under Marshall had done far more.

The Supreme Court

John Marshall (1755–1835) was born far out on the Virginia frontier in what became a few years later Fauquier County. His father, Thomas Marshall, was a man of good education who did what he could to communicate to his son his own love of history and literature. Young Marshall early determined upon a legal career, but when the Revolution broke out he left off the study of law to enter the army, where for a time he fought against the British as a member of his father's regiment. Toward the end of the war, when the fighting had died down, he attended some lectures on law at William and Mary College, and in 1781 he began to practice in Fauquier County. When presently he won an important land title case for the tenants of Lord Fairfax, his reputation was made, and he was soon recognized as the leader of the Virginia bar. His legal labors, however, did

John Marshall

not prevent him from playing an important part in politics. He was chosen eight times to the Virginia legislature, sat in the Virginia convention called to ratify the Constitution, served as one of the three commissioners whom Adams sent to make peace with France in 1797, represented his state in Congress for one term, and became Secretary of State during the last year of the Adams administration.

Marshall, like Adams, was identified with the more moderate wing of the Federalist Party, but he had a deep distrust of the radical democracy preached by Thomas Jefferson and the Republicans. After the election of 1800, when Adams thought it his patriotic duty to save the judiciary, if possible, from the menace of Jeffersonian control, he made the young and energetic Marshall Chief Justice of the United States. Marshall served only thirty days under a Federalist president, but for thirty-four years after the Federalists lost control of Congress and the Presidency he guided the Supreme Court in a thoroughly Federalist interpretation of the Constitution. So great was the power of his personality and so convincing his logic that, to the despair of Republican Presidents, the new judges they appointed were soon following Marshall's lead. Next to the Chief Justice himself, Joseph Story of Massachusetts, whom Madison appointed to the Court in 1811, was most responsible for the trend of the Court's decisions. The growth of the national spirit during and after the War of 1812, however, served to bring the Court and the dominant political party more closely together than they had ever been before. The nationalistic decisions of Marshall and his colleagues now aroused respect and approval, particularly among the young Republicans, rather than condemnation.

The foundations of American constitutional law were carefully laid. Many important opinions were written by Marshall himself. They were ably reasoned and forcefully stated, and, since precedents were being made rather than followed, were unencum-

John Marshall of Virginia, fourth Chief Justice, although a "child of the wilderness" and severely limited in his educational opportunities, laid the principal foundations of American constitutional law. Fortunately, with British legal traditions out of favor, he was able to strike out along new and original lines. With a rare gift, according to one observer, for "putting his own ideas into the minds of others, unconsciously to them," he dominated the Court throughout the thirty-five years he headed it. The portrait is by Gilbert Stuart. At right is the Capitol at Washington in 1824, in which the Court was housed; aquatint after an original drawing of the architect, Benjamin Latrobe.

---

bered by tedious citations. They became, as Marshall intended, a guide to public opinion as well as to lawyers. As the importance of the Court came to be fully recognized, the best lawyers in the country were retained to appear before it. Such men as Luther Martin and William Pinkney of Maryland, William Wirt of Virginia, and Daniel Webster of Massachusetts contributed from their wisdom and research many of the arguments upon which the Court drew in formulating its opinions.

Marshall's decision in the case of *Marbury vs. Madison*, already noted, and the

Marshall's opinions utter failure of the Republicans to undo it, added greatly to the prestige of the Court. Its power to declare null and void an act of Congress out of harmony with the Constitution was repeatedly reasserted, and, in spite of the fact that the actual exercise of such authority was not again attempted in an important case until the Dred Scott decision, the doctrine of judicial review soon won general acceptance. A few years later in the case of the *United States vs. Judge Peters* (1809), the Court found opportunity to show that its power, in case of conflict, transcended that of a state legislature. It happened that a federal district court in Pennsylvania had awarded some prize money obtained from the sale of a British sloop, the *Active*, captured during the American Revolution, to a certain Gideon Olmstead and others. Locally this decision was extremely unpopular, and the legislature of Pennsylvania passed a law to prevent the payment that the federal judge had ordered. Finally the Attorney-General, when all other means had failed, asked the United States Supreme Court for a writ of *mandamus* directing Judge Peters to enforce his decision. Marshall not only issued the writ, but in so doing he also stated plainly the importance of the issue that had been raised. "If the legislatures of the several states," he said, "may at will annul the judgment of the courts of the United States, and destroy the rights acquired under those judgments, the Constitution becomes a solemn mockery, and the nation is deprived of the means of enforcing its laws by the instrumentality of its own tribunals." The Pennsylvania authorities did not yield gracefully, and made use of the state militia to defy the federal decision, but force was met with force, and when the state militia were confronted with a federal *posse comitatus* of two thousand men, plans for resistance were abandoned. Olmstead was allowed to collect his prize money, and the immunity of the federal courts from state interference was singularly vindicated.

The Supreme Court presently took occasion to demonstrate in two notable decisions,

Superiority of federal courts *Martin vs. Hunter's Lessee* (1816) and *Cohens vs. Virginia* (1821), that its power was also superior to that of the state courts whenever federal rights were involved. In Virginia, where these cases originated, the idea that a decision by the highest tribunal of the state could be reviewed and reversed by an outside authority was deeply resented. John Taylor of Caroline, in a series of pamphlets, *Construction Construed* (1820), *Tyranny Unmasked* (1822), and *New Views of the Constitution* (1823), came powerfully to the defense of the state courts, and public opinion in Virginia was with him. But his efforts, and all others like them, were unavailing. Litigants began to make use of federal rather than state courts whenever the former would accept jurisdiction, since the finality of a state decision was so frequently open to question. This influx of new business into the federal courts added greatly to their prestige, and particularly to that of the Supreme Court of the United States, which now in so large a number of instances became the court of last resort.

In the two Virginia decisions and in others also the Court was at pains to defend not only its own prerogatives as a court, but also the supremacy of the national government over the states. The classic expression of this point of view came in the case of *McCulloch vs. Maryland* (1819). The state of Maryland had attempted to tax out of existence the Baltimore branch of the Bank of the United States, and the bank had refused to pay the tax. The state courts naturally found against the bank and ordered it to pay, but an appeal was taken to the Supreme Court of the United States. Here was a clear-cut issue between state and nation, and Marshall made the most of it. He upheld the constitutionality of the act of Congress by which the bank was created, and in so doing gave the approval of the Court to Hamilton's doctrine of implied powers. "Let the end be legitimate, let it be within the scope of the Constitution, and all means which are appropriate, which are plainly adapted to that end, which are not prohibited, but consist with the letter and spirit of the Constitution, are constitutional." He held also that the state of Maryland had exceeded its authority in attempting to tax the notes of the Baltimore branch. "The power to tax," he reasoned, involved the "power to destroy," which, if conceded in this case, would leave the states free to undo such strictly constitutional laws of Congress as they disliked. In the course of his argument Marshall took occasion to speak out plainly against the theory that the Constitution emanated from the states, and that the government established by it was therefore merely a creature of the states. "The government of the Union," he maintained, "is emphatically, and truly, a government of the people. In form and in substance it emanates from them. Its powers are granted by them, and are to be exercised on them, and for their benefit. . . . If any one proposition could command the universal consent of mankind, we might expect it would be this — that the government of the Union, though limited in its powers, is supreme within its sphere of action. . . ." No better statement of the supremacy of the nation over the states has ever been made.

The Court made an honest attempt, nevertheless, to draw a line between the powers that were granted exclusively to **States' rights** the national government and those that were reserved wholly or in part to the states. In the case of *Gibbons vs. Ogden* (1824), it held that a law of the state of New York which granted to one company a monopoly upon the use of the waters of the state was unconstitutional, because it interfered with the complete control which Congress had been given over interstate commerce. Obviously, commerce among the states could not be construed as stopping at the borders of any one state. On the other hand, in the case of *Ogden vs. Saunders* (1827), the Court conceded that it was within the province of a state to pass a bankruptcy law, although Congress had similar authority. It is significant, however, that this decision drew from Marshall the only dissenting opinion that he ever wrote on a constitutional case. The Chief Justice was willing to protect the states in the exercise of their rightful powers, but he made no secret of his intention to exalt the power of the nation whenever he could find warrant for it in the Constitution.

The framers of the Constitution, fearful lest the states might lack either the power or the disposition to defend adequately the rights of private property, had consciously endeavored to make of the national government in this particular a great bulwark of strength. They specifically prohibited the states from passing any law "impairing the obligation of contracts," and in this clause Marshall found opportunity to range the Court as definitely as the framers of the Constitution could have wished on the side of property rights. In the case of *Fletcher vs. Peck* (1810), already noted, the Court had held that even so dishonest an act as that by which the state of Georgia had granted lands to the Yazoo companies could not be repealed without "impairing the obligation of contract." In the case of *Dartmouth College vs. Woodward* (1819), it maintained that a charter of incorporation was also a contract within the meaning of the Constitution. The state of New Hampshire had attempted to revise by law the old colonial charter under which Dartmouth College had been founded. The change was resented by the trustees of the college, who brought suit to retain their powers. When the case came to the United States Supreme Court, Daniel Webster, a Dartmouth alumnus, represented his *alma mater*, and won the Court not only to his reasoning, but even to the very wording of his argument. In vain did counsel for the state of New Hampshire plead that the framers of the Constitution had never intended the word "contract" to be so broadly construed. Marshall held that it was "necessary to go farther, and to say that, had this particular case been suggested, the language would have been so varied as to exclude it, or it would have been a special exception." Marshall's Dartmouth College decision was used later on to secure for business corporations an immunity from state control that he could hardly have foreseen. Thanks to the precedents he set, special privileges, obtained sometimes by wholesale corruption, were held inviolate long after public opinion demanded their limitation or repeal. In recent years, as a means of self-protection, states ordinarily reserve in all charters they grant the right to modify the terms of the charter at will.

Marshall's decisions, with their tremendous emphasis upon the power and importance of the national government, fitted in well with the temper of the American people in the years immediately following the War of 1812. The country was young and growing, conscious of its strength, confident of the future. Even the decisions with respect to property rights were not so out of harmony with the democratic trend of the times as they now seem. The opportunities for the acquisition of private property were not then limited to a few, but were the prerogative of the many. Marshall's decisions, while later used to build up a specially favored propertied class, were in their time meant to protect the small property-holder no less than the great.

Bibliography

Carman, *Social and Economic History of the United States*, II, covers admirably the rise of industrialism in the United States following the War of 1812. This subject receives careful attention also in all the standard textbooks on American economic history such as E. C. Kirkland, *A History of American Economic Life* (1939), and the similar works cited for Chapter 10, p. 183. Katherine Coman, *The Industrial History of the United States* (1920); and C. D. Wright, *The Industrial Evolution of the United States* (1902), were written from a somewhat closer perspective, but are still useful. Particular subjects of economic history are covered in Ralph C. H. Catterall, *The Second Bank of the United States* (1903); F. W. Taussig, *The Tariff History of the United States* (1888, 8th ed., 1931); Edward Stanwood, *American Tariff Controversies in the Nineteenth Century* (2 vols., 1903).

On the political side, Babcock, *Rise of American Nationality*, remains useful. J. W. Burgess, *The Middle Period* (1897), was an early successful effort to draw these years together into one synthesis. Allen Johnson, *Union and Democracy* (1915), while brief, is readable and perspicacious. The various lives of Madison cited for Chapter 16, p. 280, may be supplemented by W. P. Cresson, *James Monroe* (1946); and D. C. Gilman, *James Monroe* (1883). J. Q. Adams, *Parties in the United States* (1941), by the sixth President, discusses the rise and fall of the Federalist party. In this connection, see also D. R. Fox, *The Decline of Aristocracy in the Politics of New York* (1919).

On the all-important subject of transportation, A. B. Hulbert, *The Paths of Inland Commerce* (1920), is brief and to the point. T. B. Searight, *The Old Pike, A History of the National Road, with Incidents, Accidents and Anecdotes Thereon* (1894), is all that its title implies. The illuminating narratives of those who used the roads provide the sources for Jane L. Mesick, *The English Traveller in America, 1785–1835* (1922). Excerpts from travel literature are collected in *American Social History as Recorded by British Travellers*, edited by Allan Nevins (1931). *Early Western Travels*, 1748–1846, edited by R. G. Thwaites (32 vols., 1904–07), reprints nearly all of the important books of this nature for the period covered.

On the judicial contribution to nationalism, Beveridge, *Life of John Marshall*, III–IV, are of fundamental importance, but may be supplemented by such early biographies as: John P. Kennedy, *Memoirs of the Life of William Wirt* (2 vols., 1856); W. W. Story, *Life and Letters of Joseph Story* (2 vols., 1851); G. T. Curtis, *Life of Daniel Webster* (2 vols., 1870). A. C. McLaughlin, *A Constitutional History of the United States* (1935), covers the work of the Court under Marshall in great detail. E. T. Mudge, *The Social Philosophy of John Taylor of Caroline; A Study in Jeffersonian Democracy* (1939), makes Taylor's ideas easily available. J. T. Horton, *James Kent: A Study in Conservatism, 1763–1847* (1939), examines the reasoning of a prominent state jurist. See also references for Chapter 15, p. 268.

On social and intellectual history the literature is voluminous. V. L. Parrington, *The Romantic Revolution in America* (*Main Currents in American Thought*, II, 1927), covers the years 1800 to 1860. Merle Curti, *The Growth of American Thought* (1943), is an admirable one-volume synthesis of the whole period of American history. Van Wyck Brooks, *The World of Washington Irving* (1944), portrays "American arts, letters and life from 1800 to 1840." Dixon Wecter, *The Saga of American Society: A Record of Social Aspiration, 1607–1937* (1937), is an entertaining study of the American quest for social prestige. Other books of pertinence on special subjects include F. L. Mott, *A History of American Magazines* (3 vols., 1930–38); E. P. Cubberley, *Public Education in the United States* (1934); E. G. Dexter, *A History of Education in the United States* (1904); E. E. Slosson, *The American Spirit in Education* (1921); E. M. Coulter, *College Life in the Old South* (1928); W. W. Manross, *The Episcopal Church in the United States, 1800–1840* (1938); A. M. Schlesinger, *Learning How to Behave: A Historical Study of American Etiquette Books* (1946).

19

The Rise of the New West

Why people went West — Western banking — Panic of 1819 — Land Law of 1820 — Slavery and Sectionalism — The Missouri Compromise — Purchase of Florida — Long's Expedition — The northwestern fur trade — American isolation — Latin America — European doctrine of intervention — Canning's proposals to Rush — The Monroe Doctrine

"THE rise of the new west," according to Frederick Jackson Turner, "was the most significant fact in American history in the years immediately following the War of 1812."[1] Applied to a period in which so many important developments were taking place, this is a broad statement, yet only a few critics appear to have questioned it. Certainly the rapidity with which the frontier was advanced during these years set a new record. During the thirty-six years that elapsed between the signing of the Declaration of Independence and the outbreak of the War of 1812, only five new states were added to the original thirteen: Vermont, Kentucky, Tennessee, Ohio, and Louisiana. But during the half-dozen years following the War of 1812, six new states, all of them frontier and five of them definitely western, were added to the Union: Indiana (1816), Mississippi (1817), Illinois (1818), Alabama (1819), Maine (1820), and Missouri (1821).

The opening up of new western states was undoubtedly promoted by the war itself. **Why people went west** Both in the Northwest and in the Southwest the war made an end to the Indian menace, so that now, wholly without risk, new western lands could be acquired as rapidly as the advance of settlement demanded. Moreover, the war served greatly to advertise the West. Throughout the nation the western campaigns were followed with intense interest, an interest which often carried over from the fighting to the region in which the fighting was taking place. Soldiers who participated in the western campaigns observed, as frontier soldiers had always done, the fertility of the lands over which they fought, and when the war was over they frequently returned to the West as emigrants, taking many of their friends and neighbors with them. The business dislocations produced by the conflict also stimulated westward migration. In the Northeast unemployment crises developed, first as a result of the commercial restrictions that preceded and accompanied the war, and secondly, as a result of the British policy of "dumping" their surplus manufactured goods in America to compete with the expensive products of American infant industries. These crises materially increased the volume of migration to the West. So also did the destruction of the Bank of the United States in 1811, and the outbreaks of wildcat banking which recurred from that time until 1817 — developments which unsettled business generally, inflated the currency, and promoted a reckless speculation in western lands.

[1] F. J. Turner, *Rise of the New West* (1906), p. 67. Quoted by permission of Harper and Brothers, Publishers.

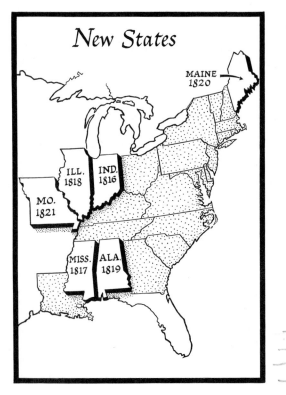

New States

MAINE
1820

ILL.
1818

IND.
1816

MO.
1821

MISS.
1817

ALA.
1819

Long-distance emigration to the West was made easier by the completion of the Cumberland Road, and by the in-
The river steamboats creasing success with which steamboats were able to conquer the "western waters." The first river steamboat to be launched in the West, the *New Orleans*, was the work of Nicholas J. Roosevelt, a Pittsburgh agent of the famous firm of Fulton and Livingston, which had sponsored in 1807 the epochal trip of the steam-driven *Clermont* up the Hudson from New York to Albany and back again in sixty-two hours. The *New Orleans* was launched at Pittsburgh in 1811, and next spring it reached the city after which it was named. It lacked the power to return against the current, but in 1816 the *Enterprise* steamed from New Orleans to Louisville in twenty-five days. By the end of the decade not less than sixty steamboats were in operation on the Mississippi and its tributaries. Most of the early boats harbored defects that brought them to untimely ends, but the reports of such disas-

ters did little to discourage the use of the boats, and much to make the rest of the nation better aware of the West.

To such unconscious advertising as the blowing up of steamboats, and the earthquake which shook the Mississippi Valley in 1811, were added the reports of the European travelers in America, whose books were read with much greater interest on this side of the Atlantic than on the other. Comparatively few Europeans responded to the call of opportunity in the American West which the travelers almost invariably made clear, for during the years 1812 to 1821 the annual immigration into the United States averaged only about eight thousand. But that many Americans were quickened to action by the tales of European travelers can hardly be questioned. Many others, no doubt, were set in motion by the reports of such explorers as Zebulon M. Pike, whose memoirs were published just before the War of 1812, and Lewis and Clark, whose *Journals* appeared just after it. These accounts, to be sure, described a farther West than that which was now open to settlement. But they bespoke a new field of activity for the trapper and the fur-trader, and they were probably more influential than seems reasonable in inducing undecided Americans to make up their minds to join the advance of the agricultural frontier.

The phenomenal growth of cotton culture in the years following the War of 1812 added a strong southern element to the **Southern** stream of westward migration. **migration** The lands of the new Southwest were in large part ideally fitted for the production of cotton, whereas the cotton lands of the Southeast soon showed signs of wearing out. Sometimes well-established planters sold their eastern lands in order to purchase more fertile acres in Mississippi, or Alabama, or Louisiana, and by transferring themselves and their slaves to the West they contributed directly to the westward movement. Frequently, however, eastern planters sought to enlarge their holdings in accordance as their yield per acre declined. In the latter event

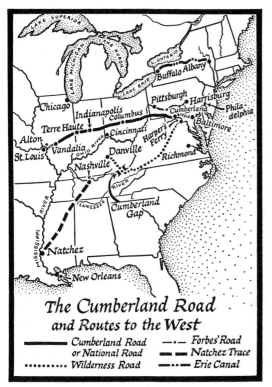

The Cumberland Road
and Routes to the West

———— Cumberland Road
      or National Road
—·— Forbes' Road
═ ═ Natchez Trace
·········· Wilderness Road
—··— Erie Canal

where slavery was legalized but for climatic reasons could never flourish.

This rapid assault upon the West was not without its unfortunate aspects. The great majority of those who went West, whether they came from the South or from the North, were men of very slender means. More often than otherwise they were compelled to go into debt for the cost of their migration, for the price of the land they settled on, and for the expense of making their new land over into productive farms. Western farmers had developed

Western banking

GROWTH OF THE WEST, 1810–1830

	1810	1820	1830
Kentucky....	406,511	564,317	687,917
Tennessee....	261,727	422,823	681,904
Ohio.........	230,760	581,434	937,903
Louisiana....	76,556	153,407	215,739
Indiana......	24,520	147,178	343,031
Illinois......	12,282	55,211	157,445
Mississippi....	{40,352}	75,448	136,621
Alabama......		127,901	157,445
Missouri......	20,845	66,586	140,455

they contributed indirectly to the westward movement by buying out neighboring planters and farmers, whose best recourse was to re-establish themselves somewhere in the West. Members of the non-slaveholding class often displayed great eagerness to escape from an environment dominated by the great planters. In such a society only the planters made money; the free laborer barely made a living. Moreover, wherever slaves were employed in large numbers it was natural to assume that manual labor was beneath the dignity of free men. Some of the poorer southern whites in their retreat from the slavery system went directly West, felled the timber, grubbed the stumps, tilled the fields until the cotton grower's frontier caught up with them, and then sold out to move farther West and repeat the process. Others, unwilling to live where slavery existed, crossed the Ohio River into the Northwest to swell the populations of such frontier states as Illinois and Indiana. Still others crossed the Mississippi River into Missouri,

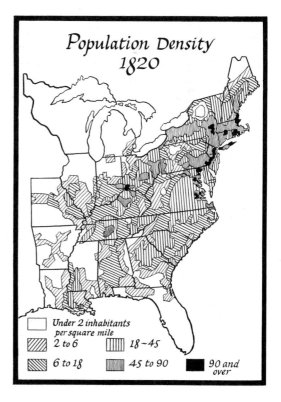

Population Density 1820

☐ Under 2 inhabitants
     per square mile
▨ 2 to 6   ▥ 18~45
▧ 6 to 18   ▦ 45 to 90   ■ 90 and over

The way west involved the use of both land and water routes. Turnpike companies, usually corporations that were privately owned but made possible by state aid, provided improved highway facilities through the more settled areas, but the emigrants were required to pay tolls at all-too-frequent intervals. Access to the western-flowing rivers, however, was free to all who cared to launch their boats and to risk the freakish behavior of the currents.

HIGHWAY TOLL GATE. Covered wagons going west on the Baltimore-Reistertown Road. Engraved from a drawing by F. B. Mayer.

OHIO RIVER FLATBOAT. Illustration from Croft, *Pioneers in the Settlement of America*, 1876.

the habit of borrowing a large part of the funds they needed from banks, a practice which was greatly facilitated by the multiplication of state banks after the year 1811, when the first Bank of the United States ceased to exist. Between 1811 and 1815 the number of state banks throughout the country rose from eighty-eight to two hundred and eight, and by 1820 to three hundred and seven. The new banks, particularly those in the West, operated under few legal restraints, and their officers were apt to be grossly ignorant of good banking practice. They tried to meet the heavy demand upon them for loans by issuing paper money, often far in excess of their resources. They lent for long terms on land and other securities for which a ready sale could not always be found. They failed to discriminate carefully among would-be borrowers, and rarely kept an adequate supply of cash on hand. With specie payments generally suspended during and after the War of 1812, their reckless inflation of the currency brought on for business in general an unhealthy "boom," and for the

West an orgy of land speculation. By 1815 the government was selling as much as a million acres of new land each year; by 1817, nearly two million acres; and by 1819, over five million acres. Rapid as was the migration of population into the West, the opening up of new lands was even more rapid, and the dangers in the situation were not difficult to see.

The second Bank of the United States, which began to operate in 1817, unfortunately sought at first to outdo **Panic** the state banks in the quest of **of 1819** speculative profits, and its Baltimore branch failed in 1818 because of mismanagement. Furthermore, the bank began an attack on the state banks, not so much because of the type of business they did as because of its desire to take their business away from them. To this end it used its power ruthlessly to force all competitors to an immediate resumption of specie payments. Notes of a given bank would be accumulated by the Bank of the United States and then suddenly presented for payment in specie.

STEAM FERRY. Crossing the Mississippi to St. Louis, 1832. Lithograph after a painting by L. Pomarede.

The western rivers played an enormously significant part in the settlement of the West. Steamboats, so modified as to make their use feasible on shallow rivers, solved many transportation problems of the West. Steam ferries helped the emigrant across the Mississippi, and river cities grew prosperous. With the means of communication continually improving, the much-fabled life of the western rivermen receded gradually into legend.

THE WESTERN STEAMBOAT. Scene on the Ohio. Illustration by Charles Bodmer, 1832, for Maximilian de Wied, *Travels in . . . North America*, 1843.

THE RIVERMEN. "The Jolly Flatboatmen," painted by George Caleb Bingham.

CINCINNATI, 1835. Front street, lined with river steamers. Watercolor by J. C. Wild.

Thereupon the bank so attacked would be compelled to call in its loans, while individuals who had borrowed from it would be forced in turn to raise what they owed by selling their property for whatever it would bring. With such a policy generally pursued, speculation was effectively, although perhaps unintentionally, arrested, and a general liquidation followed. Bankers, merchants, manufacturers, and farmers, as well as speculators, went down in the general collapse; indeed, a new management for the Bank of the United States barely saved that institution from the same disaster that overtook so many other businesses in the panic of 1819. To add to the country's distress the price of cotton fell from thirty-two cents a pound in 1818 to eighteen cents in 1820, and the prosperity of even the cotton planter seemed for the moment to have vanished. For more than two years the people of the United States were caught in the throes of a serious economic depression.

The political power of the new West was made manifest during these years by the success which attended its efforts to secure a change in the land policy of the United States. The Harrison Land Law of 1800 had permitted the purchaser of government land to pay only one fourth of the purchase price in cash, and the remainder in three annual installments. In practice the collection of these debts owing to the government had proved exceedingly difficult. With that over-optimism so characteristic of the frontier, land purchasers had used up all their resources in making their first payment, and had trusted to the future for the funds with which to meet later payments. Then followed the slow and expensive process of clearing the land, the inevitable accidents and disappointments of a new environment, and the discovery that markets were so hard to reach that profits, even when crops were good, were practically non-existent. If the pioneer farmer had borrowed the money to make his "start," he found difficulty in paying the high interest exacted, and as for paying the annual installments due on his land, he found that quite impossible. Year by year the arrears due the government for land mounted, and demands for relief began to be heard. Politicians, quick to realize that evictions would cost votes, readily responded by introducing bills into Congress postponing the date of payments due. Such measures became almost an annual affair; the first was passed in 1806, and by 1820 twelve more had been placed on the statute books. Meanwhile the West was more and more confirmed in its belief that money payments should not be required at all; that the land was valueless except for the labor put in upon it; and that in return for his labor the pioneer farmer was entitled to the land without price.

The panic of 1819 called serious attention to this situation. Overbuying had been particularly in evidence during **Land Law** the preceding years, and the **of 1820** customary relief bill was at hand. But Congress was now easily persuaded to put an end to the unworkable credit system. In 1820 a law was passed which reduced the size of the tract that an individual might buy to eighty acres, and fixed the price per acre at $1.25 in cash. Thus for one hundred dollars a man could become the owner of a farm. This was not quite the free gift of land to which the Westerners felt they were entitled, but it approximated that goal closely. To supplement the new land law a Relief Act was passed in 1821, according to the terms of which the man who had bought more land on credit than he could pay for was permitted to turn back to the government a part of his land in lieu of further payments. If, for example, he had purchased three hundred and twenty acres of land and had made only the first of the four payments due, he might keep whichever eighty acres he chose and return the other two hundred and forty to the government. If, however, he chose to keep all of his land, he was permitted one of two alternatives, either a cash payment with a discount of thirty-seven and one half per cent, or eight annual installments instead of four, with all

WILDERNESS CLEARING

FRONTIER FARM

The growing West is well illustrated by these four pictures drawn of the same site at intervals over a generation's time. The log cabin doubles in size, the cleared area grows; houses and barns of sawed lumber, surrounded by fences, replace the primitive cabins; finally a veritable mansion, flanked by bigger and better barns, looks out over broad treeless fields. Meantime, the growing cities assume an established orderliness reminiscent of the Eastern towns from which the Western settlers emigrated.

SETTLED COUNTRY

THE FOUR STAGES OF THE FRONTIER. Illustration from Turner, *Pioneer History of Western New York*, 1847.

PROSPEROUS ESTATE

CLEVELAND, OHIO. Southwestern corner of the Public Square. Painting by S. Heine, 1839.

interest remitted. The Land Law of 1820 and the Relief Act of 1821 gave much satisfaction to the people of the West, and facilitated materially the transition of that region from depression to normal conditions.

The rapid expansion of the West soon made the country acutely aware of an impending conflict, hitherto hardly suspected, between the North and the South. Fundamentally the issue upon which these sections came to divide was whether slavery in the United States was to be a temporary or a permanent institution, but for the moment the difference of opinion was restricted to the question of what limits, if any, should be set for the expansion of slavery in the territory west of the Mississippi River. Under French and Spanish rule slavery had been legal in the whole of Louisiana, a situation which the American occupation did not at first disturb. Most of the pioneers who crossed the Mississippi came from the southern states, and while the newcomers, particularly in the St. Louis area, were rarely slaveholders, they were accustomed to slavery and showed no disposition whatever to interfere with it. Once northerners fully realized, however, that the entire trans-Mississippi West was in danger of being appropriated for slavery, they were ready to call a halt.

Slavery and sectionalism

When Jefferson purchased Louisiana from France, he acquired for the United States not only a vast area of land but about fifteen thousand new citizens as well, most of whom were of French or Spanish descent. The chief center of Louisiana settlement was along the lower Mississippi in the vicinity of New Orleans, but a somewhat smaller population was located near the confluence of the Missouri and the Mississippi, with St. Louis as its principal city. Soon after the purchase had taken place, American settlers began to enter the lower Mississippi region in numbers, and by the time of the War of 1812 thousands of them each year were crossing also in the vicinity of St. Louis to thrust a firm wedge of settlement up the valley of the Missouri.

The size of the Louisiana Purchase insured that, once its settlement was actively begun, numerous subdivisions would have to be made. Accordingly, in 1804, Congress created the Territory of Orleans out of the region adjacent to New Orleans, and the District of Louisiana out of all the rest. In 1812 the Territory of Orleans became the state of Louisiana, but meantime the District of Louisiana had been repeatedly reorganized. Temporarily it was attached to Indiana Territory; in 1805 it became an entirely separate territory with a government of its own; in 1812 its name was changed to Missouri; and in 1819 it was materially reduced in size by the creation of the Territory of Arkansas. At this time the population of Missouri closely approximated the sixty thousand which, according to precedents set in the Old Northwest, made a territory eligible to statehood. Successive Missouri legislatures petitioned Congress on the subject, and in 1819 the House Committee on Territories reported favorably a bill enabling Missouri, with its boundaries still further restricted, to draw up a constitution and make ready for statehood.

Missouri Territory

It was at this juncture that Representative James Tallmadge of New York raised the question of setting limits to the expansion of slavery in the Louisiana Purchase. He proposed to amend the bill reported from committee by providing that the further introduction of slavery into Missouri should be forbidden, and that all children born of slave parents after the admission of the state should be free upon reaching the age of twenty-five years.

The Tallmadge amendment

Until the introduction of the Tallmadge amendment, the slavery question had played little part in national politics. The problem of how slaves should be counted when apportioning representatives in Congress or assessing direct taxes on the states had been satisfactorily settled in the federal convention by the three-fifth compromise. Also, an early Congress had exercised its constitutional authority to pass a fugitive slave act,

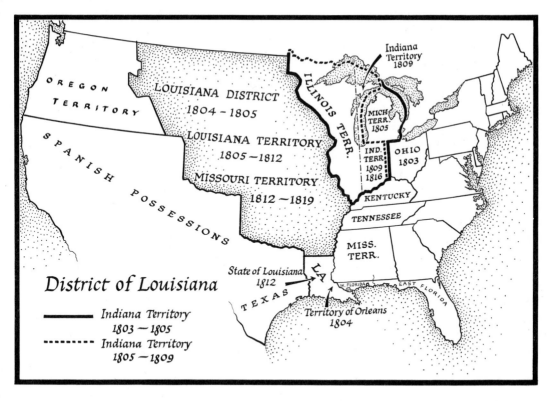

District of Louisiana

——————— Indiana Territory
              1803 — 1805
- - - - - - - - Indiana Territory
              1805 — 1809

and the administration of this measure had so far provoked little criticism. Moreover, slavery had long been regarded as a dying institution. The founders of the American nation had almost unanimously so considered it, Southerners no less than Northerners. Many of them were eager to speed the day when slavery should cease to exist throughout the whole country. Washington emancipated his slaves by his will; Alexander Hamilton and Benjamin Franklin were prominent in the work of emancipation societies; Thomas Jefferson's anti-slavery views were written into the Northwest Ordinance of 1787. Almost by common consent the slave trade was forbidden in 1808, the earliest date possible under the Constitution. Indeed, this act was mistakenly supposed by many contemporaries to insure the decline and ultimate disappearance of the institution of slavery itself.

Hostility to slavery during these early years of the republic was firmly grounded on the fact that the institution had ceased to be economically profitable. For this reason, even before the American Revolution, many of the colonies would have taken some anti-slavery action had not the British government been so insistent on protecting the profits of British merchants engaged in the slave trade. Jefferson's original draft of the Declaration of Independence actually listed British disallowance of colonial acts aimed at the slave trade as one of the chief grievances from which the colonies suffered, but out of deference to the pro-slavery views of South Carolina and Georgia this clause was suppressed. As soon as independence became a fact, one state after another took action against slavery, and after 1804, the date when New Jersey voted to do away with it, not a slave state remained north of the Mason and Dixon's line. The chief obstacle to abolition in the South, where the slaves were far more numerous than in the North, was the perplexity felt about what to do with the freed slaves, but southern emancipation societies were deeply concerned with this problem and were hopeful of finding a solution.

The discovery that cotton could be grown profitably by means of slave labor served to **Cotton and** revive the institution of slavery **slavery** just at the time when it had seemed destined to disappear. Cotton-growing was a simple process that the minds of illiterate blacks could comprehend, and yet it was a long-continued process that kept workers busy from early in the spring until late in the fall. Furthermore, cotton-growing furnished adequate employment for women and children as well as men, and it lent itself so easily to supervision that one overseer could be entrusted with as many as forty slaves. The profits that could be made from slave labor were revealed in the rapidly mounting price of slaves; whereas two hundred and fifty dollars would buy a good field hand in 1815, twenty years later an equally good man would cost no less than six hundred dollars. Free labor was correspondingly debased, for the small farmer who had few slaves or no slaves at all soon found that he could not raise cotton profitably in competition with the great planters. As already pointed out, it was in part this situation that led so many of the poorer whites to leave the Old South and move on into the West.

When the question of admitting Missouri came up, there were eleven free states and ten slave states, but the impending admission of Alabama would soon restore the balance of the sections that Americans had come to regard as normal. Of the original thirteen states, seven had abolished slavery and six had retained it, while of the new states four had been admitted without slavery, and five (counting Alabama) were slave. This would mean an equal number of United States senators from each section, a balance which the South, always sensitive on the slavery question, wished to maintain.

In the House of Representatives there was no such equality. In population the South had lagged far behind the North; in fact, the Northwest had been peopled in large

SLAVE STATES AND FREE STATES, 1820

ORIGINAL THIRTEEN

Slave	Free
Delaware	New Hampshire
Maryland	Massachusetts
Virginia	Rhode Island
North Carolina	Connecticut
South Carolina	New York
Georgia	New Jersey
	Pennsylvania

NEW STATES

Slave	Free
Kentucky (1792)	Vermont (1791)
Tennessee (1796)	Ohio (1803)
Louisiana (1812)	Indiana (1816)
Mississippi (1817)	Illinois (1818)
Alabama (1819)	

part by emigrants from the South. Whereas in 1790 the two sections had been almost equal in population (1,968,000 for the North to 1,925,000 for the South), by 1820 the North had forged far ahead (5,144,000 to 4,372,000). This difference was reflected in the number of representatives which the free and the slave states sent to the lower house of Congress, a difference made even more marked by the fact that five slaves counted only as three free men in making the apportionment of seats. Thus in 1790 there had been fifty-seven representatives from the states north of the Mason and Dixon line to forty-eight south of it, but by 1820 there were one hundred and twenty-three representatives from the free states to only eighty-nine from the slave states.

And now the Tallmadge amendment proposed further to curtail the weight of the slaveholding South in the Union. When, only a few years before, a government for the Louisiana Purchase was under consideration, probably little objection would have been raised to the adoption for the whole new region of just such a measure as Tallmadge now proposed, but by 1820 the cotton planters of the South were alive to the need of protecting slavery from any further assaults. Should Missouri and other states from the Louisiana Purchase be admitted as free states, then the balance of the sections in the Senate would be lost, and future Congresses might act, not only to exclude the slave-owner from the West in favor of the free farmer, but even to interfere with the now profitable institution of slavery where it had long existed. Actuated by these motives, southern members of Congress maintained that the Tallmadge amendment was unconstitutional because it put restrictions on a state as a condition of its admission to the Union; that it was contrary to the treaty of purchase from France, inasmuch as that document implied that the states created out of Louisiana should be admitted to the Union on an equal footing with the other states; that it was unfair, since it would open settlement in Missouri to all free state men while closing it to such Southerners as owned slaves; and that it was unwise, because the people of Missouri wanted to legalize slavery within the borders of the proposed state, and the question was one for them, and not for Congress to decide.

Not for years had there been so heated a debate in Congress, nor one that had so aroused the interest of the country at large. To the pro-slavery arguments those who favored the Tallmadge amendment retorted that the measure was no more unconstitutional than the Northwest Ordinance, under the terms of which slavery had been excluded from the Old Northwest; that the treaty with France required the United States to accord only the same treatment to the states west of the Mississippi River that was accorded to the states east of it, many of which had been compelled to enter the Union as free states; that slavery itself was a moral and political evil contrary to the spirit of the Declaration of Independence; that it had been tolerated in the Constitution only by necessity and ought now to be restricted. These arguments satisfied a small majority in the House, which on February 16, 1819, voted for the amendment, but eleven days later the Senate rejected it, 22 to 16, five northern senators voting on the side of the South.

In the next Congress, which met in December, 1819, the situation was somewhat altered when Maine, with the approval of Massachusetts, applied for admission to the Union as a free state. Sensing the possibilities of compromise, the Senate combined into one measure the bill to admit Maine as a free state and the bill to admit Missouri as a slave state, and listened with much interest to an amendment introduced by Senator J. B. Thomas of Illinois which proposed that for the rest of the Louisiana Purchase, exclusive of Missouri, the line of 36° 30′ should serve to divide free territory from slave territory. A solution of the vexatious problem seemed to have been found, and a joint committee of the two houses was appointed to work out the details. This committee recommended that the Senate abandon its plan for combining in one bill the fortunes of Maine and Missouri; that the House give up its attempt to exclude slavery from Missouri; and that both houses agree to the dividing line between slave and free territories advocated by Senator Thomas. Finally the requisite majorities were found, but the House vote to rescind its restrictions on slavery in Missouri was only 90 to 87. The President seriously questioned the constitutionality of the exclusion of slavery from an organized territory, but on this point his Cabinet unanimously reassured him, and he gave his approval (March 6, 1820). Strictly speaking, the "Missouri Compromise" has usually been regarded as that portion of the Missouri Enabling Act which provided "that in all territory ceded by France to the United States . . . which lies north of thirty-six degrees and thirty minutes north latitude, not included within the limits of the state [of Missouri], . . . slavery . . . shall be, and is hereby, forever prohibited."

The Missouri Compromise offered a natural solution to the problem of slavery expansion. East of the Mississippi River,

The Missouri Compromise

the Mason and Dixon's line and the Ohio River had long been accepted as the proper dividing line between slave and free states, and the idea of continuing such a line west of the Mississippi could readily be accepted. The Missourians, however, were somewhat irritated at the efforts which had been made in Congress to limit their control over slavery within the borders of their state. Hence, in spite of the fact that slavery seemed destined never to prosper so far north, they drew up a constitution which was as aggressively pro-slavery as possible. One of its provisions forbade the state legislature ever to pass a law emancipating slaves without the consent of their masters, and another forbade the entrance of free Negroes into the state on any pretext whatever. Obviously, since the latter clause was out of harmony with Article IV, Section 2, of the national Constitution, which required that the citizens of each state should "be entitled to all privileges and immunities of citizens of the several states," it could not be operative, but the very presence of such a statement in the proposed constitution caused the debate to break out in Congress anew. For a time it seemed that the admission of Missouri would have to be postponed, but through the efforts of Henry Clay a second Missouri Compromise was arranged. By its terms the state was admitted under the constitution it had written, but the Missouri legislature was required to pledge itself never to construe the offensive clause in such a way as to deny any citizen of any state the privileges which he enjoyed under the Constitution of the United States.

Once more the dispute died down, and for many years the two Missouri Compromises served to hold the slavery question in abeyance. Far-seeing men were deeply disturbed, however, at the acute difference of opinion between North and South that the discussions over the admission of Missouri had revealed. They knew full well that some day the nation must face squarely the problem it had just evaded, and that out of the ensuing conflict might come civil war or even the dissolution of the Union.

Meantime the advance of population in the Southwest had brought forcibly to the attention of the government the long-standing menace of Spanish impotence in Florida, and the great desirability of acquiring this territory from Spain for the use of American settlers. Spanish occupation had dwindled down to little more than the maintenance of garrisons at St. Marks, Pensacola, and St. Augustine, while the greater part of Florida was a kind of "no man's land" in which Indians, runaway Negroes, and ruffians of every description held sway. In July, 1816, a "Negro fort" on the Apalachicola, which had been established by a renegade Englishman known as Colonel Edward Nicolls, was blown up by some American troops, and shortly afterward war broke out between the United States and the unruly Seminole Indians. The task of restoring order was entrusted to General Andrew Jackson, who was authorized, in case he deemed it expedient, to pursue the Seminoles into their Florida retreats. Jackson, fully convinced that the administration had at last made up its mind to seize Florida, considered it his duty to prepare the way for the American occupation. By the spring of 1818 he had won an easy victory over the Indians, had taken St. Marks and Pensacola, had executed two white men whom he blamed in part for the Seminole outbreak, and had sent the Spanish governor and all his soldiers to Havana.

Jackson's exploits were immensely popular with the American people, but they embarrassed the administration, which in reality was working for the acquisition of Florida by peaceful means. Angry protests were registered at Washington by the Spanish government against the gross insults Jackson had offered Spanish sovereignty. Also, the two white men Jackson had put to death turned out to be British, and British complaints had to be reckoned with. The Secretary of War, John C. Calhoun, was in favor of censuring Jackson openly for ex-

The second Missouri Compromise

Florida

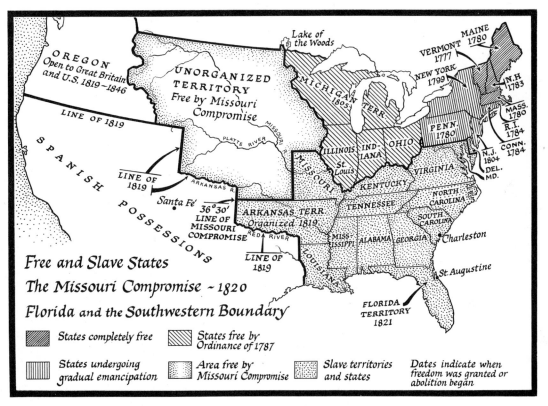

Free and Slave States
The Missouri Compromise - 1820
Florida and the Southwestern Boundary

States completely free	States free by Ordinance of 1787	
States undergoing gradual emancipation	Area free by Missouri Compromise	Slave territories and states — Dates indicate when freedom was granted or abolition began

ceeding his instructions, but the Secretary of State, John Quincy Adams, defended Jackson's course as incidental to his main duty of crushing the Seminoles. The discussions of the Cabinet were kept secret, and Jackson did not learn of Calhoun's hostile attitude for years, but resolutions of censure were introduced into both houses of Congress, and although not adopted by either, their proposal gave Jackson great offense. Adams finally straightened matters out with the foreign powers by offering to restore St. Marks and Pensacola to Spain whenever the Spanish government stood ready to occupy the posts with adequate garrisons, and by convincing the British government that the two subjects in question were unworthy of support.

Moreover, negotiations for the acquisition of Florida were soon pushed to a successful **Purchase of Florida** conclusion. Adams insisted that Spain must either police Florida adequately or turn the province over to the United States, and he drove home his point

so successfully that in 1819 the Spanish agreed to the cession on condition that claims of American citizens against Spain, amounting in all to five million dollars, should be met by the United States. On July 17, 1821, Jackson himself, acting now as the duly appointed governor of the territory of Florida, received for a second time the surrender of the Spanish province to the United States.

The same treaty that transferred Florida from Spain to the United States marked off also the boundary line between **The southwestern boundary** the United States and Spanish-American possessions west of the Mississippi River. Adams believed that the boundary line should have been placed at the Rio Grande, but the administration was eager to make sure of the Florida cession, and forced him to make an offer more favorable to Spain. As a result, all of what later became Texas was left in Spanish hands, and the western boundary of the United States was placed at the Sabine River, "up that

FORT UNION, 1833. At the junction of the Yellowstone and Missouri Rivers, Fort Union was one of the largest outposts of Astor's American Fur Company. Lithograph after a drawing made by Charles Bodmer for Maximilian de Wied, *Travels in . . . North America*, 1843.

The fur trade country lay well to the west of the farmers' frontier, in a vast wilderness pin-pointed with a few trading posts and forts. The furs were usually brought in to these forts by Indians who received in return the white man's much coveted goods. Official explorers, such as Long, treated with the Indians and paved the way for trade expansion.

INDIANS PORTAGING FURS. Painting by Cornelius Krieghof, 1838. By permission of the Governor and Committee of the Hudson's Bay Company.

INDIAN COUNCIL. Major Long meeting with the Pawnee Indians near Council Bluffs. Illustration from James, *Account of an Expedition . . . to the Rocky Mountains*, 1823.

river along the western bank to the thirty-second parallel, thence due north to the Red River, up that river to the one-hundredth meridian, thence due north to the Arkansas, up that river along its southern bank to its source, thence due north to the forty-second parallel, and then along that parallel to the 'South Sea.'" This article clearly gave over to the United States whatever claim Spain had previously held to the Oregon country, and it furnished for the first time since the purchase of Louisiana an authentic southwestern boundary.

Curiosity with respect to the unsettled portions of the trans-Mississippi West, to which American title was again confirmed, led to another ex- **Long's expedition** ploring expedition similar to the expeditions under Lewis and Clark, and Pike, that Jefferson had authorized earlier in the century.

Major Stephen H. Long, who had gained some experience in 1817 on a trip up the Mississippi in search of suitable sites for forts, was put in charge. For his use shipbuilders constructed at Pittsburgh a steamboat, the *Western Engineer*, which, in accordance with the latest designs, was a flat-bottomed stern-wheeler with a draught of only nineteen inches of water — too much, experience proved, for some portions of the Missouri. To impress the Indians the prow of the boat was shaped into a dragon's head through which steam might be exhausted. Major Long was instructed to explore the sources of the Platte River, after which he was to turn southward and follow along the mountains to the valleys of the Arkansas and the Red. The *Western Engineer* left St. Louis in June, 1819, and arrived at Council Bluffs, near the mouth of the Platte, the following September. Here the expedition halted until the next spring, when, reinforced by a detachment which had marched overland from St. Louis, it advanced by land along the north bank of the Platte. When the forks were reached, Long led his men to the south bank of the south fork, and followed it out to the mountains. Long's Peak was sighted and named, but the sources of the Platte were not found. The expedition skirted the mountains to the Arkansas and a small party pushed on to what was mistaken for the Red River, but was actually the Canadian, a branch of the Arkansas. The return trip was attended by great hardship, and Long's report was full of pessimism. Beyond the Missouri he believed the country he had visited wholly unfit for cultivation, and thus uninhabitable by a people dependent upon agriculture. Probably Long's report did more than any other single document to fix in the American mind the legend of the "Great American Desert."

Meantime the region north and west of the route taken by Long was being penetrated with singular completeness by fur-traders rather than by official explorers. In 1808 William Clark, Manuel Lisa, and others

The northwestern fur trade

joined in the formation of the Missouri Fur Company, through which they hoped to exploit the fur trade of the upper Missouri and its tributaries. After about a dozen years of bad management and inadequate capital the company collapsed, but the knowledge its agents had gained was not lost on its successor, the Rocky Mountain Fur Company, which in 1823 began a series of brilliant explorations by sending Jedediah S. Smith to the Green River Valley and the Great Salt Lake.

Other fur-trade activities of the period centered about the name of John Jacob Astor, a New York fur dealer who dreamed of bringing the whole American fur trade under one control, and even of connecting it up with the trade with China. His American Fur Company, organized a few years before the outbreak of the War of 1812, was designed to extend his interests in the Great Lakes region, while a subsidiary, the Pacific Fur Company, was to pioneer the way into the far Northwest. In 1810 Astor sent out two expeditions to the Oregon country, one by sea and the other by land. The seafarers arrived at the Columbia River early in 1811 and founded Astoria. Next year they were joined by the "Overlanders." Both parties encountered many harrowing experiences, but they would probably have succeeded in establishing the Pacific fur trade on a sound basis had the second war with England not intervened. This event frightened the Astorians into the sale of their outpost, including all the furs they had gathered, to the Canadian "Northwesters," who had also decided to enter the region. Astoria was rechristened Fort George, and under the powerful Hudson's Bay Company, which in 1821 took over the privileges of the Northwesters, it became the chief center of British influence in the Oregon country. In 1825, however, Fort George was abandoned in favor of the better-located Fort Vancouver.

Astor was never able to revive his Pacific interests, but after the War of 1812 was over he induced Congress to prohibit aliens from carrying on the fur trade within the

United States. This law enabled him to purchase at his own price British trading-posts south of the international border. By the year 1830 he had virtually monopolized the fur trade within the United States, although the Rocky Mountain Fur Company long kept its separate identity, and its agents, rather than Astor's, were chiefly responsible for the exploration of the West. According to Frederick Jackson Turner, they "revealed the sources of the Platte, the Green, the Yellowstone, and the Snake Rivers, and the characteristics of the Great Salt Lake region; they pioneered the way to South Pass, descended Green River by boat, carried cannon into the interior basin; showed the practicability of a wagon route through the Rockies, reached California from Salt Lake, crossed the Sierras and the deserts of Utah and Nevada, and became intimately acquainted with the activity of the British traders of the northwest coast." [1]

The rapid settlement of the Mississippi Valley and the penetration of the farther West emphasized the feeling of aloofness from Europe that had come to characterize the United States during the period of the War of 1812. The American people were now content to concern themselves chiefly with the development of their own country, and they viewed with increasing pride their native manufactures, their expanding agriculture, and particularly the westward advance of their population. They were aware, almost for the first time, of the physical basis of greatness with which, thanks to the size of the West, their nation was endowed; and, reasonably enough, they wished to exploit as their interests might direct the magnificent opportunities that confronted them. Thus absorbed in their own affairs, they were less concerned than formerly with what was going on in Europe, but they were willing to challenge instantly any tendency on the part of European nations to limit the natural course of development of the United States.

American isolation

[1] *Rise of the New West*, p. 122. By permission of Harper and Brothers, Publishers.

Out of this attitude of mind came a significant statement of American foreign policy, the Monroe Doctrine.

To understand this declaration of policy it is necessary to note briefly what had been happening in that portion of the New World which lay to the south of the United States. Here Spain had reared a mighty empire, with colonies more numerous and riches far greater than had fallen to the British in North America. The Spanish monopoly of South America and the southern parts of North America was not quite complete, for the Portuguese held Brazil, while the Dutch, French, and British each had small colonies bordering on the Caribbean and in the West Indies. But the leadership in colonial affairs, from the Sabine River to the southernmost tip of South America, lay definitely with Spain, whose colonial policy, like that of Great Britain, sought to benefit the mother country in every possible way, and sometimes worked to the serious detriment of the colonies. Particularly was the restriction of colonial trade to Spain a matter of great hardship, for Spain herself had little to exchange, and other European countries, notably Great Britain, not only coveted the raw produce of the Spanish colonies, but were prepared also to offer a wide variety of manufactured articles in return. Naturally the Spanish-Americans wished to establish direct trade relations with England, and they resented to the point of disobedience the roundabout system, required by law, of trading almost exclusively through Spain. In a general way the grievances of the Spanish colonies were duplicated in Brazil, with Portugal in the rôle of the offending mother country.

Latin America

When, during the years 1807 and 1808, Napoleon Bonaparte, seeking to tighten up his unfortunate continental system, overran with his armies both Portugal and Spain and converted them into satellite states of France, their American colonies, one after another, began to revolt. The situation in Brazil was unique, for the Portuguese ruler himself fled to

Revolutions

America and reigned for the time being as a monarch of the New World. Eventually he returned to Portugal (1822), and his eldest son became the emperor of an independent Brazil. In the Spanish colonies revolutionary *juntas* took control, at first in the name of Ferdinand VII, whom Napoleon had deprived of the Spanish throne and held captive in France, but later, when the collapse of Napoleon's empire enabled Ferdinand to regain his throne, as the founders of independent republics. Invariably the revolting colonies established close and mutually lucrative trade relations with England, and in the wars of liberation through which, under the leadership of Simon Bolivar and José de San Martin, the Spanish-American republics maintained their independence, they received much unofficial British encouragement, and from individual Englishmen, direct aid. By the year 1822 the Spanish Empire in the New World had dwindled down to little more than the Caribbean

islands of Cuba and Porto Rico, although Ferdinand VII consistently refused to acknowledge his defeat.

The successful revolt of the Spanish-American colonies was viewed with undisguised approval by the people **United** of the United States, who saw **States** in the actions of their neighbors **Recognition** to the south full vindication of the principles enunciated in their own Declaration of Independence. Moreover, the Spanish-American republics, while unable to combine into a single union, copied in other respects the form of government which had been developed in the United States. Duly flattered by this further evidence of esteem, public opinion in the United States called so strongly for recognition of the Spanish-American governments that John Quincy Adams, the Secretary of State, was able only with great difficulty to postpone such action until after his negotiations with Spain for the purchase of Florida were completed. By

March, 1822, with Florida safely in hand, President Monroe was able to announce that the time for recognition had come.

European nations also were interested in the course of events in Spanish America, **The Euro-** although with the exception of **pean system** Great Britain they were far from pleased with what had happened. Following the defeat of Napoleon, the great powers of Europe had been closely associated in an effort to preserve the peace and prevent the return of Napoleon to power. At first the Quadruple Alliance, composed of the nations which had overthrown Napoleon — Great Britain, Austria, Russia, and Prussia — sought to direct the course of European affairs, but in 1818 France, whose conservatism was by that time no longer open to question, was admitted to full fellowship in the counsels of the powers. The leading statesman of Europe during this period was Metternich, the prime minister of Austria, whose hostility to democracy in government was extreme. In his opinion democracy was a kind of communicable disease that must be stamped out, wherever found, if the peace of the world was to be maintained. A conference held at Aix-la-Chapelle in 1818 considered seriously the request made by Ferdinand VII of Spain for aid in the recovery of his revolting American colonies, but Great Britain was able to block any such action. A year later Ferdinand, whose devotion to absolutist principles equaled that of Metternich himself, was having trouble at home. A mutiny of some soldiers collected at Cadiz for service against the American revolutionists grew to the proportions of a revolt, and early in 1820 the King was compelled to accept the liberal constitution of 1812 which, on his restoration to the Spanish throne in 1814, he had promptly abrogated. The Spanish revolution served also to stimulate sympathetic outbursts in two Italian kingdoms, Naples and Piedmont, where, since the overthrow of Napoleon, reactionary monarchs had ruled with small regard for the welfare of their people.

Faced by this situation, Metternich persuaded Russia and Prussia to agree to the principle that revolution in any **The doc-** European state might properly **trine of** be suppressed by the great **intervention** powers. Great Britain strongly dissented, and France at first held aloof, but at Laibach in 1821 Austria was commissioned in the name of Austria, Russia, and Prussia (the three allies were sometimes called incorrectly the "Holy Alliance") to suppress the revolutions in Italy; and a year later at Verona France was authorized to do the same for Spain. British opinion of this high-handed policy was stated clearly by George Canning, the British foreign secretary, who sent word to Verona that "while England was no friend to revolution, she did emphatically insist on the right of nations to set up for themselves whatever form of government they thought best, and to be left free to manage their own affairs, so long as they left other nations to manage theirs." But Austrian troops in Italy, and French troops in Spain, stamped out the revolutions, and revived in each offending state the old system of autocracy.

While the doctrine of intervention stated at Laibach was confined specifically to European countries, the possibility of European intervention to suppress the revolts in Spanish America was a subject of much speculation. It was an open secret that Ferdinand VII would be deeply grateful for any such aid, and it was supposed that he might even be generous to any nation or nations from which aid might come. France at Verona actually proposed intervention in Spanish America as well as in Spain, and while the conference confined itself to the problem of suppressing European revolts, there was reasonable ground for fear that some future congress might not show such restraint. To the British government the possibility that the Spanish-American republics might be restored to Spain was alarming, for such a development would mean in all probability the revival of the old colonial trade-barriers and the consequent restriction of English trade. Moreover, if France should help subdue Spanish America, she could hardly be expected to do it for nothing. What pay could Ferdinand give other than an American colony for France? Could Great Britain stand idly by while France prepared to revive her empire in the New World?

All this diplomatic gossip in due time reached the United States, where it produced a reaction somewhat similar to that in Great Britain. Dare the United States permit Spain, presumably with the help of France, blot out the liberty of one American republic after another? Dare the United States risk the revival of a French empire in America, perhaps at her very doors? If it became the fashion for European absolutist governments to suppress democracy south of the United States, what guaranty was there that the same tactics would not presently be tried on the United States itself? Moreover, if European rivalries were once more let loose in America, could the United States hope to hold aloof from them? Would she not be drawn into the whirlpool of European diplomacy and war, and away from her strictly domestic program of internal development conditioned upon western expansion? President Monroe was keenly aware of the dangers of the situation, and long before the publication of the famous doctrine which bears his name he was seeking to forestall intervention by urging Spain to recognize the independence of her revolted colonies, and he repeatedly brought to the attention of the British government the desirability of joint Anglo-American action on the subject.

The similarity of the views held in Great Britain and the United States on the **Canning's proposals to Rush** Spanish-American question was not lost on the British foreign secretary, Canning. As the situation stood, his country was at odds with all the great powers of Europe, and in real need of an ally to stand with her against a policy which might jeopardize her valuable Spanish-American trade. Why not enlist the aid of the United States? Canning decided to try. In a "private and confidential" com-

munication to Richard Rush, the American minister to Great Britain, he suggested that it might be "expedient for ourselves, and beneficial for all the world" if the common principles held by the two nations "should be clearly settled and plainly avowed." Obviously Spain could not recover her lost colonies, hence recognition, which the United States had accorded but Great Britain had not, was only a matter of time and circumstance. As for Great Britain, she would not object to any amicable agreement reached by the mother country with her revolting colonies. On the other hand, while the British government did not itself aim at the possession of any Spanish-American territory, it could not look with indifference upon the transfer of such sovereignty to any other power. If these were also the sentiments of the United States, why should the two nations not unite in announcing their stand to the world?

Rush promptly referred this communication to President Monroe, who recognized its importance and gave it im- **The Monroe** mediate attention. At the out- **Doctrine** set he felt inclined to accept the British proposal, although the departure involved from the policy set by Washington and Jefferson against entangling the United States in European affairs gave him much concern. On this matter, however, the counsel he received from the two Republican ex-Presidents, Jefferson and Madison, tended to reassure him. Jefferson, who regarded the question raised as the most momentous since independence, wrote to Monroe in part as follows:

Our first and fundamental maxim should be, never to entangle ourselves in the broils of Europe. Our second, never to suffer Europe to intermeddle with cis-Atlantic affairs. America, North and South, has a set of interests distinct from those of Europe, and peculiarly her own. She should therefore have a system of her own, separate and apart from that of Europe. While the last is laboring to become the domicil of despotism, our endeavor should surely be, to make our hemisphere that of freedom. One nation, most of all, could disturb us in this pursuit; she now offers to lead, aid, and accompany us in it. By acceding to her proposition, we detach her from the bands, bring her mighty weight into the scale of free government, and emancipate a continent at one stroke, which otherwise might linger long in doubt and difficulty. Great Britain is the nation which can do us the most harm of any one, or all on earth; and with her on our side we need not fear the whole world.

Madison agreed with Jefferson, but was ready to go even further. He would protest also against French invasion of Spain, and against any attempt to interfere with the progress toward independence of the Greeks, who had lately undertaken a revolt against Turkey.

In his Cabinet Monroe found a contrary opinion. John Quincy Adams, his Secretary **Opposition** of State, objected strenuously **of Adams** to the proposed joint declaration with Great Britain, and insisted instead that the United States issue a wholly independent statement. He had no desire to see the United States appear merely as a "cock-boat in the wake of a British man-of-war"; he had caught, perhaps from Henry Clay, the vision of a Pan-American system in which the United States would play a leading part; he was by no means certain that the United States should bind itself not to add more American territory to its boundaries; and he knew that Great Britain would do as much to prevent European intervention in Spanish America without an alliance with the United States as with it. "The ground that I wish to take," he said, "is that of earnest remonstrance against the interference of the European powers by force with South America, but to disclaim all interference on our part with Europe; to make an American cause and adhere inflexibly to that."

Monroe at length came around to the Adams point of view. In reaching this decision he was perhaps influenced by the fact that, although several months had elapsed, he had received no further word from Canning on the subject. Had Canning's ardor cooled? As a matter of fact, although

Monroe could probably have had no definite information to this effect, Canning's interest in American co-operation had declined. He had hoped originally that Rush might join him, without referring the matter to President Monroe, in an immediate declaration, and when Rush refused had turned to other expedients. From the French ambassador in England Canning now sought and obtained assurance that the French government had no idea of using force against the revolting Spanish colonies, and this statement, privately communicated to the other European powers, completely eased his mind on the subject.

It must have occasioned the British foreign secretary, and many another European statesman, much surprise when the message which President Monroe sent Congress in December, 1823, reached Europe. Two widely separated statements in that document set forth clearly the position of the United States on the subject of European intervention in America. The first was aimed specifically at Russia, whose aggressions in the Pacific Northwest had already drawn protests from Secretary Adams, and asserted "as a principle in which the rights and interests of the United States are involved, that the American continents, by the free and independent condition which they have assumed and maintain, are henceforth not to be considered subjects for future colonization by any European powers." The second statement, much more elaborate, pointed out that the United States had taken no part in the wars of European powers relating to themselves, and did not intend to do so. But in matters relating to "this hemisphere we are of necessity more immediately connected."

The political system of the allied powers is essentially different . . . from that of America. This difference proceeds from that which exists in their respective Governments; and to the defense of our own, which has been achieved by the loss of so much blood and treasure, and matured by the wisdom of their most enlightened citizens, and under which we have enjoyed unexampled felicity, this whole nation is devoted. We owe it, therefore, to candor and to the amicable relations existing between the United States and those powers to declare that we should consider any attempt on their part to extend their system to any portion of this hemisphere as dangerous to our peace and safety. With the existing colonies or dependencies of any European power we have not interfered and shall not interfere. But with the Governments who have declared their independence and maintained it, and whose independence we have, on great consideration and on just principles, acknowledged, we could not view any interposition for the purpose of oppressing them, or controlling in any other manner their destiny, by any European power in any other light than as the manifestation of an unfriendly disposition toward the United States.

Canning's subsequent claim to authorship of the Monroe Doctrine — "I called the New World into existence to redress the balance of the Old" — was somewhat absurd, in view of his failure to obtain the joint declaration he had sought and in view of his private negotiations with France. Probably no country was more annoyed at the Monroe Doctrine than Great Britain, whose own claim to pre-eminence in American affairs it summarily denied. Furthermore, Monroe's contention that Europe had one system of government and America another was somewhat far-fetched in view of the fact that constitutional governments existed in several European countries, notably Great Britain, while Brazil, the largest country in South America, was still a monarchy.

The Monroe Doctrine had no immediate consequences. Even before it was announced Russia had already called a halt in the Northwest and France had definitely given up all thought of intervention in Spanish America. Nor were the ambitions of Adams and Clay for the United States to assume hegemony in a great Pan-American system soon to be realized. But the statement did register once more the emphatic determination of the United States to maintain the doctrine of isolation. What the United States most needed, with its industries developing, its frontiers expanding, and its democratic government serving well the purpose for which it had been formed, was to be let alone. European interference anywhere on the western continent might endanger this cherished position and divert the new nation from its chosen course. Therefore Europe for the future must keep out of American affairs. It is obvious, of course, that in 1823, and for many years thereafter, the United States could not possibly have enforced against serious European attack the doctrine it had declared. But, thanks to the similarity of British and American interests, the British navy could be trusted to do what the United States could not do, and ultimately the United States would grow up to the doctrine she had declared. It is quite possible, also, that Monroe did not assume that he had said the last word on the subject, and even looked forward to open collaboration between the two English-speaking nations on American affairs.

Bibliography

F. J. Turner, *Rise of the New West* (1906), covers the decade 1819 to 1829, not only with reference to the West but also with reference to the various other sections, and the nation as a whole. This volume takes high rank in the literature of American history. All of the general histories, McMaster, IV–V, Channing, V, and Schouler, III, are detailed at this point, particularly with reference to the sectional split over slavery. On the Missouri Compromise, F. C. Shoemaker, *Missouri's Struggle for Statehood, 1804–1821* (1916), is an excellent special study. Useful background may also be found in Mary S. Locke, *Anti-Slavery in America, 1619–1808* (1901); Alice D. Adams, *The Neglected Period of Anti-Slavery in America, 1808–1831* (1908); W. E. B. DuBois, *The Sup-*

pression of the African Slave Trade to the United States of America, 1638–1870 (1896).

On transportation, Seymour Dunbar, *A History of Travel in America* (4 vols., 1915), is valuable particularly because of its excellent illustrations. L. C. Hunter, *Steamboats on the Western Rivers: An Economic and Technological History* (1949), follows this theme with abundant detail. L. D. Baldwin, *The Keelboat Age on Western Waters* (1941), deals effectively with the pre-steamboat age. G. M. Capers, *The Biography of a River Town; Memphis: Its Heroic Age* (1939), is a good case study. J. T. Flexner, *Steamboats Come True: American Inventors in Action* (1944), records the early steamboating experiments.

On economic history, besides the general works cited for Chapter 10, p. 183, W. B. Smith and A. H. Cole, *Fluctuations in American Business, 1790–1860* (1935), is particularly useful. Other books of significance for these years are Harry E. Miller, *Banking Theories in the United States before 1860* (1927); and D. R. Dewey, *State Banking before the Civil War* (1910). Land legislation is covered by the books cited for Chapter 10, p. 182.

On the Far West, Cardinal Goodwin, *The Trans-Mississippi West, 1803–1853* (1922), furnishes a convenient summary of explorations and expansion. L. R. Hafen and C. C. Rister, *Western America* (1941), is similarly useful. Constance Lindsay Skinner, *Adventurers of Oregon* (1920), is excitingly told. Everett Dick, *Vanguards of the Frontier* (1941), is another tale of adventure and adventurers.

On the diplomacy of expansion, see for Florida: H. B. Fuller, *The Purchase of Florida* (1906); S. W. Martin, *Florida during the Territorial Days* (1944); Marquis James, *Andrew Jackson: The Border Captain* (1933). On the Latin-American situation: F. L. Paxson, *The Independence of the South American Republics* (1903); A. P. Whitaker, *The United States and the Independence of Latin America, 1800–1830* (1941). On the European background of the Monroe Doctrine: W. P. Cresson, *The Holy Alliance* (1922). On the Monroe Doctrine itself three books by Dexter Perkins, *The Monroe Doctrine, 1823–1826* (1927); *The Monroe Doctrine, 1826–1867* (1933); and *Hands Off: A History of the Monroe Doctrine* (1941), best summarize recent historical scholarship. Brief, but excellent, is J. H. Latané, *From Isolation to Leadership* (1918, new ed., 1925). See also J. H. Powell, *Richard Rush: Republican Diplomat, 1780–1859* (1942); and S. F. Bemis, *John Quincy Adams and the Foundations of American Foreign Policy* (1949).

20

Sectional Cross-Currents

Sectionalism in the United States — Sectional candidates for the Presidency in 1824 — Clay's American System — Election of Adams — A new party alignment — The Panama Congress — Indian affairs — The "Tariff of Abominations" — Internal improvements — The Erie Canal — The Pennsylvania System — The Chesapeake and Ohio Canal — The Canal Age

IN SPITE of the strongly nationalistic spirit that still pervaded the United States in the **Sectionalism** eighteen-twenties, the beginning of a three-cornered sectional struggle between Northeast, South, and West was plainly in evidence. Boundary lines between these three sections could not always be clearly drawn, but their points of view, determined respectively by the needs of the northern manufacturer, the southern cotton-planter, and the western free farmer, were fairly obvious. Intra-sectional conflicts, such as the struggle for mastery in New England between the commercial and the manufacturing classes, sometimes blurred the picture, but usually not for long. National politics became, in the main, a resultant of certain definite sectional forces acting upon it. Often, as in the case of the Monroe Doctrine, a community of interests made easy the task of charting the nation's course. But bitter strife between the sections also developed, and compromise solutions had to be found, such, for example, as those that made possible the admission of Missouri.

The Federalist Party, which in its day had ministered primarily to the needs of the commercial classes, was by the third decade of the century fast becoming only a memory. Manufacture now mattered more to the Northeast than commerce, and Republicans, not Federalists, had enacted the protective tariff law of 1816. In 1820 the Federalists made no effort to oppose the re-election of President Monroe, who won every vote but one in the electoral college; by 1824 the Federalist Party had virtually ceased to exist. The complete triumph of Republicans during these years led contemporaries to characterize the period as an "era of good feelings," but the phrase is misleading. Within the dominant party factionalism was rife, and by the time of the election of 1824 no less than four candidates, each claiming to be a good Republican, contested for the Presidency. Two of these candidates represented the rising West, one came from the Northeast, and one from the South.

Mention has already been made of the dissatisfaction generally felt with the system of nominating presidential can- **Sectional** didates by means of a congres- **candidates** sional caucus. In 1820 such a caucus was called, but fewer than fifty members of Congress attended, and they voted not to make nominations. Monroe, therefore, was re-elected without ever having been renominated. By 1822, however, the question of the "succession" was in hot debate, and the problem of how to nominate a candidate became acute. The President was known to favor the candidacy of William H. Crawford of Georgia, his Secretary of the Treasury, whose claim to preferment rested largely on the fact that he, more nearly than any other candidate, represented the old plantation aristocracy which, through the "Virginia dynasty," had controlled the Presidency every term but one since the Constitution

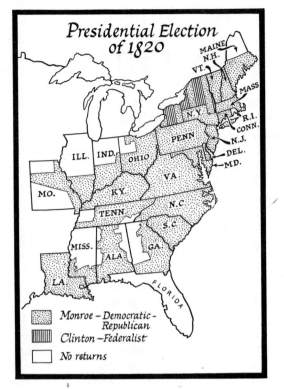

Presidential Election of 1820

Monroe – Democratic - Republican
Clinton – Federalist
No returns

went into effect. But there were other candidates. John Quincy Adams of Massachusetts, the Secretary of State, seemed to conservative New-Englanders the logical man to succeed Monroe; John C. Calhoun of South Carolina, the Secretary of War, was openly ambitious; Henry Clay of Kentucky, several times Speaker of the House, was actively interested; and Andrew Jackson of Tennessee, the hero of New Orleans and the conqueror of Florida, commanded loyal and enthusiastic support. Besides these were many minor candidates, all of whom dropped out of the race. Calhoun, also, decided ultimately to bide his time, and in return for his withdrawal was very generally acclaimed as the proper person for the Vice-Presidency. But Crawford, Adams, Clay, and Jackson remained in the race to the end. Not often has the American electorate had the privilege of choosing a President from such a galaxy of stars.

With the congressional caucus discredited, state legislatures very generally usurped the privilege of making presidential nominations.

Crawford's name was presented by the legislature of Virginia; Adams was nominated by the legislatures of Massachusetts and other New England states; Clay was first brought forward by the Kentucky legislature, then endorsed by many others; Jackson was supported by the lower house of the Tennessee legislature, and by mass conventions in various parts of the country. Crawford's candidacy won the approval of the customary congressional caucus, but on this occasion only sixty-nine members attended the meeting, and probably the support of the caucus did its nominee more harm than good. Prophetic of the future were some resolutions passed by a meeting of Republicans in Lancaster County, Pennsylvania, which asserted that "the best and most unexceptionable method" of nominating a candidate would be by "a convention of delegates from all the States of the Union," a system, however, that was admittedly "impracticable, from the immense extent of the country, and from the great expense . . ."

William H. Crawford (1772–1834) was a Virginian by birth and a lawyer by profession. He had long been a resident of Georgia, where as a member of the state legislature he had stoutly defended the interests of the great planters against the back-country farmers, and had won for himself a seat in the United States Senate. In 1813 he was appointed by President Madison to be minister to France, a post which he gave up two years later to become Secretary of the Treasury. By discreet use of the patronage that went with his office he won a large following in Congress, and almost obtained the presidential nomination over Monroe in 1816. Like Albert Gallatin, Crawford stayed on at the treasury long after the President who originally appointed him had retired, but his political strength, unlike that of Gallatin, grew with his years of service. He was a man of his own mind, and had not hesitated to criticize party measures of which he did not approve; indeed, he was not always on the best of terms with Monroe. In his earlier

William H. Crawford

career a strong nationalist, by the eighteen-twenties he seems to have felt that the pendulum had swung too far in the direction of nationalism, and must now swing back toward strict construction and states' rights. An able politician, and assured of the President's support, Crawford was far out in the lead until September, 1823, when he suffered what was probably a stroke of paralysis. His partial recovery permitted his candidacy to continue, but much of the early advantage he had gained was lost.

John Quincy Adams (1767–1848) was the son of the second President, and in many

John Quincy Adams respects an even abler man. In addition to his rare inheritance, no less from his mother, Abigail Adams, than from his father, he had received a rigorous training for public life. At eleven he was taken by his father to Europe, where under private tutors and in a variety of countries his education was carried on assiduously. He learned to speak French and Dutch fluently, and was once reprimanded by his father for writing better in a foreign language than in his own. At fourteen he went to Russia as private secretary to the American envoy, and at fifteen he returned alone from St. Petersburg to The Hague, a six month's winter journey by way of the Scandinavian countries. At twenty he was graduated from Harvard, and soon after began the practice of law; at twenty-seven he began a diplomatic career that took him on important missions to Portugal, Prussia, England, Holland, Russia, and Sweden. During all these years he read voluminously and wrote extensively. He had been trained by his father to keep a diary, and the information that he thus preserved from his early youth to the time of his death is of great value, not only because of the light it throws upon his character, but also because of his penetrating observations on public events. Indeed, this diary and other writings by members of the Adams family have been relied upon so extensively by historians that, according to some critics, American history needs to be "de-Adamsized."

When Jefferson became President, Adams returned to the United States, and after a short term in the Massachusetts state legislature was elected in 1803 to the United States Senate. This seat he resigned in 1808 because his conscience bade him approve the embargo, while the legislature of Massachusetts opposed it; and thereafter he became a member of the Republican Party, to which his diplomatic experience proved a valuable asset. In 1809 he was sent as minister to Russia; in 1814 he was chosen to be a member of the peace commission that drew up the treaty of Ghent; and when the war ended he was selected to represent the United States at London. When he took office as Monroe's Secretary of State, he was doubtless better fitted for that post by training and experience than any other American. He was almost painfully eager to crown his career by becoming President, but his demeanor was cold and forbidding, and the number of friends upon whom he could count was few. Moreover, he was belligerently incorruptible in all his dealings, and yet inclined to ascribe the worst motives to all who disagreed with him. New England accepted him as its candidate for the Presidency in 1824 with reluctance, but the obvious superiority of the man would have made any other candidacy from that part of the country seem ridiculous.

Henry Clay (1777–1852) never attained the Presidency, but his name is far better known than that of many of the men who did. He was of no **Henry Clay** such distinguished lineage as Adams, for his father was only a Baptist preacher of back-country Virginia; and his education was as limited as Adams's was extensive. But Clay had a warm, magnetic personality, and won friends as easily as Adams lost them. He made the most of his meager opportunities, read law under a distinguished jurist, Chancellor Wythe, and when he was twenty years old opened a law office in Lexington, Kentucky. His legal career was successful from the start, not because he was learned in the law, but because of a native shrewdness that proved to be of greater value in the frontier courts than any amount of book learning. Within a few years he was a member of the state legislature, then for a short time, beginning even before he had attained the constitutional age of thirty years, of the United States Senate. On the eve of the War of 1812 he entered the House, where he was repeatedly chosen Speaker. He served with Adams on the commission that made peace with Great Britain after the war, and acquired from the experience an acquaintance with Europe that he sorely needed. Likeable, and desiring to be liked, Clay could usually be counted on to reflect his surroundings. In his youth he was a man of the West, tempestuous and aggressive — a leading "War Hawk" when the West wanted war. As he grew older, contacts with the East and with Europe had a sobering influence upon him, and a discreet moderation took the place of his former recklessness. He saw intuitively the need of a political program that would satisfy all sections — a national program — and early set himself the task of finding one. He saw, too, the necessity of compromise when conflicting interests were involved, and his willingness to strike bargains that would satisfy all concerned won him the title, not undeservedly, of the "Great Compromiser." His persuasive oratory, once it was enlisted in any cause, was a potent influence in shaping public opinion. Few American statesmen have ever maintained, through victory and defeat, a larger or more devoted personal following.

Andrew Jackson (1767–1845), like Henry Clay, was a product of the upland South, a **Andrew Jackson** South Carolinian[1] whose parents had emigrated from the north of Ireland to the American frontier. In spite of his extreme youth he saw service during the later years of the American Revolution, and out of his wartime experiences emerged with a bitter hatred of England. With the faintest of qualifications he began

[1] Both North and South Carolina claim (or disclaim, as the case may be) to have furnished the birthplace of Andrew Jackson.

the practice of law in western North Carolina when he was only twenty years of age, but within a year he followed the course of migration into Tennessee and settled at Nashville. Here he was soon public prosecutor, then in turn a member of the national House of Representatives and of the United States Senate, then a judge of the Tennessee Supreme Court. But it was as a warrior that he won his chief renown. His successful campaign against the Creeks in 1814, his triumph next year over Pakenham at New Orleans, and his subsequent exploits against the Seminoles and the Spanish in Florida made him the outstanding military hero of the time. As a fitting reward he was chosen in 1823 to represent the state of Tennessee once more in the United States Senate. The pride of the West at having produced so great a man was unbounded, particularly when the great man had attained his eminence because he possessed in marked degree those qualities that the West most highly esteemed. Jackson was a veritable personification of the western democratic ideal which held that common men were as good as aristocrats and deserved to play quite as important a part in the affairs of the nation. He exhibited, too, the contentious individualism of the frontier, its unreasoning hatreds, its rashness, and its resourcefulness. He was an ardent patriot, and identified with patriotism the Westerner's desire to obtain expanded boundaries for the nation and unlimited opportunities for its citizens. He was not at first politically ambitious, but designing politicians saw the powerful appeal his candidacy would make to the masses, and pushed him into the race.

While the election of 1824 turned to a great extent upon the personalities of the candidates, it showed also the interplay of sectional forces. John Quincy Adams, the only candidate from a non-slaveholding state, and unmistakably associated with the Northeast, developed his greatest strength in New England and New York; Crawford, but for his physical condition, would probably have been a universal favorite in the older states of the South; Jackson and Clay divided the West. Many of Crawford's adherents turned reluctantly to Jackson, who after all was a Southerner and a slaveholder as well as a Westerner; and the hero of New Orleans was aided also by the fact that he alone among the candidates was a newcomer to national politics. The government of the United States ever since its inception had been in the hands of a relatively small group of aristocrats, and Jackson's managers argued cleverly that the time had come for the introduction of new blood. This appeal won a hearty response from Westerners imbued with frontier ideals of democracy, from Easterners of the farmer and laborer classes who were just beginning to be conscious of their political power, and from back-country Southerners who had long struggled within their respective states against the domination of an eastern planter aristocracy. To a considerable degree Jackson thus became the candidate of the masses, while his opponents were the candidates of the classes.

All of the candidates professed to be members of the same political party, hence opposing political principles were hardly in order. The views of Henry Clay, however, were widely known, and they constituted an

Clay's American system

intelligible program which in a later age would have been embodied in the customary resolutions. Clay, more than any other candidate, was conscious of the divergent sectional interests of the nation, and was seeking eagerly for a solution that would benefit all sections equally. His "American system" — a "planned economy," a century ahead of "economic planning" — was the result. The War of 1812 had revealed the risk involved in the too great dependence of the United States upon the outside world, either for markets or for manufactures. Clay hoped, therefore, to build up home industries by a generous tariff policy, which would make the United States to a greater extent than ever before independent of the rest of the world, in time of peace no less than in time of war. Not only would the nation be encouraged to manufacture many articles that it had previously been forced to buy abroad, but the existence of a larger number of factory operatives would tend to insure also a more satisfactory home market for the produce of the American farm. The industrial East could sell to the agricultural West and South; the agricultural West and South could sell to the industrial East. Nor need lack of transportation facilities constitute a drawback. With

The "American System." A contemporary illustration of one of Clay's frequent arguments in favor of higher tariffs to protect American industry, showing American shelves stocked with foreign wares.

the heavy revenues that a tariff could be made to produce, the government would have the means to aid all worthy works of internal improvement and to insure that a complete network of roads and canals would soon cover the nation. To carry through such a program much remained to be done. Those who favored increased tariffs, after a failure in 1820, won a modest victory in 1824, but Monroe's constitutional scruples still effectively blocked the efforts of Clay and his friends to turn any great part of the national revenue toward internal improvements.

The fact that Clay had a definite program forced the other candidates to declare themselves on the issues he raised. **Campaign of 1824** Crawford sought to appear as the only true heir to the Jeffersonian tradition, and won the approval of Jefferson himself, who regarded some of the other candidates as little better than Federalists. But Crawford dared not oppose too frankly a policy of tariff protection, for he hoped to win many votes in Pennsylvania and the other middle states where protection had its strongest appeal. On internal improvements he trimmed also, and like Monroe called for a constitutional amendment before the national government should proceed further along that line. Adams favored the tariff duties of 1824, although in some items he thought they might reasonably be lowered, and agreed with Clay heartily as to the desirability of internal improvements at national expense. Jackson as a member of the Senate had voted for the Tariff of 1824 and for internal improvements, but his managers sought to keep all such controversial matters in the background, and featured rather his opposition to the caucus system and the right of the common people to a larger share in governmental affairs.

The sectional character of the American nation was clearly apparent in the election results. Adams won the electoral votes of New England and most of the votes of New York. Crawford led only in Virginia and Georgia. Clay carried Kentucky, Ohio, and Missouri. Jackson alone had a large enough following to win electoral votes outside the section which he directly represented. He divided the West with Clay, obtained every electoral vote in North Carolina, South Carolina, Pennsylvania, and New Jersey, won seven out of the eleven votes of Maryland, and even received a single vote in New York. In the South he was helped materially by the support he received from Calhoun, who thought he had an understanding with Jackson that after four years the General would stand aside and allow Calhoun to capture the Presidency. The final vote stood: Jackson 99, Adams 84, Crawford 41, Clay 37. Statistics on the popular vote cast are misleading, for in some states the legislature still chose electors, while in only a few states were electoral tickets for every candidate in the field. Calhoun received more than two thirds of the electoral votes for Vice-President.

The failure of the electoral college to choose a President threw the election into the House of Representatives. **Election of Adams** Clay was now out of the race, for the Constitution restricted the choice of the House to the three highest on the list, but if he could not be President he could at least decide which one of his rivals should have the honor. His choice fell naturally upon Adams, who approved more fully than any of the others Clay's American system, and with the Speaker's influence powerfully at work in his behalf Adams won an easy victory. In addition to the votes of New England and New York he received the support of five western states and Maryland, 13 in all, as against Jackson's 7 and Crawford's 4.

Clay worked for Adams without much enthusiasm, and there is not the slightest evidence to show that a bargain had been struck between the two whereby Adams was to become President and Clay his Secretary of State. But the fact remains that Adams, also without enthusiasm, decided that Henry Clay was the right man for first place in the new Cabinet, and offered him the appointment. Already the cry of "bargain and corruption" had been raised, and when Clay accepted the proffered post all who so desired could believe the worst. Both Adams and Clay produced ample evidence to show that the accusation was false, and Clay even fought a duel with John Randolph of Roanoke about it, but the charge would not down. Andrew Jackson, who at the outset had taken his own defeat in good part, was at last convinced that this corrupt bargain had kept him out of the Presidency, and became an open enemy of the Adams administration. Before the year was out he had been renominated for the Presidency by the legislature of Tennessee, and had resigned his seat in the United States Senate in order to be free to carry on a three years' campaign.

Once more a two-party political division seemed in sight. Adams offered to retain **A new party alignment** Crawford as his Secretary of the Treasury, but the offer was declined and the Georgian passed out of public life. The followers of Adams and Clay, with some recruits from those who had once favored Crawford, combined to support the administration, while all others looked to Jackson as their leader. Such shrewd politicians as William B. Lewis of Tennessee, Martin Van Buren of New York, Thomas Hart Benton of Missouri, and the newly chosen Vice-President joined hands to oppose the administration and to advance the interests of their candidate. In 1826 a Missourian named Duff Green was brought to Washington to establish an anti-administration paper, the *Telegraph*, which repeatedly rang the changes on the "bargain and corruption" charge, and in a thousand petty ways criticized the conduct of the President and his supporters. Adams's title to the Presidency was even called into question on the ground that Jackson had received more electoral and popular votes than any other candidate, and should therefore have been chosen by the House in order to uphold the will of the people.

Faced by this kind of opposition, Adams

John Quincy Adams

BRILLIANT MEMBER of an illustrious family, and sixth President of the United States, Adams achieved his greatest successes outside the Presidency. As Secretary of State under Monroe, he reached an agreement with Great Britain over Oregon, acquired Florida from Spain, and helped formulate the Monroe Doctrine. As ex-President he served notably for seventeen years in the House of Representatives. Portrait by Stuart, completed by Sully.

might well have used the power he possessed as President to weld together a strong political machine that would uphold his administration, but his strict New England conscience would tolerate no such tactics. Instead, he consistently refused to remove his political opponents from appointive offices, and he sometimes even chose Jackson adherents to fill important vacancies. One such appointee was the Postmaster-General, John McLean of Ohio, who made it a point to dispense such patronage as he could command to Jackson men rather than to Adams men. The President's hope was to perpetuate the "era of good feelings" that was popularly supposed to have characterized the administration of James Monroe, but a better politician would have seen that such a course was impossible.

Adams's long experience with diplomacy made it seem reasonable that his administration should be distinguished for **The Panama Congress** its record in dealing with foreign affairs. Such, however, could hardly have been the case, for the problems that the

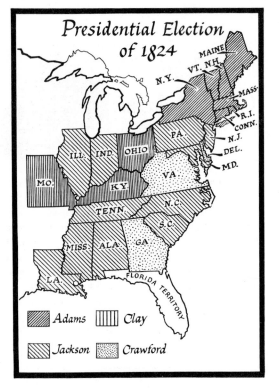

Presidential Election of 1824

Adams | Clay
Jackson | Crawford

country now faced were primarily domestic in nature. Clay understood, perhaps better than Adams, the determination with which the United States had turned its back upon Europe, but he had visions of an increasing pan-American co-operation, and he hoped to follow up the Monroe Doctrine by making the United States the acknowledged protector of all the lesser American nations. An opening soon appeared for the introduction of this policy. When, at the suggestion of Bolivar, the Spanish-American states decided to hold a congress at Panama to consider a union of forces by which they might compel Spain to recognize their independence, Mexico and Colombia inquired if the United States would care to send delegates. Clay was eager to accept the invitation, but Adams at first hesitated, for he feared that the war might be carried into Cuba and Porto Rico, and believed that the interests of the United States would be best served if those islands remained for the time being the colonies of Spain. One important consider-

ation was that their separation from Spain would doubtless involve, as it had elsewhere in Spanish America, the abolition of slavery, and the turbulence of the black republic of Haiti aroused grave doubts as to the wisdom of such a course. But Adams was won over by Clay's representations, and sent to the Senate for confirmation the names of two delegates to attend the Panama Congress. Unfortunately the subject was not considered on its merits, either in the Senate or in the country at large. The opposition sought merely to discredit the administration, and while it did not succeed in preventing the mission from being sent, it did delay proceedings so long that the Panama Congress had adjourned before the delegates of the United States arrived. The results of the Congress were inconsequential, and perhaps the participation of the United States would not have altered its course, but the incident put the administration in a bad light before the country, quite as the Jackson leaders had intended.

Adams also aroused undeserved antagonism by his handling of Indian affairs. The expansion of the cotton South **Indian** led to an insistent demand from **affairs** the Southwest that the lands held by the now semi-civilized Creeks, Cherokees, Choctaws, and Chickasaws be made available for settlement. In response to this demand a treaty was signed at Indian Springs, just before Adams took office, by which the Creeks gave up all their holdings in Georgia. This treaty was duly ratified by the Senate, but it was promptly repudiated by the great majority of the Creek nation, and one of its chief negotiators was put to death. Adams, on investigation, found that the treaty had been obtained by fraud, refused to proclaim it in effect, and ordered that new negotiations should be begun. This assumption that the Indians had rights which the national government was bound to respect profoundly irritated the frontier, where the doctrine that "there is no good Indian but a dead Indian" was in the ascendancy; and it also provoked the wrath of the southern cotton planters, who were delayed in their acquisition of the valuable Indian lands. The governor of Georgia claimed that the lands acquired by the treaty became immediately upon its ratification a part of the sovereign state of Georgia, and that the government of the United States had no ight to reopen the question. Adams maintained with warmth that he was justified in defending the good faith of the nation towards the Indians by "all the means under his control." A glaring difference of opinion on the old question of states' rights versus national powers was thus revealed, a difference which the subsequent negotiation of a satisfactory treaty failed to obscure. Under Adams's administration the practice of obtaining from the Indians such lands as were coveted by the whites continued without abatement, but the scruples displayed by the President gave the states'-rights South and the nationalistic West a common grievance that they did not soon forget.

Sectional differences on the tariff question had become acutely apparent well before Adams entered the White **The tariff** House. The tariff of 1816 had received support from every section, although the commercial elements in the Northeast and a majority of the southern planters had opposed it. The depression of 1819–20 led to a movement, emanating chiefly from the middle Atlantic states, for increased duties as an aid to languishing manufacturing interests, and a bill to raise the duties on woolen and cotton manufactures, forged iron bars, and many other articles passed the House with a good majority. The West, particularly Kentucky, was favored by a high duty on hemp, and revenue duties on sugar, molasses, coffee, and salt were intended to relieve the embarrassment of the treasury. But the opposition of the South to protective duties had stiffened since 1816, and in the Senate the bill failed by a single vote. In 1824 the advocates of protection returned to the fray with a measure similar to that which had failed in 1820, but with a tariff on raw wool

to win the support of the sheep-growing interests. The vote in the House was even closer than in 1820, but a slender majority was obtained in the Senate, and the measure carried. The representatives of the West, charmed by the arguments of Clay and by the agricultural duties, were almost solidly for the bill. "The merchants and manufacturers of Massachusetts, New Hampshire, the province of Maine and Sagadahock," said John Randolph in fine irony, "repel this bill, whilst men in hunting shirts, with deerskin leggings and moccasins on their feet, want protection for manufactures."

The woolen interests were not entirely satisfied with the Tariff of 1824, for the duties on raw wool cut deeply **Protectionist** into the profits of manufactur- **demands** ing. British competition was acute, for American laborers, with the leverage of cheap lands in the West to help them, demanded and received higher wages than the British operatives could obtain. Moreover, the British duty on raw wool had been reduced in 1824, and the British manufacturers profited accordingly. The contradiction between a tariff on raw wool and a tariff on manufactured woolens was sufficiently apparent, but American wool-growers, who had found the duties levied in 1824 of great advantage, were determined to secure increased protection. A bill designed to satisfy both the wool-growers and the woolens manufacturers by increasing duties all around failed of adoption in 1827 only by the casting vote of the Vice-President, John C. Calhoun, who thus made clear his complete retreat from the protective principle he had so warmly espoused in 1816. It now seemed obvious that if the wool and woolens interests could get together with other interests desiring protection, a generally higher schedule of duties could be enacted. To promote this cause a hundred delegates from thirteen states met at Harrisburg, Pennsylvania, in July, 1827, and strongly urged their combined wishes upon Congress.

The mid-term election of 1826, however, had given a majority in the lower house of

Congress to the anti-administration forces,

The "Tariff of Abomina-tions" and when the tariff question came up, a few of the Jacksonian leaders determined to make political capital of it. They knew that Jackson, in order to be elected in 1828, must win support from the South, which opposed a protective tariff, and from the Northeast and the West, where a strong majority favored it. Their plan, afterward fully revealed by John C. Calhoun himself, was to present a bill which placed such excessively high rates on raw materials that some of the manufacturers of the Northeast would join with the commercial interests and the South to defeat the measure. Amendments which would make the bill more satisfactory to the manufacturers were to be voted down, and thus the Jackson men could claim credit in the North for having introduced a high-tariff measure, and in the South for having defeated it. The bill, according to the sharp-tongued John Randolph, related "to manufactures of no sort or kind but the manufacture of a President of the United States." As it turned out, the ruse failed to work, for enough northern support for the bill was obtained to enact the "Tariff of Abominations," as it was generally called, into law. Among those who unexpectedly favored the measure was Daniel Webster of Massachusetts. In preceding tariff debates Webster had always led the fight against protection, and as late as 1824 he had held that it was "the true policy of government to suffer the different pursuits of society to take their own course and not to give excessive bounties or encouragements to one over another." His change of front reflected the growing importance of manufacturing in New England, just as Calhoun's change of front had indicated the complete conversion of the South to low-tariff principles. The Northwest, as in previous tariff debates, was still hypnotized by the arguments Clay presented for an American system, and particularly by the high duties proposed on such items as wool, flax, and hemp.

Adams was an enthusiastic believer in

TARIFF VOTES IN THE HOUSE OF REPRESENTATIVES

	1816		1820		1824		1828	
	For	Against	For	Against	For	Against	For	Against
New England....	17	10	18	17	15	23	16	23
Middle Atlantic*...	42	5	55	1	57	9	56	6
South Atlantic....	16	35	5	49	4	56	4	47
Southwest..	3	3	0	7	2	14	0	16
Northwest†.	10	1	12	3	29	0	29	1

* Includes Delaware.
† Includes Kentucky and Missouri.

internal improvements at national expense, and was unhandicapped by the **Internal improve-ments** constitutional scruples that had restrained Madison and Monroe in their dealings with this subject. In 1824 Monroe had given his approval to a General Survey Act which authorized the President to conduct such surveys of canal and turnpike routes as would serve an important national interest. Undoubtedly Adams hoped to use this power to lay out a great national system of transportation, and his efforts along this line were not entirely unavailing. During his term of office army engineers were detailed freely to survey prospective transportation routes, and the sums actually expended in aid of internal improvements grew by leaps and bounds. But almost the only strictly national project that the administration was able to carry on was the continuation westward of the Cumberland Road. Beginning in 1825 liberal appropriations were made for this purpose, and with Jefferson City, Missouri, as its intended western terminal the National Road, as it came to be called, progressed slowly across central Ohio, and then on through Indiana and Illinois. By 1838 contruction reached Vandalia, Illinois, but was discontinued because of the hard times that followed the panic of 1837, and was not resumed because of the increasing evidence that railroads, not turnpikes, would soon carry the commerce of the country.

Adams's dream of a carefully planned national system of roads and canals had little chance to come true. At the close of the War of 1812 the national government might possibly have seized the leadership in developing such a system, but its failure to act quickly when the need was first keenly felt left the solution of the problem to the states and to private initiative. By the time Adams became President there was little left that the government could do except to aid enterprises already undertaken under other auspices. For such works Congress voted frequent subsidies, usually in the form of generous subscriptions of stock, but local rather than national interests determined the nature of the improvements made and the routes followed.

Undoubtedly the most spectacular development in transportation during this period **The Erie** was the building of the Erie **Canal** Canal, a project which DeWitt Clinton had persuaded the state of New York to undertake. Early in the nineteenth century Clinton served several terms as mayor of the city of New York, and he was among the first to catch the vision of what it would mean to that city if the Hudson River could only be connected by a canal with the Great Lakes. In 1812 he was the leading member of a commission that sought to interest the United States government in the idea, but neither at that time nor at any later time could Congress be persuaded to help. Finally Clinton decided that the state of New York must sponsor the work, and in 1816, with the canal as his ultimate objective, he won the governorship. So well were his efforts rewarded that the first excavation was made in 1817, soon after he took office, while only eight years later the canal was open for business. This waterway, when completed, extended from Troy on the Hudson to Buffalo on Lake Erie, a distance of three hundred and sixty-three miles. It was

forty feet wide at the top, twenty-eight feet at the bottom, and carried four feet of water. Eighty-one locks overcame a grade of about 700 feet. The cost ran to $7,602,000. Canals before this time were by no means uncommon, but Clinton's "big ditch" taxed the engineering resources of the period and the financial resources of New York to the limit. In revolt against the heavy expenditures, the people of the state turned Clinton out of office in 1822, but two years later he was triumphantly re-elected, and when the canal was opened he, as governor, took the leading part in an elaborate set of ceremonies. Accompanied by a number of distinguished guests, he boarded a canal boat, the *Seneca Chief*, at Buffalo, October 26, 1825, and ten days later, after witnessing enthusiastic celebrations all along the route, arrived at New York City. Thereupon he poured a keg of water taken from Lake Erie into the Atlantic Ocean, and the "marriage of the waters" was complete.

Clinton was not merely optimistic when he staged this celebration, for the canal, thanks to a lucrative local **Success of** traffic that was making cities of **the canal** such points along the route as Syracuse, Rochester, and Utica, was already a financial success. A branch canal from Albany to Lake Champlain, completed in 1824 at a cost of two million dollars, was similarly successful, and the tolls produced by the two canals were so heavy that by 1837 their original cost had been entirely repaid. The Erie Canal was also of immense significance in linking the East to the West. Before it was built the cost of transporting a ton of freight from New York City to Buffalo had been about one hundred dollars, and the time required, about twenty days. The canal at once reduced the cost to ten dollars and the time to eight days, and as the volume of business increased the cost of transportation went steadily down. Steamboats on the Great Lakes made possible a cheap all-water route to the shores of Lake Huron and Lake Michigan as well as Lake Erie, and with the problem of transportation no longer a serious barrier to settlement, pioneers by the tens of thousands took up vacant lands in the northern parts of Ohio, Indiana, and Illinois. Michigan Territory grew so rapidly in population that by 1836 the eastern half was ready for statehood, while the western half, known later as Wisconsin, seemed likewise destined to an early maturity. Moreover, as Clinton had foreseen, the tremendous volume of trade that flowed through the Erie Canal–Great Lakes route to and from the West paid a generous tribute to New York City. In population New York grew from less than one hundred and twenty-five thousand in 1820 to over two hundred thousand by 1830; during the same time the value of its real and personal property rose sixty per cent; and the increasing volume of its import and export trade soon made it the leading American city.

The success of New York in making connections with the West led to quick emulation The "Pennsylvania System" by her chief rivals, Philadelphia and Baltimore. The prosperity of Philadelphia was based to a great extent upon the growth of manufacturing and agriculture in eastern Pennsylvania, but the city had long felt the need of better communications with the West. Early in the century, when a system of turnpikes was built across the mountains to Pittsburgh, she had enjoyed a temporary triumph, but the Cumberland Road and steamboats on the Ohio had quickly diverted much of the trade of western Pennsylvania to Baltimore and New Orleans, respectively. In 1825, with the superiority of canal communications to all others seemingly apparent, the legislature authorized the construction of an elaborate system of canals to unite the various sections of the state. Unfortunately the route to the Ohio through Pennsylvania was far more difficult than the Mohawk Valley route through New York, so that when the "Pennsylvania System" finally reached its western goal in 1834 a portage railway thirty-six miles in length, for which the power was furnished by stationary engines on the inclines and horses on

the leveler stretches, was necessary to carry the canal traffic across the mountains. The new route to the West did a flourishing business, but it never became a serious rival to the Erie Canal, and Philadelphia never seriously challenged the lead of New York in the race for the western markets.

Baltimore, meantime, saw all the advantages which the Cumberland Road had once given her slipping fast away. Chesapeake and Ohio Canal Engineers reported that a canal could not be built from Baltimore across the mountains, but incorrigible optimists began in 1828, with state backing, the construction of the Chesapeake and Ohio Canal, for which President John Quincy Adams at a Fourth-of-July celebration lifted the first shovelful of earth. On the same day, however, Charles Carroll of Carrollton, the sole surviving signer of the Declaration of Independence, broke ground for the building of the Baltimore and Ohio Railroad, a project upon which a few far-sighted men had set their hearts. Twenty years of labor and ten million dollars expenditure brought the canal no farther west than Fort Cumberland, but the railroad, in 1853, finally reached its destination.

The craze for canals in the twenties and thirties went to unreasonable lengths. In the East feeders to the main The Canal Age canals, and connecting links between arms of the Atlantic, were built with little regard to costs involved and possible earning power. In the new western states the task of connecting the Ohio–Mississippi River system with the Great Lakes was eagerly embraced. Ohio led the way in 1825 by authorizing the building of two such canals, the Ohio and Erie from Portsmouth to Cleveland, and the Miami and Erie from Cincinnati to Toledo. The former was completed in 1832, and for a little while did a thriving business; the latter was finished in considerable part by 1835, but by 1845, when it was opened the whole way through, railroads were rapidly making canals obsolete. Not to be outdone by Ohio, Indiana began in 1832 and completed in 1843 the Wabash

The Erie Canal was the fabulously successful example of the benefits of a continuous waterway to the West. Built at an expense that had seemed staggering in prospect, Clinton's "big ditch" began immediately to pay for itself far in excess of expectations. Passengers and cargo of every description poured into the West as never before, while a wealth of western produce flowed east at a fraction of the overland cost.

EXCAVATION FOR THE CANAL. Hand- and horse-powered hoists devised to meet unprecedented engineering problems. Lithograph by Anthony Imbert, from Colden, *Memoir . . . of New York Canals*, 1825.

A SYSTEM OF LOCKS. The junction of the Erie and Northern (Champlain) Canals, near Troy, N. Y. Aquatint by J. W. Hill, 1835.

SCENE ON THE ERIE CANAL. During 1826, the year after its opening, nearly 20,000 such barges passed one toll point on the canal. Watercolor drawing by J. W. Hill, about 1830.

BUFFALO, N. Y., 1836. Within a few years of the opening of the Canal, Buffalo grew from a village to a prosperous city of some 25,000. View of the city from Lake Erie. Aquatint by Bennett, after J. W. Hill.

Erie Canal commerce made New York City the great American metropolis, and Buffalo an important interior port. Pennsylvania, eager to duplicate New York's successful thrust into the West, met the obstacle of the Alleghenies by a canal system which included a railway device for transporting sectional canal boats over the mountains from Hollidaysburg to Johnstown.

CANAL NAVIGATION COMPANY. Four shares of stock, at $100 a share, issued May 22, 1821.

CROSSING THE ALLEGHENIES. The Portage Railway, Pennsylvania, completed in 1834.

RAILROAD AND CANAL. The Tonnewanta Railroad Bridge, crossing the Erie Canal at Rochester, N.Y. Illustration from O'Reilly, *Sketches of Rochester*, 1838.

and Erie Canal, while Illinois between 1832 and 1848 built the Illinois and Michigan Canal. In the fifties Wisconsin succeeded in opening a waterway from Green Bay to the Mississippi by way of the Fox and Wisconsin Rivers, and Michigan, by building a canal around St. Mary's Falls, greatly facilitated through traffic on the Great Lakes. Except for Maryland, there was little canal construction in the South, where the mountain barriers were obstinate and the highways of the rivers and the ocean still furnished fairly adequate means of transportation. Charleston, South Carolina, was eager for connections with the West that would give her a better chance to compete with her new western rival, New Orleans, but for topographical reasons she was compelled to turn to a railroad rather than to a canal. By 1850 the total canal mileage in the United States had reached thirty-two hundred miles.

The Canal Age continued for many years after John Quincy Adams left the Presi-

dency, but it was during his term of office that this type of internal improvement won its first great popularity. Adams urged Congress to vote aid for many such works, and the total appropriations made for internal improvements during his administration reached many millions. On roads and harbors his administration spent more than twice as much as had been appropriated for such enterprises during the administrations of all his predecessors taken together. Ordinarily such benefactions by the national government won the hearty approval of the Northeast and the Northwest, but many Southerners saw little to applaud in a policy from which their section could profit so little. John Randolph as early as 1824, in the debate on the General Survey Bill, pointed out also the constitutional risk involved. He argued that if Congress could pass such a measure it could also emancipate every slave in the United States, "and with stronger color of reason than it can exercise the power now contended for." Moreover, Clay's linking of the obnoxious protective tariff with the program of internal improvements tended to make the two equally unpalatable to a section that was coming more and more to see in the high duties on manufactured articles a body blow at its prosperity.

Bibliography

F. J. Turner, *The Significance of Sections in American History* (1932), strongly upholds the theory that American party politics arise from the interplay of sectional interests. This is also the thesis of an admirable survey of American political history by Herbert Agar, *The Price of Union* (1950). Since individuals tended to reflect the attitudes of the sections they represented, biographies are of great importance in this connection. One of the best is G. G. Van Deusen, *The Life of Henry Clay* (1937). The chapter on the sixth President in J. T. Adams, *The Adams Family* (1930), is also excellent. J. T. Morse, Jr., *John Quincy Adams* (1917); and B. C. Clark, *John Quincy Adams, "Old Man Eloquent"* (1932) are appreciative biographies. Jackson has attracted innumerable biographers: W. G. Sumner, *Andrew Jackson* (1910); James Parton, *Life of Andrew Jackson* (3 vols., 1860); J. S. Bassett, *The Life of Andrew Jackson* (2 vols., 1928). Of these three, Bassett's is best from the critical point of view, but Parton contains the greatest amount of picturesque detail. J. E. D. Shipp, *Giant Days; or, The Life and Times of William H. Crawford* (1909), is of some value. C. M. Wiltse, *John C. Calhoun, Nationalist, 1782–1828* (1944), is a careful reappraisal of the great southern statesman's early career. C. M. Fuess, *Daniel Webster* (2 vols., 1930), presents the shifting point of view of the Northeast on such matters as the tariff.

Other books with a strong sectional implication are C. S. Sydnor, *The Development of Southern Sectionalism, 1819–1848* (1948); T. P. Abernethy, *From Frontier to Plantation in Tennessee* (1932); R. G. Albion and Jennie B. Pope, *The Rise of New York Port, 1815–1860* (1939); S. J. Folmsbee, *Sectionalism and Internal Improvements in Tennessee, 1796–1845* (1939); J. M. Miller, *The Genesis of Western Culture: The Upper Ohio Valley, 1800–1825* (1938); A. L. Kohlmeier, *The Old Northwest as the Keystone of the Arch of American Federal Union* (1938); R. C. Buley, *The Old Northwest: Pioneer Period, 1815–1840* (2 vols., 1950). *History of the State of New York*, edited by Alexander C. Flick (10 vols., 1933–37), is a notably successful cooperative state history.

The Canal Age has been much written about. N. E. Whitford, *History of the Canal System of the State of New York* (2 vols., 1906), tells the story of the Erie Canal. W. S. Sanderlin, *The Great National Project* (1947), deals with the Chesapeake and Ohio. See also C. P. McClelland and C. C. Huntington, *History of the Ohio Canals, Their Construction, Cost, Use and Partial Abandonment* (1905); E. L. Bogart, *Internal Improvements and State Debt in Ohio* (1924); E. J. Benton, *The Wabash Trade Route in the Development of the Old Northwest* (1903); T. C. Pease, *The Frontier State, 1818–1848* (*Centennial History of Illinois*, II, 1918). A. F. Harlow, *Old Towpaths, The Story of the American Canal Era* (1926), is more general.

For the part played by the Great Lakes waterways, see Edward Channing, *The Story of the Great Lakes* (1909); Harlan Hatcher, *The Great Lakes* (1944); M. M. Quaife, *Lake Michigan* (1944); Fred Landon, *Lake Huron* (1944); Grace Lee Nute, *Lake Superior* (1944); Arthur Pound, *Lake Ontario* (1945); Harlan Hatcher, *Lake Erie* (1945).

21

The Revolution of 1828

THE defeat of Adams and the election of Jackson to the Presidency in 1828 was long foreseen, even by Adams himself. The President and his chief advisers represented incontestably the old aristocracy of brains and wealth that had always, regardless of party, held most of the offices and governed the country. Jackson's candidacy was nothing else so much as a challenge to this type of governmental control. A new concept of democracy was abroad in the land. No longer were the people satisfied, as Jefferson had supposed they would be, to fill the offices from among their betters. Popular rule had come to mean that the common people should choose their rulers from among themselves, and by 1828 the extension of the suffrage had gone to such lengths that an aristocratic Adams in a contest with a democratic Jackson had not the remotest chance to win.

Popular sovereignty, as set forth in the doctrines of the American Revolution and **Suffrage** the French Revolution, logi-**extension** cally demanded that every man should have the right to vote. This principle the ruling classes in the United States had been slow to concede, but by 1828 the advocates of manhood suffrage had won battle after battle. In these contests the frontier states, now eleven in number, played an important part. Whereas, to begin with, not one of the original thirteen states had failed to place formidable restrictions upon the suffrage, the new states had with one accord either granted manhood suffrage outright, or else had put up such slight barriers against it as amounted to the same thing. Gradually the older states fell into step with this march of democracy. The example of the western states was before them, and the demands of their own disfranchised classes were insistent. The growth of the factory system increased the number of workmen who could scarcely hope to amass enough property to be able to vote, and who yet stood more in need of the protection of the state than any other class. To obtain desired legislation they must have a voice on election day. Designing politicians, themselves often risen from the masses, saw in a widened electorate the chance for personal advancement that under the old régime they might have waited for in vain. Each potential party boss was a noisy and effective advocate of the principle that the people must have the right to rule. One after another the citadels of aristocracy fell before the attack, until by the time the election of 1828 was held three of the original states, New Hampshire, Maryland, and Connecticut, had abolished all property qualifications for voting, while two others, Massachusetts and New York, had made them only nominal. Thus by 1828 the masses in a good majority of the states had the ballot, and, what is even more significant, they had acquired the will to use it. In Pennsylvania, for example, only forty-seven thousand votes were cast in the election of 1824, whereas with no changes of consequence in the election laws one hundred and fifty thousand votes were cast in 1828.

After Jackson became President the suffrage movement continued to win victories,

Constitutional changes and ultimately the principle of manhood suffrage was established in every state. The most exciting contest occurred in Rhode Island, where the popular forces won in 1843 only after they had staged a demonstration known as Dorr's Rebellion. Virginia and North Carolina were slowest to yield to the trend of the times. Not until the eighteen-fifties did they give up their requirement that only the owners of land might vote. The process by which these and other constitutional changes were made is in itself a remarkable revelation of the hold that democracy in government had taken upon the American people. Constitutional conventions, chosen by the people, were held during the years 1820 to 1850 in nearly every state. Ordinarily these conventions made the recommendations, and the changes were adopted by the people at the polls. In keeping also with the spirit of democracy was the tendency to make more and more officials elective rather than appointive. Even judges came to be numbered among the popularly elective officials. Experience led, however, to the substitution of biennial for annual elections, and to the placing of closer restrictions upon the power of the legislatures. Governors, on the other hand, seemed to have grown in popular estimation, and the narrow interpretation of their rights and duties, so common during the era of the American Revolution, was generally abandoned.

The movement for greater democratization in the state government was accompanied by a movement to put **Popular choice of electors** the Presidency more directly into the hands of the people. The constitution left to the various legislatures the right to decide how the presidential electors should be chosen, and the decision promptly made was in most cases that the legislatures themselves should choose the electors. But the advocates of more democracy in government were soon insisting that the choice should be made by popular vote. By 1824 only six states still permitted the legislatures to choose electors; by 1828, only two, Delaware and South Carolina. In most of the states the people voted for a general electoral ticket, so that ordinarily all the votes of a given state would be cast for one candidate; but in a few states the electors were chosen by districts, and the vote of the state might be split. Since the latter system was at best somewhat complicated, and served also to reduce the importance in the election of the state that adhered to it, the choice of electors on a state-wide ticket was ultimately adopted by all the states.

The campaign of 1828 gave a foretaste of what might be expected when an appeal had to be made to "King Numbers." **Campaign of 1828** Issues were lost sight of, and personalities held the center of the stage. Adams was portrayed by the opposition as a place-seeker who had lived almost his entire life at public expense, and had drawn hundreds of thousands of dollars from the national treasury. In spite of his well-known New England frugality, he was accused of unbridled extravagance, and even of purchasing from public funds "gambling tables and gambling furniture" for the White House. The old cry of "bargain and corruption" between Adams and Clay was relentlessly repeated, and other bargains and other corruptions were invented to suit the taste of Jacksonian orators and editors. Adams himself, while pouring out his spleen in his diary, maintained in public a correct aloofness, but his supporters did not hesitate to descend to the methods of their ad-

Andrew Jackson of Tennessee, seventh President of the United States, was the first American President who was not either a Virginia or a Massachusetts aristocrat; his parents were poor Scotch-Irish immigrants. In his earlier years Jackson lived the life of a southwestern frontiersman, but eventually he became the owner of a fine estate, "The Hermitage," near Nashville, which marked him as a southern country gentleman. His earlier record, together with his war-time prominence, made him the focal center of the movement for greater democracy in government. The portrait is by Asher B. Durand, 1835, and "The First State Election in Detroit, Michigan, 1837," which shows one aspect of popular rule, is from a painting by T.O.H.P. Burnham.

---

versaries. Jackson's personal life was above reproach, but a mighty scandal was made of the fact that he had married a divorced woman, and indeed had married her, although quite innocently, before the divorce from her former husband had been granted. Much was made also of the crude frontier fights in which the General had participated, and of his abysmal ignorance of public affairs.

Jackson's election was not accomplished, however, without the assistance of many

Classes supporting Jackson voters to whom an excess of democracy did not appeal. Calhoun, as the Jacksonian candidate for the Vice-Presidency, hoped to wield a great influence in the new administration and to succeed the General after four years. This consideration weighed heavily with the aristocratic element in the South, who could hardly have supported Adams anyway because of his well-known attitude on the tariff. An alliance of the West, the South, and the lower classes of the Northeast won the election for Jackson. Every western state supported him, and every southern state except Maryland, which divided its vote, 5 for Jackson to 6 for Adams, and Delaware. Pennsylvania cast all its electoral votes for Jackson, New York gave him 20 out of 36, and even in Maine, where electors were still chosen by districts, 1 vote out of 9 went to Jackson. The total electoral vote stood 178 to 83, and the popular vote, as nearly as it could be ascertained, 647,276 to 508,064.

The day of Jackson's inauguration brought to Washington a "noisy and disorderly rabble" bent on celebrating the rescue of the government from the hands of the aristocrats. The capital city, which still had far to go before it could grow up to the ambitious pattern L'Enfant had cut for it, was taxed to the limit to care for the huge crowd

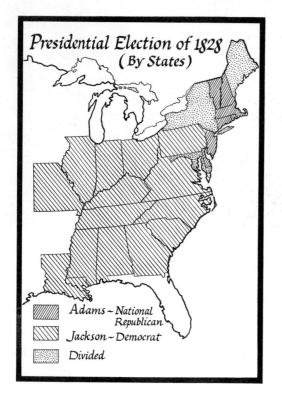

Presidential Election of 1828
(By States)

Adams ~ National Republican
Jackson ~ Democrat
Divided

henchmen. Once he had made his cabinet, however, the President had little use for it, beyond the usual administrative duties for which each member was legally responsible. There were two exceptions to this rule. Martin Van Buren, the Secretary of State, was close in the confidence of the President, and so also was John H. Eaton, the Secretary of War. Van Buren was the leader of the New York Democracy, a man of humble antecedents who had risen to power because he knew how to control the votes of the masses. Eaton was an old friend from Tennessee.

Jackson soon made it evident that a "kitchen cabinet" composed of men even less renowned than his official **The "kitchen** advisers would wield the chief **cabinet"** influence in his administration. Ablest among these men was Amos Kendall, a New Englander who had removed to

of celebrants that overflowed the boarding-houses, lined the streets to cheer the President-elect uproariously as he walked to the capitol, followed him in frenzied droves as he rode down the Avenue after taking the oath of office, surged through the White House like the Paris mob at the Tuileries, upset the presidential punch, trampled under muddy feet the presidential carpets, and in a thousand other ways gave free vent to their joy that the people had at last taken possession of their government.

Jackson's cabinet appointments showed that he had little disposition to minimize the **Jackson's** revolution that had taken place. **cabinet** Instead of the men of distinction who had usually been chosen to such positions, he selected mediocrities for the most part, men who were as new to national politics as the President himself, and who represented primarily the factions that had made his triumph possible. Half the appointments went to the friends of Calhoun, but the other half went to Jackson's own

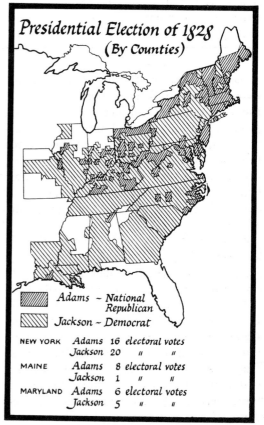

Presidential Election of 1828
(By Counties)

Adams ~ National Republican
Jackson ~ Democrat

NEW YORK	Adams 16 electoral votes	
	Jackson 20 " "	
MAINE	Adams 8 electoral votes	
	Jackson 1 " "	
MARYLAND	Adams 6 electoral votes	
	Jackson 5 " "	

Jackson's inauguration symbolized for many the triumph of the common man. "All Creation Going to the White House" (for the inaugural reception), is an amiably satirical drawing by the English cartoonist Cruickshank, about 1830.

Kentucky and had once been closely associated with Henry Clay. Kendall was a graduate of Dartmouth, had edited a paper at Frankfort, Kentucky, and was possessed of considerable literary skill. His facile pen phrased many Jacksonian state papers, and provided besides a stream of pro-Jackson propaganda for the press. William B. Lewis of Tennessee was probably the President's closest friend. It was Lewis who had made Jackson a formidable candidate for the Presidency, who had directed his campaign, and who now lived at the White House to offer sagacious counsel on the petty ways of politics. Another of Jackson's intimates was Isaac Hill, a crippled, rebellious, vituperative editor from New Hampshire. The Senate refused to confirm Hill's appointment to a minor administrative office, but in 1830 a Jacksonian majority in the New Hampshire legislature, with fine irony, made Hill a member of the Senate itself. Others generally connected with the "kitchen cabinet" were Andrew Jackson Donelson of Tennessee, the President's nephew and private secretary, Duff Green, the vitriolic editor of the *United States Telegraph*, an administration paper published in Washington, and Francis P. Blair, who after 1830, when the *Telegraph* became too friendly to Calhoun, edited a

new administration organ, the *Globe*. Undoubtedly this little coterie of friends, especially Kendall and Lewis, had great influence with the President, but he was himself the dominating figure of his administration, and was quite as capable of ignoring their advice as of taking it.

Jackson's decision to remove from office a large number of the men whom his predecessors had appointed was quite **The "spoils** in keeping with the revolt **system"** against aristocracy in government that had brought him to power. Appointments before his time had gone to needy members of the upper strata of society and only rarely to the common people. Moreover, once an individual obtained an office, he could usually count upon retaining it for life. This was not because earlier Presidents had been above partisan appointments, for Washington himself had been careful, after a few unhappy experiments, to appoint only Federalists to office, while Jefferson during his eight years in the White House had gradually replaced most Federalists with Republicans. The next three Presidents after Jefferson were also Republicans, and they (with the exception of John Quincy Adams, whose conscience restrained him) lacked the incentive to remove office-holders for purely partisan reasons. When Jackson became President it was no doubt true that the efficiency of the public service was crippled by the presence within it of many aged and incompetent relics of an earlier day. Jackson held that the duties of all public officers were "so plain and simple that men of intelligence may readily qualify themselves for their performance." He professed also to believe that "more is lost by the long continuance of men in office than is generally to be gained by their experience." Furthermore, no one man had "any more intrinsic right to official station than another." Professing such views, the new President began immediately after his inauguration a proscription of office-holders that soon weeded out of the service hundreds of men who had supposed that they were to retain their positions indefinitely. Naturally the outcries from those who had been dispossessed and from their friends rent the skies, but Jackson's conduct was hardly as ruthless as they tried to pretend. During his first year and a half in office he made only about nine hundred removals from among civil servants numbering about ten thousand, and some of his removals could be accounted for on grounds that were not strictly partisan. Most of the men who lost office, however, were Adams men, and all of their successors were Jackson men.

Already the practice of rewarding the victors with the "spoils of office" had been tried out by local politicians in **The party** such states as New York and **"machine"** Pennsylvania with phenomenal results. The hope of obtaining office spurred party workers to far greater endeavor than could have been expected of them out of mere devotion to principle. The fear of losing an office, once obtained, proved likewise a powerful incentive to fighting the party's battles. On the basis of carefully distributed spoils, it was possible to build up a party "machine" which could raise money, wage campaigns, reward loyalty, punish disobedience, and perpetuate itself in power for long periods of time. Since such a machine could not function smoothly without a single directing genius to guide it, the party "boss" came into being. Sometimes he was honest; sometimes he was not. The opportunity for what a later generation called "graft" lay wide open.

The kitchen cabinet which Jackson gathered around him knew well the advantages that accrued in the states from the use of offices as rewards for party service, and they insisted that Jackson should accept the same system in making appointments to national offices. The President was nothing loath, and his conviction that any intelligent American was capable of filling practically

The spoils system aroused the wrath of those who lost office and the enthusiasm of those who gained it. Here an anonymous cartoonist ridicules Jacksonian "Office Hunters for the Year 1834."

any office furnished a ready defense for appointing those most useful politically, regardless of other tests. When it became necessary to replace one party worker with another from the same party, the doctrine of "rotation in office" was devised. Politicians argued soberly that the valuable training in citizenship that went with office-holding ought to be widely diffused by passing the offices around. However specious these arguments may appear to a later generation, they were then accepted cheerfully by the great majority of the electorate, and for the next forty years the "spoils system" went practically unchallenged.

Jackson's interpretation of the Presidency also offered something new to American **Jackson's** politics. The overwhelming ma-
view of the jority by which he was ushered
Presidency into office, coupled with the fact that the American people themselves were responsible for the result, not a party caucus nor a college of electors nor a series of favorable legislatures, gave rise to the theory that the executive was endowed with greater authority than any other branch of the government. Jackson as the chosen representative of the whole American people sought actively to secure the passage of the laws he favored, and he lectured Congress with regard to its duties in a fashion that Washington and Jefferson would have regarded as unbecoming, if not actually unconstitutional. Moreover, he made far more extensive use of the veto power than any other President had seen fit to do. All six of his predecessors in office together had vetoed only nine bills that Congress had passed, whereas Jackson during his two terms vetoed twelve measures, and used freely also the "pocket veto," a device which no previous President had dared to invoke. The pocket veto was made possible by a provision in the Constitution that unless the President vetoed a bill within ten days after it reached him, the bill would become a law anyway, "unless Congress by their adjournment prevent its return, in which case it shall not be a law." Since many im-portant measures were passed in the closing days of a session, the President might, if he chose, defeat legislation by a mere failure to act, or in popular parlance "pocketing" the bill. Jackson's feeling of superiority extended even to his relations with the Supreme Court, and on one occasion he is reported to have said: "John Marshall has made his decision; now let him enforce it."

This clash with the Supreme Court arose out of Jackson's attitude on the Indian question. The quarrel between **The Georgia** the state of Georgia and the **Indians** Creeks, already alluded to, was paralleled by a somewhat similar conflict between the same state and the Cherokees. This tribe, like the Creeks, had attained a fairly high degree of civilization, and desired merely to be left alone in the possession of its land and customs. Treaties with the United States existed that seemed fully to guarantee these rights, and in 1827 the Cherokees went so far as to adopt a constitution in which they declared pointedly that they were not subject to the jurisdiction of any other state or nation. This declaration the state of Georgia took as a direct affront, and the Georgia legislature promptly extended the authority of the state over all the inhabitants within its borders, both white and Indian. The position taken by Georgia was not without some legal basis, for the United States had promised in 1802 to extinguish all Indian titles within the state "as early as the same can be obtained on reasonable terms," and if the Indians were allowed to have their way it seemed likely that no more of their lands would be ceded. The matter was finally brought to the Supreme Court in the case of the *Cherokee Nation vs. the State of Georgia*, but the Court, although complimenting the Indians on their successful efforts at self-government, refused to take jurisdiction on the ground that the Cherokees were a "domestic dependent nation" rather than a "foreign state," as the suit contended. Later, however, in the case of *Worcester vs. Georgia*, the Court held that the laws of Georgia were of no effect within

American Indians attracted the attention of George Catlin, a distinguished artist and writer. He portrays here a meeting between Colonel Henry Dodge of the United States Dragoons and a Comanche chieftain, 1834.

the Cherokee borders. This decision was openly flouted by the Georgians, and the President, whatever the precise phrases that may have sprung to his lips, made no effort to enforce it.

As a matter of fact the Indian question had passed the bounds of a simple dispute between some Indians and a state. Who first caught the vision it would be hard to determine, but for a long time the idea had been afloat that a kind Providence had arranged for this vexing problem an easy solution. Explorers had reported with great unanimity that the western half of the continent would never be useful to white men; on the other hand, because of its abundance of game, it was an ideal home for Indians. Why not accept this divinely ordained plan, and colonize the Indians in the West where they need never fear the encroachments of the whites? As early as 1825, John C. Calhoun, then Secretary of War, had outlined this plan in an able state paper, and had urged it upon President Monroe, who in return had urged it upon Congress. Few objections could be raised to so natural a solution, and from that time forward the removal of the Indians to the region west of the western

The policy of Indian removal

borders of Missouri and Arkansas was regarded as settled policy. Thus Jackson did not inaugurate this policy, but he fell in line with it cheerfully, and under his administration it was successfully carried through. His irritation that the Supreme Court should dare to interfere with so benign a project is understandable, if not wholly defensible.

During Jackson's administration ninety-four Indian treaties were signed, most of which were treaties of cession; and under the steady pressure of the United States government even the Cherokees left sullenly for the West. Two disciplinary wars had to be fought in order to subject the Indians wholly to the white man's will. The Black Hawk War with the Sauk and Foxes, whose departure from northern Illinois was too slow to satisfy the frontiersmen, was fought in 1832; the Seminole War, which became necessary when most of that tribe refused to leave their homes, even after they had agreed to go, was an unhappy legacy that Jackson left to his successor, Van Buren, and that ended in the forties only when most of the Seminoles had been hunted down and killed. Jackson's Indian policy did not fail to arouse the sincere criticism of humanitarians like the Quakers, and the pretended criticism of many of his political adversaries, but the West as a whole approved it heartily, and the country in general was content to let events take their natural course. What is perhaps most remarkable is the restraint with which Jackson, himself a veteran of many Indian wars, dealt with the red men. For the most part the removals, although tragic enough, were carried out without bloodshed and with the consent of the tribes themselves.

Perhaps many of those who supported Jackson in 1828 could have predicted the nature of his handling of the Indian question, but on most matters of public policy his views were at that time far from clear. One such issue was that of federal assistance to works of internal improvement. While he was a member of the United States Senate, he had cast his vote in favor of internal improvements, and yet he had written a letter of commendation to Monroe on the occasion of the latter's veto of the Cumberland Road Tolls Bill of 1822. As a Westerner he might be expected to favor internal improvements; as a Southerner, to oppose them. He gathered about him as his chief advisers men who held precisely opposite views on the subject, Calhoun, for example, who, in spite of his right-about-face on the tariff, still favored internal improvements, and Martin Van Buren, who opposed them. In his first inaugural the President conceded that internal improvements, "so far as they can be promoted by the constitutional acts of the Federal Government, are of high importance," but so vague a statement left him free to take almost any stand he chose.

A shrewd observer might have guessed that Jackson's attitude toward internal improvements would be quite at variance from the views of Adams and Clay. While Adams was President, Congress, with much encouragement from the executive, granted federal aid liberally for the building of roads and canals, the improvement of ports and harbors, and the clearing of obstructions from the chan-

The Maysville veto

nels of navigable streams. But Jackson, who in this matter seems to have leaned heavily upon the advice of Van Buren, was not long in concluding that many such expenditures were neither constitutional nor expedient. An opportunity to state his position came in May, 1830, when Congress sent him a bill which authorized federal assistance for the building of a road from Maysville, Kentucky, to Lexington, in the same state. Although this road was in reality a link in the famous route from Zanesville, Ohio, on the National Road, to the Tennessee River at the Muscle Shoals, and thence to Natchez on the lower Mississippi, the measure as it stood provided merely for a strictly intra-state road. Half the stock in the turnpike company that was to do the work was to be subscribed by the United States government, and the other half in equal parts by the state of Kentucky and by private individuals. Jackson refused his signature to the bill, and in an able veto message defended the position he had taken. He doubted its constitutionality and, like Madison and Monroe, believed that a constitutional amendment should be adopted if federal aid to roads and canals was to be continued; but his chief objection to the measure was the local character of the internal improvement it proposed to aid. The Maysville road, he declared, had "no connection with any established system of improvements; it is exclusively within the limits of a State, starting at a point on the Ohio river and running out sixty miles to an interior town, and even as far as the State is interested conferring partial instead of general advantages." He pointed also to the drain on the treasury entailed by lavish expenditures for internal improvements, and suggested that Congress might better reduce the revenue if it could spare the funds, or use its surplus to pay off the national debt.

The Maysville veto was the subject of acrimonious debate in Congress and in the country at large, but the veto was sustained, and Jackson clung tenaciously to the position he had taken. Other vetoes and pocket

vetoes of similar measures soon followed.
Convinced, as time went on, that the national revenues were likely to remain larger
than the legitimate expenditures of the government would warrant, he urged that all
surplus funds should be distributed to the
states according to their ratio of representation in Congress. Should such a course be
deemed unconstitutional, he suggested the
adoption of an amendment to the Constitution that would grant to Congress the necessary authority. Then the states, provided
with an adequate revenue and freed from the
danger of national interference, might construct whatever works of internal improvement they saw fit. Jackson often pointed
out that there was nothing necessarily final
about his stand on internal improvements,
and that the people, if they chose, might
reverse it by a constitutional amendment.
But their failure so to do convinced him
that the weight of public opinion lay on his
side of the argument, and he persisted in
his course.

It should not be assumed, however, that
Jackson's vetoes rang the death-knell of
internal improvements at national expense.
The President showed no disposition to interrupt work on the National Road, he
signed many bills for federal assistance to
road-building in the territories, and he
offered no very effective opposition to federal
grants in aid of river and harbor improvement. But the appropriation of national
funds for the construction of roads and
canals within and among the several states
he did hold down to a minimum. The
adoption of such a policy at such a time was
of even greater significance than Jackson
knew. Before his administration ended
canals and turnpikes were giving place to
railroads, and the enormous capacity of this
new variety of internal improvements for
absorbing federal funds was not hard to
see. Jackson's policy, however, set a strong
precedent against such expenditures, and for
many years the railroads were unable to
induce Congress to aid them, even by
grants of land.

Scarcely less important than the problem
of internal improvements was the enduring
problem of the public lands. **The public**
Flushed with the victories they **lands**
had won by the Land Law of 1820, western
representatves were soon demanding an
even further liberalization of the public land
policy. Many of them felt particularly
aggrieved that the government insisted on
collecting a minimum of $1.25 for each acre
of the land it sold, regardless of quality.
The best lands in a newly opened plot were
quickly sold, although sometimes to speculators who held them for a rise in value
rather than to actual settlers. But the poorer
lands were apt to remain vacant for many
years. Why not, therefore, reduce the price
of these left-over lands to a figure commen-
surate with their value? The low prices
would in themselves attract new settlers to
the West, and they would also serve to beat
down the figure at which speculators held
their lands. Senator Benton of Missouri,
ever the mouthpiece of the West, repeatedly
pressed "graduation" bills upon Congress.
Let the price of vacant lands be reduced each
year by twenty-five cents an acre. Any lands
that remained unsold after their price had
declined to fifty cents an acre might thereafter be donated outright to actual settlers.
Any lands that fell to twenty-five cents an
acre, but remained unsold or untaken, were
to be donated to the states in which they
were located for use as they saw fit. Some
extremists went even further than Benton's
proposition suggested. Why not, they
argued, give the public lands outright to the
states in which they lay? Only by such an
act could the new states be placed on an
equal footing with the old, who had originally
owned their own lands. Needless to say, if
the disposition of the public lands could thus
be thrown into the hands of the western
states, the terms for the settlers would lack
nothing in liberality.

Another western demand was for a generous right of pre-emption. With increasing
frequency pioneers, either because they
lacked the means to pay for lands or because

Time and Distance 1830

Principal
Highways
1825 – 1830

they were unwilling to await the slow process of extinguishing Indian titles

Pre-emption
and completing surveys, rushed
far out into the West and selected for themselves the best lands they could find. Such
foresight and energy the West was eager to
reward, and it resented, sometimes to the
point of armed resistance, the attempts of
speculators and others to acquire for little
or nothing the improvements that a "squatter" had made on his "claim." Westerners
urged that the government should grant to
the man who had braved the dangers of the
far frontier first chance at the purchase of the
land he had appropriated. One proposition,
rejected in 1820 but by no means forgotten,
was that the squatter should be given the
chance, up to two weeks before land sales in
any particular district began, to purchase
at the ordinary minimum price one hundred
and sixty acres adjacent to his house and
improvements. The long-continued failure
of Congress to recognize the right of pre-
emption, or as it was more frequently called
in the West, "squatters' rights," led to the

formation in many frontier communities of
"claims clubs," or "claims associations."
Groups of settlers in a given community
banded themselves together, elected a secretary or other official with whom they listed
their claim, and, when land sales began, prevented by force the purchase of a member's
land by anyone other than the squatter who
lived upon it.

The continued growth of manufactures in
the Northeast made the representatives of
that section extremely wary **The Foot**
about granting to the West the **Resolution**
easy land terms it desired. Ever more favorable terms for western lands tended unmistakably to drain off the surplus population of the East into the West. Also,
laborers could, and did, demand higher
wages than they could ever have hoped to
receive had they not had the alternative of a
move to the West with which to threaten
their employers. "It cannot be overlooked,"
wrote Richard Rush, Secretary of the Treasury under John Quincy Adams, "that the
prices at which fertile bodies of land may be

bought of the Government ... operate as a perpetual allurement of their purchase. It must, therefore be taken in the light of a bounty, indelibly written in the text of the laws themselves, in favor of agricultural pursuits." Far from desiring to increase this subsidy to the western agricultural states, representatives of the Northeast were by Jackson's time beginning to talk of a reversal of policy. They were ready, as Benton charged, to attempt the regulation of land sales in such a way "as to create and preserve, in certain quarters of the Union, a population suitable for conducting great manufacturing establishments." They spurned angrily the plan for squatter's rights. They refused to reduce the price of lands long surveyed but left unsold. They scoffed at the idea that the federal government should turn over public lands that had been won by the "blood and treasure" of all the people to the western states in which those lands happened to be located. And in a famous resolution Senator Samuel Augustus Foot of Connecticut even proposed "That the Committee on Public Lands be instructed to inquire into the expediency of limiting for a certain period the sales of the public lands to such lands only as have heretofore been offered for sale, and are subject to entry at the minimum price. And also, whether the office of Surveyor General may not be abolished without detriment to the public interest." In other words, had the time not come when the growth of the West must be checked, "for who would remove to a new country if it were not to get new lands?"

Inevitably politicians made the effort to reconcile the opposing interests of the Northeast and the West on the land question. **"Distribution"** Why not permit the sale of public lands to go on, and even encourage it, but distribute the revenue derived therefrom among all the states? Probably this idea did not originate with Henry Clay, but he was quick to seize upon it and to fit it into his increasingly complicated American system. In April, 1832, he

suggested that a small portion (later set at one eighth) of the revenue from the public lands be given to the states in which the sales were made, and that the remainder be divided among all the states "according to their federal representative population, to be applied to education, internal improvements, or colonization, or to the redemption of any existing debt contracted for internal improvements, as each state, judging for itself, shall deem most conformable with its own interests and policy." Early in 1833 a measure drawn along these lines passed both houses of Congress, but received a pocket veto from the President, who for the moment preferred, in common with many other Westerners, that the public lands should "cease as soon as practicable to be a source of revenue," and should be sold to actual settlers at a price barely sufficient to reimburse the United States for the cost of acquiring them from the Indians and conducting the necessary surveys.

During Jackson's administration the

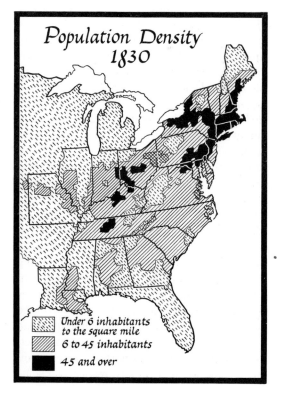

Population Density 1830

☐ Under 6 inhabitants to the square mile
▨ 6 to 45 inhabitants
■ 45 and over

South consistently stood with the West to prevent the Northeast from placing new strictures on western land sales. Southerners, at least those who were moving into the Southwest, saw point to the expansion westward of the cotton-growing frontier, and they were not averse to the growth of an agricultural Northwest that might serve them well as a counterbalance to the industrial Northeast. "Distribution," as the scheme Clay favored was labeled, the South was also inclined to oppose, in part because it meant a too generous subsidy from the national government to the populous eastern states, and in part because what Clay really intended to do by distribution, as Benton took pains to point out, was to divert "the land revenue from the support of the Government," and thus "to create a vacuum in the treasury, which must be filled up by duties on imported goods." If distribution meant high tariffs, the South had little choice but to oppose it. On the other hand, Benton was unable to muster sufficient support to enact his "graduation" plans into law; and pre-emption, while foreshadowed by the passing of several special laws to meet the needs of particular groups of squatters, was delayed for a number of years.

Benton was not the only one to observe the close relation between public land policy **The treasury** and the tariff. The rapid growth **surplus** of the West had led to steadily mounting receipts from the sales of public lands, and the treasury was by Jackson's time actually embarrassed by the surplus revenue it collected each year. Appropriations for internal improvements could readily take care of this surplus, but the Maysville veto had checked such expenditures, even if it had not completely stopped them. Both Jackson's plan for distributing the surplus among the states and Clay's plan for distributing the proceeds from the sales of public lands would have relieved the treasury, but the South, which had come to believe that its prosperity was imperiled by the high duties on imports, insisted upon tariff reduction as the only reasonable solu-

tion. But the Tariff of Abominations had apparently shown that any considerable lowering of the tariff schedules was politically impossible. The Northeast demanded high duties, not only to protect its manufactures from European competition, but also as a fitting offset to the advantage which accrued to agriculture because of cheap lands in the West. And the West, except where cotton-planting throve, while deeply resentful of all eastern suggestions that one way to reduce the revenue was to throw no more new lands on the market, still agreed with the Northeast that a protective tariff was a good thing. The South thus found itself in a permanent minority whenever the question of the tariff was broached. However much it might try to rid itself of this handicap, it was sure to fail, for the Northwest and the Northeast by standing together were able, as they had repeatedly demonstrated, to command a comfortable majority in favor of the high duties.

South Carolina, of all the southern states, felt most aggrieved at this situation. The decline in her fortunes that had **South** lately set in was unmistakable. **Carolina** Like the rest of the lower South, she had devoted herself to cotton culture almost to the exclusion of other pursuits. For a while the profits were good, but as the cotton-growing area spread farther and farther into the West the great quantities of cotton that were thrown on the market beat down the price. From one hundred and sixty million pounds produced by the South in 1820 the annual output had grown by 1830 to three hundred and fifty million pounds. Naturally the price fell. The crop of 1820 brought $27,200,000, whereas that of 1830, although more than twice as large, brought only $35,000,000. And South Carolina, whose lands could not compete in richness with the newly opened lands of the Southwest, saw her profits dwindle steadily away. In this respect the older states of the South were all alike. Western planters made money in spite of the drop in price of cotton, but eastern planters struggled in vain to keep their incomes up to the standard of living to which in more prosperous times they had become accustomed.

Other factors than the decline of cotton prices entered into the situation. Slavery as a labor system was in reality inefficient, and at best made only a few rich while leaving the bulk of the population permanently poor. Moreover, the existence of slavery practically forced upon the South the one-sided development to which it had succumbed. Manufacturing establishments, worked perhaps by slave labor, had been one of Calhoun's dreams, but as long as slavery existed the factories failed to appear. And no doubt the tariff did hurt the South. Three fourths or more of the cotton crop was exported, and from 1825 until the time of the Civil War the value of the cotton exported from the United States was greater than the combined value of all the other commodities that the country exported. Could the South have bought the manufactures it needed directly from Europe, the saving would have been considerable. Instead, it must pay high prices for northern goods, while the cotton it sent abroad was used to redress the balance of trade for the whole country. Southerners complained, not without some color of truth, that the tariff-protected profits of the northern manufacturers were paid out of the pockets of the southern planters. But the tendency to blame all the troubles of the South upon the tariff overlooked facts that were far more important. The Southwest was prosperous in spite of the tariff, while the Southeast suffered far more from its poor lands and the low price of cotton than from an unfair tariff policy.

Circumstances combined to make South Carolina take the lead in voicing protests against the tariff. The state possessed a unity that in many other southern states had not yet been achieved. Political differences between the seaboard and the back country had been adjusted by a compromise that gave control of one house of the legislature to each section. Moreover, Charleston, the only city of consequence in the old South, was to South Carolina, in a sense, what Paris was once supposed to be to France. At Charleston all the planters gathered for the social season, and here public opinion for the whole state was made. Nothing could be more apparent than that the fortunes of Charleston were, at least relative to other great cities, on the decline. The chief trouble, as thoughtful men must have known, was that New Orleans with its richer hinterland and better means of communication with the interior, was replacing Charleston as the metropolis of the South. But the fashion in Charleston was to blame everything on the tariff, and here the assembled planters, harassed by their mounting debts, railed against the tyranny of a government in which the prosperity of one section could be bought at the price of adversity for another.

Extremists flirted dangerously with the doctrine of secession, for in spite of Marshall's decisions there were **The doctrine** many who still adhered to the **of secession** theory that sovereignty resided wholly with the states. The Constitution, they contended, provided merely for a partnership of sovereign and independent states, joined together merely to accomplish certain specified ends; and therefore if any state chose for any reason to withdraw at any time from the partnership, it had full power to do so. There was nothing necessarily southern about the doctrine of secession, for many New England Federalists had once regarded it as their last defense against the tyranny of Jeffersonian democracy. The Hartford Convention, held during the War of 1812, had been restrained with difficulty from asserting secessionist views. Now the southern leaders, because their states were destined apparently to remain forever an oppressed minority section, boldly reasserted the right of a state to secede. Some of them, South Carolinians in particular, held that the time had about come when arguments should give way to deeds, and the oppressed states should leave the Union.

To the most distinguished statesman of the Old South, John C. Calhoun (1782–1850), himself a South Carolinian, the disruption of the Union which secessionists had in mind was a disaster that must somehow be avoided. Calhoun had always been an ardent nationalist. He was a product of the back country, and his parents, like Jackson's, were of Scotch-Irish immigrant stock. He had been subjected in his youth to the nationalizing influence of the frontier, he had shared with Henry Clay the leadership of the expansionist "War Hawks" who had brought on the War of 1812, he had taken the lead when the war was over in demanding an extensive program of nationalistic legislation. A lawyer and, thanks in part to a marriage into the tidewater aristocracy, a rich planter, he had naturally made politics his career, but it was in the national arena that he had found his chief interest. From 1811 to 1817 he was a member of Congress, from 1817 to 1825 he was Secretary of War in Monroe's Cabinet, and after that he was Vice-President with a strong title to the "succession." If South Carolina should leave the Union, not only the nation but also the career of John C. Calhoun would be ruined. His every instinct and interest was therefore to preserve the existing Union, and not to destroy it. But a politician may not break away too far from his constituency. Calhoun could take the risk, perhaps, of supporting internal improvements at national expense, but he had no choice but to agree with the dominant sentiment of his state and section on the tariff. Nor could he disagree with the doctrine of secession now so stoutly held.

But he could, and did, take steps to prevent secession from being put into practice. A profound thinker and a clever dialectician, he had soon evolved the alternative doctrine of nullification. He supported with irreproachable logic the contention that sovereignty is indivisible, and must reside either with the states or with the nation. He saw eye to eye with those who held that the sovereignty of the states was unimpaired by the formulation of the Constitution and the establishment of a federal government. He conceded that a state might withdraw from the Union in precisely the same manner it had entered the Union. But he also maintained that a less drastic course of action was available which might make secession unnecessary. Just as the states themselves, acting individually and separately through conventions especially called to ratify or reject the Constitution, had originally conferred certain powers on the federal government, so in the same fashion each state might at any later time through conventions of the same type decide whether and to what extent the federal government had exceeded the authority conferred upon it. Should such a convention find the federal government guilty of an unconstitutional act "so deliberate, palpable, and dangerous, as to justify the interposition of the State to protect its rights," it might declare the act "null and void within the limits of the State; which solemn declaration, based on her rights as a member of the Union, would be obligatory, not only on her citizens, but on the General Government itself; and thus place the violated rights of the State under the shield of the Constitution."

This doctrine was not wholly new, for it followed in the main the arguments of the Kentucky and Virginia Resolutions. Calhoun, however, in advocating that each state alone might invoke the right of nullification, took a more radical stand than Jefferson and Madison had contemplated, for the resolutions of 1798 had presumed merely that there should be joint action by the several states. The new doctrine of nullification, by which Calhoun hoped to avert secession and save the Union, was first authoritatively stated in a document known as the "South Carolina Exposition," which the legislature of South Carolina adopted in December, 1828, as part of a protest against the Tariff of Abominations. Calhoun's connection with the "Exposition"

John C. Calhoun

The doctrine of nullification

was not known at the time, but later on he elaborated his arguments in various speeches and documents, particularly in an essay entitled *A Disquisition on Government.* While undoubtedly he was concerned to preserve for himself a political future, he saw clearly and wrestled intelligently with the problem, still unsolved, of how in a democracy the rights of a minority are to be protected against the tyranny of a majority.

Calhoun's doctrine was readily accepted throughout the South, but the support, or **Southern** at least the tolerance, of a **overtures** majority of the states must be **to the West** obtained if nullification was to be anything more than an empty gesture or a prelude to secession. Nothing, certainly, was to be hoped from the industrial Northeast, to which the advantages of a strong central government were increasingly obvious. But the West, although it in part favored a protective tariff, had a well-developed grievance against the Northeast because some representatives from the latter section wished to bar settlers from the free and easy access to the public domain that they had come to look upon as their right. During the debate on the Foot resolution, which suggested that no further surveys of public lands be undertaken, Senator Robert Y. Hayne of South Carolina seized the opportunity to set forth to the irritated Westerners what advantages the doctrine of nullification might hold for them. He was promptly answered by Daniel Webster of Massachusetts, who upheld brilliantly the supremacy of the Union. The doctrine of nullification was on trial, and the West was to be the jury.

Daniel Webster (1782–1852), like Jackson and Calhoun, was not far removed from the **Daniel** frontier. The son of a New **Webster** Hampshire pioneer farmer, he had surmounted many obstacles to obtain an education, and had won distinction as a lawyer no less because of the superb rhetoric in which his arguments were couched and the impassioned oratory with which they were presented than because of his able

reasoning. For two terms, 1813–17, he served as a New Hampshire representative in the lower house of Congress, and devoted himself to the defense of the commercial interests with which his home city, Portsmouth, was then closely identified. He opposed the War of 1812 with all the vehemence at his command, and he charged Madison's wartime government with being 'more tyrannical, more arbitrary, more dangerous, more allied to blood and murder, more full of every form of mischief, most productive of every sort and degree of misery than has been exercised by any civilized government, with a single exception, in modern times.'' He opposed, also, with similar vigor the nationalistic measures that followed the war, most of which were damaging to the commercial interests of New England. In 1817 he changed his residence to Boston, and did not reappear in Congress until 1823. By this time the particularistic sentiments that had satisfied commercial New England began to be supplanted by sentiments of extreme nationalism that pleased the manufacturing classes. First in the House, then after 1827 in the Senate, Webster led the friends of the nationalistic Adams administration, and when Calhoun's doctrine of nullification was proclaimed in the Senate, it was to Webster that all eyes turned for an answer.

The Webster-Hayne debate was not an affair of an afternoon or an evening, but of nearly two weeks' duration. **The Web-** The debate on the Foot resolu- **ster-Hayne** tion began on January 13, with **debate** Benton of Missouri doing most of the talking. On January 19 Hayne made his first address, and from that time until the end of the month either Hayne or Webster had the floor the greater share of the time. Calhoun, as Vice-President and presiding officer of the Senate, could take no part in the debate, but he heard his views adequately, even admirably, set forth by Hayne. Webster's oratory rose to new heights, indeed, his orations on this occasion are generally conceded to be the greatest ever delivered in an American forum. He attacked point blank the theory that the states were sovereign under the Constitution, or were ever meant to be. The Constitution, he maintained, was created primarily to impose certain restrictions on state sovereignty, and the states were left sovereign only "so far as their sovereignty is not affected by the supreme law." He cited the plain historical fact that if once the thirteen states had created the nation, the nation had since that time created nearly as many new states, and might yet create many more. He pointed out the impracticability of a doctrine which left to each of the twenty-four states individually the right to pass on the constitutionality of an act of Congress, and to the eminent practicability of leaving this power where, as he contended, the Constitution placed it, in the hands of the federal courts, with a right of appeal to the Supreme Court. He warned the South that the nation could never admit that its laws might constitutionally be defied by a state, and that nullification, if attempted, could lead only to a fratricidal war or the disruption of the Union. Finally, in a magnificent peroration, he appealed to the patriotism of the whole American people:

When mine eyes shall be turned to behold for the last time the sun in heaven, may I not see him shining on the broken and dishonored fragments of a once glorious Union; on States dissevered, discordant, belligerent; on a land rent with civil feuds, or drenched, it may be, in fraternal blood! Let their last feeble and lingering glance rather behold the glorious ensign of the republic, now known and honored throughout the earth, still full high advanced, its arms and trophies streaming in their original lustre, not a stripe erased or polluted, not a single star obscured, bearing for its motto, no such miserable interrogatory as "What is all this worth?" nor those other words of delusion and folly, "Liberty first and Union afterwards"; but everywhere, spread all over in characters of living light, blazing on all its ample folds, as they float over the sea and over the land, and in every wind under the whole heavens, that **other** sentiment, dear to every true American

heart — Liberty *and* Union, now and forever, one and inseparable!

The South had spoken through Hayne, the Northeast through Webster. What would be the verdict of the West? **The attitude** Would it align itself in a natural **of the West** partnership with the agricultural South and support nullification? Or would it throw itself into the arms of the industrial Northeast and admit the supremacy of the Union? The answer was not long in coming. The Union, after all, had been of service to the West. Through repeated and insistent appeals to the national government it had generally obtained nearly everything it had sought. Even on the matter of the public lands the West was by no means ready to despair, for the obnoxious Foot resolution was soon voted down. No one knew better than Jackson the attitude of the West toward the Union, and no one shared its sentiments more fully. In a cleverly staged incident he made himself the mouthpiece of the section he best represented, and of all those who stood for national supremacy. An anniversary dinner was set for Jefferson's birthday, April 13, 1830, which all the leading Democrats were to attend. The nullificationists, with curious lack of insight, believed that the President was with them, and they arranged a program filled with nullification sentiments that they expected him in some fashion to approve. Well advised as to their plans, and fully decided as to what part he would play, the President rose at an opportune moment, and with his eyes on Calhoun proposed a toast:

"Our Federal Union — it must be preserved!"

Calhoun countered skillfully:

"The Union — next to our liberty, the most dear! May we all remember that it can only be preserved by respecting the rights of the states and distributing equally the benefits and burdens of the Union."

But the President's speech had made it clear that his states'-rights views went to no such lengths as those of Calhoun and Hayne.

HENRY CLAY

JOHN C. CALHOUN

DANIEL WEBSTER

Notable Americans of the Middle Period, Henry Clay,

John C. Calhoun and Daniel Webster all served with distinction in both Houses of Congress. Each was deeply concerned over the growing problem of sectionalism. Clay, although a Westerner, saw that to achieve any truly national policy western interests must be reconciled with the interests of the other sections. He was well called "the Great Compromiser." Calhoun, the Southerner, urged that "concurrent majorities" of all the sections be required for great national decisions, thus providing each section with a kind of veto power over actions it deemed inimical to its interests. Webster, a New Englander who fully realized that the prosperity of his section was closely identified with the indivisibility of the Union, rang the changes on that theme with great resourcefulness. The portraits shown here are, top to bottom, by Samuel S. Osgood, Charles B. King, and George P. A. Healy. Above is Samuel F. B. Morse's painting of "The Old House of Representatives," 1822.

Nor could the attitude of the West, which the President could be depended upon to reflect with rare accuracy, be longer open to doubt. The South must stand alone in its support of nullification; the North and the West would stand together against it.

Such an alliance in defense of the Union could be accomplished, however, only at the **Party dissensions** cost of a rift in the Democratic Party. From the first, trouble between the supporters of Jackson and the supporters of Calhoun had plagued the administration. Jackson's appointment of his good friend John H. Eaton to be Secretary of War had served as an opening wedge, for Eaton's wife was socially unacceptable to Mrs. Calhoun and the Washington hostesses who took their cue from her. Only a short time before his appointment Eaton, then a Senator from Tennessee, had shocked the prudish by his marriage to Peggy O'Neill, the lively daughter of an Irish tavern-keeper. Jackson's wife, who died before the inauguration, had found no fault with the new Mrs. Eaton, and Jackson as President treated her with marked consideration. So also did

Peggy Eaton's scandal is the subject of this cartoon published by Robinson in 1836, "The Celeste-Al Cabinet." Seated are the cabinet members, three to each side of the President. Standing are O'Neill and "Celeste."

Van Buren, who, like the President, was a widower and therefore free to do as he chose. To this strained social situation was soon added the clash of opinions at the Jefferson Day dinner, and finally an open rupture between Jackson and Calhoun. This event came in May, 1830, when Jackson, spurred on by his kitchen cabinet, reminded Calhoun that as Secretary of War under Monroe he had warmly advocated the censure of Jackson for the course the latter had pursued in Florida. For this behavior the President now demanded an explanation. Calhoun explained at length, but, to the delight of the kitchen cabinet, the President refused to have anything further to do with him. The chief political significance of the break was that Van Buren, not Calhoun, would receive the President's support for the succession when Jackson's term of office came to a close.

To clear the now badly overheated atmosphere, Van Buren and Eaton resigned from
Cabinet re- the Cabinet, and left the Cal-
construction houn members no choice but to follow their example. Jackson then appointed a cabinet composed entirely of his own friends, and retained only one member of the first Cabinet. Among the new appointees were at least three men of some distinction, Secretary of State Edward Livingston of Louisiana, Secretary of War Lewis Cass of Michigan, and Attorney-General Roger B. Taney of Maryland, but the

President still looked mainly to his kitchen cabinet for counsel. Jackson sought to reward Van Buren's magnanimity by an appointment as minister to England, but the Senate, with Vice-President Calhoun casting the deciding vote, refused to confirm the nomination. This rebuke was the more pointed because Van Buren had already sailed for England, but Benton of Missouri read the future aright when he remarked, "You have broken a minister and elected a Vice-President." Eaton was made governor of Florida, then minister to Spain. During the rest of Jackson's administration the hostility between the adherents of Jackson and the adherents of Calhoun was bitter and unconcealed.

Calhoun soon had occasion to marshal his forces for a final test of the doctrine of nullification. In December, 1831, Jackson urged Congress, in view of the rapid reduction of the national debt that the heavy revenues had made possible, to undertake a revision of the tariff. The South insisted upon radically lower duties, but the Northeast and the Northwest, standing together under the leadership of John Quincy Adams, now a member of the House, and Henry Clay, now a member of the Senate, achieved in July, 1832, another victory for protection. Most of the abominations that had characterized the Tariff of 1828 were removed, however, and the measure was so much better than the old that many representatives from Virginia and North Carolina supported it. Nevertheless, the South Carolina delegation in Congress promptly issued an address of protest to the people of their state. Since protection must "now be regarded as the settled policy of the country," they insisted that the time had come to use the weapon that Calhoun had forged, to decide whether "the rights and liberties you received as a precious inheritance from an illustrious ancestry shall be tamely surrendered, or transmitted undiminished to your posterity." The response of the state was all that Calhoun could have asked. Nullification became the issue upon which a legislature was chosen in the fall of 1832, and, upon the recommendation of the governor, the new legislature promptly called a convention to deal with the emergency that confronted the state. Delegates were chosen, the convention met, and on November 19, 1832, by a vote of 136 to 26, it declared the tariffs of 1828 and of 1832 "null, void, and no law, nor binding upon this State, its officers, or citizens." Furthermore, federal officers were forbidden to collect customs in South Carolina after February 1, 1833, and any federal action designed to coerce the state into obedience of the nullified laws was declared to be not only null and void, but also "inconsistent with the longer continuance of South Carolina in the Union." Calhoun now resigned as Vice-President, was promptly chosen to the Senate, and made ready to defend the course of action that he had led his state to pursue.

Jackson did not hesitate to take up the gauntlet that the nullificationists had thus

Jackson and the nullifiers thrown down. He sent a warship and seven revenue cutters to Charleston Harbor, reinforced the garrisons of the forts that commanded it, and even let it be known that in case a clash came he might take the field personally. On December 10, 1832, he issued a proclamation that left no slightest doubt as to his constitutional views. "I consider" he said, "the power to annul a

law of the United States, assumed by one State, incompatible with the existence of the Union, contradicted expressly by the letter of the Constitution, unauthorized by its spirit, inconsistent with every principle on which it was founded, and destructive of the great object for which it was formed." A month later he asked Congress for more specific authority to deal with the crisis, and a "force bill," enabling him, if he saw fit, to change the location of customs houses and to enforce federal law and the decisions of federal courts by the use of military might, was promptly introduced in the Senate. Here it met the inflamed opposition of Calhoun, Tyler, and other states'-rights advo-

States' Rights at issue in South Carolina, 1832. The Union party, whose candidates from the Charleston District are listed on this broadside, was defeated by the Nullifiers.

cates, and its passage was delayed until the crisis was over.

It was not Jackson's intention, however, to use force if he could help it. His De-

The Compromise Tariff cember proclamation had contained a long appeal to the South Carolinians to reconsider their action, and in the interest of national harmony to "snatch from the archives of your State the disorganizing edict of its convention." Moreover, he was ready to concede that the existing tariff rates, although constitutional, were inexpedient, and he encouraged his friends in Congress to seek a revision downward. It was not, however, until Henry Clay, arch-protectionist and leading exponent of the "American system," assumed leadership of the movement for tariff reduction that any real progress was made. On February 12, 1833, he introduced a compromise tariff bill, which was rushed through Congress in three weeks' time. This measure, which even Calhoun supported, somewhat enlarged the free list, and provided for the gradual reduction of such duties as remained until at the end of nine years no rate should exceed twenty per cent. This compromise, it was generally conceded, would satisfy South Carolina and put an end to nullification, but on the same day that it was signed by the President the force bill also became law.

A peaceful solution of the controversy was now possible. Nothing had yet been done by the South Carolina authorities toward the enforcement of the nullification ordinance, and on March 11, 1833, it was formally withdrawn by the same convention, reassembled for the purpose, that had passed it. The convention, however, to show that it was making no retraction of the constitutional rights it claimed, formally nullified the force bill that had just been passed. Both sides now claimed the victory. The nullificationists pointed out that their firm stand had won a concession on the tariff that could otherwise never have been obtained. The nationalists maintained that through Jackson's firm course the doctrine of the supremacy of the Union had been singularly vindicated. In a sense both contentions were correct. But it was the threat of secession and the danger of Civil War rather than the resort to nullification that had led to the passage of the Compromise Tariff; while Jackson's ardent defense of the Union was somewhat qualified by his increasingly evident desire to interpret strictly the powers conferred upon it by the Constitution.

Bibliography

The classic portrait of American democracy during this period is Alexis de Tocqueville, *Democracy in America* (4 vols., 1935–40, new ed., 2 vols., 1945). For a later evaluation of Tocqueville's contribution, see G. W. Pierson, *Tocqueville and Beaumont in America* (1938). Claude Bowers, *The Party Battles of the Jackson Period* (1922), gives an unrestrained account of the inauguration, and of the events that succeeded it. The book is intensely pro-Jackson. More dependable accounts are contained in F. J. Turner, *The United States, 1830–1850* (1935); William MacDonald, *Jacksonian Democracy* (1906); and F. A. Ogg, *The Reign of Andrew Jackson* (1919). Marquis James, *Andrew Jackson: Portrait of a President* (1937), is brilliantly written, and especially useful on the personal side. M. Ostrogorski, *Democracy and the Organization of Political Parties* (2 vols., 1902), is a classic of American party history. Dorothy G. Fowler, *The Cabinet Politician: The Postmasters-General, 1829–1909* (1943), sheds light on the problem of patronage disposal. McMaster, V, VI; Schouler, III, IV; and Channing, V, deal in whole or in part with this period.

On the important subjects of state political and constitutional development, F. N. Thorpe, *A Constitutional History of the American People, 1776–1850* (1898), is most illuminating. A. B.

Darling, *Political Changes in Massachusetts, 1824–1848* (1925), serves a similar purpose for a single state. K. H. Porter, *A History of Suffrage in the United States* (1918), gives a good account of the movement for suffrage extension.

On the Indian problem, particularly with reference to Indian removal, Annie H. Abel, *The History of Events Resulting in Indian Consolidation West of the Mississippi* (1908), is scholarly and detailed. Relevant chapters exist also in F. L. Paxson, *The Last American Frontier* (1910); and Angie Debo, *The Road to Disappearance* (1941). See also Grant Foreman, *Indian Removal: The Emigration of the Five Civilized Tribes* (1932); and, by the same author, *Indians and Pioneers* (1930); *Advancing the Frontier* (1933); *The Five Civilized Tribes* (1934). George D. Harmon, *Sixty Years of Indian Affairs* (1941), is also useful. For aspects of the Indians' removal from Georgia, the best work is U. B. Phillips, *Georgia and State Rights* (1902).

On the public lands, the general histories by Hibbard, and by Robbins, may be supplemented by a special study: R. G. Wellington, *The Political and Sectional Influence of the Public Lands, 1828–1842* (1914), a book which reveals how greatly sectional interests and jealousies affected the course of events. See also A. M. Sakolski, *The Great American Land Bubble* (1932). Thomas Hart Benton, *Thirty Years' View; or, A History of the Working of the American Government, 1820–1850* (2 vols., 1854–56), presents the western view on the land question, and nearly every other.

On nullification there are many illuminating studies. Among the best of them are E. P. Powell, *Nullification and Secession in the United States* (1897); D. F. Houston, *A Critical Study of Nullification in South Carolina* (1896); C. S. Boucher, *The Nullification Controversy in South Carolina* (1916); Frederic Bancroft, *Calhoun and the South Carolina Nullification Movement* (1928). Two excellent biographies of Calhoun exist: Gaillard Hunt, *John C. Calhoun* (1908); and W. M. Meigs, *The Life of John Caldwell Calhoun* (2 vols., 1917). The distinguished German historian, Hermann Eduard von Holst, showed a pronounced anti-southern bias, both in his *John C. Calhoun* (1882), and in his *The Constitutional and Political History of the United States* (8 vols., 1876–92). For a more balanced judgment, see C. B. Swisher, *American Constitutional Development* (1943).

Other useful biographies for the period include several on Webster: H. C. Lodge, *Daniel Webster* (1883); J. B. McMaster, *Daniel Webster* (1902); F. A. Ogg, *Daniel Webster* (1914); and Fuess, *Daniel Webster*, already mentioned. T. D. Jervey, *Robert Y. Hayne and His Times* (1909), is a useful southern counterweight. W. B. Hatcher, *Edward Livingston: Jeffersonian Republican and Jacksonian Democrat* (1940), is scholarly and unbiased.

22

The Reign of Andrew

Jackson

The Bank of the United States — A new charter vetoed — Anti-Masonry — Election of 1832 — Jackson's war on the Bank — Speculation in lands — The "Specie Circular" — Distribution of the surplus — State extravagance — Panic of 1837 — "Shirt-sleeve" diplomacy — British West Indian trade opened — The French spoliation claims — Recognition of Texas

ALMOST as spectacular as his conflict with the Nullificationists was Jackson's war on the **Bank of the United States.** This institution, operating after 1822 under the presidency of Nicholas Biddle, a wealthy and aristocratic Philadelphian, was in a flourishing condition when Jackson took office. Its cautious conservatism satisfied the eastern industrialists and silenced the criticism of many states'-rights Southerners, who on principle could not bring themselves to approve it. Its charter rights would last until 1836, and the chances that the privileges it enjoyed would be renewed for another twenty years seemed excellent. The bank, however, did not lack for critics, particularly in the West. It had unhesitatingly made use of its powerful position to restrain state banks from indulging in dubious practices, such as issuing more paper money than their resources warranted and lending freely on insufficient security. This restrictive policy won the deep resentment of all potential "wildcatters," whose resources were meager and whose profits were being curtailed. It won the resentment also of the many disappointed customers of state banks, who were given to understand that the real reason they could not renew old loans or negotiate new ones lay in the policy of the Bank of the United States. The bank was itself a good collector, and by its numerous foreclosures had raised up an equally numerous company of enemies.

Indeed, many people who had had unhappy experiences with banks had begun to think that the whole banking business was essentially dishonest. State banks, in spite of the watchful attitude of the Bank of the United States, sometimes closed their doors and inflicted heavy losses on their depositors. All banks, by virtue of the special privileges the law conferred upon them, were prone to charge unreasonable interest rates and to exact unreasonable profits. Furthermore, there was no such thing as "free banking"; that is to say, a man, simply because he had the means, could not become a banker. In the states political influence, doubtless reinforced at times by downright bribery, was necessary to obtain the special law of incorporation under which, and under which only, a bank was permitted to do business; while the Bank of the United States was an outright monopoly. By the terms of its charter no other such bank was to be permitted. Jackson represented a fairly well-defined anti-bank sentiment when he told Biddle: "I do not dislike your bank more than all banks, but ever since I read the history of the South Sea Bubble, I have been afraid of banks." [1]

[1] The South Sea Company was an English corporation, chartered in 1711, with a monopoly on the Spanish-American trade. It attempted in 1720 to underwrite the British national debt in return for a guaranteed interest rate of 5 per cent. This introduced a period of unbridled speculation, not only in stocks of the South Sea Company, but in all sorts of

When he first took office, however, Jackson did not seem disposed, whatever his private views, to make immediate trouble for the Bank of the United States. In his first three annual messages to Congress he pointed out the wisdom of deciding early upon the expediency of rechartering the bank, and he made it clear enough that he would prefer an institution whose powers would be confined primarily to handling the business of the United States government. But he issued no declaration of war, while among his supporters, both in the Cabinet and in Congress, there were many outspoken friends of the bank. Twice in 1830 congressional committees controlled by Democrats upheld the constitutionality of the bank, and urged its continuance.

Nevertheless, Biddle found it impossible to view the future without anxiety. Not only did Jackson consistently refuse to state precisely the terms of a new charter which he would be willing to sign, but he also made thinly veiled hints that places for good Jacksonian Democrats should be found on the bank's pay-roll. Biddle did not hesitate to make a number of Jackson men directors of branch banks, but he was unwilling to subject the welfare of the bank more fully to the hazards of the spoils system. His nervous apprehension, however, led him to seek the favor of Congress in a way almost equally open to question. Previous to the election of Jackson, the bank had lent to congressmen only when such a course seemed warranted as a strictly business proposition; but, beginning with 1829, this policy was unmistakably relaxed. That year thirty-four members of Congress found it possible to borrow a total amount of $192,161 from the bank; in 1830 fifty-two congressmen borrowed a total of $322,199; in 1831 fifty-nine congressmen borrowed a total of $478,069. Thus the bank was almost as definitely in politics as even the introduction of the spoils system could

The bank in politics

have made it. Also, it lent with similar freedom to powerful newspaper editors, and it paid each year a generous retainer to Daniel Webster, who, as its attorney and a member of its board of directors, saw nothing improper in representing its interests both in and out of Congress.

Jackson's war on the bank was precipitated by the ill-advised action of Webster and Clay, who persuaded Biddle to bring forward a request for the recharter of the bank along existing lines well before the election of 1832. They were convinced — correctly, as the event proved — that Congress would pass such a bill, and they thought it shrewd politics to force upon Jackson the alternative of signing a measure he disliked, or taking the responsibility for what, in their opinion, would be an unpopular veto. Clay was early in the field as the candidate of the National Republican Party in 1832, and he felt especially confident of victory in case he could make an issue of the President's antagonism to the bank. All went substantially as the conspirators had planned. In the summer of 1832 the Senate, by a vote of 28 to 20, and the House by a vote of 109 to 79, passed the bank bill, and Jackson's veto was quickly forthcoming. The bank, he argued, was un-American, undemocratic, and unconstitutional.

A new charter vetoed

More than a fourth part of the stock is held by foreigners and the residue is held by a few hundred of our own citizens, chiefly of the richest class. . . . Should the stock of the bank principally pass into the hands of the subjects of a foreign country, and we should unfortunately become involved in a war with that country, what would be our condition? . . . If we must have a bank with private stockholders, every consideration of sound policy and every impulse of American feeling admonishes that it should be purely American.

In support of this contention that the bank was undemocratic, he pointed to the dangers which "might flow from such a concentration of power in the hands of a few men irresponsible to the people," and deplored the requests of rich men to be made "richer by act of Congress." He professed alarm at

stocks also. The "Bubble" burst in November, 1720, with disastrous consequences to a host of investors.

the way in which the bank made profits from the debtor West for the benefit of eastern and European creditors, and he denounced all further "grants of monopolies and exclusive privileges" for the "advancement of the few at the expense of the many." He maintained, also, that the President and Congress, no less than the Supreme Court, were entitled to an opinion on the constitutionality of laws, and he made it clear that on this score the President, at least, felt the gravest doubts about the measure before him.

Jackson's message, with its ringing appeal to the patriotism and self-interest of the masses, and its deliberate deference to the states'-rights prejudices of the South, may not have shown a keen understanding of banking and finance, but it was far shrewder politics than the more elaborate schemes of Webster and Clay. The issue in the election became for the ordinary voter not so much the success or failure of the bank, as Clay had intended, but rather the success or failure of Andrew Jackson, champion of the common man. Jackson and his advisers had grasped the fact, far more clearly than their opponents, that elections were won by the votes of the people rather than by the good opinion of thoughtful men. Issues must be dramatized and simplified. The great importance of a national bank to the financial system of the country, a tenet which Clay now welcomed into his ever expanding American system, could not possibly compete in popular appeal with the Democratic demand that Andrew Jackson, the people's friend, should be sustained in his struggle to defend their rights against the attacks of rich aristocrats.

In this campaign, for the first time in American history, an organized third party **Anti-** put in its appearance. The **Masonry** Anti-Masonic Party, as it was called, originated in western New York, a region still distinctly frontier in character. Secret societies in this democratic community were regarded with much disfavor, partly, no doubt, because only a few could

afford membership in such organizations, and partly because of the fantastic exaggerations that gained currency with regard to the oaths sworn and the secrets kept. In 1826 one William Morgan, a citizen of Batavia, New York, and a former Mason, published a pamphlet in which he claimed to have revealed the secrets of Masonry. When, shortly afterwards, he disappeared under conditions that suggested foul play, the Masons were held responsible and a furor of protest arose against the Masonic fraternity in particular and, for good measure, all other secret societies also. The contagion spread rapidly throughout central and western New York, across the borders into Pennsylvania and Vermont, as far east as Massachusetts and as far west as Ohio. For a time Anti-Masonry was a social upheaval rather than a political movement, but shrewd politicians — former Federalists, defeated National Republicans, and unrewarded Democrats — were not slow to make it serve their purposes. They found flaws in state and local administrations that were dominated by Masons. They appealed to religious prejudice, and saw in even the small number of Catholic immigrants who were coming to the United States (most of whom voted the Democratic ticket) a menace to the liberty of the Republic. They further widened their program to advocate assistance for "domestic manufacture, internal improvements, the abolishment of imprisonment for debt, repeal of our militia system, and all other measures calculated to promote the general interest and welfare of the people." Some of these principles were taken over bodily from Henry Clay's American system, but they had a strong popular appeal in the sections where Anti-Masons were most numerous.

The democratic spirit that had given rise to Anti-Masonry should normally have drawn it toward the support of Jackson and the national administration, but circumstances decreed otherwise. In the first place, success for the politicians who headed the movement, such men as Thurlow Weed and

William H. Seward in New York, and Thaddeus Stevens in Pennsylvania, depended upon their ability to overthrow the existing Democratic control of their respective states; and, secondly, Jackson was himself a Mason who consistently refused to forswear an innocent allegiance he had long avowed. Cheered by many local victories, the Anti-Masonic leaders were eager to enter the arena of national politics, and as the election of 1832 approached they began an intensive search for a presidential candidate around whom they might rally all the forces opposed to Jackson. They would gladly have supported Clay, but he like Jackson was a Mason who refused to retract. Perhaps also he underestimated the strength of the Anti-Masonic movement, and showed it too little deference. At length the Anti-Masonic leaders took the unprecedented step of calling a national nominating convention to select their candidate for the Presidency, and in September, 1831, their convention, meeting at Baltimore, chose William Wirt of Virginia to lead them, and Amos Ellmaker of Pennsylvania for second place. Wirt's friendship and admiration for Clay were well known, and it was the Anti-Masonic hope that all anti-Jackson men would support him.

But the Anti-Masonic movement failed completely to divert attention from the **Election of 1832** main contest, which was between the National Republicans, with Clay as their candidate, and the Democrats, with Jackson as theirs. Both parties, however, followed an Anti-Masonic precedent in calling together national nominating conventions for the selection of presidential and vice-presidential candidates. Such a direct consultation of the popular will was quite in line with the current conception of democracy, and neither party dare overlook the opportunity of thus cultivating the favor of "King Numbers." In December, 1831, the National Republicans, also meeting at Baltimore, nominated Clay for President, and John Sergeant of Pennsylvania for Vice-President; and in May, 1832,

the Democrats, at the same place, endorsed the "repeated nominations" which Jackson had received "in various parts of the Union," and chose Martin Van Buren of New York as their candidate for Vice-President. The nomination of Van Buren was in strict accordance with Jackson's desires, but was so lacking in popular appeal that in the hope of giving a contrary impression, a rule was devised whereby a candidate to be nominated must receive "two thirds of the whole number of votes in the convention." Van Buren, thanks to the persuasive efforts of the President's friends, received well over this number, and for a hundred years the "two-thirds rule" remained the practice of Democratic national conventions. Each state, in these early conventions, was assigned as many delegates as it had senators and representatives in Congress, but the methods employed for the choosing of delegates were somewhat irregular. In time a complete system of state and local conventions was devised which, theoretically, at least, made the voters of any given party the ultimate source of all party authority.

The election resulted in an overwhelming victory for Jackson. In New York, Ohio, and elsewhere the National Republicans and the Anti-Masons **Jackson's victory** supported the same electoral tickets, and in general the Wirt candidacy was used to promote Clay's chances of victory. Nevertheless, in the popular vote Jackson triumphed by 687,502 to 530,189 for Clay and Wirt combined, while in the electoral college the vote was 219 for Jackson to 49 for Clay. Only half the states of New England stood by Clay; Vermont cast her seven votes for Wirt, while Maine and New Hampshire gave comfortable majorities for Jackson. In South Carolina, where the legislature still chose presidential electors, the Nullificationists retained their majority, and gave the eleven votes of the state to John Floyd of Virginia. Jackson's re-election was essentially an endorsement of the popular principles of government for which he stood. This was not due to any lack of specific issues, for the Anti-Masonic and the Democratic conventions had made sufficiently definite commitments in formal addresses to the people, while the National Republicans had set the precedent for party platforms by adopting a series of resolutions that embodied the whole "American system" of Henry Clay. Furthermore, during the campaign both major parties gave much attention to Jackson's veto of the bank bill, and doubtless swayed some voters by the arguments over this issue. Nevertheless, it seems reasonable to suppose that Jackson would have won by about the same majority had he signed the bill instead of vetoing it. The common people liked him as an individual, they believed in him as the peculiar champion of their rights, and his political lieutenants had already learned how to "get out the vote." Among the innovations in campaigning used by both sides was the political cartoon, which was quite as intelligible even to the voters who could not read as to those who could.

Jackson naturally interpreted his re-election as a mandate against the recharter of **Jackson's war on the bank** the bank, but he was far too impatient to await its orderly demise in 1836, the year in which its charter rights expired. He feared, too, that Biddle might somehow use the power of the bank to rebuild its popularity, and to force its continuance, even over the opposition of the President. Jackson determined, therefore, to cripple the bank by withdrawing from it the deposits of the United States government — a truly formidable blow, for the treasury balance was rarely less than ten or twelve million dollars. Power to withdraw the deposits was vested, however, not in the President, but in the Secretary of the Treasury, who was authorized to take such action only in the event that he considered the bank an unsafe place for the government's funds. Jackson's current Secretary of the Treasury, Louis McLane of Delaware, refused to remove the deposits, whereupon Jackson made him Secretary of State to succeed Livingston, who

became minister to France. Jackson assumed that his new Secretary of the Treasury, William J. Duane of Pennsylvania, knew why he had been appointed and would take action against the bank at once, but Duane, too, refused to remove the deposits and was summarily dismissed. His successor, Roger B. Taney of Maryland,[1] was a states'-rights Jeffersonian Democrat of the old school who believed the bank unconstitutional, and did not hesitate to issue the order which Jackson desired. Thereafter the United States drew upon its deposits in the bank to meet its obligations, but placed all newly collected tax money in selected state banks — "pet banks," as they were called — whose importance increased as that of the Bank of the United States declined. Jackson's action was received with a storm of criticism from the National Republicans, and the Senate actually passed a resolution of censure, which, however, Benton at length induced it to expunge from the record.

Jackson's war on the bank ushered in a period of great financial uncertainty. Biddle did not entirely give up hope of securing a recharter before 1836, but the withdrawal of government deposits obliged him to curtail his business drastically. This, in turn, caused serious embarrassment to many of his former customers in the Northeast, for a disproportionate number of the pet banks were located in the agricultural West, while the industrial centers found it extremely difficult for a time to obtain the money and credit they needed. During the year 1834 this money famine in the Northeast was so acute as to cause a sharp panic, but the West prospered as never before. The administration made an effort to select only the soundest state banks as federal depositories and to hedge them about with strict regulations, but the urgent pleas

---

[1] Taney was later chosen by Jackson to succeed Marshall as Chief Justice. His stand on the Bank almost cost him confirmation by the Senate, but he eventually showed himself to be a worthy successor to Marshall. His decisions somewhat modified the extremely nationalistic trend of the Court under Marshall, and limited a little more the prerogatives of private property.

for funds made by state bankers who had supported Jackson were hard to ignore. Too many of these bankers were Westerners; too much federal money drifted into the West. Moreover, the declining power of the Bank of the United States emboldened state bankers of wildcat tendencies to indulge their long-suppressed desires to issue more currency and to extend their loans. Eastern state bankers were for the most part conservative, and refused to expand their business more than their resources warranted, but the number of wildcatters in the West steadily increased. Here many new state banks were chartered, some of them with the flimsiest of financial backing, but they nevertheless added generously to the amount of money and credit available. What was happening can best be set forth as follows:

STATE BANKING IN THE UNITED STATES

Year	Number of Banks	Capital*	Circulation*	Loans*
1829	329	110.2	48.2	137.0
1834	506	200.0	94.8	324.1
1836	718	251.9	140.3	457.5
1837	788	290.8	149.2	525.1

*In millions of dollars.

So marked an inflation of money and credit was certain to result in some form of **Speculation in land** speculation, and with the chief incidence of inflation in the West this meant primarily speculation in land. Even before inflation set in, western land prices were on the rise. The demand for new cotton land in the Southwest steadily increased, while throughout the interior the improved means of transportation promised such profits from western agriculture as had never been known before, and at the same time greatly facilitated long-distance migration. Land speculators bought up choice locations far in advance of settlement, and sold their holdings at a good profit to actual settlers, or to other speculators. The effect of inflation on such a situation was certain to be disastrous. Purchases of government land far outran any reasonable demand, and the same plots were often sold and resold several times without once being held by anyone who expected to till them. There is no way of measuring the full scope of the speculation, but a fair idea of what was going on can be gathered from the fact that the government sales of public lands rose from four million acres in 1834 to fifteen millions in 1835, and to twenty millions in 1836. It was during this period that the phrase "doing a land-office business" entered the American vernacular.

The changed banking habits of the United States government served to add unneeded fuel to the flames. Receipts from public lands had contributed to the treasury only $4,857,000 in 1834; but in 1835 this item rose to $14,757,000, and in 1836 to $24,877,000. To care for these funds more and more pet banks were designated, until instead of the twenty-nine depositories of January, 1835, the government by November, 1836, had its accounts distributed among eighty-nine state banks. These banks had nothing better to do with the funds that poured into their vaults than to lend them out again, and in far too many instances the borrowers were mere speculators who bought more land. Thus an endless chain was fashioned; payments made by the speculators to the United States were deposited in pet banks, then lent again to other speculators to buy more land, then paid once more into the treasury, then redeposited, then lent again, and so on in a vicious circle.

The unhealthiness of a situation which, as Jackson said, served "to transfer to speculators the most valuable public **The "Specie Circular"** lands and pay the government by a credit on the books of the banks," could not long be ignored. Jackson finally decided that the universal practice among government land agents of accepting bank notes in payment for public lands must stop, and in July, 1836, his Secretary of the Treasury embodied this policy in an official statement known as the "Specie Circular." This document announced that after August 15 land purchased of the government would have to be paid for in gold or silver, except in the case of actual settlers who were permitted until December 15, on purchases of three hundred and twenty acres or less, "the same indulgences heretofore extended." The Specie Circular, timed carefully to take effect after, rather than before, the election of 1836, virtually ended for a number of years the purchase of land directly from the government.

Meantime the treasury was seriously embarrassed by its mounting receipts. In 1835 the last dollar of the public debt was paid off, and the treasury needed only enough money to pay current expenses. At the peak of the speculation, however, the revenues from the public lands were alone sufficient to meet the entire cost of the national government, but by that time the tariff was also bringing in startlingly large sums. The Compromise Tariff of 1833, because it provided for a gradual scaling-down of rates, was expected to produce less revenue as time went on rather than more; but the exact reverse proved to be true. The huge speculative profits that were being made in western lands, and the stimulating effects of inflation on business generally, fostered a spirit of extravagance that was reflected in the heavy purchases of foreign goods. Such a luxury item as silk, for example, rose from an import value of under six millions in 1831 to over ten millions in 1834, and in 1836 to nearly twenty-three millions. Tariff receipts which had stood at only about sixteen millions in 1834 were half again as large by 1836, and therefore, like the receipts from the public lands, sufficient in themselves to pay the full costs of the national government. A reduction in the revenue from public lands seemed impracticable, for eastern sentiment strongly opposed any further cut in the sale price, while western sentiment was equally hostile to the restriction of land sales. Likewise, a reduction in tariff receipts could not easily be made, for such a plan would involve a revision of the rates agreed upon in the Compromise Tariff of 1833, a course which all who had supported that measure wished earnestly to avoid. Furthermore, schemes for extravagant spending by the government were sure to be opposed by the President on some such grounds as he advanced in his Maysville veto.

Various projects were brought forward to rid the treasury of its surplus revenue. Most debated was Clay's plan for the distribution of the proceeds of the sales of public lands among **Distribution of the surplus** all the states, but the President's known antagonism to such a measure prevented its adoption. Others took seriously a suggestion that Jackson himself had once made, and urged that all the surplus funds of the government, regardless of their origin, should be distributed among the states; but again the President objected, not because he opposed such a course on principle, but because he questioned whether Congress had the necessary authority under the Constitution to take such action. Finally, to satisfy the President, it was agreed that the money should be distributed among the states as a loan rather than as a gift, and in June, 1836, such a bill became law. According to this act, whatever money in excess of five million dollars was in the treasury on January 1, 1837, was to be apportioned among the states in accordance with their representation in the electoral college, and paid over to them during the year in four quarterly installments.

The national government might far better have held on to its funds. Already many of the states, particularly the new states in the West, had embarked upon extensive programs of internal **State extravagance** improvement, and had borrowed heavily for this purpose. Unfortunately they found a ready market for their securities among foreign investors, who were misled by the excellent credit of the United States government into thinking that the credit of the various American states was equally good. As a matter of fact, some of the states had not only contracted obligations for far more than their taxable resources warranted, but had also lent their credit freely in aid of dubious private enterprises. Now, dazzled by the prospect of receiving generous subsidies from the national government, many of them were tempted to increase their extravagance; by 1837 the total of state indebtedness had reached $170,000,000, for the times a prodigious sum.

English exporters, who furnished the bulk of the goods sent to the United States, were among the first to observe that the phenomenal prosperity of their customers might have a disastrous ending. By 1836 the balance of trade was running strongly against the United States, for in addition to much extravagant spending by Americans on manufactured articles, a crop failure in 1835 necessitated the heavy importation of high-priced European wheat. When, as a result of the unfavorable trade balance, American drafts and bills of exchange began to sell at a discount in England, the Bank of England promptly raised its discount rates. Thereupon exporters took fright, refused new credits to American customers, and demanded the immediate settlement of old accounts. To meet their foreign obligations American importers in turn tried to make immediate collections, and, since the foreign balance could be met only in hard money, the American banks were deluged with requests for specie, requests they could not possibly hope to meet.

For the American banking system, even without this blow, was tottering to its fall. **The panic of 1837** Unaccustomed to doing business with gold and silver, neither the banks nor the public they served had been fully aware of the fact that much of the nation's slender store of specie had already gone abroad to redress unfavorable trade balances. But the inadequacy of the bank reserves was made abundantly apparent by Jackson's Specie Circular. Thereafter land speculators who tried to get hard money from the banks found out that the banks had no hard money to lend; moreover, Jackson's order also revealed clearly that the United States treasury no longer regarded state bank notes as of face value. To make matters

still worse, the pet banks, supposedly the strongest in the country, were given a body blow by the Distribution Act, which required them to return the surplus government funds they held on deposit. Payment of the first installment, January 1, 1837, caused them great embarrassment, and the second, on April 1 following, brought almost immediate disaster. Bank failures now came thick and fast, and in May, 1837, every bank in the United States suspended specie payment. Notes of the failed or failing banks became virtually worthless, and the public took enormous losses. Meantime, many English exporters, unable to collect on the debts owed them by Americans, had also been forced into bankruptcy. Their failure brought down, in turn, the English merchants and manufacturers who furnished goods for the American market. Soon both Great Britain and the United States were plunged into the depths of a thoroughgoing economic depression. English cotton mills closed down, and the American planter saw his best market evaporate. The ensuing distress of the cotton planter similarly affected the western farmer, who had sold great quantities of foodstuffs to the South. The loss of buying power in the South and West meant the strangulation of manufacturing in the Northeast. By the summer of 1837 business was almost at a standstill, and for many years its normal activity was not resumed.

It would not be fair to say that Jackson's war on the Bank of the United States was wholly responsible for the panic **Causes of** of 1837. Doubtless the West **the panic** would have developed with dangerous rapidity under any circumstances; internal improvements, particularly the building of canals, were already an obsession when the "war" began; over-expansion of cotton planting in the South and of manufacturing in the Northeast could hardly have been forestalled. But Jackson's crude handling of public finance certainly stimulated the boom, and accentuated the crash. Fortunately for his popularity, he left office a few

FAIRVIEW INN. Scene on the National Road, Maryland. Painting by T. C. R.

The National Road, according to its historian, Searight, often looked "more like a leading avenue of a great city than a road through rural districts." It was alive with traffic, emigrants going West, drovers bringing their herds to eastern markets, wagoners carrying traffic both ways. Inns of varying degrees of comfort served the needs of the travelers, and in many of them land speculators lay in wait for the unwary.

THE LAND SPECULATOR. Painting by James H. Beard, about 1840.

weeks before the panic broke. As for the Bank of the United States, it secured a charter from the state of Pennsylvania, and continued in operation until 1841, when it failed. Its management during these later years showed little of the restraint for which the bank had once been famous, and the speculations that it promoted probably served to prolong the depression.

Jackson's administration witnessed an abrupt break with the past in the handling of American foreign relations. "Shirt-sleeve" diplomacy Most of Jackson's predecessors in the Presidency had represented their country for long periods abroad, and were thoroughly versed in the arts of diplomacy, but neither Jackson nor many of the men whom he appointed to office had had the benefit of any such training. By 1833 the state department was cleared of all but two of the officials who had served before Jackson took office, while diplomatic posts were parceled out as the exigencies of party politics required. The resulting lack of finesse in dealing with foreign countries has sometimes been described as "shirt-sleeve" diplomacy; but the new methods, if exasperating to Europeans, were often singularly effective.

Among the diplomatic problems that Jackson inherited was the impasse between the United States and Great Britain over Ameri-

THE WHITE WATER CANAL, INDIANA. The canal, built in 1836–41 with state funds, is shown passing the home of William Henry Harrison. Illustration from *The Ladies' Repository,* July, 1841.

A "SAFETY COACH" ON THE PHOENIX LINE. Lithograph after a drawing by M. Swett, about 1834.

Internal improvements, except for the National Road, were usually promoted by the states rather than by the national government, although national aid was often sought and obtained. The success of the Erie Canal ushered in a Canal Age, but state turnpikes, abounding in Concord coaches, ran everywhere. Western states benefited greatly from transportation improvements, and rapidly grew to statehood size.

MISSOURI STATE CAPITOL. Jefferson City about 1840. Illustration from Meyer, *Universorum,* 1851.

can trade with the British West Indies.

British West Indian trade Repeated efforts to secure for American shippers the same rights to trade with these islands as British subjects enjoyed had failed to produce results, and during the administration of John Quincy Adams irritating reprisals had been adopted by both governments. Jackson was determined to secure the opening of the West Indian trade on the best terms he could get, and he lost no time in notifying the British authorities that a new administration was in power which was ready to adopt a new policy. Such a reference to internal politics, however precisely in accordance with the facts, was regarded by experienced diplomats as extremely improper, but Jackson soon found out that he could make good progress if only the law discriminating against British trade could be eliminated. Accordingly, he asked from Congress, and in May, 1830, received, authority to withdraw the existing discriminations against British ships coming from the West Indies to the United States, and to admit them upon whatever terms West Indian ports were open to American ships. This satisfied the British, and in a short time an agreement was reached that gave the United States full freedom of trade with the British West Indies, although the right of American ships to trade between these islands and Great Britain was still withheld. Probably, however, the British concession was not so much a victory for Jacksonian diplomacy as a revelation that the British government was about ready to remove the last of the shackles it had once placed on colonial trade.

Another problem that confronted Jackson was the non-payment by France of the so-called "spoliation claims."

The "spoliation claims" These the United States had long held against France in consideration of the losses which Napoleon, in his vain effort to enforce the Continental System, had inflicted upon American shipping. French governments after Napoleon were usually willing to acknowledge the justice of the American demand, but they pleaded poverty and asked for delay. Also, they advanced counterclaims for American damages to French shipping, and for the failure of the United States to grant to French vessels in the ports of the Louisiana Purchase the "most-favored nation" treatment stipulated by the treaty of cession. Under strong pressure from Jackson an agreement was reached in July, 1831, whereby the United States was to be paid twenty-five million francs, less one and one half millions for the French claims against the United States, in six equal installments beginning in February, 1833. Also, the French gave up their interpretation of the Louisiana treaty in return for a ten-year reduction of the American duty on French wines. This settlement fully satisfied American public opinion, and Congress made prompt provision for carrying it out, but the payments required were so strongly resented in France that the French Chamber refused to appropriate the necessary funds. Completely disgusted, Jackson, in a message to Congress, denounced the French government in plain words for its failure to live up to a solemn agreement, and asked for authority to make reprisals if necessary. Among European nations so frank a statement was generally regarded as a prelude to war, and throughout France the already heated feeling against the United States was fanned to a flame. Responsible French officials were honestly desirous of meeting the American obligation in full, but the popular clamor forced them to break off diplomatic negotiations with the United States and to make ready for war. Finally, however, the Chamber was induced to vote the necessary sums on condition that a suitable apology should be made for the President's blunt threats. Jackson was not given to apologies, but a statement he made to Congress that he had no desire to harm, insult, or menace France was construed in that light, and the money was at length paid over.

Jackson also was confronted with the difficult task of maintaining peaceful relations with Mexico while the independent state of

Texas was in process of formation. Unfortunately the southwestern boun-
dary of the United States, as
defined by the treaty of 1819 with Spain, was
set at the Sabine River just at a time when
the southwestern pioneers were beginning to
look with longing upon the practically unoc-
cupied lands of Texas, lands which for a good
third of the way to the Rio Grande were
admirably suited to cotton-growing.   In
Spanish times Moses Austin, a resident of
Missouri, sought and obtained permission
to lead a group of colonists to Texas, and a
few years later his son, Stephen F. Austin,
won from the new revolutionary government
of Mexico confirmation of the privileges the
Spanish had extended to his father.   A nucleus of settlement from the United States
speedily appeared at San Felipe de Austin,
and in 1824 a general colonization law welcomed other American settlers in.   By 1830
about twenty thousand former citizens of the
United States, owners of perhaps a thousand
Negro slaves, were residents of Texas.

Inevitably trouble developed between the
Texans and their Mexican overlords.   The
former were constantly irritated by the fact
that Texas was not a separate and self-governing state of Mexico, but was joined to
the neighboring state of Coahuila on terms
that insured to the native Mexicans a permanent majority in the state legislature.   They
were skeptical, too, of Mexican land titles,
which were semi-feudal in character, and
beyond the comprehension of the ordinary
American pioneer.   Also they were presumed
by the terms of the law under which they
were admitted to Texas to be good Catholics,
whereas only occasionally was this the case.
But most important of all, the sentimental
attachment of the Texans for their native
land was not destroyed merely because they
had crossed an international border, and a
great many of them looked forward confidently to the time when Texas would become
a part of the United States.   With this ambition the government of the United States
seemed fully sympathetic, for it made repeated efforts, both before and after Jackson

Texas

Stephen F. Austin, called "the
founder of Texas," devoted his life to
"redeeming Texas from its wilderness
state."

became President, to purchase Texas from
Mexico.   These efforts, however, the Mexicans deeply resented, and, far too late, the
Mexican government began to repent of
having admitted so large a foreign element
within the borders of its country.   In 1830
further immigration into Texas was prohibited and the importation of Negro slaves
was forbidden.   Practically prohibitive duties were placed on imports from the United
States, and Mexican officials supported by
Mexican soldiers were sent to the border to
enforce the regulations.

Inasmuch as during this period Americans
within the United States were not above attempts to nullify the acts of **The Texan**
their own Congress, it is not **revolt**
difficult to understand how their kinsmen in
Texas were ready to revolt against the far
more unpopular rule of Mexico.   At first the
Texans took sides with a Mexican revolutionist, Santa Anna, whose promises seemed
fair enough, but when he triumphed they
found themselves no better off than they
had been before.   Finally, they decided to
follow the well-known precedents of the
American Revolution, and in March, 1836,

The Texan revolt against Mexican authority was successfully concluded with Santa Anna's surrender to General Sam Houston at San Jacinto, the subject of this painting by W. H. Huddle.

declared their independence of Mexico. By this time war had already begun, and Santa Anna was sweeping northward with so many troops at his command that the Texans should have been easily overwhelmed. But at San Jacinto, on April 21, 1836, Santa Anna was disastrously defeated by a Texas army under the command of General Sam Houston, and from this time forward Mexican authority in Texas was at an end.

The government of the United States, meanwhile, preserved an air of neutrality, but made little effort to restrain the American public from giving great aid and comfort to the Texans. American volunteers joined the Texan army, and American money and supplies kept the war for independence going. There is little reason to doubt that, had Santa Anna rather than Houston won at San Jacinto, public opinion in the United States would have forced the administration to come openly to the defense of the Texans. Indeed, for a little time, on the pretense of danger from the Indians, a detachment of American troops under General Edmund P. Gaines was actually on Texas soil, and because of this and other allegedly unneutral acts of the United States, the Mexican minister left Washington.

Annexation, however, proved to be a different matter. The Texans, supported by many citizens of the United States, urged it strongly, and probably Jack- **Recognition** son would have been glad to **of Texas** comply with their wishes. He was restrained by the growing opposition both within and without his party to such a course. Annexation meant the ultimate admission from the new territory of one or more slave states, and many Northerners, among them ex-President John Quincy Adams, were by this time on record against the acquisition of any new territory open to slavery. Also, there was the practical certainty that annexation would involve the United States in a war with Mexico, and many Southerners as well as Northerners were eager to avert such a calamity. Jackson, therefore, with an eye to the effect of anything he might do on the Democratic chances of victory in 1836, wisely decided to take no action whatever on this subject. He even delayed the opening of diplomatic relations with Texas until after he could consult Congress, and not until the day before he left office was the Republic of Texas officially recognized by the United States.

When Jackson became President there was little agreement as to the policies for which his party stood, but by the end of his administration he had committed both himself and his followers on a wide variety of issues. His

EAST VS. WEST. "A New Map of the U. S. with Additional Territories on an Improved Plan." Anonymous cartoon, about 1829.

KING ANDREW THE FIRST Anonymous cartoon, about 1832.

Political cartoons were used freely to discredit or support the Jackson administration. In one of the three shown here, Jackson becomes an alligator (a familiar symbol for Jackson and his party), while Adams and the eastern Whigs are represented by a tortoise. In another, Jackson, whose autocratic actions were much deplored, appears in the robes and trappings of royalty. In the third, "Zek Downing," a popular pro-Jackson cartoonist, celebrates the destruction of the United States Bank.

"THE DOWNFALL OF MOTHER BANK." Cartoon "draw'd off from Natur by Zek Downing," about 1836.

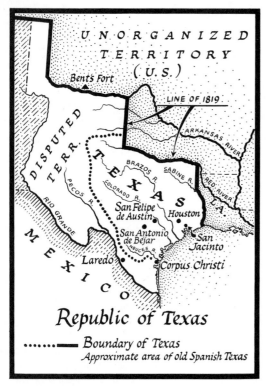

U N · O R · G A N I Z E D
T E R · R · I T O R Y
(U. S.)
Bent's Fort
LINE OF 1819

DISPUTED TERR.

BENT'S FORT
ARKANSAS RIVER

DISPUTED TERR.
BRAZOS R.
SABINE R.
RED RIVER
COLORADO R.
PECOS R.
RIO GRANDE
T E X A S
LA.
San Felipe
de Austin
Houston
San Antonio
de Bejar
San
Jacinto
NEUCES R.
Laredo
Corpus Christi

M E X I C O

Republic of Texas

········ Boundary of Texas
Approximate area of old Spanish Texas

interpretation of the slogan, "Let the people rule," had led to the adoption of the spoils system with its useful corollary, rotation in office. His whole-hearted espousal of Calhoun's plan for the removal of the Indians to the trans-Mississippi West had constituted in effect a party pledge that the settled portions of the United States must become a "white man's country." His conflict with the South Carolinians over nullification had left no doubt that under his leadership the Democratic Party proposed to maintain the supremacy of the Union at all costs; but his Maysville veto and his war on the Bank of the United States had set equally strong precedents in favor of the drastic limitation of the scope of national powers. On the critical questions of the public lands and the tariff, the clash of sectional interests had forced upon him compromise solutions, but the unmistakable trend of his administration had been toward the generous treatment of actual settlers on the public domain, and the reduction of the tariff to a strictly revenue basis.

In his conduct of foreign affairs he had taken an aggressive, strongly nationalistic attitude, and had seemed at times on the verge of plunging his country into war. These various commitments won for the President and his party much support, but also much opposition.

The National Republicans, led by Henry Clay, unceasingly denounced the administration and sought to encompass its defeat. This party included within its membership the "better classes" of the Northeast — the aristocratic and the moderately well-to-do — most of whom were interested, directly or indirectly, in manufactures, and were therefore in favor of a high protective tariff. Moreover, they believed, practically to the last man, in a strong banking system, headed by just such a national bank as Jackson had made it his business to destroy. The National Republicans had also a strong following in the West, where Jackson's Maysville veto was extremely unpopular and his attitude toward the bank by no means universally admired.

Jackson's opponents

Anti-Masons, following the failure of their party to achieve national prominence in the election of 1832, very generally went over to the National Republicans. Indeed, the doctrines of Anti-Masonry, except on the subject of secret societies, were from the beginning the doctrines of Henry Clay. This accretion to the National Republican strength was of great importance, for it gave the party an enthusiastic rural following and an atmosphere of democracy that it otherwise would have lacked.

Southerners who were opposed to Jackson were somewhat at a loss to know what to do. Conservatives for the most part, they resented the open flouting of states' rights that had characterized Jackson's utterances during the nullification controversy, they regarded his inept handling of public finance as an even worse calamity than an unconstitutional Bank of the United States, and they objected strenuously to the excesses of democracy that the spoils system introduced. On the other hand, they could have little sympathy for National Republicanism as long as its cardinal tenets were a national bank, a protective tariff, and a national program of internal improvements.

As the election of 1836 approached, it became the fashion for Jackson's opponents, who had long denounced as "Tory" the autocratic powers the President had assumed, to refer to themselves as "Whigs." The Whigs, to be sure, had little in common except their hostility to "King Andrew I," but they at least agreed that another such "reign" must be prevented. They accused the President of desiring to found a dynasty; for he was determined that the Vice-President, Martin Van Buren, should succeed to the Presidency, and practically dictated his nomination to the Democratic National Convention. The weakness of the Whigs lay in their lack of cohesion. They did not themselves dare to have a national convention, for their leaders doubted whether they could agree either on candidates or on platform. Ultimately they decided, almost of necessity, that there should be many candidates, as in 1824, and that each section should be encouraged to support its favorite son. In this fashion enough electoral votes might be drawn from Van Buren to insure his defeat, and the House of Representatives could choose Jackson's successor.

Thus the election of 1836 became a kind of free-for-all. Before the Democratic National Convention met, the Tennessee legislature had presented Judge Hugh L. White as a candidate for the Presidency, and in spite of the action of the convention, White's name was not withdrawn. Whether White was a Whig or an Independent Democrat was open to speculation, but two years later he declared himself to be a Whig. The legislature of Massachusetts nominated Daniel Webster, and a Pennsylvania state convention, William Henry Harrison. In South Carolina, where the legislature still chose electors, the Nullificationists would indubitably support some anti-Jackson Democrat. Hence there were to all intents and purposes four candidates in the field against Van Buren. But in the fall of 1836 the country was still prosperous. Jackson was still popular, and Van Buren won with 170 electoral votes against 73 for Harrison, 26 for White, 14 for Webster, and 11 (from South Carolina) for Willie P. Mangum. The selection of the Vice-President, for the first and only time in the history of the United States, went to the Senate, which chose Richard M. Johnson of Kentucky, the Van Buren candidate. Jacksonian Democracy had triumphed, but the margin of victory was uncomfortably narrow.

Election of 1836

Bibliography

A. M. Schlesinger, Jr., *The Age of Jackson* (1945), is a brilliant re-evaluation, which finds the sources of Jackson's power in the urban working classes rather than in the frontier farmers. The book suffers somewhat from a forced parallelism with the age of Franklin D. Roosevelt. For other general references on the Jackson administration, see Bibliography for the preceding chapter, p. 384.

For Jackson's "War on the Bank," Catterall, *Second Bank of the United States*, already cited, is excellent. See, in addition: J. T. Holdsworth and D. R. Dewey, *The First and Second Banks of the United States* (1910); W. L. Royall, *Andrew*

Jackson and the Bank of the United States (1880); and von Holst, *Constitutional and Political History of the United States*, III. *The Correspondence of Nicholas Biddle Dealing with National Affairs, 1807–1844*, edited by R. C. McGrane (1919), supplements admirably the numerous secondary accounts that deal with the Bank. On Taney's role as Secretary of the Treasury, see C. B. Swisher, *Roger B. Taney* (1936); C. W. Smith, Jr., *Roger B. Taney: Jacksonian Jurist* (1936); and Bernard C. Steiner, *Life of Roger Brooke Taney* (1922).

The financial unsettlement that followed Jackson's success in overthrowing the Bank is treated

with commendable directness and brevity in R. C.
McGrane, *The Panic of 1837* (1924). See also
A. M. Sakolski, *The Great American Land Bubble*
(1932), already cited; M. S. Wildman, *Money In-
flation in the United States: A Study in Social Pa-
thology* (1905); E. G. Bourne, *The History of the
Surplus Revenue of 1837* (1885); W. J. Schultz and
M. R. Caine, *Financial Development of the United
States* (1937); Sister M. Grace Madeleine, *Mone-
tary and Banking Theories of Jacksonian Democ-
racy* (1943). On the activities of the state banks,
see Leonard C. Helderman, *National and State
Banks* (1931); E. L. Bogart, *Financial History of
Ohio* (1912); G. W. Dowrie, *The Development of
Banking in Illinois, 1817–1863* (1913); Logan
Esarey, *State Banking in Indiana* (1912); A. C.
Bryan, *History of State Banking in Maryland*
(1899); C. A. Campbell, *The Development of Bank-
ing in Tennessee* (1932); S. A. Caldwell, *A Bank-
ing History of Louisiana* (1935); W. B. Worthen,
Early Banking in Arkansas (1906); J. R. Cable,
The Bank of the State of Missouri (1923).

For new political developments, see Charles
McCarthy, *The Antimasonic Party: A Study of
Political Antimasonry in the United States, 1827–
1840* (1903); S. R. Gammon, *The Presidential
Campaign of 1832* (1922); E. M. Carroll, *Origins
of the Whig Party* (1925); G. R. Poage, *Henry Clay
and the Whig Party* (1936); A. C. Cole, *The Whig
Party in the South* (1913).

On expansion and diplomacy there are several
first-rate special works: E. C. Barker, *Mexico and
Texas, 1821–1835* (1928), and *The Life of Stephen
F. Austin, Founder of Texas, 1793–1836* (1925);
F. L. Benns, *The American Struggle for the British
West India Carrying Trade, 1815–1830* (1923);
G. A. King, *The French Spoliation Claims* (1912).

EXPANSION AND ITS

CONSEQUENCES

1837 - 1850

Periods in history cannot actually be marked off with exact precision. One era flows into another. Jackson left the Presidency in 1837, but in many ways the Jackson era was by no means at an end. Jackson was succeeded as President by Martin Van Buren, a strong Jackson supporter, and Jackson's choice for the Presidency. And Van Buren's administration was plagued throughout by the depression that Jackson's policies had helped to create. Moreover, those remarkable social and economic transformations that had begun in the 1820's and 1830's were most of them still in process of evolution throughout the 1840's and 1850's. Sometimes with good reason, all the years from the Revolution to the Civil War are lumped together as "The Middle Period of American History."

From the economic point of view, the Jacksonian Era had introduced forces that were greatly to exaggerate the sectionalism from which the United States was never able fully to escape. The Northeast became increasingly industrialized; the ever-expanding Northwest found its chief interest in food production at the hands of small free farmers; the South concentrated more and more on the production of cotton and tobacco, and leaned heavily on slavery for its labor supply. These three great sections were as unlike in their interests as three separate nations. Policies that were helpful to one might be damaging to the other two; policies that drew any two together were almost certain to alienate the one that was excluded. The task of holding the three sections together politically strained to the breaking-point the capacities of the politicians of the period. While Jackson was President, the West, supported with some reluctance by the South, but with growing enthusiasm by the common people of the Northeast, was in the ascendancy. But during the 1840's the leadership passed to the South, with only lukewarm support from the West, and with fairly solid opposition from the Northeast. Political tension filled the air.

Such times of stress and strain perhaps served to promote rather than to discourage the intellectual and humanitarian activities of the period. At any rate during these years the United States came of age in journalism and literature; it made extraordinary strides in science and invention; it showed traces of progress in art, architecture, and music; it recognized and tackled with some success the labor problem that grew out of the industrial revolution; and it produced a group of energetic reformers who overhauled the nation's educational system, demanded equal rights for women, sponsored a temperance movement, a prison-reform movement, a peace movement, and, most significant of all, embarked upon an abolitionist crusade.

Once the South had tended to feel apologetic about slavery, but the growing profits of the slave-manned cotton plantation system, coupled with the intemperate attacks upon slavery by the northern abolitionists, brought many able Southerners to the defense of the South's "peculiar institution." No longer did Southerners regard slavery as a necessary evil; more and more they came to think of it as a benevolent institution, ordained of God, and good alike for master and slave. The South as a section sprang to the defense of slavery, and resented with intense emotion the efforts of Northerners to attach a stigma of evil to so important a part of the Southern way of life.

If slavery was good there was no reason why it should not be permitted to grow; if it was evil, there was every reason why its growth should be held at a minimum, or if possible stopped altogether. The conflict between the sections tended more and more to center on this issue. Manifest destiny was marching relentlessly along. The United States was finding out the possibilities of the western half of the continent, and was preparing to take it over. Texas became the Lone Star Republic during the 1830's and a state in the Union during the 1840's. The Santa Fe trade opened the way to New Mexico. The California and Oregon trails revealed the boundless possibilities of the Far West. The United States must round out its boundaries, if need be, even at the cost of war. And war came, a war of expansion with Mexico in 1846–48. But when the coveted land was won, the query, Should it be slave or free, still had to be faced. For a while the compromise of 1850 kept the issue in abeyance, but the day of decision could not be long postponed.

23

A Period of Depression

Martin Van Buren — The Independent Treasury —
Whigs and "Loco-Focos" — Banking reform — Repudiation of state debts — State withdrawals from
business — Attacks on Van Buren — Campaign and
election of 1840 — Death of Harrison — John Tyler —
Failure of the Whig program — Foreign policy — The
Caroline affair — Webster-Ashburton Treaty

MARTIN VAN BUREN (1782–1862), to whose
lot fell the task of guiding the United States
Martin   government through the period
Van Buren   of depression, was by no means
lacking in political experience. He was of
Dutch descent, but hardly of the Hudson
Valley aristocracy, for his father was only a
poor farmer and tavern-keeper of Kinderhook, New York. Young Van Buren's
formal education was confined to such instruction as he could obtain from the common schools of Kinderhook and from a local
academy. He read law, however, under a
prominent New York City lawyer, and he
won such success as a practitioner that his
financial independence was quickly assured.
Unusually adroit in his dealings with men, he
was irresistibly drawn into the factional
political struggles of his native state, and
held a succession of minor offices. After
1816 he made Albany his residence, and was
soon recognized as the leader of a little group
known as the "Albany Regency" which dictated the policies of the Republican, or as it
was later known, the Democratic Party, in
the whole of New York. The Regency made
good use of such political devices as the
spoils system to maintain its hold upon the
party, and the party's hold upon the state;
indeed, Van Buren's clever manipulations
won for him a title that followed him all his
life — "the Little Magician." In 1821 he
went to the United States Senate, where,
however, he made no very profound impres-

sion. He lacked the gift of dramatic oratory,
then deemed so essential to success as a senator; moreover, his chief interest still lay in
state rather than national politics, and his
attitude toward such national issues as the tariff and internal improvements was vacillating.

In 1824 Van Buren supported Crawford
for President, but shortly afterward he identified himself with the partisans of Andrew
Jackson, and had much to do with the successful termination of Jackson's campaign
in 1828. That same year Van Buren was
elected governor of New York, but he resigned in order to enter Jackson's Cabinet
as Secretary of State. In his personal relationships he was far more conciliatory than
his chief, and he made fewer enemies among
the professional politicians; but he lacked the
popular appeal that made so many votes for
Jackson, and it was only because of the President's favoritism that the Little Magician
could be chosen Vice-President in 1832 and
President in 1836. Indeed, the popular vote
in the latter contest was extremely close, for
Van Buren's majority over all his opponents
was less than twenty-seven thousand out of
a total vote cast of over a million and a half.

Jackson left the Presidency in a blaze of
glory, but Van Buren had barely taken
office when the panic of 1837 broke, and his
whole administration was affected by the
economic depression that gripped the country. Brought up, however, on the Jeffersonian principle of the "less government the

Martin
Van Buren

EIGHTH PRESIDENT of the United States, Van Buren of New York had served four years as Vice-President before attaining the Presidency. He owed his office largely to the favor of his predecessor, Andrew Jackson, but unfortunately he fell heir to a depression that Jackson had helped produce. Jackson had sown the wind, some said, and Van Buren had reaped the whirlwind. Portrait by Henry Inman.

better," he regarded the afflictions of the business world as entirely removed from the proper scope of governmental activity. His chief concern as President, therefore, was not to restore prosperity to the people of the United States as a whole, but rather to put the United States government on a sound financial basis. Business would have to look out for itself.

To deal with the situation Van Buren called a special session of Congress for September, 1837. With the rev-enues of the government at the vanishing point, the law calling for the distribution of the surplus was quickly repealed, and an issue of treasury notes to meet current expenses was authorized. But Van Buren's most cherished plan, the estab-lishment of an independent treasury, was violently opposed, and its adoption long de-layed. Van Buren recommended that for the future the United States Treasury should have no dealings whatever with banks, whether national or state. Strong vaults, or

Independent Treasury Bill

sub-treasuries, should be constructed in various cities and placed in charge of govern-ment officials, who should receive and dis-perse government funds on a strictly specie basis. Thus the government would run no risk of losing its money by depositing it in banks, nor would it contribute indirectly and unintentionally to such an overexpansion of bank credit as had preceded the panic of 1837.

The Sub-Treasury Bill, as it was popu-larly called, furnished the Whigs a much-needed issue. Some of them believed that a third Bank of the United States should be chartered, and some of them did not, but they could all agree that the sub-treasury system would merely deal one more disastrous blow to the already reeling business interests of the country. Partisans of the state banks de-clared that Van Buren's measure, if adopted, would affect not only the deposit banks (that is, the pet banks), but all other state banks also, for their notes would no longer be receivable by the United States government. Henry Clay thought that the sub-treasury system would drive the country to the use of a strictly metallic currency, "reduce all property in value two thirds," and force the debtor to pay back in effect three times as much as he had borrowed. Webster un-leashed his eloquence against a measure that was designed exclusively for the relief of the United States government, and contained not one single clause for the relief of the American people. Nevertheless, the bill passed the Senate in 1837 and again in 1838, only to meet defeat both times at the hands of a hostile House of Representatives.

Whig opposition

Van Buren's championship of a "divorce bill" that would sever the connection be-tween the government of the United States and the banking business did not lack for popular appeal. Among the first to come to his support was a noisy popular faction in the Democratic Party of New York State, known as the Loco-Focos, whose activities had for several years been a thorn in the flesh of conserva-tive citizens. The Loco-Focos blamed the

The "Loco-Focos"

panic of 1837 upon the reckless activities of banks and bankers, and they looked upon Jackson's war on the Bank of the United States as only the beginning of a war against all banks and monopolies. Their curious name came from an episode that occurred in 1835 when the conservatives at a Democratic convention in New York City put out the lights to prevent a radical victory, only to be discomfited in turn when the radicals produced a new invention called "loco-focos," or matches, and rekindled the lights. Anti-banking sentiment was not confined to New York, but was strong wherever individuals had lost heavily from bank failures, and in all such circles the news that Van Buren had gone "loco-foco" was received with great enthusiasm. More than ever the Democratic Party could claim to be the party of the people, and could charge that the Whigs were out to obtain special privileges for the favored few. Finally, in 1840, the advocates of the Sub-Treasury Bill succeeded in obtaining a majority in both houses of Congress, and the long-debated measure became a law.

With the national government completely removed from the banking field, it became necessary for the states and private individuals to work out a banking system that could meet the needs of the country. Several western states experimented with state-owned banks, patterned after the Bank of the United States, but with a few exceptions these banks soon met disaster. They were too easily involved in partisan politics, they were rarely well managed, and their provisions for redeeming note issues were generally inadequate. Better results were obtained by instituting reforms in the existing system of privately owned state banks. Indeed, many precedents for reform were set even before the panic of 1837. New England, for example, through the "Suffolk Bank system," so called from the bank that first introduced it, had succeeded fairly well in establishing a currency of standard value throughout that section. The notes of the smaller country banks, which tended ordinarily to circulate at a varying discount away from home, were redeemed at par by the large Boston banks

Banking reform

"*The Times — July 4, 1837.*" An elaborate cartoon by E. W. Clay depicting the evils of the panic and depression that followed Jackson's issuance of his famous "Specie Circular."

out of funds deposited with them for the purpose by the country banks. Thus a kind of clearing-house system was evolved which insured, at least for the region concerned, that one bank's notes would ordinarily be as good as another's.

To New York, however, goes the credit for the most important innovations in the state banking system. There, ever since 1829, a state law had required each newly chartered bank to contribute a certain percentage of its income to a common safety fund, the purpose of which was primarily to insure that all the notes of failed banks should be redeemed at par. When the panic of 1837 proved that the amounts so collected were apt to be inadequate, another law was passed, which obliged every bank in the state to deposit with the comptroller sufficient United States, state, or other designated bonds to protect all the notes it proposed to circulate. If the bank failed, then the securities so deposited could be sold, and the note-holders indemnified. More important still was the adoption in 1838 of the principle of free banking. Before that time the only way an individual or company could enter the banking business was to secure from the legislature a special law granting the desired privilege. But the New York statute now specified certain conditions which, if properly met, permitted any individual or group of individuals to establish a bank. Free banking appealed strongly to the democratic sentiment of the time, and was very generally adopted by other states. By thus substituting a general law of incorporation for special laws, and by insisting on such devices as safety funds and bond deposits, the states were soon able to provide a banking system which, if not wholly satisfactory, at least enabled the country to carry on its business.

Many of the states, however, were long troubled by the debts they had incurred **Repudiation** during the boom period. Little **of state** of the money they had so freely **debts** lavished upon canals and other works of internal improvement had been raised by taxation; most of it had been bor-

rowed on the assumption that profits from the works undertaken would ultimately pay off the debt. Also, some western and southern states, notably Louisiana, Alabama, and Mississippi, had borrowed the capital for their ill-fated state-owned banks. As previously noted, the credit of the American states among English investors was excellent, and little difficulty was experienced in floating these huge loans. Repayment, however, with the depression persisting year after year, was a different matter. Indeed, many of the states found themselves unable so much as to meet the interest on their indebtedness. Heavy taxation for this purpose was politically inexpedient, and in many instances such a policy would have availed little because of the inadequacy of the state's taxable resources. With a few exceptions the projects upon which the borrowed money had been spent failed to bring in a revenue. Some of these projects had to be abandoned half finished and entirely unproductive, while others proved all too frequently to be unnecessary and premature and could be operated only at a loss. Overwhelmed by their calamities, several states, notably Mississippi, Louisiana, Maryland, Pennsylvania, Indiana, and Michigan, frankly repudiated their indebtedness. The blow which this action dealt to American credit abroad was long felt. Some of the defaulting states repented and paid off their obligations in whole or in part, but others remained obdurate, and their debts were never paid. Urgent pleas, emanating mainly from the solvent states, that the federal government save American credit by assuming all state debts, came to nothing.

The reverses experienced by the states in their efforts to finance banks and internal improvements made a lasting **State with-** impression upon the public **drawal from** mind. One after another the **business** projects so initiated found their way into private hands or were abandoned altogether. The conviction grew that the state might better withdraw completely from the field of business, and leave the carrying-out of even such expensive enterprises as canals and railroads to private initiative. Prior to the panic of 1837 sentiment generally regarded state sponsorship of such large projects as preferable to the formation of powerful private corporations, but during the depression a complete reversal of opinion took place. Provisions were inserted in the constitutions of many states which limited to a specified sum the total indebtedness that the state might incur, and forbade outright the lending of the state's credit for any purpose whatsoever. On the other hand, less objection was raised than formerly to the formation of private corporations large enough to finance needed projects. Indeed, the public had little choice but to encourage private capital to do the work which both nation and state now refused to do. General laws of incorporation, not only to extend banking privileges but for other purposes as well, became increasingly common, the principle of limited liability for stockholders was reluctantly conceded, and in a general way the corporation came to enjoy the same rights and immunities before the law that generations of precedents had built up for the protection of the individual.

The political effect of depression is usually adverse to the party in power, whichever it **Attacks on** is and whatever it does. The **Van Buren** Whig orators, led by Clay, Adams, and Webster, pointed to the hundreds of closed factories, the thousands of unemployed men, the collapse of cotton prices in the South and of land prices in the West as evidence of the mistaken policies that the Democratic Party had pursued. Not an opportunity was lost to discredit the unfortunate Van Buren. For his advocacy of an independent treasury he was likened to the captain of a ship at sea who seizes the lifeboats to save himself and his crew, but permits the passengers to drown. The corruption of government officials, mostly land agents who had speculated with the funds that passed through their hands, was charged against the administration, and the cry raised that the "Goths and Vandals" must

be driven from power. An expensive Indian war, fought to effect the removal of the Seminoles from Florida, was branded as a pro-slavery extravagance, designed mainly to punish runaway Negroes who had joined the Indians. On the other hand, the President's failure to work for the annexation of Texas was cited as unmistakable proof of his anti-slavery views.

The success of the Whig propaganda was already apparent in the elections of 1838, when the administration lost control of both houses of Congress; hence the Whig leaders looked forward with confidence to a complete victory in 1840. Northern and southern Whigs were as far apart as ever on political principles, but they had discovered some interests in common. The northern manufacturers of cotton, for example, had necessary business contacts with the southern producers of cotton. Both types were essentially conservative, and socially they got on well together. Moneyed men everywhere tended to unite under the Whig banner as a means of protecting themselves from further Democratic experimentation in the realm of banking and finance. Agreement upon a Whig platform might still be impossible, but the results of the campaign of 1836, when the Whig policy of encouraging many favorite-son candidacies served only to bring about the election of Van Buren, indicated clearly the necessity of agreement upon a common candidate. To do this a national convention was essential, and accordingly one was called to meet at Harrisburg, Pennsylvania, in December, 1839.

At this gathering union and harmony were the watchwords. Henry Clay was the outstanding Whig leader, but his **The Whig** chances were sacrificed upon the **nominees** altar of availability. His long political career had netted him many enemies, and his political principles were too well known. He himself sensed these facts, and well in advance of the convention he advised his friends to "discard all attachment or partiality to me, and be guided solely by the motive of rescuing our country from the

TEXTILE MANUFACTUR-ING. View of Lowell, Mass., 1833. Litho-graph by Pendleton after E. A. Farrar.

The Industrial Revolution was rap-idly gaining momentum in the United States during the second quarter of the nineteenth century. Such cities as Lowell, Mass., which had been only a country village in 1800, grew prodigiously — by 1836 Lowell had a population of 18,000, and taxable property worth some $5,000-000. Housing accommodations for the growing numbers of factory workers pro-duced a difficult problem, not always ideally solved. To turn the factory wheels both steam and water-power were used.

POWER LOOM WEAVING. Slater's mill, Pawtucket, R. I. Illustration from White, *Memoir of Samuel Slater*, 1836.

ELI WHITNEY'S GUN FAC-TORY. Employee living quarters are visible be-yond the factory build-ings, near New Haven, Conn., 1828. Painting by W. G. Munson.

FLOUR MILLS. Scene on the Genesee River Falls, Rochester, N. Y., 1835. Lithograph by Bufford after J. Young.

SHIPBUILDING. The Smith & Dimon shipyard in New York, from which came many of the great American clippers. Painting by James Pringle, 1833.

RETAILING. Fashionable beaver hats, "terms cash," at Bond's, New York. Water color by Alexander J. Davis, about 1828.

American business in the pre-Civil War period exploited energetically every opportunity that seemed to promise a profit. Ship-builders produced the clipper ship, noted alike for its grace and beauty and for the speed with which it sailed the seas. The fur trade lived on, contributing its bit to the hat industry as long as high hats, commonly called "beavers," continued in demand. Whalers in the year 1846 — before the petroleum age — sent out no less than 736 ships from New England ports alone.

WHALING. "The Rotch Fleet" after sperm whales off Hawaii. Painting by J. Stuart Black, about 1833.

dangers which now encompass it." If the
convention decided to name another candidate, Clay promised that, "far from feeling
any discontent, the nomination will have my
best wishes and receive my cordial support."
The delegates, perhaps somewhat to his surprise, took Clay at his word, and cast about
for a man whose name would arouse the least
possible opposition. Daniel Webster obviously would not do, for he was too closely
identified with the conservative East to have
much vote-getting power in the West. John
Tyler of Virginia was satisfactory to the
southern Whigs, but to no one else. Once
Clay was passed by, the choice seemed to lie
between two military heroes, General Winfield Scott, whom Thurlow Weed had persuaded the New York delegation to favor,
and General William Henry Harrison. Both
candidates had seen service in the War of
1812 and in Indian wars, but the greater
glamour had come to attach to the name of
Harrison, and in the campaign of 1836 his
ability to win support had already been
demonstrated. Clay led in the early balloting, but the convention finally turned to

Popular appeal was the keynote of the presidential campaign of 1840. Painting by Francis
H. Schell.

Harrison. For Vice-President, John Tyler
was chosen, not only as an appropriate concession to the South, but also as a gesture of
friendship to his close personal friend, Henry
Clay, whose disappointment at being passed
over in favor of Harrison was extreme.

William Henry Harrison (1773–1841) was
the son of Benjamin Harrison, an early governor of Virginia and a signer of   William
the Declaration of Independ-   Henry
ence. The younger Harrison's   Harrison
whole career, however, was associated with
the West. He was one of General Wayne's
aides during the campaign against the Northwest Indians, and at the close of that struggle was placed in command of Fort Washington, near Cincinnati. He married a
daughter of John Cleves Symmes, the purchaser of the Symmes tract. He was made
secretary of the Northwest Territory in 1797,
delegate to Congress in 1799, and governor
of Indiana Territory — an office which he
held for a dozen years — in 1800. His clash
with the Indians at Tippecanoe, and his participation in the Canadian campaign which
ended in the battle of the Thames, have
already been noted. After the War of 1812,
for short periods each, he represented an
Ohio district in Congress, served in the Ohio
State Senate, and was a United States Senator from Ohio. In 1828 he was appointed
by President Adams minister to Colombia,
but was promptly recalled at the beginning
of the Jackson administration. Throughout
his long career he had distinguished himself
for little else than his dealings with the Indians, both in peace and in war, but his reputation as an Indian fighter was second only
to that of Jackson himself, and constituted
an unmistakable political asset. After Jackson became President, Harrison retired to
his farm at North Bend, Ohio, and would
doubtless have been content to stay there
had not the Whig leaders determined to
capitalize upon the popular enthusiasm
which they believed his name would evoke.

The Democrats renominated Van Buren
and in a long series of resolutions stood by
the record he and his predecessor in office

had made. They were thus subject to attack in a fashion that the Whigs, who had **The Whig** no platform, escaped. But is- **strategy** sues of any sort or kind were soon forgotten. It was a part of the Whig strategy to commit their party only in the matter of opposition to the Democrats. "If General Harrison is taken up as the candidate," Nicholas Biddle had said in 1835, "it will be on account of the past. Let him say not one single word about his principles, or his creed — let him say nothing — promise nothing. Let no committee, no convention, no town meeting ever extract from him a single word about what he thinks now or will do here-after. Let the use of pen and ink be wholly forbidden." This advice was followed in so far as it was humanly possible, not only by Harrison but also by the Whig orators. Their campaign speeches were long and nu-merous, but confined primarily to denuncia-tions of Van Buren and laudations of Har-rison. The observation of a disappointed adherent of Henry Clay's, that if Harrison could only be given a pension and a barrel of cider he would gladly retire to a log cabin for the rest of his days, produced a text for the Whig orators. This quip, repeated in a Democratic paper, made it possible for Har-rison's supporters to feature the plainness of their candidate in comparison with the fastidiousness of Van Buren. The votes of common men, many of whom themselves still lived in log cabins and drank cider, were solicited for the "log-cabin, hard-cider candi-date." Van Buren was attacked as a lover of old silver and good wine, who wore cologne-scented whiskers and laced up in corsets. Daniel Webster regretted that he himself had not been born in a log cabin, but rejoiced that his brothers and sisters had had that advantage. Seward campaigned the country districts of New York State in a green farm wagon. Log cabins, cider barrels, and coonskin caps furnished the *motifs* for in-numerable badges, floats, and songs. Enthu-siasm replaced argument, and emotion put reason to flight. In this bizarre fashion the Whig candidates, "Tippecanoe and Tyler

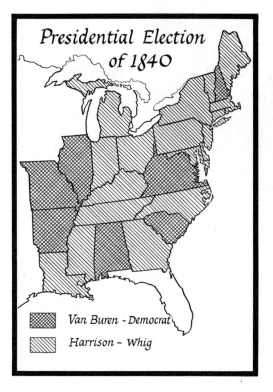

Presidential Election of 1840

Van Buren - Democrat

Harrison - Whig

too," came to be identified, as once the name of Andrew Jackson had been, with the com-mon man's crusade against the aristocrats.

Let Van from his coolers of silver drink wine,
And lounge on his cushioned settee;
Our man on his buckeye bench can recline
Content with hard cider is he!

The success of the Whig tactics was com-plete, and Van Buren was defeated by an electoral vote of 234 to 60. The popular vote, however, was surprisingly close, for Harrison received less than 150,000 majority out of over 2,400,000 votes cast.

The frank abandonment of principle in favor of expediency, so characteristic of the Whig campaign, has aroused perhaps greater ridicule and criticism at the hands of later generations of Americans than it deserved. As Herbert Agar, a keen observer of Ameri-can politics, has pointed out, this course of action, followed to a greater or lesser degree throughout the nation's history by both major parties, is the "price of union" for **a**

William Henry Harrison

NINTH PRESIDENT of the United States, Harrison of Ohio rose to fame as a general in the War of 1812. His availability largely influenced his nomination, for his political views were neither extreme nor deeply held. At sixty-eight Harrison was the oldest man ever to take the oath of office as President, and he died one month after his inauguration. Portrait by E. D. Marchon.

country so vast, and with so many diverse sectional interests. Only by compromise and conciliation, even to the point occasionally of dodging issues that seem to many people to be fundamental, can American political parties continue to exist as national rather than sectional organizations. When, a few years later, the Republican party came into being as a strictly sectional party, stressing principle above expediency, and refusing to compromise in the face of southern intransigence, the result was the disruption of the Union, and Civil War.

The leaders of the northern Whigs, particularly Webster and Clay, in spite of the **Death of Harrison** concessions they had made during the campaign to the southern element in the party, took it for granted that they would be called upon to guide the new administration, and all started off well enough. Harrison chose Webster to be Secretary of State, and gave most of the other places in his Cabinet to the friends of Henry Clay. Clay himself retained his seat in the Senate, and prepared to push through a Congress that the election had made overwhelm-

ingly Whig his long-delayed American system. Unfortunately, however, the President, who was more than sixty-eight years of age at the time of his inauguration, did not long survive that event. Thousands of Whig office-seekers, bent upon replacing the "rascally Democrats" at once, thronged into the capital and gave him no peace. With his strength thus overtaxed, he failed to throw off a severe cold contracted the day of his inauguration, and a month later he was dead.

John Tyler (1790–1862) was a Virginia aristocrat who had long been known for the pronounced views he held and **John Tyler** the determination with which he held them. As a member of the Virginia state legislature, of the national House of Representatives, and finally of the United States Senate, he had gone on record repeatedly on all the important issues of the day. He was uncompromisingly opposed to a protective tariff, to a national bank, and to internal improvements at national expense; and he was equally ardent in his defense of states' rights, slavery, nullification, and expansion. He had, too, a kind of vanity in his views and a touchiness about them that made it extremely difficult for him to compromise. In 1838, for example, he had resigned from the Senate rather than obey instructions sent him by the Virginia legislature. Possibly no man of his generation was less fitted to play the rôle of figurehead for which his predecessor, Harrison, had been cast. Dismayed at the prospect before them, some of the Whig leaders hoped to restrict Tyler's powers on the theory that he was merely a Vice-President acting as President. But Tyler promptly assumed the same title and the same prerogatives as had always been accorded to elected Presidents. He retained Harrison's Cabinet, however, and was as conciliatory toward the Whig leaders as he knew how to be.

The Whigs had been elected to save the country from the depression, and with this in view a special session of Con- **The Whig program** gress was called to meet the last of May, 1841. Unfortunately, there was no platform to which either the President or the Whig members of Congress could be held, but Clay attempted to supply this deficiency by an elaborate series of resolutions which he presented to the Senate. The Whig program, according to these resolves, would be (1) repeal of the Sub-Treasury Bill, (2) a third Bank of the United States, (3) a higher tariff to produce a revenue adequate to the needs of the government, and (4) the distribution among the states of the proceeds from the sales of public lands. That Clay stated accurately the views of the National Republican wing of the Whig Party there can be no doubt, and Whigs of this persuasion probably constituted a majority in Congress. But there was much about the program that the southern Whigs did not relish, and unfortunately for harmony Tyler was a southern Whig. He had never been a National Republican, and never could have been one. Clay was hopeful, nevertheless. "Tyler dares not resist me," he is reputed to have said. "I will drive him before me."

But Tyler was not so easily driven. He had always opposed the Independent Treasury Act, and in August, 1841, he readily signed the measure for its repeal that Clay carried through Congress. That same month, however, he refused to sign a bill for a "fiscal bank," which would have established in actual fact a new Bank of the United States. Efforts to meet the President's objections resulted in the passage of another bank bill, this time for what was called a "fiscal corporation," but the second measure met the same fate as the first. Since a two-thirds majority could not be obtained to override the veto, all hope of chartering a national bank was now at an end. The distribution bill which Clay sponsored fared little better than the bank bills. For the national government, which had to float frequent loans in order to meet its current obligations, to deprive itself of any of its revenue seemed unreasonable; moreover, distribution had long been opposed by low-tariff men, of whom the President was one, on the ground that it would

Tyler and the Whigs

John Tyler

TENTH PRESIDENT of the United States, Tyler of Virginia was a man of strong political opinions, unlike Harrison whom he succeeded in office. Indeed, he had once resigned from the Senate rather than obey a demand from the Virginia legislature that he vote for some resolutions of which he disapproved. He was a Whig only in his opposition to many Jacksonian policies. Daguerreotype by Mathew B. Brady.

merely create a "vacuum in the treasury," and so prepare the way for a high tariff. Finally Clay agreed to an amendment which stipulated that distribution should cease whenever it became necessary to levy higher duties than the twenty per cent maximum provided for by the Compromise Tariff of 1833; and so modified, the bill became a law. Clay believed that he could later induce Congress to strike out the objectionable amendment, but in this he failed. On the other hand, Congress did raise the tariff. Clay and the protectionists strongly favored such a course, and even Tyler was persuaded to agree to the higher rates because of the great necessity of increasing the revenue. The Tariff of 1842 restored duties to about the level of the Act of 1832, and was thus decidedly protective in character. It was the one conspicuous success which Clay scored in his effort to turn his American system into law, but it remained in force only a few years, and its enactment rang the death-knell of distribution.

Most of Clay's program was of long stand-

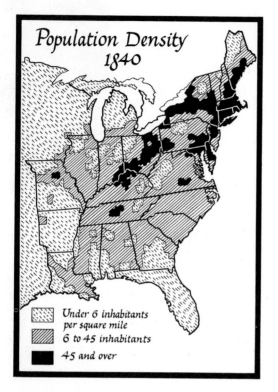

Population Density
1840

▨ Under 6 inhabitants
per square mile
▨ 6 to 45 inhabitants
■ 45 and over

ment offered the land for sale, buy it in at the minimum price. By this measure not only was the stigma of law-breaker removed from the squatters but in reality a bid was made for more squatters to go West and seek new homes. The old theory that the land was to be so administered as to produce a revenue received a fatal blow, and the western theory that the land should be used to provide homes for the needy millions was tacitly acknowledged. Pre-emption had been advocated often enough before 1841, but it was adopted at that particular time primarily as a means of encouraging those who suffered from the depression to seek their salvation in a move to the West.

The West as a haven of refuge was discovered, however, long before it received this legislative blessing. During the boom period two new western states, Arkansas (1836) and Michigan (1837), were admitted to the Union, and in the next few years their population increased with great rapidity. So also did the population of all the western states where cheap lands were still available. But the most startling development occurred in the territories that were soon to become the states of Wisconsin, Iowa, and Minnesota. Here land was still to be found that government surveyors had not entered, and here squatters by the thousands took claims which for the time being cost them nothing. Also, the new territories had escaped the heavy expenditures for internal improvements that had characterized the boom period, and their rates of taxation were low. Steamboats on the Mississippi River and the Great Lakes, and covered wagons across the prairies brought the population in. The rapid growth of the West during the early forties, of which this movement into the New Northwest was an important part, had much to do with alleviating the distress felt by the country as a whole. Here many of the unemployed found employment, and at the same time created by their efforts a new market for the goods which the older sections so much needed to sell.

Growth of the West

ing, and had been advocated by him and his adherents as earnestly in time of prosperity as in adversity. But the Whig Congress passed two important measures that were designed primarily to alleviate the existing economic distress. One was a bankruptcy act, under the terms of which some 39,000 persons wiped out $441,000,000 of debt with assets of only $44,000,000. The law turned out to be immensely unpopular, and many individuals who might have gone into bankruptcy refused to take advantage of terms which seemed to them dishonorable. Subsequently the same Congress that had passed the law repealed it. A pre-emption act, however, which western members of Congress succeeded in attaching to Clay's distribution bill, was generally regarded as a reasonable measure of relief. This law made legal at last the pioneer practice of settling upon public lands in advance of their being offered for sale. Pre-emptors, or squatters, were assured that, in case they were actual residents on their claims and had made slight improvements, they might, when the govern-

Tyler's obstinate refusal to sign a bank bill brought disaster not only to Clay's program **Whig dissensions** but to the Whig Party itself. All pretense of party harmony was now thrown to the winds. At Clay's behest Tyler's entire Cabinet, with the exception of Webster, resigned, and the President was formally read out of the party. Naturally the unseemly dissension at Washington had an adverse effect on the voters, and in the elections of 1842 the Whigs lost their majority in the House of Representatives, although they still controlled the Senate. Clay himself dramatically retired to private life. His farewell speech to the Senate moved many of his auditors to tears, and even won a warm handclasp from his arch-enemy, Calhoun. Everyone knew, however, that in spite of his apparent renunciation of politics he would be a candidate for the Presidency in 1844. Meanwhile, with Congress divided, Clay in retirement, and John Tyler still President, legislation, except on routine matters, was at a standstill.

Webster's decision to remain in Tyler's Cabinet was due in part, no doubt, to his **Foreign policy** unwillingness to have it appear that Clay could tell him what to do; but he also believed that he was well fitted to effect a settlement of the serious difficulties that had arisen between the United States and Great Britain. During the year 1839 he had spent several months in England, and had met many notables, including Carlyle, Dickens, Hallam, Channing, and, possibly more important still, Lord Ashburton, with whom he was soon to negotiate. On Carlyle, Webster made a profound impression:

Not many days ago I saw at breakfast the notablest of your notabilities, Daniel Webster. He is a magnificent specimen. You might say to all the world, "This is our Yankee Englishman; such limbs we make in Yankeeland!" As a logic fencer, or parliamentary Hercules, one would be inclined to back him at first sight against all the extant world. The tanned complexion, that amorphous crag-like face; the dull black eyes under the precipice of brows, like dull anthracite

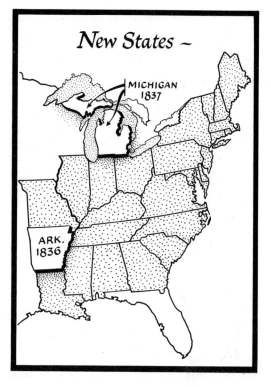

New States —

MICHIGAN
1837

ARK.
1836

furnaces, needing only to be blown; the mastiff mouth accurately closed; I have not traced so much of silent Berserkir rage that I remember in any man.

Beginning with the Canadian insurrection of 1837, the relations between the United States and Great Britain had taken an unfortunate turn. Thereafter for a number of years disorder and unrest rather than actual revolt marked the history of Canada, but many American citizens expressed freely their hope that the great British colony to the north would become first independent of the mother country, and then a part of the United States. Some Americans went so far as to assist the Canadian revolutionists in every possible way to obtain money, men, and supplies. Under the strain of this situation, chronic and long-standing diplomatic differences between the United States and Great Britain became suddenly matters of vital consequence, and were magnified, particularly on this side of the Atlantic, out of all reasonable proportion to their importance.

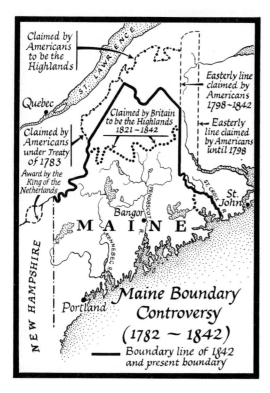

Claimed by Americans to be the Highlands

Quebec

Claimed by Americans under Treaty of 1783

Award by the King of the Netherlands

Claimed by Britain to be the Highlands 1821–1842

Easterly line claimed by Americans 1798–1842

Easterly line claimed by Americans until 1798

St. John

Bangor

M A I N E

NEW HAMPSHIRE

Portland

St. John

Maine Boundary Controversy (1782 – 1842)

Boundary line of 1842 and present boundary

Fortunately, Sir Robert Peel, who became the British Prime Minister in 1841, was eager to restore good relations between the two countries, and sent as special envoy to Washington Lord Ashburton, a man well versed in American matters with whom Webster found it easy to cooperate.

The *Caroline* affair, a particularly disconcerting incident of the Canadian insurrection, occurred late in 1837. Some Canadian rebels, with headquarters at Navy Island on the Canadian side of the Niagara River, had chartered a small American steamship, the *Caroline*, to bring to their rendezvous volunteers and supplies from the United States. The Canadian authorities planned to seize and destroy the vessel while she was at the island, and therefore in Canadian waters, but owing to some miscalculation they sent troops for the purpose when the vessel was tied up at a wharf on the American side. Undeterred by this development, the troops crossed the river, boarded the *Caroline*, and overpowered her

The Caroline affair

crew, killing one man and injuring several others. They then set fire to the craft and turned her adrift to float over the falls. The United States government, which was really making an effort to maintain a correct neutrality, took the *Caroline* incident seriously, and demanded an explanation of the British government. When the British reply proved unsatisfactory, President Van Buren let it be known that he was determined to seek redress.

The matter was further complicated in November, 1840, when a Canadian named Alexander McLeod boasted in a New York saloon that he had been a member of the party which had boarded the *Caroline*, and that it was he who had killed a member of her crew. Thereupon McLeod was promptly arrested, indicted for murder, and brought to trial in a New York state court. The British minister to the United States made it clear that his government accepted full responsibility for what had happened to the *Caroline*, and demanded that McLeod be released; also the American minister in London was told that the execution of McLeod would mean war. This was the situation when Webster became Secretary of State. Unfortunately, the new secretary was almost powerless to act in the matter, for the state of New York had complete jurisdiction in the McLeod case; but he kept a watchful eye on the proceedings, and was not surprised when the prisoner was acquitted on an alibi. The international tension was further eased by concessions on both sides. The United States officially agreed that the British were right in contending that in military affairs individuals were not responsible for carrying out orders issued by their government, and Congress, at Webster's request, passed a law which provided that in the future the accused in all such cases should have the right of appeal to the federal courts. The British, on the other hand, while maintaining that their part in the *Caroline* affair was strictly defensible, expressed regret that it had ever occurred.

Another dispute which Lord Ashburton

and Webster were called upon to settle concerned the boundary line be-
The Canadian boundary tween the United States and
Canada. The northeastern, or
Maine, boundary had been fixed by the
Treaty of 1783 at "the Highlands which
divide those rivers which empty themselves
into the St. Lawrence from those which fall
into the Atlantic Ocean." Unfortunately,
there were several sets of highlands that
answered this description, and an area of
approximately twelve thousand square miles
was claimed by both countries. In 1827 this
dispute had been referred to the King of the
Netherlands, who suggested a compromise
line, but his decision had been rejected by
the United States. In the eighteen-thirties
American and Canadian lumberjacks began
to clash in the disputed territory, and by the
end of the decade the so-called "Aroostook
War" had broken out. For a time the situation threatened to get out of hand. Maine
voted several hundred thousand dollars for
forts, Congress authorized the President to
call out the militia and accept fifty thousand
volunteers, and General Winfield Scott was
sent to the border. Fortunately, however,
the governors of Maine and New Brunswick
were able in 1839 to agree upon a *modus
vivendi*, pending the settlement of the dispute, and early in 1842 Webster and Ashburton began their negotiations. After much
jockeying they agreed upon a settlement
which gave approximately seven twelfths of
the disputed area to the United States, and
five twelfths to Great Britain. These terms
were included in the famous Webster-Ashburton Treaty, signed August 9, 1842, and
subsequently ratified by both nations.

Two minor boundary disputes were also
settled by the treaty. The forty-fifth parallel, which supposedly marked the northern
boundary of the United States between the
Connecticut and St. Lawrence Rivers, had
been incorrectly surveyed in 1774 to swing
northward over a considerable part of the
distance, as much as three quarters of a mile.
This inaccurate line, which had long been
regarded as the correct boundary, was con-

firmed as such by the treaty. Also, the
boundary west from Lake Superior to the
Lake of the Woods, inadequately defined by
earlier negotiations, was brought into harmony with existing geographic information.
The Canadian-American boundary from the
Atlantic Ocean to the Rocky Mountains thus
took the form that it still retains. It was
perhaps unfortunate that Webster and Ashburton felt no call to extend their efforts to
include a settlement of the Oregon question.

Probably as a result of the *Caroline* affair,
it was decided to include in the treaty an
article on extradition. Jay's
treaty had provided for the **Extradition**
mutual return of fugitives who were accused
of murder or forgery, but after its expiration
there had been no agreement whatever on
the subject. As a consequence, criminals
on both sides of the Canadian-American
boundary found it altogether too easy to
escape from punishment by flight across the
international border. The Webster-Ashburton Treaty listed seven crimes, "murder,
or assault to commit murder, or piracy, or
arson, or robbery, or forgery, or the utter-
ance of forged paper," for which extradition
was to be required. Embezzlement, unfortunately, was not included, and for a long
time the phrase "gone to Canada," implied
in the American vernacular that the traveler
was guilty of this crime. Later, however, the
list of extraditable offenses was greatly
extended.

Another subject that the treaty dealt with
was the international slave trade. In 1807
Great Britain, and the following **The slave
trade** year the United States, had declared this trade illegal, and in a short time
practically all the other civilized nations of
the world had done likewise. But as long
as slavery existed anywhere, there were
bound to be those who were willing to take
the risk of breaking the law. Ships designed
to engage in the slave trade were elaborately
outfitted with concealed slave decks, carried
falsified papers, and used at will the flags of
all nations. Slave cargoes could be easily
and cheaply obtained at the numerous sta-

tions along the western coast of Africa where native chiefs brought in their captives, and exchanged them for liquor and trinkets. The slaver, if he escaped capture on the high seas, could then dispose of his booty at a stiff profit in Porto Rico, Cuba, Brazil, or the United States. Great Britain, with a navy far superior to that of any other power, took the lead in efforts to suppress this nefarious trade, and succeeded in obtaining from many countries permission to visit and search suspected vessels, regardless of the flag they happened to fly. This policy, however, ran counter to a strong American prejudice, and when American ships were so molested the United States entered vigorous protests. Repeatedly the British government tried to come to an understanding with the United States on the subject, but all such efforts ended in failure, and the Stars and Stripes became, in consequence, the chief protection of the slaver. Webster and Ashburton at first wrestled in vain with this knotty problem, but at length they agreed to a suggestion made by President Tyler that both powers should keep strong naval forces off the coast of Africa, the two squadrons to cooperate whenever occasion demanded. This agreement was reasonable enough, but the United States failed to maintain its proper quota of ships in African waters, and until the time of the Civil War the American flag continued, unfortunately, to be used freely by ships engaged in the slave trade.

Webster and Ashburton were also forced by circumstances to try to smooth out irrita-

The Creole affair tions that had arisen because of the practice, common along the Atlantic seaboard, of transporting slaves by sea from one part of the United States to another. On several occasions ships engaged in this maritime domestic slave trade were compelled because of storms or other exigencies to put in at some British West Indian port, whereupon the slaves they carried were promptly set free by the British authorities. In 1841 the *Creole* case brought this matter to a dramatic head. The *Creole* was an American ship bound from Virginia to New Orleans with a cargo of one hundred and thirty-five slaves. During the voyage the slaves engaged in a successful mutiny, killing one person and wounding several others, and then took the ship into the British port of Nassau, where, with the exception of those held responsible for the murder, they were given their freedom. In the United States this incident aroused great excitement, and Webster voiced in no uncertain terms the American objection to what the British had done. The ship, he argued, had entered the British port in distress, and under such circumstances the laws of the United States were not suspended. The slaves were therefore still slaves, and should be returned to their owners. Lord Ashburton claimed that he had no authority to deal with the *Creole* case, and asked that it be excluded from the scope of the treaty. He agreed, however, that for the future "there shall be no officious interference with American vessels driven by accident or by violence" into British ports. There the matter rested for the time being, but in 1853 the case was submitted to the arbitration of a British umpire, Joshua Bates, who upheld Webster's reasoning, and awarded to the United States damages of $110,330.

Bibliography

All the general economic histories, Kirkland, Faulkner, McGrane, and Shannon, are useful for the depression years. W. B. Smith and A. H. Cole, *Fluctuations in American Business, 1790–* *1860* (1935); and Dewey, *Financial History of the United States*, also cover this period with care. On special problems relating to banking, Horace White, *Money and Banking, Illustrated by Ameri-*

can History (1895, new ed., 1936), is excellent. It has been repeatedly revised, and has gone through many editions. David Kinley, *The Independent Treasury of the United States and its Relations to the Banks of the Country* (1910), deals effectively with the national situation. On state banking, Dewey, *State Banking before the Civil War*, is particularly good on banking methods. This subject is further elaborated in H. W. Lanier, *A Century of Banking in New York, 1822–1922* (1922); J. J. Knox, *A History of Banking in the United States* (1900); N. S. B. Gras, *The Massachusetts-First National Bank of Boston, 1784–1934* (1937). On state debts, see W. A. Scott, *The Repudiation of State Debts* (1893); and R. C. McGrane, *Foreign Bondholders and American State Debts* (1935).

On politics, there is a brilliant chapter on the Whig party in John Fiske, *Essays Historical and Literary* (2 vols., 1902), I. See also A. C. Cole, *The Whig Party in the South* (1913); H. R. Mueller, *The Whig Party in Pennsylvania* (1922); O. D. Lambert, *Presidential Politics in the United States, 1841–44* (1936). *The Autobiography of Martin Van Buren*, edited by John C. Fitzpatrick (1920), is a document of great value, although it was never completed. An old, but still useful biography of Van Buren is E. M. Shepard, *Martin Van Buren* (1888). See also Holmes Alexander,

The American Talleyrand; The Career and Contemporaries of Martin Van Buren (1935). Two biographies of Harrison, J. A. Green, *William Henry Harrison: His Life and Times* (1941); and Freeman Cleaves, *Old Tippecanoe: William Henry Harrison and His Time* (1939), both attempt, without notable success, to build up the old general. O. P. Chitwood, *John Tyler, Champion of the Old South* (1939), is a judicial and scholarly biography. Van Deusen, *Henry Clay;* and Poage, *Henry Clay and the Whig Party*, both continue useful.

On the public lands question the books by Hibbard and by Robbins should be supplemented by G. M. Stephenson, *The Political History of the Public Lands from 1840 to 1862* (1917). Shosuke Sato, *History of the Land Question in the United States* (1886), was an early, less detailed study.

On Anglo-American relations during this period the following books should be consulted: O. E. Tiffany, *The Relations of the United States to the Canadian Rebellion of 1837–1838* (1905); J. F. Sprague, *The Northeastern Boundary Controversy and the Aroostook War* (1910); H. S. Burrage, *Maine in the Northeastern Boundary Controversy* (1919); H. G. Soulsby, *The Right of Search and the Slave Trade in Anglo-American Relations, 1814–1862* (1933); A. B. Corey, *The Crisis of 1830–1842 in Canadian American Relations* (1941).

24

The Awakening of the American Mind

THE United States during and immediately following the Jacksonian era was the scene of a series of remarkable transformations. Democracy in government became for the nation and for most of the states a fact as well as a theory; the multiplication of canals, turnpikes, steamboats, and railroads wrought a revolution in transportation; the industrialization and consequent urbanization of the Northeast progressed with startling rapidity; the triumph of "King Cotton" was duly celebrated in the South; the advance of the western frontier continued through good times and bad. Quite as striking, and quite as characteristic of the age, were the stirrings that the new scene awakened in the American intellect. During this period inventive genius was strangely stimulated, literary talent rose to unprecedented heights, and many crusades for the righting of ancient wrongs swept through the land.

It is easier to produce evidence of this spiritual ferment than to explain how it came **Intellectual** about. The growing wealth of **activity** the young nation may have had something to do with it. Wealth meant, at least for a few, freedom from ordinary labor, and the leisure to read and think. And yet comparatively little of consequence was ac-

complished directly by the leisure class; most of the striking achievements of the period were made by men and women who had to earn their own livings. Possibly the chief contribution of the well-to-do was to create demands, spiritual no less than material, that others less favored would seek to supply. Closer contacts with European culture had also an invigorating influence upon trends of thought in the United States. Foreign travel, which had been at low ebb from the time of the American Revolution to the close of the War of 1812, slowly revived; more European books were imported and read; European criticisms of the United States, while seemingly scorned, were nevertheless taken deeply to heart; European ideas that were applicable to American conditions were quickly detected and freely appropriated. But the seething, restless, growing American nation was, after all, its own irresistible challenge to thought. The physical needs of so vast and so new a country commanded the best that inventive genius could supply; and the unique character of the American experiment insured that alert and inquiring minds would seek to understand it, to explain its implications, to direct its course for the future.

Fortunately the United States was not

wholly without an intellectual tradition.

Leadership of New England New England from its beginning had had a high regard for learning; it had taken great pride in its schools and colleges; it had required its clergy to become masters of an intricate system of theology. New Englanders, moreover, were not confined to New England, for in every generation their migratory propensities had taken some of them to nearly every part of the country. Tenacious of their views and born propagandists, they introduced wherever they went New England ideas, New England ways of doing things. Particularly in the West, where a materialistic point of view was naturally prevalent, the New England emigrants exerted a strong leavening influence. Nor were they content merely to uphold the cultural traditions they had inherited; they kept in constant touch with developments in their old homes, and passed on to the rest of the country the new impulses they received. Thus New England became a kind of intellectual capital toward which the whole country looked for leadership.

The thoroughgoing democratization of the newspaper, which took place during this period, helped immeasurably to **Newspapers** facilitate the spread of new ideas. In an earlier age only the upper classes could afford the luxury of a newspaper subscription, but from the eighteen-thirties on almost anyone who could read could enjoy that privilege. No one editor could claim the chief credit for this revolutionary change, but a New Yorker named Benjamin H. Day, who began in 1833 to sell his paper, the *Sun*, at a penny a copy, had something to do with it. Day further extended his subscription list by making the *Sun* sensational enough to interest even the dullest-witted reader, and because his paper reached so many people he could exact a heavy tribute from the advertisers. His methods were imitated by James Gordon Bennett, who in 1835 began the publication of the *New York Herald*, and by Horace Greeley, who six years later established the *New York Tribune*. Conservative editors and readers at first held the penny papers in great contempt, but the efforts of the latter to increase their circulation led them to present controversial news with an impartiality that even the intelligent public came to respect. In time the higher-priced newspapers were forced either to suspend publication or to reduce their prices. It is also worth noting that the rapid improvement of the national system of transportation enabled the leading papers to extend greatly the radius of their circulation. Not only the New York journals, but such papers also as the *Boston Evening Transcript*, the *Philadelphia Ledger*, and the *Springfield* (Massachusetts) *Republican* exerted far more than a merely local influence. Very often for the distant readers weekly editions took the place of the ordinary daily.

Magazines as well as newspapers enjoyed an astonishing vogue. Possibly a hundred such publications existed in 1825, but a generation later **Magazines** there were six or eight times that number. Most of these periodicals, like their predecessors, were both local in character and extremely short-lived, but a few of them, *Graham's Magazine*, the *Knickerbocker Magazine*, and the *Southern Literary Messenger*, for example, were during many years widely read. They printed articles of nearly every sort and kind — critical essays, sermons, stories, poems, and travel accounts — and played an important part in the formulation of American taste and opinion. Through the magazines American readers made the acquaintance of such writers as Edgar Allan Poe, William Cullen Bryant, Henry Wadsworth Longfellow, and James Fenimore Cooper, not to mention many contemporary English authors whose works, for lack of an international agreement as to copyrights, were frequently pirated. Of especial appeal to American women was *Godey's Lady's Book*, founded in 1830, which supplied not only a somewhat saccharine type of literature, but also the latest word on feminine fashions, good morals, and good manners.

Its literary editor, Mrs. Sarah Josepha Buell Hale, became a kind of arbiter of propriety for American womanhood, and its publisher, Louis A. Godey, for his times was soon a very rich man. His magazine and many others, also, were plentifully supplied with really excellent woodcut or metal illustrations.

Lyceums vied with newspapers and magazines in giving the public something to think and talk about. Inaugurated at Millburg, Vermont, in 1826, the lyceum movement soon became nation-wide in its scope, and successfully stimulated the presentation of lecture courses far and wide. Some of the lyceums — for example, the Lowell Institute of Boston, which received in 1836 a bequest of a quarter of a million dollars — were well supplied with funds, but most of them depended for their support upon the willingness of large numbers of citizens to pay small sums to hear the addresses of famous men and women. The stipends which the lecturers received, while often extremely modest, were sufficient to aid many intellectuals in the sometimes difficult task of eking out a living. Naturally not every lecturer had a worth-while contribution to make, but such a man as Ralph Waldo Emerson, whose lecture tours were frequent and extensive, was known to accept as little as five dollars for delivering an address in some remote frontier village. It is difficult to estimate the influence of the lyceum movement, but it must have been considerable. The lyceums offered a platform to every celebrity with a talent for public speaking, and to every earnest apostle of reform. Like the newspapers and the magazines, they were both a cause and a result of the intellectual and moral awakening that was so characteristic of the age.

Lyceums

Not in America alone, but throughout the civilized world, this period was remarkable for its inventions. One by one the machines that were necessary to complete the Industrial Revolution were brought to a fair degree of perfection and started on their course. In this work Americans, well aware of the need

Inventions — the telegraph

of annihilating distance in a country so large as their own, and faced by a chronic shortage of labor, played an honorable and important part. Outstanding among them was Samuel F. B. Morse, a painter and sculptor of New England origin who had twice spent long periods abroad. In 1832, as he was returning to the United States the second time, he talked with his fellow passengers aboard the ship *Sully* about some electrical experiments then being made in France, and conceived the idea of the electromagnetic telegraph. On his arrival in the United States he assumed a professorship of painting and sculpture, to which he had recently been elected in the University of the City of New York, but he spent much of his time in experimentation. By 1835 he had a mile of telegraph wire in a room at the university, over which he was transmitting messages successfully. It was not until 1843, however, that he obtained an appropriation of thirty thousand dollars from Congress to build an experimental line from Washington to Baltimore. On May 1, 1844, with the line complete to Annapolis, the first news message was sent over the wires. The invention met so obvious a need that its use became general almost at once. By 1850 the settled portions of the country were well supplied with telegraphic communications, and in 1858 a cable was successfully laid across the Atlantic.

Of tremendous importance to agriculture was the work of Cyrus Hall McCormick, a back-country Virginian of Scotch-Irish descent, who in 1831 produced a successful reaper. His father, Robert McCormick, had long sought to construct an improved harvesting machine, and had made extensive experiments which his more successful son had been able to utilize. In 1834 young McCormick patented his device, but he was not well enough satisfied with it to attempt its manufacture and sale until he had worked for several years upon improvements. With better business ability than is given to most inventors, he succeeded ultimately in putting on the market a machine which contributed greatly to

The McCormick reaper

"DAY ON THE MOUNTAINS." Title page of *Graham's Magazine*, January, 1849.

Popular literature in the Middle Period was suited to every taste and interest. Graham's Magazine was the first American periodical to pay its contributors generously; through its columns such writers as Bryant, Longfellow and Cooper became known to the public. Almanacs, ever since Franklin's Poor Richard's, had been an American staple, but toward midcentury the comic almanac became extraordinarily popular, especially in the West. Newspapers sometimes achieved more than a local circulation and a few of them, such as Bennett's daily Herald, greatly influenced public opinion.

PARIS FASHIONS. Engraved plate from *Graham's Magazine*, October, 1849.

WESTERN TALL TALES. A scene from the life of Davy Crockett, in Davy Crockett's Almanac, 1846.

THE "HERALD" IN THE COUNTRY. Engraving by Thielly, after a painting by William S. Mount.

the revolution in methods of farming that characterized the middle years of the nineteenth century. Sound judgment led him to establish his headquarters in the West, first at Cincinnati (1845) and then at Chicago (1847), where the demand for agricultural machinery would be greatest and the opposition to new devices least. By 1850 he was manufacturing three thousand machines each year, and by 1860 twenty thousand. Nor was the reaper the only new tool that during this period inventors provided for the farmer. Dozens of other useful devices were constructed, each of which in time was to play a part in freeing the farmer from the bondage of hand labor. It should be observed, however, that the full effect of these inventions was long delayed. Not until the time of the Civil War did the life of the average American farmer begin to be seriously affected by the new machines.

Another American invention of great importance was the sewing machine, which **The sewing** Elias Howe, a manufacturer of **machine** cotton-mill machinery at Lowell, Massachusetts, produced in 1845. While Howe was in England, seeking to obtain financial backing for the manufacture and sale of his machine, some American capitalists put just such a device as he had invented on the market. Fortunately, however, Howe had taken out a patent in 1846, and he was able to protect his rights by legal processes. By the early fifties the manufacture of sewing machines was being carried on extensively, and a decade later the extraordinary demands of the Civil War made the industry extremely prosperous. Ultimately Howe, who himself engaged in the business and received also a royalty on the machines made by other manufacturers, reaped a rich reward. But the sewing machine, like the reaper, was of far greater benefit to a subsequent generation than to the one that produced it.

Several other products of the American inventive genius deserve to be mentioned. In 1830 Samuel Colt, a sixteen-year-old Connecticut lad who had shipped as a sailor from Boston to Calcutta, whiled away his time on the voyage by whittling out a wooden model of a revolving pistol. In 1835 he patented his "revolver" in England, and next year in the United States. By 1838 a company at Paterson, New Jersey, had begun its manufacture. It is difficult to imagine what the history of the Great Plains, just then beginning, would have been like without Colt's invention. In 1836, another Connecticut Yankee, Charles Goodyear, made his first important discovery of an improved treatment for the surface of India-rubber products. Some years later he perfected the vulcanizing process, and thus "gave a substantial basis to an industry built on American brains rather than material resources." In 1846 Richard M. Hoe, a New York City manufacturer of printing materials, produced for the use of the *Philadelphia Ledger* the first steam cylinder press. Faster presses were an absolute necessity if the demand for more and more newspapers was to be met, and improvements upon Hoe's invention made during the next few years, enabled the publishers to print an almost incredible number of papers in a minimum length of time.

Americans also showed great resourcefulness in improving and adapting to different conditions inventions that were introduced from abroad. This was true of the English locomotive, which had to be made lighter and speedier to meet American needs, and of numerous details in the way of railroad equipment. It was true of most of the machinery used in American factories and foundries, of the development of the photograph from the French "daguerreotype," of the "loco-focos," or friction matches, which were invented in Europe but first patented in America. Heating and cooking stoves, which had ancestors on both sides of the Atlantic, were made sufficiently practical during the period to cause the closing-off of many handsome fireplaces. By the middle of the century furnaces and plumbing were being installed, whale-oil lamps were replacing candles, gas-lighting systems were spreading from city to city, tinware was being substituted for costlier copper and iron kitchen utensils, woven carpets were sharing the honors with the old-fashioned rag rugs, and wallpaper was coming into general use. At least for the city dweller, life was becoming increasingly comfortable.

Most American inventions were made to meet an obvious need, and the inventors **Scientific advances** achieved results, as a rule, only by a persistent application of the trial-and-error method. More scientific advances, however, were by no means lacking. Chief among these should be listed the use of anesthetics in surgery, which a Georgia physician, Doctor Crawford W. Long, proved to be practicable as early as 1842. He did not publish his findings for some years, however, and in the meantime two New England dentists, Doctor Horace Wells of Hartford, Connecticut, and Doctor W. T. G. Morton of Boston, achieved similar results. Useful descriptive data were also made available by American scientists. During these years Louis J. R. Agassiz, a French-Swiss immigrant who became a Harvard professor, made important contributions, based upon observations in America, to the world's knowledge of geology and zoology. J. J. Audubon, born in Haiti, the son of a French naval officer, and educated as an artist in France, made the United States his home, and devoted his life to the observation and description of the birds of America. Notable also was the work of Joseph Henry, a physicist, and the first head of the Smithsonian Institution, a foundation made possible by an Englishman's eccentric bequest of a half million dollars to the United States government "for the increase and diffusion of knowledge among men." Other American scientists who won distinction were Asa Gray in botany, James Dwight Dana in mineralogy, Ormsby M. Mitchell in astronomy, and Benjamin Silliman in geology. Silliman, a professor at Yale, was not content merely with his teaching and research, but carried to the country by means of popular lectures information about the work the scientists were trying to do.

The period witnessed also a remarkable outburst of literary activity. Foremost among the writers of the time was Ralph Waldo Emerson **Emerson** (1803–82), a philosopher and poet whose influence upon his fellow men was little short of phenomenal. Emerson was descended on his father's side from a long line of New England preachers, and was thus "born to be educated." He attended the Boston Latin School, was graduated in 1821 from Harvard College, taught school, studied theology, and accepted a Unitarian pulpit. He was soon convinced, however, that "to be a good minister one must leave the ministry," and acted accordingly. Late in 1832 he sailed for Europe, where he met many prominent men of letters, among them Coleridge, Wordsworth, and Carlyle. On his return to America a few years later he began to formulate, first in sermons and lectures, and then in books of essays, his doctrine that "God is in every man." Through his reading and his European contacts he had absorbed the philosophy of the German idealists. Like them, he deduced from the teachings of Kant that the world of experience revealed a realm of the spirit. The visible world of the senses was, as he expressed it, only an "apparition of God." There was much to be learned from nature, for whose teachings he sought to be a "transparent eyeball." The deepest truths, he held, came unbidden and unsought to the receptive human soul. "To believe in your own thought . . . is genius." Always professing confidence in the infinite possibilities of man, Emerson found a firm basis for his reasoning in the society he saw about him. Here man was accomplishing new things, building a new civilization. Material progress must be matched by spiritual progress. American thinkers, like American men of action, must strike out for themselves along original lines. "Our day of dependence, our long apprenticeship to the learning of other lands, draws to a close," he told the Phi Beta Kappa Society of Cambridge in 1837. "Let us have done with Europe and

American inventors were ever quick to make practical application of scientific knowledge discovered by others. Although Americans did little for pure science, their skill at adapting general principles to useful ends was outstanding. Pictured to the left are: Morton, Bogardus, Colt, McCormick, Saxton, Goodyear, Cooper, Henry, Mott, Ericsson, Sickels, Morse, Burden, Hoe, Bigelow, Blanchard, and Howe.

AMERICAN INVENTORS. "Men of Progress," a composite portrait by C. Schussele, lithographed for a wide public sale by Sartain, 1861.

McCORMICK'S REAPER. A later painting of the first public testing of McCormick's invention, 1831.

MORSE IN HIS WORKSHOP. Illustration from Prime, *Life of Samuel F. B. Morse*, 1855.

dead cultures, let us explore the possibilities of our own new world."

Other young Americans of this generation were profoundly influenced by German idealism, some from having read Coleridge and Carlyle, its leading English proponents, some from having studied in the German universities. In Boston, from 1836 to 1843, a small group of these like-minded men, Emerson among them, met together informally in what they called the Symposium, or sometimes, after Henry Hedge, their leader,

The "transcendentalists"

"Hedge's Club." To outsiders, however, members of the group were generally known as "transcendentalists," and their version of Kant's philosophy as "transcendentalism." In 1838 they brought out a series of volumes known as *Specimens of Foreign Standard Literature*, and in 1840 they began the publication of a magazine called the *Dial*, through which many of Emerson's writings reached the public. Nearly all of the original transcendentalists became nationally prominent: Henry Thoreau as one of the few really great masters of English prose; Bronson Alcott,

Scientific advances played significant but varied rôles in American history. Colt's revolver was first "the perfect weapon for the horsemen who waged war on the Plains Indians," then later became an inseparable part of the cowboy's equipment. The sewing machine happened along just in time to make possible mass production of uniforms and other items of equipment needed by the Civil War armies. Audubon's birds and beasts set new standards in art as well as in descriptive science.

THE COLT PISTOL. Advertising sheet showing the scenes engraved on the gun cylinders, about 1850.

THE SEWING MACHINE. Illustration from the title page of a song sheet, published by J. L. Peters, New Jersey, 1860's.

AN AUDUBON STUDY. An original watercolor by the natural scientist of the *Brown Pelican.*

James Freeman Clarke, and Theodore Parker as preachers and lecturers; George Ripley and Margaret Fuller as editors and literary critics; George Bancroft as historian. The transcendentalists dreamed of an America which should live up to its opportunities, and, because they thought that it so often failed to do so, they criticized it scathingly. In 1840 some of them, hoping to show how "a system of brotherly co-operation" might be substituted for "one of selfish competition," took part in the establishment of Brook Farm, near West Roxbury, Massachusetts. Here all property was held in common, labor was equally shared, and much time was allotted to social and literary activities. The experiment lasted for several years, and, because of the prominence of its

RALPH WALDO EMERSON

EMERSONIAN CARICATURE. Sketch by Christopher P. Cranch, a friend and colleague of the writer, based on lines from Emerson's *Nature;* "Standing on the bare ground, — my head bathed by the blithe air, & uplifted into infinite space, — all mean egotism vanishes. I become a transparent Eyeball."

The Transcendentalists of New England long dominated philosophical thought in the United States. They believed in man's infinite capabilities, and provided a basis in reason for the democratic spirit of the age. Emerson as essayist and lecturer was their outstanding leader, but Thoreau expressed transcendentalist ideas in some of the finest prose ever written by an American. Hawthorne spent a brief period at Brook Farm.

HENRY DAVID THOREAU

NATHANIEL HAWTHORNE

originators, it attracted much attention. The transcendentalists, however, should not be thought of as communists. Their interest was primarily in the individual, and in the full development of his capabilities. Their emphasis upon the dignity of human nature and the perfectibility of man was generally regarded with favor by the public, for it was easy enough to see in such doctrines a kind of justification of American democracy.

The writings of the transcendentalists constituted only a fraction of the literary achievements of New England during the middle decades of the nineteenth century. Indeed, the contrast in this respect between the years before and the years following 1830 was so striking that the term "New England Renaissance" soon came to

"New England Renaissance"

be applied to the literary activities of the period. The blight of Calvinistic theology, which assured mankind of its total depravity and its helplessness without the saving grace of God, is generally regarded as the chief reason for the stifling of nearly every creative impulse in the earlier years of the century. So Emerson maintained when he wrote that "from 1790 to 1820 there was not a book, a speech, a conversation or a thought" in the whole state of Massachusetts. But Emerson exaggerated. New England under the sway of the Calvinists may have reflected chiefly upon its sins, but at least it reflected. Out of these reflections came the Unitarian and Universalist revolts in religion, the New England renaissance in literature, and a remarkable drive for social reform. New England minds may have been slow to open to new ideas, but at least the minds were there, and ultimately some of them did open. The soil which produced such men as Emerson, Thoreau, Longfellow, Whittier, Holmes, Hawthorne, Lowell, Bancroft, Prescott, Motley, Garrison, and Phillips could hardly have been as barren as it has been pictured.

Whatever Americans of the present time may think, Henry Wadsworth Longfellow (1807–82) was a great poet to Americans of his own age. Long-
Longfellow
fellow was born in Portland, Maine, and was graduated from Bowdoin College, where he soon became a professor of modern languages. In 1835 he was appointed to a similar post at Harvard University, and from that time on he was closely identified with the aristocracy of Cambridge and "Back Bay" Boston. Longfellow's poetry was much affected by the cloistered life he led. Twice he made long visits to Europe, but most of his time he spent in the spacious mansion at Cambridge which Washington had used as headquarters during the first year of the American Revolution. In his poetic forms Longfellow followed European precedents, and he often made use of European themes; indeed, some of his best work is to be found in his translations of European writers. But he also used American themes, such, for example, as in *Evangeline, The Courtship of Miles Standish*, and *Hiawatha*, although in such a restrained, drawing-room manner that the principals concerned could hardly have recognized themselves. Longfellow's incurable romanticism, his aloofness from the sometimes painful realities of life, and his gentle, soothing rhymes appealed greatly to the American masses. His poetry matched exactly the popular conception of what poetry should be; ordinary men were deeply gratified to see how easily they could understand and appreciate it.

Less able than Longfellow, but freer from the charge of artificiality, was the Quaker poet John Greenleaf Whittier
Whittier
(1807–92). He was born in Haverhill, Massachusetts, of Quaker parents, and he was himself a lifelong member of the Society of Friends. As a boy he worked on his father's farm and sometimes sent verses to the local newspaper. His first publication of consequence, *Legends of New England* (1831), exploited themes with which he had a natural intimacy, but he was soon caught up in the anti-slavery crusade, and turned his talent to the furthering of that cause. He advocated, as a Quaker would, the overthrow of slavery by pacific means, but he portrayed its evils in verse vivid enough to gratify the most earnest believer in more direct action. His "Ichabod," a scathing denunciation of Webster for supporting the Compromise of 1850, reveals clearly his intransigeance. Once the battle for abolition was won, Whittier grew pleasantly reminiscent of by-gone days in New England, and preserved his memories in such poems as *The Barefoot Boy, Snow-Bound*, and *The Tent on the Beach*. His output was more limited than Longfellow's, and his poetic competence less marked, but his influence upon the course of events was far greater.

Among the other outstanding writers of the New England Renaissance were Nathaniel Hawthorne (1804–64), Oliver
Hawthorne,
Wendell Holmes (1809–94), and
Holmes,
James Russell Lowell (1819–91).
Lowell
Hawthorne began his literary career with *Twice-Told Tales*, the first series of which, published in 1837, exploited American themes, although for most people the title calls to mind the modern versions of classical myths which he published later. In *The Scarlet Letter*, a story of early New England Puritanism, he drew a powerful indictment of the moral values of his ancestors; in *The House of the Seven Gables* and *The Blithedale Romance* he dealt with the influences that had shaped the lives of those about him. His artistry with words and his deep psychological insight gave his writings a permanent value, although he was unable to make a living from them, and had to piece out his income by holding minor political offices. Holmes is known for his poetry no less than for his prose, but for his wit and humor most of all. He hated Calvinism cordially, but he

could still celebrate its collapse in the perennially amusing *Wonderful One-Hoss Shay*. His *Autocrat of the Breakfast-Table*, and its numerous sequels, showed him to be a past master of the worldly lore and native drollery of the Yankees. Lowell, like Holmes, was remarkable for his versatility. A New England Brahmin, he nevertheless expressed himself admirably in dialect poems, such as the *Biglow Papers*, many of which, like the poems of Whittier, had a definite anti-slavery bias. But Lowell was also a political essayist of note, a professor in Harvard University, editor for several years of the *Atlantic Monthly*, and later one of the editors of the *North American Review*. His services to letters and politics were recognized after the Civil War by two diplomatic appointments, first as minister to Spain, and later as minister to Great Britain.

Any survey of literary New England during the middle period would be incomplete

New England historians

without mention of its able group of historians. The name of Jared Sparks (1789–1866) naturally heads this list. Like so many scholars of his time, Sparks turned his hand to many things. He occupied a Unitarian pulpit, edited the *North American Review*, was for ten years a professor of history at Harvard University and for three years its president. He was one of the first to recognize in the history of the United States a theme of consequence that must no longer be neglected, and he early set himself the task of collecting the records from which at least an important part of this history could be written. In 1830 he published twelve volumes of the *Diplomatic Correspondence of the American Revolution*; several years later twelve more, the *Writings of George Washington*; then within the decade another dozen, the *Works of Benjamin Franklin*. He also found time during his busiest years to edit a twenty-five-volume *Library of American Biography*, for which he himself wrote many of the sketches, and later in life to bring out four valuable volumes of *Correspondence of the American Revolution*. As

an editor he took greater liberties with an original text than would now be regarded as proper, but the debt historians owe him is very great.

George Bancroft (1800–91), like Sparks, saw significance in the history of his own country. A graduate of Harvard, he spent five years in the universities of Germany and came back to the United States well grounded in the principles of historical method. But Bancroft's love of country, and his devotion to the principle of democracy in government for which it stood, led him to saturate his work with a patriotic fervor that today would be regarded as bad form. For half a century he occupied himself with the writing of a monumental *History of the United States*, which from the first volume, published in 1834, to the twelfth, published in 1882, idealizes and overstates the American case on nearly every page. Throughout the colonial period, with which Bancroft was chiefly concerned, the colonists in all contentions with the mother country were always right, the British always wrong. The reader gets the unmistakable impression that Bancroft wrote primarily to justify American democracy, to prove the success of the American experiment. For historians of a later generation such a work has little value; but for Americans of Bancroft's time this flattering point of view gave great satisfaction, and Bancroft's popularity was tremendous.

Two other New England historians, William H. Prescott (1796–1859) and John Lothrop Motley (1814–77), looked beyond the borders of the United States in search of more romantic materials than the history of their own country afforded. Prescott found what he wanted in the history of Spain and of the Spanish empire in America. His *History of Ferdinand and Isabella*, published in 1838, won him an enviable reputation both at home and abroad, a reputation which grew as one important work — the *Conquest of Mexico*, the *Conquest of Peru*, and a *History of Philip II of Spain* — succeeded another. Motley interested himself in the his-

"LEATHERSTOCKING." The first representation of James Fenimore Cooper's hero, by Henry Inman, 1823.

"THE LEGEND OF SLEEPY-HOLLOW." Illustration for Washington Irving's tale, by Felix O. C. Darley, 1849.

HERMAN MELVILLE

EDGAR ALLAN POE

American writers testified unconsciously to the growing importance of the United States by devoting their attention increasingly to strictly American themes. *Irving's* Sketch Book, *Cooper's* Leatherstocking Tales, *and Whitman's* Leaves of Grass *were almost "one hundred per-cent American." Melville and Poe, however, dealt with subjects more universal in their appeal.*

WALT WHITMAN

tory of Holland, and after a long period of research produced in 1856 his *History of the Rise of the Dutch Republic,* and in 1861 the first half of his *United Netherlands.* Greater than either was Francis Parkman (1823–93), who, after an initial work, the *Oregon Trail* (1836), in which he related his own experiences during a trip to the West, fixed upon the French in North America as the theme he wished to develop. But most of Parkman's books were written and published in the years following the Civil War, and they belong, therefore, in point of time, if not in spirit, to the later period.

While the leadership of New England in **Writers of** the world of American letters **the middle** was incontestable, writers of dis-**states** tinction were also to be found in other parts of the country. Washington

Irving (1783–1859), who returned to New York in 1832 after a residence of seventeen years abroad, sought with some success to catch the spirit of the untamed West in his *Tour of the Prairies, Astoria,* and *Adventures of Captain Bonneville.* During his later years he wrote a monumental *Life of Washington,* which was more admired by his contemporaries than by their descendants. James Fenimore Cooper (1789–1851), another New-Yorker, found a field for his imagination in the North American Indian, and his *Leather-Stocking Tales* are still read. William Cullen Bryant (1794–1878), a New England boy who won fame in New York and for half a century was editor of the New York *Evening Post,* wrote verse of enduring charm. Herman Melville (1819–91) told with rare vividness tall tales of the sea. His *Moby Dick,* the story of a "strange, fierce white whale" and his enemy, Captain Ahab, is one of the world's greatest romances. Walt Whitman (1819–92) more than any other writer caught the spirit of his times, and reflected it in verse forms that were as new and unpredictable as the civilization he delighted to honor. His *Leaves of Grass* registered a more complete break with European tradition than anything that had come out of New England, and the freedom and gusto with which he expressed himself set important precedents for the coming age.

Edgar Allan Poe (1809–49) defies classification both as to time and place. He was **Edgar Allan Poe** not much concerned with the problems of his own, or any other, generation, and while the South claims him, he was born in Boston and spent much of his time in New York. Virginia was his home, however, as nearly as he had one, and for a number of years he edited the *Southern Literary Messenger.* Undoubtedly a psychopathic case himself, he was interested in the weird and abnormal to a startling degree, but he had such a sure eye for beauty and for perfection of form that he ultimately won the admiration of even the most conventional. Although he mastered better than any of his predecessors the technique of the short story, particularly the detective story, his chief title to fame rests upon his poetry. Such poems as *The Raven, The Bells,* and *Annabel Lee* remain unsurpassed for their haunting melodies and their technical perfection.

The ante-bellum South produced no other writer even faintly comparable to Poe, but it **Southern writers** did not lack for stars of a lesser magnitude. William Gilmore Simms (1806–70), a persistent and often successful imitator of such English writers as Byron and Scott, published over a hundred volumes of verse and prose before the Civil War. Like so many other Southerners of his time, he turned whatever talent he possessed to a militant defense of the institution of slavery. Henry Timrod (1829–67) and Paul Hamilton Hayne (1830–86) wrote enchanting, but not very enduring, poetry. William J. Grayson (1788–1863) defended slavery in a long poem, *The Hireling and the Slave,* which effectively contrasted the unhappy lot of the wage-slave in the northern mines and factories with the carefree life of the bond-slave of the South. John Pendleton Kennedy (1795–1870) revealed in vivid prose pictures the charm of plantation life in Old Virginia, but he held no brief for slavery.

It is a curious fact that the literary activities of the years following 1830 were in nowise paralleled by similar successes in the realm of the arts. Indeed, the period witnessed a definite decline in such fields as painting and architecture, fields in which during the early years of the Republic promising beginnings had seemingly been made. The blame for this state of affairs is usually placed on the triumph of democracy — a triumph which exalted the taste of the ordinary man, however execrable it might be, to a parity with the taste of the élite. But this explanation is not entirely satisfying, for by the same reasoning a dearth of good literature should also have developed. One might rather suppose that the artists found it more difficult than the men of letters to keep abreast of the Industrial Revolution. The traditions that bound them were more rigid than literary forms; the materials they worked with were less plastic than words. Not only in the United States, but throughout the civilized world, the arts were at low ebb during the middle decades of the nineteenth century. Everywhere those who looked only to the past for guidance failed to catch the spirit of the new age, while those who broke with the past and began to experiment made many false starts.

American architecture throughout this period was strikingly free from originality. The classical vogue that Jefferson had done so much to intro- **Architecture** duce still flourished, and totally irrelevant replicas of early Greek temples were everywhere in evidence. For public buildings the favorite design was a combination of dome and portico that was not often strikingly successful. Dwelling-houses were apt to reveal the old Georgian influence of the colonial period, although there was much rule-of-thumb modification, and, as time went on, an unmistakable tendency to copy anything that anybody had ever done anywhere. About the middle of the century American builders began to follow European architects in a furious revolt against classicism. Gothic forms were revived, excessive ornamentation replaced simplicity, and a kind of general pandemonium broke loose. This freedom was necessary, no doubt, if any really important new note was to be struck, but at least until well toward the end of the century the search was conducted in vain.

Buildings are a necessity, and architecture of a kind is therefore indispensable in any

Painting and sculpture age, but the same can hardly be said of painting and sculpture, which throughout the period under review were almost non-existent in the United States. Portrait painters there were, but they showed little of the distinction that had characterized the post-Revolutionary artists, and the beginnings of photography soon dealt their craft a serious blow. A group of landscape painters, known generally as the "Hudson River School," called attention to the beauty of American scenes, and genuinely sought to reproduce what they saw rather than what artists were traditionally supposed to see. But their technique was European, not American, and their achievements hardly above mediocrity. American sculptors had even less to their credit. What few of them there were clung tenaciously to the classical traditions, and did their best to make American politicians look like Roman emperors in disguise. Horatio Greenough, ablest American sculptor of his time, carved from Italian marble a heroic statue of Washington, scantily clad and seated on a throne, which fortunately was soon relegated to storage in the Smithsonian Institution. The "Greek Slave" by Hiram Powers attracted much attention, mainly perhaps because it was a nude female figure, and most Americans had been taught to identify nudity with naughtiness. Powers's extraordinary daring came doubtless from his long residence in Florence, Italy. A fad for waxwork was widely followed, and some really exquisite modeling was done, mostly by women of leisure, who also busied themselves successfully with many other varieties of "fancy work."

Americans of the period were by no means uninterested in music, although in this respect dependence on Europe remained marked. Musical so- **Music** cieties were common to the larger cities, European artists often made American tours, a few symphony orchestras were organized, and attempts to produce opera, mainly Italian, were not unknown. But American composers of music were neither numerous nor of profound ability, although some of their work lives on. The hymns of Lowell Mason (1792–1872), for example, are familiar to nearly every American churchgoer, and their publication contributed materially to the popularity of congregational singing. Mason is also to be remembered for his success in introducing the teaching of music into the public schools. Stephen C. Foster (1826–64), a native of Pennsylvania who knew little of the South or, for that matter, of formal music, wrote both the melodies and the words of dozens of songs which reflected admirably the tempo of southern plantation life, and won an enduring popularity in all parts of the country. Foster's songs, and many others like them, frequently reached the public first through black-face minstrel shows, which then enjoyed a great vogue. The Negroes themselves, who sang while they worked, and whose talent for music was very great, were doubtless the originators of many of the melodies that these song-writers exploited.

Owing partly to frontier conditions and partly to the hostility of New England Puritanism, the American theater was slow to develop. During **The theater** the colonial period small beginnings were made in some of the coast cities, but both the plays and the players were English, and the

A COUNTRY HOME. An American version of an Italian villa. Lithograph by Currier and Ives, about 1855.

The arts in America during the romantic period reflected the idealism and optimism that characterized the times, but they produced little of originality or lasting value. At best, architecture displayed a jumble of overdecorated, imitative styles. Painting, much of it widely popularized by the Currier and Ives lithographs, concentrated on peaceful, panoramic landscapes, or on the homely scenes of a comfortable, often idealized, existence.

GENRE PAINTING. "Bargaining for a Horse," by William Sydney Mount, 1835.

THE HUDSON RIVER SCHOOL. "In the Catskills," by Thomas Doughty, about 1840.

"THE GREEK SLAVE." Hiram Powers' controversial sculpture first shown at the Düsseldorf Galleries in New York. Engraving by R. Thew, 1858.

FOSTER'S MELODIES. Title page of the sheet music for *Jeanie With the Light Brown Hair*, about 1850.

Sculpture, music and the theater in America had many obstacles to overcome, among them both ignorance and indifference on the part of the public. Hiram Powers finished his "Greek Slave" in 1843, and later made no less than six marble copies of it, but it was not greatly appreciated. Foster's melodies, on the other hand, caught on immediately and live with us still. Americans liked the theater and produced a few great stars, but dramatic productions still suffered from religious opposition in many localities.

SHAKESPEARIAN DRAMA. Charlotte and Susan Cushman in *Romeo and Juliet*. Engraving, about 1847.

response to their efforts was not always cordial. Even after the Revolution the theater in the United States was for a long time an alien rather than a native institution. By the thirties and forties, however, most of the large towns and cities had stock companies with which well-known actors or actresses on tour co-operated in the produc-

tion of plays. The tendency to rely mainly upon English stars was a serious handicap to the development of native talent, but a few Americans rivaled the best of the visitors in popularity. Chief among the American stars were Edwin Forrest and Edwin Booth, whose greatest successes were in Shakespearean rôles, and Charlotte Cushman, whom the public liked best as Lady Macbeth or Meg Merrilies.

The theater of this period was more famous for its actors than for its playwrights. Ears attuned to the resonant oratory of Daniel Webster and Henry Clay asked nothing better than to listen to the long declamations of Shakespearean characters, and the steady devotion of theatrical patrons to the classics tended to discourage the writing of new plays. To this rule, however, there were important exceptions. George Henry Boker's *Francesca da Rimini*, for example, won an enduring place in dramatic literature, and Cora Mowatt's *Fashion, or, Life in New York*, burlesqued so successfully the social pretensions of the times that it has had numerous popular revivals. Current English plays also enjoyed a considerable popularity in the United States. One of them, Tom Taylor's *Our American Cousin*, ran one hundred and forty nights at Laura Keene's New Theater in New York. It was during a performance of this play at Ford's Theater in Washington that Abraham Lincoln was. assassinated. His assassin, John Wilkes Booth, a younger brother of Edwin Booth, and also an actor, fancied that by this deed he would redress the wrongs done the South.

Possibly an acute sensitiveness to music and the arts was too much to expect of an age that centered so much attention upon the lot of the common man. Above all else this was a period which proclaimed his importance and sought to meet his needs. Jacksonian democracy was founded on the principle that one man was as much worth while as another; Unitarian theology saw in even the humblest of God's children a spark of the divine; and, long before the publication of Darwin's *Origin of Species* in 1859, the idea of evolution, at least in so far as it implied the doctrine of human progress, was beginning to find able defenders on both sides of the Atlantic. "Progressive development does not end with us," wrote Theodore Parker, the transcendentalist divine, "we have seen only the beginning;

The idea of progress

the future triumphs of the race must be vastly greater than all accomplished yet." Society in an age that believed so intensely in the capacity of mankind for improvement could not fail to become increasingly aware of the evils with which it was afflicted, and to seek for remedies. In precisely the same spirit religion discarded some of its formalism and "otherworldliness" in order to concern itself more with the necessity of making this world "a better place to live in." Writers developed their talents, more often than otherwise, as the advocates of worthy causes. Humanitarian reformers of every kind got a hearing, and with surprisingly few exceptions a following as well.

The rapid advance of the factory system in the American Northeast presented the country with a serious labor problem. Under the vanishing domestic system apprentices and journeymen could hope to rise ultimately to the status of master craftsmen and employers, but only rarely was it possible under the new system for a workman to climb into the capitalist class. As the number of employees under a single management grew greater, the line of cleavage between the two classes grew deeper. Moreover, the employer was no longer aware of the conditions under which his employees lived, and he was often little concerned about the conditions under which they worked, so long as the profits of the factory remained good. Competition among manufacturers was keen, and the need of keeping down labor costs led frequently, especially in the textile mills, to the employment of women and children. Long hours of labor were required in the early factories — "from dawn to dark," or from thirteen to fifteen hours a day, was not unusual. Since most of the original "hands," or operators, had been recruited from the farms, where these long working hours had been the rule, the laborers at first saw no reason to protest. But some of them, at least, soon came to realize that the varied outdoor labor of the farm was one thing, and the monotonous indoor labor of the factory quite another.

The labor problem

Many of the factories were badly lighted, poorly ventilated, and dangerous to life and limb. Children were given little if any opportunity for schooling, women were kept away from the duties of the home, heads of families were often unemployed because of the unfair competition of women and children.

As the lot of the laborer grew harder, the strength of the employer grew greater. During the decade of the twenties American manufacturers increased their output six times over, while by 1830, with a total investment about one fifth as great as that of all the southern plantations combined, they were turning out goods worth one and one half times as much. Their importance to the society in which they lived won quick acclaim. To the wealthy manufacturers the lawyers looked for fees, the ministers for salaries, the colleges for endowments, the shopkeepers for goods on credit. For all such dependents the prosperity of the manufacturers was a matter of vital importance. Even the farmers, who supplied the foodstuffs to the factory towns, and the laborers themselves, who had no other means of subsistence than their factory jobs, generally accepted the manufacturer's point of view. His will became the will of the community. If protective tariffs were required to make him prosperous, then protective tariffs must be obtained. If the cost of labor must be cut, then the laborer must somehow bear the burden.

Such a thoroughgoing denial in practice of the democratic tenets of the age should have aroused criticism sooner than it did. But the right of individual freedom was a heritage no less prized by Americans than democracy itself. An employer, according to this tradition, must be left free to conduct his business as he chose; an employee must be equally free to accept or reject the contract he was offered. When, early in the nineteenth century, artisans in some of the larger cities sought through unions to force their employers to raise wages, public opinion rallied strongly to the support of the employers. Courts which made use of the English common law to punish strikers for "conspiracy to raise wages" were applauded. Labor organizations of every kind were bitterly condemned, but associations of employers, designed to keep the laborers in their places, won hearty approval.

In spite of these obstacles the country witnessed during the decade that preceded the panic of 1837 a well-defined and relatively successful labor movement. The leadership of this movement came from the artisans rather than from the factory hands, but the benefits were shared quite generally by all types of laborers. Prior to 1827 a few labor organizations patterned upon those of England had been formed in the United States, but they were merely local trades unions; that is, membership in a union was confined to a single city and a single craft. But in the year mentioned the failure of a carpenter's strike in Philadelphia led to the formation of the Mechanics' Union of Trade Associations, a federation of many trades unions. By thus combining forces the Philadelphia workingmen found that their power to exert pressure upon their employers was enormously increased. Strikes, when supported by the city federation, had a good chance to win, and the political influence of so large a group of voters was not to be despised. Soon other cities were similarly organized, and from 1834 to 1837 a somewhat imperfect national federation held annual meetings.

The city federation revealed a strong penchant for political action. The recent widening of the suffrage had made voters of the workingmen, and the possibility of turning this newly won weapon to good purpose was too obvious to be overlooked. The laws, laboring men held, had long been made by the well-to-do, or by their satellites, and the lawmakers had shown little concern for the workers. Mechanics' lien laws, free schools supported by public taxes, the abolition of imprisonment for debt, and the abolition of chartered monopolies were among the demands of the Philadelphia workingmen, who for four years, beginning in 1828, regularly nominated candidates for office. During the same period a Workingman's Party was active in New York, and in 1830 its candidate for governor polled a total of three thousand votes. Not only in Philadelphia and New York, but in many other cities also, workingmen's parties existed, and steps were even taken toward the formation of a national labor party. This promising third-party movement was undermined and defeated by the old parties only at the cost of taking over and putting into effect many of the reforms which the workingmen demanded.

To supplement their political activities the workingmen resorted also to strikes. **Strikes** These were particularly numerous during the four years of lush prosperity, 1833–37, when, according to Professor Channing, there were no less than one hundred and sixty-eight such conflicts in the United States. Of this number one hundred and three were held to secure higher wages, and twenty-six for a ten-hour day. Strikers also demanded what came later to be called the "closed shop"; that is, the employment of union men only, and the exclusion of non-union men. Even the factory operatives, who had at first taken little part in the labor movement, now began to strike. Through these direct methods the workingmen gained some victories, although the courts remained on the whole hostile, and could be used by employers to hamper the strikers. In 1842, however, the Massachusetts Supreme Court relaxed the rule of conspiracy to the extent of holding that labor organizations might legally seek to advance wages "by rules binding solely on members." By this time, however, strikes were infrequent and the labor movement at low ebb; indeed, lack of employment after the panic of 1837 led to the disintegration of many unions and the temporary cessation of labor activities.

The untimely decline of this first American labor movement did not prevent it from winning many substantial victories for the workingmen. A number of the strikes for a ten-hour day were successful, **Labor reforms** and the demand for shorter hours attracted much favorable comment, even outside labor circles. Politicians were not slow to catch the drift of public opinion. In 1840 President Van Buren proclaimed the ten-hour day in effect on all public works conducted by the national government. In 1847 the state of New Hampshire legalized the ten-hour day "except in pursuance of an express contract requiring greater time." Other states followed this precedent, employers reluctantly swung into line, and by the time of the Civil War the ten-hour day was general throughout the country, although longer hours were by no means unknown, particularly in New England, where in most of the factories a twelve-hour day was still required. During these same years several other labor demands were materially advanced. In nearly all the states new mechanics' lien laws were passed which gave the claims of laborers for wages precedence over the claims of those who merely furnished materials. Imprisonment for debt, a practice still so common that in 1830 there were, according to reliable estimates, no less than seventy-five thousand persons thus imprisoned in the United States, was abolished throughout the North by 1840, although in the South it continued down to the time of the Civil War. Also, laws designed to safeguard the life and health of factory workers were enacted with increasing frequency.

Many thoughtful Americans (among them most of the New England transcendentalists), although not themselves of the laboring class, sympathized deeply with the efforts of the workers to help themselves, but feared that the remedies proposed would prove to be mere palliatives, and of no permanent value. These high-minded observers sought instead to find some formula by which society could be remade with the evils from which it suffered left out. Since the Industrial Revolution, which was mainly responsible for the existing state of affairs, had come sooner to

Europe than to America, Europeans had anticipated Americans in thinking and writing about this problem. American reformers, therefore, were not obliged to rely wholly upon their own observation and reflection in the formulation of their ideas. Borrowing freely from such European theorists as Saint-Simon, Fourier, Robert Owen, and Karl Marx, they attacked the principle of competitive individualism, and sought to substitute for it some collectivist scheme that would improve the lot of the ordinary man. They watched with eager eyes the results of the communistic experiments which Robert Owen staged at New Lanark, Scotland, New Harmony, Indiana, and elsewhere. They tried many experiments of their own, such, for example, as the one at Brook Farm, already noted. As utopian reformers they failed, but as agitators for the amelioration of the workingman's lot they made a notable impression. Individualism was too deeply rooted in the American mind to be eradicated, but Emerson's contention that "a man has a right to be employed, to be trusted, to be loved, to be revered," was quite in keeping with the currents of the age.

Both the workingmen and their allies, the humanitarian reformers, were earnest advocates of free public education. **The demand for free schools** To the workingmen the necessity of equal educational opportunities for the children of rich and poor alike seemed absolutely essential; otherwise the caste lines between the two classes, already marked, would soon become complete and thoroughgoing barriers. The ordinary workingman, however, could not afford to pay for the education of his children; indeed, he often found it necessary to put them to work because he needed their wages, and thus to compound the evils from which he suffered. For child labor, at least in certain industries, kept wages low, and even deprived adults of the opportunity to labor. Workingmen, therefore, united in the demand that the state accept the full responsibility of providing schools at public expense. Taxes for such a purpose, they claimed, were quite as

just a public obligation as taxes for any other purpose. The humanitarian reformers carried the argument even further. From their point of view, every man had a right to an education; moreover, in a democracy such as the United States, where, at least in theory, the people ruled, obviously the government must take pains to insure that its rulers were educated. On the strength of this argument even taxpayers were persuaded that the taking of one man's property to educate another man's children was not so bad as it seemed.

As a matter of fact, the old idea that education was a class prerogative to which ordinary men had no right to aspire had always been somewhat on the defensive in America. Even in the seventeenth century, the Puritans in New England, the Dutch in New York, and the Quakers in Pennsylvania had in varying degrees accepted the responsibility of providing education for the masses, and had passed the tradition down to later generations. In the time of the Confederation the original states had not hesitated to include in the Northwest Ordinances of 1785 and 1787 provisions that obliged the new western states to establish, at least on paper, systems of free public schools. But in every part of the country the difference between precept and practice was considerable. Elementary schools, supported in whole or in part, did exist in the Northeast, particularly in Massachusetts and New York, but they were rarely as good as the private schools to which those whose means permitted preferred to send their children. Moreover, the public schools were often regarded as charity, or "pauper," schools, provided out of tax money (as also were poorhouses) only for those who had no alternative but to use them. In the South, country life made the problem of schooling difficult at best, and the planters were usually content to solve it in their own way for their own children, and to let the rest do without. In the West, the generous grants of school lands were received with much favor, and the obligation to provide free schools was cheerfully accepted, but the schools were slow to materialize. School lands brought slender revenues, and the taxable resources of the new states were always overstrained.

There was need, therefore, of a crusade to secure free public instruction, in fact as well **Educational** as in theory, and the crusaders **reformers** were not lacking. Two principles had to be established; first, that the maintenance of a school system must be required of every community; and second, that the schools so established must be equally open to all children, regardless of the ability or the inability of their parents to pay tuition. The second principle was embodied in a law which passed the legislature of Pennsylvania in 1834, and which the young Anti-Masonic leader, Thaddeus Stevens, helped save from repeal. The first principle, long established in Massachusetts, was there made thoroughly effective by the work of Horace Mann, who from 1837 to 1848 was secretary of the state board of education. Henry Barnard of Connecticut pioneered in the study of European educational systems with a view to their application in the United States. From such beginnings as these, particularly from the activities of Horace Mann, whose annual reports were studied far and wide, the American system of public schools was soon to grow. Well before the Civil War every northern state was attempting to provide elementary schools at public expense in every community, and important experiments were being made with public high schools. In general, however, private "academies" bridged the gap between elementary and college education, while the zeal of religious denominations, more often than otherwise, provided the colleges. In the South, where both elementary and secondary schools were frequently lacking, the efforts of Thomas Jefferson in behalf of nonsectarian higher education bore fruit when the University of Virginia opened its doors in 1825. Not until 1842, however, was the first of the western state universities, Michigan, able to

receive students. By 1850 no less than fifteen such universities had been founded, nearly all of them in the South or the West.

No less important than the wider extension of educational opportunities was the change in the content of the instruction **Schoolbooks** offered. Except for Noah Webster's *American Speller*, published in 1783, and Jedediah Morse's *American Geography*, published in 1789, the schools of the United States had been compelled to rely mainly upon reprints of European textbooks. When, therefore, a Connecticut Yankee named Samuel Griswold Goodrich began to publish in 1827 his definitely American "Peter Parley" texts, they filled a real need. Goodrich, according to Professor Channing, wrote or edited about one hundred and seventy volumes, most of which bore the name Peter Parley in the title. Among his collaborators was Nathaniel Hawthorne, whose authorship of *Peter Parley's Universal History on the Basis of Geography*, which appeared in 1837, is well attested. The Peter Parley books were not notable, as a rule, either for literary merit or for high standards of scholarship, but they covered a wide variety of subjects, and they provided a medium of instruction precisely fitted to the requirements of the times. Goodrich estimated that not less than seven million copies of his books were sold in the United States, a record that would seem more startling but for the fact that the total sales of Webster's *Speller* probably reached fifty millions.

Competition for the Peter Parley readers was soon furnished by the *Eclectic Series*, compiled by William Holmes McGuffey. These readers not only introduced the youth of America to the best in English and American literature, but contrived at the same time to drive home deftly the moral precepts of the Victorian Age. So popular were the selections that they were repeated in other series, such as the *National Readers* and *Lippincott's Readers*, and probably Mark Sullivan is correct in his opinion that they did much to set the pattern of American thought far down into the twentieth century. In 1828 Noah Webster, whose standardization of English spelling was already taking effect, published his great two-volume *Dictionary of the English Language*. This work, revised and republished in 1840, defined thousands of words that had never before been noted in any English dictionary, and set important precedents in pronunciation. Armed with these new tools of instruction, American teachers, particularly in the elementary schools, became increasingly effective. Largely through the leadership of Horace Mann, who in 1839 induced the state of Massachusetts to establish a normal school at Lexington, efforts were even begun to provide at state expense for the professional training of teachers.

The strongly classical bent of the academies, high schools, and colleges was destined to endure with but slight **Higher** variation until the time of the **education** Civil War. Classes in Latin, Greek, and mathematics absorbed the bulk of the student's time, although such new subjects as modern languages and natural science won places of importance in some curriculums. The instruction was often mediocre or worse. College students, eager to concern themselves with topics of current interest, sometimes learned more from the debates and oratorical contests which literary societies and fraternities delighted to sponsor than from their classroom exercises. Few went to college except those who wished to enter one of the three learned professions, the ministry, the law, and medicine; and many entered these professions without the benefit of college, or even secondary, training. Separate divinity, law, and medical schools were fairly common among the older colleges and universities by the middle of the century, but the instruction offered, particularly for the medical students, was extremely meager. In general, the importance of higher education was not fully recognized by Americans before the Civil War. Students with a real thirst for learning found it necessary, as a rule, to spend some time in Europe.

The emancipation of women from the restrictions that a man-made world had placed about them enlisted the efforts **Women's** of a notable company of Amer- **rights** ican reformers. On both sides of the Atlantic custom had long decreed that woman's place was in the home. The education of women, therefore, except in so far as it might be of use in better fitting them for their domestic duties, was regarded as unnecessary, and even unwise. Girls who were fortunate enough to receive more than an elementary education attended female seminaries or finishing schools, where religion, morality, and the social graces, including music and art, were given primary consideration. Before the eighteen-thirties not a college or university in the United States had opened its doors to women, and every other approach to the learned professions was similarly restricted to men. Also, the legal status of woman was definitely inferior to that of man: she might not vote; control of her property passed at the time of marriage to her husband; in certain matters the husband answered to the law for the conduct of his wife; legal responsibility for the children of a marriage was vested exclusively in the father.

While American men treated women with a deference that excited the comment of European travelers, the women **Women as** themselves had to take the lead **reformers** in the crusade for women's rights. And of these women many were led to embrace the feminist cause mainly through their interest in other reforms. So deep-seated was the prejudice against women in any public capacity that male reformers sometimes refused to accept the assistance of women, except in a definitely humble and secondary capacity. For example, eight women delegates to a World's Anti-Slavery Convention, held in London in 1840, were denied admission solely because they were women. Two of the excluded delegates were Lucretia Mott and Elizabeth Cady Stanton, both of whom then realized that if women were ever to accomplish anything as reformers they must first achieve a more honorable status **for**

Outstanding social reformers, Dorothea Dix and Margaret Fuller attracted much noteworthy attention to the feminist cause. Miss Fuller was for two years editor of the Transcendentalist paper, *The Dial.* Engraved portraits by R. G. Tietze and H. B. Hale, Jr.

themselves. In this sentiment they were supported strongly by such other able women as Frances Wright, a Scotswoman who on her second trip to America in 1825 had remained to work against slavery and on behalf of the emancipated slave; Lucy Stone, one of the first to demand equal suffrage; Margaret Fuller, the brilliant literary editor of the *New York Tribune,* who in 1844 published a scandalously frank book, *Woman in the Nineteenth Century;* Doctor Elizabeth Blackwell, who won admission to the medical profession against almost insuperable obstacles; Dorothea L. Dix, whose primary passion was the reform of prisons and insane asylums; and Mrs. Antoinette Louisa Brown Blackwell, pioneer woman preacher.

While the feminist movement was greeted with much ridicule and was not wholly successful until well into the twentieth century, some promising beginnings were made. High schools and normal schools for girls became increasingly common, and teaching in the elementary schools was soon recognized as almost a woman's monopoly. In 1833 Oberlin College, a Congregationalist institution, recognized two reform movements at once by opening its doors to women and Negroes. Coeducation was permitted by

Antioch College in 1853, by the University of Iowa in 1858, and in due time by most of the state-supported schools. A little later, following the example of Mount Holyoke Seminary, which opened at South Hadley, Massachusetts, November 8, 1837, under the guidance of Mary Lyon, many strictly women's colleges were founded. Women also made definite headway against the prejudice which had so long barred them from appearance on the public platform. A few of them were licensed to preach; and by persistent effort many more won toleration, then approval, as lecturers. In their contest for equality before the law the women scored victories in a few states, mainly with respect to the right of married women to hold property separately from their husbands. For the most part, however, the reforms they sought were delayed until after the Civil War, and the suffrage cause was not won until the adoption of the Nineteenth Amendment in 1920.

Among the causes, other than that of their own emancipation, to which the women reformers were deeply devoted **Temperance** was temperance. Hard drinking **reform** was an English tradition which had been easily transplanted to America and had flourished in the new environment. There was some variation, however, in the types of beverages consumed. English ale, which was of limited potency and required considerable skill to brew, was discarded in favor of the remarkably effective whiskey, which almost any frontiersman knew how to distill. Likewise imported wines, except for the use of the very rich, gave way to more primitive drinks, such as hard cider. Statistics on the consumption of liquor in the United States during these early years are not available, and the testimony of temperance reformers is not to be trusted, but it is safe to say that drinking was almost universal, among women as well as men, and that public drunkenness, at least for men, was no disgrace. Even ministers were apt to exhibit a degree of conviviality at ordination ceremonies, conferences, and college commencements that later generations would have regarded with astonishment.

In its early phases the temperance movement was directed against obvious excesses. Scripture was abundantly available for quotation against drunkenness, and preachers, particularly in the evangelical churches, were fond of quoting it. Women who suffered because of the intemperance of their mates, or who saw the suffering which intemperance inflicted upon other women, bestirred themselves against the evil. A few far-seeing humanitarians connected drunkenness with poverty and crime, and sought by promoting temperance to effect a more fundamental reform. Even before 1830 many local temperance societies had been formed, particularly in New England, and by 1833 a United States Temperance Union joined these locals into one national organization. These early reformers, as the name they took indicated, were primarily interested in temperance rather than in total abstinence; but views of so moderate a nature could hardly survive in an age which responded so cordially to the teachings of extremists. During the eighteen-thirties the temperance movement was practically taken over by the teetotalers. For more than

twenty years orators such as John B. Gough and Father Theobald Mathew denounced drinking as a crime against society; writers such as Lucius M. Sargent, with his six volumes of *Temperance Tales*, and Timothy Shay Arthur, with his even more effective *Ten Nights in a Bar-Room*, portrayed the decay of the individual who indulged in drink; and artists, more numerous than talented, provided pictures and cartoons that left nothing to the imagination. This campaign of education was strikingly successful. Individuals by the tens of thousands gave up the use of liquor, churches set more rigorous standards of conduct for the clergy and often also for the laity, and excessive drinking fell into general disrepute.

Efforts to diminish the temptation that led to the downfall of so many youths, and that made so difficult the regeneration of addicts, suggested **Prohibition** naturally an appeal to the power of the state. To the New Englanders, who stood in the vanguard of the movement, such an appeal was no confession of failure. Brought up, as most of them were, on the tradition that the state was properly charged with the duty of protecting the morals of the people, they could not overlook so effective an ally. Laws were demanded, and were frequently obtained, to license the liquor traffic, to hamper it with heavy taxation, and even to prohibit it altogether. State-wide prohibition of a sort was first adopted by Maine in 1846, under the influence of Neal Dow. Ohio followed in 1850, and perhaps a dozen other northern states had enacted prohibition laws before the Civil War. None of these laws was as effective as its advocates had hoped, and most of them were repealed during the Civil War period. The South, which in later years was to champion the prohibition cause so enthusiastically, was at this time totally uninterested.

It would be difficult to call the roll of the reform movements of the eighteen-thirties and forties with any assurance **A reform** that all of them would be in- **era** cluded. During these years the very word

LABOR GROUPS. Title page of a series of essays written by the "factory girls" of the Lowell, Mass., textile mills, 1840.

EDUCATION FOR WOMEN. The George B. Emerson School, Boston, Mass. Daguerreotype, about 1850.

Cultural self-betterment became an obsession with many Americans during the 1830's and 1840's. Labor was not content merely to seek through organization to obtain higher wages, shorter hours, and better working conditions, but also made valiant efforts to improve the intellectual level of the workers. Labor insistence had much to do with the success of the movement for free public schools. Women demanded educational facilities equal to those provided for men, and utopias such as New Harmony multiplied throughout the land.

PUBLIC SCHOOLS. Painting by George W. Harvey, about 1840.

UTOPIAN COMMUNITY. New Harmony, Indiana, colony founded by Robert Owen. Sketch by Charles A. Leseuer, 1831.

The DRUNKARD'S PROGRESS,
OR THE DIRECT ROAD TO POVERTY, WRETCHEDNESS & RUIN.

The MORNING DRAM.   The GROG SHOP.   The CONFIRMED DRUNKARD.   CONCLUDING SCENE.

TEMPERANCE MESSAGE. "The Drunkard's Progress" from the morning dram to the poorhouse. Broadside published by J. W. Barber, 1826.

FEMINISM. "The speaker of the day denouncing the lords of Creation." Cartoon published in *Harper's Weekly*, 1859.

Reform movements engaged the interest of great numbers of Americans. The temperance crusade paralleled and almost equalled in intensity the abolitionist crusade; Americans were heavy drinkers, and the evils of intoxication were painfully apparent. The feminist movement cut through all reform agitations; women not only objected to being treated as inferior beings; they objected also to the indifference to humanitarianism of a man-made world.

"reform" had an almost irresistible charm for multitudes of Americans, and the mere adoption of that label was sufficient to secure a following. Not only in the United States, but throughout the civilized world, the "man of sensibility" was at the crest of his power, seeking out wrongs, striving earnestly to right them. Many reform movements came to America from Europe; others originated on both sides of the Atlantic at about the same time. The rigors of penal codes, although much modified since colonial times, were still open to attack by reformers, who objected to the long sentences meted out for trivial offenses, and to the overfree use of the death penalty. The barbarities common to prisons, insane asylums, and almshouses needed only to be revealed to arouse a feeling of horror, and a demand for change. Probably Dorothea L. Dix, the leading advo-

cate in the United States of this type of reform, saw more of her ambitions realized than any other reformer of the period. New plans of dealing with convicts, designed not so much to punish as to reform them, were tried out with some success, and the idea that the mentally afflicted were entitled to hospitalization and medical treatment was almost universally accepted.

The sufferings incidental to war, while somewhat disguised by the glamor of patriotism, were also recognized, and **The peace** the problem attacked at its **movement** source by concerted efforts to prevent the outbreak of war. As early as 1815, the formation of local organizations devoted to the cause of peace had begun in the United States, and in 1828 about fifty of them joined hands to found the American Peace Society, which for decades not only carried on within the United States a steady propaganda for peace, but co-operated also with similar organizations abroad. An American peace plan was formulated which called for regular world congresses to codify international law, and a world court to apply it. Unhappily the peace movement was unable to sustain the shock of the wars which soon engulfed both Europe and America, and naturally the interest of reformers turned during the war-torn decades of the eighteen-fifties and sixties from the highly academic problem of world peace to the more pressing necessity of ameliorating the horrors of the battlefield.

With the spirit of humanitarian reform so thoroughly unleashed, it was unthinkable

Slavery a natural target that the continued existence of African slavery in the American South could long be overlooked. Ever since the time of the French Revolution slavery had been generally frowned upon by world opinion, and its extinction had proceeded with such rapidity that by the middle of the nineteenth century the southern states of the United States shared only with Brazil and the Spanish colonies the doubtful honor of being the last strongholds of slavery in the civilized world. That many people in the United States were opposed to slavery became abundantly apparent during the debate on the admission of Missouri, and the Missouri Compromise, which actually permitted the further spread of slavery, by no means satisfied them. Benjamin Lundy, a Quaker emancipationist, published from 1812 to 1839 a periodical known as *The Genius of Universal Emancipation*. Lundy's Fabian tactics and mild manners, however, did not satisfy William Lloyd Garrison, a young enthusiast of Newburyport, Massachusetts, who proposed instead a crusade "as harsh as truth" and "as uncompromising as justice." With the first issue of Garrison's newspaper, the *Liberator*, published in Boston on January 1, 1831, the abolitionist movement may properly be said to have begun. So completely did this reform take the center of the stage that all others soon seemed insignificant in comparison; indeed, the slavery issue was destined to shape the course of American politics for more than a generation, and to leave a legacy of unsolved problems that were to plague many generations to come.

Bibliography

The subjects covered in this chapter have attracted much attention. Curti, *The Growth of American Thought*, surveys the whole history of ideas in the United States, but is especially useful here. R. H. Gabriel, *The Course of American Democratic Thought* (1940) is a series of admirably conceived essays. Harvey Wish, *Society and Thought in Early America: A Social and Intellectual History of the American People through 1865* (1950), begins a promising series, *Society and Thought in America*, I. R. G. Gettell, *History of American Political Thought* (1928), is confined to one important aspect of American thinking. For more specialized studies, see A. A. Ekirch, *The Idea of Progress in America, 1815–1860* (1944); and Albert Post, *Popular Freethought in America, 1825–1850* (1943). A general picture of the period is given in C. R. Fish, *The Rise of the Common Man, 1830–1850* (1927). More colorful, but marred somewhat by their flippant style, are E. Douglas Branch, *The Sentimental Years, 1836–1860* (1934); and Meade Minnigerode, *The Fabulous Forties, 1840–1850* (1924).

Observations of the American scene by foreigners are described in Pierson, *Tocqueville and Beaumont in America*, already mentioned; and Max Berger, *The British Traveller in America, 1836–1860* (1943). Harriet Martineau, *Retrospect of Western Travel* (2 vols., 1838), has been recently reissued in the original format.

On literature, Van Wyck Brooks, *The Flowering of New England, 1815–1865* (1936), is a vivid presentation of the great age in New England's literary history. More comprehensive is *The Cam-*

bridge *History of American Literature*, edited by
W. P. Trent and others (4 vols., 1917–1921). For
a brief account, see Bliss Perry, *The American
Spirit in Literature* (1918). On Emerson, the
Journals of Ralph Waldo Emerson, edited by E. W.
Emerson and W. E. Forbes (10 vols., 1909–14);
and *The Letters of Ralph Waldo Emerson*, edited by
Ralph L. Rusk (6 vols., 1939), will repay scrutiny,
but O. W. Firkins, *Ralph Waldo Emerson* (1915);
and R. L. Rusk, *The Life of Ralph Waldo Emerson*
(1949), will satisfy the cursory student. Dorothy
Waples, *The Whig Myth of James Fenimore
Cooper* (1938), is devoted principally to Cooper's
political ideas. H. S. Canby, *Walt Whitman*
(1943), is a satisfactory biography. On drama
and the theater: A. H. Quinn, *A History of the
American Drama from the Beginning to the Civil
War* (2d edition, 1943); O. S. Coad and Edwin
Mims, Jr., *The American Stage* (*The Pageant of
America*, XIV, 1929). On the historians of the
period, the best general work is J. S. Bassett, *The
Middle Group of American Historians* (1917). See
also R. B. Nye, *George Bancroft, Brahmin Rebel*
(1944).

On science and invention: George Iles, *Leading American Inventors* (1912); Holland Thompson, *The Age of Invention* (1921); Carleton
Mabee, *The American Leonardo: A Life of Samuel
F. B. Morse* (1943); W. T. Hutchinson, *Cyrus Hall
McCormick* (2 vols., 1930–35); W. B. Kaempffert,
A Popular History of American Invention (1924);
Robert Hoe, *A Short History of the Printing Press
and the Improvements in Printing Machinery*
(1902); Bernard Jaffe, *Men of Science in America*
(1944); R. H. Shryock, *American Medical Re-
search, Past and Present* (1947); R. L. Thompson,
*Wiring a Continent: The History of the Telegraph
Industry in the United States, 1832–1866* (1947).

On art and architecture: Suzanne LaFollette,
Art in America (1929); Samuel Isham and Royal
Cortissoz, *The History of American Painting*
(1936); Virgil Barker, *American Painting; History
and Interpretation* (1950); Lorado Taft, *The His-
tory of American Sculpture* (1930); A. T. Gardner,
*Yankee Stonecutters: The First American School of
Sculpture, 1800–1850* (1945); Porter Butts, *Art in
Wisconsin* (1936); T. E. Tallmadge, *The Story of
Architecture in America* (1927); O. W. Larkin,
Art and Life in America (1949).

On music: J. T. Howard, *Our American Music,
Three Hundred Years of It* (1946); N. I. White,
American Negro Folk-Songs (1928); Carl Wittke,
Tambo and Bones (1930); A. L. Rich, *Lowell

Mason, "The Father of Singing among the Children"*
(1946).

On magazines and newspapers, F. L. Mott,
*American Journalism: A History of Newspapers in
the United States* (1941), is an excellent summary.
See also, by the same author, *A History of American Magazines, 1741–1850* (1930); and Algernon
de Vivier Tassin, *The Magazine in America* (1916).
Useful manuals are W. G. Bleyer, *Main Currents
in the History of American Journalism* (1927);
and J. M. Lee, *History of American Journalism*
(1917). On the value of newspapers as historical
sources, see Lucy M. Salmon, *The Newspaper and
the Historian* (1923). Oliver Carlson, *The Man
Who Made News: James Gordon Bennett* (1942),
is better on the journalistic than on the historical
side.

On education: S. L. Jackson, *America's Strug-
gle for Free Schools: Social Tension and Education
in New England and New York, 1827–42* (1941), is
a good preliminary study. See also Paul Monroe,
Founding of the American Public School System
(1940); B. A. Hinsdale, *Horace Mann and the Com-
mon School Revival in the United States* (1898);
Will S. Monroe, *The Educational Labors of Henry
Barnard* (1893); H. H. Vail, *A History of the
McGuffey Readers* (1910). On higher education:
C. F. Thwing, *A History of Higher Education in
America* (1906); D. G. Tewksbury, *The Founding
of American Colleges and Universities before the
Civil War* (1932); S. E. Morison, *Three Centuries
of Harvard, 1636–1936* (1936); T. J. Wertenbaker,
Princeton, 1746–1896 (1946); R. S. Fletcher, *A
History of Oberlin College from its Foundation
through the Civil War* (2 vols., 1943); Albea God-
bold, *The Church College of the Old South* (1944);
W. F. Norwood, *Medical Education in the United
States before the Civil War* (1944); M. J. L. O'Con-
nor, *Origins of Academic Economics in the United
States* (1944).

Books on reforms and reformers are legion, and
only a few can be cited. More general in nature
than most of them is Alice Felt Tyler, *Freedom's
Ferment: Phases of American Social History to 1860*
(1944). R. E. Riegel, *Young America, 1830–1840*
(1949) includes something on nearly all the reform
movements of the decade. The feminist movement may be best approached through its plentiful biographic and autobiographic literature.
See, for example, Katharine S. Anthony, *Margaret Fuller: A Psychological Biography* (1920),
Margaret Fuller [Ossoli], *Woman in the Nineteenth Century* (1845); Elizabeth Blackwell,

Pioneer Work for Women (1914); Elizabeth Cady Stanton, Susan B. Anthony, and others, *History of Woman Suffrage* (6 vols., 1889–1922). The last mentioned is an important source-book for all the major reform movements of the nineteenth century. A. E. Bestor, *Backwoods Utopias: The Sectarian and Owenite Phases of Communitarian Socialism in America: 1663–1829* (1950), introduces the New Harmony experiment. Blake McKelvey, *American Prisons: A Study in American Social History Prior to 1915* (1936), covers a single aspect of the reform movement with care. Among the better biographies of reformers are R. W. Leopold, *Robert Dale Owen: A Biography* (1940); Helen E. Marshall, *Dorothea Dix, For-gotten Samaritan* (1937); Francis Tiffany, *Life of Dorothea Lynde Dix* (1890); W. R. Waterman, *Frances Wright* (1924); Alice J. G. Perkins and Theresa Wolfson, *Frances Wright, Free Enquirer* (1939); A. M. Schlesinger, Jr., *Orestes Brownson: A Pilgrim's Progress* (1939).

On Labor, a useful summary is to be found in Mary R. Beard, *A Short History of the American Labor Movement* (1920); and Selig Perlman, *A History of Trade Unionism in the United States* (1922). For fuller accounts, see J. R. Commons and associates, *History of Labour in the United States* (4 vols., 1918–35). Channing, V., ch. 4, is especially good on this subject.

25

Slavery and Abolition

The "Cotton South" — Growth of slavery — The plantation system — The slave trade — Abolitionism — Opposition to the abolitionists: in the North; in the South — The pro-slavery argument — The economics of slavery — Effect of slavery on the Southern whites

By the time Garrison had opened his abolitionist crusade the institution of slavery, The "Cotton South" which had once seemed well on the way toward extinction, was more deeply entrenched in the South than ever before. The chief reason for this change, as already noted, was the insatiable demand for American cotton, an article which, as experience had amply demonstrated, could be profitably grown by means of slave labor. Under pressure of the world's need for cotton, the South produced nearly twice the amount of that commodity in 1830 that it had produced in 1820, fully twice the amount in 1840 that it had produced in 1830, and more than three times the amount in 1860 than it had produced in 1840. Cotton exports during these years showed similar gains, until by the time of the Civil War well over half the value of American goods shipped abroad was in cotton. A broad belt of southern land, ranging in width from about five hundred miles in the Carolinas and Georgia to six or seven hundred miles in the Mississippi Valley, was devoted primarily to cotton culture. Other crops were grown in this region, particularly foodstuffs, and not all the land was suited to cotton-growing; but the chief wealth of the "lower

South" came from cotton. In this region, too, the majority of the Negro slaves were congregated. Such states as Virginia and Kentucky, for example, which depended far more upon tobacco-growing and general agriculture for their prosperity than upon cotton, sold great numbers of their slaves "down South," where the demand for "cotton hands" was always good. Slaves were used profitably also, although in smaller numbers, in the Carolina-Georgia rice fields along the coast, and in the production of Louisiana sugar cane.

The demand for slave labor in the lower South led both to an increase in the southern slave population and to an ad- Growth of vance in the price of slaves. slavery Between 1820 and 1860 the number of slaves in the South grew from about a million and a half to nearly four million, but in spite of the increased supply the price of a good field hand mounted in the same years from three or four hundred dollars to a thousand dollars or more. So great, indeed, was the demand for slaves that their importation, although forbidden by law, was carried on surreptitiously until the outbreak of the Civil War, while freed Negroes living in the South were in some danger of being kidnaped and sold back into slavery. The greatest increases in slave population were naturally in the states of the new Southwest, where cotton culture was making its most rapid strides.

The ownership of slave property in the South was confined to a relatively small number of whites. On the eve of the Civil War probably not more than four hundred thousand southern families — approximately one in four — held slaves. Furthermore, at least two thirds of these families held fewer than ten slaves each. The number of great planters — men who owned fifty or more slaves and proportionately large holdings of land — was probably not above six or seven thousand. Some planters numbered their slaves by the thousand and their acres by the tens of thousands, although such instances were the exception rather than the rule.

The small farmers who lived in the cotton belt, both those who owned slaves and those who did not, raised a considerable part of the cotton crops; but the chief profits of the industry were reserved for the great planter. He was in a far better position than his less prosperous neighbors to practice scientific agriculture, his expenditures bulked less than theirs in proportion to his receipts, and he generally owned the most fertile lands. The farmers, however, saw eye to eye with the planters in all matters pertaining to slavery. Poor men looked forward to the time when they would become slaveholders; and the owners of a few slaves aspired to be the owners of many. What seemed good to the great planter seemed good, therefore, to the rank and file of southern farmers, for they tended to think of themselves not so much as what they were but as what they aspired to become. Thus the great planter and his ways occupy a place in the history of the South quite out of proportion to the numerical strength of the planter class.

The plantation owner was first and foremost a manager. Ordinarily a single plantation, which rarely exceeded a thousand acres in size, commanded his entire energies; but if, as sometimes was the case, he owned many planta-

The plantation system

tions, he delegated authority to a hierarchy of stewards and overseers who carried out his orders. Altogether too many of these underlings possessed faults of character which unfitted them to be farmers and planters in their own right, and the relations between master and slave were apt to be far more pleasant than the relations between these white employees and the slaves whose work they supervised. Practically all of the manual labor of a plantation was done by the slaves. Most of the slaves, of course, were field hands, but every plantation had its quota of skilled workers, such as blacksmiths and carpenters, while a favored few were selected for domestic service in and about the master's house. Sometimes Negro foremen, or "slave drivers," were placed in charge of small gangs of slaves. Frequently these drivers, themselves freed from the necessity of labor and empowered to inflict corporal punishment upon those who worked under them, were more oppressive than the whites. Field labor was accomplished by the gang system, in which a driver kept a group of slaves at work on a given task under fear of the lash, or by the task system, in which each individual was given a certain amount of work to do in a given period of time and left free to finish it as he chose, provided only that he did his work well. Any extra time the slave earned by rapid work was his to while away.

The lot of the slave on the southern plantation was ordinarily quite tolerable. As a valuable piece of property, his good health was a matter of **The slave** considerable consequence to his master. He was well fed, although no particular pains were taken to vary his diet from the standard corn bread and fat pork that was regarded as entirely adequate to sustain life. In case of illness he was usually cared for by the same physician that attended the master and his family. His living quarters, usually located not far from the "big house" of the planter, were apt to be primitive, but they afforded protection from the wind and the rain, and were ordinarily provided with fireplaces and

THE OLIVIER PLANTATION, LOUISIANA. Painting by Adrian Persac, 1860.

COTTON PICKING ON A SOUTHERN PLANTATION. Illustration from Sala, *America Revisited*, 1888.

The Cotton South has suffered much at the hands of prejudiced writers. Southern apologists have thrown about it a romantic aura that tends to obscure the harsh reality of slavery; northern humanitarians, revolted by the very thought of human bondage, have painted the picture blacker than it was. Plantation life was not without its lavender and old lace, but there was plenty of "blood, toil, tears, and sweat."

LOW WATER ON THE MISSISSIPPI. Currier and Ives lithograph, 1860's.

a plentiful supply of fuel for use in cold weather. The slave's clothing was coarse enough, and in summer he was not expected to wear very much, but he was about as well clad as southern whites of the lower class. By and large, the conditions of his life represented a distinct advance over the lot that would have befallen him had he remained in Africa.

Indeed, the slaves got much positive enjoyment out of life. Extremely gregarious, they delighted in the community life of the plantation, and on special occasions were permitted to indulge in picnics, barbecues, and various other types of celebration. They loved to sing and dance, and contributed ideas along both lines that the whites, at least of a later generation, were not too proud to appropriate. They were generally blessed with a keen sense of humor; they rarely fretted, when treated well, because of their state of bondage; and they were often deeply devoted to their master and his family. Small children, regardless of color, played together freely, and the affection of white boys and girls for their Negro nurses, or "mammies," was proverbial. The slaves were deeply religious, and almost universally accepted Christianity, usually as interpreted by one of the more emotional denominations, such as the Methodists and the Baptists, whose camp meetings, revivals, and baptizings gave them unbounded joy. A few Negroes were taught to read, but most of them acquired by word of mouth rather than by reading a considerable knowledge of the Bible and of Christian theology. Their devotions were extremely picturesque, and their moral standards sufficiently latitudinarian to meet the needs of a really primitive people. Heaven to the Negro was a place of rest from all labor, the fitting reward of a servant who obeyed his master and loved the Lord. Negroes sometimes worshiped separately from the whites, and sometimes they were assigned seats in the galleries of the white people's churches. More or less formal marriages among slaves were encouraged by some masters, although cohabitation with-

out marriage was regarded as perfectly normal, and a certain amount of promiscuity was taken for granted. Slave women were at the mercy of predatory white males, as their numerous mulatto progeny abundantly attested.

Nevertheless, the privileges of the slave were strictly limited. Each southern state had a "slave code," which gave **Slave** the sanction of law to the prac- **discipline** tices that experience had proved to be of value in keeping the slave population in order. Even minor offenses were punishable by law, but in all save the most exceptional cases the master usually chose to mete out justice himself. Whippings were permissible at his discretion, or at the discretion of those to whom he delegated authority, although it was a punishable crime to beat a slave to death. Some masters, and many of their subordinates, were excessively cruel, although punishment so severe as to unfit the slave for labor was an expensive indulgence which not many masters would either practice or permit. Slave crimes of a serious nature, such as murder, rape, theft, and conspiracy to revolt, were punishable by death, but their concealment by masters who feared the inconvenience and possible property loss involved was not uncommon. Exacting masters were much troubled by runaways, or so the advertisements in southern papers seem to show. Attempts at insurrection were extremely rare, although in the regions where the blacks far outnumbered the whites, the latter sometimes suffered acutely from an unconfessed fear of what their slaves might do. In 1831 a serious slave uprising, led by a trusted Negro preacher named Nat Turner, occurred in Virginia. Some fifty-five whites, mostly women and children, were killed. Turner, and nearly all the other participants in this insurrection, suffered death or worse for their crime, but the incident served to unsettle the good relations between many southern masters and their slaves for years to come.

Undoubtedly the most unlovely aspect of slavery was the slave trade. As already noted, the international slave trade was out- **The slave** lawed in 1808, and after 1820 it **trade** was punishable as piracy, but the right to buy and sell slaves within the United States, and to transport them from one slave state to another, remained unimpaired. During the years that the cotton lands of the newer South — from Alabama to Texas — were being opened up, this domestic slave trade came to assume extraordinary importance. Not only did the planters of the Gulf states need more and more slaves, but it was also a fact that the upper South was being confronted with an oversupply of slave labor. Tobacco raisers in such states as Maryland, Virginia, and Kentucky were suffering from the continued exhaustion of the soil, from the decline of their export trade which began with the embargo and the War of 1812, and from the competition of Latin-American producers. Under such circumstances the natural increase of their slave population would have amounted almost to tragedy except for the opportunity to sell their surplus hands down South to work in the cotton fields. Except in the case of refractory and objectionable slaves, however, reputable masters often hesitated to dispose of their human property by sale, and many cases are on record where planters allowed themselves to become "slave poor." Other slaveholders were not so squeamish, and bankruptcy or death often accomplished what the best-intentioned master hoped to avoid. Sometimes planters or farmers went as permanent emigrants from the old South to the new, and took their slaves along to be disposed of in whole or in part as necessity required; but far more frequently the slaves were transported from the one region to the other by slave traders, who bought and sold them strictly with an eye to profit. In 1836, the peak year of this traffic, the number of slaves sold South, or taken there by their masters, from Virginia alone reached the astounding figure of one hundred and twenty thousand. In the eighteen-forties and fifties a revival of agriculture took place in the upper South, due in part to the discovery of better methods of curing tobacco, and in part to the introduction of new and superior varieties. This served to check the domestic slave trade to some extent, but by no means to destroy it. Down to the time of the Civil War there were many planters in the upper South who, whether they would admit it or not, were engaged primarily in the business of raising slaves for sale.

The slave-trader was nevertheless an object of well-nigh universal disdain throughout the South. His business was **The** brutalizing in the extreme, for he **slave-trader** was called upon constantly to engage in the separation of families, and to maintain discipline under adverse circumstances over slaves who in many instances were selected for sale precisely because they were hard to discipline. Few high-minded men would engage in such a business, and those who did were usually corrupted by its demands. The typical slave trader was coarse and ill-bred, intemperate of speech and habits, and callous to the opinions of his fellow men. To succeed among ruthless competitors he learned to drive close bargains and became as adept at covering up the defects of his Negroes as ever was the Yankee horse-trader in making light of blemishes in horseflesh. Slave traders were rarely accepted into polite southern society; indeed, they were treated as outcasts even by those who had to deal with them. The social status of bootleggers during the prohibition era was, on the whole, well above that of the slave-trader in the pre-Civil War South.

The collection of a group of slaves and their shipment to the lower South afforded many painful spectacles. Pending shipments, they might be herded together in stockades, locked up in warehouses, or jails, or occasionally cared for decently in taverns. Frequently they were marched overland in coffles to their destination, although the trader also made good use of river steamers and ships engaged in the coastwise trade.

In the final disposal of slaves, the auction-block was frequently resorted to. The slave-trader availed himself, however, of every opportunity to sell, and stops along the route of march, or at wharves, were duly utilized for the cultivation of purchasers. Sometimes slaves were hired out for long or short periods of service, in which case the employer succeeded to the disciplinary authority of the master. Hired slaves were more frequently overworked and mistreated than slaves directly under the control of their masters.

Such was the institution upon which Garrison and the abolitionists opened their attack. They knew little about it at first hand, but they sought and found an abundance of ammunition to use. Stories of atrocities committed against slaves, such as brutal whippings, the breaking up of slave homes, enforced immorality, and the like were constantly drifting northward, stories which lost nothing in the telling. These tales were picked up indiscriminately by abolitionist editors and orators who were eager to believe the worst about slavery and who used, as if they were typical, stories which had to do with highly exceptional occurrences. The abolitionists were not limited, however, to the recital of wrongs done the slaves. They regarded the institution at its best as morally indefensible. Slaves were men, and no man, according to the abolitionist argument, had the right to hold a fellow man in bondage. On this ground the abolitionists rejected totally the idea of compensated emancipation. The slaveowner was a criminal; why pay him for his crime?

The abolitionist doctrines struck a responsive chord in many northern hearts. Humanitarian reformers could not logically resist them. Many New Englanders, angered by the vicious attacks upon their section that nullificationist orators delighted to make, retaliated, perhaps unconsciously, by going over to the abolitionist camp. The Quakers had always regarded slavery as immoral, and great numbers of them found the transition from passive to active opposition extremely easy to make. Most of the northern evangelical churches, particularly the Methodist and the Baptist, began to lean in the direction of abolition. Among the abolitionist orators, Wendell Phillips, scion of an aristocratic Boston family, was preeminent. Not since the days of Patrick Henry had American audiences been treated to such fervid appeals as fell from his lips. Two South Carolinians, Sarah and Angelina Grimké, went North to Philadelphia, joined the Society of Friends, and devoted their lives to the anti-slavery crusade. Theodore Dwight Weld, a Westerner who became the husband of Angelina, is thought by many to have done more for the cause of abolition than Garrison himself. Lucretia Mott, a Philadelphia Quakeress, overcame valiantly the obstacles placed in the way of women orators, and lectured far and wide in behalf of abolition. Gerrit Smith, an up-state New-Yorker of considerable wealth, devoted both his time and his fortune to the cause. Escaped slaves, such as Frederick Douglass and Harriet Tubman, lifted up eloquent voices on behalf of freedom. Unnamed hundreds of workers spread the abolitionist doctrines among their neighbors, and, translating word into deed, established many lines of secret stopping-places, or "underground railroads," by means of which fugitive slaves could be passed along from the southern states to Canada and freedom.

The abolitionists lost no time in perfecting an organization. Their first local association was formed in 1831. The next year a New England Anti-Slavery Society was functioning, and in 1833 a convention at Philadelphia launched the American Anti-Slavery Society. A division in this society occurred in 1840, however, mainly because Garrison and a few other extremists were unwilling to stoop to the level of party politics. Slavery was recognized by the Constitution of the United States, a fact which, according to Garrison, made that document "a covenant with death and an agreement with hell." Theodore Parker, ardent abolitionist and the most eminent preacher of his time, prided himself on his unwillingness even to cast a vote

SLAVE-PEN AT NEW ORLEANS. "Before the auction. A sketch of the past." Illustration from *Harper's Weekly*, Jan. 24, 1863.

KIDNAPPING SLAVES. Illustration from *A Portraiture of Domestic Slavery*, 1817, an early anti-slavery tract.

SLAVES IN THE FIELDS. Cutting sugar cane, Louisiana, *circa* 1860.

Abolitionist propaganda made much of the horrors of buying and selling slaves, and the break-up of families it involved. Labor under cruel task-masters was also featured, although not many slaveowners could have found it profitable to beat or work their slaves to death. The kidnaping of free Negroes for sale as slaves had its counterpart in the spiriting away of slaves to freedom through the Underground Railroad.

THE UNDERGROUND RAILROAD. "The resurrection of Henry Box Brown at Philadelphia." Lithograph by Rosenthal after a drawing by Kramer, about 1860.

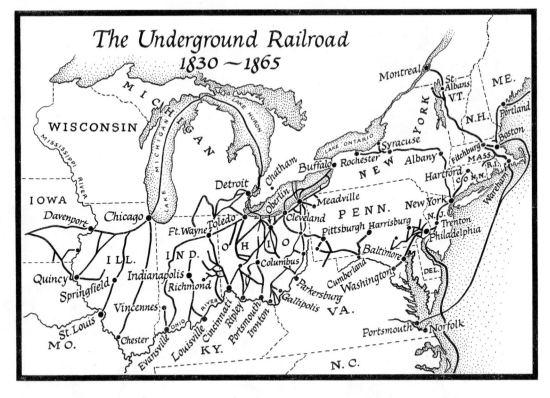

The Underground Railroad
1830 ~ 1865

under the authority of such a government. But to the rank and file of abolitionists, the obvious way to promote their cause was through united political action. The actual abolition of slavery was conceded to depend upon the individual states where anti-slavery majorities could not soon be achieved, but the national government had authority to abolish slavery in the District of Columbia and to put an end to the interstate slave trade. To promote these ends, as well as to work toward the eventual abolition of slavery in every state, the Liberty Party was formed shortly before the election of 1840, and James G. Birney was selected as its candidate for President. Birney was a Kentuckian by birth, who, after spending many years as a planter in Alabama, had freed his slaves and come North to work against slavery. For a time he published an abolitionist paper, *The Philanthropist*, at Cincinnati, but in 1837 he became secretary of the American Anti-Slavery Society and removed to New

York. In the election of 1840 he polled a total of about seven thousand votes.

The abolitionists had made greater progress, however, than this small vote seemed to indicate. Their arguments had stirred up much feeling against slavery throughout the North, and had convinced many people who were unwilling to vote the abolitionist ticket that the slavery system must ultimately be overthrown. Furthermore, the prestige of the southern planters, who traditionally had occupied a prominent place in national affairs, was seriously damaged. Northern farmers came to suspect southern leadership of working against the interests of the small free farmer and solely for the interests of the slaveholding planter. More and more the conviction grew that slavery at least ought not to expand, that the newly opened lands of the West should be reserved for the use of free farmers and should be denied forever to slaveholders. Partly with this idea in view, and partly also because of the obvious evils it bred, opponents of the domestic slave trade also increased steadily in numbers.

Perhaps the abolition of slavery in the District of Columbia won more support than any other abolitionist tenet. Northern members of Congress were increasingly sensitive to the existence of slavery in the national capital, and to the necessity of witnessing day by day the public buying and selling of slaves. Floods of abolitionist petitions, most of them praying that slavery be abolished in the District, cluttered up their mail, and many congressmen took pleasure in presenting them. The southern members, however, were deeply offended at these memorials, and in 1836 they persuaded the House to pass a "gag rule" that required all such petitions to be laid on the table without debate. This action was construed by ex-President John Quincy Adams, who still represented a Massachusetts district in Congress, as a direct violation of the constitutional right of petition, and he fought against it with all his might. While not himself actually an abolitionist, his constant appearance as a defender of abolitionist petitions tended to identify him with the anti-slavery movement, and to clothe it with increasing respectability. In 1844 his efforts were crowned with success, and by a vote of 108 to 80 the obnoxious rule was repealed. But the abolition of slavery in the District of Columbia awaited the verdict of the Civil War.

Regardless of the headway they made, the abolitionists were cordially disliked in the North as well as in the South. As individuals they were, like so many professional reformers, apt to be extremely irritating to their less conscience-smitten fellow men. Moreover, the indifference of the extremists among them to the Constitution, and their openly expressed willingness to see the slave-owning South outside the Union, were thoroughly resented by a generation which held both the Constitution and the Union in the deepest reverence. Business interests took

fright at the abolitionist propaganda. Northern manufacturers were making good profits from southern trade; with higher tariffs, they stood a chance to make even better profits. Abolitionist activities might imperil the trade relations between the sections, lessen the chance of raising duties against foreign goods, destroy the business value of the Union. Many Northerners, moreover, were themselves ex-Southerners or the descendants of Southerners, and they agreed wholeheartedly with the southern contention that the only proper status for the Negro was slavery. With this view many other Northerners, not themselves of southern descent, were inclined to agree, because of unpleasant contacts they had had with freed Negroes in the North. In fact, most of the anti-slavery crusaders, particularly in the early years of the movement, were subjected to frequent outrages, the offices of abolitionist newspapers were repeatedly sacked, and at least one abolitionist editor, Elijah P. Lovejoy of Alton, Illinois, was put to death at the hands of a pro-slavery mob.

But the unpopularity of the abolitionists in the North was a mild thing indeed compared with the venomous hatred they provoked in the South. Losses from runaway slaves became increasingly serious, and for these losses southern masters, with good reason, held the abolitionists responsible. Abolitionist literature, some of which deliberately suggested to the slaves, by means of cartoons and otherwise, the possibility of running away, flooded the South in spite of the best efforts of Southerners to keep it out. The efficiency of the underground railroad, over which unnumbered thousands of Negroes traveled to freedom every year, was spread assiduously by word of mouth. Southerners believed also that the abolitionists were doing their best to promote Negro insurrections in the South, and occasional unguarded utterances on the part of a few extremists gave color to this charge. The *Liberator*, for example, once wished "success to all slave insurrections," and quoted approvingly the

WILLIAM LLOYD GARRISON

THEODORE DWIGHT WELD

FREDERICK DOUGLASS

ELIZABETH CADY STANTON

The Abolitionist crusade absorbed the energies and interests of a large number of humanitarian reformers, both men and women, Negro and white. William Lloyd Garrison was the fiery leader of the eastern Abolitionists; Theodore Dwight Weld, the more moderate leader of the Westerners. Mrs. Stanton, Miss Wright, and Miss Mott were all earnest advocates of both women's rights and abolition. Two escaped slaves who became leaders in the anti-slavery movement were Frederick Douglass, who spoke widely and published an abolitionist paper, and Harriet Tubman, who led hundreds of other slaves over the underground railroad.

LUCRETIA MOTT

FRANCES WRIGHT

HARRIET TUBMAN

statement of an Englishman who said, "Southern slaves ought, or at least have a right, to cut the throats of their masters." Nat Turner's Rebellion, occurring as it did at about the same time that the abolitionist crusade began, was soon very generally, although quite incorrectly, ascribed to northern anti-slavery propaganda. But more galling even than property losses or the fear of insurrection were the abolitionist denunciations of slaveholders as the lowest type of criminals. Slavery, according to Garrison, was a "damning crime," and slaveholders were the "meanest of thieves and the worst of robbers. . . . We do not acknowledge them to be within the pale of Christianity, of republicanism, or humanity." The southern planter, who was traditionally proud of his reputation and resented hotly any charge against his personal honor, could not let such epithets pass unchallenged; and he was particularly incensed to have them flung at him by un-Christian Unitarians from a region notorious for its tightfisted money-changers.

Coincident with the rise of abolitionism came the almost complete subsidence of southern interest in emancipation. It was generally alleged that this change of sentiment in the South was due mainly to resentment against the northern anti-slavery propaganda, but a better argument can be made in support of the theory that the increasing profits of slavery had already sapped the vitality of southern emancipationism. Whatever the reason, such projects as compensated emancipation and the return of freed Negroes to Africa no longer received southern approbation. The last significant southern debate on the subject of slavery occurred in the Virginia legislature of 1832, immediately following Nat Turner's Rebellion, an incident which few Southerners had as yet thought to blame on the northern abolitionists. During the debate the institution of slavery was subjected to the most searching criticism; slavery, according to one member, was "the heaviest calamity which has ever befallen any portion of the human race," and according to another was "a curse upon him

who inflicts as upon him who suffers it." But the legislature finally refused to take action, and within a few years hardly a Southerner of consequence could be found who would not spring to the defense of slavery.

Furthermore, every possible effort was made throughout the South to suppress all agitation in favor of emancipation, and in particular to prevent the delivery of the abolitionist tracts that the mails of the United States brought in. In 1835, after a Charleston, South Carolina, mob had burned a sack of abolitionist literature, the Postmaster-General ruled that local postmasters might refuse to deliver such mail if they believed it to be of an incendiary nature. Although this ruling was soon rescinded, many southern postmasters continued to abide by it, and many other obstacles to the spread of abolitionist propaganda in the South were devised. The individual who failed to destroy such literature immediately on its receipt was subjected to social ostracism, northern states were threatened with an economic boycott if they permitted its publication within their borders, and efforts were made, more spectacular than successful, to secure the extradition for trial in the South of objectionable northern editors.

At length, arguments were adduced to prove that slavery, far from being an evil, was actually a positive good. **The pro-slavery argument** Of all the pro-slavery philosophers probably Thomas Roderick Dew, professor of history, metaphysics, and political law in the College of William and Mary, and afterwards its president, was the most systematic and effective. Dew had obtained his education in Germany, where he was impressed by the open recognition of the inequalities of man, and the inevitability of a stratified society. Instead of apologizing for what he found in the South, he defended it. The great planters, because of their superior education, ability, and property, stood rightly at the head of southern society; next to them in rank were the small landowners, the traders, and free laborers at the bottom of the ladder were the slaves. "It is the order of nature and of God," he claimed, "that the being of superior faculties and knowledge, and therefore of superior power, should control and dispose of those who are inferior. It is as much the order of nature that men should enslave each other as that other animals should prey upon each other." Dew's arguments were set forth in pamphlet form as early as 1832, and were repeatedly reprinted. He was ably seconded by Chancellor William Harper of the Supreme Court of South Carolina, who published in 1838 a *Memoir on Slavery* that was quoted as authority throughout the South. About the same time John C. Calhoun gave it as his opinion that the South had no reason to be ashamed of slavery, and added that "There never has yet existed a wealthy and civilized society in which one portion of the community did not in fact live on the labor of the other." Professional men of every kind, particularly the preachers and the politicians, took up the argument, and boldly proclaimed the virtues of the South's most distinctive institution.

The idea that slavery was ordained of God was particularly comforting to the people of the South, most of whom were devoutly orthodox in their religious views. The Fourth and the Tenth Commandments, which referred to man-servants and maid-servants as of the same status as slaves, clearly gave the stamp of divine approval to slavery. Abraham, Isaac, and the other patriarchs had held slaves. The apostle Paul had enjoined servants to be obedient to their masters. Moreover, it was a particularly happy dispensation of Providence which brought heathen Africans to America, where they might learn the truths of Christianity. But for the institution of slavery they might still be outside the pale of Christian influence.

Slavery was also defended as a benevolent institution in which the relationship between capital and labor was more kindly than could be found anywhere else in the world. The master must care for the slave in sickness as well as in health, in childhood and old age no less than in his prime. The master must not overwork his slave, for to do so would impair the slave's value. Compared with the wage-slave system of the industrial North and of Europe, where, it was asserted, men, women, and children were worked to death in mines and factories, and where the aged, the ill, and the incompetent were ruthlessly discharged, the slavery system could be made to appear as "a beautiful example of communism, where each one receives not according to his labor, but according to his wants."

The claim that slavery as an economic device was also ideally suited to the South was continually made. Dew was not in the least embarrassed by the fact that Virginia piled up excellent profits each year from slave-breeding. Without that prop to its economic structure, he maintained that the Old Dominion would soon become a "howling wilderness." Less specious were the arguments of the eminent southern agriculturalist, Edmund Ruffin, who pointed out the economic advantage in large-scale production and in the wholesale purchasing of supplies made possible by the slavery plantation system. Furthermore, slave labor could be specialized at the will of the planter and in accordance with the aptitudes of the slaves, while the expensive struggles between capital and labor that had come to be characteristic of the free-labor system could be avoided. Some insisted that the drudgery required for the production of tobacco, rice, sugar-cane, and cotton could never be provided in sufficient amount by free men; and according to one observer, the North was as much benefited by the slave-labor system of the South as ever was the South itself. Northern manufacturers could count on the plantation South both as a steady source of supply for raw materials and as a market for northern goods.

As a matter of fact, the economic disadvantages of slave labor were becoming plain enough to those who wished to observe them.

The economics of slavery

The South, thanks in considerable part to the limitations of the slave, was overspecialized. It produced only what the slave could produce profitably, and to an increasing extent this meant cotton. Even foodstuffs, which could be, and ordinarily were, grown on every southern farm and plantation, were frequently produced in such meager quantities that importations from the North had to be made. The prosperity of the South thus rose and fell with the proceeds from its money crops. Cotton was "King," but an off year, or a serious drop in price, meant widespread disaster. Moreover, the returns of the southern planter were far too small in proportion to his investment. Much of his capital was tied up in the ownership of labor, a situation which the northern employer of free labor did not confront. Much capital had to be invested also in land, the price of which, thanks to the competition among planters for good cotton land, soared frequently to absurd figures. On a much smaller investment the successful northern industrialist made far greater profits.

Doubtless the worst feature of the system of slavery, from the economic point of view, **Effect of slavery on the whites** was that its rather scanty profits were absorbed by so small a number of planters. Ruffin was right in his contention that large-scale production was more profitable economically than small-scale production. But the bulk of the people of the South belonged to the small planter and the farmer class. They had no choice but to compete with the large planter on terms that made him comfortable, but made them permanently poor. It was on this account that tens of thousands of Southerners who had no

slaves or only a few slaves fled to the free states of the old Northwest, or to such portions of the slave states as the plantation system was unable to follow them. Many of them apparently agreed with Jesse Grant, the father of the General, who once said: "I would not own slaves and I would not live where there were slaves and not own them." Not only did the South lose a steady stream of emigrants to the North; it failed also, because of slavery, to attract immigrants in large numbers, as the North was doing, from outside the United States. The effect of slavery upon the rank and file of the native southern whites was also unfortunate. They tended to regard physical labor, because it was the customary lot of slaves, as essentially menial and degrading. The leisure class thus came to include many who might have fared far better had they been less opposed to work, and who made little or no contribution to the welfare of their section.

Undoubtedly the flaws in the slave-labor system were too numerous and too serious for slavery to have survived indefinitely. The leaders of southern opinion were temporarily deceived, however, by the advent of King Cotton, and as a consequence came boldly to the defense of the South's "peculiar institution." The attack of the abolitionists gave them an excellent opportunity to transform their apologies for slavery into a determined insistence on its righteousness and the desirability of its permanence. Thus the scene was being rapidly set for an "irrepressible conflict" between North and South — a conflict that would soon rock the Union to its very foundations.

Bibliography

The importance of slavery in the southern economy is admirably set forth in M. B. Hammond, *The Cotton Industry* (1897). More recent studies include W. E. Dodd, *The Cotton Kingdom* (1919); R. S. Cotterill, *The Old South* (1936); E. Q. Hawk, *Economic History of the South* (1934); Clement Eaton, *A History of the Old South* (1949); F. P. Gaines, *The Southern Plantation* (1924);

R. H. Taylor, *Ante-Bellum South Carolina* (1942). On slavery the best general treatise, from the Negro's point of view, is J. H. Franklin, *From Slavery to Freedom: A History of American Negroes* (1947), but see also U. B. Phillips, *American Negro Slavery* (1918); and *Life and Labor in the Old South* (1929). A good state history is J. B. Sellers, *Slavery in Alabama* (1950). L. E. Atherton, *The Southern Country Store, 1800–1860* (1949), rescues from oblivion an important subject in the old southern economy. Frederic Bancroft, *Slave-Trading in the Old South* (1931), covers one unlovely aspect of the slavery system. Frank Tannenbaum, *Slave and Citizen: The Negro in the Americas* (1947), is a comparative treatment of North and South America. On the freed Negro see L. P. Jackson, *Free Negro Labor and Property Holding in Virginia* (1942); and J. H. Franklin, *The Free Negro in North Carolina, 1790–1860* (1943). An important aspect of the problem, little noted at the time, is discussed in Avery O. Craven, *Soil Exhaustion as a Factor in the Agricultural History of Virginia and Maryland, 1606–1860* (1926).

The Abolitionist movement has attracted the attention of a host of writers. The work of Garrison is told in detail, and probably with over-emphasis on his importance to the movement, by Wendell Phillips Garrison and Francis Jackson Garrison, *William Lloyd Garrison* (4 vols., 1885–1889). The significance of the western group of abolitionists is set forth, perhaps with equal overemphasis, by Gilbert H. Barnes, *The Anti-Slavery Impulse, 1830–1844* (1933); and Dwight L. Dumond, *Antislavery Origins of the Civil War in the United States* (1939). For further evidence on this subject, see also the *Letters of Theodore Dwight Weld, Angelina Grimké Weld, and Sarah Grimké, 1822–1844,* edited by Gilbert H. Barnes and Dwight L. Dumond (2 vols., 1934). Nearly

all of the abolitionist leaders have been the subjects of biographies. See, for example, Lorenzo Sears, *Wendell Phillips, Orator and Agitator* (1909); Catherine H. Birney, *The Grimké Sisters, Sarah and Angelina Grimké* (1885); Anna D. Hallowell, *James and Lucretia Mott, Life and Letters* (1884); Ralph V. Harlow, *Gerrit Smith* (1939); H. S. Commager, *Theodore Parker* (1936); William Birney, *James G. Birney and His Times* (1890). For more general accounts, see A. B. Hart, *Slavery and Abolition* (1906); and Jesse Macy, *The Anti-Slavery Crusade* (1919); W. H. Siebert, *The Underground Railroad from Slavery to Freedom* (1898); Benjamin Quarles, *Frederick Douglass* (1948); F. B. Simkins, *The South Old and New: A History, 1820–1947* (1947); C. A. Madison, *Critics and Crusaders: A Century of American Protest* (1947), Ralph Korngold, *Two Friends of Man: The Story of William Lloyd Garrison and Wendell Phillips and their Relationship with Abraham Lincoln* (1950).

On the pro-slavery side, W. S. Jenkins, *Pro-Slavery Thought in the Old South* (1935), best covers the subject, but see also Harvey Wish, *George Fitzhugh: Propagandist of the Old South* (1943); and Clement Eaton, *Freedom of Thought in the Old South* (1940). W. G. Brown, *The Lower South in American History* (1902), is highly emotional. A. Y. Lloyd, *The Slavery Controversy, 1831–1860* (1939), seeks to revive the pro-slavery argument. Avery O. Craven, *Edmund Ruffin, Southerner, A Study in Secession* (1932), is of broader scope and interest than the title indicates. Everett Dick, *The Dixie Frontier: A Social History of the Southern Frontier* (1947), is concerned with the everyday life of southern pioneers. R. W. Shugg, *Origins of Class Struggle in Louisiana* (1939), deals with the problems of white farmers and laborers during slavery and after.

26

Manifest Destiny

The Santa Fe trade — Anglo-American rivalry for the Oregon country — American interest in California; in Texas — The issue of annexation — Presidential campaign and election of 1844 — James K. Polk — Acquisition of Oregon — The Slidell mission — The Mexican War — Conquest of New Mexico and California — The Mormons in Utah

UNTIL the late eighteen-thirties and the early eighteen-forties, the people of the **The American frontier** United States took it for granted that the growth of the populated area of their country would be hedged in by certain obvious limits. They had foreseen for some time that the frontier of population would advance steadily into the upper Mississippi Valley and that it would reach, and perhaps cross, the international border to the southwest, but they had no idea that the region west of Missouri, which was labeled on the maps the "Great American Desert," would ever be desired for settlement. Indeed, it was because of this conviction that the policy of Indian removals, carried out in Jackson's time, met with such whole-hearted approval. Public opinion demanded that the eastern half of the continent be cleared for the use of the white man, but the Indian was welcome to the rest of it. To be sure, the boundaries of the United States might still be altered, and what they would ultimately become no one was ready to say. The title to the Oregon country was in dispute between the United States and Great Britain, and the settlement of the southwestern boundary, made in 1819, might, owing to the Texas problem, be subjected to generous revision. But the idea that any considerable number of persons would soon have their hearts set upon making their homes in the Far West seemed palpably absurd.

One of the circumstances that served to provide Americans with a new vision of expansion was the opening of the Santa Fe Trail. On the up- **New Mexico** per Rio Grande, separated by a long desert trip from Mexico City, the Spanish had established outposts at about the same time the English were founding Jamestown. Settlement in such a faraway spot, however, had been extremely slow to take root, and two hundred years later the American explorer, Zebulon M. Pike, found Santa Fe only a cluster of one-story adobe houses that reminded him of a "fleet of flatboats . . . descending the Ohio," and that offered shelter for a "supposed population" of only forty-five hundred. These people, and the inhabitants of the lesser Spanish villages of the region, depended mainly upon agriculture, particularly cattle raising, for their subsistence, but they carried on a far-flung trade with the Indians, and they sent each year a large shipment of their own and the Indians' products by caravan down the long trail toward Mexico City to be exchanged for greatly needed articles of European manufacture.

Pike was quick to observe, and to point

INDEPENDENCE, MISSOURI. The Court House Square. Illustration from Dana, *The United States Illustrated*, 1853.

The Santa Fe Trail ran from Independence, Missouri, to Santa Fe, New Mexico, through vast stretches of lonely territory where clashes with the wandering Indian tribes were so frequent that military escorts were sometimes required. The events of the journey and the rugged scenery of the West, reported by many artists, were of considerable interest back in the East where enthusiasm for western expansion was high.

INDIAN ATTACK. Engraving after a sketch by Didier for Gregg, *Commerce of the Prairies*, 1844.

ARRIVAL OF THE CARAVAN AT SANTA FE. Engraving after a sketch by Didier for Gregg, *Commerce of the Prairies*, 1844.

SANTA FE, NEW MEXICO. Illustration from Abert, *Expedition to New Mexico*, 1847–48.

EMIGRANT TRAIN. Prairie schooners fording a river. Painting by Samuel Colman, 1872.

The far Northwest was the goal of an increasing number of emigrants and fur traders who set out from Independence, Missouri, on the long and hazardous Oregon Trail. Steamboats, which navigated the western rivers far into the interior to pick up furs for shipment to New Orleans, also provided access to the distant territories for emigrants.

A STEAMBOAT AT THE GORGE OF THE ST. CROIX RIVER. Detail from a painting by Henry Lewis.

out for the benefit of his countrymen, that a thriving trade might be established between the American and the Spanish frontiers. Imports into Mexico came by way of Vera Cruz, fifteen hundred miles distant from Santa Fe, and the cost of transportation so far into the interior was prohibitive except for the barest necessities. The distance to the bend of the Missouri, on the other hand, to which steamboats could easily bring articles needed for the trade, was not half as great. Thus an excellent market seemed only to await the taking. Early efforts on the part of the Americans to seize this opportunity were thwarted by the Spanish authorities in New Mexico, who rigorously enforced the regulations of the home government against colonial trade with foreign nations, but all this was changed by the Mexican Revolution. After 1822, when William Becknell returned to the Missouri settlements from the first profitable trip to Santa Fe, the caravans of American traders crossed the "Desert" each year for more than two decades. Sometimes their profits were excellent. The expedition of 1824, for example, consisting of eighty-one men with thirty thousand dollars' worth of merchandise in twenty-five wagons, brought back one hundred and eighty thousand dollars in gold and silver, in addition to ten thousand dollars' worth of furs, and some mules.

The men who engaged in the Santa Fe trade were as a rule merely pioneer farmers or merchants with a taste for adventure. Each individual outfitted one or more wagons with hardware, needles and thread, cotton and silk goods,

The Santa Fe trade

The Western Trails

The "Pony Express"
⎫
⎬ Routes of the "Forty-Niners"
⎭
Santa Fé Trail

mirrors, glassware, china, and dozens of other articles that his frontier experience recommended as easily salable. For convenience and protection the traders united soon after leaving the "jumping-off place," which most of the time was Independence, Missouri, and traveled as a caravan. A leader, elected by the traders for the purpose, then took command, assigned to each man his duties, and, unless deposed, guided the long procession of wagons to its destination. When, however, after a journey of about six weeks, the goal was near at hand, all pretense of order was given up, and a mad rush began to see who could arrive first. Import duties as high as sixty per cent were levied against the trade by the Mexican government, but because the Mexican officials could usually be bribed, such high charges were rarely paid. For the inhabitants of Santa Fe the arrival of the caravan was the event of the year, and the goods

brought were quickly disposed of. Most of the traders made all possible haste to return to the United States, but a very few stayed on, the forerunners of the American occupation.

The total volume of trade down the Santa Fe Trail was never very large, and the number of traders engaged in it probably did not average many more than a hundred a year. Nevertheless, the opening of a new trail into the Far West was, at least to the people of the Mississippi Valley, an event of real significance. Traders who were themselves farmers were not slow to observe that the land along the first lap of the journey was good land, and that heavy rainfall sometimes impeded their progress. In 1825, Thomas Hart Benton persuaded Congress to appropriate funds for the survey of the trail, and ardent believers in internal improvements talked even of extending the National Road far out along this new southwestern route. Military escorts that cost the government sums almost as large as the annual profits of the traders occasionally accompanied the caravan to the international border, and United States Commissioners to the Indians, blissfully unconcerned about the promise that the Far West was never to become a white man's country, attempted to purchase immunity for the white man's trade. Nor was the romance of the Santa Fe Trail lost upon a people that had long looked to the West for its tallest tales. In 1843, when Santa Anna, the Mexican leader, put a stop to the trade, the country was ready to be shocked, and even its reopening a year or two later did not serve to destroy the impression that "manifestly" this whole region ought to be a part of the United States.

Meantime, the Oregon Trail had opened to American eyes a new vision of the possibilities of the Far Northwest. **The Oregon Trail** The origins of this route to the West are far more obscure than the origins of the Santa Fe Trail. After the explorations of Lewis and Clark and the journey of Astor's Overlanders, numbers of Indian traders had found their way by a variety of routes into the Northwest, and by the eighteen-thirties they had settled upon the Oregon Trail as the easiest way through. This route led, not without many variations, from the bend of the Missouri to the bend of the Platte, out the latter stream and its north fork to what is now southern Wyoming, through South Pass, an easy divide in the mountains, to the Snake Valley, then by a cut-off to the Columbia. This journey was three times as long as the Santa Fe Trail, it penetrated the lands of many more Indians, and for years it led only to a wilderness. An alternative route into the interior, used frequently after 1832 by the American Fur Company, was by steamboat up the Missouri River. Incredible as it may now seem, these river boats reached the mouth of the Yellowstone each year, and sometimes they went much farther.

Ownership of the Oregon country, to which both these routes pointed, was officially a matter of dispute. **The Oregon country** Under the convention of 1818 between the United States and Great Britain, as subsequently revised and renewed, citizens of both nations were still permitted to occupy the region jointly, but whose territory they occupied was undetermined. Whatever claims Spain might once have had, the United States had acquired by the Florida Treaty of 1819; and whatever rights Russia might once have had, the British had acquired by an agreement as to the Alaskan boundary in 1825. Thanks to these various understandings the borders of the Oregon country were clear — the forty-second parallel to the south, the line of 54° 40′ to the north, the Pacific Ocean to the west, and the crest of the Rockies to the east. But should it all go to the United States, or all to Great Britain? Or should it be divided between the two?

For a long time no one much cared. Here British fur-trading interests, united after 1821 under the exclusive control of the Hudson's Bay Company, carried on practically without opposition a profitable trade. So great was the influence of the company's chief factor, Doctor John McLoughlin, that he has since been correctly described as the "King of Old Oregon." He kept order among his subordinates, carried on agriculture so that they would never lack for food, and won by his fairness and generosity the fealty of the Indians. As long as his rule went unchallenged the profits of the trade were good, and no one felt the need of a more formal government.

Rivalry between English and American fur-traders, however, could not long be delayed. McLoughlin's agents on their **Anglo-American rivalry** adventures eastward into the Rockies were soon reporting contacts, and even conflicts, with traders sent out by the American Fur Company and its ruthless competitor, the Rocky Mountain Fur Company. McLoughlin would not permit the use of rum in dealing with the Indians, but the Americans, particularly the Rocky Mountain traders, had no scruples on this score, and the Indians were corrupted accordingly. Private adventurers also, among them Captain Benjamin L. E. Bonneville, a regular army officer on leave, and Nathaniel J. Wyeth, a Boston ice merchant, both of whom led expeditions into the Far Northwest, brought to McLoughlin's attention the imminence of strenuous American competition. By the year 1832 it was abundantly evident that "joint occupation" was soon to be given a real test.

And yet the conflict, when finally it came, was less the work of fur-traders than **Missionaries** of missionaries. By the eight-**to Oregon** een-thirties most American religious denominations had developed a keen interest in foreign missions, and had recognized, somewhat belatedly, that the Indian tribes offered a suitable field for such labors. So far as the Indians of the Far Northwest were concerned, a clear call to action was sounded when the news came out that a deputation of Flatheads had crossed the plains to St. Louis and had asked General William Clark to send them a Bible and a "black-robe." Whether such a request was ever made is a matter of doubt, but the Methodists, undeterred by the obvious reference to the garb of a Catholic priest, promptly responded, and in 1834 sent out their first missionary to the Oregon country, Jason Lee. Close on the heels of the Methodists came the Presbyterians, whose ablest representative, Marcus Whitman, appeared on the scene in 1836. By the end of the decade the American Catholics also were represented in the Rocky Mountain country by Father Pierre Jean de Smet, a Belgian Jesuit from St. Louis.

McLoughlin extended to all good men a hearty welcome, but since the Methodists had established a mission in the Willamette Valley, he strongly advised the Presbyterians to make their headquarters much farther in the interior at the junction of the Columbia and the Snake. Father de Smet of his own accord confined his activities largely to the Indians of the mountains and the western plains, who lived still farther to the east. Thus conflict between the American missionaries was largely avoided. The great majority of McLoughlin's traders, however, were Catholics, and the French-Canadian priests who came out at about this same time to minister to their needs worked at will among all the Indians. Religious rivalry thus began to take on a nationalistic bias. In a general sort of way the British subjects were Catholic and favorable to the Catholic missions, while the Americans were mostly Protestants.

The real trouble, however, came from the fact that many of the Methodist and Presbyterian missionaries, who were nearly all married men with families, soon became actively engaged in agriculture. In this they had the example of McLoughlin himself; but McLoughlin had no desire to carry on agriculture except as a necessary adjunct to his main business, the fur trade, whereas the missionaries sometimes became so absorbed in their farms that they almost forgot the spiritual needs of the Indians. In 1844 the Methodists, convinced that the sending of missionary money to Oregon under these circumstances was a scandal, closed down their Willamette mission. Well before this time, however, the far more interesting news that there was good farming land in Oregon had been spread far and wide, and after 1841 hundreds of emigrants gathered each spring at Independence, Missouri, to make the long journey by covered wagon into the new frontier. Such of them as completed it were often cared for considerately by McLoughlin himself, who in welcoming in the Americans was actually giving the country away. In 1842 the United States government sent out Doctor Elijah White, ostensibly as an Indian agent, but actually to take charge of the growing American colony in Oregon. That same year John C. Frémont, son-in-law of Thomas Hart Benton, began a survey of the Oregon Trail, and a year later the Americans in Oregon held a convention to inaugurate the well-known frontier process of establishing a means of local self-government. By the next election year, 1844, the whole United States was aware of the Oregon question. Joint occupation had run its course. Should Oregon be British or American?

Even in California the workings of "manifest destiny" were becoming apparent. Here California the Spanish outposts were not so old as in New Mexico, but even so they dated back to the period when Daniel Boone was leading the advance guard of American settlement into the Ohio Valley. At about that time Spanish officials in the New World, fearful that Russian and British traders might advance too far down the Pacific coast toward Mexico, sought to forestall them by sending missionaries, soldiers, and colonists from Mexico to California. Before the American Revolution had come to a close, these Mexican frontiersmen had established themselves firmly at San Diego, Santa Barbara, Monterey, and San Francisco. Mexico had few colonists to spare, however, and the number of civilians who made California their home during the next half-century was not very great. Those who came prospered in a fashion, for the climate was easy and the soil was rich. They adopted ranching as their chief occupation, but they had no adequate market for the vast herds they could raise, and the lives they led, while picturesque, were fairly primitive.

The missions, under the able direction of Franciscan friars, fared rather better. Not The missions only did the friars win the Indians over to the Christian religion; they also persuaded great numbers of them to give up their tribal ways, and to attach themselves as laborers to the missions. Thus it was possible for each mission to expand its grainfields, to plant vineyards, olive groves, and orchards, to raise great herds of cattle, horses, and sheep, and to build the handsome churches and living quarters that in some instances still stand. A score of prosperous missions soon dotted the fertile coast valleys from San Diego to San Francisco. The natives also learned numerous arts and crafts from the friars, whose benevolent rule they accepted with increasing contentment.

To some extent before and to a greater extent after the Mexican Revolution, the Californians suffered from the ineptitude of their political rulers. Governors and their subordinates were usually venal, and their authority was supported by garrisons of unsavory soldiers who corrupted the Indians, hampered the work of the missionaries, and sometimes drove the civilians to revolt. Moreover, both the Spanish and the Mexican governments insisted upon regarding the missions as merely temporary affairs which, whenever the Indians were sufficiently civilized, should be broken up. When that time came the lands and the herds that the friars had amassed were to be divided among the Indians and the religious duties of the friars were to be taken over by parish priests. Soon after the revolt from Spain the Mexican government attempted to put this policy into effect, but the Indians, who failed to see that they were to be its chief beneficiaries, shared the resentment of the friars and resisted vigorously. So great was the disorder that the government finally tried to restore the old system, but in this also it failed. Many of the missions were abandoned, their livestock destroyed, and their land appropriated by anyone who chose. Deprived of the protection of the friars, the Indians were ultimately forced to revert to the wild life whence they had come.

The uneasiness of California society was not lessened by the presence of a constantly increasing number of non-Mexican Americans in California residents. Some of these came in to profit from the overseas trade which, regardless of hampering regulations, soon began to enliven the remote harbors of the Pacific coast. One such was Thomas O. Larkin, a former citizen of Massachusetts and of South Carolina, who in 1832 opened a store in Monterey. Larkin from the first seems to have cherished the hope that the United States would some day annex California, but he was careful to keep in the good graces of the Mexican officials, even at the cost of lending money to the governor at twelve per cent interest. Occasionally, also, the whalers and merchantmen that put into California harbors left behind deserters who preferred the salubrious climate of that region to the long voyage around the Horn or across the Pacific. More important still were the emigrants from the American frontier who were lured in by the spreading tales of California's fertile unclaimed acres. In 1841, a caravan of forty-eight left the Missouri border with California instead of Oregon as their goal. Following the Oregon Trail to the vicinity of the present Wyoming-Idaho boundary line, they successfully pushed southwestward through the alkaline plains and the Sierra Nevada mountains to their destination. They were not the first to find such a way through, but after their well-advertised journey the trail to California was as much a fact as the trail to Oregon. By 1845 there were no less than seven hundred Americans in California out of a total white population of about ten times that number.

After 1839 Sutter's Fort on the American River, a tributary of the Sacramento, furnished a convenient haven of refuge for the American emigrants. Johann Augustus Suter was a German by birth who served for several years in the Swiss army, emigrated in 1834 to the American frontier, and shortened his name to John A. Sutter. In five years' time he had engaged in the Santa Fe trade, had made the long trip overland to Oregon, had sold at a comfortable profit in Alaska a shipload of freight acquired in the Sandwich Islands, and had sailed into San Francisco Bay seeking yet another world to conquer. By embracing Mexican citizenship he made himself eligible to hold land, and obtained a magnificent grant of eleven square leagues, which he determined to transform into a kind of feudal barony. Here he gathered about him such of the Indians as would accept his protection, supervised their prosecution of the fur trade so successfully that

Sutter's Fort

he was soon a recognized rival of the Hudson's Bay Company factor in Oregon, taught his wards many useful skills such as the weaving of baskets and blankets, and gave them charge over his lands and his increasing herds of cattle, horses, and sheep. Besides his "fort," Sutter built himself a capacious house, a blacksmith shop, a grist mill, and even a tannery and a distillery. These evidences of civilization were ordinarily the first of their kind to greet the Americans who had successfully crossed the Sierra Nevada, and Sutter never failed to give the tired travelers the aid and encouragement they needed. He even pointed out to them the lands they might safely appropriate, regardless of the Mexican regulations designed to prevent alien landownership. Sutter himself was more or less above all law. Armed retainers of an astonishing variety of nationalities protected him from the wrath of the constituted authorities, who sat idly by while he parceled out the lands of California to the American invaders.

Naturally, the American government was not unmindful of the prospect that California might some day become a part of the United States. In 1841, Commodore Thomas ap Catesby Jones, commander of the American squadron in the Pacific, was instructed to seize Monterey in the event of war between the United States and Mexico. Excited by rumors that a British fleet also had designs on California, and convinced that the United States was already at war with Mexico, Commodore Jones decided in October, 1842, that the time had come to carry out his instructions. Accordingly he landed a force at Monterey, took possession of the public property, and ran up the American flag. When Larkin produced evidence to show that Jones's fear of the British was groundless and that the United States and Mexico were still at peace, there was nothing for the American officer to do but apologize and withdraw. His precipitate action revealed, however, all too plainly the ultimate goal of his government. By 1844 Larkin had been

American interest in California

designated American consul at Monterey, and the responsiveness of the American colony in California to the idea of annexation was abundantly apparent.

Much as the American public was interested in New Mexico, Oregon and California, **Texas** the place where "manifest destiny" was most clearly at work was Texas. Here in the "Lone Star State" lived far more Americans than in all the other coveted regions combined. Furthermore, the United States had had a claim to Texas before 1819, and had renounced it only in order to obtain Florida. The issue could therefore be made to appear not so much annexation as reannexation. Texas had made good its independence, and had been recognized by the other governments as well as by the United States. It was in actual fact no longer a part of Mexico, whatever the Mexican officials might claim. The Texans themselves, with relatively few exceptions, desired annexation, and stood ready to see it accomplished on any reasonable terms. Why should the United States hesitate to add to the wealth and resources of the nation a region that ought never to have been alienated? Still further point was given to this argument by the fear, not wholly groundless, that an alliance between Texas and Great Britain might be consummated that would not only give preference in English ports to Texas cotton, but might also encourage Texas to expand her borders west and south to such an extent as to create for the United States a dangerous southwestern rival.

Probably the annexation of Texas would have been accomplished without serious op- **Slavery** position but for the growing dis- **and Texas** taste in the North for slavery and the conviction that no more slave territory should be added to the Union. These considerations were sufficient to restrain Van Buren, who refused throughout his term of office to give the slightest encouragement to the annexationists. John Tyler, however, was ardently in favor of annexation, and was undeterred by opposition.

Accordingly, as soon as Webster had retired from the State Department Tyler reopened negotiations with Texas, first through Abel P. Upshur, Webster's successor as Secretary of State, and later, after Upshur's untimely death, through John C. Calhoun, whose appointment to the State Department was due mainly to his well-known interest in annexation. On April 12, 1844, a treaty between the United States and the Republic of Texas was signed which provided that Texas should become a territory of the United States, but not yet a state. This treaty, however, was overwhelmingly rejected by the United States Senate. The Mexican government had made it clear that the annexation of Texas would be regarded as good grounds for war, and some senators who might otherwise have favored the treaty voted against it on this account. Moreover, the election of 1844 was close at hand, and it seemed proper to await the verdict of the people; for, even at the time the Senate took its vote, annexation had become a dominant issue in the campaign.

The emergence of this issue took place, however, in spite of the best efforts of Henry Clay, the prospective **The issue of** Whig candidate, and Martin **annexation** Van Buren, the prospective Democratic candidate, to head it off. Shortly before the nominating conventions met, Clay and Van Buren issued separate statements on the subject so similar as to leave little doubt that their action had been previously agreed upon. Both opposed the annexation of Texas without the consent of Mexico on the ground that it would be dishonorable and would lead to war. Clay went even further, and pointed to the financial obligations that the acquisition of Texas, with its large war debt, would entail, and to the strong opposition to annexation among the people of the North. But the conventions were by no means satisfied with these pronouncements. The Whigs nominated Clay unanimously, but they made no mention of Texas in their platform, while the Democrats, after much fruitless balloting, passed over Van Buren

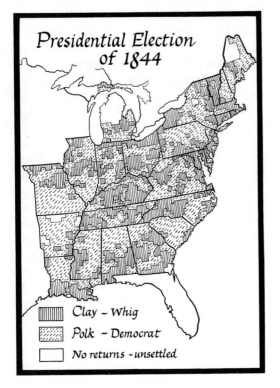

Presidential Election of 1844

Clay – Whig

Polk – Democrat

No returns – unsettled

in favor of James K. Polk of Tennessee, whose devotion to the cause of annexation was unquestioned. Their platform maintained, moreover, that "our title to the whole of the territory of Oregon is clear and unquestionable," and urged both "the reoccupation of Oregon and the reannexation of Texas." The introduction of the Oregon question was shrewdly devised to appeal to the people of the Northwest, whose interest in Oregon was as great as, or greater than, their interest in Texas. Also, by advocating the acquisition of free territory as well as slave territory, the Democrats freed themselves from the charge of sectionalism. With Oregon no less coveted than Texas, they could not so easily be denounced as seeking merely to promote the spread of slavery. Unmentioned, but by no means overlooked, was the further possibility of acquiring New Mexico and California.

As the campaign wore on, it became evident that the Democratic strategy had been wisely planned. To many voters, North-

erners as well as Southerners, but to Westerners most of all, it seemed   **Campaign** both reasonable and in line with   **of 1844** precedent that the borders of the United States should now be expanded. No one was seriously deceived by the pretense of campaign orators that the United States wished only to obtain what was already rightfully hers. The real issue was whether or not the electorate was willing to follow the dictates of "manifest destiny," beginning with Texas and Oregon, and ending no one knew quite where. Clay himself soon realized that he had underestimated the strength of the annexationists, and began to qualify his prenomination statement. Ultimately his position became so equivocal that neither side knew precisely where he stood, and a number of anti-slavery men who had expected to support him turned instead to James G. Birney, the Liberty Party candidate. The attitude of the Democrats, on the other hand, was so plainly revealed throughout the campaign that they attracted practically all the expansionists to their standard. Their battle-cry, "The reannexation of Texas and the reoccupation of Oregon," struck the popular fancy, and was reinforced by such threatening slogans as "Fifty-four-forty or fight," and "All of Oregon or none."

When the votes were counted, it was apparent that Polk had won, although by so narrow a margin that the change   **Polk's** of a few thousand votes in New   **victory** York State would have insured his defeat. The statement is sometimes made that Clay's trimming, which cost him the support of many Liberty men in New York State, lost him the election. This is not entirely clear. Had he not trimmed, it is possible that he might have lost some of the states which he carried — Tennessee, for example, which voted for him in preference to its native son, Polk, by a majority of less than a thousand. But Polk's victory, in spite of his slender majority, was complete. Not only had he defeated a man whose personal following was probably greater than that of any other politician in the country, but he had received a further endorsement of his principles by the selection of a Congress that was Democratic in both branches. The mandate of the electorate in favor of expansion was perfectly clear.

With this reassuring popular verdict, steps were taken toward the annexation of **Annexation** Texas even before Polk became **of Texas** President. Prior to the election Tyler had already suggested to Congress the possibility of annexation by joint resolution instead of by treaty, and in this position he had received the enthusiastic support of the venerable ex-President, Andrew Jackson. Such a course would avoid the almost impossible task of obtaining the two-thirds majority in the Senate necessary for the ratification of a treaty. After the election, annexation by joint resolution was again pressed by the President upon a Congress now willing to comply. By a vote of 120 to 98 in the House and 27 to 25 in the Senate, Texas was invited to become a state in the Union on condition that (1) it should present a constitution acceptable to Congress, (2) agree that at some future time it might be subdivided into as many as five states, (3) pay its own war debt, and (4) retain its own public lands. Assurance that the institution of slavery would not be disturbed was given by extending the terms of the Missouri Compromise to apply to Texas as well as to the Louisiana Purchase. Three days before he left office, March 1, 1845, Tyler signed this resolution, and at once dispatched a courier to notify the Texas authorities. It was not long before the Lone Star State had signified its willingness to exchange independence for membership in the American Union, but formal admission was not accomplished until December 29, 1845.

The new President, James Knox Polk (1795–1849), was a North-Carolinian by **James** birth, of Scotch-Irish ancestry. **K. Polk** He was not widely known, and for the preceding three or four years had been out of office, but his obscurity was much overemphasized by his contempo-

James K. Polk

ELEVENTH PRESIDENT of the United States, Polk of Tennessee owed his nomination in 1844 to the fact that Martin Van Buren, the "logical" Democratic candidate, had come out against the annexation of Texas. This greatly offended many southern Democrats, including ex-President Jackson, who threw their support to James K. Polk, an ardent annexationist. Photo by Mathew B. Brady.

raries, who had never before witnessed the nomination of a "dark horse" — that is, a candidate for the Presidency who had not been long groomed for the race. For fourteen consecutive years, 1825–39, Polk had represented a Tennessee constituency in the House of Representatives, and during much of that time he was the recognized leader of the Democratic forces. The last four years he was Speaker of the House. From 1839 to 1841 he was governor of Tennessee, and, although he twice failed of re-election, his prominence in the political life of the state was hardly surpassed by any other man. Thanks to the fact that during the time he was President Polk kept a detailed diary, which subsequently was published, historians now know far more than his contemporaries knew about him. He was a hard-working, conscientious executive who believed it his foremost duty to carry out the will of the people as expressed in the late election. He had no taste for war, and earnestly sought to avoid it; but the annexation of Texas he regarded as both a necessity and a right. The United States and Texas, he maintained, were "independent powers competent to contract, and foreign nations have no right to interfere with them or to take exceptions to their reunion." As for Oregon, he pointed out that

But eighty years ago our population was confined on the west by the ridge of the Alleghanies. Within that period — within the lifetime, I might say, of some of my hearers — our people, increasing to many millions, have filled the eastern valley of the Mississippi, adventurously ascended the Missouri to its headsprings, and are already engaged in establishing the blessings of self-government in valleys of which the rivers flow to the Pacific. The world beholds the peaceful triumphs of the industry of our emigrants. To us belongs the duty of protecting them adequately wherever they may be upon our soil.

The virtual certainty of trouble with Mexico over the annexation of Texas led **The Oregon** Polk to trim his sails materially **settlement** with regard to Oregon. As early as 1826, plans for the division of the

Oregon country had been discussed between the United States and Great Britain, and at that time the American government had indicated its willingness to accept an extension to the Pacific of the forty-ninth parallel as the international boundary line. This was more than the British were then willing to concede, for the Hudson's Bay fur trade had long centered in the region south of the proposed line. Polk, however, hopefully renewed the offer, for Americans were now entering the Columbia Valley by the thousands, and the Oregon fur trade, whether British or American, had seen its best days. When the British again rejected this plan of division, Polk asked Congress for permission to give notice, in accordance with the terms of the treaty, that after one year joint occupation must come to an end. He wished also the right to erect forts in the American zone and to extend the laws of the United States over Oregon. Probably the President had in mind only to threaten the British and so hasten negotiations along, but Congress feared he might involve the country in war, and agreed only to the termination of joint occupation, refusing the rest. More drastic action was unnecessary, however, for the British then offered to accept the line Polk had so recently proposed. After some diplomatic sparring, this was done; a treaty was signed on June 15, 1846, which extended the forty-ninth parallel as proposed in the negotiations, but gave to Great Britain all of Vancouver Island, to which the British fur-traders had recently shifted their headquarters. The Hudson's Bay Company retained also full freedom to navigate the Columbia River.

Meantime the relations between the United States and Mexico had grown steadily worse. Mexican pro- **Relations** tests against the proposed an- **with Mexico** nexation of Texas came thick and fast, and when her admission as a state was finally accomplished the Mexican government once again, as in 1836, withdrew its representative at Washington. The situation was still further complicated by the extravagant boundaries that the Texans claimed. While Texas was a part of Mexico, its southwestern border was generally conceded to be the Nueces River, but on becoming independent the new state laid claim to a new border, the Rio Grande from its mouth to its source, and thence due north to the forty-second parallel. This meant that much of New Mexico, including Santa Fe itself, would fall within Texas, a claim so palpably without foundation that the United States in the resolution offering statehood to Texas had definitely reserved the right to adjust "all questions of boundary that may arise." Nevertheless, Polk, in June, 1845, as soon as he had received assurance that Texas would accept statehood, had promptly ordered General Zachary Taylor to occupy territory "on or near the Rio Grande del Norte" in order to be able to "protect what, in event of annexation, will be our western frontier." The United States had also a list of grievances against Mexico that were not connected with Texas. For years the Mexican government had persistently hampered the easy interchange of commerce between the two countries; it had failed miserably to protect the lives and the property of American citizens in Mexico; and it had habitually disregarded its promises to pay damages for the losses Americans had suffered. Unfortunately, Polk was wholly ignorant of Mexican psychology, and failed to realize that the Mexican leaders were really eager for war. They genuinely doubted that the people of the United States would adequately support a war of invasion, and they felt confident that in a defensive contest they would win.

Polk hoped for peace, but he was determined to obtain not only the part of New **The Slidell** Mexico claimed by Texas, but **mission** all the rest of it as well, and in addition California. Accordingly he sent a minister to Mexico, John Slidell of Louisiana, with orders to acquire the desired territory by purchase if he could. For full acknowledgment of the Texas boundary claim, the United States would assume all

Texas Boundary Controversy

Claimed by Texas by Statute Dec. 19, 1836

Claimed by Texas, 1836~1850 Ceded to U.S. 1850

damages due American citizens from Mexico. For the rest of New Mexico, the United States would pay five million dollars in cash. As for California, "money would be no object," and the United States stood ready to pay from twenty to twenty-five millions, depending upon the exclusion or inclusion of Lower California. But Slidell's mission was doomed to disappointment. He arrived in Mexico just as a revolution was about to take place, and with public opinion intensely anti-American neither Herrera, who was in office when Slidell reached Mexico, nor Paredes, the successful revolutionist, dared receive him. Accordingly, in March, 1846, he returned to the United States with nothing accomplished.

Long before Slidell's return, Polk had decided that war was inevitable, and in January, 1846, Taylor's troops, which for several months had been encamped just west of the Nueces River, were ordered to the Rio Grande. This movement was regarded by the Mexican President as an act of war, but he was unable to make a formal declaration to that effect until the Mexican Congress should meet. Polk, however, grew tired of delay, and early in May, 1846, he prepared a message to Congress in which he recited the failure of the Slidell mission, and recommended war to bring the Mexicans to terms. Before this message was sent, news arrived in Washington that fighting had broken out between Taylor's troops and the Mexicans along the border. Polk, therefore, rewrote his message in such a way as to put the blame for starting hostilities upon the enemy. On May 11, 1846, he told Congress that

The cup of forbearance had been exhausted even before the recent information from the frontier of the Del Norte. But now, after reiterated menaces Mexico has passed the boundary of the United States, has invaded our territory and shed American blood upon the American soil . . . war exists, and, notwithstanding all our efforts to avoid it, exists by the act of Mexico herself.

Congress came with alacrity to the President's support. A declaration of war was **War declared** carried in the Senate by a vote of 40 to 2 and in the House by 174 to 14. To insure the successful prosecution of the war, Congress appropriated ten million dollars and authorized a volunteer army of fifty thousand men. At first the country seemed genuinely enthusiastic about the war, but before many months strenuous opposition began to develop. The attack upon a weaker neighbor was criticized as unworthy of the national honor. The Democrats were charged with fomenting war in order to gain glory enough to enable them to win the next election. Antislavery men, already deeply distressed at the annexation of Texas, were sure that a southern conspiracy existed to extend still further the area open to slavery. The Whig Party, always in danger of dissolution because of the discordant views of its members, found a new source of dissension. The "cotton" Whigs, mostly from the West and South, supported the war now that it had begun, while the "conscience" Whigs, mainly from the Northeast, branded it as an inexcusable blunder that ought to be abandoned at once, with apologies and reparations to Mexico.

To Zachary Taylor, known in the army as "Old Rough and Ready," was assigned the task of advancing south- **Taylor's** westward into Mexico from the **campaign** Texas border. He captured Matamoras without much difficulty, then with a handful of regulars and several thousand volunteers he advanced toward Monterrey. Hampered not only by the enemy, but also by the out-

"*Uncle Sam's Taylorifics,*" a cartoon by Edward W. Clay, 1846, indicates the strong southern and western support for Taylor's actions in Texas, with allusions to John Bull fishing for Oregon and California.

Campaigns
of the Mexican War
1846 — 1847

break of disease among his poorly conditioned recruits, and by almost insuperable obstacles in the matters of transportation and supplies, Taylor nevertheless pushed on to his objective and in three days' hard fighting, September 21–23, took it; although to the intense disgust of President Polk he did not insist on unconditional surrender, and permitted the enemy troops to evacuate. From this time forward Polk lost all confidence in Taylor, but because the General, in the eyes of the people, had become a hero, his removal was politically impossible. Meantime Santa Anna, whose return to Mexico from exile in Cuba Polk had unwisely facilitated, had once again emerged as the Mexican President and war leader. With an army which outnumbered Taylor's by three to one, he marched rapidly northward to repel the invader. Taylor prepared for the attack at Buena Vista, and owing far less to his strategy, which was singularly defective, than to the superior morale of the

American soldiers, the Mexicans were repulsed (February 22–23, 1847).

But Polk had already determined to shift the main attack on Mexico from the international border to Vera Cruz Scott's on the eastern coast. To carry campaign out this plan, General Winfield Scott was placed in charge of an expeditionary force at New Orleans, and Taylor was notified, shortly before the battle of Buena Vista, that henceforth he must subordinate himself to Scott. Before Santa Anna could recover from his defeat by Taylor, Scott had successfully invested Vera Cruz, and with an army of more than ten thousand men was working his way westward, without much opposition, toward Mexico City. Not until the expedition had neared Jalapa, well up in the mountains, did Santa Anna appear with a newly collected army to dispute its advance. But Scott was a far better general than Taylor, and Santa Anna's troops were not very dependable. At Cerro Gordo the Mexicans

Gen. Winfield Scott's entrance into the Grand Plaza of Mexico City, Sept. 14, 1847, is from an illustration in G. W. Kendall, *The War Between the U. S. and Mexico*, 1851.

suffered a disastrous defeat (April 17–18, 1847), Jalapa was soon occupied, and then Puebla. Here Scott rested for several months in preparation for the final climb to Mexico City, but by the middle of August he was again on the march. To the surprise of the Americans, who expected to be attacked in the difficult mountain passes, Santa Anna offered no resistance until the central plateau on which Mexico City is located had been reached. Then he fought, and fought hard, but he was no match for Scott, who won a succession of victories: Contreras (August 19), Churubusco (August 20), Molino del Rey (September 8), and Chapultepec (September 13). On September 14, 1847, the Americans were in possession of the Mexican capital.

The war was won by the campaigns of Taylor and Scott, but the conquest of New **Conquest of** Mexico and California clearly **New Mexico** foreshadowed the terms of the peace. Early in the summer of 1846, Colonel Stephen W. Kearny left Fort Leavenworth, near the Missouri border, bound for Santa Fe. He had with him a

force of about seventeen hundred men, but he made no effort to maintain a line of communications, and carried only enough supplies to last until he reached his objective. He counted on a minimum of opposition and, as he had anticipated, the city was abandoned to him without a battle, August 18, 1846. After proclaiming all New Mexico a part of the United States, he set out with a small force for California, leaving the greater part of his troops at Santa Fe with orders to proceed southward under the command of Colonel A. W. Doniphan to jom Taylor in Mexico. The garrison left at Santa Fe was soon reinforced by the arrival of a regiment from Missouri under Colonel Sterling Price, who took command. In 1847 Price had to put down a small revolt, but his adventures were slight in comparison with those of Doniphan and Kearny. The former, after weeks of wandering and much irregular warfare, established connections with Taylor's right wing; the latter arrived in southern California in time to bear the brunt of the fighting in that area, and to carry on an interesting dispute with the

American officers who had preceded him as to which was in supreme command.

Certainly California had no dearth of conquerors. On the eve of the war an officer of the United States **Conquest of California** Army, John C. Frémont, who was already famed as the "Pathfinder of the West," had led a party of explorers across the Sierra Nevada into California, only to be warned out by the Mexican authorities. At first Frémont was defiant and refused to go, but at length he withdrew northward to Oregon, although slowly and with obvious reluctance. Here he was overtaken by a dispatch-bearer from Washington, A. H. Gillespie, who had already delivered messages to Commodore J. D. Sloat, commander of the American squadron in California waters, and to T. O. Larkin, the American consul at Monterey. All these documents were subsequently published, and they sound harmless enough; but something persuaded Frémont to advance once more into California. At about this same time a number of Americans who resided in the Sacramento Valley became excited by rumors that they were to be driven out, and precipitated the so-called "Bear Flag Revolution" at Sonoma (June 14, 1846). They asked Frémont to lead them, but this he refused to do until he learned, some two weeks later, that war had been declared between the United States and Mexico. He then enlisted most of the revolters in a "California battalion," and continued his advance. On July 7 Commodore Sloat hoisted the American flag over Monterey and proclaimed the annexation of California to the United States. Soon afterward Sloat was succeeded by Commodore R. F. Stockton, whose instructions gave him authority over "the forces and operations on shore." Stockton accepted Frémont as his subordinate, and even appointed him military governor of California. But Kearny, who after some sharp skirmishes with the Californians, had appeared on the scene, claimed that he was rightfully in command and had documents to prove it. Kearny finally forced Stockton and Frémont to

accede to his authority, and took the latter back to Washington virtually a prisoner. Presently a court-martial found the Pathfinder guilty of insubordination and ordered him dismissed from the army, and although pardoned by the President he resigned his commission.

Thus, long before Mexico City had fallen, the United States was in possession of the territory Polk had sought to **Treaty of** purchase before the war began. **Guadalupe** Indeed, while Scott was on his **Hidalgo** way from Vera Cruz to the Mexican capital, he was joined by Nicholas P. Trist, an employee of the state department whom the President had authorized to open negotiations for peace on terms only a little less generous than those once offered through Slidell. As a diplomat Trist left much to be desired, and his sole accomplishment up to the time Mexico City was taken was a contribution of ten thousand dollars to Santa Anna, the price demanded by the wily Mexican for his co-operation, something that failed to materialize. Polk was so incensed by the failure of his emissary that he deprived him of all authority and ordered him to return to the United States. But Trist cheerfully disregarded the President's instructions, and, with the war finally won, negotiated the treaty of Guadalupe Hidalgo, February 2, 1848. By its terms Mexico accepted the Rio Grande boundary, and ceded New Mexico and California, including all the territory that lay between them, to the United States. The United States, in return, made a cash payment of fifteen million dollars to Mexico, and agreed to the cancellation of all claims due from Mexico to American citizens, claims which the United States government itself now undertook to satisfy to the extent of three and a quarter million dollars. It was an expensive peace, considering that the United States was in position to demand what it liked, but Polk accepted it, and sent the treaty to the Senate, where it was ratified by a vote of 38 to 14. Among those who voted against the treaty was Daniel Webster, who was

Mormon emigrants, led by Joseph Smith and then Brigham Young, settled finally at Salt Lake, Utah, in 1847. View of the city engraved from a photograph for *Harper's Weekly,* July, 1857.

opposed to the addition of any foreign territory, and E. A. Hannigan of Indiana, who believed that the United States should annex all of Mexico. A majority of the members of both parties voted for the treaty.

It was the irony of fate that the treaty added to the United States a colony of religious refugees who had sought to put persecution behind them **The Mormons** by crossing the American border into Mexico. The Mormons had originated in western New York during the late eighteen-twenties when that region was still sparsely settled. The prophet of the new religion, Joseph Smith, proclaimed doctrines that differed only a little from the numerous other Christian sects that during this same period were springing up all along the frontier. His "Church of Jesus Christ of the Latter Day Saints" accepted the teachings of the Bible, but received added inspiration from the *Book of Mormon,* which had been revealed to Smith in a miraculous fashion, and from other "revelations" which came to him from time to time. The chief distinction of the church was its centralized economic life, which contrasted markedly

with the "rugged individualism" of the ordinary frontiersmen. Indeed, the close cooperation of the Mormons gave them a certain economic advantage over their neighbors that was resented far more than their religious idiosyncrasies. Retreating before this opposition, the Mormons first made Kirtland, Ohio, their residence, then Independence, Missouri, then a station they called "Far West" in Clay County, Missouri, then Nauvoo, Illinois, a small city on the left bank of the Mississippi River nearly opposite the mouth of the Des Moines. At Nauvoo the Mormons prospered quite consistently until 1844, when Smith announced himself a candidate for the office of President of the United States. This annoyed both Whigs and Democrats, for each party had counted on Mormon support, and the customary outbreak of antagonism was soon in evidence. To add to the confusion, there was talk of polygamy among the Mormon leaders, and schism rent the church. Smith was arrested, then taken from jail by a mob and shot. His successor, Brigham Young, decided, reasonably enough, that the only hope of peace for the Mormons lay outside the boundaries of the United States.

The Mormon migration is one of the outstanding episodes of American frontier history. **Migration to Utah** During the spring and summer of 1846, about twelve thousand of the Mormons, four fifths of their total membership, left their homes, including such of their property as they were unable to take with them, and crossed through Iowa to the Council Bluffs, a place-name then given to the region on both sides of the Missouri River adjacent to the present city of Omaha. Early in 1847 Young and a small company of his associates pushed on farther west to "spy out the land," and determined on the Great Salt Lake basin as the best available site for the colony they meant to establish. In September, 1847, the first detachment arrived, 1553 in number, and others followed with such rapidity that by 1850 the Salt Lake settlement numbered over eleven thousand. The "Mormon Trail" usually followed the north bank of the Platte River, continued westward through what is now Wyoming to South Pass, then turned southward to the Great Salt Lake. It was not so long or so difficult as either the Oregon or the California Trail, but the endurance of Mormon emigrants was nevertheless severely taxed, and the large volume of the migration made necessary the most systematic organization. Salt Lake City grew with astonishing rapidity, and soon became, to the very great profit of the Mormons, a convenient stopping-point on the way to California. The success of the colony, however, was due primarily to the sound judgment and the extraordinary executive ability of its leader, Brigham Young.

He it was who planned the migration, supervised the settlement of the newcomers, introduced irrigation, and in many other ways warded off the misfortunes that might otherwise have befallen so large a company in so difficult an environment. His dictatorship was virtually unquestioned.

Polk's policy of expansion was carried through well before his term of office was over, and without a serious **Polk's** failure. He obtained all of **achievement** Oregon to which he could reasonably lay claim, insured the permanence of the annexation of Texas, and took one third of the territory of Mexico in order to advance the boundary of the United States to the Pacific in the Far Southwest, as it had already been advanced in the Far Northwest. Important settlements had been made in every section of the new acquisitions — in Oregon, in California, in New Mexico, and, thanks to the Mormon migration, in what was soon to be known as Utah. Well-defined trails crossed the continent to the Southwest, to the Northwest, and in between. Much of the western country was still regarded as uninhabitable, but such guides as Kit Carson, who accompanied Frémont on some of his explorations and showed Kearny the way from Santa Fe to California, and Jim Bridger, who helped Brigham Young locate the Great Salt Lake basin, were fast dispelling its mysteries. Polk was a man of mediocre ability somewhat lacking in imagination, but by his persistence in the face of obstacles, and by his unconcern for other people's scruples, he had accomplished a work in which many an abler man might have failed.

Bibliography

Three general histories of the frontier, not previously cited, which cover in considerable detail the various aspects of "manifest destiny," are D. E. Clark, *The West in American History* (1937); R. E. Riegel, *America Moves West* (1930, new ed., 1947); and E. Douglas Branch, *Westward* (1930). Paxson, *History of the American Frontier*, and Billington, *Westward Expansion*, are similarly useful. A. K. Weinberg, *Manifest Destiny* (1935), traces American expansionism from its earliest beginnings. G. P. Garrison, *Westward Extension* (1906); and W. E. Dodd, *Expansion and Conflict* (1915), are good period studies. Hafen and Rister, *Western America;* and Goodwin, *The Trans-Mississippi West*, give careful attention to the subjects discussed in this chapter. Bernard De Voto, *The Year of Decision, 1846* (1943), besides being dramatic and exciting, is broader in scope than the title indicates. T. M. Marshall, *A History of the Western Boundary of the Louisiana Purchase, 1819–1841* (1914), touches many aspects of western expansion. W. C. Macleod, *The American Indian Frontier* (1928), views the subject from the Indian angle.

On New Mexico and the Santa Fe trail, Josiah Gregg, *Commerce of the Prairies: or, The Journal of a Santa Fe Trader* (1844), is a classic. For a popular secondary account, see R. L. Duffus, *The Santa Fe Trail* (1930). There is material on the pre-American period in three books by H. E. Bolton, *The Spanish Borderlands* (1921); *Rim of Christendom* (1936); and *The Padre on Horseback* (1932).

There is a wealth of literature on Oregon and the Pacific Northwest. Much background material can be found in H. M. Chittenden, *The American Fur Trade of the Far West* (3 vols., 1902). Joseph Schafer, *A History of the Pacific Northwest* (1918); and O. O. Winther, *The Great Northwest* (1947), furnish excellent guides to the history of the section. Katharine Coman, *Economic Beginnings of the Far West* (2 vols., 1912), is interesting and informative. Francis Parkman, *The California and Oregon Trail* (1849), has gone through innumerable editions under a shorter title, *The Oregon Trail*, and is as authentic as it is interesting. More recent accounts are M. C. Jacobs, *Winning Oregon* (1938); and W. J. Ghent,

The Road to Oregon (1929). Useful biographies are C. M. Drury, *Marcus Whitman, M. D.* (1937); K. W. Porter, *John Jacob Astor, Business Man* (2 vols., 1931); F. V. Holman, *Dr. John McLoughlin, The Father of Oregon* (1907).

California before the Forty-Niners is well portrayed in C. E. Chapman, *A History of California: The Spanish Period* (1921). Mention should also be made of the voluminous writings of H. H. Bancroft, whose *History of California* (7 vols., 1884–1890) is but a fraction of his total output. Bancroft's interest in western history spread from California to the regions north, east, and south of it. Much of his writing was done for him by subordinates, and it is unequal in value. His interesting career is well portrayed in J. W. Caughey, *Hubert Howe Bancroft, Historian of the West* (1946). T. H. Hittell, *History of California* (4 vols., 1885–97); and Zoeth S. Eldredge, *History of California* (5 vols., 1915), are also extremely detailed, especially on the early period. Other useful volumes include R. G. Cleland, *From Wilderness to Empire: A History of California, 1542–1900* (1944); J. W. Caughey, *California* (1940); Irene Paden, *The Wake of the Prairie Schooner* (1943); J. H. Kemble, *The Panama Route, 1848–1869* (1943); Julian Dana, *Sutter of California* (1936); Vincent Carosso, *The California Wine Industry, 1830–1895* (1951).

The historians of Texas have also been busy. R. N. Richardson, *Texas, The Lone Star State* (1943), is an interesting general account. W. R. Hogan, *The Texas Republic* (1946), is good, especially on social and economic history. N. W. Stephenson, *Texas and the Mexican War* (1921), covers the subject for the *Chronicles of America* series. On the diplomatic side, there are several elaborate studies, G. L. Rives, *The United States and Mexico, 1821–1848* (2 vols., 1913); Justin H. Smith, *The Annexation of Texas* (1911); Jesse S. Reeves, *American Diplomacy under Tyler and Polk* (1907); and J. W. Schmitz, *Texas Statecraft, 1836–1845* (1941). A special phase of the subject is treated in E. D. Adams, *British Interests and Activities in Texas, 1838–1846* (1910). Jim Dan Hill, *The Texas Navy* (1937), explores a little known subject.

On the Mexican War, Justin H. Smith, *The*

War with Mexico (2 vols., 1919), is at pains to show that the United States was not wholly to blame for the outbreak of hostilities. R. S. Henry, *The Story of the Mexican War* (1950); and A. H. Bill, *Rehearsal for Conflict: The War with Mexico, 1846–1848* (1947), are readable and objective accounts. E. J. McCormac, *James K. Polk* (1922), is a model biography of the war President, but the careful student will wish to examine also *The Diary of James K. Polk during his Presidency, 1845 to 1849*, edited by M. M. Quaife (4 vols., 1910). Biographies of value include Holman Hamilton, *Zachary Taylor* (1941); Brainerd Dyer, *Zachary Taylor* (1946); C. W. Elliott, *Winfield Scott* (1937); Allan Nevins, *Frémont, The West's Greatest Adventurer* (2 vols., 1928), and *Frémont, Pathmarker of the West* (1939); L. M. Sears, *John Slidell* (1925).

On Utah and the Mormons Nels Anderson, *Desert Saints: The Mormon Frontier in Utah* (1942), is both interesting and impartial. An earlier account, not always friendly to the Mormons, is W. A. Linn, *The Story of the Mormons* (1902). M. R. Werner, *Brigham Young* (1930); and Fawn M. Brodie, *No Man Knows my History; The Life of Joseph Smith, the Mormon Prophet* (1945), are entertaining biographies of the great Mormon leaders. L. H. Creer, *The Founding of an Empire: The Exploration and Colonization of Utah, 1776–1856* (1947), is meticulous and detailed. G. O. Larson, *Prelude to the Kingdom: Mormon Desert Conquest, A Chapter in American Cooperative Experience* (1947), is a laudatory view.

27

The Compromise of 1850

Legislation under Polk — The debate over slavery expansion — The Wilmot Proviso — Plans of compromise — Election of 1848 — The Free-Soil Party — Gold in California — The "Forty-Niners" — Taylor and state sovereignty — The Compromise of 1850 — Northern opinion on the Compromise — Southern opinion — Election of 1852

POLK's main concern as President was expansion, but during the first half of his administration he was able to redeem two of his party's pledges that had to do primarily with domestic affairs. The first of these was the enactment of a lower tariff than the measure Clay had persuaded Tyler to accept in 1842. Polk's Secretary of the Treasury, Robert J. Walker of Mississippi, had so much to do with the framing of the new law that it became known as the Walker Tariff. It met the customary opposition from the industrial interests in New England and the middle Atlantic states, but it was warmly supported in the South and in the West, passed both houses of Congress with comfortable majorities, and was signed by the President, July 30, 1846. Walker was deeply impressed with the success Great Britain was having in abandoning protection, and looked forward confidently to a world movement for free trade. The tariff which bore his name, however, proved to be an excellent revenue measure, for it produced on an average nearly forty per cent greater receipts than the Whig Tariff of 1842. The second of the Democratic pledges which Polk carried through was the re-establishment by act of Congress, signed August 6, 1846, of the independent, or subtreasury, system that had

Legislation under Polk

been discontinued early in the preceding administration. Not until the time of the Civil War did the national government abandon its policy of complete aloofness from the banking business, and the subtreasury system as a means of handling treasury receipts continued in force until the passage of the Federal Reserve Act in 1913.

The outbreak of the Mexican War soon provided the country with a much more exciting issue than either the tariff or the subtreasury. It was obvious that the success of the United States in the war would mean the acquisition of more territory; the administration made not the slightest pretense to the contrary. Naturally, therefore, the question was raised, Should slavery be permitted to expand into the territory soon to be acquired? The anti-slavery forces were convinced that only for this express purpose had the war been precipitated; the southern slaveholders, in spite of their success in annexing Texas, were not yet satisfied. As Lowell wrote,

The debate over slavery expansion

> They just want this Californy,
> So's to lug new slave states in.

When in August, 1846, Polk asked Congress to appropriate two million dollars to be used in purchasing territory from Mexico, David

Wilmot, an anti-slavery Democrat from Pennsylvania, introduced in the House a resolution that "as an express and fundamental condition" to any such acquisition "neither slavery nor involuntary servitude shall ever exist in any part of said territory." After heated debate the House passed the resolution, but the Senate refused to concur.

The "Wilmot Proviso," as it came universally to be called, was debated, not only **The Wilmot** in Congress, where for years it **Proviso** was proposed as an amendment to any relevant measure, but with equal ardor throughout the country. In the North, Wilmot Proviso Leagues were organized to work for the exclusion of slavery from all further territorial acquisitions; in the South, mass meetings were held to denounce the Northerners for the stand they were taking. The issue was one which tended to become strictly sectional; party lines had nothing to do with it. Northern anti-slavery men maintained that Congress was legally competent to exclude slavery from the territories of the United States, and should exercise its right at once. Southern extremists took the opposite view, and held that the Constitution, because it recognized and protected slavery in some of the states, must be construed to protect slavery also in the territories, for otherwise the property rights of slave-owners would be discriminated against in a region which was the joint possession of all the states. According to this argument neither Congress, nor a territorial legislature that derived its authority from Congress, had any right to interfere with slavery in any territory of the United States. Congress should therefore keep hands off, and slave-owners should be permitted to take their slaves at will into any of the territories.

There were many, however, who were ready to compromise. One such group ac- **Plans of** cepted the doctrine of "squatter **compromise** sovereignty" that Lewis Cass of Michigan had first suggested, but that came later to be intimately associated with the name of Stephen A. Douglas of Illinois, who

renamed it "popular sovereignty." Adherents of this theory argued that the people of a territory had the right to decide for themselves whether the territory should be free or slave, and that Congress should concede that privilege to whatever new territories it might create. Still another group had no constitutional argument, but pointed merely to the practical wisdom of dividing the acquired territory between the slave states and the free states. This could be done conveniently, and with good historical precedent, by extending the line of the Missouri Compromise to the Pacific.

But evidence accumulated, month by month and year by year, that the North as a section was determined to prevent the expansion of slavery. Practically every northern legislature urged Congress to prohibit slavery in the territories; some of them urged also that slavery be abolished in the District of Columbia; some even went so far as to prohibit state officials from aiding in the return of fugitive slaves. At the same time the South, stung by the implication in the northern attitude that slavery was morally wrong, and fearful that the increasing weight of the North in the Union might lead to an attack on slavery where it already existed, was equally determined that slavery should expand. Southern fears were not wholly without foundation. In population the North was drawing farther and farther away from the South, while unless new territory open to slavery could be acquired, the balance of the sections in the Senate would soon be broken. Iowa and Wisconsin, admitted in 1846 and 1848, respectively, would serve as numerical offsets to Florida and Texas, admitted in 1845, but Minnesota could not long be held out of the Union, and the Oregon country offered a still further opportunity for the creation of new free states. Southern members of Congress, in a vain attempt to extend the Missouri Compromise line to the Pacific, held up the organization of a territorial government in Oregon for two years, but were at length compelled to capitulate, and Oregon became

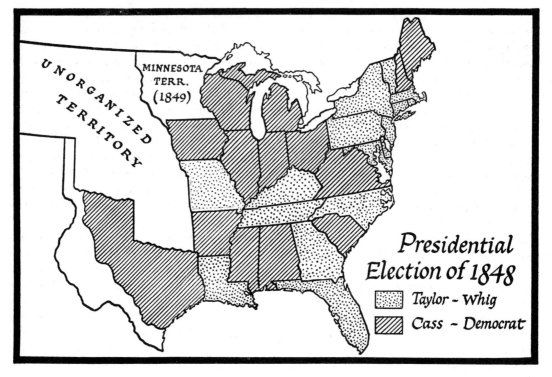

Presidential
Election of 1848

▨ Taylor - Whig

▧ Cass - Democrat

a free territory in 1848, with no pledges given. Thereafter threats of secession were made with ever-increasing boldness.

The debate on the Wilmot Proviso was interrupted to some extent by the election **Election of 1848** of 1848. Both parties were threatened with disruption by the one issue in which the country seemed genuinely interested. For the Democrats to come out openly in favor of the expansion of slavery meant the alienation of a large northern element in the party; for the Whigs to embrace the free-soil doctrine meant for them equally serious losses in the South. Moreover, many sincere patriots in both parties were alarmed at the rapid deepening of the sectional line of cleavage between North and South, and they feared for the safety of the Union if the two major parties lost their national character and became sectional. It was not merely expediency that led both Whigs and Democrats to avoid the slavery issue in the campaign of 1848; it was also the sincere desire on the part of their most influential leaders to keep the Union intact. The Democrats, therefore, made no reference in their platform to the status of slavery in the territory acquired from Mexico, and turned to the North for their presidential candidate, Lewis Cass of Michigan. The Whigs, even more cautious, adopted no platform, and presented as their candidate General Zachary Taylor, the "hero of Buena Vista," who by a lucky chance happened to be from Louisiana, and owned over a hundred slaves. Before his Mexican exploits brought him into the limelight, General Taylor had apparently taken no interest in politics, and his willingness to accept the Whig nomination was at first conditioned upon his being left free to maintain his independence of parties. Later, however, under pressure from the politicians, he admitted that he was a "Whig, but not an ultra Whig." For second place on their ticket the Whigs chose Millard Fillmore, an obscure politician from western New York.

However well-intentioned the actions of the old party leaders may have been, **Agitation for a third party** the situation that they created called insistently for the formation of a new third party. All anti-slavery men, whether outright abolitionists, or moderates who would be content to prevent the expansion of slavery, could agree to the Wilmot Proviso, which both Democrats and Whigs had so completely ignored. It seemed only reasonable, therefore, that with this as their platform the various dissatisfied groups should join forces. Two abolitionist candidates were early in the field, John P. Hale of New Hampshire, whom the Liberty Party had nominated in 1847, and Gerrit Smith of New York, the choice of a somewhat visionary "Liberty League." At the other extreme was the faction of New York Democrats once known as "Loco-Focos," but now generally termed "Barnburners," because in their determination to overcome all opposition they were willing, some said, to imitate the Dutchman who burned down his barn to get rid of the rats in it. The Barnburners were the devoted followers of Martin Van Buren, whose defeat by Polk for the Democratic nomination in 1844 they had never been able to forgive. Since Van Buren's failure had been due chiefly to his refusal to countenance the annexation of Texas, he and his followers were regarded, more or less correctly, as the element in the Democratic Party most opposed to the expansion of slavery. During the Polk administration the Barnburners were denied all patronage favors, and the federal offices in New York went instead to the opposing faction, or "Hunkers," so called because of their notorious "hunkering" after office. When the Democratic National Convention of 1848 assembled, the Barnburners and the Hunkers sent contesting delegations. The convention, although essentially friendly to the Hunkers, sought to compromise by dividing the vote of the state between the two factions, but this offer was indignantly rejected by the Barnburners, who returned home to hold a convention of their own, and to nominate their leader, Martin Van Buren, for the Presidency. Obviously, if the abolitionists and the Barnburners could unite, a strong third party could be formed.

The effort was made at a convention held in Buffalo, August 9, 1848, and presided over by Charles Francis Adams, the **The Free-son of ex-President John Quincy Soil Party** Adams. The convention adopted a ringing set of resolutions which insisted that "there must be no more compromise with slavery," that "the soil of our extensive domains" must be "ever kept free for the hardy pioneers of our own land, and the oppressed and banished of other lands," and that the free grant of land "to actual settlers, in consideration of the expenses they incur in making settlements in the wilderness . . . is a wise and just measure of public policy." The clear intent of the platform was to emphasize the contest between the slaveholder and the small free farmer for the lands of the West. There was no lack of moral indignation against slavery, but the strength of the economic appeal, particularly among the working classes of the East, whose interest in free lands was tremendously accentuated by the panic of 1837, was not overlooked. As a final resolve the convention voted to "inscribe on our banner 'Free Soil, Free Speech, Free Labor and Free Men,'" and the new party became known, accordingly, as the "Free-Soil" Party. The nomination of Martin Van Buren over John P. Hale was a further gesture in the direction of expediency, for Van Buren's opposition to slavery was of the most moderate variety. For Vice-President, however, Charles Francis Adams was named, and the ticket received the enthusiastic support of practically all the anti-slavery men.

The strength of the Free-Soil movement was revealed when the election returns came in. The new party had polled nearly three hundred thousand votes, had won the balance of power in a dozen states, and, for good or ill, had drawn enough votes from the Democratic column in New York to throw that state, and the election, to Taylor. The thirteen Free-Soilers chosen to the National House of Representatives were a power to be reckoned with, for no party had a majority in that branch of Congress. In the Senate, which was Democratic, John P. Hale already represented New Hampshire, and the legislature of Ohio sent Salmon P. Chase, whose anti-slavery views were almost equally radical, to join him. The one lesson that the election seemed to teach was that the effort to avoid the slavery issue could not long be successful.

Nor was it. The nation was at last face to face with the necessity of deciding upon the status of slavery in the territory acquired from Mexico. Already the unreasonable delay of Congress in providing civil government for the regions annexed was causing difficulty. In California and New Mexico the military conquerors, under authority of the President of the United States as commander-in-chief of the army, kept order and, with the assistance of the former Mexican *alcaldes*, or local magistrates, carried on the most essential of the peace-time duties of government. But the arrangement was extremely unsatisfactory: land titles were in dispute, and the legality of any important action was open to question. The Mormons,

by means of their closely knit church organization, were adequately governed, but the existence of this peculiar frontier theocracy was hardly compatible, to say the least, with the American democratic tradition.

The discovery of gold in California and the subsequent "gold-rush" introduced a new element into the situation. **Gold in** Early in 1848, James Marshall, **California** a carpenter whom Sutter had employed to construct a sawmill not far from his fort, found flakes of gold in the mill-race, and immediately reported the fact to his employer. Sutter tried to keep the news from spreading, for he feared the effect of a gold-rush upon his industries, and believed that the quantity of gold must be small. His efforts were unavailing, however, and by the end of the summer the whole world knew that there was gold — much gold — in California. Polk himself, in his annual message to Congress, December, 1848, confirmed the news. Long before this, Californians had dropped whatever work they were doing and rushed to the gold-fields. They were speedily joined by other residents of the Far West, by sailors who deserted their ships in San Francisco Bay, and even by pioneers who had heard the news on their way to Oregon and had "branched off" on

"*The Modern Colossus,* 8th Wonder of the World," a cartoon of 1848, shows Van Buren, the Free Soiler, trying to bridge the gap between the two old parties.

the California Trail. While the "free gold" lasted, anyone, however inexperienced, with only a pick, a shovel, and a wash-pan as tools, could become a successful miner. Claims were staked out, informal records were made, and rules of ownership based upon common sense rather than upon legal precedents were agreed upon.

Comparative peace reigned in the "diggings" until the inrush of the "Forty-Niners" The "Forty-Niners" made good claims scarce. Then everything was changed. Thousands of men in every part of the United States left for California at the earliest possible opportunity. Those who could not afford to do otherwise took the long journey overland by covered wagon; others took ship around Cape Horn; still others went expensively and with great danger to their health by way of the Isthmus of Panama. Not the United States alone, but the whole world caught the gold-fever, and a huge polyglot population descended upon California. San Francisco, a city of tents and shacks, grew prodigiously; burned down, and grew again. To handle so bewildering a situation, the temporary military government was totally inadequate. Men went armed as a matter of course, fatal shootings were common and rarely investigated, voluntary associations kept what order they could. The need of an adequate and authoritative civil government was obvious, and was keenly felt.

It devolved naturally upon the new President, Zachary Taylor (1784–1850), to take the initiative in seeking a solution for this pressing problem. Taylor was a Virginian by birth, but he grew to manhood in frontier Kentucky, whither, as an infant, he had accompanied his father on the customary move to the West. Early in his twenties he was commissioned a lieutenant in the United States Army, and for forty years before his election to the Presidency he was a soldier. He had fought with vigor in the War of 1812, the Black Hawk War, and the Seminole War, as well as in the war with Mexico. He was not a great tactician, as his record in the Mexican War abundantly proved, but he was honest and forthright, well accustomed to meeting emergencies, and unembarrassed by the necessity of making a sudden decision. As President, he had a somewhat exaggerated opinion of the confidence that the nation reposed in him, and showed little respect for the opinions of Henry Clay, who had long since come to identify the Whig Party with himself. Taylor's Louisiana residence was acquired in 1840 when the General, as commander of the Department of the Southwest, had purchased a sugar plantation near Baton Rouge.

With reference to the problem of government in the newly acquired territory Taylor was ready to act. His solution Taylor and was to encourage the organiza- state tion of state governments that sovereignty would decide for themselves on the question of slavery, and with this end in view he urged both the Californians and the New Mexicans to draw up state constitutions at once and to seek admission to the Union. This advice the Californians promptly followed. Indeed, by the end of 1849 they had not only drawn up a constitution, but they had also elected a full quota of state officers, who, with the consent of the military governor, had taken over the government of the self-created "state." To the great chagrin of pro-slavery politicians, the California constitution definitely excluded slavery. The New Mexicans, with less reason for haste, were not ready with their constitution until May, 1850, but when it appeared, the chagrin of the pro-slavery men was still greater, for New Mexico, like California, proposed to enter the Union as a free state. Even the Mormons drew up an anti-slavery constitution for a proposed state of Deseret, and with Brigham Young as their duly elected governor applied for admission to the Union.

When, in December, 1849, Congress assembled for the first time after Taylor's inauguration and listened to Threats of the President's recommenda- secession tion that California and New Mexico be promptly admitted, regardless of what their

SAN FRANCISCO, 1847. View "from the back hill" by Hutton.

"THE ROCKET LINE." Detail from a lithograph, "The Way They Go," 1849, cartooning Easterners setting out for California by every conceivable means.

PACKET SHIP FOR THE GOLD REGION. Ship notice, New Bedford, Mass., October, 1849.

constitutions might say on slavery, the anger and resentment of the southern extremists knew no bounds. Said Robert Toombs of Georgia:

I do not hesitate to avow before this House and the country, and in the presence of the living God, that if by your legislation you seek to drive us from the territories of California and New Mexico, purchased by the common blood and treasure of the whole people, and to abolish slavery in this District, thereby attempting to fix a national degradation upon half the states of this Confederacy, *I am for disunion.*

Many genuine patriots, both Northerners and Southerners, on listening to such outbursts felt grave doubt for the safety of the Union.

Possibly the President might better have consulted Congress before committing himself so freely. Had he lived, however, there is some reason to believe that his capacity

for decisive action might have preserved the Union, even without the compromise measures of 1850, some of which he would doubtless have refused to sign. On one occasion, when it was intimated that the Texans might seek by force to maintain their claims to the upper Rio Grande boundary, and so add materially to the territory open to slavery, the President announced that if any such effort were made he would take the field in person at the head of the United States Army to prevent it.

The Thirty-First Congress was one of the ablest that had ever been chosen. This was in part due to the fact that it was a kind of meeting-point of two generations. In it sat the three great statesmen of the preceding era: Daniel Webster, John C. Calhoun, and Henry Clay. But its roster contained also the names of many men whose careers were before them, such as Salmon P. Chase,

SAN FRANCISCO, 1851. View from Telegraph Hill, after Bainbridge and Casilear.

The Gold Rush to California was one of the most exciting episodes of all American history. As Seward observed, in the spring of 1849 the world seemed to be divided into two classes — "those who are going to California in search of gold, and those going to Washington in quest of office." San Francisco became a city overnight, mining camps rose and fell, all to the theme song of the gold seekers:

We'll scrape the mountains clean, old girl, we'll drain the rivers dry.
We're off to Californy. Susannah, don't you cry!
Oh, Susannah, don't you cry for me!
I'm off to Californy with my wash-pan on my knee.

A FORTY-NINER. Watercolor drawing by John W. Audubon, 1849.

AT THE DIGGINGS. Illustration from *Ballou's Pictorial Drawing-Room Companion*, May 3, 1856.

Zachary Taylor

TWELFTH PRESIDENT of the United States, Taylor of Louisiana won renown as a general in the War with Mexico. His interest in politics was so slight that he had never in his life voted for President, but the Whigs decided nevertheless to capitalize on his popularity and nominated him in 1848. Portrait by John Vanderlyn.

William H. Seward, Thaddeus Stevens, Stephen A. Douglas, Jefferson Davis, Alexander H. Stephens, and Robert Toombs. That so distinguished a group would sit idly by while a military hero with no experience in politics settled offhand the gravest problem, perhaps, that had ever confronted the nation was more than could be expected. Congress proposed to have a hand in the matter, and all eyes turned naturally to the aged Henry Clay, whose reputation as a compromiser was justly great. Throughout his life he had never held so tenaciously to any principle that under sufficient pressure he had found himself unable to give it up.

It is not fair, however, to assign the whole credit for the Compromise of 1850 **The** to Henry Clay. Other men, **Compromise** notably Stephen A. Douglas, **of 1850** had an important part in its making, and during the long debate over the Wilmot Proviso a multitude of political theorists had set forth the various possibilities of compromise. It was Clay, however, who presented to the Senate the elaborate series of resolutions that was to form the

basis of compromise, and it was Clay's well-established reputation that won for them an instant hearing. The resolutions sensibly did not stop with the question of slavery extension, but included also all the other phases of the slavery problem with which the public mind was vexed. Clay hoped that his plan would restore "the peace, concord, and harmony of the Union" for another thirty years, the length of time that the Missouri Compromise had lasted. On January 29, 1850, he asked the Senate to consider the following suggestions:

1. Permit California to enter the Union as a free state.
2. Establish territorial governments without any restriction as to slavery in the rest of the territory acquired from Mexico.
3. Set reasonable limits to the western boundary of Texas.
4. Assume the public debt of Texas contracted prior to annexation, on condition that Texas relinquish her claim to any part of New Mexico.
5. Agree that slavery in the District of Columbia may not be abolished without the consent of Maryland, and of the people of the district, and without just compensation to the owners of slaves.
6. Prohibit the slave trade in the District of Columbia.
7. Enact a more stringent fugitive slave law.
8. Assert that Congress has no power to interfere with the slave trade between the states.

The debate that these resolutions precipitated in the United States Senate ranks justly as one of the greatest in American legislative history. Clay led off in defense of the Compromise with a speech which for the most part was eminently conciliatory. He pointed out that the admission of California under the free-state constitution already proposed was entirely in line with historical precedent and could scarcely be avoided. He urged that the organization of territorial governments in the rest of the territory acquired from Mexico be no longer delayed by insistence on the Wilmot Proviso, and reminded the North that it could count on "what is worth a thousand Wilmot provisos.

You have got Nature itself on your side."
As for the other provisions, they offered a
sensible solution of the Texas boundary dispute, they made balanced concessions to
both sides in dealing with slavery in the
District of Columbia, and they assured the
South that the rights of slave-owners should
no longer be threatened, either by the inadequacy of the present laws for the rendition
of fugitive slaves, or by the continued threat
of congressional interference with the domestic slave trade. Possibly because so much
of the Compromise was favorable to the
North, possibly because he was himself from
the upper South, where the problem was
most acute, Clay was particularly outspoken
as to the necessity of a stricter fugitive slave
law. Upon this subject he declared that he
was ready to "go with the senator from the
South who goes furthest." On the whole,
however, his speech was less an exposition of
the provisions of the Compromise than an
appeal to Congress and the country to quiet
the clamor over slavery, and thus to save the
nation from the unnecessary chaos of civil
war.

Clay's appeal was insufficient, however, to
win over the southern extremists. John C.
Calhoun, so old and ill that his
Southern views on the Compromise address against the Compromise
had to be read to the Senate by
a colleague, Senator Mason of Virginia, recited the repeated encroachments of the North
upon the South, and declared that the admission of California would serve notice that the
North intended to destroy "irretrievably the
equilibrium between the two sections." In
a posthumous essay he proposed that two
Presidents should be elected, one from the
North and one from the South, each with a
veto on congressional legislation, but his
address on the Compromise asked only that
a constitutional amendment be submitted
"which will restore to the South, in substance, the power she possessed of protecting
herself before the equilibrium between the
two sections was destroyed by the action of
this government." This vague proposal,
while courteously received by the other

southern extremists, left them unsatisfied.
Most of them believed in the doctrine of non-
intervention, according to which all the property of emigrants to new territories, including their slave property, was entitled to
equal protection; but Jefferson Davis probably reflected their sentiments accurately
when he announced his willingness to "agree
to the drawing of a line of 36° 30′ through
the territories acquired from Mexico, with
the condition that in the same degree as
slavery is prohibited north of that line, it
shall be permitted to enter south of the
line."

The ablest northern defender of the Compromise was Daniel Webster, whose "Seventh of March speech" on the **Northern**
subject ranks among the great- **views**
est of American orations. Webster, like
Clay, appealed to the North to forego its
insistence on the Wilmot Proviso. By the
"law of nature," he maintained, it was
settled forever, "with a strength beyond all
terms of human enactment, that slavery
cannot exist in California or New Mexico.
... I would not take pains uselessly to reaf-
firm an ordinance of nature, nor to re-enact
the will of God. I would put in no Wilmot
Proviso for the mere purpose of a taunt or
reproach." Webster also denounced the abolitionists for the furor they were creating
throughout the country, and conceded that
"the injunction of the Constitution for the
delivery of fugitive slaves" had not been
properly obeyed. He wished above all else
to save the Union. Peaceable secession he
branded as a delusion:

Sir, he who sees these states, now revolving in
harmony around a common center and expects
them to quit their places and fly off without con-
vulsion, may look the next hour to see the heav-
enly bodies rush from their spheres, and jostle
against each other in the realms of space, without
causing the wreck of the universe.

His peroration closed with a solemn charge:

Never did there devolve on any generation of
men higher trusts than now devolve upon us for
the preservation of this constitution, and the har-

mony and peace of all who are destined to live under it. Let us make our generation one of the strongest and brightest links in that golden chain which is destined, I fondly believe, to grapple the people of all the states to this Constitution for ages to come.

If Clay was unable to win over the southern extremists to the compromise, Webster was no more successful with those of the North. Probably the speech of William H. Seward, the young Senator from New York, best represents the northern opposition to the Compromise. Seward was a Whig, but his views on slavery were as radical as those of many Free-Soilers. "Slavery can be limited to its present bounds," he told an audience in 1848, "it can be ameliorated; it can and must be abolished, and you and I can and must do it." In his speech on the Compromise he urged the immediate admission of California, and objected strenuously to the delays which came from connecting this question with any other. He charged, also, that the failure of the existing Fugitive Slave Law was not due to any fault of the law, but rather to a hostile public sentiment in the North, something that a more drastic

law would tend only to aggravate. He professed to believe, in spite of Webster's argument, that slavery might actually be transplanted to New Mexico, and he invoked "a higher law than the Constitution" as the authority of Congress to prevent so great a calamity. "The territory is a part, no inconsiderable part, of the common heritage of mankind, bestowed upon them by the creator of the universe. We are his stewards, and must so discharge our trust as to secure in the highest attainable degree their happiness." Emancipation he held to be inevitable and near, and its peaceful consummation would be made more difficult if new laws for the strengthening of slavery should be passed. Unwarrantedly optimistic, he declared that "there will be no disunion and no secession."

Meantime, majority sentiment throughout the country began to assert itself unmistakably in favor of some sort of compromise. Business men, thanks to the flow of gold from California and the increasing demand for railways, enjoyed a degree of prosperity unparalleled since the panic of 1837. Farmers benefited materially from the strong foreign

Sentiment for the Compromise

Compromise on California was the result of heated debate in Congress. Henry Clay is shown here addressing the Senate on February 5, 1850. Engraved from a painting by P. F. Rothermel.

demand for American grain that followed the repeal of the Corn Laws in England, and commercial interests, already flourishing because of the pre-eminence of the American-built clipper ship, were still further stimulated by the low rates of the Walker Tariff. Laborers drew high wages and could count on steady employment. Such prosperity was far too precious to be disturbed by an academic dispute over slavery. Particularly were the northern manufacturers eager to insure the permanence of their southern markets by conciliating the South; while southern producers were by no means happy at the prospect of secession, with its inevitable disruption of their normal lines of trade. A convention of southern delegates, called together on the advice of Calhoun, met at Nashville, Tennessee, in June, 1850, but failed to display the radicalism in its resolutions that had been expected of it, and adjourned to await the final action of Congress. Webster's Seventh of March speech made a powerful impression on the public mind, and brought many to the support of the Compromise who might otherwise have wavered. Abolitionists, not without some reason, branded him as a traitor to their cause, and read with approval the lines of Whittier's *Ichabod:*

> All else is gone; from those great eyes
>   The soul has fled:
> When faith is lost, when honor dies,
>   The man is dead!

Consideration of the Compromise occupied the chief attention of Congress from the end of January to the middle of September. The Senate referred the proposals to a select committee of thirteen, headed by Clay, which reported back three separate measures. The first, which was promptly termed the "Omnibus Bill," provided for the admission of California as a free state, the creation out of the rest of the Mexican cession of two new territories, New Mexico and Utah, without the Wilmot Proviso, and the payment of ten million dollars to Texas as an indemnity for her surrender of title to New Mexi-

Millard Fillmore

THIRTEENTH PRESIDENT of the United States, Fillmore of New York had started his political career as an Anti-Mason and a protégé of Thurlow Weed. With Weed he moved over into the Whig party in 1834, and in general supported the policies of Henry Clay. His anti-slavery views were not strong enough to keep him from signing the compromise measures of 1850. Photo by Mathew B. Brady.

can territory. The second measure proposed the drastic fugitive slave law that the South demanded. The third prohibited the slave trade in the District of Columbia. As the favorable reaction of the country was sensed, the desire of Congress to accept the Compromise became increasingly apparent. Even so, there were serious obstacles to be surmounted. Most baffling, apparently, was the unrelenting opposition of President Taylor, who seemed determined to pursue his own course without regard for the wishes of Congress. But in July, 1850, the President was taken suddenly ill, probably of cholera morbus or typhoid fever, and within a few days he was dead.

The new President, Millard Fillmore (1800–74), was known only as a successful lawyer from Buffalo, New York, Millard who had served several terms Fillmore in the state legislature and in Congress. Early in his career he had won some distinction by pushing through the New York legislature an act for the abolition of im-

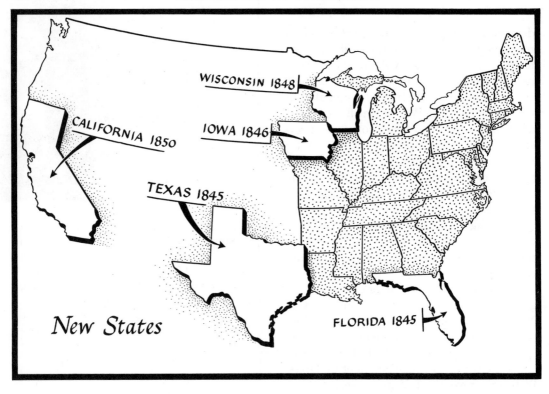

WISCONSIN 1848

CALIFORNIA 1850

IOWA 1846

TEXAS 1845

New States

FLORIDA 1845

prisonment for debt; later, as a member of Congress, he had much to do with the writing of the Tariff of 1842. When nominated for the Vice-Presidency he was generally regarded as an anti-slavery man, but the debates in the Senate on the Compromise measures, to which he listened as presiding officer, seem to have impressed upon him the urgent necessity of conciliating the South. On succeeding to the Presidency he at once put himself into the hands of Clay, formed a new cabinet with Webster at its head, and gave his undivided support to the proposed plan of compromise.

But opposition in Congress to various features of the Omnibus Bill also threatened **The Compromise accepted** for a time to wreck the Compromise. Fortunately, however, while passage of the measure as a whole would probably have been impossible, its friends soon observed that if it were properly subdivided different majorities could be obtained for its several component parts. It thus came about that the Compro-

mise of 1850, as finally passed by Congress and signed by the President, was complete in five laws: (1) California was admitted as a free state; (2) New Mexico was created a territory without the Wilmot Proviso, and the claim of Texas to New Mexican territory was indemnified by the payment of ten million dollars from the federal treasury; (3) Utah was created a territory without the Wilmot Proviso; (4) more stringent provision was made for the rendition of fugitive slaves; and (5) the slave trade was abolished in the District of Columbia. Actually only four senators voted for every one of the five measures, although several others, including Clay and Douglas, would have done so had they not been unavoidably absent when some of the votes were taken. Indeed, in both houses of Congress the majorities in favor of the various compromise bills were in no two instances identical.

For a time it seemed that the Compromise might fail to conciliate the South. Particularly did the admission of California, an

"*Conquering Prejudice,* or Fulfilling a Constitutional Duty with Alacrity," ridicules Webster and other Northerners for supporting the Fugitive Slave Act on high constitutional grounds. Cartoon by P. Kramer, about 1850.

act which definitely upset the balance of slave and free states in the Union, arouse resentment and alarm. The adjourned session of the Nashville convention, held in November, 1850, condemned the Compromise, and urged that a general convention of the southern states should be called to safeguard southern rights within the Union, if possible, but if that could not be done, to prepare the way for independence. In four states, Georgia, Mississippi, Alabama, and South Carolina, special state conventions were held to consider the advisability of immediate secession. On second thought, however, the people of the South decided in favor of the Compromise. The recommendation of the Nashville "rump" convention — it was attended by only one third as many delegates as had composed the original session — went virtually unheeded, and not one of the state conventions came out in favor of secession. Except in South Carolina, those who wished to give the Compromise a trial were in the majority, and the South Carolinians were unwilling to risk secession without the support of other southern states. "To secede now," as one of them observed, "would be to secede from the South." Probably the "Georgia Platform," as the resolutions adopted by the Georgia convention were generally called, best expressed the southern point of view. This document admitted freely that Georgia derived many advantages

Reception in the South

"from her adherence to the confederacy"; it accepted the Compromise "as a permanent adjustment of the sectional controversy"; and it warned the North that "upon the faithful execution of the Fugitive Slave Bill depends the preservation of our much-loved union."

In the North the chief obstacle to acceptance of the Compromise was the harshness of the Fugitive Slave Act. Even legally free Negroes had good reason to fear for their safety when its provisions went into effect. Under the new law the fugitive, or anyone accused of being a fugitive, was denied the right of trial by jury and his status was determined either by a United States judge, or by one of the many commissioners appointed by the federal circuit courts for the more rapid disposal of such cases. In this hearing the fugitive, who was not allowed to testify in his own behalf, might be turned over to his claimant on no other evidence than the affidavit of his supposed master, or his master's attorney or agent. The act, moreover, was *ex post facto,* for its provisions applied to slaves who had fled from their masters at any time in the past; and it contained an outright bribe, for if the commissioner decided in favor of the master, his fee was to be ten dollars, whereas if he decided in favor of the fugitive, it was to be only five dollars. Federal marshals and their deputies were required, under threat of heavy

The Fugitive Slave Act

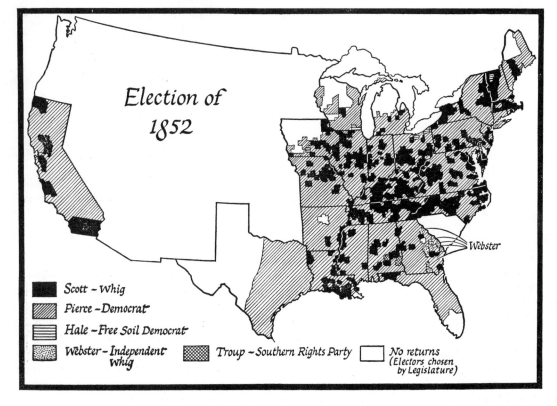

Election of 1852

Scott – Whig
Pierce – Democrat
Hale – Free Soil Democrat
Webster – Independent Whig   Troup – Southern Rights Party   No returns (Electors chosen by Legislature)

Webster

penalties, to make unusual exertions to capture fugitives, and anyone aiding in the escape of a slave was liable to a fine of not more than one thousand dollars or imprisonment not to exceed six months, in addition to civil damages of one thousand dollars to the owner of the slave. These terms, quite obviously, were not dictated merely by the desire to secure the return of fugitive slaves. They were, and they were meant to be, as Rhodes says, "a taunt and reproach to that part of the North where the anti-slavery sentiment ruled supremely."

But even this thoroughly obnoxious act was insufficient to keep the North from

Northern support of Compromise

rallying to the support of the Compromise. "Business interests," says Rhodes, "were well satisfied with the conclusion of the matter, for trade loves political repose." Mass meetings were held in Boston, New York, Philadelphia, and elsewhere to voice enthusiastic approval of the Compromise. The Fugitive

Slave Act was defended by able lawyers as constitutional throughout, and was generally accepted as a necessary, if irritating, part of the price of peace. Partisans of the Compromise shrewdly proclaimed it as a *final* settlement of the slavery dispute. The question was, by common consent, to be forever outlawed from politics. In January, 1851, forty-four members of Congress, representing both major parties and both North and South, signed a pledge to oppose any candidate for public office who did not accept the Compromise as a *finality*. More Southerners than Northerners signed the pledge, but to Northerners this was especially gratifying, for it put the South even more clearly on record than the North as favorable to a plan which was designed primarily to end the southern threat of secession.

The presidential election of 1852 served as a kind of popular referendum on the Compromise. The Democratic National Convention accepted the Compromise without Election of 1852 equivocation, and announced its determination to "resist all attempts at renewing, in Congress or out of it, the agitation of the slavery question, under whatever shape or color the attempt may be made." The Democratic nominee, Franklin Pierce of New Hampshire, was another "dark horse" who captured the nomination after three more prominent leaders, Cass, Buchanan, and Douglas, had each failed in a prolonged contest to win the necessary two-thirds majority. But Pierce's unqualified endorsement of the Compromise measures was well known, and with this in mind the stampede of the convention to his support had been carefully planned. The Whigs, on the other hand, were unable to present so united a front. Many of their ablest leaders in the North had opposed the Compromise, and at heart were still opposed to it. The Whig platform announced that it "acquiesced in" the Compromise laws "as a settlement in principle and substance of the dangerous and exciting questions which they embrace," and promised to "maintain them . . . until time and experience shall demonstrate the necessity of further legislation." Even this lukewarm statement was opposed by one fourth of the delegates, whereas the Democratic convention had adopted its ringing resolutions by an almost unanimous vote. Moreover, the Whigs refused to nominate Millard Fillmore, whose support had so greatly contributed to the adoption of the Compromise, and turned instead to their one remaining Mexican War hero, General Winfield Scott of Virginia, whose views on the Compromise were unknown.

The issue before the electorate was thus primarily Franklin Pierce and the Compromise, or General Scott and uncertainty. A third alternative was offered by the Free-Soil candidacy of John P. Hale, but four

Franklin Pierce

FOURTEENTH PRESIDENT of the United States, Pierce of New Hampshire could hardly be described as a successful President, although he was an able lawyer, a fine orator, and possessed great personal charm. He did not seek the Presidency, and had retired from national politics long before 1852 when the Democrats selected him as the "dark horse" nominee. Photo by Mathew B. Brady.

years of Whig supremacy had brought the Van Buren Democrats back into the party fold, so that the Free-Soilers polled little more than half the number of votes in 1852 that they had polled four years before. The popular verdict was plain. The Democrats carried twenty-seven states, and the Whigs only four: Massachusetts, Vermont, Kentucky, and Tennessee. Pierce's electoral vote was 254 to Scott's 42. Indeed, the Whig Party, which throughout its existence had rarely been more than an "organized incompatibility," collapsed under the blow, and was never again strong enough to contest a presidential election. For the time being an overwhelming majority, both North and South, chose to believe that the slavery question was permanently settled.

Bibliography

Allan Nevins, *Ordeal of the Union* (2 vols., 1947), reviews in extraordinary detail the events of the decade immediately following the war with Mexico. At this point also the scholarly and exhaustive work of James Ford Rhodes, *History of the United States from the Compromise of 1850* (9 vols., 1893–1922), begins to be of use. An excellent single volume, up to date in point of view, is W. B. Hesseltine, *The South in American History* (1943). The persistence of secessionist sentiment is well set forth in the following treatises: P. M. Hamer, *The Secession Movement in South Carolina, 1847–1852* (1918); M. J. White, *The Secession Movement in the United States, 1847–1852* (1916); and R. H. Shryock, *Georgia and the Union in 1850* (1926). The part played by the anti-slavery elements is well stated in T. C. Smith, *The Liberty and Free-Soil Parties in the Northwest* (1897).

In addition to the works on California cited for the previous chapter, page 484, R. G. Cleland, *A History of California: The American Period* (1922), is excellent. S. E. White, *The Forty-Niners* (1920), is readable, but perhaps overdrawn. A. B. Hulbert, *Forty-Niners* (1931), provides a sympathetic diary of the trails. J. H. Jackson, *Anybody's Gold* (1941), recovers admirably the atmosphere of the old mining towns.

Biographies of the principals in the Compromise of 1850 are important. Fuess, *Daniel Webster*, is particularly good. Sympathetic views of Calhoun are given in W. E. Dodd, *Statesmen of the Old South* (1911); and Margaret L. Coit, *John C. Calhoun: American Portrait* (1950). U. B. Phillips, *The Life of Robert Toombs* (1913), is admirably done. A. C. McLaughlin, *Lewis Cass* (1891), is competent. G. F. Milton, *The Eve of Conflict: Stephen A. Douglas and the Needless War* (1934), gives due credit to Douglas for the part he played in bringing about the Compromise of 1850. See also Allen Johnson, *Stephen A. Douglas: A Study in American Politics* (1908).

All the general histories are full of the subject of the Compromise of 1850: Schouler, V; McMaster, VIII; Channing, VI. A. C. Cole, *The Irrepressible Conflict, 1850–1865* (1934), is especially useful for social history. A. O. Craven, *The Repressible Conflict, 1830–1861* (1939), takes a strongly southern point of view.

THE SECTIONAL

CONTROVERSY

1850 - 1877

At first the Compromise of 1850 seemed to be serving the purpose which its framers had designed. Politicians of both major parties made it a point to talk as if the slavery issue were dead, and to exclude it rigorously from party platforms. They even sought new issues, such as expansion at the expense of Cuba or Mexico, overseas commercial expansion in the Far East, the dangers implicit in the arrival of new hordes of German and Irish immigrants. They were aided by an unbounded prosperity which flowed in part from the great gold discoveries in California, in part from the expansion of the railroads, in part from the mounting profits of manufactures, cotton growing, and agriculture in general. Boom days are poor days for agitators, and the Abolitionist Crusade was at low ebb, although a third party, the Free-Soil Party, tried to keep alive the idea that the expansion of slavery must be checked. And Harriet Beecher Stowe wrote *Uncle Tom's Cabin.*

The Kansas-Nebraska Act of 1854 was credited with having revived the slavery issue, but no doubt it could not long have been kept dormant anyway. Stephen A. Douglas of Illinois, as able a politician as the times had yet produced, argued that each new territory should decide for itself whether it should be slave or free. When this principle was enacted into law for Kansas and Nebraska, it was supposed that Nebraska would vote free and Kansas, slave. But a great battle was joined for Kansas that resulted in much local bloodshed, and the birth of the Republican Party. Like the Free-Soilers, the Republicans argued that slavery should not be permitted to expand. They drew to their standards those who believed that slavery was morally wrong and should be checked; those who believed that the lands of the west should be reserved to small free farmers, and not turned over to the southern planters; and those who were tired of southern leadership in the national government, with its persistent obstruction of protective tariffs, its reluctance to grant aid to railroad building, particularly in the Far West, and its general support of policies that favored agriculture rather than manufactures.

The issue was in fact sectional. The Republicans virtually supplanted the northern Whigs and drew many northern Democrats into their ranks. But the Republican party made no headway south of the Mason and Dixon line. It became a strictly sectional party, representing a sectional point of view. Could the union of the Northeast and the Northwest that it had achieved impose its will upon the South? The defense of "Southern Rights," however, was founded constitutionally on states'-rights rather than on sectional rights. The states had made the Union, Southerners declared, and they could also unmake it. If the North persisted in imposing its policies upon the South, then the South, state by state, would secede from the Union.

With the panic of 1857, and the beginning of hard times in the North, the restraint of prosperity disappeared. To the South, the fact that the depression was less marked in the "Cotton Kingdom" seemed a vindication of its economy, and southern determination to resist northern aggression mounted year by year. When in 1860 the strictly sectional Republican party was able to elect a President, Abraham Lincoln, some, but not all, of the southern states put their threat into effect. And the Confederate States of America was born.

There followed a devastating Civil War, the worst war the United States had ever yet known, and the worst it was ever to know at least until the Second World War. The North with superior numbers, and with what counted even more, industrial supremacy, won the war, and forced the seceding states to return to the Union. The constitutional issue of secession was settled, not by argument, but by bullets. Slavery, the institution that lay back of the tumult that had produced the war, was illegalized by a constitutional amendment. And the Northeast, in which the industries of the nation centered, emerged as the leader among the sections, a leadership that was not to be challenged successfully for many decades to come. The ravages of war hurt the South most, but physically and psychologically, the whole nation, victors no less than vanquished, was deeply wounded by the struggle, and the process of recovery was sure to be slow.

Unfortunately reconstruction was badly done. The hatreds of the war lived on after the fighting ended, and the victors chose to wreak unwarranted vengeance upon the vanquished. The death of Lincoln robbed the nation of an astute and experienced leader, and his successor, Johnson, quarreled endlessly with Congress. The northern Radicals, in order to insure Republican supremacy in the South, forced Negro suffrage prematurely upon the former Confederate states, and aggravated the racial problem to such an extent that a "solid South" emerged, which for many decades voted the Democratic ticket in all elections. For eight years after the war the North, with industry increasingly predominant, was prosperous, while the South struggled merely to survive. The hard times that began in 1873 helped pave the way for a more moderate southern policy. Diplomatic reconstruction, little appreciated at the time, set the stage for major developments in the twentieth century.

28

Peace and Prosperity

The railway age — Ocean transportation — Manufacturing — The tariff — Southern agriculture — The Northwestern farmer — Exploitation of mineral resources — Immigration — Native Americanism — Expansion as a political issue — Commerce with the Orient — Persistence of the dispute over slavery — *Uncle Tom's Cabin* — The transcontinental railroad idea — Douglas and the Kansas-Nebraska Act

THE prominent place that the slavery dispute occupied in American politics during the two decades preceding the Civil War has tended to divert the attention of historians from other subjects of equal, or even greater, significance. During these same years transportation was revolutionized by the construction of railways, industry and commerce expanded with phenomenal rapidity, agriculture began its far-reaching shift from traditional to more business-like methods, a new flood of European immigrants swept over the country, and the final conquest of the Far West was definitely assured. Contemporary political leaders, who, in the light of these momentous changes, sought to bury the slavery issue, hardly deserve the scorn that some historians have heaped upon them. Could their efforts have been crowned with success instead of failure, the public mind would have been left free to recognize and wrestle with the issues precipitated by the economic revolution, while slavery in time might well have disappeared without resort to war.

Undoubtedly the greatest factor in transforming American society during this period **The railroad** was the railroad. Up to about 1840 this means of transportation was still in the experimental stage, and the building of a railroad was a choice of desperation to be resorted to only where engineering difficulties made a canal impossible. Among these unwilling experiments were the Baltimore and Ohio, which opened a few miles to traffic in 1830, and the Charleston and Hamburg, which in 1833, with its 137 miles of track across the state of South Carolina, was the longest railroad in the world. Short lines were built, also, to facilitate trade between the principal cities of the country and their respective outlying districts. Philadelphia, for example, was soon connected by rail with the coal-mining regions of central Pennsylvania. By the year 1840 the total railroad trackage of the country had reached 2818 miles.

From the operation of these early railroads, short and disconnected as they were, many valuable lessons were learned. The use of horses and sails for motive power was quickly discarded in favor of steam locomotives similar to those built by George Stephenson, the English inventor, but lighter and speedier. Unsubstantial wooden rails, protected only by thin iron straps, gave way to far more durable iron rails. Dizzy curves and steep grades, so characteristic of the early roadbeds, tended to disappear, while wooden cross-ties, designed to insure that the two lines of rails should remain at all times equidistant, replaced the more uncertain separate foundations. Low four-wheeled trucks, pivoted beneath each end of a freight or passenger car, made the rounding of curves less hazardous, and pointed the way to a complete abandonment of the stage-coach and rail-wagon appearance of the first

THE "WEST POINT," 1830. One of the first trains to carry passengers and freight. Illustration from Brown, *First Locomotives in America*, 1874.

PASSENGER TRAIN IN MICHIGAN, ABOUT 1840. "Balloon-stacked" engine on the Erie and Kalamazoo Railroad.

THE STARUCCA VIADUCT. Part of the Erie Railroad. Illustration from Dana, *The United States Illustrated*, 1853.

The railroad so successfully met the problem of overland travel that it fanned out quickly from East to West. Difficult terrain was soon bridged by viaducts and trestles, sometimes too hastily for safety, in the general eagerness to "get there" — everywhere. The experimental trains of the 1830's gave way to ever-better locomotives and rolling stock, and even sleeping cars were soon attempted.

AN AMERICAN EXPRESS TRAIN. Lithograph by Currier and Ives, 1850's.

SLEEPING CAR ON THE NEW YORK CENTRAL. Illustration from *Frank Leslie's Illustrated Weekly*, April 30, 1859.

'rolling-stock." Coal began to replace wood as fuel, partly to save the time consumed in "wooding-up" at frequent intervals, partly to allay the irritation of passengers whose clothing caught fire from the steady stream of sparks that a wood-burner always emitted. Also, the necessity of railroad companies to manage the traffic was quickly demonstrated. On some of the early roads anyone with a proper conveyance was permitted to use the rails just as he might have used a toll road, but endless confusion resulted; moreover, the cost of locomotives and cars was beyond the means of the ordinary individual. It soon became the practically universal custom, therefore, for the owners of the road also to own and operate the equipment. For this service they exacted whatever charges they saw fit, but as "common carriers" they were under obligation to accept for shipment anything within reason presented to them for that purpose.

The second decade of railroad history saw the mistrust with which the new means of **Through routes** transportation had at first been viewed replaced by a deep and abiding faith. Accidental connections — such, for example, as made possible all-rail transportation from Boston to Albany after 1841 — added tremendously to the business of the connecting lines, and pointed the way to future development. The significant part that the railroads might play in linking the East and the West together became apparent in 1842, when a series of seven or eight local lines furnished an alternative route to the Erie Canal across the state of New York. The combinations of all such roads into one through route, while delayed in this case until the emergence of the New York Central in 1853, was a logical next step. By that year three other lines connected the eastern seaboard with the West: the Erie, completed through southern New York in 1851; the Pennsylvania, opened all the way to Pittsburgh in 1852; and the Baltimore and Ohio, which reached its western objective in 1853. Within the West itself the railroad was hailed as the long-sought solution to the problem of land transportation, and innumerable ambitious projects were begun. Such cities as Memphis, Chicago, and St. Louis, eager to become important as railroad centers, held railroad "conventions" to arouse enthusiasm. Hastily built local lines were soon succeeded by through routes, such as the Michigan Central and the Michigan Southern, which reached Chicago in 1852, and the Rock Island and Chicago, which connected the Great Lakes with the Mississippi River in 1854. Next year through rail connections were established between New York and St. Louis.

The task of providing funds for these extensive enterprises taxed the resources of the railroad promoters to the limit. **Railroad finance** The earlier roads, when not actually owned and operated by some state, could ordinarily depend upon a loan of the state's credit or a generous state subscription to railroad stock. But as already noted, this policy was very generally discredited after the financial disasters that overtook the states during the panic of 1837. Railroad lobbyists were able, however, to get direct aid from a few states, and they became extremely adept at securing from all the states valuable privileges and immunities for the companies they represented. They also induced cities and counties that lay along the route of a proposed line to vote large sums to the coveted railroad, either as outright gifts, or as loans, or as subscriptions to stock. Skillful, if none too scrupulous, salesmen persuaded private investors, foreigners as well as Americans, to buy large blocks of railroad securities. Finally, the politicians who sympathized with the aims of the railroads won from Congress grants of federal land to be used in aid of railroad-building. The first such grant was obtained in 1850 for the Illinois Central Railroad by Senator Stephen A. Douglas. According to this act, three square miles of land in alternate sections on each side of the proposed line were granted to the state of Illinois for transfer to the railroad as fast as construction was completed. To secure the necessary

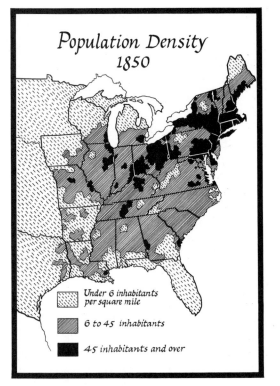

Population Density
1850

[ ] Under 6 inhabitants
    per square mile

[ ] 6 to 45 inhabitants

[■] 45 inhabitants and over

Practically all the important eastern cities were connected by rail, and many of them had also direct connections with the West. The most feverish building, however, had taken place in the Northwest. By 1860 this section, which before the panic of 1837 had hardly a mile of railroad in effective operation, had 11,078 miles to its credit, more than one third of the total trackage of the country. Chicago, thanks mainly to its natural advantages as a railroad center, had grown from a town of 4000 inhabitants in 1840 to 29,000 in 1850, and to 109,000 in 1860. Inland cities, such as Indianapolis, had achieved an importance that without the railroads could scarcely have been imagined. Railroad connections between the Great Lakes and the Ohio–Mississippi River system put the western canals virtually out of business, and stimulated tremendously the growth of such cities as Cleveland, Cincinnati, and Milwaukee, which could serve as links between the waterways and the rails. By 1855 the Mississippi River had been bridged; by 1857 the railroad frontier had reached the Missouri River at St. Joseph. In the South, railroad-building lagged perceptibly. This section, with its extensive coastline and its numerous navigable rivers, stood far less in need of railroads than the Northwest; moreover, whatever surplus capital the South could command was generally invested in plantations and slaves. Nevertheless many short lines were built, and a few of sectional importance. By 1860, both Norfolk, Virginia, and Charleston, South Carolina, were connected through Chattanooga, Tennessee, with the Mississippi River at Memphis; and the Mississippi itself was paralleled from the Ohio to the Gulf. With 10,048 miles of railroads the South was slightly ahead of the Northeast in total mileage, although, in view of its greater distances, the effectiveness of its railroads was far less marked. The Northeast on the eve of the Civil War had about twice as much railroad trackage per square mile of land as the Northwest, and four times as much as the South.

political support for this measure, similar grants had to be made available for a railroad from the Ohio River to Mobile; and thereafter land grants were generally allotted to any railroad projected in a region where the government still owned land. Many of the western states had at their disposal, also, great tracts of overflowed and swamp lands, which Congress had voted to them in 1849, and which they often regranted to the railroads. Between 1850 and 1860 about twenty million acres of public lands found their way, in one fashion or another, into the hands of the railroads.

Under these circumstances the conquest of the country by the railroads proceeded **Railroad** with astonishing rapidity. The **expansion** amount of trackage increased from 2818 miles in 1840 to 9021 miles in 1850 and to 30,626 miles in 1860. By the last-mentioned year the Northeast alone had 9500 miles of railroads, more than the whole country had possessed ten years before.

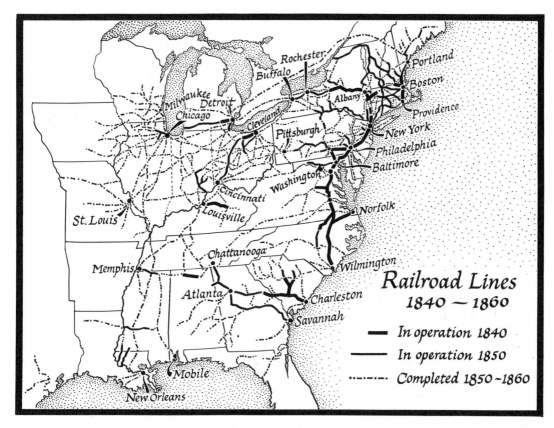

Railroad Lines
1840 — 1860

▬▬ In operation 1840
▬▬▬ In operation 1850
·····-· Completed 1850-1860

RAILROAD MILEAGE IN THE
UNITED STATES, 1830–1865

Year	Miles	Year	Miles
1830	32	1850	9,021
1835	1,098	1855	18,374
1840	2,818	1860	30,626
1845	4,663	1865	35,085

One of the most striking developments that a railroad map of 1860 reveals is the drawing together of the Northeast and the Northwest. So closely connected, indeed, were the railroads of these two sections that they appear to be, as to all practical purposes they were, one network. With ever-increasing ease the produce of the Northwest found its way to the consumers of the East and to the eastern seaports for transshipment to Europe. Similarly the eastern manufacturers found in the expanding Northwest a gratifying market for the output of their factories. The southern railroads, on the other hand, were not yet integrated with the railroads of the rest of the country. Because so many of them had been built primarily as a means of supplementing the southern waterways, they lacked even sectional unity, and they made contact with the northern railroad system at only three widely separated points.

In spite of the mounting significance of the railroads, the western waterways long remained a major factor in the communications system of the country. Until the railroads appeared, the river steamboats had no transportation rivals in the West, and for years after the coming of the roads the Mississippi River continued to carry an enormous volume of traffic. Great shipyards were located at St. Louis, Cincinnati, and Louisville which turned out huge and speedy craft to carry grain and merchandise downstream, cotton, rice, and sugar upstream, and a

Western steamboating

steady flow of passengers both ways. By means of these boats the northern farmers found a needed outlet for their produce in the South; southern cotton-planters saved money by buying foodstuffs from the Northwest instead of raising their own; both farmers and planters had more funds to use in the purchase of eastern manufactured goods. Some of the boats were incredibly swift — the best of them made the twelve or thirteen hundred miles from New Orleans to St. Louis in four days, or even less. By the fifties well over a thousand steamboats plied the Mississippi and its tributaries, and since the cost of the larger boats ran to about fifty thousand dollars each, this represented a sizable investment. Cargoes valued at two hundred and fifty thousand dollars each were not unknown. To the upper Mississippi and its tributaries, steamboats brought the blessings of swift transportation long before the railroads arrived, and far out on the upper Missouri fur-traders, too, had their steamboats. Indeed, this elaborate system of river communications seemed so essential to the life of both the Northwest and the South that the prospect of its separation from New Orleans, the head of the river traffic, was one of the worst of the nightmares associated with secession. But the steamboats not only solved a problem of transportation for the West; they created also a way of life and a cast of characters that happily Mark Twain's *Life on the Mississippi* has preserved intact for the wonderment of posterity.

Steamboats on the rivers flowing into the Atlantic had been common from the time of Robert Fulton, and the mid-century rush of settlement to the Pacific coast brought them there also. The Sacramento and San Joaquin Rivers, which, with their tributaries, opened easy routes to the gold fields, were soon alive with "paddle-wheelers." By the end of the 1850's there were not less than twenty-eight steamboats plying the waters of the Sacramento and Feather Rivers, while schedules had been cut to such short hours that steamboat disasters were a common oc-

currence. Up in the Far Northwest, the Columbia and its tributaries furnished additional unneglected opportunities for the use of steamboats.

The revolution in means of communication that took place during this period was almost as marked on the high seas as on the land. To this end American shipbuilders contributed during the eighteen-forties the fleet clipper ship, which with a fair breeze could make better time than the early steamships, and under normal circumstances could make three trips to Europe while an ordinary ship was making two. Partly because of the superiority of these ships, partly because of recurring wars both in Europe and in Asia, American ships for a few years carried a far greater proportion of the world's commerce than had ever been the case before. During the decade 1850–60, about seventy per cent of the total foreign trade of the United States was carried in ships that flew the American flag, while in the year 1853 alone, according to a reliable estimate, the total tonnage carried by American ships exceeded that of the British by no less than fifteen per cent. About 1855, however, the American clipper ship began to be superseded by the British-built iron steamer, which could cross the Atlantic in less than two weeks' time. Backed by adequate government subsidies, the British steamers soon made heavy inroads upon the American carrying trade. To meet this competition several American steamship companies, which had been organized during the forties, were for a few years voted subsidies by Congress, but they proved to be unable to hold the trans-Atlantic trade against the British. Their importance in the coastwise trade, however, which was closed to foreign vessels, became very great. From the point of view of efficiency in transportation, it mattered little whether the commerce of the United States was carried in British or American bottoms. What was of far greater significance was the fact that ocean lanes were being multiplied, and the time of transit was being lessened. Just as

Ocean transportation

"The War News from Mexico."
Engraving by A. Jones, after a painting by R. C. Woodville, 1851.

Ocean Steamers. "Commodore Perry carrying
the 'Gospel of God' to the Heathen," 1853. Painting by J. G. Evans.

The Pony Express Meets the Telegraph. Illustration from *Harper's Weekly*, 1861.

Improved communications brought the United States closer together and closer to the rest of the world. Such makeshift experiments as the Pony Express soon gave way to the electric telegraph which, together with the transatlantic cable, provided newspapers with information that would otherwise have been denied them for days or weeks. The cable laid in 1858 did not last long, but it was followed by others that endured.

Transatlantic Cable. Engraving commemorating messages exchanged by Queen Victoria and President Buchanan, August 16, 1858, from *Leslie's Illustrated Weekly*.

the railroads within the country were bringing its various sections closer together, so the clipper ships and the steamers tended to bring the United States into closer contact with the outside world.

Easier means of communication had much to do with the growth of industry in the **Manufacturing** United States during this same period. The use of power machinery in manufacturing had made steady progress during the first four decades of the nineteenth century, but the difficulties experienced in transporting goods to market had kept down the size of American factories and the amount of their output. Not until the advent of the steam locomotive did the full effects of the Industrial Revolution begin to be felt in the United States. Then factories that had previously depended on serving only a local market began suddenly to expand, while others, less fortunately situated, began to decline materially in importance, and even to disappear. Regardless of the number of factories, the total annual output of manufactured goods mounted rapidly. By 1850, the first year in which the federal census attempted to ascertain accurately the amount of manufacturing that went on in the United States, the total value of manufactured goods, $1,055,500,000, exceeded slightly the total value of agricultural products, $994,000,000. Ten years later the figures were $1,885,862,000 for manufacturing and $1,910,000,000 for agriculture; but the ascendancy that agriculture thus seemed to have regained proved short-lived, for all subsequent census statistics showed manufacturing far in the lead.

Not only improved means of transportation, but many other factors also tended to promote the growth of American industry. The liberal patent system of the United States, which guaranteed to patent-holders a long-time monopoly upon the manufacture, use, and sale of their inventions, encouraged American inventors to devise many labor-saving machines for use in the factory or on the farm, as well as a great variety of articles for the comfort and satisfaction of individ-

uals. A rising standard of living meant also the manufacture and sale in quantities to the ordinary man of the one-time luxuries of the rich. Moreover, the United States was growing rapidly in population, both from the ordinary natural increase and from a new wave of immigration; hence the needs of ever greater numbers of people had to be met. Prosperity meant that nearly everyone had the means with which to buy. Wages were good; agricultural products, thanks in part to the repeal of the Corn Laws in England and in part also to the mid-century European wars, brought high prices; newly mined gold and silver paid the bills of the Far West.

American manufacturing, in spite of its rapid growth, still showed many of the characteristics of youth. The **Manufacturing practices** concentration of factories at strategic centers had only begun, and there was in consequence a far greater diffusion of manufacturing industries than was later the case. While New England and the Middle Atlantic States maintained their early lead in manufacturing, small factories of one kind or another were apt to be found in any part of the country, even in the South and along the frontier. A second characteristic of youth was the close restriction of American manufacturing to the use of such raw materials as were produced within the country: comparatively little was imported in order to be manufactured. American grain was turned into flour and meal, American forests into sawed lumber, American cotton into cotton goods, American wool into woolen goods, American iron ore into iron products, and so on. Also, with some minor exceptions, the entire output of the American factories was consumed in the United States, and that without fully satisfying the demand. American cotton mills turned out enough cotton goods of the coarser grades, and a little to spare, but the finer grades still had to be imported from Europe. American woolens fell still further short of supplying the domestic demand, for the American woolens manufacturers were handicapped not only by their inability to compete with the English in producing fine fabrics, but also by an inadequate American supply of raw wool. The use of anthracite coal and of coke as fuel greatly stimulated the iron industry and pointed the way to a phenomenal development, but the heavy demands of the railway age were greater than the American supply could meet. With reference to many minor industries the situation was not far different.

The high degree of prosperity that American manufacturers enjoyed during these years was achieved in spite of the relatively low duties of the Walker Tariff. Naturally, the fact that importers were able to throw upon the American market a plentiful supply of foreign-made goods was not at all relished by the manufacturing interests. Demands for higher duties in order to promote the more rapid expansion of American industry were persistently voiced, particularly by representatives of the northeastern states, where most of the factories were located. Until the time of the Civil War, however, all such demands were foredoomed to failure. Both the South and the West profited from the low duties, and a coalition of southern and western politicians ruled the country. Indeed, in 1857 the rates of the Walker Tariff were still further reduced.

The tariff

Circumstances conspired to make this period one of extraordinary prosperity for the cotton-growers of the South. The steady fall in the price of cotton that had at first accompanied the expansion of cotton-growing was arrested in the forties and reversed in the fifties. From an all-time low of less than six cents a pound in 1845, the price of cotton rose to an average of between ten and eleven cents throughout the fifties, and to nearly fourteen cents in 1857. Nor was this change in price due to any curtailment of production, for each year saw a sizable increase in the acreage devoted to cotton culture. Rather, the world demand for cotton had been immensely accelerated. Improve-

The profits of cotton-growing

ments in textile machinery now made possible the manufacture of cotton goods for sale at so low a price that even the humblest Asiatic or African could afford to buy. American manufacturers, after meeting practically the entire domestic demand for cheap cotton cloth, were able to export a considerable excess to the Orient; English manufacturers, insured by the repeal of the Corn Laws against the danger of having to pay high wages to their operatives, sought and found new markets everywhere in the world; French manufacturers, while definitely less flourishing than their British competitors, were by no means idle. Manufacturers everywhere turned to the American South for their raw cotton, for nowhere else could they find an abundant supply of comparable quality. To meet this tremendous demand practically all the land of the South that was suited to cotton culture was used for that purpose. Indeed, except for cotton and tobacco the production in the South of every important crop failed during the fifties to keep pace with the growth of the population. But the cotton crop, which had risen from 1,500,000 bales in 1840 to 2,500,000 bales in 1850, reached the enormous total of 5,300,000 bales in 1860 — seven eighths of the world's supply.

Less frequently noted is the fact that during these same years a renaissance of tobacco-growing made the states of the upper South more prosperous than they had been for years. This was due in part to the increased demand of a growing world population, in part to the introduction of new species and to improved methods of cultivation and manufacture. In 1849 the tobacco crop of the United States amounted to less than 200,000,000 pounds; ten years later it was nearly 430,000,000 pounds. Virginia and Kentucky were the greatest tobacco-growing states, but other states also, notably Maryland, Tennessee, and Missouri, contributed large quotas. Indeed, every state in the Union, North as well as South, grew some tobacco, although the cotton states during this decade grew pro-

Tobacco-growing

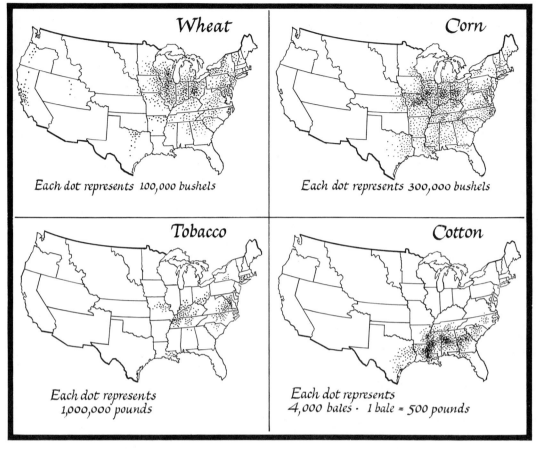

Agricultural Products in the United States in 1859

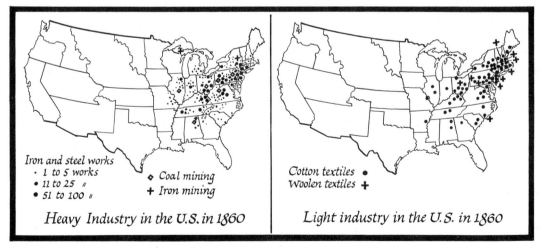

Industry in the United States in 1860

portionately less tobacco than they had ever grown before.

While tobacco was second in value only to cotton among the crops that the South produced, it was a rather poor second. Throughout that section the saying that "Cotton is King!" went unchallenged. Southerners were proud of the fact that the world depended upon them almost exclusively to supply one of the primary necessities of civilization; they relished the thought that without their help the wheels of industry in the North and in England would scarcely turn; they never forgot that the export of cotton paid more than half the bills contracted by the United States abroad. On one score, however, they confessed some embarrassment. The world's need for cotton would continue to mount, but by the end of the fifties the South's ability to meet that need would be taxed to the limit. Practically all available cotton-growing land was already in use, and in the older states continual planting of the same crop had almost exhausted the soil. New cotton lands must be found. If they did not exist within the United States, why not expand the national borders to include them?

In the general reign of plenty the small farmer of the Northwest was by no means forgotten. The steady growth in population meant for him, too, an increased demand to satisfy. Eastern farmers were unable to meet in full the needs of their new industrial centers for foodstuffs, but the western farmer, thanks to the improved means of transportation that the railway age introduced, was able to flood the eastern markets with his produce. Southerners, also, owing to their increasing concentration upon cotton and tobacco, consumed an ever-growing quantity of northwestern farm products. For this intersectional trade the Mississippi and its tributaries still furnished a cheap and easy means of transportation; and it is worth noting that nearly all the northern goods sent down the river in the years immediately preceding the Civil War found a market in the South itself. The export of northern grain and flour from New Orleans, once deemed so important a factor in the economic life of the Northwest, dwindled to insignificance in comparison to the domestic trade. This did not mean, however, that exports of northwestern products were not being made, for during the middle years of the century the need of Europe for American foodstuffs was considerable. But grain and flour destined for a foreign market now went by rail to the eastern ports for transshipment, instead of by river boat, as formerly, to New Orleans. These overseas sales, while not very great in comparison to the total output of the American farms, were sufficient most of the time to absorb the excess not needed for domestic consumption. Particularly during the Crimean War, 1853-56, the European demand was great and the prices paid were correspondingly high. Stimulated by the new prosperity, the population of the Northwest grew with amazing rapidity. Frontier conditions in central Illinois, Missouri, Iowa, and southern Wisconsin tended to disappear, and in 1858 a new northwestern state, Minnesota, was added to the Union.

That a revolution in agriculture had begun — a revolution soon to be particularly significant for the new Northwest — was perhaps less apparent to contemporaries than to later generations. Farmers were no longer so strictly concerned, as they once had been, to produce upon their own farms all the necessities of life for themselves and their families. In earlier times they had taken their own corn and wheat to a near-by mill to be ground into the very flour from which the bread they ate was to be made. They had shot or butchered their own meat, had clipped with their own hands the wool that ultimately through home manufacture provided the clothes they wore, had built their own houses, sheds, and fences from timber cut on their own property, and in a great variety of other ways also had met their own needs without help from the outside. But the

The Northwestern farmer

The revolution in agriculture

THE MARSH HARVESTER. Illustration from an advertisement, about 1845.

READY-TO-WEAR. Advertisement for Kelly's department store, Milledgeville, Illinois, 1855.

A COAL BREAKER. Illustration from Bowen, *Pictorial Sketch Book of Pennsylvania*, 1854.

Peace and prosperity keynoted the early 1850's. Farmers profited greatly from the use of new agricultural machinery; retailers could count on quantities of machine-made goods, such as ready-made clothes, to stock their shelves; coal could be shipped long distances to furnish power for the new factories. New York, imitating London, had an International Exhibition in 1853 to show off the nation's progress.

THE NEW YORK CRYSTAL PALACE, 1853. "For the exhibition of the industry of all nations." Lithograph by N. Currier after F. F. Palmer.

CASTLE GARDEN. Immigration center at New York. Painting by Samuel Waugh, about 1847.

City development following the growth of the factory system and the influx of immigrants, proceeded at a rapid rate. The new cities, with their population constantly increasing, had to give more attention to police and fire protection. Early in the 1850's New York put its policemen into uniforms, and organized its fire department into a professional, salaried, full-time force. Note the presence of both policemen and firemen in the picture to the left.

BROADWAY, N.Y. Detail from a painting by H. Sebron, about 1857.

self-sufficient farmer was rapidly becoming a thing of the past. New agricultural machines, such as the reaper, enabled him to produce far more of certain commodities than he could hope to use. New means of transportation, especially the railroads, enabled him to ship his excess to market. With the proceeds from the sale of his crop he could now buy many of the things he had formerly found it necessary to make for himself or go without. He could, and did, begin to specialize in farming, even to the extent of producing only one kind of crop. His farm became a kind of factory from the profits of which he lived. No longer was he independent of the rest of the world, for he must sell to it, and he must buy from it. His purchases stimulated manufacturing, and the growth

of manufacturing provided him with new markets. Northwestern farmers, while grateful for the markets that the cotton- and tobacco-growers of the South were also providing, were increasingly conscious of the greater purchasing power of the industrial Northeast. The bond of union that was being cemented between these two sections would soon be strong enough to meet the test of civil war.

The rich natural resources of the United States were already contributing generously to what President Pierce chose **Exploitation** to call "the light of our pros- **of mineral** perity." Precious metals had **resources** much to do, although by no means everything, with making the population of California four times as great in 1860 as it had been in 1850. California prospectors pushed throughout the Rocky Mountain area in search of other gold-fields, and made some strikes. In 1859 the Pike's Peak gold-rush duplicated many of the scenes of ten years before in California, and laid the foundations of the future state of Colorado. That same year discoveries along the famous Comstock Lode made Nevada possible. Magnificent virgin forests in the upper Mississippi Valley furnished an almost limitless supply of lumber to the prairie states below. The lead mines of northwestern Illinois and southwestern Wisconsin, once worked by the Indians, now made profits for the whites. Coal and iron ore were found conveniently close together in central and western Pennsylvania. The first oil well was drilled in 1859, near Titusville in northwestern Pennsylvania.

It is not surprising that the United States, as "the land of opportunity," attracted during these prosperous years a **Immigration** great host of European immigrants. The impact of the Industrial Revolution upon Europe had not been without its unfortunate aspects. Those left unemployed by the introduction of labor-saving devices found great difficulty in obtaining re-employment. Also, profound political disturbances, such as the Chartist movement in England and the Revolutions of 1848 on the Continent, accompanied the changing economic order. For those who wished to flee this turmoil, Europe had no adequate outlet of its own, but this defect the United States was fortunately in good position to remedy. Its industries were new, and could profitably absorb both skilled and unskilled European workmen. Its frontier, capable seemingly of an almost indefinite expansion, could give homes not only to its own needy millions, but to millions of Europeans as well. Before 1840 the number of immigrants who came to the United States each year was an almost negligible figure, twenty-three thousand in 1830, and eighty-four thousand in 1840; but between 1845 and 1855 the average number of newcomers admitted annually had risen to not less than three hundred thousand. They came from many lands, but, owing to special circumstances, from Ireland and Germany far more than from all other countries combined.

Unlike the Scotch-Irish who came to the United States from the north of Ireland during the eighteenth century, **The Irish** the new Irish immigrants came from the southern counties of Ireland; they were Celtic in origin rather than Teutonic, and Roman Catholic in religion rather than Presbyterian. Their incentives for leaving Ireland were numerous: political oppression, whether real or fancied, absentee landlordism, overpopulation, and above all a series of devastating famines that began with the failure of the potato crop in 1845. Deaths by starvation during these hard seasons were pitifully frequent, and those who were able to leave for a land of plenty such as America availed themselves of the first opportunity. Shipping companies cut the cost of transportation to a figure lower than had ever been known before, herded the immigrants together in stifling holds, and made a rich harvest from their enterprise. The Irish landed virtually destitute at Boston, New York, and other eastern ports, and went to work at small wages in the factories, on the railroads, or wherever their help was needed. Thousands of Irish girls found employment as domestics. Soon nearly every city had its "Shantytown" where the newly arrived Irish lived in quarters even more squalid than those they had known in Ireland, and rejoiced on incomes that to the native Americans seemed ridiculous.

The reasons for the German migration were somewhat analogous. In the vanguard were the political refugees, lib- **The Germans** erals who had taken a part in the revolutions of 1848 only to lose out in the end before the forces of reaction. Some men of this type, Carl Schurz and Franz Sigel, for example, soon achieved a greater prominence in their adopted land than they had ever known in Germany. Still others left to avoid the compulsory military service required by most German princes, and others to get away from distressing economic conditions for which no remedy seemed available. The success of the English manufacturers with factory-made textiles brought ruin to the numerous German household producers of linen, while crop failures in the Rhine Valley and a losing struggle to hold the English grain market meant critical times for agriculture.

The average German immigrant was a little higher in the social scale than his Irish contemporary, and had often saved enough money to get a start in the new land. Sometimes he went into business, and whole cities, such as Cincinnati, St. Louis, and Milwaukee, soon exhibited many of the characteristic qualities of the Germans. More frequently he bought himself a farm and, unaccustomed to the thriftless methods into which an abundance of rich soil had betrayed the native Americans, he farmed carefully and prospered inordinately. Unlike the Irish, the Germans rarely settled in the East, but went instead to the Middle West, where lands were cheaper and opportunity more abundant. For a generation or more they continued to speak the German language, and they clung tenaciously to the manners and customs of their European homes. Great lovers of music and of good-fellowship, each German community was apt to have its *Liederkranz*, its *Turnverein*, and its *Biergärten*. In Wisconsin the German influence was so pronounced that there was talk of making the state over into an ideal German commonwealth.

Politicians in search of new issues, after the Compromise of 1850 had made a truce over slavery, were quick to discover in the immigrant a menace to American institutions. Port cities and the districts adjacent to them complained bitterly of the pauper population that the immigrant tide forced upon them. Religious zealots professed alarm at the presence of a rapidly growing Roman Catholic element in a country that had always before been dominantly Protestant. American workmen complained that their wages were being

Native Americanism

Carl Schurz, a German immigrant of liberal tendencies, became an outstanding anti-slavery leader.

beaten down and their jobs actually taken away from them by their alien competitors. Southerners were deeply concerned because the foreigners, unaccustomed to slavery in their former homes, generally avoided the slaveholding South and helped to swell the already alarming lead of the North in population. Good citizens generally recognized the natural prejudices that must be overcome in order to assimilate fully the clannish Irish and the self-sufficient Germans. Not only must the difficult barriers of race and religion be surmounted, but different political traditions must somehow be reconciled. Some of the Germans, thoroughly imbued with the revolutionary doctrines that had precipitated the revolutions of 1848, even dared to propose radical changes in the American form of government.

The first impulse of the politicians, however, was to cater to the foreign vote. In many states the law permitted aliens to vote if they had resided in the United States for a year and had declared their intention of becoming citizens, but the lax polling system of the time made the restrictions in practice even less consequential. To curry favor with the foreigners, German and Irish names were often placed on the ballots, while naturalized citizens were showered with political favors. In the contest for foreign support, however, the Democrats completely eclipsed the Whigs, who were convincingly portrayed by their opponents as the American conservatives. The Irish, almost to the last man, accepted the Democratic Party as the "poor man's party," and therefore their rightful place. Similarly, the liberals among the German leaders saw little to hope for from the Whigs, and encouraged their countrymen to vote for Democratic candidates.

Logically the Whigs might well have seized upon the anti-foreigner issue, but **The Know-Nothings** their party was already too moribund to take a pronounced stand upon anything. It fell out, therefore, that a new party was formed precisely for this purpose. Its origins lay in a succession of secret societies, such as the American Brotherhood, the American Protestant Association, the Order of United Americans, and finally the Order of the Star-Spangled Banner, the purpose of which was to combat the alien menace. While not at first admittedly political, these organizations soon sought to correct such "evils" as alien voting or office-holding, too easy means of naturalization, and the admission of foreigners to the same advantages as natives in the acquisition of public lands. Fear of Roman Catholic interference with the public school systems, then being formed, led also to a demand that no Roman Catholic should ever be elected to any public office. Decisions of the anti-foreigner groups were kept secret, and members who were asked what they intended to do replied simply, "I know nothing," whereupon they were promptly dubbed "Know-Nothings." On election days the Know-Nothing vote, particularly in Massachusetts, Pennsylvania, and New York, sometimes assumed astonishing proportions, and candidates were elected whose chances had been regarded as poor. By the middle fifties openly announced Know-Nothing, or American Party, tickets were winning many local victories.

In their search for an attractive issue to keep the mind of the public off the slavery question, the Democrats tried **Expansion as a political issue** repeatedly to rekindle the interest in expansion that had brought them such success in the election of 1844. This was a favorite idea with President Pierce, who declared in his inaugural address that the policy of his administration would "not be controlled by any timid forebodings of evil from expansion." "Indeed," he continued, "it is not to be disguised that our attitude as a nation and our position on the globe render the acquisition of certain possessions not within our jurisdiction eminently important for our protection."

Most coveted by Pierce and his advisers was the island of Cuba, which still belonged to Spain, and in spite of the **Cuba** efforts of many filibustering expeditions from the United States declined to take an abiding interest in revolt. Pierce probably hoped to make the acquisition of Cuba the outstanding achievement of his administration, even if it cost a war with Spain. In 1854 the seizure by Cuban officials of an American merchantman, the *Black Warrior*, on the charge that the vessel had violated some port regulation, almost gave the President the opportunity he needed, but the island authorities receded from their position too soon to permit him to take any drastic action. Disorders in Spain that same year, however, seemed to offer a better pretext, and the ministers from the United States to Great Britain, France, and Spain (James Buchanan, John Y. Mason, and Pierre Soulé) were charged with the task of formulating the American program. Their handiwork, the so-called "Ostend Manifesto," proposed that Spain should be offered one hundred and twenty million dollars for Cuba. If this offer were refused, the United States would be justified in taking the island by force on the ground that "our internal peace and the existence of our cherished union" would otherwise be threatened. But this bit of international bad manners came to nothing. Spain refused to sell, and the United States, already embroiled with the slavery issue and in no position to fight a foreign war, disavowed the action of its ministers.

Efforts were also made to acquire more territory on the mainland. James Buchanan, to **The Gadsden Purchase** whose advice Pierce usually listened with respect, had favored the annexation of all of Mexico in 1848, and many others had felt that at best Trist's failure to obtain Lower California had been an inexcusable blunder. Some ardent expansionists felt that the United States should even have a foothold in Central America, and they especially deplored the terms of the Clayton-Bulwer Treaty of 1850 by which the United States conceded to Great Britain an equal interest in any interoceanic canal that might there be built. But the sole tangible result of this expansionist propaganda was the purchase in 1853 from Mexico for ten million dollars of a sandy triangle south of the Gila River. Surveyors claimed that this territory, generally called the "Gadsden Purchase," would be needed in case the United States ever wished to construct a railroad along a southern route to California.

More successful were the efforts of the administration to smooth the way for American traders in the Far East. **Commerce with the Orient** Ever since 1784, when the *Empress of China* set sail under the Stars and Stripes from New York for Canton, a small but lucrative oriental trade had been maintained, and in 1844, following the Opium War between Great Britain and China, the United States had been accorded by formal treaty the same commercial privileges that the British had won by force. But American trade in China had always operated at a disadvantage in competition with the long-established connections maintained by Europeans; and it was in part to offset this handicap that the American government determined to open up a new field for commercial exploitation in the so-called "Hermit Kingdom" of Japan. Except for the Dutch, who were allowed limited privileges of trade

at Nagasaki, Japan was virtually closed to the outside world, and so mistrustful were the natives of foreigners that shipwrecked sailors were often treated with extreme cruelty. To end this unfortunate situation, Commodore Matthew Perry visited Japan in 1854 with the largest fleet the United States had ever assembled in Asiatic waters. Overawed by so great a show of force, the Japanese government agreed to open two ports to American traders, to permit an American consul to reside at one of them, and to accord protection to American seamen left in distress upon Japanese shores. Elsewhere in the Pacific also the administration sought new advantages for American traders. A treaty with Siam, concluded in 1856, enlarged upon trade privileges that had been obtained twenty years earlier; and an attempt to annex Hawaii, although unsuccessful, called attention to the dominance of American influence in the Middle Pacific.

Meantime, the impossibility of keeping the vexatious slavery question in abeyance was becoming increasingly apparent. **Persistence of the debate over slavery** Know-Nothingism won a foothold in the South, where there were no foreigners, because the inrush of immigrants was strengthening the free states, and loomed up, therefore, as a possible menace to slavery. Expansion was ardently championed in the South, particularly with respect to Cuba, for only in such a fashion could new lands suited to the slave-labor system be obtained; but expansion was quite as heatedly denounced in the North, where it was correctly regarded as a thinly veiled disguise for the acquisition of more slave territory. Efforts to enforce the newly enacted Fugitive Slave Law added to the difficulties of the situation, and Charles Sumner in a four-hour address to the United States Senate called eloquently for its repeal. Abolitionists brought forth evidence to prove that under the terms of this act free Negroes were being kidnaped from their northern homes and sold into slavery; but Southerners had quite as convincing evidence of the success with which anti-slavery men in the North were assisting runaway slaves from the South over the underground railroad to Canada. In spite of the Compromise of 1850 the debate over the morality of slavery did not cease. On this question the leading Protestant churches had already split — the Presbyterians in 1838, the Methodists in 1844, and the Baptists in 1845 — and seemingly the more pronounced the views of any given sect on the slavery question, the more it prospered.

Doubtless the most important document in the history of the anti-slavery crusade "Uncle was Harriet Beecher Stowe's Tom's *Uncle Tom's Cabin, or, Life* Cabin" *Among the Lowly,* a simple and moving story of Negro life. Mrs. Stowe was the daughter of one New England clergyman, Lyman Beecher, the wife of another, and the sister of seven others, among whom

"Uncle Tom's Cabin," by Harriet Beecher Stowe, was one of the most influential books ever published.

UNCLE TOM'S CABIN;

OR,

LIFE AMONG THE LOWLY.

BY

HARRIET BEECHER STOWE.

VOL. I.

BOSTON:
JOHN P. JEWETT & COMPANY.
CLEVELAND, OHIO:
JEWETT, PROCTOR & WORTHINGTON.
1852.

was Henry Ward Beecher. For many years her husband, Calvin Stowe, taught at Lane Theological Seminary in Cincinnati, Ohio, and it was here that she came into intimate contact with the institution of slavery, as it existed across the river in Kentucky. She saw something, too, of the plight of the fugitive slave, and with the strong humanitarian urge that was her birthright she felt impelled to attack what she believed to be an unmitigated evil. Her weapon was her pen, for by her writing she added each year a few hundred dollars to the family income. In 1850 her husband became a professor in Bowdoin College, Brunswick, Maine, and it was here, far removed from the scenes of which she wrote, that *Uncle Tom's Cabin* took form. Published first as a serial in the *National Era,* an anti-slavery paper of Washington, D.C., it attracted little attention, but in 1852 when it appeared in book form its popularity was immediate and great. Three thousand copies were sold the first day, and three hundred thousand copies before the end of a year. As a novel, the book left much to be desired, but as a moral indictment of slavery it was tremendous. Dramatized, and played before enthusiastic audiences throughout the North, it made converts for the anti-slavery cause even among those who could not or would not read. Years later when President Lincoln first met Mrs. Stowe he is said to have remarked, "So you're the little woman who wrote the book that made this great war!" For the popularity which the book achieved in the North was matched only by its unpopularity in the South.

Under these circumstances it is hardly fair to place the entire blame for the reopening of the slavery dispute upon the shoulders of Stephen A. Douglas of Illinois. It is a fact, however, that in 1854 Douglas did sponsor a measure, the Kansas-Nebraska Act, which embodied a plan for the further expansion of slavery, and which could therefore be construed as unsettling the delicate balance that the compromise measures of 1850 had established. But the time was ripe for such a step, and if Douglas had not been

Stephen A. Douglas of Illinois, the "Little Giant," was an effective public speaker, and a resourceful politician. Although of New England birth and ancestry, he was completely identified with the West, and devoted to its expansion. He was quick to recognize the importance of railroads to his section, and in a later generation would have been called a "rail- road senator." He saw clearly the disruptive forces unleashed by the slavery dispute, and fought valiantly for a compromise solution that would save the Union and keep the peace. The portrait is from a photograph by Mathew B. Brady, and the second picture shows the build- ing of a railroad across the western plains.

the first to suggest it, in all likelihood some- one else would have done so at a not much later date.

Stephen A. Douglas (1813–61) was born in Brandon, Vermont, but at the age of twenty **Stephen A.** he went to Illinois, where he be- **Douglas** gan the practice of law. Law led naturally to politics, an occupation for which Douglas had great natural aptitude. He knew how and when to be shrewd and calcu- lating, he mastered easily the oratorical technique required by his time, and he put no restraints upon his ambition. By 1847 he was a member of the United States Senate, and the idol of the boastful, untutored, ex- pansionist Illinois Democracy. Sensitive to the necessity of keeping the southern and western wings of his party together, he sup- ported the Compromise of 1850 with telling effectiveness, and that same year he won the consent of both sections to his policy of lib- eral land grants to the states in aid of rail- road-building. Thereafter the rapid con- struction of the Illinois Central and other western roads greatly enriched the state of Illinois, converted Chicago from a frontier village into the "metropolis of the West," and made it abundantly clear to Douglas

that in befriending the railroads he had made no mistake. Short of stature, but possessed of a magnificent head and massive shoulders, he was called by his admirers the "Little Giant."

The idea of a transcontinental railroad was almost as old as railroads in the United States. In the thirties Asa **The trans-** Whitney, a merchant who was **continental** engaged in the China trade, had **railroad** begun to advocate that such a **idea** road should be built as a means of shortening the route to the Orient. Whitney had also suggested that the government might aid in financing the project by endowing the road with a strip of land sixty miles wide along the right of way. Even before the Mexican War Whitney's arguments had won some support in Congress; after the war, with Cali- fornia a part of the United States and gold discovered in the newly acquired territory, converts came thick and fast. It soon be- came apparent, however, that there would be grave difficulty in choosing the route over which such a road was to be built. Every enterprising city in the Mississippi Valley aspired to become its eastern terminus, and the claims of New Orleans, Vicksburg, St.

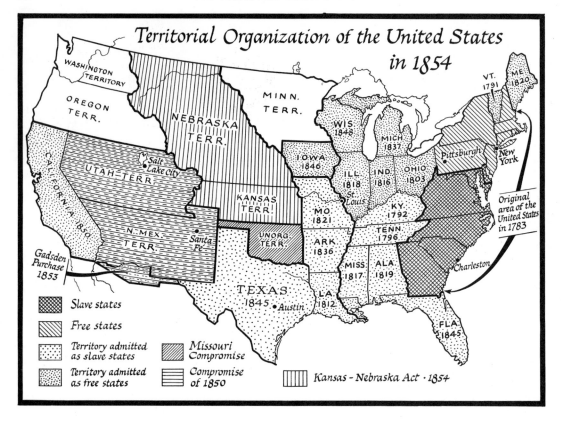

Territorial Organization of the United States in 1854

Louis, Chicago, and Milwaukee were elaborately set forth. In 1853 Congress, unwilling and unready to choose among so many aspirants, appropriated one hundred and fifty thousand dollars to be used by the Secretary of War in surveying a number of alternative railroad routes across the western half of the continent. In due time the surveyors reported that, at least so far as the engineering problem was concerned, a northern, a southern, and one or more central routes were equally feasible.

Douglas naturally hoped that Chicago, his official residence and the center of his **Objections to a northern route** somewhat extensive real-estate speculations, would be in line with the route to the West finally selected. But unfortunately there were serious objections to every northern or central way through. Such a route necessarily traversed much unorganized Indian territory, where the savages were none too

tractable, and where the government owned no lands to grant. The proposed southern route, on the other hand, led through the state of Texas and the now fully organized territory of New Mexico. No serious Indian menace embarrassed the advocates of this route, and land grants, either from the state of Texas or from the United States, would be available for its entire length. But there was an obvious way to overcome the serious handicap from which partisans of a northern or central route suffered. The legend of the "Great American Desert" was fast breaking down, and demands that the good agricultural lands directly west of the bend of the Missouri should be opened to settlement were already insistent. Indeed, by the summer of 1853 the Commissioner of Indian Affairs had begun negotiations for the removal of the Indians from the coveted region, and a bill for the erection of the unorganized Indian country into the territory of Nebraska had passed the House of Representatives. If the Senate could only be persuaded to concur in this measure, the relative advantages of the southern railway route would be materially lessened.

Douglas, who as chairman of the Senate Committee on Territories, was beyond a doubt fully conversant with this situation, championed, early in January, 1854, the creation of the new territory. His views were set forth in an elaborate report to the Senate, a report that was fraught with far graver consequences than he could have dreamed. Knowing full well that the South would never favor the creation of a new territory without some concession to slavery, he artfully suggested that the Compromise of 1850, which had left New Mexico and Utah free to decide for themselves whether they would or would not legalize slavery, had superseded the Missouri Compromise of thirty years before. The proposed new territory might, therefore, be free or slave, not as Congress should determine, but as the people of the territory should determine. Douglas's championship at this juncture of "popular sovereignty," as he called it, was shrewdly conceived, for it appealed both to

The Kansas-Nebraska Act

the democratic instincts of the West and to the persistent hopes of the South for the extension of slave territory. Nevertheless, before the bill could pass its sponsor had to accept important amendments. Instead of one territory, two were authorized, Kansas to the west of Missouri, which presumably would be slave, and Nebraska to the west of Iowa, which presumably would be free. Also, the repeal of the Missouri Compromise, which Douglas would have preferred merely to take for granted, was specifically stated.

The debate over the Kansas-Nebraska Bill revived all the bitterness that had preceded the Compromise of 1850. Southern members of Congress, almost to the last man, supported the measure, while practically all the northern Whigs and many northern Democrats opposed it. Douglas was accused of deliberately undoing the sectional truce in order to obtain support from the South for his presidential candidacy in 1856, and it would be difficult to prove that no such thought ever crossed his mind. He had no aversion to slavery or to slavery extension, and his first wife, a North-Carolinian, held slaves. Moreover, he must have foreseen that the truce

The undoing of the sectional truce

The County Election. Voters in a western town casting spoken ballots on the courthouse steps. Painting by George Caleb Bingham, 1851, courtesy of The Boatmen's National Bank of St. Louis.

over slavery could not last long, and he may well have believed that the principle of popular sovereignty would furnish a better solution of the problem of slavery extension than the Missouri Compromise. Perhaps a grateful country might make its proponent President. But there is good reason to believe that the idea of a Pacific railroad west from Chicago was never long absent from his mind. Probably, too, he was no less impressed by the demands of pro-slavery Missourians, who were greatly concerned lest their state be surrounded on three sides by free territory, than by the wishes of the South as a whole.

Whatever Douglas's motives may have been (a subject upon which historians seem destined never to agree), the fires of sectional controversy once more burned bright. The Democratic Party of the North was rent violently in twain. Those who defended the act were known as Pro-Nebraska Democrats; those who opposed it as Anti-Nebraska Democrats. The Whig Party lost its last vestige of unity. Northern Whigs were almost unanimously anti-Nebraska; southern Whigs were quite as unanimously pro-Nebraska. Even the Know-Nothings were forced to take sides, and anti-Nebraska and pro-Nebraska factions brought discord to their lodges. Division of opinion, however, was for the time being confined to the North. Southerners, whether Whigs, Democrats, or Know-Nothings, stood solidly together in favor of the act.

Bibliography

All the various economic histories, such as Faulkner, Shannon, McGrane and Kirkland, are full at this point.

On the railroad activities, an excellent short history is John Moody, *The Railroad Builders* (1919). An early assessment, still useful, is C. F. Adams, Jr., *Railroads: Their Origins and Problems* (1878). See also B. H. Meyer, C. H. MacGill, and others, *History of Transportation in the United States before 1866* (1917); Edward Hungerford, *The Story of the Baltimore and Ohio Railroad, 1827–1897* (1928); F. W. Stevens, *The Beginnings of the New York Central Railroad* (1926); U. B. Phillips, *A History of Transportation in the Eastern Cotton Belt to 1860* (1908).

On water transportation there are many books of interest. William J. Petersen, *Steamboating on the Upper Mississippi* (1937), recovers much of the glamour of the old river days. Jerry MacMullen, *Paddle-Wheel Days in California* (1944), is interesting and colorful. On ocean going shipping, the following are useful: A. H. Clark, *The Clipper Ship Era, 1843–1869* (1910); C. C. Cutler, *Greyhounds of the Sea: The Story of the American Clipper Ship* (1930); Ralph D. Paine, *The Old Merchant Marine* (1919); J. G. B. Hutchins, *The American Maritime Industries and Public Policy, 1789–1914* (1941); R. G. Albion, *Square Riggers on Schedule* (1938); W. J. Lane, *Commodore Vanderbilt: An Epic of the Steam Age* (1942).

On the history of agriculture, there are several important works. L. C. Gray, *History of Agriculture in the Southern United States to 1860* (2 vols., 1933), is elaborate and satisfactory. It may be supplemented by Meyer Jacobstein, *The Tobacco Industry in the United States* (1907). P. W. Bidwell and J. I. Falconer, *History of Agriculture in the Northern United States, 1620–1860* (1925), is the companion volume to Gray. A. H. Sanford, *The Story of Agriculture in the United States* (1916), is a convenient one-volume summary. Joseph Schafer, *The Social History of American Agriculture* (1936), approaches the subject from an interesting point of view. Leo Rogin, *The Introduction of Farm Machinery in its Relation to the Productivity of Labor in the Agriculture of the United States during the Nineteenth Century* (1931), is excellent. For more specialized studies, see D. M. Ellis, *Landlords and Farmers in the Hudson-Mohawk Region, 1790–1860* (1946); J. P. Pritchett, *The Red River Valley, 1811–1849: A Regional Study* (1942); W. C. Neely, *The Agricultural Fair* (1935); A. L. Demaree, *The American Agricultural Press, 1819–1860* (1941).

On industrial development, V. S. Clark, *History of Manufactures in the United States* (2 vols.,

1916–28), Vol. I, *1607–1860*, is a good general account. T. C. Cochran and William Miller, *The Age of Enterprise, A Social History of Industrial America* (1942), is interpretative. Particular industries have also attracted writers, for example: M. T. Copeland, *The Cotton Manufacturing Industry of the United States* (1912); J. V. Woodworth, *American Tool Making and Interchangeable Manufacturing* (1905); J. M. Swank, *History of the Manufacture of Iron in all Ages* (1892). On the rise of a great industrial city, see Bessie L. Pierce, *A History of Chicago*, Vol. I (1937), Vol. II (1940).

On the immigrant and immigrant problems, G. M. Stephenson, *A History of American Immigration* (1926); and Carl Wittke, *We Who Built America* (1939), are both excellent. T. C. Blegen, *Norwegian Migration to America* (2 vols., 1931–1940), treats of the influences that made for emigration as well as of the movement itself. Other useful books on the subject include M. L. Hansen, *The Immigrant in American History* (1940); L. M. Larson, *The Changing West and Other Essays* (1937), and *The Log Book of a Young Immigrant* (1939); Oscar Handlin, *Boston's Immigrants, 1790–1865* (1941); Frank Freidel, *Francis Lieber, Nineteenth Century Liberal* (1947); Robert Ernst, *Immigrant Life in New York City, 1825–1863* (1949). On the nativist reaction, the best general treatment is R. A. Billington, *The Protestant Crusade, 1800–1860* (1938). See also Sister M. Evangeline Thomas, *Nativism in the Old Northwest, 1850–1860* (1936); and Sister Agnes Geraldine McGann, *Nativism in Kentucky in 1860* (1944).

On the renewal of the sectional controversy, T. C. Smith, *Parties and Slavery* (1906), presents the traditional view. P. O. Ray, *The Repeal of the Missouri Compromise* (1909), challenged this interpretation; but his views were in turn attacked by F. H. Hodder, "The Genesis of the Kansas-Nebraska Act," in Wisconsin State Historical Society, *Proceedings*, 1912, pp. 69–86. G. R. Gaeddert, *The Birth of Kansas* (1940), is a valuable revisionist treatment. Robert Forrest Wilson, *Crusader in Crinoline: The Life of Harriet Beecher Stowe* (1941), is a satisfactory biography. J. N. Norwood, *The Schism in the Methodist Episcopal Church, 1844* (1923), shows the disruptive forces at work in a single denomination. For the others, see H. K. Rowe, *The History of Religion in the United States* (1924). On the hope for American annexation of Cuba, see J. M. Callahan, *Cuba and International Relations* (1899); and Basil Rauch, *American Interest in Cuba, 1848–1855* (1948).

The frontier theme is variously treated in J. T. Flanagan, *America Is West: An Anthology of Middlewestern Life and Literature* (1945); H. C. Hubbart, *The Older Middle West, 1840–1880* (1936); T. D. Clark, *The Rampaging Frontier* (1939); Madge E. Pickard and R. Carlyle Buley, *The Midwest Pioneer: His Ills, Cures, Cares and Doctors* (1945).

29

Coordinate with Lectures.

The House Divided

Birth of the Republican Party — Popular sovereignty in Kansas — The Sumner-Brooks episode — Election of 1856 — James Buchanan — The Dred Scott case — Panic of 1857 — Elections of 1858 — The Lincoln-Douglas debates — John Brown at Harper's Ferry — *The Impending Crisis* — Presidential campaign and election of 1860

THE united front achieved by the opponents of slavery extension during the debate on the

Birth of the Republican Party
Kansas-Nebraska Act was not destined to disappear. In fact, the men who had fought together against the opening of new territory to slavery were about ready, as events proved, to forsake their old party loyalties, and to join in the formation of a new party that would reflect accurately the stand they had taken. So general was this sentiment that it is somewhat difficult to designate an exact time and place for the birth of the Republican Party. The superior claims of the Middle West, however, must be conceded, for in this section action was both immediate and vigorous. Here opposition to slavery on moral grounds was rife, but the western small farmers felt also that the lands of the new frontier should belong to them and their kind, and not to the southern slaveholders. At Ripon, Wisconsin, February 28, 1854, an "Anti-Nebraska" mass meeting revived the name Republican; at Jackson, Michigan, July 6, 1854, the first state-wide Republican organization was launched. By November, when the mid-term state and congressional elections were held, Republican tickets, or their equivalent under a different name, challenged the Democrats in every northwestern state, and won far more often than they lost.

In the Northeast, although both Maine and Vermont voted Republican in 1854, the emergence of the new party was not quite so speedily accomplished. The decision of Seward, who was up for re-election to the United States Senate from New York and feared to change his party alliance, did much to postpone a little longer the day of Whig dissolution. Also Know-Nothingism, by an astonishing victory in Massachusetts and a large vote in Pennsylvania and New York, proved that the anti-foreigner issue had not yet run its course. Shortly after the election the Republican tide set in. By the fall of 1855 Seward, who was generally recognized as the outstanding leader of the anti-slavery Whigs, was safe in the new party fold, and although the Whig Party in the Northeast died hard, it died. Know-Nothingism likewise was unable to survive the inevitable split upon the rock of slavery extension, and ultimately the bulk of the northern Know-Nothings became Republicans. Eastern Republicans, it should be noted, while embracing within their number many former abolitionists, were often quite as much motivated by their resentment against the existing southern domination of the national government as by their dislike of slavery as an institution. New slave states meant more pro-southern votes in Congress, votes that were certain to be used in favor of policies desired by the agricultural South — the low tariff, for example — but against such policies as would enhance the prosperity of the industrial Northeast.

In all sections of the North the rise of the Republican Party did serious damage to the **Decline of the northern Democracy** Democrats. According to a compilation made by the *National Intelligencer*, the northern wing of the Democratic Party polled nearly three hundred and fifty thousand fewer votes in 1854 than in 1852. Of the forty-two northern Democrats who voted for the Kansas-Nebraska Act in the House, only seven were re-elected. Both in 1854 and in 1855 states that had once been Democratic strongholds elected Republican legislatures and Republican state officers. Eager to clear himself of responsibility for the calamity that had befallen his party, Douglas blamed these results mainly upon the rise of the Know-Nothings. But the statistics did not bear him out; neither did his own alarming loss of popularity throughout the North. Denounced as a traitor for his reopening of the slavery dispute, he was compared to Benedict Arnold and Judas Iscariot. He could have traveled, he later admitted, "from Boston to Chicago by the light of his own burning effigies." In Chicago, where his popularity had once been unbounded, he was greeted with groans and hisses by an unruly audience that finally drove him in a temper from the platform.

Democratic losses in the North, however, were not duplicated in the South. There the passage of the Kansas-Nebraska Act was regarded as a defeat for the hated abolitionists, and a timely recognition of southern rights. Even if Kansas did not become a slave state, as some Southerners had begun to fear, the doctrine of popular sovereignty might be used to advantage elsewhere, in Cuba, for example. Not only did the southern Democrats hold their party lines intact after the passage of the act; they made substantial gains. The Whig Party of the South, like the Whig Party of the North, was in process of liquidation, and many southern Whigs be-

came Democrats. Others, unable to join hands so suddenly with their traditional enemies, broke the fall by becoming Know-Nothings, or "Americans," for a season. Some of the Know-Nothing leaders were shrewd enough to try to make a new issue for their party by requiring of their members an oath to protect and defend the union of the states. Most Southerners, however, chose to interpret this oath as meaning merely that the North should cease its opposition to slavery expansion, hence the difference in principle between southern Democrats and southern Know-Nothings was slight. Perhaps the "Solid South" had not yet arrived, but it was on the way.

The real test of popular sovereignty as a remedy for the sectional controversy over slavery came in Kansas. Under **Kansas and Nebraska** the terms of the Kansas-Nebraska Act territorial governments were set up both in Kansas and in Nebraska, but the beginnings of Nebraska Territory attracted little attention. Southerners as well as Northerners conceded that the Iowans who were moving over into Nebraska would be certain to exclude slavery from the territory; and this they promptly did. Nor did many settlers come; indeed, for a time Nebraska was less a place of abode than a highway to the Far West. From its river towns — Omaha, Plattsmouth, and Nebraska City — traders and emigrants set off for Oregon, Utah, and California, but only a few remained to take lands and settle down. With Kansas it was quite otherwise. No sooner was this territory authorized than rivalry broke out between North and South to see which section should settle it, and thus be in position to determine whether it should be free or slave. In the normal course of events Missourians would have taken the lead in the settlement of Kansas, just as Iowans without much outside interference were moving slowly into Nebraska. And, whether correctly or otherwise, it was generally assumed that these Missourians would make Kansas a slave territory and ultimately a slave state. But northern anti-slavery men set themselves the task of heading off this "normal course of events." Organizations to aid emigrants were formed in New England and elsewhere with the avowed intention of putting enough anti-slavery men in Kansas to insure the defeat of the pro-slavery element when the new government should be organized. In such a competition the South was at a distinct disadvantage, for it had far less man-power to mobilize than the North. Pro-slavery Missourians, however, organized themselves into secret lodges and prepared to march over into Kansas, whenever occasion should demand, to stuff the ballot-boxes. With instinctive common sense the pro-slavery and anti-slavery emigrants to Kansas settled at a considerable distance from each other. Most of the pro-slavery men settled close to the Missouri River, and founded such towns as Atchison and Leavenworth. The anti-slavery men, on the other hand, went farther into the interior of the state, where they founded Lawrence and Topeka.

Unfortunately, the man Franklin Pierce chose for the governorship of Kansas, Andrew H. Reeder, a Douglas Democrat from Pennsylvania, turned out to be much more interested in land speculation than in the question of whether Kansas should be slave or free. He called an election for territorial delegate in November, 1854, which the pro-slavery faction, ably assisted by the votes of several hundred Missourians who crossed the border for the purpose, won easily. The following March Reeder ordered the election of a territorial legislature, and again the Missourians appeared, this time five thousand strong, to carry all before them. When Reeder canvassed the returns, as was his privilege, he ordered re-elections in a few instances; also, while en route to Washington a little later he told a Pennsylvania audience that the election in Kansas had been rotten with fraud. Naturally this made him extremely unpopular with the pro-slavery men chosen to the Kansas legislature, and their hostility was by no means lessened when Reeder called them to meet at Pawnee City, a virtually uninhabited town-site he himself

had laid out as a speculative venture, far up the Kansas River. At that obscure point, however, the legislature was obliged to meet and organize, but it adjourned at once to a more convenient place, petitioned President Pierce to remove Reeder from office, and adopted the slave code then current in Missouri.

Franklin Pierce (1804–69) was hardly to be depended upon in such an emergency. Handsome, a good lawyer, and a polished public speaker, he had entered the Presidency with the hearty good-will of almost the entire American public. Judging from his record as a member for short terms each in both houses of Congress and as a volunteer officer in the Mexican War, there was some reason to hope that, in spite of his relative obscurity, he would rise to the requirements of his high office. But these expectations were doomed to quick disappointment. Eager to please, he was always in an agony of indecision, for whichever way he decided someone would be offended: he was known, on occasion, to promise the same office to two different applicants. Such a weakling was bound to be at the mercy of the strongest-willed among his advisers. When the Kansas-Nebraska Act was before Congress, the pressure exerted by Douglas and his friends had brought the President, after much wavering, to the support of the measure. Later, with the southern influence strongly dominant among his advisers, he decided to remove Reeder from office, and to give the pro-slavery cause in Kansas his full support. When Reeder, after a long correspondence with the President, refused to resign, the President removed him to make way for an Ohio politician, Wilson Shannon, whose pro-slavery sympathies were well known. Reeder now went over completely to the anti-slavery side. Whatever his merits and demerits, his brief term as governor had proved that the pro-slavery interests were determined to have their way in Kansas, regardless of the methods used.

When the anti-slavery Kansans realized

Franklin Pierce on Kansas

the hopelessness of trying to win a territorial election, they decided to follow the precedent recently set by California for establishing a state government in advance of congressional permission. Accordingly they elected delegates to a constitutional convention which met at Topeka, October 23, 1855, and drew up a free state constitution. Before the end of the year this document was submitted to the people at the polls, and, since the pro-slavery faction did not participate in the election, was adopted by a one-sided vote. Under its terms a governor and legislature were promptly chosen, and Congress was petitioned to admit Kansas as a state. This action President Pierce denounced as treasonous. The pro-slavery territorial government, he told Congress, was the only lawful government in Kansas, and as such was deserving of the full support of the United States.

Douglas had claimed that popular sovereignty would exile the debate over slavery

The Sumner–Brooks episode from the halls of Congress, and put it where it belonged, in the territories concerned. The speciousness of his reasoning was now fully apparent, for in spite of Pierce's contention Congress, not the President, had authority over the admission of new states, and Congress, not the President, must decide whether to leave the pro-slavery territorial government in control, or heed the request of the free-state party and admit Kansas as a state. After a prolonged struggle over the Speakership, the House of Representatives voted in March, 1856, that the new Speaker, a Republican, should appoint a committee of three to inquire into the trouble in Kansas, and report back to the House. In midsummer the committee presented majority and minority reports, neither of which helped toward a solution of the vexing problem, and both of which added fuel to the flames. The debate on Kansas in the Senate reached its climax on May 19-20, when Charles Sumner of Massachusetts spoke at great length on the "Crime against Kansas." During this address he denounced Senator Andrew P.

Butler of South Carolina in the most offensive language, and charged the state he represented with "shameful imbecility" during the American Revolution. For such abuse, according to the southern code, he might possibly have deserved a caning, but the attack made upon him afterward by Preston Brooks, a relative of Butler's and a member of the House, far exceeded any code of proprieties. Brooks, who was a young man, approached Sumner while the latter was seated at his desk in the Senate Chamber, upbraided him for his libelous language, and then, while the Senator was still sitting, beat him over the head with a heavy gutta-percha cane until he fell to the floor covered with blood. The injuries inflicted were so serious that Sumner was unable to resume his regular duties for five years, and his health was permanently impaired.

While the futility of popular sovereignty as a remedy for the dispute over slavery expansion was thus being revealed **Violence in Kansas** in Washington, its results in Kansas were no less unfortunate. There the "border ruffians" who crossed over from Missouri from time to time in order to carry elections did not hesitate to use violence, and they were soon met in kind by the free-state men from the North. Collections were taken up at public meetings throughout the northern states, not only to send more anti-slavery emigrants to Kansas, but also to arm them with the rifles they might need to defend themselves. According to Henry Ward Beecher, who addressed many such meetings, these Sharps rifles might be "a greater moral agency" in Kansas than the Bible, hence such weapons were generally referred to as "Beecher's Bibles." The day before the assault on Sumner a pro-slavery posse of about a thousand men, consisting mainly of border ruffians, was assembled by the federal marshal for Kansas territory to assist him in serving writs upon the "treasonous" anti-slavery officers of the free-state government at Lawrence. The arrests were made without resistance, but the "posse" did not withdraw until it had destroyed all the local newspaper offices, set fire to a number of buildings, and thoroughly sacked the city.

The self-appointed avenger of this outrage was John Brown of Osawatomie, an abolitionist fanatic whose family was strongly tainted with insanity. Brown reckoned that from first to last five free-state men had been killed in Kansas by their opponents, and that an equal number of pro-slavery men must die. Three days after the raid on Lawrence he and four of his sons, a son-in-law, and two neighbors murdered in cold blood five pro-slavery settlers who lived along Pottawatomie Creek. This wild deed most of the free-state men in Kansas were at pains to disavow, but reprisals were in order, and they were not long in coming. Attempts to arrest Brown failed, but soon armed bands of free-staters and border ruffians were wandering about, attacking each other at sight, and making life for the peaceful settler a nightmare. The "Civil War in Kansas" which thus began was ended presently by a new

governor, John White Geary, who did not hesitate to invoke the proffered aid of federal troops. But altogether probably two hundred lives were lost.

It was in an atmosphere surcharged with excitement over the attack on Sumner and "Bleeding Kansas" that the presidential campaign and election of 1856 took place. The logic of the situation demanded that the Democrats should renominate Pierce, who had stood as firmly by popular sovereignty as he was ever able to stand by anything; or, if not Pierce, then Douglas, the foremost champion of the doctrine. But both Pierce and Douglas had made a host of enemies, particularly among the Democrats of the North; hence the nomination went to James Buchanan of Pennsylvania, whose absence as minister to England had saved him from too close identification with any point of view. Despite the overwhelming evidence from Kansas to the contrary, the Demo-

Presidential campaign of 1856

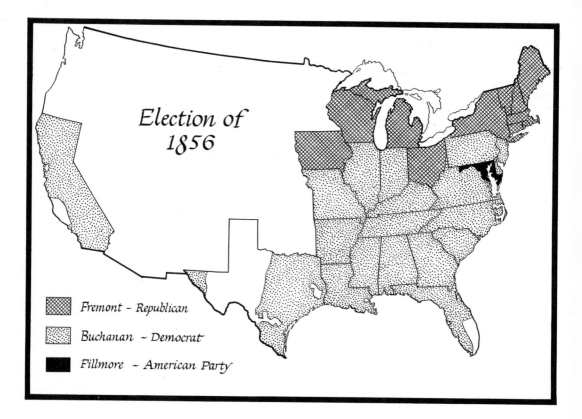

Election of 1856

Fremont ~ Republican
Buchanan ~ Democrat
Fillmore ~ American Party

cratic National Convention maintained in its platform that the doctrine of popular sovereignty was "the only sound and safe solution of the slavery question." The Republicans, as eager to serve availability as the Democrats, overlooked the claims of Seward and Chase, their best-known leaders, to choose as their standard-bearer John C. Frémont, the glamorous "Pathfinder of the West." Their platform revived the Free-Soil doctrine that Congress had the constitutional right and the moral duty to prohibit the expansion of slavery into any of the territories of the United States. The Americans, or Know-Nothings, and a remnant of the Whigs held separate conventions, but nominated the same candidate, ex-President Fillmore, and adopted platforms that sought in the main to avoid sectionalism by an insistent demand for the preservation of the Union.

The Democrats won an unexpectedly easy victory. Their party alone, as events soon proved, was truly national, and it profited materially from that fact. The Republican Party was so definitely a northern organization that in eleven southern states the names of its candidates did not even appear on the ballot. The Know-Nothings were almost as strictly southern, for their convention, under pressure from the southern delegates, had declared that territories should be permitted "to regulate their domestic and social affairs in their own mode." This could mean only one thing; popular sovereignty. Northerners who believed in Douglas's doctrine generally preferred to vote the Democratic ticket, while those who were opposed to it lined up with the Republicans. Overconfident as a result of their successes in 1854, the Republicans really expected to win. They made a whirlwind campaign, patterned on the Whig tactics of 1840, with "Bleeding Kansas" as their principal issue. But the country was frightened by the specter of disunion, and preferred a national party to one that represented only a section. Eleven northern states cast 114 votes for Frémont, but five northern states and every southern

James Buchanan

FIFTEENTH PRESIDENT of the United States, Buchanan of Pennsylvania was nominated in 1856 by the Democrats in an effort to promote party harmony. He was generally liked, and although a northerner had won popularity in the South by his support of the Ostend Manifesto (p. 520). Buchanan won the election easily. Portrait after a photo by Mathew B. Brady.

state but one cast a total of 174 votes for Buchanan. While the American Party furnished strong opposition to the Democrats in the South, Fillmore carried only one state, Maryland, with 8 electoral votes. Both houses of Congress were safely Democratic.

James Buchanan (1791–1868) was nearly sixty-six years of age when he assumed the Presidency, and, unlike Pierce, James he had had ample experience in Buchanan politics. Curiously, he had begun his political career as a Federalist, and had moved over into the Democratic Party only when the Federalist Party had ceased to exist. After he had served for ten years in the House as a representative from Pennsylvania, he was sent by President Jackson in 1832 as minister to Russia, but returned two years later to enter the United States Senate. Here he remained for more than two decades. Afterward he was Secretary of State under Polk, minister to England under Pierce, and at all times a persistent aspirant to the Presidency. His opposition to the Wilmot Proviso and his ardent championship of expansion marked him as a "dough-face," that is, a "northern man with southern principles." Beyond a doubt he was devoted to the Union, but the conservatism of old age tended to confirm him in the belief that the only way to preserve the Union was to permit the southern leaders to have their way.

Two days after Buchanan's inauguration the Supreme Court of the United States **The Dred** handed down a decision in the **Scott case** case of *Dred Scott vs. Sanford* [1] that put a new aspect upon the dispute over slavery in the territories. This decision did not come unsolicited. The Kansas-Nebraska Act had assumed that the Supreme Court might have a final word to say on the subject; and Southerners, confident that the Court would be on their side, were eager for its pronouncement. Even the President-elect, shortly before his inauguration, seems to have used his influence to swing a wavering justice into line. Seven of the justices were Democrats, one was a Whig, and one a Republican; and of the seven Democrats five were from the South. Surely such a Court would end for all time the Republican pretension that Congress had a right to exclude slavery from the territories. No doubt the majority of the Court, including the venerable Chief Justice Taney, were genuinely persuaded that the weight of their opinion would be sufficient to bring the heated controversy to an end.

The Dred Scott case offered a satisfactory opportunity for the Court to declare itself. Dred Scott was a Negro who until 1834 had legally been held in bondage in the slave state of Missouri. After that date his master, an army surgeon, removed, taking Dred with him, first to Illinois, a free state, and then to Minnesota Territory, where, under the terms of the Missouri Compromise, slavery was also forbidden. Ultimately Dred was brought back to Missouri. Here he was induced by some interested abolitionists to bring suit for his freedom on the ground that his residence in free territory had set him

[1] Curiously, in the official report of this decision, 19 Howard, 393, Sanford's name is misspelled, and the case appears as *Dred Scott vs. Sandford*.

free. Evidence that there was connivance between the defense and the prosecution appears from the fact that during the litigation the ownership of Dred was transferred to a New Yorker named Sanford. A federal court was then asked to assume jurisdiction on the ground that the suit lay between the citizens of different states. Thus the case could be, and was, promptly passed on up to the United States Supreme Court, where it was argued first in the spring of 1856, and, because of the sharp divergence of views it evoked among the justices, a second time in December of the same year. Naturally these proceedings had won for the case much publicity, and President Buchanan, who knew in advance what the decision would be, saw nothing improper about venturing the hope in his inaugural address that the forthcoming opinion of the Court would settle with finality the status of slavery in the territories.

Chief Justice Taney spoke for the seven Democratic justices. First of all, he denied emphatically the right of the **Taney's** lower federal court to assume **opinion** jurisdiction in the case. Dred Scott, said the Chief Justice, was not a citizen of Missouri within the meaning of the Constitution; hence he could neither sue nor be sued in the federal courts. This opinion the Court might have based, as some of the assenting justices would have been more content to do, on the ground that Dred Scott, whatever his status in Illinois or Minnesota, was at the time he brought suit a slave in Missouri, and so not a citizen. But the Chief Justice had no notion of dodging what to him appeared to be an important issue. Negroes who were of the African race and the descendants of slaves, he asserted, were not and could not become citizens of a state in the sense in which the word citizen was used when the Constitution of the United States was adopted. At that time, according to the Chief Justice, such persons were commonly regarded as of an inferior order of beings who had no rights that a white man need respect. So far as the Constitution of the United States was con-

The extension of slavery as a moral and political issue of national consequence was intensified rather than abated by Chief Justice Roger B. Taney's ruling on the Dred Scott case. Portrait of Taney by M. B. Brady; of Scott by Louis Schultze.

cerned, their status had not changed during the intervening years. The inference was clear, therefore, that Dred Scott's suit would have been thrown out even if he had been free, and not a slave.

But the Chief Justice took great pains to point out that Dred was not free, that neither his residence in a free state nor in territory north of the Missouri Compromise line could possibly have made him free. Precedent was cited to prove that each state had the right to determine for itself the status of a slave who had resided temporarily in a free state, and the Missouri courts had held that Dred was still a slave. As for the territorial residence, the Chief Justice aligned himself and the Court with the most extreme of the southern extremists. Congress, he said, had exceeded its authority in forbidding slavery in that part of the Louisiana Purchase north of 36° 30′. Slave property in the territories was as much protected by the Constitution as any other kind of property. The Missouri Compromise was therefore unconstitutional, and Dred Scott had been no less a slave in Minnesota than in Missouri.

While the opinion of the Chief Justice was officially regarded as the opinion of the Court, each of the nine justices submitted a separate argument. Five of the Democratic members agreed in the main with the reasoning of the Chief Justice, but one of them, Justice Nelson of New York, held that the case should have been decided strictly on the ground that the highest court of Missouri, by ruling that Dred was a slave and not a citizen, had already settled the only point that the Court need consider. Justice Curtis of Massachusetts and Justice McLean of Ohio in dissenting opinions presented much historical evidence to controvert the argument that Negroes had not been regarded as eligible to citizenship at the time the Constitution was adopted, and cited also a long list of precedents to uphold the right of Congress to forbid slavery in the territories. Indeed, the certainty that Justice McLean, who was known to be an ardent Republican with presidential ambitions, would include in his dissenting opinion the contentions of his party on the subject of slavery in the territories had undoubtedly had much to do with persuading the majority of the Court to present the other side of the argument.

Lack of unanimity in the Court

It was idle to suppose that a decision so partisan from a Court so divided could settle anything with finality. The Republicans refused to concede that the status of slavery in the territories had actually been before the Court at all. If Dred Scott was not a citizen, that fact alone required demonstration. All the rest of the argument was irrelevant and gratuitous, or as the lawyers put it, *obiter dicta.* Thus the opinion of the Court that slavery in the territories was protected by the Constitution had no legal standing, and could not be regarded as binding precedent. According to a writer for the strongly Republican *New York Tribune* the arguments of the Chief Justice deserved "no more respect than any pro-slavery stump-speech made during the late presidential canvass." Some future Court should, and must, decide otherwise. The duty of the Republicans was clear. They must obtain control of the national government, and then so alter the personnel of the Court as to make sure of a correct decision.

Southern Democrats, on the other hand, were greatly elated by the stand the Court had taken. They denied indignantly, and with fair logic, the argument that the status of slavery in the territories had not properly been before the Court. The decision, they insisted, had settled that matter for all time. The Republicans, in standing out against the highest court in the land, were showing their true colors. To gain their partisan ends they would willingly subvert the Constitution itself. Slavery, said the Southerners, must now be allowed to spread. It must henceforth be regarded as legal in Kansas and in every other territory of the United States. Northern Democrats were by no means so pleased with the decision. Many of them realized that Douglas's doctrine of popular sovereignty, to which they had pinned their faith, could not easily be reconciled with the Dred Scott decision. If slavery could not be excluded from a territory by law of Congress, how then could the legislature of a territory, which owed its authority to Congress, exclude slavery? For the moment, however, they refused to admit the contradiction and said little about it.

Southern approval of the decision

Once more the attention of the country turned to Kansas. Eager to prevent a recurrence of trouble in that quarter, President Buchanan persuaded Robert J. Walker of Mississippi, a man of far greater ability than could ordinarily be obtained for such a post, to accept the governorship of the new territory. Walker promptly called an election for delegates to a constitutional convention, and urged the free-state men to participate. This, however, they refused to do, for they felt little confidence in the fairness of the Buchanan administration, whose agent Walker was. In consequence, the pro-slavery element carried the election overwhelmingly, and in October, 1857, a convention held at Lecompton framed a pro-slavery constitution. Determined to take no chances, the Lecompton convention failed to give the voters an opportunity to reject the document it had framed, but provided merely that they might vote for or against the further introduction of slaves. Whichever way the vote went, slavery in Kansas would be fully protected. Undeceived by this ruse, the free-state men again refused to vote, so that the constitution was carried with the more extreme pro-slavery clause. In the fall elections for a territorial legislature, however, the free-state men not only voted, but thanks to the rejection by Governor Walker and the territorial secretary of many fraudulent votes, they won. Thereupon the legislature resubmitted the Lecompton constitution, this time with the full alternative of adoption or rejection. Now the pro-slavery men refused to vote, so that the constitution that had just been so easily ratified was almost unanimously rejected. But the relative strength of the two sides was clearly revealed. In support of the Lecompton constitution the pro-slavery forces had cast only 6226 votes, whereas the free-state men only a few weeks later had cast 10,226 votes against it. That Kansas wished to be free and not slave was fully apparent to any unprejudiced observer.

Unhappily, President Buchanan could not

Events in Kansas

be so described. His most trusted advisers Douglas on Kansas were Southerners, and ordinarily he reflected their views. In November, 1857, he forced Walker out of office because the governor's rejection of fraudulent pro-slavery votes had given the legislature of Kansas to the free-state men. Moreover, in December, 1857, when Congress convened, the President made clear his desire to see Kansas admitted promptly as a slave state. Two months later he submitted to Congress the now thoroughly discredited Lecompton constitution, and urged its acceptance. All this was too much for Douglas. His doctrine of popular sovereignty rested upon the assumption that a majority, even in a territory, had the right to decide for or against slavery, and now the President proposed to make Kansas a slave state against its clearly expressed will. This travesty upon popular sovereignty Douglas denounced with all the vigor at his command. Such a course required courage of a high order, for it meant for the Illinois senator not only a break with the administration, but also the certain loss of his recently won popularity in the South. Many other northern Democrats agreed with him, however, and while the President was able to force his policy upon the Senate, he failed with it in the House.

At length a compromise measure, known as the English Bill, was adopted. According to its terms Kansas might vote for a third time on the Lecompton constitution, and in case a majority of the voters approved that document, might be immediately admitted as a state. In case the constitution was rejected, statehood would be delayed until the population of Kansas should reach the figure set by the congressional ratio for a representative in Congress, then 93,600. This unsavory threat was insufficient to overawe the free-staters in Kansas, who again voted down the Lecompton constitution, and in consequence saw their chance of winning statehood delayed until after a number of southern states had withdrawn from the Union.

The Panic of 1857. "Wall Street, 2:30 P.M., Oct. 13, 1857," a painting by Cafferty and Rosenberg, shows how news of the failure of the Ohio Life Insurance and Trust Company fell "like a thunderbolt" on the Street.

Meantime the panic of 1857 had burst upon the country, and had left in its train a trying period of economic depression. The prosperity of the The panic of 1857 early years of the decade had carried with it the germs of its own dissolution. The success of the railroads tempted them to an unreasonable overexpansion. Lines were built into unsettled areas where for years to come there could be little hope of profits. Manufacturers, likewise, eager to keep pace with the ever-growing markets, were soon well ahead of them. Producers of foodstuffs were lulled into a false sense of security by the abnormal demand of a war-torn Europe for American grain. At best the prices that the farmers received were none too good, and the loss of the European market when the Crimean War came to an end was calamitous. Moreover, the boom period, like every other of its kind, was accompanied by an enormous amount of speculation. To a great extent this took the same form that it had taken before the panic of 1837, speculation in land. Town sites along the lines of projected railroads, city lots in the rapidly growing industrial centers, desirable farm lands everywhere, but particularly in the West, tempted investors to over-buy.

The situation was seriously aggravated by the weakness of the banking system upon **Weakness of the banking system** which the country was forced to depend. Ever since Jackson's successful war on the Bank of the United States, the country had been without a national bank, and while numerous state-chartered banks existed, they were of widely varying merit. While some of the banks were sound, most of these were eastern institutions, and even in that section the reserves required by law were often too small and the credit extensions too great. There was much confusion, too, because of the plentiful, variegated, and easily counterfeited bank-note currency. A *Bank-Note Reporter*, issued at frequent intervals, undertook to keep subscribers posted on the fluctuating values of the numerous issues of state bank-notes, but with indifferent success. That the currency of the country, as a whole, was seriously inflated, no one could doubt. During the winter of 1856–57 business interests became acutely conscious of the economic breakers ahead, and when in August, 1857, a supposedly powerful financial house, the Ohio Life Insurance and Trust Company, closed its doors, the panic was on. The news of this failure, and of the numerous others that followed it, was spread more rapidly than could have been possible but for the electric telegraph, and a truly "psychological" panic developed. Even financially sound businesses went into bankruptcy. The panic was soon over, but the depression lasted for several years. During this period railroad-building was at a standstill, many factories remained closed, speculators took heavy losses, farmers were unable to pay their debts, and unemployed workmen thronged the city streets.

Strange as it may seem, the economic depression accentuated to an extraordinary degree the bitterness of the sectional controversy. Because of the hard times the pro-southern administration of President Buchanan lost ground throughout the North. Particularly aggrieved were the northeastern industrialists, to whose demand that the hard-pressed American manufacturer should be aided by a higher tariff the southern leaders turned deaf ears. Southerners generally regarded the additional revenues that such a tariff would bring as unnecessary and undesirable, for the government had accumulated a surplus during the period of prosperity and these funds, locked safely away in subtreasury vaults while the panic was on, seemed sufficient to outlast the lean years. More and more the conservatives of the North, who had long tolerated the leadership of the South only because it had seemed the only way to secure national harmony, swung their support to the new and sectional Republican Party. But if the North drew more closely together, so also did the South. Strangely, the Cotton Kingdom had almost escaped the depression. Naturally some economic distress was felt in the South, but all through the years that brought such calamity to the North, the world demand for cotton continued to mount, and the price of cotton remained high. Mindful of the reproaches that had long been hurled against them, the southern leaders now claimed that the superiority of their economic system had won singular vindication. "The wealth of the South," said *De Bow's Review*, a New Orleans journal, "is permanent and real, that of the North fugitive and fictitious." And yet the uneasiness of the South at the continued expansion of the North, in spite of the depression, was ill-concealed. The advance of the northern frontier went on through good times and bad. Minnesota was admitted to the Union early in 1858, statehood for Oregon could not possibly be long postponed, and northern emigrants seemed destined to take both Kansas and Nebraska.

The mid-term elections of 1858 revealed

clearly how deep the sectional line of cleavage had become. Throughout
the North the pro-southern
national administration was disastrously defeated. In Pennsylvania, the President's
own state, a coalition of Republicans, Know-
Nothings, and anti-Lecompton Democrats
carried all but three of the twenty-five congressional districts, a loss of twelve seats for
the administration. This result was due in
considerable part to the stagnation in the
Pennsylvania iron industry, a condition
which, according to the Republicans, the low
rates of the Democratic Tariff of 1857 had
made inevitable. In New England, New
York, and the Northwest, where the tariff
issue was not so prominent, the rebuke to
the administration was more pointedly upon
its handling of affairs in Kansas. In the
South, however, the President's pro-slavery
policy was cordially supported. "The abolitionists," said Senator Hammond of South
Carolina during the campaign, "have at
length . . . compelled us into a union — a
union not for aggression, but for defense."
Nevertheless, the solid support of the South
was not enough to save the day. While the
Senate remained safely Democratic, the administration lost its majority in the House.

Undoubtedly the most spectacular contest
of the campaign took place in Illinois, where
Stephen A. Douglas fought desperately to retain his seat in the
United States Senate. Doug-
las's break with the Buchanan administration over its policy in Kansas had served to
rehabilitate his reputation in the North.
Popular sovereignty, it appeared, would, if
honestly applied, insure that Kansas, and
practically every other western territory
also, would be free. What more could even
a Republican ask? So pleased were many
of the eastern Republicans with Douglas's
new stand that they openly urged their Illinois
friends not to oppose him for re-election.
Some went so far as to say that Douglas
would ultimately join the Republicans, and
that he might possibly be their candidate for
the Presidency in 1860. But the Illinois Re-

Elections of 1858

The senato-rial contest in Illinois

publicans, who knew Douglas for himself as
well as for the enemies he had made, had no
notion of permitting the election to go by de-
fault. To oppose Douglas they settled upon
Abraham Lincoln, a Springfield lawyer who
was well known throughout the state for his
political sagacity and his forceful public
speaking. Lincoln had served one term in
Congress during the Polk administration,
he had barely missed election to the United
States Senate by an anti-Nebraska legislature
in 1855, and he had received strong support
for the vice-presidential nomination on the
Frémont ticket in 1856. Far from being an
obscure backwoodsman, he was the best man
the Republicans of Illinois could put forward
against Douglas, as the Senator himself well
knew.

The choice of Douglas's successor rested,
of course, with the Illinois legislature, and so
deep was the antagonism of the Buchanan
administration for Douglas that administration Democrats were nominated to oppose
the Douglas candidates in nearly every legislative district of the state. Ostensibly the
administration sought to win seats enough to
hold the balance of power in the legislature,
and thus be in position to force the election
of some other Democrat than Douglas. But
no one was deceived. The Buchanan following in Illinois was negligible, and, except for
the patronage at the disposal of the President, would have been non-existent. Actually, the only possible effect of the administration tickets upon the contest would be to
draw enough votes from the Douglas candidates to insure that in a majority of the districts their Republican opponents would
win. Had the administration openly announced its support of Lincoln, it could
hardly have helped him as much.

Lincoln, in accepting his nomination, made
a prophetic statement:

"A house divided against itself cannot stand."
I believe this government cannot endure permanently half slave and half free. I do not expect
the Union to be dissolved — I do not expect the
house to fall — but I do expect it will cease to be
divided. It will become all one thing or all the

other. Either the opponents of slavery will arrest the further spread of it, and place it where the public mind shall rest in the belief that it is in the course of ultimate extinction; or its advocates will push it forward till it shall become alike lawful in all the States, old as well as new — North as well as South.

The radicalism of this statement pleased Douglas greatly, and on his return to Illinois, after a "magnificent welcome" in Chicago, he accused Lincoln of urging a "war of sections until one or the other shall be subdued." As against this fratricidal doctrine Douglas reaffirmed his faith in "the great principle of the Kansas-Nebraska Bill, the right of the people to decide for themselves." Lincoln was at once put on the defensive, and the better to cope with his skillful adversary he challenged Douglas to a series of joint debates. The challenge was promptly accepted, and arrangements were made for seven different meetings, one in each of the seven congressional districts of the state.

The Lincoln-Douglas debates attracted widespread notice, not only in Illinois, where **The Lincoln–Douglas debates** eager throngs attended them, but throughout the nation at large. Douglas was the outstanding northern Democrat, and his political life was at stake. More than that, if he lost, the northern Democracy had little chance to retain a place in the party councils; if he won, his title to the Democratic nomination in 1860 could scarcely be denied. Lincoln was hardly known outside of Illinois, but his bold words, and his temerity in challenging the able Douglas to a joint debate, awakened an interest in him that grew as the debate went on. Accounts of its progress, and long excerpts from the speeches delivered, appeared in nearly every metropolitan paper, and in many lesser journals as well. Douglas, in his immediate effect upon an audience, clearly had the advantage, and his re-election to the Senate occasioned no surprise. On the other hand, the smashing attacks that Lincoln made upon his opponent's "great principle" carried conviction to many thoughtful hearers and readers.

Two points Lincoln succeeded in making with telling effectiveness. One was that Douglas did not regard slavery as morally wrong. Repeatedly Lincoln forced from his adversary the statement, "I don't care whether slavery is voted down, or voted up." The Republican Party did care. If Douglas did not care, if he could not agree that slavery was an evil that must not be allowed to spread, then he had no title whatever to consideration for the Republican presidential nomination in 1860. With uncanny skill Lincoln also brought to the attention of the country the contradiction between the doctrine of popular sovereignty and the Dred Scott decision. "Can the people of a United States territory," he asked Douglas at Freeport, "against the wish of any citizen of the United States, exclude slavery from its limits prior to the formation of a state constitution?" If popular sovereignty meant anything at all, Douglas must answer in the affirmative, and this he promptly did. By "unfriendly legislation" or even by a refusal to enact friendly legislation, he declared, a territorial legislature might effectively exclude slavery, whatever the Supreme Court might say "as to the abstract question whether slavery may or may not go into a territory." In short, the Dred Scott decision in its practical effect meant nothing at all.

Douglas's "Freeport Doctrine" satisfied the northern Democrats and had much to do with his success in winning re-election to the Senate, but the South, already deeply incensed by his stand on the Lecompton constitution, was now completely alienated. To the pro-slavery leaders popular sovereignty had been pleasing enough when it furnished an unexpected avenue for the expansion of slavery, but popular sovereignty as an obstacle in the way of the far more gratifying doctrine of the Dred Scott decision was wholly devoid of charm. "We have a right of protection for our slave property in the territories," Senator Brown of Mississippi maintained. "The Constitution, as expounded by the Supreme Court,

A RIDE FOR LIBERTY. "The Fugitive Slaves." Painting by Eastman Johnson, 1861.

BORDER RUFFIANS INVADING KANSAS, 1856. Drawing by Felix O. C. Darley.

THE DISPUTE IN CONGRESS, 1858. On-the-spot sketches of an argument between Representatives Keitt (S.C.) and Grow (Pa.).

The slavery dispute aroused a spirit of violence almost from its inception. The escape of fugitive slaves was perilous, for federal marshals and posses did what they could to block the road to freedom. In Kansas pro-slavery men from Missouri fought against anti-slavery men from the North. In Congress pistols and bowie knives were ill concealed. John Brown, an anti-slavery fanatic who went too far, met death on the gallows.

THE LAST MOMENTS OF JOHN BROWN, DEC. 2, 1859. Painting by Thomas Hovenden, 1884.

awards it. We demand it, and we mean to have it." Perhaps unwittingly, Lincoln had driven home the wedge between the northern and the southern wings of the Democratic Party that was to make Republican victory a certainty in the next presidential election.

After the elections were over, the sectional dispute raged on with ever-increasing acri-

The sectional dispute more intense

mony. Whatever the North desired, Congress, unchanged in personnel until after the fourth of March, was at great pains to deny. President Buchanan, deeply impressed by the defeat his party had received in Pennsylvania, urged a revision of the tariff upward, but southern opposition prevented the adoption of such a conciliatory course. The Pacific railroad project, upon which the North had now set its heart, was likewise done to death, for the South feared that such a measure might result in the further aggrandizement of the North. A homestead bill, long demanded by the small farmers and free laborers of the North, met an identical fate, for Southern leaders contended that its primary purpose was to promote the emigration of free-state settlers to the territories. In the House the bill passed with only three southern members voting for it; in the Senate southern influence prevented it from coming to a vote at all. Southern orators waxed eloquent over the fact that throughout the North the Fugitive Slave Law had virtually become a dead letter. In many northern states "personal liberty laws," artfully contrived by Republican legislatures to "nullify" the federal law, hampered the federal officers; nearly always a hostile public opinion did the rest. In Oberlin, Ohio, several respectable citizens cheerfully stood trial and went to jail for their open rescue of a fugitive from his captors. Northern orators found cause for alarm at the repeated violations in the South of the federal law against the importation of slaves. Douglas placed the number of slaves illegally brought into the country during the preceding year at fifteen thousand. A convention of prominent Southern-

ers, held in May, 1859, at Vicksburg, warmly advocated the reopening of the African slave trade.

As if matters were not already bad enough, John Brown of Osawatomie now re-emerged. By one means or another he had

John Brown at Harpers Ferry

escaped arrest for the Pottawatomie murders, and had even conducted a successful expedition into Missouri to liberate some slaves who were about to be sold. A far more ambitious project now took form in his ill-balanced mind. He would put himself at the head of a small body of trusted men, fortify a rendezvous in the mountains of western Virginia, and from time to time make raids into the neighboring plantation area to free slaves. These slaves would then be armed, and from this small beginning would grow at length a powerful war on slavery throughout the South. Slave property would soon lose its value; all the slaves would have to be freed. The scheme was fantastic, and destined to certain failure, but to every criticism Brown would reply, "If God be for us, who can be against us?" He traveled East, laid his plans before some of the leading abolitionists, and actually got from them considerable financial aid. Without their consent or knowledge, however, he finally decided to make his first blow an attack on the United States Arsenal at Harpers Ferry. The capture of this well-known arsenal, he reasoned, would not only provide him with arms, but would serve also "as a trumpet" to rally the slaves to his standard. On the night of October 16, 1859, with only eighteen followers, he struck, and since the arsenal was virtually without military defense succeeded easily in taking it. Next morning fighting broke out between Brown and the citizens of Harpers Ferry. Soon militia companies from neighboring towns joined in the fray, and presently Colonel Robert E. Lee, with a detachment of United States marines, restored order by capturing Brown and four of his men. Ten others of the attacking party lay dead, and four had escaped.

The reaction of the country to this extraordinary event was ominous in the extreme.

Reaction of the country   The South refused to regard it as the act of an irresponsible madman, but insisted instead that such an outrage was precisely what was to be expected from the teachings of the abolitionists and their Republican allies. Stories that influential members of the Republican Party had been in conference with Brown were assiduously circulated. The North, on the other hand, was less shocked than it should have been. To incite slave insurrection with all its attendant horrors was indefensible, and yet John Brown's plan, despite his protestations to the contrary, could at best have succeeded in nothing else. When Brown, after a fair if somewhat early trial for treason, was found guilty, sentenced, and executed, he became to thousands of Northerners a martyr to the anti-slavery cause. In some towns bells were tolled and guns fired in honor of the dying saint, while many agreed with the verdict of Emerson that Brown's death would "make the gallows glorious like the cross." Responsible Republican leaders, however, gave voice to no such expressions. Seward, who a few months before had foretold "an irrepressible conflict" between the systems of slave and free labor, now denounced Brown for his resort to violence, and pointed to the ballot-box as the only proper avenue of reform in a democracy, while the next Republican national platform classed Brown's exploit as "among the gravest of crimes." That there existed in the North, nonetheless, a powerful undercurrent of sympathy for Brown seems evident from the fact that within so short a time northern soldiers were marching south to the tune of

John Brown's body lies a-mouldering in the grave,
  But his soul goes marching on.

On December 5, 1859, three days after the death of John Brown, the Congress elected

Helper's "Impending Crisis"   in 1858 convened for its first session. In the House of Representatives, where the Republicans had a plurality but not a majority, a contest for the Speakership developed that lasted for nearly two months. After the first ballot Representative John B. Clark of Missouri introduced a resolution, aimed at John Sherman of Ohio, the leading Republican candidate, to the effect that anyone who had endorsed a book by Hinton R. Helper, *The Impending Crisis of the South*, was unfit to be Speaker of the House. Helper was a non-slaveholding white of North Carolina, and his book, published in 1857, was an attempt to demonstrate by means of somewhat unreliable statistics that the deep poverty of the class to which he belonged was due to slavery. Naturally the slaveholders were outraged by such an argument, coming as it did from the South itself, and when in 1859 the obnoxious book was reprinted with approval from high Republican quarters for circulation as an anti-slavery tract their anger knew no bounds. The Republican Party had always claimed that its policy was merely to prevent the expansion of slavery, and not to attack it where it already existed. But Helper's book urged both the abolition of slavery in the southern states and the overthrow of the "oligarchical despotism," based on slavery, that ruled the South. To the pro-slavery leaders it was an incendiary document "precisely in the spirit of the act which startled us a few weeks since at Harpers Ferry." During the contest for the Speakership they could think or talk of little else. Sectional feeling became increasingly tense. According to one congressman, "The members on both sides are mostly armed with deadly weapons, and it is said that the friends of each are armed in the galleries." According to another, "I believe every man in both houses is armed with a revolver — some with two — and a bowie-knife." At length the Speakership went to a conservative Republican from New Jersey, William Pennington, but the contest had aroused much bad blood, and southern threats of secession had become almost commonplace.

The session of Congress that began thus tempestuously enacted few measures of consequence. Only a presidential veto, however, prevented the passage of a homestead

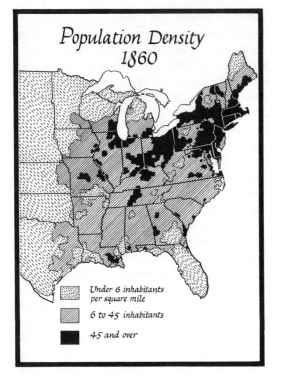

Population Density 1860

Under 6 inhabitants per square mile

6 to 45 inhabitants

45 and over

act. With the election of 1860 in sight, even
the southern Democrats hesita-
A homestead act vetoed ted to antagonize further the
northern wing of their party, which was as
fully committed to the homestead policy as
the Republicans themselves. At least one
Southerner, Senator Andrew Johnson of Tennessee, had long urged the granting of homesteads because of the benefit the poor whites
of the South might derive from such a policy;
but Johnson was a man of humble antecedents, and no more representative of the
plantation aristocracy than the author of
The Impending Crisis. During the summer
of 1860 both the Senate and the House
agreed to a measure that would permit heads
of families, whether citizens of the United
States or aliens who had declared their intention of becoming citizens, to occupy one
hundred and sixty acres of government land
for five years, and then buy it at the nominal
price of twenty-five cents per acre. But
Buchanan promptly denounced the bill in a
veto message that recited all the traditional
arguments against it. Such a measure, he

claimed, would depopulate the older states,
strike a blow at the frontiersman's "noble
spirit of independence," and "proclaim to all
the nations of the earth" that a farm awaited
every immigrant to American shores, virtually free of charge, if he would only declare
his intention of becoming a citizen.

Few presidential campaigns have aroused
the intense interest that extended to every
section of the country during **Democratic
dissensions**
nearly the entire year of 1860.
From the outset the likelihood of a split in
the Democratic Party was well understood.
Senator Jefferson Davis of Mississippi,
speaking for the southern wing of the party,
had served notice on Douglas that if he
wished southern support for his candidacy
he must agree to the enactment by Congress
of a territorial slave code. This complete
abandonment of popular sovereignty, designed to protect slavery in every territory
whether the people of the territory wanted
it or not, Douglas refused utterly to make.
When, therefore, the Democratic convention
met at Charleston, South Carolina, in April,
1860, the battle was on. Douglas, it
transpired, controlled a majority of the delegates and could write the platform, but he
lacked the two-thirds majority necessary to
achieve the nomination. As soon as the
platform was adopted, the delegations of four
southern states withdrew from the convention, and were followed by most of the
delegates from four other states. After ten
days of fruitless balloting, with Douglas far
in the lead on every ballot and sometimes in
a clear majority, the convention adjourned
to meet again in Baltimore on the eighteenth
of June. But the adjourned session was no
more successful than the original in reconcil-
ing northern and southern delegates, so after
a few preliminaries the convention divided.
One faction, composed mainly of northern
delegates, nominated Douglas and stood by
popular sovereignty. The other, composed
almost exclusively of Southerners, nominated John C. Breckinridge of Kentucky,
and called for the protection of slavery in
all the territories.

During the interval between the Democratic sessions at Charleston and at Baltimore the Republicans met at Chicago — a significant recognition of the rôle the West was expected to play in the coming election. Their platform was intensely nationalistic, not only in its denunciation of southern threats of disunion, but also in its advocacy of national action to satisfy the demands of its adherents. The advance of slavery into the West must be halted, imposts "to encourage the development of the industrial interests" must be levied, a satisfactory homestead law must be enacted, the existing liberal naturalization policy must be maintained, and a railroad to the Pacific (advocated also by both Democratic platforms) must be built — all by authority of the national government. While the "right of each state to order and control its own institutions according to its own judgment" was expressly affirmed, the Chicago platform clearly served notice on the South that, according to Republican principles, a minority section had neither the right to rule the nation nor the right to withdraw from it. If, on the other hand, the new party by uniting the industrial Northeast and the agricultural Northwest could command a majority, it proposed to make full use of the national power for the benefit of the interests it represented.

The Republicans at Chicago

The nomination of Abraham Lincoln for the Presidency was to a considerable extent a surrender to expediency. The foremost Republican of the time was William H. Seward of New York, who confidently expected the nomination. But Seward had been long in the public eye, and had won the reputation of being an extremist. Everyone knew that he had predicted "an irrepressible conflict," and that in his speech against the Compromise of 1850 he had appealed to "a higher law than the Constitution." Lincoln's utterances, particularly in his "house divided" speech, were equally radical, but they were not so widely known. Lincoln also represented the West, which was regarded as

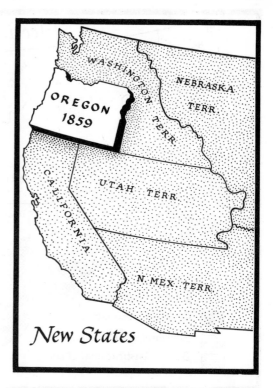

New States

far more debatable territory than the East, and he came from the same state as Stephen A. Douglas, who would be his chief opponent. Deals made by Lincoln's subordinates to give Indiana and Pennsylvania representation in the Lincoln Cabinet, and the packing of the galleries of the improvised "Wigwam" where the convention was held with ardent Lincoln men, also had some part in the result. Seward had a lead on the first ballot, but on the third ballot Lincoln won the nomination.

A fourth-party ticket was placed in the field by the remnant of the Whig-Know-Nothing combination that had supported Fillmore in 1856. Meeting at Baltimore early in May, they gave their organization a new name, the Constitutional Union Party, and a new platform that was chiefly notable because it recognized "no political principle other than the Constitution of the country, the union of the States, and the enforcement of the laws." To this negative standard they sought to rally all those who wished to pre-

The Constitutional Union Party

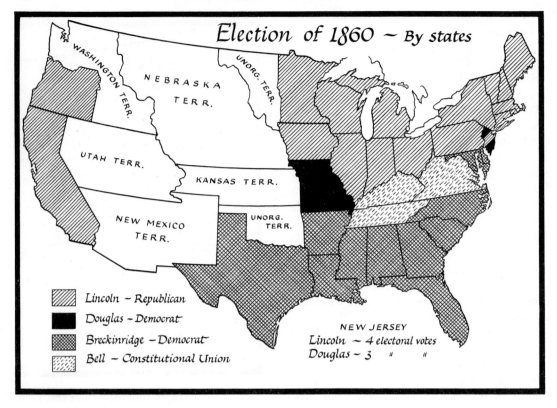

Election of 1860 ~ By states

Lincoln ~ Republican
Douglas ~ Democrat
Breckinridge ~ Democrat
Bell ~ Constitutional Union

NEW JERSEY
Lincoln ~ 4 electoral votes
Douglas ~ 3 " "

serve the Union by compromise and conciliation — the way it had always been preserved before. In order to insure an intersectional appeal, they chose as their candidate for the Presidency a Southerner, John
Bell of Tennessee, and as their candidate
for the Vice-Presidency a Northerner, Edward Everett of Massachusetts. Much ridicule was heaped upon the "Bell-Everetts," or
the "Bell-Ringers," as they were generally
called, during the campaign, but the party
had a strong appeal for thoughtful conservatives who could see in a more forthright stand
only disunion and conflict.

The campaign and election served only
to emphasize how deep the line of cleavage
The contest between the sections had be-
in the North come. For all practical purposes two separate contests were being held,
one in the North and another in the South.
The only candidates to figure seriously in the
northern balloting were Lincoln and Douglas, and the issue between them was clearly:

Should the North use its numerical majority
to force upon the South the nationalistic
program called for in the Republican platform? With this program Douglas and the
northern Democrats found little fault. Their
doctrine of popular sovereignty had proved
to be only another way of preventing the
spread of slavery into the territories; they had
little objection to a higher tariff; they believed in the Homestead Law; they had long
defended the immigrants from the attacks of
the Know-Nothings; they, too, favored a
Pacific railroad. But Douglas and his followers realized, as seemingly the Republicans
did not, the serious consequences that might
result from forcing the northern point of view
upon the South. They knew that the
southern threats of secession were far from
meaningless, and that if the North insisted
upon pressing its advantage a disruption of
the Union was in sight. Sobered by the
calamity that had overtaken the Democratic
Party at Baltimore, they were now ready,

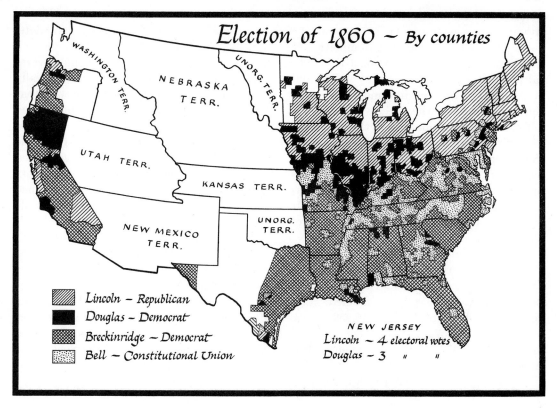

Election of 1860 ~ By counties

Lincoln ~ Republican
Douglas ~ Democrat
Breckinridge ~ Democrat
Bell ~ Constitutional Union

NEW JERSEY
Lincoln ~ 4 electoral votes
Douglas ~ 3 " "

like the Constitutional Unionists, to use caution, restraint, and denial in order to preserve an undivided nation.

In contrast with this attitude, the Republicans stood ready to give the North what it wanted. They denounced with the utmost intemperance the "slave-power" that with the aid of conscienceless "dough-faces" had so long ruled the country. They offered tariffs to please the industrial East, "homes for the millions" to please the agricultural West, and equality of treatment for aliens and citizens to please the immigrants. Against such a forthright attack Douglas fought valiantly, but in vain. Even the generous contributions of a few northern men of means, who feared the disastrous effects of secession on business, availed him nothing. Lincoln carried every northern state but one, New Jersey, and from that state he received four out of seven electoral votes. With the admission of Oregon in 1859, the free states numbered three more than the slave states and cast half again as many electoral votes. Thus Lincoln was elected, even though he had received not a single electoral vote from a southern state. In ten southern states his name had not appeared on the ballot.

In the South the contest lay between Breckinridge on the one hand and either Bell or Douglas on the other. **The contest in the South** Here the question at issue was, Should "southern rights" be maintained, even at the cost of secession and possible civil war? "Southern rights" meant vaguely whatever the individual who used the term wished it to mean, but the fundamental idea was the right of the South to some kind of constitutional protection from the tyranny of a northern majority. The election of Lincoln, southern extremists contended, would in itself constitute so flagrant an invasion of "southern rights" as to justify the southern states in seceding immediately from the Union. The party that supported

Lincoln lay wholly in the North, and its triumph, they genuinely believed, would be but a prelude to the complete domination of the South by the North. Against this radical point of view the adherents of Bell and of Douglas urged an intermediate course that would insure the preservation of the Union. But in the South as in the North the more aggressive policy won. Eleven out of the fifteen slave states voted for Breckinridge; only four, all in the Upper South, for his opponents. The verdict of the South was almost as clear as that of the North. It would insist upon its "rights" at whatever cost.

With so many candidates in the field, and the North and the South holding virtually separate elections, it was inevitable that the popular vote should be badly divided. Lincoln received a total of 1,866,452 votes, Douglas 1,376,957, Breckinridge 849,781, and Bell 588,879. Thus Lincoln's clear majority in the electoral college, 180 to 123 for all his opponents combined, was obtained

with only forty per cent of the popular vote being cast for the Republican candidate. Lincoln's opponents actually received all together nearly a million more popular votes than their successful rival. But the really significant fact about the election was that both the North and the South had voted decisively for radical action. Except for a few states of the upper South, the whole nation was in a radical mood. The combined vote of the extremists, Lincoln and Breckinridge, was 2,716,233, while the combined vote of the candidates who urged a middle course, Douglas and Bell, was only 1,965,331.

Could a house so divided against itself hope to stand? Many feared that it could not, but others pointed out that the Republicans had failed to capture a majority in either house of Congress, and that the Supreme Court still had its southern majority. Thus the North was not yet in a position to force its views upon the South, and the fears of the southern "fire-eaters" might for a season be allayed.

Bibliography

Many of the books cited for Chapter 28, pp. 526–527, are equally useful for this chapter. The general histories all cover it, Rhodes, I–III; Channing, VI; McMaster, VIII; Schouler, V. Allan Nevins, *The Emergence of Lincoln* (2 vols., 1950), begins where his *Ordeal of the Union* leaves off, and is significant for its great mass of well-documented detail. Avery O. Craven, *The Coming of the Civil War* (1942), emphasizes the southern point of view. H. H. Simms, *A Decade of Sectional Controversy* (1942), blames the war mainly on political factors. Three excellent books by R. F. Nichols, *Franklin Pierce* (1931); *The Democratic Machine, 1850–1854* (1923); and *The Disruption of American Democracy* (1948), concentrate primarily on the growing split in the Democratic party. A. W. Crandall, *The Early History of the Republican Party, 1854–1856* (1930), shows from the northern angle the rapid development of sectionalism. The first Republican campaign is

well described in Ruhl J. Bartlett, *John C. Frémont and the Republican Party* (1930). H. C. Hockett, *The Constitutional History of the United States, 1826–1876* (1939), centers principally on the sectional dispute over slavery. L. M. Ganaway, *New Mexico and the Sectional Controversy, 1846–1861* (1944), is an able monograph on a peripheral subject. E. C. McGavin, *U. S. Soldiers Invade Utah* (1937), deals, from a Mormon point of view, with the ill-fated Mormon war.

On the Buchanan administration and its problems, the most sympathetic treatment comes from Philip G. Auchampaugh, *James Buchanan and his Cabinet on the Eve of Secession* (1926). *Robert Tyler, Southern Rights Champion, 1847–1866*, edited by Philip G. Auchampaugh (1934), presents many interesting letters bearing on the Buchanan administration. G. T. Curtis, *Life of James Buchanan* (2 vols., 1883), is still useful. G. W. Van Vleck, *The Panic of 1857: An An-*

alytical Study (1943), explains the economic background which added to Buchanan's troubles. W. N. Brigance, *Jeremiah Sullivan Black* (1934), gives a good account of one of Buchanan's most loyal advisers.

On the Kansas situation, Eli Thayer, *A History of the Kansas Crusade* (1889), greatly overemphasizes the part played by the New England Emigrant Aid Society. James C. Malin, *John Brown and the Legend of Fifty-Six* (1942), does much to set the record straight. Older, and less dependable on controversial matters are W. E. Miller, *The Peopling of Kansas* (1906); and L. W. Spring, *Kansas, The Prelude to the War for the Union* (1885). Of the many biographies of John Brown the best are probably O. G. Villard, *John Brown, 1800–1859* (1910); and Robert P. Warren, *John Brown, The Making of a Martyr* (1929).

The Dred Scott case has received much attention, and original interpretations of it have been much revised. Carl B. Swisher, *American Constitutional Development* (1943), presents the more recent point of view, but the careful student will be interested in the brilliant articles by F. H. Hodder, "Some Phases of the Dred Scott Case," in the *Mississippi Valley Historical Review*, vol. XVI, pp. 3–22; and by E. S. Corwin, "The Dred Scott Decision," in the *American Historical Review*, vol. XVII, pp. 52–69. The biographies of Taney by Swisher, and by Charles W. Smith, cited on p. 401, are also useful. See also the biography of one of Taney's associates by Francis P. Weisenburger, *The Life of John McLean* (1937). B. W. Palmer, *Marshall and Taney, Statesmen of the Law* (1939), is popular rather than scholarly, but good for general reading.

On the rise of Lincoln, A. J. Beveridge, *Abraham Lincoln, 1809–1858* (2 vols., 1928), is scholarly and detailed. The local situation which produced the Lincoln-Douglas debates is analyzed by A. C. Cole, *The Era of the Civil War* (1919). On the election of 1860, R. H. Luthin, *The First Lincoln Campaign* (1944); E. D. Fite, *The Presidential Campaign of 1860* (1911); and Ollinger Crenshaw, *The Slave States in the Presidential Election of 1860* (1945), present somewhat differing opinions. Philip Kinsley, *The Chicago Tribune: Its First Hundred Years*, Vol. I, *1847–1865* (1943), studies the policy of an anti-slavery and pro-Lincoln newspaper. H. L. Stoddard, *Horace Greeley: Printer, Editor, Crusader* (1946), is a journalistic account of the great anti-slavery editor. J. A. Isely, *Horace Greeley and the Republican Party, 1853–1861* (1947), is scholarly, and directed at the period under review in this chapter. J. H. Parks, *John Bell of Tennessee* (1950), throws light on the attitude of the upper South toward the sectional controversy.

30

Secession

The doctrine of secession invoked — The Confederate
States of America — Jefferson Davis — The Confeder-
ate Constitution — Northern opinion on secession —
Fort Sumter — The proposed Crittenden compromise
— Other efforts at compromise — Abraham Lincoln —
His policy toward the South — Bombardment of
Sumter — The border slave states — Division of forces
— Robert E. Lee

THAT every state possessed the constitutional right to secede at will from the Union
The doctrine had long been regarded as sound
of secession doctrine throughout the South.
The argument in support of this contention,
simplified and standardized by constant rep-
etition, was by no means illogical. History
was recited to prove that the states were
sovereign, not the nation; and just as the
individual states, each acting in its sovereign
capacity, had once joined the Union, so now,
if they chose, they might leave it. A precise
formula by which secession could be accomplished had been evolved. The legislature
of a state that contemplated withdrawal
from the Union must call for the election of
a constituent convention — the same kind
of convention that had been held in the
original states to ratify the Constitution.
On assembling, such a convention might by
a majority vote recall all the powers that the
state had delegated to the central government, and so declare the state outside the
Union.

Was the election of Lincoln a serious
enough violation of "southern rights" to
justify resort to secession? After the returns
were known, this was the question above all
others that agitated the South. Many felt
that the day of expostulation and protest

was done, and that the time had come for
action. The North, they said, had harbored
and protected the abolitionists, it had openly
flouted the Fugitive Slave Act, it had sung
the praises of John Brown and his "band of
midnight assassins," and it proposed now
through a sectional party and a sectional
President to subordinate the South to northern interests. The southern states ought not,
therefore, even to await Lincoln's inauguration. They should leave the Union at once.
But there were many Southerners also who
counseled a more moderate course. Why not
wait, they asked, until the new régime had
actually committed some overt act of oppression? After Lincoln's inauguration,
only one out of the three departments of government would be in Republican hands, and
years might well elapse before any direct
invasion of southern rights could take place.
In the meantime constitutional changes or
legislative compromises might be adopted
that would satisfy the South. At the very
least, individual states ought not to secede
one by one, and so precipitate a series of
crises. Time should be taken for all the
southern states to consult together, and to
plan for concerted action.

The overwhelming vote that the states of
the lower South gave Breckinridge in the

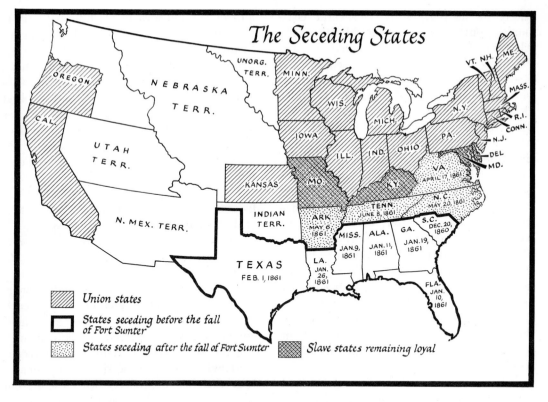

The Seceding States

Union states

States seceding before the fall of Fort Sumter

States seceding after the fall of Fort Sumter

Slave states remaining loyal

election indicated clearly that in this region the counsels of moderation would not prevail. Nor did they. In South Carolina, traditionally the most radical of the southern states, the legislature, in order to be ready to take prompt action, had remained in session until after the election was over. Without the slightest hesitation it summoned a convention which, at a meeting held in Charleston, December 20, decided by a vote of 169 to 0 to dissolve the ties that bound the state of South Carolina to the Union. Within six weeks similar action had been taken by all the states that bordered on the Gulf of Mexico: Mississippi on January 9, Florida on January 10, Alabama on January 11, Georgia on January 19, Louisiana on January 26, and Texas on February 1.[1] Only in South Carolina, however, was the vote in

favor of immediate secession unanimous. In every other state convention a determined minority stood out steadfastly for delay. Doubtless these minorities might in some cases have been majorities had not the precipitate action of South Carolina tended to identify the theory and the practice of secession. On this account southerners who heartily regretted that South Carolina had left the Union felt obliged to work for the secession of other states. Obviously one small state, acting alone, could not maintain its independence, and if a seceding state should be forced back into the Union, the whole doctrine of secession would be correspondingly discredited.

The seceding states left the Union one by one, but none of them had the slightest intention of maintaining a separate existence. Secession was but a means to an end, and the end was a united southern confederacy. Early in February a "congress" of delegates,

The Confederate States of America

---

[1] The decision of the Texas convention was referred to a popular vote taken February 23, so that technically Texas was not out of the Union until that time.

chosen for the purpose by the several secessionist conventions, met at Montgomery, Alabama, to establish the new nation. On February 8 this congress adopted for the Confederate States of America a hastily devised provisional constitution; next day it chose as President and Vice-President, respectively, Jefferson Davis of Mississippi and Alexander H. Stephens of Georgia; and thereafter it remained in session long enough to act as a legislature for the provisional government and to draw up a permament constitution. Throughout these proceedings the delegates were acutely conscious of the parallel between what they were doing and what their forefathers had done in severing the ties that had bound the colonies to the mother country. They issued no common declaration of independence, but in spite of their lip service to the doctrine of secession they found the real justification of their course in the right of an oppressed people to revolt.

Jefferson Davis (1808–89), upon whose shoulders now devolved the political leader- **Jefferson** ship of the Confederacy, was a **Davis** Kentuckian by birth, a graduate of West Point who had seen active military service on the frontier and in the war with Mexico, and a Mississippi cotton planter who shared most of the prejudices of his class. As United States Senator from 1847 to 1851, and again from 1857 to 1861, he had participated in the two great debates of the decade on the preservation of the Union. His views on southern rights had thus been fully stated, and they were known to be far less radical than those of many other Southerners, notably R. B. Rhett of South Carolina, who as one of the most persistent advocates of secession was bitterly disappointed not to be the first President of the Confederacy. But Davis, far more than Rhett, was a southern nationalist. Although the Confederate President believed in states' rights and accepted the doctrine of secession as good constitutional law, he set himself the task of building a new nation. His failure was due in part, no doubt, to his own shortcomings. He had

an exaggerated idea of his military ability, and often gravely handicapped his generals by dictating to them, or interfering with their plans. He was not a good judge of men, and surrounded himself with mediocre subordinates when he could have had the best talent of the South for the asking. He was proud to the point of arrogance, and his overbearing attitude toward those who held opinions at variance from his own often cost him dear.

The permanent constitution of the Confederacy turned out to be a frank adaptation of the Constitution of the United **The** States. The familiar preamble **Confederate** was revised to read, "We, the **Constitution** people of the Confederate States, each State acting in its sovereign and independent character," but instead of guaranteeing to each state the right of secession, the new federal government was described as "permanent." Several provisions were reminiscent of recent sectional disputes. The right of citizens to take their slave property with them from state to state, and to hold it anywhere as such, was expressly affirmed; Congress was granted full authority to acquire new territory, but in any such territory the institution of slavery must be "recognized and protected"; new states could be admitted only by a two-thirds majority of both houses of Congress; bounties, protective tariffs, and appropriations for internal improvements were forbidden. A few changes, dictated by experience, were made in the machinery of government. The presidential term was lengthened to six years, and the President was made ineligible for re-election; single items in appropriation bills could be separately vetoed by the President; cabinet members, at the option of Congress, might be permitted seats upon the floor of either house; and a modified executive budget was contemplated. On March 11 the constitution was submitted to the seven seceding states, and by the end of April it had been ratified by all of them.

The North, meantime, observed what was going on in the South without fully compre-

Jefferson Davis, a Kentuckian by birth, served in the Northwest for several years after his graduation from West Point, then returned to his home in Mississippi to live for ten years the life of a southern gentleman and planter. He entered politics in 1845 as a member of the national House of Representatives, but resigned to accept a regimental command in the Mexican War. He became Senator from Mississippi in 1847, and was prominent in national politics until his state left the Union. The portrait above was painted by Enoch W. Perry in the year of Davis' inauguration as President of the Confederacy, February 18, 1861, at Montgomery, Alabama, pictured at the right in a painting by James Massalon.

---

hending it. Many Northerners refused utterly to believe that the secessionists meant what they said. Southern tempers, always easily overheated, would presently cool off, and the states that now seemed so determined to leave the Union would soon be trying to forget their folly. Others maintained, not without some justification in southern opinion, that a reconstruction of the Union would soon take place. This might possibly be accomplished through the calling of a constitutional convention, or more likely through some great congressional compromise as in 1850. Throughout the winter of 1860–61 northern sentiment definitely rejected the idea of coercion. Greeley's powerful *New York Tribune* repeatedly set forth this point of view. "If the fifteen slave States," ran a typical *Tribune* editorial, "or even the eight cotton States alone, shall quietly, decisively, say to the rest, 'We prefer to be henceforth separate from you,' we shall insist that they be permitted to go in peace. War is a hideous necessity at best, and a civil conflict — a war of estranged and embittered fellow-

Northern opinion on secession

countrymen — is the most hideous of all wars." Abolitionists professed delight to see the Union purged of so many slave states, and agreed with Greeley that the best policy was to "let the erring sisters go in peace." Quakers and other pacifists read with approval the lines penned by John Greenleaf Whittier:

> They break the bonds of Union: shall we light
> The fires of hell to weld anew the chain
> On that red anvil where each blow is pain?

Nevertheless, most Northerners were deeply dissatisfied with the weakness displayed by the national administration in its handling of the secessionist movement. When in earlier years Andrew Jackson and Zachary Taylor had been confronted by somewhat similar situations, they had met the southern threats, although themselves from the South, with equally bold words, and even with deeds. Had James Buchanan shown less timidity, had he talked back to the secessionists in their own language, many felt that the headlong flight of the southern states from the

Buchanan on secession

Union might have been checked. But the President, old and ill, and the discredited representative of a discredited party, showed himself to be utterly incapable of aggressive action. When, early in December, 1860, he sent his annual message to Congress, not a state had left the Union, although the intentions of South Carolina were well enough known. This was the time, if ever, for the President to warn the South of the grave consequences that might result from secession. Instead, he told them that while secession, in his opinion, was unconstitutional, so also was the coercion of a state. If, therefore, the southern states seceded, they need fear nothing as long as Buchanan remained in office, for, as Seward rephrased the presidential pronouncement, "It is the duty of the President to execute the laws — unless somebody opposes him; and . . . no State has the right to go out of the Union — unless it wants to."

Buchanan did not fail to tell Congress, however, what it should do. The whole blame for the existing sectional controversy he placed upon the North, and the only way to make amends, as he saw it, was for the North to yield completely to the southern contentions. Let Congress submit an "explanatory amendment" to the Constitution on the subject of slavery. Let this amendment guarantee in so many words the right to hold slave property in all the states where slavery then existed, and in all the territories of the United States as well. Let it also definitely recognize the right of the master "to have his slave who had escaped from one state to another restored and 'delivered up' to him." Then, for good measure, let it declare the existing Fugitive Slave Law valid, and the existing "personal liberty" laws of the northern states invalid. Perhaps with these assurances the South might be persuaded to remain in the Union.

With the secession of South Carolina an accomplished fact, the President was faced **Fort Sumter** by a situation in Charleston Harbor that called insistently for action. Such of the property of the United States within South Carolina as was undefended was promptly taken over by the seceding state, but the forts that protected Charleston Harbor were occupied by a small federal garrison under the command of Major Robert Anderson. Foreseeing the probable course of events, Anderson had long urged the authorities in Washington to reinforce him, and in this request he had been strongly supported by General Scott. The President, however, fearful of irritating the South Carolinians, sought to maintain the *status quo* in the harbor, and left Anderson to his own devices. A few days after the ordinance of secession was adopted, Anderson, on his own authority, abandoned the indefensible Fort Moultrie and removed his entire garrison to Fort Sumter, an island fortification in the mouth of the harbor. This action deeply enraged the South-Carolinians, who interpreted it as a threat of war, but the President sustained Anderson.

For a time, indeed, it seemed that Buchanan might attempt to play the Jacksonian rôle that some of his advisers desired. A reorganization of his Cabinet brought strong Unionists to the fore, particularly Jeremiah Sullivan Black, the new Secretary of State, and Edwin M. Stanton, the new Attorney-General. Under their urging, Buchanan finally decided to reinforce Sumter and on January 8 he sent the *Star of the West*, a merchant steamer, to Charleston Harbor, with two hundred soldiers aboard. But when three days later the vessel attempted to enter the harbor, she was met by the fire of state batteries, and turned back to New York without discharging her errand. This attack on the *Star of the West* was in reality an act of war, but the President chose to ignore it, and during the remainder of his administration he made no further effort to aid Anderson.

Congress, meantime, was hard at work on a plan of compromise by which the Union might be preserved. This movement was led, appropriately, by Senator John J. Crittenden of Kentucky, the successor to Clay's seat in **The Crittenden compromise** the Senate, and to the Clay tradition of compromise. Two days before the secession of South Carolina, Crittenden introduced into the Senate an elaborate set of resolutions not unlike those Clay had presented to the same body ten years before. By amendment to the Constitution he proposed that:

1. Slavery should be prohibited in all the territory of the United States now held, or hereafter acquired, north of 36° 30', and protected south of that line.
2. Congress should have no power to abolish slavery in places under its exclusive jurisdiction, and situate within the limits of states that permitted the holding of slaves.
3. Congress should have no power to abolish slavery within the District of Columbia without compensation, and without the consent of Maryland, Virginia, and the people of the District.
4. Congress should have no power to prohibit or hinder the transportation of slaves between slaveholding states and territories.
5. The owners of rescued fugitive slaves were to be compensated for their losses by the United States government.

Additional recommendations urged (1) the faithful observance and execution of the Fugitive Slave Law, which, however, should be made less obnoxious to the North, (2) the repeal of all "personal liberty" laws, and (3) the thorough suppression of the African slave trade.

A Senate committee of thirteen, headed by Crittenden, was at once constituted to consider these and other plans of compromise. Care was taken in the selection of the committee to give representation to every section and party. Six members, including Crittenden and Douglas, were open advocates of compromise; Seward, Wade, and three other Republicans spoke for the northern extremists; Toombs and Davis, whose states had not yet seceded, effectively represented the lower South. At first it seemed probable that the committee might agree upon substantially the plan of compromise that Crittenden had proposed. The chief bone of contention was the 36° 30'

dividing line between free and slave territory, a proposition that Toombs and Davis were known to be ready to accept, provided only that a majority of the Republicans would also agree to it. Seward seems to have flirted with the idea, but before committing himself definitely he sent his friend, Thurlow Weed, to Springfield, Illinois, for a conference with the President-elect. Weed reported that Lincoln was willing to make almost unlimited concessions with regard to the enforcement of the Fugitive Slave Law and the repeal of the "personal liberty" laws, but that he was unalterably opposed to any yielding on the question of slavery expansion. Lincoln's opinion seems to have been conclusive, for the Republicans voted unanimously against the proposed dividing line, and the committee reported back to the Senate that it could not agree.

Later Crittenden and his supporters argued that the compromise in which they were interested should be submitted to the people of the country for approval or rejection at the polls. But the machinery for obtaining such a referendum vote did not exist, and all efforts looking toward its creation failed, largely because of Republican opposition. Had there been such a possibility, however, there is some reason to suppose that during the winter of 1860–61 a popular majority for the compromise might have been obtained. The vote of November, 1860, showed the extremists in the majority, both North and South, but at that time the actual specter of secession was not before the voters as they marked their ballots. Faced by the direct alternative of compromise or secession, many who had voted for Lincoln or Breckinridge a few weeks before might well have changed their minds and voted for Crittenden's solution.

If so eminent and representative a group as the Senate committee of thirteen could not propose a successful plan of **House** compromise, it seemed unlikely **efforts at** that any other group could do **compromise** so. Nevertheless, a House committee of thirty-three continued to struggle with the problem, and early in January, 1861, it brought forth an alternative plan, which had substantial support even among the Republicans. The House plan called for (1) an amendment to the Constitution that would safeguard slavery in the states where it already existed, (2) a recommendation that the "personal liberty" laws be repealed, and (3) the admission of New Mexico, "with or without slavery." That this last-mentioned provision would mean a new slave state, few could deny, for in 1859 the territorial government of New Mexico, under pressure from the South, had definitely legalized slavery. But not many slaves were held in the territory, and even Lincoln admitted that he did not "care much about New Mexico." Neither, it seemed, did the representatives of the cotton states, for they were as quick to reject the House plan as the Republicans had been to reject the Crittenden plan; and so nothing came of it. Both houses of Congress voted, however, by two-thirds majorities, to submit a thirteenth amendment to the Constitution that would forever deny to Congress the right to abolish or interfere with slavery in any of the states. This amendment was never ratified, although Lincoln in his inaugural address expressly approved of it. By a curious irony the Thirteenth Amendment that presently was ratified abolished slavery.

Convinced as time went on that Congress would not succeed in working out a satisfactory compromise, the legislature of Virginia invited the various states to send delegates to a great peace convention to be opened in Washington, February 4. Twenty-one states responded favorably, and with ex-President Tyler in the chair the convention made a sincere effort to save the Union. After three weeks of deliberation it recommended to Congress an amendment to the Constitution that would have made latitude 36° 30′ the dividing line between slave and free territories, but would also have provided that in the acquisition of any new territory by the United States concurrent majorities of the free-state senators

The peace convention

and of the slave-state senators should be required. Unfortunately this provision received far from unanimous support in the convention, and it reached Congress at a time when the secession movement had proceeded too far to be turned back. The resolves of the peace convention were duly presented to the Senate by Senator Crittenden, but they were promptly rejected.

As the time for Lincoln's inauguration approached, all eyes turned toward the ungainly Westerner upon whose shoulders the crisis was so soon to devolve. Abraham Lincoln (1809–65) was born in Kentucky, the descendant of several generations of American frontiersmen. His father, Thomas Lincoln, was only a child when his grandfather, Abraham Lincoln, met death at the hands of the Indians. Grown and married, Thomas Lincoln made two typical pioneer "moves" to the West, first to Indiana, and later to Illinois. Thus repeatedly transplanted, the boy Abraham obtained only the slightest schooling, but he read all the books he could get hold of, and he ultimately learned enough law to meet the modest requirements of the West for admission to the bar. He possessed a native shrewdness that stood him in good stead on all occasions, and he developed a capacity for logical thinking and for the accurate expression of his thought that would have been remarkable in any age or place. On the frontier, politics and law went hand in hand, and Lincoln's political ambitions were not slow in materializing. At first as a Henry Clay Whig, and later as a Republican, he demonstrated his skill in state and local politics; later, particularly by his utterances during the Lincoln-Douglas debates, he won recognition throughout the nation as a leading exponent of Republican doctrine. A thoroughgoing Westerner, he instinctively idealized both nationalism and democracy, and he resented deeply the determination of the southern leaders to rule the nation with or without a majority, or else to ruin it. Well above the average height and homely to the point of fascination, he affected the stoop-

Lincoln

Abraham Lincoln, of Kentucky and Illinois, was schooled in the rough and tumble of western debate, and became a magnificent stump speaker. He had the gift of phrasing his utterances in simple but forceful language, and he drove home his points with relentless logic. The close attention given by the press to his debates with Douglas in 1858 made him a national figure. Lincoln, who was smooth-shaven until after becoming President, grew his beard at the suggestion of a little girl who thought it would help his looks. The portrait photograph above of Lincoln as the Republican presidential candidate was taken by Alexander Hesler in June, 1860, for use in the campaign. At the right, "Stump Speaking" is a painting by George Caleb Bingham, 1854, unique artist-reporter of the nineteenth-century American midwest. Courtesy of the Boatmen's National Bank of St. Louis.

shouldered posture and the loose-jointed shambling gait that western lawyers generally mistook for dignity. He knew little or nothing of the polite usages of eastern society, and to those who were more sophisticated the essential gentility of his nature was often obscured by his uncouth manners, his off-color jokes, and his easy familiarity.

During his months as President-elect, Lincoln had studiously avoided any public expression of opinion, and the country awaited eagerly his announcement of policy. This statement he properly decided to reserve for his inaugural address, but when crowds gathered around his train on the long journey to Washington he unfortunately felt obliged to talk to them. Unskilled in the art of concealing his thoughts, and yet strongly desirous of setting the public mind at ease, he resorted to ambiguous and sentimental remarks that made some men wonder if he really understood the situation at all. Also,

Lincoln's inaugural address

he was persuaded by those responsible for his personal safety to deviate from his announced schedule in order to enter Washington at a time when he was not expected. Was Lincoln afraid? This suspicion seemed to receive confirmation on Inauguration Day, for on that occasion the city of Washington fairly bristled with bayonets. But the President's inaugural address was reassuring. He reviewed the history of the crisis in such a way as to leave no doubt that he fully understood it, and he presented a calm, cogent argument against the constitutional right of secession that could scarcely have been improved upon. More than that, he left the South no alternative but to return to the Union, or else fight to stay out. He declared it his intention to execute the federal laws in all the states, to "hold, occupy, and possess the property and places" belonging to the United States, and to collect as usual the duties and imposts. "In doing this," he reasoned, "there needs to be no bloodshed or violence; and there shall be none, unless it be forced upon the national authority."

Lincoln had stated his policy with perfect candor, but for the first few weeks after the inauguration his administration was in a too chaotic condition to do more than mark time. The President himself, never an efficient administrator, allowed office-seekers and their sponsors to throng the White House, and to interfere seriously with his consideration of graver matters. Moreover, the election and the subsequent secession of the lower South had worked a veritable revolution in the official personnel of Washington; new and inexperienced hands had hold of every important post. Members of the Cabinet, whom Lincoln had chosen primarily to appease the various elements that made up the Republican Party, were not only lacking in experience, but what was far worse, some of them were not fully loyal to their chief. Four out of the seven, Secretary of State Seward, Secretary of the Treasury Chase, Secretary of War Cameron, and Attorney-General Bates, had hoped for the nomination that Lincoln had won. Two of them, Seward and Chase, were fully convinced that in ability they far outranked the new President; and Seward, in an amazing document written four weeks after the inauguration, actually offered to take over the government. "We are at the end of a month's administration," he told the President, "and yet without a policy, either domestic or foreign." Then, after suggesting that the domestic crisis might be cleared by declarations of war against both France and Spain, he demanded that "whatever policy we adopt, there must be an energetic prosecution of it. Either the President must do it himself, or devolve it on some member of his cabinet. It is not in my especial province. But I neither seek to evade nor assume responsibility." Fortunately Lincoln did not choose to abdicate his duties to Seward, and with that extraordinary magnanimity for which he soon became famous he made no effort to discipline his presumptuous subordinate.

Lincoln's policy

But Lincoln could not much longer postpone action. Either he must furnish Major Anderson at Fort Sumter with supplies or else permit the evacuation of the post; and approximately the same situation existed at Fort Pickens in the harbor of Pensacola, Florida. Increasingly it became clear that any attempt to relieve these garrisons would precipitate war, while the failure to do so, with their consequent surrender, would amount to a tacit recognition of the Confederacy. At length Lincoln, in spite of the disapproval of most of his Cabinet, ordered relief expeditions to both garrisons. The one sent to Fort Pickens was entirely successful, and that southern outpost was retained by the North all through the War, but the mere news that Sumter was to be reprovisioned led the Davis government to order its bombardment. On the morning of April 12 this order was executed, and after defending his post gallantly for more than a day Major Anderson surrendered. On Sunday afternoon, the fourteenth of April, with the relief ships standing helplessly by, he abandoned the fort "with colors flying and drums beating, bringing away company and private property, and saluting my flag with fifty guns." No one had been killed on either side, but the South had served notice by the incident that it meant to accept Lincoln's challenge, and would fight to stay out of the Union.

The bombardment of Sumter

The reception in the North of the news from Charleston made it equally apparent that the North would fight to keep the South in. Three months before, when under almost identical circumstances the *Star of the West,* flying the national flag, had drawn the fire of Charleston batteries, there had been no answering wave of resentment from the North, and no uprising of the masses. Now there were both. Almost with one voice the people of the free states, irrespective of party, proclaimed their approval of the call for seventy-five thousand militia that Lincoln issued the day after Sumter fell. Douglas sought an

Response of the North

"The Secession Movement." Northern cartoon showing southern states, led by South Carolina, heading for the breakers. Lithograph published by Currier and Ives, 1861.

The northern view of secession as an accomplished fact was at first confused and uncomprehending. Many Northerners felt that the South, having acted impetuously, might soon be made to see the folly of her ways, and be persuaded to remain in the Union; others felt that the South should be allowed to leave immediately and peacefully. The inevitable problem of United States property claimed by the Confederacy necessitated decisive action, however, and by the time Fort Sumter was taken Northern opposition was strong and it was apparent that each side would fight — the North to prevent, the South to enforce, secession.

"Uncle Sam's Way of Letting Traitors Alone." Northern reaction to Fort Sumter. Lithograph published by C. A. Evans, Boston, Mass, 1861.

The Bombardment of Fort Sumter, April 13, 1861. Engraving printed in *Harper's Weekly*, 1861.

interview with the President, and then came out with the ringing statement: "There are only two sides to the question. Every man must be for the United States government or against it. There can be no neutrals in this war; only patriots or traitors." Edward Everett accused the South of inaugurating an "unprovoked and unrighteous war." Ex-Presidents Pierce and Buchanan let their sympathy for the Union cause be known, and Benjamin F. Butler of Massachusetts, an ardent Breckinridge supporter in the campaign of 1860, proclaimed dramatically: "Our faces are set South, and there shall be no footstep backwards. The day of compromise is past."

During the first three months of 1861 the North had thought the problem of secession through, and like Lincoln had made up its mind to prevent it, even at the cost of war. Not every individual had been swayed by the same considerations. To some the economic argument was strong. The Northeast needed southern cotton for its mills, southern markets for its manufactured goods. Both might be imperiled if the South were permitted to leave the Union. The Northwest drove a thriving intersectional trade with the South, and believed, although there was no longer good ground for such an impression, that the Mississippi outlet was essential to its economic life. Many thoughtful men were convinced of the impracticability of secession. After all, it would settle none of the problems that had harassed the good relations of North and South. The territorial question would remain, for how would the two nations divide the territories between them? The fugitive slave problem would be more irritating than ever before. Furthermore, if secession were permitted, to what extent might it not go? Why not next a Pacific confederacy, or a northwestern confederacy? Fernando Wood, mayor of New York City, had actually suggested the desirability of that city's leaving the Union — a project that Lincoln described as not unlike "the front-door setting up housekeeping by itself."

There were numerous other arguments in favor of the North's supporting the war. Some saw in the coming struggle a long-coveted opportunity to strike a death-blow to African slavery. Probably some were influenced by fear of the diplomatic weakening that the division of the United States into two nations would involve. Such a separation would put an end to American isolation, promote alliances with European nations, destroy the Monroe Doctrine. But possibly more potent than anything else was the pride which so many people felt in the American democratic experiment. The United States was practically the only successful republic in the world. Could it survive in the face of such internal dissension as that from which it now suffered? Was democracy a failure? Certainly this question agitated Lincoln far more than any other.

For my own part [he told his private secretary], I consider the central idea pervading this struggle is the necessity of proving that popular government is not an absurdity. We must settle this question now, whether, in a free government, the minority have the right to break up the government whenever they choose. If we fail, it will go far to prove the incapability of the people to govern themselves.

Before the bombardment of Sumter the eight slave states of the upper South had steadfastly refused to leave the Union. Ties of blood and of interest bound them no less to the North than to the South; war, if it came, would surely make them a battle-ground. From their point of view the retention of the Union as it was, or its "reconstruction" in such a way as to satisfy the seceding members, was far preferable to dismemberment. In all of them, however, the right of secession was generally conceded, and a strong minority favored putting the right into practice. When war between North and South became a certainty, this minority was quickly transformed into a majority in four of the border states — Virginia, North Carolina, Tennessee, and Arkansas. Three others — Delaware, Maryland, and Missouri — decided definitely to remain with the North. Kentucky for a time attempted an impossible neutrality, but Lincoln, with excellent judgment, allowed the Confederacy to trespass first upon its soil, whereupon Kentucky also fell to the Union. Another important victory for the North was won when a block of forty-six counties in the mountains of northwestern Virginia refused to follow the rest of the state out of the Union, and by somewhat irregular methods became the independent loyal state of West Virginia, which Congress in June, 1863, belatedly admitted to the Union.

It must not be supposed that these decisions of the border states reflected in every instance the will of the majority. The federal government took pains to insure that Maryland, whose territory surrounded the District of Columbia on three sides, had no chance to secede; and the little state of Delaware had perforce to do what Maryland did. Similarly, the Confederacy could not risk the loss of Tennessee because of its important railroad connections, and with the earnest co-operation of the governor and other state officials, made its secession a certainty. In all the border states sentiment was divided, and most of them furnished recruits for the armies of both North and South. While in a general way it is not inaccurate to speak of the struggle as a "war between the states,"

in the border area it was a true "civil war," with brother sometimes pitted against brother, and father against son.

In the division of forces the North fared far better than the South. Eleven states left the Union; twenty-two (or counting West Virginia, twenty-three) remained loyal to it. Of the territories, only New Mexico and the Indian country to the west of Arkansas fell to the South, and this whole region was quickly reconquered. The North got all the rest, and from it admitted Kansas (1861) and Nevada (1864) to statehood. In population the North outnumbered the South, 22,000,000 to 9,500,000, while the relative fighting power of the South was still further lessened by the fact that about 3,500,000 of its people were slaves. As events proved, however, nearly all of the slaves remained loyal to their masters throughout the war, and, although they were not used by the South as soldiers, their labor, both at home and at the front, released a far larger proportion of southern white population for military service than could otherwise have been available.

A disproportionately large share of the economic resources of the nation lay in the northern states and territories. The known mineral deposits of the country — coal, iron, copper, precious metals — were located almost entirely in the North. Ninety-two per

Harpers Ferry, Virginia. The United States arsenal at Harpers Ferry was one of the few strategic pieces of government property taken over by the South at the outbreak of the Civil War. Engraving by Moran.

cent of the manufacturing of the country was carried on in the North, and its iron foundries, textile mills, tanneries, etc., had only to be expanded to meet the unusual demands of war. The South, on the other hand, expected to import the greater part of its manufactures, including the *matériel* of war, a task that would have been easy enough had the North done nothing to prevent the exportation of cotton in payment; for, as already noted, the South had a virtual monopoly on the world's supply of raw cotton. Neither side suffered for lack of foodstuffs, although southern armies and southern cities sometimes went hungry because of transportation difficulties. Of tremendous importance in determining which side would win the war was the railroad supremacy of the North. With nearly two and a half times as many miles of railroad as the South, and with the northern railroads far more strategically located than the southern, the advantage of the North in this all-essential factor was decisive.

Nearly all of the property of the United States government that possessed military value went to the North. The South took over the Norfolk navy yard, Harpers Ferry, and the other southern arsenals, the sub-treasury and mint at New Orleans, and a few coast defenses; but the North got practically all the rest, including almost every ship in the United States Navy. It was long charged that John B. Floyd of Virginia, who was Buchanan's Secretary of War until the closing days of 1860, deliberately transferred enough arms from northern to southern arsenals to give the South an undue advantage in this particular. Some such transfers were made, but it is improbable that Floyd, who until close to the end of his term was strongly opposed to secession, could have had the motive imputed to him. Furthermore, the transfers that took place actually left the southern states short of their proper proportion of federal weapons. Just before he left office Floyd did issue some unreasonable, and possibly treasonous, orders for the shipment of ordnance from

northern factories to points in the South' but these orders were immediately countermanded by his successor. In point of fact, neither side possessed enough reliable weapons at the time the war broke out to constitute any real menace to the safety of the other.

The United States had a regular army at the beginning of the war of about sixteen thousand men, and a navy of ninety ships manned by a total of perhaps nine thousand men. The enlisted men in both branches of the national defense remained, with but rare exceptions, loyal to the North, but at least one fourth of the officers resigned their commissions and tendered their services to the South. Unfortunately for the North, the officers who resigned were as a group superior in ability to those who did not, for southern planters had long been proud to send their sons to West Point or Annapolis, while among Northerners of comparable talent the military life was but little esteemed.

Any assessment of the relative strength of North and South would be incomplete without some reference to the personal characteristics of the men who were to do the fighting. The Southerners were convinced that in this respect they far outshone their adversaries. The statement that "any Southerner could lick five Yankees" was as sincerely believed as it was common. Undoubtedly the population of the South had preserved more of the primitive fighting spirit than the population of the North. Southerners were the more habituated to outdoor life, they were better skilled in the use of firearms, they were far superior as horsemen and in a much shorter space of time produced good cavalry, they were already accustomed to caste lines and adjusted themselves more easily to army discipline. Northerners, on the other hand, while difficult to weld into an army because of their unwillingness to recognize and follow leaders, possessed far more individual resourcefulness. The northern privates were as a whole far better educated than their southern opponents, they were drawn from a wider range of occupations, they possessed greater mechanical skill, they were less embarrassed by an unusual situation. All of which was hardly sufficient to overcome the handicap of fighting in an alien climate and over terrain that neither they nor their officers knew anything about.

The "preponderating asset of the North" turned out to be Lincoln himself. This

Lincoln was not because he possessed any intuitive military understanding that was of use to his generals; indeed, his ideas on strategy were quite as naïve as those of any other civilian. Nor was he at first a notably good judge of military men. His strength lay in his extraordinary understanding of the feelings and prejudices of the masses, without whose support the war could never have been won. He realized, more fully than most of his advisers, that when a democracy goes to war military efficiency is of no avail without the backing of public opinion. Every such war has, therefore, its political no less than its military side; and it was in the management of the political side of the struggle that Lincoln's genius was mostly clearly manifest.

What Abraham Lincoln, the politician, was to the North, Robert E. Lee, the sol-

Lee dier, was to the South. The two men could hardly have stood in greater contrast with each other. Lee was of the Virginia gentry, a patrician to his fingertips, and a military genius. The son of General Henry Lee, who had served under Washington during the Revolution, his "strong hereditary claims on the country" had helped him obtain a cadetship at West Point in 1825, where four years later he was graduated, second in his class. As Captain Lee, he was General Scott's chief of staff in Mexico, and out of that campaign he won no less than three brevets — major, lieutenant-colonel, and colonel — for gallant service in the field. Always a favorite with General Scott, who believed him the ablest officer in the army, he was undoubtedly the first choice of both Scott and Lincoln for the active command of the United States Army; a week before the bombardment of Sumter, Francis P. Blair, speaking unofficially for the President, actually offered Lee this post. But Lee, to use his own words, "declined the offer he made me, stating as candidly and as courteously as I could, that though opposed to secession and deprecating war, I could take no part in an invasion of the Southern States." He was deeply distressed at the thought of fighting against the United States, but he regarded it as his duty, in case Virginia seceded, to draw his sword in defense of his native state. As handsome as Lincoln was homely, and steeped in the chivalry of the Old South, he was the perfect embodiment of the rôle he was chosen to play. Had he cast his lot with the North instead of the South, it is hard to see how the struggle could have been so long drawn out.

Bibliography

Kenneth M. Stampp, *And the War Came: The North and the Secession Crisis, 1860–1861* (1950), brilliantly analyzes northern opinion on the crisis. The equivalent southern approach is presented in a number of state-wide studies: H. S. Schultz, *Nationalism and Sectionalism in South Carolina, 1852–1860: A Study of the Movement for Southern Independence* (1950); J. G. Van Deusen, *Economic Bases of Disunion in South Carolina* (1928); J. C. Sitterson, *The Secession Movement in North Carolina* (1939); H. T. Shanks, *The Secession Movement in Virginia, 1847–1861* (1934); J. C. McGregor, *The Disruption of Virginia* (1922); C. H. Ambler, *West Virginia, The Mountain State* (1940). The subject as a whole is given scholarly and sympathetic treatment by Dwight L. Dumond, *The Secession Movement, 1860–1861* (1931); and U. B. Phillips, *The Course of the South to Secession; An Interpretation* (1939). P. S. Foner, *Business and Slavery: The New York*

Merchants and the Irrepressible Conflict (1941), shows the fear of disunion felt by northern business leaders. Other useful special accounts include J. T. Carpenter, *The South as a Conscious Minority, 1789–1861; A Study in Political Thought* (1930); Madeleine H. Rice, *American Catholic Opinion in the Slavery Controversy* (1944); Mary Scrugham, *The Peaceable Americans of 1860–1861* (1921).

Books on Lincoln are legion. The best on the period under review is J. G. Randall, *Lincoln, the President: Springfield to Gettysburg* (2 vols., 1945). The most voluminous, but written as a sustained paean of praise, is John G. Nicolay and John Hay, *Abraham Lincoln: A History* (10 vols., 1890). Carl Sandburg, *Abraham Lincoln, The Prairie Years* (2 vols., 1926), and *The War Years* (4 vols., 1939) show a poetic indifference to accuracy of detail, but taken as a whole are convincing. The best single-volume biography is Lord Charnwood, *Abraham Lincoln* (1916). This may be supplemented on the personal side by N. W. Stephenson, *Lincoln* (1922); and W. E. Barton, *The Life of Abraham Lincoln* (2 vols., 1925). B. P. Thomas, *Portrait for Posterity: Lincoln and His Biographers* (1947), is an interesting attempt to evaluate the work of Lincoln's biographers. Special aspects of Lincoln's activities are treated in the following: W. E. Baringer, *Lincoln's Rise to Power* (1937), and *A House Dividing: Lincoln as President Elect* (1945); D. M. Potter, *Lincoln and his Party in the Secession Crisis* (1942); J. S. Tilley, *Lincoln Takes Command* (1941), and *The Coming of the Glory* (1949); R. S. Harper, *Lincoln and the Press* (1951). W. E. Dodd, *Lincoln or Lee* (1928), is an interesting interpretation.

Biographies of Lee are almost as numerous as biographies of Lincoln, but most of them have been supplanted by the excellent and exhaustive work of Douglas Southall Freeman, *R. E. Lee: A Biography* (4 vols., 1934–35). Sir Frederick B. Maurice, *Robert E. Lee, The Soldier* (1925), is useful on the military side. B. J. Hendrick, *The Lees of Virginia* (1935), is an interesting effort to write the biography of an illustrious family. C. C. Rister, *Robert E. Lee in Texas* (1946), examines Lee's career just prior to the Civil War.

Biographies of Jefferson Davis are also numerous. W. E. Dodd, *Jefferson Davis* (1907), is excellent. R. M. McElroy, *Jefferson Davis, The Unreal and the Real* (2 vols., 1937), is more detailed. B. J. Hendrick, *Statesmen of the Lost Cause: Jefferson Davis and His Cabinet* (1939), explains in human terms the fall of the South. See also Jefferson Davis, *The Rise and Fall of the Confederate Government* (2 vols., 1881).

Biographies of those associated with Lincoln or Davis are numerous and in many instances of great value. Frederic Bancroft, *The Life of William H. Seward* (2 vols., 1900); and A. B. Hart, *Salmon Portland Chase* (1899), deal with two of Lincoln's leading advisers. L. F. Crippen, *Simon Cameron: Ante-Bellum Years* (1942), attempts to rehabilitate a somewhat tarnished reputation. Rudolph Von Abele, *Alexander H. Stephens: A Biography* (1946), is a discriminating portrait of the great southern leader. J. B. Ranck, *Albert Gallatin Brown, Radical Southern Nationalist* (1937), shows the attitude of the southern small farmer toward division. Others are cited at the end of Chapter 31, pp. 594–595.

31

The Civil War

Lack of preparedness HAD lack of preparedness alone been a sufficient deterrent, there would have been no war between North and South in 1861. In a military sense neither side was ready for war; indeed, except for some eleventh-hour activities in the South, it could almost be said that neither side had given any very serious consideration to the military problem. The regular army of the United States was not only insignificant in size; it was divided up into a multitude of tiny garrisons, most of which were located along the Indian frontier, and could be withdrawn only at the risk of an Indian uprising. The organized state militia, which was the second line of defense for the North and the beginning and end of southern preparedness, consisted of a few companies of volunteers to each state, imperfectly armed and inadequately drilled. Probably the total number of such militiamen in the loyal states on the eve of the war was less than ten thousand, and in the seceding states even less than that. When Lincoln, on April 15, 1861, issued his call for seventy-five thousand state militia, and Davis shortly afterward countered with a somewhat similar request for one hundred thousand, both men knew that they were asking for units that did not exist. Before there could be any war, volunteers must be obtained, armed, and organized into armies. This situation, more than anything else, accounts for the slow beginning of military operations, and the uncertainty and delay that characterized the first campaigns. Not until well toward the middle of the war did the armies of North and South confront each other as dependable fighting machines.

Lincoln's first call for troops, issued under an antiquated militia law, asked for a specified number of regiments from each state. Since none of the **How the armies were** states had anywhere nearly **raised** enough organized militia to fill its assigned quota, each loyal governor was forced in turn to issue his own state-wide call for troops. He was in no better position, however, than the President to accept individual volunteers, so he in turn passed on this task to the various communities of the state. There local leaders promptly assumed the responsibility thrust upon them, called patriotic mass meetings where "muster-rolls" could be started, and as soon as a company was filled offered its services to the state. Company officers were invariably elected by the volunteers themselves, but regimental officers were usually chosen by the governor. At the state capital, or some other prescribed rendezvous, the companies were assembled into regiments, furnished with whatever equipment the state was able to obtain, and then promptly turned over to the national government. Within a remarkably short space of time the troops thus raised far exceeded the number Lincoln had called for; but in spite of frantic purchases abroad by both state and national governments, the supply of arms was totally inadequate, and the uniforms, whenever they existed at all, presented an astonishing variety of colors and patterns. Few of the recruits knew even the barest rudiments of military drill, and the officers, selected usually because of their political or social prominence, were almost as ignorant of military matters as the men they attempted to command.

The law cited by Lincoln to authorize his call for state militia limited their term of national service to ninety days, but the President was not so short-sighted as to believe that in that time the war would be over. Encouraged by the response of the country to his first call, he issued another on the third of May following which asked for forty-two thousand volunteers to serve for three years, and directed an increase of eighteen thousand men in the regular army. Since the Constitution gives to Congress, rather than to the President, the right to raise armies, it is hard to see how this second call could have been constitutional. Lincoln himself was under no illusions about his action, and when Congress met on July 4 he asked (and subsequently received) its official ratification of what he had done. Convinced by that time more than ever that the war would be a serious struggle, he asked also for a volunteer army of at least four hundred thousand three-year men. Congress granted him five hundred thousand.

The public, however, expected a speedy conclusion of the war, and called for a battle **"On to Richmond"** to end it. With the secession of Virginia, the Confederate capital was removed to Richmond, about a hundred miles from Washington, while Confederate soil was no farther away than just across the Potomac. Only a few weeks were required to assemble at Washington a Union

army of some thirty-six thousand men, and inevitably the battle-cry was raised, "On to Richmond!" General Scott, who in spite of his seventy-five years was still in high command of the Union forces, counseled delay until the troops could be better trained, but Lincoln felt compelled to yield to the popular pressure for action. Most of the Union troops were three-months men whose term of enlistment would be over before the end of July; moreover, sadly in need of training as they were, they were little if any worse off in this respect than the enemy. A council of war, held in the White House on June 29, decided in favor of an immediate battle, and assigned to General Irvin McDowell, a West Point graduate, the task of striking the blow.

Meantime General Robert E. Lee, first as the commander-in-chief of the Virginia militia, and later as the chief military adviser of President Davis, had made what preparations he could for the defense of his native state. The methods used by the South in raising an army did not vary markedly from the methods of the North, and a plentiful supply of raw recruits was available. General Pierre G. T. Beauregard, with about twenty-two thousand men, was stationed at Manassas Junction, an important railway point some thirty miles to the west of Washington. Half as many men under General Joseph E. Johnston were at Winchester, not less than fifty miles to the northwest of Manassas, guarding the entrance to the Shenandoah Valley. That these two forces might be united in case of an emergency was a part of the Confederate strategy. Knowing full well the limitations of his untrained troops, Lee refused to consider taking the offensive.

McDowell's plan was to attack Beauregard, but in accepting the command he expressly stipulated that the **The Union** two Confederate forces must not **advance** be permitted to unite. This seemed easy to prevent, for General Robert Patterson had a Union army of at least fourteen thousand men at Martinsburg, Virginia, only a few miles from Winchester, and was already under orders to keep Johnston fully engaged. On the sixteenth of July, amidst almost indescribable confusion and with no slightest attempt at concealment, McDowell's columns began to advance. Only six miles were made the first day, most of the second day was spent in rounding up stragglers, and five days altogether were consumed in reaching the enemy's lines. Unaccustomed to discipline, and oppressed by the delays, the dust, and the heat, the men wandered away in search of water, stopped along the roadside to pick blackberries, and generally followed their own devices. Baggage-wagons in charge of unruly civilians brought up the rear, and throngs of sight-seers, including newspapermen, politicians, and even Washington society matrons, all of whom were determined to witness the impending battle, got in everyone's way.

Since McDowell had not less than thirty thousand men under his command, he counted on an easy victory. But unfortunately for these hopes, Johnston was able to give his none-too-clever opponent, Patterson, the slip, and thanks to a conveniently located railroad succeeded in joining forces with Beauregard on the eve of the Union attack. On the morning of the twenty-first, with the contestants nearly equal in numbers, the battle opened at Bull Run, a few miles north of Manassas. The Confederates had meant to be the first to attack, but an unhappy confusion in orders delayed them and permitted McDowell to develop his admirably devised plan of battle. The men on both sides fought bravely, in spite of their lack of training, and for a time it seemed that the northern troops must surely win. At about three o'clock in the afternoon, however, a Confederate charge, in which the last of Johnston's troops to arrive were just in time to participate, threw the Union right into confusion. Still further dismayed by the rumor, all too true, that the enemy had been heavily reinforced, the same men that had stood their ground bravely all day long now broke and

Bull Run

Bull Run
21 July 1861

ran. In less than an hour the whole Union army was utterly demoralized, and in full retreat toward Washington. Except for a few hundred regulars, who covered the retreat, all semblance of order was lost, and it was as a panic-stricken mob rather than as a defeated army that McDowell's troops returned to the capital.

On the whole the North was fortunate to have lost at Bull Run. The fear expressed by some of Lincoln's advisers that the Confederates would follow up their victory by the destruction of the Union army and the capture of Washington was wholly unwarranted, for, to use the words of Johnston himself, "the Confederate army was more disorganized by victory than that of the United States by defeat." What the North learned from the humiliating experience was that the war was not to be won by untrained volunteers in a short summer campaign. Only by careful preparation could ultimate success be assured. The South, on the other hand, suffered from a feeling of overconfidence. The southern leaders were not deceived. "I have no idea that the North will give up," wrote Stephens. "Their defeat will increase their energy." But among the masses the conviction grew that the Yankees could not or would not fight. After Bull Run some of the Confederate soldiers went home thinking the war was over.

The "second uprising of the North," which followed closely on the heels of the battle, soon gave Lincoln all the three-year men he asked for, and many more. In raising and organizing these troops, the precedents already set in calling out the state militia were closely followed. Quotas were assigned to the various states, upon whom the primary task of ob-

The Union volunteers

Recruiting broadside, advertising for volunteers to fill up vacancies in "The Clinton Rifles" regiment, encamped on Staten Island, N.Y., to "Rescue our Glorious Union," 1861.

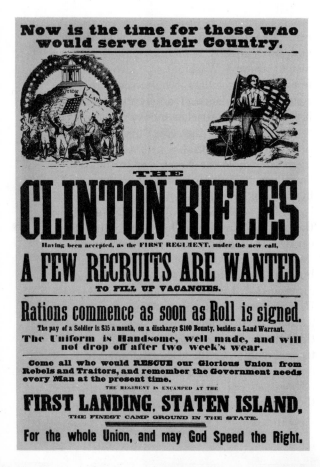

taining recruits thus devolved. Communities then vied with one another in the heartiness of their response to the governor's call. Officers from the grade of colonel down were commissioned by the governors, although in practice company officers were usually chosen by the men themselves, and their choices merely ratified by the governor. Care was taken to obtain if possible at least one officer to a regiment who had had some military training, and for this purpose the presence in the northern states of many immigrants who had seen service in Europe proved to be a great advantage. General officers were appointed by the President, by and with the advice and consent of the Senate. This system of recruiting was admirably devised to capitalize fully the existing mass enthusiasm, for the young men of each community could enlist together with the knowledge that they would probably serve together throughout the war. Often they even knew in advance the officers under whom they would serve. But the system also had its disadvantages. When, as frequently happened, certain units took most of the punishment in a given engagement, it followed that the communities from which the men came were correspondingly hard hit. Had the men for each unit been drawn from many different places, the losses would have been more evenly distributed. The problem of replacements was still more perplexing. New companies and new regiments, with a whole new complement of officers, were far easier to raise than an equal number of men for old units that had been decimated by battle losses or disease. Another misfortune was that the War Department chose to keep the regular army intact rather than to distribute it among the volunteer troops to assist in their training. But the President chose many regular army officers for high command in the volunteer army, and it was due mainly to their work that the raw recruits ultimately attained a fair degree of military efficiency. By the spring of 1862, with well over six hundred thousand volunteers accepted, the War Department felt that enough troops had been raised to win the war, and stopped recruiting.

To reorganize the badly beaten "Grand Army of the Potomac," General George B. McClellan was called to Washington. McClellan was a former regular army officer who as a major-general of Ohio volunteers had scored some small but spectacular successes in the occupation of West Virginia. He proved to be an admirable drill-master, and in a short time brought order out of chaos. By the end of the summer he had no less than one hundred thousand men at his disposal, all well disciplined, well equipped, and reasonably well drilled. The pride of the North in its new army, and in the general who had produced it, was very great. When Scott resigned in November, McClellan was made commander-in-chief of all the Union forces, and confidence that he would soon bring the war to a successful conclusion was high. But as month after month wore on, and nothing was accomplished, the watchword "All quiet along the Potomac" began to sound like a reproach to the entire country. McClellan's great defect, it soon appeared, was his excess of caution. While he was developing a Union army, General Johnston was doing the same thing over in Virginia for the Confederates. But whereas Johnston's army was never anywhere nearly as strong as his own, McClellan always insisted that the exact opposite was true, and, fearful of another Bull Run, he steadfastly refused to move. Not until the spring of 1862, after the President had issued express orders commanding it, did he begin his advance.

The general strategy of the war soon became fairly obvious to all the participants. Since the South could ask nothing better than to be left alone, the North, in order to win, must take the aggressive and wage a war of conquest. The existence of the Appalachian mountain barrier insured that there would be two battle-fronts, one to the east, and one to the west. A third, and extremely important, theater of war lay on the high seas. The South, because of its primarily agricultural economy, must depend to a great extent for its munitions of war upon importations from Europe. To pay for these supplies, it would seek to export cotton, and possibly to a lesser extent tobacco and sugar. If, therefore, the North could blockade the South, and could effectively prevent trade between the Confederacy and the outside world, victory would soon crown the northern arms. The armies of the East and of the West, advancing simultaneously into the lower South, would ultimately join forces, crush out the last vestige of opposition, and restore the supremacy of the Union. The hope of

In the field. President Lincoln visiting General McClellan in his headquarters at Antietam. Photograph by Mathew B. Brady, October 3, 1862.

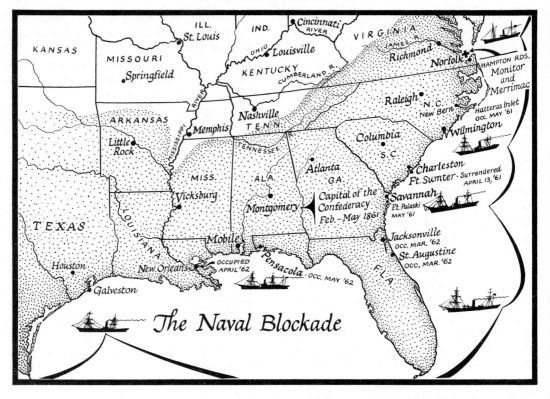

The Naval Blockade

the South, on the other hand, lay in breaking the blockade, and in maintaining armies in the field large enough to hold the invaders at bay. The South did not so much need to win victories as to keep the North from winning victories.

Events on the western front during the first year of the war strikingly paralleled **The western front** what went on in the East. About a month before Bull Run, General Nathaniel Lyon with a handful of regulars drove the Confederates from the Missouri state capital and defeated a small secessionist force under General Sterling Price at Boonville, Missouri. This victory virtually insured control of the northern half of Missouri for the Union, but Lyon's valiant efforts to expel the enemy from the southern part of the state ended with his defeat and death at the battle of Wilson's Creek, on August 10 following. Thereafter the fighting ceased, and in the West as in the East the main concern was the creation of an army. For this purpose two headquarters were

established, one at St. Louis on the Mississippi, the other at Cincinnati on the Ohio. Unfortunately the command at St. Louis was given to one of Lincoln's "political" generals, John C. Frémont, who in spite of his former connection with the army had far more exploration than military training to his credit, and proved to be totally lacking in administrative ability. In November, 1861, when his incompetence and the corruption it bred could no longer be tolerated, Lincoln removed him; and a little later he gave the post to General Henry W. Halleck, a middle-aged and uninspiring West Pointer, who had left the army to become a lawyer. Halleck's administration was business-like, but in his excess of caution he was more than a match for McClellan. General Don Carlos Buell, whom Lincoln placed in charge of the "Army of the Ohio," was a more fortunate choice, although Buell regarded his command as wholly independent of Halleck's, and friction between the two became chronic. Fortunately for the North, the decision of Kentucky to remain loyal enabled the Union forces to occupy Louisville, Frankfort, and most of the northern part of that state, and lost for the Confederacy the highly defensible boundary of the Ohio River. But until the spring of 1862 the amount of actual fighting on this front was negligible.

The blockade of the southern coast was decided on immediately after the fall of **The** Sumter. Davis conveniently **blockade** prepared the way for the introduction of this policy by a proclamation of April 17, 1861, in which he authorized privateers to prey upon the commerce of the United States. Two days later Lincoln retaliated by declaring a blockade of all the ports from South Carolina to Texas, and when Virginia and North Carolina seceded, he added their ports also. With a total of only ninety ships in the United States Navy, and a Confederate coastline of over three thousand miles to be guarded, this proclamation amounted at first to nothing more serious than a "paper blockade." But the Secretary of the Navy, Gideon Welles of Connecticut, although totally ignorant of nautical affairs, developed executive ability of a high order, while his Assistant Secretary, Gustavus Vasa Fox, had been a naval officer, and possessed the necessary technical qualifications. Ships of every sort and kind were converted into blockaders, and before the war was six months old the South had begun to feel the results. Such items as tea, coffee, soap, candles, and matches brought extremely high prices, and were hard to get at any price. Medical supplies fell desperately short of the demand. Because of the lack of print paper, newspapers found it necessary to reduce the size of their issues, and sometimes to print them on brown wrapping paper. Because of the shortage of drygoods, homespun gained steadily in popularity, and women accepted as a patriotic duty the necessity of wearing out-of-date garments.

To make the blockade one hundred per cent effective was, until the very close of the war, wholly outside the realm of possibility.

Fleet blockade-runners, usually of British origin, repeatedly got through **Blockade-** the blockading squadrons under **runners** cover of night or fog, and easily outsailed the nondescript ships that the North had pressed into service. Muskets, ammunition, artillery, and nearly all the necessary *matériel* of war were obtained by the South in this fashion. At first, ports in the West Indies and the Bahamas served admirably as headquarters for the blockade-runners, for here the produce of the Confederacy could readily be exchanged for European goods. Irritated by this procedure, the United States government finally advanced the theory that the shipment of goods from European ports to the Confederacy was one "continuous voyage," even if the goods were unloaded and reloaded at neutral ports on this side of the Atlantic. American sea-captains were therefore given orders to seize ships suspected of being engaged in this traffic whether they were found on the "long lap" or the "short lap" of the voyage. This ruling served to tighten up the blockade to some extent, but certainly not to make it entirely effective. Otherwise Lee at Gettysburg, after two years of war, would not have had almost, if not quite, as good artillery as his northern opponent.

Another method used by the North to increase the effectiveness of the blockade was the capture of southern ports **Amphibious** and coast fortifications. As **expeditions** early as August, 1861, the Confederate forts at Hatteras Inlet, which controlled the best entrance to the waters of North Carolina, were taken by a joint army and navy expedition. The following November a similar attack lost for the Confederacy Port Royal, South Carolina, one of the finest harbors on the southern coast. These "amphibious" expeditions, kept up for the duration of the war, finally closed every Confederate port except Charleston and Wilmington. Although far less spectacular than the great land engagements, they were of tremendous significance; for the success of the blockade, more than any other single factor, brought about the breakdown in southern military efficiency and the collapse in southern civilian morale that enabled the North to win.

Hopeful that the need of the outside world for cotton would bring European nations, **The clash of** particularly Great Britain, to **ironclads** their aid, the Confederate leaders were at first inclined to regard the blockade with a certain degree of equanimity. The old illusion that cotton was king died hard; surely the British and French navies must soon break the blockade and open the southern ports. When this hope failed to materialize, however, and the pressure of the blockade became increasingly irksome, the South began to take steps to help herself. The hasty, and probably quite unnecessary, abandonment by the North of the Norfolk navy yard had involved the firing and sinking of the *Merrimac*, a forty-gun steam frigate. This hulk the Confederates raised, remodeled into a low-lying ironclad with ten guns and a cast-iron ram, and dispatched (renamed the *Virginia*, but rarely so called) in March, 1862, against the blockading squadron at Hampton Roads. There on the afternoon of March 8 the *Merrimac* sank the *Cumberland*, a sloop-of-war, forced the *Congress*, a sailing frigate, to strike her colors, and planned to finish off the remaining Union warship, the *Minnesota*, next morning. Well advised from the beginning of the work being done on the *Merrimac*, the Union navy had long had under construction at Brooklyn an ironclad of its own, the *Monitor*, designed by John Ericsson, a Swedish engineer. By an extraordinary coincidence the *Monitor* reached Hampton Roads the night of March 8, so that when the *Merrimac* resumed the fray on the following morning she was met by another ironclad. The *Monitor* was much smaller than the *Merrimac*, and in appearance resembled a "cheese-box on a raft," or a "tin can on a shingle." Her flat, heavily armored deck was surmounted only by a revolving iron tower that carried two powerful guns. In the duel that followed neither ship was able to do serious damage to the other, and the *Merrimac* at length

withdrew, never again to figure in the war. The engagement marked a turning-point in naval history, for it proved that the old-fashioned wooden ships were obsolete. But it did nothing to aid the Confederacy, for the North was able to multiply the number of *Monitors* at will, while the South could not produce another *Merrimac*.

The South did succeed, however, in harassing the trade of the North by means of commerce-destroyers. Nine- **Commerce-** teen of these vessels, of which **destroyers** the most famous was the *Alabama*, got to sea. Nearly all of them were British-built, manned chiefly by British subjects and outfitted from British ports, but they were officered by the Confederacy, and, acting on its authority, they destroyed a total of over two hundred and fifty northern merchant ships. Their exploits struck an almost fatal blow to the American merchant marine, for the risk of destruction and the consequent high insurance rates led American shipowners to dispose of the bulk of their holdings to foreigners, whereupon the ships were transferred to foreign registry. Commerce between the United States and the outside world was not seriously interrupted, but because of the commerce-destroyers such trade tended increasingly to be carried on under a foreign flag.

The commerce-destroyers were built for speed rather than for heavy fighting, and they proved to be of no value in **The Laird** breaking the blockade. In the **rams** spring of 1863, however, it became known that the same British firm that had built the *Alabama* for the Confederacy was now engaged in the building of two heavy ironclad rams for use in bringing the blockade to an end. Had these "Laird rams" been permitted to sail, they might well have succeeded in opening up a number of southern ports, but the vigorous protests that the United States launched with the British government, backed up by the threat of a war that the British ministry had decided to avoid, caused orders to be issued for their restraint. With the failure of this scheme

HAMPTON ROADS, MARCH 9, 1862. The engagement between the *Monitor* and the *Merrimac* Engraving by J. C. McRae after Momberger.

Iron-clad warships *were first used in actual naval engagements during the Civil War, although both England and France had undertaken the construction of "armor plated" ships in the late 1850's. After the battle between the* Monitor *and the* Merrimac, *it was generally admitted that wooden ships would soon be obsolete. When the United States undertook to build a fleet of "monitors," the respect of the British government for the North noticeably increased. Iron-clad gunboats on the western rivers had much to do with the winning of the river war by the North.*

THE DECK OF THE "MONITOR." Photograph by Mathew B. Brady, probably about 1862.

RIVER FIGHTING ON THE MISSISSIPPI. Lithograph published by Currier and Ives, 1863.

the last serious effort of the South to break the blockade came to nought.

The impatience of the northern public with the slow start of the war finally vented itself upon the person of the Secretary of War, Simon Cameron, a Pennsylvania politician whom Lincoln had felt obliged to include in his Cabinet. While Cameron was by no means wholly, or even chiefly, to blame for the existing inertia, his shortcomings as an administrator were soon painfully apparent. Contracts were awarded to political hacks at fantastic figures, the efficiency of the army was threatened by the acceptance of inferior goods, and railroads were permitted to make ridiculous overcharges for their services. In January, 1862, Lincoln removed Cameron from office and nominated him to be minister to Russia, an appointment which he accepted and held for a time. Among the loudest of the critics of the administration was another Pennsylvanian, Edwin M. Stanton, who talked freely of "the painful imbecility of Lincoln" and the discreditable record of his subordinates. Stanton was a Democrat, and had served as Attorney-General under Buchanan, but his loyalty to the Union was unquestioned and his ability to serve it had already been demonstrated. Lincoln by a master stroke made him Secretary of War, in which capacity, despite his incorrigibly bad manners, his dangerous habit of interfering in strictly military matters, and his deep-seated personal prejudices, he became a tower of strength to the northern cause. His opinion of Lincoln soon changed.

Less than ten days after Stanton took office, news of active fighting on the western **Fighting in** front began to come in. Lincoln **the West** had long urged that something should be done to free the mountaineer Unionists of eastern Kentucky and eastern Tennessee from Confederate control. From the military point of view, this seemed scarcely worth the pains, for railroads to facilitate such a movement were lacking, whereas farther to the West the existence of navigable waterways, as well as railroads,

made the transportation problem much simpler. Nevertheless, a small detachment of Buell's army under General George H. Thomas penetrated as far south as Mill Springs, in southeastern Kentucky, and on January 19–20 won a decisive victory over a slightly superior Confederate force. The way was now open to Cumberland Gap, but the difficulties of maintaining a line of communications into this region were so great that Thomas's victory was not followed up, and his command was soon withdrawn.

Of far greater importance was the beginning of the "river war" in western Tennessee. General Albert Sidney Johnston, whom Davis had placed in supreme command of all the Confederate forces in the West, was an abler officer than either Halleck or Buell, and was unharassed by any conflict in authority. He had fewer troops than his opponents, however, and was compelled to fight mostly on the defensive. The natural line of the Union advance was by way of the Mississippi, the Tennessee, and the Cumberland, which almost parallel each other for nearly a hundred miles south of the Ohio. At Columbus and Island No. 10 on the Mississippi, at Fort Henry on the Tennessee, and at Fort Donelson on the Cumberland, Johnston had made every effort to prepare for the Union attack. Early in February General Ulysses S. Grant, supported by a Union flotilla of gunboats under Flag-Officer Andrew H. Foote, advanced against Fort Henry. On February 6, after hard fighting, the fort surrendered to Flag-Officer Foote an hour and a half before Grant's army arrived on the scene. On February 16 another joint army and gunboat attack under the same officers brought a like fate to Fort Donelson. These victories forced Johnston to abandon his northernmost hold on the Mississippi River at Columbus, and his headquarters at Nashville on the Cumberland. The way seemed well prepared for a Union invasion of western Tennessee. Meantime, far out in the Ozarks at Pea Ridge, Arkansas, March 5–8, another Union victory drove the Confederates from south-

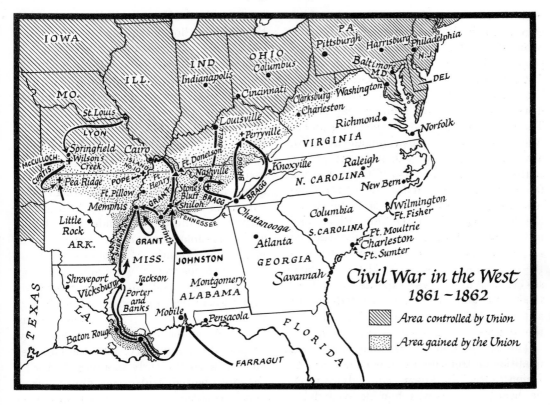

Civil War in the West
1861 - 1862

Area controlled by Union

Area gained by the Union

ern Missouri and northern Arkansas. The North was overjoyed at the success of its arms, and took particular pride in General Grant, whose victory at Fort Donelson was regarded as a kind of offset for the defeat at Bull Run the year before.

Ulysses S. Grant (1822–85) was the son of an eccentric and unprosperous Ohio tanner.

Grant

Accident rather than ability won him an appointment to West Point in 1839, where, to use his own words, he "never succeeded in getting squarely at either end of my class, in any one study, during the four years." Among the thirty-nine members of the graduating class of 1843, reputed to have been unusually weak as a whole, he ranked twenty-first. Commissioned a second lieutenant of infantry, he planned soon to leave the army, but changed his mind with the outbreak of the Mexican War. That conflict, however, brought him only the rank of first lieutenant, and no such distinction as came to Lee,

Davis, and many others. The monotony of army life in the Far West, to which he was assigned soon after the war was over, drove him to drink, and in 1854 rather than face a court-martial on the charge of drunkenness he resigned his commission. The year before he had been made a captain. Years of poverty and failure followed, and when the war broke out in 1861 Grant was a clerk at fifty dollars a month in a leather store owned by his two brothers at Galena, Illinois.

In spite of the lack of confidence in himself that had deepened with the years, Grant hoped that his military training and experience fitted him for a colonelcy, and for that rank he applied both at Washington and at Springfield. His applications were ignored until a regiment of Illinois volunteers grew mutinous under its "political" colonel and Governor Richard Yates asked Grant, who was almost the only military man available, to accept its command and straighten it out. This task he gladly undertook, and accomplished with ease. Shortly after, when Lincoln asked the Illinois congressmen to make nominations for the rank of brigadier-general, Elihu B. Washburne, from whose district Grant came, sent in Grant's name because Grant was the only colonel from his district who had had military experience. The commission was soon forthcoming, and in August, 1861, Grant took command at Cairo, a village in Frémont's department at the southern tip of Illinois. Without waiting for instructions, Grant forestalled the Confederates in the occupation of Paducah, on the Kentucky side of the Ohio River, and in November, 1861, he successfully attacked a Confederate outpost on the west bank of the Mississippi at Belmont, Missouri, opposite Columbus. These exploits, as well as the location of his command, pointed him out as the natural leader when the time came for the attacks on Forts Henry and Donelson.

The test of time proved that Grant had qualities of tremendous importance to the Union cause. He knew sound advice when he heard it, and was humble enough to accept it. He had a dogged determination, amounting almost to an obsession, never to turn back once he had decided on a given course of action. He chose his subordinates with skill, made his decisions with a degree of speed and accuracy that increased as the war wore on, and accepted without hesitation every new responsibility that was thrust upon him. A member of his staff, General John A. Rawlins, supplemented Grant's qualities admirably, and did much to bring out the best that was in his chief. Among other things, Rawlins saw to it that Grant did not fall again into the liquor habit, which had caused him such sorrow years before. Grant's victory at Donelson, where he refused to accept any terms except "unconditional surrender," won him a sobriquet that followed him all through the war. In "Unconditional Surrender" Grant the North found its first and most authentic hero. He was promptly promoted to the rank of major-general.

Grant seems to have thought that the river war in the West could be won in 1862. He was for following up his initial victory at once, and while **Shiloh** somewhat handicapped in this resolve by the cautious and now thoroughly jealous Halleck, he was permitted to advance up the Tennessee River to Pittsburg Landing, a point near the Tennessee-Mississippi border where the river makes a sharp turn to flow north instead of west. With perhaps as many as forty-five thousand men spread out between the river and Shiloh Meeting House, two miles to the southwest, he awaited the arrival of reinforcements under Buell before attacking Johnston's army, known to be near-by at Corinth, Mississippi. Many of Grant's troops were raw recruits, and more attention was paid to making them over into soldiers than to preparing the encampment for an attack. Grant himself spent the nights at Savannah, seven miles away. Sensing the opportunity, Johnston launched an attack on the early morning of April 6 that by nightfall had driven Grant's army out of its camp and to the very banks of the river. The Confederate triumph, however, was short-lived. The death of Johnston, whose refusal to leave the field at the time he was wounded doubtless cost him his life, was a severe blow to Confederate morale, and the arrival of Buell's troops in time to participate in the next day's fighting gave Grant a decided advantage. Beauregard, who had succeeded Johnston in command of the Confederates, was forced back in an orderly retreat to Corinth. But Grant's battle-scarred troops were unable to pursue the retreating enemy, and both sides claimed the victory. The battle of Shiloh, as this engagement is generally called, was a serious setback to Grant's hope of concluding the river war in a single season. A Confederate army of forty thousand men had almost defeated a Union army of sixty thousand, and had inflicted injuries so serious that the advance could not be immediately resumed.

General Halleck, with ill-concealed satisfaction at Grant's discomfiture, now announced that he would take personal command of the army at the front. Grant was

Evacuation of Corinth supposed to be second in command, but he was studiously snubbed by his superior, who prepared cautiously for an advance on Corinth. Here Beauregard collected all the troops he could get, for the capture of the village meant not only the cutting of the important railroad connection between the Confederate capital in Virginia and the port of Memphis on the Mississippi, but also the loss of another link in the north-and-south railroad from the Ohio to the Gulf. But by the end of May he had only sixty thousand men to oppose Halleck's army, which was now swollen to more than double that number. Convinced that to offer battle would be to take unreasonable chances on the loss of his army, Beauregard decided on retreat. When at last Halleck was ready to move, he crawled forward at the rate of a mile a day, and gave Beauregard ample time to withdraw in safety. On the thirtieth of May the Union forces occupied Corinth without a battle.

While all this was taking place, an effort was being made to clear the Mississippi

River fighting River of Confederates for its entire length. The same day that Grant was driving Beauregard's troops from the Shiloh battlefield, Flag-Officer Foote and his gunboats, aided by troops under General John Pope, forced the Confederates to abandon Island No. 10. Soon after this Foote retired from the command because of injuries, but his successor, Flag-Officer Charles Henry Davis, continued the campaign, and won a spectacular victory over a Confederate flotilla near Memphis, which became Grant's headquarters. Meantime a naval squadron under Admiral David Glasgow Farragut ran the strong defenses that guarded the mouth of the Mississippi, took New Orleans on April 28 (while Halleck was advancing toward Corinth), and penetrated up the river as far as Vicksburg. That important point, however, and some others, could not be taken without a larger number of troops than Farragut had at his disposal. Nor did it prove to be of great avail to have

swept the Confederates from a large part of the river as long as the river banks remained in Confederate hands. One of the chief purposes of this campaign was to cut off the Confederate states west of the Mississippi from any chance of aiding the Confederate armies east of the river. That purpose, the northern government tardily learned, could never be realized by the activities of river boats, here today and gone tomorrow. The ports along the river had also to be occupied, and before this could be done the Confederate "Army of the Mississippi" would have to be reckoned with.

After these spring and early summer campaigns, the river war in the West reached a stalemate. Halleck dispersed his troops over so wide an area and under so many different commands that aggressive tactics were out of the question. Fortunately, however, his presence was soon required elsewhere than in the West. By accepting full credit for the successes of his subordinates, and by blaming them for his failures, he had made for himself an excellent reputation in Washington, whither he was called in July to become general-in-chief of all the Union armies. The offensive now passed to the Confederates, who made two brilliant efforts to regain the territory they had lost. General Braxton Bragg advanced from Chattanooga through Tennessee and Kentucky with the Ohio River as his goal, but at Perryville, Kentucky, October 8, 1862, he was checked by a Union army under Buell. Although neither side won a victory, the Confederate leader felt obliged to retreat toward Chattanooga. The other Confederate attack was made in western Tennessee, where Generals Earl Van Dorn and Sterling Price sought to oust the Union army from its hold on the railroad from Corinth to Memphis. This campaign ended with a Confederate defeat, October 4, near Corinth. Late in the year Grant resumed the offensive, with the Confederate army before Vicksburg as his goal, but he accomplished nothing, and the year ended with the Union-Confederate lines about where they had been in midsummer.

Civil War in the East 1862

-------- Confederate forces ——— Union forces

East of the mountains the North had far less to congratulate itself upon. While **The eastern front** Grant was moving on Donelson, McClellan, with two hundred thousand men at Washington to Johnston's fifty thousand at Manassas Junction, let slip the opportunity to strike his adversary a telling blow. Even when ordered by the President to begin an advance on February 22, in honor of Washington's birthday, he delayed long enough on account of bad roads to permit Johnston to withdraw his army to the south bank of the Rappahannock. The middle of March had passed before the cautious Union commander got under way. His plan was to transport his army by sea to Fortress Monroe at the mouth of the Chesapeake, and then to advance up the peninsula between the York and the James Rivers toward Richmond. To satisfy Lincoln and his civilian advisers, who feared that, with McClellan's army gone, the Confederates might somehow attack Washing-

ton, McDowell with an army of forty thousand men was to march overland to the peninsula, keeping between Washington and the enemy. At first everything went as planned, but Lee suggested to General "Stonewall" Jackson, who commanded a few thousand "foot cavalry" in the Shenandoah Valley, that a diversion was needed in his area to create the impression that Washington might soon be attacked. On guard in the lower Shenandoah was General Nathaniel P. Banks with at least twenty thousand Union troops, and more near at hand. Nevertheless, Jackson brought on an engagement at Kernstown, March 23, and, although he failed to win the battle, he created the impression that he had with him a powerful army. Fear that Washington might be in danger led Lincoln to cancel McDowell's marching orders and keep him close at hand, near Centreville, Virginia.

McClellan, always overestimating his enemy, was much discomfited at this turn of events, and delayed accordingly. Not until the end of April, when he had 110,000 men on the peninsula, did he dare to begin his advance. Then for a time it seemed as if nothing could stop him. The Confederates, unable to muster more than 65,000 men to meet the invader, evacuated Yorktown on May 3, lost a rear-guard engagement at Williamsburg two days later, and by the middle of the month were preparing to remove their government from Richmond. McDowell, once again on the march, had reached Fredericksburg. But Lee, meantime, had decided to try the same strategy that had worked so well two months before. He increased Jackson's little army in the Shenandoah to 17,000 men, and ordered it to make another diversion. Once more Jackson rose to the occasion. He marched first toward an army of 9000 men under Frémont that was advancing through West Virginia to join Banks, and on May 8, at the village of McDowell, won a decisive victory over its advance guard. Then, after destroying the bridges and blocking the roads over which Frémont meant to march, he returned to the Valley, and in three days' hard fighting, May 23–25, decisively defeated Banks at Winchester. Again the civilian strategists at Washington were sure that the Union capital was in danger, and again, as Lee had hoped, McDowell was called back to protect it. Every effort was then made to entrap Jackson, but repeatedly he defeated in detail the superior forces sent against him, and escaped in safety to the upper Shenandoah.

While all this was going on, the Union army on the peninsula stood still, awaiting **The peninsular campaign** the time when McDowell's corps could join it. Richmond was only four and a half miles away and the Union forces were overwhelmingly superior, but McClellan dared not attack. Finally the offensive passed to the Confederates. On May 31 Johnston attacked a part of the Union army at Seven Pines, and on the first day's fighting seemed to have won. But on the second day the Union

Jackson's Campaigns in the Shenandoah Valley 1862

Jackson's route →

0 5 10 20 MILES

superiority in numbers asserted itself, and he fell back on Richmond. In this battle Johnston himself was severely wounded, and Lee left his post as chief adviser to Davis to become the active commander of the "armies in eastern Virginia and North Carolina." Davis should have made him commander-in-chief of all the Confederate armies, but he long failed to realize that Lee's genius far outmatched his own. On the twelfth of June Lee sent his ablest cavalry officer, J. E. B. Stuart, with twelve hundred men to reconnoiter the Union positions. Finding his retreat cut off, Stuart accomplished the remarkable feat of riding clear around the Union army. Fortified with the information Stuart had brought him, Lee sent word to Jackson to join him for a combined attack on McClellan's army. Jackson obeyed with alacrity, and even succeeded in keeping his destination unknown to the Union scouts. Then, beginning on June 25, there followed the famous Seven Days' Battles, in which Lee forced McClellan to retreat twenty miles to the protection of the Union gunboats on the James River.

PENNSYLVANIA Gettysburg York
Chambersburg   [1–3 July '63]
Hagerstown   •Hanover
POTOMAC RIVER   MARYLAND
Sharpsburg   •Frederick
Harpers Ferry   •Baltimore
Winchester   —Balls Bluff
        Leesburg
Front   Washington
Royal   •Alexandria
    Manassas• Fairfax
Sperryville Warrenton
    Culpeper
Orange • Chancellorsville Falmouth
Charlottesville Spotsylvania Fredericksburg
•

Civil War
in the East-1863

JAMES RIVER
                •Richmond
- - - - - Confederate forces
———— Union forces

This reverse need not have been so serious, for McClellan's army was in good condition and ready to continue the campaign. McClellan now suggested a plan that Grant was to follow successfully later on. He wished to remove his army to the south of the James River, and, by threatening the railroads that brought supplies from the south into Richmond, force the Confederates to abandon the city. But by this time Halleck was in Washington as general-in-chief, and his advice, rather than McClellan's, was followed. Halleck brought with him from the West the brash and boastful General John Pope, whose services in the capture of Island No. 10 both he himself and his superior had much overrated. Pope superseded McDowell; and McClellan, without actually being removed from command, was ordered to embark his army at Harrison's Landing for Aquia Creek on the Potomac. He was then to join Pope, whose "Army of Virginia" lay along the Rappahannock with its principal base at Manassas.

No greater blunder could have been made. By a single stroke the pressure on Richmond was removed and McClellan's army was tied up in an operation that would last for a month. Naturally Lee turned his attention to Pope, whom he completely outmaneuvered and defeated at the second battle of Bull Run, August 30. The rout of the Union forces was almost as complete as McDowell's army had suffered at the same place the year before.

Lee now decided that the time had come to carry the war into the enemy's territory, and early in September he **Battle of** crossed the Potomac from Lees- **Antietam** burg, Virginia, to Frederick, Maryland. He had no intention of attacking Washington, but meant rather to cut some of the important railroad connections between the East and the West and then invade Pennsylvania. McClellan, who after Pope's disaster resumed command of all the troops about Washington, was compelled to give chase, and on September 12, two days after the Confederates had withdrawn to the northwest, Union troops occupied Frederick. Next day by a lucky chance one of McClellan's soldiers found, wrapped around three cigars, a copy of Lee's "Special Orders No. 191" to his division commanders. These orders divulged the fact that Lee had sent a part of his army back across the Potomac to capture Harpers Ferry and Hagerstown, so that if McClellan had been capable of prompt action he might have won a magnificent victory. But Lee soon found out what had happened, took up a strong position on Antietam Creek, and trusted that McClellan's caution would give him time to reunite his army. In this he was not disappointed, and when the battle came, on September 17, it could hardly be said that either side had won. On September 19, Lee crossed back into Virginia unpursued. Three weeks later Stuart repeated his previous performance, and rode completely around McClellan's army. It was on this occasion that Lincoln remarked: "When I was a boy we used to play a game called 'Three times round and out.' Stuart has been round McClellan twice. The third time McClellan will be out."

But McClellan never had his third time, for in November he was superseded by one **Fredericks-** of his corps commanders, Gen- **burg** eral Ambrose E. Burnside. It was a choice of desperation, and Burnside himself not only protested his unfitness for so great a responsibility, but soon proved it. His plan was to advance southward from a secure base on navigable water at Aquia Creek. But Lee forestalled him in the occupation of Fredericksburg, only twelve miles from Aquia, and from an impregnable position beat off the rash frontal attack that Burnside launched on December 13. Before the winter was over, Burnside followed McClellan into the discard, and like his predecessor was succeeded by one of his own subordinates. This time Lincoln's choice fell on "Fighting Joe" Hooker, an able soldier whom the men liked, but a caustic critic of his superiors. Lincoln's letter to Hooker, entrusting him with the command, set forth clearly the President's misgivings:

I have heard, in such a way as to believe it, of your recently saying that both the army and the government needed a dictator. Of course it was not for this, but in spite of it, that I have given you the command. Only those generals that gain successes can set up dictators. What I now ask of you is military success, and I will risk the dictatorship. . . . And now beware of rashness. Beware of rashness, but with energy and sleepless vigilance go forward and give us victories.

Hooker took hold with vigor, and by spring had instilled into the discouraged and **Chancel-** defeated Army of the Potomac **lorsville** a feeling of confidence and buoyancy. His numbers were overwhelming: against Lee's 62,000 still encamped at Fredericksburg, he had fully 130,000 men spread out along the left bank of the Rappahannock. By the end of April the Union army was on the move. Fully conscious of his superiority, Hooker thought it safe to divide his forces. General John Sedgwick with 35,000 men was ordered to attack

Chancellorsville
May 1863

1st Position 3 May
●●●●●● Confederate forces
⌇⌇⌇⌇ Union forces
2ND Position 3 May
■ ■ ■ ■ Confederate forces
▬▬▬ Union forces

0 ½ 1   2 Miles

below Fredericksburg, while Hooker himself with the rest of the army crossed the Rappahannock above the city, near the village of Chancellorsville, and prepared to turn Lee's left flank. The Union cavalry had now reached a fair degree of efficiency, and in imitation of Stuart's tactics General George Stoneman was sent on a raid back of Lee's lines to cut his communications with Richmond. Stoneman succeeded in his task, but his raid was a mistake, for the damage he did was soon repaired, and, as events proved, he was absent when Hooker needed him most. Lee was not deceived by Hooker's plans, and met the Union attack at Chancellorsville, May 2, with all but 10,000 of his troops. A brilliant fourteen-mile march by Jackson's command around the rear of the Confederate army and then across the Union front enabled the Confederates to surprise the Union right wing and win an astounding victory. On May 5 Hooker, defeated and dazed, retired to his own side of the Rappa-

Gettysburg
1 – 3 JULY 1863
----- Confederate
—— Union
0   ¼   ½   Miles

hannock. The Confederate victory, however, was dearly bought, for Jackson himself was mortally wounded.

Once more Lee determined on taking the war into the enemy's country. Early in **Lee again crosses the Potomac** June he left Fredericksburg, crossed the Blue Ridge into the Shenandoah Valley, and marched northward toward Maryland and Pennsylvania. Hooker curiously wanted to invest Richmond at once, but Lincoln, who had learned something with the years, wisely observed that "Lee's army and not Richmond is your sure objective point"; so Hooker's army advanced in a northerly direction almost parallel with Lee's, but on the east side of the Blue Ridge. Crossing the Potomac above Harpers Ferry, Lee advanced through the Maryland panhandle, and by the end of June had his entire army, now seventy-five thousand men, on Pennsylvania soil. Both the Confederate

and the Union cavalry did excellent work during these weeks in screening the movements of each army from the other. Lee probably blundered, however, in permitting Stuart to make one of his famous distant raids, for while the cavalry was gone, Lee was virtually in the dark as to his opponent's whereabouts. He did not know for three days that on June 27 Hooker had crossed the Potomac, and was hard-by at Frederick. Throughout this trying period Hooker had conducted himself well, but he had constant trouble with Halleck, still general-in-chief, and on the very eve of what turned out to be the most important battle of the war he resigned his command. Almost as surprising, Lincoln accepted his resignation, and gave the command to another Army of the Potomac corps commander, General George G. Meade.

Both Lee and Meade had selected other sites for the impending battle, but the convergence of the roads they must **Gettysburg** use on the little village of Gettysburg, Pennsylvania, took the decision out of their hands. Here on the first of July two brigades of Union cavalry under General John Buford were driven back by a detachment of the Confederate advance guard under General A. P. Hill. Before noon the Union troops were reinforced by the First Corps under General John F. Reynolds, who stemmed the tide of the Confederate advance and chose the positions that the Union army must defend. Reynolds was shot dead long before the day was over, but General Winfield S. Hancock, whom Meade sent forward to replace him, fell in with his plans and established the Union lines along Cemetery Ridge, to the southeast of Gettysburg. By this time both Lee and Meade were concentrating their forces on the scene of the battle. The Confederates occupied Seminary Ridge, to the west of the Union lines, and almost parallel with them. Both battle-lines ran almost directly north and south, and both had natural heights to defend. The advantage, however, lay with the Union army, for it had a numerical superiority of over twenty thousand men, and it could afford to fight on the defensive. Lee, on the other hand, must attack and win, or else order a rapid retreat to Confederate soil.

The battle of Gettysburg lasted two days more. Meade speedily proved himself to be by far the most dangerous adversary Lee had met, and handled his troops with skill and precision. His subordinates, too, executed his orders faithfully and well, while Lee sorely missed the brilliant support of Stonewall Jackson and was hampered by the half-hearted co-operation of Longstreet. Of the fighting on July 2, Lee reported: "We attempted to dislodge the enemy, and, though we gained some ground, we were unable to get possession of his position." Next day at three o'clock, after an extensive artillery preparation, Lee sent General George E. Pickett with ten thousand men directly against the Union center. But Pickett's valiant troops suffered frightful losses from the Union artillery, and were turned back after a brief period of hand-to-hand fighting at the top of Cemetery Ridge. Three fourths of Pickett's men fell dead or wounded, and only a pitiful remnant reached the shelter of the Confederates lines. Next day Lee began his retreat to the Potomac. Forty per cent of his men were killed or wounded, but his cavalry was able to cover his movements, and Meade, whose losses were about thirty per cent of his command, was unable to follow up the victory he had won. Still it was a victory, and with the failure of Pickett's charge at Gettysburg the scales seemed to have tipped definitely in favor of the North.

From the West also came news of a Union triumph. There Grant had been wrestling **Vicksburg** for months with the difficult problem of taking Vicksburg, the most serious obstacle to northern control of the Mississippi River. After all other means had failed, he finally transported his army, in April, 1863, to the west bank of the river above the city, then marched it thirty miles to the south, where, with the

Vicksburg 1863

---- Confederate forces
—— Union forces   0   5   10 Miles

help of a flotilla of Union gunboats that had successfully passed the Confederate batteries at Vicksburg for the purpose, he recrossed to the east bank of the river. Then, after dislodging the Confederates from Port Gibson on May 1, he marched northward to invest the city. This movement gave the Union troops the advantage of high ground on which to operate, but it meant that for weeks Grant was without a secure land base, and that his men had to live off the country.

Opposed to Grant's army of forty-three thousand men were forty thousand Confederates under General J. C. Pemberton at Vicksburg, and nearly fifteen thousand more under General J. E. Johnston at Jackson, Mississippi. Perceiving the necessity of defeating Johnston before he could join Pemberton, Grant turned aside from his main objective, and in two battles, at Raymond, May 12, and at Jackson, May 14, won decisive victories. With the city of Jackson now safely in Union hands, Grant headed again toward Vicksburg, only to meet Pem-

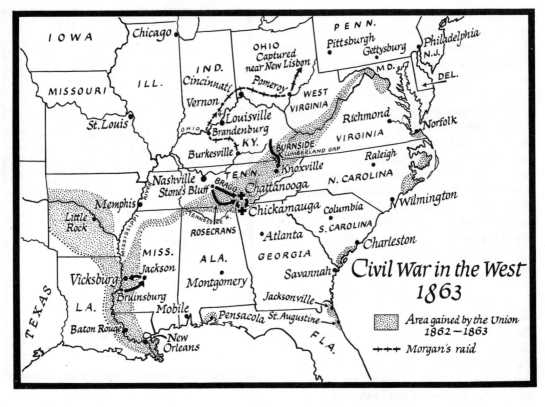

Civil War in the West
1863

Area gained by the Union
1862–1863
+++ Morgan's raid

berton, who was vainly seeking to cut his adversary's non-existent line of communications. At Champion's Hill on May 16, and at Big Black River on May 17, Grant won easily, and on the eighteenth Pemberton took refuge within the defenses of Vicksburg. Then followed a long, wearisome siege with Grant's army on one side of the city and the Union gunboats on the other. On July 3, while Meade was winning at Gettysburg, Pemberton met Grant and arranged terms for the surrender of Vicksburg next day — the "Glorious Fourth." On the eighth following, when the news of Grant's victory at Vicksburg had reached Port Hudson, Louisiana, its commander surrendered to General N. P. Banks, who had brought troops up from New Orleans to invest it. A few days later the safe descent of a commercial steamboat from St. Louis to New Orleans justified Lincoln's observation that "the Father of Waters again goes unvexed to the sea." More important still, the Confederate states

to the west of the Mississippi were now virtually out of the war.

Meantime General William S. Rosecrans, who had succeeded Buell after the battle of Perryville, was campaigning with another Union army in eastern Tennessee. The Union objective was Chattanooga, which, if taken, would cut squarely in two the only continuous railroad from the East to the West that the Confederacy possessed. At the desperate and bloody battle of Murfreesboro, fought on the last day of 1862 and the first two days of 1863, a Confederate army under General Braxton Bragg successfully halted the Union advance, although Rosecrans claimed the victory. Then, during the rest of the winter and on into the spring and summer, the two armies did little more than keep a close watch on one another. In June Bragg sent General John H. Morgan with twenty-five hundred cavalry on a raid into Kentucky, Indiana, and Ohio that caused some physical

Murfrees-
boro

The Northern Commanders, pictured with Lincoln in a composite photographic portrait of the 1870's. Left to right behind Lincoln are Admiral Farragut, and Generals Sherman, Thomas, Meade, Grant, Hooker, Sheridan and Hancock.

and much mental anguish to the loyal civilians along the line of march. Morgan was ultimately captured, and his raid had no military significance, except, perhaps, to divert attention from the retreat of Bragg's army into the strong defenses of Chattanooga. By somewhat the same type of maneuvers that Grant had used at Vicksburg, Rosecrans almost trapped Bragg in Chattanooga, but the Confederate general chose rather to abandon the city to his opponent, who entered it on September 9. Shortly before, General Burnside with a much smaller army had occupied Knoxville, so that Lincoln's hope of rescuing the loyal Unionists of the Tennessee mountains from Confederate control seemed at last to have been realized.

But Bragg was not the man to give up without a battle. Collecting reinforcements **Chicka-** from every possible source, he **mauga and** soon had under his command or **Chattanooga** on the way to join him no less than sixty-six thousand men, while Rosecrans had only fifty-eight thousand. In-

deed, the tables were soon completely turned, for Rosecrans was badly beaten at Chickamauga, September 19–20, and his communications with the outside world cut off, except for one narrow wagon-road through the mountains. Real want descended upon the Union camp in Chattanooga, but the administration acted with celerity in coming to the rescue. The discredited Rosecrans was succeeded by General George H. Thomas, whose conduct during the recent battle had won him undying fame as the "Rock of Chickamauga." A division under Hooker was detached from the Army of the Potomac and sent by rail to the West. More important still, General Grant, whose success at Vicksburg had captured the national imagination, was given supreme command in the West, and on October 23 arrived at Chattanooga, soon to be followed by his former army, now under General William T. Sherman. Grant and Thomas quickly opened a road over which the greatly needed supplies could be obtained, and before long, with the troops of Sherman and Hooker

The Southern Commanders, pictured in a composite photographic portrait by G. E. Matthews. General Robert E. Lee is the white-haired figure in the foreground; at his right, hat on arm, is General Joseph E. Johnston; to Lee's left, hand on sword, is General "Stonewall" Jackson.

converging on his lines, it was Bragg's turn to be beleaguered. The battle of Chattanooga, which followed on November 23–25, was a decisive Union victory, and Bragg was sent in full retreat toward Atlanta. Once again Grant had opened a way to the lower South.

Grant's victories at Vicksburg and Chattanooga marked him as the man so sorely needed to take supreme command of all the Union armies, East as well as West. Congress, therefore, promptly revived the grade of lieutenant-general, and Lincoln as promptly nominated Grant for the place. By March, 1864, the nomination had been confirmed, and the new commander-in-chief was in Washington to assume his responsibilities. His modesty and tact won him many friends. Halleck was consoled for the loss of his title as general-in-chief by being made Grant's chief of staff, and Meade, who after Gettysburg had spent the rest of the year in a fruitless game of hide and seek with Lee, was left in command of the Army of the Potomac. Grant made it clear, however, that he had no intention of remaining in Washington as an "armchair" general, and the first hard fighting of the spring found him riding side by side with Meade to direct the operations of the Army of the Potomac. If the war was to be won, Lee must be beaten, and Grant rightly concluded that his first duty was to match his wits with Lee's.

The first results were far from reassuring. Grant, with more than one hundred and twenty thousand men to Lee's **Grant** sixty-five thousand, felt justified **vs. Lee** in advancing overland directly toward Richmond. On May 3 he crossed the Rapidan at the Germanna Ford and entered a tangled thicket generally known as the Wilderness. His plan was to cross through this region before fighting a battle, but Lee decided that the now definitely superior Union artillery would be less effective at such a spot than elsewhere, and on May 5 opened the battle of the Wilderness, which raged on for two days, with appalling losses on both sides. Unable to dislodge Lee's army, Grant first wheeled his columns to the left, and then, amidst shouts of joy from troops that had known so many retreats, began again the southward march. But Lee, disregarding the damage that General Phil Sheridan with ten thousand Union cavalry was doing in the Confederate rear, again blocked Grant's way. For five days more, May 8–12, the two armies fought desperately near Spotsylvania. Both here and in the Wilderness Grant's losses far exceeded Lee's, but Grant could count confidently on his government for replacements, whereas Lee could not. Conscious of this advantage, the Union commander unhesitatingly forced the fighting. On May 11 he sent back word to Halleck, "I propose to fight it out along this line if it takes all summer." After Spotsylvania, beaten or not, he advanced again, only to find that in three weeks' intermittent fighting Lee's "living screen" was always between the Union army and Richmond. At Cold Harbor the Confederate army occupied a position so impregnable that Grant's order to attack, as he afterward admitted, was sheer folly. But the defeat he suffered, June 1–3, did not cause him to give up, nor did the administration at Washington supersede him, as it had so frequently done with his predecessors when they were beaten. The heavy fighting, after all, had not been wholly in vain, for Lee's battered army was never the same again, while Grant, in spite of battle losses of over fifty thousand men in a month's campaign, could and did remake his army. For future fighting, however, he chose the south bank of the James, to which he removed his army with such skill and celerity that Lee for a long time did not know what his adversary was about, and made no move to check him. Grant then began the advance toward Richmond by way of Petersburg that McClellan had once recommended in vain, and that ultimately was to end the war.

Grant's plans for the campaigns of 1864 had called for a concerted Union attack on all fronts. While he himself reckoned with Lee's main army, Butler was to lead a small force up the James River and strike at Richmond from the rear, Banks was to co-

Civil War in the East · 1864
◄——— GRANT · May–July 1864

operate with Farragut in the capture of Mobile, the only Gulf port still remaining in Confederate hands, and Sherman was to advance southeastward from Chattanooga toward Atlanta. Butler had a brilliant opportunity, for his movement was unsuspected, but he was not a good enough general to take full advantage of the situation, and was soon completely checked. Banks, unfortunately, was in no position to play the part assigned to him, for his army, before Grant took command, had been sent by the civilian authorities in Washington on an ill-starred and wholly unnecessary expedition up the Red River, and had not yet returned. Only Sherman succeeded measurably in carrying out the orders he had received.

Indeed, Sherman had already made an extensive raid through Mississippi before the time set for his advance on **The Atlanta** Atlanta. Wherever his troops **campaign** went, public property was destroyed, railroads were torn up, and many buildings were burned. Later he was given credit for

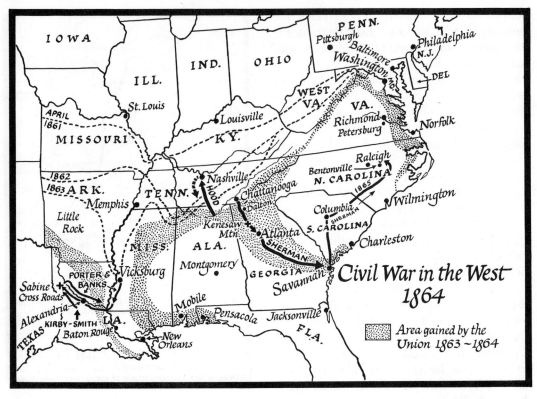

Civil War in the West 1864

Area gained by the Union 1863 ~ 1864

the statement, "War is hell," and whether or not he used precisely that phrase, it well describes his tactics. One of the best ways to shorten the war, he believed, was to bring its horrors home to the people of the lower South, who, for the most part, knew war only at a distance. In May, 1864, acting under orders from Grant, he advanced with 100,000 men along the railroad line that led from Chattanooga to Atlanta. His adversary, General J. E. Johnston, who had succeeded Bragg after the battle of Chattanooga, artfully impeded the invader's progress; but Johnston had only 55,000 men at his command, and he wisely avoided a general engagement. Sharp fighting occurred from time to time as Johnston clung tenaciously to carefully prepared positions, and at Kenesaw Mountain, June 27, the exasperated Sherman lost 3000 men in a rash frontal attack. Ordinarily, however, he used his superior numbers to outflank the Confederates, and in two months' time his battle losses were only 16,800 men to 14,500

for Johnston — heavy enough, except when compared with what was going on in Virginia. Bleak desolation accompanied the Union advance, and Johnston's defensive tactics, while wholly justified, soon aroused a storm of criticism in the South. With the Union army almost in sight of Atlanta, President Davis removed Johnston on the ground that he had "failed to arrest the advance of the enemy," and put in his place General John B. Hood, who promptly gave battle at Peach Tree Creek, July 20, near Atlanta, July 22, and at Ezra Church, July 28. Each time he lost, but it was not until September 2 that he abandoned Atlanta to the enemy.

Sherman speedily expelled the civilian population from Atlanta, and made the city over into a fortified Union camp. "If the people raise a howl about my barbarity and cruelty," he told the authorities at Washington, "I will answer that war is war, and not popularity-seeking. If they want peace, they and their relatives must stop the war."

Sherman's march to the sea

Hood's army was still intact, and was used by its commander with great skill to threaten Sherman's long line of communications with Chattanooga. Finally Sherman, with Grant's consent, embarked upon a bold course of action. Thomas, with headquarters at Nashville, and an army that was soon strengthened by new recruits to seventy thousand men, was left behind to account for Hood. Atlanta, which not only because of Hood's activities, but also because of the desolation that surrounded it had become a liability rather than an asset, was abandoned and destroyed; and Sherman, with sixty thousand picked men, cut loose from his base and started southeastward toward Savannah, where the United States Navy had already taken Fort Pulaski. "I propose," he said, "to demonstrate the vulnerability of the South and make its inhabitants feel that war and individual ruin are synonymous terms." On the fifteenth of November Sherman left on his long march "from Atlanta to the sea"; on the tenth of the following month he arrived at Savannah. He had been as good as his word. In his wake lay a devastated area nearly three hundred miles long and sixty miles wide. While his army invested the city, news came that on December 15–16 Thomas had defeated and scattered Hood's army near Nashville. Four days after Thomas's victory Sherman received the surrender of Savannah.

The utter hopelessness of the Confederate cause was now apparent. Just as the operations of Grant and Farragut had served the year before to isolate the trans-Mississippi West, so now the campaigns of Sherman and Thomas had taken the lower South out of the war. Only the Carolinas and a part of Virginia remained to be conquered. Moreover, the relative superiority of the North in man-power grew steadily as time went on. By 1865 the southern armies totaled less than two hundred thousand men all told, and the South had no reserves from which to replace battle losses and desertions. The North, on the other hand, had a million men under arms and at least an additional

Civil War in the East · 1865
······· Confederate forces   —— Union forces

million subject to call. But neither Davis nor Lee was ready to give up. Finally, a few months before the end of the war, Davis made Lee commander-in-chief of all the Confederate forces. This action came far too late to do much good, but Lee promptly restored Johnston to his command, and the two together did what could be done to impede the progress of the northern armies.

Sherman now turned northward with his sixty thousand men to march through the Carolinas and join Grant in Virginia. "God pity South Carolina!" he wrote, as he entered the state **Sherman in the Carolinas** which his thoroughly efficient army of pillagers regarded as responsible for the war. Columbia, the capital, was burned, and the depredations along the march generally exceeded those done by his "dashing Yankee boys" in Georgia. As he advanced, he obtained reinforcements, whereas his opponent, Johnston, who could muster a Confederate army of only forty thousand men, was utterly unable to replace his losses. Sherman's march through the Carolinas, however, was no such easy promenade as his march through Georgia. The country was much more difficult, and in Johnston he had a worthy opponent. At Bentonville, North Carolina, March 19–21, Johnston gave battle, but with such odds against him that he had no chance to win. A few days later Sherman had made Goldsboro, North Carolina, his headquarters. He was now within one hundred and fifty miles of Grant's army in Virginia, and had more than twice as many men as Johnston.

Ever since the summer of 1864 Grant had been engaged in the dreary business of besieging Petersburg and Richmond. For a while Lee used the Shenandoah Valley successfully for diversions, but General Phil Sheridan, acting under Grant's orders, finally put an end to that. Twice, at Opequon Creek, September 19, 1864, and at Cedar Creek, exactly a month later, he won notable victories over his opponent, General Jubal Early, but his chief contribution was the devastation of the Shenandoah Valley. On October 7, 1864, he reported to Grant: "I have destroyed over 2000 barns filled with wheat, hay, and farming implements; over 70 mills filled with flour and wheat; have driven in front of the army over 4000 head of stock, and have killed and issued to the troops not less than 3000 sheep. . . . Tomorrow I will continue the destruction of wheat, forage, etc., down to Fisher's Hill. When this is completed, the Valley from Winchester up to Staunton, ninety-two miles, will have but little in it for man or beast." Not only was it impossible for the Confederate cavalry to operate in a region so denuded of forage, but it was likewise impossible for Lee to depend any longer upon the Valley to furnish supplies for his army at Richmond.

Sheridan in the Shenandoah

Only because the Union lines about Richmond and Petersburg did not encircle the cities had Lee been able to withstand Grant's siege so long. Railway connections leading to the west were still open, and over them

The Petersburg campaign

came the supplies on which the Confederate army lived. By the spring of 1865, however, Lee's position had become extremely precarious. He had less than 50,000 men to Grant's 113,000, and with Sherman approaching from the South the odds threatened soon to be even worse. Late in March Grant began to extend his lines to the west from below Petersburg. A battle followed at Five Forks, April 1, in which the Confederates were badly beaten, and next day Lee abandoned both Petersburg and Richmond. Lee's plan was to get away to the mountains, where he thought he might continue the war indefinitely, but he experienced great difficulty in obtaining supplies and moved too slowly. By the seventh Grant's army was upon him; two days later Sheridan's cavalry, well supported by infantry, was in front of him. "There is nothing left me but to go and see General Grant," he said, when he heard the news, "and I would rather die a thousand deaths."

The same day in the village of Appomattox Court House, Lee and Grant met for a conference that virtually ended the war. Grant, who had discussed with Lincoln a few days before the terms on which Lee's surrender should be accepted, was magnanimous. All the Confederate troops, officers as well as men, were to be paroled under promise not to serve against the United States again until exchanged; all military stores and arms, except the sidearms of officers, were to be surrendered; the mounted Confederates, who unlike the Union cavalry owned the horses they rode, were to be allowed to keep their mounts. Learning that Lee's men were desperately short of food, Grant also ordered that rations for twenty-five thousand men, approximately the number of troops Lee had surrendered, should be sent to the former enemy at once. Johnston, whose army was now "melting away like snow before the sun," realized that further resistance was useless and soon surrendered to Sherman on the same terms that Grant had given Lee. One by one the lesser bodies

Lee's surrender

of Confederate troops laid down their arms, and on May 10 Jefferson Davis himself was captured. The Confederate States of America had ceased to exist.

The Union was saved, but at a fearful cost. For four years great numbers of men had **Losses of** been taken by both sides from **the war** productive employment and had been turned into efficient engines of destruction. The total number of enlistments in the Union army had been about 2,900,000; in the Confederate army about 1,300,000. But because these figures take no account of short-term enlistments they fail to give an accurate picture of the relative strength of the two armies. A careful student of the subject, Thomas L. Livermore, computes that the Union army was equivalent to about 1,500,000 men serving for three years, and the Confederate army on the same basis, to about 1,000,000 men. These statistics are doubtless inaccurate, and the confused state of the records makes it virtually impossible to estimate the actual number of individuals who served on one side or the other. The death-toll was terrific. For the Union army, counting those killed or mortally wounded in battle, and those who died from sickness or other causes, Livermore sets the figure at about 359,000 and for the Confederate army at about 258,000. Among the survivors were thousands who were maimed for life, and other thousands whose health was permanently undermined.

In spite of the enthusiasm that had at first moved more men to join both armies than the two governments were able to make over into soldiers, the volunteering principle failed, unaided, to supply the huge armies that had somehow to be raised. Loath to resort to conscription, both North and South first tried to encourage enlistments by offering bounties. Many of the southern troops had enlisted for one year only, and late in 1861 they were offered a bounty of fifty dollars and a sixty-day furlough to re-enlist. The North went much further. From the beginning of the war it offered a cash bounty of one hundred dollars to every

volunteer, and in 1863 it raised the sum to three hundred and two dollars for new recruits, and four hundred and two dollars for veterans who would re-enlist. Even so, conscription was not to be forestalled for long.

The South invoked it first. Comparatively few of the twelve-months troops accepted the bounty-furlough offer, and **Conscription** in the spring of 1862, with the **in the South** northern drives beginning, something had to be done to keep them in the army. Accordingly, on March 28, 1862, President Davis was authorized to disregard all short-term enlistments and retain everyone then in the service for three full years from the date of his original enlistment. Also, he might conscript for a like period all white males between the ages of eighteen and thirty-five. Six months later the age limit was raised from thirty-five to forty-five, and in February, 1864, conscription was made applicable to all between seventeen and fifty. In the closing months of the war many Southerners, including General Lee, believed that the slaves should be offered their freedom to enlist, and on March 13, 1865, the Confederate Congress actually passed such a law. But the measure came too late to be of any use. In the earlier conscription laws, liberal exemptions were permitted, but toward the end these were whittled down to extremely narrow limits.

The North was a year later than the South in resorting to conscription, and when on March 3, 1863, a draft act was **The northern** finally passed, it differed ma- **draft** terially from the southern conscription laws. The purpose of the northern act was primarily to stimulate enlistments. Only when a given district had failed to produce its assigned quota of troops by volunteering was the draft to be applied. It was thus made a point of honor for a state or a city or a county to supply all the soldiers required of it by means of volunteering, and without resort to the draft. All the able-bodied citizens, and all aliens who had declared their intention of becoming citizens, be-

THE BATTLE OF FREDER-
ICKSBURG, December 13,
1862. Painting by John
Richards, about 1870.

WAR CORRESPONDENTS. A. R. Waud
doing an on-the-spot sketch for *Harper's
Weekly* magazine of a battle in progress.
Photograph by Mathew B. Brady.

*Civil War scenes appeared in every illus-
trated periodical. Photography was still in its
infancy, but Mathew B. Brady and his assistants, with official permission, accompanied the
Northern armies in the field and took thousands
of photographs, showing conditions that existed
in camp, on the march, and in actual battle.
Drawings from photographs, sketches made at
the front, and paintings more or less fanciful,
brought the war home to the people far more forcibly than would ever have been possible through
strictly written accounts.*

A SHARPSHOOTER OF THE ARMY OF THE POTOMAC. Drawing by
Winslow Homer, artist-correspondent, for *Harper's Weekly*, November 15, 1862.

Southern defeat was accomplished only after the most devastating punishment to many parts of the South. Cities such as Richmond lay in ruins, the places where houses had once stood were often marked only by blackened chimneys, the sites of army-camps and battlefields long defied cultivation. Lee's surrender at Appomattox came only when the brilliant southern general had lost the power to fight further.

SHERMAN'S MARCH THROUGH GEORGIA, 1864.
A northern view, painted by A. B. Carlin, 1871.

THE RUINS OF RICHMOND. Photograph by MATHEW B. BRADY, 1865.

THE SURRENDER AT APPOMATTOX, APRIL 9, 1865. Painting by Alonzo Chappel, 1865.

tween the ages of twenty and forty-five were enrolled by districts, roughly resembling the congressional districts, and in assigning quotas to each district the President was to take into consideration the number of volunteers it had already furnished. Many whole states were able to escape the draft altogether, and the number of men forcibly inducted into the northern army was trifling.

But the stimulation to enlistment was very real. Bounties were raised to fantastic figures as states, counties, and cities vied with one another for volunteers. In some districts the total amount of bounty-money that a man who enlisted could claim ran to over a thousand dollars. Immigrants, particularly those coming from Ireland, were often persuaded to enter the army as a means of getting a start in the new land. So generous were the rewards that a class of "bounty-jumpers" arose, whose business it was to enlist and collect the bounty, then desert and re-enlist as often as possible. Lincoln's tender-heartedness caused him to pardon many such deserters, and deeply irritated the draft authorities. But whatever the defects of the system, the draft and the bounties worked relentlessly to keep the Union armies full. Generous exemptions were allowed, and at first a man who was drafted could escape service either by pay-

ing three hundred dollars or by hiring a substitute. This provision, which led to the charge that the struggle was a "rich man's war but a poor man's fight," was soon abolished, and a like provision in the southern conscription law went the same way.

In both North and South the attempts to enforce conscription met forcible resistance. In the North serious "draft riots" occurred in New York City and elsewhere during the summer of 1863. In the South resistance was strongest in the mountain regions where the Confederate cause was never popular, and among the states'-rights extremists, who thought that in conscripting an army the southern government was exceeding its powers. In several southern states, particularly in Georgia, where Governor J. E. Brown definitely branded the conscription law as unconstitutional, and in North Carolina, where the legislature added at will to the exempted classes, the execution of the law was somewhat impeded. On the whole, however, resistance to conscription, both North and South, was ineffective. Thanks to these measures the South put practically its entire man-power into the field, and the North drew as heavily upon its man-power as was necessary to win the war.

Resistance to conscription

Bibliography

On all aspects of the Civil War, the best single volume is J. G. Randall, *The Civil War and Reconstruction* (1937). C. R. Fish, *The American Civil War* (1937), is a brilliant interpretation. G. F. Milton, *Conflict: The American Civil War* (1941), is an excellent popular account.

On the creation of the armies that fought the war, F. L. Huidekoper, *The Military Unpreparedness of the United States* (1915), is amply convincing on the point that in this case preparedness was certainly not a cause of war. For the creation of the armies, see F. A. Shannon, *The Organization and Administration of the Union Army, 1861–*

1865 (2 vols., 1928); and A. B. Moore, *Conscription and Conflict in the Confederacy* (1924). B. I. Wiley, *The Life of Johnny Reb* (1943), describes the lot of the common soldier of the Confederacy. Ella Lonn, *Desertion during the Civil War* (1928), shows the difficulties experienced in keeping the armies intact.

The military history of the Civil War is graphically covered in Fletcher Pratt, *Ordeal by Fire; An Informal History of the Civil War* (1935). O. L. Spaulding, *The United States Army in War and Peace* (1937), covers the whole period from colonial times to 1920. Barron Deaderick,

Strategy in the Civil War (1946), is a guide to eleven major campaigns. The best technical history of the battles and campaigns of the war is J. C. Ropes and W. R. Livermore, *The Story of the Civil War* (4 vols., 1894–1913). The Comte de Paris, *History of the Civil War in America* (4 vols., 1876–88), is the work of an experienced military observer. Briefer, but also strictly military, are T. A. Dodge, *A Bird's Eye View of Our Civil War* (1883); and W. B. Wood and J. E. Edmonds, *A History of the Civil War in the United States* (1905). T. L. Livermore, *Numbers and Losses in the Civil War in America, 1861–1865* (1901), provides figures that are hotly contested. Probably it would be impossible to compile anything like exact statistics on this conflict.

McClellan's career as commander in the East has been subjected to painstaking examination. His autobiography, *McClellan's Own Story* (1887), tends to confirm Lincoln's doubts about him. Favorable to McClellan is H. J. Eckenrode and Bryan Conrad, *George B. McClellan, The Man who Saved the Union* (1941). An interesting character sketch is in W. S. Myers, *A Study in Personality: George Brinton McClellan* (1934). Bruce Catton, *Mr. Lincoln's Army* (1951), also contains an appraisal of McClellan.

The best picture of Grant's military career is given in his own story, *The Personal Memoirs of U. S. Grant* (2 vols., 1885–86). K. P. Williams, *Lincoln Finds a General: A Military Study of the Civil War* (2 vols., 1949), is excellent. A good biography, both military and political, is L. A. Coolidge, *Ulysses S. Grant* (1917). W. B. Hesseltine, *Ulysses S. Grant, Politician* (1935), is primarily concerned with the period after the war, but it contains an excellent chapter on Grant's career as a soldier. A. H. Burne, *Lee, Grant, and Sherman: A Study in Leadership in the 1864–65 Campaign* (1938), concentrates on the final phases of the war in the East.

Biographies of other northern generals include: Lloyd Lewis, *Sherman, Fighting Prophet* (1932); W. H. Hebert, *Fighting Joe Hooker* (1944); Free-man Cleaves, *Rock of Chickamauga, The Life of General George H. Thomas* (1948); F. H. Harrington, *Fighting Politician: Major General N. P. Banks* (1948); Joseph Hergesheimer, *Sheridan; A Military Narrative* (1931); G. G. Meade, *The Life and Letters of George Gordon Meade, Major-General, United States Army* (2 vols., 1913).

On the southern side, in addition to Freeman's *R. E. Lee*, the following are worthy of note: D. S. Freeman, *Lee's Lieutenants* (3 vols., 1942–44); W. W. Blackford, *War Years with Jeb Stuart* (1945); John C. Pemberton, *Pemberton, Defender of Vicksburg* (1942); R. S. Henry, *"First with the Most" Forrest* (1944); C. F. Holland, *Morgan and His Raiders* (1942); G. F. R. Henderson, *Stonewall Jackson and the American Civil War* (2 vols., 1898); J. P. Dyer, *The Gallant Hood* (1950), and *"Fightin' Joe" Wheeler* (1941); Richard O'Connor, *Hood: Cavalier General* (1949).

On the naval side *Diary of Gideon Welles, Secretary of the Navy under Lincoln and Johnson* (3 vols., 1911), is indispensable. R. S. West, Jr., *Gideon Welles: Lincoln's Navy Department* (1943), and *The Second Admiral: A Life of David Dixon Porter* (1937), are also useful. On ironclads the definitive work is J. P. Baxter, 3d, *The Introduction of the Ironclad Warship* (1933). On Farragut and the Union Navy, see C. L. Lewis, *David Glasgow Farragut* (2 vols., 1941–43); A. T. Mahan, *Admiral Farragut* (1892). On the Naval activities of the Confederacy, see J. T. Scharf, *History of the Confederate States Navy* (1887); F. B. C. Bradlee, *Blockade Running during the Civil War and the Effect of Land and Water Transportation on the Confederacy* (1925); W. A. Roberts, *Semmes of the Alabama* (1938).

Miscellaneous. Louise B. Hill, *Joseph E. Brown and the Confederacy* (1939), views the war through the eyes of a states' rights governor of Georgia. F. P. Summers, *The Baltimore and Ohio in the Civil War* (1939), deals with a significant chapter of railroad history. A. H. Bill, *The Beleaguered City: Richmond, 1861–1865* (1946), is interesting and colorful.

32

Behind the Lines

Wartime prosperity of the North — The Morrill Tariff — Downfall of "King Cotton" — Financial problems, North and South — English neutrality — The *Trent* affair — French intervention in Mexico — Spanish neutrality — Russia — The Emancipation Proclamation — Elections of 1862 and 1864 — Death of Lincoln — Significance of the Civil War

WHEN the Civil War broke out the North had not fully recovered from the depression that had followed the panic of 1857, and for a time business interests were more frightened than stimulated by the clash of arms. By the summer of 1862, however, a surge of prosperity had put in its appearance that was to outlast the war. The returns of agriculture were phenomenally good, manufactures flourished as never before, railroads rolled up huge wartime profits, and business generally enjoyed a "boom."

Prosperity for the northern farmer was in part a result of the abnormal demands of **War and** war. With millions of men **prosperity** under arms the government became a dependable and generous purchaser of every kind of foodstuff, and its equally great need of woolen goods and leather strengthened the market also for raw wool and hides. Probably the sales that the farmers made directly or indirectly to the government more than offset the losses sustained by wartime interference with sales to the South. And, as a matter of fact, much of this intersectional trade persisted in spite of the war, and in spite of the half-hearted efforts of the government to suppress it.

Almost equally important, however, was the chance that forced Great Britain during these critical years to import from the United States a large proportion of its wheat. For some time the British farmer had failed to supply the United Kingdom with all the wheat it needed, but in the early years of the Civil War a succession of crop failures made the deficiency abnormally large. Ordinarily the British shortage in wheat had been made up by importations from the Continent, from South America, or from Egypt, but these sources of supply now proved to be insufficient, and the importation of wheat from the United States became a virtual necessity. During the three-year period 1861–63, northern farmers actually furnished more than forty per cent of the wheat and flour imported into Great Britain, and the total export of wheat from the United States rose to well above fifty million bushels annually, three times the normal amount.

Several circumstances conspired during these same years to make possible the needed expansion of American agricul- **Agricultural** ture. In the first place, it was **expansion** possible to increase the acreage under cultivation almost at will. All along the frontier, and elsewhere, good land that had remained unworked or unappropriated was pressed into service. Moreover, with the South out of the Union, a homestead law, so long the goal of believers in free land, was speedily enacted (1862). Thereafter any person who was the head of a family, or had arrived at the age of twenty-one years, whether a citizen of the United States or an alien who had declared his intention of becoming a citizen, might take up a quarter section of public land, and, after having lived upon it for five years and improved it, might receive full title to it virtually free of charge. Comparatively little use was made of this law during the war, although under its terms thousands of acres of new land were placed under cultivation, immediately after the war ended, all along the "middle border," in Iowa, Kansas, Nebraska, and Minnesota.

Very important also was the rapid introduction of labor-saving farm machinery. Such valuable aids to farming as the improved plow, the corn-planter, the two-horse cultivator, the mower, the reaper, and the steam thresher had all been invented before the Civil War, but it took the acute shortage of man-power that resulted from placing millions of men under arms to induce farmers to give up their old-fashioned methods and make use of the new tools. Before the war, with farm labor relatively cheap and plentiful, the farmer had seen little point to labor-saving machinery. But when he was faced with the alternative of losing his crops or using the machines, he used the machines. A reaper operated by one man could cut ten or twelve acres of grain in a day, whereas the best a man could hope to do with an old-fashioned back-breaking cradle was an acre and a half. By utilizing the new implements the northern farmer was able to take care of a vastly increased acreage without serious difficulty. Even women and children could operate many of the machines, and in innumerable instances they were called upon to do so. By 1865 it was estimated that not less than two hundred and fifty thousand reapers were in use in the United States.

Of some assistance also was the trend toward more scientific methods of farming.

The Morrill Land Grant Act The states that lay to the east of the virgin lands of the frontier were soon aware that they suffered from certain obvious disadvantages.

Their soil would not, unaided, grow such crops as the newer states could produce. In the older states, particularly, much of the land had been "cropped to death." Discerning men, mostly Easterners, had begun well before the Civil War to advocate the scientific study and teaching of agriculture, but legislative response to their pleas, curiously, came at the outset more from the West than from the East. In 1857 Michigan established the first state college of agriculture, only to be emulated in quick succession by Iowa in 1858, and Minnesota in 1859. By the latter date Justin S. Morrill of Vermont, chairman of the House Committee on Agriculture, had pushed through Congress a measure for the granting of public lands to each of the states as an endowment for agricultural education. But Buchanan vetoed the bill, and it was not until 1862, with Lincoln in the presidential chair, that the Morrill Act was placed on the statute-books. Each state, according to the new law, was granted as many times thirty thousand acres of public land as the number of senators and representatives it elected to Congress. Thus stimulated, the establishment of agricultural colleges, or of agricultural departments in state-supported universities, spread rapidly from state to state. The wartime character of the Morrill Act is attested by the fact that the measure required that courses in military training be offered by each of the educational institutions that received benefits under the terms of the act.

Another factor, probably of far greater importance than agricultural education in promoting the welfare of northern agriculture during the Civil War, was the weather. Year after year ideal climatic conditions prevailed over the greater part of the North. The total wheat production of the loyal states and territories rose from 142,000,000 bushels in 1859 to 187,000,000 in 1862, and to 191,000,000 in 1863. This was the banner year for wheat, but the general level of production for all agricultural commodities remained high throughout the entire war. With inflated prices, and with adequate transportation facilities available both by land and by sea, the American farmer enjoyed a degree of prosperity that he had never known before.

Much as agriculture profited from the war, the stimulus given by the struggle to manu-
Wartime manufacturing facturing was even greater. The armies required huge quantities of manufactured goods of every sort and kind — clothing, boots and shoes, hats and caps, blankets, wagons, arms and ammunition, ready-to-eat rations, and innumerable other items. To meet these needs old factories were remodeled and expanded and new factories were built. As was the case with the farmer, the manufacturer had only to make use of inventions already at hand in order to increase his output. Possibly of all machines the sewing machine helped him most. By use of it whole uniforms, and many other types of garments, could be turned out in far greater quantity and with far less hand labor than had ever been possible before. The war, indeed, changed the clothing habits of masculine America completely. For the average male citizen ready-made suits permanently replaced suits made at home or at the local tailor shop. Out of the war, too, came the habit of using such factory-made items as shoes, caps, socks, and prepared foods. It is not too much to say that the war brought to an end the last remaining survivals of the domestic system of manufacture in the United States. Manufacturers whose fortunes were founded on government contracts saw their wealth continue to increase after the war, for the changes in customs that the war promoted enabled them to sell with equal advantage to the civilian population.

What came in later times to be called the "heavy industries" profited enormously from the war. Purchases of munitions abroad practically ceased after the first year because of the rapidity with which American factories supplied the government's needs. The new iron works, gun factories, and powder plants that came into existence were for the most part the results of private initiative, but the government itself went as deeply into the business of manufacturing war materials as public opinion would permit. Before the end of the war, for example, the government arsenal at Springfield, Massachusetts, was producing a thousand rifles a day. Railroad-building, which was resumed in the North after the outbreak of the war, and the continual need for railroad repairs, did much for the manufacturers of iron and steel. They were helped, also, by the demand for ironclads that set in after the battle between the *Monitor* and the *Merrimac*.

High tariffs insured the northern manufacturers against the dangers of European competition. A protectionist **The Morrill Tariff Act** policy had been demanded by the Republican national platform of 1860, and a higher schedule of tariffs, sponsored by the same Justin S. Morrill who gave his name to the act for the stimulation of agricultural education, was placed upon the statute-books two days before Buchanan left office. This speedy answer to the prayers of the protectionists was made possible by the withdrawal from Congress of the delegations from the seven seceding states of the lower South, and by the fact that President Buchanan was no longer unmindful of the wishes of the manufacturers within his home state. The original Morrill Tariff Act was repeatedly revised upward during the war, until by 1864 the average of duties levied on imports had reached forty-seven per cent, the highest thus far in the history of the nation. The significance of this development can scarcely be overemphasized. A policy which the South had persistently blocked in the years preceding the war became an actuality during it, and, as subsequent events were to prove, remained as a permanent fixture in American political and economic life.

An important component part of northern wartime prosperity was the pro- **Exploitation of natural resources** duction of a sufficient quantity and variety of raw materials to satisfy the needs of the northern manufac-

HEAVY INDUSTRY. The Nashua
Iron Company, New Hampshire,
makers of forged iron "for steam
marine work, for ship work, and
upon railroads." Lithograph from
a photograph by J. S. Miller.

*The strength of the North grew with
the struggle, while that of the South
dwindled steadily away. The Civil War
was the first war in history to make extensive use of railroads, and the overwhelming advantage of the North in railroad mileage and efficiency was one of the
principal reasons for Northern victory.
The North had a tremendous superiority,
too, in both heavy and light industries,
and in mineral resources, especially coal
and iron.*

MASS-PRODUCED CLOTHING.
Thomson's Skirt Manufactory,
New York. Engraving from
Harper's Weekly, 1859.

NATURAL RESOURCES.
Mining Coal, illustrated
in *Harper's Weekly*,
about 1860.

turers. The mining of coal, which was not only a lucrative industry in itself but served also as a kind of measuring-stick for the progress of the factory system, increased threefold, and the production of such basic items as iron ore, copper, salt, and petroleum reached unprecedented heights. Lumber also was in great demand, and the forests of the Great Lakes region, of Maine, and of New York were exploited as never before. Wool-growers found a ready market for all the wool they could grow, and by 1865 were producing annually two and one third times as much wool as in 1860. The only commodity that the northern manufacturers experienced serious difficulty in obtaining was cotton, and there was enough trading through the lines, both licensed and illicit, to hold this shortage to a minimum.

Another important source of northern prosperity lay in the output of the gold and silver mines of the Far West. While the flow of precious metals from the mines of California was somewhat diminished during the war, new mines were opened up in various parts of the Rocky Mountains area — particularly in the regions later known as Colorado, Nevada, Arizona, and Montana — that more than made up for this loss. Millions of dollars' worth of gold and silver thus flowed into the national mints at a time when the nation's need for hard money was greatest.

Indeed, from whatever angle the subject is viewed, the wartime prosperity of the

Business activities North was phenomenal. Its railroads, overbuilt during the fifties, were turned into profitable investments by the heavy traffic of the war, and the railroad mileage of both the Northeast and the Northwest had to be substantially increased to carry the load. Internal waterways — the Great Lakes, the western rivers, and the canals — did an enormous volume of business. Financial institutions, which at the outset of the war had seriously missed the patronage of the South, found a more than adequate compensation for this loss in the expanding commercial activity of the

northern states. The northern merchant marine, as already noted, was virtually ruined by the war; but this involved little loss of capital, for most of the ships were sold, not sunk, and the proceeds from their sale were invested in such lucrative securities as government bonds, manufacturing concerns, and railroads. From one point of view, American shippers were fortunate in leaving the field of ocean transportation at this particular time. Wooden ships were soon to be replaced by ships of iron and steel, and many American firms sold out just in time to escape the cost of extensive replacements.

The profits of war bred a spirit of extravagance and frivolity among the non-combatants of the North that **Wartime** contrasted oddly with the long **extravagance** casualty lists displayed as a regular part of the daily news. Social life reached a dizzy whirl, with more parties and dances, theaters and circuses, minstrel shows and musicales than ever had been known before. Public interest in sports tended to grow rather than to diminish, and to such standard outlets of the sporting instinct as horse-racing and prize-fighting were added the crude beginnings of baseball, soon to be the favorite game of the nation. The *nouveaux riches*, of whom every community had its quota, spent so lavishly as to win the contempt of more sober-minded citizens. Their purchases of foreign luxuries, rather than imports needed for the prosecution of the war, resulted in an unfavorable balance of trade with Europe that sent $54,000,000 of American gold abroad in 1863 and $91,000,000 in 1864. Prosperity, however, was not evenly divided and labor in particular failed to obtain its proportionate share. With prices rising steadily throughout the war, wages rose also, but never rapidly enough to keep pace with the cost of commodities. According to a statement published by the *Springfield Republican* in 1864, many of the factories whose profits during the war had been "augmented beyond the wildest dreams of their owners"

AT THE WHITE HOUSE. "Grand Reception of the Notabilities of the Nation, 1865." Lithograph by Major and Knapp, N.Y.

Gaiety and extravagance characterized the society of the North during the Civil War, in spite of the long lists of casualties that poured in after each battle. People seemed eager to forget the horrors of war, while high wages and war profits provided the means for lavish spending. Social activities continued even in the White House. Note the elaborate styles affected by both men and women.

HIGH FASHION. Parisian styles in day and evening wear for young ladies. Illustration from a "Supplement to *Harper's Bazaar*," about 1861.

SKATING IN THE CENTRAL PARK, N. Y. Watercolor by Winslow Homer, 1860.

A "FOUR-IN-HAND." Lithograph by Currier and Ives, 1861.

paid their laborers only from twelve to twenty per cent more than before the war. "There is absolute want in many families, while thousands of young children who should be at school are shut up at work that they may earn something to eke out the scant supplies at home." As a consequence of such tactics on the part of employers labor disorders were frequent, and a strong impetus was given to labor organization.

If the war brought prosperity to the North, it brought little but adversity to the South. With the welfare of the section so intimately bound up with cotton culture, the failure of southern cotton to find a normal market was simply catastrophic. The southern government, gambling on the hope that European nations would come to the aid of the South whenever European mills faced a serious enough cotton shortage, tried in the early months of the war to prevent the shipment of cotton abroad. Cotton-planters were even urged to destroy their crops as the best insurance against exportation, and it is estimated that this mistaken policy cost the South about a million bales of cotton. Had exportation been stimulated rather than discouraged, the South might have built up credit abroad for subsequent use, but faith in the power of "King Cotton" clouded the judgment of the southern leaders. By 1862 the southern government was ready to reverse its cotton policy, but by that time the northern blockade held shipments to a minimum. The effectiveness of the blockade may be estimated from the fact that the price of cotton in Liverpool rose from fourteen cents in 1861 to fifty cents in 1865. Trade between the lines helped the South and the cotton-planter to some extent, especially after the northern armies had penetrated far into the southern states. In exchange for cotton and tobacco, southern traders received salt, clothing, foodstuffs, and even war materials. Naturally much of this trade was accomplished by means of the most demoralizing bribery and corruption.

Downfall of "King Cotton"

The break with the North, followed by the blockade, forced the South to attempt a far greater diversity of economic life, both agricultural and industrial, than it had known before the war. Foodstuffs were grown instead of cotton, salt-works were established wherever the resources justified, while cotton mills, boot and shoe factories, munitions plants, and the like were started up in spite of inadequate capital, defective machinery, and poorly trained workers. The difficulties experienced by the South in its effort to achieve self-sufficiency, however, were too great to be overcome in a short space of time, and as the war wore on, both soldiers and civilians were frequently called upon to endure the greatest extremes of privation. While the North was pushing forward relentlessly to the factory system, the South was compelled to resort more and more to household manufacture. The breakdown of southern transportation, particularly the railroads, which the South was utterly unable to keep in repair, served to compound the confusion. The suffering endured by northern prisoners in southern prison-camps was due far more to this confused economic situation than to any deliberate intent on the part of the jailers.

Southern manufacturing

But even the hard-pressed South was not without its war profiteers. Most of those who made money out of the war were associated in some fashion or other with blockade-running, from which the returns were frequently spectacular. Money inflation tempted also to speculation, a passion which, according to Jefferson Davis, "seduced citizens of all classes from a determined prosecution of the war." The southern *nouveaux riches*, while more limited in their opportunities than those of the North, did not hesitate to make whatever vulgar display of their wealth they could, and the social life of such cities as Charleston and Richmond kept up an appearance of gaiety to the very end.

Southern profiteers

Once prosperity was in the saddle, the North had little difficulty in financing the war. At the outset, however, the credit of the northern government was at low ebb, the treasury was empty, and the banks of the country were so skeptical of the outcome that they soon suspended specie payments. Secretary of the Treasury Chase had little acquaintance with finance, and was so fearful of the political effects of taxation that he proposed to pay the cost of the war mainly from loans. At first he was compelled to pay ruinous rates to obtain money — on one occasion as high as 7.3 per cent — but with the assistance of Jay Cooke, a Philadelphia banker, he succeeded in floating loans that totaled by the end of the war well over two billion dollars. Cooke popularized the bond issues, and besides making the public see that they were a good investment, he played most successfully upon the patriotic motive. People bought bonds to help the government as well as to help themselves. Cooke himself profited considerably from his undertaking, for the government allowed him a commission of one half of one per cent on all the sales he made up to ten million dollars, and three eighths of one per cent on all sales above that amount.

Northern wartime finance

While loans were the chief reliance, the government resorted also to far heavier taxation than the people of the United States had ever before been called upon to pay. In 1862 excises were levied upon a remarkable variety of articles, businesses, occupations, and activities. This tax levy, according to James Ford Rhodes, "might be briefly described with a near approach to accuracy as an act which taxed everything." Even lawyers, physicians, and dentists were required to buy licenses, and such articles as liquor, tobacco, carriages, yachts, billiard-tables, and plate carried heavy duties. Manufacturers were required to pay a tax for the privilege of manufacturing, and the articles they manufactured were also taxed. Railroads, steamboats, toll-bridges, savings banks, insurance companies, and the like paid a three per cent duty on their gross receipts. Multifold as

Northern taxation

these taxes were, they did not produce a great revenue. Even with the help of increased rates, levied in 1864, the total receipts from all such sources during the war barely passed the $300,000,000 mark. An income tax, which began in 1861 as a three per cent tax on all incomes above $800, and was later so modified as to tax incomes between $600 and $5000 at the rate of five per cent, and all higher incomes at the rate of ten per cent, was even less successful as a revenue measure, for it brought in a total of only $55,000,000. Still these were large sums to a people quite unused to federal taxation. Tariff levies, pushed steadily upward as an offset to the internal taxes that protected interests were required to pay, also netted the government more than $305,000,000 during the last four years of the war.

But neither the loans nor the taxes sufficed to keep the government supplied at all times with ready cash, and as a result several issues of paper money were authorized by Congress. Between February, 1862, when the first of the "legal tender" acts was passed, and March, 1863, the date of the last, a total of no less than $450,000,000 in fiat money was ordered printed. Of this sum $431,000,000 was outstanding at the close of the war. Back of the "greenbacks," as the public promptly dubbed these notes, there lay no gold reserve, but only the good faith of the government. Since they were by law made legal tender for all debts, public and private, except duties on imports and interest on the public debt, they constituted in fact a forced non-interest-bearing loan that the government as an emergency measure exacted from the people.

Greenback issues

A National Bank Act, passed in 1863 and amended in 1864, provided the nation with yet another type of paper money; the national bank-note. According to this measure, any association desiring to do a national banking business and possessed of the minimum capital ($50,000 for cities of less than 6000 inhabitants, $100,000 for cities of from 6000

The National Bank Act

to 50,000, and $200,000 for larger cities) was entitled to a national charter of incorporation. Partly as a means of stimulating the market for United States bonds, the law provided that one third of the capital of such a bank must be invested in national securities, but it was also stipulated that, by depositing these bonds with the United States Treasurer as security, the bank should be entitled to receive in exchange "circulating notes equal in amount to ninety per centum of the current market value of the United States bonds so transferred and delivered." It was hoped at first that the state banks would quickly convert themselves into national banks, but when this failed to materialize, Congress levied in 1865 a ten per cent tax on all state bank-notes. While this law did not destroy state banking, it did, as was intended, tax state bank-notes out of existence, so that one of the legacies of the Civil War was a national currency, composed in part of greenbacks and in part of national bank-notes. By the end of 1865 the national bank-note circulation had reached more than $200,000,000. The bank-notes were not "legal tender," as were the greenbacks, but the two types of paper money depended in the last analysis upon the credit of the national government, and circulated at the same value.

Since the government had been forced to suspend specie payments early in the war, **Currency depreciation** none of this paper money was worth its face value in gold. Two main factors controlled the value of a paper dollar: (1) the amount of paper in circulation, and (2) the success or failure of the Union armies at the front. During the dark days of 1864, when it appeared that even the tenacity of Grant might prove insufficient to win the war, the value of the paper dollar, as expressed in terms of gold, dropped to thirty-nine cents, and even at the close of the war it stood at only sixty-seven cents. Even fractional currency was driven out of circulation as the premium on precious metals mounted, and the Treasury was forced to issue paper half-dollars, quarters,

dimes, five-cent and three-cent "shinplasters," as the small-sized notes were called. The paper dollars themselves, as well as the notes of larger denominations, were of generous dimensions — about twice the size of the currency now in circulation. Their fluctuating value caused an equivalent fluctuation in prices that netted huge fortunes to speculators. While the wages of laborers rose slowly toward the new price-levels, the salaries of "white collar" workers proved to be extremely resistant to change. Soldiers, also, fought on at thirteen dollars a month until late in the war, when their pay was raised to sixteen dollars. The generous bounties paid for enlistments served, however, to correct this inequality.

In addition to the official expenditures of the United States government for the winning of the war there was an **Private benevolence** unknown amount of assistance given to the cause by private individuals. In the early weeks of the struggle the outfitting of soldiers was often paid for by patriotic men or groups, some of whom neglected to bill the government for their expenditures. The families of soldiers were in innumerable instances cared for by relatives and neighbors. Ladies' Aid Societies in nearly every village sewed and knit and made bandages for the "boys in blue." A group of humanitarians, led by Henry W. Bellows and Frederick Law Olmstead, organized early in 1861 the United States Sanitary Commission to aid in the care of the sick and wounded. This society, which the United States government recognized with some reluctance, co-operated effectively with the hopelessly overworked Medical Bureau of the army, and raised millions of dollars in gifts for the purpose. "Sanitary fairs" were held all over the country to stimulate the collection of funds, and from the larger cities and from California huge sums were obtained. Pacific coast communities consciously atoned in this way for their inability to contribute their proper proportion of men to the northern armies. So sustained, the Commission became "a great machine running side by side with the Medical Bureau wherever the armies went." Another private organization, the United States Christian Commission, sought to promote the spiritual well-being of the soldiers by distributing tracts, holding religious services, and relieving in numerous practical ways the "intolerable ennui" of camp life.

The South, in its efforts to finance the war, was driven rapidly from one makeshift to **Southern** another. The United States **finance** mint at New Orleans and the United States custom-houses that were seized provided the Confederacy with perhaps a million dollars in greatly needed specie, and the confiscation of private debts owed by southern citizens to northern creditors also helped. Bond issues were floated, both by the Confederacy and by the several Confederate states, but the limited credit resources of the South were soon dried up. The best results were obtained when the bonds were made payable in produce. In this fashion the southern government came into possession of large quantities of cotton, tobacco, and other staple commodities, some of which it was able to market, and some of which it pledged as security for a small loan floated in Europe in 1863. Taxation turned out to be almost as fruitless as borrowing. An attempt to levy a direct tax through the instrumentality of the states netted as little real money as the similar efforts of the United States Congress during the Confederation period. Thereafter, the example set by the northern government of levying excises, licensing occupations, and taxing incomes was tried, but with comparatively slight success. One unique feature of the southern taxation program, a ten per cent tax on farm produce, to be paid in kind, proved to be of great assistance to the Confederate armies. It was excessively unpopular, however, and the charge of unconstitutionality was persistently hurled at this and all other effective means of taxation. The total receipts of the Confederacy from all tax sources has been estimated at about one hundred million dollars.

The inadequacy of the sums realized from bond issues and taxation drove the Confederacy early in the war to a chief reliance upon printing-press money. Notes were issued by the Confederate Treasury in a steadily increasing volume until before the end of the war more than a billion dollars of such money was in circulation. In addition, states, municipalities, and private corporations also put out issues of paper that passed for money. The depreciation that inevitably set in as the amount of fiat money increased, and the prospect of Confederate victory dimmed, far outran the depreciation of the northern greenback. By the summer of 1863 the Confederate dollar was worth only twenty-five cents in gold; a year later it was worth less than five cents; by the end of the war it was valueless. Southerners of small incomes suffered the acute distress usually attendant upon such extremes of money inflation, but a few skillful speculators made comfortable fortunes. Northern greenbacks, smuggled through the lines, were eagerly received, and circulated at a tremendous premium.

The confidence of the South that European intervention on behalf of "King Cotton" would be the decisive factor in **"King** the war made diplomacy a major **Cotton"** concern on the part of both bel- **diplomacy** ligerents from the very beginning. Every move of the southern government was designed to promote intervention, while the fondest hope of the northern government was to prevent it. In the diplomatic battle of wits the South, with leaders more experienced in international relations than the northern Republicans could command, should have had the advantage, but the southern government failed to live up to its opportunities. Davis's two secretaries of state, R. M. T. Hunter and Judah P. Benjamin, were second-rate men who had no particular aptitude for the post assigned them, and were quite outmatched by Seward. William L. Yancey, the first Confederate commissioner to Great Britain, quickly lost heart and came home. He was succeeded

THE WAR SPIRIT AT HOME. "Celebrating the Victory at Vicksburg, July 4, 1863." Painting by Lilly Martin Spencer, 1866.

Behind the lines at home, as in every war, patriotism ran high among the relatives of fighting men, both North and South. The progress of the war was closely followed in newspaper reports, and nearly every woman was engaged in some form of war work. The unprecedented casualties suffered by both sides brought up new problems of hospitalization, and a great deal was learned about care of the sick and wounded.

THE LADIES' LOYAL UNION LEAGUE. Certificate of membership, published by Currier and Ives, N.Y., 1863.

IN THE HOSPITAL. Painting by William L. Sheppard, 1861.

by James M. Mason, who was well received by the British aristocracy, but made little headway with the British government. In France, John Slidell did better, but there was little that France could do to aid the Confederacy without the approval of Great Britain, who as "mistress of the seas," and the chief foreign consumer of southern cotton, had to make the decision for or against European intervention in the American war.

British sympathy at the outset of the war seemed definitely to lean toward the South. The Tory aristocracy, which understood and appreciated the kindred southern planter class, looked forward with satisfaction to the possible downfall of democracy anywhere. Many British liberals also favored the South,

English attitude toward Civil War

for their favorite doctrine was then free trade, and the South seemed to be definitely committed to a free-trade policy, while the North had just inaugurated a program of protection. Moreover, the right of revolution was a part of the Whig tradition. By the "Glorious Revolution" Great Britain had been freed from the tyranny of the Stuarts, and by the American Revolution the colonies had rightfully won their independence, while at the same time bringing deserved discredit upon the attempt of a British king to establish personal rule. If, therefore, the southern people wished to be free, they had the right to be free. Possibly among Whig manufacturers this argument was duly strengthened by the reflection that a direct exchange of southern cotton for

British manufacturers would be greatly facilitated by the success of the southern arms. Diplomats of both parties saw a probable advantage for Great Britain in the division of the United States into two contending powers.

The North, however, was not without its friends in Great Britain. Such reformers as John Bright and Richard Cobden, although distressed at the newly adopted tariff policy of the United States, saw clearly that a northern victory must result in the abolition of slavery. With the issue thus reduced to a struggle between free labor and slave labor, their sympathies could lie only with the North. Lincoln's early insistence that the war was one for the preservation of the Union, and not for the abolition of slavery, was somewhat confusing to many British subjects, but when at last he issued his Emancipation Proclamation, the number of northern sympathizers was greatly increased, particularly among the lower classes. The workingmen of Manchester, in spite of the suffering that the failure of the American cotton supply had caused them, congratulated Lincoln upon his stand, and urged him to complete "the erasure of that foul blot upon civilization and Christianity — chattel slavery." To some extent, perhaps, British sympathy for the North was purchased by the greater need for northern wheat than for southern cotton; and there can be no doubt that the profits of neutrality were widely regarded as preferable to a hazardous war on behalf of southern independence. At all events, well before the end of the war the weight of British opinion had shifted to the side of the North.

Northern anxiety as to the course Great Britain meant to pursue became acute as **Recognition of southern belligerency** early as May, 1861, when the British government issued a proclamation of neutrality with respect to the American war. This action, because it accorded to the South the status of belligerent, was regarded by the North as deliberately unfriendly, for at the time the northern government still maintained that the uprising in the South was no more than an insurrection, and was therefore of no concern to outside nations. The British contention, however, that the struggle was in reality a war was in closer accord with the facts. Indeed, Lincoln himself, in ordering a blockade of the southern coast, had already unwittingly recognized the belligerency of the South. Probably the British proclamation was not meant to be unfriendly, but was designed merely to serve notice that the two contending parties would be expected to observe the customary rules of war. Nevertheless the fact that it was issued just as Charles Francis Adams, whom Lincoln had sent as minister from the United States, was arriving in England, confirmed Northerners in their suspicion that the sympathies of the British government lay with the South. Otherwise, they argued, Adams would at least have been given an opportunity to present the northern point of view. Northern fears that the recognition of southern belligerence would ultimately be followed by the recognition of southern independence proved to be unfounded.

Late in 1861 an incident occurred that almost precipitated war between the United States and Great Britain. When **The Trent affair** the news reached Captain Charles Wilkes of the United States frigate *San Jacinto* that the two Confederate commissioners, Mason and Slidell, were aboard a British mail steamer, the *Trent*, bound from Havana to Southampton, he promptly intercepted the neutral ship, arrested the Confederate commissioners, and took them to Boston. Wilkes's action was totally without official authorization, and was much the same sort of high-handed procedure that the United States had protested against when practiced by Great Britain before the War of 1812. But the northern public went wild with joy at the news, and Congress voted Wilkes the thanks of the nation for his exploit. What he had done seemed, in a sense, a fair offset to Great Britain's hasty proclamation of neutrality.

In view of the record of its own admiralty

during the Napoleonic wars, the British government should not have been deeply shocked at the capture of Mason and Slidell. But immediately on hearing the news, the Cabinet decided that Wilkes's action was "a clear violation of the law of nations, and one for which reparation must be at once demanded." The British public, also, was fully aroused, and there was much loose talk to the effect that this "insult to the flag" must be avenged. Fortunately for the friends of peace, the Queen's husband, Prince Albert, was enough of an outsider to take a somewhat objective view of the incident. When the ultimatum that the Ministry framed came to the Queen for her approval, he successfully urged that its tone be softened so that the United States might the more easily yield to its demands. The British minister to the United States, Lord Lyons, who was friendly to the North, still further eased the tension by neglecting to refer to the British note as an ultimatum, although he made it clear that Mason and Slidell must be released, and a suitable apology made, or there would be war. To emphasize the gravity of the situation, the British government ordered the navy to be put on a war footing, and sent eight thousand troops to Canada.

Secretary Seward seems to have realized from the first that, in case Great Britain so demanded, the prisoners would have to be released, but because of the superheated state of American public opinion and the divergent views of his colleagues in the Cabinet he was obliged to delay action as long as possible. When at length he replied to the British ultimatum, he neglected to include a formal apology for Wilkes's action, but argued somewhat trickily that the persons of Mason and Slidell were "contraband of war." As such they were justly liable to capture, although Wilkes, Seward held, was clearly at fault in failing to bring the *Trent* as well as its passengers into port. On this account the American government stood ready to deliver up the Confederate envoys to the proper British authorities. Seward's

argument, however specious it may have been, served its purpose well, for public opinion on both sides of the Atlantic was appeased, and so the crisis passed.

The blockade of the southern coast that the North maintained caused far less friction with the British government than might have been expected. After all, Great Britain dared **England and the blockade** not raise too serious objections to practices that she herself could follow to excellent advantage as a belligerent. Even the American doctrine of continuous voyages, which led at times to the capture of British ships bound from one British port to another, was allowed to stand unchallenged. After 1914, when Great Britain was a belligerent and the United States was a neutral, the precedents of the American Civil War were followed by the British Admiralty with telling effect.

The lax interpretation that the British government placed upon its neutral duties sorely taxed the patience of the United States. Commerce-destroyers were built in British ports for the use of the Confederacy, and were allowed to attack the shipping of the United States without ever having visited a Confederate port. Damaging as this practice was to northern commerce, the northern government contented itself with protests that could be, and were, made the basis for collecting damages later on. The Laird rams, however, which might possibly have raised the blockade had they sailed, were quite another thing. On hearing in September, 1863, that one of them was about to leave port, Charles Francis Adams wrote to Lord John Russell, the British foreign minister: "It would be superfluous for me to point out to your Lordship that this is war." But the British government, well aware of this fact without being told, had already given orders that the rams be detained. From this time until the close of the war there was no further danger of British intervention.

Had the British government approved, there is little reason to doubt that Napoleon

III of France would gladly have come to the aid of the South. His chief reason for desiring a Confederate victory lay in his hope that by this means the Monroe Doctrine might be eliminated, and the expansion of French influence on the American continent made possible. Shortly after Burnside's crushing defeat at Fredericksburg, Napoleon offered mediation between North and South, and when it was indignantly rejected by the North, he toyed long with the idea of recognizing southern independence. Objections from Great Britain held him back, however, and he was compelled to content himself with the working-out of his project for the virtual acquisition of Mexico.

The way was paved for Napoleon's Mexican adventure when in October, 1861, Great Britain, France, and Spain agreed to a joint intervention in Mexico to secure "protection for the persons and properties of their subjects, as well as the fulfillment of obligations." In accordance with this program the allies sent troops into Mexico and seized several Mexican custom-houses. By April, 1862, Great Britain and Spain had come to a satisfactory agreement with the Mexican government, and withdrew, but Napoleon ordered his army to Mexico City, called an assembly of pliant "Notables," and with their consent placed the Archduke Maximilian of Austria upon an imperial Mexican throne. A more complete violation of the Monroe Doctrine could scarcely have been imagined, but as long as the United States was torn by civil strife Napoleon knew that he had nothing to fear from north of the Rio Grande. Secretary Seward did not fail to register a vigorous protest, however, and after the defeat of the South, Napoleon found it expedient to recall his troops from Mexico. The fall of Maximilian's government then followed as a matter of course.

French intervention in Mexico

Spain, too, attempted to profit from the temporary weakness of the United States, first, by the reannexation of the Dominican Republic, and, secondly, by the occupation of some valuable

Spanish neutrality

guano islands off the coast of Peru. These actions were taken in spite of Seward's warning that anything of the kind would meet "with a prompt, persistent, and, if possible, effective resistance" from the United States. The Dominican venture, however, aroused such active native opposition that by 1865 the Spanish were ready to abandon it, while a pointed remonstrance from the United States brought to an end a little later the trespass upon the property of Peru.

Other European nations showed comparatively slight interest in the American Civil War, although the American public got the impression that Russia was strongly sympathetic with the northern cause. This opinion was borne out to some extent by the anti-slavery sentiments of the Tsar Alexander II, which led him in 1861 to emancipate the Russian serfs, and by the common assumption that both Russia and the United States were in the bad graces of the British government. In anticipation of war with Great Britain, the Russian government, late in 1863, dispatched two fleets to American waters, one to New York and the other to San Francisco. The purpose of this maneuver was to have the Russian ships in readiness for an instant attack on British commerce in case war between Russia and Great Britain should be declared, but the Americans very generally interpreted the presence of the Russian fleet as a gesture of friendship to the North. Several years later the purchase from Russia of Alaska, at a price supposed to be far above its actual value, was justified in the United States on the ground that Russia had once been a friend in time of need.

Russia

Left practically alone by European nations, the two American belligerents found problems of even graver consequence than diplomacy in their own internal dissensions. While the South was far more united than the North, the Davis government lost steadily in popularity, particularly after the defeats at Gettysburg and Vicksburg, and was seriously handicapped by the opposition it encountered behind the lines. In the North, opposition to the Lincoln government was open and defiant almost from the beginning.

One of the most persistent of the problems that arose within the Confederacy was the age-old contest between states' rights and nationalism. Were the southern nationalists, led by Jefferson Davis, merely trying to establish a new tyranny to replace the central government at Washington against which the southern states had revolted? Accusations that the Davis administration was strongly nationalistic were not without plausibility, for each step that it took in the direction of military efficiency led it farther and farther away from states' rights. Reasonable wartime precaution demanded that the President should have authority to suspend the writ of habeas corpus in the war zones, and yet, when the Confederate Congress granted him this privilege, his opponents accused him of seeking to establish a centralized despotism upon the ruins of the states. Conscription, also, which was assuredly a necessity if southern resistance was to be maintained at all, led to a violent clamor against the administration for its encroachments upon the reserved rights of the states. Likewise, each effective tax measure raised up a crop of enemies who took refuge behind the wellworn screen of unconstitutionality. Party lines were not clearly drawn in the Confederacy, but the congressional elections held in the fall of 1863 placed the Confederate Congress definitely in the hands of the antiadministration forces.

States' rights in the Confederacy

But Davis, in his effort to establish a new nation, had more than merely political opposition to meet. A small proportion of the southern population, probably not above ten per cent, was actually opposed to the war from the beginning, and consistently sought to evade military service and other unpleasant duties. Most such individuals were of the lowest class of southern whites, whose imaginations were incapable of grasping

Southern opposition to the war

either the idea of states' rights or of southern nationalism, and whose interests were strictly local. Moreover, as the horrors of war multiplied and came closer home, the futility of the struggle grew apparent to an increasing number of every class. Why fight on, or hope on, when there was no chance to win? Many did so, loyally and valiantly, but others made ready to give up, and even to place the blame on Jefferson Davis that their cause was lost.

The unity of northern opinion that had been so apparent immediately after the bombardment of Sumter was not maintained for long. Had the war lasted only for a summer, as many seemed to anticipate, and had Bull Run been a resounding northern victory instead of a defeat, the outburst of patriotic ardor in which the war was launched might have been of sufficient duration to see it through. As matters turned out, discontent with Lincoln's administration, and dismay at the prospect of a long fratricidal war, had become abundantly apparent well before the first summer was over. While such sentiments were by no means entirely confined to Democratic circles, the Republicans were generally pro-war, even when anti-Lincoln, and urged that all Union men, regardless of party convictions, stand together. In the fall of 1861, Union rather than Republican tickets were nominated wherever important state elections were to be held, and in New York and Ohio these tickets were even headed by War Democrats. This strategy, while unavailing as a means of heading off the nomination of separate Democratic tickets, did enable the Republicans and their pro-war allies to win by satisfactory majorities.

Northern opposition to the war

Opponents of the Lincoln administration were quick to charge the President with indulgence in unconstitutional practices that made him little less than a dictator. His orders of May, 1861, for the increase of the regular army and for the organization of a volunteer army composed of three-year men clearly

Criticism of the President

Copperheads 4

transcended his constitutional authority. About the same time he suspended the writ of habeas corpus without previously obtaining the consent of Congress, and he deliberately defied the ruling of Chief Justice Taney in *Ex Parte Merryman* (1861) that the President had no right to take such action on his own authority. Also, he permitted citizens to be arrested by military orders and tried by courts-martial, without as well as within the regions where hostilities existed. By such means no less than thirteen thousand arbitrary arrests and imprisonments were made during the war, although, according to a subsequent decision of the Supreme Court (1866), military courts had no lawful authority over civilians where regular civil courts were open for business. In May, 1863, Lincoln even approved of the arrest and trial by military commission of Clement L. Vallandigham of Ohio, his leading Democratic critic, on the charge that Vallandigham's utterances tended to "weaken the power of the government in its efforts to suppress an unlawful rebellion." In this case, however, the President ordered that the court-martial sentence of close confinement until the end of the war should be commuted to banishment, and directed that Vallandigham be sent beyond the Union lines to the Confederacy. On the question of freedom of the press, the President's course was less open to criticism. When the military authorities attempted to suppress the New York *World* and the Chicago *Times*, he promptly reversed their orders.

The administration was criticized also for its inefficiency in waging the war. Members **Committee on the Conduct of the War** of the President's own party were free with criticism on this score, and a strongly Republican Congress created, early in 1862, a joint Committee on the Conduct of the War, the duty of which was to point out to the administration its mistakes, and also, if possible, to force the President to allow Congress a greater voice in the direction of military affairs. The vast amount of waste and corruption that characterized the early months of the war played into the hands of this committee, and the failure of the northern arms to win victories, particularly in the East, helped it still more. But Lincoln refused to be intimidated, and persisted in his assumption that the conduct of the war was an executive, not a legislative, function. Judging from the temper of his "radical Republican" critics, it seems probable that his "presidential dictatorship" was far milder than the "congressional dictatorship" they would have set up had they had the opportunity.

Beyond a doubt the most perplexing problem of public opinion that the administration faced was the debate over Negro **The problem of emancipation** emancipation. Abolitionists argued with increasing effectiveness that the war had been caused by slavery, and that to fight on without removing the root of the evil was ridiculous. They were promptly joined by a host of radical Republicans who were out to punish the "rebels" for carrying secession into effect, and saw in the abolition of slavery a convenient tool. More conservative Republicans, however, were for a considerable time reluctant to abandon the official attitude of their party, which had always been to oppose only the expansion of slavery, and to leave the institution itself alone where it already existed. Sentiment in the loyal slave states, and in Democratic circles generally, was strongly against emancipation, and in many regions merely to suggest that the war was being fought as an "anti-slavery crusade" was a sure means of provoking trouble.

With opinion so divided, Lincoln wisely emphasized the preservation of the Union as the fundamental war aim of the North, for on this ground he could appeal to a far larger number of people than on any other. As late as the summer of 1862, he wrote to Horace Greeley:

My paramount object in this struggle is to save the Union. If I could save the Union without freeing any slaves, I would do it; if I could save it by freeing some and leaving others alone, I would also do that. I shall do less whenever I shall believe what I am doing hurts the cause, and I shall do more whenever I shall believe doing more will help the cause. I shall adopt new views as fast as they shall appear to be true views.

Nevertheless, when Lincoln penned these words he had already made up his mind that emancipation would have to come. From the first of the war the northern government had been perplexed with the problem of what to do with the Negroes that came through the lines from the South. When they were ordinary fugitives, orders were usually given, although not always obeyed, for their return. But sometimes Negroes that had been employed in building fortifications or in digging trenches, or in aiding the enemy directly in some such way, either escaped to the Union lines or were captured by Union troops. It was manifestly absurd to return such valuable property to the enemy, and nothing of the kind was done. But what was the legal status of such Negroes? Were they free or slave? If slave, whose property were they? General Benjamin F. Butler answered this question by calling them "contraband of war," but while the term tickled the public fancy, it had little legal significance. Probably before, and certainly after August, 1861, when Congress passed an act for the confiscation of any property, including slaves, that was being used for an insurrectionary purpose, the captured slaves were technically the property of the United States government. To put an end to such an anomalous situation, Congress in July, 1862, passed a second confiscation act, one clause of which specifically declared that whenever the slaves of "rebel" masters should fall into Union hands they should be "forever free of their servitude." Ultimately about one hundred and fifty thousand freed Negroes were enlisted in the Union army, and many of them saw active service.

Meantime the radical Republicans, steadily augmented in numbers as the war wore on, pressed insistently for complete and thoroughgoing emancipation. Two of Lin-

Slaves as "contraband"

coln's generals, John C. Frémont and David Hunter, early yielded to this pressure, the first with a proclamation issued in August, 1861, which freed the slaves of disloyal citizens in Missouri, and the second with a proclamation issued in May, 1862, which performed a like service for all the slaves in North Carolina, Georgia, and Florida. Both orders were revoked by the President, who understood far better than his subordinates the opposition within the North that such a course was sure to arouse. Lincoln would have much preferred a system of graduated emancipation, with compensation to the owners of slaves. In April, 1862, Congress adopted such a policy for the District of Columbia, and at Lincoln's suggestion also offered federal funds to the loyal slave states — which were not accepted — to aid them in working out a similar policy. But to the radicals the idea of waiting until the end of the war to effect the abolition of slavery within the Confederacy was intolerable, and the prospect of compensating former "rebels" for the loss of their slave property was utterly unthinkable.

Ultimately the time came when Lincoln had either to emancipate the slaves or alienate the majority of his own party. He knew, too, that if he proclaimed to the world that the war was being fought to free the slaves, there would be an immediate end to the danger of foreign intervention. His mind made up, he waited two full months longer before he acted, so that the winning of a Union victory (Antietam, September 17, 1862) could be cited as proof that his course was not a choice of desperation. Then, on September 22, 1862, he issued his preliminary Emancipation Proclamation. Claiming the right as commander-in-chief of the army and navy, he promised that "on the 1st day of January, A.D. 1863, all persons held as slaves within any state or designated part of a state the people whereof shall then be in rebellion against the United States shall be then, thenceforward, and forever free."

Growing emancipation sentiment

Emancipation proclaimed

The elections of 1862, which took place immediately after this proclamation was **Opposition to the administration** issued, offered an opportunity for the voters of the North to express their sentiments with respect to the administration. While the Republicans were able, as in 1861, to induce many Democrats to co-operate with them in the support of "Union" tickets, the Democratic party organization had remained intact, and now furnished vigorous opposition. Among the Democrats there were many ardent supporters of the war. Some of these, indeed, had no serious objection to the course the administration was following, but were for sentimental reasons unable to break from the party to which they had always belonged. Others, while definitely favorable to the war, objected strenuously to Lincoln's dictatorial course, and criticized the administration freely for its failure to achieve military success. Still others, a large and vociferous minority, were definitely opposed to the war and wished to see it brought to an immediate conclusion. In the Emancipation Proclamation this faction had a strong talking point. The war, they said, had ceased to be a struggle to save the Union. If the administration so desired, it could have peace at once with the old Union fully restored. The trouble was that the abolitionists were in control, and were shedding the best blood of the North merely to set free a rabble of Negro slaves.

The death of Douglas, in June, 1861, was a great misfortune, not only for the Democrats, but also for the whole nation. Had Douglas lived, there is little reason to doubt that he would have remained a Democrat, and would have led his party along a course of intelligent and useful criticism of the administration. Unfortunately, after his death no Democrat of like ability arose to take his place. General McClellan, who, on his loss of favor with the administration in the fall of 1862, became a kind of Democratic rallying-point, totally lacked political flair. Horatio Seymour, Democratic candidate for the governorship of New York, was probably the ablest of the Democratic leaders, but he was little known beyond the confines of his own state. Clement L. Vallandigham of Ohio was a more astute politician than either, but he was among the most extreme of the opponents of the war, and for that reason was practically disqualified for a position of national leadership.

With its pacifist element well to the fore, the Democratic Party made an excellent showing in the elections of 1862. **The elections of 1862** Helped along by the failure of the armies in the East to win a decisive victory, and by the near escape Grant had had at Shiloh, they easily took the ascendancy in New York, New Jersey, Pennsylvania, Ohio, Indiana, Illinois, and Wisconsin, all of which, with the exception of New Jersey, had voted for Lincoln in 1860. Fortunately for the Unionists, the border slave states, together with New England, the Far West, Michigan, Iowa, Minnesota, and Kansas, supported the administration; otherwise the Democrats would have won a majority in the national House of Representatives. As it was, some of the Democratic legislatures that were chosen gave the administration serious trouble. The virtual withdrawal of Indiana and Illinois from the support of the war was prevented only by the resourcefulness of the two governors concerned, Oliver P. Morton of Indiana and Richard Yates of Illinois, each of whom proved to be more than a match for his recalcitrant legislature.

The passage of the Draft Act in the spring of 1863 added fresh fuel to the flames of discontent. Peace-at-any-price **"Copperheadism"** men banded together into secret societies with such high-sounding names as "Knights of the Golden Circle," "Order of American Knights," "Order of the Star," and "Sons of Liberty." Thus organized, they plotted much mischief, and performed a little. They were accused of assassinating enrolling officers, of fomenting draft riots, of encouraging soldiers to desert, of giving aid and information to the Confederacy, of helping captured Confederate prisoners to

"COMPROMISE WITH THE SOUTH." Cartoon by Thomas Nast, dedicated to the Chicago convention, from *Harper's Weekly*, September 3, 1864.

Northern pacifists and other opponents of the war provoked the venomous hatred of those whose sons, husbands, fathers or brothers had died to save the Union. Peace-at-any-price men were called "copperheads," possibly after a snake as deadly as the rattlesnake, but without rattles to give warning that it was about to strike. The cartoon above, satirizing compromise, was one of the first by Thomas Nast, and enjoyed extraordinary popularity.

THE COPPERHEAD PARTY. "In favor of a vigorous prosecution of Peace!" Cartoon from *Harper's Weekly*, 1863.

UNION AND LIBERTY! AND UNION AND SLAVERY!

THE CAMPAIGN OF 1864. Pro-administration cartoon depicting Lincoln as the champion of the workman and emancipation, while McClellan is shown making peace with Jefferson Davis and slavery. Lithograph published by M. W. Siebert, 1864.

escape. To counteract such activities, "Union Leagues" were formed, and during the last two years of the war an unknown number of individual assaults and reprisals took place. Democrats who were opposed to the war, or lukewarm toward it, were generally called "Copperheads" by the Unionists, and, inasmuch as the Democratic Party as a whole was somewhat tinctured with "Copperheadism," the terms Democrat and Copperhead tended, on hostile lips, to be regarded as synonymous.

The occasional elections that were held in the fall of 1863 revealed, however, an unmistakable trend back to the support of the administration. In nearly every instance the Unionists showed greater strength than **The effect** the Democrats, although by **of Union** majorities that were not always **victories** large. This change of sentiment was due primarily to the victories at Gettysburg and Vicksburg, but even those successes were insufficient to quiet the peace-at-any-price men, whose numbers, particularly in the states that bordered on the Ohio River, were very great. In Ohio a governor had to be chosen, and Vallandigham himself, still an exile but by that time in Canada, won the Democratic nomination. To oppose him the Unionists chose John Brough, a War Democrat, who won the election by a vote of 288,000 to 187,000. Inasmuch as Vallandigham consistently denounced the war and called for an immediate armistice, this vote furnished a fair test of the pacifist forces in the Middle West. The eastern wing of the Democratic Party, which looked to Seymour rather than to Vallandigham for leadership, was far less imbued with pacifist principles.

The dark days of 1864, with their long casualty lists and their infrequent victories, **Presidential** led the critics of Lincoln's ad-**nominations,** ministration to redouble their **1864** efforts. Among them were the radicals within his own party, who had always objected to his moderation, and now plotted to deprive him of a renomination. At a mass convention held in Cleveland,

May 21, 1864, they called for the suppression of the rebellion "by force of arms and without compromise," urged the "confiscation of the lands of the rebels, and their distribution among the soldiers and actual settlers," and nominated an opposition Republican ticket headed by John C. Frémont. But Frémont's candidacy failed to develop the popular support for which its backers had hoped, and Frémont presently withdrew. The Democratic National Convention, under the control of the Vallandigham element, went to an opposite extreme in its platform by denouncing the war as a failure, and urging an immediate cessation of hostilities as a prelude to a convention of the states which should restore the federal Union. For their nominee, however, they turned to General McClellan, who accepted the nomination, but denounced the platform. The Union, he declared, must be saved before there could be peace: "no peace can be permanent without union."

The administration forces, to make clear that they represented an alliance of Republicans and War Democrats, not only retained the Union label that had served them so well before, but also nominated as Lincoln's running-mate Andrew Johnson of Tennessee, a War Democrat who had no Republican connections whatever. But for a while it seemed as if the re-election of the President would be impossible. Later generations, accustomed to the veneration of Lincoln, find it difficult to realize that his popularity dates from the end rather than from the beginning of the war, and that many of his contemporaries had the gravest doubt as to his ability. On one occasion during the campaign Lincoln himself went on record as convinced that he could not win. At an August Cabinet meeting he asked the members present to endorse unopened a document he had written. Then, several weeks later when the election was over, he read it to them: "This morning," it ran, "as for some days past, it seems exceedingly probable that this administration will not be re-elected. Then it will be my duty to so co-operate with the President-elect as to save the Union between the election and the inauguration, as he will have secured his election on such grounds that he cannot possibly save it afterwards."

But victories changed the situation again, and the Union ticket won. Three states, **Election results** New Jersey, Delaware, and Kentucky, cast together only 21 electoral votes for McClellan, while all the other states that voted were carried by Lincoln, whose total reached 212. In nearly every state, however, McClellan's share of the popular vote was only a little less than Lincoln's, so that the change of a comparatively small number of votes would have given the Democrats the election. In New York, for example, Lincoln's majority was less than 7000 votes out of a total of 730,000.

By Inauguration Day, March 4, 1865, the war was nearly over, and Lincoln promised, **Death of Lincoln** "with malice toward none, with charity for all ... to bind up the nation's wounds." But he was not permitted to have a part in the work of restoration, for on the following April 15, six days after Appomattox, he died from an assassin's wounds. This tragic event, coming as it did at the very hour of victory, forced a reappraisal of his capacities, with the result that his name and fame were soon coupled in the public mind with Washington's. Even *Punch*, the English periodical, which had repeatedly heaped ridicule upon him, made the following graceful recantation:

> Beside this corpse that bears for winding sheet
> The Stars and Stripes he lived to rear anew,
> Between the mourners at his head and feet,
> Say, scurrile jester, is there room for you?
>
> Yes, he had lived to shame me from my sneer,
> To lame my pencil and confute my pen;
> To make me own this hind of princes peer,
> This rail-splitter a true-born king of men.

Lincoln and his contemporaries interpreted the victory of the North as primarily **Significance of the Civil War** a triumph of nationalism over states' rights, or perhaps, more accurately, state sovereignty.

That the Union was now in fact "one and indivisible," whatever theoretical views some individuals might continue to hold, was generally acknowledged, even by the defeated South. Incidentally, the institution of slavery, which had made the doctrine of state sovereignty its chief constitutional defense, was also brought to an end. While the Emancipation Proclamation had applied only to those states and parts of states that on January 1, 1863, were still at war with the United States, the momentum that Lincoln's action gave to the abolition movement was too great to be stopped. State action in Missouri, West Virginia, Maryland, Tennessee, and Louisiana had abolished slavery within their respective borders by the time the war was over. Meantime, a movement to write abolition into the national Constitution had gathered headway, and on February 1, 1865, Congress submitted to the states the Thirteenth Amendment, which forbade slavery or involuntary servitude,.except as a punishment for crime, within the United States, or any place subject to its jurisdiction. By the end of the year this amendment had become a part of the Constitution. Whether a long civil war was necessary to secure the triumph of nationalism over state's rights and of abolitionism over slavery may well be doubted. Probably, with more skillful handling of a few crises, both ends might ultimately have been achieved without resort to war.

A factor not fully understood at the time, and possibly overemphasized today, was the commanding importance that **Industrial supremacy** the new industrial interests won during the course of the struggle. War profits compounded the capital of the industrialists and placed them in a position to dominate the economic life, not only of the Northeast where they were chiefly concentrated, but also of the nation at large. With the southern planters removed from the national scene, the government at Washington tended more and more to reflect the wishes of the industrial leaders. The protective tariff, impossible as long as southern influence predominated in national affairs, became the corner-stone of the new business edifice, for by means of it the vast and growing American market was largely restricted to American industry. Transcontinental railroads, designed to complete the national transportation system, were likewise accorded the generous assistance of the government, while a national banking act and a national currency facilitated still further the spread of nation-wide business.

The Northwest, where industry was definitely subordinate to agriculture, profited less from the war than the Northeast, but the Westerners applauded the passage of the Homestead Act, which threw the national domain wide open to settlers, and they were for a time as eager as the Easterners to accelerate the expansion of the railroads. By assisting in the defeat of the South, however, the Northwest had unknowingly sacrificed a valuable ally. Before the war the two agricultural sections had repeatedly stood together, first against the commercial, and later against the industrial, Northeast. Now, with the weight of the South in the Union immensely lessened, the Northwest was left to wage its battles virtually alone. For more than a generation after the war, with eastern men and eastern policies in the ascendancy, American industry steadily consolidated the gains it had made.

Bibliography

Many of the books cited for Chapters 29 and 31, pp. 548–549 and 594–595, continue useful. All civilian aspects of the struggle, but with the emphasis on politics, are covered in Channing, VI; Rhodes, III–V; Schouler, VI; and J. B. McMaster, *A History of the People of the United States during Lincoln's Administration* (1927). Useful short accounts are contained in F. L. Paxson, *The Civil War* (1911); J. F. Rhodes, *History of the Civil War* (1917); N. W. Stephenson, *Abraham Lincoln and the Union* (1918), and *The Day of the Confederacy* (1919). E. D. Fite, *Social and Industrial Conditions in the North during the Civil War* (1910), is an excellent analysis of the causes of northern prosperity. E. M. Coulter, *The Confederate States of America, 1861–1865* (1950), covers the non-military aspects of Confederate history. L. M. Hacker, *The Triumph of American Capitalism* (1940), construes the Civil War as a victory for industrial capitalism. Constitutional problems evoked by the war are covered for the North in J. G. Randall, *Constitutional Problems under Lincoln* (1926); and for the South in F. L. Owsley, *State Rights in the Confederacy* (1925).

On financial aspects of the war, E. P. Oberholtzer, *Jay Cooke, Financier of the Civil War* (2 vols., 1907), is indispensable. For the South, an important but difficult book is J. C. Schwab, *The Confederate States of America, 1861–1865: A Financial and Industrial History of the South during the Civil War* (1901). On northern inflation, see W. C. Mitchell, *A History of the Greenbacks with Special Reference to the Consequence of their Issue, 1862–1865* (1903).

There is a considerable literature on northern opposition to the war. An excellent discussion of Copperheadism is contained in W. D. Foulke, *Life of Oliver P. Morton* (2 vols., 1899); but this account should be checked with the more objective views expressed in K. M. Stampp, *Indiana Politics during the Civil War* (1949). This is also the subject of chief interest in G. F. Milton, *Abraham Lincoln and the Fifth Column* (1942); and Wood Gray, *The Hidden Civil War* (1942). Stewart Mitchell, *Horatio Seymour of New York* (1938), reveals Seymour's moderating influence among northern Democrats. C. F. Dunham, *The Attitude of the Northern Clergy toward the South, 1860–1865* (1942), shows the part played by the clergy in the formation of war aims. S. A. Pleasants, *Fernando Wood of New York* (1948), rescues the Civil War mayor of New York from a not altogether undeserved oblivion. E. C. Kirkland, *The Peacemakers of 1864* (1927); and E. J. Benton, *The Movement for Peace without Victory during the Civil War* (1918), deal with pacifist activities. One aspect of the controversy over civil rights is treated in R. S. Harper, *Lincoln and the Press*

(1951). Interesting illustrations relating to the campaign and election of 1864 appear in Stefan Lorant, *The Presidency* (1951).

Lincoln's difficulties with various other problems of the home front have called forth a number of books. T. Harry Williams, *Lincoln and the Radicals* (1941), shows the trouble Lincoln had with the Joint Committee on the Conduct of the War. H. J. Carman and R. H. Luthin, *Lincoln and the Patronage* (1943), is a useful and detailed study of an important subject. W. B. Hesseltine, *Lincoln and the War Governors* (1948), calls attention to an especially difficult problem of wartime administration. George Fort Milton, *The Use of Presidential Power, 1789–1943* (1944), is of further value in this connection. Lloyd Lewis, *Myths after Lincoln* (1929), shows the beginning of the apotheosis of Lincoln; and Roy P. Basler, *The Lincoln Legend* (1935), its continuation.

On the Confederate side, see the books on Lee and Davis, cited for Chapter 30, page 564. R. W. Patrick, *Jefferson Davis and His Cabinet* (1944) comes to the defense of Davis. J. K. Bettersworth, *Confederate Mississippi* (1943), studies the people and policies of a cotton state in wartime. Ella Lonn, *Foreigners in the Confederacy* (1940), counters the generally held theory that immigrants to the United States would not go to the South. Two useful biographies are H. H. Simms, *Life of Robert M. T. Hunter* (1935); and R. D. Meade, *Judah P. Benjamin, Confederate Statesman* (1943). On the death throes of the Confederacy, see C. H. Wesley, *The Collapse of the Confederacy* (1922); and R. S. Henry, *The Story of the Confederacy* (1943).

On the diplomacy of the war, the texts by Bemis and by Bailey are excellent. Other books of value include: E. D. Adams, *Great Britain and the American Civil War* (2 vols., 1925); Donaldson Jordon and E. J. Pratt, *Europe and the American Civil War* (1931); W. R. West, *Contemporary French Opinion on the American Civil War* (1924); J. M. Callahan, *The Diplomatic History of the Southern Confederacy* (1901); F. L. Owsley, *King Cotton Diplomacy* (1931); James A. B. Scherer, *Cotton as a World Power; A Study in the Economic Interpretation of History* (1916); C. F. Adams, Jr., *Charles Francis Adams* (1900); T. L. Harris, *The Trent Affair* (1896); B. P. Thomas, *Russo-American Relations, 1815–1867* (1930).

Certain aspects of social history have been well covered. Margaret Leech, *Reveille in Washington, 1860–1865* (1941), gives a vivacious account of Washington society during the war. Charles J. Stillé, *History of the United States Sanitary Commission* (1866), is excellent, although almost a contemporary account. Useful in this connection also is W. E. Barton, *The Life of Clara Barton, Founder of the American Red Cross* (1922). The trials of the war-torn South are well told in M. P. Andrews, *The Women of the South in War Times* (1920); B. I. Wiley, *The Plain People of the Confederacy* (1943); and, by the same author, *Southern Negroes, 1861–1865* (1938). One aspect of the southern shortages is treated in Ella Lonn, *Salt as a Factor in the Confederacy* (1933). On the moot question of southern treatment of war prisoners, see W. B. Hesseltine, *Civil War Prisons: A Study in War Psychology* (1930); on hospitals and surgery, G. W. Adams, *Doctors in Blue* (1952).

33

Reconstruction[1]

The Radicals — President Johnson — Theories of reconstruction — The "black laws" — The Freedmen's Bureau — The President vs. Congress — "Thorough" reconstruction — The carpetbag governments — The Ku Klux Klan — The redemption movement — Elections of 1872 and 1876 — Economic reconstruction — The post-war North — Panic and depression — Diplomatic reconstruction

THE "road to reunion" after the Civil War proved to be far more difficult than either North or South could foresee in 1865. One might say as General Grant said later, "Let us have peace," but there were forces at work that the mere cessation of hostilities could not destroy. Long before the war broke out the two sections had begun to hate and distrust each other, and the four years of strife had whipped these sentiments to a white heat of intensity. Not everyone on either side was really ready for peace, whatever he might say, and the years of reconstruction, so-called, were in a sense only a continuation of conflict.

In the North the "Radicals," a faction in the Republican party that had opposed Lincoln throughout the war, soon **The Radicals** made havoc of the conciliatory policies adopted by the new President, Andrew Johnson, and pressed with all their might to compound the ruin that the war had brought to the South. Lincoln, in his second inaugural address, had urged that the work of restoration should proceed "with

malice toward none" and "with charity for all," but the Radical program came closer to being with malice for all and with charity for none; none, that is, save the ex-slaves and such others in the South as were willing to collaborate with their conquerors. The Radicals stood ready to give the Negroes all civil and political rights, including especially the right to vote, a program which, as they saw it, would not only do justice to the freedmen, but would also serve as a suitable rebuke to the southern whites for having started the war. Naturally, too, the Negroes would tend to support the party that had freed and favored them, and, with the ex-Confederates still further punished by wholesale confiscation and disfranchisement, the southern states, when finally reconstructed, could be counted on to provide the Republicans with comfortable majorities for many years to come.

The South, on its part, was defeated, but in no sense convinced that there was anything wrong about the stand it **The South** had taken. It was obliged to accept the fact of Negro emancipation, but the number of southerners who believed that emancipation was really a good thing was few indeed. Most of the men who had fought in the southern armies were not slave-

---

[1] This chapter is provided primarily for classes which wish to include reconstruction in the first semester's work. For a fuller account, see the second volume of this series, John D. Hicks, *The American Nation* (3d ed., 1955), pp. 1–53.

holders, but the poorer they were in terms of property the more they cherished the idea of white superiority — every white man could at least belong to the master race. Most southerners, therefore, had no slightest intention of permitting the freedmen to rise in status to anything like equality with the whites; moreover, as the Radical program unfolded, the South felt an ever greater compulsion to "keep the Negro in his place." Southern whites could not strike directly at the northern Radicals, for they were out of reach; but they could, and they sometimes did, strike at the southern Negroes, who were close at hand and in a sense represented the Radicals. Negro lynchings were by no means unknown in slavery times, but the Negro then could make no pretensions of equality, and he was further protected by his property value. During and after reconstruction such acts of violence became distressingly commonplace. As for the states'-rights doctrine the South had so steadfastly maintained, four years of war, in which the soldiers of every southern state mingled with those of every other, had tended to nationalize — or, in defeat, to sectionalize — the southern point of view. It was southern rights now, rather than states' rights, for which the South stood; the "solid South" was in plain sight. Even if the war had turned out to be a failure, the people of the South were determined that the southern way of life must somehow be preserved. The South could not again secede from the Union, but it had a vision of remaining in effect a "nation within a nation."

Andrew Johnson (1808–1875), the Vice-President who succeeded to the Presidency **President** when Lincoln was assassinated, **Johnson** might have served well the cause of reunion had the two sections really wished to get together. He was a southern Democrat who had remained loyal to the Union during the war, and precisely on that account had been placed on the Union party ticket with Lincoln in 1864. Born in North Carolina, he had lived most of his life in the mountain country of eastern Tennessee, and

was about as far removed in spirit from the planter aristocracy of the South as any southerner could be. He had grown up in poverty as grinding as that which surrounded Lincoln, and he had received no formal schooling, although learning much from his school-teacher wife. A tailor by trade, he early discovered an aptitude for politics and for oratory, which he indulged freely. As a firm defender of the workingman and a bitter opponent of the southern aristocrats, he mounted the political ladder step by step. When only twenty-one years of age he became an alderman in his home city, Greeneville, Tennessee, after which he won elections that made him successively mayor, member of the state legislature, member of Congress, governor, United States Senator, and Vice-President. Thickset and dark complexioned, he had about him an air of contentiousness and belligerence in marked contrast with the mild-mannered Lincoln. The Radicals thought at first that they could use him against the southern leaders, but they were soon disillusioned, for Johnson shared with Lincoln, whatever their external differences, the belief that the best way to heal the nation's wounds was to deal generously with the defeated South. As for the southern aristocrats he had once hated, he soon saw that they had suffered much for their sins and were no longer to be feared.

Johnson did not have to invent a plan by which the southern states could be restored to the Union, for Lincoln had **Lincoln's** already wrestled with the prob- **plan of re-** lem, and had given some indi- **construction** cations of what he had intended to do had he lived. As the war progressed, northern armies overran one after another of the seceded states, and thus posed for the President, as commander-in-chief, the alternative of continuing the conquered states under military rule, or somehow providing for the revival within their borders of civilian government. Lincoln chose the latter course in what was sometimes called mockingly his "ten per cent plan." For each of the liberated states he appointed a military governor, whose duty it was to reestablish normal civilian government as soon as at least one-tenth of the number of citizens who had voted in 1860 had taken a prescribed oath of allegiance to the United States. Presidential pardons were freely promised, and only the highest military and civilian officers of the Confederacy were deemed ineligible to take the oath. At the time Johnson became President, Lincoln had already recognized three loyal state governments, each established under his plan, in Tennessee, Louisiana, and Arkansas, respectively. But the easy treatment of the South which the President's terms portended greatly angered the Radicals, who in answer pushed through Congress during the summer of 1864 a plan of their own embodied in the Wade-Davis bill. According to this plan, the President should appoint a provisional governor for each of the Confederate states, who should then take a census of white male citizens. If a majority (rather than ten per cent) of these potential voters should take the oath of allegiance, the provisional governor might then allow them to choose delegates to a constitutional convention, the duty of which would be to accept for themselves and to include in a new constitution three provisions: (1) the denial of political rights to all high-ranking civil and political officers of the Confederacy; (2) the abolition of slavery; and (3) the outlawing of state or Confederate debts incurred in the war against the Union. With this document duly approved by the voters at the polls, the President, *after obtaining the consent of Congress*, might recognize the state government established under its provisions.

Since the Wade-Davis bill passed Congress during the last ten days of a session, Lincoln was able to give it a pocket veto, but this did not mean that he was necessarily opposed to all its provisions. In fact, he issued a formal proclamation, calling attention to the Congressional plan as well as his own, and inferring that, while he was as yet uncommitted to any one plan for every state, the ideas set forth in the Wade-Davis bill were well worth considering. The fundamental difference between Lincoln's plan and the Congressional plan lay in whether the President or the Congress should take charge of the process of reconstruction. If the President could maintain the control he had assumed, the way was open for a relatively simple means of reviving state government in the South; but if Congress was to have the last word, then the Radicals might substitute (as indeed they did) a far harsher plan than they had proposed in the Wade-Davis bill. Undoubtedly Lincoln was well aware of the Radical intent, and had he lived might have made the best possible bargain he could get with Congress. He was a much shrewder politician than Johnson, and would certainly have sought to avoid the complete break between the executive and the legislative branches that developed during Johnson's administration.

Lincoln was far less interested in theory than in action, but his plan of reconstruction was predicated upon the assumption that a state, once created, could neither be destroyed nor destroy itself, and that secession, being illegal, a state could never actually have left the Union. It was now, therefore, as if secession had never been; the state was still in the Union, and all that was needed was to restore its government to normal functioning. This the President believed he was entirely competent to do as Commander-in-Chief, without especial authority from Congress, although only Congress could create a new state. With any such line of argument the Radicals in Congress had little patience. According to Thaddeus Stevens, their most influential member in the House, the southern states since the war were only "conquered provinces," over which Congress had full authority, as over any other unorganized territory of the United States; while to Charles Sumner, leader of the Senate Radicals, the former Confederate states, by the very act of secession, had committed suicide, and were no longer in existence. Congress, and only Congress, might therefore create

Theories of reconstruction

out of their former territory new states if it chose, and meantime Congress, and only Congress, had authority under the Constitution to provide for their government.

Under Johnson's leadership the issue was soon joined in practice as well as in theory. **Johnson's plan** Drawing both upon Lincoln's plan of reconstruction and the Wade-Davis bill, he elaborated a plan of his own which pointedly ignored the pretensions of Congress to a part in reconstruction. First, he accepted as fully restored to their place in the Union the states that Lincoln had recognized. These included, in addition to Tennessee, Louisiana, and Arkansas, a loyal government in Virginia which early in the war had exerted full authority in the northwestern counties of the state, but after the admission of West Virginia in 1863 had continued in virtual impotence at Alexandria. For the seven other ex-Confederate states Johnson promptly appointed provisional governors, who differed in name only from the military governors of Lincoln's plan, and whose salaries in most instances came from War Department funds. For each governorship he chose a local man who had shown sympathy for the Union during the war; none of them had fought on the Union side, and only one, Judge Benjamin F. Perry of South Carolina, had ever served the Confederacy in any way. Each governor was then to call for elections to a constitutional convention under the same suffrage provisions that had existed before the war, provided that such voters were eligible to take, and had taken, the prescribed oath of allegiance to the United States. There was thus no provision for Negro suffrage, and high Confederate leaders, including those whose property exceeded $20,000 in value, were still denied pardons and political rights. The conventions must invalidate the various ordinances of secession, abolish slavery, and repudiate all debts contracted to help the Confederacy; otherwise they were free to write into their constitutions such provisions as they chose. Meantime, most of the old local and state officials, after taking the oath

of allegiance, continued to discharge their customary duties. Thus the road to restoration seemed easy indeed. All that remained to be done, after the conventions had finished their work, was to hold new elections, and choose new officials.

It was probably a mistake for Johnson to have tried to carry through this program without consulting Congress. Whatever the truth might be about the legal status of the seceded states, it was too much to expect that the Republican politicians in the Senate and the House would permit an accidental President such as Johnson, who was both a Democrat and a southerner, to carry through the whole program of reconstruction on his own. With the war ended, party politics was bound to reappear, and did. The Republicans promptly turned their backs on the Union coalition they had formed for the election of 1864, and operated strictly as Republicans. Moreover, with Lincoln's restraining hand no longer available, the party tended increasingly to fall under the domination of the Radicals. Johnson should have realized the necessity of making terms with his opponents. Instead, he kept on Lincoln's cabinet, most of whom held moderate views; he refused to call Congress into special session as he might well have done; and he planned to have the whole process of reconstruction completed by December, 1865, when the next regular session of Congress would begin. Indeed, with more or less enthusiastic cooperation in the South, he seemed by that time in easy sight of his goal.

Under the circumstances it was not surprising that Congress returned to Washington for the long session of 1865–66 with blood in its eye. The southern state governments that Johnson was reconstructing were little different in spirit, or even in personnel, from those that had destroyed the Union. In defiance of the President's regulations, prominent ex-Confederates, some of whom were not yet even pardoned, were among those chosen to high state office, and, still more incredible, to Congress — one such was Alexander H. Stephens, formerly Vice-Presi-

KU KLUX KLAN DISGUISES. *Harper's Weekly*, December 19, 1868.

NEGROES IN THE LEGISLATURE. A civil rights speech in South Carolina, 1874.

Negro status after the bonds of slavery had been loosed was one of the South's greatest reconstruction problems. Sudden freedom rocketed Negroes into state legislatures and even Congress. Liberty often turned to license, and for a while Southerners defended themselves by vigilante organizations like the Ku Klux Klan.

"CUTTING HIS OLD ASSOCIATES." *Harper's Weekly*, January 17, 1863.

dent of the Confederacy.[1]   The fact that

[1] To the everlasting credit of the victors, there were no executions for treason after the war. Surrendering officers and troops received military paroles which protected them, and high-ranking civilians, while sometimes imprisoned for a time, eventually were released. The execution of Henry Wirz, who had been in command of Andersonville prison, was ordered after trial before a military commission on the charge that he was personally responsible for atrocities that occurred within the prison walls, and for the death of 12,000 Union prisoners.

under the Constitution each house was the judge of its own elections made it possible for the northern Senators and Representatives to refuse to seat the new southern delegations, and this was the action they took, thus registering their emphatic disapproval of the President's decision to go it alone. But more than principle was involved in this move. If the eleven ex-Confederate states, as reconstructed by Lincoln and Johnson, should be allowed their former quotas of seats in Congress, they would at once reduce the Republican majorities in both Senate and House to slender margins, with the chances strong that in future elections a combination of southern and northern Democrats would not only win control of the two legislative branches, but also of the electoral college and the Presidency. To the Radicals this looked very much like turning the national government back to the very forces that had sought to destroy it. By establishing in December, 1865, a Joint Committee on Reconstruction, with membership drawn from both the House and the Senate, they made it clear that Congress, as well as the President, intended to have its say on the subject.

Representation in Congress was less important to the South than the effective functioning of the reconstructed **The "black** state governments, a task to **codes"** which their newly-elected legislatures turned painstaking attention. Of the many pressing problems that confronted them, the most perplexing, no doubt, was how to deal with the Negroes. The South understood far better than the North the great distance that lay between slavery and freedom; it would take far more than a presidential proclamation and a Constitutional amendment to bridge the gap. Although Johnson and some other southerners favored the enfranchisement of educated Negroes, in part, no doubt as a sop to the Radicals, the southern people as a whole were not prepared for any such move; not one of the reconstructed states gave the Negroes the right to vote. Furthermore, most of them enacted "black codes," defining the civil rights of the ex-slaves, and prescribing for them a status definitely inferior to that of the whites. Of these codes the most severe and the most quoted was that of Mississippi, but they all denied to Negroes the privilege of sitting on juries, and usually rejected Negro testimony in case a white defendant was involved. Among the provisions most criticized in the North (mainly from the Mississippi code) were those requiring labor contracts to be in writing, and if broken the wages not to be payable; those

directing that Negroes under eighteen years of age whose parents could not support them be apprenticed to some white "master," preferably their former owner; those prescribing stiff fines for vagrancy, which if not paid might be collected by selling the services of the offender; and those forbidding Negroes "to carry fire arms or other deadly weapons, to make seditious speeches, to treat animals cruelly, to sell liquors, or to preach without a license." [1]

However well intentioned these provisions may have been, to many northerners, particularly the Radicals, they **The** seemed little less than a di- **Freedmen's** rect defiance of the Thirteenth **Bureau** Amendment, and a conscious effort to retain slavery in fact if not in form. In general, however, they never went into effect, principally because of the presence throughout the South of Union troops who made the welfare of the Negroes an object of especial solicitude, and the work of a national agency, the Freedmen's Bureau, created in March, 1865, to provide relief and guidance for the Negroes and other refugees who had concentrated around the army camps and in the southern towns and cities. Under the leadership of General O. O. Howard the Bureau was doing an excellent work, distributing rations, and generally caring for the needy, but its existence, by the law creating it, was to terminate a year after the end of the war. Here was a test case made to order for the Radicals. Should the Freedmen's Bureau, with its program of national supervision of the freed slaves be continued, or should the Negro problem be turned over to the reconstructed states to handle as they chose? Johnson, a states' rights Democrat by training and conviction, favored the latter course, but Congress, with overwhelming majorities, sent up for his signature a law continuing the Freedmen's Bureau, with greatly increased powers. Thus challenged, Johnson responded with an anticipated veto, which to his delight the Senate sustained by a small

[1] E. M. Coulter, *The South during Reconstruction, 1865–1877* (1947), p. 40 n.

majority. Unfortunately his rejoicing was far more public than was wise, and included heated denunciations of the Radical leaders, the net result of which was to lose him the votes he needed to continue his policies.

What the Radicals required in order to overturn Johnson's plan of reconstruction was a two-thirds majority in each house of Congress, and this, it developed, Johnson's indiscreet action had given them. A Civil Rights bill, which declared the Negro to be a citizen and gave him the same civil rights as were enjoyed by the whites, passed Congress over the President's veto. This was followed by a somewhat different version of the Freedmen's Bureau bill, which was again vetoed, but this time won repassage by the requisite majorities. Thus the leadership in reconstruction had passed from the President and the moderates to Congress and the Radicals. By this time — the summer of 1866 — the Joint Committee on Reconstruction was ready to report a Congressional substitute for the President's plan. Its recommendations, after slight modification, were embodied in the Fourteenth Amendment to the Constitution, and submitted to the states for ratification. The first section repeated the provisions of the Civil Rights bill, and forbade any state to "deprive any person of life, liberty, or property without due process of law," or to "deny to any person within its jurisdiction the equal protection of the laws." The second dealt with Negro suffrage, but refrained from requiring it outright, providing instead that to the extent that any state should deny eligible males over twenty-one the right to vote, to the same extent the representation of such a state in Congress and in the electoral college should be reduced. The third section was designed to repudiate the free bestowal of Presidential pardons upon persons who had broken an oath of allegiance to the United States in order to serve the Confederacy. Only Congress, by a two-thirds vote of each house, could remove such a disability. A fourth section asserted that the debt of the United

The First Congressional Plan

States, incurred for any cause, including the suppression of rebellion, should never be questioned, and at the same time denied both to the United States and to the several states the right to assume any debts incurred in aid of rebellion, or for losses due to the emancipation of slaves. All this Congress was given full authority to enforce by appropriate legislation.

Despite the Radical contention that the seceded states were no longer in the Union, Congress had submitted the Thirteenth Amendment to them for ratification,[1] and now also submitted to them the Fourteenth, with the implication that they must ratify, or be reconstructed all over again. Of the eleven states concerned, however, only Tennessee complied; all the rest turned the Amendment down, an act of questionable wisdom in view of subsequent events, but understandable enough at the time, especially since President Johnson had counseled such a course. Congress now declared Tennessee, ostensibly for its cooperation, to be fully restored to the Union, but the state was already in the hands of a Radical government, and it was probably this fact, rather than ratification merely, that won it Congressional recognition. Had the other ten states followed Tennessee's example, there is no certainty that Congress would have readmitted them; nevertheless, it would have had less excuse for the brutal program it finally adopted. To add to the generally bad impression made in the North by southern rejection of the Fourteenth Amendment, race riots had occurred during the year in Memphis and New Orleans, proof, according to the Radicals, of what the South meant to do to the Negro if left to its own devices.

The contest between the President and Congress came to a head in the elections of 1866. If the President's friends could win one more than one-third of the seats in either house

The President vs. Congress

[1] The Thirteenth Amendment, submitted by Congress February 1, 1865, was proclaimed in effect December 18, 1865, after being ratified by twenty-seven states, among them several that were still in the process of Presidential reconstruction.

of Congress, he could make his vetoes stand, and prevent the Radicals from pushing their program further; on the other hand, if the Radicals could win a two-thirds majority in each house, they could devise their own program, and drive the President before them. Johnson seems at first to have thought that he could make use of the Union coalition that had elected him in 1864, and gave earnest support to a National Union Convention, held during the late summer of 1866, which southern as well as northern delegates attended. But he was eventually to learn that he could count on more help from the Democrats than from any other quarter, and that only a few of the more moderate Republicans were willing to stand by him. The Radicals, on the other hand, had not only the advantage of the growing anti-southern sentiment they were building up in the North, but they had also won enormously useful support from financial and business circles. Here the fear was genuine that a revived Democratic party, composed of the old alliance of northern and southern Democrats, might if it took over the government do something to deflate the business boom that had engulfed the North during and after the war. Business leaders of this period showed none of the fear of national powers that came to characterize them later, when the specter of national regulation appeared. So far the national government had served only to aid them in their plans. They wanted, and were obtaining from the Radicals, lower internal taxes, a continuation of the high wartime tariffs, a benevolent attitude toward the holders of national bonds, a sound currency, and generous subsidies for the building of western railroads. Why risk all this by making it possible for the Democrats to return to power? The preferable policy, obviously, was to delay the course of reconstruction until the Radicals could build up in the South, on Negro votes if necessary, a Republican wing strong enough to keep the businessman's party in power.

Had Johnson remained in Washington and kept quiet during the campaign, he might have won the one-more-than-one-third in either the House or the Senate that he needed. But he essayed instead a "swing around the circle" to Chicago, where he laid the cornerstone for a monument to the late Stephen A. Douglas, and back again to Washington. His intemperate utterances to many audiences, well-advertized by a hostile press, lost rather than gained him votes, and as a result of the elections the Radicals obtained far more than the two-thirds majority they required in each house of Congress. Furthermore, a law passed during the preceding session over the President's veto required the new Congress to convene on March 4, 1867, instead of in December, as would otherwise have been the case. The new Congress would thus be on hand without delay to carry on the Radical program, which by this time was abundantly clear: (1) to impeach the President and remove him from office, and (2) to inflict on the South a new and far harsher plan of reconstruction than the one outlined for campaign purposes in the Fourteenth Amendment.

Elections of 1866

By the Tenure of Office Act, passed like so many laws over Johnson's veto, Congress had sought to lay a trap for the President. This measure, which made it a misdemeanor for the President without the consent of the Senate to remove civil office-holders whose original appointment had required Senate confirmation, was in Johnson's opinion (and later the Supreme Court's) unconstitutional, but the only way he could test it was ostensibly to violate it. For a long time Edwin M. Stanton, the Secretary of War Lincoln had appointed in part to appease the Radicals, had been a thorn in the flesh to Johnson. Finally, in defiance of the Tenure Act, the President removed Stanton from office, while Stanton, in his turn, defied the President's order, and stayed on. The Radicals, thus presented with the opportunity they had craved, acted with alacrity; the House brought the necessary impeachment charges to the Senate, and the Senate, sitting as a

Impeachment of Johnson

"THE VETO GALOP." Lithograph cover for sheet music. Louisville, 1866.

"MY POLICY." The wreck of Johnson's hopes in 1868.

IMPEACHMENT OF JOHNSON. The Senate in session. Sketch by Theodore R. Davis.

Johnson's policies of forbearance toward the South followed Lincoln's, but collided with the desires of the Radical Republicans, who wanted to chastise the vanquished and make the seceded states pay dearly for their actions. A series of vetoes of Radical measures brought retaliation in the form of a move to impeach the President. This failed, but Johnson's own policies were wrecked.

trial court with Chief Justice Chase presiding, heard the case. Since the Republicans had more than the two-thirds majority necessary for a conviction, the Radicals were confident they would win, but seven Republicans risked (and lost) their political lives to stand by the President. The case against him, as good lawyers knew, was not sound. There was grave doubt that the law was intended to apply to one of Lincoln's cabinet appointees whom Johnson had merely inherited, and that Congress had the right to limit the President's power of removal so drastically. The final vote stood 35 to 19, so by a single vote the President kept his office. The anger of the Radicals at having failed to wreak their vengeance on the President was intense, but Johnson finished out his term, and was later again elected to the Senate from Tennessee.

Meantime Congress had worked out a second and more "thorough" plan of reconstruction, which wiped out as nearly as possible everything that Lincoln and Johnson had done, and started all over again. As an

"Thorough" reconstruction

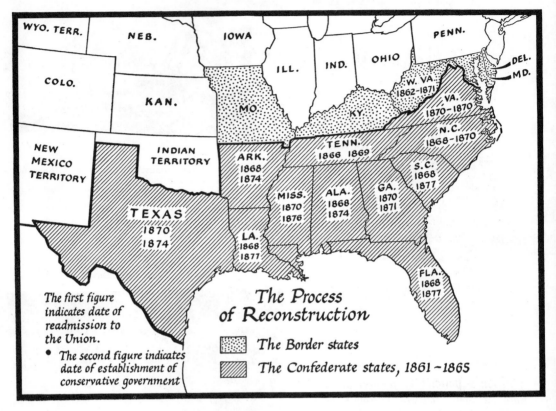

WYO. TERR.   NEB.   IOWA   PENN.
COLO.   KAN.   ILL.   IND.   OHIO   DEL.   MD.
NEW MEXICO TERRITORY   INDIAN TERRITORY   MO.   KY   W. VA. 1862-1871   VA. 1870-1870
   ARK. 1868 1874   TENN. 1866 1869   N.C. 1868-1870
   MISS. 1870 1876   ALA. 1868 1874   GA. 1870 1871   S.C. 1868 1877
TEXAS 1870 1874   LA. 1868 1877   FLA. 1868 1877

The first figure indicates date of readmission to the Union.
• The second figure indicates date of establishment of conservative government

The Process of Reconstruction

[dotted] The Border states

[hatched] The Confederate states, 1861–1865

intended rebuke to the idea of "state perdurance," Congress divided the ten states involved into five military districts, over each of which it required the President to place a general. These military officers must then call for the election of a constitutional convention in each state, to be chosen by the male citizens "of whatever race, color, or previous condition," except such as were disfranchised by the Fourteenth Amendment. The convention must then frame a constitution granting the suffrage to male citizens "of whatever race, color, or previous condition," which would then be submitted to the same electorate for ratification. If this document should be approved by the people and by Congress, the state should then hold elections, and the newly chosen legislature must ratify the Fourteenth Amendment. With this process duly completed, the state might confidently expect readmission.

The key to the new system of reconstruction was of course Negro suffrage. With numerous whites disfranchised, and with all the Negroes voting, there was **Negro suffrage** every reason to suppose that the new southern electorates would be dominantly Republican. This would hardly have been a certainty immediately after the war, for at that time the Negroes, totally untutored in politics as they were, might well have deferred to the judgment of their former masters. But in the two years since Appomattox new leaders, "carpetbaggers," "scalawags," and a few native Negroes, had arisen to teach the ex-slaves the meaning of freedom. The "carpetbaggers" were northerners who had come south as governmental agents, or as army officers, or as officials of the Freedmen's Bureau, or as religious or educational missionaries, or as agricultural, or business, or political adventurers seeking new worlds to conquer. They were as a rule fully imbued with the Radical point of view, and many of them were members of the Union League, which, now that the war was over, took as its principal duty the political indoctrination of the Negroes. The "scalawags" were southern whites, or northerners long resident in the South, who for the most part were motivated by hope of office or of private gain. They stood ready to collaborate with the agents of "thorough" reconstruction, and to contribute to the Radical cause whatever influence they might be able to exert over the Negroes. The native Negro leaders were mostly pre-Civil War freedmen who had long occupied a recognized place in the southern social structure. They were more numerous than most northerners supposed, but they were probably less influential with the more recently freed slaves than the carpetbaggers and the scalawags, for Negro deference to white superiority was of long standing and hard to eradicate. Under the intense political pressure of this new leadership, the great mass of the Negroes tended to believe as they were taught, that the Republican party had freed them, and that to keep their freedom they must vote Republican at every opportunity. Thanks to the carefully devised provisions of the second Congressional plan and to the protective presence of Union troops in the South, the Negro often found it easier to vote as the Radicals wished him to vote than to abstain from voting.

Down to the time that the new electorates took over in 1867, reconstruction in the South had proceeded without undue tension. Military government was usually efficient in keeping order, and even when locally elected civilian officials disagreed with their military overlords, and were removed from office by them, the effect on the ordinary citizen was likely to be insignificant. The Lincoln and Johnson governments had built upon such remnants of the former secessionist governments as they found in existence, and the military authorities who administered the second Congressional plan had made similar use of the Johnson governments. But when the new constitutions were drawn and went into effect, the control of state government in the South passed from the hands of the local southern leaders into the hands of the carpetbaggers, the scalawags, and such Negroes as were able to participate. By this time the Union League had perfected a propaganda organization throughout the southern states that appealed irresistibly to the freedman, making him virtually "the emotional and intellectual slave" of the white Radicals. Regardless of the number of Negro delegates, it was the white Radicals who dominated every constitutional convention, and wrote their views into every new constitution. These included, besides complete civil and political equality for Negroes with whites, many provisions aimed at social equality, and many provisions, borrowed from northern constitutions, that greatly improved the antiquated systems of taxation and finance, and of local and judicial administration, that had prevailed in the Old South. Also, the new constitutions tended to liberalize the legal status of women, to accept the principle of protecting homesteads up to a certain minimum value against creditors, and to provide for free educational systems such as the South in slavery times had never known. For this latter innovation the Negro delegates were far more than passively responsible.

The issue of adoption or rejection of the new constitutions drew a political line in the South that had long been on the way. Before the war southern whites had divided on politics between Whigs and Democrats, or when the Whigs faded out, between Know-Nothings, or Americans, or Constitutional Unionists, and Democrats. Immediately after the war, to avoid the memory of past differences, some southerners made use of the designation Conservatives, in opposition to the Radicals, whose views they so greatly feared. But as time went on most of the southern whites tended, whatever their pre-war affiliations, to accept the Democratic label. Their best friends in the North were the Democrats, and their worst enemies everywhere were the Republicans, now almost completley dominated by the Radicals.

Conservatives vs. Radicals

Opposed to the Democratic party in the South was the carpetbagger-scalawag-Negro combination that had not only framed the new constitutions, but now also voted for their ratification, and under their provisions elected governors, legislatures, and other officials to carry on the business of government. While the terms Radicals and Conservatives long persisted in the South, Radical became virtually synonymous with Republican, and Conservative with Democrat.

The struggle to delay the day of carpetbag rule lasted longer in some of the southern states than in others, and sometimes required the direct intervention of Congress. In Alabama, for example, when the new Radical constitution failed to secure a majority of the registered voters, as the Reconstruction Act required, Congress reversed its former stand by decreeing that a majority of those voting would be sufficient. Also, to insure the general eligibility to vote of Negroes, who in the early days of freedom often wandered aimlessly from place to place, Congress decided that residence anywhere for a period of ten days prior to an election was adequate, and that, if the voter happened to have lost his certificate of registration, he might by an affidavit or "other satisfactory evidence," establish his right to cast his ballot. The first state to complete the process of "thorough" reconstruction was Arkansas, which Congress readmitted to the Union in June, 1868, and the last was Georgia, readmitted in July, 1870. All the others but three (Virginia, Mississippi, and Texas) won full restoration to the Union in time to participate in the election of 1868, and most of them cast their electoral votes for General Grant, whom the Republicans had nominated for President, and Schuyler Colfax, Republican candidate for Vice-President. Two of the reconstructed states, Louisiana and Georgia, in spite of the most valiant efforts of the Radicals, voted Democratic. It came as something of a shock to the Radicals that Grant's popular majority, which was only about 300,000, was made possible by the casting of some 450,000 Negro ballots; a majority of the nation's white voters opposed him. In an understandable effort to insure that Negro voting should not be curtailed, Congress in February, 1869, therefore submitted the Fifteenth Amendment, which forbade the states to deny or abridge the right to vote "on account of race, color, or previous condition of servitude." Furthermore, states still undergoing reconstruction must ratify this amendment as a condition of readmission. Thirteen months later the Amendment was declared in force.

In the election of 1868 the Democrats might logically have nominated President Johnson as their candidate to succeed himself, for they made **Election of 1868** his attitude toward reconstruction their own. But they passed him by for Horatio Seymour of New York, and chose for Vice-President Francis P. Blair, Jr., of Missouri. With so many southern states legislated into the Republican column, Grant won an easy triumph in the electoral college, 214 to 80, although his margin of victory in many northern states was surprisingly narrow. Democratic flirtation with the "Ohio idea," a scheme advocated by George H. Pendleton, an Ohio Democrat, for the payment of the national debt in greenbacks, failed to win Seymour's support, but tended to confirm the business world of the North in its adherence to Republican principles. By this time Grant had gone wholeheartedly over to the Radicals, and his election was expected to end the deadlock between the President and Congress, in both houses of which the Radicals retained control. Among the Republican senators and representatives there were now many carpetbaggers and scalawags, and a few Negroes. Local officials in the newly reconstructed states showed a similar distribution, with the Radical whites usually absorbing for themselves most of the important offices, and leaving only the less consequential for the Negroes.

It took Grant some time as President to adjust to the ways of the political world, and during his term of office the Presidency never at any time really offered a threat to the leadership of Congress. On recon-

Congres-
sional
supremacy

struction he was a willing tool of the legislative branch, and backed it up in every extreme. As rapidly as possible he replaced Johnson's appointees in the South with uncompromising Radicals; even the Federal judges he chose displayed unbecoming zeal in furthering the Radical cause. If the President during these years was no match for Congress, neither was the Supreme Court, which came in for severe discipline. During the war Congress had raised the number of Supreme Court justices to ten, but when a vacancy occurred under Johnson the Senate refused to confirm his appointee, while Congress, partly in retaliation for a decision the Radicals disliked — *Ex parte Milligan,* which condemned military trials where civilian courts were open for business — provided that new vacancies on the Court should not be filled until the number of justices should be reduced to seven. When Grant became President, however, Congress raised the number again to nine, with results that the famous Legal Tender Cases soon made apparent. Before Grant's appointees took office, the Supreme Court held in a split decision, *Hepburn vs. Griswold* (1870), that the Legal Tender Acts of 1862 and 1863, in so far as they concerned the fulfillment of contracts entered into *before* their passage, were unconstitutional. But the very next year the two new judges that Grant had chosen joined with the minority in the Hepburn case to reverse this decision, and to hold that the Legal Tender Acts were justifiable under the emergency powers of the government, and were therefore valid in every respect. The new decision was far more palatable to the Radicals than the one it supplanted, but the Court's quick reversal, seemingly under political pressure, of a stand it had just taken detracted seriously from its prestige.

As for the newly reconstructed governments of the southern states, they rested frankly on Federal bayonets; only the presence of Union troops, acting under the President's orders, enabled them to survive against the overwhelming majority of the native whites. Carpetbaggers and scalawags, to a greater or lesser degree, were everywhere in control; it is a complete misnomer to speak of the period as one of Negro rule. Only two states, South Carolina and Louisiana, ever had Negro majorities in their legislatures, and here as elsewhere the freedmen were dominated by their new white leaders. What the new governments did was by no means all evil. Following out the provisions of the new constitutions, they made many useful administrative innovations, and they sought also to better the lot of the ordinary man, whether Negro or white. They gave generous support to the cause of public education; they redistributed the tax burden with an eye to the welfare of the less well-to-do; they provided perhaps more amply than their resources justified for poor relief; and they replaced as rapidly as possible the public buildings, roads, and bridges that the war had left in ruins.

The worst aspect of "alien rule," as the South called the new regimes, lay in the venality of many of the white leaders who had come to power. Reconstruction governments piled up extravagant debts for later generations to deal with, and the money they borrowed far too frequently went in large part to enrich corruptionists. Faithless officials sold state and municipal bonds at a fraction of their value; they backed with public credit dubious or frankly dishonest financial enterprises, railroad and otherwise; they levied taxes upon landowners so burdensome as greatly to depreciate land values; and they often showed as great disdain for personal as for property rights. Some of the states organized Negro militia, which in general served more to promote than to quell violence and disorder. But blame for the excesses of Radical reconstruction rests far less upon the Negroes than upon the white carpetbaggers and scalawags who misled them, and upon the Congressional majority in Washington that sponsored the system.

Now then Jim—
No jockeying you know!

LET EM RIP
COMMODORE—!
BUT DONT STOP TO
WATER OR YOU'LL BE
BEAT

HUDSON RIVER R.R.

N.Y. CENTRAL R.R.

ERIE R.R.

COMMODORE VANDERBILT AND JIM FISK. The race to link east and midwest. Currier and Ives, 1870.

Corruption was rampant under Grant's administration, though he himself was never deliberately involved. Graft in politics, in the Indian service, in government salaries, the "Whiskey Ring," and in railroad building made this perhaps the most lurid era in our national history.

"STONE WALLS DO NOT A PRISON MAKE." Cartoon of Boss Tweed, *Harper's Weekly*, January 6, 1872.

Let us have peace.

Let us have a piece.

Let us have a piece.

Let us have a piece.

GOVERNMENT CAKE.

"A NICE FAMILY PARTY." The Grant scandals. Currier and Ives, 1872.

The freedmen, encouraged by their new leaders to believe

De bottom rail's on de top,
An' we's gwine to keep it dar,

eventually found themselves at the bottom again, and obliged to pay a heavy penalty for the misdeeds of others. Negro legislators and officials were sometimes guilty of ridiculous and child-like behavior, but these faults were of little moment in comparison with the very real crimes of those who betrayed them.

In extenuation, if the term is not too generous, it should be said that the reconstruction period was one of gross corruption, North as well as South. There was little that the carpetbaggers and scalawags did that could not be duplicated elsewhere. The Tweed Ring, which operated in New York City during the very years that Radical reconstruction was doing its worst in the South, took from the taxpayers of the nation's greatest city an estimated $100,000,000 in loot. The scandals of the Grant administration were similarly devastating. The "gold conspiracy," engineered by Jay Gould and Jim Fisk, two unprincipled business buccaneers, involved President Grant himself, whom Gould persuaded to stop the regular sales of govern-

Northern corruption

ment gold. Since the currency of the time consisted of depreciated greenbacks and national bank notes, worth far less than their value in gold, the latter, in terms of paper money, sold at a considerable premium, by 1869, when the "conspiracy" occurred, about 140 to 100. For certain necessary transactions, such as the payment of customs duties and the settlement of international trade balances, only gold would serve, hence when the conspirators were able to corner the privately-owned gold supply, they managed to drive the price from 140 to $163\frac{1}{2}$, thus making a tremendous profit. Eventually Grant, who was innocent of intentional wrong-doing, permitted the sale of government gold, but not until a disastrous panic had gripped the stock-market, and brought heavy losses to many legitimate businesses. There was a scandal, too, connected with the Union Pacific railroad, which Congress had chartered to build the eastern half of the first great transcontinental, providing for the purpose a heavy subsidy in government lands and government bonds. The Crédit Mobilier was a construction company, which consisted of the principal Union Pacific stockholders. As Union Pacific stockholders they voted the Crédit Mobilier, which they also owned, enormously profitable contracts, but to insure that the government subsidies would keep coming they offered Crédit Mobilier stock to members of Congress on bargain terms. Many prominent Congressmen, and the Vice-President also, accepted this ill-concealed bribe. A similar company, organized by the Central Pacific railroad, which was charged with the building of the western half of the same transcontinental, was equally fraudulent, but did not involve members of Congress. The new road to the Pacific, completed in 1869, was a great asset to the nation, but the profits taken by its builders were notoriously excessive.

These were only a beginning; there were others, such as the Sanborn contracts, by which the Treasury Department allowed a fifty per cent commission to a favored contractor for the collection of back taxes; and the Whiskey Ring, which defrauded the government of millions of dollars in excise taxes on liquor; and the Salary Grab Act, by which Congress in March, 1873, voted its members an additional $2500 a year, with back pay for two years; and wholesale graft in the Indian service, where, for example, one Indian trader who was making a good thing of his post sought to keep it by paying a stipulated sum each year to the wife of the Secretary of War. And it may be safely assumed that for every fraud exposed many others occurred that were never made public, while for every dishonest act that involved government there were hundreds that did not. Thus the crimes committed by the reconstruction governments in the South were quite in keeping with the peculations that so generally disgraced the times. There was this difference, however. The South was being victimized to a large extent by outsiders, and the resentment its people felt was the greater because the misdeeds were associated with "alien rule."

Republican hopes of building up in the seceded states a new and dependable wing of the party were soon doomed **The Ku** to disappointment. The first **Klux Klan** substantial successes of the southern opponents of Congressional reconstruction came with the activities of the Ku Klux Klan, a secret order that grew up in the South after the war, and made its influence felt by vigilante methods. Members of the Klan wore white gowns and hoods which both concealed their identity and struck terror to the hearts of the superstitious Negroes. Operating mainly at night, gangs of Klansmen beat up Negro militiamen, terrorized freedmen who had the temerity to vote, broke up Union League meetings, and committed innumerable other depredations aimed in general at alien rule. The Klan was widely imitated by similar orders, and its method of disguise was freely utilized by bands of ruffians who belonged to no order and knew no restraint — whippings, fiendish torture, and outright murder, particularly of Negroes, became all too common. Alarmed at these excesses, the

Klan leaders sought as early as 1869 to disband the order, but they had little control over the forces they had unleashed, and Congress felt obliged to take a hand. A series of Enforcement Acts, passed in 1870 and 1871, condemned as crimes the various activities for which the Klan and its imitators were held responsible, and provided drastic punishments for their perpetrators. Grant enforced these laws ruthlessly, even suspending the writ of *habeas corpus* in certain areas, as Congress had authorized him to do, and using Federal troops to see that Federal courts were unmolested because of unpopular decisions. As a consequence, vigilante activities diminished greatly, but the Negro votes on which the reconstruction governments depended were thereafter far less certain to be cast. Congress also appointed a committee, generally known as the Ku Klux Committee, to investigate what was going on in the South. This Committee through extensive hearings not only succeeded in revealing the iniquities of those who opposed the will of Congress in the South, but also, quite unintentionally, brought to light the complaints of the southerners. Widely publicized in the newspapers, and printed eventually in twelve large volumes, the hearings brought home to northerners, almost for the first time, the true plight of the South under carpetbag and scalawag rule, and prepared the way for reform.

Gradually, even with Federal troops standing guard, the native whites of the South who opposed Radical reconstruction began to take over. This "redemption movement," as it is sometimes called, found ways short of physical violence to persuade the Negroes not to vote; trickery, bribery, and economic pressure proved in many cases to be quite as effective as physical intimidation, and Negro ballots were not always counted. Radical propaganda among the Negroes, which had depended so much on unfulfilled promises, also wore thin, and the southern Radicals, sensing that their day was about done, fell

The redemption movement

to quarreling among themselves. Of great aid to the redemption movement was the growing demand in the North for a more generous treatment of the defeated South. Even Congress felt obliged in 1872 to pass an Amnesty Act, which restored the voting privileges of nearly all ex-Confederates. Thereafter in state after state the Democrats took over the offices from the Republicans, made life so uncomfortable for the carpetbaggers that most of them got out, absorbed great numbers of scalawags into the "white man's party," and ended the political importance of the Negro vote. Federal troops might hold off this eventuality for a time, but not indefinitely, and their removal invariably meant the doom of alien rule. The "solid South" at which the Radicals had connived did indeed materialize, but it turned out to be a Democratic, not a Republican, "solid South."

Unfortunately for the idea of permanent solidarity, many of the leaders of the redemption movement had other objectives than merely the restoration of home rule and white supremacy in the South. Some of them were primarily interested in the promotion of industry and commerce, and as former Henry Clay Whigs, looked forward eagerly to cooperating with northern capitalists in such profitable enterprises as the construction of new railroads and the building up of southern manufactures. Once in power they showed as little regard for the less-well-to-do whites as for the now disfranchised Negroes; they cheerfully lowered the taxes that the Radicals had levied to support better school systems and other social services; they allowed the southern school term to fall off in length by twenty per cent; and they showed little concern that illiteracy, which had begun to decline, tended as a result of their policies to increase steadily until the beginning of the twentieth century. They also promoted state constitutional changes that substituted easily-controlled appointive for elective officials, and they gerrymandered election districts in such a way as to reduce materially

The New Departure

the representation of the poorer white farming communities. Simultaneously they gave railroads and other business enterprises preferential treatment, including especially low taxes and freedom from state regulation. This business-minded movement, which some called "The New Departure," greatly disturbed many southerners, and paved the way for a vigorous protest later on; but the appearance of unity was long maintained out of deference to the real, or fancied, need for white solidarity.

When time came for the election of 1872, the opposition to Radical reconstruction that had long permeated the Democratic party had reached over also into Republican ranks. There the reformers, in order to distinguish themselves from the Radicals, adopted the designation "Liberals," and even threatened to leave the Republican party altogether if they could not convert it to their point of view. The Liberal movement began in Missouri as an attack on the rabidly anti-southern provisions of a state constitution adopted in 1865, and in the elections of 1870 it won substantial victories. Many prominent citizens helped to make Liberal Republicanism national, among them Carl Schurz, who became United States Senator from Missouri, Horace Greeley, editor of the powerful New York *Tribune*, and Charles Francis Adams, Lincoln's minister to Great Britain during the Civil War. With some Liberals, opposition to "Grantism" went much further than mere denunciation of the administration's southern policy. Civil service reformers hoped for the day when appointments would be made on merit, and tariff reformers were determined that through Liberal auspices they should scale down the unreasonably high protective duties that had lasted on after the Civil War. A good many Liberals, moreover, were opposed to the increasing and often corrupt connection between big business and government, and hoped for the end of government subservience to business.

Unable to dent the hard shell of Radical Republicanism, the Liberals determined in the election of 1872 to go it alone, with such Democratic support as they could muster. But the convention they held in Cincinnati, May 1, 1872, unfortunately chose Horace Greeley as their candidate for the Presidency, a mistake little rectified by the nomination of the relatively unknown B. Gratz Brown of Missouri for Vice-President. Greeley was a firm believer in high tariffs, and to please him the Liberal tariff plank had to be made thoroughly innocuous; further, he was a life-long enemy of the Democratic party, for the support of which the Liberals meant to bid. He had, to be sure, signed Jefferson Davis's bail bond, when the former President of the Confederacy was under arrest for treason, and he had been outspoken in his criticism of Radical reconstruction. And so the Democrats, with what grace they could muster, accepted the Liberal Republican candidates as their own, and endorsed the Liberal platform, which on the treatment of the defeated South echoed views they had long expressed. The Republicans, of course, renominated Grant, but they dropped Colfax for second place on the ticket in favor of Henry Wilson of Massachusetts. At the time of the election most of the scandals that were later to be associated with the Grant regime had not yet come to light, and there were still those who believed that "To doubt Grant is to doubt Christ." Moreover, Greeley's many idiosyncracies made him an easy target for Republican campaigners, and for the Republican cartoonist, Thomas Nast, who heaped every ridicule upon him. In the election Greeley carried only two states from the lower South, Georgia and Texas (Congress rejected the Democratic returns from Arkansas and Louisiana), and four border states, Missouri, Tennessee, Maryland, and Kentucky. Three weeks afterward Greeley died, and the Liberal Republican party he had headed lasted little longer. What the election results might have been had the Liberals and the Democrats united on a suitable candidate, one can only guess, but undoubtedly many disappointed adherents of both factions failed to vote.

Election of 1872

Pressure on Negroes to prevent them from voting was common throughout the South. "I shall discharge every nigger who votes to adopt this Radical Yankee Constitution" was the caption of this newspaper sketch by V. Karst.

Despite this Republican triumph, Radical reconstruction was soon on the rocks. The **Election of 1876** Grant scandals began to come out, one after another, to the great chagrin of even the most devoted Republicans. Worse still, the Panic of 1873 dried up the abounding prosperity that the North, if not the South, had enjoyed since the war, and for five long years hard times gripped the nation. In the mid-term elections of 1874 the Democrats scored notable victories, winning the ascendancy in nine northern and five southern states, and taking easy control of the national House of Representatives. Fearful of a complete Democratic triumph in 1876, the agonized Republican leaders sought to draw the Liberals back into the party ranks by nominating for the Presidency that year a moderate of unimpeachable integrity, Rutherford B. Hayes, three times governor of Ohio; while the Democrats, equally desirous of attracting Liberal voters, chose the man who had done most to break up the Tweed Ring in New York, Governor Samuel J. Tilden. As the votes came in, it appeared that Tilden had scored an easy victory, but double returns from three southern states, South Carolina, Louisiana, and Florida — the last three in which Federal troops were still stationed — enabled the Republicans to claim victory for Hayes, 185 to 184, in spite of a Tilden majority in the popular vote of about 250,000. Eventually the Republicans succeeded in counting their man in, but the House of Representatives remained Democratic, and the new President, early in 1877, whether in response to the trend of the times, or because of a deal that enabled him to take office unopposed, or both, removed the Federal troops from the three states without whose votes he could not possibly have won. By this time a Democratic administration had already taken over in Florida, and the withdrawal of Federal troops ended Republican rule in South Carolina and Louisiana — when the troops moved out, Democratic state officials moved in without a struggle. The year 1877 can therefore be taken as the end of military and political reconstruction, including, for most of the South, Negro suffrage. As for the civil discriminations forbidden by the Fourteenth Amendment, the Supreme Court in the Civil Rights cases ruled six years later that only the states, and not individuals, were so restrained; discriminations of every sort or kind, provided only that they were the work of individuals and not of a state, were not to be regarded as illegal. Thus after many years of turmoil and controversy, the status of the Negro settled down to about where it had been under the Johnson governments of 1865, while the greatly-desired southern wing of the Republican party existed only in shadow rather than in substance.

Important as political reconstruction was, the average southerner was no doubt far

Economic reconstruction more interested in the problems of economic reconstruction. The war had dealt heavy blows to the South; huge armies had surged back and forth within its borders, burned many of its cities, laid waste untold acres of farm land, disrupted communications, paralyzed normal business relationships, and demoralized economic life generally. The wholesale destruction wrought by war is a commonplace of twentieth century history, but not for centuries before the American Civil War had any part of the western world done itself such stupendous damage. In addition there was the colossal loss of life that the South had suffered — not less than a quarter of a million men — to say nothing of the probably far larger number who had suffered irreparable damage to mind and body, but lived on as a burden to themselves and to society. Above and beyond that was what had happened to the Negroes, approximately one-third of the population of the South. By the Emancipation Proclamation and the Thirteenth Amendment they had ceased to be property, an economic loss to their owners for which there was no compensation. But they were still there, if only they could be taught to work as free men. Without the labor of the Negroes the South could hardly hope to resume its place in the national economy; but the Negro labor problem involved was baffling in the extreme. Many of the ex-slaves had little thought but to "enjoy their freedom," which to their naive minds meant primarily freedom from work.

As if all this were not enough, substantial confiscations of southern property accom-

Confiscation panied or followed the war. All the savings that southern investors had put into Confederate bonds, or into state securities floated to aid the southern cause, were irretrievably lost. The efforts of United States Treasury agents to seize all property that had belonged to the extinct Confederate government also cost many private individuals heavily, for these agents made little distinction between public and private property, and took everything they could get their hands on, particularly cotton, which the Confederacy had supposedly held in large quantity. The small amounts turned over to the Federal Treasury from these seizures by no means measured their extent, for Treasury agents were notably corrupt, and kept most of the loot for themselves. What they did under semblance of law, others did on their own. According to Johnson's Secretary of the Treasury, Hugh McCulloch, "lawless men, singly and in organized bands, engaged in general plunder; every species of intrigue and peculation and theft were resorted to." Fortunately land confiscations, although repeatedly threatened, were in practice not very extensive. Lincoln virtually ignored the Confiscation Act of 1862, which called for the seizure of all "rebel" property, while Johnson in his amnesty proclamation of May, 1865, declared such seizures at an end. But confiscations of land did take place, both by order of commanders in the field during the war, and by Treasury agents at its close. The reasons given were that the owners had forfeited their land because they had aided the Confederacy, or that they had abandoned it, or that they must surrender it to satisfy the unpaid direct tax that the Federal government had levied on the states at the beginning of the war. The Freedmen's Bureau, which under its grant of power from Congress took over the administration of all such land, actually acquired only about 800,000 acres, a comparatively small amount. Furthermore, Johnson's Attorney-General ruled that a presidential pardon carried with it the return of confiscated property, while later the Courts sometimes gave to the heirs of the original owners title to such land, citing the Constitutional provision that "no attainder of treason shall work corruption of blood, or forfeiture except during the lifetime of the person attainted." But if private owners did not in fact lose much land, they suffered much from the uncertainties of Federal policy, and from the depressing effect it had on land values.

Aid to the prostrate South from the prosperous North would have been the best **Federal aid** investment the nation could have made, but in this respect the nineteenth century differed markedly from the twentieth. What the United States and the United Nations have done for the defeated and devastated people of the world since the Second World War was a virtual impossibility in the 1860's, for *laissez-faire* philosophy still dominated economic thought, and the people of the South, as individuals, were expected to work out their own destinies. This is not to say that nothing whatever was done by the North for the South. The armies of occupation, undesirable to southerners as they might seem, brought much-needed money to the South, and soldier generosity provided many persons of both races with food, clothing, and shelter. Negro troops, numerous in the South at the end of the war, were particularly generous in helping their own people, but their presence gave such offense to southern whites that by the end of 1866, on the advice of General Grant, they were practically all removed. Army activities, such as the restoration of essential railroads, the replacement of destroyed bridges, and the clearing of waterways, did much toward providing the South with a normal system of transportation.

Among the most important of the northern contributions to southern recovery was the Freedmen's Bureau, which, despite many proved irregularities on the part of its agents, accepted during the first hard years the chief responsibility for relief of the needy, both white and black. It aided liberally efforts to educate the freedmen; tried to help them solve the problem of unemployment; supervised the contracts under which they went to work; and sometimes placed them on the confiscated or abandoned land it administered. Unfortunately this latter process helped along a rumor, started probably by soldiers in the Union army, that the government intended to give each freedman "forty acres and a mule." There was far more foundation for this idea than idle gossip. Thaddeus Stevens, for example, advocated earnestly that Congress confiscate the lands of all Confederates owning more than two hundred acres, and use them for distribution among the freedmen in forty acre plots, as well as for sale to help pay pensions and to reduce the national debt. Many Negroes, awaiting the glad day when they would have their own land, were persuaded only with difficulty to go to work on any other terms. But the number of Radicals who were prepared to support the Stevens program was comparatively few; most of them cherished strong views as to the sanctity of private property, and were unwilling in any way to undermine the legal conceptions that protected it. Federal aid in the form of buying up land for use in enabling the more capable Negroes to become independent farm owners might have paid off well, but the idea scarcely crossed the minds of the makers of reconstruction policy. Most of them thought they were doing enough in trying to fit the ex-slaves to become free laborers and voters.

The role of northern benevolence in providing assistance to the South should not be ignored. Religious and humanitarian groups of great diversity **Northern benevolence** raised funds to promote Negro education, and sent many northern schoolteachers and missionaries into the South. All such help was eagerly welcomed by the Freedmen's Bureau, which gave protection to the newcomers, provided quarters in which they could teach, and actually met most of their educational expenses out of its own funds. When religious workers from the North found that the reunion of northern and southern wings of their denominations was all but impossible, they tended to encourage the freedmen to form separate churches of their own, and so began the process of religious segregation. Individual northerners, such as George Peabody, who set up the Peabody Education Fund for "the suffering South," contributed significantly to work among both Negroes and whites. The interest of the freedmen in education was touching in the extreme; this was one of the ways in which they most obviously differed from the whites, and many of them thought that through it lay the route toward greater equality.

What the South needed most to promote recovery was capital, and that the Federal **Southern self-help** government might have provided directly, or by giving suitable encouragement to private investors. But the hatreds engendered by the war, coupled with the prevailing adherence to *laissez-faire* views, made any such program impossible. The South was therefore left to go it alone as best it could. Northern investors did help some, particularly with railroads, but there was abundant opportunity for northern capital in the North, and most of it stayed there. The South, to restore its agricultural economy, needed cotton-seed, tools, farm animals, machinery, and enough credit to make possible mere survival while production got under way. By borrowing on whatever terms they could get, and by securing advances from prospective purchasers, both European and American, southern planters made slow but steady progress. A decade and a half after the war the production of cotton was back to pre-war levels, with other crops, particularly tobacco, showing similar improvement. Many southerners, however, as already noted, were less interested in the restoration of agriculture than in the promotion of industry. Northern industry, they reasoned correctly, had played a principal part in the defeat of the South; to be strong again the South must imitate its conquerors. Soon cotton and tobacco were not only grown but also processed, while as fast as capital could be found for the purpose the abundant natural resources of the South in lumber, coal, and iron began to be exploited.

The development of a labor system to replace slavery was perhaps the hardest of the problems the South had to solve. Despairing of ever getting the Negroes back to work, some southerners toyed **The labor problem** with the idea of sending them back to Africa or to the West Indies, and obtaining a new labor supply through immigration. But there were no facilities, legal or otherwise, for Negro deportation, and European immigrants preferred the prosperous North to the shattered South. Talk of importing Chinese coolies likewise came to nothing, although actually a few Chinese were used in the canefields of Louisiana and in railroad construction. The introduction of Chinese also met strong opposition in northern labor circles, and in the South itself, where sober second thought cast grave doubts upon the wisdom of thus compounding the color problem. Actually there was no alternative to getting the Negro back to work, and this eventually was accomplished. Regular wages rarely served the purpose; if the freedmen had money they saw no reason to work, and in practice it proved almost impossible to hold them to the contracts they made. Gang labor after the old plantation system also tended to fail; whether the pay was in wages or in a share of the profits, this was all too suggestive of the methods of slavery. In the end the "forty-acres-and-a mule" idea won out, although not exactly as the Negro had hoped. Experience proved that he was willing to work for a share of the crop he raised, if provided with a plot of land, a cabin to live in, a mule, a plow, the necessary seed, and food for the year. Landlords, conscious of what might happen to any food crops their tenants might raise, usually reserved the right to determine what should be planted, and in cotton-growing areas it was mainly cotton. In return for the use of the land, the tenant turned over from one-third to one-half of his crop to the landlord, and to obtain the supplies he needed he gave a lien on the rest of it to some country merchant, who might, or might not, also be the landlord. At the end of the year the sharecropper usually had nothing whatever to show for his labor, but he and his family had survived after a fashion, and could start the cycle all over again. Many impoverished whites as well as Negroes were drawn into this vicious system of near-peonage, but whatever its faults it worked, and variously modified, tended to become dominant throughout the South. Some of both races took advantage of the low price of land to buy farms of their own, but not all who bought were able to hold their land, and tenancy became the rule rather than the exception.

In dealing with the complicated problems of the South after the Civil War, it is all too **The post-** easy to overlook the North, **war North** where the industrial basis of what Lincoln called "a new nation" was being laid. The shift from a preponderant interest in agriculture to a preponderant interest in manufacturing began before the Civil War, grew phenomenally with the needs of the war, and continued unabated at its close. Naturally the dominant economic interest tended with time to rule also in politics, and to replace the old alliance between the agricultural South and the agricultural West which had controlled the nation before the war. The historian, Charles A. Beard, perhaps identifying these changes with the war itself more fully than the facts really warrant, renamed that struggle the "Second American Revolution." But if the name overstates for the war, it by no means overstates for the transformation that occurred during the Civil War and Reconstruction period. Railroads had come into their own, and the nation was united as never before by an effective transportation network. New machines had put an end to the old domestic system of manufacturing, and had made the factory system everywhere triumphant. Even agriculture had participated in the revolution, for agricultural machinery and the new means of transportation had changed its pattern from production mainly for use to production mainly for sale; the very farms themselves were on the way to becoming factories.

The contrasts between North and South at the close of the war could hardly have been more marked. All that the South lacked the North had in great abundance. Huge capital gains, piled up during the war, provided the means for further business expansion. Unlike those of the Confederacy, the debts of the United States, although contracted for the most part in depreciated paper currency, were paid in gold; not only did the lender get back far more in value than he lent, but the interest also was paid in gold. The greenbacks themselves, with the war won, rose steadily in value; thus every dollar one had was worth more, and every debt one collected, private as well as public, carried with it a neat built-in profit. The exploitation of the gold and silver mines of the Far West, so helpful to the North during the war, continued actively at its close. American credit, except for the South, was good abroad, and bankers found that they could easily float overseas such industrial loans as American investors failed to absorb. Rich natural resources added to the nation's wealth. The Old and the New Northwest furnished lumber; the Pittsburgh area furnished coal and oil; the surface mines of the Lake Superior region were the world's richest in iron-ore; and the mines of the Far West were by no means confined to the production of precious metals. Heavy industries, with a growing emphasis on steel rather than iron, turned without difficulty from manufacturing the *matériel* of war to supplying necessities for the expanding western railroads, and for the construction required to keep pace with the rapidly growing cities. Factories that had made boots and shoes, or uniforms, or blankets, or other items needed by soldiers, found an ample civilian market for the same or similar goods. The textile mills of New England, the flour mills of Minnesota, the meat-packing plants of the Middle Border, the makers of agricultural machinery in and about Chicago, these and scores of other industries participated in the northern postwar boom. Even agriculture did well; production throughout the North continued at a generally high level, and soon came to include the output of the Great Plains cattle industry. Much of this the burgeoning American economy itself was able to absorb, while the outbreak of the Bismarckian wars in Europe provided another war market to replace the one lost by the ending of the Civil War.

And yet, as already indicated, the business cycle was still at work; the Panic of 1873 **Panic and depression** ended the boom and began the depression. Excessive railroad building, particularly in unsettled portions of the West where a population adequate to pay the necessary rates did not yet exist, bore much of the blame, but by no means all, for overexpansion was general. Business confidence, shattered with the failure of the great banking firm of J. Cooke and Company in September, 1873, did not return fully for the next five years, while agriculture, with production mounting and the world market declining, was also in serious trouble. Throughout the "dreadful decade" of the seventies unemployment was rife, labor difficulties were frequent, farmer protests rose loud and long, despair and discouragement were the order of the day. But as usual the prophets of doom were not to have it all their own way for long. By 1879 the evidence of returning prosperity was overwhelming, both in industry and in agriculture, and the nation soon began to resume its normal economic behavior. By this time, too, the South, with a "new South" devoted to industry, had begun to add to the national economy rather than to subtract from it. The excesses of reconstruction were over, and home rule had replaced alien rule. Even so, it would take time, much time, before the once seceded states could see eye to eye with the rest of the Union on the civil and political rights of the Negro, or could feel themselves full partners in the new nation.

So absorbed were most Americans in their domestic problems that they possibly took **Diplomatic reconstruction** less interest in foreign affairs than the facts now seem to justify. There was a significant diplomatic aspect to reconstruction. While the nation was divided, its strength in dealing with foreign countries was seriously curtailed; it could not even prevent the outright challenge to the Monroe Doctrine of French intervention in Mexico. But at the close of the war, with the American army and navy among the strongest in the world, and with 50,000 Union troops under General Sheridan poised ominously on the Mexican border, the protests that the American State Department had merely voiced before took on a more commanding tone. Also, Napoleon III could now no longer ignore the progress of Prussian aggression in Europe, and needed all his troops at home. So when Secretary Seward delivered an ultimatum in February, 1866, demanding the withdrawal of French forces from Mexico, the results were as satisfactory as they had been previously unsatisfactory. By the spring of 1867 the French were out of Mexico, leaving their puppet, Maximilian I, to face a Mexican firing squad. Later, had President Grant had his way, he might have gone further, and turned the Monroe Doctrine into an instrument of aggression by absorbing Santo Domingo, where the Spanish had sought unsuccessfully during the Civil War to resume their sway. But happily his efforts were frustrated by Charles Sumner, Chairman of the Senate Committee on Foreign Relations, who blocked ratification of the necessary treaty of annexation.

The reconstruction era, however, did witness significant additions to the territory of the United States. Secretary Seward, who was as ardent an expansionist as Grant, had in his time sought but failed to acquire the Danish West Indies. But he was completely successful in obtaining Alaska from Russia by a treaty signed early in 1867. The purchase price for "Seward's Folly," as the new territory was sometimes called, $7,200,000, seemed to many excessive, and the House of Representatives might not have passed the necessary appropriation bill except for the activities of the Russian Minister to the United States, Baron Edoard de Stoeckl, who influenced certain House members by bribery. What the history of the United States and the world might have been in the twentieth century had Alaska remained a part of Russia, one may only surmise. It is also worth noting that the Midway Islands, which an American sea captain had discovered in 1859, were officially occupied in 1867.

The most important diplomatic stroke of the period in the eyes of contemporaries was **Treaty of Washington** no doubt the settlement of the claims by the United States against Great Britain, arising from alleged British laxness in enforcing the duties of a neutral during the war. By the Treaty of Washington, signed in 1871, the British government agreed to submit to arbitration the *Alabama* Claims, so-called, which the United States demanded as compensation for the

damages done to American shipping by certain Confederate commerce destroyers that had operated during the war from British ports. As a result an international tribunal of arbitration, meeting at Geneva, Switzerland, in 1872, awarded the United States the sum of $15,500,000, which the British government paid. Also, under the terms of the Treaty of Washington, other outstanding differences between the two nations were settled amicably. The United States had as yet no premonition of the role it was to play later in international affairs, but it had shown the strength it needed to deal with the problems it then faced, and it had reinforced the already significant precedent for the settlement short of war of all diplomatic differences with Great Britain.

Bibliography

Probably the best single volume on the postwar South is E. M. Coulter, *The South during Reconstruction, 1865–1877* (1947), but many older volumes continue to be useful, among them J. G. Randall, *The Civil War and Reconstruction* (1937); W. L. Fleming, *The Sequel of Appomattox* (1919); W. A. Dunning, *Reconstruction, Political and Economic* (1907); Claude G. Bowers, *The Tragic Era* (1929); and George Fort Milton, *The Age of Hate* (1930). There are many good books dealing with various aspects of political reconstruction such as Charles H. McCarthy, *Lincoln's Plan of Reconstruction* (1901); Howard K. Beale, *The Critical Year; a Study of Andrew Johnson and Reconstruction* (1930); C. H. Coleman, *The Election of 1868* (1933); R. W. Winston, *Andrew Johnson, Plebeian and Patriot* (1928); L. P. Stryker, *Andrew Johnson* (1929); R. N. Current, *Old Thad Stevens* (1942); W. B. Hesseltine, *Ulysses S. Grant, Politician* (1935); E. D. Ross, *The Liberal Republican Movement* (1919); T. S. Barclay, *The Liberal Republican Movement in Missouri, 1865–1871* (1926); Glyndon C. Van Deusen, *Horace Greeley, Nineteenth Century Crusader* (1953); and Malcolm Moos, *The Republicans* (1956).

There are numerous state histories of reconstruction, some far better than others. Among

the best is F. B. Simkins and R. H. Woody, *South Carolina during Reconstruction* (1932), which is far sounder than James Pike, *The Prostrate State: South Carolina under Negro Government* (1874, new ed., 1935). Louisiana, like South Carolina, played a colorful part in reconstruction, and has been fortunate in its historians: Willie Malvin Caskey, *Secession and Restoration of Louisiana* (1938); Ella Lonn, *Reconstruction in Louisiana after 1868* (1918); G. W. McGinty, *Louisiana Redeemed: the Overthrow of Carpetbag Rule, 1876–1880* (1941); and of especial merit, Roger W. Shugg, *Origins of Class Struggle in Louisiana: a Social History of White Farmers during Slavery and after, 1840–1875* (1939). The somewhat unusual situation in Tennessee is taken care of adequately by C. R. Hall *Andrew Johnson, Military Governor of Tennessee* (1916); J. W. Patton, *Unionism and Reconstruction in Tennessee* (1934); E. M. Coulter, *William G. Brownlow, Fighting Parson of the Southern Highlands* (1937); and Thomas B. Alexander, *Political Reconstruction in Tennessee* (1950). Other state histories worth mentioning are H. J. Eckenrode, *Political History of Virginia during Reconstruction* (1904); Charles H. Ambler, *Francis H. Pierpont, Union War Governor of Virginia and Father of West Virginia* (1937); J. G. de R. Hamilton, *Reconstruction in North Carolina* (1914); E. M. Coulter, *Civil War and Readjustment in Kentucky* (1926); W. W. Davis, *The Civil War and Reconstruction in Florida* (1913); W. L. Fleming, *Civil War and Reconstruction in Alabama* (1905, new ed., 1949); C. M. Thompson, *Reconstruction in Georgia, Economic, Social, Political, 1865–1872* (1915); J. W. Garner, *Reconstruction in Mississippi* (1901); T. S. Staples, *Reconstruction in Arkansas* (1923); and C. W. Ramsdell, *Reconstruction in Texas* (1910).

On the special problems of the Negro, the best general treatment is John Hope Franklin, *From Slavery to Freedom* (1947), but there is also much of value in F. B. Simkins, *The South Old and New, 1820–1947* (1947). W. E. B. DuBois, *Black Reconstruction* (1935), is full of understandable bitterness. Other useful studies are V. L. Wharton, *The Negro in Mississippi, 1865–1900* (1947); W. F. Nowlin, *The Negro in American National Politics* (1931); Charles S. Johnson, *The Negro in American Civilization* (1930); J. C. Furnas, *Goodbye to Uncle Tom* (1956); Kenneth M. Stampp, *The Peculiar Institution* (1956); and three books by A. A. Taylor, *The Negro in the Reconstruction of Virginia* (1926); *The Negro in South Carolina during Reconstruction* (1924); and *The Negro in Tennessee, 1865–1880* (1941). On the work of the Freedmen's Bureau, see P. S. Peirce, *The Freedmen's Bureau* (1904); Laura J. Webster, *The Operation of the Freedmen's Bureau in South Carolina* (1916); and George R. Bentley, *A History of the Freedmen's Bureau* (1955). On the problem of Negro education, see Henry Lee Swint, *The Northern Teacher in the South, 1862–1870* (1941); and E. W. Knight, *The Influence of Reconstruction on Education in the South* (1913). On the Ku Klux

Klan there are many books, but possibly the best are S. L. Davis, *Authentic History, Ku Klux Klan, 1865–1877* (1924); and S. F. Horn, *Invisible Empire: the Story of the Ku Klux Klan* (1939).

On the social and economic aspects of reconstruction an old book, M. B. Hammond, *The Cotton Industry* (1897), is still useful, and may be supplemented by the still older Charles Nordhoff, *The Cotton States in the Spring and Summer of 1875* (1876), a contemporary study. Holland Thompson, *The New South* (1919), features the introduction of industry. Paul H. Buck, *The Road to Reunion, 1865–1900* (1937), deals with the prolonged difficulties in allaying intersectional dislikes. C. Vann Woodward, in two excellent books, introduces the post-reconstruction era, *Reunion and Reaction* (1951); and *Origins of the New South, 1877–1913* (1951). Allan Nevins, *The Emergence of Modern America, 1865–1878* (1927), concerns both North and South; and Thomas C. Cochran and William Miller, *The Age of Enterprise* (1942), gives a good picture of the rise of industry. On financial subjects, see Henrietta M. Larson, *Jay Cooke, Private Banker* (1936); M. S. Wildman, *Money Inflation in the United States* (1905); W. C. Mitchell, *History of the Greenbacks* (1903); and Frederick Lewis Allen, *The Great Pierpont Morgan* (1949).

On reconstruction diplomacy, Allan Nevins, *Hamilton Fish: the Inner History of the Grant Administration* (1936), is extremely illuminating. This may be supplemented by E. D. Adams, *Great Britain and the American Civil War* (2 vols., 1925); C. F. Adams, *Charles Francis Adams* (1900); and S. F. Bemis (ed.), *The American Secretaries of State and their Diplomacy* (10 vols., 1927–29), VII.

APPENDIX

THE DECLARATION OF INDEPENDENCE

In Congress, July 4, 1776,

THE UNANIMOUS DECLARATION OF THE THIRTEEN UNITED STATES OF AMERICA.

WHEN, in the course of human events, it becomes necessary for one people to dissolve the political bands which have connected them with another, and to assume, among the powers of the earth, the separate and equal station to which the laws of nature and of nature's God entitle them, a decent respect to the opinions of mankind requires that they should declare the causes which impel them to the separation.

We hold these truths to be self-evident, that all men are created equal; that they are endowed by their Creator with certain unalienable rights; that among these, are life, liberty, and the pursuit of happiness. That, to secure these rights, governments are instituted among men, deriving their just powers from the consent of the governed; that, whenever any form of government becomes destructive of these ends, it is the right of the people to alter or to abolish it, and to institute a new government, laying its foundation on such principles, and organizing its powers in such form, as to them shall seem most likely to effect their safety and happiness. Prudence, indeed, will dictate that governments long established, should not be changed for light and transient causes; and, accordingly, all experience hath shown, that mankind are more disposed to suffer, while evils are sufferable, than to right themselves by abolishing the forms to which they are accustomed. But, when a long train of abuses and usurpations, pursuing invariably the same object, evinces a design to reduce them under absolute despotism, it is their right, it is their duty, to throw off such government and to provide new guards for their future security. Such has been the patient sufferance of these colonies, and such is now the necessity which constrains them to alter their former systems of government. The history of the present King of Great Britain is a history of repeated injuries and usurpations, all having, in direct object, the establishment of an absolute tyranny over these States. To prove this, let facts be submitted to a candid world: —

He has refused his assent to laws the most wholesome and necessary for the public good.

He has forbidden his governors to pass laws of immediate and pressing importance, unless suspended in their operation till his assent should be obtained; and, when so suspended, he has utterly neglected to attend to them.

He has refused to pass other laws for the accommodation of large districts of people, unless those people would relinquish the right of representation in the legislature; a right inestimable to them, and formidable to tyrants only.

He has called together legislative bodies at places unusual, uncomfortable, and distant from the depository of their public records, for the sole purpose of fatiguing them into compliance with his measures.

He has dissolved representative houses repeatedly for opposing, with manly firmness, his invasions on the rights of the people.

He has refused, for a long time after such dissolutions, to cause others to be elected; whereby the legislative powers, incapable of annihilation, have returned to the people at large for their exercise; the state remaining, in the meantime, exposed to all the danger of invasion from without, and convulsions within.

He has endeavored to prevent the population of these States; for that purpose, obstructing the laws for naturalization of foreigners, refusing to pass others to encourage their migration hither, and raising the conditions of new appropriations of lands.

He has obstructed the administration of justice, by refusing his assent to laws for establishing judiciary powers.

He has made judges dependent on his will alone, for the tenure of their offices, and the amount and payment of their salaries.

He has erected a multitude of new offices, and sent hither swarms of officers to harass our people, and eat out their substance.

He has kept among us, in time of peace, standing armies, without the consent of our legislatures.

He has affected to render the military independent of, and superior to, the civil power.

He has combined, with others, to subject us to a jurisdiction foreign to our Constitution, and unacknowledged by our laws; giving his assent to their acts of pretended legislation:

For quartering large bodies of armed troops among us:

For protecting them by a mock trial, from punishment, for any murders which they should commit on the inhabitants of these States:

For cutting off our trade with all parts of the world:

For imposing taxes on us without our consent:

For depriving us, in many cases, of the benefit of trial by jury:

For transporting us beyond seas to be tried for pretended offences:

For abolishing the free system of English laws in a neighboring province, establishing therein an arbitrary government, and enlarging its boundaries, so as to render it at once an example and fit instrument for introducing the same absolute rule into these colonies:

For taking away our charters, abolishing our most valuable laws, and altering, fundamentally, the powers of our governments:

For suspending our own legislatures, and declaring themselves invested with power to legislate for us in all cases whatsoever.

He has abdicated government here, by declaring us out of his protection, and waging war against us.

He has plundered our seas, ravaged our coasts, burnt our towns, and destroyed the lives of our people.

He is, at this time, transporting large armies of foreign mercenaries to complete the works of death, desolation, and tyranny, already begun, with circumstances of cruelty and perfidy scarcely paralleled in the most barbarous ages, and totally unworthy the head of a civilized nation.

He has constrained our fellow citizens, taken captive on the high seas, to bear arms against their country, to become the executioners of their friends, and brethren, or to fall themselves by their hands.

He has excited domestic insurrections amongst us, and has endeavored to bring on the inhabitants of our frontiers, the merciless Indian savages, whose known rule of warfare is an undistinguished destruction of all ages, sexes, and conditions.

In every stage of these oppressions, we have petitioned for redress, in the most humble terms; our repeated petitions have been answered only by repeated injury. A prince, whose character is thus marked by every act which may define a tyrant, is unfit to be the ruler of a free people.

Nor have we been wanting in attention to our British brethren. We have warned them, from time to time, of attempts made by their legislature to extend an unwarrantable jurisdiction over us. We have reminded them of the circumstances of our emigration and settlement here. We have appealed to their native justice and magnanimity, and we have conjured them, by the ties of our common kindred, to disavow these usurpations, which would inevitably interrupt our connections and correspondence. They, too, have been deaf to the voice of justice and consanguinity. We must, therefore, acquiesce in the necessity which denounces our separation, and hold them, as we hold the rest of mankind, enemies in war, in peace, friends.

We, therefore, the representatives of the United States of America, in general Congress assembled, appealing to the Supreme Judge of the world for the rectitude of our intentions, do, in the name, and by the authority of the good people of these colonies, solemnly publish and declare, that these united colonies are, and of right ought to be, free and independent states: that they are absolved from all allegiance to the British Crown, and that all political connection between them and the state of Great Britain is, and ought to be, totally dissolved; and that, as free and independent states, they have full power to levy war, conclude peace, contract alliances, establish commerce, and to do all other acts and things which independent states may of right do. And, for the support of this declaration, with a firm reliance on the protection of Divine Providence, we mutually pledge to each other our lives, our fortunes, and our sacred honor.

THE CONSTITUTION OF
THE UNITED STATES

WE the people of the United States, in order to form a more perfect union, establish justice, insure domestic tranquillity, provide for the common defense, promote the general welfare, and secure the blessings of liberty to ourselves and our posterity, do ordain and establish this Constitution for the United States of America.

ARTICLE I

SECTION 1

All legislative powers herein granted shall be vested in a Congress of the United States, which shall consist of a Senate and House of Representatives.

SECTION 2

1. The House of Representatives shall be composed of members chosen every second year by the people of the several States, and the electors in each State shall have the qualifications requisite for electors of the most numerous branch of the State legislature.

2. No person shall be a representative who shall not have attained to the age of twenty-five years, and been seven years a citizen of the United States, and who shall not, when elected, be an inhabitant of that State in which he shall be chosen.

3. Representatives and direct taxes [1] shall be apportioned among the several States which may be included within this Union, according to their respective numbers, which shall be determined by adding to the whole number of free persons, including those bound to service for a term of years, and excluding Indians not taxed, three fifths of all other persons.[2] The actual enumeration shall be made within three years after the first meeting of the Congress of the United States, and within every subsequent term of ten years, in such manner as they shall by law direct. The number of representatives shall not exceed one for every thirty thousand, but each State shall have at least one representative; and until such enumeration shall be made, the State of New Hampshire shall be entitled to choose three, Massachusetts eight, Rhode Island and Providence Plantations one, Connecticut five, New York six, New Jersey four, Pennsylvania eight, Delaware one, Maryland six, Virginia ten, North Carolina five, South Carolina five, and Georgia three.

4. When vacancies happen in the representation from any State, the executive authority thereof shall issue writs of election to fill such vacancies.

5. The House of Representatives shall choose

[1] Revised by the 16th Amendment.
[2] Revised by the 14th Amendment.

their speaker and other officers; and shall have the sole power of impeachment.

SECTION 3

1. The Senate of the United States shall be composed of two senators from each State, chosen by the legislature thereof,[1] for six years; and each senator shall have one vote.

2. Immediately after they shall be assembled in consequence of the first election, they shall be divided as equally as may be into three classes. The seats of the senators of the first class shall be vacated at the expiration of the second year, of the second class at the expiration of the fourth year, and of the third class at the expiration of the sixth year, so that one third may be chosen every second year; and if vacancies happen by resignation, or otherwise, during the recess of the legislature of any State, the executive thereof may make temporary appointments until the next meeting of the legislature, which shall then fill such vacancies.[1]

3. No person shall be a senator who shall not have attained to the age of thirty years, and been nine years a citizen of the United States, and who shall not, when elected, be an inhabitant of that State for which he shall be chosen.

4. The Vice President of the United States shall be President of the Senate, but shall have no vote, unless they be equally divided.

5. The Senate shall choose their other officers, and also a president pro tempore, in the absence of the Vice President, or when he shall exercise the office of the President of the United States.

6. The Senate shall have the sole power to try all impeachments. When sitting for that purpose, they shall be on oath or affirmation. When the President of the United States is tried, the chief justice shall preside: and no person shall be convicted without the concurrence of two thirds of the members present.

7. Judgment in cases of impeachment shall not extend further than to removal from office, and disqualifications to hold and enjoy any office of honor, trust or profit under the United States: but the party convicted shall nevertheless be liable and subject to indictment, trial, judgment and punishment, according to law.

SECTION 4

1. The times, places, and manner of holding elections for senators and representatives, shall be prescribed in each State by the legislature thereof; but the Congress may at any time by law make or alter such regulations, except as to the places of choosing senators.

[1] Revised by the 17th Amendment.

2. The Congress shall assemble at least once in every year, and such meeting shall be on the first Monday in December, unless they shall by law appoint a different day.

SECTION 5

1. Each House shall be the judge of the elections, returns and qualifications of its own members, and a majority of each shall constitute a quorum to do business; but a smaller number may adjourn from day to day, and may be authorized to compel the attendance of absent members, in such manner, and under such penalties as each House may provide.

2. Each House may determine the rules of its proceedings, punish its members for disorderly behavior, and, with the concurrence of two thirds, expel a member.

3. Each House shall keep a journal of its proceedings, and from time to time publish the same, excepting such parts as may in their judgment require secrecy; and the yeas and nays of the members of either House on any question shall, at the desire of one fifth of those present, be entered on the journal.

4. Neither House, during the session of Congress, shall, without the consent of the other, adjourn for more than three days, nor to any other place than that in which the two Houses shall be sitting.

SECTION 6

1. The senators and representatives shall receive a compensation for their services, to be ascertained by law, and paid out of the Treasury of the United States. They shall in all cases, except treason, felony, and breach of the peace, be privileged from arrest during their attendance at the session of their respective Houses, and in going to and returning from the same; and for any speech or debate in either House, they shall not be questioned in any other place.

2. No senator or representative shall, during the time for which he was elected, be appointed to any civil office under the authority of the United States, which shall have been created, or the emoluments whereof shall have been increased during such time; and no person holding any office under the United States shall be a member of either House during his continuance in office.

SECTION 7

1. All bills for raising revenue shall originate in the House of Representatives; but the Senate may propose or concur with amendments as on other bills.

2. Every bill which shall have passed the House of Representatives and the Senate, shall, before it becomes a law, be presented to the President of the United States; if he approves he shall sign it, but if not he shall return it, with his objections to that House in which it shall have originated, who shall enter the objections at large on their journal, and proceed to reconsider it. If

after such reconsideration two thirds of that House shall agree to pass the bill, it shall be sent, together with the objections, to the other House, by which it shall likewise be reconsidered, and if approved by two thirds of that House, it shall become a law. But in all such cases the votes of both Houses shall be determined by yeas and nays, and the names of the persons voting for and against the bill shall be entered on the journal of each House respectively. If any bill shall not be returned by the President within ten days (Sundays excepted) after it shall have been presented to him, the same shall be a law, in like manner as if he had signed it, unless the Congress by their adjournment prevent its return, in which case it shall not be a law.

3. Every order, resolution, or vote to which the concurrence of the Senate and the House of Representatives may be necessary (except on a question of adjournment) shall be presented to the President of the United States; and before the same shall take effect, shall be approved by him, or being disapproved by him, shall be repassed by two thirds of the Senate and House of Representatives, according to the rules and limitations prescribed in the case of a bill.

SECTION 8

The Congress shall have the power

1. To lay and collect taxes, duties, imposts, and excises, to pay the debts and provide for the common defense and general welfare of the United States; but all duties, imposts, and excises shall be uniform throughout the United States;

2. To borrow money on the credit of the United States;

3. To regulate commerce with foreign nations, and among the several States, and with the Indian tribes;

4. To establish a uniform rule of naturalization, and uniform laws on the subject of bankruptcies throughout the United States;

5. To coin money, regulate the value thereof, and of foreign coin, and fix the standard of weights and measures;

6. To provide for the punishment of counterfeiting the securities and current coin of the United States;

7. To establish post offices and post roads;

8. To promote the progress of science and useful arts, by securing for limited times to authors and inventors the exclusive right to their respective writings and discoveries;

9. To constitute tribunals inferior to the Supreme Court;

10. To define and punish piracies and felonies committed on the high seas, and offenses against the law of nations;

11. To declare war, grant letters of marque and reprisal, and make rules concerning captures on land and water;

12. To raise and support armies, but no ap-

propriation of money to that use shall be for a longer term than two years;

13. To provide and maintain a navy;

14. To make rules for the government and regulation of the land and naval forces;

15. To provide for calling forth the militia to execute the laws of the Union, suppress insurrections and repel invasions;

16. To provide for organizing, arming, and disciplining the militia, and for governing such part of them as may be employed in the service of the United States, reserving to the States respectively, the appointment of the officers, and the authority of training the militia according to the discipline prescribed by Congress;

17. To exercise exclusive legislation in all cases whatsoever, over such district (not exceeding ten miles square) as may, by cession of particular States, and the acceptance of Congress, become the seat of the government of the United States, and to exercise like authority over all places purchased by the consent of the legislature of the State in which the same shall be, for the erection of forts, magazines, arsenals, dockyards, and other needful buildings; and

18. To make all laws which shall be necessary and proper for carrying into execution the foregoing powers, and all other powers vested by this Constitution in the government of the United States, or in any department or officer thereof.

SECTION 9

1. The migration or importation of such persons as any of the States now existing shall think proper to admit, shall not be prohibited by the Congress prior to the year one thousand eight hundred and eight, but a tax or duty may be imposed on such importation, not exceeding ten dollars for each person.

2. The privilege of the writ of habeas corpus shall not be suspended, unless when in cases of rebellion or invasion the public safety may require it.

3. No bill of attainder or ex post facto law shall be passed.

4. No capitation, or other direct, tax shall be laid, unless in proportion to the census or enumeration hereinbefore directed to be taken.[1]

5. No tax or duty shall be laid on articles exported from any State.

6. No preference shall be given by any regulation of commerce or revenue to the ports of one State over those of another: nor shall vessels bound to, or from, one State be obliged to enter, clear, or pay duties in another.

7. No money shall be drawn from the treasury, but in consequence of appropriations made by law; and a regular statement and account of the receipts and expenditures of all public money shall be published from time to time.

8. No title of nobility shall be granted by the

[1] Revised by the 16th Amendment.

United States: and no person holding any office of profit or trust under them, shall, without the consent of the Congress, accept of any present, emolument, office, or title, of any kind whatever, from any king, prince, or foreign State.

SECTION 10

1. No State shall enter into any treaty, alliance, or confederation; grant letters of marque and reprisal; coin money; emit bills of credit; make anything but gold and silver coin a tender in payment of debts; pass any bill of attainder, ex post facto law, or law impairing the obligation of contracts, or grant any title of nobility.

2. No State shall, without the consent of the Congress, lay any imposts or duties on imports or exports, except what may be absolutely necessary for executing its inspection laws: and the net produce of all duties and imposts laid by any State on imports or exports, shall be for the use of the treasury of the United States; and all such laws shall be subject to the revision and control of the Congress.

3. No State shall, without the consent of the Congress, lay any duty of tonnage, keep troops, or ships of war in time of peace, enter into any agreement or compact with another State, or with a foreign power, or engage in war, unless actually invaded, or in such imminent danger as will not admit of delay.

ARTICLE II

SECTION 1

1. The executive power shall be vested in a President of the United States of America. He shall hold his office during the term of four years, and, together with the Vice President, chosen for the same term, be elected as follows:

2. Each State shall appoint, in such manner as the legislature thereof may direct, a number of electors, equal to the whole number of senators and representatives to which the State may be entitled in the Congress: but no senator or representative, or person holding an office of trust or profit under the United States, shall be appointed an elector.

The electors shall meet in their respective States, and vote by ballot for two persons, of whom one at least shall not be an inhabitant of the same State with themselves. And they shall make a list of all the persons voted for, and of the number of votes for each; which list they shall sign and certify, and transmit sealed to the seat of the government of the United States, directed to the president of the Senate. The president of the Senate shall, in the presence of the Senate and House of Representatives, open all the certificates, and the votes shall then be counted. The person having the greatest number of votes shall be the President, if such number be a majority of the whole number of electors appointed; and if there be more than one who have such majority, and have an equal number of votes, then the House of Representatives shall immediately choose by ballot one of them for President; and if no person have a majority, then from the five highest on the list the said House shall in like manner choose the President. But in choosing the President, the votes shall be taken by States, the representation from each State having one vote; a quorum for this purpose shall consist of a member or members from two thirds of the States, and a majority of all the States shall be necessary to a choice. In every case, after the choice of the President, the person having the greatest number of votes of the electors shall be the Vice President. But if there should remain two or more who have equal votes, the Senate shall choose from them by ballot the Vice President.[1]

3. The Congress may determine the time of choosing the electors, and the day on which they shall give their votes; which day shall be the same throughout the United States.

4. No person except a natural born citizen, or a citizen of the United States, at the time of the adoption of this Constitution, shall be eligible to the office of President; neither shall any person be eligible to that office who shall not have attained to the age of thirty-five years, and been fourteen years a resident within the United States.

5. In case of the removal of the President from office, or of his death, resignation, or inability to discharge the powers and duties of the said office, the same shall devolve on the Vice President, and the Congress may by law provide for the case of removal, death, resignation, or inability, both of the President and Vice President, declaring what officer shall then act as President, and such officer shall act accordingly, until the disability be removed, or a President shall be elected.

6. The President shall, at stated times, receive for his services a compensation, which shall neither be increased nor diminished during the period for which he shall have been elected, and he shall not receive within that period any other emolument from the United States, or any of them.

7. Before he enter on the execution of his office, he shall take the following oath or affirmation: —
"I do solemnly swear (or affirm) that I will faithfully execute the office of President of the United States, and will to the best of my ability, preserve, protect and defend the Constitution of the United States."

Section 2

1. The President shall be commander in chief of the army and navy of the United States, and of the militia of the several States, when called into the actual service of the United States; he may require the opinion, in writing, of the principal officer in each of the executive departments, upon any subject relating to the duties of their respective offices, and he shall have power to grant reprieves and pardons for offenses against the United States, except in cases of impeachment.

2. He shall have power, by and with the advice and consent of the Senate, to make treaties, pro-

[1] Voided by the 12th Amendment.

vided two thirds of the senators present concur; and he shall nominate, and by and with the advice and consent of the Senate, shall appoint ambassadors, other public ministers and consuls, judges of the Supreme Court, and all other officers of the United States, whose appointments are not herein otherwise provided for, and which shall be established by law: but the Congress may by law vest the appointment of such inferior officers, as they think proper, in the President alone, in the courts of law, or in the heads of departments.

3. The President shall have power to fill up all vacancies that may happen during the recess of the Senate, by granting commissions which shall expire at the end of their next session.

Section 3

He shall from time to time give to the Congress information of the state of the Union, and recommend to their consideration such measures as he shall judge necessary and expedient; he may, on extraordinary occasions, convene both Houses, or either of them, and in case of disagreement between them with respect to the time of adjournment, he may adjourn them to such time as he shall think proper; he shall receive ambassadors and other public ministers; he shall take care that the laws be faithfully executed, and shall commission all the officers of the United States.

Section 4

The President, Vice President, and all civil officers of the United States, shall be removed from office on impeachment for, and conviction of, treason, bribery, or other high crimes and misdemeanors.

ARTICLE III

Section 1

The judicial power of the United States shall be vested in one Supreme Court, and in such inferior courts as the Congress may from time to time ordain and establish. The judges, both of the Supreme and inferior courts, shall hold their offices during good behavior, and shall, at stated times, receive for their services, a compensation, which shall not be diminished during their continuance in office.

Section 2

1. The judicial power shall extend to all cases, in law and equity, arising under this Constitution, the laws of the United States, and treaties made, or which shall be made, under their authority; — to all cases affecting ambassadors, other public ministers and consuls; — to all cases of admiralty and maritime jurisdiction; — to controversies to which the United States shall be a party; — to controversies between two or more States; — between a State and citizens of another State;[1] — between citizens of different States; — between citizens of the same State claiming lands under grants of different States, and between a State, or

[1] Revised by the 11th Amendment.

the citizens thereof, and foreign States, citizens or subjects.

2. In all cases affecting ambassadors, other public ministers and consuls, and those in which a State shall be party, the Supreme Court shall have original jurisdiction. In all the other cases before mentioned, the Supreme Court shall have appellate jurisdiction, both as to law and to fact, with such exceptions, and under such regulations as the Congress shall make.

3. The trial of all crimes, except in cases of impeachment, shall be by jury; and such trial shall be held in the State where the said crimes shall have been committed; but when not committed within any State, the trial shall be at such place or places as the Congress may by law have directed.

Section 3

1. Treason against the United States shall consist only in levying war against them, or in adhering to their enemies, giving them aid and comfort. No person shall be convicted of treason unless on the testimony of two witnesses to the same overt act, or on confession in open court.

2. The Congress shall have power to declare the punishment of treason, but no attainder of treason shall work corruption of blood, or forfeiture except during the life of the person attainted.

ARTICLE IV

Section 1

Full faith and credit shall be given in each State to the public acts, records, and judicial proceedings of every other State. And the Congress may by general laws prescribe the manner in which such acts, records and proceedings shall be proved, and the effect thereof.

Section 2

1. The citizens of each State shall be entitled to all privileges and immunities of citizens in the several States.[1]

2. A person charged in any State with treason, felony, or other crime, who shall flee from justice, and be found in another State, shall on demand of the executive authority of the State from which he fled, be delivered up to be removed to the State having jurisdiction of the crime.

3. No person held to service or labor in one State under the laws thereof, escaping into another, shall, in consequence of any law or regulation therein, be discharged from such service or labor, but shall be delivered up on claim of the party to whom such service or labor may be due.[2]

Section 3

1. New States may be admitted by the Congress into this Union; but no new State shall be formed or erected within the jurisdiction of any other State; nor any State be formed by the junction of two or more States, or parts of States,

without the consent of the legislatures of the States concerned as well as of the Congress.

2. The Congress shall have power to dispose of and make all needful rules and regulations respecting the territory or other property belonging to the United States; and nothing in this Constitution shall be so construed as to prejudice any claims of the United States, or of any particular State.

Section 4

The United States shall guarantee to every State in this Union a republican form of government, and shall protect each of them against invasion; and on application of the legislature, or of the executive (when the legislature cannot be convened) against domestic violence.

ARTICLE V

The Congress, whenever two thirds of both Houses shall deem it necessary, shall propose amendments to this Constitution, or, on the application of the legislatures of two thirds of the several States, shall call a convention for proposing amendments, which in either case, shall be valid to all intents and purposes, as part of this Constitution when ratified by the legislatures of three fourths of the several States, or by conventions in three fourths thereof, as the one or the other mode of ratification may be proposed by the Congress; Provided that no amendment which may be made prior to the year one thousand eight hundred and eight shall in any manner affect the first and fourth clauses in the ninth section of the first article; and that no State, without its consent, shall be deprived of its equal suffrage in the Senate.

ARTICLE VI

1. All debts contracted and engagements entered into, before the adoption of this Constitution, shall be as valid against the United States under this Constitution, as under the Confederation.[1]

2. This Constitution, and the laws of the United States which shall be made in pursuance thereof; and all treaties made, or which shall be made, under the authority of the United States, shall be the supreme law of the land; and the Judges in every State shall be bound thereby, anything in the Constitution or laws of any State to the contrary notwithstanding.

3. The senators and representatives before mentioned, and the members of the several State legislatures, and all executive and judicial officers, both of the United States and of the several States, shall be bound by oath or affirmation to support this Constitution; but no religious test shall ever be required as a qualification to any office or public trust under the United States.

ARTICLE VII

The ratification of the conventions of nine States shall be sufficient for the establishment of

---

[1] Elaborated by the 14th Amendment, Sec. 1.
[2] See the 13th Amendment, abolishing slavery.

[1] See the 14th Amendment, Sec. 4, for additional provisions.

this Constitution between the States so ratifying the same.

Done in Convention by the unanimous consent of the States present the seventeenth day of September in the year of our Lord one thousand seven hundred and eighty-seven, and of the independence of the United States of America the twelfth. In witness whereof we have hereunto subscribed our names.

AMENDMENTS

First Ten Amendments submitted by Congress Sept. 2ʳ, 1789. Ratified by three-fourths of the States December 15, 1791.

ARTICLE I

Congress shall make no law respecting an establishment of religion, or prohibiting the free exercise thereof; or abridging the freedom of speech, or of the press; or the right of the people peaceably to assemble, and to petition the government for a redress of grievances.

ARTICLE II

A well regulated militia, being necessary to the security of a free State, the right of the people to keep and bear arms, shall not be infringed.

ARTICLE III

No soldier shall, in time of peace be quartered in any house, without the consent of the owner, nor in time of war, but in a manner to be prescribed by law.

ARTICLE IV

The right of the people to be secure in their persons, houses, papers, and effects, against unreasonable searches and seizures, shall not be violated, and no warrants shall issue, but upon probable cause, supported by oath or affirmation, and particularly describing the place to be searched, and the persons or things to be seized.

ARTICLE V

No person shall be held to answer for a capital, or otherwise infamous crime, unless on a presentment or indictment of a grand jury, except in cases arising in the land or naval forces, or in the militia, when in actual service in time of war or public danger; nor shall any person be subject for the same offense to be twice put in jeopardy of life or limb; nor shall be compelled in any criminal case to be a witness against himself, nor be deprived of life, liberty, or property, without due process of law; nor shall private property be taken for public use without just compensation.

ARTICLE VI

In all criminal prosecutions, the accused shall enjoy the right to a speedy and public trial, by an impartial jury of the State and district wherein the crime shall have been committed, which district shall have been previously ascertained by law, and to be informed of the nature and cause of the accusation; to be confronted with the witnesses against him; to have compulsory process for obtaining witnesses in his favor, and to have the assistance of counsel for his defense.

ARTICLE VII

In suits at common law, where the value in controversy shall exceed twenty dollars, the right of trial by jury shall be preserved, and no fact tried by a jury shall be otherwise reëxamined in any court of the United States, than according to the rules of the common law.

ARTICLE VIII

Excessive bail shall not be required, nor excessive fines imposed, nor cruel and unusual punishments inflicted.

ARTICLE IX

The enumeration in the Constitution of certain rights shall not be construed to deny or disparage others retained by the people.

ARTICLE X

The powers not delegated to the United States by the Constitution, nor prohibited by it to the States, are reserved to the States respectively, or to the people.

ARTICLE XI

Submitted by Congress March 5, 1794. Ratified January 8, 1798.

The judicial power of the United States shall not be construed to extend to any suit in law or equity, commenced or prosecuted against one of the United States by citizens of another State, or by citizens or subjects of any foreign State.

ARTICLE XII

Submitted by Congress December 12, 1803. Ratified September 25, 1804.

The electors shall meet in their respective States, and vote by ballot for President and Vice President, one of whom, at least, shall not be an inhabitant of the same State with themselves; they shall name in their ballots the person voted for as President, and in distinct ballots, the person voted for as Vice President, and they shall make distinct lists of all persons voted for as President and of all persons voted for as Vice President, and of the number of votes for each, which lists they shall sign and certify, and transmit sealed to the seat of the government of the United States, directed to the President of the Senate; — The President of the Senate shall, in the presence of the Senate and House of Representatives, open all the certificates and the votes shall then be counted; — The person having the greatest number of votes for President, shall be the President, if such number be a majority of the whole number of electors appointed; and if no person have such majority, then from the persons having the highest numbers not exceeding three on the list of those voted for as President, the House of Representatives shall choose immediately, by ballot, the President. But in choosing the President, the votes shall be taken by States, the representation from each State having one vote; a quorum for this purpose shall consist of a member or members from two thirds of the States, and a majority of all the States shall be necessary to a choice. And if the House of Representatives shall not choose a President whenever the right of choice shall devolve upon them, before the fourth day of March next following, then the Vice President shall act as President, as in the case of the death or other constitutional disability of the President. The person having the greatest number of votes as Vice President shall be the Vice President, if such number be a majority of the whole number of electors appointed, and if no person have a majority, then from the two highest numbers on the list, the Senate shall choose the Vice President; a quorum for the purpose shall consist of two thirds of the whole number of Senators, and a majority of the whole number shall be necessary to a choice. But no person constitutionally ineligible to the office of President shall be eligible to that of Vice President of the United States.

ARTICLE XIII
Submitted by Congress February 1, 1865. Ratified December 18, 1865.

SECTION 1
Neither slavery nor involuntary servitude, except as punishment for crime whereof the party shall have been duly convicted, shall exist within the United States, or any place subject to their jurisdiction.

SECTION 2
Congress shall have power to enforce this article by appropriate legislation.

ARTICLE XIV
Submitted by Congress June 16, 1866. Ratified July 28, 1868.

SECTION 1
All persons born or naturalized in the United States, and subject to the jurisdiction thereof, are citizens of the United States and of the State wherein they reside. No State shall make or enforce any law which shall abridge the privileges or immunities of citizens of the United States; nor shall any State deprive any person of life, liberty, or property, without due process of law; nor deny to any person within its jurisdiction the equal protection of the laws.

SECTION 2
Representatives shall be apportioned among the several States according to their respective numbers, counting the whole number of persons in each State, excluding Indians not taxed. But when the right to vote at any election for the choice of electors for President and Vice President of the United States, representatives in Congress, the executive and judicial officers of a State, or the members of the legislature thereof, is denied to any of the male inhabitants of such State, being twenty-one years of age, and citizens of the United States, or in any way abridged, except for participation in rebellion, or other crime, the basis of representation therein shall be reduced in the proportion which the number of such male citizens shall bear to the whole number of male citizens twenty-one years of age in such State.

SECTION 3
No person shall be a senator or representative in Congress, or elector of President and Vice President, or hold any office, civil or military, under the United States, or under any State, who having previously taken an oath, as a member of Congress, or as an officer of the United States, or as a member of any State legislature, or as an executive or judicial officer of any State, to support the Constitution of the United States, shall have engaged in insurrection or rebellion against the same, or given aid or comfort to the enemies thereof. But Congress may by a vote of two thirds of each House, remove such disability.

SECTION 4
The validity of the public debt of the United States, authorized by law, including debts incurred for payment of pensions and bounties for services in suppressing insurrection or rebellion, shall not be questioned. But neither the United States nor any State shall assume or pay any debt or obligation incurred in aid of insurrection or rebellion against the United States, or any claim for the loss or emancipation of any slave; but all such debts, obligations, and claims shall be held illegal and void.

SECTION 5
The Congress shall have power to enforce, by appropriate legislation, the provisions of this article.

ARTICLE XV
Submitted by Congress February 27, 1869. Ratified March 30, 1870.

SECTION 1
The right of citizens of the United States to vote shall not be denied or abridged by the United States or by any State on account of race, color, or previous condition of servitude.

SECTION 2
The Congress shall have power to enforce this article by appropriate legislation.

ARTICLE XVI
Submitted by Congress July 12, 1909. Ratified February 25, 1913.

The Congress shall have power to lay and collect taxes on incomes, from whatever source derived, without apportionment among the several States, and without regard to any census or enumeration.

ARTICLE XVII

Submitted by Congress May 16, 1912. Ratified May 31, 1913.

The Senate of the United States shall be composed of two senators from each state, elected by the people thereof, for six years; and each senator shall have one vote. The electors in each State shall have the qualifications requisite for electors of the most numerous branch of the State legislature.

When vacancies happen in the representation of any State in the Senate, the executive authority of such State shall issue writs of election to fill such vacancies: *Provided*, That the legislature of any State may empower the executive thereof to make temporary appointments until the people fill the vacancies by election as the legislature may direct.

This amendment shall not be so construed as to affect the election or term of any senator chosen before it becomes valid as part of the Constitution.

ARTICLE XVIII [1]

Submitted by Congress December 17, 1917. Ratified January 29, 1919.

After one year from the ratification of this article, the manufacture, sale, or transportation of intoxicating liquors within, the importation thereof into, or the exportation thereof from the United States and all territory subject to the jurisdiction thereof for beverage purposes is hereby prohibited.

The Congress and the several States shall have concurrent power to enforce this article by appropriate legislation.

This article shall be inoperative unless it shall have been ratified as an amendment to the Constitution by the legislatures of the several States, as provided in the Constitution, within seven years from the date of the submission hereof to the states by Congress.

ARTICLE XIX

Submitted by Congress June 5, 1919. Ratified August 26, 1920.

The right of citizens of the United States to vote shall not be denied or abridged by the United States or by any State on account of sex.

The Congress shall have power by appropriate legislation to enforce the provisions of this article.

ARTICLE XX

Submitted by Congress March 3, 1932. Ratified January 23, 1933.

Section 1

The terms of the President and Vice President shall end at noon on the 20th day of January, and the terms of Senators and Representatives at noon on the 3d day of January, of the years in which such terms would have ended if this article had not been ratified; and the terms of their successors shall then begin.

[1] Repealed by the 21st Amendment.

Section 2

The Congress shall assemble at least once in every year, and such meeting shall begin at noon on the 3d day of January, unless they shall by law appoint a different day.

Section 3

If, at the time fixed for the beginning of the term of the President, the President-elect shall have died, the Vice President-elect shall become President. If a President shall not have been chosen before the time fixed for the beginning of his term, or if the President-elect shall have failed to qualify, then the Vice President-elect shall act as President until a President shall have qualified; and the Congress may by law provide for the case wherein neither a President-elect nor a Vice President-elect shall have qualified, declaring who shall then act as President, or the manner in which one who is to act shall be selected, and such person shall act accordingly until a President or Vice President shall have qualified.

Section 4

The Congress may by law provide for the case of the death of any of the persons from whom the House of Representatives may choose a President whenever the right of choice shall have devolved upon them, and for the case of the death of any of the persons from whom the Senate may choose a Vice President whenever the right of choice shall have devolved upon them.

Section 5

Sections 1 and 2 shall take effect on the 15th day of October following the ratification of this article.

Section 6

This article shall be inoperative unless it shall have been ratified as an amendment to the Constitution by the legislatures of three-fourths of the several States within seven years from the date of its submission.

ARTICLE XXI

Submitted by Congress February 20, 1933. Ratified December 5, 1933.

Section 1

The Eighteenth Article of amendment to the Constitution of the United States is hereby repealed.

Section 2

The transportation or importation into any State, Territory, or possession of the United States for delivery or use therein of intoxicating liquors in violation of the laws thereof, is hereby prohibited.

Section 3

This article shall be inoperative unless it shall have been ratified as an amendment to the Constitution by conventions in the several States, as provided in the Constitution, within seven years from the date of the submission thereof to the States by the Congress.

ARTICLE XXII

Submitted by Congress March 12, 1947.   Ratified March 1, 1951.

No person shall be elected to the office of the President more than twice, and no person who has held the office of President, or acted as President, for more than two years of a term to which some other person was elected President shall be elected to the office of the President more than once.

But this article shall not apply to any person holding the office of President when this article was proposed by the Congress, and shall not prevent any person who may be holding the office of President, or acting as President, during the term within which this article becomes operative from holding the office of President or acting as President during the remainder of such term.

This article shall be inoperative unless it shall have been ratified as an amendment to the Constitution by the legislatures of three-fourths of the several states within seven years from the date of its submission to the states by the Congress.

THE STATES OF THE UNION, 1787-1877

(with dates of ratification of the Constitution or admission to the Union)

1. Delaware	Dec. 7, 1787	20. Mississippi	Dec. 10, 1817
2. Pennsylvania	Dec. 12, 1787	21. Illinois	Dec. 3, 1818
3. New Jersey	Dec. 18, 1787	22. Alabama	Dec. 14, 1819
4. Georgia	Jan. 2, 1788	23. Maine	Mar. 15, 1820
5. Connecticut	Jan. 9, 1788	24. Missouri	Aug. 10, 1821
6. Massachusetts	Feb. 6, 1788	25. Arkansas	June 15, 1836
7. Maryland	Apr. 28, 1788	26. Michigan	Jan. 26, 1837
8. South Carolina	May 23, 1788	27. Florida	Mar. 3, 1845
9. New Hampshire	June 21, 1788	28. Texas	Dec. 29, 1845
10. Virginia	June 25, 1788	29. Iowa	Dec. 28, 1846
11. New York	July 26, 1788	30. Wisconsin	May 29, 1848
12. North Carolina	Nov. 21, 1789	31. California	Sept. 9, 1850
13. Rhode Island	May 29, 1790	32. Minnesota	May 11, 1858
14. Vermont	Mar. 4, 1791	33. Oregon	Feb. 14, 1859
15. Kentucky	June 1, 1792	34. Kansas	Jan. 29, 1861
16. Tennessee	June 1, 1796	35. West Virginia	June 19, 1863
17. Ohio	Mar. 1, 1803	36. Nevada	Oct. 31, 1864
18. Louisiana	Apr. 30, 1812	37. Nebraska	Mar. 1, 1867
19. Indiana	Dec. 11, 1816	38. Colorado	Aug. 1, 1876

OTHER GOVERNMENTAL UNITS IN 1877

(with dates of creation)

District of Columbia	July 16, 1790	Territory of Arizona	Feb. 24, 1863
Indian Territory (unorganized)	June 30, 1834	Territory of Idaho	Mar. 3, 1863
Territory of New Mexico	Sept. 9, 1850	Territory of Montana	May 26, 1864
Territory of Utah	Sept. 9, 1850	Alaska (by treaty)	Mar. 30, 1867
Territory of Washington	Mar. 2, 1853	Territory of Wyoming	July 25, 1868
Territory of Dakota	Mar. 2, 1861		

PRESIDENTS, VICE-PRESIDENTS,

President	Vice-President	Secretary of State	Secretary of Treasury
1. George Washington, Federalist.1789 Virginia	John Adams, Federalist..........1789 Massachusetts	T. Jefferson.....1789 E. Randolph....1794 T. Pickering.....1795	Alex. Hamilton..1789 Oliver Wolcott ..1795
2. John Adams, Federalist.......1797 Massachusetts	Thomas Jefferson, Republican....1797 Virginia	T. Pickering.....1797 John Marshall...1800	Oliver Wolcott ..1797 Samuel Dexter...1801
3. Thomas Jefferson, Republican .1801 Virginia	Aaron Burr, Republican.........1801 New York George Clinton, Republican......1805 New York	James Madison..1801	Samuel Dexter...1801 Albert Gallatin ..1801
4. James Madison, Republican...1809 Virginia	George Clinton, Republican......1809 New York Elbridge Gerry, Republican......1813 Massachusetts	Robert Smith ...1809 James Monroe...1811	Albert Gallatin ..1809 G. W. Campbell .1814 A. J. Dallas.....1814 W. H. Crawford .1816
5. James Monroe, Republican....1817 Virginia	D. D. Tompkins, Republican.....1817 New York	J. Q. Adams.....1817	W. H. Crawford .1817
6. John Quincy Adams, Nat'l Rep. Massachusetts..........1825	John C. Calhoun, Republican.....1825 South Carolina	Henry Clay.....1825	Richard Rush ...1825
7. Andrew Jackson, Democratic ..1829 Tennessee	John C. Calhoun, Democratic....1829 South Carolina Martin Van Buren, Democratic...1833 New York	M. Van Buren...1829 E. Livingston ...1831 Louis McLane...1833 John Forsyth....1834	Sam D. Ingham .1820 Louis McLane...1831 W. J. Duane....1833 Roger B. Taney .1833 Levi Woodbury..1834
8. Martin Van Buren, Democratic.1837 New York	Richard M. Johnson, Democratic.1837 Kentucky	John Forsyth....1837	Levi Woodbury..1837
9. William H. Harrison, Whig....1841 Ohio	John Tyler, Whig..............1841 Virginia	Daniel Webster..1841	Thos. Ewing.....1841
10. John Tyler, Whig and Democratic Virginia.................1841		Daniel Webster..1841 Hugh S. Legare .1843 Abel P. Upshur..1843 John C. Calhoun 1844	Thos. Ewing ....1841 Walter Forward .1841 John C. Spencer .1843 Geo. M. Bibb....1844
11. James K. Polk, Democratic....1845 Tennessee	George M. Dallas, Democratic....1845 Pennsylvania	James Buchanan.1845	Robt. J. Walker .1845
12. Zachary Taylor, Whig........1849 Louisiana	Millard Fillmore, Whig..........1849 New York	John M. Clayton 1849	Wm.M.Meredith 1849
13. Millard Fillmore, Whig........1850 New York		Daniel Webster..1850 Edward Everett.1852	Thomas Corwin .1850
14. Franklin Pierce, Democratic...1853 New Hampshire	William R. D. King, Democratic .1853 Alabama	W. L. Marcy....1853	James Guthrie...1853
15. James Buchanan, Democratic..1857 Pennsylvania	John C. Breckinridge, Democratic.1857 Kentucky	Lewis Cass......1857 J. S. Black......1860	Howell Cobb....1857 Philip F. Thomas 1860 John A. Dix.....1861
16. Abraham Lincoln, Republican .1861 Illinois	Hannibal Hamlin, Republican....1861 Maine Andrew Johnson, Unionist.......1865 Tennessee	W. H. Seward...1861	Salmon P. Chase.1861 W. P. Fessenden.1864 Hugh McCulloch.1865
17. Andrew Johnson, Unionist.....1865		W. H. Seward...1865	Hugh McCulloch.1865
18. Ulysses S. Grant, Republican..1869	Schuyler Colfax, Republican......1869 Henry Wilson, Republican........1873	E. B. Washburne 1869 Hamilton Fish...1869	Geo. S. Boutwell.1869 W. A. Richardson 1873 Benj. H. Bristow.1874 Lot M. Morrill...1876
19. Rutherford B. Hayes..........1877 Republican	William A. Wheeler, Republican..1877	W. M. Evarts...1877	John Sherman...1877

AND CABINET MEMBERS

Secretary of War	Attorney-General	Postmaster-General*	Secretary of Navy	Secretary of Interior
Henry Knox....1789 T. Pickering....1795 Jas. McHenry...1796	E. Randolph.....1789 Wm. Bradford....1794 Charles Lee......1795	Samuel Osgood....1789 Tim. Pickering....1791 Jos. Habersham...1795	Established April 30, 1798	Established March 3, 1849
Jas. McHenry...1797 John Marshall...1800 Sam'l Dexter....1800 R. Griswold.....1801	Charles Lee......1797 Theo. Parsons....1801	Jos. Habersham...1797	Benj. Stoddert......1798	
H. Dearborn....1801	Levi Lincoln......1801 Robert Smith.....1805 J. Breckinridge...1805 C. A. Rodney.....1807	Jos. Habersham...1801 Gideon Granger...1801	Benj. Stoddert......1801 Robert Smith......1801 J. Crowninshield.....1805	
Wm. Eustis.....1809 J. Armstrong....1813 James Monroe ..1814 W. H. Crawford.1815	C. A. Rodney.....1809 Wm. Pinkney....1811 Richard Rush....1814	Gideon Granger...1809 R. J. Meigs, Jr....1814	Paul Hamilton.....1809 William Jones.......1813 B. W. Crowninshield.1814	
Isaac Shelby....1817 Geo. Graham....1817 J. C. Calhoun...1817	Richard Rush.....1817 William Wirt.....1817	R. J. Meigs, Jr....1817 John McLean.....1823	B. W. Crowninshield.1817 Smith Thompson....1818 S. L. Southard......1823	
Jas. Barbour....1825 Peter B. Porter..1828	William Wirt.....1825	John McLean.....1825	S. L. Southard......1825	
John H. Eaton..1829 Lewis Cass......1831 B. F. Butler.....1837	John M. Berrien..1829 Roger B. Taney ..1831 B. F. Butler......1833	Wm. T. Barry....1829 Amos Kendall....1835	John Branch........1829 Levi Woodbury......1831 Mahlon Dickerson...1834	
Joel R. Poinsett.1837	B. F. Butler......1837 Felix Grundy.....1838 H. D. Gilpin.....1840	Amos Kendall....1837 John M. Niles....1840	Mahlon Dickerson...1837 Jas. K. Paulding.....1838	
John Bell.......1841	J. J. Crittenden...1841	Francis Granger ..1841	George E. Badger....1841	
John Bell.......1841 John McLean...1841 J. C. Spencer....1841 Jas. M. Porter...1843 Wm. Wilkins....1844	J. J. Crittenden...1841 Hugh S. Legare...1841 John Nelson......1843	Francis Granger 1841 C. A. Wickliffe....1841	George E. Badger....1841 Abel P. Upshur....1841 David Henshaw.....1843 Thomas W. Gilmer ..1844 John Y. Mason......1844	
Wm. L. Marcy..1845	John Y. Mason ...1845 Nathan Clifford...1846 Isaac Toucey.....1848	Cave Johnson.....1845	George Bancroft.....1845 John Y. Mason......1846	
G. W. Crawford.1849 C. M. Conrad...1850	Reverdy Johnson .1849 J. J. Crittenden...1850	Jacob Collamer...1849 Nathan K. Hall...1850 Sam D. Hubbard .1852	Wm. B. Preston.....1849 Wm. A. Graham...1850 John P. Kennedy...1852	Thomas Ewing...1849 A. H. Stuart.....1850
Jefferson Davis..1853	Caleb Cushing....1853	James Campbell.. 1853	James C. Dobbin...1853	R'bt. McClelland.1853
John B. Floyd...1857 Joseph Holt....1861	J. S. Black.......1857 Edw. M. Stanton.1860	Aaron V. Brown...1857 Joseph Holt......1859	Isaac Toucey....... 1857	Jacob Thompson .1857
S. Cameron.....1861 E. M. Stanton ..1862	Edward Bates....1861 Titian J. Coffey...1863 James Speed......1864	Horatio King.....1861 M'tgomery Blair..1861 Wm. Dennison....1864	Gideon Welles.......1861	Caleb B. Smith...1861 John P. Usher....1863
E. M. Stanton ..1865 U. S. Grant.....1867 L. Thomas......1868 J. M. Schofield...1868	James Speed......1865 Henry Stanbery ..1866 Wm. M. Evarts...1868	Wm. Dennison...1865 A. W. Randall....1866	Gideon Welles.......1865	John P. Usher....1865 James Harlan....1865 O. H. Browning...1866
J. A. Rawlins*...1869 W. T. Sherman..1869 W. W. Belknap..1869 Alphonso Taft...1876 J. D. Cameron...1876	E. R. Hoar.......1869 A. T. Ackerman ..1870 Geo. H. Williams .1871 Edw. Pierrepont..1875 Alphonso Taft....1876	J. A. J. Creswell ..1869 Jas. W. Marshall..1874 Marshall Jewell...1874 James N. Tyner...1876	Adolph E. Borie.....1869 Geo. M. Robeson....1869	Jacob D. Cox....1869 C. Delano.......1870 Zach. Chandler...1875
G. W. McCrary ..1877	Chas. Devens.....1877	David M. Key....1877	R. W. Thompson....1877	Carl Schurz......1877

* Not in Cabinet until 1829.

CHIEF JUSTICES OF THE UNITED STATES SUPREME COURT

John Jay, New York	1789–1795	Roger B. Taney, Maryland	1836–1864
John Rutledge, South Carolina	1795	Salmon P. Chase, Ohio	1864–1873
Oliver Ellsworth, Connecticut	1796–1799	Morrison R. Waite, Ohio	1874–1888
John Marshall, Virginia	1801–1835		

SPEAKERS OF THE HOUSE OF REPRESENTATIVES

F. A. C. Muhlenberg, Pennsylvania	1789–1791	James K. Polk, Tennessee	1835–1839
Jonathan Trumbull, Connecticut	1791–1793	R. M. T. Hunter, Virginia	1839–1841
F. A. C. Muhlenberg, Pennsylvania	1793–1795	John White, Kentucky	1841–1843
Jonathan Dayton, New Jersey	1795–1799	John W. Jones, Virginia	1843–1845
Theodore Sedgwick, Massachusetts	1799–1801	John W. Davis, Indiana	1845–1847
Nathaniel Macon, North Carolina	1801–1807	R. C. Winthrop, Massachusetts	1847–1849
Joseph B. Varnum, Massachusetts	1807–1811	Howell Cobb, Georgia	1849–1851
Henry Clay, Kentucky	1811–1814	Linn Boyd, Kentucky	1851–1855
Langdon Cheves, South Carolina	1814–1815	N. P. Banks, Massachusetts	1856–1857
Henry Clay, Kentucky	1815–1820	James L. Orr, South Carolina	1857–1859
John W. Taylor, New York	1820–1821	William Pennington, New Jersey	1860–1861
Philip P. Barbour, Virginia	1821–1823	Galusha A. Grow, Pennsylvania	1861–1863
Henry Clay, Kentucky	1823–1825	Schuyler Colfax, Indiana	1863–1869
John W. Taylor, New York	1825–1827	James G. Blaine, Maine	1869–1875
Andrew Stevenson, Virginia	1827–1834	Michael C. Kerr, Indiana	1875–1876
John Bell, Tennessee	1834–1835	Samuel J. Randall, Pennsylvania	1876–1881

THE SOVEREIGNS OF ENGLAND AND GREAT BRITAIN DURING THE COLONIAL ERA

ENGLAND, 1485–1707

Henry VII, 1485–1509
Henry VIII, 1509–1547
Edward VI, 1547–1553
Mary, 1553–1558
Elizabeth, 1558–1603
James I (VI of Scotland), 1603–1625
Charles I, 1625–1649
(Protectorate, 1649–1660)
  Oliver Cromwell, 1650–1658
  Richard Cromwell, 1658–1659)
Charles II, 1660–1685
James II (VII of Scotland), 1685–1688
William III and Mary II, 1689–1694

William III, 1694–1702
Anne, 1702–1714 (Queen of Great Britain after 1707)

GREAT BRITAIN, 1707–1801

Anne, 1707–1714
George I, 1714–1727
George II, 1727–1760
George III, 1760–1820 (King of Great Britain and Ireland after 1800)

POPULATION OF THE UNITED STATES, 1790-1870

Division and State	1790	1800	1810	1820	1830	1840	1850	1860	1870
UNITED STATES	3,929,214	5,308,483	7,239,881	9,638,453	*12,866,020	*17,069,453	23,191,876	31,443,321	39,331,183
GEOGRAPHIC DIVISIONS									
New England	1,009,408	1,233,011	1,471,973	1,660,071	1,954,717	2,234,822	2,728,116	3,135,283	3,487,924
Middle Atlantic	952,632	1,402,565	2,014,702	2,699,845	3,587,664	4,526,260	5,898,735	7,458,985	8,810,806
South Atlantic	1,851,806	2,286,494	2,674,891	3,061,063	3,645,752	3,925,299	4,679,090	5,364,703	5,853,610
East South Central	109,368	335,407	708,590	1,190,489	1,815,969	2,575,445	3,363,271	4,020,991	4,404,445
West South Central			77,618	167,680	246,127	449,985	940,251	1,747,667	2,029,965
East North Central		51,006	272,324	792,719	1,470,018	2,924,728	4,523,260	6,926,884	9,124,517
West North Central			19,783	66,586	140,455	426,814	880,335	2,169,832	3,856,594
Mountain							72,927	174,923	315,385
Pacific							105,871	444,053	675,125
NEW ENGLAND									
Maine	96,540	151,719	228,705	298,335	399,455	501,793	583,169	628,279	626,915
New Hampshire	141,885	183,858	214,460	244,161	269,328	284,574	317,976	326,073	318,300
Vermont	85,425	154,465	217,895	235,981	280,652	291,948	314,120	315,098	330,551
Massachusetts	378,787	422,845	472,040	523,287	610,408	737,699	994,514	1,231,066	1,457,351
Rhode Island	68,825	69,122	76,931	83,059	97,199	108,830	147,545	174,620	217,353
Connecticut	237,946	251,002	261,942	275,248	297,675	309,978	370,792	460,147	537,454
MIDDLE ATLANTIC									
New York	340,120	589,051	959,049	1,372,812	1,918,608	2,428,921	3,097,394	3,880,735	4,382,759
New Jersey	184,139	211,149	245,562	277,575	320,823	373,306	489,555	672,035	906,096
Pennsylvania	434,373	602,365	810,091	1,049,458	1,348,233	1,724,033	2,311,786	2,906,215	3,521,951
SOUTH ATLANTIC									
Delaware	59,096	64,273	72,674	72,749	76,748	78,085	91,532	112,216	125,015
Maryland	319,728	341,548	380,546	407,350	447,040	470,019	583,034	687,049	780,894
Dist. of Columbia		14,093	24,023	33,039	39,834	43,712	51,687	75,080	131,700
Virginia	747,610	880,200	974,600	1,065,366	1,211,405	1,239,797	1,421,661	1,596,318	1,225,163
North Carolina	393,751	478,103	555,500	638,829	737,987	753,419	869,039	992,622	1,071,361
South Carolina	249,073	345,591	415,115	502,741	581,185	594,398	668,507	703,708	705,606
Georgia	82,548	162,686	252,433	340,989	516,823	691,392	906,185	1,057,286	1,184,109
Florida					34,730	54,477	87,445	140,424	187,748
EAST SOUTH CENTRAL									
Kentucky	73,677	220,955	406,511	564,317	687,917	779,828	982,405	1,155,684	1,321,011
Tennessee	35,691	105,602	261,727	422,823	681,904	829,210	1,002,717	1,109,801	1,258,520
Alabama				127,901	309,527	590,756	771,623	964,201	996,992
Missisippi		8,850	40,352	75,448	136,621	375,651	606,526	791,305	827,922
WEST SOUTH CENTRAL									
Arkansas			1,062	14,273	30,388	97,574	209,897	435,450	484,471
Louisiana			76,556	153,407	215,739	352,411	517,762	708,002	726,915
Texas							212,592	604,215	818,579
EAST NORTH CENTRAL									
Ohio		45,365	230,760	581,434	937,903	1,519,467	1,980,329	2,339,511	2,665,260
Indiana		5,641	24,520	147,178	343,031	685,866	988,416	1,350,428	1,680,637
Illinois			12,282	55,211	157,445	476,183	851,470	1,711,951	2,539,891
Michigan			4,762	8,896	31,639	212,267	397,654	749,113	1,184,059
Wisconsin						30,945	305,391	775,881	1,054,670
WEST NORTH CENTRAL									
Minnesota							6,077	172,023	439,706
Iowa						43,112	192,214	674,913	1,194,020
Missouri			19,783	66,586	140,455	383,702	682,044	1,182,012	1,721,295
Dakota								4,837	
North Dakota									2,405
South Dakota									11,776
Nebraska								28,841	122,993
Kansas								107,206	364,399
MOUNTAIN									
Colorado								34,277	39,864
New Mexico							61,547	93,516	91,874
Utah							11,380	40,273	86,786
Nevada								6,857	42,491
PACIFIC									
Washington								11,594	23,955
Oregon							13,294	52,465	90,923
California							92,597	379,994	560,247

* Includes 5,318 persons in 1830 and 6,100 in 1840 on public ships in U.S. service, not credited to any division or state.

THE GENEALOGY OF AMERICAN POLITICAL PARTIES

Federalist **Anti-federalist**

1788 — *Washington* (FEDERALIST)

1792 — *Washington* (FEDERALIST) — **Republican** — (Sometimes called Federal Republicans or Democratic Republicans)

1796 — *Adams* (FEDERALIST)

1800 — *Jefferson* (REPUBLICAN)

1804 — *Jefferson* (REPUBLICAN)

1808 — *Madison* (REPUBLICAN)

1812 — *Madison* (REPUBLICAN)

1816 — *Monroe* (REPUBLICAN)

1820 — *Monroe* (REPUBLICAN)

} "Era of Good Feelings"

1824 — *Adams* (REPUBLICAN)

National Republican **Democrat**

1828 — *Jackson* (DEMOCRAT)
Anti-Mason (1830) **Anti-Jackson Democrat**

1832 — *Jackson* (DEMOCRAT)

Whig (1834)

1836 — *Van Buren* (DEMOCRAT)

Harrison (WHIG)
1840
Tyler (WHIG and DEMOCRAT) **Liberty (1840)**

1844 — *Polk* (DEMOCRAT)

Taylor
1848 — (WHIG) **Free-Soil**
Fillmore **Know-Nothing**

1852 — *Pierce* (DEMOCRAT)

American **Republican**

1856 — *Buchanan* (DEMOCRAT)
Constitutional Union **Democrat (North)** **Democrat (South)**

1860 — *Lincoln* (REPUBLICAN)
War Democrats

1864 — *Lincoln* (UNION) **Union (1862)** **Democrat**
Johnson (UNION and DEM.) **Republican**

1868 — *Grant* (REPUBLICAN) **Democrat** **Prohibitionist**
Liberal Republican **Anti-Monopoly (*Granger*)**

1872 — *Grant* (REPUBLICAN)

Greenback
1876 — *Hayes* (REPUBLICAN)

LIST OF BOOKS CITED

(With page references to original citations in chapter bibliographies. Books cited in the Bibliography at the end of Chapter 33 are not included in this list.)

Abbott, Wilbur C. *New York in the American Revolution.* 1929. 164.

Abel, Annie H. *The History of Events Resulting in Indian Consolidation West of the Mississippi* (American Historical Association, *Annual Report*, 1906, I). 1908. 384.

Abernethy, Thomas P. *From Frontier to Plantation in Tennessee; A Study in Frontier Democracy.* 1932. 149, 362.

—— *Western Lands and the American Revolution.* 1937. 108.

Adams, Alice D. *The Neglected Period of Anti-Slavery in America, 1808–1831.* 1908. 345.

Adams, Charles Francis, Jr. *Charles Francis Adams* (American Statesmen, XXIX). 1900; new ed., 1917. 618.

—— *Railroads: Their Origins and Problems.* 1878. 526.

—— *Studies Military and Diplomatic, 1775–1865.* 1911. 301.

Adams, Ephraim D. *British Interests and Activities in Texas, 1838–1846.* 1910. 484.

—— *Great Britain and the American Civil War.* 2 vols. 1925. 617.

Adams, George W. *Doctors in Blue.* 1952. 618.

Adams, Henry. *The Formative Years: A History of the United States during the Administrations of Jefferson and Madison.* 2 vols. 1947. 252.

—— *History of the United States of America . . . 1801–1817.* 9 vols. 1889–1891. 252, 280, 302.

—— *John Randolph* (American Statesmen, XVI). New ed., 1917. 269.

—— *The Life of Albert Gallatin.* 1879. New ed., 1943. 215.

—— *The War of 1812.* 1944. 301.

Adams, Hubert B. *Maryland's Influence upon Land Cessions to the United States* (Johns Hopkins University, *Studies in Historical and Political Science*, 3rd series, I). 1885. 182.

Adams, James Truslow. *The Adams Family.* 1930. 229, 361.

—— *Atlas of American History.* 1943. 21.

—— *The Founding of New England.* 1921. 37, 77.

—— *New England in the Republic, 1776–1850.* 1926. 164.

—— *Provincial Society, 1690–1763* (A History of American Life, III). 1927. 79.

—— *Revolutionary New England, 1691–1776.* 1923. 77, 126.

——, ed. *Dictionary of American History.* 6 vols. 1940. 2nd ed. (5 vols.), 1942. 37.

Adams John. *The Works of John Adams.* Ed. by C. F. Adams. 10 vols. 1850–56. 183.

Adams, John and John Quincy Adams. *The Selected Writings of John and John Quincy Adams.* Ed. by A. Koch and W. Peden. 1946. 229.

Adams, John Quincy. *Parties in the United States.* 1941. 324.

Agar, Herbert. *The Price of Union.* 1950. 361.

Albion, Robert. *Square Riggers on Schedule.* 1938. 526.

Albion, Robert G. and Jennie B. Pope. *The Rise of New York Port, 1815–1860.* 1939. 362.

Alden, Carroll S. and A. Westcott. *The United States Navy: A History.* 1943. Rev. ed., 1945. 302.

Alden, John R. *General Charles Lee, Traitor or Patriot.* 1951. 149.

Alexander, Holmes M. *The American Talleyrand; The Career and Contemporaries of Martin Van Buren, Eighth President.* 1935. 421.

Allen, Gardner W. *Our Naval War with France.* 1909. 229.

—— *Our Navy and the Barbary Corsairs.* 1905. 268.

Alvord, Clarence W. *The Illinois Country, 1673–1818* (Centennial History of Illinois, I). 1920. 108.

—— *The Mississippi Valley in British Politics.* 2 vols. 1917. 108.

Ambler, Charles H. *George Washington and the West.* 1936. 108.

—— *West Virginia, The Mountain State.* 1940. 563.

Anderson, Nels. *Desert Saints: The Mormon Frontier in Utah.* 1942. 485.

Anderson, Troyer S. *The Command of the Howe Brothers during the American Revolution.* 1936. 148.

Andrews, Charles M. *The Colonial Background of the American Revolution.* 1924. Rev. ed., 1931. 125.

—— *The Colonial Period* (Home University Library of Modern Knowledge, no. 47). 1912. 37.

—— *Colonial Folkways* (Chronicles of America, IX). 1919. 77.

—— *The Colonial Period of American History.* 4 vols., 1934–1938. 36.

—— *Colonial Self-Government, 1652–1689* (American Nation, V). 1904. 92.

Andrews, Charles M. *The Fathers of New England* (*Chronicles of America*, VI). 1919. 37.

Andrews, Matthew. *The Founding of Maryland.* 1933. 51.

——— *The Soul of a Nation: The Founding of Virginia and the Projection of New England.* 1943. 37.

——— *The Women of the South in War Times.* 1920. 618.

Anthony, Katharine S. *Margaret Fuller: A Psychological Biography.* 1920. 449.

Ashe, Samuel A. *History of North Carolina.* 2 vols. 1908–25. 51.

Atherton, Lewis E. *The Southern Country Store, 1800–1860.* 1949. 464.

Atkins, Gaius S. and F. L. Fagley. *History of American Congregationalism.* 1942. 78.

Atwood, Wallace W. *The Physiographic Provinces of North America.* 1940. 20.

Auchampaugh, Philip G. *James Buchanan and his Cabinet on the Eve of Secession.* 1926. 548.

——— *Robert Tyler, Southern Rights Champion, 1847–1866.* 1934. 548.

Babcock, Kendric C. *The Rise of American Nationality, 1811–1819* (*American Nation*, XIII). 1906. 301, 324.

Bailey, Kenneth P. *Thomas Cresap, Maryland Frontiersman.* 1944. 108.

Bailey, Thomas A. *A Diplomatic History of the American People.* 4th ed., 1950. 148, 228, 280, 617.

Bakeless, John E. *Lewis and Clark, Partners in Discovery.* 1947. 269.

Baldwin, Leland D. *The Keelboat Age on Western Waters.* 1941. 346.

——— *Whiskey Rebels, The Story of a Frontier Uprising.* 1939. 215.

Bancroft, Frederic. *Calhoun and the South Carolina Nullification Movement.* 1928. 385.

——— *The Life of William H. Seward.* 2 vols., 1900. 564.

——— *Slave-Trading in the Old South.* 1931. 464.

Bancroft, Hubert Howe. *History of California.* 7 vols., 1884–1890. 484.

Barclay, Wade C. *Early American Methodism, 1769–1844* (*History of Methodist Missions*, pt. I). 1949. 252.

Baringer, William E. *A House Dividing: Lincoln as President Elect.* 1945. 563.

——— *Lincoln's Rise to Power.* 1937. 563.

Barker, Charles A. *The Background of the Revolution in Maryland* (*Yale Historical Publications, Miscellany*, XXXVIII). 1940. 126.

Barker, Eugene C. *The Life of Stephen F. Austin, Founder of Texas, 1793–1836.* 1925. 402.

——— *Mexico and Texas, 1821–1835.* 1928. 402.

Barker, Virgil. *American Painting: History and Interpretation.* 1950. 252, 449.

Barnes, Gilbert H. *The Anti-Slavery Impulse, 1830–1844.* 1933. 464.

Barnes, Viola F. *The Dominion of New England, A Study in British Colonial Policy* (*Yale Historical Publications, Miscellany*, XI). 1923. 92.

Barrett, J. A. *Evolution of the Ordinance of 1787; with an Account of the Earlier Plans of Government of the Northwest Territory* (University of Nebraska, Departments of History and Economics). 1891. 183.

Barry, Richard. *Mr. Rutledge of South Carolina.* 1942. 149.

Bartlett, Ruhl J. *John C. Frémont and the Republican Party.* 1930. 548.

Barton, William E. *The Life of Abraham Lincoln.* 2 vols. 1925. 563.

——— *The Life of Clara Barton, Founder of the American Red Cross.* 2 vols. 1922. 618.

Basler, Roy P. *The Lincoln Legend.* 1935. 617.

Bassett, John Spencer. *The Constitutional Beginnings of North Carolina, 1663–1729* (Johns Hopkins University, *Studies in Historical and Political Science*, Twelfth Series, III). 1894. 51.

——— *The Federalist System, 1789–1801* (*American Nation*, XI). 1906. 215.

——— *The Life of Andrew Jackson.* 2 vols. 1911. New ed., 1931. 362.

——— *The Middle Group of American Historians.* 1917. 449.

Baxter, James P., 3d. *The Introduction of the Ironclad Warship.* 1933. 595.

Beard, Charles A. *An Economic Interpretation of the Constitution of the United States.* 1913. New ed., 1935. 196, 215.

——— *Economic Origins of Jeffersonian Democracy.* 1915. New ed., 1949. 215.

——— *The Supreme Court and the Constitution.* 1912. New ed., 1938. 196.

Beard, Charles A. and Mary R. *The Rise of American Civilization.* 2 vols. 1927. New ed., 1949. 196.

Beard, Mary R. *A Short History of the American Labor Movement.* 1920. 450.

Becker, Carl L. *Beginnings of the American People* (*Riverside History*, I). 1915. 21.

——— *The Declaration of Independence; A Study in the History of Political Ideas.* 1922. New ed., 1942. 148.

——— *The Eve of the Revolution* (*Chronicles of America*, XI). 1918. 125.

Beer, George L. *British Colonial Policy, 1754–1765.* 1907. New ed., 1933. 92, 108.

——— *The Origins of the British Colonial System, 1578–1660.* 1908. New ed., 1933. 37, 92.

Beer, George L. *The Commercial Policy of England toward the American Colonies* (Columbia University, *Studies in History, Economics, and Public Law*, III). 1893. 92.

—— *The Old Colonial System, 1660–1754.* 1912. New ed., 1933. 92.

Belden, Albert D. *George Whitefield, the Awakener; A Modern Study of the Evangelical Revival.* 1930. 79.

Bemis, Samuel F. *The Diplomacy of the American Revolution.* 1935. 148.

—— *A Diplomatic History of the United States.* 3rd ed. 1950. 148, 228, 280, 617.

—— *Jay's Treaty: A Study in Commerce and Diplomacy.* 1923. 228.

—— *John Quincy Adams and the Foundations of American Foreign Policy.* 1949. 346.

—— *Pinckney's Treaty; A Study of America's Advantage from Europe's Distress, 1783–1800.* 1926. 228.

——, ed. *The American Secretaries of State and Their Diplomacy.* 10 vols. 1927–29. 228, 280.

Benns, Frank L. *The American Struggle for the British West India Carrying Trade, 1815–1830* (*Indiana University Studies*, X). 1923. 402.

Benton, Elbert J. *The Movement for Peace without Victory during the Civil War* (Western Reserve Historical Society, *Collections*, no. 99). 1918. 617.

—— *The Wabash Trade Route in the Development of the Old Northwest* (Johns Hopkins University, *Studies in History and Political Science*, series xxi, nos. 1–2). 1903. 362.

Benton, Thomas Hart. *Thirty Years' View; or, A History of the Working of the American Government, 1820–1850.* 2 vols. 1854–56. 385.

Berger, Max. *The British Traveller in America, 1836–1860.* 1943 (Columbia University, *Studies in History, Economics, and Public Law*, no. 502).

Bernstein, Harry. *Origins of Inter-American Interest, 1700–1812.* 1945. 280.

Bestor, Arthur E. *Backwoods Utopias: The Sectarian and Owenite Phases of Communitarian Socialism in America, 1663–1829.* 1950. 450.

Bettersworth, John K. *Confederate Mississippi, The People and Policies of a Cotton State in Wartime.* 1943. 617.

Beveridge, Albert J. *Abraham Lincoln, 1809–1858.* 2 vols. 1928. 549.

—— *The Life of John Marshall.* 4 vols. 1916–19. 229, 268, 324.

Beverley, Robert. *The History and Present State of Virginia.* Ed. by Louis B. Wright. 1947. 37.

Bidwell, Percy and John I. Falconer. *History of Agriculture in the Northern United States, 1620–1860.* 1925. 526.

Biesele, Rudolph L. and others, eds. *Readings in American History, 1492 to 1865.* 1952. 21.

Bigelow, John, ed. *The Life of Benjamin Franklin Written by Himself.* 3 vols., 1874. 78.

Bill, Alfred H. *The Beleaguered City: Richmond, 1861–1865.* 1946. 595.

—— *Rehearsal for Conflict: The War with Mexico, 1846–1848.* 1947. 485.

Billington, Ray A. *The Protestant Crusade, 1800–1860.* 1938. 526.

—— *Westward Expansion: A History of the American Frontier.* 1949. 78, 484.

Birney, Catherine H. *The Grimké Sisters, Sarah and Angelina Grimké, The First American Women Advocates of Abolition and Woman's Rights.* 1885. 464.

Birney, William. *James G. Birney and His Times.* 1890. 464.

Bittinger, Lucy F. *The Germans in Colonial Times.* 1901. 78.

Blackford, William W. *War Years with Jeb Stuart.* 1945. 595.

Blackwell, Elizabeth. *Pioneer Work for Women.* 1941. 450.

Blegen, Theodore C. *Norwegian Migration to America.* 2 vols. 1931–1940. 526.

Bleyer, Willard G. *Main Currents in the History of American Journalism.* 1927. 449.

Bloom, Sol, ed. *History of the Formation of the Union under the Constitution.* 1940. 196.

Boardman, Roger Sherman. *Roger Sherman, Signer and Statesman.* 1938. 196.

Bogart, Ernest L. *Financial History of Ohio* (University of Illinois, *Studies in the Social Sciences*, Vol. 1, nos. 1–2). 1912. 402.

—— *Internal Improvements and State Debt in Ohio.* 1924. 362.

Bolton, Charles K. *The Private Soldier under Washington.* 1902. 148.

Bolton, Herbert E. *The Padre on Horseback; A Sketch of Eusebio Francisco Kino, S.J., Apostle to the Pimas.* 1932. 484.

—— *Papers of L. M. Pike, 1806–07* (*American Historical Review*, XIII, pp. 798–827). 269.

—— *Rim of Christendom.* 1936. 484.

—— *The Spanish Borderlands* (*Chronicles of America*, XXIII). 1921. 484.

Bolton, Herbert E. and T. M. Marshall. *The Colonization of North America, 1492–1783.* New ed., 1936. 37.

Bond, Beverley W., Jr. *The Civilization of the Old Northwest. A Study of Political, Social and Economic Development, 1788–1812.* 1934.

—— *The Monroe Mission to France, 1794–1796* (Johns Hopkins University *Studies in Historical and Political Science*, Series XXV, nos. 2–3). 1907. 228.

—— *The Quit-Rent System in the American Colonies* (*Yale Historical Publications, Miscellany*, VI). 1919. 51, 182.

Boorstin, Daniel J. *The Lost World of Thomas Jefferson.* 1948. 252.

Boucher, Chauncey S. *The Nullification Controversy in South Carolina.* 1916. 385.

Bourne, Edward G. *The History of the Surplus Revenue of 1837.* 1885. 402.

——— *Spain in America, 1450–1580 (American Nation,* III). 1904. 21.

Bowen, Catherine D. *John Adams and the American Revolution.* 1950. 126.

Bowers, Claude. *Jefferson and Hamilton; The Struggle for Democracy in America.* 1925. 214.

——— *Jefferson in Power; The Death Struggle of the Federalists.* 1936. 252.

——— *The Party Battles of the Jackson Period.* 1922. 384.

——— *The Young Jefferson, 1743–1789.* 1945. 148.

Bowman, Allen. *The Morale of the American Revolutionary Army.* 1943. 148.

Bradlee, Francis B. C. *Blockade Running during the Civil War and the Effect of Land and Water Transportation on the Confederacy.* 1925. 595.

Branch, E. Douglas. *The Sentimental Years, 1836–1860.* 1934. 448.

——— *Westward; The Romance of the American Frontier.* 1930. 484.

Brant, Irving. *James Madison: The Nationalist, 1780–1787.* 1948. 280.

——— *James Madison: The Virginia Revolutionist.* 1941. 280.

Bridenbaugh, Carl. *Cities in the Wilderness: The First Century of Urban Life in America, 1625–1742.* 1938. 77.

——— *The Colonial Craftsman.* 1950. 78.

——— *Seat of Empire; The Political Role of Eighteenth-Century Williamsburg.* 1950. 77.

Bridenbaugh, Carl and Jessica. *Rebels and Gentlemen: Philadelphia in the Age of Franklin.* 1942. 78.

Brigham, Albert P. *Geographic Influences in American History.* 1903. 20.

Brigance, William N. *Jeremiah Sullivan Black.* 1934. 549.

Brockunier, Samuel H. *The Irrepressible Democrat: Roger Williams.* 1940. 37.

Brodie, Fawn M. *No Man Knows My History; The Life of Joseph Smith, the Mormon Prophet.* 1945. 485.

Brooks, Van Wyck. *The Flowering of New England, 1815–1865.* 1936. Rev. ed., 1940. 448.

——— *The World of Washington Irving.* 1944. 324.

Brown, Ralph H. *Historical Geography of the United States.* 1948. 20.

Brown, William G. *The Lower South in American History.* 1902 Reprinted, 1930. 464.

Browne, William H. *George Calvert and Cecilius Calvert.* 1890. 51.

——— *Maryland, The History of a Palatinate.* 1884. New ed., 1904. 51.

Bruce, Henry A. *Daniel Boone and the Wilderness Road.* 1910. 108.

Bruce, Philip A. *The Colonial Period, 1607–1763 (American Historical Society, History of Virginia,* I). 1924. 77.

——— *Economic History of Virginia in the Seventeenth Century.* 2 vols. 1896. New ed., 1935. 37.

——— *Institutional History of Virginia in the Seventeenth Century.* 2 vols. 1910. 37.

——— *Social Life of Virginia in the Seventeenth Century.* 1907. New ed., 1927. 37.

Bruce, William C. *John Randolph of Roanoke, 1773–1833.* 2 vols. 1922. New ed., 1939. 269.

Brunhouse, Robert L. *The Counter-Revolution in Pennsylvania, 1776–1790.* 1942. 164.

Bryan, Alfred C. *History of State Banking in Maryland.* 1899. 402.

Buley, R. Carlyle. *The Old Northwest: Pioneer Period, 1815–1840.* 2 vols. 1950. 362.

Burgess, John W. *The Middle Period, 1817–1858.* 1897. 324.

Burne, Alfred H. *Lee, Grant, and Sherman: A Study in Leadership in the 1864–65 Campaign.* 1939. 594.

Burnett, Edmund C. *The Continental Congress.* 1941. 147.

Burns, Edward M. *James Madison, Philosopher of the Constitution (Rutgers University, Studies in History,* I). 1938. 196.

Burrage, Henry S. *The Beginnings of Colonial Maine, 1602–1658.* 1914. 37.

——— *Maine in the Northeastern Boundary Controversy.* 1919. 421.

Burson, Caroline M. *The Stewardship of Don Esteban Miró, 1782–1792.* 1940. 183.

Burt, Alfred L. *The United States, Great Britain, and British North America from the Revolution to the Establishment of Peace after the War of 1812.* 1940. 183, 280.

Butts, Porter. *Art in Wisconsin; The Art Experience of the Middle-West Frontier.* 1936. 449.

Butts, R. Freeman. *The American Tradition in Religion and Education.* 1950. 252.

Cable, John R. *The Bank of the State of Missouri (Columbia University, Studies in History, Economics, and Public Law,* no. 232). 1923. 402.

Calder, Isabel M. *The New Haven Colony (Yale Historical Publications, Miscellany,* XXVIII). 1934. 37.

Caldwell, Lynton K. *The Administrative Theories of Hamilton and Jefferson; Their Contribution to Thought on Public Administration.* 1944. **214.**

Caldwell, Stephen A. *A Banking History of Louisiana* (Louisiana State University, *Studies*, XIX). 1935. 402.

Callahan, James M. *Cuba and International Relations; A Historical Study in American Diplomacy* (Johns Hopkins University, *Studies*, extra vol. XXI). 1899. 527.

—— *The Diplomatic History of the Southern Confederacy.* 1901. 618.

Campbell, Claude A. *The Development of Banking in Tennessee.* 1932. 402.

Canby, Henry S. *Walt Whitman, an American; A Study in Biography.* 1943. 449.

Capers, Gerald M. *The Biography of a River Town; Memphis: Its Heroic Age.* 1939. 346.

Carlson, Oliver. *The Man Who Made News, James Gordon Bennett.* 1942. 449.

Carman, Harvey J. *Social and Economic History of the United States.* 2 vols. 1930–34. 77, 252, 324.

Carman, Harry J. and R. H. Luthin. *Lincoln and the Patronage.* 1943. 617.

Carosso, Vincent P. *The California Wine Industry, 1830–1895; A Study of the Formative Years.* 1951. 484.

Carpenter, Edmund J. *Roger Williams; A Study of the Life, Times and Character of a Political Pioneer* (Grafton Historical Series). 1909. 37.

Carpenter, Jesse T. *The South as a Conscious Minority, 1789–1861; A Study in Political Thought.* 1930. 563.

Carroll, E. M. *Origins of the Whig Party* (Duke University, *Publications*). 1925. 402.

Carter, Clarence E., ed. *The Territorial Papers of the United States.* 17 vols. 1934–50. 182.

Catterall, Ralph C. H. *The Second Bank of the United States.* 1903. 324, 401.

Catton, Bruce. *Mr. Lincoln's Army.* 1951. 594.

Caughey, John W. *California.* 1940. 484.

—— *Hubert Howe Bancroft, Historian of the West.* 1946. 484.

Channing, Edward. *A History of the United States.* 6 vols. 1905–30. 21, 92, 126, 215, 252, 302, 345, 384, 450, 502, 548, 618.

—— *The Jeffersonian System, 1801–1811* (*American Nation*, XII). 1906. 252.

—— *The Story of the Great Lakes.* 1909. 362.

Chapman, Charles E. *A History of California: The Spanish Period.* 1921. 484.

Charnwood, Lord. *Abraham Lincoln.* 1916. 563.

Cheyney, Edward P. *European Background of American History, 1300–1600* (*American Nation*, I). 1904. 21.

Chinard, Gilbert. *Honest John Adams.* 1933. 215.

—— *Thomas Jefferson, The Apostle of Americanism.* 1929. 252.

Chittenden, Hiram M. *The American Fur Trade of the Far West* 3 vols. 1902. 484.

Chitwood, Oliver P. *A History of Colonial America.* 1931. New ed., 1948. 37, 77.

—— *John Tyler, Champion of the Old South.* 1939. 421.

Chumbley, George L. *Colonial Justice in Virginia; The Development of a Judicial System, Typical Laws and Cases of the Period.* 1938. 92.

Clark, Arthur. *The Clipper Ship Era, 1843–1869.* 1910. 526.

Clark, Bennett C. *John Quincy Adams, "Old Man Eloquent."* 1932. 362.

Clark, Dan E. *The West in American History.* 1937. 484.

Clark, George L. *A History of Connecticut, Its People and Institutions.* 1914. 37.

Clark, Thomas D. *The Rampaging Frontier; Manners and Humors of Pioneer Days in the South and Middle West.* 1939. 527.

Clark, Victor S. *History of Manufactures in the United States, 1607–1914* (Carnegie Institute of Washington, *Publication*, no. 2153). 2 vols. 1916–1928. 526.

Cleaves, Freeman. *Old Tippecanoe: William Henry Harrison and His Time.* 1939. 421.

—— *Rock of Chickamauga, The Life of General George H. Thomas.* 1948. 594.

Cleland, Robert G. *From Wilderness to Empire: A History of California, 1542–1900.* 1944. 484.

—— *A History of California: The American Period.* 1922. 502.

Cleveland, Catharine C. *The Great Revival in the West, 1797–1805.* 1916. 252.

Coad, Oral S. and Edwin Mims, Jr. *The American Stage* (*The Pageant of America*, XIV.) 1929. 449.

Cobb, Sanford H. *The Rise of Religious Liberty in America.* 1902. 78.

—— *The Story of the Palatines.* 1897. 78.

Cochran, Thomas C. and William Miller. *The Age of Enterprise, A Social History of Industrial America.* 1942. 526.

Coit, Margaret L. *John C. Calhoun, American Portrait.* 1950. 502.

Coker, Francis W., ed. *Democracy, Liberty, and Property: Readings in the American Political Tradition.* 1942. 21.

Cole, Arthur C. *The Era of the Civil War, 1848–1870* (*Illinois Centennial Publications*, III). 1919. 549.

—— *The Irrepressible Conflict, 1850–1865* (*A History of American Life*, VII). 1934. 502.

—— *The Whig Party in the South.* 1913. 402, 420.

Coleman, Roy V. *The First Frontier.* 1948. 21.

Coman, Katharine. *Economic Beginnings of the Far West.* 2 vols. 1912. New ed., 1925. 484.

—— *The Industrial History of the United States.* 1905. New ed., 1920. 324.

Comfort, William W. *William Penn, 1644–1718.* 1944. 51.

Commager, Henry Steele. *Majority Rule and Minority Rights.* 1943. 269.

—— *Theodore Parker.* 1936. 464.

——, *Documents of American History.* 5th ed., 1949. 21.

Commons, John R. and associates. *History of Labour in the United States.* 4 vols. 1918–1935. 450.

Coolidge, Louis A. *Ulysses S. Grant (American Statesmen, XXXII).* 1917. New ed. 1922. 594.

Copeland, Melvin T. *The Cotton Manufacturing Industry of the United States (Harvard Economic Studies, VIII).* 1912. 526.

Corey, Albert B. *The Crisis of 1830–1842 in Canadian-American Relations.* 1941. 421.

Corwin, Elwood S. "The Dred Scott Decision," *American Historical Review,* vol. XVII, pp. 52–69. 549.

—— *The Doctrine of Judicial Review.* 1914. 196.

—— *French Policy and the American Alliance of 1778.* 1916. 148.

—— *John Marshall and the Constitution; A Chronicle of the Supreme Court (Chronicles of America, XVI).* 1919. 268.

Cotterill, Robert S. *The Old South; The Geographic, Economic, Social, Political and Cultural Expansion, Institutions, and Nationalism of the Ante-Bellum South.* 1936. 463.

Coulter, Ellis Merton. *College Life in the Old South.* 1928. 2nd ed., 1951. 324.

—— *The Confederate States of America, 1861–1865 (A History of the South, VII).* 1950. 617.

—— *Georgia, A Short History.* 1947. 51.

Coupland, Reginald. *The American Revolution and the British Empire.* 1930. 126.

Cox, Isaac J. *The West Florida Controversy, 1798–1813.* 1918. 269.

Crandall, Andrew W. *The Early History of the Republican Party, 1854–1856.* 1930. 548.

Crane, Verner W. *Benjamin Franklin, Englishman and American.* 1936. 78.

—— *The Southern Frontier, 1670–1732.* 1929. 51.

Craven, Avery O. *The Coming of the Civil War.* 1942. 548.

—— *Edmund Ruffin, Southerner, A Study in Secession.* 1932. 464.

—— *The Repressible Conflict, 1830–1861.* 1939. 502.

—— *Soil Exhaustion as a Factor in the Agricultural History of Virginia and Maryland, 1606–1860.* 1926. 77, 464.

Craven, Wesley F. *The Southern Colonies in the Seventeenth Century, 1607–1689.* 1949. 37.

Creer, L. H. *The Founding of an Empire: The Exploration and Colonization of Utah, 1776–1856.* 1947. 485.

Creighton, Donald G. *Dominion of the North: A History of Canada.* 1944. 108.

Crenshaw, Ollinger. *The Slave States in the Presidential Election of 1860.* 1945. 549.

Cresson, William P. *The Holy Alliance; The European Background of the Monroe Doctrine.* 1922. 346.

—— *James Monroe.* 1946. 324.

Crippen, Lee F. *Simon Cameron, Ante-Bellum Years (Men of America, III).* 1942. 564.

Cross, Arthur Lyon. *The Anglican Episcopate and the American Colonies (Harvard Historical Studies, IX).* 1902. 78.

Crowl, Philip A. *Maryland during and after the Revolution (Johns Hopkins University, Studies in Historical and Political Science. Ser. LXI, no. 1).* 1943. 164.

Cubberley, Ellwood P. *Public Education in the United States.* 1919. New ed., 1934. 324.

Curti, Merle E. *The Growth of American Thought.* 1943. New ed., 1950. 77, 252, 324, 448.

—— *The Roots of American Loyalty.* 1946. 229.

Curtis, Edith R. *Anne Hutchinson.* 1930. 37.

Curtis, Edward E. *The Organization of the British Army in the American Revolution (Yale Historical Publications, Miscellany, XIX).* 1926. 148.

Curtis, George T. *Life of Daniel Webster.* 2 vols. 1870. 324.

—— *Life of James Buchanan.* 2 vols. 1883. 548.

Cushing, Harry A. *History of the Transition from Provincial to Commonwealth Government in Massachusetts (Columbia University, Studies in History, Economics, and Public Law, VII).* 1896. 164.

Cutler, Carl C. *Greyhounds of the Sea: The Story of the American Clipper Ship.* 1930. 526.

Dana, Julian. *Sutter of California.* 1936. 484.

Darling, Arthur B. *Our Rising Empire, 1763–1803.* 1940. 183.

—— *Political Changes in Massachusetts, 1824–1848; A Study of Liberal Movements in Politics (Yale Historical Publications, Miscellany, XV).* 1925. 385.

Davidson, Marshall. *Life in America.* 2 vols. 1951. 77.

Davidson, Philip G. *Propaganda and the American Revolution, 1763–1783.* 1941. 148.

Davis, Jefferson. *The Rise and Fall of the Confederate Government.* 2 vols., 1881. New ed., 1938. 564.

Deaderick, Barron. *Strategy in the Civil War.* 1946. 594.

Debo, Angie. *The Road to Disappearance* (*The Civilization of the American Indian Series*). 1941. 385.

Decker, Malcolm. *Benedict Arnold, Son of the Havens*. 1932. 148.

Demaree, Albert L. *The American Agricultural Press, 1819–1860* (Columbia University, *Studies in the History of American Agriculture*, VIII). 1941. 526.

DeMond, Robert O. *The Loyalists in North Carolina during the Revolution* (Duke University, *Publications*). 1940. 149.

DeVoto, Bernard. *The Year of Decision, 1846*. 1943. 484.

Dewey, Davis R. *Financial History of the United States* (*American Citizen Series*). 1903. 12th ed., 1936. 183, 420.

———— *State Banking before the Civil War*. 1910. 346, 420.

Dexter, Edwin G. *A History of Education in the United States*. 1904. 324.

Dick, Everett. *The Dixie Frontier: A Social History of the Southern Frontier*. 1948. 464.

———— *Vanguards of the Frontier, A Social History of the Northern Plain and Rocky Mountains from the Earliest White Contacts to the Coming of the Homemaker*. 1941. 346.

Dickerson, Oliver Morton. *American Colonial Government, 1696–1765: A Study of the Board of Trade in its Relation to the American Colonies*. 1912. 92.

Dodd, William E. *The Cotton Kingdom* (*Chronicles of America*, XXVII). 1919. 463.

———— *Expansion and Conflict* (*Riverside History*, III). 1915. 484.

———— *Jefferson Davis* (*American Crisis Biographies*). 1907. 564.

———— *Lincoln or Lee; Comparison and Contrast of the Two Greatest Leaders in the War Between the States*. 1928. 564.

———— *The Old South: Struggles for Democracy*. 1937. 77.

———— *Statesmen of the Old South; From Radicalism to Conservative Revolt*. 1911. 502.

Dodge, Theodore A. *A Bird's Eye View of Our Civil War*. 1883. Rev. ed., 1897. 594.

Dole, Esther M. *Maryland during the American Revolution*. 1941. 149.

Donaldson, Thomas C. *The Public Domain, Its History*. 1884. 269.

Dorfman, Joseph. *The Economic Mind in American Civilization, 1606–1865*. 2 vols. 1946. 78.

Downes, Randolph C. *Council Fires on the Upper Ohio*. 1940. 183.

———— *Frontier Ohio, 1788–1803* (Ohio State Archaeological and Historical Society, *Ohio History Collections*, III). 1935. 183, 269.

Dowrie, George W. *The Development of Banking in Illinois, 1817–1863*. 1913. 402.

Doyle, John A. *English Colonies in America*. 5 vols. 1882–1907. 36.

Drake, Thomas E. *Quakers and Slavery in America*. 1950. 78.

Drury, Clifford M. *Marcus Whitman, M.D., Pioneer and Martyr*. 1937. 484.

DuBois, William E. B. *Suppression of the African Slave Trade to the United States of America, 1638–1870* (*Harvard Historical Studies*, I). 1896. 346.

Duffus, Robert L. *The Santa Fe Trail*. 1930. 484.

Dumbauld, Edward. *The Declaration of Independence and What it Means Today*. 1950. 148.

Dumond, Dwight L. *Antislavery Origins of the Civil War in the United States*. 1939. 464.

———— *The Secession Movement, 1860–1861*. 1931. 563.

Dunaway, Wayland F. *A History of Pennsylvania*. 1935. 2nd ed., 1948. 51, 164.

———— *The Scotch Irish of Colonial Pennsylvania*. 1944. 78.

Dunbar, Louise B. *A Study of "Monarchical" Tendencies in the United States from 1776–1801* (University of Illinois, *Studies in the Social Sciences*, X, No. 1). 1923. 215.

Dunbar, Seymour. *A History of Travel in America*. 4 vols. 1915. New ed., 1937. 346.

Dunham, Chester F. *The Attitude of the Northern Clergy toward the South, 1860–1865*. 1942. 617.

Dunning, William A. *The British Empire and the United States*. 1914. 302.

Dwight, Theodore. *History of the Hartford Convention*. 1833. 302.

Dyer, Brainerd. *Zachary Taylor* (*Southern Biography Series*). 1946. 485.

Dyer, John P. *"Fightin'" Joe Wheeler* (*Southern Biography Series*). 1941. 595.

———— *The Gallant Hood*. 1950. 595.

Earle, Alice Morse. *Child Life in Colonial Days*. 1899. 78.

———— *Colonial Dames and Goodwives*. New ed., 1924. 78.

———— *Colonial Days in Old New York*. 1896. 78.

———— *Customs and Fashions in Old New England*. 1893. 78.

———— *Home Life in Colonial Days*. New ed., 1913. 78.

———— *The Sabbath in Puritan New England*, 1891. 78.

———— *Stage Coach and Tavern Days*. New ed., 1935. 78.

East, Robert A. *Business Enterprise in the American Revolutionary Era*. 1938. 164.

Eaton, Clement. *Freedom of Thought in the Old South* (*Duke University Publications*). 1940. 464.

—— *A History of the Old South.* 1949. 463.

Eckenrode, Hamilton J. *The Randolphs, The Story of a Virginia Family.* 1946. 301.

Eckenrode, Hamilton J. and Bryan Conrad. *George B. McClellan, The Man Who Saved the Union.* 1941. 594.

Egerton, Hugh E. *The Causes and Character of the American Revolution.* 1923. 125.

—— *A Short History of the British Colonial Policy 1606–1909.* 9th ed. 1932. 51.

Eggleston, Edward. *The Beginners of a Nation.* 1896. 37.

—— *The Transit of Civilization from England to America in the Seventeenth Century.* 1901. 77.

Egleston, Melville. *The Land System of the New England Colonies.* 1886. 78.

Ekirch, Arthur A. *The Idea of Progress in America, 1815–1860.* 1944. 448.

Eldredge, Zoeth S. *History of California.* 5 vols. 1915. 484.

Elliott, Charles W. *Winfield Scott, the Soldier and the Man.* 1937. 485.

Elliot, Jonathan, ed. *The Debates on the Federal Constitution.* 5 vols. 1827–1845. 196.

Ellis, David M. *Landlords and Farmers in the Hudson-Mohawk Region, 1790–1860.* 1946. 526.

Emerson, Ralph Waldo. *Journals of Ralph Waldo Emerson, 1820–1872.* Ed. by E. W. Emerson and W. E. Forbes. 10 vols. 1909–14. 449.

—— *The Letters of Ralph Waldo Emerson.* Ed. by Ralph L. Rusk. 6 vols. 1939. 449.

Ernst, Robert. *Immigrant Life in New York City, 1825–1863.* 1949. 526.

Esarey, Logan. *State Banking in Indiana, 1814–1873.* 1912. 402.

Ettinger, Amos A. *James Edward Oglethorpe, Imperial Idealist.* 1936. 51.

Faris, John T. *The Romance of Old Philadelphia.* 1918. 78.

Farrand, Livingston. *Basis of American History, 1500–1900* (*American Nation*, II). 1904. 21.

Farrand, Max. *The Fathers of the Constitution* (*Chronicles of America*, XIII). 1921. 196.

—— *The Framing of the Constitution of the United States.* 1913. 196.

—— *Records of the Federal Convention of 1787.* 4 vols. 1911–1937. 196.

Faulkner, Harold U. *American Economic History.* 6th ed. 1949. 183, 420, 526.

Faust, Albert B. *The German Element in the United States.* 2 vols. 1909. New ed. (1 vol.) 1927. 78.

Faÿ, Bernard. *Franklin, The Apostle of Modern Times.* 1929. 149.

—— *The Revolutionary Spirit in France and America.* 1927. 148.

Firkins, Oscar W. *Ralph Waldo Emerson.* 1915. 449.

Fish, Carl Russell. *The American Civil War.* 1937. 594.

—— *American Diplomacy.* 1915; 5th ed., 1938. 148.

—— *The Civil Service and the Patronage* (*Harvard Historical Studies*, XI). 1905. 268.

—— *The Rise of the Common Man, 1830–1850* (*History of American Life*, VI). 1927. 448.

Fisher, Sydney G. *The Making of Pennsylvania.* 1896. New ed., 1932. 51.

—— *Pennsylvania; Colony and Commonwealth.* 1897. 51.

—— *The Quaker Colonies* (*Chronicles of America*, VIII). 1919. 51.

—— *The Struggle for American Independence.* 2 vols. 1908. 147.

—— *William Penn, A Biography.* 1932. 51.

Fiske, John. *The American Revolution.* 2 vols., 1891. 147.

—— *The Critical Period of American History.* 1888. New ed., 1916. 164.

—— *The Beginnings of New England.* 1889. 37.

—— *The Dutch and Quaker Colonies in America.* 2 vols. 1899. 51.

—— *Essays Historical and Literary.* 2 vols. 1902. 420.

—— *The Historical Writings of John Fiske.* 12 vols. 1902. 37.

—— *New France and New England.* 1902. New ed., 1930. 108.

—— *Old Virginia and her Neighbours.* 2 vols. 1897. 37.

Fite, Emerson D. *The Presidential Campaign of 1860.* 549.

—— *Social and Industrial Conditions in the North during the Civil War.* 1910. 617.

Fitzpatrick, John C. *George Washington Himself.* 1933. 214.

Flanagan, John T. *America Is West: An Anthology of Middlewestern Life and Literature.* 1945. 527.

Fletcher, Robert S. *A History of Oberlin College from its Foundation through the Civil War.* 2 vols. 1943. 449.

Flexner, James T. *America's Old Masters: First Artists of the New World.* 1939. 252.

—— *Steamboats Come True: American Inventors in Action.* 1944. 346.

Flick, Alexander C., ed. *History of the State of New York.* 10 vols. 1933–37. 362.

Folmsbee, Stanley J. *Sectionalism and Internal*

Improvements in Tennessee, 1796–1845. 1939. 362.

Foner, Philip S. *Business and Slavery: The New York Merchants and the Irrepressible Conflict.* 1941. 563.

Ford, Amelia C. *Colonial Precedents of our National Land System as it Existed in 1800* (University of Wisconsin, *History Series*, II). 1910. 182.

Ford, Henry Jones. *Alexander Hamilton.* 1920. 214.

——— *The Scotch-Irish in America.* 1915. 78.

——— *Washington and his Colleagues* (*Chronicles of America*, XIV). 1918. 215.

Ford, Paul L. *The True George Washington.* 1896. New ed., 1903. 214.

———, ed. *Pamphlets on the Constitution of the United States.* 1888. 196.

Foreman, Grant. *Advancing the Frontier.* 1933. 385.

——— *The Five Civilized Tribes.* 1934. 385.

——— *Indian Removal: The Emigration of the Five Civilized Tribes.* 1932. 385.

——— *Indians and Pioneers.* 1930. 385.

Forman, Samuel E. *The Rise of American Commerce and Industry.* 1927. 78.

Fortescue, John W. *A History of the British Army.* 13 vols. 1899–1930. 148, 301.

Foster, John W. *A Century of American Diplomacy.* 1900. 183.

Foulke, William D. *Life of Oliver P. Morton.* 2 vols. 1899. 617.

Fowler, Dorothy G. *The Cabinet Politician: The Postmasters-General, 1829–1909.* 1943. 384.

Fox, Dixon Ryan. *The Decline of Aristocracy in the Politics of New York* (Columbia University, *Studies in History, Economics, and Public Law,* LXXXVI). 1919. 324.

——— *Ideas in Motion.* 1935. 164.

——— *Yankees and Yorkers.* 1940. 78.

Franklin, Benjamin. *Autobiography.* SEE Bigelow, John, ed.

Franklin, John H. *The Free Negro in North Carolina, 1790–1860.* 1943. 464.

——— *From Slavery to Freedom: A History of American Negroes.* 1947. 464.

Freeman, D. S. *George Washington.* 4 vols. 1948–51. 214.

——— *Lee's Lieutenants.* 3 vols. 1942–44. 595.

——— *R. E. Lee: A Biography.* 4 vols. 1934–35. 564, 595.

Freidel, Frank. *Francis Lieber, Nineteenth Century Liberal.* 1947. 526.

Friedenwald, Herbert. *The Declaration of Independence: An Interpretation and an Analysis.* 1904. 148.

Frothingham, Richard. *The Rise of the Republic of the United States.* 10th ed., 1910. 37.

Fry, William H. *New Hampshire as a Royal Province* (Columbia University, *Studies in History, Economics, and Public Law,* XXIX). 1908. 37.

Fuess, Claude M. *Daniel Webster.* 2 vols. 1930. 362, 385, 502.

Fuller, Hubert B. *The Purchase of Florida.* 1906. 346.

Fuller [Ossoli], Margaret. *Woman in the Nineteenth Century.* 1855. 449.

Gabriel, Ralph H. *The Course of American Democratic Thought.* 1940. 448.

Gabriel, Ralph H. and others, eds. *The Pageant of America.* 15 vols. 1929. 77.

Gaeddert, Gustave R. *The Birth of Kansas.* 1940. 527.

Gaines, Francis P. *The Southern Plantation* (Columbia University, *Studies in English and Comparative Literature*). 1924. 463.

Galpin, William Freeman. *The Grain Supply of England during the Napoleonic Period* (University of Michigan, *Publications, History and Political Science,* VI). 1925. 280.

Gammon, Samuel R. *The Presidential Campaign of 1832* (Johns Hopkins University, *Studies in Historical and Political Science,* ser. XL, no. 1). 1922. 402.

Ganaway, Loomis M. *New Mexico and the Sectional Controversy, 1846–1861* (Historical Society of New Mexico, *Publications in History,* Vol. XII). 1944. 548.

Gardner, Albert T. *Yankee Stonecutters: The First American School of Sculpture, 1800–1850.* 1945. 449.

Garrison, George P. *Westward Extension, 1841–1850* (*American Nation,* XVII). 1906. 484.

Garrison, Wendell Phillips and Francis Jackson Garrison. *William Lloyd Garrison.* 4 vols. 1885–89. 464.

Gay, Sydney H. *James Madison* (*American Statesmen*). 1884. 280.

Geiger, Sister Mary Virginia. *Daniel Carroll: A Framer of the Constitution.* 1943. 196.

Getell, Raymond G. *History of American Political Thought.* 1928. 448.

Ghent, William J. *The Road to Oregon.* 1929. 484.

Gilman, Daniel Coit. *James Monroe* (*American Statesman,* XIV). 1883. 324.

Gilmore, James R. *John Sevier as a Commonwealth Builder.* 1887. 182.

Gipson, Lawrence H. *The British Empire before the American Revolution.* 7 vols. 1936–49. 92.

Godbold, Albea. *The Church College of the Old South.* 1944. 449.

Goebel, Dorothy B. *William Henry Harrison.* 1926. 301.

Gooch, George P. *English Democratic Ideas in the Seventeenth Century.* 1927. 92.

Goodwin, Cardinal. *The Trans-Mississippi West, 1803–1853.* 1922. 346.

Goodwin, Edward L. *The Colonial Church in Virginia.* 1927. 77.

Goodwin, Maud W. *Dutch and English on the Hudson (Chronicles of America, VII).* 1919. 51.

Gordy, John P. *Political History of the United States with Special Reference to the Growth of Political Parties.* 2 vols. 1903. 215.

Gottschalk, Louis. *Lafayette and the Close of the American Revolution.* 1942. 148.

—— *Lafayette Comes to America.* 1935. 148.

—— *Lafayette Joins the American Army.* 1937. 148.

Graeff, Arthur D. and others. *The Pennsylvania Germans.* 1942. 78.

Grant, Ulysses S. *The Personal Memoirs of U. S. Grant.* 2 vols. 1885–86. 594.

Gras, Norman S. B. *The Massachusetts-First National Bank of Boston, 1784–1934.* 1937. 420.

Gray, Lewis C. *History of Agriculture in the Southern United States to 1860.* 2 vols. 1933. 526.

Gray, Wood. *The Hidden Civil War.* 1942. 617.

Green, James A. *William Henry Harrison: His Life and Times.* 1941. 421.

Greene, Evarts B. *The Foundations of American Nationality.* 1922. New ed., 1935. 37.

—— *Provincial America (American Nation, VI).* 1905. 92.

—— *The Provincial Governor in the English Colonies of North America.* 1898. 92.

—— *The Revolutionary Generation, 1763–1790 (History of American Life, IV).* 1943. 164.

Greene, Francis V. *The Revolutionary War.* 1911. 148.

Greene, Lorenzo J. *The Negro in Colonial New England.* 1942. 78.

Greenslet, Ferris. *The Lowells and Their Seven Worlds.* 1946. 252.

Gregg, Josiah. *Commerce of the Prairies, or, The Journal of a Santa Fe Trader.* 1844. 484.

Griffith, Ernest S. *History of American City Government: The Colonial Period.* 1938. 92.

Guttridge, George H. *English Whiggism and the American Revolution.* 1942. 126.

Hacker, Louis M. *The Triumph of American Capitalism.* 1940. 617.

Hacker, Louis M. and Helène S. Zahler, eds. *The Shaping of the American Tradition.* 1947. 21.

Hafen, LeRoy R. and Carl C. Rister. *Western America.* 1941. 346, 484.

Haiman, Miecislaus. *Kosciuszko in the American Revolution.* 1943. 149.

Haines, Charles Grove. *The Role of the Supreme Court in American Government and Politics, 1789–1835.* 1944. 215.

Hallowell, Anna D. *James and Lucretia Mott, Life and Letters.* 1884. 464.

Hamer, Philip M. *The Secession Movement in South Carolina, 1847–1852.* 1918. 502.

Hamilton, Holman. *Zachary Taylor.* 1941. 485.

Hammond, Matthew B. *The Cotton Industry.* 1897. 463.

Handlin, Oscar. *Boston's Immigrants, 1790–1865.* 1941. 526.

Hanna, Charles A. *The Scotch Irish.* 1902. 78.

Hansen, Marcus Lee. *The Atlantic Migration, 1607–1860.* 1940. 37.

—— *The Immigrant in American History.* 1940. 526.

Harding, Samuel B. *The Contest over the Ratification of the Federal Constitution in the State of Massachusetts (Harvard Historical Studies, II).* 1896. 196.

Harlow, Alvin F. *Old Towpaths, The Story of the American Canal Era.* 1926. 362.

Harlow, Ralph V. *Gerrit Smith.* 1939. 464.

—— *Samuel Adams, Promoter of the American Revolution.* 1923. 126.

Harmon, George D. *Sixty Years of Indian Affairs.* 1941. 385.

Harper, Lawrence A. *The English Navigation Laws.* 1939. 92.

Harper, Robert S. *Lincoln and the Press.* 1951. 563, 617.

Harrington, Fred H. *Fighting Politician: Major General N. P. Banks.* 1948. 595.

Harris, Thomas L. *The Trent Affair.* 1896. 618.

Hart, Albert B. *Salmon Portland Chase (American Statesmen, XXVIII).* 1899. 564.

—— *Slavery and Abolition, 1831–1841 (American Nation, XVI).* 1906. 464.

——, ed. *The American Nation: A History.* 28 vols. 1904–28.

Hart, Albert B., and H. E. Bolton. *American History Atlas.* 1930. New ed., 1949. 21.

Hart, Freeman H. *The Valley of Virginia in the American Revolution.* 1942.

Hatch, Louis C. *The Administration of the American Revolutionary Army (Harvard Historical Studies, X).* 1904. 148.

Hatcher, Harlan. *The Great Lakes.* 1944. 362.

—— *Lake Erie.* 1945. 362.

Hatcher, William B. *Edward Livingston: Jeffersonian Republican and Jacksonian Democrat.* 1940. 385.

Havighurst, Walter. *Land of Promise: The Story of the Northwest Territory.* 1946. 182.

Hawk, Emory Q. *Economic History of the South.* 1934. 463.

Haynes, George H. *The Senate of the United States: Its History and Practice.* 2 vols. 1938. 215.

Hazelton, John H. *The Declaration of Independence: Its History.* 1906. 148.

Hebert, Walter H. *Fighting Joe Hooker.* 1944. 594.

Helderman, Leonard C. *National and State Banks.* 1931. 402.

Henderson, Archibald. *Conquest of the Old Southwest, 1740–1800.* 1920. 78.

Henderson, George F. R. *Stonewall Jackson and the American Civil War.* 2 vols. 1898. 595.

Hendrick, Burton J. *The Lees of Virginia.* 1935. 564.

—— *Statesmen of the Lost Cause: Jefferson Davis and His Cabinet.* 1939.

Henry, Robert S. *"First with the Most" Forrest.* 1944. 595.

Henry, Robert S. *The Story of the Confederacy.* 1943. 617.

—— *The Story of the Mexican War.* 1950. 485.

Henry, William W. *Patrick Henry.* 3 vols. 1891. 126.

Hergesheimer, Joseph. *Sheridan; A Military Narrative.* 1931. 595.

Hermannsson, Halldór. *The Problem of Wineland.* 1936. 21.

Hesseltine, William B. *Civil War Prisons: A Study in War Psychology.* 1930. 618.

—— *Lincoln and the War Governors.* 1948. 617.

—— *The South in American History.* 1943. 502.

—— *Ulysses S. Grant, Politician.* 1935. 594.

Hibbard, Benjamin H. *A History of the Public Land Policies.* 1924. 183, 269, 385, 421.

Hill, Charles E. *Leading American Treaties.* 1922. 164, 269.

Hill, Helen D. *George Mason, Constitutionalist.* 1938. 196.

Hill, Jim Dan. *The Texas Navy.* 1937. 484.

Hill, Louise B. *Joseph E. Brown and the Confederacy.* 1939. 595.

Hinsdale, Burke A. *Horace Mann and the Common School Revival in the United States.* 1898. 449.

Hinsdale, Burke A. *The Old Northwest.* 1888. 182.

Hirsch, Arthur H. *The Huguenots of Colonial South Carolina.* 1928. 77.

Hittell, Theodore H. *History of California.* 4 vols. 1885–97. 484.

Hockett, Homer C. *The Constitutional History of the United States, 1776–1876.* 2 vols. 1939. 196, 548.

—— *Western Influences on Political Parties to 1825* (Ohio State University, *Contributions in History and Political Science*, no. 4). 1917. 268.

Hodder, Frank H. "The Genesis of the Kansas-Nebraska Act," Wisconsin Historical Society, *Proceedings*, 1912, pp. 69–86. 526.

—— "Some Phases of the Dred Scott Case," *Mississippi Valley Historical Review*, vol. XVI, pp. 3–22. 549.

Hodges, George. *William Penn.* 1901. 51.

Hoe, Robert. *A Short History of the Printing Press and the Improvements in Printing Machinery.* 1902. 449.

Hogan, William R. *The Texas Republic.* 1946. 484.

Holand, Hjalmar R. *The Kensington Stone.* 1932. 21.

—— *Westward from Vinland.* 1940. 21.

Holbrook, Stewart H. *Ethan Allen.* 1940. 149.

Holdsworth, John T. and Davis R. Dewey. *The First and Second Banks of the United States.* 1910. 401.

Holland, Cecil F. *Morgan and His Raiders.* 1942. 595.

Holman, Frederick V. *Dr. John McLoughlin, The Father of Oregon.* 1907. 484.

Holst, Hermann Eduard von. *The Constitutional and Political History of the United States.* 8 vols. 1876–92. 385, 401.

—— *John C. Calhoun (American Statesmen).* 1882. 385.

Horton, John T. *James Kent: A Study in Conservatism, 1763–1847.* 1939. 324.

Hosmer, James K. *The History of the Louisiana Purchase.* 1902.

—— *The Life of Thomas Hutchinson.* 1896. 126.

Houston, David F. *A Critical Study of Nullification in South Carolina (Harvard Historical Studies, III).* 1896. 385.

Hovgaard, George W. *The Voyages of the Norsemen to America.* 1914. 21.

Howard, George E. *Preliminaries of the American Revolution (American Nation, VIII).* 1905. 125.

Howard, John T. *Our American Music, Three Hundred Years of It.* New ed., 1946. 449.

Hubbart, Henry C. *The Older Middle West, 1840–1880.* 1936. 527.

Hughes, Rupert. *George Washington.* 3 vols. 1926–30. 108, 148, 214.

Huidekoper, Frederic L. *The Military Unpreparedness of the United States.* 1915. 594.

Hulbert, Archer B. *Braddock's Road (Historic Highways of America, IV).* 1903. 108.

—— *Forty-Niners.* 1931. 502.

—— *The Paths of Inland Commerce (Chronicles of America, XXI).* 1920. 324.

Hungerford, Edward. *The Story of the Baltimore and Ohio Railroad, 1827–1897.* 1928. 526.

Hunt, Gaillard. *John C. Calhoun.* 1908. 385.

——— *The Life of James Madison.* 1902. 280.

Hunt, George T. *The Wars of the Iroquois.* 1940. 51.

Hunter, Louis C. *Steamboats on the Western Rivers: An Economic and Technological History.* 1949. 346.

Huntington, Ellsworth. *The Red Man's Continent (Chronicles of America,* I). 1919. 21.

Hutchins, John G. B. *The American Maritime Industries and Public Policy, 1789–1914.* 1941. 526.

Hutchinson, William T. *Cyrus Hall McCormick.* 2 vols. 1930–35. 449.

Iles, George. *Leading American Inventors.* 1912. 449.

Isley, Jeter A. *Horace Greeley and the Republican Party, 1853–1861.* 1947. 549.

Isham, Samuel and Royal Cortissoz. *The History of American Painting.* 1936. 449.

Jackson, Joseph H. *Anybody's Gold.* 1941. 502.

Jackson, Luther P. *Free Negro Labor and Property Holding in Virginia.* 1942. 464.

Jackson, Sidney L. *America's Struggle for Free Schools: Social Tension and Education in New England and New York, 1827–1842.* 1941. 449.

Jacobs, James R. *The Beginning of the U.S. Army, 1783–1812.* 1947. 215, 301.

——— *Tarnished Warrior: Major General James Wilkinson.* 1938. 269.

Jacobs, Melvin C. *Winning Oregon.* 1938. 484.

Jacobstein, Meyer. *The Tobacco Industry in the United States.* 1907. 526.

Jaffe, Bernard. *Men of Science in America.* 1944. 449.

James, James A. *The Life of George Rogers Clark.* 1928.

——— *Oliver Pollock; The Life and Times of an Unknown Patriot.* 1937. 148.

James, Marquis. *Andrew Jackson: Portrait of a President.* 1937. 384.

——— *Andrew Jackson: The Border Captain.* 1933. 346.

Jameson, John Franklin. *The American Revolution Considered as a Social Movement.* 1926. 164.

———, ed. *Original Narratives of Early American History.* 19 vols., 1906–17. 36.

Jenkins, William S. *Pro-Slavery Thought in the Old South* (University of North Carolina, *Social Study Series*). 1935. 464.

Jensen, Merrill. *The Articles of Confederation.* 1940. 164.

——— *The New Nation: A History of the United States during the Confederation, 1781–1789.* 1950. 164.

Jernegan, Marcus W. *The American Colonies (Epochs of American History,* I). 1929. 77.

Jervey, Theodore D. *Robert Hayne and His Times.* 1909. 385.

Johnson, Allen. *Jefferson and His Colleagues (Chronicles of America,* XV). 1921. 252.

——— *Stephen A. Douglas: A Study in American Politics.* 1908. 502.

——— *Union and Democracy.* 1915. 324.

———, ed. *The Chronicles of America Series.* 50 vols. 1918–21. 21.

Johnson, Allen and Dumas Malone, eds. *Dictionary of American Biography.* 21 vols. 1928–1944. 37.

Johnson, Amandus. *The Swedish Settlements on the Delaware, 1638–1664.* 2 vols. 1911. 51.

Johnson, Cecil. *British West Florida, 1763–1783.* 1943. 149.

Johnson, Gerald W. *Randolph of Roanoke, A Political Fantastic.* 1929. 269.

Johnson, Ida A. *The Michigan Fur Trade.* 1919. 183.

Johnston, Mary. *Pioneers of the Old South (Chronicles of America,* V). 1918. 51.

Jones, Edward A. *The Loyalists of New Jersey.* 1927. 149.

——— *The Loyalists of Massachusetts.* 1930. 147.

Jones, Matt Bushnell. *Vermont in the Making, 1750–1777.* 1939. 164.

Jones, Rufus M. *The Faith and Practice of the Quakers.* 1927. 51.

——— *The Quakers in the American Colonies.* 1911. 51.

Jordan, Donaldson and Edwin J. Pratt. *Europe and the American Civil War.* 1931. 618.

Kaempffert, Waldemar B. *A Popular History of American Invention.* 1924. 449.

Kellogg, Louise P. *The British Régime in Wisconsin and the Northwest.* 1935. 182.

———. *The French Régime in Wisconsin and the Northwest.* 1925. 108.

Kemble, John H. *The Panama Route, 1848–1869.* 1943. 484.

Kennedy, John P. *Memoirs of the Life of William Wirt.* 2 vols. 1856. 324.

Kimball, Marie. *Jefferson: The Road to Glory, 1743 to 1776.* 1943. 148, 252.

——— *Jefferson: War and Peace, 1776 to 1784.* 1947. 252.

——— *Jefferson: The Scene of Europe, 1784 to 1789.* 1950. 252.

King, George A. *The French Spoliation Claims*

(*American Journal of International Law*, VI). 1912. 402.

King, Rufus. *Ohio: First Fruits of the Ordinance of 1787*. 1888. 269.

Kinley, David. *The Independent Treasury of the United States and its Relations to the Banks of the Country*. 1910. 420.

Kinnaird, Lawrence, ed. *Spain in the Mississippi Valley, 1765–1794* (*Annual Report of the American Historical Association*, 1945, II–IV). 1946–49. 183.

Kinsley, Philip. *The Chicago Tribune: Its First Hundred Years, 1847–65*. 1943. 549.

Kirkland, Edward C. *A History of American Economic Life*. 1939. 324, 420, 526.

——— *The Peacemakers of 1864*. 1927. 617.

Klees, Frederic. *The Pennsylvania Dutch*. 1950. 78.

Klett, Guy S. *Presbyterians in Colonial Pennsylvania*. 1937. 78.

——— *The Scotch-Irish in Pennsylvania*. 1948. 78.

Klingberg, Frank J. *The Morning of America*. 1941. 37, 125.

Knollenberg, Bernhard. *Washington and the Revolution*. 1940. 148.

Knorr, Klaus E. *British Colonial Theories, 1570–1850*. 1944. 37.

Knox, John J. *History of Banking in the United States*. 1900. 420.

Kobre, Sidney. *The Development of the Colonial Newspaper*. 1944. 77.

Koch, Adrienne. *Jefferson and Madison: The Great Collaboration*. 1950. 252.

——— *The Philosophy of Thomas Jefferson*. 1943. 148.

Kohlmeier, Albert L. *The Old Northwest as the Keystone of the Arch of American Federal Union*. 1938. 362.

Korngold, Ralph. *Two Friends of Man: The Story of William Lloyd Garrison and Wendell Phillips and Their Relationship with Abraham Lincoln*. 1950. 464.

Krout, John A. and D. R. Fox. *The Completion of Independence, 1790–1830* (*History of American Life*, V). 1944. 215.

LaFollette, Suzanne. *Art in America*. 1929. 449.

Lambert, Oscar D. *Presidential Politics in the United States, 1841–1844*. 1936. 421.

Landon, Fred. *Lake Huron*. 1944. 362.

Lane, Wheaton J. *Commodore Vanderbilt: An Epic of the Steam Age*. 1942. 526.

Lanier, Henry W. *A Century of Banking in New York, 1822–1922*. 1922. 420.

Larkin, Oliver W. *Art and Life in America*. 1949. 449.

Larson, Gustive O. *Prelude to the Kingdom: Mormon Desert Conquest; A Chapter in American Cooperative Experience*. 1947. 485.

Larson, Laurence M. *The Changing West and other Essays*. 1937. 526.

——— *The Log Book of a Young Immigrant*. 1939. 526.

Latané, John H. *From Isolation to Leadership*. 1918. New ed., 1925. 346.

Latané, John H. and David W. Wainhouse. *A History of American Foreign Policy*. 1940. 148.

Lecky, William E. H. *The American Revolution, 1763–1783*. Edited by James A. Woodburn. 1898. 126.

Lee, James M. *History of American Journalism*. 1917. New ed., 1923. 449.

Leech, Margaret, *Reveille in Washington, 1860–1865*. 1941. 618.

Leopold, Richard W. *Robert Dale Owen: A Biography* (*Harvard Historical Studies*, XLV). 1940. 450.

Lester, William S. *The Transylvania Colony*. 1935. 108.

Levermore, Charles H. *The Republic of New Haven*. 1886. 37.

Lewis, Charles L. *David Glasgow Farragut*. 2 vols. 1941–43. 595.

——— *The Romantic Decatur*. 1937. 302.

Lewis, Lloyd. *Myths after Lincoln*. 1929. 617.

——— *Sherman, Fighting Prophet*. 1932. 594.

Lewis, Meriwether and William Clark. *Original Journals of the Lewis and Clark Expedition*. Ed. by R. G. Thwaites. 8 vols. 1904–1905. 269.

Libby, Orin G. *The Geographical Distribution of the Vote of the Thirteen States on the Federal Constitution*. 1894. 196.

Lincoln, Charles H. *The Revolutionary Movement in Pennsylvania, 1760–1776* (University of Pennsylvania, *Series in History*, No. 1). 1901. 126.

Linn, William A. *The Story of the Mormons*. 1902. 485.

Livermore, Thomas L. *Numbers and Losses in the Civil War in America, 1861–1863*. 1901. 594.

Lloyd, Arthur Y. *The Slavery Controversy, 1831–1860*. 1939. 464.

Locke, Mary S. *Anti-Slavery in America, 1619–1808* (*Radcliffe College Monographs*). 1901. 345.

Lodge, Henry Cabot. *Alexander Hamilton*. 1882. New ed., 1917. 214.

——— *Daniel Webster*. 1883. 385.

——— *George Washington*. 2 vols. 1889. 214.

——— *Life and Letters of George Cabot*. 1877. 302.

Long, Morden H. *A History of the Canadian People*. 1942. 108.

Lonn, Ella. *The Colonial Agents in the Southern Colonies*. 1945. 92.

Lonn, Ella. *Desertion during the Civil War.* 1928. 594.

——— *Foreigners in the Confederacy.* 1940. 617.

——— *Salt as a Factor in the Confederacy.* 1933. 618.

Lorant, Stefan. *The Presidency.* 1951. 617.

Lord, Clifford and Elizabeth H. *Historical Atlas of the United States.* 1944. 21.

Lorenz, Lincoln. *John Paul Jones.* 1943. 149.

Lucas, Charles P. *The Canadian War of 1812.* 1906. 301.

Lundin, Leonard. *Cockpit of the Revolution: The War for Independence in New Jersey.* 1940. 149.

Luthin, Reinhard H. *The First Lincoln Campaign.* 1944. 549.

Lyon, Elijah Wilson. *Louisiana in French Diplomacy, 1589–1804.* 1934. 183, 269.

——— *The Man Who Sold Louisiana, The Life of François Barbé-Marbois.* 1942. 269.

Mabee, Carleton. *The American Leonardo: A Life of Samuel F. B. Morse.* 1943. 449.

McBain, Howard L. *The Living Constitution.* 1927. 196.

McCain, James R. *Georgia as a Proprietary Province.* 1917. 51.

McCaleb, Walter F. *The Aaron Burr Conspiracy.* 1903. New ed., 1936. 269.

McCarthy, Charles. *The Antimasonic Party: A Study of Political Anti-masonry in the United States, 1827–1840* (American Historical Association, *Annual Report*, 1902). 1903. 402.

McClellan, George B. *McClellan's Own Story.* 1887. 594.

McClellan, William S. *Smuggling in the American Colonies at the Outbreak of the Revolution.* 1912. 126.

McClelland, Cloys P. and C. C. Huntington. *Ohio Canals, Their Construction, Cost, Use and Partial Abandonment.* 1905. 362.

McCormac, Eugene I. *Colonial Opposition to Imperial Authority during the French and Indian War* (University of California, *Publications in History*, I). 1911. 126.

——— *James K. Polk.* 1922. 485.

McCrady, Edward. *The History of South Carolina under the Proprietary Government, 1670–1719.* 1897. 51.

MacDonald, William. *Jacksonian Democracy, 1829–1837* (*American Nation*, XV). 1906. 384.

McElroy, Robert M. *Jefferson Davis, The Unreal and the Real.* 2 vols. 1937. 564.

——— *Kentucky in the Nation's History.* 1909. 182.

McGann, Sister Agnes Geraldine. *Nativism in Kentucky in 1860.* 1944. 526.

McGavin, Elmer C. *U. S. Soldiers Invade Utah.* 1937. 548.

McGrane, Reginald C. *The Economic Development of the American Nation.* 1950. 183, 420, 526.

——— *Foreign Bondholders and American State Debts.* 1935. 420.

——— *The Panic of 1837.* 1924. 402.

———, ed. *The Correspondence of Nicholas Biddle Dealing with National Affairs, 1807–1844.* 1919. 401.

McGregor, James C. *The Disruption of Virginia.* 1922. 563.

McIlwain, Charles H. *The American Revolution; A Constitutional Interpretation.* 1923. 126.

——— *The High Court of Parliament and its Supremacy,* 1910. 92.

McInnis, Edgar W. *The Unguarded Frontier: A History of American-Canadian Relations.* 1942. 302.

McKelvey, Blake. *American Prisons: A Study in American Social History Prior to 1915.* 1936. 450.

McLaughlin, Andrew C. *The Confederation and the Constitution, 1783–1789* (*American Nation*, X). 1905. 164.

——— *A Constitutional History of the United States.* 1935. 324.

——— *Lewis Cass.* 1891. 502.

McLaughlin, A. C. and others. *Source Problems in United States History.* 1918. 148.

Maclay, William. *The Journal of William Maclay.* Ed. by E. S. Maclay. 1890. New ed., 1927. 214.

MacLear, Anne B. *Early New England Towns* (Columbia University, *Studies in History, Economics, and Public Law*, XXIX). 1908. 78.

Macleod, William C. *The American Indian Frontier.* 1928. 484.

McMaster, John B. *The Acquisition of Political, Social, and Industrial Rights of Man in America.* 1903. 164.

——— *Daniel Webster.* 1902. 385.

——— *A History of the People of the United States from the Revolution to the Civil War.* 8 vols. 1883–1913. 164, 215, 252, 302, 345, 384, 502, 548.

——— *A History of the People of the United States during Lincoln's Administration.* 1927. 617.

MacMullen, Jerry. *Paddle-Wheel Days in California.* 1944. 526.

McNemar, Richard. *The Kentucky Revival.* 1807. 252.

Macy, Jesse. *The Anti-Slavery Crusade* (*Chronicles of America*, XXVIII). 1919. 464.

Madeleine, Sister M. Grace. *Monetary and Banking Theories of Jacksonian Democracy.* 1943. 402.

Madison, Charles A. *Critics and Crusaders: A Century of American Protest.* 1946. 464.

Madison, Dolly. *Memoirs and Letters of Dolly Madison.* Ed. by Lucia B. Cutts. 1911. 301.

Mahan, Alfred T. *Admiral Farragut.* 1892. 595.

—— *The Influence of Sea Power upon History, 1660–1783.* 1890. 108.

—— *The Major Operations of the Navies in the War of American Independence.* 1913. 148.

—— *Sea Power in its Relation to the War of 1812.* 2 vols. 1905. 280, 302.

Maitland, Frederic William. *The Constitutional History of England.* 1908. 92.

Major, Howard. *The Domestic Architecture of the Early American Republic.* 1926. 252.

Malin, James C. *John Brown and the Legend of Fifty-Six.* 1942. 549.

Malone, Dumas. *Jefferson and his Time.* 4 vols. (projected). 1948– . 148, 252.

Manross, William W. *The Episcopal Church in the United States, 1800–1840.* 1938. 324.

Marshall, Helen E. *Dorothea Dix, Forgotten Samaritan.* 1937. 450.

Marshall, Thomas M. *A History of the Western Boundary of the Louisiana Purchase, 1819–1841.* 1914. 484.

Marshall, Thomas M., and H. E. Bolton. *The Colonization of North America, 1492–1783* (1920).

Martin, S. W. *Florida during the Territorial Days.* 1944. 346.

Martineau, Harriet. *Retrospect of Western Travel.* 2 vols. 1838. 448.

Mason, Edward C. *The Veto Power (Harvard Historical Monographs, no. 1).* 1890. 196.

Mason, Kathryn H. *James Harrod of Kentucky.* 1951. 108.

Mathews [Rosenberry], Lois Kimball. *The Expansion of New England.* 1909. 78.

Maurice, Sir Frederick B. *Robert E. Lee, The Soldier.* 1925. 564.

Mayo, Bernard. *Henry Clay, Spokesman of the New West.* 1937. 301.

Mayo, Lawrence S. *John Endicott: A Biography.* 1936. 37.

Meade, George Gordon. *The Life and Letters of George Gordon Meade, Major-General, United States Army.* 2 vols. 1913. 595.

Meade, Robert D. *Judah P. Benjamin, Confederate Statesman.* 1943. 617.

Meigs, William M. *The Life of John Caldwell Calhoun.* 2 vols. 1917. 385.

Melvin, Frank E. *Napoleon's Navigation System.* 1919. 280.

Mereness, Newton D. *Maryland as a Proprietary Province.* 1901. 51.

Meriwether, Robert L. *The Expansion of South Carolina, 1729–1765.* 1940. 51.

Merriam, Charles E. *A History of American Political Theories.* 1936. 126.

Mesick, Jane L. *The English Traveller in America, 1785–1835* (Columbia University, Studies in English and Comparative Literature). 1922.

Meyer, Balthasar, Caroline E. MacGill, and others. *History of Transportation in the United States before 1866.* 1917. 526.

Miller, Harry E. *Banking Theories in the United States before 1860 (Harvard Economic Studies, XXX).* 1927. 346.

Miller, James M. *The Genesis of Western Culture: The Upper Ohio Valley, 1800–1825.* 1938. 362.

Miller, John C. *Crisis in Freedom: The Alien and Sedition Acts.* 1951. 252.

—— *Origins of the American Revolution.* 1943. 125.

—— *Sam Adams, Pioneer in Propaganda.* 1936. 126.

—— *Triumph of Freedom, 1775–1783.* 1948. 148.

Miller, Perry. *Jonathan Edwards.* 1949. 79.

—— *The New England Mind: The Seventeenth Century.* 1939. 78.

Miller, Wallace E. *The Peopling of Kansas.* 1906. 549.

Milton, George F. *Abraham Lincoln and the Fifth Column.* 1942. 617.

—— *Conflict: The American Civil War.* 1941. 594.

—— *The Eve of Conflict: Stephen A. Douglas and the Needless War.* 1934. 502.

—— *The Use of Presidential Power, 1789–1943.* 1944. 617.

Miner, Clarence E. *The Ratification of the Federal Constitution by the State of New York* (Columbia University, Studies in History, Economics, and Public Law, XCIV). 1921. 196.

Minnigerode, Meade. *The Fabulous Forties, 1840–1850.* 1924. 448.

Minot, George R. *The History of the Insurrections in Massachusetts in the Year 1786.* 1788. 183.

Mitchell, Stewart. *Horatio Seymour of New York.* 1938. 617.

Mitchell, Wesley C. *A History of the Greenbacks with Special Reference to the Consequence of their Issue, 1862–1865.* 1903. 617.

Monaghan, Frank. *John Jay, Defender of Liberty.* 1935. 228.

Monaghan, Frank, and Marvin Lowenthal. *This was New York: The Nation's Capital in 1789.* 1943. 215.

Monroe, Paul. *Founding of the American Public School System.* 1940. 449.

Monroe, Will S. *The Educational Labors of Henry Barnard.* 1893. 449.

Montross, Lynn. *The Reluctant Rebels: The Story*

of the Continental Congress, 1774–1789. 1950. 126.

Moody, John. *The Railroad Builders* (*Chronicles of America*, XXXVIII). 1919. 526.

Moore, Albert B. *Conscription and Conflict in the Confederacy.* 1924. 594.

Moore, John Bassett. *The Principles of American Diplomacy.* 1918. 148, 228.

Morgan, John H. and Mantle Fielding. *The Life Portraits of Washington.* 1931. 214.

Morison, Samuel E. *Admiral of the Ocean Sea.* 2 vols., 1942. 21.

—— *Builders of the Bay Colony.* 1930. 37.

—— *The Life and Letters of Harrison Gray Otis.* 2 vols. 1913. 302.

—— *Three Centuries of Harvard, 1636–1936.* 1936. 449.

Morris, Richard B. *Government and Labor in Early America.* 1946. 78.

——, ed. *The Era of the American Revolution.* 1939. 148.

Morse, James K. *Jedidiah Morse: Champion of New England Orthodoxy* (*Columbia Studies in American Culture*, no. 2). 1939. 164.

Morse, John T., Jr. *John Adams* (*American Statesmen*, VI). 1884. New ed., 1917. 149.

—— *John Quincy Adams* (*American Statesmen*, XV). 1882. New ed., 1917. 361.

—— *The Life of Alexander Hamilton.* 2 vols. 1876. 214.

—— *Thomas Jefferson* (*American Statesmen*, XI). 1883. New ed., 1917. 252.

Mott, Frank L. *American Journalism: A History of Newspapers in the United States.* 1941. 449.

—— *A History of American Magazines.* 3 vols., 1930–38. 324, 449.

—— *Jefferson and the Press.* 1943. 252.

Mowat, Charles L. *East Florida as a British Province, 1763–1784* (*University of California Publications in History*, XXII). 1943.

Mowat, Robert B. *The Diplomatic Relations of Great Britain and the United States.* 1925. 302.

Mudge, Eugene T. *The Social Philosophy of John Taylor of Caroline; A Study in Jeffersonian Democracy* (*Columbia Studies in American Culture*, no. 4). 1939. 324.

Muelder, Hermann R., and David M. Delo. *Years of this Land.* 1943. 21.

Mueller, Henry R. *The Whig Party in Pennsylvania* (*Columbia University, Studies in History, Economics, and Public Law*, CCXXX). 1922. 421.

Munro, William B. *The Seigneurs of Old Canada* (*Chronicles of Canada*, V). 1914. 108.

Murdock, Kenneth B. *Increase Mather, The Foremost American Puritan.* 1925. 77.

—— *Literature and Theology in Colonial New England.* 1949. 79.

Muzzey, David S. *Thomas Jefferson.* 1918. 252.

Myers, William S. *A Study in Personality: George Brinton McClellan.* 1934. 594.

Namier, Lewis B. *England in the Age of the American Revolution.* 1930. 126.

Neely, Wayne C. *The Agricultural Fair.* 1935. 526.

Nettels, Curtis P. *George Washington and American Independence.* 1951. 126.

—— *The Money Supply of the Colonies before 1720* (*University of Wisconsin, Studies in the Social Sciences and History*, no. 20). 1934. 92.

—— *The Roots of American Civilization.* 1936. 37, 77.

Nevins, Allan. *The American States during and after the Revolution, 1775–1789.* 1924. 164.

—— *The Emergence of Lincoln.* 2 vols. 1950. 548.

—— *Frémont, Pathmarker of the West.* 1939. 485.

—— *Frémont, The West's Greatest Adventurer.* 2 vols. 1928. 485.

—— *Ordeal of the Union.* 2 vols. 1947. 502, 548.

——, ed. *American Social History as Recorded by British Travellers.* 1923. New ed., 1931. 324.

Nichols, Roy F. *The Democratic Machine, 1850–1854* (*Columbia University, Studies in History, Economics and Public Law*, CXI). 1923. 548.

—— *The Disruption of American Democracy.* 1948. 548.

—— *Franklin Pierce.* 1931. 548.

Nicolay, John G. and John Hay. *Abraham Lincoln: A History.* 10 vols. 1890. 563.

Nissenson, Samuel A. *The Patroon's Domain* (*New York State Historical Association Series*, V). 1937. 51.

Nock, Albert J. *Jefferson.* 1926. 252.

Norwood, John N. *The Schism in the Methodist Episcopal Church, 1844: A Study of Slavery and Ecclesiastical Politics* (*Alfred University, Studies*, I). 1923. 527.

Norwood, William F. *Medical Education in the United States before the Civil War.* 1944. 449.

Notestein, Wallace. *The Winning of the Initiative by the House of Commons.* 1924. 92.

Nussbaum, Frederick L. *Commercial Policy in the French Revolution.* 1923. 280.

Nute, Grace Lee. *Caesars of the Wilderness: Medard Chouart, Sieur des Groseilliers, and Pierre Esprit Radisson, 1618–1710.* 1943. 108.

—— *Lake Superior.* 1944. 362.

Nye, Russel B. *George Bancroft, Brahmin Rebel.* 1944. 449.

Oberholtzer, Ellis P. *Jay Cooke, Financier of the Civil War.* 2 vols. 1907. 617.

Oberholtzer, Ellis P. *Robert Morris*. 1903. 149.

O'Connor, Michael J. L. *Origins of Academic Economics in the United States*. 1944. 449.

O'Connor, Richard. *Hood: Cavalier General*. 1949. 595.

Ogg, Frederick A. *Daniel Webster*. 1914. 385.

—— *The Old Northwest* (*Chronicles of America*, XIX). 1919. 182.

—— *The Opening of the Mississippi*. 1904. 183.

—— *The Reign of Andrew Jackson*. (*Chronicles of America*, XIX). 1919. 384.

Osgood, Herbert L. *The American Colonies in the Eighteenth Century*. 4 vols. 1924–25. 92.

—— *The American Colonies in the Seventeenth Century*. 3 vols. 1904–1907. 36.

Ostrogorski, Moiseĭ. *Democracy and the Organization of Political Parties*. 2 vols. 1902. 384.

Owsley, Frank L. *King Cotton Diplomacy*. 1931. 618.

—— *State Rights in the Confederacy*. 1925. 617.

Paden, Irene. *The Wake of the Prairie Schooner*. 1943. 484.

Padover, Saul K. *Jefferson*. 1942. 252.

Paine, Ralph D. *The Fight for a Free Sea* (*Chronicles of America*, XVII). 1920. 280.

—— *The Old Merchant Marine* (*Chronicles of America*, XXXVI). 1919. 526.

Palfrey, John G. *History of New England*. 5 vols. 1858–90. 37.

Palmer, Benjamin W. *Marshall and Taney, Statesmen of the Law*. 1939. 549.

Paris, Comte De. *History of the Civil War in America*. 4 vols. 1876–88. 594.

Parkman, Francis. *The California and Oregon Trail*. 1849. 484.

—— *The Conspiracy of Pontiac*. 2 vols. 1866. 107.

—— *Count Frontenac and New France under Louis XIV*. 1877. 107.

—— *A Half Century of Conflict*. 2 vols. 1892. 107.

—— *LaSalle and the Discovery of the Great West*. 2 vols. 1879. 107.

—— *Montcalm and Wolfe*. 2 vols. 1884. 107.

—— *The Oregon Trail*. 1886. 484.

—— *Pioneers of France in the New World*. 1865. 107.

—— *The Works of Francis Parkman*. 12 vols. 1922. 107.

Parks, Joseph H. *Felix Grundy, Champion of Democracy*. 1940. 301.

—— *John Bell of Tennessee*. 1950. 549.

Parrington, Vernon L. *Main Currents in American Thought*. 3 vols. 1927–30. 77, 324.

Parton, James. *Life of Andrew Jackson*. 3 vols. 1860. 362.

Patrick, Rembert W. *Jefferson Davis and His Cabinet*. 1944. 617.

Patterson, Samuel W. *Horatio Gates: Defender of American Liberties*. 1941. 149.

Paullin, Charles O. *Atlas of the Historical Geography of the United States*. 1932. 21.

—— *Commodore John Rodgers*. 1910. 268.

—— *Diplomatic Negotiations of American Naval Officers*. 1912. 268.

—— *The Navy of the American Revolution*. 1906. 148.

Paxson, Frederic L. *The Civil War*. 1911. 617.

—— *A History of the American Frontier, 1763–1893*. 1924. 78, 484.

—— *The Independence of the South American Republics*. 1903. 346.

—— *The Last American Frontier*. 1910. 358.

Pease, Theodore C. *The Frontier State, 1818–1848* (*Centennial History of Illinois*, II). 1918. 362.

Pease, Theodore C. and Ernestine Jenison. *Illinois on the Eve of the Seven Years' War, 1747–1755*. 1939. 108.

Pease, Theodore C. and A. S. Roberts, eds. *Selected Readings in American History*. New ed., 1940. 21.

Peckham, Howard H. *Pontiac and the Indian Uprising*. 1947. 108.

Pellew, George. *John Jay* (*American Statesmen*, IX). New ed., 1917. 149.

Pemberton, John C. *Pemberton, Defender of Vicksburg*. 1942. 595.

Perkins, Alice J. G. and Theresa Wolfson. *Frances Wright, Free Enquirer*. 1939. 450.

Perkins, Dexter. *Hands Off: A History of the Monroe Doctrine*. 1941. 346.

—— *The Monroe Doctrine, 1823–1826*. 1927. 346.

—— *The Monroe Doctrine, 1826–1867*. 1933. 346.

Perkins, James B. *France in the American Revolution*. 1911. 148.

Perlman, Selig. *A History of Trade Unionism in the United States*. 1922. 450.

Perry, Bliss. *The American Spirit in Literature* (*Chronicles of America*, XXXIV). 1918. 449.

Petersen, William J. *Steamboating on the Upper Mississippi*. 1937. 526.

Phillips, Ulrich B. *American Negro Slavery*. 1918. 464.

—— *The Course of the South to Secession: an Interpretation*. 1939. 563.

—— *Georgia and State Rights* (American Historical Association, *Annual Report*, 1901, II). 1902. 385.

—— *A History of Transportation in the Eastern Cotton Belt to 1860*. 1908. 526.

—— *Life and Labor in the Old South*. 1929. 464.

Phillips, Ulrich B. *The Life of Robert Toombs*. 1913. 502.

Pickard, Madge E. and R. Carlyle Buley. *The Midwest Pioneer: His Ills, Cures, Cares and Doctors*. 1945. 527.

Pierce, Bessie L. *A History of Chicago*. 2 vols. 1937-40. 526.

Pierson, George W. *Tocqueville and Beaumont in America*. 1938. 384, 448.

Pike, Zebulon M. *The Expeditions of Zebulon Montgomery Pike . . . during the years 1805-6-7*. Ed. by Elliott Coues. 3 vols. 1895. 269.

—— *Zebulon Pike's Arkansaw Journal*. Ed. by S. H. Hart and A. B. Hulbert. 1932. 269.

Pleasants, Samuel A. *Fernando Wood of New York* (Columbia University, *Studies in History, Economics, and Public Law*, no. 536). 1948. 617.

Poage, George R. *Henry Clay and the Whig Party*. 1936. 402, 421.

Polk, James K. *The Diary of James K. Polk, during His Presidency, 1845 to 1849*. Ed. by M. M. Quaife, 4 vols. 1910. 485.

Pollard, Albert F. *The Evolution of Parliament*. 1920. 92.

Porter, Kirk H. *A History of Suffrage in the United States*. 1918. 385.

—— *John Jacob Astor, Business Man*. 2 vols. 1931. 484.

Posey, Walter B. *The Development of Methodism in the Old Southwest, 1783-1824*. 1923. 252.

Post, Albert. *Popular Freethought in America, 1825-1850*. 1943. 448.

Potter, David M. *Lincoln and His Party in the Secession Crisis* (*Yale Historical Studies*, XIII). 1942. 563.

Pound, Arthur. *Lake Ontario*. 1945. 362.

Powell, Edward P. *Nullification and Secession in the United States*. 1897. 385.

Powell, John H. *Richard Rush: Republican Diplomat, 1780-1859* (Pennsylvania Lives). 1942. 346.

Pratt, Fletcher. *The Navy: A History*. 1938. 302.

—— *Ordeal by Fire; An Informal History of the Civil War*. 1935. 594.

—— *Preble's Boys: Commodore Preble and the Birth of American Sea Power*. 1950. 302.

Pratt, Julius W. *Expansionists of 1812*. 1925. 301.

Priestley, Herbert I. *The Coming of the White Man* (*History of American Life*, I). 1929. 21.

—— *France Overseas through the Old Régime*. 1939. 108.

Pritchett, John P. *The Red River Valley, 1811-1849: A Regional Study*. 1942. 526.

Quaife, Milo M. *Chicago and the Old Northwest, 1673-1835*. 1913. 301.

—— *Lake Michigan*. 1944. 362.

—— "The Myth of the Kensington Rune Stone," *New England Quarterly*, VII, 1934, pp. 613-645. 21.

Quarles, Benjamin. *Frederick Douglass*. 1948. 464.

Quinn, Arthur H. *A History of the American Drama from the Beginning to the Civil War*. 2nd ed., 1943. 449.

Ragatz, Lowell J. *The Fall of the Planter Class in the British Caribbean*. 1928. 51.

Ranck, James B. *Albert Gallatin Brown, Radical Southern Nationalist*. 1937. 564.

Randall, Emilius O. and D. J. Ryan. *History of Ohio*. 5 vols. 1912. 269.

Randall, James G. *The Civil War and Reconstruction*. 1937. 594.

—— *Constitutional Problems under Lincoln*. 1926. 617.

—— *Lincoln, the President: Springfield to Gettysburg*. 2 vols. 1945. 563.

Raper, Charles L. *North Carolina, A Study in English Colonial Government*. 1904. 51.

Rauch, Basil. *American Interest in Cuba, 1848-1855*. 1948. 527.

Ray, P. Orman. *The Repeal of the Missouri Compromise*. 1909. 526.

Reeves, Arthur M. *The Finding of Wineland the Good*. 1890. 21.

Reeves, Jesse S. *American Diplomacy under Tyler and Polk*. 1907. 484.

Rhodes, James Ford. *History of the Civil War*. 1917. 617.

—— *History of the United States from the Compromise of 1850*. 9 vols. 1893-1922. 502, 548, 617.

Rice, Madeleine H. *American Catholic Opinion in the Slavery Controversy*. 1944. 563.

Rich, Arthur L. *Lowell Mason, "Father of Singing among the Children."* 1946. 449.

Richardson, Rupert N. *Texas, The Lone Star State*. 1943. 484.

Richman, Irving B. *Rhode Island, Its Making and Meaning*. 2 vols. 1902. 37.

Riegel, Robert E. *America Moves West*. 1930. New ed., 1947. 484.

—— *Young America, 1830-1840*. 1949. 449.

Rippy, J. Fred and Angie Debo. *The Historical Background of the American Policy of Isolation*. 1924. 229.

Rister, Carl C. *Robert E. Lee in Texas*. 1946. 564.

Rives, George L. *The United States and Mexico, 1821-1848*. 2 vols. 1913. 484.

Robbins, Roy M. *Our Landed Heritage: The*

Public Domain, 1776–1936. 1942. 183, 269, 385, 421.

Roberts, Walter A. *Semmes of the Alabama.* 1938. 595.

Robinson, Howard. *The Development of the British Empire.* 1922. New ed., 1936. 51.

Rogin, Leo. *The Introduction of Farm Machinery in its Relation to the Productivity of Labor in the Agriculture of the United States during the Nineteenth Century* (University of California, Publications in Economics, IX). 1931. 526.

Roosevelt, Theodore. *The Naval War of 1812.* 1882. 302.

—— *The Winning of the West.* 4 vols. 1894–96. 108.

Ropes, J. C. and W. R. Livermore. *The Story of the Civil War.* 4 vols. 1894–1913. New ed. (4 vols. in 3), 1933. 594.

Roseboom, Eugene H. and F. P. Weisenburger. *A History of Ohio.* 1934. 269.

Rosenberger, Jesse L. *The Pennsylvania Germans.* 1923. 78.

Rowe, Henry K. *The History of Religion in the United States.* 1924. 527.

Royall, William L. *Andrew Jackson and the Bank of the United States.* 1880. 401.

Rusk, Ralph L. *The Life of Ralph Waldo Emerson.* 1949. 449.

Russell, Nelson V. *The British Régime in Michigan and the Old Northwest.* 1939. 183.

Sakolski, Aaron M. *The Great American Land Bubble.* 1932. 385. 402.

Salmon, Lucy M. *The Newspaper and the Historian.* 1923. 449.

Sandburg, Carl. *Abraham Lincoln, The Prairie Years.* 2 vols. 1926.

—— *Abraham Lincoln, The War Years.* 4 vols. 1939. 563.

Sanderlin, W. S. *The Great National Project; A History of the Chesapeake and Ohio Canal* (Johns Hopkins University, Studies in Historical and Political Science, LXVI, no. 1). 1947. 362.

Sanford, Albert H. *The Story of Agriculture in the United States.* 1916. 526.

Sato, Shosuke. *History of the Land Question in the United States* (Johns Hopkins University, Studies in Historical and Political Science, IV). 1886. 421.

Savelle, Max. *The Diplomatic History of the Canadian Boundary, 1749–1763.* 1940. 108.

—— *The Foundations of American Civilization.* 1942. 37.

Schachner, Nathan. *Aaron Burr: A Biography.* 1937. 269.

—— *Alexander Hamilton.* 1946. 214.

—— *Thomas Jefferson: A Biography.* 2 vols. 1951. 252.

Schafer, Joseph. *A History of the Pacific Northwest.* 1905. New ed., 1918. 484.

—— *The Social History of American Agriculture.* 1936. 526.

Scharf, John T. *History of the Confederate States Navy from its Origin to the Surrender of its Last Vessel.* 1887. 595.

Scherer, James A. B. *Cotton as a World Power; A Study in the Economic Interpretation of History.* 1916. 618.

Schlesinger, Arthur M. *The Colonial Merchants and the American Revolution, 1763–1776* (Columbia University, Studies in History, Economics, and Public Law, LXXVIII). 1917. 125.

—— *Learning How to Behave: A Historical Study of American Etiquette Books.* 1946. 324.

—— *New Viewpoints in American History.* 1922. 78, 126.

Schlesinger, Arthur M. and Dixon Ryan Fox, eds. *A History of American Life.* 12 vols. 1929–1949. 21.

Schlesinger, Arthur M., Jr. *The Age of Jackson.* 1945. 401.

—— *Orestes Brownson: A Pilgrim's Progress.* 1939. 450.

Schmitz, Joseph W. *Texas Statecraft, 1836–1845.* 1941. 484.

Schouler, James. *History of the United States of America under the Constitution.* 7 vols. 1880–1913. 164, 302, 345, 384, 502, 548, 617.

Schultz, Harold S. *Nationalism and Sectionalism in South Carolina, 1852–1860: A Study of the Movement for Southern Independence.* 1950. 563.

Schuyler, Robert L. *Parliament and the British Empire.* 1929. 126.

—— *The Constitution of the United States.* 1923. 196.

Schwab, John C. *The Confederate States of America, 1861–1865: A Financial and Industrial History of the South during the Civil War.* 1901. 617.

Scott, William A. *The Repudiation of State Debts.* 1893. 420.

Scrugham, Mary. *The Peaceable Americans of 1860–1861; A Study in Public Opinion* (Columbia University, Studies in History, Economics, and Public Law, XCVI). 1921. 563.

Searight, Thomas B. *The Old Pike, A History of the National Road, with Incidents, Accidents and Anecdotes Thereon.* 1894. 324.

Sears, Louis M. *George Washington.* 1932. 214.

—— *A History of American Foreign Relations.* 1927. New ed., 1938. 183.

—— *Jefferson and the Embargo.* 1927. 280.

—— *John Slidell.* 1925. 485.

Sears, Lorenzo. *Wendell Phillips, Orator and Agitator.* 1909. 464.

Sellers, Charles C. *Charles Willson Peale.* 2 vols., 1947. 252.

Sellers, James B. *Slavery in Alabama.* 1950. 464.

Sellery, George C. *The Renaissance, its Nature and Origins.* 1950. 21.

Sellery, George C. and August C. Krey. *Medieval Foundations of Western Civilization.* 1929. 21.

Semmes, Raphael. *Crime and Punishment in Early Maryland.* 1938. 92.

Semple, Ellen C. *American History and its Geographic Conditions.* 1903. New ed., 1933. 20.

Shaler, Nathaniel S. "Physiography of North America," in *Narrative and Critical History of America,* IV, ed. by Justin Winsor. 20.

———— *Nature and Man in America.* 1891. 20.

Shanks, Henry T. *The Secession Movement in Virginia, 1847–1861.* 1934. 563.

Shannon, Fred A. *The Organization and Administration of the Union Army, 1861–1865.* 2 vols. 1928. 594.

———— *America's Economic Growth.* 1940. 183, 420, 526.

Shepard, Edward M. *Martin Van Buren.* 1888. 421.

Shipp, John E. D. *Giant Days; or, The Life and Times of William H. Crawford.* 1909. 362.

Shipton, Clifford K. *Roger Conant: A Founder of Massachusetts.* 1944. 37.

Shoemaker, Floyd C. *Missouri's Struggle for Statehood, 1804–1821.* 1916. 345.

Shryock, Richard H. *American Medical Research, Past and Present.* 1947. 449.

———— *Georgia and the Union in 1850.* 1926. 502.

Shugg, Roger W. *Origins of Class Struggle in Louisiana.* 1939. 464.

Shultz, William J., and M. R. Caine. *Financial Development of the United States.* 1937. 402.

Siebert, Wilbur H. *The Underground Railroad from Slavery to Freedom.* 1898. 464.

Simkins, Francis B. *The South Old and New: A History, 1820–1947.* 1947. 464.

Simms, Henry H. *A Decade of Sectional Controversy.* 1942. 548.

———— *Life of Robert M. T. Hunter.* 1935. 617.

Sitterson, Joseph C. *The Secession Movement in North Carolina.* 1939. 563.

Skinner, Constance Lindsay. *Adventurers of Oregon (Chronicles of America, XXII).* 1920. 346.

———— *Pioneers of the Old Southwest (Chronicles of America, XVIII).* 1919. 78.

Slosson, Edwin E. *The American Spirit in Education (Chronicles of America, XXXIII).* 1921. 324.

Small, Albion W. *The Beginnings of American Nationality (Johns Hopkins University, Studies in Historical and Political Science, VIII).* 1890. 164.

Smith, Abbot E. *James Madison, Builder: A New Estimate of a Memorable Career.* 1937. 280.

Smith, Charles W., Jr. *Roger B. Taney: Jacksonian Jurist.* 1936. 401, 549.

Smith, Ellen H. *Charles Carroll of Carrollton.* 1942. 196.

Smith, Justin H. *The Annexation of Texas.* 1911. New ed., 1941. 484.

———— *Our Struggle for the Fourteenth Colony, Canada and the American Revolution.* 1907. 148.

———— *The War with Mexico.* 2 vols., 1919. 485.

Smith, Theodore C. *The Liberty and Free-Soil Parties in the Northwest (Harvard Historical Studies, VI).* 1897. 502.

———— *Parties and Slavery, 1850–1859 (American Nation, XVIII).* 1906. 526.

Smith, Walter B. and A. H. Cole. *Fluctuations in American Business, 1790–1860.* 1935. 346, 420.

Smith, William Henry, ed. *The St. Clair Papers.* 2 vols. 1882. 215.

Soulsby, Hugh Graham. *The Right of Search and the Slave Trade in Anglo-American Relations, 1814–1862 (Johns Hopkins University, Studies in Historical and Political Science, LI, no. 2).* 1933. 421.

Spaulding, Ernest W. *His Excellency, George Clinton, Critic of the Constitution.* 1938. 196.

Spaulding, Oliver L. *The United States Army in War and Peace.* 1937. 594.

Sprague, John Francis. *The Northeastern Boundary Controversy and the Aroostook War.* 1910. 421.

Spring, Leverett W. *Kansas, The Prelude to the War for the Union.* 1885. 549.

Sprout, Harold and Margaret. *The Rise of American Naval Power, 1776–1918.* 1939. 302.

Spruill, Julia C. *Women's Life and Work in the Southern Colonies.* 1938. 77.

Stampp, Kenneth M. *And the War Came: The North and the Secession Crisis, 1860–1861.* 1950. 563.

———— *Indiana Politics during the Civil War.* 1949. 617.

Stanton, Elizabeth Cady, Susan B. Anthony, and others. *History of Woman Suffrage.* 6 vols. 1889–1922. 450.

Stanwood, Edward. *American Tariff Controversies in the Nineteenth Century.* 2 vols. 1903. 324.

———— *A History of the Presidency.* 2 vols. 1898. New ed., 1916. 215.

Starkey, Marion L. *The Devil in Massachusetts: A Modern Inquiry into the Salem Witch Trials.* 1949. 79.

Steiner, Bernard C. *Beginnings of Maryland.* 1903. 51.

—— *Life of Roger Brooke Taney.* 1922. 401.

Stephenson, Carl. *Medieval History.* New ed., 1943. 21.

Stephenson, George M. *A History of American Immigration.* 1926. 526.

—— *The Political History of the Public Lands from 1840 to 1862.* 1917. 421.

Stephenson, Nathaniel Wright. *Abraham Lincoln and the Union* (*Chronicles of America,* XXIX). 1918. 617.

—— *The Day of the Confederacy* (*Chronicles of America,* XXX). 1919. 617.

—— *Lincoln.* 1922. 563.

—— *Texas and the Mexican War* (*Chronicles of America,* XXIX). 1921. 484.

Stephenson, N. W. and W. H. Dunn. *George Washington.* 2 vols. 1940. 214.

Stevens, Frank W. *The Beginnings of the New York Central Railroad.* 1926. 526.

Stevens, Wayne E. *The Northwest Fur Trade, 1763–1800.* 1928. 183.

Stewart, George R. *Names on the Land.* 1945. 21.

Stillé, Charles J. *History of the United States Sanitary Commission.* 1866. 618.

—— *The Life and Times of John Dickinson.* 1891. 126.

Stoddard, Henry L. *Horace Greeley: Printer, Editor, Crusader.* 1946. 549.

Stoddard, Theodore L. *The French Revolution in San Domingo.* 1914. 269.

Story, William W. *Life and Letters of Joseph Story.* 2 vols. 1851. 324.

Summers, Festus Paul. *The Baltimore and Ohio in the Civil War.* 1939. 595.

Sumner, William Graham. *Alexander Hamilton.* 1890. 214.

—— *Andrew Jackson.* 1910. 362.

—— *The Financier and the Finances of the Revolution.* 2 vols. 1891. 149.

Sutherland, Stella H. *Population Distribution in Colonial America.* 1936. 78.

Swank, James M. *History of the Manufacture of Iron in all Ages.* 1892. 526.

Sweet, William W. *Methodism in American History.* 1933. 78.

—— *Religion in Colonial America.* 1942. 78.

—— *Revivalism in America.* 1944. 78.

—— *The Story of Religion in America.* 1930. Rev. ed., 1950. 78.

——, ed. *The Baptists.* 1931. 252.

Swisher, Carl B. *American Constitutional Development.* 1943. 385, 549.

—— *Roger B. Taney.* 1936. 401, 549.

Sydnor, Charles S. *The Development of Southern Sectionalism, 1819–1848.* 1948. 362.

Taft, Lorado. *The History of American Sculpture.* 1903. 449.

Tallmadge, Thomas E. *The Story of Architecture in America.* 1927. 449.

Tannenbaum, Frank. *Slave and Citizen: The Negro in the Americas.* 1947. 464.

Tanner, Edwin P. *The Province of New Jersey, 1664–1738* (Columbia University, *Studies in History, Economics, and Public Law,* XXX). 1908. 51.

Tansill, Charles C., ed. *Documents Illustrative of the Union of the American States.* 1927. 196.

Tassin, Algernon de Vivier. *The Magazine in America.* 1916. 449.

Taussig, Frank W. *Tariff History of the United States.* 1888. 8th ed., 1931. 324.

Taylor, Rosser H. *Ante-Bellum South Carolina* (*James Sprunt Studies in History and Political Science,* vol. 25, no. 2). 1942. 464.

Tewksbury, Donald G. *The Founding of American Colleges and Universities before the Civil War.* 1932. 449.

Thayer, Eli. *A History of the Kansas Crusade.* 1889. 549.

Thayer, William R. *George Washington.* 1922. 214.

Thomas, Benjamin P. *Portrait for Posterity: Lincoln and His Biographers.* 1947. 563.

—— *Russo-American Relations, 1815–1867* (Johns Hopkins University, *Studies in Historical and Political Science,* XLVIII). 1930. 618.

Thomas, Charles M. *American Neutrality in 1793; A Study in Cabinet Government* (Columbia University, *Studies in History, Economics, and Public Law,* no. 350). 1931. 228.

Thomas, Sister M. Evangeline. *Nativism in the Old Northwest, 1850–1860.* 1936. 526.

Thompson, Charles M. *Independent Vermont.* 1942. 164.

Thompson, Holland. *The Age of Invention* (*Chronicles of America,* XXXVII). 1921. 449.

Thompson, Robert L. *Wiring a Continent: The History of the Telegraph Industry in the United States, 1832–1866.* 1947. 449.

Thorndike, Lynn. *The History of Medieval Europe.* 3rd ed., 1949. 21.

Thorpe, Francis Newton. *A Constitutional History of the American People, 1776–1850.* 1898. 384.

Thwaites, Reuben Gold. *The Colonies* (*Epochs of American History,* I). 1891. 77.

—— *Daniel Boone.* 1902. 108.

—— *France in America, 1497–1763* (*American Nation,* VII). 1905. 108.

——, ed. *Early Western Travels, 1748–1846.* 32 vols. 1904–07. 324.

——, ed. *The Jesuit Relations, 1610–1701* (73 vols., 1896–1901). 107.

Thwaites, R. G. and Louise P. Kellog, eds. *Documentary History of Dunmore's War, 1774.* 1905. 108.

Thwing, Charles F. *A History of Higher Education in America.* 1906. 449.

Tiffany, Francis. *Life of Dorothea Lynde Dix.* 1890. 450.

Tiffany, Orrin E. *The Relations of the United States to the Canadian Rebellion of 1837–1838* (Buffalo Historical Society, *Publications*, VIII). 1905. 421.

Tilley, John S. *The Coming of the Glory.* 1949. 563.
——— *Lincoln Takes Command.* 1941. 563.

Tinkcom, Harry M. *The Republicans and Federalists in Pennsylvania, 1790–1801: A Study in National Stimulus and Local Response.* 1950. 215, 252.

Tocqueville, Alexis de. *Democracy in America.* 4 vols. 1835–40. New ed., 2 vols. 1945. 384.

Torbet, Robert G. *A History of the Baptists.* 1950. 252.

Tower, Charlemagne. *Marquis de La Fayette in the American Revolution.* 2 vols. 1895. 148.

Treat, Payson J. *The National Land System, 1785–1820.* 1910. 182, 269.

Trent, William P., and others, eds. *The Cambridge History of American Literature.* 4 vols. 1917–1921. 449.

Trevelyan, Sir George Otto. *The American Revolution.* 4 vols. 1905–12. 147.
——— *George the Third and Charles Fox.* 2 vols. 1912–1914. 147.

Tryon, Rolla M. *Household Manufactures in the United States, 1640–1860.* 1917. 78.

Turner, Frederick J. *The Frontier in American History.* 1921. 21, 78.
——— *Rise of the New West, 1819–1826.* (*American Nation*, XIV). 1906. 325.
——— *The Significance of Sections in American History.* 1932. 182, 215, 361.
——— *The United States, 1830–1850.* 1935. 384.

Turner, Francis M. *Life of General John Sevier.* 1910. 182.

Tyler, Alice Felt. *Freedom's Ferment: Phases of American Social History to 1860.* 1944. 449.

Tyler, Lyon G. *England in America, 1580–1652* (*American Nation*, IV). 1904. 37.

Tyler, Moses C. *The Literary History of the American Revolution, 1763–1783.* 2 vols. 1897. 148.
——— *Patrick Henry* (*American Statesmen*, III). 1887. New ed., 1917. 126.

Updyke, Frank A. *The Diplomacy of the War of 1812.* 1915. 280.

Vail, Henry H. *A History of the McGuffey Readers.* 1910. 449.

Van Alstyne, Richard W. *American Diplomacy in Action: A Series of Case Studies.* 1944. 148, 228.

Van Buren, Martin. *The Autobiography of Martin Van Buren.* Ed. by John C. Fitzpatrick. 1920. 421.

Van Deusen, Glyndon G. *The Life of Henry Clay.* 1937. 361, 421.

Van Deusen, John G. *Economic Bases of Disunion in South Carolina* (Columbia University, *Studies in History, Economics, and Public Law*, no. 305). 1928. 563.

Van Doren, Carl C. *Benjamin Franklin.* 1938. 78.
——— *The Great Rehearsal: The Story of the Making and Ratifying of the Constitution of the United States.* 1948. 196.
———, ed. *The Letters of Benjamin Franklin and Jane Mecom.* 1951. 78.

Van Doren, Carl C. and others. *Meet Dr. Franklin.* 1943. 78.

Van Tyne, Claude H. *The American Revolution, 1776–1783* (*American Nation*, IX). 1905. 147.
——— *The Causes of the War of Independence.* 1922. 125.
——— *The Loyalists in the American Revolution.* 1902. 147.
——— *The War of Independence.* 1929. 147.

Van Vleck, George W. *The Panic of 1857: An Analytical Study.* 1943. 548.

Vignaud, Henry. *Toscanelli and Columbus.* 1902. 21.

Villard, Oswald Garrison. *John Brown, 1800–1859.* 1910. 549.

Volwiler, Albert T. *George Croghan and the Westward Movement, 1741–1782.* 1926. 108.

Von Abele, Rudolph. *Alexander H. Stephens: A Biography.* 1946. 564.

Wallace, David D. *The Life of Henry Laurens.* 1915. 149.

Wallace, Willard M. *Appeal to Arms: A Military History of the American Revolution.* 1951. 148.

Wandell, Samuel H., and Meade Minnegerode. *Aaron Burr.* 2 vols. 1925. 269.

Waples, Dorothy. *The Whig Myth of James Fenimore Cooper.* 1938. 449.

Ward, Adolphus William, ed. *The Cambridge History of British Foreign Policy.* 3 vols., 1922–23. 302.

Ward, Christopher. *The Dutch and Swedes on the Delaware, 1609–1664.* 1930. 51.

Warfield, Ethelbert D. *The Kentucky Resolutions of 1798.* 1887. 252.

Warren, Charles. *The Making of the Constitution.* 1928. 196.
——— *The Supreme Court in United States History.* 2 vols. New ed., 1937. 268.

Warren, Robert P. *John Brown, The Making of a Martyr.* 1929. 549.

Waterman, William R. *Frances Wright* (Columbia University, *Studies in History, Economics and Public Law,* no. 256). 1924. 450.

Webb, Walter P. *The Great Plains.* 1931. 21.

Wecter, Dixon. *The Saga of American Society: A Record of Social Aspiration, 1607–1937.* 1937. 324.

——— *When Johnny Comes Marching Home.* 1944. 164.

Weeden, William B. *Economic and Social History of New England.* 2 vols. 1891. 77.

Weinberg, Albert K. *Manifest Destiny.* 1935. 484.

Weisenberger, Francis P. *The Life of John McLean.* 1937. 549.

Weld, Theodore, Angelina Grimké Weld, and Sarah Grimké. *Letters of Theodore Dwight Weld, Angelina Grimké, and Sarah Grimké, 1822–1844.* Ed. by Gilbert Barnes and Dwight L. Dumond. 2 vols. 1944. 464.

Welles, Gideon. *Diary of Gideon Welles, Secretary of the Navy under Lincoln and Johnson.* 3 vols. 1911. 595.

Wellington, Raynor G. *The Political and Sectional Influence of the Public Lands, 1828–1842.* 1914. 385.

Werner, Morris R. *The Admirable Trumpeter: A Biography of General James Wilkinson.* 1941. 269.

——— *Brigham Young.* 1930. 485.

Wertenbaker, Thomas J. *Father Knickerbocker Rebels: New York City during the Revolution.* 1948. 149.

——— *The First Americans, 1607–1690* (*A History of American Life,* II). 1927. 37, 77.

——— *The Founding of American Civilization: The Middle Colonies.* 1938. 78.

——— *The Golden Age of Colonial Culture,* 1942. 78.

——— *The Old South: The Founding of American Civilization.* 1942. 77.

——— *Princeton, 1746–1896.* 1946. 449.

——— *The Puritan Oligarchy: The Founding of American Civilization.* 1947. 78.

——— *Torchbearer of the Revolution: The Story of Bacon's Rebellion and its Leader.* 1940. 37.

Wesley, Charles H. *The Collapse of the Confederacy* (Howard University, *Studies in History,* no. 2). 1922. 617.

West, Warren R. *Contemporary French Opinion on the American Civil War* (Johns Hopkins University, *Studies in Historical and Political Science,* Series XLII). 1924. 618.

West, Richard S., Jr. *Gideon Welles: Lincoln's Navy Department.* 1943. 595.

——— *The Second Admiral: A Life of David Dixon Porter, 1813–1891.* 1937. 595.

Westcott, Allan, ed. *American Sea Power since 1775.* 1947. 302.

Wheat, Col. Clayton E., ed. *The Democratic Tradition in America.* 1943. 21.

Whitaker, Arthur P. *The Mississippi Question, 1795–1803.* 1934. 269.

——— *The Spanish-American Frontier, 1783–1795.* 1927. 183.

——— *The United States and the Independence of Latin America, 1800–1830.* 1941. 346.

White, Charles Langdon and E. J. Foscue. *Regional Geography of Anglo-America.* 1943. 21.

White, Horace. *Money and Banking, Illustrated by American History.* 1895. New ed., 1936. 420.

White, Leonard D. *The Federalists: A Study in Administrative History.* 1948. 214.

White, Melvin J. *The Secession Movement in the United States, 1847–1852.* 1916. 502.

White, Newman I. *American Negro Folk Songs.* 1928. 449.

White, Stewart Edward. *The Forty-Niners* (*Chronicles of America,* XXV). 1920. 502.

Whitford, Noble E. *History of the Canal System of the State of New York.* 2 vols. 1906. 362.

Whitlock, Brand. *La Fayette.* 2 vols. 1929. 148.

Wildes, Harry E. *Anthony Wayne.* 1941. 149.

Wildman, Murray S. *Money Inflation in the United States: A Study in Social Pathology.* 1905. 402.

Wiley, Bell I. *The Life of Johnny Reb.* 1943. 594.

——— *The Plain People of the Confederacy.* 1943. 618.

——— *Southern Negroes, 1861–1865.* 1938. 618.

Williams, Kenneth P. *Lincoln Finds a General: A Military Study of the Civil War.* 2 vols. 1949. 594.

Williams, Samuel C. *History of the Lost State of Franklin.* 1924. 182.

——— *Tennessee during the Revolutionary War.* 1944. 149.

Williams, Thomas H. *Lincoln and the Radicals.* 1941. 617.

Wilson, Robert Forrest. *Crusader in Crinoline: The Life of Harriet Beecher Stowe.* 1941. 527.

Wiltse, Charles M. *John C. Calhoun, Nationalist, 1782–1828.* 1944. 362.

Winslow, Ola. *Jonathan Edwards, 1703–1758.* 1940. 79.

Winsor, Justin. *The Westward Movement.* 1897. 182.

———, ed. *Narrative and Critical History of America.* 8 vols. 1884–1889. 20.

Winther, Oscar O. *The Great Northwest.* 1947. 484.

Wish, Harvey. *George Fitzhugh: Propagandist of the Old South.* 1943. 464.

Wish, Harvey. *Society and Thought in Early America: A Social and Intellectual History of the American People through 1865.* 1950. 79, 448.

Wittke, Carl. *A History of Canada.* 1941. 108.

———— *Tambo and Bones.* 1930. 449.

———— *We Who Built America.* 1939. 526.

————, ed. *The History of the State of Ohio.* 6 vols. 1941–1944. 182.

Wood, Walter B. and James E. Edmonds. *A History of the Civil War in the United States.* 1905. 594.

Wood, William C. H. *Elizabethan Sea-Dogs* (*Chronicles of America*, III). 1918. 21.

———— *The War with the United States.* 1915. 301.

Woodward, William E. *George Washington, The Image and the Man.* 1926. 214.

Woodworth, Joseph V. *American Tool Making and Interchangeable Manufacturing.* 1905. 526.

Worthen, William B. *Early Banking in Arkansas.* 1906. 402.

Wright, Carroll D. *The Industrial Evolution of the United States.* 1902. 324.

Wright, Louis B. *The Atlantic Frontier: Colonial American Civilization.* 1947. 77.

Wrong, George M. *The Conquest of New France* (*Chronicles of America*, X). 1918. 108.

———— *The Rise and Fall of New France.* 2 vols., 1928. 108.

———— *Washington and His Comrades at Arms* (*Chronicles of America*, XII). 1921. 148.

Young, Eleanor. *Forgotten Patriot: Robert Morris.* 1950. 149.

Zeichner, Oscar. *Connecticut's Years of Controversy, 1750–1776.* 1949. 126.

Zimmerman, James F. *Impressment of American Seamen* (Columbia University, *Studies in History, Economics, and Public Law*, CXVIII). 1925. 280.

PICTURE CREDITS

In the following page-by-page list of credits, page numbers appear in bold face. Where there is more than one picture on a page, the pictures are referred to from left to right, top to bottom. The following abbreviations have been used for a few sources from which a great many illustrations have been obtained: *Bettmann* — The Bettmann Archive; *Culver* — Culver Service; *Field Collection* — The William B. Osgood Field Collection, Houghton Library, Harvard University; *Hist. Soc. of Pa.* — The Historical Society of Pennsylvania; *N-Y Hist. Soc.* — The New-York Historical Society; *N.Y.P.L.* — The New York Public Library.

3 Marginal sketch from Columbus' *Letter to Santangel*, Paris, 1493 — N.Y.P.L. **7** Smithsonian Institution. **8** Metropolitan Museum. **11** Portrait by Sebastiano del Piombo, 1519, Metropolitan Museum; N.Y.P.L. **12** From the *Codice Florentino*, American Museum of Natural History. **16** California Historical Society. **22** From John Smith's *Generale Historie*, London, 1624 — N.Y.P.L. **23** N.Y.P.L. **26** Bettmann; Bettmann; Perkins Press. **27** Bettmann; except lower right, Yale Univ. Library. **29** American Antiquarian Society. **32** Rhode Island Historical Society; State Street Trust Co., Boston. **38** Playing card, from a collection owned by Worcester College, Oxford. **39** Enoch Pratt Free Library, Phila. **42** Model based on the Castello Plan of New Amsterdam, 1660, Museum of the City of New York. **45** Hist. Soc. of Pa.; Pennsylvania Academy of Fine Arts. **47** From *The Salzburger Collection of Tracts*, 1732, N.Y.P.L. **50** N.Y.P.L. **52** Colonial Church, Sudbury, Mass. — Photo by William Sargent. **54** Duke Univ.; N.Y.P.L.; John Carter Brown Library; Historic American Buildings Survey, Library of Congress. **59** Essex Institute; formerly in possession of Knoedler Galleries; Bettmann; N.Y.P.L. **61** N.Y.P.L. **72** Metropolitan Museum; Bowdoin College Museum of Fine Arts; Brooklyn Museum; Historic American Buildings Survey, Library of Congress; N.Y.P.L. **73** Philadelphia Museum of Art; Wells Historical Museum, Old Sturbridge Village; Metropolitan Museum; Library Company of Philadelphia. **74** Collection of Col. and Mrs. Edgar W. Garbisch; Theatre Collection, Harvard Univ.; Clements Library, Univ. of Michigan; N.Y.P.L.; N.Y.P.L. **75** Yale Univ. Art Gallery. **76** Metropolitan Museum; Mabel Brady Garvan Institute, Yale Univ. Art Gallery. **80** Device from ten-shilling note, New York Colony, 18th century — N-Y Hist. Soc. **81** Bettmann. **83** N-Y Hist. Soc.; Culver; Colonial Williamsburg, Inc. **85** N.Y.P.L. **93** Detail from colonial flag, carried at the siege of Louisbourg, 1745. — N-Y Hist. Soc. **96** N.Y.P.L.; except upper right, Bett-

mann. **98** Brown Brothers; Washington and Lee Univ. **99** N-Y Hist. Soc. **105** Library of Congress; except upper left, N.Y.P.L.; lower right, Washington Univ., and City Art Museum of St. Louis. **111** Liberty device from masthead of *The Massachusetts Spy*, 1784 — Boston Public Library. **113** Culver. **115** N.Y.P.L.; Emmet Collection, N.Y.P.L.; Metropolitan Museum. **118** Museum of Fine Arts, Boston. **120** Stokes Collection, N.Y.P.L.; Metropolitan Museum. **121** Metropolitan Museum; Chicago Historical Society. **123** N-Y Hist. Soc. **127** American soldiers of the Revolutionary War, drawn for a German calendar, 1784. — Metropolitan Museum. **131** N.Y.P.L.; N.Y.P.L.; Hist. Soc. of Pa. **132** Library of Congress. **134** Fort Ticonderoga Museum; Metropolitan Museum, courtesy of Mrs. Charles A. Pfeffer, Jr.; Independence Hall Collection. **135** Art Commission, N.Y.C.; Bettmann; Yale Univ. Art Gallery. **144** Bancroft and Stokes collections, N.Y.P.L. **145** Hist. Soc. of Pa.; U. S. Naval Academy Museum; courtesy of The State Street Trust Company. **150** The United States Seal, adopted 1782 — N.Y.P.L. **151** Culver. **160** Hist. Soc. of Pa. **161** Hist. Soc. of Pa. **163** Trinity College; Georgetown Univ.; Drew Theological Seminary. **165** Decoration from a view of the capitol, about 1800, by William Birch — N.Y.P.L. **168** Tennessee Historical Society, both. **170** Enoch Pratt Free Library, Baltimore; N-Y Hist. Soc. **171** Chase National Bank Collection of Monies of the World; N.Y.P.L. **178** Hist. Soc. of Pa. **180** Museum of Fine Arts, Boston. **184** Detail from "Adoption of the Constitution" painted by J. B. Stearns — Courtesy of Mr. Clarence Dillon. **186** Courtesy of Mr. Clarence Dillon. **192** Clements Library, Univ. of Michigan. **193** N-Y Hist. Soc. **194** N-Y Hist. Soc. **199** Detail from an engraving of Washington's Inauguration in Federal Hall, N.Y. by Amos Doolittle — Stokes Collection, N.Y.P.L. **201** Brown Brothers; Hist. Soc. of Pa. **202** Brooklyn Museum; N-Y Hist. Soc. **205** Museum of Fine Arts, Boston; Culver. **209** Corcoran Gallery of

Art, Collection of Col. & Mrs. Edgar W. Garbisch; Chicago Historical Society. **212** N-Y Hist. Soc.; Free Library of Philadelphia. **216** Sketch of an American Seaman, 1797. — Naval Records and Library. **218** Peabody Museum of Salem; Hist. Soc. of Pa.; N-Y Hist. Soc. **220** National Gallery of Art, courtesy of Mrs. Arthur Iselin and Mr. Wm. Jay Iselin. **225** N-Y Hist. Soc. **227** Hist. Soc. of Pa.; American Antiquarian Society; Huntington Library; Corcoran Gallery of Art, courtesy of Musée Nationale de la Cooperation Franco-Americaine, Blérancourt. **230** Monticello, Jefferson's home, designed by himself — Bettmann. **231** N-Y Hist. Soc. **233** N-Y Hist. Soc.; Old Print Shop. **234** Bettmann; Stokes Collection, N.Y.P.L. **237** N.Y.P.L.; Bella C. Landauer Collection, N-Y Hist. Soc.; Penna. Academy of Fine Arts. **238** Metropolitan Museum; N.Y.P.L.; N.Y.P.L.; N-Y Hist. Soc. **239** American Antiquarian Soc.; Metropolitan Museum; American Antiquarian Society; N-Y Hist. Soc. **241** N.Y.P.L.; Penna. Academy of Fine Arts; Smithsonian Institution; N.Y.P.L. **246** Historical Society of York County, Pa.; N.Y.P.L.; N.Y.P.L.; Provincial Archives, Moravian Church, North. **248** Yale Univ. Art Gallery; Philadelphia Museum of Art; Index of American Design, National Gallery of Art. **249** Virginia State Library; Boston Athenaeum. **253** Woodcut by Alexander Anderson, 19th century — N.Y.P.L. **254** Peabody Museum of Salem. **256** Huntington Library. **259** N.Y.P.L.; except lower right, Chicago Historical Society. **262** Wildenstein & Co. **270** Detail from broadside announcing end of Embargo, 1809 — N-Y Hist. Soc. **272** Essex Institute; N-Y Hist. Soc. **274** N.Y.P.L.; N-Y Hist. Soc.; N-Y Hist. Soc.; Hist. Soc. of Pa. **277** Bowdoin College Museum of Fine Arts; N-Y Hist. Soc. **281** Boat flag used by Decatur as Commodore — Truxtun-Decatur Museum. **291** Hist. Soc. of Pa. **294** Maryland Historical Society; N.Y.P.L.; Irving Olds, *Bits & Pieces of American History*. **295** N-Y Hist. Soc.; except center, Chicago Historical Society. **299** N-Y Hist. Soc. **305** Detail from

"Fourth of July, 1819" painted by J. L. Krimmel — Hist. Soc. of Pa. **307** N.Y.P.L.; except upper right, Culver. **308** Metropolitan Museum from the collection of the late Harry T. Peters, Jr.; American Antiquarian Society; Metropolitan Museum. **310** Hist. Soc. of Pa.; Yale Univ. Art Gallery; N.Y.P.L. **312** Museum of Fine Arts, Boston; N–Y Hist. Soc.; Boston Public Library; Old Print Shop. **319** Chappel Studio, Philadelphia. **321** Harris & Ewing; Library of Congress. **325** Mile-post on the Cumberland Road — Uniontown (Pa.) Free Public Library. **328** Metropolitan Museum; N.Y.P.L. **329** Mariners' Museum; N.Y.P.L.; City Art Museum of St. Louis; Historical and Philosophical Society of Ohio. **331** N.Y.P.L.; except lower right, Western Reserve Historical Society. **338** N.Y.P.L.; except center, Hudson's Bay Co., London. **347** Detail from "View of Buffalo, N.Y.," 1836, by Bennett after J. W. Hill — N–Y Hist. Soc. **351** N.Y.P.L. **353** Fogg Art Museum, Harvard Univ. **359** Metropolitan Museum; N–Y Hist. Soc.; Stokes Collection, N.Y.P.L. **360** N–Y Hist. Soc.; Collection of Regional Art, Cornell Univ.; Baltimore & Ohio RR.; N.Y.P.L. **363** Detail from States' Rights *versus* Union Party broadside, 1832 — South Carolina Historical Society. **365** N–Y Hist. Soc.; Detroit Institute of Arts. **367** L. C. Handy Studio. **368** Field Collection. **370** N.Y.P.L. **381** Portraits: N–Y Hist. Soc.; Corcoran Gallery of Art; Brown Brothers. Upper right, Corcoran Gallery of Art. **382** Library of Congress. **383** South Carolina Historical Society. **386** Detail from "King Andrew the First," anonymous cartoon, about 1832 — Library of Congress. **394** Maryland Historical Society; Edward Eberstadt. **395** N.Y.P.L.; Old Print Shop; Brown Brothers. **397** San Jacinto Museum and Monument. **398** Texas State Library. **399** N.Y.P.L.; Library of Congress; American Antiquarian Society. **405** Detail from "The Times," cartoon by E. W. Clay, 1837 — N–Y Hist. Society. **408** Bettmann. **407** N–Y Hist. Soc. **410** Goodspeed Collection, Worcester Art Museum; N.Y.P.L.; Yale Univ. Art Gallery; N–Y Hist. Soc. **411** State N.Y.

Historical Association; Museum of the City of New York; Marine Historical Association. **412** Old Print Shop, courtesy of the owner. **414** L. C. Handy. **415** L. C. Handy. **422** Detail from title page of *Graham's Magazine*, 1849 — N.Y.P.L. **424** N.Y.P.L.; American Antiquarian Society; N.Y.P.L.; Old Print Shop. **428** Courtesy of Mr. Orson D. Munn; International Harvester; N.Y.P.L. **429** Colt's Manufacturing Co.; American Antiquarian Society; N–Y Hist. Soc. **430** Brown Brothers; except upper right, from L. C. Scott, *Christopher P. Cranch*. **433** Huntington Library; Boston Public Library; Brown Brothers; Poe and Whitman from prints in possession of the publisher. **436** Old Print Shop; N–Y Hist. Soc.; Addison Gallery of Amer. Art. **437** N.Y.P.L.; Foster Hall Collection, Univ. of Pittsburgh; Bettmann. **444** Culver Service; Chicago Historical Society. **446** Huntington Library; Metropolitan Museum; N–Y Hist. Soc.; American Antiquarian Society. **447** N–Y Hist. Soc.; N.Y.P.L. **451** Detail from "Low Water on the Mississippi," lithograph by Currier & Ives, 1860's — Old Print Shop. **453** Louisiana State Museum; N.Y.P.L.; Old Print Shop. **457** N.Y.P.L.; except lower right, Huntington Library. **460** Bettmann; N.Y.P.L.; Chicago Historical Society; Brown Brothers; Brown Brothers; Bettmann; N.Y.P.L. **465** Detail from "Emigrant Train," painting by Samuel Colman, 1872 — Metropolitan Museum. **466** N.Y.P.L. **467** Metropolitan Museum; Minneapolis Institute of Arts. **475** L. C. Handy. **478** N–Y Hist. Soc. **480** N.Y.P.L. **482** Culver. **486** Detail from "San Francisco Quadrilles," songsheet about 1852 — Foster Hall Collection, Univ. of Pittsburgh. **490** Library of Congress. **492** Bettmann; except upper right, Huntington Library. **493** Old Print Shop; Southwest Museum; Culver. **494** Art Commission, N.Y.C. **496** N–Y Hist. Soc. **497** L. C. Handy. **499** Goodspeed Collection, Worcester Art Museum. **501** L. C. Handy. **505** Detail from "An American Express Train," lithograph by Currier & Ives, 1850's — Old Print Shop. **506** N–Y Hist. Soc.; Transportation Library, Univ. of Michi-

gan; N.Y.P.L.; Old Print Shop; N.Y.P.L. **511** N–Y Hist. Soc.; Chicago Historical Society; N.Y.P.L. **516** McCormick Collection, Wisconsin State Hist. Soc.; Old Print Shop; N.Y.P.L.; Library of Congress. **517** Metropolitan Museum; J. Clarence Davis Collection, Museum of the City of New York. **519** Brown Brothers. **522** N.Y.P.L. **523** Left, in possession of the publisher; N.Y.P.L. **525** Boatmen's National Bank of St. Louis. **528** Detail from "Uncle Sam's Way," lithograph published C. A. Evans, Boston, 1861 — Field Collection. **533** Brown Brothers. **535** National Archives; Missouri Historical Society. **537** Museum of the City of New York. **541** Brooklyn Museum; Mabel Brady Garvan Collection, Yale Univ. Art Gallery; courtesy of Mr. Chalmers Roberts, *Washington, Past and Present*, Public Affairs Press; Metropolitan Museum. **550** Detail from "The 'Secession Movement,'" lithograph by Currier & Ives, 1861 — Field Collection. **553** Wide World; Alabama State Department of Archives and History. **557** Left in possession of the Publisher; Boatmen's National Bank of St. Louis. **559** Field Collection; except bottom, N.Y.P.L. **561** N.Y.P.L. **565** "The Spirit of '61," lithograph published by M. W. Siebert, N.Y., 1861 — Field Collection. **568** N–Y Hist. Soc. **569** Library of Congress. **573** Culver; Mariners' Museum; Old Print Shop. **585** National Archives. **587** National Archives. **592** Collection of Mr. Nelson A. Rockefeller; L. C. Handy; N.Y.P.L. **593** Collection of Mrs. McCook Knox; Library of Congress; Collection of Mr. Harry MacNeill Bland. **596** Detail from "Platforms Illustrated," lithograph published in 1864. — Field Collection. **599** National Gallery of Art; Old Print Shop; N.Y.P.L.; N.Y.P.L. **601** Library of Congress; Brown Brothers; City Art Museum of St. Louis; Old Print Shop. **606** Newark Museum, Purchase 1944, W. M. Scudder Bequest; Field Collection; Confederate Museum. **614** N.Y.P.L.; Culver; Field Collection. **Title page** "Georgetown and Federal City, or City of Washington," engraved from a drawing by G. Beck, 1801 — Library of Congress.

623 N–Y Hist. Soc.; N–Y Hist. Soc.; Library of Congress
627 N–Y Hist. Soc.; Library of Congress; N–Y Hist. Soc.
632 Library of Congress   **633** Library of Congress   **636** Library of Congress

LIST OF MAPS

INDEX OF PLACE NAMES ON MAPS

INDEX OF ILLUSTRATIONS

GENERAL INDEX

Marion, Francis, Patriot officer, 143
Marquette, Father Jacques, Catholic
missionary, 93
Marshall, James, discovers gold in
California, 490
Marshall, John, supports Constitution
in Virginia convention, 195; member mission to France, 225; becomes
Secretary of State, 228; becomes
Chief Justice, 233; *Marbury vs.
Madison*, 256; presides over trial of
Burr, 266; sketch of, 320; opinions
of, 321–323; succeeded by Taney,
390
Martin, Luther, delegate to Federal
Convention, 185; constitutional lawyer, 321
Martin vs. Hunter's Lessee, supremacy
of federal over state courts, 322
Marx, Karl, German radical, 441
Mary, Queen of England, 16
Mary of Modena, wife of James II, 88
Maryland, founded, 38; Germans in,
65; government of, 82; overthrows
proprietor, 89; on western land
claims, 157, 159; Alexandria Conference, 180; ratifies Federal Constitution, 195; furnishes militia to
suppress Whiskey Rebellion, 206;
abolishes property qualifications for
voting, 363; repudiates state debt,
408; tobacco growing in, 513; remains with the Union, 560; northern determination to retain, 561;
votes for Greeley (1872), 635
Mason, Capt. John, founder of New
Hampshire, 35
Mason, George, delegate to Federal
Convention, 185
Mason, James M., Confederate commissioner to Great Britain, 606; captured by Wilkes, 607; freed by Seward, 608
Mason, John, minister to France, 520
Mason, Lowell, hymn writer, 435
Mason and Dixon's Line, divides political parties in 1800, 232; no slave
states north of, 333; extended westward, 336
Masonry, attacked politically, 388
Massachusetts, the Massachusetts-
Bay Company, 29; church and
state in, 31; emigration from, 33;
education in, 62; as corporate colony, 81; General Court, 82; charter
annulled, 88; calls Stamp Act Congress, 114; opposition to Townshend
Acts, 117–118; government reformed (1774), 122; defies Gage's
authority, 127; efforts to continue
royal charter, 152; new constitution, 153; process of constitutional
amendment, 155; western land
claims, 159; citadel of Puritanism,
162; Shays' Rebellion, 179; ratifies
Federal Constitution, 195; calls
Hartford Convention, 298; church
disestablishment in, 313; votes Federalist (1816), 319; liberalizes suffrage, 364; Anti-Masonry in, 388;
Know-Nothings in, 520; carried by
Know-Nothings, 528
Matamoras, captured by Taylor, 478

Mathematics, in early American education, 243
Mather, Cotton, Puritan preacher,
60
Mathew, Father Theobald, temperance reformer, 445
Maumee River, British outpost on,
209; Americans forced back to, 288
Maximilian I, executed, 641
May-Flower, flat-boat on Ohio River,
174
Mayas, in Mexico, 3
Mayflower, sails for America, 26
Maysville Veto, states Jackson's policy on internal improvements, 371
Meade, Gen. George G., at Gettysburg, 582; commands under Grant,
586
Mechanic's lien laws, demanded, 439
Mechanics' Union of Trade Associations, labor federation, 439
Mediterranean, trade on, 8; Barbary
warfare in, 255
"Mediterranean Fund," to replace
frigate *Philadelphia*, 255
"Melting-pot," American frontier, 68
Melville, Herman, writings of, 433
Memphis, Tenn., railroad center, 507;
connected with Chattanooga, 508;
riots of 1866, 625
Menéndez, Pedro, conquers Huguenots in Florida, 13
Mennonites, reasons for emigration, 65
Mercantilism, inspires English policy,
19; under Board of Trade, 86
Merchant marine of U.S., clipper ship
era, 510; during Civil War, 600
Merry, Anthony, British minister, 265
Methodists, found Methodist Episcopal Church, 162; western point of
view, 182; frontier revivals of, 247;
in national period, 313; among the
slaves, 454; on slavery, 456; missions to Oregon, 470; split over
slavery, 522
Metternich, Prince, Austrian statesman, 342
Mexico, conquest of, 12; invites U.S.
to Panama Congress, 354; relations
with U.S. concerning Texas, 396–
400; trade with Santa Fe, 467; control of California, 471; opposes annexation of Texas by U.S., 473,
476; negotiations with U.S., 477;
U.S. war with, 478–481; treaty of
Guadalupe-Hidalgo, 481; French
intervention in, 609; revolts against
French rule, 641
Mexico (City), Burr's proposed attack
on, 266; trail from Santa Fe, 465;
captured by Scott, 480
Miami and Erie Canal, from Cincinnati to Toledo, 358
Michigan, becomes a territory, 281;
builds canal around St. Mary's
Falls, 360; repudiates state debt,
408; admitted to the Union, 416;
establishes first college of agriculture, 597
Michigan Central Railroad, reaches
Chicago, 507
Michigan Southern Railroad, reaches
Chicago, 507

Michilimackinac, captured by British,
288
Middle Ages, trade during, 8
Middle Atlantic States, leadership in
manufacturing, 512
Middle colonies, as a section, 52;
geographic nature of, 63; variety of
peoples in, 66; opposition to British
control, 124
Middle Period, of American History,
403; writers of, 428–434; architecture of, 434–435; the arts during,
435–438; reform movements of,
438–448
Middle West, birthplace of Republican Party, 528
Midway Islands, occupied by U.S., 642
Milan Decree, issued by Napoleon,
271; revoked, 279
Milford, Conn., founded, 34
Military Academy. *See* West Point
Militia, state, used in Whiskey Rebellion, 206; during war of 1812, 286;
refuse to cross into Canada, 289;
failure before Washington (1814),
293; Anti-Mason opposition to, 388;
on eve of Civil War, 565
Millburg, Vt., Lyceum center, 425
Mills Springs, battle of, 574
Milwaukee, Wis., Germans in, 519;
proposed transcontinental terminal,
524
Minnesota, created a territory, 416;
aspires to statehood, 487; admitted
to the Union, 515, 538; establishes
college of agriculture, 597; flour-milling in, 640
Miranda, Don Francisco de, Spanish-
American revolutionist, 226
Mississippi (state), admitted, 325; expansion into, 326; growth of, 327;
banking in, 408; considers secession
(1850), 499; secedes, 551; Civil War
fighting in, 577, 583; black codes in,
624; readmitted, 630
Mississippi River, western boundary
of U.S., 151; free navigation of in
dispute, 176–177; Spanish unwilling
to open, 207; crossed by emigrants,
327; slavery west of, 335; steamboats on, 416; bridged, 508; traffic
on, 509; Confederate defeats on,
572; Union efforts to clear, 577; in
Union control, 584
Mississippi Valley, importance of, 6;
Anglo-French rivalry for, 93; fur
trade in, 95; in peace negotiations,
150–151; earthquake in (1811), 326;
settlement of, 340; cotton culture in,
451; advance of frontier in, 465;
looks to Far West, 468; lumbering in
upper regions of, 518; interest in
transcontinental railroad, 523
Missouri, admitted as state, 325;
growth of, 327; problem of slavery
in, 332; enabling act for, 332; Compromise of 1820, 335; Compromise
of 1821, 336; western boundary, 370;
tobacco growing in, 513; end of
frontier in, 515; migration from to
Kansas, 529; "border ruffians," 531;
remains with the Union, 560; Liberal Republicanism in, 635

Pacific
Ocean

Coast Ranges
Valley of California
Sierra Nevada
Great Basin
Great Salt
Lake Wasatch
Mts.
Wyoming
Basin
Park Range
Rocky Mts.
Great Plains

GENERALIZED EAST